Public-Private Partnerships in Emerging Economies

Over the years, a shortage of funds has resulted in a huge deficit in government budgets for infrastructure, especially in developing and emerging economies. It is no longer feasible for governments to bear the entire burden of funding public infrastructure. Given that an inadequate supply of public infrastructure poses a challenge for the economic development of any country, partnerships with the private sector to fund public infrastructure procurement have started to be relied on as an alternative to traditional public procurement. Public-private partnerships (PPP) are arrangements that allow private entities to fund, design, manage and operate public infrastructure for a term in exchange for the payment of tolls by users or the government, and they may well be the solution to the infrastructure crisis in many developing economies.

This book examines the role of law in the adoption, implementation and regulation of PPP in selected developing economies, including Brazil, India, Nigeria and South Africa. It seeks to address how to deal with overlapping laws and how the law can protect assets invested in PPP in order to attract private-sector interests in infrastructure financing in developing and emerging markets. This book also shows how law can be used to create, sustain and promote PPP frameworks that take into account local circumstances in developing economies.

Dr Augustine Edobor Arimoro is a Lecturer in Law at the Nottingham Law School, Nottingham Trent University, United Kingdom and an affiliate of the Centre for Comparative Law in Africa, University of Cape Town, South Africa. He was previously an Associate Lecturer in Law, St Mary's Law School, St Mary's University Twickenham, London. Dr Arimoro is a Barrister and Solicitor of the Supreme Court of Nigeria.

Routledge Research in Finance and Banking Law

Trust and Distrust in Digital Economies
Philippa Ryan

Credit and Creed
A Critical Legal Theory of Money
Andreas Rahmatian

Housing and financial stability
Mortgage Lending and Macroprudential Policy in the US and UK
Alan Howard Brener

Conceptualizing the Regulatory Thicket
China's Financial Markets After the Global Financial Crisis
Shen Wei

Banking Bailout Law
A Comparative Study of the United States, United Kingdom and the European Union
Virag Blazsek

Public-Private Partnerships in Emerging Economies
Augustine Edobor Arimoro

International Investment Protection within Europe
The EU's Assertion of Control
Julien Berger

Regulation and the Global Financial Crisis
Impact, Regulatory Responses and Beyond
Daniel Cash and Robert Goddard

For more information about this series, please visit: www.routledge.com/Routledge-Research-in-Finance-and-Banking-Law/book-series/FINANCIALLAW

Public-Private Partnerships in Emerging Economies

Augustine Edobor Arimoro

Routledge
Taylor & Francis Group
LONDON AND NEW YORK

First published 2021
by Routledge
2 Park Square, Milton Park, Abingdon, Oxon OX14 4RN

and by Routledge
52 Vanderbilt Avenue, New York, NY 10017

Routledge is an imprint of the Taylor & Francis Group, an informa business

British Library Cataloguing-in-Publication Data
A catalogue record for this book is available from the British Library

Library of Congress Cataloging-in-Publication Data
Names: Arimoro, Augustine Edobor, author.
Title: Public-private partnerships in emerging economies / Augustine Edobor Arimoro.
Description: 1 Edition. | New York : Routledge, 2020. | Series: Routledge research in finance & banking law | Includes bibliographical references and index.
Identifiers: LCCN 2020026872 (print) | LCCN 2020026873 (ebook) | ISBN 9780367901110 (hardback) | ISBN 9781003105701 (ebook)
Subjects: LCSH: Public-private sector cooperation—Developing countries—Case studies. | Public-private sector cooperation—Law and legislation—Developing countries—Case studies.
Classification: LCC HD3872.D44 A75 2020 (print) | LCC HD3872.D44 (ebook) | DDC 338.87—dc23
LC record available at https://lccn.loc.gov/2020026872
LC ebook record available at https://lccn.loc.gov/2020026873

ISBN: 978-0-367-90111-0 (hbk)
ISBN: 978-1-003-10570-1 (ebk)

Typeset in Bembo
by Apex CoVantage, LLC

Qing Li • Yiu-Wing Mai
Editors

Biomaterials for Implants and Scaffolds

Springer

Editors
Qing Li
School of Aerospace, Mechanical
& Mechatronic Engineering
The University of Sydney
Sydney, NSW
Australia

Yiu-Wing Mai
School of Aerospace, Mechanical
& Mechatronic Engineering
The University of Sydney
Sydney, NSW
Australia

ISSN 2195-0644 ISSN 2195-0652 (electronic)
Springer Series in Biomaterials Science and Engineering
ISBN 978-3-662-53572-1 ISBN 978-3-662-53574-5 (eBook)
DOI 10.1007/978-3-662-53574-5

Library of Congress Control Number: 2016960306

Printed on acid-free paper

This Springer imprint is published by Springer Nature
The registered company is Springer-Verlag GmbH Germany
The registered company address is: Heidelberger Platz 3, 14197 Berlin, Germany

Preface

Contemporary biomaterials signify a class of synthetised materials to replace or support lost/damaged living tissues for restoring proper functionality. Over the past few decades, biomaterials have made enormous impacts on improvement of quality of life for millions of patients. Many leading causes of death, such as cardiovascular diseases, cancer, musculoskeletal trauma and injury, etc., have been alleviated by using substitutive biomaterials devices. Strong motivation to further advance healthcare and lower socioeconomic burden has continuously fuelled new breakthrough and innovation of biomaterials, making it one of the most exciting fields of research recently. The latest generation of biomaterials encompasses interdisciplinary sciences and cutting-edge technologies in materials, medicine, cellular and molecular biology, biochemistry, nanotechnology, multiscale modelling, advanced design and biomanufacturing, largely expanding materials knowledge and broadening biomedical applications.

Biomaterials have seen fast growth in two major areas on implantable prostheses and scaffold tissue engineering. Traditional implants aim to replace or support damaged and/or lost tissues, and as substituted, implanted devices stay with the living system temporarily or permanently. Rapid increase of implant recipients and life expectancy has been stimulating continuous inventions of new implant materials and novel treatment protocol. Modern implantable biomaterials, such as alloys, polymers and composites, possess enhanced mechanical, chemical and biological properties, enriched functionality and augmented biomedical performance, allowing them to be tailored in a particular application and for a specific patient. As a class of bio-products, implants have now evolved into a mature industry that employs more than 300,000 people and counts for over US$200 billion revenue globally.

By contrast, tissue engineering provides a relatively new therapeutical strategy to generate functional tissues or organs for the human body. As a fast emerging interdisciplinary area, tissue engineering offers great promise in solving the issue of significant shortage of organs or tissues facing healthcare nowadays. A landmark of tissue engineering has been the development of scaffolds, which use structured biomaterials to guide cells to generate neotissue under proper conditions. The current status of tissue engineering bears an overwhelming resemblance to that of implants in the 1970–1980s. The concept of repair or replacing with regenerated tissues/organs is being widely accepted in medical fields, and the demand has been becoming surprisingly high. It is for this reason that the biomedical industry is spawning a new revolution at present, where tissue engineering is rendering the next generation of implants that offers enormous potential to healthcare.

While being used for different therapeutical strategies, implants and tissue scaffolds share considerable commonality from a biomaterials perspective. First, biomaterials remain a central vehicle in both treatments by enabling materialised devices to interact with biological systems properly. Second, they both necessitate certain mechanical, chemical and physical properties of materials for support of and integration with surrounding tissues. Third, the boundary between them is becoming less distinguishable as witnessed by the developments of implants that are porous and degradable as well as scaffolds that are non-degradable for various treatment applications. In this book, we introduce the critical issues and challenges of biomaterials for both implants and tissue scaffolds.

This volume comprises 14 chapters with the balanced foci on both implantable and scaffolding biomaterials, each part consisting of 7 chapters. Just as the nature of biomaterials per se, the expertise of the authors in this book spans from a wide range of disciplines, including materials science, biochemistry, nanotechnology, biomedical engineering and clinical sciences. For understanding the sophistication of biomaterials development, the methodologies outlined in this volume range from computational modelling and design analysis (in silico), fabrication and laboratory tests (in vitro) to animal and human trials (in vivo). Each chapter offers a succinct but comprehensive discussion of fundamental concepts, research approaches and scientific data relevant to a particular area of applications, such as orthopaedics, prosthetic dentistry, interventional cardiology, vascular system and hard and soft tissue regeneration, while it is more a material-orientated, rather than application-orientated, volume.

For better understanding on the interaction of implants or scaffolds with hosting tissue, Chap. 1 introduces multiscale modelling of musculoskeletal tissues through micro-CT images, which provides an effective approach to analysing osseointegration of implants and bone ingrowth in scaffold. The comprehensions of structural details of tissues would potentially help optimise implant morphology and scaffold microstructures for creating a desired microenvironment. To surgically place an implant or scaffold to its host site in vivo, drilling or sectioning of bone or other tissues is often required. Chapter 2 introduces a computational procedure for modelling the insertion process of dental implant, allowing the assessment of the initial outcome of implantation by quantifying the biomechanical responses of bone, aiming to improve implantation surgery for short- and long-term outcomes.

Metals and alloys, as the most common constitutive materials for implants, have been long used and extensively studied. The latest progress seen in this area includes surface modification for promoting osseointegration. Chapter 3 proposes a novel mechanobiological framework for multiscale analysis and topographical design of implant in silico. Following this, Chap. 4 discusses different treatment techniques for desired surface properties and further describes cellular and molecular responses to surface topography and surface chemistry through the in vitro and in vivo studies.

Bioglass and ceramic materials have been widely used in prostheses, implants and scaffolds for their desired biocompatibility and mechanical properties. Chapter 5 provides a comprehensive overview in the advances in bioglass and glass ceramics from a materials perspective, which portrays the effects of different constituents, synthesis approaches as well as biochemical and biomechanical properties with an outline of broad clinical applications. Chapter 6 describes a specific application of glass ceramics in prosthetic dentistry, where in situ preparation and clinical resurfacing of glass ceramic prosthesis are studied through multiscale analyses in vitro and in silico, aiming to provide an in-depth understanding of their mechanical behaviours when delivering such materials to clinical use. Chapter 13, on the other hand, introduces bioglass to tissue engineering by developing novel bioactive scaffolds with multifunctional properties and desired nano-/microstructural features. It also explores the additive manufacturing approach for fabricating bioglass-based scaffolds. The in vitro and in vivo studies exemplify the capacity and advantages of such materials in tissue regeneration.

Polymer signifies another class of important biomaterials which have been extensively used in both implants and scaffolds. Polymer has been seen as a trend to replace metals and ceramics in many biomedical applications attributable to its versatility and flexibility in physical and chemical properties. Chapter 7 depicts two key applications of polymeric composites in arterial stents and tissue scaffolds. Arterial stents have been traditionally metal dominated, and the introduction of polymeric materials in this field has shown considerable potential for rendering the next generation of stents. Polymeric scaffolds featured in this chapter cover several important aspects of materials, microstructures, fabrication and in vitro and in vivo studies. Chapters 8 and 9 introduce the electrospinning technologies, further demonstrating the versatility of polymer materials in tissue engineering. Chapter 8 concentrates on biomechanical and biochemical properties of electrospun polymer scaffolds with a broad range of applications, such as bone. Chapter 9 focuses on tailoring materials properties specifically for soft tissue regeneration, such as wound healing. Chapter 10 explores differently structured polymeric scaffolds for periosteum tissue engineering, further demonstrating the flexibility for compositional and structural design. Chapter 14 also outlines the applications in cartilage tissue engineering. Following these in vitro and in vivo studies, Chap. 12 provides a series of computational design approaches for optimising scaffold structures made of polymers or other biomaterials, in which tissue ingrowth is modelled to predict the outcome in silico.

Hydrogel has seen extensive applications in tissue engineering in recent years for its compelling chemical and biological properties. Chapter 11 outlines the characterisation procedures of hydrogel scaffolds and provides some important biomechanical data through monotonic and fatigue tests. The damage assessment methods outlined in this chapter enable further understanding of scaffolding behaviours of the materials. Chapter 10 discusses the role of co-deposited hydrogel in polymeric scaffolds for periosteum tissue regeneration. Chapter 14 provides an overview in a range of naturally derived and synthesised injectable hydrogels for scaffold cartilage tissue engineering with substantial in vitro and in vivo data.

The book is expected to be of interest to the readers who are willing to become familiar with biomaterials knowledge and research methodologies for broad implant and/or scaffold applications. The style and language used in this book are intended to appeal to senior students, practising engineers and materials and biomedical scientists from a diverse background in materials synthesis and cellular and molecular studies to computational biomechanics. Substantial overviews are also provided for better appreciation to the background and progress in the field.

The book would not be possible without the tremendous contributions from all the authors, who are recognised experts and active researchers in the related fields. To them we sincerely apologise for the lengthy delay in seeing their manuscripts in print after rigorous reviews and final revisions. We would like to particularly thank Professor Min Wang, the series editor of Springer, of the University of Hong Kong for giving us this excellent opportunity and technical guidance to edit this volume. We would also like to extend our gratitude to the Springer Beijing Office, especially Ms June Tang and Mr Heather Feng, for their patience and professional work during the entire process of publication.

Sydney, Australia
March 2016

Qing Li
Yiu-Wing Mai

Contents

Contributors

Clayton J. Adam School of Chemistry, Physics and Mechanical Engineering, Faculty of Science and Engineering, Queensland University of Technology, Brisbane, Australia

A. Au Smith & Nephew, Andover, MA, USA

Besim Ben-Nissan University of Technology, Broadway, NSW, Australia

D. Bhattacharyya Centre for Advanced Composite Materials, The University of Auckland, Auckland, New Zealand

Nishant Chakravorty Institute of Health & Biomedical Innovation, Queensland University of Technology, Brisbane, QLD, Australia

Che-Cheng Chang School of Aerospace, Mechanical & Mechatronic Engineering, The University of Sydney, Sydney, NSW, Australia

Jiang Chang State Key Laboratory of High Performance Ceramics and Superfine Microstructure, Shanghai Institute of Ceramics, Chinese Academy of Sciences, Shanghai, People's Republic of China

Dave Wei-Chih Chen Chang Gung Memorial Hospital, Taoyuan City, Taiwan

Junning Chen School of Aerospace, Mechanical & Mechatronic Engineering, The University of Sydney, Sydney, NSW, Australia

Yuhang Chen School of Engineering & Physical Sciences, Mechanical, Process & Energy Engineering, Heriot-Watt University, Edinburgh, UK

Andy H. Choi University of Technology, Broadway, NSW, Australia

A. Cossey Spire Portsmouth Hospital, Portsmouth, UK

Ross Crawford Institute of Health and Biomedical Innovation, Queensland University of Technology, Kelvin Grove, QLD, Australia

Fariba Dehghani School of Chemical and Biomolecular Engineering, The University of Sydney, Sydney, Australia

Wei Fan Institute of Health and Biomedical Innovation, Queensland University of Technology, Kelvin Grove, QLD, Australia

Ali Fathi School of Chemical and Biomolecular Engineering, The University of Sydney, Sydney, Australia

Hong Guan Griffith School of Engineering, Griffith University, Nathan, QLD, Australia

Y-H Hsu School of Engineering, University of Portsmouth, Portsmouth, UK

Dietmar W. Hutmacher Institute of Health and Biomedical Innovation, Queensland University of Technology, Kelvin Grove, QLD, Australia

Saso Ivanovski School of Dentistry and Oral Health, Griffith Health Institute, Griffith University, Gold Coast, QLD, Australia

Anjali Jaiprakash Institute of Health & Biomedical Innovation, Queensland University of Technology, Brisbane, QLD, Australia

Newell W. Johnson Menzies Health Institute Queensland, Griffith University, Nathan, QLD, Australia

L. Kimble Centre for Advanced Composite Materials, The University of Auckland, Auckland, New Zealand

Qing Li School of Aerospace, Mechanical & Mechatronic Engineering, The University of Sydney, Sydney, NSW, Australia

Wei Li School of Aerospace, Mechanical & Mechatronic Engineering, The University of Sydney, Sydney, NSW, Australia

Gui-Ying Liao China University of Geosciences, Wuhan, China

S.T. Lin Centre for Advanced Composite Materials, The University of Auckland, Auckland, New Zealand

Shih-Jung Liu Chang Gung University, Tao-Yuan, Taiwan

Yew-Chaye Loo Griffith School of Engineering, Griffith University, Nathan, QLD, Australia

Innocent Macha University of Technology, Broadway, NSW, Australia

K. Madi School of Engineering, University of Portsmouth, Portsmouth, UK

Yiu-Wing Mai School of Aerospace, Mechanical & Mechatronic Engineering, The University of Sydney, Sydney, NSW, Australia

Chaiy Rungsiyakull School of Aerospace, Mechanical & Mechatronic Engineering, The University of Sydney, Sydney, NSW, Australia

Xiao-Fei Song School of Mechanical Engineering, Tianjin University, Tianjin, China

Richard Stoll College of Medicine and Dentistry, James Cook University, Cairns, QLD, Australia

Michael V. Swain School of Aerospace, Mechanical & Mechatronic Engineering, The University of Sydney, Sydney, NSW, Australia

J. Tong School of Engineering, University of Portsmouth, Portsmouth, UK

Rudi C. van Staden College of Engineering and Science, Structural Mechanics and Sustainable Materials Research Group, Victoria University, Melbourne, VIC, Australia

Chengtie Wu State Key Laboratory of High Performance Ceramics and Superfine Microstructure, Shanghai Institute of Ceramics, Chinese Academy of Sciences, Shanghai, People's Republic of China

Yin Xiao Institute of Health & Biomedical Innovation, Queensland University of Technology, Brisbane, QLD, Australia

Xiao-Lin Xie School of Chemistry and Chemical Engineering, Huazhong University of Science and Technology, Wuhan, China

Ling Yin College of Science and Engineering, James Cook University, Townsville, QLD, Australia

Shiwei Zhou Centre for Innovative Structures and Materials (CISM), RMIT University, Melbourne, Australia

Xing-Ping Zhou School of Chemistry and Chemical Engineering, Huazhong University of Science and Technology, Wuhan, China

Chapter 1
Multiscale Modelling and Simulation of Musculoskeletal Tissues for Orthopaedics

Clayton J. Adam

Abstract Successful development of implants for orthopaedic surgical procedures depends on a comprehensive understanding of the interaction between implant biomaterials and the host tissues of the musculoskeletal system. Mechanical factors are a key part of this interaction. This chapter investigates the potential of computational modelling and simulation approaches at multiple length scales to elucidate the response of musculoskeletal tissues to orthopaedic implants, leading to improved treatment outcomes. To a large extent, musculoskeletal tissues derive their load-bearing function from their hierarchically arranged structure; therefore we pay particular attention to modelling of the musculoskeletal tissues themselves from the nano- and micro-scales to the macro-scale. The most well-characterised musculoskeletal tissue are bone, and this chapter covers recent work on micro- and nanoscale modelling of bone and collagen and on defining the elasto-plastic constitutive response of the bone extracellular matrix using finite element models of bone nanoindentation combined with atomic force microscopy to map the inelastic deformation of the tissues. The use of serial milling and block face imaging techniques to determine soft tissue anatomy at multiple length scales for definition of model geometry is also covered. The potential for further development of multiscale computational biomechanics through modelling cell and tissue mechanobiology is discussed, including more detailed mechanical characterisation of the tissue–implant interface, modelling the strain fields experienced by cells within the extracellular matrix and within scaffolds and coupled modelling of other physical and biological phenomena within tissues and biomaterials.

Keywords Biomechanics • Computational mechanics • Elasto-plastic constitutive model • Extracellular matrix • Finite element method • Mechanobiology • Multiscale modelling • Nanoindentation • Orthopaedic implant

C.J. Adam (✉)
School of Chemistry, Physics and Mechanical Engineering, Faculty of Science and Engineering, Queensland University of Technology, GPO Box 2434, 2 George St, Brisbane Q4000, Australia
e-mail: c.adam@qut.edu.au

Q. Li, Y.-W. Mai (eds.), *Biomaterials for Implants and Scaffolds*, Springer Series in Biomaterials Science and Engineering 8, DOI 10.1007/978-3-662-53574-5_1

1.1 Introduction

In the same way that computational mechanics has revolutionised the design and analysis of manufactured objects in many industries, the rapidly growing subfield of computational biomechanics (CB) offers much promise in using modelling and simulation to better understand degenerative processes in the musculoskeletal system and to improve orthopaedic treatments for musculoskeletal disorders. Since the function of the musculoskeletal system is predominantly a load-bearing one, it follows that the mechanics of interaction between an implant and its surrounding host tissues are of key importance in the design of orthopaedic implants and surgical procedures. This holds true both at the scale of whole bones, joints and implants (here designated the macro-scale) and at the micro- and nanosized scales of the implant surface and its mechanical interaction with hierarchically structured host tissues. From a biological perspective, the microenvironment within tissues and at the interface between tissues and implants is extremely important because this is the scale at which cells sense and respond to mechanical signals to control gene expression for tissue growth, repair and remodelling.

A key advantage of mechanics-based modelling in orthopaedic biomechanics is the ability to model many different design variants of an implant, with the aim of finding optimal design characteristics of that implant. This would be impossible in human trials and would be prohibitively time consuming and expensive in either in vitro or in vivo animal studies. Models also allow the same implant design to be simulated following virtual placement into a wide variety of different patients. A third possibility in computational biomechanics, and the focus of this chapter, is the ability to model biomechanical processes over a range of length and timescales, providing insights into the coupling between macro-scale loading and the micro- and nano-mechanical processes occurring within the tissues themselves. These micro- and nanoscale physical processes are the drivers of the biological response to mechanical loading and therefore affect the responses of the musculoskeletal system to orthopaedic implants. To date, cell-mediated processes such as tissue modelling and remodelling have been treated phenomenologically in macro-scale simulations of tissue response to implants; however, modelling at finer scales has the potential to provide a deeper physics-based mechanistic understanding of tissue response to loading.

With these considerations in mind, this chapter highlights the use of biomechanical modelling and simulation approaches to investigate the loading response of musculoskeletal tissues and orthopaedic implants at multiple scales. It is important to note that although the biomaterials used in an orthopaedic implant may themselves be intricate in geometry and surface topography, the much greater challenge is modelling host tissue responses to loading, because natural tissues are much more sophisticated than their synthetic replacements [1]. Therefore the focus of this chapter is on modelling of tissues as 'natural biomaterials' rather than modelling the metals, polymers and ceramics used for implants or scaffolds. Furthermore, the focus here is on the passive osseo-ligamentous tissues, bone, cartilage, ligament and tendon, i.e. excluding the muscle. While many of the considerations that follow are also relevant to muscle, its active contractile force-generating ability introduces additional complexities in modelling which are beyond the scope of this discussion.

It is also important to note that due to the complexities of modelling living tissues [2,3] and the resulting nascent (although rapidly developing) state of multiscale modelling in the musculoskeletal system, the use of the term 'multiscale' here does not carry the same emphasis on bridging between scales and on algorithms and strategies for the concurrent solution of multiscale problems as in some other literature on the topic. The focus here can be expressed in terms of firstly a recognition that scales other than the macro-scale (which has been the scale mostly modelled in orthopaedic biomechanics) are important, especially when attempting to model the biological response, and secondly a consideration of how to define models at these other scales of interest, including what information is required at each scale and how this information might be obtained using existing imaging and measurement technologies. Scale bridging is clearly an important consideration in tissue modelling [4], but must necessarily come after efforts to define and model the scales of relevance for cellular and extracellular matrix loading response.

1.1.1 Orthopaedic Implants and Treatment Outcomes

The aim of orthopaedic surgery is to correct problems which arise in the human musculoskeletal system. Disorders of the musculoskeletal system are a major contributor to the global burden of disease, and there is intense interest in developing new treatments for musculoskeletal disease. In childhood, bone deformities during growth can require major corrective surgery. In adults, disorders such as osteoarthritis and intervertebral disc degeneration cause immobility, pain and lost productivity. In the elderly, osteoporosis causes increased fracture risk with subsequent loss of mobility and high mortality rates after a fracture. At all ages, cancer, trauma and infectious disease can lead to bone, joint and soft tissue destruction.

The dominant paradigm in orthopaedic practice today is the use of non-biodegradable implants which may have various surface treatments or coatings applied to enhance osseointegration with host bone (Fig. 1.1), although we note that there is also intensive research underway in the field of tissue engineering, in which the implanted load-bearing structure is in fact a temporary scaffold which is designed to resorb in the body and eventually be replaced by host tissue.

The course of degeneration of musculoskeletal tissues is itself a topic of intense research, because prevention of bone and joint diseases with conservative treatments is a preferable goal to surgical procedures. However, at present there are no effective conservative treatments for musculoskeletal disorders such as osteoarthritis, degenerative disc disease and progressive spinal deformity, so that arthrodesis (joint immobilisation) and arthroplasty (joint replacement) using implants are the only treatment options in progressive cases. Orthopaedic procedures are expensive and invasive; therefore once the decision has been made to operate, it is crucial that

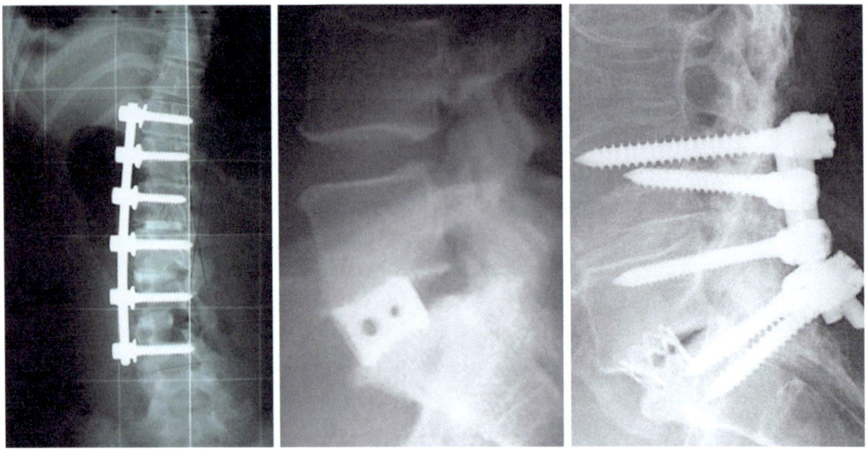

Fig. 1.1 Orthopaedic implants used in spinal surgery. In each case, significant rates of implant loosening are reported in the literature; (*left*) single anterior rod for scoliosis correction, (*centre*) anterior lumbar interbody fusion implant, (*right*) pedicle screw and posterior rod fusion construct with anterior interbody spacer in the L5-S1 disc space

the design of the surgical intervention (including the implant) is optimal to achieve the desired corrective outcome. From a structural point of view, orthopaedic surgery represents an interesting challenge, because the aim is to instantaneously correct a biological structure which has been degenerating over years or even decades and which will continue to adapt to the newly placed surgical implant for several years after the operation. The challenge is to ensure successful integration of the implant with host tissues after surgery so that joint stability and/or function is restored.

While some orthopaedic surgical procedures have a high success rate (most notably hip and knee replacement), there are other disorders for which procedures involving implant placement are risky and the postoperative response of the implant constructed within the host tissue environment is poorly understood. For example, previous studies have shown that bone resorption around implants is a potential cause of loosening following surgery [5] and that when loosening occurs, failed bone fusion is more likely to be the result [6]. In the field of orthopaedic spine surgery, a meta-analysis covering 82 studies and 5780 procedures for scoliosis treatment by Hawes and O'Brien [7] revealed an overall complication rate of 20 %, with nine of the studies in the meta-analysis reporting complication rates of 40 % or higher.[1]

[1]We note that it is not possible to deduce from this meta-analysis which of the complications were directly implant related or which were due to other causes.

1.1.2 Load-Bearing Tissues of the Musculoskeletal System

Derived from the embryonic mesoderm, the human musculoskeletal system is a complex assembly of 206 bones, 360 joints and 640 muscles. The role of the musculoskeletal system is mechanical, exerting and bearing the forces associated with movement and body weight. Each of the tissues in the musculoskeletal system is exquisitely adapted to its particular mechanical role. The bone achieves light-weight stiffness and strength through a hierarchical assembly of mineralised collagen fibres, built from the nanoscale up [8]. In addition to its mechanical role, the bone also acts as a calcium reservoir and a host for bone marrow. The ligaments which connect one bone to another are tough, collagenous tension-bearing structures with nonlinear force versus stretch characteristics, and variable elastic energy storage capacity according to their biomechanical role is conferred by the presence of elastic fibres together with the collagen [9]. Smooth articulating movement under high contact pressures between adjacent bones occurs between the lubricated sliding surfaces of articular cartilage, which is comprised of a network of graduated zones of self-assembled type II collagen fibres pre-strained by physicochemical swelling of hydrophilic proteoglycan molecules within the network [10]. The intervertebral discs of the spine are the largest avascular structures in the body, resisting forces of up to nine times the body weight, and are comprised of a series of annular rings of collagenous fibres criss-crossed in alternating orientations, surrounding a gel-like inner nucleus pulposus which is pressurised to about 70kPa due to pre-stretch in the ligamentum flavum within the annular outer layers [11]. The skeletal muscle is comprised of a repeated hierarchical assembly of actin and myosin fibres again held in place by a collagen network (the endomysium) [12]. The muscles are attached to the bone via flexible tendons. The tendon is a tough and resilient collagenous tissue with a highly aligned longitudinal fibrous structure which allows transmission of high forces from the muscles to their bony attachment points [13].

At the microstructural level, the defining characteristic of musculoskeletal tissues is their dense, tough extracellular matrix (ECM) comprised of hierarchically assembled fibrous proteins. The ECM is built and maintained by a network of living cells both within the tissue and on its surface. Cellular activity is in turn controlled by soluble signaling molecules, as well as by biophysical and biochemical signals from the ECM itself, so that the ECM acts as both a substrate for cell attachment and a signaling source to control cell activity [14]. Within this general framework, musculoskeletal tissues exhibit a diverse range of morphologies and mechanical properties specifically adapted for their structural role, and tissue adaptation to changing loading conditions occurs throughout the lifespan.

The general form of this adaptation response in skeletally mature adults is an increase in ECM density and size (hypertrophy) in response to increased mechanical load and loss of ECM (atrophy) in regions of decreased loading. For example, it is well known that rapid bone loss occurs during extended bed rest and space flight or on a local scale adjacent to a stiff, metallic load-bearing implant after surgical implantation [15–18]. The change in ECM composition in response to increased loading is achieved through cell-mediated 'remodelling', in which damaged ECM is resorbed [19] and new ECM is deposited by cells. Because highly loaded tissues, such as the ligament, tendon and the intervertebral disc, are avascular (presumably for reasons of structural integrity and limitations on blood flow in the presence of high hydrostatic ECM stresses), cellular repair and remodelling activity must rely on nutrient and oxygen diffusion through dense ECM, so that healing responses can be slow.

The hierarchical structure of musculoskeletal tissues has been defined according to various schemas [20–22]. For simplicity here we adopt a three-level nomenclature as follows: the term 'nanoscale' is used when referring to either anatomical structures or computational models of these structures with characteristic dimensions of less than 1 μm; 'micro-scale' covers the range 1–100 μm; and 'macro-scale' refers to structural features and characteristic element dimensions above 100 μm. We note that other authors have defined 'meso-scales' as intermediate levels between other scales; however, due to the variability in the usage of the term, we avoid it here.

1.2 Macro-scale Modelling in Orthopaedic Biomechanics

In any mathematical model, the aim is to capture the salient features of the system being modelled using as simple a representation of the system as possible. Overly complicated models incur computational expense and the required input data may not be available, while overly simplistic models miss important features of system response. In structural mechanics, spatiotemporal representations of the structure are usually defined and solved using the finite element (FE) method, and so in what follows we are referring to FE modelling unless otherwise stated. In orthopaedic biomechanics, the starting point is often a 'top-level' whole bone/joint/implant FE model where the surgical procedure is simulated under quasi-static loading using relatively simple material constitutive properties. The geometry of bones and joints is not known a priori; therefore, the ability to prescribe model geometry is dependent on state-of-the-art scanning and imaging technologies.

1.2.1 3D Imaging and Medical Image-Based Modelling

Since the geometries of musculoskeletal tissues are not known in advance, three-dimensional biomechanical models rely on digital data from scanners. At present, clinical whole-body computed tomography (CT) and magnetic resonance imaging (MRI) scanners are limited to maximum resolutions of approximately 250 μm. These resolutions are usually sufficient to define macrostructure, although we note that they may be only marginally acceptable when defining the thickness of certain anatomical structures such as the cartilage in articulating joints or the cortical wall in the spinal vertebrae. Also, scans for clinical purposes are usually performed at lower resolution than this and do not usually involve 3D acquisition protocols, necessitating special ‘research scans’ to obtain submillimetre voxel dimensions in 3D. In the case of CT scans of the bone, voxel sizes of several hundred microns are one or two orders of magnitude coarser than the resolution needed to represent tissue microstructure. Therefore, the top-level models of bones and joints derived from medical image datasets are limited to macro-scale.

There are several possible approaches to geometric generation of macro-scale models and FE meshing from 3D medical image datasets; image voxels can be directly converted into hexahedral finite elements; or the surface of an implant or organ can be calculated using image processing techniques, which then forms the boundary of a solid that is meshed using volumetric meshing techniques (e.g. [23]). Mesh matching between implants and surrounding host tissues is an important part of model generation; and various approaches have been proposed to ensure mesh compatibility across tissue–implant interfaces [24] (Fig. 1.2). Even at the macro-scale, models based on medical scan image data can be too complex to solve using current computational power. For example, a voxel-based FE model of a whole femur with 0.25-mm voxel size would contain in the order of 15 million hexahedral elements.

1.2.2 Continuum Representation of Tissues and Constitutive Relations

In such macro-scale models, the structure being modelled is the bone, joint or implant in question, and the tissues are treated as continua. This top-down, ‘organ equals structure, tissue equals continuum material’ approach has been widely used in orthopaedic biomechanics [25]. Using this approach, mechanical property characterisation for each ‘material’ (the cortical bone, trabecular bone, cartilage, ligament, tendon) can be performed using either direct experimental measurements (e.g. a four-point bending test of a sample of cortical bone) or inverse characterisation where, for example, an FE model of a complex bone anatomy is built and then the material properties in the model are iteratively adjusted to obtain agreement with the experiment. In this approach, the effects of the hierarchical structure and inhomogeneity of the tissues at scales below that of the geometry being modelled are ‘built into’ the material properties in a statistical sense. Furthermore, a degree of material inhomogeneity can be introduced (at least for the bone) by taking advantage of the effect of bone density on X-ray beam attenuation, so that radiographically derived bone models can be assigned specimen-specific inhomogeneous material properties based on the greyscale values of each voxel in the CT scan used to build the model.

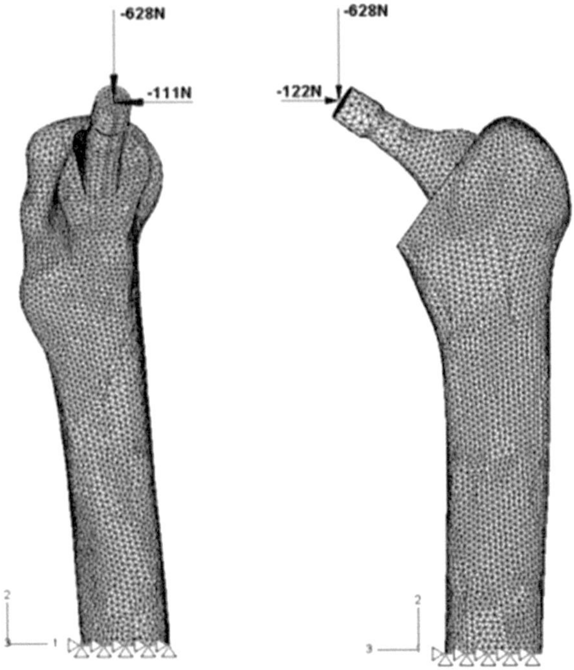

Fig. 1.2 Macro-scale FE model of a hip replacement implant showing applied loads and boundary conditions. The outer cortical bone of the femur, inner cancellous bone, poly (methyl methacrylate) bone cement and implant are each modelled using different sets of homogeneous material properties (From [24], used with permission)

Although it is well known that musculoskeletal tissues exhibit nonlinear stress–strain phenomena such as creep, rate dependence and hyperelasticity, many models use linear elastic (isotropic or orthotropic) material properties for bone and cartilage, and tendons and ligaments are sometimes modelled as linear or nonlinear springs with properties defined from in vitro tensile tests [26]. Assumptions of linearity enable much faster computational solutions (since the stiffness matrix need only be assembled and inverted once); however, they are also valid over a limited range of tissue responses. To provide just one example, it is well known that relaxation of surrounding tissues after orthopaedic implant insertion can cause large decreases in the loading experienced by the implant after surgery [27]. Such time-dependent, nonlinear behaviour is missed by linear quasi-static material constitutive models. Of course it is a matter of engineering judgement as to the importance of including such behaviours in macro-scale models of tissue–implant interaction. Having said this, a large body of work has also been performed on the development of nonlinear, macro-scale continuum constitutive relations for musculoskeletal tissues. Detailed coverage of all the constitutive relations which have been developed and employed is beyond the scope of this chapter; however, in light of the focus on trabecular bone in Sect. 1.3, we note that Carretta et al. [28] provide a useful overview of apparent-level constitutive models developed for trabecular bone.

Having defined macro-scale geometry and material properties, prescription of loads and boundary conditions must be applied. Due to the difficulties of direct load measurement in living humans, rigid body dynamics approaches have been used in conjunction with clinical or laboratory data to estimate loads during various postoperative activities. Here the musculoskeletal system is represented mathematically as an assembly of structural elements (beams, struts, springs and joints) in which forces generated by the muscles acting against gravity and body mass generate motion. Solving the inverse problem, in which motion is known (using motion tracking systems), allows calculation of internal forces[2] which can in turn be used as inputs to the macro-scale continuum FE models. In more trivial cases than gait, simple statics calculations may provide a reasonable estimate of the loads on the musculoskeletal system for input to macro-scale FE models. In a few cases, in vivo loads have been directly measured using strain gauges or pressure needles during daily activities, thus providing useful reference data for biomechanical models [29–31].

1.2.3 Phenomenological Treatment of Biological Processes

So far, nothing has been said regarding the main distinguishing feature of musculoskeletal tissues, that they are *living* structural entities. Tissues grow, remodel and self-heal over the course of an organism's lifespan. These behaviours are characteristic of a complex living biological system. The primary function of a musculoskeletal tissue may indeed be load bearing, but the means by which these tissues are built and adapted to the changing environment of an organism over a lifetime involves cell-mediated physiological processes of great complexity.

In recent years the role of mechanical loading in governing tissue growth and remodelling has been increasingly studied. This research field at the interface of mechanics and biology has been coined 'mechanobiology' and is an active field with particular interest in understanding how cells transduce mechanical signals. The use of spatiotemporal modelling in mechanobiology spans both phenomenological macro-scale continuum descriptions of tissue remodelling and differentiation and micro-scale simulations (discussed further in Sect. 1.3.1) designed to provide greater insight into the cellular processes behind tissue growth and remodelling. An example of a macro-scale mechanobiological model is the incorporation of 'Frost's mechanostat' [32] into a trilinear model to simulate bone response to altered loading around an orthopaedic implant after insertion. Such models are solved iteratively by defining bone density as a state variable and iteratively increasing density in regions of high strain energy and decreasing it in regions of low strain energy (e.g. [33]). Elastic properties are in turn defined as a

---

[2]Even in this supposedly simple case of modelling the body as a multi-jointed mechanism, modelling uncertainties abound: muscle lines of action are complex and involve wrapping and contact with other muscles; joints are polycentric, the axis of rotation changing with the degree of rotation. Intra-abdominal pressure affects trunk stiffness, and muscle activation strategies vary during repeated performance of the same task.

function of bone density. The resulting models can reproduce aspects of the radiographically observed remodelling response around the implant following insertion [34].

Another example of phenomenological modelling of a mechanically mediated biological process is the differentiation of newly formed tissue in a haematoma (e.g. in a fracture site or adjacent to a newly placed implant) into various mature tissue types according to the stress or strain state in the callus tissue. Several groups have developed empirically based mechanobiological FE models to describe the differentiation of newly formed tissue into different types depending on the stress–strain state in the tissue [35–38].

Thus biological processes of growth and remodelling have been incorporated to some extent in top-down continuum models of bones and joints, but the phenomenological relations on which they are based afford little insight into the finer scale biological processes which drive them, and they are therefore of unknown value outside the range of experimental conditions for which they were calibrated.

1.2.4 Rationale for Multiscale Modelling

This issue of phenomenological versus physics-based, mechanistic modelling is at the heart of the question regarding the need for multiscale approaches in modelling tissues and tissue–implant interaction. If a macroscopic model with appropriately defined continuum material properties (in other words a phenomenological relationship which is an adequate statistical representation of the relationship between stress and strain in the tissue without considering the finer scale processes which result in this relationship) can satisfactorily predict the outcomes of a particular implant being inserted, is it necessary to make additional effort to model processes mechanistically at finer spatial or temporal resolution?

The response to this question is that there are a host of processes occurring at the micro- and nanoscales in musculoskeletal tissues which are relevant to tissue–implant interaction and for which a mechanistic[3] rather than a purely phenomenological understanding could potentially improve implant design. Biological structures are built and maintained from the bottom-up, not from the top-down [40], and phenomenological rules, such as Frost's mechanostat, although conceptually useful, represent a simplification of actual growth and remodelling processes. Furthermore, even if a phenomenological model could provide equivalent predictive ability to a mechanistic model across the current problem space, the understanding provided by mechanistic modelling at finer scales may provide new insights into the

[3]The physics-based, mechanistic models we refer to here are spatio-temporal models, i.e. they represent tissues and implants as structures in three-dimensional space. Pivonka and Komarova [39] provide an overview of other types of (temporal only) mathematical models used in bone biology.

problem which may in turn allow new design paradigms outside of current design space. Finally, phenomenological models calibrated to represent the response of healthy tissues provide no insight into the micro- and nanoscale aspects of disease processes, and similarly empirical tissue responses based on measurements in patients with a particular pathology provide no clues as how to best prevent or treat that pathology from a biological perspective. They tell us 'what' without any insight into the 'how' or 'why' of musculoskeletal mechanobiology.

Having established that micro- and nanoscale processes are crucial in understanding musculoskeletal tissue loading response to implants, we go further and state that computational modelling and simulation have a valuable role to play in elucidating these. Observation and hypothesis testing through laboratory-based experiments and clinical studies are essential, but are also expensive and inherently limited in the range of tissue states and implant designs which can be investigated. Cost and ethical considerations combine to severely limit the scope of in vivo (large animal or human) studies on living musculoskeletal tissues relevant to orthopaedics. Small animal (mouse and rat) studies of orthopaedic implant designs are possible and are performed; however, these raise questions regarding the transferability of outcomes across species varying by three orders of magnitude in mass. Therefore modelling and simulation can play a key role in studying micro- and nanostructure aspects of tissue loading response and tissue–implant interaction at various levels of the structural hierarchy.

One way to classify the processes of interest for micro- and nanoscale modelling in orthopaedics is by dividing them into processes related to the extracellular matrix (ECM) and cells, respectively. ECM processes are those micro- and nanoscale activities which govern the response of the implant extracellular matrix construct to loading, including noncellular processes which alter the structure and composition of the ECM in certain ways (e.g. ECM damage or non-enzymatic glycation). The cellular processes are those by which cells mediate the addition or removal of extracellular matrix to change ECM structure during growth and remodelling. Note that in the passive musculoskeletal tissues, the ECM is the key structural element. The cells themselves do not play a significant load-bearing role, rather they act as autonomous agents which sense the conditions within the ECM and modify extracellular matrix structure accordingly. Therefore the mechanics of cell deformation are still of interest, but from the perspective of mechanotransduction of ECM loading and the resulting response. Using this ECM/cell division, some key processes are listed below.

Extracellular matrix physicochemical processes (structural response to load and noncellularly mediated structural modifications)

- Micro- and nanostructural basis of ECM force–displacement response (elasticity and plasticity as well as time-dependent behaviours; creep, viscoelasticity)
- Micro- and nanoscale fracture in the ECM
- Coupled fluid flow and diffusion within the micro- and nanoporosity of ECM

- Physicochemical swelling in proteoglycan-rich tissues as a function of ion concentration
- Piezoelectricity and streaming potentials induced during ECM deformation
- Biomineralisation of bone
- Non-enzymatic glycation

Cellular processes (ECM modifying physicochemical processes)

- ECM synthesis by cells during growth and tissue remodelling
- Mesenchymal cell differentiation according to stress and fluid flow conditions
- ECM self-assembly outside the cell
- ECM resorption via enzymatic digestion
- Membrane strain experienced by cells attached to the ECM
- Fluid flow-induced mechanotransduction by cells within the ECM
- Cell metabolism (nutrient, oxygen and waste product transport to and from cells)
- Intercellular signaling within the ECM

In addition, it is possible to add several more micro- and nanoscale processes specifically related to tissue interaction with an implant.

Implant-related physicochemical processes

- Microscopic damage and wear particle formation from implant surfaces
- Protein adsorption on implant surfaces
- Surface chemistry of implant biomaterials in body fluids

It should be clear from the lists above that the complexity of the micro- and nanoscale processes occurring within tissues is daunting from a modelling perspective. Even if the problem is reduced to solely considering physical structure–function relationships of the ECM (without any cell-mediated matrix modification and without any ECM chemical modification processes such as mineralisation or glycation), then the problem of modelling load–deformation behaviour in a hierarchically arranged, nanostructured, hydrated matrix of biological macromolecules and its interaction with a metallic, polymeric or ceramic implant is highly challenging. Note also that although the extracellular matrix is the key structural element in musculoskeletal tissue response to loading, it is clear from the last four points in the list of cell-mediated processes above that understanding how cells transduce physical signals from the matrix is a vital step in revealing how cells modify the matrix in response to these signals.

In summary, a full understanding of how the body responds to an orthopaedic implant involves multiple lengths and timescales: the macro-scale (that of the whole bone or joint) and its physiological loads, the micro-scale (the level of cells, tissue microarchitecture and implant surface roughness) and the nanoscale (the level of proteins and individual molecules of the implant material). Associated timescales range from years (for tissue growth and remodelling, i.e. the clinical timescale), to hours (for fluid diffusion in musculoskeletal tissues), to seconds (for gait). It is these complexities that necessitate multiscale approaches to the study of orthopaedic implants, both from experimental and modelling perspectives. Macroscopic studies of orthopaedic implants, whether in vitro, in vivo or more recently in silico, have led to many advances in the development of orthopaedic implants to date, but without coupling a proposed implant design to the micro- and nanoscale processes which occur within the host tissue and at the implant–tissue interface, the macro-scale descriptions of tissue response remain phenomenological, so that proposed new designs (which may depart substantially from the existing designs upon which heuristic 'rules' have been developed) cannot be adequately assessed and refined. Similarly, a micro- or nanoscale biological or materials-based approach to implant characterisation can be successful only insofar as it is also cognisant of the macro-scale mechanics of the problem, since it is at this level that the overall forces and motions to which the construct is subjected are determined.

1.3 Micro- and Nanoscale Modelling in Orthopaedic Biomechanics

Having summarised the dominant top-down continuum mechanics paradigm which has been used in much orthopaedic biomechanics modelling to date and pointed out the rationale for multiscale biomechanical modelling in the musculoskeletal system, this section now provides a more detailed overview of existing models of passive musculoskeletal tissues at the micro- and nanoscales. The focus in Sects. 1.3.1–1.3.3 is on trabecular bone, which is chosen for three reasons: (i) because its highly porous and heterogeneous microstructure provides challenges to macro-scale continuum representations, (ii) because it has been intensively imaged and modelled at the micro-scale and (iii) because trabecular bone is a metabolically active tissue and high rates of cell-mediated remodelling at certain anatomical sites provide a good example of the challenges faced when incorporating biological activity into multiscale FE models. Multiscale models of collagenous tissues more generally are discussed in Sect. 1.3.4, including the models at the atomistic scale because they provide important insights into the macromolecular nano-mechanics underpinning musculoskeletal tissue load response.

1.3.1 Micro-scale Modelling of Trabecular Bone

Trabecular bone is the spongy, porous tissue which lies within whole bones, providing lightweight structural support, participating in calcium homeostasis and acting as a reservoir for bone marrow. Trabecular bone is metabolically active [41] and is the tissue at most risk of loss in postmenopausal osteoporosis. The role of trabecular bone loss in reducing overall bone stiffness and strength in osteoporosis has been extensively studied [42]. Although trabecular bone has been mechanically characterised in terms of its 'apparent-level' macroscopic constitutive behaviour (i.e. neglecting the porous microstructure, see Sect. 1.2.2), apparent level continuum representations of trabecular bone which are not informed by finer-scale models only provide limited insight into the deformation processes of interest because the underlying porous microstructure plays a key role in defining the deformation and damage mechanics of the tissue. Therefore modelling at the micro-scale is a necessity for understanding trabecular bone function. Once such models have been developed, they can, if desired, be used to upscale to macro-scale continuum representations. Harrigan et al. [43] suggested that the use of apparent-level continuum models for trabecular bone is suspect when close to an interface or in regions where stress gradients of more than 20–30 % occur across a distance of 3–5 trabeculae.

The importance of microstructure in trabecular bone mechanics is further reinforced by the limited correlation found clinically between radiographic measures of bone quantity and fracture risk in osteoporosis [44]. That is to say, it is not just the quantity of bone lost in osteoporosis that determines bone strength, but its microstructure, the level and type of pre-existing in vivo microdamage and the properties of the mineralised tissue itself. These factors have been collectively referred to as 'bone quality' (in contrast to bone quantity) [45]. In osteoporosis, the initially plate-like structure of healthy trabecular bone gradually changes to a rod-like structure during bone loss. In rod-like trabecular bone, longitudinally oriented 'trabeculae' or struts (oriented parallel to the principal physiological loading direction) act as columns in compression and are susceptible to buckling, and transverse struts act as tensile stabilisers and are susceptible to microfracture.

Given the importance of the porous microstructure, micro-scale FE modelling has been extensively used to explore the structural response of trabecular bone to load.[4] High-resolution imaging techniques, in particular micro-computed tomography, have played a key role in the development of micro-FE models of trabecular bone, because they allow image-based models of actual bone specimens to be generated, such as those shown in Fig. 1.3. With regard to material constitutive relations, note that because the microstructure is represented explicitly in micro-scale FE models, the material constitutive response is moved down a level relative to macro-scale models as described in Sect. 1.2.2, so that the constitutive relation now represents the 'tissue level', i.e. the mineralised bone matrix rather than the 'apparent level'.

Early image-based linear elastic micro-FE analyses of small regions of trabecular bone were performed with element sizes of several hundred microns in the mid-1990s [47,48]. By adjusting the tissue elastic modulus in the model so that the predicted specimen stiffness agreed with the experimentally measured specimen stiffness, tissue level elastic properties for trabecular bone could be inversely determined [49], and the resulting models correctly predicted the anisotropic elastic

[4]Micro-scale FE models of bone are sometimes described in the literature as 'high-resolution finite element models' (see, e.g. [46]).

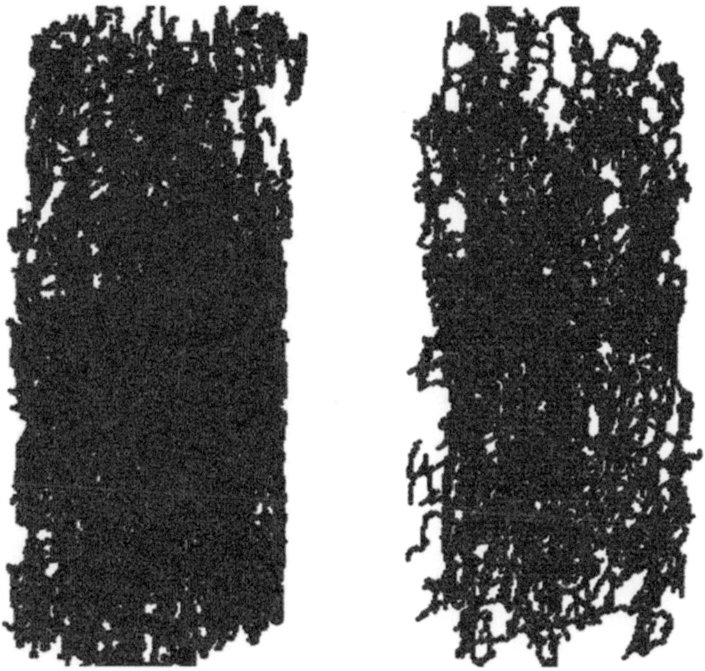

Fig. 1.3 Voxel-based FE meshes of cylindrical vertebral trabecular bone cores generated from micro-CT scans of (*left*) a 91-year-old male and (*right*) a 97-year-old female. Hexahedral element sizes are 100 × 100 × 100 μm. The 91-year-old model has approximately 135,000 elements, and the age 97 model has approximately 45,000 elements (From [128], used with permission)

behaviour of trabecular bone at the apparent level [50,51]. In order to predict strength as well as stiffness, isotropic (von Mises) yield criteria were then added to the micro-FE models [52,53]. In order to improve the prediction of apparent strength (which was limited by the assumption of isotropic yield), Niebur et al. [46] performed a 3D voxel-based FE study in which the material constitutive relation incorporated tensile-compressive yield strength asymmetry (0.61 % tensile and 1.01 % compressive yield strains, respectively). This tensile-compressive yield asymmetry allowed the microstructural FE models to capture apparent trabecular bone strength to 'an outstanding level of accuracy'.

Having established that apparent trabecular bone stiffness and strength could be accurately predicted using micro-FE models with relatively simple homogenous tissue properties, several groups then attempted to model the post-yield response of trabecular bone by incorporating material nonlinearity [54,55]. Stolken and Kinney [56] pointed out the need to include geometric nonlinearity in such solutions. Verhulp et al. [57] used voxel-based micro-FE models of 5.35-mm-diameter cylinders of bovine proximal tibia trabecular bone to simulate the post-yield compressive response and compared the simulation results with actual experiments up to 5 % apparent compressive strain. These simulations incorporated both material and geometric nonlinearity. The authors found that although element size effects were minimal, element type (linear vs. quadratic) and the material model used (bilinear elastic, elasto-plastic with isotropic Hill yield function, elasto-plastic with von Mises yield surface) both had significant effects. However, none of the three material models investigated provided satisfactory prediction of the experimentally observed post-yield strain softening. As an indication of the solution time required to perform these nonlinear simulations, a full analysis with 156,000 elements took 1.7 GB of memory and 14 h on a single processor. The authors estimated that running the same model with quadratic elements would require approximately 8 GB of memory and take 130–140 h on a single processor.

Numerous subsequent studies have utilised voxel-based micro-FE models to investigate different aspects of trabecular bone loading response, including models based on in vivo images of trabecular bone obtained using peripheral quantitative computed tomography (pQCT) [58]. A recent study by Vilayphiou et al. [59] demonstrated the use of pQCT-based micro-FE analysis in large groups of patients. Micro-FE-derived stiffness, stress and failure load of distal radius and tibia were assessed in 185 men with prevalent fragility fractures and compared to 185 age-, height- and weight-matched controls. The micro-FE-derived stiffness and failure load were found to be 8–9 % lower in the fracture group ($P < 0.01$), suggesting that microarchitecturally derived mechanical properties at anatomical sites which can be accessed using pQCT are relatively representative of bone properties at less accessible fracture sites. A recent multiscale study used homogenisation to determine apparent macro-scale (orthotropic) trabecular bone properties based on microstructure and isotropic elasticity at the micro-scale and then applied progressive meshing and a porosity-based modification of material properties to allow rapid model generation at intermediate scales [60]. Another recent multiscale study [61] used homogenisation together with stochastic incorporation of uncertainties in apatite crystal orientation and image-based modelling to derive distributions of trabecular bone stiffness at the apparent level from the underlying microstructure.

These studies suggest that by using two scales (micro and macro), both of which have scanning technologies available to derive the 3D geometry, the apparent level, quasi-static stiffness and strength of trabecular bone can be satisfactorily modelled. However, as mentioned above, current micro-FE models still do not adequately capture the post-yield softening response. Post-yield behaviour in trabecular bone is important not only because of its role in reducing apparent-level compressive load-bearing ability but also because cell-mediated bone remodelling is triggered in response to the formation of microcracks within the tissue. Therefore there is both a structural imperative and a biological imperative for studying the post-yield mechanics of trabecular bone.

It is now widely accepted that the primary role of bone remodelling is to repair microscopic cracks formed during physical loading before they can grow to a dangerous size [62]; therefore post-yield and continuum-to-discrete fracture mechanics in trabecular bone tissue are important in elucidating the remodelling response.

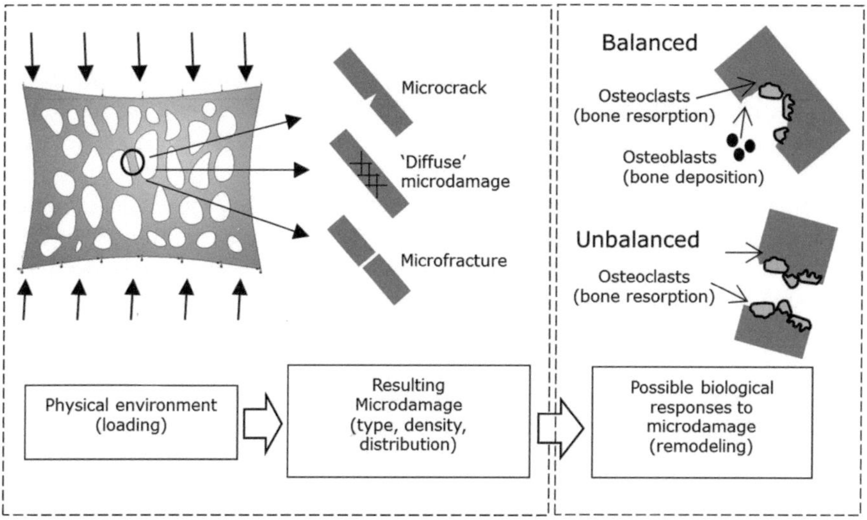

Fig. 1.4 The role of mechanically induced microdamage in the bone remodelling process. The remodelling response is dependent on the type of microdamage. Balanced remodelling maintains bone mass, while imbalance leads to bone loss. The *left dotted box* represents the mechanics of damage formation, while the *right dotted box* represents the biological response

Three[5] types of microcracks have been observed in trabecular bone: (i) discrete microcracks up to about 100 microns in length; (ii) ultra microcracks smaller than 1 micron, usually described as diffuse microdamage [63]; and (iii) trabecular microfractures, in which an entire trabecular strut is broken. Microcracks formed by physical loading activate the cellular remodelling response [64]. Microfractures can lead to aggressive resorption of the broken strut by osteoclasts because of the loss of strain signal within the disconnected trabecular strut [65,66]. This in turn reduces the integrity of the trabecular bone network [67,68]. Figure 1.4 shows the three types of microdamage schematically in vertebral trabecular bone and the possibility for either balanced (no net bone loss) or unbalanced (bone loss) cellular responses depending on the nature of the microdamage.

In order to model the onset of microdamage within trabecular bone under compression, Yeh and Keaveny [68] developed a 3D lattice beam FE model, again using asymmetrical tensile (0.67 %) and compressive (1.1 %) yield strains to explore microdamage formation under simulated compressive loading. Eighty percent of trabecular struts developed microdamage at 2 % apparent compressive strain. Nagaraja [69] used micro-CT and image-based FE of bovine tibial trabecular cores loaded in compression to register experimentally observed regions of microdamage with estimated microstructural stresses, strains and strain energy. Significant positive relationships between microdamage and estimated tissue stress and strain were found. Jungmann et al. [70] developed idealised (cylindrical) linear

[5]We note that several studies refer to four types of microcracks rather than three.

elastic FE models of a single trabecular strut undergoing three-point bending in order to correlate experimentally observed stress whitening (indicative of microscopic damage accumulation) with predicted local tissue strains. Predicted maximum tensile strain at the lower surface of the three-point bending sample ($\varepsilon_x^{max} = 0.03$ for 66μm mid-span displacement of a 2.5-mm long, 480-μm diameter strut with 2-mm support span) was around three times less than the value measured experimentally using digital image correlation ($\varepsilon_x^{max} = 0.09$), a discrepancy which the authors attributed to sample heterogeneity. Attempts to explicitly model crack formation in bone using cohesive zone FE methods have been made by Ural and Vashishth [71] for cortical bone and by Tomar [72] for trabecular bone, although we note that both of these models were limited to 2D with homogenous tissue properties. Rather than modelling cracks explicitly, other studies have incorporated damage mechanics (modulus reduction) approaches in 2D micro-FE models of trabecular bone [73,74]. Although the focus here is on trabecular bone, studies by Budyn [75] (using the extended finite element method, XFEM) and by Yang et al. [76] pointing out the need for nonlinear fracture models when modelling cracks in cortical bone are also noteworthy.

When considering the formation and growth of cracks in trabecular bone tissue from a mechanical modelling perspective, it is clear that the use of homogenous tissue properties in micro-FE models, although suitable for predicting apparent stiffness and strength, can only provide a simplified view of the plastic and crack formation processes occurring in the tissue. In actual bone tissue the variations in mineralisation, inter-lamellar cement lines and osteocyte lacunae which can all be clearly seen under the microscope will influence the mechanics of the tissue at the scale at which damage occurs. Several studies [77,78] have explored the biomechanical effects of mineral heterogeneity by comparing the predictions of homogenous and heterogeneous FE models of trabecular bone. In these studies, the models which included the observed gradient of mineralisation from centre to edges of a trabecular strut (by incorporating graded material properties) predicted substantially different stress distributions throughout the trabecular thickness compared to those assuming homogenous properties.

In addition to the formation of damage within trabecular tissue, FE models have also been used to study the cellular remodelling which occurs in bone's response to damage. A key question in bone remodelling is how bone cells sense extracellular matrix strain, and micro-FE modelling studies in this area necessarily bridge the micro- and nanoscales because osteocyte lacunae are in the order of 10 μm in size, whereas the fluid-filled canalicular processes which connect osteocyte lacunae are only a few hundred nanometres in diameter [79]. Several models have been developed to calculate the strain magnification which occurs between tissue level apparent strain and local matrix strains adjacent to an osteocyte lacuna which acts as a 'stress raiser' [80]. Deligianni and Apostolopoulos [81] used a four-scale FE analysis to conclude that strain amplification of matrix could account for local strains of 10,000με adjacent to osteocyte lacunae during apparent level tissue level strains of only 2,000 με.

Other models have been developed to explore the extent to which interstitial fluid flow driven by extracellular matrix deformation may be responsible for osteocyte mechanotransduction. The review articles by Knothe-Tate [79] and Jacobs et al. [82] provide the lists of models. It is important to keep in mind that until recently, there were few experimental studies quantifying flow within the lacuno-canalicular system (see [83] for a thorough overview), so that bone fluid flow models generally use idealised geometry, and have not usually been validated by comparison with experiments to date. We also note that the existing fluid flow models focus on osteonal bone with Haversian canals [84,85]; therefore fluid flow in the lacuno-canalicular system of trabecular bone (with its absence of Haversian canals) remains unexplored. Rémond et al. [86] modelled fluid flow within an idealised osteon and demonstrated that spatially varying permeability and elastic properties had a significant effect on model results. Cowin et al. [87] developed governing equations for fluid flow in the bone with hierarchical permeability using an analytical approach with idealised cylindrical geometries for the whole bone and for the osteon. This theoretical formulation provides a promising basis for multi-scale numerical modelling with more realistic anatomy, which highlights the importance of accounting for the vascular porosity in bone fluid flow models. Nguyen et al. [88] modelled the bone as a periodic osteonal structure with anisotropic elastic properties using frequency domain poroelastic finite element analysis. Lemaire et al. [89,90] developed a multiscale model of coupled electro-osmotic and osmotic diffusion in addition to Darcy flow occurring within the canalicular and collagen–apatite matrix porosity of the osteon. Upscaling was performed using periodic homogenisation. Given the uncertainties in many of the parameters required to generate such models, the same group [91] recently published a sensitivity study to identify key parameters for further analytical and experimental investigations. Verbruggen et al. [92] recently used fluid–structure interaction modelling with model geometry based on confocal imaging of actual osteocytes to investigate fluid velocities and shear stresses experienced by the cells during physiological loading. The model indicated that the greatest stimulation occurred in the region of the osteocytic cell processes and that these flows were in the range known to generate osteogenic responses by osteoblastic cells in vitro. Although the focus in this section is on micro-scale models, for completeness we note that poroelastic models of the bone have also been developed at the macro-scale, effectively smearing the effects of the lacuno-canalicular porosity into a continuum tissue permeability, in which the vascular permeability may either be modelled explicitly [93] or omitted due to the perceived primary importance of the lacuno-canalicular porosity [94].

With respect to the effect of microcracks on fluid flow in bone, Galley et al. [85] developed a 2D (non-coupled) fluid flow model and found that the presence of a fatigue microcrack in Haversian bone affected fluid velocities up to a distance of 150 μm from the crack. Nguyen et al. [95] used poroelastic models to determine that the presence of an interstitial crack could dramatically reduce fluid flow/pressure in neighbouring osteons.

Once cellular activity has been initiated, bone remodelling involves removal of damaged bone by osteoclasts, followed by deposition of new osteoid tissue by osteoblasts. The newly formed osteoid then mineralises over time. This subtractive and additive process changes the bone microstructure over time, and as already illustrated in Fig. 1.4, unbalanced remodelling can lead to net bone loss. Computational mechanics approaches have again been used to simulate both the end result of the remodelling process in trabecular bone and the process itself. In an early 2D model with idealised trabecular microstructure, Silva and Gibson [96] showed that when net bone loss occurs in osteoporosis, loss of a few struts had a much more important effect than thinning of many struts in terms of reducing the apparent stiffness and strength of trabecular bone. Langton et al. [97] incorporated stochastic bone remodelling in a 2D micro-FE of trabecular bone remodelling, observing simulated trabecular perforation. The same authors used a similar approach to simulate anabolic treatment following various degrees of bone resorption [98]. Another example of stochastic remodelling simulation was done by Huiskes et al. [99,100], in which 2D models of small regions of trabecular bone were simulated and elements in the model were assigned a relative bone density between 0.01 (no bone) and 1.0 (fully mineralised). Strain energy density (SED) rate was used as the mechanical stimulus driving remodelling, such that mineralisation was reduced in the elements with low SED rate and increased in regions with high SED rate. The resulting simulations of metabolic activity demonstrated qualitatively plausible adaptation of trabecular orientation to altered loading direction and increases or decreases in bone mass which were approximately proportional to the amount of increased or decreased loading, respectively. The approach was later extended to 3D simulations [101]. In subsequent studies by the same group [102,103], the 2D modelling approach was extended to incorporate damage accumulation, as well as modelling the action of individual osteoclasts and the ability of osteoclasts to both deposit new bone and act as bone lining cells. These more recent simulations suggested that cell-mediated remodelling is beneficial under moderate fatigue, but has a detrimental effect under intense fatigue because resorption cavities create more damage than they remove. Again using the concept of trabecular bone as an optimised structure, Chen et al. [104] adopted the evolutionary structural optimisation algorithm to predict bone remodelling around an implant.

Several authors have based their remodelling simulations on micro-CT data of actual trabecular bone samples. Van der linden et al. [105] performed 3D simulation of age-related trabecular remodelling based on the micro-CT scans of human vertebral trabecular bone specimens. Remodelling parameters were based on biological data, including partial refilling of resorption cavities to simulate age-related imbalances in bone metabolism. The predicted bone loss rates varied between 0.3 and 1.1 % per year. Hernandez et al. [106] studied the effect of resorption cavities on bone strength by adding idealised resorption cavities to image-based micro-FE models of trabecular bone. Cavities added in the regions of high strain (targeted remodelling) caused significantly greater decreases in bone stiffness and strength than when resorption cavities were randomly located (nontargeted remodelling).

Smit and Burger [107] investigated the strain distributions in the immediate vicinity of remodelling cavities using micro-FE models. A secondary osteon in cortical bone was idealised as a 700-μm diameter cylinder with a 200-μm diameter tunnel, while a Howship lacuna in trabecular bone was modelled as a 200-μm diameter pit in a single cylindrical trabecula of diameter 200 μm. The FE results showed that reduced strains occur in front of the osteonal tunnel tip (where osteoclasts are active), and elevated strains occur at the flanks of the tunnel behind the tip (where osteoblasts are active). For the trabecular model, high strains were found at the base and transverse border of the lacunar cavity (which would inhibit further osteoclast activity), whereas lower strains were found on the surface of the trabeculae. The authors concluded that strain fields within the tissue could be related to osteoclast and osteoblast remodelling activity.

McNamara et al. [108,109] used a 2D poroelastic FE model of an axially loaded trabecular strut containing a resorption cavity to simulate remodelling in response to both strain and damage stimuli. The simulation results showed that there was a critical resorption pit depth beyond which remodelling was incapable of refilling the cavity; therefore trabecular perforation occurred. The authors concluded that a system which can respond to either strain or microdamage, but which prioritises removal of damaged bone after a damage threshold is reached, was the only process which provided plausible remodelling predictions. A subsequent study [110] suggested that a rule governing osteoblast attachment was required to produce realistic remodelling cycles.

Ryser et al. [111] developed a 2D spatiotemporal simulation of microfracture remodelling in the bone, incorporating mathematical descriptions of biochemical regulation of cellular activity through OPG and RANKL signaling. This model shows a different approach to remodelling simulation, since it is entirely biochemical and cell based, with no consideration of the mechanics of the bone matrix being modelled. The study also demonstrates the difficulties in parameter estimation for even relatively idealised models, since 21 separate model parameters had to be estimated.

Adachi et al. [112] developed a 2D plane strain poroelastic FE model of a single trabecula which incorporated fluid flow-induced shear stresses acting on the osteocyte mechanosensory system as a remodelling stimulus. They suggested that the simulated trabecular orientation coincided with in vivo observations of trabecular remodelling. Gerhard et al. [113] provided a useful and relatively more recent overview of bone remodelling simulations. Hambli et al. [114–116] used a novel approach combining FE simulation with neural network computation to link the macro- and micro-scale mechanics of damage accumulation and repair in trabecular bone. Neural networks were trained based on the result of voxel-based micro-FE simulations, and macro-scale continuum mechanical properties were updated based on the neural network computations.

The above-mentioned work on microcracks in bone and the subsequent remodelling response provided valuable insight into normal bone physiology in its own right. However, it is also clearly relevant to orthopaedics because implant insertion causes a sudden change in the biomechanical environment of the bone in the vicinity of the implant, and an intensive remodelling response then follows. Some regions of the bone are overloaded by the implant, and other regions are 'stress shielded' due to the presence of a stiff structure. In a recent micro-FE study of trabecular bone response to an orthopaedic implant, Mann and Miller [117] modelled an idealised trabecula interdigitated with a mass of bone cement and performed fluid–structure analysis of the flow conditions at the bone–cement interface under load. The analysis suggested that supra-physiologic fluid velocities and shear stresses could occur in thin spaces between bone and implant and that these unnatural flow conditions could be responsible for osteolysis (bone resorption at the interface with implants). Although beyond the remit of this discussion, we note that a relevant body of micro-scale modelling work, including detailed bone remodelling simulation, has also been performed in the field of dental biomechanics to study implant osseointegration.

In summary, micro-FE models have been used to explore how the apparent stiffness and strength of trabecular bone are related to its porous microstructure, attempting to simulate damage and post-yield deformation of trabecular bone, to explore crack formation and mechanisms of mechanotransduction in bone and to simulate bone remodelling. There is recognition that tissue heterogeneity is important in post-yield damage processes, but there has been very limited incorporation of heterogeneity in micro-FE models to date. The need for better understanding of damage processes therefore provides an incentive to develop models with element sizes in the order of a few microns to better capture tissue level heterogeneity. We note that although these would still be micro-scale FE models, such models would be 1–2 orders of magnitude finer than the ~100-μm voxel-based element sizes which are now routinely derived from micro-CT scans. The use of nanoindentation to provide local tissue properties for such models is discussed in Sect. 1.3.3. With regard to the link between the micro and macro-scales, there has been limited upscaling between micro- and macro-scale FE models of trabecular bone to date [60,118]. Because of the wide variations in trabecular bone porosity and microstructure which occur even within the same anatomical site, there is limited benefit in building a micro-FE model of a single small region of bone and then upscaling the resulting properties for use in macro-scale continuum models. However, because micro-CT scanners now allow high-resolution imaging of large (~100 mm) regions of bone, it should be possible to perform nonlinear micro-FE analyses in small regions of bone and then upscale these to accurately define heterogeneous apparent tissue properties at the macro-scale, so that whole implant–tissue interactions can be studied. Such studies, although computationally challenging, would provide valuable insight into the response of trabecular bone to orthopaedic implants taking both micro- and macro-scale deformation response of the implant and surrounding bone into account.

1.3.2 Microbeam Models of Trabecular Bone Applied to Vertebroplasty Simulation

Although micro-CT and peripheral quantitative CT scanners now allow routine non-destructive imaging of large regions of bone at the micro-scale, voxel-based FE modelling from these scans is still severely constrained with regard to computational power, especially when nonlinear material and geometric or contact effects are to be included in the analysis. One way to model large regions of trabecular bone at the micro-scale is to represent the struts and plates of the tissue using beam and shell elements rather than continuum solid elements [119]. This maintains a level of (idealised) microstructural representation while greatly reducing the number of degrees of freedom of the problem compared to continuum analysis. Here we describe the application of one such approach to investigate the compressive loading response of osteoporotic vertebrae to a poly(methyl methacrylate) (bone cement) augmentation process known as vertebroplasty. The work described here is based on a doctoral thesis performed within the author's group and extends the approach reported in [120] to the case of modelling a vertebroplasty intervention. Briefly, a perturbed hexagonal lattice of microbeam elements is used to represent the trabecular bone microstructure. A perturbation factor is used to randomly displace lattice junctions from their regular positions, and several previous studies have suggested that a perturbation factor of 0.3 is appropriate for representing rod-like trabecular bone [121,122].

By using average trabecular microstructural indices obtained from micro-CT scan post-processing (bone volume-to-total volume ratio, strut thickness, strut spacing, degree of anisotropy, structure modal index and others [123,124]) to define microbeam diameter, length and spacing, the microstructural parameters of the microbeam model can be prescribed to represent a particular specimen, even though the locations and dimensions of individual struts are not being reproduced exactly. For example, Fig 1.5 shows microbeam meshes based on microstructural parameters for three age groups of patients based on microstructural indices reported in Mosekilde [125].

The use of microbeam models under simulated compressive loading immediately highlights the importance of strut bending and buckling mechanisms in osteoporotic trabecular bone [126]. For dense, healthy bone, the predominant compressive failure mode is plastic collapse [127], whereas for osteoporotic bone with more slender struts, elastic buckling plays a more significant role. Since the slenderness ratio and degree of end support of the struts in trabecular bone can vary widely, it is

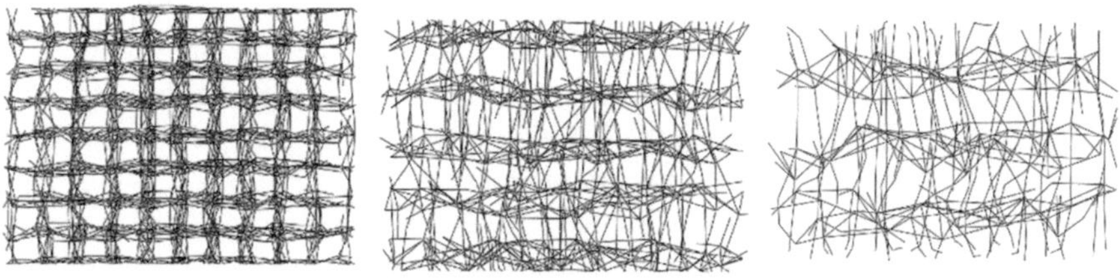

Fig. 1.5 Microbeam models of trabecular bone (age < 50, age 50–75 and age > 75) based on the microstructural indices from Mosekilde et al. [125]. The perturbation factor is 0.3 in all the cases, but the age < 75 model appears more perturbed because of its increased strut spacing (From [128], used with permission)

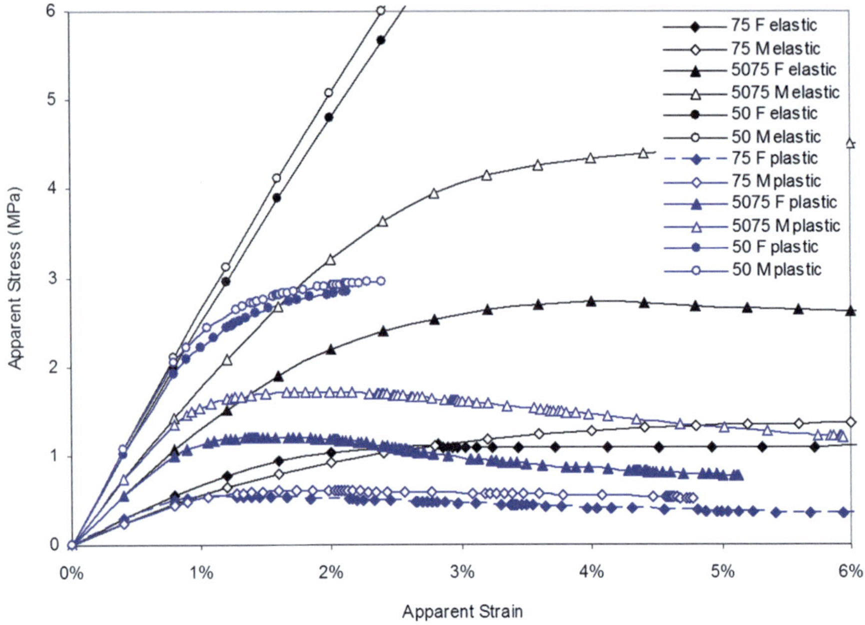

Fig. 1.6 Microbeam FE models of cylindrical cores of trabecular bone under uniaxial compression for differing age and gender (F/M) groups based on microstructure from Mosekilde et al. [125]; age less than 50 years, age 50–75 years and age greater than 75 years. For each core, both elastic only ($E = 8GPa$, $\nu = 0.3$) and elastic–perfectly plastic analyses were performed ($E = 8GPa$, $\nu = 0.3$, $\sigma_y = 0.8\,\%$). Note that even for the elastic analyses, strong nonlinearity is introduced at the apparent level due to strut buckling (From [128], used with permission)

important that microbeam models are able to capture both elastic and plastic buckling modes accurately. Mesh- and element-type sensitivity analysis showed that the use of two quadratic elements per strut was sufficient to capture experimentally observed elastic–plastic and/or analytical (Euler) buckling behaviour with a mean error of 8 % [128]. The graph in Fig. 1.6 shows apparent compressive stress vs. strain results for microbeam simulations of a 7-mm-diameter cylindrical core of trabecular bone, in which either isotropic linear elastic ($E = 8GPa$, $\nu = 0.3$) or elastic perfectly plastic material behaviour was modelled ($E = 8GPa$, $\nu = 0.3$, $\varepsilon_y = 0.8\,\%$) using the age < 50, age 50–75 and age > 75 microstructures illustrated above. In addition to the loss of load-bearing capacity in vertebral trabecular bone with age, the key point with regard to Fig. 1.6 is that even for purely elastic material constitutive behaviour, elastic buckling of microbeams introduces a strong geometric nonlinearity in the compressive loading response at the apparent (macro) level.

Having established a suitable meshing and solution strategy for capturing elastic and plastic buckling mechanisms in trabecular bone, the microbeam representation was then used to mesh large regions of trabecular bone and integrated with shell element representations of the cortical shell of the anterior vertebral body. Figure 1.7 shows a mesh of an L3 osteoporotic vertebral body with dimensions based

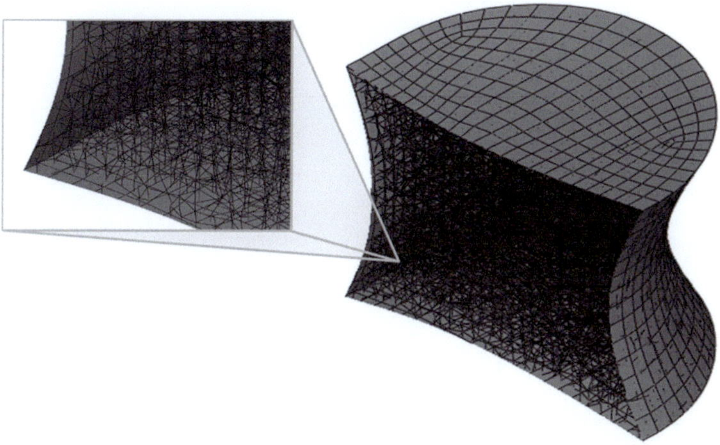

Fig. 1.7 Sectioned view of an idealised L3 lumbar vertebra with trabecular microstructure from Mosekilde et al. [125] with an age > 75 female. Overall vertebral body dimensions from Mizrahi et al. [129] with cortical shell thickness of 200 μm (From [128], used with permission)

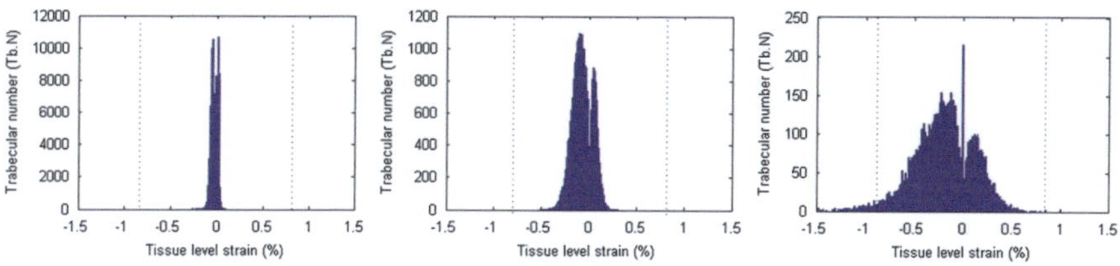

Fig. 1.8 Result histograms showing the distribution of predicted principal strain (-ve compressive, +ve tensile) in all struts of L3 vertebra microbeam FE models for (*left*) healthy, (*centre*) mildly osteoporotic and (*right*) severely osteoporotic L3 vertebral bodies (From [128], used with permission)

on [129], where the vertebral cortical shell has been meshed using four-node shell elements and the inner trabecular core is meshed using the microbeam approach. The cortical shell and trabecular core are connected using tied constraints in the FE model.

Because of the large number of beam elements in the model, it is convenient to report the stress and strain state within the trabecular centrum (under compressive loading) statistically using histograms such as those shown in Fig 1.8. In Fig 1.8, the trabecular microstructure has been altered to represent increasingly severe osteoporosis. The progression of osteoporosis shifts the strain distribution from a relatively optimised structure where all struts are similarly loaded to a more uneven distribution. Struts with zero principal strain are generally those attached to and shielded by the vertebral cortical shell.

The microbeam vertebral body FE model was then used to investigate the biomechanics of a surgical procedure known as vertebroplasty, in which polymethyl

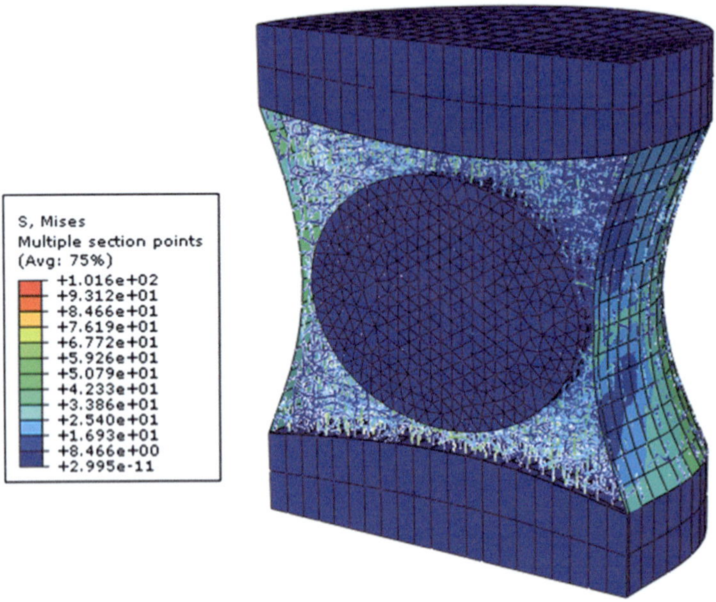

Fig. 1.9 Contour plot of predicted von Mises stress (MPa) in an age 78 T11 vertebroplasty model with microbeam trabecular bone architecture, shell elements representing the cortical shell and spherical cement inclusion (From [128], used with permission)

methacrylate bone cement is injected into the vertebral body in an attempt to stabilise and/or restore the height to an osteoporotic vertebra. Figure 1.9 shows a contour plot of predicted von Mises stresses within the trabecular microbeam network of an osteoporotic vertebra with an embedded sphere of bone cement.

By performing simulations with different volumes of vertebroplasty cement, it was possible to demonstrate that the percentage of trabecular struts that exceeded tissue level yield strain of 0.8 % during a physiological compressive load on the vertebra increased as the volume of bone cement increased. For example, the model predicted that yield occurred in 3.6 % of the struts under physiological compressive load with a 2-ml volume of cement, where for a 6-ml volume of cement the percentage of struts yielding increased to 8.5 %. Therefore, for the same compressive loading, more microdamage and more subsequent bone remodelling activity would be expected with greater volumes of cement. The microbeam models of vertebrae described above are 'multiscale' in the sense that they represent two levels of the bone structural hierarchy (microstructure and macrostructure) in one model, which differentiates them from the purely 'microstructural' FE models described in Sect. 1.3.1 where a small region of trabecular bone of simplified geometry (usually a cylinder or cube) was modelled. However, they are not multiscale in the sense of requiring separately solved models at different scales and information passing between the scales.

1.3.3 Nano-mechanical Modelling of Trabecular Bone Post-yield Mechanics

Micromechanical models of trabecular bone such as those discussed in Sects. 1.3.1 and 1.3.2 still use continuum mechanics representations of the 'tissue', except that the definition of 'tissue' from the perspective of material constitutive relations has now been pushed down a scale compared to the macro-scale models. In micro-FE models the voxel-based element dimensions may be only a few tens of microns, but the tissue is still assumed to be a homogenous continuum for the prescription of constitutive relations. One troublesome issue with the voxel-based micro-FE models discussed in Sect. 1.3.1 is that the elastic modulus required in the models to match experimentally measured overall compressive stiffness tends to be much lower than direct experimental measurements of bone tissue elastic modulus. For example, Chevalier et al. [130] found that elastic moduli derived from voxel-based FE models exhibited 'surprisingly low values when compared to nanoindentation results'. This discrepancy, together with the difficulty in accurately modelling trabecular bone post-yield response mentioned earlier, hints at the fact that characterising micro-scale and nanoscale heterogeneity in bone tissue properties is important for understanding all aspects of the loading response.

Nanoindentation has emerged as an important experimental tool to probe the deformation response of bone at the nanoscale and, when combined with FE modelling, can provide insights into the tissue-level response at submicron scales. Here we discuss the use of FE models of bone nanoindentation to inform the development of elasto-plastic constitutive relations for bone tissue at scales small enough to study heterogeneity due to lamellar structure and varying mineralisation levels. The principle of nanoindentation is simple; an indenter tip with dimensions in the order of several hundred nanometres is pushed into the material to be measured with a known force. The force versus tip displacement profile is measured during both the loading and unloading phases of the indentation. By using the load–displacement curve and knowing in advance the geometry of the indenter tip, material properties such as elastic modulus (E) and hardness (H) can be obtained.

Nanoindentation has been used to measure bone modulus and hardness in a large number of experimental studies. However, nanoindentation has the potential to provide further valuable information on the post-yield mechanics of bone tissue at the nanoscale [131]. Firstly, by modelling the nanoindentation process using nanoscale continuum FE models and using an atomic force microscope (AFM) to measure the shape of the residual indent left after indenter removal, model predictions can be assessed directly against AFM measurements with regard to the amount of elastic recovery of the tissue after indenter removal and with respect to the presence or absence of phenomena such as 'pile up' or 'sink in' adjacent to the indenter flank (Fig. 1.10). Secondly, by modelling time-dependent effects during indentation (creep under constant load and relaxation under constant displacement), material properties governing viscous and poroelastic [132] behaviour at the nanoscale can again be inversely estimated by comparison of model predictions with

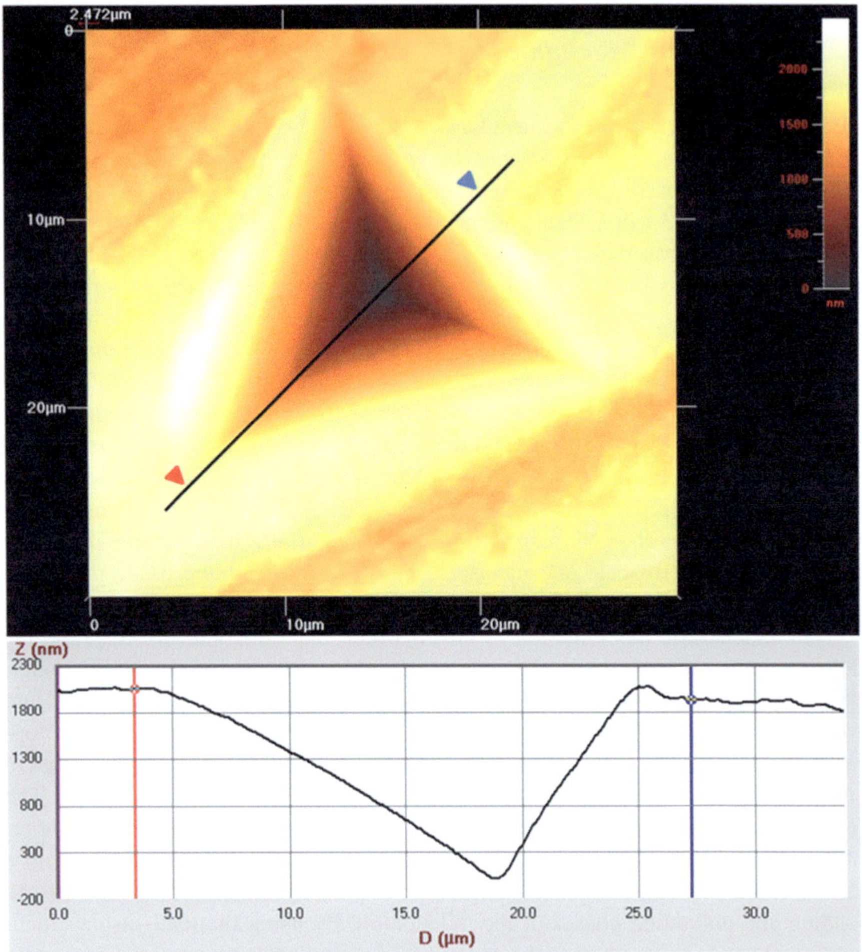

Fig. 1.10 Atomic force microscope image of the impression left by a Berkovich indenter on a sample of trabecular bone. The line profile beneath the image shows a cross section through the indent (z-axis in nm, y-axis in µm), showing a small degree of pile up to the right of the indent in this case (From [131], used with permission)

experimental results. Thirdly, because nanoindentation is highly localised, the material composition at the indent site (e.g. the degree of mineralisation of bone tissue as measured by quantitative back-scattered electron imaging, qBEI) can be imaged and correlated with the mechanical properties measured using indentation [133].

A number of authors have developed FE models of bone nanoindentation [134–146] and explored the effect of various elasto-plastic constitutive relations on the predicted force and deformation response. Wang et al. [136] identified material parameters for a Mohr–Coulomb material model of canine vertebral trabecular bone following bisphosphonate therapy. Mullins et al. [137] reported an extended Drucker–Prager model which can more accurately predict deformation and load–displacement response than a von Mises yield surface. A recent model by the author [147] pointed out that including friction between the bone and indenter could strongly affect predictions of pile up adjacent to the indenter. Carnelli et al. [141,144] used constitutive models with anisotropic elasticity and anisotropic plasticity (tensile-compressive yield asymmetry) to simulate nanoindentation of cortical bone. Schwiedrzik et al. [148] developed and applied a general anisotropic quadric yield criterion to model nanoindentation of lamellar bone.

Figure 1.11 shows the contours of maximum (most tensile) and minimum (most compressive) logarithmic principal strains in the FE model of nanoindentation developed by the author [147]. The model used in this case was a 2D axisymmetric representation of a spheroconical indenter with tip radius 600 nm and tip angle 90°. The material constitutive model in this case was based on the values used by Mullins et al. [137] (isotropic linear elasticity $E = 13.56$GPa, $\nu = 0.3$ with a Drucker–Prager yield surface, cohesion 122 MPa and friction angle 46°). At the instant shown in the figure, the indenter penetration into the material is 0.63 μm, and it can be seen from the contour plots that the maximum (tensile) principal strains are slightly below 20 %, while the minimum (compressive) principal strains reach nearly 80 %. This figure demonstrates that the nanoindentation experiments together with tightly integrated modelling are able to probe bone tissue mechanical response well into the post-yield region. Although the strain states in the tissue cannot be directly extracted from the experimental data, the tissue stress and strain state can be inferred by modelling the indentation process. We envisage that future combined modelling–experimental studies using a range of different tip types (including cube corner tips designed to induce cracks in the tissue) will further elucidate the elasto-plastic constitutive response of bone tissue at the

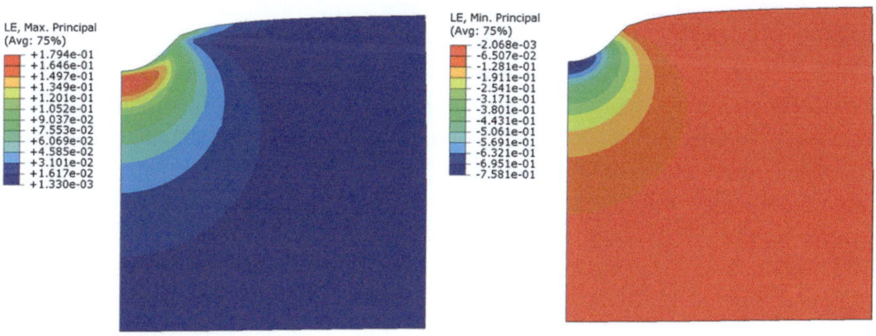

Fig. 1.11 Contours of (*left*) the maximum and (*right*) minimum (logarithmic) principal strains in the axisymmetric FE models of bone nanoindentation for an indenter vertical displacement of 0.63 μm. Note that only a subsection of the total mesh is shown for visualisation purposes so that the lower boundaries appear tilted

nanoscale [148]. Furthermore, imaging of the mineral and organic matrix composition at the indent site will allow nanoindentation-based constitutive properties to be correlated with tissue composition, providing a basis for models which incorporate heterogeneity of both elastic and inelastic constitutive responses at the micro-scale.

Bone modelling at the nanoscale also covers bone response to loading at the level of interactions between the organic matrix and plate-like apatite crystals with dimensions in the order of 2–100 nm [149]. Various collagen–apatite models have been developed to explore the mechanics of this interaction and how it confers higher level stiffness and strength. To date, given the paucity of experimental data, such models have tended to assume simple stiffness properties and idealised geometry for the mineral and organic phases [150–153]. Only one atomistic simulation of mineralised collagen in the bone has been published to date [154], which suggested that mineral crystals bear up to four times more stress than the collagen fibrils. With respect to the dynamics of bone–implant interactions at the nanoscale, Ganazzoli and Raffaini [155,156] and De Nardo et al. [157] describe atomistic and coarse-grained molecular dynamics simulations of protein absorption onto the surfaces of implant biomaterials.

1.3.4 Multiscale Models of Non-mineralised Tissues

Orthopaedic implants are usually anchored to bone; however, joint function and stability also depend on the mechanical response of ligaments and cartilage. Compared to the amount of modelling work on bone, there have been relatively fewer micro-scale modelling studies on non-mineralised musculoskeletal tissues to date. One limiting factor is the ability to perform the 3D high-resolution imaging across large regions of non-mineralised tissue which is necessary for image-based micro-FE modelling (to be discussed further in Sect. 1.4.1). Shim et al. [158] used a micro-FE model of the bone–cartilage interface to explore the initiation of osteoarthritis, in which a macro-model was used to derive input strains to a micro-model, which in turn drove a set of ordinary differential equations governing cellular remodelling activity, which in turn altered matrix structure. The model was run iteratively in this fashion to simulate three months of loading and remodelling. Further, a cartilage damage prediction model linked peak cartilage strains to pro-inflammatory response. Lavagnino et al. [159] developed a multiscale FE tendon model to explore the role of fluid flow-induced shear stresses and ECM-induced cell deformation in governing the cellular remodelling response. Hadi and Barocas [160] developed a multiscale FE model consisting of stochastically generated networks of type I collagen fibres to study damage and failure in collagen gel tissue analogues. Reese et al. [161] developed a micromechanical FE model to study force transfer across scales in a collagen gel containing extruded collagen fibres under tension. The results showed strong heterogeneity at the micro-scale due to size and boundary effects, and the authors concluded that traditional continuum assumptions were not valid for describing the macro-scale load–deformation response. We note that 1D (mathematical rather than finite element) multiscale models of the tendon have also recently been developed, with a two-step homogenisation technique being used to bridge between the scales [162,163]. Gronau et al. [164] reviewed multiscale approaches to the design of biopolymers (elastin, silk and collagen), finding that although there are difficulties in relating the disparate length and timescales of relevance, bottom-up multiscale approaches integrating both experiment and computational modelling offer much promise in biomaterial design.

In order to better understand the molecular basis of the load–deformation response in collagenous tissues, atomistic simulations of triple-helical tropocollagen molecules have also been performed [165–168]. Models at the molecular scale have been successful in elucidating the mechanisms which confer extensibility, strain hardening and toughness at the fibril scale through twisting, stretching and uncoiling of individual molecules. Having said this, it is challenging to contemplate bridging between nano- and micro-scales because of the limitations on nano (molecular)-scale imaging in 3D across microns of tissue.

1.4 Future Directions for Multiscale Modelling in Orthopaedics

1.4.1 Serial Milling and Block Face Imaging Techniques

Micro-scale models of musculoskeletal tissues require 3D imaging modalities which can accurately characterise structure at these scales. As already mentioned, micro-CT scanners now allow resolutions of a few microns to be achieved with large (~100 mm) bone specimens. However, micro-CT relies on X-ray attenuation by the mineral phase of bone to provide contrast and therefore is not capable of imaging non-mineralised tissues in their native state. One possible solution for micro-CT imaging of non-mineralised musculoskeletal tissues is the use of osmium tetroxide (OsO_4) as a radiographic contrast agent [169]; however, OsO_4 is highly poisonous. Another possibility for soft tissue imaging at the micro-scale is micro-MRI, which can achieve resolutions of 30 microns, i.e. sufficient to image the upper end of tissue microstructure. However, scan times at this resolution are in the order of 30 h, and the cost of such scanners is prohibitive [169]. Higher resolutions (~200 nm) are possible with 3D light microscopy techniques such as laser scanning confocal microscopy and multiphoton microscopy. However, these techniques can only image small volumes of tissue sample in a single field of view. More importantly, the penetration depth of these modalities into tissues is limited to ~100 μm for the confocal microscope and ~1 mm for two-photon microscopy. Optical coherence tomography (OCT) allows 3D imaging with resolutions less than 10 μm, but again the penetration depth is limited to a few millimetres. Therefore imaging intact microstructure deep within a musculoskeletal soft tissue is not readily achievable at present.

The field of view of an imaging modality relative to its resolution is an important issue in musculoskeletal imaging for model generation, because the tissues are not generally self-similar, and therefore it is not sufficient to image a small region of the structure at high resolution and assume that this is representative of the entire structure. Therefore imaging modalities are required which can image large (several centimetre) regions of tissue at high resolution.

One such technique, which is not limited to solely imaging mineralised tissues, is serial sectioning and block face imaging. The technique is conceptually simple; the structure to be imaged is embedded in a rigid block, and one surface of the block is either sliced or milled away layer by layer, using a microscope with a motorised stage to perform multi-pass imaging of each successive block face. The grid of microscope images taken on a particular block face slice can be stitched together using image post-processing software to form one large image of each block face, and the series of block face images with known separation forms a 3D z-stack. The advantage of the technique is that it allows high-resolution imaging for large regions of tissue, effectively decoupling resolution from specimen size [170]. Also, both soft and mineralised tissues can be imaged together, including tissues with implants when using appropriate milling cutters. The technique is also flexible in regard to which various stains and microscopy modalities (white light, polarised light, fluorescence, even spectroscopy) can be used to obtain the desired specimen contrast. The resolution of the technique is limited by the microscope used to perform the block face imaging and by the mechanical resolution of the sectioning/milling tool used to cut the block face together with the cutting properties of the embedding medium. The limitations of the technique are that it is destructive and that the imaging is performed on the block face so that reflected incident (rather than transmitted) light microscopy must be performed. Also, opacifier must be added to the embedding medium to prevent light reflection or fluorescence from subsurface structures from reducing image contrast. We note that previous authors have developed similar systems to examine both bone and non-mineralised tissues, particularly in the field of embryology and developmental biology (e.g. [171–175]). As pointed out by Viceconti [176], serial sectioning techniques fell into relative disuse for bone imaging following the development of desktop micro-CT scanners, but for the reasons given above, they have continuing potential for imaging musculoskeletal soft tissues and joints, where both cells and matrix can be imaged and used as a basis for micro-FE modelling.

Here we briefly describe a custom-designed serial milling and block face imaging system developed by the author in order to allow high-resolution 3D imaging of the intervertebral disc for use in multiscale biomechanical models of healthy and degenerative intervertebral discs. The focus here is on the capability of the imaging technique to enable high-resolution mapping of the entire anatomical structures rather than on the subsequent modelling, which is a work in progress.

The system comprised a Proxxon MF70 micro-miller (Proxxon, Germany) which was converted to computer numerical control (CNC) through the addition of stepper motors on all three axes. A digital microscope with inbuilt reflected white light illumination and adjustable polarisation was mounted to the head of the mill. Custom code was written to control the mill and microscope camera, in order to perform a milling and imaging sequence in which each milling pass was followed by multiple microscope images of the resulting block face, which were later stitched together to produce a single high-resolution image of the entire milled surface. Milling was performed using 3-mm-diameter, two-flute tungsten carbide end mills (Kyocera Corporation, Kyoto, Japan) at a feed per tooth of approximately 1–2 μm. By using a new end mill for each specimen, a surface finish in the order of 5 μm can be achieved, which is less than the depth of field of the microscope. Vacuum and compressed air were used during milling to safely collect dust and particles of embedding resin and organic matter and to clear milling debris from the block face prior to imaging.

The resolution of the image dataset in the z-direction is controlled by the depth of each milling pass and was typically 10–20 μm. The resolution in the x–y plane was controlled by the microscope camera which had a maximum 5MP resolution (2592 × 1944 pixels) at 240× magnification, corresponding to 0.66-μm minimum pixel size. Since the technique produces very large datasets, images were often taken at a lower in-plane resolution. When imaging a block face, each microscope image was taken with approximately 100-μm overlap with the boundaries of the neighbouring images, in order to facilitate more accurate stitching of the reconstructed image during post-analysis (ImageJ software, version 1.47b, National Institutes of Health, USA). Background correction was also performed using ImageJ in order to correct for nonuniformities in illumination by the microscope light source. Other than the image stitching and background correction, no post-alteration or digital enhancement of the raw microscope images was performed.

Figure 1.12 shows a resulting single block face image of a bovine tail intervertebral disc in the sagittal plane. The stitched image is comprised of 15 × 17 = 255 reflected polarised light microscope images, covering a total disc cross section of 25.6 × 16.6 mm with 1.5-μm resolution. The full image size is 15823 × 10727 pixels. In this specimen a small (<0.1 %) amount of Sudan black opacifier was added to the epoxy embedding media. Other than that, the tissue is unstained.

The ability to image microstructure in 3D through an entire disc using a technique such as this forms a basis for multiscale model generation. Clearly it is not possible in this situation to simply convert voxels to finite elements due to computing power constraints; however, using combined imaging modalities, it should be possible to obtain the necessary contrast between tissue types to segment the collagen and elastic fibre networks in the annulus fibrous of the disc, the bony and cartilaginous endplates and the proteoglycan-rich nucleus pulposus and thereby to generate microstructural models of the disc based on actual (rather than idealised) specimen anatomy. As an example of the ability to differentiate between tissue types using multimodal block face imaging, the strongly reflecting fibrous network in the annulus fibrous (outer region) of the disc shown in Fig. 1.12 is the elastic fibre network, since the amorphous molecular structure of elastic tissue is a strong

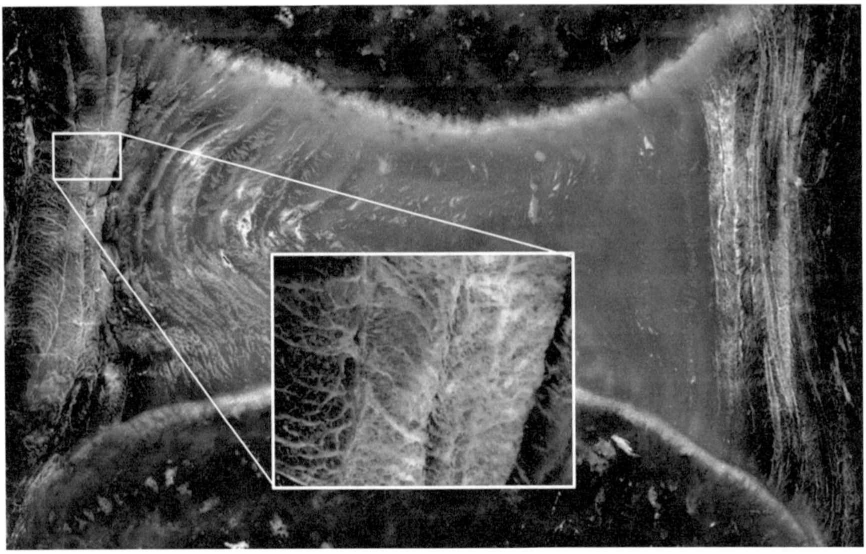

Fig. 1.12 High-resolution block face reflected polarised light image of bovine tail intervertebral disc

diffuse reflector. However, by performing complementary fluorescent block face imaging on the same block face (not shown here), it is possible to see more detail of the collagen fibre bundles in the annulus, since collagen and elastin fluoresce at similar intensities under the 365-nm excitation used for the fluorescence imaging used in our pilot work to date.

In principle therefore, the 3D morphologies of the collagen and elastic fibre networks could be defined and biomechanically modelled, either by physically embedding networks of beam elements within a 'macro-scale' representation of the proteoglycan-rich disc ground substance or by homogenisation of subregions of the image dataset. Clearly there are challenges with attempts to develop image-based microstructural models such as these: fibres smaller than the imaging resolution will not be visible; it will not be possible to know whether touching fibres are physically joined or just touching, and tissue processing during embedding may alter the microstructure from its native state. Notwithstanding, the potential of such approaches to improve our biomechanical understanding of non-mineralised fibrous tissues by coupling the micro- and macro-scales is significant.

1.4.2 Modelling Cells Within the Cellular Microenvironment

As mentioned above, the response of cells within musculoskeletal tissues is crucial to understanding disease states and the effect of orthopaedic treatments. Although the cells themselves in musculoskeletal tissues do not contribute appreciably to the short-term load–deformation response of the extracellular matrix, their importance lies in their ability to modify the ECM in response to physicochemical cues throughout the lifespan. The common theme underlying the studies discussed in Sect. 1.3.1 was that they came from the perspective of matrix mechanics, i.e. they were concerned with modelling strains, cracks, fluid pressures and velocities within the ECM from a biomechanics perspective. The models that attempted to include bone remodelling also used a matrix-centred approach, incorporating phenomenological descriptions of matrix alteration according to various candidate stimuli in the ECM such as strain energy density or fluid flow. However, several recent attempts to explicitly model cell behaviour within the ECM microenvironment have been made. Fernandez et al. [177] coupled synchrotron-based micro-FE and smoothed particle hydrodynamics models (2-μm voxel size) with cell models from the CellML repository. The cells were not modelled mechanically in the spatio-temporal framework of the ECM model, but outputs from the ECM mechanical model drive biochemical ODE-based models of cell response via the RANK–RANKL–OPG pathway, which in turn drives remodelling of the matrix. Thus cell and matrix behaviour were coupled in both directions. The previously mentioned study by Verbruggen et al. [92] explicitly modelled osteocytes and their cellular processes subject to pericellular fluid flow within the lacuno-canalicular system. This study is significant which mechanistically couples cell and matrix mechanics via fluid–structure interaction simulation. From a mechanobiological perspective, such coupling is 'one way' at present, but there is much potential for further multiphysics-based modelling of intercellular signaling and subsequent matrix remodelling.

We note that multiscale, multiphysics approaches, in which cells and matrix are both explicitly modelled, are also being adopted in the field of tissue engineering to better understand matrix formation on artificial cartilage constructs grown in dynamically perfused bioreactors (e.g. [178,179]). FE models of cell attachment to tissue engineering scaffolds were developed by Stops et al. [180], in which both scaffold and cells were modelled structurally. This model predicted that for uniaxial strains of 10 % in a collagen–GAG scaffold, cell strains as high as 49 % were generated, though the majority of cells experienced less than 5 % strain. Again, the next stage with such models is to link cell membrane stress or strain to cellular signaling and subsequent ECM modification from a spatiotemporal, coupled structural–biochemical perspective.

1.5 Conclusions

The main challenge in modelling orthopaedic procedures lies in modelling the musculoskeletal tissues within which the implant is placed. While implants themselves and the biomaterials used in their construction can be complex in topography and microstructure, the response of the cells and extracellular matrix of the host tissue is far more challenging to simulate. Due to the recognition that cellular and matrix deformation, flow and damage processes on the micro- and nanoscale drive the tissue remodelling response, modelling efforts in recent years have shifted from the traditional top-down macro-scale approach to a bottom-up approach. While top-down approaches use phenomenological descriptions of tissue behaviour, bottom-up approaches attempt to gain a more fundamental understanding of the system by incorporating mechanistic descriptions of tissue behaviour as much as possible. The potential rewards of such bottom-up multiscale modelling are high, though the models must be informed by imaging and experimental data at the scales of interest.

Multiscale modelling and experimentation are thus intricately related. In fact, for multiscale models to have true explanatory power, they should ideally be derived from 3D imaging datasets of individual tissue specimens and then be validated against experimental (flow, deformation, remodelling, etc.) measurements on these same specimens wherever possible. This is a challenging requirement, but is becoming increasingly possible due to rapid development and wide availability of micro-scale imaging technologies which can be used both in vitro and in vivo. As micro-scale models become more advanced in their ability to represent tissue-level heterogeneity and spatially varying mechanical properties across large regions of tissue, micro/macro-scale bridging methodologies will become increasingly important. Even with massively parallel computing, it will not be possible to model clinically relevant regions of tissue using voxel-based meshing. Also, as mechanistically driven descriptions of cell behaviour are incorporated in such models, the issue of short- and long-term temporal timescales will become increasingly important, coupling deformation, fluid flow and diffusion events in the order of milliseconds with tissue healing and adaptation over months and years.

The design of treatments for musculoskeletal disease and degeneration is a multidisciplinary field, and spatiotemporal, mechanics-based computer modelling is just one approach among the armoury of expertise which can be brought to bear on the problem. The problems which multiscale modelling attempts to address should be informed by clinicians, biologists, biochemists and materials scientists, especially with regard to the behaviour of the cell within the ECM in response to the physical signals captured by computational simulations. Clearly, the issues of biocompatibility, wear, degeneration and degradation of the implants themselves are also important. In the emerging field of tissue engineering, the physico-chemistry of controlled scaffold degradation is a highly complex problem which again will benefit from computational modelling approaches.

While nanoscale mechanics of musculoskeletal tissues at the molecular level are clearly important, it is the author's opinion that the most pressing current issue in this field is the development of micro–macro frameworks which can incorporate micro-scale mechanistic models of ECM deformation and cellular response with macro-scale continuum models of whole implant–tissue constructs. Such models will need to take account of micro-scale heterogeneity to better describe nonlinear deformation and fracture behaviour, will need to be coupled with mathematical models of cell signaling and will need to be verified and validated against an integrated program of experimental measurements. All of these are challenging;

however, the potential to drive genuine improvements in the outcomes of orthopaedic procedures is worth the effort.

Acknowledgements The author wishes to acknowledge Dr Victoria Toal, Dr Katrina McDonald and Dr Cameron Bell for providing images.

References

1. Whitesides G, Wong A (2006) The intersection of biology and materials science. MRS Bulletin 31:19–27
2. Hunter PJ, Borg TK (2003) Integration from proteins to organs: the Physiome Project. Nat Rev Mol Cell Biol 4:237–43
3. Horstemeyer MF (2010) Multiscale modelling: a review. In: Leszczynski J, Shukla MK (eds) Practical aspects of computational chemistry. Springer, New York, pp 87–135
4. Fish J (ed) (2010) Multiscale Methods: Bridging the scales in science and engineering. Oxford University Press, Oxford
5. Tsubota K, Adachi T, Tomita Y (2003) Effects of a fixation screw on trabecular structural changes in a vertebral body predicted by remodelling simulation. Ann Biomed Eng 31: 733–40
6. Ebraheim NA, Rupp RE, Savolaine ER et al (1994) Use of titanium implants in pedicular screw fixation. J. Spinal Disord 7:478–86
7. Hawes MC, O'Brien JP (2008) A century of spine surgery: what can patients expect? Disabil Rehabil 30:808–17
8. Paris O, Zizak I, Lichtenegger H et al (2000) Analysis of the hierarchical structure of biological tissues by scanning X-ray scattering using a micro-beam. Cell Mol Biol 46: 993–1004
9. Mandel U, Dalgaard P, Viidik A (1986) A biomechanical study of the human periodontal ligament. J Biomech 19:637–45
10. Maroudas A (1976) Balance between swelling pressure and collagen tension in normal and degenerate cartilage. Nature 260:808–809
11. Evans JH, Nachemson AL (1969) Biomechanical study of human lumbar ligamentum flavum. J Anat 105:188–9
12. Borg TK, Caulfield JB (1980) Morphology of connective tissue in skeletal muscle. Tissue Cell 12:197–207
13. Rigozzi S, Müller R, Snedeker JG (2010) Collagen fibril morphology and mechanical properties of the Achilles tendon in two inbred mouse strains. J Anat 216:724–31
14. Kim SH, Turnbull J, Guimond S (2011) Extracellular matrix and cell signalling: the dynamic cooperation of integrin, proteoglycan and growth factor receptor. J Endocrinol 209:139–51
15. Chen JH, Liu C, You L et al (2010) Boning up on Wolff's Law: mechanical regulation of the cells that make and maintain bone. J Biomech 43:108–18
16. Sievänen H (2010) Immobilization and bone structure in humans. Arch Biochem Biophys 503:146–52
17. LeBlanc A, Schneider V, Shackelford L et al (2000) Bone mineral and lean tissue loss after long duration space flight. J Musculoskelet Neuronal Interact 1:157–60
18. Merle C, Streit MR, Volz C et al (2011) Bone remodelling around stable uncemented titanium stems during the second decade after total hip arthroplasty: a DXA study at 12 and 17 years. Osteoporos Int 22:2879–86
19. Burr DB (1993) Remodelling and the repair of fatigue damage. Calcif Tissue Int 53:S75–80
20. Weiner S, Wagner HD (1998) The material bone: structure mechanical function relations. Annu Rev Mater Sci 28:271–298

21. Rho JY, Kuhn-Spearing L, Zioupos P (1998) Mechanical properties and the hierarchical structure of bone. Med Eng Phys 20:92–102
22. Buehler MJ (2007) Nano- and micromechanical properties of hierarchical biological materials and tissues. Mater Sci 42(21):8765–8770
23. de d'Otreppe BV (2012) From medical imaging to finite element simulations : a contribution to mesh generation and locking-free formulations for tetrahedra. Universite de Liège, PhD Dissertation
24. Bell CG (2005) A finite element and experimental investigation of the femoral component mechanics in a total hip arthroplasty. Queensland University of Technology, PhD Dissertation
25. An YH, Draughn RA (eds) (2000) Mechanical testing of bone and the bone-implant interface. CRC Press, Boca Raton
26. Little JP, de Visser H, Pearcy MJ et al (2008) Are coupled rotations in the lumbar spine largely due to the osseo-ligamentous anatomy?--a modelling study. Comp Meth Biomech Biomed Eng 11:95–103
27. Nachemson A, Elfström G (1971) Intravital wireless telemetry of axial forces in Harrington distraction rods in patients with idiopathic scoliosis. J Bone Joint Surg Am 53:445–65
28. Carretta R, Lorenzetti S, Müller R (2013) Towards patient-specific material modelling of trabecular bone post-yield behavior. Int j numer method biomed eng 29:250–72
29. Hoshaw SJ, Fyhrie DP, Takano Y et al (1997) A method suitable for in vivo measurement of bone strain in humans. J Biomech 30:521–4
30. Nachemson AL (1981) Disc pressure measurements. Spine 6:93–7
31. Wilke HJ, Neef P, Caimi M et al (1999) New in vivo measurements of pressures in the intervertebral disc in daily life. Spine 24:755–62
32. Frost HM (2003) Bone's mechanostat: a 2003 update. Anat Rec A Discov Mol Cell Evol Biol 275:1081–101
33. Dabirrahmani D, Hogg M, Kohan L et al (2010) Primary and long-term stability of a short-stem hip implant. Proc Inst Mech Eng H 224:1109–19
34. Dickinson A, Taylor A, Browne M (2012) Implant-bone interface healing and adaptation in resurfacing hip replacement. Comp Meth Biomech Biomed Eng 15:935–47
35. Geris L, Van Oosterwyck H, Vander Sloten J et al (2003) Assessment of mechanobiological models for the numerical simulation of tissue differentiation around immediately loaded implants. Comp Meth Biomech Biomed Eng 6:277–88
36. Prendergast PJ, Huiskes R, Søballe K (1997) Biophysical stimuli on cells during tissue differentiation at implant interfaces. J Biomech 30:539–548
37. Huiskes R, Van Driel WD, Prendergast PJ et al (1997) A biomechanical regulatory model for periprosthetic fibrous-tissue differentiation. J Matl Sci: Materials in Medicine 8:785–788
38. Claes LE, Heigele CA (1999) Magnitudes of local stress and strain along bony surfaces predict the course and type of fracture healing. J Biomech 32:255–266
39. Pivonka P, Komarova SV (2010) Mathematical modelling in bone biology: from intracellular signaling to tissue mechanics. Bone 47:181–9
40. Meyers MA, Chen PY, Lopez MI et al (2010) Biological materials: a materials science approach. J Mech Behav Biomed Mat 4:626–57
41. Parfitt AM (2002) Misconceptions (2): turnover is always higher in cancellous than in cortical bone. Bone 30:807–9
42. Eswaran SK, Gupta A, Adams MF, Keaveny TM (2006) Cortical and trabecular load sharing in the human vertebral body. J Bone Miner Res 21:307–14
43. Harrigan TP, Jasty M, Mann RW et al (1988) Limitations of the continuum assumption in cancellous bone. J Biomech 21:269–75
44. McDonnell P, McHugh PE, O'Mahoney D (2007) Vertebral osteoporosis and trabecular bone quality. Ann Biomed Eng 35:170–189
45. Seeman E, Delmas PD (2006) Bone quality--the material and structural basis of bone strength and fragility. N Engl J Med 354:2250–61

46. Niebur GL, Feldstein MJ, Yuen JC (2000) High-resolution finite element models with tissue strength asymmetry accurately predict failure of trabecular bone. J Biomech 33:1575–83
47. Müller R, Rüegsegger P (1995) Three-dimensional finite element modelling of non-invasively assessed trabecular bone structures. Med Eng Phys 17:126–33
48. van Rietbergen B, Weinans H, Huiskes R et al (1995) A new method to determine trabecular bone elastic properties and loading using micromechanical finite-element models. J Biomech 28:69–81
49. Jacobs CR, Davis BR, Rieger CJ et al (1999) The impact of boundary conditions and mesh size on the accuracy of cancellous bone tissue modulus determination using large-scale finite-element modelling. J Biomech 32:1159–64
50. van Rietbergen B, Kabel J, Odgaard A et al (1997) Determination of trabecular bone tissue elastic properties by comparison of experimental and finite element results. In: Sol H, Oomens CWJ (eds) Material identification using mixed numerical experimental methods. Kluwer Academic Publisher, Norwell (MA)
51. Kabel J, van Rietbergen B, Dalstra M et al (1999) The role of an effective isotropic modulus in the elastic properties of cancellous bone. J Biomech 32:673–680
52. Fyhrie DP, Hou FJ (1995) Prediction of human vertebral cancellous bone strength using non-linear, anatomically accurate, large-scale finite element analysis. Proc Bioeng Conf ASME 29:301–2
53. Van Rietbergen B, Ulrich D, Pistoia W et al (1998) Prediction of trabecular bone failure parameters using a tissue failure criterion. Trans Orthop Res Soc 23:550
54. Niebur GL, Yuen JC, Burghardt AJ et al (2001) Sensitivity of damage predictions to tissue level yield properties and apparent loading conditions. J Biomech 34:699–706
55. Pistoia W, van Rietbergen B, Lochmuller EM et al (2002) Estimation of distal radius failure load with micro-finite element analysis models based on three-dimensional peripheral quantitative computed tomography images. Bone 30:842–8
56. Stölken JS, Kinney JH (2003) On the importance of geometric nonlinearity in finite-element simulations of trabecular bone failure. Bone 33:494–504
57. Verhulp E, Van Rietbergen B, Muller R et al (2008) Micro-finite element simulation of trabecular-bone post-yield behaviour-effects of material model, element size and type. Comp Meth Biomech Biomed Eng 11:389–95
58. Pistoia W, van Rietbergen B, Laib A et al (2001) High-resolution three-dimensional-pQCT images can be an adequate basis for in-vivo microFE analysis of bone. J Biomech Eng 123:176–83
59. Vilayphiou N, Boutroy S, Szulc P et al (2011) Finite element analysis performed on radius and tibia HR-pQCT images and fragility fractures at all sites in men. J Bone Miner Res 26: 965–73
60. Podshivalov L, Fischer A, Bar-Yoseph PZ (2011) Multiscale FE method for analysis of bone micro-structures. J Mech Behav Biomed Mater 4:888–99
61. Basaruddin KS, Takano N, Nakano T (2013) Stochastic multiscale prediction on the apparent elastic moduli of trabecular bone considering uncertainties of biological apatite (BAp) crystallite orientation and image-based modelling., Comp Meth Biomech Biomed Eng, (epub ahead of print)
62. Taylor D, Hazenberg JG, Lee TC (2007) Living with cracks: Damage and repair in human bone. Nature Materials 6:263–8
63. Fazzalari NL, Forwood MR, Manthey BA et al (1998) Three-dimensional confocal images of microdamage in cancellous bone. Bone 23:373–8
64. Mori S, Burr DB (1993) Increased intracortical remodelling following fatigue damage. Bone 14:103–9
65. Mulvihill BM, McNamara LM, Prendergast PJ (2008) Loss of trabeculae by mechano-biological means may explain rapid bone loss in osteoporosis. J R Soc Interface 5:1243–53

66. Mosekilde L (1990) Consequences of the remodelling process for vertebral trabecular bone structure: a scanning electron microscopy study (uncoupling of unloaded structures). Bone and Mineral 10:13–35
67. Burr DB, Forwood MR, Fyhrie DP et al (1997) Bone microdamage and skeletal fragility in osteoporotic and stress fractures. J Bone Miner Res 12:6–15
68. Yeh OC, Keaveny TM (2001) Relative roles of microdamage and microfracture in the mechanical behavior of trabecular bone. J Orthop Res 19:1001–7
69. Nagaraja S, Couse TL, Guldberg RE (2005) Trabecular bone microdamage and microstructural stresses under uniaxial compression. J Biomech 38:707–16
70. Jungmann R, Szabo ME, Schitter G et al (2011) Local strain and damage mapping in single trabeculae during three-point bending tests. J Mech Behav Biomed Mater 4:523–34
71. Ural A, Vashishth D (2006) Cohesive finite element modelling of age-related toughness loss in human cortical bone. J Biomech 39:2974–82
72. Tomar V (2008) Modelling of dynamic fracture and damage in two-dimensional trabecular bone microstructures using the cohesive finite element method. J Biomech Eng 130:021021
73. Kosmopoulos V, Keller TS (2003) Finite element modelling of trabecular bone damage. Comp Meth Biomech Biomed Eng 6:209–16
74. Kosmopoulos V, Keller TS (2008) Predicting trabecular bone microdamage initiation and accumulation using a non-linear perfect damage model. Med Eng Phys 30:725–32
75. Budyn E, Hoca T (2006) Multiscale Modelling of Human Cortical Bone: Aging and Failure Studies. Mat Res Soc Fall Meeting 975:27–32
76. Yang QD, Cox BN, Nalla RK et al (2006) Fracture length scales in human cortical bone: the necessity of nonlinear fracture models. Biomaterials 27:2095–113
77. Renders GA, Mulder L, Langenbach GE et al (2008) Biomechanical effect of mineral heterogeneity in trabecular bone. J Biomech 41:2793–8
78. Renders GA, Mulder L, van Ruijven LJ et al (2011) Mineral heterogeneity affects predictions of intratrabecular stress and strain. J Biomech 44:402–7
79. Knothe Tate ML (2003) "Whither flows the fluid in bone?" An osteocyte's perspective. J Biomech 36:1409–24
80. McNamara LM, Van der Linden JC, Weinans H et al (2006) Stress-concentrating effect of resorption lacunae in trabecular bone. J Biomech 39(4):734–41
81. Deligianni DD, Apostolopoulos CA (2008) Multilevel finite element modelling for the prediction of local cellular deformation in bone. Biomech Model Mechanobiol 7:151–9
82. Jacobs CR, Temiyasathit S, Castillo AB (2010) Osteocyte mechanobiology and pericellular mechanics. Annu Rev Biomed Eng 12:369–400
83. Cardoso L, Fritton SP, Gailani G et al (2013) Advances in assessment of bone porosity, permeability and interstitial fluid flow. J Biomech 46:253–65
84. Swan CC, Lakes RS, Brand RA et al (2003) Micromechanically based poroelastic modelling of fluid flow in Haversian bone. J Biomech Eng 125:25–37
85. Galley SA, Michalek DJ, Donahue SW (2006) A fatigue microcrack alters fluid velocities in a computational model of interstitial fluid flow in cortical bone. J Biomech 39:2026–33
86. Rémond A, Naïli S, Lemaire T (2008) Interstitial fluid flow in the osteon with spatial gradients of mechanical properties: a finite element study. Biomech Model Mechanobiol 7: 487–95
87. Cowin SC, Gailani G, Benalla M (2009) Hierarchical poroelasticity: movement of interstitial fluid between porosity levels in bones. Philos Trans A Math Phys Eng Sci 367:3401–44
88. Nguyen VH, Lemaire T, Naili S (2010) Poroelastic behaviour of cortical bone under harmonic axial loading: a finite element study at the osteonal scale. Med Eng Phys 32:384–90
89. Lemaire T, Naïli S, Rémond A (2006) Multiscale analysis of the coupled effects governing the movement of interstitial fluid in cortical bone. Biomech Model Mechanobiol 5:39–52
90. Lemaire T, Capiez-Lernout E, Kaiser J (2011) What is the importance of multiphysical phenomena in bone remodelling signals expression? A multiscale perspective. J Mech Behav Biomed Mater 4:909–20

91. Sansalone V, Kaiser J, Naili S et al (2012) Interstitial fluid flow within bone canaliculi and electro-chemo-mechanical features of the canalicular milieu : A multi-parametric sensitivity analysis., Biomech Model Mechanobiol, (epub ahead of print)
92. Verbruggen SW, Vaughan TJ, McNamara LM (2013) Fluid flow in the osteocyte mechanical environment: a fluid-structure interaction approach., Biomech Model Mechanobiol, (epub ahead of print)
93. Goulet GC, Hamilton N, Cooper D (2008) Influence of vascular porosity on fluid flow and nutrient transport in loaded cortical bone. J Biomech 41:2169–75
94. Steck R, Niederer P, Knothe Tate ML (2003) A finite element analysis for the prediction of load-induced fluid flow and mechanochemical transduction in bone. J Theor Biol 220:249–59
95. Nguyen VH, Lemaire T, Naili S (2011) Influence of interstitial bone microcracks on strain-induced fluid flow. Biomech Model Mechanobiol 10:963–72
96. Silva MJ, Gibson LJ (1997) Modelling the mechanical behavior of vertebral trabecular bone: Effects of age-related changes in microstructure. Bone 21:191–199
97. Langton CM, Haire TJ, Ganney PS et al (1998) Dynamic stochastic simulation of cancellous bone resorption. Bone 22:375–80
98. Langton CM, Haire TJ, Ganney PS et al (2000) Stochastically simulated assessment of anabolic treatment following varying degrees of cancellous bone resorption. Bone 27:111–8
99. Huiskes R, Ruimerman R, van Lenthe GH, Janssen JD (2000) Effects of mechanical forces on maintenance and adaptation of form in trabecular bone. Nature 405:704–6
100. Ruimerman R, Van Rietbergen B, Hilbers P et al (2003) A 3-dimensional computer model to simulate trabecular bone metabolism. Biorheology 40:315–20
101. Ruimerman R, Van Rietbergen B, Hilbers P (2005) The effects of trabecular-bone loading variables on the surface signaling potential for bone remodelling and adaptation. Ann Biomed Eng 33:71–8
102. van Oers RF, Ruimerman R, Tanck E et al (2008) A unified theory for osteonal and hemi-osteonal remodelling. Bone 42:250–9
103. van Oers RF, van Rietbergen B, Ito K et al (2011) Simulations of trabecular remodelling and fatigue: is remodelling helpful or harmful? Bone 48:1210–5
104. Chen G, Pettet GJ, Pearcy M et al (2007) Modelling external bone adaptation using evolutionary structural optimisation. Biomech Model Mechanobiol 6:275–85
105. Van Der Linden JC, Verhaar JA, Weinans H (2001) A three-dimensional simulation of age-related remodelling in trabecular bone. J Bone Miner Res 16:688–96
106. Hernandez CJ, Gupta A, Keaveny TM (2006) A biomechanical analysis of the effects of resorption cavities on cancellous bone strength. J Bone Miner Res 21:1248–55
107. Smit TH, Burger EH (2000) Is BMU-coupling a strain-regulated phenomenon? A finite element analysis. J Bone Miner Res 15:301–7
108. McNamara LM, Prendergast PJ (2005) Perforation of cancellous bone trabeculae by damage-stimulated remodelling at resorption pits: a computational analysis. Eur J Morphol 42:99–109
109. McNamara LM, Prendergast PJ (2007) Bone remodelling algorithms incorporating both strain and microdamage stimuli. J Biomech 40:1381–91
110. Mulvihill BM, McNamara LM, Prendergast PJ (2008) Loss of trabeculae by mechano-biological means may explain rapid bone loss in osteoporosis. J R Soc Interface 5:1243–53
111. Ryser MD, Nigam N, Komarova SV (2009) Mathematical modelling of spatio-temporal dynamics of a single bone multicellular unit. J Bone Miner Res 24:860–70
112. Adachi T, Kameo Y, Hojo M (2010) Trabecular bone remodelling simulation considering osteocytic response to fluid-induced shear stress. Philos Trans A Math Phys Eng Sci 368: 2669–82
113. Gerhard FA, Webster DJ, van Lenthe GH et al (2009) In silico biology of bone modelling and remodelling: adaptation. Philos Trans A Math Phys Eng Sci 367:2011–30
114. Hambli R (2010) Application of neural networks and finite element computation for multi-scale simulation of bone remodelling. J Biomech Eng 132:114502

115. Hambli R, Katerchi H, Benhamou CL (2011) Multiscale methodology for bone remodelling simulation using coupled finite element and neural network computation. Biomech Model Mechanobiol 10:133–45
116. Hambli R (2011) Apparent damage accumulation in cancellous bone using neural networks. J Mech Behav Biomed Mater 4:868–78
117. Mann KA, Miller MA (2013) Fluid-structure interactions in micro-interlocked regions of the cement-bone interface., Comput Methods Biomech Biomed Engin, (epub ahead of print)
118. Hollister SJ, Fyhrie DP, Jepsen KJ et al (1991) Application of homogenization theory to the study of trabecular bone mechanics. J Biomech 24:825–39
119. van Lenthe GH, Stauber M, Müller R (2006) Specimen-specific beam models for fast and accurate prediction of human trabecular bone mechanical properties. Bone 39:1182–9
120. McDonald K, Little J, Pearcy M et al (2010) Development of a multi-scale finite element model of the osteoporotic lumbar vertebral body for the investigation of apparent level vertebra mechanics and micro-level trabecular mechanics. Med Eng Phys 32:653–61
121. Yeh OC, Keaveny TM (1999) Biomechanical effects of intraspecimen variations in trabecular architecture: A three-dimensional finite element study. Bone 25:223–228
122. Jensen KS, Mosekilde L, Mosekilde L (1990) A model of vertebral trabecular bone architecture and its mechanical properties. Bone 11:417–423
123. Hildebrand T, Rüegsegger P (1997) Quantification of Bone Microarchitecture with the Structure Model Index. Comput Methods Biomech Biomed Engin 1:15–23
124. Odgaard A (1997) Three-dimensional methods for quantification of cancellous bone architecture. Bone 20:315–328
125. Mosekilde L (1989) Sex differences in age-related loss of vertebral trabecular bone mass and structure-biomechanical consequences. Bone 10:425–432
126. Pugh JW, Rose RM, Radin EL (1973) A structural model for the mechanical behavior of trabecular bone. Journal of Biomechanics 6:657–670
127. Gibson LJ, Ashby MF, Schajer GS, et al. (1982) The mechanics of three-dimensional cellular materials. In: Proceedings of the Royal Society of London. Series A, Mathematical and physical sciences A 382
128. McDonald K (2009) An experimental and finite element investigation of the biomechanics of vertebral compression fractures. Queensland University of Technology, PhD Dissertation
129. Mizrahi J, Silva MJ, Keaveny TM et al (1993) Finite-element stress analysis of the normal and osteoporotic lumbar vertebral body. Spine 18:2088–2096
130. Chevalier Y, Pahr D, Allmer H et al (2007) Validation of a voxel-based FE method for prediction of the uniaxial apparent modulus of human trabecular bone using macroscopic mechanical tests and nanoindentation. J Biomech 40:3333–40
131. Toal V (2013) The mechanics of microdamage and microfracture in trabecular bone. Queensland University of Technology, PhD Dissertation
132. Galli M, Oyen ML (2009) Fast identification of poroelastic parameters from indentation tests. Comp Model Eng Sci 48:241–268
133. Fratzl-Zelman N, Roschger P, Gourrier A et al (2009) Combination of nanoindentation and quantitative backscattered electron imaging revealed altered bone material properties associated with femoral neck fragility. Calcif Tissue Int 85:335–43
134. Tai K, Qi HJ, Ortiz C (2005) Effect of mineral content on the nanoindentation properties and nanoscale deformation mechanisms of bovine tibial cortical bone. J Mater Sci Mater Med 16: 947–959
135. Tai K, Ulm FJ, Ortiz C (2006) Nanogranular origins of the strength of bone. Nano Letters 6: 2520–2525
136. Wang X, Allen MR, Burr DB et al (2008) Identification of material parameters based on Mohr-Coulomb failure criterion for bisphosphonate treated canine vertebral cancellous bone. Bone 43:775–780
137. Mullins LP, Bruzzi MS, McHugh PE (2009) Calibration of a constitutive model for the post-yield behaviour of cortical bone. J Mech Behav Biomed Mater 2:460–70

138. Oyen ML, Ko CC (2007) Examination of local variations in viscous, elastic, and plastic indentation responses in healing bone. J Mater Sci Mater Med 18:623–8
139. Brockaert H, Mazerain PE, Rachik M, Ho Ba Tho MC (2009) Nanoindentation on isotropic and anisotropic materials confrontation with FEM simulations. Comp Meth Biomech Biomed Eng 12:63–64
140. Paietta R, Campbell SE, Ferguson VL (2011) Influences of spherical tip radius, contact depth and contact area on nanoindentation properties of bone. J Biomech 44:285–90
141. Carnelli D, Gastaldi D, Sassi V et al (2010) A finite element model for direction-dependent mechanical response to nanoindentation for cortical bone allowing for anisotropic post-yield behavior of the tissue. J Biomech Eng 132:081008
142. Wolfram U, Wilke HJ, Zysset PK (2010) Valid micro finite element models of vertebral trabecular bone can be obtained using tissue properties measured with nanoindentation under wet conditions. J Biomech 43:1731–7
143. Reisinger AG, Pahr DH, Zysset PK (2011) Elastic anisotropy of bone lamellae as a function of fibril orientation pattern. Biomech Model Mechanobiol 10:67–77
144. Carnelli D, Lucchini R, Ponzoni M et al (2011) Nanoindentation testing and finite element simulations of cortical bone allowing for anisotropic elastic and inelastic mechanical response. J Biomech 44:1852–8
145. Lucchini R, Carnelli D, Ponzoni M et al (2011) Role of damage mechanics in nanoindentation of lamellar bone at multiple sizes: experiments and numerical modelling. J Mech Behav Biomed Mater 4:1852–63
146. Vaughan TJ, McCarthy CT, McNamara LM (2012) A three-scale finite element investigation into the effects of tissue mineralisation and lamellar organisation in human cortical and trabecular bone. J Mech Behav Biomed Mater 12:50–62
147. Adam CJ, Swain MV (2011) The effect of friction on indenter force and pile-up in numerical simulations of bone nanoindentation. J Mech Behav Biomed Mater 4:1554–8
148. Schwiedrzik JJ, Wolfram U, Zysset PK (2013) A generalized anisotropic quadric yield criterion and its application to bone tissue at multiple length scales., Biomech Model Mechanobiol, (epub ahead of print)
149. Currey JD (2002) Bones: Structure and mechanics. Princeton University Press, Oxfordshire
150. Jäger I, Fratzl P (2000) Mineralized collagen fibrils: a mechanical model with a staggered arrangement of mineral particles. Biophys J 79:1737–46
151. Nikolov S, Raabe D (2008) Hierarchical modelling of the elastic properties of bone at submicron scales: the role of extrafibrillar mineralization. Biophys J 94:4220–32
152. Siegmund T, Allen MR, Burr DB (2008) Failure of mineralized collagen fibrils: modelling the role of collagen cross-linking. J Biomech 41:1427–35
153. Hambli R, Barkaoui A (2012) Physically based 3D finite element model of a single mineralized collagen microfibril. J Theor Biol 301:28–41
154. Nair AK, Gautieri A, Chang SW et al (2013) Molecular mechanics of mineralized collagen fibrils in bone. Nat Commun 16:1724
155. Ganazzoli F, Raffaini G (2005) Computer simulation of polypeptide adsorption on model biomaterials. Phys Chem Chem Phys 7:3651–63
156. Raffaini G, Ganazzoli F (2007) Understanding the performance of biomaterials through molecular modelling: crossing the bridge between their intrinsic properties and the surface adsorption of proteins. Macromol Biosci 7:552–66
157. De Nardo L, Raffaini G, Ebramzadeh E et al (2012) Titanium oxide modelling and design for innovative biomedical surfaces: a concise review. Int J Artif Organs 35:629–41
158. Shim VB, Hunter PJ, Pivonka P et al (2011) A multiscale framework based on the physiome markup languages for exploring the initiation of osteoarthritis at the bone-cartilage interface. IEEE Trans Biomed Eng 58:3532–6
159. Lavagnino M, Arnoczky SP, Kepich E et al (2008) A finite element model predicts the mechanotransduction response of tendon cells to cyclic tensile loading. Biomech Model Mechanobiol 7:405–16

160. Hadi MF, Barocas VH (2013) Microscale fiber network alignment affects macroscale failure behavior in simulated collagen tissue analogs. J Biomech Eng 135:021026
161. Reese SP, Ellis BJ, Weiss JA (2013) Micromechanical model of a surrogate for collagenous soft tissues: development, validation and analysis of mesoscale size effects., Biomech Model Mechanobiol, (epub ahead of print)
162. Maceri F, Marino M, Vairo G (2010) A unified multiscale mechanical model for soft collagenous tissues with regular fiber arrangement. J Biomech 43:355–63
163. Maceri F, Marino M, Vairo G (2012) An insight on multiscale tendon modelling in muscle-tendon integrated behavior. Biomech Model Mechanobiol 11:505–17
164. Gronau G, Krishnaji ST, Kinahan ME et al (2012) A review of combined experimental and computational procedures for assessing biopolymer structure-process-property relationships. Biomaterials 33:8240–55
165. Israelowitz M, Rizvi SW, Kramer J et al (2005) Computational modelling of type I collagen fibers to determine the extracellular matrix structure of connective tissues. Protein Eng Des Sel 18:329–35
166. Buehler MJ (2006) Nature designs tough collagen: explaining the nanostructure of collagen fibrils. Proc Natl Acad Sci 103:12285–90
167. Buehler MJ (2008) Nanomechanics of collagen fibrils under varying cross-link densities: atomistic and continuum studies. J Mech Behav Biomed Mater 1:59–67
168. Gautieri A, Vesentini S, Redaelli A et al (2011) Hierarchical structure and nanomechanics of collagen microfibrils from the atomistic scale up. Nano Lett 11:757–66
169. Kim JS, Min J, Recknagel AK et al (2011) Quantitative three-dimensional analysis of embryonic chick morphogenesis via microcomputed tomography. Anat Rec 294:1–10
170. Kazakia GJ, Lee JJ, Singh M et al (2007) Automated high-resolution three-dimensional fluorescence imaging of large biological specimens. J Microsc 225:109–17
171. Bigley RF, Singh N, Hernandez CJ et al (2008) Validity of serial milling-based imaging system for microdamage quantification. Bone 42:212–15
172. Odgaard A, Andersen K, Melsen F et al (1990) A direct method for fast three-dimensional serial reconstruction. J Microsc 159:335–42
173. Ewald AJ, McBride H, Reddington M et al (2002) Surface imaging microscopy, an automated method for visualizing whole embryo samples in three dimensions at high resolution. Dev Dyn 225:369–75
174. Boyde A, Lovicar L, Zamecnik J (2005) Combining confocal and BSE SEM imaging for bone block surfaces. Eur Cell Mater 26:33–8
175. Slyfield CR Jr, Niemeyer KE, Tkachenko EV et al (2009) Three-dimensional surface texture visualization of bone tissue through epifluorescence-based serial block face imaging. J Microsc 236:52–9
176. Viceconti M (2012) Multiscale modelling of the skeletal system. Cambridge University Press, Cambridge
177. Fernandez JW, Shim VB, Hunter PJ (2012) Integrating degenerative mechanisms in bone and cartilage: a multiscale approach. In: Proceedings of IEEE Engineering in Medical and Biology Society 6616–6619.
178. Causin P, Sacco R, Verri M (2012) A multiscale approach in the computational modelling of the biophysical environment in artificial cartilage tissue regeneration., Biomech Model Mechanobiol, (epub ahead of print)
179. Sacco R, Causin P, Zunino P et al (2011) A multiphysics/multiscale 2D numerical simulation of scaffold-based cartilage regeneration under interstitial perfusion in a bioreactor. Biomech Model Mechanobiol 10:577–89
180. Stops AJ, McMahon LA, O'Mahoney D et al (2008) A finite element prediction of strain on cells in a highly porous collagen-glycosaminoglycan scaffold. J Biomech Eng 130:061001–1

Chapter 2
Performance Evaluation of Bone–Implant System During Implantation Process: Dynamic Modelling and Analysis

Rudi C. van Staden, Hong Guan, Newell W. Johnson, and Yew-Chaye Loo

Abstract Inappropriate choice of dental implant type in relation to the detailed structure of bone at the site, and inadequate surgical technique has led to 5 % failure of dental implants worldwide. By using the finite element method, three typical implant insertion scenarios are modelled and evaluated in this chapter. The scenarios are implant thread forming, cutting and the combination of forming and cutting. The bone–implant system is modelled using three-dimensional finite element technique which incorporates realistic material properties in simulating the cancellous and cortical bone. The bone–implant contact is defined using 'surface-to-surface' discretisation and the arbitrary Lagrangian–Eulerian adaptive meshing scheme. In current practice many implant companies recommend thread cutting for normal bone and forming for compact bone so that implant stability can be ensured. Based on the findings of the present study, the combination of forming and cutting may also be recommended for clinical practice because it best matches the specified ideal stress level resulting in positive bone stimulation with minimum resorption. Stress information obtained in these three implant insertion scenarios will advance the understanding of bone response at an early stage of the osseointegration process and primary stability.

Keywords Dental implant • Implant insertion • Bone–implant system • Finite element modelling technique • Stress analysis

R.C. van Staden
College of Engineering and Science, Structural Mechanics and Sustainable Materials Research Group, Victoria University, Melbourne, VIC, Australia

H. Guan (✉) • Y.-C. Loo
Griffith School of Engineering, Griffith University, Gold Coast, QLD, Australia
e-mail: h.guan@griffith.edu.au

N.W. Johnson
Menzies Health Institute Queensland, Griffith University, Gold Coast, QLD, Australia

Q. Li, Y.-W. Mai (eds.), *Biomaterials for Implants and Scaffolds*, Springer Series in Biomaterials Science and Engineering 8, DOI 10.1007/978-3-662-53574-5_2

2.1 Introduction

2.1.1 Background

Development of an ideal substitute for missing teeth has been a major aim of dentistry for millennia [1]. Mouths which have missing teeth are frequently restored by 'conventional' prostheses (partial or total), fabricated from plastic and/or metal alloys supported by the remaining teeth and/or the soft tissues. In many cases, however, removable prostheses will not be satisfactory, e.g. because of the lack of retention and/or psychological inability to accept such an appliance. In these cases, dental prostheses retained by an implant are an attractive alternative. A dental implant is a biocompatible 'fixture', usually screw-like and commonly made from titanium which is surgically placed into a jawbone to support a crown which forms an artificial tooth. Implants made of commercially available pure titanium have established a benchmark in osseointegration, against which no other materials can compare in a number of ways. Osseointegration is defined as the formation of bony interface which links bone to the implant surface [2].

The long-term benefits of dental implants include restored oral functions, improved appearance, comfort, speech clarity and self-esteem. With the implant, the patient can eat more conveniently, and the associated inconvenience of removable partial or full dentures does not exist. In addition, an implant is able to protect the remaining natural teeth, stop bone loss and restore facial skeletal structure. As far as the cost is concerned, implants have been shown to be comparable or even less expensive overall than conventional prostheses such as crown and bridge restorations [3]. Although the cost of an implant is generally higher than that of a crown or a bridge, the life time of an implant can be longer [4].

Worldwide implant statistics show a high success rate: in excess of 95 % retention over a 5-year period if the devices are correctly designed, manufactured and inserted [5–12]. Implants are expected to function for life, and this may well be possible in many cases, given that the retention rate at 15 years has been reported to be as high as 90 % if proper and professional care was taken by the practitioner and patient [13]. Despite all these advantages, only 10 % of Australian patients have received single or multiple dental implants [14]. This is mainly due to the initial high costs. However, it has been suggested [14] that another reason of low implant usage in Australia could be the lack of clinical skills [15] and knowledge of comparatively more complicated and less well-known implantation techniques. This is because the failure mechanisms consequential to the stress distribution characteristics in the jawbone during the implantation process itself, as well as the healing and maintenance phases, are poorly understood. Inaccurate implant manufacturer guidelines and inadequate surgical techniques also contribute to the 5 % failure of implants.

2.1.2 Implantation Procedure and Scenarios

Prior to commencement of implant placement, careful and detailed planning is required to identify the shape and dimensions of the bone to correctly orientate the implant. Periapical, panoramic and tomographic radiographs or computer tomography (CT) scans are often taken to assist in identifying these anatomical details and also to locate the nerve. The implantation process is initiated by making a small incision into the gingival tissue at the proposed implantation site. After the bone is made visible, a pilot hole is drilled into the cortical bone using a round bur. Drills of diameters 2.2, 3.0, 3.6 and 3.9 mm may be used successively, to create the implantation site in the cortical and cancellous bone, when inserting a single implant of diameter 4.5 mm [12]. Other operations, such as countersinking or screw tapping, may be a further stage before the implant is placed into the jawbone. The entire operation is performed under local anaesthesia, and a constant supply of physiological saline during the procedure reduces heat and flushes away blood and bone fragments.

The implant is finally inserted manually, using a ratchet or using a surgical micromotor mechanically. Manual insertion of the implant generally requires an increased torque with insertion depth as a result of the relatively low insertion velocity. On the other hand, mechanical insertion is performed at increased velocity, and thus the torque remains constant regardless of the insertion depth. Generally, 1 week after surgery, the implantation site is checked by the clinician for complete soft tissue healing around the healing abutment (one-stage implants) or over the implants (two-stage healing) [12]. The healing period for osseointegration varies and is dependent on criteria such as primary stability of implant at time of placement, bone quality, the use of any grafted bone or otherwise, overall patient health and the expected masticatory forces.

The bone strength and cortical thickness are generally the determining factors for the insertion drill sizes and finally the implant diameter. As such, three typical implant insertion scenarios are often adopted clinically. They are implant thread forming (scenario one, S1), thread cutting (scenario two, S2) or forming and cutting (scenario three, S3). If the bone cavity is 0.25 mm smaller in diameter than the implant, S1 takes place. Sennerby and Meredith [16] have shown that stability is reduced at sites of S1, thereby increasing the possibility of implant failure. For a bone cavity that is 0.6 mm smaller in diameter than the implant, S2 occurs. S2 is ideal in which the implant cuts a new thread pattern into the bone around a cavity of smaller diameter. In this case, optimum implant stability can be achieved through the entire length of the implant. In practice, S2 is often recommended by implant companies [12, 17, 18]. Note that if an implant is placed into a cavity created by a newly extracted tooth, the diameter of the cavity will vary. Generally, this cavity will be of a larger diameter at the top than the bottom. Therefore S3 takes place during insertion [12]. The amount of forming or cutting would ultimately contribute to the biological response of the bone and subsequently the outcome of the implantation procedure.

2.1.3 Finite Element Technique

While inserting the implant, elevated compressive stress can obstruct blood supply and damage the cells particularly for dense bone which in turn would affect osseointegration. On the other hand, inadequate stress cannot stimulate bone remodelling properly, thereby compromising implant stability. An optimal stress level and distribution must therefore be sought during and after implantation for the jawbone to remain strong and healthy.

There have been limited publications available on the response of bone cells to mechanical forces [19]. Limited data from animal studies suggest a large range of stress–strain values for the mandible [20]. Furthermore, bone densities and the local cell and tissue responses are also dependent on the general health and systematic responses of the patient. As such, the stress condition in the jawbone will change accordingly. The effects of such a phenomenon on bone resorption or healing has not been researched adequately, and the long-term effects of such stresses are still unclear.

The finite element method (FEM) is showing overwhelming capability and versatility in its application to dentistry [21–26]. The FEM has proven to be a reliable tool in analysing stress levels and distributions in biological bone tissues and in tissue-implant interacting structures. The primary difficulties in simulating the mechanical behaviour of dental implants are the complex finite element meshing process and the modelling of living human bone tissue and its response to applied mechanical forces. In an attempt to reduce the potential risks of clinical failure, research has been mainly directed towards finding the most biocompatible materials with which the dental implants are manufactured.

Despite the considerable research efforts on finite element analysis (FEA) of implant-mandible structure under a condition of full osseointegration, research into the modelling of the entire implantation process is non-existent. The purpose of this study is to model the insertion process in a dynamic manner, including further advancement on the bone–implant contact modelling. The major implantation scenarios to be considered are S1, S2 and S3. The aim of this study is to advance the work of van Staden et al. [27] on stepwise simulation of the implantation process. This will help provide an improved understanding of how various thread forming or cutting processes affect the outcome of implantation.

2.2 Dynamic Modelling

Summarised herein are the bone–implant geometry and material properties, modelling details and contact simulation for simulating the implantation process. The dynamic modelling of the implantation process requires the definition of complex bone–implant contact behaviour and material properties.

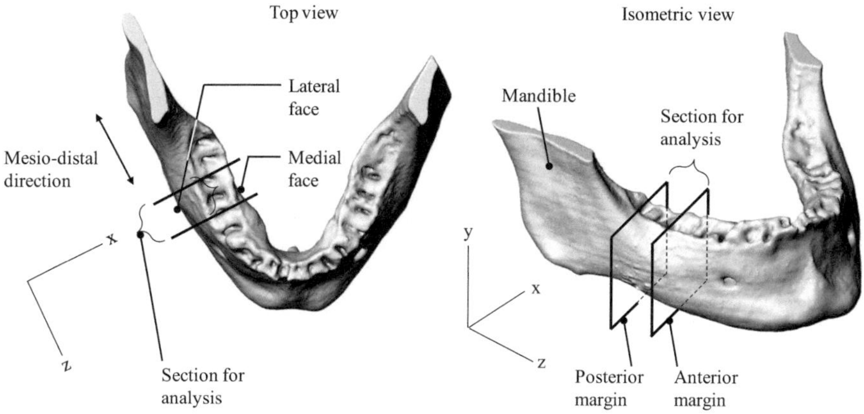

Fig. 2.1 Location of three-dimensional slice in a mandible

2.2.1 Bone–Implant System Geometry and Material Properties

All the modelling and analyses are carried out using ABAQUS in this study [28]. Data acquisition for bone dimensions are based on computed tomography (CT) scanned images. From these images, a section from the human mandible is taken as illustrated in Fig. 2.1. The bone is categorised as 'soft quality' or type IV bone.

The geometry of the sectioned bone structure for analysis, as identified in Fig. 2.1, has been smoothed out with geometrical discontinuities removed. This model is illustrated in Fig. 2.2 with different dimensions of bone cavities. S1, S2 and S3 take place, respectively, for bone cavity diameters of 4.25, 3.9 mm and the combination of these two. Note that for S3 the bone cavity has a 1.5° taperage due to the difference in the top (4.25 mm) and bottom (3.9 mm) diameters of the cavity, as shown in Fig. 2.2 (b). A conical implant is considered herein with 2° of taper angle, a helical thread and three primary cutting faces. A typical implant of 4.5 mm in diameter and 11 mm in length is presented in Fig. 2.3.

Realistic material behaviour of the cancellous bone requires the definition of elastic and plastic properties. Plastic behaviour is defined because it is expected that the bone would exceed its maximum yield stress during implantation. Note that the stress–strain relationship for the bone is defined up to the point of fracture (see Fig. 2.4), as obtained by Burstein et al. [29] from human femur and tibia specimens. The detailed material properties of the bone adopted in this study are listed in Table 2.1. The friction coefficient between the surfaces of bone and commercially available pure titanium was obtained from Choubey et al.'s [30] fretting wear tests performed in a salt solution. Young's modulus, Poisson's ratio and density of the implant are, respectively, 102GPa, 0.3 and 4.54×10^{-6} kg/mm^3.

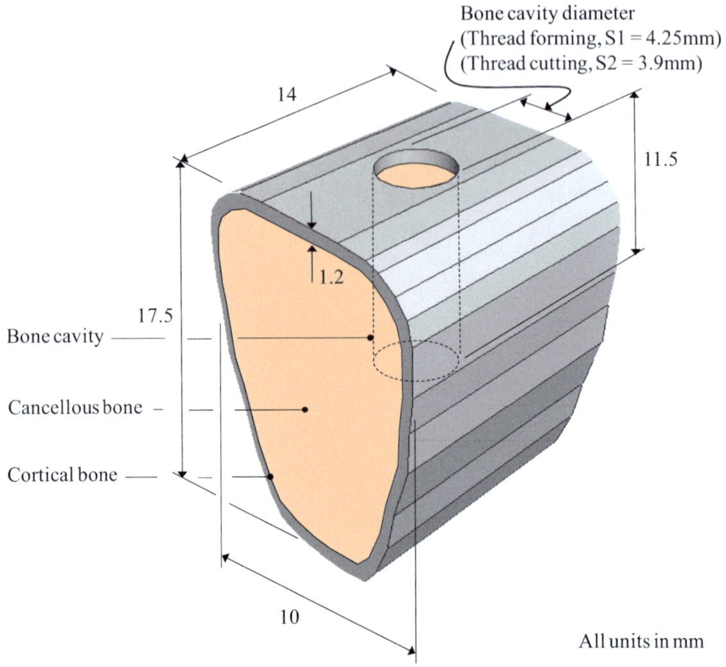

a) Thread forming, S1 or cutting, S2

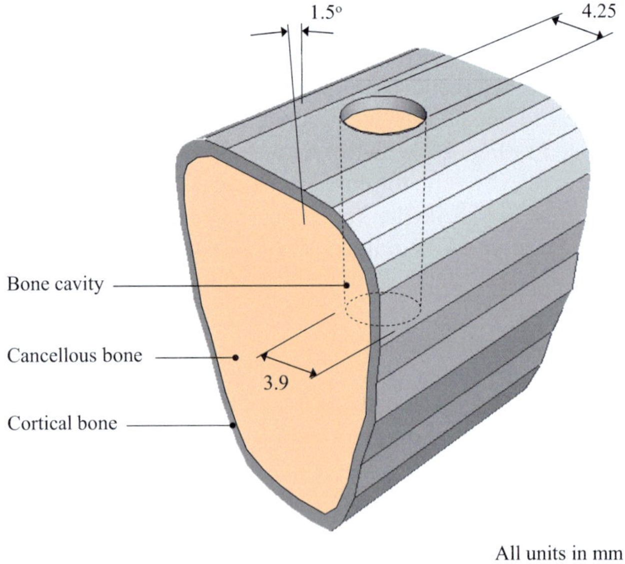

b) Thread forming and cutting, S3

Fig. 2.2 Details of mandibular bone and cavity

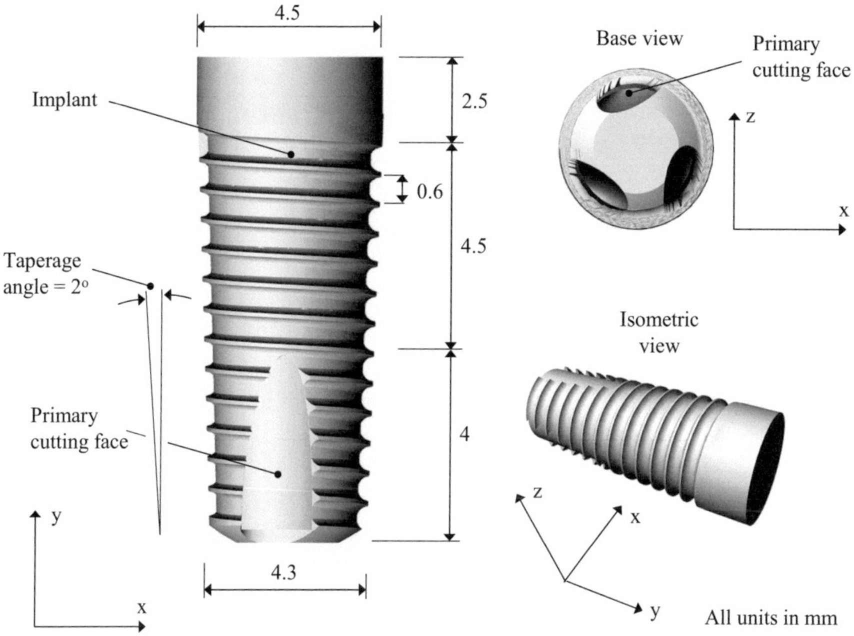

Fig. 2.3 Details of a typical implant design

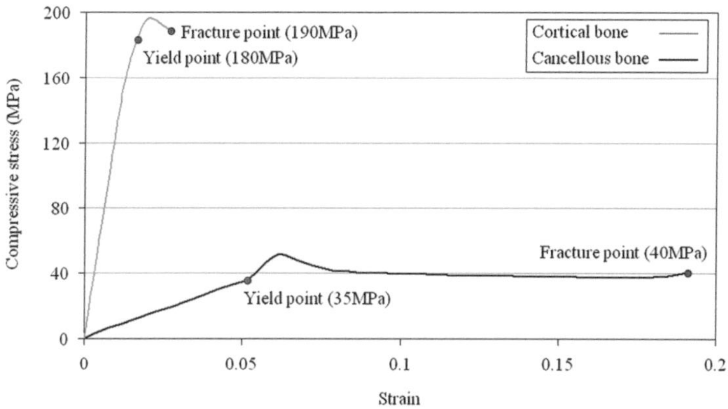

Fig. 2.4 Stress–strain behaviour [29]

2.2.2 *Modelling Details*

During implantation, the implant can be inserted manually or mechanically. A manual insertion process was modelled previously [27] in a stepwise manner with a torque applied to the implant that increases with time. The present study

Table 2.1 Material properties of cancellous and cortical bone

		Cancellous bone	Cortical bone	Sources	Specimen details
Elastic	Young's modulus, E ($\times 10^3$ N/mm^2)	0.7	9	[29]	Human femur and tibia (type IV)
	Poisson's ratio, v	0.35	0.3		
	Density, ρ ($\times 10^{-7}$ kg/mm^3)	5.3	18		
Plastic	Yield stress (N/mm^2)	35	180	(Fig. 2.4)	
	Plastic strain	0.135	0.015		
Contact	Friction coefficient	0.61		[30]	Human femur

deals with mechanical insertion whereby the process of implantation is continuous with a constant torque.

Figure 2.5 illustrates a constant torque of 450 Nmm with an insertion velocity of 0.31 mm/s applied to the top of the implant. The velocity is based on an insertion depth of 11 mm over a total period of 36 s. Note that the bone cavity is 11.5 mm in depth, thereby leaving 0.5 mm between the bottom of the implant and bone to store blood and bone fragments. Shown in Fig. 2.5 are the fixed constraints on the bone surfaces (anterior and posterior) along the mesiodistal direction of such a hypothetical human mandible.

The finite element models of the bone and implant are meshed automatically within the program by using tetrahedral elements. As an example, for the bone and implant models of S2, the total numbers of elements and nodes are 85,234 and 67,567, respectively. The elements on the entire cavity surface are refined to 40 % of the average mesh size on the anterior and posterior faces. This would enable to obtain more accurate results during implant insertion. Mesh convergence was undertaken on the similar models in our previous work [31].

2.2.3 Contact Simulation

Interaction between the bone and implant during dynamic simulation of the implantation process is complex and requires proper definition of contact conditions. In the present study, the contact is defined in ABAQUS [28] using 'surface-to-surface' discretisation because it provides more accurate stress and pressure results than node-to-surface discretisation. Surface-to-surface contact is incorporated in the modelling by using the constraint enforcement methods where the surfaces do not require matching meshes (i.e. node-to-node contact). This is because ABAQUS [28] enforces conditional constraints on each surface to simulate contact conditions. In addition, the contact interaction properties are also required to be defined for the contact pair.

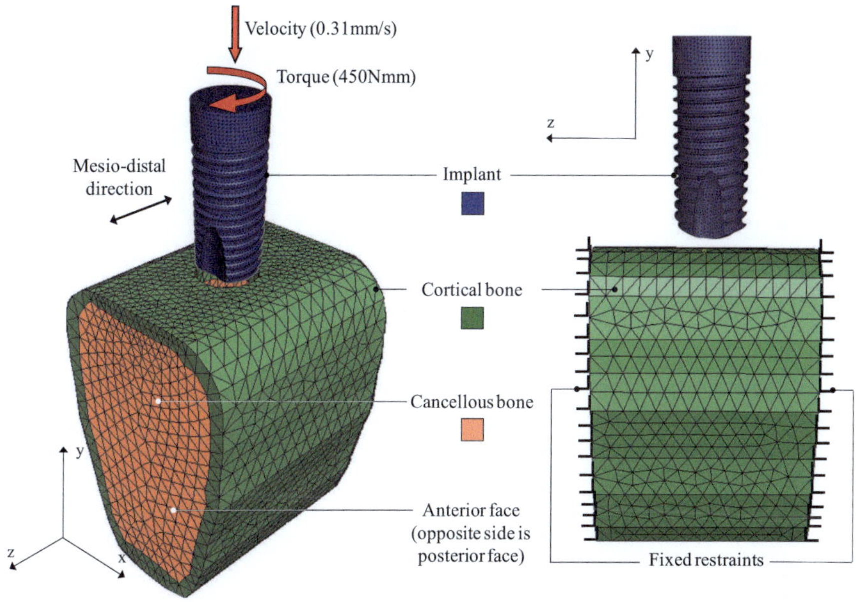

Fig. 2.5 Loading and restraint conditions applied to the bone and implant

As illustrated in Fig. 2.6, the definition of the two contact surfaces is achieved by setting the side and bottom surfaces of the implant as the master surface. The slave surface includes the entire inner surface of the bone cavity and the top ring area of 0.5 mm width on the cortical surface. This top ring area defines the contact between the implant and the top of cortical bone because the implant diameter is larger than the cavity. In accordance with the surface-to-surface definition, contact constraints are enforced in an average sense over the slave surface, rather than at discrete points, such as at slave nodes in the case of node-to-surface discretisation. Therefore, penetration of individual master nodes into the slave surface is allowed; however, the reverse is not permitted.

Defining the contact is yet to be completed because under large deformation, ABAQUS [28] defaults the slave surface to be penetrated by the master nodes, as illustrated in Fig. 2.7 (a). As such, the material properties of the slave surface cannot be properly defined after deformation. Therefore, adaptive meshing technique must be employed so that the material moves with the slave surface mesh at all times during the insertion simulation.

The adaptive meshing scheme specified in ABAQUS [28] is termed 'arbitrary Lagrangian–Eulerian' (ALE) because it combines the Lagrangian and Eulerian methods. The Lagrangian method is used to track the path of the element so that no nodal penetrations occur. However, this method alone still allows material to move independently of the mesh. The Eulerian method, on the other hand, takes into account conservation of mass so that the material is conserved within the elements. The ALE combines these two methods so that if nodal penetrations occur,

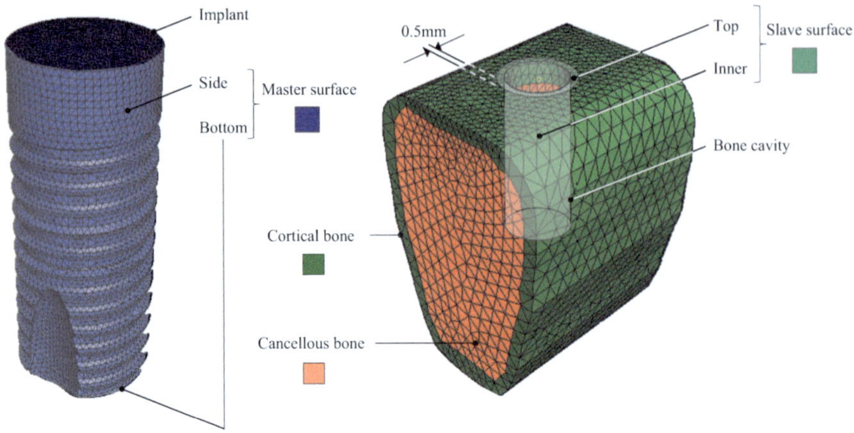

Fig. 2.6 Master and slave surfaces

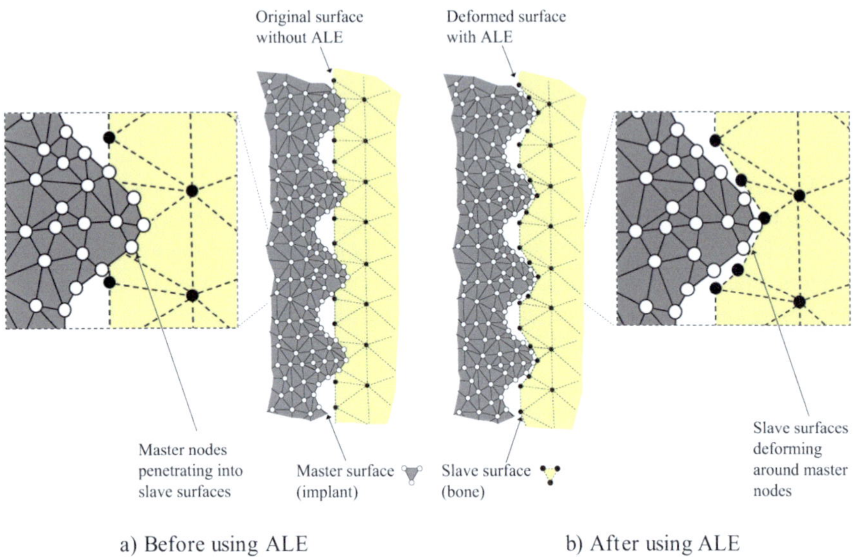

Fig. 2.7 Adaptive meshing

forces that are a function of the penetration distance are applied to the master nodes to counteract the penetration, with equal and opposite forces acting on the slave surface at the penetration points. Detailed in Fig. 2.7 (b) is an example of the slave surface deforming around the master nodes after ALE is applied.

The next step in defining a surface-based contact is to model the contact interaction properties. In this study, the tangential properties of the surface are defined using friction coefficient (see Table 2.1) and the normal properties defined as hard contact. Hard contact is implemented to ensure that the master nodes are in

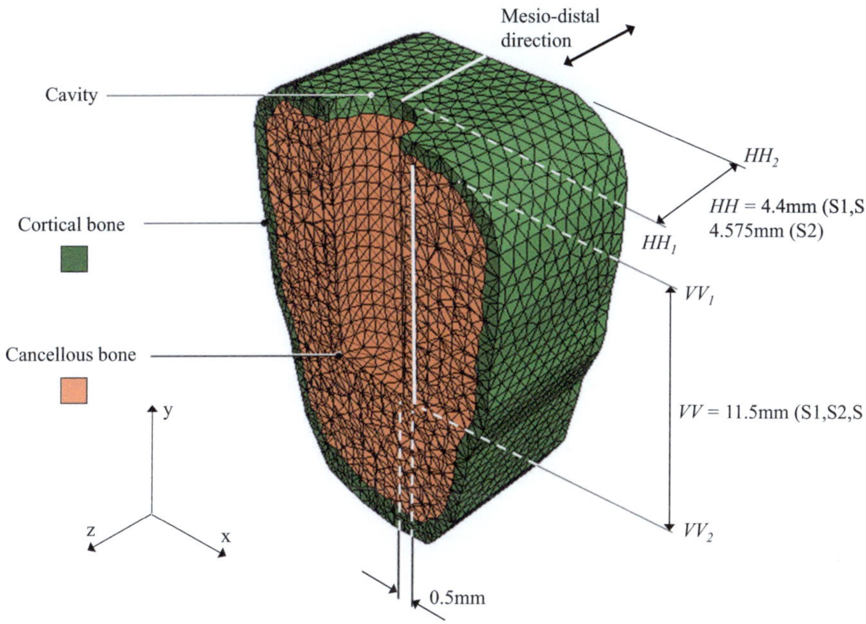

Fig. 2.8 Stress measurement within cancellous and cortical bone

complete contact with the slave surface therefore not allowing transfer of any tensile stresses across the interface.

2.2.4 Criteria for Stress Measurements

The stress within the bone are considered to be the determining factor for understanding both bone fracturing during insertion and subsequent bone resorption. The von Mises stresses are measured along the lines *VV* in the cancellous bone and *HH* in the cortical bone, as shown in Fig. 2.8. Line *VV* is 11.5 mm in length for all bone cavity diameters; however, the length of *HH* is dependent on the bone cavity dimensions. The length of line *HH* is 4.4 mm for S1 and S3 and 4.6 mm for S2. Due to the irregularity of the mesh, a straight line of nodes at which the stress is measured is only approximated for both *VV* and *HH*. The distance of *VV* away from the bone cavity surface is fixed at 0.5 mm. The stress measurement line, *HH*, is positioned to capture the most severe stress levels. The beginning and end points of *VV* (i.e. V_1 and V_2) and *HH* (i.e. H_1 and H_2) are also identified in Fig. 2.8 for ease of discussion.

2.3 Results and Discussion

The following subsections detail the von Mises stresses in both cancellous and cortical bone, each with discussions for the three insertion scenarios (S1, S2 and S3). The stresses are measured along the lines *VV* and *HH* during the entire insertion process. Sections 2.3.1 and 2.3.2 present the stress characteristics within the cancellous and cortical bone, respectively, for S1, S2 and S3. The stress profile within the cancellous and cortical bone for the selected stages of insertion is presented followed by stress contour plots in subsequent figures illustrating the stress characteristics. It is assumed that the implant tip is pushed slightly into the top surface of cortical bone prior to the application of the torque. This corresponds to 1.8 s or 0.5 mm insertion depth where the stresses are measured from the stress profiles shown in Figs. 2.9, 2.10, 2.12, 2.13, 2.14 and 2.15 (a). For ease of discussion, stress profiles produced for 3.6–36 s at 10.8 s time steps (Figs. 2.9, 2.10, 2.12, 2.13, 2.14 and 2.15 (b), (c), (d), (e) and (f)) are detailed in Sections 2.3.1 and 2.3.2.

2.3.1 Cancellous Bone

2.3.1.1 Thread Forming, S1

For most of the time steps, it is evident that when the insertion depth increases, the stress level also increases. This is because the surface area of contact between the bone and implant increases, and therefore a larger amount of the applied torque is transferred to the bone.

As seen in Fig. 2.9 (a) and (b), when the implant is inserted 0.5 mm into the cortical bone, the stress level within the cancellous bone is relatively low (0.07 MPa) because the implant and cancellous bone are not yet in direct contact. At this stage, the only stresses experienced in the cancellous bone are those transferred from the cortical bone. Figure 2.9 (c) also indicates that for an insertion depth of 1.1 mm, the global stress peak occurs at VV_1. This peak is caused by the primary cutting faces together with the stresses transferred from the cortical bone.

At a depth of 4.4 mm, the cancellous bone experiences an increase in the stress further away from VV_1 because the implant is inserted deeper into the bone (Fig. 2.9 (d)). At 7.7 mm depth, the stress increases slightly compared to the previous stages (i.e. average from 0.93 to 1.24 MPa). The stress contour distributes more evenly throughout the bone adjacent to the implant as the insertion depth increases, as illustrated in Fig. 2.9 (e).

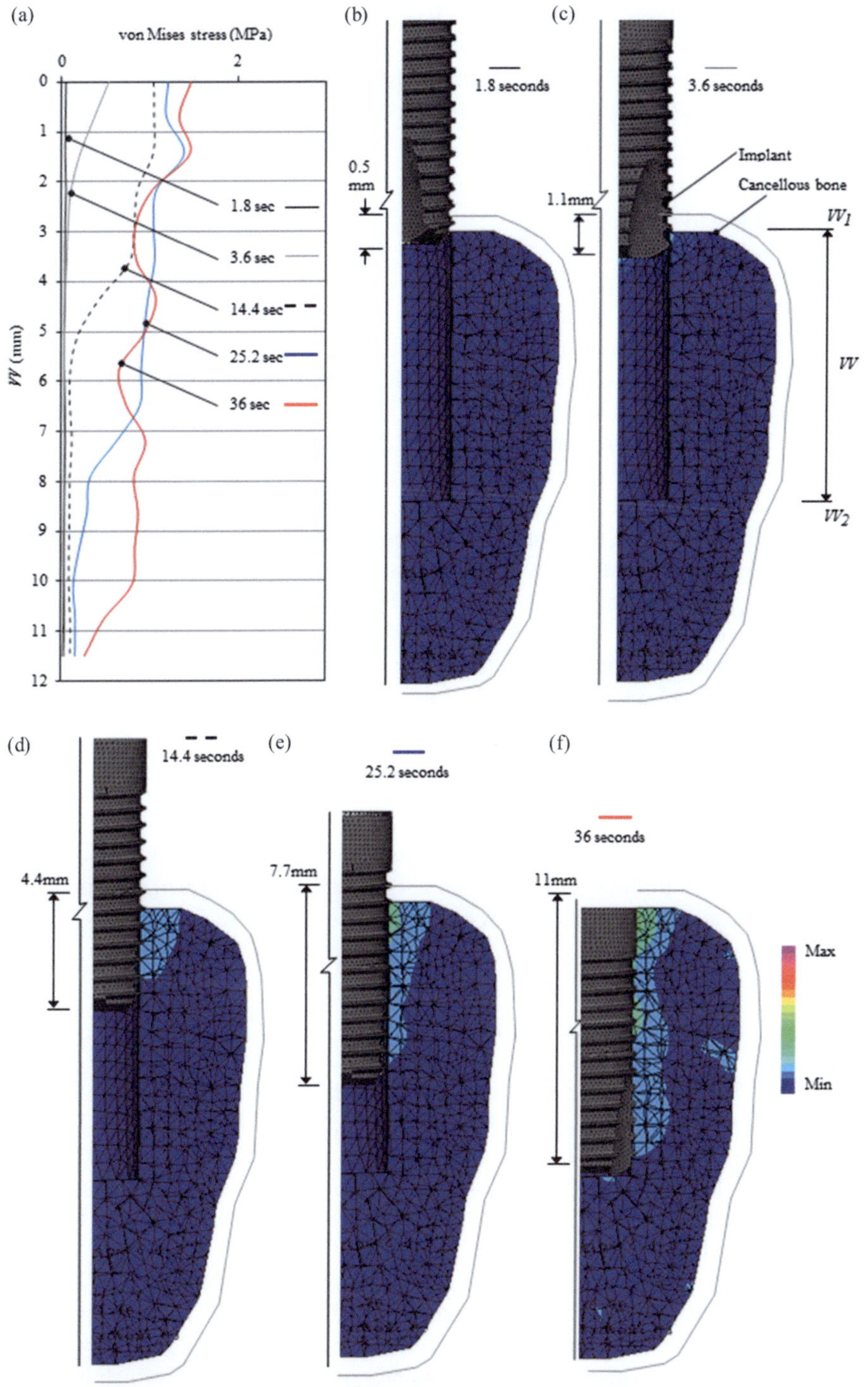

Fig. 2.9 Stress characteristics in cancellous bone at five insertion stages during thread forming

At the final stages of insertion (Fig. 2.9 (f)), the stress at 11 mm insertion depths increase (1.48 MPa) compared to all the previous stages. The global stress peak for this insertion step is a result of the abrupt change in implant geometry where the implant neck establishes contact with the cancellous bone.

2.3.1.2 Thread Cutting, S2

Similar to S1, S2 also causes increased stresses when the insertion depth increases. From the time periods 1.8 and 3.6 s, the stresses (0.3 and 1.2 MPa) are significantly higher than those found during S1 (0.07 and 0.51 MPa, correspondingly), as illustrated in Fig. 2.10. This is because the diameter of the bone cavity is reduced in S2. This also results in a larger stressed region towards the outer edge of the cortical bone, as evident in the stress contour plots (Fig. 2.10 (b), (c), (d), (e) and (f)). It is also found that stress peaks occur at the same locations as found for S1.

At 14.4 s, as detailed in Fig. 2.10 (d), the increased stresses move further down and away from VV_1 due to the increased insertion depth. The stress contours show to be more unevenly distributed when compared to the previous stages. The stress peak at VV_1 is much higher (4.0 MPa) than that found in S1.

At the final insertion stages, the stress profile and contour are shown to be more evenly distributed as compared to the corresponding ones in S1. The stress peak occurs at 4.7 mm (5.34 MPa) from VV_1 for the insertion depth of 11 mm. Similar to S1, this stress peak is again a result of the implant neck commencing contact with the cancellous bone.

Figure 2.11 illustrates, as an example, the progressive stress contours within the cancellous bone during the entire implantation process for the thread cutting scenario (S2). The corresponding time, insertion depth and implant revolutions are also indicated in the figure. Note that only the exterior surface of the implant is shown for ease of viewing the stress contours within the bone.

2.3.1.3 Thread Forming and Cutting, S3

Similar to S1 and S2, when the insertion depth increases, the stresses within the cancellous bone also increase for S3. From 1.8 to 3.6 s, as presented in Fig. 2.12 (a), the stress levels (0.09 and 0.4 MPa) are similar to those of S1 (0.07 and 0.5 MPa) but smaller than those for S2 (0.3 and 1.2 MPa). This is due to the geometrical changes of the bone cavity. The stress contours are also more comparable to those of S1, as detailed in Fig. 2.12 (b) and (c).

At 14.4 s, as illustrated in Fig. 2.12 (d), the stress level (1.3 MPa) is slightly higher than that of S1 (1.0 MPa) but significantly lower than S2 (4.0 MPa). A global stress peak at 14.4 s occurs along the line VV because of the geometry of the primary cutting faces and the reduced diameter of the bone cavity which induce a slight change in the stress contour when compared to S1.

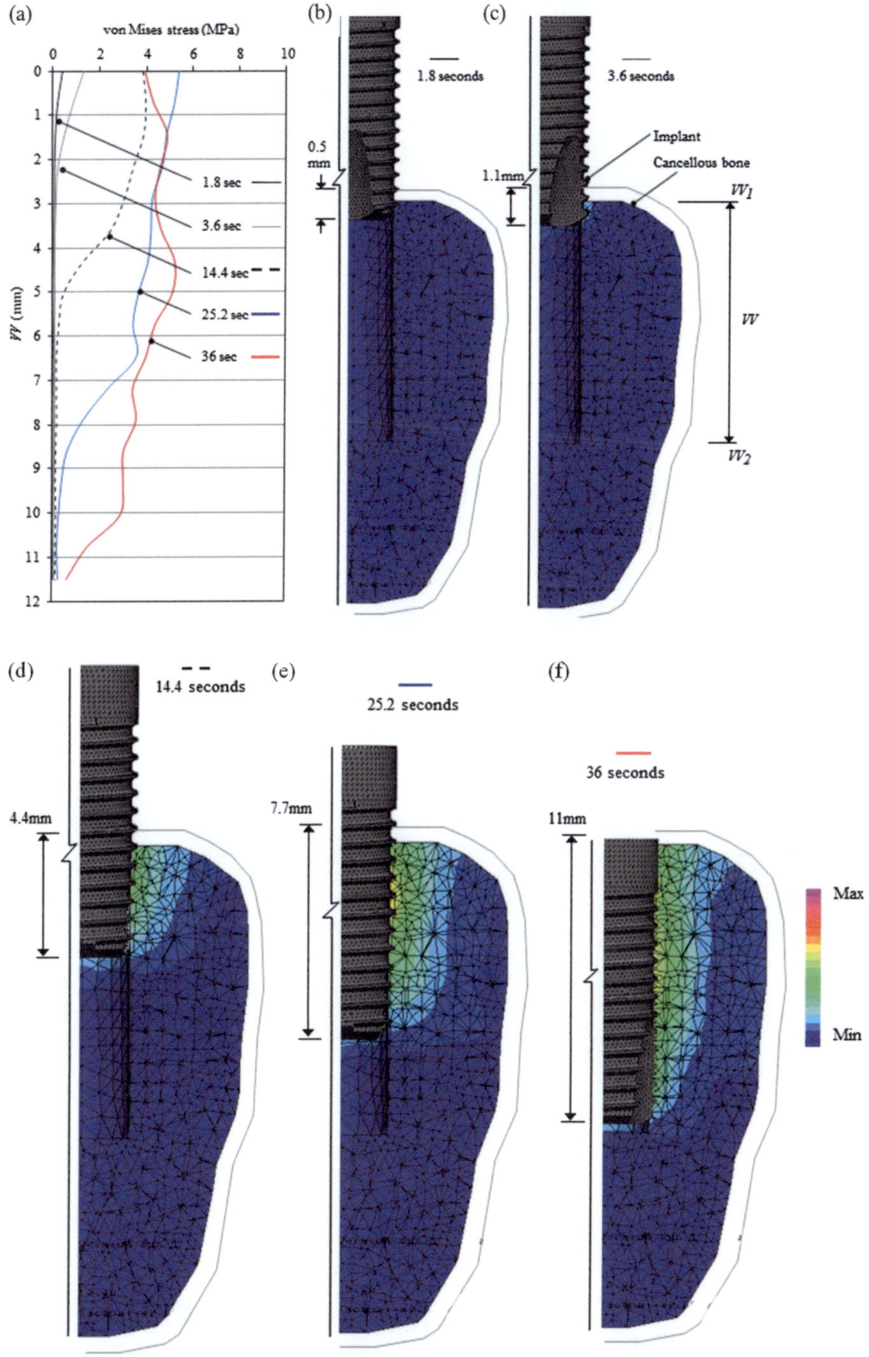

Fig. 2.10 Stress characteristics in cancellous bone at five insertion stages during thread cutting

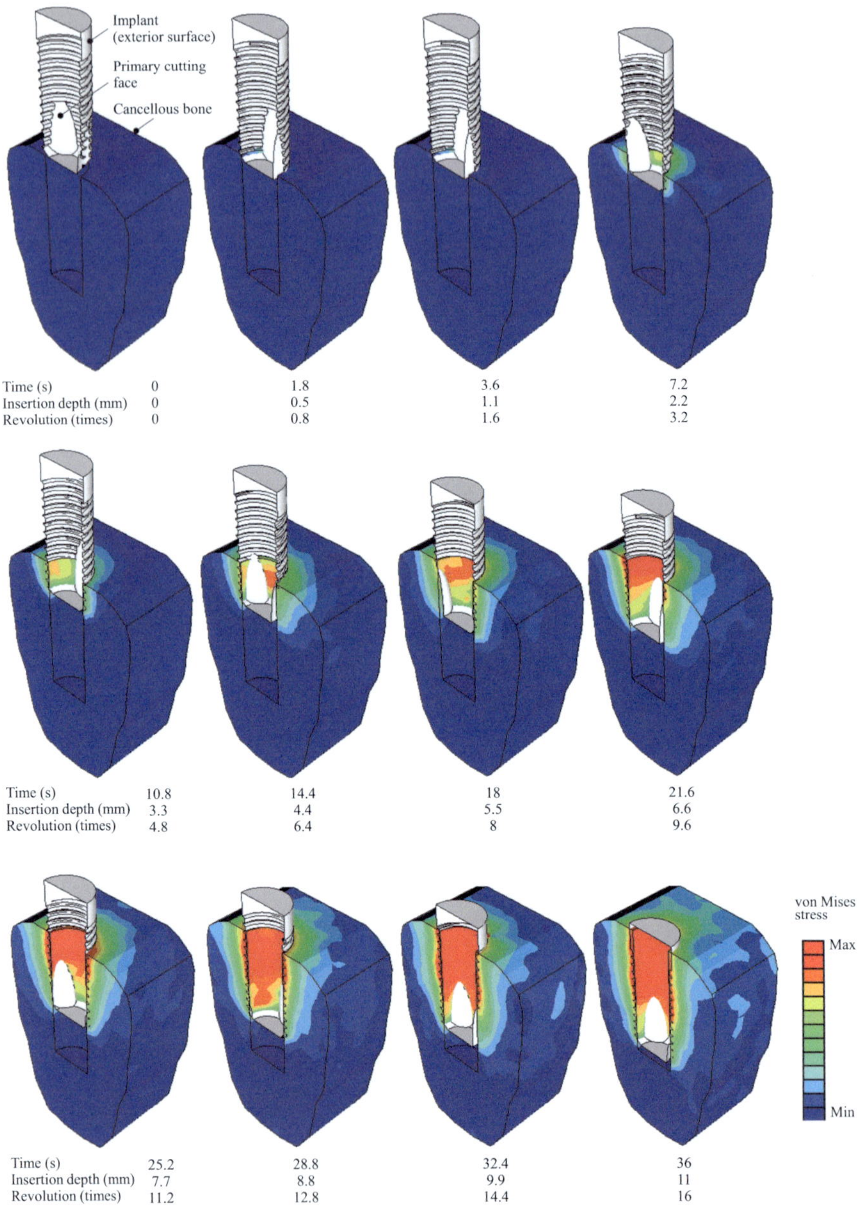

Fig. 2.11 Progressive stress contours in cancellous bone during the entire implantation process (thread cutting, S2)

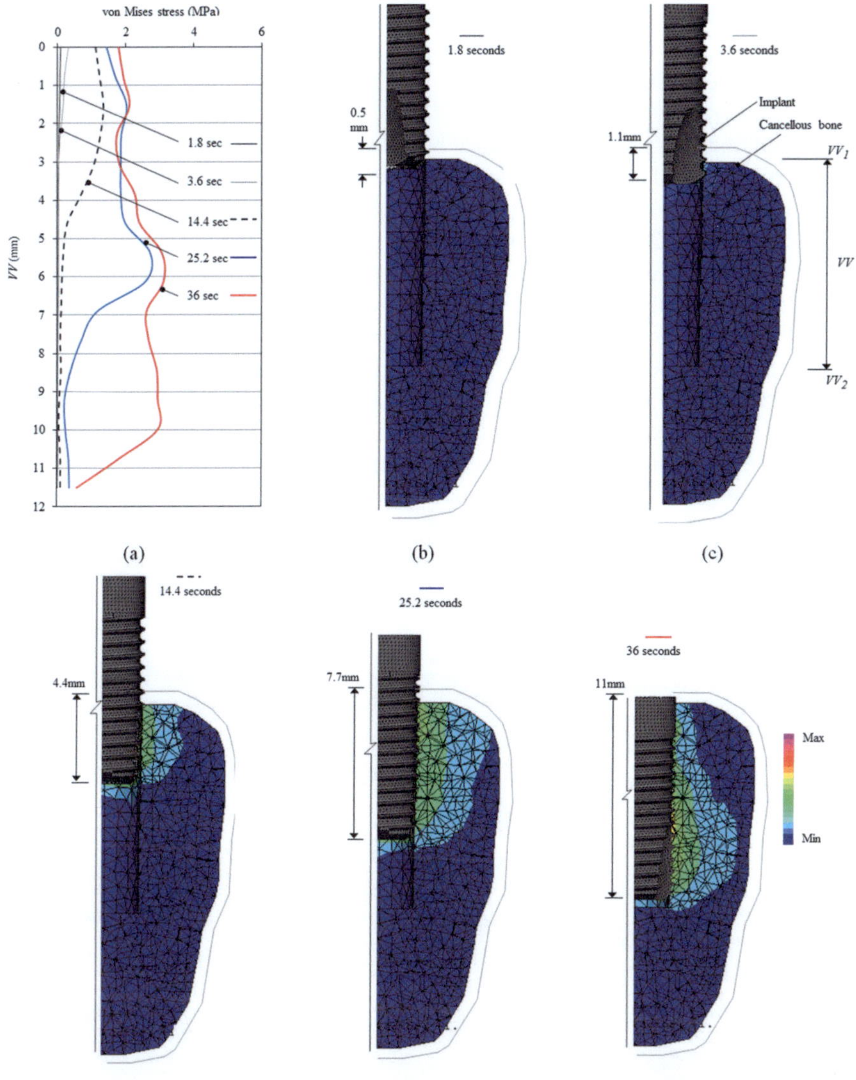

Fig. 2.12 Stress characteristics in cancellous bone at five insertion stages during thread forming and cutting

The stress characteristics at 25.2 s show an increase in magnitude (2.7 MPa) when compared to that of S1 (1.4 MPa) and a decrease as compared to S2 (5.2 MPa). The stress profile shown in Fig. 2.12 (a) indicates that a stress peak occurs at a region close to the primary cutting faces. A reduction in bone cavity diameter gives a stress contour that is more comparable to that of S1 than S2.

At 11 mm insertion depth, the stress shows a significant increase; however, the stress at VV_1 remains comparable to that found for S1. The increase in stress is a result of the reduced cavity diameter. Note also that the stress contour is more comparable to S2.

2.3.2 *Cortical Bone*

2.3.2.1 Thread Forming, S1

In general, the stress within the cortical bone decreases from HH_1 towards HH_2 for all insertion steps. The stress profiles presented in Fig. 2.13 (a), shows a significant stress increase at point HH_1 from 1.6 MPa (1.8 s, before the primary cutting faces are in contact) to 9.2 MPa (3.6 s, when contact is established). Such a large variation in stress is particularly evident in the contour plots (Figs. 2.13 (b) and (c)).

For 14.4 s, the stress next to the implant increases to 14.4 MPa. Such an increase is due to the increased cortical bone to implant contact as a result of the narrowing gaps between the cutting faces as the insertion step increases.

At 25.2 s, the stress contour only exhibits a marginal increase in stress (i.e. 16.4 MPa) because the cutting faces are no longer in contact with the cortical bone at HH_1. For the 36 s, an increase in stress (i.e. 20.4 MPa) is found when compared to 25.2 s because the implant neck is in contact with the cortical bone at this stage.

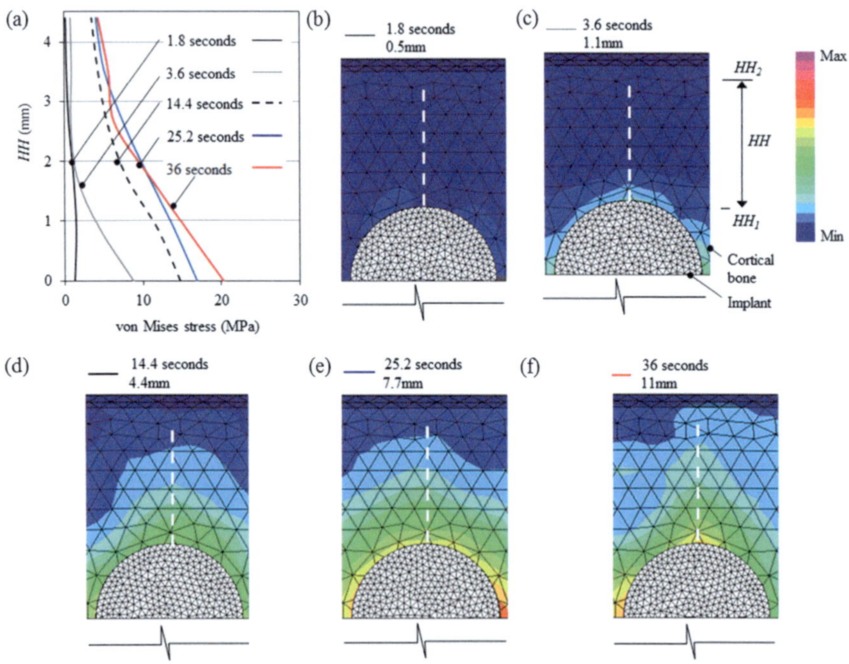

Fig. 2.13 Stress characteristics in cortical bone at five insertion stages during thread forming

2.3.2.2 Thread Cutting, S2

Similar stress characteristics are found for S2 as with S1. However, S2 induces significantly higher stresses within the cortical bone, with a maximum of 11.4 MPa compared to 9.2 MPa at 3.6 s, as illustrated in Fig. 2.14 (a). At an insertion depth of 4.4 mm, a maximum stress of 20.1 MPa occurs at the implant neck, which is significantly higher than that found at the same insertion step during S1 (14.4 MPa). The stress contours shown in Figs. 2.14 (b) to (f) also confirm such an increase in stresses.

2.3.2.3 Thread Forming and Cutting, S3

The stress characteristics are again comparable to those found for S1 or S2, as detailed in Fig. 2.15. In general, the stress characteristics are between those of S1 and S2, but closer to the S1 scenario. This is because the stresses are only measured at the top of the bone cavity where its diameter is identical to that of forming (i.e. S1).

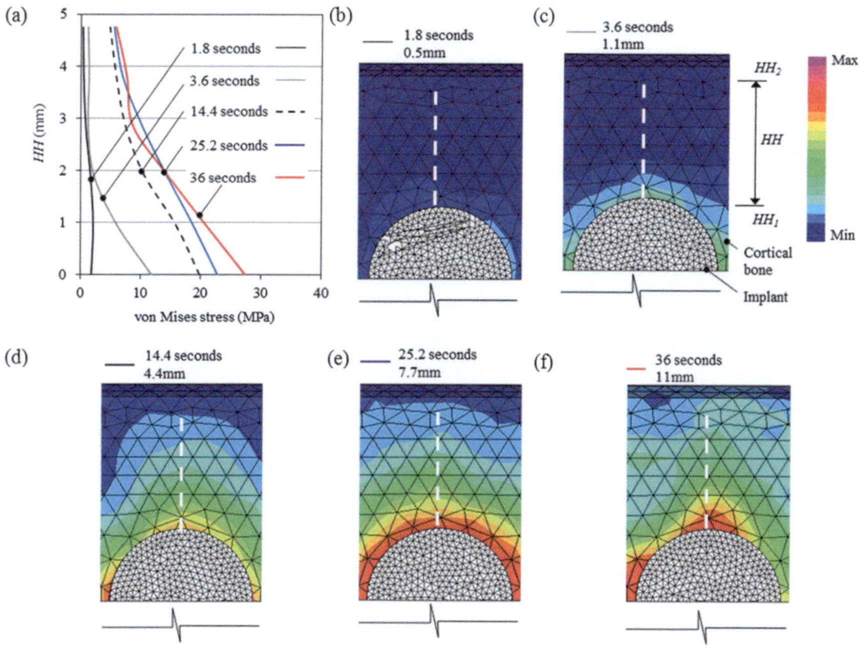

Fig. 2.14 Stress characteristics in cortical bone for five insertion stages during thread cutting

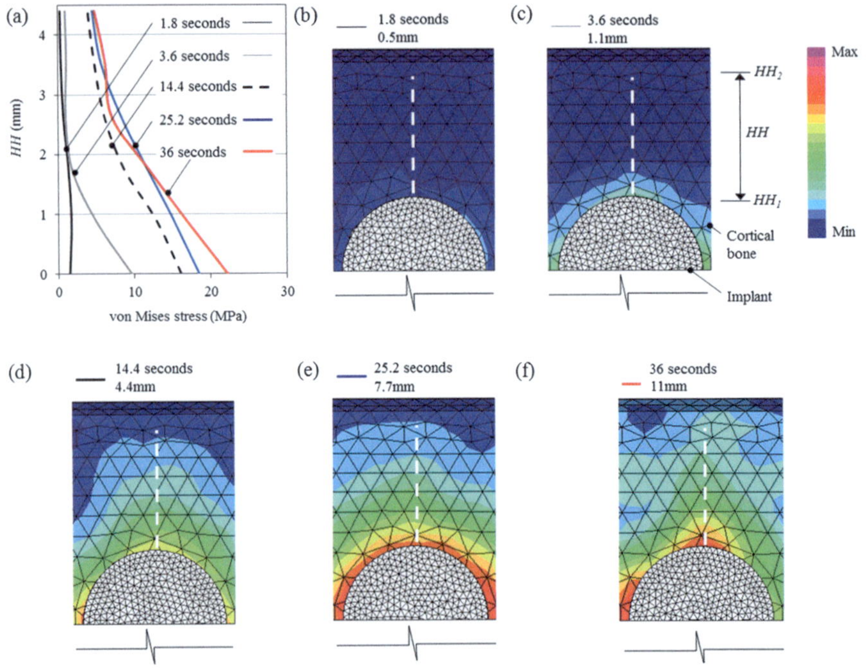

Fig. 2.15 Stress characteristics in cortical bone for five insertion stages during thread forming and cutting

2.3.3 *Maximum Stresses in Different Implantation Scenarios*

This subsection summarises the maximum von Mises stresses for 11 selected insertion depths of the S1, S2 and S3 scenarios. Based on the data shown in Figs. 2.9, 2.10, 2.11, 2.12, 2.13, 2.14 and 2.15, the maximum stresses along lines *VV* and *HH* are summarised in Table 2.2. As the insertion depth increases, the maximum stress along the line *VV* takes place at varied distances, *dv* away from VV_1. However for cortical bone, the maximum stresses always occur at HH_1.

Table 2.2 reveals that for the cancellous bone, the maximum stresses for S3 are closer in magnitude to those of S1 at initial insertion depths. This is because the upper bone cavity diameters are similar to each other for these two case scenarios. As the insertion depth increases, the maximum stress of the combined scenario (S3) approaches a magnitude which is approximately halfway between the S1 and S2 scenarios. This is due to the reduction in bone cavity diameter in the lower region which is approaching to that of the S2 scenario. In the initial insertion depths in general, the maximum stresses along the line *VV* occur on or close to VV_1. However, for the insertion depths 8.8–11 mm, the maximum stresses occur further away from VV_1 due to the decrease in the bone cavity diameter. For the cortical bone, the maximum stresses at HH_1 for S3 are in between those of S1 and S2 from 0.5 to 2.2 mm insertion depths. For the insertion depths from 3.3 to 11 mm, the

Table 2.2 Maximum von Mises stresses (MPa) along line *VV* and at point HH_1

	Forming, S1			Cutting, S2			Forming and cutting, S3		
Insertion depth (mm)	*VV*	*dv*	HH_1	*VV*	*dv*	HH_1	*VV*	*dv*	HH_1
0.5	0.07	0.0	1.6	0.3	0.0	2.1	0.09	0.0	2.06
1.1	0.51	0.0	9.2	1.2	0.0	11.44	0.44	0.0	9.8
2.2	0.96	0.7	9.9	3.92	0.71	12.1	0.99	0.82	10.9
3.3	0.8	0.0	14.37	2.5	0.0	20.3	1.09	1.48	16.1
4.4	1.08	0	14.4	4.02	0.79	20.1	1.34	1.66	16.14
5.5	0.9	1.47	23.4	4.8	0	32	1.11	0.87	26.3
6.6	1.09	0	22.1	4.57	0.97	30.2	1.48	1.59	24.7
7.7	1.46	1.41	16.4	5.2	0	22.6	2.76	5.6	18.4
8.8	1.18	1.65	20.7	5.24	2.75	28.5	2.21	3.91	22.9
9.9	1.94	3.62	17.2	5.1	4.07	22.8	2.32	7.52	19
11	1.48	1.47	20.4	5.34	4.61	28.1	3.02	9.77	22.2

dv in mm

stress levels of S3 are closer in magnitude to S1 than S2, because the cavity diameters at the top of the cortical bone are the same for S2 and S3.

2.3.4 Clinical Significance

The optimal or desirable stress levels to be experienced by local bone during implantation have not yet been firmly established. However, according to Rieger et al. [32] and O'Mahony et al. [33], the desirable stress level lies between 1.72 and 2.76 MPa. The material structure of the cancellous bone makes it more sensitive to fracture than the cortical bone. The minimum and maximum stress profiles along the line *VV* produced by S1, S2 and S3 are plotted in Fig. 2.16 together with an ideal stress range (presented by the lower and upper limits) for cancellous bone growth and repair. Note that the minimum stress profiles are obtained at 1.8 s and the maximum at 36 s. On the basis of present knowledge, if the stress falls below 1.72 MPa, bone may not be stimulated adequately for effective healing and osseointegration. On the other hand, if the stress exceeds 2.76 MPa, bone resorption may occur, which contributes to loosening and potential failure of the implant. The ideal bone response will be achieved when the stress remains between these limits.

For all three insertion scenarios, the minimum stress profiles at 1.8 s are considerably below the lower limit of the stimulation stress (i.e. 1.72 MPa). For S1 (forming), the maximum stress profile (at 36 s) still does not reach the lower stress limit of 1.72 MPa. The low stress level produced by S1 may adversely affect initial retention of the implant which confirms the findings of Sennerby and Meredith [16] in that thread forming reduces implant stability. For S2 (cutting), the maximum stress profile at 36 s shows that bone resorption may occur around the implant because the upper stress limit of 2.76 MPa is exceeded for most of the

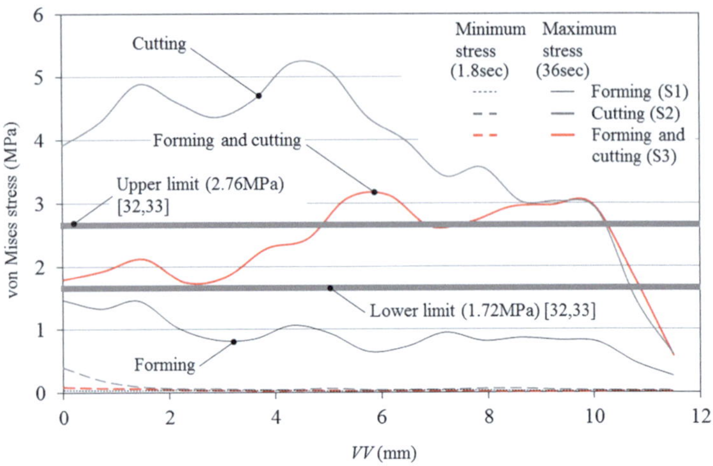

Fig. 2.16 Maximum and minimum stress profiles during implantation

locations along line *VV*. Overall, S3 (forming and cutting) best satisfies the ideal level of stress suggested in the literature. In current practice, many implant companies [12, 17, 18] generally recommend S2 for normal bone (i.e. type III or IV [34]) and S1 for compact bone (i.e. type I or IV) so that implant stability can be compromised. Based on the findings of this study, S3 may also be recommended for clinical practice.

It is important to note, however, that these findings have not modelled the fracture of bone through element deletion nor the effects of blood flow which influences contact friction. Incorporating such aspects into the finite element analysis merits further investigation.

2.4 Conclusion

2.4.1 Research Outcomes

The von Mises stress characteristics within the cancellous and cortical bone are evaluated for thread forming (scenario one, S1), cutting (scenario two, S2) and combined forming and cutting (scenario three, S3). With the adaptive meshing and contact interaction properties available in ABAQUS [28], realistic stress characteristics are modelled. The continuous dynamic simulation and implant cutting faces prove to be the major factors that distinguish the present results from those achieved in the stepwise simulation [14].

For S1, the stress levels within the cancellous and cortical bone are less than those in S2 and S3 because of the reduced bone to implant surface contact area. However, the stresses within the cancellous bone are only slightly reduced for S3 during the initial insertion steps. Then at later insertion steps, the stress within the cancellous bone (at any location along the line *VV*) increases to be at a level approximately halfway between those of S1 and S2. For cortical bone, the magnitude increases less significantly as the implant insertion depth progresses. The minor variation is due to the geometrical differences of the bone cavity. In both cancellous and cortical bone, the primary cutting faces induce stress peaks during the initial insertion stages (0.55–2.2 mm). This is because of the abrupt changes in geometry of the cutting faces. For the final insertion stages (9.9 and 11 mm) the change in implant section (i.e. implant neck establishes a contact with the cancellous bone) results in stress peaks within the cancellous bone.

The innovation of this research lies in the increased understanding of the stress characteristics in bone during the implantation process. This is likely to advance biomechanics of implantation surgery appreciably. Mechanical loosening after implantation is a significant challenge for most endoprosthetic procedures, and this research presents useful insights.

2.4.2 Recommendations for Further Developments

Optimisation techniques such as the application programming interface and/or design of experiment and response surface function of commercial software may be used to determine the highs and lows and the sensitivities of the stresses to a range of bone and implant parameters during implantation. Parameters that can be considered include element deactivation, contact friction, optimum combination of insertion torque/speed, implant diameter, length, tapers, thread design and primary cutting face and secondary cutting flute dimensions for each bone type.

References

1. Irish JD (2004) A 5,500 year old artificial human tooth from Egypt: a historical note. Int J Oral Maxillofac Implants 19(5):645–647
2. Brånemark PI (1983) Osseointegration and its experimental background. J Prosthet Dent 50(3):399–410
3. Bragger U, Krenander P, Lang NP (2005) Economic aspects of single-tooth replacement. Clin Oral Implants Res 16(3):335–341
4. van der Wijk P, Bouma J, van Oort RP, van Waas MA, van't Hof MA, Rutten FF (1996) Cost-effectiveness analysis of dental implants. Ned Tijdschr Tandheelkd 103(10):382–385
5. Albrektsson T, Dahl E, Enbom L, Engevall S, Engquist B, Eriksson AR, Feldmann G, Freiberg N, Glantz PO, Kjellman O (1988) Osseointegrated oral implants. A Swedish multicenter study of 8139 consecutively inserted Nobelpharma implants. J Periodontol 59(5): 287–296
6. Arvidson K, Bystedt H, Frykholm A, von Konow L, Lothigius E (1992) A 3-year clinical study of Astra dental implants in the treatment of edentulous mandibles. Int J Oral Maxillofac Implants 7:321–329

7. Spiekermann H, Jansen VK, Richter EJ (1995) A 10-year follow-up study of IMZ and TPS implants in the edentulous mandible using bar-retained overdentures. Int J Oral Maxillofac Implants 10:231–243
8. Mericski-Stern R, Schaffner TS, Marti P, Geering AH (1994) Peri-implant mucosal aspects of ITI implants supporting overdentures: a five-year longitudinal study. Clin Oral Implants Res 5:9–18
9. Fritz ME (1996) Implant therapy. II. Ann Periodontol 1:796–815
10. Jemt T, Johansson J (2006) Implant treatment in the edentulous maxillae: a 15-year follow-up study on 76 consecutive patients provided with fixed prostheses. Clin Implant Dent Relat Res 8(2):61–69
11. Nobel Biocare (2012) http://www.nobelbiocare.com/. Accessed 12 July 2012
12. Neoss, Pty Ltd (2009) Neoss implant system surgical guidelines. Neoss, Pty Ltd, Harrogate
13. O'Brien WJ (1989) Dent mats: properties and selection. Quintessence Publishing, Chicago/London
14. McClarance E (2004) Close to the cutting edge. Brånemark and the development of Osseointergration. Quintessence Publishing, London
15. Porter JA, von Fraunhofer JA (2005) Success or failure of dental implants? A literature review with treatment considerations. Gen Dent 53(6):423–432
16. Sennerby L, Meredith N (2008) Implant stability measurements using resonance frequency analysis: biological and biomechanical aspects and clinical implications. Periodontol 47(1): 51–66. doi:10.1111/j.1600-0757.2008.00267.x
17. 3i (2013) 3i implant innovations Inc. http://biomet3i.com/. Accessed 13 Apr 2013
18. Lambert FE, Weber HP, Susarla SM, Belser UC, Gallucci GO (2009) Descriptive analysis of implant and prosthodontic survival rates with fixed implant-supported rehabilitations in the edentulous maxilla. J Periodontol 80(8):1220–1230. doi:10.1902/jop.2009.090109
19. Mullender M, El Haj AJ, Yang Y, van Duin MA, Burger EH, Klein-Nulend J (2004) Mechanotransduction of bone cells in vitro: mechanobiology of bone tissue. Med Biol Eng Comput 42:14–21
20. Miyata T, Kobayashi Y, Araki H, Ohto T, Shin K (2002) The influence of controlled occlusal overload on peri-implant tissue. Part 4: a histologic study in monkeys. Int J Oral Maxillofac Implants 17(3):384–390
21. Tada S, Stegaroiu R, Kitamura E, Miyakawa O, Kusakari H (2003) Influence of implant design and bone quality on stress/strain distribution in bone around implants: a 3-dimensional finite element analysis. Int J Oral Maxillofac Implants 18(3):357–368
22. Petrie CS, Williams JL (2005) Comparative evaluation of implant designs: influence of diameter, length, and taper on strains in the alveolar crest. A three-dimensional finite-element analysis. Clin Oral Implants Res 16(4):486–494
23. Kitagawa T, Tanimoto Y, Nemoto K, Aida M (2005) Influence of cortical bone quality on stress distribution in bone around dental implant. Dent Mater J 24(2):219–224
24. Satoh T, Maeda Y, Komiyama Y (2005) Biomechanical rationale for intentionally inclined implants in the posterior mandible using 3D finite element analysis. Int J Oral Maxillofac Implants 20(4):533–539
25. Perez del Palomar A, Arruga A, Cegonino J, Doblare M (2005) A finite element comparison between the mechanical behaviour of rigid and resilient oral implants with respect to immediate loading. Comput Meth Biomech Biomed Eng 8(1):45–57
26. Sevimay M, Turhan F, Kiliçarslan MA, Eskitascioglu G (2005) Three-dimensional finite element analysis of the effect of different bone quality on stress distribution in an implant-supported crown. J Prosthet Dent 93(3):227–234
27. van Staden R, Guan H, Johnson NW, Loo YC, Meredith N (2008) Step-wise analysis of dental implant insertion process using finite element technique. Clin Oral Implants Res 19(3): 303–313
28. ABAQUS (2013) http://www.simulia.com. Accessed 5 Feb 2013

29. Burstein AH, Reilly DT, Martens M (1976) Aging of bone tissue: mechanical properties. J Bone Joint Surg Am 58(1):82–86
30. Choubey A, Basu B, Balasubramaniam R (2004) Tribological behaviour of Ti-based alloys in simulated body fluid solution at fretting contacts. Mater Sci Eng A 379(1–2):234–239. doi: http://dx.doi.org/10.1016/j.msea.2004.02.027
31. van Staden R (2008) Finite element analysis of dental implant-bone system during and after implantation, PhD thesis. Griffith University, Australia
32. Rieger MR, Mayberry M, Brose MO (1990) Finite element analysis of six endosseous implants. J Prosthet Dent 63(6):671–676
33. O'Mahony A, Bowles Q, Woolsey G, Robinson SJ, Spencer P (2000) Stress distribution in the single-unit osseointegrated dental implant: finite element analyses of axial and off-axial loading. Implant Dent 9(3):207–218
34. Rho JY, Ashman RB, Turner CH (1993) Young's modulus of trabecular and cortical bone material: ultrasonic and microtensile measurements. J Biomech 26(2):111–119

Chapter 3
Multiscale Remodelling and Topographical Optimisation for Porous Implant Surface Morphology Design

Wei Li, Junning Chen, Chaiy Rungsiyakull, Michael V. Swain, and Qing Li

Abstract Solid titanium and its alloys have been the most prevalent materials for dental and orthopaedic implants attributable to their advantageous mechanical and biocompatible properties. Nevertheless, there still is a range of biomechanics and biomaterials issues with titanium implants, such as delayed/insufficient osseointegration and limited shear-load bearing capacity in clinic. In order to tackle these problems, various physical and chemical treatment technologies have been developed to modify surface morphology of such implantable dental prostheses. Fully porous coating (FPC) is one of such techniques, where beads or particles are sintered to bond onto a solid core of implants under specific conditions. This process forms a layer of porous structure on the surface of the implant, whose morphology relies on the bead size, volume fraction and pattern of distribution. Given the critical roles that porous surface could play to enhance osseointegration, a major interest consists in how to optimise morphological parameters. This chapter aims to address this issue through a new multiscale modelling and design framework for optimising the surface morphology to enhance bone–implant interface stability and osseointegration in a biomechanics context. Four different measurements in the microscopic model are used as the design criteria to assess osseointegration outcomes: (1) peri-implant bone density, (2) uniformity of peri-implant bone density, (3) bone–implant contact (BIC) ratio, and (4) Tresca stress (maximum shear). To achieve these osseointegrative criteria, multiobjective optimisation is formulated with respect to the design variables of particle size, volume fraction and gradient. The optimised surface morphology allows creating a better microenvironment for cell attachment, differentiation and proliferation. While cells are seeded in a passive way during implantation in vivo, the tailored surface topography enables to better engage cellular activities in both biomechanical and biochemical aspects, thereby generating better short- and long-term clinical outcomes.

W. Li (✉) • J. Chen • C. Rungsiyakull • M.V. Swain • Q. Li
School of Aerospace, Mechanical & Mechatronic Engineering, The University of Sydney, Sydney, NSW 2006, Australia
e-mail: wei.li@sydney.edu.au

Q. Li, Y.-W. Mai (eds.), *Biomaterials for Implants and Scaffolds*, Springer Series in Biomaterials Science and Engineering 8, DOI 10.1007/978-3-662-53574-5_3

Keywords Multiscale remodelling • Surface topography • Osseointegration • Implant • Functionally graded coating • Computational biomechanics

3.1 Introduction

Titanium and its alloys have been one class of the most prevalent implantable materials achieving considerable success in orthopaedic, prosthodontic and cardiological applications, for their advantageous mechanical and biocompatible properties [1–6]. This broad range of applications signified a main concern on the strength of implant anchorage onto host tissues, and a series of biomechanics and biomaterials challenges remain with titanium implants, including poor or delayed osseointegration and limited shear-load bearing capacity [1, 5–9].

In order to enhance osseointegration, various physical and chemical surface treatment technologies have been developed to modify the external surfaces of an implant, to achieve desirable morphologies [6, 7, 9–12]. A rough or porous implant surface has been reported to provide more space and favourable biomechanical microenvironment to facilitate cell attachment and tissue ingrowth, thereby promoting a higher level of bone–implant interaction with improved cell migration and osteoblast adhesion to the implant surfaces [5–7, 12–18]. Fully porous coating (FPC) is one of such approaches, in which beads or particles are sintered onto a solid substrate core of implants to form desirable surface morphology [19, 20]. A layer of porous structure forms on the surface of the implant through such a process, and the topographical characteristics largely depend on the bead/particle sizes, volume fraction and internal bindings [21, 22]. Accordingly, the shear stress can be more evenly transferred across the interface, leading to better stimulation to the surrounding tissues for the establishment of osseointegration and biomechanical binding [9, 23, 24].

Several in vivo studies have been conducted to investigate the effects of these morphological factors on osseointegration and to examine the advantages in using the porous-coated endosseous implants [5, 6, 9, 12–14, 25–32]. Among these reports, the implants with the greater porosities were found to stabilise the healing more quickly than those with less porous ones, based upon radiographic analysis on the bone remodelling on dogs [31]. Further analysis confirmed these observed advantages of porously coated implants over a bare threaded design by using a histological comparison of harvested dental implants from the dogs [33]. In general, increasing porosity to a certain extent can provide a greater space to enable more efficient nutrient delivery and metabolite removal for cellular activities, thereby better promoting bone mineralisation and stabilisation over a shorter period [5, 9, 28–30].

The topographical characteristics of a porous surface are believed to be the critical determinants to the implant performance. Certain pore sizes were reported to facilitate the adhesion of fibrin blood clots and to promote osteoid formation, as well as the subsequent mineralisation, thereby helping develop a stable connection of implant with the surrounding bony tissues [34, 35]. One study [29] suggested that the pore sizes between 50 and 120 μm would allow bone ingrowth, while another orthopaedic study [34] suggested a minimum pore size of 100–150 μm for bone ingrowth into a porous ceramic scaffold. Marginal differences of the stabilisation rates were shown between pore sizes up to 100 μm and in excess of 100 μm, on porously coated cobalt-base alloy implants [36].

Given the important role of a porous surface in enhancing osseointegration, an optimal morphology remains a major interest in implant research. Despite indicative relations between morphological parameters and osseointegration rates that were revealed in these above-mentioned in vivo studies, the empirical approaches are often quite invasive and can be very difficult (if not impossible) to precisely define important details in the biomechanical interaction for the development of proper porous implants. As an alternative, computer modelling (namely, in silico) provides a non-destructive means to understanding the effect of pores and capturing time-dependent process of osseointegration for predicting the possible outcomes of bone remodelling, which has proven to be efficient and low risk to complement in vivo studies [37]. For example, Shen and Brinson developed computational models to determine the effects of porosity and particle sizes of porous titanium [3], and their further study modelled the bone's responses to surface morphology [38]. Few in silico studies have, however, addressed the computational design of implant topography for optimising treatment outcomes [6].

Most of these in silico studies have considered nearly uniform morphology across the porous thickness except for microscopic randomness. A major concern associated with such uniformly coated implants is the ability of gradually transferring load from implant core to the surrounding bony tissue. A potential upgrade to such uniform coatings is a specially designed graded surface morphology [6, 39–43]. For this purpose, some attempts have been made to develop functionally graded implants for a lower mismatch of mechanical properties and to further improve osseointegration between the implant and bone with different morphological gradients [7, 41, 44]. A few experimental studies have actually been carried out to evaluate the advantages of graded surfaces in promoting osseointegration [7, 42, 43, 45]. Computationally, Lin et al. [39] developed the finite element (FE) models at a macroscopic level for the axially graded hydroxyapatite–titanium implants; and some indicative results were obtained to seek an optimal material gradient for bone remodelling [39, 41, 46]. Nevertheless, most of these graded implant studies focused on either a macroscopic length scale or an axial gradient. However, a macroscopic FEA may not be adequate to capture the biomechanical details within the microstructural features; few reports have been available to model a graded porous surface morphology in radial direction of an implant through examining microscopic responses and none has genuinely searched for an optimal radial gradient to date.

This chapter aims to introduce a multiscale finite element framework of simulating bone remodelling activities and quantifying the effects of different surface morphological parameters. In order to evaluate the osseointegration and interface stability, four critical indicators to implant success have been considered here, including the average apparent bone density, uniformity of density distribution, bone–implant contact (BIC) ratio and averaged peak Tresca shear stress (PTS) through the porous layer and peri-implant regions. Based upon the remodelling results obtained, the response surface method (RSM) will be employed to formulate the relation between these above-mentioned remodelling indicators and the morphological parameters, thereby deriving an optimal configuration of surface coating through a multiobjective optimisation approach.

3.2 Materials and Methods

3.2.1 Finite Element Modelling

With state-of-the-art fabrication technologies, a range of desired nano- and/or microstructured materials can be generated. In this context, traditional mono-scale finite element analysis (FEA) is facing significant challenge as it is inadequate to capture detailed interaction between biomaterials and host tissues at different scales in an effective way. In order to tackle this problem, multiscale analysis techniques have been developed by bridging macro-scale (global) homogenised materials to micro-scale (local) heterogeneous structures with more insightful information [39, 41, 46]. Typical examples in this area include simulating bone internal structures and implant compositions [47, 48], trabecular bone remodelling for correlation to empirical data [49] and implant morphological effects on bone biomechanics and remodelling [50].

In this chapter, the threaded and non-threaded implant configurations are considered as two typical examples in dental implants. In both cases, the implant core is coated with beads at different sizes by sintering [9]. The macroscopic (global) model herein is based upon a 3D solid model created from a set of computerised tomography (CT) data at a human mandibular canine section. The image in DICOM format is firstly segmented in ScanIP (Simpleware Ltd, Exeter, UK) and then processed in Rhinoceros 3D (Robert McNeel & Associates, Seattle, USA). To avoid the structural complexity of the 3D multiscale model and associative high computational costs for remodelling analyses [6, 21, 51], a 2D demonstrative model is adopted in this study, capable of capturing the major biomechanical features under the occlusal loading scenario of mandible section [52]. In essence, a 2D model facilitates capturing many randomly located particles/beads and pores in a reasonably dense mesh, requiring relatively lower computational cost for iterative remodelling simulations compared to the 3D version of multiscale models. Other computational pros and cons between 2D and 3D models can be consulted from literature [6, 51, 53–56]. Therefore, the complete 3D solid model is then converted into a 2D macro-scale model by sectioning in a bucco-lingual plane as shown in Fig. 3.1. A typical implantation is adopted, which consists of a metallic abutment, a

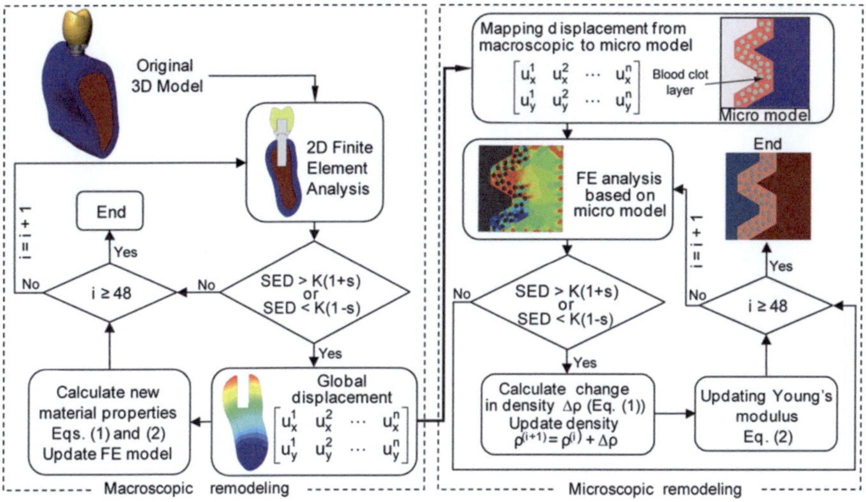

Fig. 3.1 Multiscale remodelling algorithm on a threaded implant with a homogenous porous surface morphology by randomness (Reprinted from Ref. [6], Copyright 2010, with permission from Elsevier)

ceramic crown and a metallic screw body (threaded or non-threaded types). A 202.23 N load is applied vertically to the crown cusp with a 2-mm horizontal offset from the centre to the buccal side [6, 39, 51]. It must be noted that such a macroscopic model is not capable of presenting the microscopic details of either bone or implant surface morphology, just like other mono-scale FE studies.

To capture microscopic morphological features, micro-scale models are created by selecting a region of interest (ROI) with a size of 1 mm × 1 mm (Fig. 3.1). The microscopic model consists of bone, implant substrate (core) and a layer of 200-μm transitional region between them. This transitional layer presents a mixture of pores formed by the implant surface morphology and blood clot that will gradually turn into connective tissues and form host bone [14, 57]. In this chapter, two types of surface morphological patterns, namely homogeneous and gradient, are considered to explore the effect of the coating topography on osseointegration.

For the homogeneous pattern (Case 1), a threaded implant is considered, with sintered (fully bonded) Ti6A14V alloy particles in spherical shapes, in a randomised manner. Forty microscopic models are created to represent different coating scenarios for the localised cortical and cancellous ROIs (20 models each, Fig. 3.1). Two key topological parameters, the particle diameters and volume fractions, are considered to create different morphological configurations. The former varies at 30, 50, 75 and 100 μm, and the latter adopts 15, 20, 25, 30 and 35 % [6, 19, 21, 22], resulting in 20 microscopic models for both the cortical and cancellous ROIs.

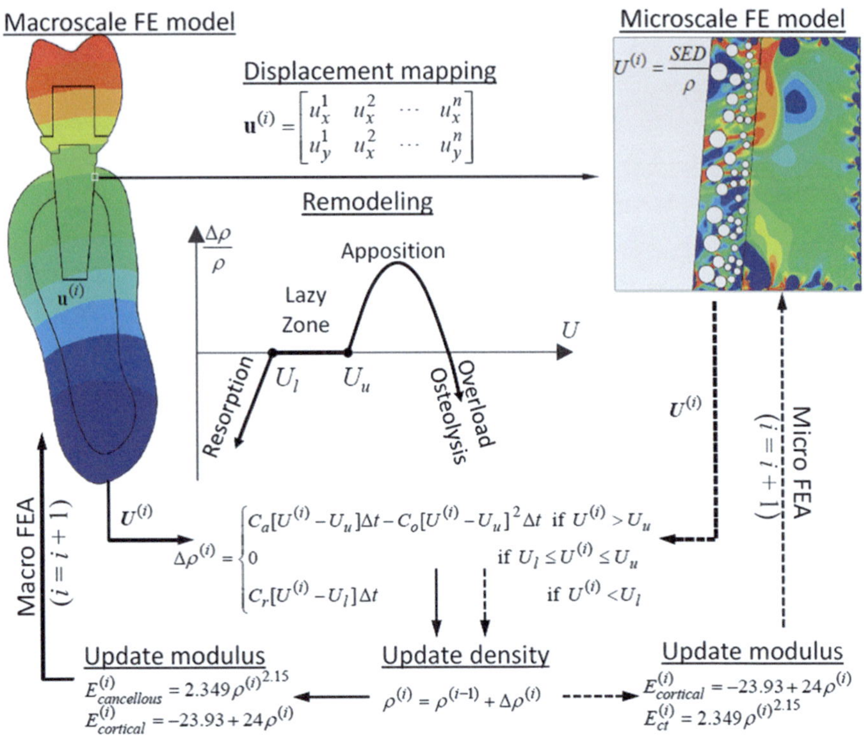

Fig. 3.2 Multiscale remodelling procedure considering overload resorption on a non-threaded implant with a gradient porous surface morphology (Reprinted from Ref. [52], Copyright 2013, with permission from Elsevier)

For the gradient pattern (Case 2), a non-threaded implant surface is considered for another common implant body type (Fig. 3.2). The surface morphological gradient is created by dividing the transitional zone into three sub-layers with different combinations of particle sizes of 30, 50 and 70 μm in diameter [6, 14, 19, 57]. The volume fractions of particles are kept constant at 30 %, equivalent to a porosity of 70 %; so our attention can be focused on the net effects from the particle sizes and morphological gradients. For Case 2, 27 microscopic models are created for the cortical ROI, to represent all possible gradients determined from the given design parameters.

Both macro-scale and micro-scale models are meshed in ABAQUS Ver. 6.9.2 (Dassault Systemes, USA) with three-node linear triangular plain strain elements (CPE3). Verified by a convergence test [6, 51, 53, 58–66], the global adaptive mesh size is set at 1.0×10^{-6} with a curvature deviation factor of 0.01, resulting in an average mesh density of 1.7 elements per μm^2 to ensure a sufficient numerical accuracy. All the finite element analyses are performed using ABAQUS.

3.2.2 Material Properties

The mechanical properties for different materials in this chapter are adopted from literature data; and they are assumed to be linear elastic and isotropic for the sake of simplification in the remodelling analysis [51, 53, 61–63, 67, 68]. In the macroscopic models, the screw body and the abutment are made of titanium alloy [9, 69], and the crown is made of zirconia [53, 69]. The initial properties of the cortical and cancellous bones are obtained from the experimental results reported in the literature [9, 69, 70]; and the remodelling activities will be simulated based on these initial statuses. Poisson's ratios of the same types of tissues are assumed to remain constant during remodelling. The microscopic models adopted the same material properties for the implant region, and the bone region adopts as those in the macroscopic models. The transitional region is assumed to be fully filled by blood clot after 30 min of implantation [71] as its initial status, which will gradually turn into connective tissues, immature bone and mature bone with the corresponding material property changes [70, 72, 73]. Through the remodelling activities, both the existing bone and the transitional area will turn into a heterogeneous status with different bone mineral densities over the cross-sectional plane. All the material properties used in this simulation are summarised in Table 3.1. Following the literature, the densities of cancellous and cortical bones are assumed to be limited by an upper limit of 1.2 and 2.0 g/cm^3, respectively [6, 51, 53, 54].

Table 3.1 Initial properties of multiscale models for remodelling simulation

<table>
<tr><td colspan="7">Macro-scale model</td></tr>
<tr><td></td><td colspan="2">Implant core and abutment</td><td>Crown</td><td>Cortical bone</td><td colspan="2">Cancellous bone</td></tr>
<tr><td>Young's modulus (MPa)</td><td colspan="2">110,000</td><td>201,000</td><td>1,970</td><td colspan="2">14.8</td></tr>
<tr><td>Poisson's ratio</td><td colspan="2">0.35</td><td>0.28</td><td>0.33</td><td colspan="2">0.33</td></tr>
<tr><td colspan="7">Micro-scale model</td></tr>
<tr><td></td><td>Native bone</td><td>Implant core and particles</td><td>Host tissue (blood clots)</td><td>Mature bone</td><td>Immature bone</td><td>Soft tissues</td></tr>
<tr><td rowspan="2">Young's modulus (MPa)</td><td>1,970 (cortical)</td><td rowspan="2">110,000</td><td rowspan="2">0.001</td><td rowspan="2">6,000</td><td rowspan="2">1,000</td><td rowspan="2">1</td></tr>
<tr><td>14.8 (cancellous)</td></tr>
<tr><td>Poisson's ratio</td><td>0.33</td><td>0.3</td><td>0.33</td><td>0.33</td><td>0.33</td><td>0.167</td></tr>
</table>

Adapted from Ref. [52], Copyright 2013, with permission from Elsevier

3.2.3 Multiscale Remodelling Algorithm

The remodelling activities are occurring in both these two length scales. The macroscopic model determined the bone response in terms of the apparent mineral density change in the global scale; and the microscopic model stimulated the detailed tissue ingrowth in the ROIs specified from the macroscopic models. The widely accepted Wolff's rule is used to model the turnover of cortical and cancellous bones and connective tissues for both scales [6, 51, 54, 63, 74–76]. In the remodelling simulation, the apparent density ($\Delta\rho$) is set to change over a time increment (Δt) and is proportional to the mechanobiological stimulus. The time increment is chosen at a month here, and the stimulus is defined as the difference between an instant strain energy density (SED) per unit mass (i.e. $U = 0.5\boldsymbol{\sigma} : \boldsymbol{\varepsilon}$) and either upper or lower reference [53, 54, 74, 77–80]. This governing remodelling equation can be mathematically formulated in Eq. (3.1) as below.

$$\Delta\rho = \begin{cases} C_a\left[\dfrac{U}{\rho} - K(1+s)\right]\Delta t, & \text{if } \dfrac{U}{\rho} > K(1+s) \\ 0 & \text{if } K(1-s) \le \dfrac{U}{\rho} \le K(1+s) \\ C_r\left[\dfrac{U}{\rho} - K(1-s)\right]\Delta t, & \text{if } \dfrac{U}{\rho} < K(1-s) \end{cases} \tag{3.1}$$

In this equation, ρ is the local apparent density, and C_a and C_r are the remodelling rate constants [6, 51, 63]. K is the median of the stimulus over the lazy zone, determined at 0.036 mJ/g/cm^3 from the in vivo data [53]. $2s$ is the width of the lazy zone where we adopt $s = 10\,\%$ as suggested in the literature [76]. Bone resorption can also be induced by mechanical overload once the stimulus level exceeds the physiological limit [12, 81–83]. To represent this factor, a quadratic term can be added to the remodelling equation for an adjusted Wolff's rule [51, 54, 84].

The change in apparent density will lead to the changes in consequential mechanical property, and the empirical relationships between Young's modulus of elasticity (E in GPa) and apparent density (ρ in g/cm^3) are used here [85, 86] as in Eq. (3.2):

$$E = \begin{cases} -23.93 + 24\rho, & \text{for cortical bone} \\ 2.349\rho^{2.15}, & \text{for cancellous bone} \end{cases} \tag{3.2}$$

The bone remodelling simulation is initially conducted on the macroscopic model. The displacement fields are extracted around the ROI boundaries at each time step of this global remodelling simulation. These time-dependent displacement fields are then mapped onto the microscopic models as the loading conditions at each time step. The strain energy density (SED) determined in the microscopic model interpolates the microscopic remodelling responses for further design analysis and optimisation.

Both macroscopic and microscopic remodelling simulations are implemented in ABAQUS system by using FORTRAN user-defined subroutines. This multiscale bone remodelling algorithm is summarised in a flowchart for a threaded implant in Fig. 3.1 and for a non-threaded implant in Fig. 3.2.

3.2.4 Evaluation of Osseointegration

To evaluate the degree of osseointegration, there are several different indicative measures. A primary indicator for the extent of tissue ingrowth is the apparent density in the peri-implant region, which is often calculated by using an area (or volume for 3D) average in a finite element context [3, 87], as formulated in Eq. (3.3). In this equation, A_e is the area of element e, NE is the total number of elements in this region, ρ_e is the apparent density in element e, and $\mathbf{x}$ denotes design variables, such as particle size and volume fraction, namely, $\mathbf{x} = (\alpha, \upsilon)^{\mathrm{T}}$. A higher bone density typically represents better osseointegration.

$$F_1(\mathbf{x}) = \widetilde{\rho} = \frac{1}{A}\int_A \rho dA \approx \frac{1}{\sum_{e=1}^{NE} A_e}\sum_{e=1}^{NE} \rho_e A_e \tag{3.3}$$

There is an alternative indicator for the amount of tissue ingrowth considering bone–implant contact (BIC) ratio, which has been widely used in literature to measure how the bone anchors into and becomes mature in the pore space of the transitional porous region [72, 88]. The BIC ratio can be determined by the proportion of elemental areas with Young's modulus higher than the threshold of mature bone (MB) to the total element area (AE) of connecting tissues, as in Eq. (3.4).

$$\begin{aligned} F_1'(\mathbf{x}) = f_{BIC} = \%BIC &= \frac{\text{Mature Bone Area}}{\text{All Elemental Areas}} \times 100\% \\ &= \frac{\sum_{i=1}^{MB} A_i}{\sum_{i=1}^{AE} A_i} \times 100\% \end{aligned} \tag{3.4}$$

In conjunction with the primary indicators, the homogeneity of the final bone density can be a secondary indicator for quantifying a successful osseointegration and stability. It can be represented by the standard deviation of apparent density in the distribution of established bone density in the region. The less the standard deviation, the more uniform the apparent density. The standard deviation ($\widetilde{\varepsilon}$) concerned is defined as in Eq. (3.5).

$$F_2(\mathbf{x}) = \widetilde{\varepsilon} = \sqrt{\frac{1}{NE}\sum_{e=1}^{NE}(\rho_e - \overline{\rho})^2} \tag{3.5}$$

Similar to the primary indicator, the secondary indicator can also be interpreted in an alternative way, as the capability of the consequential implant–bone interface structure to withstand mechanical loading without debonding. In practice, a pull-out test is a common method to test the degree of shear resistance [19, 89–91]. The Tresca stress is adopted to assess how well the shear stress concentration can be avoided. Nevertheless, the peak Tresca stress may occur in a single element, leading to the misinterpretation of the shear failure for entire transitional region; therefore, the elemental Tresca stress is averaged out over 10 % of the total volume with the highest stress level to provide more statistical meaning. The overall risk of shear failure is thus measured in Eq. (3.6), where n is the number of elements counting for 10 % the total volume that withstands the peak Tresca stresses (PTS).

$$F'_2(\mathbf{x}) = f_{PTS} = \frac{\sum_{e=1}^{n} \sigma^e_{10\%\ Peak\ Tre} \times V^e_{10\%\ Peak\ Tre}}{\sum_{e=1}^{n} V^e_{10\%\ Peak\ Tre}} \tag{3.6}$$

3.2.5 Response Surface Method (RSM)

It is often very difficult to establish analytical functions for these above-mentioned multiple biological indicators, especially in complex nonlinear mechanobiological processes, such as osseointegration. The surrogate modelling techniques such as RSM are considered an effective and sometimes unique, alternative approach to modelling these responses [6, 46, 51, 92]. Through RSM, an approximated function $f(\mathbf{x})$ is formulated in terms of a series of simple basis functions [92, 93]. Eq. (3.7) denotes a typical example, where $\widetilde{f}(\mathbf{x})$ stands for the surrogate model that is used to approximate the true function $f(\mathbf{x})$, and N denotes the number of the basis functions $\varphi_j(\mathbf{x})$.

$$\widetilde{f}(\mathbf{x}) = \sum_{j=1}^{N} a_j \varphi_j(\mathbf{x}) \tag{3.7}$$

To determine the unknown parameters $\mathbf{a} = (a_1, a_2, \ldots, a_N)^{\mathrm{T}}$ in Eq. (3.7), M ($M > N$) sampling points $\mathbf{x}^{(i)}$ ($i = 1, 2, \ldots, M$) are needed, which is often not linearly proportional to N. If the remodelling results for each sample point are obtained to form a response vector $f = (f^{(1)}, f^{(2)}, \ldots, f^{(M)})^{\mathrm{T}}$, the typical least-square method can be applied to determine the unknown parameter vector $\mathbf{a}$ by minimising

$$E(\mathbf{a}) = \sum_{i=1}^{M} \left[\mathbf{f}^{(i)} - \mathbf{a}^{\mathrm{T}} \varphi_i \left(\mathbf{x}^{(i)} \right) \right]^2 \tag{3.8}$$

thereby determining the unknown vector, $\mathbf{a} = (a_1, a_2, \ldots, a_N)^{\mathrm{T}}$ from

$$\mathbf{a} = \left(\mathbf{\Phi}^{\mathrm{T}} \mathbf{\Phi} \right)^{-1} \left(\mathbf{\Phi}^{\mathrm{T}} \mathbf{f} \right), \tag{3.9}$$

where the matrix $\mathbf{\Phi}$ denotes the values of the basis functions evaluated at these M sampling points, as

$$\mathbf{\Phi} = \begin{bmatrix} \varphi_1 \left(\mathbf{x}^{(1)} \right) & \cdots & \varphi_N \left(\mathbf{x}^{(1)} \right) \\ \vdots & \ddots & \vdots \\ \varphi_1 \left(\mathbf{x}^{(M)} \right) & \cdots & \varphi_N \left(\mathbf{x}^{(M)} \right) \end{bmatrix}_{M \times N} \tag{3.10}$$

By substituting Eq. (3.9) into Eq. (3.7), the expression of $\tilde{f}(\mathbf{x})$ can be fully defined, which mathematically relates the objective functions to the design variables.

To ensure an adequate accuracy of the response surface model, the degree of approximation to the FEA results can be evaluated by the relative error (*RE*) as,

$$RE = \frac{\tilde{f}(\mathbf{x}) - f(\mathbf{x})}{f(\mathbf{x})} \tag{3.11}$$

3.2.6 Design Optimisation

With multiple indicators for osseointegration, we introduce multiobjective optimisation techniques to address the above-mentioned design issue. Three types of optimisation algorithms are considered in this chapter, namely, linear weighted average (LWA), geometrical average (GA) and multiple objective particle swarm optimisation (MOPSO) methods [92, 94–96].

In Case 1, the particle size (diameter) α and associated volume (or the area in the 2D model) fraction υ are the key design variables, i.e. $\mathbf{x} = (\alpha, \upsilon)^{\mathrm{T}}$, to the homogeneous porous morphology on the threaded implant surface. For this typical case, we employ the primary and the secondary indicators (F_1 and F_2) to measure the overall osseointegration. From a clinical perspective, successful osseointegration expects the maximised (or the minimised reciprocal of) bone mineral density gain in the peri-implant region as the first indicator. Meanwhile, it is also expected to minimise the variance of bone mineral density distribution as the second indicator as per the standard deviation in the apparent density. In order to achieve both these two objects simultaneously, the multiobjective optimisation problem can be formulated using the linear weighted average method [94], as in Eq. (3.12), where f°_{avg} and f°_{std} are the normalising values. By varying the weights w_1 and w_2 systematically, a Pareto set can be generated to include a range of the optimal design solutions for different design requirements. The Pareto set provides the entire optimal solution space for the multiobjective optimisation problem. The weights (w_1, w_2) play an important role in emphasising on these two different design objectives, differently.

$$\begin{cases} \min\ J_{u,LWA} = F_1^{-1}(\alpha, \upsilon) + F_2(\alpha, \upsilon) = w_1 \dfrac{f^{\circ}_{avg}}{f_{avg}} + w_2 \dfrac{f_{std}}{f^{\circ}_{std}} \\ s.t.:\quad w_1 + w_2 = 1,\ w \in [0, 1], \\ \qquad\quad 30\mu m \le \alpha \le 100\mu m, \\ \qquad\quad 15\% \le \upsilon \le 35\% \end{cases} \tag{3.12}$$

The geometric average (GA) method is similar to the LWA method. In this method, the cost function is formulated from the relative performance index of each objective (Eq. (3.13)). In other words, the multiobjective problem is constructed in terms of a geometric average of the relative distance of each objective to its corresponding ideal value, as in Eqs. (3.14) and (3.15), where f^L_{avg}, f^U_{avg}, f^L_{std} and f^U_{std} denote the minimum and maximum objective values of the density and standard deviation, respectively:

$$\begin{cases} \max\ J_{u,GA}(\alpha, \upsilon) = \sqrt{F_1^* F_2^*} = \sqrt{f^*_{avg}(\alpha, \upsilon) f^*_{std}(\alpha, \upsilon)} \\ s.t.:\quad 30\mu m \le \alpha \le 100\mu m \\ \qquad\quad 15\% \le \upsilon \le 35\%, \end{cases} \tag{3.13}$$

$$f^*_{avg} = \frac{f_{avg}(\alpha, \upsilon) - f^L_{avg}}{f^U_{avg} - f^L_{avg}} \le 100\% \tag{3.14}$$

$$f^*_{std} = 1 - \frac{f_{std}(\alpha, \upsilon) - f^L_{std}}{f^U_{std} - f^L_{std}} \le 100\% \tag{3.15}$$

Compared with the LWA and GA methods, the MOPSO method provides a more efficient solution to seeking for optimal solutions. MOPSO is an extended version of the particle swarm optimisation (PSO) procedure that has been successfully used in a broad range of the single-objective design problems. Coello and Lechuga [95] introduced the MOPSO algorithm by incorporating the ability to handle the multiple objectives without sacrificing typical fast convergence of PSO. This method incorporates the mechanism of crowding distance, which is specifically benefited on global best selection of dominated solutions from an external archive. More details of this algorithm can be found in the literature [95, 96]. In this case, the design problem is formulated mathematically as in Eq. (3.16).

$$\begin{cases} \min\ J_{u,PSO}(\alpha, \upsilon) = \left[F_1^{-1}(\alpha, \upsilon), F_2(\alpha, \upsilon)\right]^T = \left[f_{avg}^{-1}, f_{std}\right]^T \\ s.t.: \quad 30\mu m \le \alpha \le 100\mu m \\ \qquad\quad 15\% \le \upsilon \le 35\%, \end{cases} \tag{3.16}$$

In Case 2, the particle sizes, α_1, α_2 and α_3, in these three different sub-layers, are considered as the design variables $\mathbf{x} = (\alpha_1,\ \alpha_2,\ \alpha_3)^T$ for the graded porous surface morphology on a non-threaded implant. For this case, alternative indicators (F_1' and F_2') are adopted to evaluate the overall osseointegration and load-bearing capacity. Similar to Case 1, it is expected to maximise (or minimise the reciprocal of) the first indicator of BIC and minimise the second one in terms of averaged top 10 % Tresca stress. For this typical case, we adopted LWA and MOPSO methods for this multiobjective optimisation. The LWA method formulates the optimisation scenario in Eq. (3.17) [6, 46, 51, 92], where the normalisation by means of the minimum f_{BIC}° and maximum f_{Tre}° is used to eliminate the dimensional difference for better combining these two different objective functions.

$$\begin{cases} \min\ J_{g,LWA} = F_1'^{-1}(\alpha_1, \alpha_2, \alpha_3) + F_2'(\alpha_1, \alpha_2, \alpha_3) = w_1 \dfrac{f_{BIC}^{\circ}}{f_{BIC}} + w_2 \dfrac{f_{PTS}}{f_{PTS}^{\circ}} \\ s.t.: \quad w_1 + w_2 = 1, \quad (w_1 \ge 1,\ w_2 \ge 1) \\ \qquad\quad 30\mu m \le \alpha_1, \alpha_2, \alpha_3 \le 70\mu m \end{cases} \tag{3.17}$$

The MOPSO method, on the other hand, is also expressed directly as Eq. (3.18), similar to the homogenous case.

$$\begin{cases} \min\ J_{g,PSO} = \left[F_1'^{-1}(\alpha_1, \alpha_2, \alpha_3),\ F_2'(\alpha_1, \alpha_2, \alpha_3)\right]^T = \left[f_{BIC}^{-1},\ f_{PTS}\right]^T \\ s.t. \quad 30\mu m \le \alpha_1, \alpha_2, \alpha_3 \le 70\mu m \end{cases} \tag{3.18}$$

3.3 Results

In this chapter, both cases are simulated for bone remodelling responses with different surface morphological gradients over the 48 months, in which the host bone can grow into the void space and the corresponding osseointegration performance is measured by the different indicators. The first few months (as the first few increments) in the simulation are critical for the establishment of the secondary stability of an implant; after a certain period, bone could gradually achieve a dynamic equilibrium with both apposition and resorption occurring to a similar extent. Both the short-term and long-term implant performance assessments are considered here.

3.3.1 Homogeneous Coating Configuration with Threaded Implant (Case 1)

3.3.1.1 Bone Remodelling Responses

In Case 1, the effects of design variables, i.e. particle size and volume fraction of the coated material to void space, are first explored at month 48. The apparent densities for the cortical and cancellous bones are assumed to approach their upper limits of 2.00 and 1.2 g/cm^3, respectively, during this period as suggested in the literature [97]. As reported being a critical period for the osseointegration and stabilisation of implant, month 12 is also considered to be the initial time point to assess the remodelling outcomes in the short term, for comparing the mechanobiological responses induced by various designs in this case.

Table 3.2 summarises all the 40 ROIs in the homogenous surface morphology case, in terms of their area average density (ρ) and corresponding standard deviation (STD) after 12-month remodelling with regard to each design variable in the cortical and cancellous regions, respectively. During the first year, an increase in the volume fraction from 15 % to 35 % results in an average of 8.40 % and 8.12 % increase in density for the cortical and cancellous regions, respectively. Increasing the particle size from 30 μm to 100 μm, however, induces insignificant and fluctuating changes in the density, mainly because the location randomness of the particles may have resulted in a non-negligible effect on the biomechanical stimulation and thus leads to an inconsistent density variation.

Such finding is in good agreement with the study by Shen et al. [3], who concluded that the pore size has an insignificant effect on the stress–strain response, while the arrangement of the particles has a determinant influence on the stiffness.

Table 3.2 Area average density and standard deviation in the cortical and cancellous regions (12 months)

	30 μm		50 μm		75 μm		100 μm	
υ	ρ	STD	ρ	STD	ρ	STD	ρ	STD
Cortical region								
15 %	1.4315	0.3100	1.5172	0.3302	1.4988	0.3348	1.5074	0.3189
20 %	1.5247	0.3407	1.5687	0.3361	1.6645	0.3389	1.5739	0.3281
25 %	1.5344	0.3472	1.6638	0.3645	1.5045	0.3472	1.5424	0.3326
30 %	1.5680	0.3486	1.5879	0.3461	1.5367	0.3418	1.5896	0.3444
35 %	1.5962	0.3499	1.5948	0.3501	1.6029	0.3487	1.6590	0.3279
Cancellous region								
15 %	0.8369	0.1970	0.8716	0.2183	0.8643	0.2191	0.8680	0.2227
20 %	0.8942	0.2208	0.8959	0.2392	0.9167	0.2523	0.8758	0.2244
25 %	0.8851	0.2315	0.9236	0.2398	0.8486	0.2416	0.8763	0.2351
30 %	0.9098	0.2354	0.9084	0.2389	0.8956	0.2382	0.9122	0.2340
35 %	1.5962	0.3499	1.5948	0.3501	1.6029	0.3487	1.6590	0.3279

According to Bobyn et al. [19], the spherical particles with size ranging from 45 to 150 μm were estimated to provide the morphology with a pore size ranging from 50 to 200 μm. This range of pore size, in the adult canine (beagle) femurs, generated the maximum strength from the pull-out test at 8 weeks postoperatively. This could be another reason why there was small difference in remodelling responses when the particle size increased from 30 to 100 μm.

Table 3.2 also suggests that the surface morphologies with a greater volume fraction of spherical particles could potentially provide a better initial stability than those with a less volume fraction. This is simply due to the fact that the design containing more particles within the same volume provides a greater contact area with bone, thereby enabling it to achieve a higher interfacial or bonding force [19].

From the bone engagement perspective, the 100 μm particles are found to deliver the best bone density outcome under various volume fractions. The cortical and cancellous remodelling progressions are plotted for the design with a particle size of 100 μm in Fig. 3.3a and b, respectively, which show that the average bone density increases throughout the entire 48-month remodelling period in all different surface morphologies. Particularly in the first 12 months, the rate of density gain is very high and then gradually slows down until the end of the remodelling period considered (48 months). From the clinical perspective, it is important that bone formation is initiated at the earliest possible stage to establish sufficient stability for implant functions. In these two particular ROIs, the bone remodelling over the 48 months does not yet reach the full dynamic equilibrium status, signifying the existence of a remaining stimulus concentration in the peri-implant region, possibly resulting in further bone apposition and/or resorption.

The density contours in the transitional layer are displayed as the inserts in Fig. 3.3. In the cortical region (Fig. 3.3a), the dense bone is distributed in a way perpendicular to the inclined surface of implant threads, whereas the dense cancellous bone (Fig. 3.3b) distributes in a pattern preferentially along the horizontal direction and propagates into the implant fixture side of the bony tissues through the coated particles. This agrees with the macroscopic analysis where the occlusal loading is mainly borne by the cortical bone, while the cancellous bone stabilises the implant by accommodating the bending moments.

3.3.1.2 Response Surface Model

Based on the above remodelling results, the uniform morphological configuration can be further optimised by controlling the two topological factors, namely, the particle size (α) and the volume fraction (υ), as the design variables. To do so, a full factorial design of experiments (DoE) is first considered with these two design variables, i.e. the particle sizes at 30, 50, 75 and 100 μm and the volume fractions at 15, 20, 25, 30 and 35 %. Consequently, 20 design samples of the surface morphologies have been generated for the cortical and cancellous ROIs, respectively, evenly distributing the entire design domain. With these sampled points, several polynomial basis functions at different orders ranging from 1 to 4 are tested to

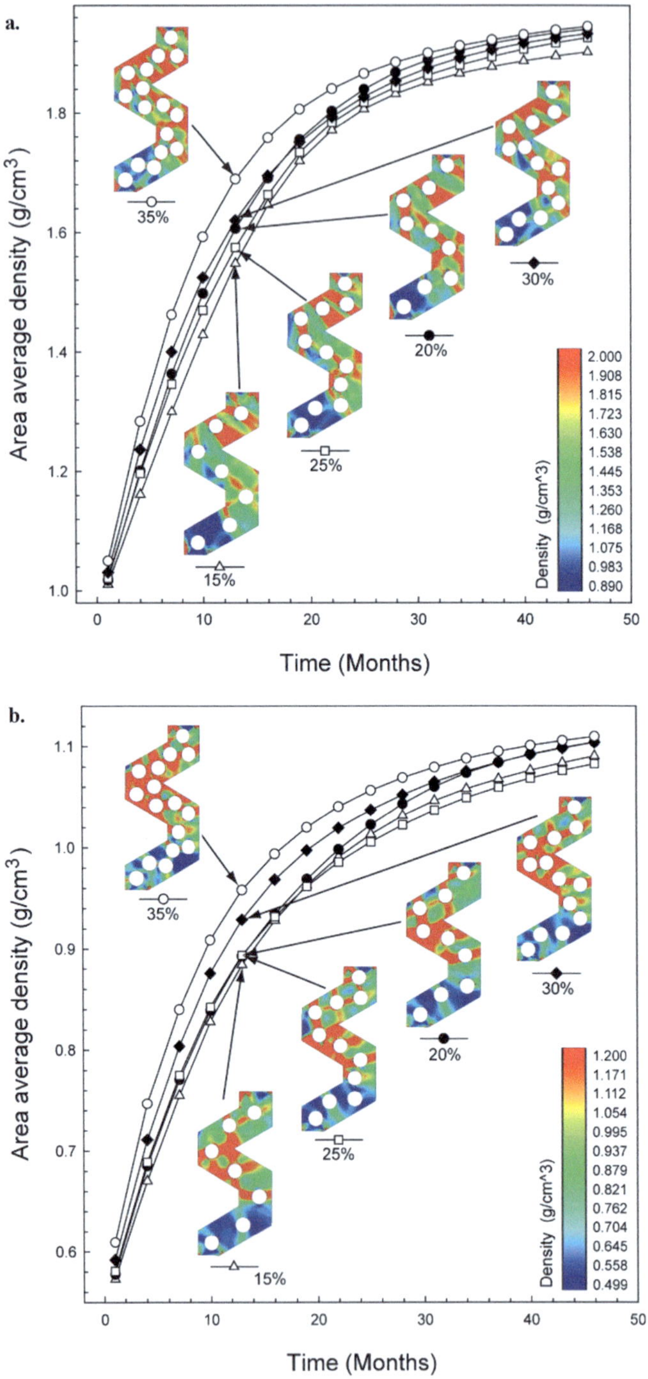

Fig. 3.3 Micro-scale remodelling progressions of area average of bone density with different volume fractions (at particle size 100 μm) at (**a**) cortical and (**b**) cancellous regions (Reprinted from Ref. [6], Copyright 2010, with permission from Elsevier)

Table 3.3 Response surface modelling accuracies for different polynomials (Reprinted from ref. [6], Copyright 2010, with permission from Elsevier)

	RS model (polynomial order)	Max RE (Cortical) (%)	Max RE (Cancellous) (%)
Density	Linear	6.38	5.47
	Quadratic	5.66	5.51
	Cubic*	4.86*	4.24*
	Quartic	558	2868
Standard deviation	Linear	7.66	11.02
	Quadratic	3.72	6.34
	Cubic*	3.37*	3.87*
	Quartic	2763	394

*The most accurate polynomial function

validate the response surface (RS) models. As evaluated by their modelling accuracies using Eq. (3.11), the outcomes are summarised in Table 3.3. Note that the smaller the relative error (RE), the better the regression for the RS model. Obviously, the cubic polynomial function provided the best overall approximation for both the cortical and cancellous regions considered.

The resulting response surfaces shown in Figs. 3.4 and 3.5 graphically illustrate the effects of particle sizes and volume fractions on the apparent density and the standard deviation in the cortical and cancellous regions, respectively. It is clear that the response surfaces of the average densities in both ROIs largely resemble each other. The least average densities in both the regions occur when the particle size and the volume fraction are at their lowest values. In contrast, the average density reaches the maximum at the largest particle size and volume fraction (i.e. 100 μm and 35 %, respectively).

3.3.1.3 Surface Morphology Design Optimisation

As mentioned in Sect. 3.2.6, two different design criteria are adopted to measure the subsequent osseointegration and bone remodelling. In the linear weighted averaged (LWA) method, the weighting factors w_1 and w_2 can be systematically varied to generate different optimal solutions from Eq. (3.12), which forms a Pareto solution set as plotted in Fig. 3.6 (blue circle). These two objective functions (F_1 and F_2), for the average bone density and its standard deviation in this case, vary from their upper to lower bounds as the results of different weights. As shown in Fig. 3.6a, three isolated optimal solution clusters (overlapping each other around 30 μm, 15 %; 100 μm, 30 %; and 100 μm, 35 %) can be determined for the cortical region. It must be noted that within the Pareto frontier, any further improvement in one objective must sacrifice the other, e.g. to increase the bone density further, and its uniformity must be compromised and vice versa. Similarly, the optimal designs for the cancellous bone are shown in Fig. 3.6b. Although the number of optimal

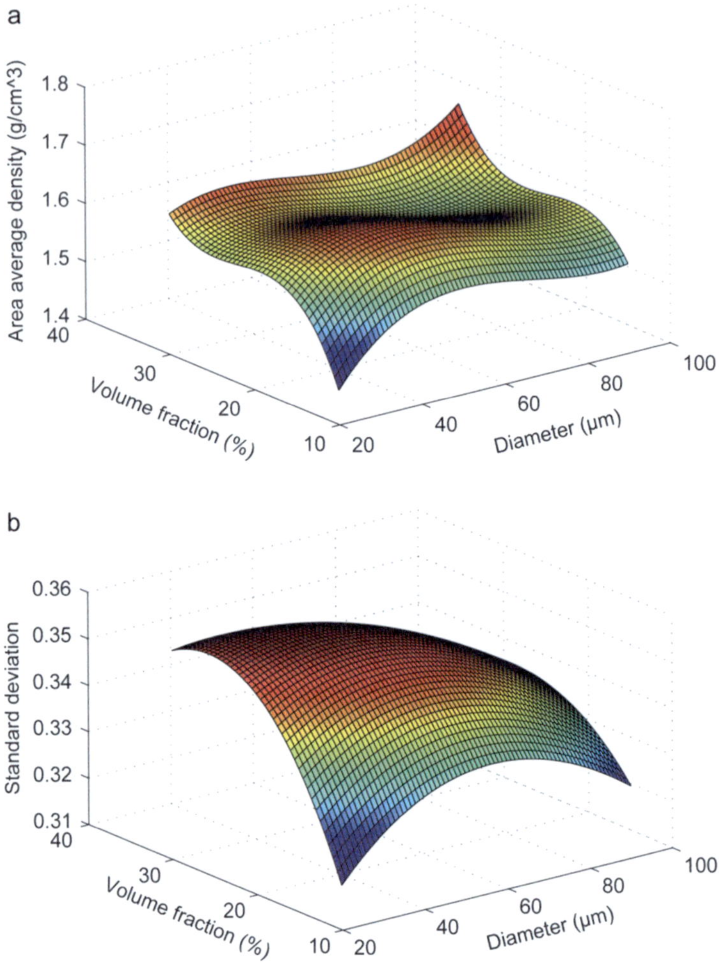

Fig. 3.4 Response surface plots showing the effects of particle size and volume fraction on the average density (**a**) and standard deviation (**b**) in the cortical regions (Reprinted from Ref. [6], Copyright 2010, with permission from Elsevier)

solutions appears more than that in the cortical bone, it would be preferable to generate more uniformly distributed optimal points in the Pareto space.

The other approach, namely multiobjective particle swarm optimisation (MOPSO) method, generates the Pareto solutions through gradually moving particles for Pareto dominance. Note that as any Pareto point denotes an optimum, which enables us to obtain the entire solution domain for the multiobjective optimisation problem. Its outcomes are plotted in the same figure as the LWA method with red dots. For the cortical ROI (Fig. 3.6a), the three isolated solution clusters are well positioned in the Pareto curves produced from the MOPSO method, showing the coincident trends as expected. Obviously, the MOPSO

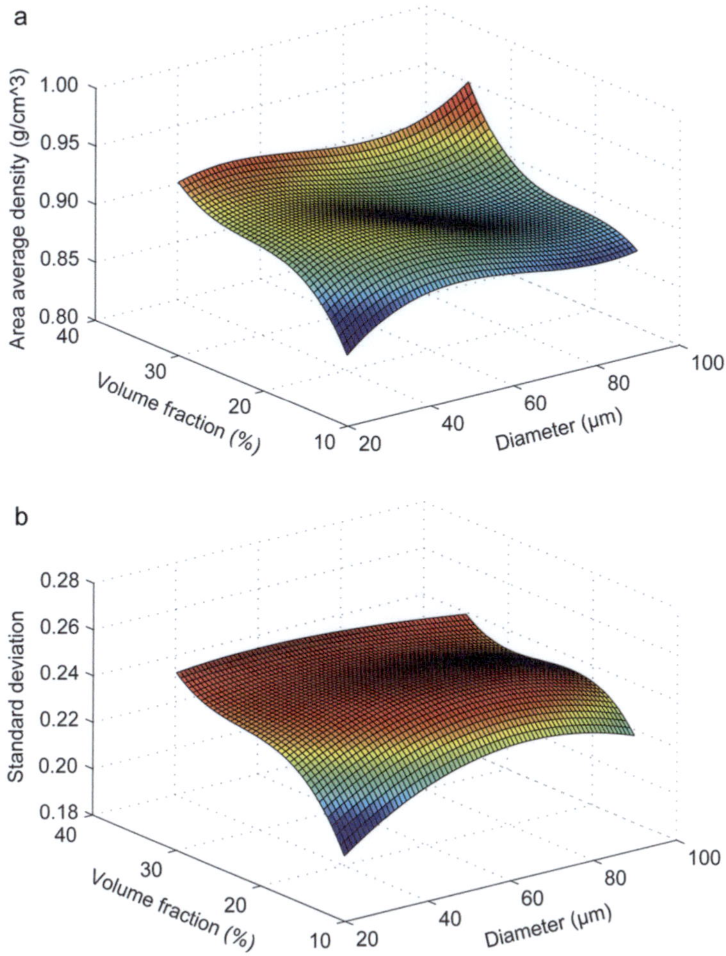

Fig. 3.5 Response surface plots showing the effects of particle size and volume fraction on the average density (**a**) and standard deviation (**b**) in the cancellous regions (Reprinted from Ref. [6], Copyright 2010, with permission from Elsevier)

method has provided much more uniform distribution of solution points, showing a significantly improved efficiency in pursuing optimal solutions, compared to the overlapped clusters of solutions from LWA. Importantly, the MOPSO method well demonstrates the competition between the two objective functions. When reaching the Pareto fronts, any further improvement in one must sacrifice the other.

Figure 3.6b plots the Pareto front for the implant design in the cancellous region, where the LWA method leads to slightly broader distribution than that in the cortical region. Again, all the optimal designs from the LWA method are well located on the Pareto frontiers resulted from the MOPSO method, indicating the

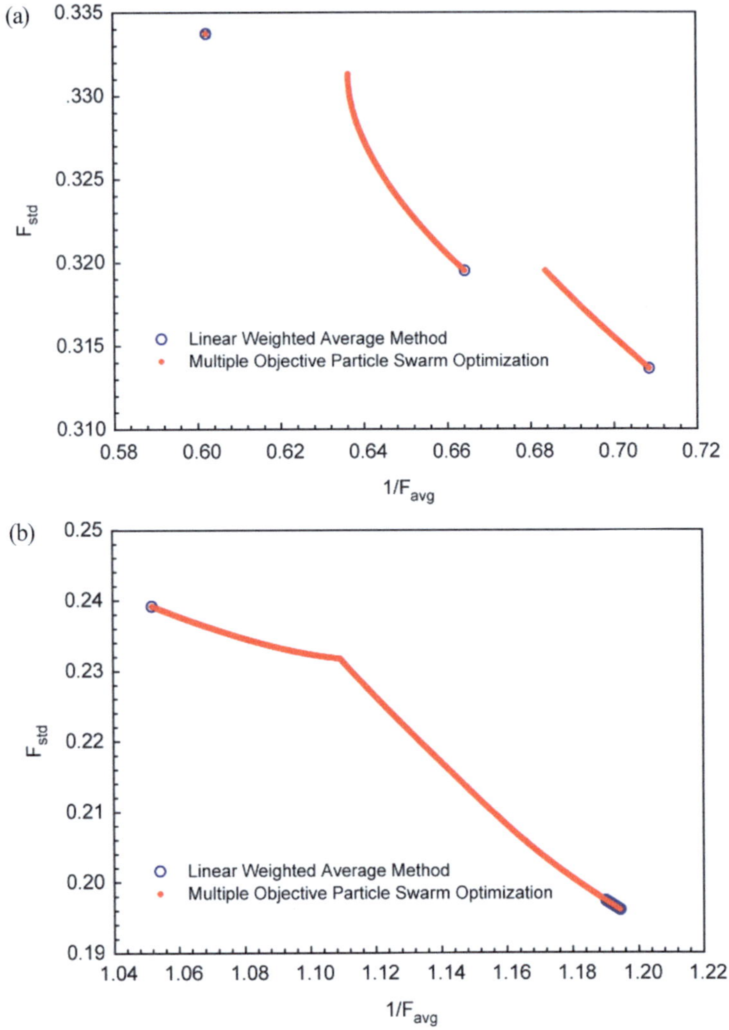

Fig. 3.6 Pareto frontiers resulted from the LWA and MOPSO multiobjective optimisation algorithms: (**a**) cortical region and (**b**) cancellous region (Reprinted from Ref. [6], Copyright 2010, with permission from Elsevier)

effectiveness of these two methods when searching for the optima in the design domain. This design further confirms that the MOPSO method is more effective by presenting much more uniform distribution of the Pareto solution points than the LWA method in the scenarios where the sophisticated nonlinear mechanobiological processes are involved.

The last optimisation method applied to this case is the geometrical average (GA) method. Different to the LWA and MOPSO methods, the GA method aims to chase a single optimal solution by minimising the relative distances of the two

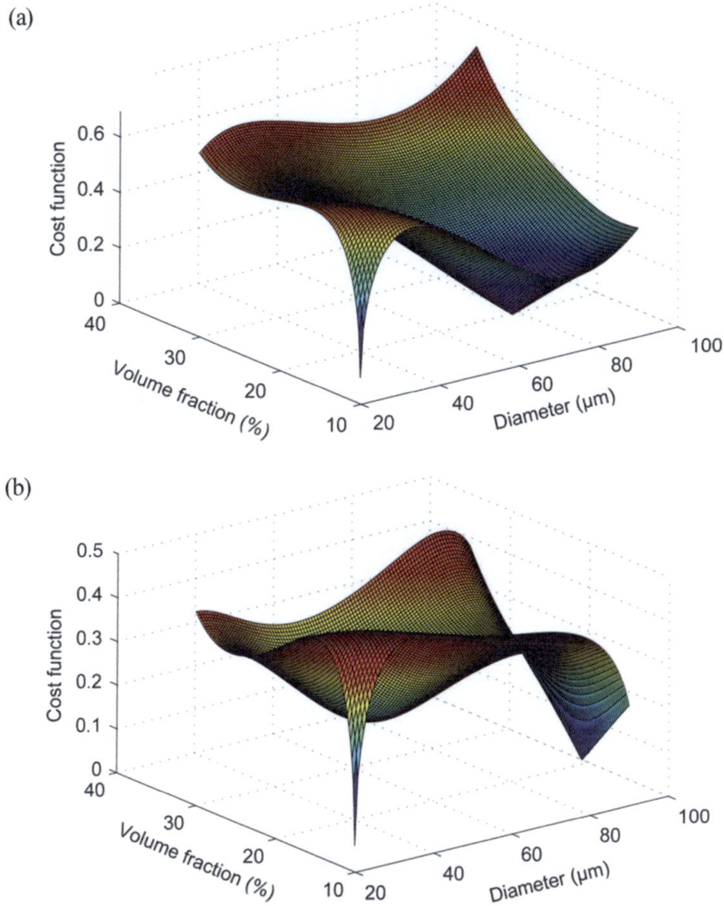

Fig. 3.7 Surface of efficiency coefficient function versus design variables of cortical region (**a**), where the optimum appears at the boundary of the design domain, and the cancellous region (**b**), where the optimum occurs around the lower bounds (Reprinted from Ref. [6], Copyright 2010, with permission from Elsevier)

objective functions from a geometric average point of view. Considering the both design criteria, the cost functions $F_g(\alpha, \upsilon)$ against the design variables are plotted in Fig. 3.7a and b for the cortical and cancellous ROIs, respectively, in which non-monotonic relationships can be seen for the both regions except at a lower volume fraction ($\upsilon < 20\,\%$) and a greater particle size ($\alpha > 60$ μm).

Table 3.4 summarises the GA optimisation outcomes, in which the performance index (f^*_{avg}, f^*_{std}) and overall cost functions $F_g(\alpha, \upsilon)$ indicate how close these functions approach to the maximum degree of optimisation. From this perspective, the greater the values of f^*_{avg}, f^*_{std} and $F_g(\alpha, \upsilon)$, the better the design. It is interesting to note that the optimal designs are somewhat different for the cortical and

Table 3.4 Optimisation results from the geometrical average method

Region	Optimal design variables (α:μm), (υ:%)	Cost function $F_g(\alpha, \upsilon)$	Performance index f^*_{avg}	Performance index f^*_{std}	Density (g/cm^3)	Standard deviation
Cortical	$\alpha = 100$, $\upsilon = 35$	0.7069	1.0000	0.5003	1.6605	0.3538
Cancellous	$\alpha = 37.7, \upsilon = 17.4$	0.6498	1.0000	0.8555	0.8827	0.2203

Reprinted from Ref. [6], Copyright 2010, with permission from Elsevier cancellous regions. The optimisations occur at the upper bound of the design domain (i.e. 100 μm – 35 %) for the cortical bone, but at the middle of design domain (i.e. 38 μm – 17.5 %) for the cancellous bone. This difference implies that, to achieve a maximum osseointegration, a functionally graded morphology of the surface coating may be needed for the different locations along the implant–bone interface.

3.3.2 *Graded Coating Configuration with Non-threaded Implant (Case 2)*

3.3.2.1 Bone Remodelling Responses

In the case of the graded porous surface morphologies, we adopt the alternative indicators (F_1' and F_2') for the bone remodelling response over the 48 months of healing, in terms of the bone–implant contact (BIC) ratio and the 10 % average peak Tresca stress (PTS), as the load-bearing capacity is more crucial for such a the non-threaded implant considered. The porosity of each sub-layer in the graded surface is kept constant at 70 % (i.e. 30 % volume fraction of particles) in this case, which provides all the models in different sub-layers with the same void space for tissue ingrowth. All the gradient configurations are presented in a form of (α_1-α_2-α_3), in which α_1 is for the sub-layer closest to the implant core, whereas α_3 is next to the host bone.

Figure 3.8 (a) compares the highest and the lowest BIC ratios in the graded surface morphologies with the three homogenous ones comprising 30, 50 and 70 μm particles. It clearly shows the evident effect of morphological gradients on osseointegration rates. All the five morphologies plotted here may have similar rates of mature bone apposition during the first 3 months of acute healing; however,

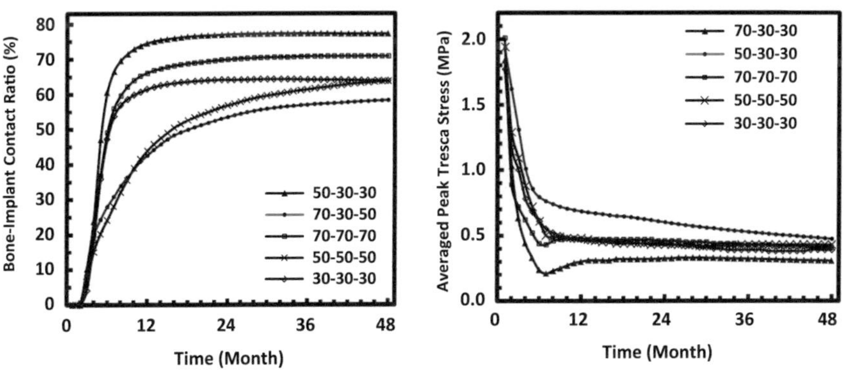

Fig. 3.8 (**a**) Highest/lowest bone–implant contact (BIC) ratios and (**b**) average peak Tresca stresses comparing to the three uniform morphologies (with porosity of 70 %) (Reprinted from Ref. [52], Copyright 2013, with permission from Elsevier)

there is a significant difference in the BIC ratio after month 6. Gradient 50-30-30 maintained a steep growth rate till the end of the first year, showing superior stimulation for bone mass growth over the entire simulation period than the others, and finally it has 6.41 % more bone mass than the best homogenous configuration of 70-70-70 by month 48. It is noted that not all graded surface morphologies increase the extent of osseointegration. Gradient 70-30-50, on the other hand, has an earlier take-off but a slower growth thereafter. It shows a reverse effect on osseous tissue ingrowth, even worse than the uniform morphologies, despite its rapid density gain in the first few months. At the end of 48 months, the best and worst gradients ended up with around 20 % difference in the BIC ratios.

Figure 3.8 (b) compares the evolutions of the highest and lowest averaged peak Tresca stress (10 %) with those three uniform morphologies. Note that the quick drops in the first 6 months indicate the rapid growth of osseous tissues, with the reductions of 86.9 % for gradient 70-30-30 and 58.5 % for gradient 50-30-30, respectively. A similar pattern is observed in all the uniform surface morphologies which fall in between the highest (worst) and lowest (best) gradient ones. It is interesting to see that in addition to its highest BIC ratio, gradient 50-30-30 delivers the highest stress concentration over the 48 month. On the other hand, gradient 70-30-30, rather than 70-30-50, has the highest averaged peak Tresca stress, indicating the highest risk of shear failure. Nevertheless, the final difference between the lowest (gradient 70-30-30) and highest (gradient 50-30-30) values at month 48 is fairly marginal (0.17 MPa, approximately 10 % of the initial stress concentration).

Different to the BIC outcomes, all the gradients show a slower and more gradual convergence for PTS. Figure 3.9 compares the trends between the best and worst performers under these two different indicators of osseointegration. The PTS

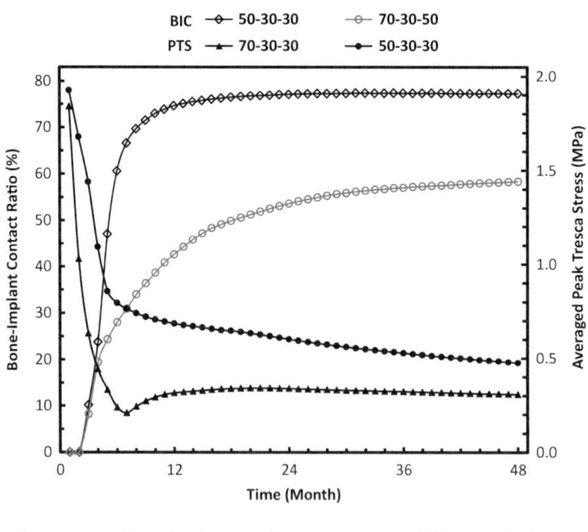

Fig. 3.9 Best and worst gradient implant performance under different design criteria

bumps back after the quick drop and then levels off to an equilibrium over time, instead of approaching to a steady state straightway as in BIC. Based on the monthly data obtained, however, it seems unclear to draw a direct relationship between BIC and PTS.

3.3.2.2 Response Surface Model

Similar to the homogeneous cases, these two alternative indicators (BIC and PTS) are also difficult to formulated with respect to the design variables. Again, RSM models are considered effective for approximating the indicators. As already observed in the bone remodelling responses, month 6 and month 48 are the two critical stages to evaluate the short-term and long-term performances of remodelling outcomes.

The sample data provides the essential information to extrapolate design analysis and optimisation. Based upon the above remodelling results, the assessment criteria, BIC and PTS, are related to the design variables of coating parameters in each layer as (α_1, α_2, α_3,). Combined with the experience in the homogeneous case, three different orders (linear, quadratic and cubic) of polynomials are attempted by the least-square method, to evaluate the fitness of response surface (RS) models. The R^2 and root–mean–square error (RMSE) between simulation and RS functions (Max and Min) are used to assess which polynomial is most accurate. As summarised in Table 3.5, the cubic polynomial functions provide the best fits to both BIC and PTS in these two selected time points for the short- and long-term osseointegration (months 6 and 48, respectively).

Table 3.5 Response surface models (polynomial) for months 6 and 48

	Time (month)	RSM	R^2	Max	RSM* Max	Min	RSM* Min	RMSE**
BIC (%)	6	1st	0.8828	60.59	45.79	21.51	27.33	8.69
		2nd	0.9035		50.54		23.02	6.21
		3rd	0.9536		59.15		21.83	4.30
	48	1st	0.9950	77.25	71.92	58.36	63.23	4.88
		2nd	0.9968		73.69		57.90	3.88
		3rd	0.9983		76.95		56.66	2.88
PTS (10^5 Pa)	6	1st	0.9417	9.14	6.50	2.38	4.09	1.35
		2nd	0.9572		8.05		3.15	1.16
		3rd	0.9647		8.89		2.84	1.06
	48	1st	0.9810	4.96	4.03	2.85	3.64	0.54
		2nd	0.9888		4.55		3.21	0.42
		3rd	0.9942		4.83		3.04	0.31

RSM* response surface method result
RMSE** root–mean–square error

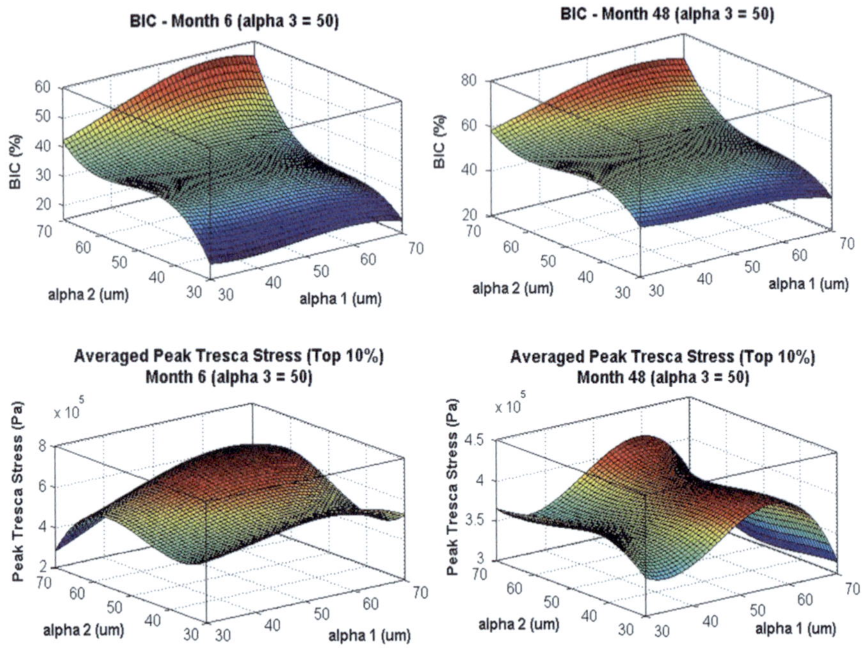

Fig. 3.10 Response surfaces showing the effects of gradient input α_1 and α_2 when α_3 is set to 50 μm on BIC (**a**, **b**) and averaged peak Tresca stress (**c**, **d**) at months 6 and 48 (Adapted from Ref. [52], Copyright 2013, with permission from Elsevier)

With the three design variables, the 'response surface' is literally a three-dimensional isometric response cube. To clearly demonstrate the responses on the surface models, α_3 is set to be 50 um representing an intermediate size of particles as an example for RSM. Figure 3.10 plots the BIC and PTS for months 6 and 48, respectively. From the BIC perspective, the combinations of medium particles in the inner layer (α_1) with large sizes in the mid-layer (α_2) show their advantages over the other configuration in both short term (month 6 as in Fig. 3.10a) and long term (month 48 as in Fig. 3.10b). The trend is also affected by α_2 (mid-layer) more significantly than α_1 (inner layer), and it drops dramatically along the reverse direction of α_2 axis, with a short level-off at the medium size range. The benefit of using a medium–large combination is being amplified in BIC as healing time progresses. Figure 3.10 (a) and (b) also reflects that gradient 70-30-50 (right bottom corner in the plots) is the worst performer in the design range over the simulation time.

On the other hand, PTS shows more distinct patterns than BIC. From Fig. 3.10 (c), α_2 plays a more important role in the short-term stability than α_1; however, this is reversed in the long term as in Fig. 3.10 (d). The minimum PTS appears in the case when small particles in the inner layer are combined with the large ones in the mid-layer in month 6, while it occurs at the medium–large combinations at month 48. Similarly to BIC, the lowest PTS occurs around gradient 70-30-50 which is close to gradient 70-30-30, likely having the least failure chance.

Based on the RS functions obtained, we can determine the gradients for either maximum BIC or minimum PTS outcomes in both months 6 and 48, respectively. It is noted that gradient 61.8-70.0-49.9 has the highest BIC ratio as 61.35 % in month 6, but at the same time has a high PTS of 0.54 MPa. In contrast, gradient 70.0-30.1-70.0 has the lowest PTS of 0.29 MPa accompanied by a lower gain of bone mass, leading to a BIC ratio of 29.81 % only. In month 48, gradient 30.0-30.0-32.1 leads to the maximum BIC ratio of 76.92 % (0.34 MPa PTS), while gradient 70-45.4-40.8 provides with the lowest PTS of 0.28 MPa (40.71 % BIC). Falling into a similar situation to the homogenous case, these two design criteria cannot be achieved concurrently.

3.3.2.3 Surface Morphology Design Optimisation

As determined from the response surfaces in Fig. 3.10, the optimal BIC and PTS are very hard to attain simultaneously. To address both design criteria, we again employ the multiobjective optimisation to maximise BIC and minimise PTS by using the linear weighted average (LWA) and the multiobjective particle swarm optimisation (MOPSO) methods to seek an optimal solution domain for various balances of these two design criteria.

To enhance the uniformity of Pareto distribution, we attempt to vary the weighting factors in a very small increment of 0.0005 in the LWA method. As plotted in Fig. 3.11 (a) and (b) for months 6 and 48, respectively, it is interesting to see that there are multiple optimal solution clusters for month 6 and three separate but highly overlapping clusters for month 48. To tackle the non-uniform distribution problem that occurred in the LWA solutions, the multiobjective particle swarm optimisation (MOPSO) method is again providing a much better distributed Pareto solution set, as already demonstrated in the homogenous case. 2000 Pareto points are generated through 1000 iterations, and 80 of them with uniform intervals are plotted in the same graph as that from the LWA method. Obviously, MOPSO is

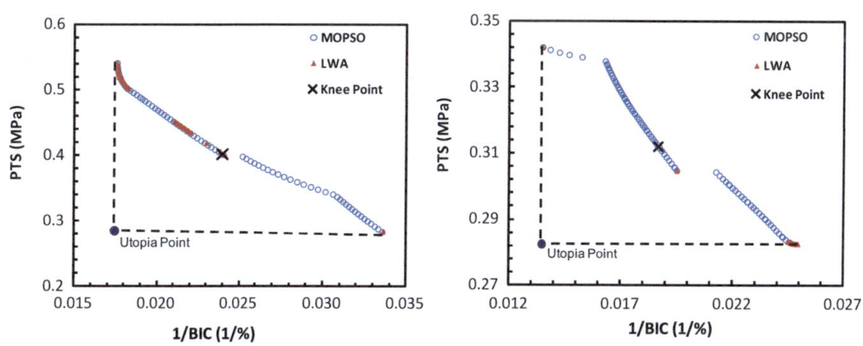

Fig. 3.11 Pareto fronts of optimal surface gradients from the two LWA and MOPSO optimisation algorithms at month 6 (**a**) and month 48 (**b**) (Reprinted from Ref. [52], Copyright 2013, with permission from Elsevier)

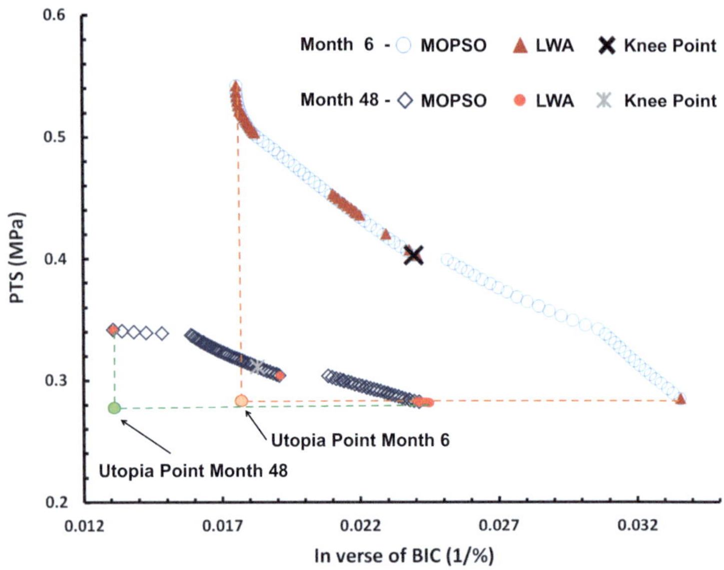

Fig. 3.12 Knee point determined based on the distances to the Utopia point for month 6 and month 48

more effective than LWA in terms of the smoothness of Pareto frontier and extent of uniformity in this design problem. As expected, MOPSO is much more widely distributed and all the LWA results are well located in the MOPSO Pareto frontier. When reflecting the effectiveness of these two approaches, their outcomes are different in the integrity. From the Pareto frontiers at these two different time points (months 6 and 48), it is also noted that further improving either BIC or PTS must sacrifice the corresponding counterpart along the Pareto frontiers.

Hypothetically, any point in the Pareto front can be a solution corresponding to a specific morphological design. Although the Pareto set provides us with multiple choices for different needs, it will be implicating if an overall optimum could be determined. The Utopia point signifies the most ideal solution that has the maximum BIC ratio and the minimum PTS at the same time (as outlined in Fig. 3.12). However, this point cannot be attained in most of design cases. As a compromise, a most 'satisfactory' solution, known as a knee point, can be chosen in the Pareto frontier. Here, we adopt the minimum distance selection method (MDSM), a similar approach as the geometric average (GA) optimisation, defined mathematically as

$$\min\ D = \sqrt{\left(\frac{f_{BIC} - f_{BIC}^{L}}{f_{BIC}^{U} - f_{BIC}^{L}}\right)^2 + \left(\frac{f_{PTS} - f_{PTS}^{L}}{f_{PTS}^{U} - f_{PTS}^{L}}\right)^2} \tag{3.19}$$

where f_{BIC} and f_{PTS} are the objective functions, while f^L and f^U are their corresponding lower and upper bounds in the design space concerned. A most 'satisfactory' solution can be determined by minimising its distance to the Utopia point.

In this case, it is found that the coating with a moderate gradient near the largest particle size (70.0-70.0-61.6) provides a most satisfactory solution in the initial healing up to month 6, giving a BIC outcome of 41.53 % and PTS of 0.40 MPa, whereas for the long-term healing (48 months), a graded coating of 37.1-70.0-67.7 is preferred, leading to a BIC ratio of 54.35 % and PTS of 0.31 MPa. Note that with other selection criteria, for instance, 'the maximum BIC ratio within a tolerated PTS range', it could lead to a different conclusion on the optimal choice.

3.4 Discussion

Despite an increasing importance, there has been a fundamental lack of predicting long-term outcome of a dental implantation in a quantitative way. The multiscale finite element analysis (FEA) framework developed in this study facilitates bone remodelling simulation in macroscopic and microscopic levels. It provides new understanding of the vital roles that biomechanics plays in characterising the time-dependent performance of dental implant that allows clinicians to formulate a more biomechanically sound treatment plan.

Osseointegration process can be affected by both implant surface morphology and physiological conditions. For the latter, age, sex, race, genetics and other medical factors all contribute on bone responses to the implantation, leading to different osseointegration outcomes. This chapter considers a particular set of remodelling parameters derived from literature to demonstrate how the surface topographical gradient of implant can be optimised for the same given mechanical and biological conditions. With sufficient patient data (e.g. from interval time history CT/MRI scans), this approach can be used to individual subject with their own remodelling parameters, aiming for a patient-specific design. For each patient, the predicted Pareto optima consists of a series of solutions at different uniform and balancing points, e.g. in between BIC ratio and PTS, and a clinic decision can be made based upon individual needs of a patient and clinical expectation.

Although this chapter takes dental implant as an example, the graded topographical configuration and corresponding design procedure can be extended to other applications of prosthetic fixation, such as orthopaedic osseointegration. A recent study [98] has examined the macroscopic remodelling outcomes in terms of bone mass density and failure possibility of different prosthetic designs in hip replacements. By applying the design procedure for graded topography proposed in this study, the microscopic surface morphology can be optimised for the hip prosthesis to meet individual patient needs.

Topology optimisation has proven an effective tool for microstructural design aiming to regulate effective material properties for bone remodelling applications

[99–102]. Another recent study [103] demonstrated how to optimise microstructural gradient of hip replacement implant for achieving minimum bone resorption and failure probability. Nevertheless, this technique is restricted to periodic microstructures and may be of limited implication to random morphology as shown in this chapter.

3.5 Conclusion

A novel application of multiscale modelling and remodelling analyses has been presented in this chapter with an aim to optimise the coated porous surface morphology. The remodelling simulation is conducted in the macroscopic level first; then the resultant displacement fields at different time steps are mapped to the microscopic representative volume element (RVE) model as loading for microscopic remodelling simulation. A layer of transitional region between host bone and implant substrate core is considered as the design domain. The osseointegration is measured in terms of four different indicators: (1) area averaged apparent density in the transitional layer, (2) standard deviation of density, (3) bone–implant contact (BIC) ratio and (4) averaged (10 %) peak Tresca stress (PTS). The response surface method (RSM) is employed to formulate these indicators with respect to the design variables. To simultaneously address several different design criteria, the multiobjective optimisation was adopted here using different approaches, including linear weighted average (LWA) and multiobjective particle swarm optimisation (MOPSO) method to provide a range of optimal solutions in a Pareto sense. In pursuing a single balanced optimal solution, the surface topographical parameters can be determined by either a geometric average (GA) method or adopting the minimum distance selection method (TMDSM).

Acknowledgement This work was supported by the fellowship grants from the Australian Research Council (ARC).

References

1. Kutty MG, Bhaduri S, Bhaduri SB (2004) Gradient surface porosity in titanium dental implants: relation between processing parameters and microstructure. J Mater Sci Mater Med 15(2):145–150
2. Brånemark PI, Adell R, Albrektsson T et al (1983) Osseointegrated titanium fixtures in the treatment of edentulousness. Biomaterials 4(1):25–28
3. Shen H, Li H, Brinson LC (2008) Effect of microstructural configurations on the mechanical responses of porous titanium: a numerical design of experiment analysis for orthopedic applications. Mech Mater 40(9):708–720
4. Dewidar MM, Lim JK (2008) Properties of solid core and porous surface Ti-6Al-4V implants manufactured by powder metallurgy. J Alloys Compd 454(1–2):442–446

5. Morra M, Cassinelli C, Cascardo G et al (2003) Surface engineering of titanium by collagen immobilization. Surface characterization and in vitro and in vivo studies. Biomaterials 24 (25):4639–4654
6. Rungsiyakull C, Li Q, Sun G et al (2010) Surface morphology optimization for osseointegration of coated implants. Biomaterials 31(27):7196–7204
7. Kunzler TP, Drobek T, Schuler M et al (2007) Systematic study of osteoblast and fibroblast response to roughness by means of surface-morphology gradients. Biomaterials 28 (13):2175–2182
8. Rosa AL, Crippa GE, de Oliveira PT et al (2009) Human alveolar bone cell proliferation, expression of osteoblastic phenotype, and matrix mineralization on porous titanium produced by powder metallurgy. Clin Oral Implants Res 20(5):472–481
9. Vaillancourt H, Pilliar RM, McCammond D (1995) Finite-element analysis of crestal bone loss around porous-coated dental implants. J Appl Biomater 6(4):267–282
10. Thelen S, Barthelat F, Brinson LC (2004) Mechanics considerations for microporous titanium as an orthopedic implant material. J Biomed Mater Res A 69A(4):601–610
11. Wen CE, Yamada Y, Shimojima K et al (2002) Processing and mechanical properties of autogenous titanium implant materials. J Mater Sci Mater Med 13(4):397–401
12. Esposito M, Hirsch JM, Lekholm U et al (1998) Biological factors contributing to failures of osseointegrated oral implants (I). Success criteria and epidemiology. Eur J Oral Sci 106 (1):527–551
13. Okazaki K, Lee WH, Kim DK et al (1991) Physical characteristics of Ti-6Al-4V implants fabricated by electrodischarge compaction. J Biomed Mater Res 25(12):1417–1429
14. Xue W, Krishna BV, Bandyopadhyay A et al (2007) Processing and biocompatibility evaluation of laser processed porous titanium. Acta Biomater 3(6):1007–1018
15. Li HL, Oppenheimer SM, Stupp SI et al (2004) Effects of pore morphology and bone ingrowth on mechanical properties of microporous titanium as an orthopaedic implant material. Mater Trans 45(4):1124–1131
16. Shen H, Oppenheimer SM, Dunand DC et al (2006) Numerical modeling of pore size and distribution in foamed titanium. Mech Mater 38(8–10):933–944
17. Mendonca G, Mendonca DBS, Aragao FJL et al (2008) Advancing dental implant surface technology – from micron- to nanotopography. Biomaterials 29(28):3822–3835
18. Park JY, Gemmelll CH, Davies JE (2001) Platelet interactions with titanium: modulation of platelet activity by surface topography. Biomaterials 22(19):2671–2682
19. Bobyn JD, Pilliar RM, Cameron HU et al (1980) The optimum pore size for the fixation of porous-surfaced metal implants by the ingrowth of bone. Clin Orthop Relat Res 150:263–270
20. Pilliar RM (1987) Porous-surfaced metallic implants for orthopedic applications. J Biomed Mater Res A 21(A1):1–33
21. Chen J, Chen L, Li W et al (2013) Porous titanium implant and micro-CT based characterization of sub-surface morphology. In: PRICM 2013. Wiley, Hoboken, pp 1579–1586
22. Chen LJ, Li T, Li YM et al (2009) Porous titanium implants fabricated by metal injection molding. Trans Nonferrous Metal Soc 19(5):1174–1179
23. Xiropaidis AV, Qahash M, Lim WH et al (2005) Bone-implant contact at calcium phosphate-coated and porous titanium oxide (TiUnite (TM))-modified oral implants. Clin Oral Implants Res 16(5):532–539
24. Geng JP, Tan KBC, Liu GR (2001) Application of finite element analysis in implant dentistry: a review of the literature. J Prosthet Dent 85(6):585–598
25. Schenk RK, Buser D (1998) Osseointegration: a reality. Periodontol 17:22–35
26. Cochran DL (1999) A comparison of endosseous dental implant surfaces. J Periodontol 70 (12):1523–1539
27. Knabe C, Howlett CR, Klar F et al (2004) The effect of different titanium and hydroxyapatite-coated dental implant surfaces on phenotypic expression of human bone-derived cells. J Biomed Mater Res A 71A(1):98–107

28. Suzuki K, Aoki K, Ohya K (1997) Effects of surface roughness of titanium implants on bone remodeling activity of femur in rabbits. Bone 21(6):507–514
29. Itala AI, Ylanen HO, Ekholm C et al (2001) Pore diameter of more than 100 mu m is not requisite for bone ingrowth in rabbits. J Biomed Mater Res 58(6):679–683
30. Bradley N (2007) The response surface methodology, in Department of Mathematical Sciences. Indiana University, South Bend, pp 36–38
31. Alsayyed A, Deporter DA, Pilliar RM et al (1994) Predictable crestal bone remodeling around 2 porous-coated titanium-alloy dental implant designs – a radiographic study in dogs. Clin Oral Implants Res 5(3):131–141
32. Anil S, Anand PS, Alghamdi H et al (2011) Chapter 4: Dental implant surface enhancement and osseointegration. In: Turkyilmaz I (ed) Implant dentistry – a rapidly evolving practice. InTech, Rijeka, pp 86–90
33. Deporter DA, Watson PA, Pilliar RM et al (1990) A histological comparison in the dog of porous-coated vs threaded dental implants. J Dent Res 69(5):1138–1145
34. Klawitter JJ, Hulbert SF (1971) Application of porous ceramics for the attachment of load bearing internal orthopedic applications. J Biomed Mater Res 5(6):161–229
35. Meyer U, Joos U, Mythili J et al (2004) Ultrastructural characterization of the implant/bone interface of immediately loaded dental implants. Biomaterials 25(10):1959–1967
36. Camron HU, Pilliar RM, Macnab I (1976) The rate of bone ingrowth into porous metal. J Biomed Mater Res 10(2):295–302
37. Magne P (2007) Efficient 3D finite element analysis of dental restorative procedures using micro-CT data. Dent Mater 23(5):539–548
38. Shen H, Brinson LC (2011) A numerical investigation of porous titanium as orthopedic implant material. Mech Mater 43(8):420–430
39. Lin D, Li Q, Li W et al (2010) Bone remodeling induced by dental implants of functionally graded materials. J Biomed Mater Res B 92B(2):430–438
40. Kim SJ, Kim MR, Rim JS et al (2010) Comparison of implant stability after different implant surface treatments in dog bone. J Appl Oral Sci 18(4):415–420
41. Yang J, Xiang H-J (2007) A three-dimensional finite element study on the biomechanical behavior of an FGBM dental implant in surrounding bone. J Biomech 40(11):2377–2385
42. Yang YZ, Tian JM, Deng L et al (2002) Morphological behavior of osteoblast-like cells on surface-modified titanium in vitro. Biomaterials 23(5):1383–1389
43. Yang YZ, Tian JM, Tian JT et al (2000) Preparation of graded porous titanium coatings on titanium implant materials by plasma spraying. J Biomed Mater Res 52(2):333–337
44. Hedia HS, Fouda N (2013) A new design of dental implant coating using functionally graded material. Mater Testing 55(10):765–771
45. Chen CC, Huang TH, Kao CT et al (2006) Characterization of functionally graded hydroxyapatite/titanium composite coatings plasma-sprayed on Ti alloys. J Biomed Mater Res B 78B (1):146–152
46. Lin D, Li Q, Li W et al (2009) Design optimization of functionally graded dental implant for bone remodeling. Compos Part B 40(7):668–675
47. Podshivalov L, Fischer A, Bar-Yoseph PZ (2011) 3D hierarchical geometric modeling and multiscale FE analysis as a base for individualized medical diagnosis of bone structure. Bone 48(4):693–703
48. Podshivalov L, Fischer A, Bar-Yoseph PZ (2011) Multiscale FE method for analysis of bone micro-structures. J Mech Behav Biomed 4(6):888–899
49. Fritsch A, Hellmich C, Dormieux L (2009) Ductile sliding between mineral crystals followed by rupture of collagen crosslinks: experimentally supported micromechanical explanation of bone strength. J Theor Biol 260(2):230–252
50. Buti F, Cacciagrano D, Corradini F et al (2010) Bone remodelling in BioShape. Electron Notes Theor Comput Sci 268:17–29
51. Chen J, Rungsiyakull C, Li W et al (2013) Multiscale design of surface morphological gradient for osseointegration. J Mech Behav Biomed 20:387–397

52. Romeed SA, Fok SL, Wilson NHF (2006) A comparison of 2D and 3D finite element analysis of a restored tooth. J Oral Rehabil 33(3):209–215
53. Lin D, Li Q, Li W et al (2010) Mandibular bone remodeling induced by dental implant. J Biomech 43(2):287–293
54. Lin D, Li Q, Li W et al (2009) Dental implant induced bone remodeling and associated algorithms. J Mech Behav Biomed 2(5):410–432
55. Field C, Li Q, Li W et al (2010) Prediction of mandibular bone remodelling induced by fixed partial dentures. J Biomech 43(9):1771–1779
56. Field C, Li Q, Li W et al (2012) A comparative mechanical and bone remodelling study of all-ceramic posterior inlay and onlay fixed partial dentures. J Dent 40(1):48–56
57. Traini T, Mangano C, Sammons RL et al (2008) Direct laser metal sintering as a new approach to fabrication of an isoelastic functionally graded material for manufacture of porous titanium dental implants. Dent Mater 24(11):1525–1533
58. Li W, Swain MV, Li Q et al (2005) Towards automated 3D finite element modeling of direct fiber reinforced composite dental bridge. J Biomed Mater Res B 74B(1):520–528
59. Li W, Swain MV, Li Q et al (2004) Fibre reinforced composite dental bridge. Part II: numerical investigation. Biomaterials 25(20):4995–5001
60. Chen J, Li W, Swain MV et al (2014) A periodontal ligament driven remodeling algorithm for orthodontic tooth movement. J Biomech 47(7):1689–1695
61. Li W, Lin D, Chen J et al (2014) Role of mechanical stimuli in oral implantation. J Biosci Med 2:63–68
62. Li W, Rungsiyakull C, Field C et al (2010) Computational biomechanics of bone's responses to dental prostheses – osseointegration, remodeling and resorption. In: Khalili N et al (eds) 9th world congress on computational mechanics and 4th Asian Pacific congress on computational mechanics. IOP Publishing, Sydney. doi:10.1088/1757-899X/10/1/012122
63. Rungsiyakull C, Chen J, Rungsiyakull P et al (2014) Bone's responses to different designs of implant-supported fixed partial dentures. Biomech Model Mechanobiol 14(2):403–411
64. Ahmad R, Chen J, Abu-Hassan MI et al (2015) Investigation of mucosa-induced residual ridge resorption under implant-retained overdentures and complete dentures in the mandible. Int J Oral Maxillofac Implants 30(3):657–666
65. Chen J, Ahmad R, Suenaga H et al (2015) A comparative study on complete and implant retained denture treatments – a biomechanics perspective. J Biomech 48(3):512–519
66. Suenaga H, Chen J, Yamaguchi K et al (2015) Mechanobiological bone reaction quantified by positron emission tomography. J Dent Res 94(5):738–744
67. Li J, Li H, Shi L et al (2007) A mathematical model for simulating the bone remodeling process under mechanical stimulus. Dent Mater 23(9):1073–1078
68. Rungsiyakull C, Li Q, Li W et al (2008) Effect of particle size of Fully Porous-Coated (FPC) implants on osseointegration. Adv Mat Res 47–50:916–919
69. O'Brien WJ (2008) Dental materials and their selection. Quintessence Pub. Co., Hanover Park
70. Carr ME, Carr SL (1995) Fibrin structure and concentration alter clot elastic-modulus but do not alter platelet-mediated force development. Blood Coagul Fibrinolysis 6(1):79–86
71. Riha P, Wang X, Liao R et al (1999) Elasticity and fracture strain of whole blood clots. Clin Hemorheol Microcirc 21(1):45–49
72. Liu XY, Niebur GL (2008) Bone ingrowth into a porous coated implant predicted by a mechano-regulatory tissue differentiation algorithm. Biomech Model Mechanobiol 7 (4):335–344
73. Isaksson H, van Donkelaar CC, Ito K (2009) Sensitivity of tissue differentiation and bone healing predictions to tissue properties. J Biomech 42(5):555–564
74. Keaveny TM (2001) Strength of trabecular bone. In: Cowin SC (ed) Bone mechanics handbook. CRC Press LLC, Danvers, p 7
75. Frost HM (2003) Bone's mechanostat: a 2003 update. Anat Rec A: Discov Mol Cell Evol Biol 275A(2):1081–1101

76. Weinans H, Huiskes R, Grootenboer HJ (1992) The behavior of adaptive bone-remodeling simulation models. J Biomech 25(12):1425–1441
77. Frost HM (1964) The laws of bone structure. C.C. Thomas, Springfield
78. Carter DR (1984) Mechanical loading histories and cortical bone remodeling. Calcif Tissue Int 36:S19–S24
79. Huiskes R, Weinans H, Grootenboer HJ et al (1987) Adaptive bone-remodeling theory applied to prosthetic-design analysis. J Biomech 20(11–12):1135–1150
80. Weinans H, Huiskes R, Grootenboer HJ (1992) Effects of material properties of femoral hip components on bone remodeling. J Orthop Res 10(6):845–853
81. Noble BS, Reeve J (2000) Osteocyte function, osteocyte death and bone fracture resistance. Mol Cell Endocrinol 159(1–2):7–13
82. Wernig F, Xu Q (2000) Mechanical stress-induced apoptosis in the cardiovascular system. Prog Biophys Mol Biol 78(2–3):105–137
83. Xie M, Yang SH, Win HL et al (2010) Rabbit annulus fibrosus cell apoptosis induced by mechanical overload via a mitochondrial apoptotic pathway. J Huazhong Uni Sci Tech Med 30(3):379–384
84. Tanaka E, Yamamoto S, Nishida T et al (1999) A mathematical model of bone remodelling under overload and its application to evaluation of bone resorption around dental implants. Acta Bioeng Biomech 1(1):117–121
85. Rho JY, Hobatho MC, Ashman RB (1995) Relations of mechanical-properties to density and Ct numbers in human bone. Med Eng Phys 17(5):347–355
86. O'Mahony AM, Williams JL, Katz JO et al (2000) Anisotropic elastic properties of cancellous bone from a human edentulous mandible. Clin Oral Implants Res 11(5):415–421
87. Shen H, Brinson LC (2007) Finite element modeling of porous titanium. Int J Solids Struct 44 (1):320–335
88. Sollazzo V, Pezzetti F, Scarano A et al (2008) Zirconium oxide coating improves implant osseointegration in vivo. Dent Mater 24(3):357–361
89. Abron A, Hopfensperger M, Thompson J et al (2001) Evaluation of a predictive model for implant surface topography effects on early osseointegration in the rat tibia model. J Prosthet Dent 85(1):40–46
90. Anderson RC, Cook SD, Weinstein AM et al (1984) An evaluation of skeletal attachment to LTI pyrolytic carbon, porous titanium, and carbon-coated porous titanium implants. Clin Orthop Relat Res 182:242–257
91. Feighan JE, Goldberg VM, Davy D et al (1995) The influence of surface-blasting on the incorporation of titanium-alloy implants in a rabbit intramedullary model. J Bone Joint Surg Am 77(9):1380–1395
92. Hou SJ, Li Q, Long SY et al (2008) Multiobjective optimization of multi-cell sections for the crashworthiness design. Int J Impact Eng 35(11):1355–1367
93. Hou S, Li Q, Long S et al (2007) Design optimization of regular hexagonal thin-walled columns with crashworthiness criteria. Finite Elem Anal Des 43(6–7):555–565
94. Athan TW, Papalambros PY (1996) A note on weighted criteria methods for compromise solutions in multi-objective optimization. Eng Optimiz 27(2):155–176
95. Coello CA, Lechuga MS (2002) MOPSO: a proposal for multiple objective particle swarm optimization. In: Proceedings of evolutionary computation 2002. Honolulu, p 1051–1056.
96. Raquel CR, Naval PCJ (2005) An effective use of crowding distance in multiobjective particle swarm optimization. In: Proceedings of the 2005 conference on genetic and evolutionary computation 2005. ACM, Washington, DC, pp 257–264
97. O'Mahony AM, Williams JL, Spencer P (2001) Anisotropic elasticity of cortical and cancellous bone in the posterior mandible increases peri-implant stress and strain under oblique loading. Clin Oral Implants Res 12(6):648–657
98. Tomaszewski PK, van Diest M, Bulstra SK et al (2012) Numerical analysis of an osseointegrated prosthesis fixation with reduced bone failure risk and periprosthetic bone loss. J Biomech 45(11):1875–1880

99. Sturm S, Zhou S, Mai Y-W et al (2010) On stiffness of scaffolds for bone tissue engineering-a numerical study. J Biomech 43(9):1738–1744
100. Chen Y, Zhou S, Li Q (2009) Computational design for multifunctional microstructural composites. Int J Mod Phys B 23(6–7):1345–1351
101. Adachi T, Osako Y, Tanaka M et al (2006) Framework for optimal design of porous scaffold microstructure by computational simulation of bone regeneration. Biomaterials 27 (21):3964–3972
102. Chen Y, Zhou S, Li Q (2011) Microstructure design of biodegradable scaffold and its effect on tissue regeneration. Biomaterials 32(22):5003–5014
103. Arabnejad Khanoki S, Pasini D (2012) Multiscale design and multiobjective optimization of orthopedic hip implants with functionally graded cellular material. J Biomech Eng 134 (3):031004

Chapter 4
Implant Surface Modifications and Osseointegration

Nishant Chakravorty, Anjali Jaiprakash, Saso Ivanovski, and Yin Xiao

Abstract Osseointegration and osteogenic differentiation are important determinants of clinical outcomes involving implants in orthopaedics and dentistry. Implant surface microstructure and hydrophilicity are known to influence these properties. Recent research has focused on several modifications of surface topography and chemistry aimed at improving bone formation to achieve faster and better healing. Topographically modified titanium implant surfaces, like the sandblasted, large-grit, acid-etched (SLA) surface and chemically modified hydrophilic SLA (modSLA) surface, have shown promising results when compared with smooth/polished titanium surfaces. Although most studies consider an average roughness (Ra) of 1–1.5 μm to be favourable for bone formation, there is no consensus regarding the appropriate roughness and chemical modifications necessary to achieve optimal osseointegration. Studies on microstructurally modified surfaces have revealed intricate details pertaining to the molecular interactions of osteogenic cells with implant surfaces. The in vivo and in vitro findings from these studies highlight the ability of modified titanium surfaces to support the establishment of a native osteogenic niche for promoting bone formation on the implant surfaces. Improved osteogenic properties of modified surfaces are evidenced in vitro by the differential regulation of the molecular transcriptome on such surfaces. Recent studies indicate that post-transcriptional modulators like microRNAs also play an important role in osteogenic regulation on implant surfaces. In this chapter, we discuss the current concepts and considerations in orthopaedic and dental implant research and the new knowledge in the field, which will assist in the development of novel approaches and designs of future implant devices.

Keywords Implants • Osseointegration • Surface modification • Surface topography • Cell signaling • Osteogenic differentiation • Molecular regulation

---

N. Chakravorty • A. Jaiprakash • Y. Xiao (✉)
Institute of Health & Biomedical Innovation, Queensland University of Technology, 60 Musk Avenue, Kelvin Grove, Brisbane, QLD 4059, Australia
e-mail: yin.xiao@qut.edu.au

S. Ivanovski
School of Dentistry and Oral Health, Griffith Health Institute, Griffith University, Gold Coast, QLD, Australia

Q. Li, Y.-W. Mai (eds.), *Biomaterials for Implants and Scaffolds*, Springer Series in Biomaterials Science and Engineering 8, DOI 10.1007/978-3-662-53574-5_4

4.1 Introduction

Orthopaedic and dental implants have become important treatment options for replacement and restoration of missing/damaged parts of bones and teeth. The science of orthopaedic and dental implants has come a long way since its beginning which possibly dates back to around 600 AD when the Mayan civilisation started using seashells and stones as endo-osseous implants. Implant structures and surfaces have subsequently undergone a multitude of modifications. The quest for superior clinical outcomes has led researchers to a continually evolving search for the ideal implantation material. The choice of materials to be used as implants depends on several properties, such as mechanical stability, elasticity, biocompatibility, hydrophilicity, corrosivity, etc. Several materials have been used as implants for the human body. The ready availability and established processing methods initially made stainless steel a popular material for orthopaedic implants. The progressive search for improved implants led to the use of alloys made out of iron and other metals like nickel, cobalt and molybdenum. Titanium with its significant potential to support bone regeneration with little evidence of rejection has been the material of choice clinically for a long time now.

The primary aim of implant research is to create materials with functional designs that serve the purpose of achieving structural and functional restoration of a body part, and in the context of bone integration, we need to understand the phenomenon known as osseointegration. The term 'osseointegration' was coined by the Swedish orthopaedic surgeon Per-Ingvar Brånemark in the 1950s, when he observed difficulty in the removal of titanium chambers implanted in animals for vital microscopic studies [1]. Osseointegration may be defined as the structural and functional amalgamation of the load-bearing surface of an implant with the surrounding bone tissue. Osseointegration is a biological process guided by a highly regulated cascade of molecular steps that lead to osteogenic differentiation and new bone formation on the implant surfaces. Several research studies have emphasised the importance of surface topography on the bone-to-implant contact [2–6]. The present chapter discusses the current knowledge and concepts pertaining to the surface topography of implants, with a focus on modified titanium implant surfaces as a model to understand the mechanisms of osteogenic differentiation and osseointegration.

4.2 Discovery of Osseointegration

A chapter on osseointegration without a tribute to Professor Per-Ingvar Brånemark and his pioneering work with the implant material titanium would be an injustice to the topic itself. Titanium was first identified as an element in 1791 by Revd. William Gregor when he was examining samples of black sands sent to him from the valley of Manaccan located in the Lizard peninsula, Cornwall, in England

[7]. Based on his experiments, Gregor was able to identify an unknown metallic substance in the samples; however, he was unable to reduce it to its metallic form. He had originally named it as 'manaccanite' after the region from where he had identified the element. Later in 1795, Martin Heinrich Klaproth from Germany isolated a metal from an abundant ore called 'rutile' and named this metal as 'titanium'. Klaproth also analysed the new element Gregor had identified and found it to be the same as titanium and recognised Gregor as the scientist who discovered the new metal. Subsequently, scientists realised the properties and significance of this material, and it is now widely utilised in various areas like aircrafts, naval ships, spacecrafts, missiles, jewellery, etc.

After one-and-a-half century of the discovery of titanium, its importance as an implant material was discovered by Professor Per-Ingvar Brånemark. During the 1950s and 1960s, Brånemark was studying the formation of blood vessels in the bone marrow using in vivo models. Micro-optical devices enveloped in titanium cases were incorporated into tissues to observe the human microcirculation. He subsequently observed extreme difficulty in removal of these devices. These were the initial observations that led to the discovery of the phenomenon of osseointegration. A modified experimental setup for the rabbit ear chamber was subsequently conducted, whereby a titanium implant with a central canal and a transverse opening was placed into the bone to enable the bone and blood vessels to grow into the chamber [1]. These observations led to the findings that the integration of titanium with live tissue could enable a prolonged fixation of dental prostheses and eventually unfolded the path to the magnanimous clinical success of titanium for dental implants and reconstructive surgeries.

On 9 April 2002 the International Society of Osseointegration and the Associated Brånemark Osseointegration Centers (ABOC) visited Manaccan and unveiled a plaque made of titanium commemorating the discovery of titanium and recognising the scientific achievements of the two great scientists – Revd. William Gregor and Professor Per-Ingvar Brånemark.

4.3 Titanium and Its Modifications

Titanium is the 22nd element in the periodic table and has an atomic mass of 47.867 and its symbol is Ti (Fig. 4.1). It is classified in group 4 (transition elements) of the periodic table along with zirconium, hafnium and rutherfordium. The element is strong and lustrous with a metallic silver shade. It is usually found in the form of its ores: rutile (TiO_2), anatase (TiO_2) and ilmenite (Fe, TiO_3). Ilmenite is the most abundant form of titanium. Four grades of commercially pure titanium and two alloys of titanium are recognised by the American Society for Testing and Materials (ASTM) Committee F04 on Materials for Surgical Implants. Commercially pure titanium is graded as between I and IV; and the ASTM recognised that titanium alloys are Ti-6Hl-4 V and Ti-6Hl-4 V extra low interstitial (ELI) [8]. Essential

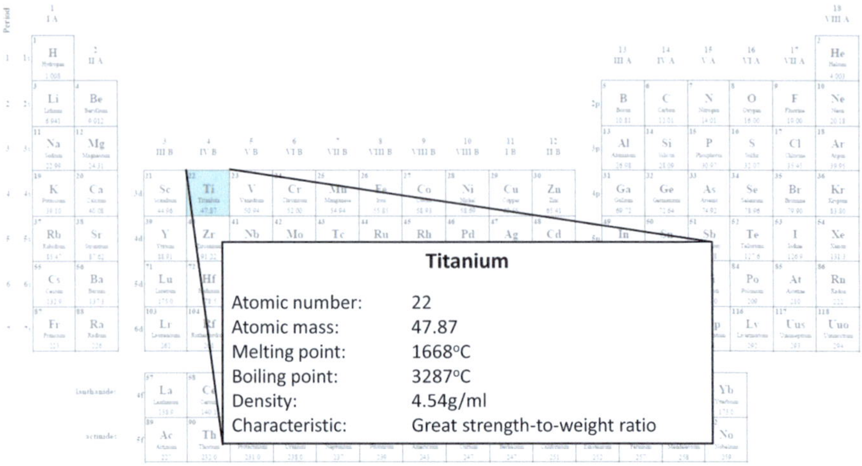

Fig. 4.1 Titanium – the element of choice for orthopaedic and dental implants

qualities that make titanium a highly compatible material in the field of implantology include:

1. High strength-to-weight ratio – titanium is 60 % the density of steel but has tensile strengths reaching as high as 63,000 psi (434.4 MPa).
2. High melting point (1668 °C) – commercial titanium alloys have the capability of safely withstanding temperatures of up to 600 °C.
3. Resistance to corrosion – usually due to the formation of a titanium dioxide layer on the surface.
4. Ability to be passivated and therefore be resistant to corrosion with acids.
5. Inert to body fluids.
6. Relatively low modulus of elasticity akin to human bone.
7. Ability to osseointegrate.

Titanium has certain shortcomings like low resistance to wear and notch sensitivity. However, its advantages outweigh the disadvantages, and therefore it is considered one of the most suitable elements for implants.

4.3.1 Surface Modifications

Implant research has focused on technologies to improve osteoinduction (ability to induce differentiation of undifferentiated cells towards osteogenic lineage), osteoconduction (allowing growth of bone on the surface of the implant) and osseointegration [9]. Surface modification techniques have been an integral part of implant research. Implant surface quality has been considered one of the most important factors implicated in successful osseointegration [3]. The most common parameters used in describing surface roughness are R_a, R_q, R_z and R_t (in - two-dimensional) and their three-dimensional counterparts: S_a, S_q, S_z and S_t.

R_a/S_a Arithmetic mean deviation (average roughness) of the roughness profile (R_a) or of a surface (S_a in 3D)
R_q/S_q Root mean square deviation of profile (R_q) or of a surface (S_q in 3D)
R_z/S_z Arithmetic mean deviation of the sum total of 10 (5 of the lowest peaks and 5 of the highest peaks) of the profile (R_z) or the surface (S_z)

Several different methods are employed to alter surface topographies. Some of the most common techniques include polishing, surface blasting, plasma spraying, anodic oxidation, etching and chemical coatings. A brief description of some of the most commonly employed techniques for modifying surfaces is outlined below.

4.3.1.1 Topographical Modifications

Polishing Polishing is a technique used to smoothen implant surfaces. The most common method of polishing is machining. Electropolishing is another technique often utilised to prepare polished surfaces, whereby metal is electrochemically removed by oxidation and subsequent dissolution into the electrolyte. Polished surfaces usually have an average roughness measuring <0.5 μm. Turning and milling are other techniques employed to modify surfaces, which would result in regular grooves on the implant surfaces and are known as 'minimally rough' surfaces.

Blasting Blasting is an abrasive technique usually employed to roughen a smooth or polished surface. The most common method of blasting surfaces is known as 'sandblasting' which is usually a dry process of thrusting a jet of abrasive media like alumina, corundum, crushed glass, silica and steel grit on to the surface at accelerated velocity. Blasting surfaces with alumina particles of 25–75 μm have been shown to create isotropic surface modifications with R_a/S_a around 1.1–1.5 μm in contrast to blasting with 250-μm particles that creates anisotropic surfaces with deviation around 2 μm [10]. Blasted surfaces have been observed to have improved cellular adhesion and osteoblastic differentiation [11]. Proper cleaning of blasted surfaces after the process is essential as retained particles of blasting materials like alumina can impair bone formation [12].

Etching	Etching is a subtractive process using strong acids or alkalis capable of eroding the surface of implants to create roughened surfaces. Hydrochloric acid, hydrofluoric acid and sulphuric acid are the most commonly used acids for etching implant surfaces. A mixture of acids is also used often to erode surfaces to make them more conducive for bone formation. Alkaline etching is commonly performed using sodium hydroxide solutions. Varying the concentration of the acid/alkali in use, time of exposure and temperature are important considerations during the process of etching.
Oxidation	Oxidation is the technique of chemically converting the titanium surface into an oxide layer, thereby increasing the surface titanium dioxide coating. This has been observed to impart improved biocompatibility to the implant surface. An oxide layer is allowed to deposit on the titanium surface placed at the anode, and this leads to a thicker layer of titanium oxide on the surface.
Bioactive coating	Several bioactive coating methods have been attempted on titanium surfaces to improve the efficacy of implants. The key property that makes bioactive coating technique an attractive modification option is their ability to exert a particular response in the biological system. The most common coatings on titanium surfaces include hydroxyapatite, calcium phosphate, bone morphogenetic proteins and collagen. Hydroxyapatite coating is a very commonly used method owing to its excellent biocompatibility and ability to bond with the surrounding bone.
Titanium plasma spraying	Plasma spraying technology is a 'non-bioactive' coating technique used to create porous titanium surfaces that can favour ingrowth of bone. A jet of molten titanium is sprayed on to the implant surface during the process of titanium plasma spraying (TPS). TPS is an additive procedure that imparts a roughened surface architecture. TPS implants have been observed to have variable R_a, and some studies have reported improved osseointegration of TPS compared to smooth surfaces [13]. Plasma spraying technique is also used to create hydroxyapatite coatings. Although plasma spraying is an established method, controlling the variables involved in the process is quite complicated, and small variations may lead to completely different properties than expected. There are several other techniques of coating implant surfaces like sputter coating, pulsed laser deposition, dip coating, electrophoretic deposition and thermal spraying. Deposition

	techniques have an inherent drawback that they take a long time.
Laser ablation	Laser ablation is a subtractive technique commonly used to create microstructures with improved physical properties like toughness, rigidity and corrosion resistance. This technique has the ability to generate nanostructures on the titanium surfaces [14].

4.3.1.2 Physicochemical Modifications

Physicochemical modifications involve changing the surface free energy, surface charge and hydrophilicity. Studies have revealed improved osseointegration and bone formation on hydrophilic surfaces [15–18]. Certain topographical modifications of surfaces also impart changes in surface charge. Sandblasting techniques have been shown to create a negative surface charge. A negative surface charge is known to improve cellular attachment [19]. Modifications of surface energy have been showing to increase the hydrophilicity and thereby help adsorption of proteins necessary for cellular growth and development [20]. Titanium is highly reactive to fluoride ions. Fluoride-treated titanium surfaces have been found to enhance osteoblastic differentiation [21].

Several combinations of these techniques have been used in the field of implantology to achieve better clinical outcomes and success. Sandblasting and acid-etching techniques have been commonly used to modify dental implants with improved clinical success. Recent research has further focused on combining the topographical methods with the physicochemical modifications leading to the development of topographically and chemically modified titanium implant surfaces like the modSLA surface.

4.3.2 Micro-roughened Surfaces

Wennerberg et al. [22–24] classified implant surfaces based on their surface topography into the following subtypes:

1. Smooth (<0.5 μm)
2. Minimally rough (0.5–1 μm)
3. Intermediately rough (1–2 μm)
4. Rough (2–3 μm)

There has been a consensus among majority of the scientific reports that suggest improved bone-to-implant contacts with higher surface roughness (micro-roughness). Wennerberg and Albrektsson's suggested guidelines for evaluation of implant surfaces based on topography [25] advocated that the positive correlation of surface roughness with bone formation works in a particular range: R_a/S_a value from 1 to 1.5 μm. However, Shalabi et al.'s systematic review on surface roughness and healing of the bone in 2006 [26] did not substantiate this. Their assessment of the literature on implant fixation/bone formation and surface roughness revealed a positive correlation between bone formation and surface roughness of implants from R_a/S_a 0.5 μm to 8.5 μm. Machined and polished titanium implant surfaces are usually used as control surfaces to test the efficacy of modified surfaces in terms of osseointegration and other improved functionalities.

Recent reports have also demonstrated the importance of nanoscale roughness to improve bone-forming properties. Newer modifications have also focused on modulating the surface free energy to enhance the wettability and hydrophilicity. Improving surface hydrophilicity has been demonstrated to increase osteogenic differentiation in vitro and osseointegration in vivo [18, 20, 27, 28]. Newer advances in implant surface technology have enabled researchers to incorporate nanostructural modifications to implant surfaces. 'Nano' modifications are conventionally defined as alterations in the range of 1–100 nm. Topographical manipulations in the nanoscale have been found to have a positive influence on the phenomenon of osseointegration and osteogenic differentiation [29].

The implication of topographical and chemical modification of titanium implants on clinical outcomes is documented by the success of micro-roughened dental implants like sandblasted, large-grit and acid-etched (SLA) surface and its successor the chemically modified hydrophilic modSLA surfaces. Both SLA and modSLA surfaces are micro-roughened surface, and the SLA surface has largely been considered the gold standard in implant dentistry. Recent studies have demonstrated the presence of nanoparticles on the modSLA surfaces [30–32]. Studies on the various implant surface modifications have enabled us to begin to unravel the molecular mechanisms of osseointegration.

4.3.3 Properties of Topographically Modified Implant Surfaces

Osseointegration is a biological phenomenon that involves the interaction of osteoblastic cells with their microenvironment. The biological response that takes place at the interface between implant surfaces and osteogenic cells is the key to the phenomenon of osseointegration. It is important to understand the physiology of the cellular response to implant surfaces, especially in light of the properties conferred on to the newer implant surfaces by virtue of their modifications. The native niche of osteoblastic cells is interspersed with proteins and structural elements at the micro- and nanoscale. Therefore modifying implant surfaces topographically (at the micro- and nanoscale) results in structural features that influence cells to directly interact with such surfaces. Micro- and nanoscale roughness allows surfaces to have an increased surface area, which allows such surfaces to adhere greater amounts of proteins and mediators necessary for growth and differentiation. Hydrophilic surfaces have the capability to attract and retain proteins necessary for growth and differentiation of cells. Cells differentiating towards an osteoblastic lineage have been observed to show higher expression of integrins and focal adhesion proteins on micro-roughened titanium surfaces, when compared to smooth surfaces [33].

4.3.4 The SLA and modSLA Titanium Surfaces

The sandblasted, large-grit and acid-etched (SLA) titanium and its successor, the chemically modified hydrophilic modSLA surfaces, designed by Institut Straumann AG (Waldenburg, Switzerland) are micro-roughened titanium implant surfaces known to have improved osseointegrative and osteoconductive properties compared to their smooth-surfaced counterparts. These surfaces have proven to be remarkable features for investigating and elucidating the mechanisms of osteogenic differentiation in vitro and osseointegration in vivo. A brief discussion about the method of preparation of these surfaces and their physical and chemical characteristics is worth detailing in this section of the chapter.

4.3.4.1 Method of Fabrication

The acronym ‘SLA’ was first used by Buser et al. in their 1991 publication [2] where they demonstrated higher bone-to-implant contact on titanium implant surfaces prepared by sandblasting using large-grit particles and etching using hydrochloric and sulphuric acid. The modSLA surface (commercially known as SLActive surface, Fig. 4.2a) was described for the first time by Buser et al. in 2004 [34], where they demonstrated increased bone apposition to modSLA surfaces compared to the SLA surfaces. The modSLA surface is essentially a physicochemically modified version of the SLA surface (Fig. 4.2b) that allows maintenance of the initial hydrophilicity of microstructured titanium surfaces after their fabrication. Both the SLA and modSLA surfaces are commercially produced by Institut Straumann (Basel, Switzerland) and have achieved the status of industry standards, with many other companies in the field of implant dentistry adopting the methods to fabricate surfaces similar to SLA and modSLA.

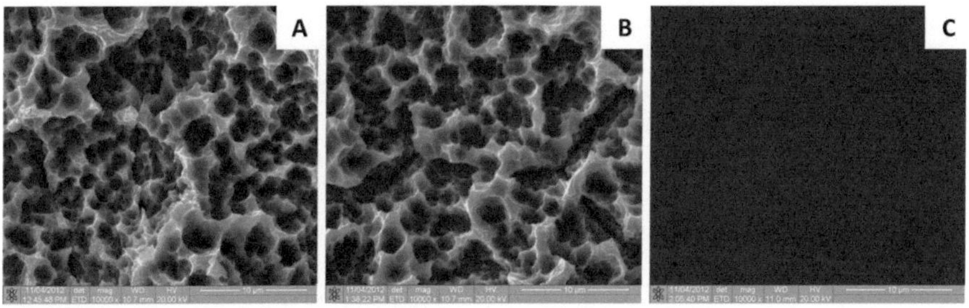

Fig. 4.2 Scanning electron microscope (SEM) images of (**a**) modSLA, (**b**) SLA and (**c**) smooth (SMO) titanium surfaces (10,000× magnification)

The SLA surface is achieved by sandblasting grade II commercially pure titanium surfaces using 250–500-μm large-grit corundum (crystalline form of Al_2O_3) and subsequently acid etching using a hot solution of hydrochloric and sulphuric acids, thereby combining the principles of blasting and acid etching. This technique gives rise to a micro-roughened topography of the titanium surface. Titanium, on exposure to air, gets converted to titanium dioxide (TiO_2) which in turn may get hydroxylated upon exposure to water. Variations in net charges may lead to ionic interactions on the surface, and exposure to air may also lead to contamination of the TiO_2, which may collectively lead to decrease in the initial hydrophilicity developed after the topographical modification [20].

The modSLA surface was introduced as a successor to the SLA surface, wherein a chemical modification was introduced to the SLA surface immediately post-production, so that the hydrophilicity generated can be maintained. Baier and Meyer's publication in 1988 on the future directions of implant surface preparations discussed the importance of surface cleaning methods on the retention of high surface energy [35]. A similar concept was employed in the creation of the modSLA titanium implant surfaces. The surfaces are produced in the same way as the SLA surface using sandblasting and acid-etching technique. Immediately after generation of the surface, they are rinsed in a nitrogen-protected environment and then stored in an isotonic sodium chloride solution in a nitrogen environment [20]. This has been observed to retain the hydrophilic properties of the surface.

4.3.4.2 Characteristic Features of modSLA and SLA Surfaces

As a result of their proven superior osseointegration properties, the modSLA and SLA surfaces have been the subject of extensive investigation. They provide us with a suitable model to study the molecular mechanisms of osteogenic differentiation and osseointegration in an in vitro setting. The essential attribute that makes these surfaces suitable for studying molecular interactions lies in the fact that they do not provoke any chemical interactions with cells and therefore provide us with physiologically relevant models to study the intricate mechanisms of osteoblastic differentiation.

Topographical features of the modSLA and SLA surfaces appear similar, when observed using conventional scanning electron microscope (SEM) and atomic force microscopy (AFM). Both the surfaces are observed to have micro-roughness with S_a values varying between 1.15 ± 0.05 μm for SLA and 1.16 ± 0.04 μm for modSLA [20]. The roughness values observed in different studies seem to vary slightly, e.g. Vlacic et al. have described an S_a value of 1.8 μm [36], whereas Olivares-Navarrete et al.'s study demonstrated R_a to be around 3.22 μm [37]. Using AFM, we observed RMS roughness values in the range of 1.6–2.1 μm for the modSLA and SLA surfaces, in contrast to mirror-finished polished titanium surfaces that showed RMS values in the range 0.006–0.009 μm [38].

The roughness features of modSLA and SLA surfaces are not seen to be distributed evenly throughout the surfaces and therefore seem to indicate that

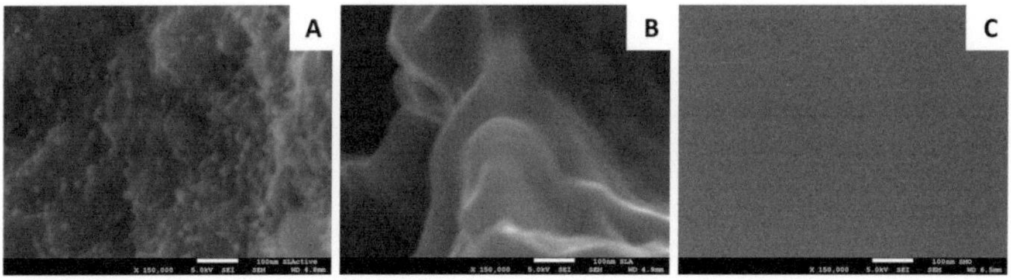

Fig. 4.3 High-resolution SEM images of (**a**) modSLA, (**b**) SLA and (**c**) smooth (SMO) titanium surfaces depicting the presence of nanostructures only on the modSLA surface (150,000× magnification)

uniformity in the topographical pattern is not a prerequisite for improved osseointegration and osteodifferentiation on implant surfaces. Recent studies using high-resolution SEM imaging techniques have observed the presence of nanostructures interspersed on the micro-roughened modSLA surface [30, 31, 39]. We also have observed similar nanostructures on the modSLA surfaces using high-resolution SEM imaging (Fig. 4.3) which corroborates with others. Chemical analysis using X-ray photoelectron spectroscopy (XPS) has confirmed that these nanostructures are not the result of crystallisation of sodium chloride present in the isotonic solution used to store the modSLA surfaces [31]. Wennerberg et al. further observed the formation of similar nanostructures when freshly prepared sandblasted and acid-etched titanium surfaces were stored in water (instead of isotonic saline solution) [31]. The impact of these nanostructures on the superior clinical outcomes of modSLA surfaces has not been established as yet.

Chemical analyses of the modSLA and SLA surfaces have demonstrated titanium, oxygen, nitrogen and carbon as the key elements present [40]. Traces of sodium and chlorine have also been observed in modSLA surfaces in some studies [28, 41] which could be a result of storing them in saline solution. The modSLA surface has a contact angle close to 0°, which exemplifies its extraordinary hydrophilic nature.

4.4 Biology of Healing on Implant Surfaces

Bone formation and healing on implant surfaces are multifaceted processes involving several factors and considerations. Several factors contribute towards successful osseointegration and bone formation on implant surfaces. Some of the key factors that play an important role in this process are summarised in Table 4.1

Insertion of any implant into the human body is akin to any other wound healing process. Bone healing starts immediately after an implant is inserted into the human body. The first tissue to come in contact with the implant surface is blood and its components. The large accessible surface area provided by micro-roughened implant surfaces allows for greater adsorption of proteins. Hydrophilic implant

Table 4.1 Key factors important for the process of osseointegration

Factors influencing osseointegration
Material biocompatibility
Implant shape and design
Surface characteristics – roughness, hydrophilicity, surface energy
Age of the patient
Pre-existing conditions – systemic diseases like diabetes, cancer, immunosuppressive conditions, hypersensitive conditions, infections, bone diseases like osteoporosis, osteomalacia, Paget's disease, etc.
Condition of the implant bed – poor bone quality, presence of debris, local infection, etc.
Surgical technique – minimal tissue damage is favourable for osseointegration
Relative mobility of implant – higher degree of movement of implant in the initial stages of healing inhibits osseointegration
Timing of loading

surfaces further improve the process of protein adsorption. The contact of blood with implants gives rise to a cascade of reactions involving coagulation, inflammation, release of chemoattractants and eventually recruitment, proliferation and differentiation of mesenchymal stem cell and pre-osteoblasts.

Coagulation of blood on the implant surface leads to the conversion of fibrinogen to fibrin. Fibrin forms a mesh-like scaffold on the implant surface that can retain other proteins and mediators to allow for appropriate progression of the healing process. Platelet activation and release of proteins like adenosine diphosphate (ADP), platelet-derived growth factor (PDGF), histamines, platelet factor 4 and transforming growth factor-β (TGF-β) and serotonin are important steps in the process of implant healing and osseointegration. The aggregation of platelets is instrumental in clot formation and eventually in the formation of the fibrin mesh network. Activated platelets have von Willebrand factor (VWF) and glycoprotein IIb/IIIa (GP IIb/IIIa) receptors on their surface. Fibrinogen binds to the GP IIb/IIIa receptors, leading to platelet aggregation. The process of activation of thrombin from prothrombin is catalysed by activated platelets. Thrombin in turn helps in the stabilisation of the fibrin network and therefore the platelet plug [42] (Fig. 4.4).

Leucocytes are next in line in the inflammatory response that happens upon the insertion of any implant. Neutrophils are the first white blood cells (WBCs) that are recruited to the site within 24–48 h. After this duration, monocytes and macrophages become the dominant cells at the implant site. Activation of leucocytes leads to release of inflammatory mediators that include cytokines like interleukin (IL)-1, IL-6, IL-8 and tumour necrosis factor (TNF)-α.

The extent and duration of the inflammatory response to any biomaterial define the biocompatibility of the material [43]. Inflammation is essentially a biological response to any injury to the body, and it may progress through the phases of acute inflammation, chronic inflammation and granulation tissue formation.

In cases of biocompatible materials, the acute inflammatory process eventually evolves into the bone formation phase of the wound healing and thereby integration of the implant material. Persistence of any inflammatory stimulus may lead to a

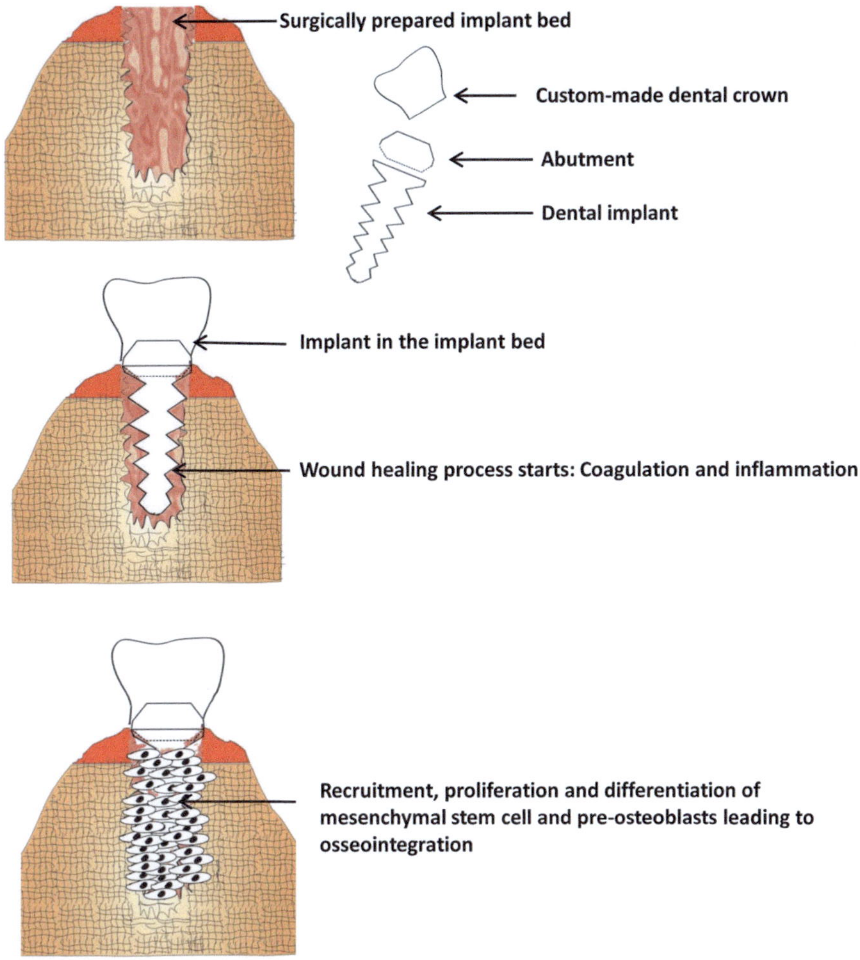

Fig. 4.4 The biology of implant healing process and osseointegration

chronic inflammatory response. The post-implantation inflammatory response may keep progressing depending on the properties of the material and may lead to a chronic inflammatory condition. The fundamental cells determining the nature of the inflammatory response are macrophages, lymphocytes and fibroblasts. Chronic inflammation may eventually lead to healing by fibrosis and scar tissue formation – an outcome not very conducive to bone formation. Higher levels of cytokines and inflammatory mediators have been observed to be deterrents to osteogenic differentiation in vitro [44] and bone formation in vivo [45].

The initial inflammatory response and haematoma formation are essential for the recruitment and differentiation of mesenchymal and osteoprogenitor cells which eventually leads to a successful osseointegration of the implant. This stage of healing leads to osteogenesis, deposition and integration of mineralised matrix on the surface of the implant. From this stage onwards, bone remodelling takes over giving rise to well-defined lamellar bone on the implant surface, thereby finally leading to bone bonding or, in other words, osseointegration.

4.5 Molecular Regulation of Osteogenic Differentiation and Osseointegration on Implant Surfaces

Multipotent mesenchymal stem cells (MSCs) have the capability to differentiate into osteogenic, chondrogenic or adipogenic cell types and other cell types such as myocytes, marrow stroma and tendons [46]. The precise cellular signaling mechanisms involved in osteogenic differentiation of progenitor cells remain indeterminate. However, before delving deeper into the phenomena of osteogenic differentiation and osseointegration on implant surfaces, it would be useful to briefly discuss normal bone architecture and physiology.

4.5.1 Bone Cells

The essential living components of bone tissue include three different types of cells – osteoblasts, osteocytes and osteoclasts. Some of the terminally differentiated osteoblast cells eventually get trapped in the lacunae of the matrix and form osteocytes.

4.5.1.1 Osteoblasts

Osteoblasts are the key bone cells that form the building blocks of the bone and are responsible for the deposition of mineralised matrix. These are mononucleate cells which have the potential to form osteoid (organised un-mineralised portion of a typical bone, characteristically composed of type I collagen). Subsequently they are also responsible for the mineralisation of the osteoid.

Osteoblasts arise from osteoprogenitor cells present in the human body (usually located in the deeper layers of the periosteum and bone marrow). Studies have demonstrated the presence of several niches of osteoprogenitor cells in the human body [47–50]. Multiple reports support the presence of mesenchymal progenitor cells with potential to differentiate into various cell types including osteoblasts. These cells under specific culturing or growing conditions give rise to osteoblasts.

Osteoprogenitor cells are known to express the RUNX2/Cbfa1 transcription factor. These osteoprogenitor cells differentiate to osteoblasts and start expressing gene markers that include Osterix, Col1, BSP, M-CSF, ALP, osteocalcin, osteopontin and osteonectin. Mature osteoblasts are cuboidal in shape. Osteoblasts have cytoplasmic projections that allow them to form communications with adjacent osteoblasts and osteocytes. Osteoblasts become flattened and elongated upon maturation. These cells usually form a single layer of cells on the surface of the bone. However, in cases where there is active bone formation, they may be present in the form of layers.

The principal function of osteoblasts is bone formation. As mentioned earlier, osteoblasts are the cells that facilitate the deposition of mineralised matrix in bones. They are also responsible for the synthesis of various bone-related proteins and polysaccharides. These cells also play an important role in bone remodelling by maintaining a balance between bone formation and resorption during new bone formation. Rarely, osteoblasts are also known to initiate the bone resorption process. Mature osteoblasts synthesise several phenotypic markers, including type I collagen, alkaline phosphatase (ALP) and osteocalcin (Fig. 4.5).

4.5.1.2 Osteocytes

Osteocytes are the most abundant type of bone cells (90–95 %) and cannot proliferate further to form new cells. They are known to function as mechanosensors of bone [51].

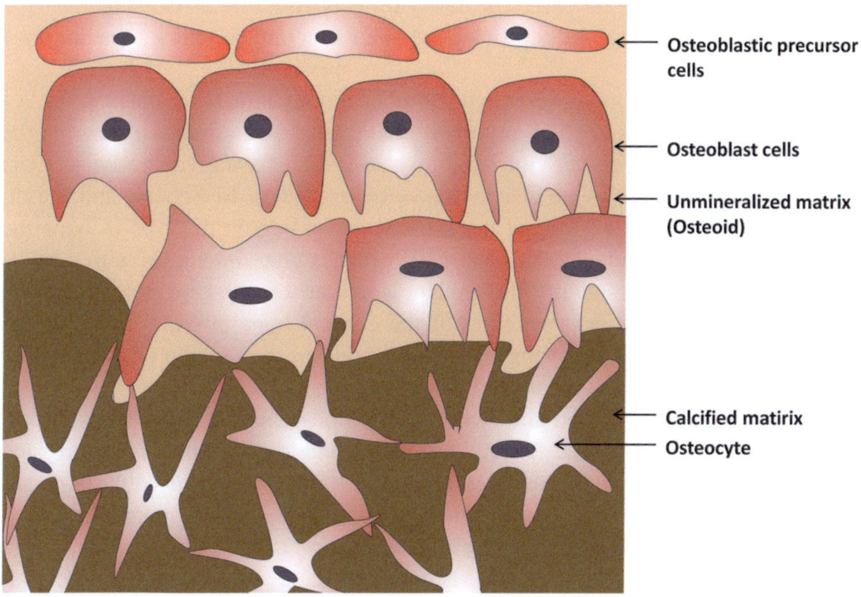

Fig. 4.5 Origin of osteoblasts in humans. The osteoblast precursors proliferate and give rise to osteoblasts which in turn lay the bone matrix and also give rise to the osteocytes

4.5.1.3 Osteoclasts

Osteoclasts are the cells responsible for bone resorption and thereby help in bone remodelling. These cells are formed by the fusion of mononuclear cells of the monocyte/macrophage lineage. The interplay between the osteoblasts and osteoclasts is responsible for maintaining normal bone homeostasis in the human body.

4.5.2 Osseointegration and New Bone Formation

The phenomenon of osseointegration is initiated simultaneously with the healing phase. Schenk and Buser have divided the process of osseointegration into three different stages [52]. Firstly, the implant surface is internalised by the formation of woven bone. They stated that the woven bone tends to form in two different patterns – 'distance osteogenesis', which occurs when the woven bone forms from the surrounding bone moving towards the implant surface, and 'contact osteogenesis', where osteogenesis occurs via direct deposition of new bone on the implant surface itself.

The second stage of osseointegration conditions the implant for its load-bearing function, wherein the woven bone laid on the implant surface slowly changes to a well-defined lamellar pattern. Lamellar bone consists of concentrically (in compact bones) or parallelly (in spongy bones) organised lamellae of collagen fibres and needs a firm base to be laid onto. The newly formed woven bone, existing bone and the implant surface supposedly provide the solid structure on which lamellar bone can be formed.

Schenk and Buser further described that bone remodelling takes place in the last stage of osseointegration which involves a balance and coordination between the osteoclastic resorptive activity and osteoblastic formative activity. The osseointegrative activities on dental implants, according to Schenk and Buser, vary with the different regions of the implant depending on the type of bone the region is in contact with. The coronal part of the implant integrates with cortical bone, whereas the remainder of the implant is in contact with cancellous bone and bone marrow. The compact structure of the cortical bone provides much of the initial stability, whereas the spongy cancellous bone ensures greater exposure to the vascular network and osteogenic cells.

Osteogenic differentiation and osteoinduction have been recognised as important processes leading to the formation of new bone during fracture healing and implant osseointegration. It has been argued that pre-existing osteoblasts play a minor role in bone formation in the regions of fracture healing or implant placement [53, 54]. The surrounding niche created in the region of the implant placement is rich in biochemical mediators that assist in recruitment and subsequent differentiation of cells towards osteogenesis, similar to fracture healing. Therefore, the process of osteogenic differentiation on implant surfaces provides important cues

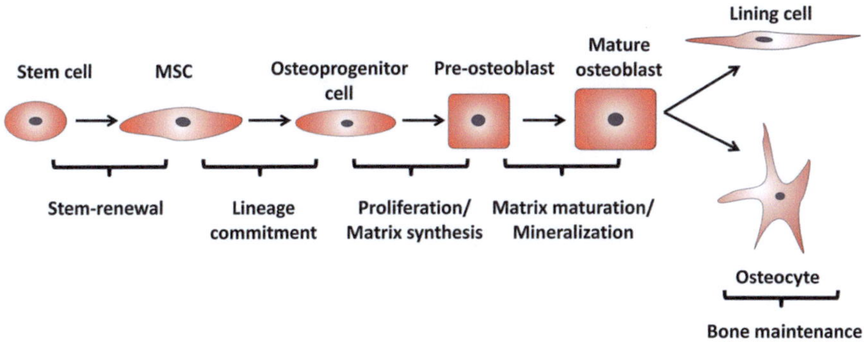

Fig. 4.6 Stages of osteoblastic differentiation (*MSC* mesenchymal stem cell)

in regard to the biocompatibility features of the material and the surface. Indeed, the implant surfaces with proven superior osseointegrative properties like the modSLA and SLA titanium surfaces have enabled us to learn some of the intricate details regarding the process of osteogenesis.

The process of osteogenic differentiation progresses through the stages of lineage commitment, pre-osteoblast cells, mature osteoblasts and ultimately forming the terminal bone cell – the osteocyte. Committed pre-osteoblasts are the first to express alkaline phosphatase (ALP-early marker of osteoblast differentiation). Mature osteoblasts express high levels of ALP and are involved in the production of extracellular matrix (ECM). Several genes and factors are involved in the process of commitment of mesenchymal stem cells to osteoblastic differentiation. The TGF-β/BMP molecules appear to play an important role in the process of commitment of MSCs to osteoprogenitor cells [55, 56] (Fig. 4.6).

4.5.3 Modulation of Molecular Pathways on Topographically Modified Implant Surface

Several studies have been conducted to observe the differences in osteogenic properties of different titanium surfaces. Most studies suggest that there is a similar initial cell attachment to all of the surfaces [40, 57]. Brett et al.'s study (2004) on the pattern of gene expression in osteoblasts cultured on different titanium surfaces (SLA, SMO and titanium plasma sprayed) revealed that surface roughness of Ti had profound effect on the pattern of gene expression by bone cells. Topographically modified titanium surfaces like the modSLA and SLA surfaces have been observed to stimulate cell signaling pathways. The BMP-2 gene is seen to be highly upregulated (greater than fivefold change) in osteoprogenitor cells as early as 24 h of culture on SLA surfaces, when compared with SMO surfaces. The osteogenic response of modSLA is considered to be better than the hydrophobic SLA surface, possibly because of the activation of WNT5A molecule [57].

4.5.3.1 Cell Signaling Pathways and Osteogenesis

Regulation of cellular interactions, differentiation and maturation are mediated by several factors, conditions and activation of different cell signaling pathways. The integrin signaling pathway is responsible for communication and adhesive interactions of cells with the implant surface, and activation of integrins leads to activation of different biological processes. Osteogenesis and osseointegration are among the various processes that become activated subsequent to stimulation of the integrin signaling pathway. Mesenchymal stem cells (MSC) undergo proliferation, and under specific conditions they become committed towards osteogenesis and thereby form mature osteoblast cells. Osteoprogenitor cells undergo a process of differentiation giving rise to osteoblasts and ultimately to osteocytes. Several cell signaling pathways are known to be instrumental in the process of osteogenic differentiation. The most important cell signaling pathways considered to be imperative to the process of osteodifferentiation are the TGF-β/BMP, Wnt, hedgehog and fibroblast growth factor (FGF) and Notch signaling.

TGF-β/BMP Pathway

The TGF-β/BMP pathway is identified as one of the most important molecular pathways that are influential in guiding the differentiation process. The bone morphogenetic proteins (BMPs) are a part of the transforming growth factor (TGF-β) superfamily of ligands, and they work through the SMAD receptors. BMP-2 and BMP-4 knockout mice do not even survive the gastrulation phase of the embryo due to failure of mesenchymal tissue induction [58]. The BMP molecules interact with the BMP receptors (BMPRs), leading to the activation of SMADs which ultimately enter the nucleus and activate several downstream transcription factors such as Dlx5, Cbfa1, Osx, etc. Several pathways have been shown to interact with the TGF-β/BMP pathway [59].

Wnt Signaling Pathway

The Wnt family of growth factors is an important pathway known to regulate growth and differentiation of tissues and organs. The canonical Wnt/β-catenin pathway has been found to be of vital significance for regulation of bone mass [60]. In fact, mutations in LRP5, a protein co-receptor in Wnt signaling, have been seen to produce osteoporosis–pseudoglioma features [61]. Moreover, the production of antagonists for the Wnt pathway, like DKK-1, is correlated with the osteolytic features seen in multiple myeloma [62].

The canonical Wnt/β-catenin pathway is probably the best understood pathway. β-catenin is a transcription factor that is central to the functioning of the pathway. The interaction of the TCF (T-cell factor) with SMAD4 potentially connects the

Wnt and the BMP signaling pathways. The canonical Wnt/β-catenin pathway has been found to be significant for regulation of bone mass [60]. The conservation of the β-catenin molecule is the prime factor responsible for the activation of downstream genes which in turn leads to the activation of SMAD4 and thereby raises the possibility of the BMP and the Wnt pathway to be closely related in the process of osteogenic differentiation.

The non-canonical Wnt pathways include the planar cell polarity (PCP) and Wnt/Ca^{2+} pathways. The distinguishing feature of the non-canonical pathways is that they are independent of β-catenin, LRP5/6 co-receptor and Dsh-DEP domain. Non-canonical Wnt pathways haven't been studied in extensive details, especially in relation to osteogenic differentiation. However, the studies on investigating interaction of osteoprogenitor cells with implant surfaces have revealed the upregulation of non-canonical Wnt pathway during osteogenic differentiation [32, 36, 63, 64].

Hedgehog Signaling Pathway

The hedgehog gene family consists of three members among which the Sonic (Shh) and Indian (Ihh) hedgehogs have been shown to be involved in skeletal development and repair. The hedgehog–BMP interaction is quite conserved in the process of differentiation [58]. Shh is seen to regulate BMP-2 expression in chicken limb buds [65]. The hedgehogs via their interaction with the BMP molecules might be important in the regulation of osteogenesis.

Fibroblast Growth Factor (FGF) Signaling Pathway

The FGF signaling pathway works through the tyrosine kinase receptors (FGFR1, FGFR2, FGFR3 and FGFR4) and leads to the activation of different cellular processes. FGFR1 signaling is known to activate osteogenic differentiation in osteoprogenitor cells. FGF ligands act on the FGF receptors and lead to downstream molecular processes. One of the key transcription factors RUNX2 is known to be phosphorylated under the influence of FGF2 ligand via the mitogen-activated protein kinase (MAPK) pathway [66].

Notch Signaling Pathway

The Notch pathway is a pathway for cellular communication that helps communication between neighbouring cells. The Notch pathway is known to work through its four receptors, NOTCH1, NOTCH2, NOTCH3 and NOTCH4. Notch signaling is believed to regulate osteogenic differentiation through its interaction with the BMP-2-mediated cell signaling pathway [67] and has been shown to induce the expression of Osterix.

4.5.3.2 Insights into the Molecular Regulation on modSLA and SLA Surfaces

Topographically modified surfaces are well recognised in the field of implant dentistry for their improved osteogenic properties. Several research groups across the world have been trying to explore the possible molecular mechanisms involved in accruing these osteogenic features. These surfaces have also been used as models to study the process of osteogenesis in vitro as they are considered to provide a substrate to osteoprogenitor cells that is akin to the native niche seen in vivo.

The SLA and modSLA surfaces have been seen to activate the integrin signaling pathway in cells capable of differentiating towards osteogenic lineage like mesenchymal stem cells and osteoprogenitor cells. Higher expression of integrins α2 and β1 has been observed on these surfaces [68, 69]. Integrin molecules are presumed to be important for anchorage of cells to surfaces, and this is possibly the first step before the process of cellular differentiations begins. We have observed higher expression of genes encoding integrins α2 (ITGA2) and β1 (ITGB1) within 24 h of culturing osteoprogenitor cells on modSLA and SLA surfaces compared to SMO surfaces [38]. Cell signaling pathways are stimulated subsequent to the activation of integrins and anchorage of cells to these surfaces. Studies on these surfaces have revealed stimulation of the key osteogenic pathways, TGF-β/BMP and Wnt [32, 36, 37, 64, 70].

The Wnt signaling pathway is subdivided into the canonical Wnt/β-catenin and the non-canonical Wnt pathways. The non-canonical Wnt is further subclassified into different pathways among which the planar cell polarity (PCP) and Wnt/Ca^{2+} pathways have been best known. The role of the Wnt/β-catenin pathway in osteogenesis and new bone formation is well established. However, the results from studies on the modSLA and SLA surfaces revealed upregulation of the Wnt/Ca^{2+} pathway during osteogenic differentiation [32, 63, 64]. Ivanovski et al.'s work assessing the transcriptional profile during osseointegration in human subjects also showed activation of the TGF-β/BMP and Wnt pathways [18]. In addition to these cell signaling pathways, their study also observed the upregulation of the Notch pathway [18]. The Notch pathway has also been shown to be important for osteogenic differentiation in other studies [67], yet it generally has received scant attention in the context of osteogenesis. Our studies exploring the differential regulation of cell signaling pathways when osteoprogenitor cells are cultured on modSLA and SLA surfaces have also shown an early stimulation of the Notch pathway along with the TGF-β/BMP and Wnt (especially the non-canonical Wnt/Ca^{2+} pathway) [32].

The modSLA and SLA surfaces have also been shown to increase the expression of osteogenic markers like alkaline phosphatase (ALP), osteocalcin (OCN), osteopontin (SPP1) and RUNX2 [57, 71–73]. These in vitro observations confirmed their in vivo osteogenic properties. The sequential stimulation of different cell signaling pathways eventually leads to the activation of osteogenic transcription factors and ultimately leads to osteogenic differentiation. We also explored the regulation of microRNAs, which are small RNA molecules that have the potential to modulate the expression of messenger RNA (mRNA) molecules, on the modSLA and SLA surfaces. Several microRNAs that are known to mediate cell development and differentiation were seen to be downregulated on both the modSLA and SLA surfaces in comparison to the SMO surfaces [38]. Bioinformatic target predictions for the downregulated miRNAs using an online tool, TargetScan, have revealed several genes of the TGF-β/BMP and Wnt/Ca^{2+} pathway as potential targets. Inhibitors of osteogenesis were found to be potential targets for miRNAs that were found to be upregulated.

4.6 Conclusion

Osseointegration is a phenomenon that is integral to the successful incorporation of orthopaedic and dental implants into the human body. In this chapter we have presented the current concepts in the field of implant surface modification and osseointegration. The modSLA and SLA micro-roughened titanium dental implant surfaces are known for their improved osteogenic and osseointegration properties, thereby highlighting the importance of topographically modified surfaces. These surfaces have been studied in-depth by researchers across the globe. Findings from such studies have enabled us to learn a great deal about the molecular mechanisms involved in osteogenic differentiation and osseointegration on micro-roughened implant surfaces. Such implant surfaces have also helped us in exploring the various signaling pathways involved in osteogenesis and therefore have provided us with a model to study the molecular mechanisms involved in osteogenic differentiation in vitro without using chemical mediators to induce differentiation.

The positive impact of micro-roughened titanium implants on osseointegration is proven. However, with the advent of nanotechnological modifications and the recent evidence from nano-topographically modified implant surfaces that show better osseointegration and bone formation, it is apparent that we haven't been able to identify all the factors and underlying mechanisms responsible for successful osseointegration and osteogenic differentiation. This in turn means that we need to explore these processes and their molecular regulation in greater depths. It is also clear that research focused on further exploring modifications of implant surfaces is ongoing, and this will likely lead to the development of different kinds of surfaces that will enable us to learn more about the process of osseointegration.

Acknowledgements The modSLA, SLA and SMO discs were supplied by Institut Straumann (Basel, Switzerland). We thank Dr. Sanjleena Singh and Dr. Mohammed Alfarsi for assisting us with the scanning electron microscope images.

References

1. Branemark R, Branemark PI, Rydevik B, Myers RR (2001) Osseointegration in skeletal reconstruction and rehabilitation: a review. J Rehabil Res Dev 38(2):175–181
2. Buser D, Schenk RK, Steinemann S, Fiorellini JP, Fox CH, Stich H (1991) Influence of surface characteristics on bone integration of titanium implants. A histomorphometric study in miniature pigs. J Biomed Mater Res 25(7):889–902
3. Albrektsson T, Branemark PI, Hansson HA, Lindstrom J (1981) Osseointegrated titanium implants. Requirements for ensuring a long-lasting, direct bone-to-implant anchorage in man. Acta Orthop Scand 52(2):155–170
4. Gotfredsen K, Wennerberg A, Johansson C, Skovgaard LT, Hjorting-Hansen E (1995) Anchorage of TiO2-blasted, HA-coated, and machined implants: an experimental study with rabbits. J Biomed Mater Res 29(10):1223–1231
5. Wennerberg A, Albrektsson T, Johansson C, Andersson B (1996) Experimental study of turned and grit-blasted screw-shaped implants with special emphasis on effects of blasting material and surface topography. Biomaterials 17(1):15–22
6. Gotfredsen K, Nimb L, Hjorting-Hansen E, Jensen JS, Holmen A (1992) Histomorphometric and removal torque analysis for TiO2-blasted titanium implants. An experimental study on dogs. Clin Oral Implants Res 3(2):77–84
7. Bristow CM, Cleevely RJ (2005) Scientific enquiry in late 18th century Cornwall and the discovery of titanium. In: Brånemark P-I (ed) The osseointegration book: from calvarium to calcaneus. Quintessenz Verlags-GmbH, Berlin, pp 1–11
8. McCracken M (1999) Dental implant materials: commercially pure titanium and titanium alloys. J Prosthodont 8(1):40–43
9. Albrektsson T, Johansson C (2001) Osteoinduction, osteoconduction and osseointegration. Eur Spine J 10(Suppl 2):S96–S101
10. Hemlata Garg GB, Garg A (2012) Implant surface modifications: a review. J Clin Diagn Res 6 (2):319–324
11. Zhu X, Chen J, Scheideler L, Reichl R, Geis-Gerstorfer J (2004) Effects of topography and composition of titanium surface oxides on osteoblast responses. Biomaterials 25 (18):4087–4103
12. Cochran DL, Nummikoski PV, Higginbottom FL, Hermann JS, Makins SR, Buser D (1996) Evaluation of an endosseous titanium implant with a sandblasted and acid-etched surface in the canine mandible: radiographic results. Clin Oral Implants Res 7(3):240–252
13. Wennerberg A, Albrektsson T (2009) Effects of titanium surface topography on bone integration: a systematic review. Clin Oral Implants Res 20:172–184
14. Zeng H, Du X-W, Singh SC, Kulinich SA, Yang S, He J, Cai W (2012) Nanomaterials via laser ablation/irradiation in liquid: a review. Adv Funct Mater 22(7):1333–1353
15. Donos N, Hamlet S, Lang NP, Salvi GE, Huynh-Ba G, Bosshardt DD, Ivanovski S (2011) Gene expression profile of osseointegration of a hydrophilic compared with a hydrophobic microrough implant surface. Clin Oral Implants Res 22(4):365–372
16. Mardas N, Schwarz F, Petrie A, Hakimi AR, Donos N (2011) The effect of SLActive surface in guided bone formation in osteoporotic-like conditions. Clin Oral Implants Res 22(4):406–415
17. Linares A, Mardas N, Dard M, Donos N (2011) Effect of immediate or delayed loading following immediate placement of implants with a modified surface. Clin Oral Implants Res 22(1):38–46
18. Ivanovski S, Hamlet S, Salvi GE, Huynh-Ba G, Bosshardt DD, Lang NP, Donos N (2011) Transcriptional profiling of osseointegration in humans. Clin Oral Implants Res 22(4):373–381
19. Guo CY, Matinlinna JP, Tang AT (2012) Effects of surface charges on dental implants: past, present, and future. Int J Biomater 2012:381535
20. Rupp F, Scheideler L, Olshanska N, de Wild M, Wieland M, Geis-Gerstorfer J (2006) Enhancing surface free energy and hydrophilicity through chemical modification of microstructured titanium implant surfaces. J Biomed Mater Res A 76(2):323–334

21. Ellingsen JE (1995) Pre-treatment of titanium implants with fluoride improves their retention in bone. J Mater Sci Mater Med 6(12):749–753
22. Wennerberg A, Albrektsson T, Andersson B, Krol JJ (1995) A histomorphometric and removal torque study of screw-shaped titanium implants with three different surface topographies. Clin Oral Implants Res 6(1):24–30
23. Wennerberg A, Hallgren C, Johansson C, Danelli S (1998) A histomorphometric evaluation of screw-shaped implants each prepared with two surface roughnesses. Clin Oral Implants Res 9 (1):11–19
24. Sykaras N, Iacopino AM, Marker VA, Triplett RG, Woody RD (2000) Implant materials, designs, and surface topographies: their effect on osseointegration. A literature review. Int J Oral Maxillofac Implants 15(5):675–690
25. Wennerberg A, Albrektsson T (2000) Suggested guidelines for the topographic evaluation of implant surfaces. Int J Oral Maxillofac Implants 15(3):331–344
26. Shalabi MM, Gortemaker A, Van't Hof MA, Jansen JA, Creugers NH (2006) Implant surface roughness and bone healing: a systematic review. J Dent Res 85(6):496–500
27. Lang NP, Salvi GE, Huynh-Ba G, Ivanovski S, Donos N, Bosshardt DD (2011) Early osseointegration to hydrophilic and hydrophobic implant surfaces in humans. Clin Oral Implants Res 22(4):349–356
28. Hamlet S, Alfarsi M, George R, Ivanovski S (2012) The effect of hydrophilic titanium surface modification on macrophage inflammatory cytokine gene expression. Clin Oral Implants Res 23(5):584–590
29. de Oliveira PT, Nanci A (2004) Nanotexturing of titanium-based surfaces upregulates expression of bone sialoprotein and osteopontin by cultured osteogenic cells. Biomaterials 25 (3):403–413
30. Wennerberg A, Galli S, Albrektsson T (2011) Current knowledge about the hydrophilic and nanostructured SLActive surface. Clin Cosmet Investig Dent 3(1):59–67
31. Wennerberg A, Svanborg LM, Berner S, Andersson M (2012) Spontaneously formed nanostructures on titanium surfaces. Clin Oral Implants Res 24(2):203–209
32. Chakravorty N, Hamlet S, Jaiprakash A, Crawford R, Oloyede A, Alfarsi M, Xiao Y, Ivanovski S (2013) Pro-osteogenic topographical cues promote early activation of osteoprogenitor differentiation via enhanced TGFbeta, Wnt, and Notch signaling. Clin Oral Implants Res 2013:1–12
33. Mathieu PS, Loboa EG (2012) Cytoskeletal and focal adhesion influences on mesenchymal stem cell shape, mechanical properties, and differentiation down osteogenic, adipogenic, and chondrogenic pathways. Tissue Eng B Rev 18(6):436–444
34. Buser D, Broggini N, Wieland M, Schenk RK, Denzer AJ, Cochran DL, Hoffmann B, Lussi A, Steinemann SG (2004) Enhanced bone apposition to a chemically modified SLA titanium surface. J Dent Res 83(7):529–533
35. Baier RE, Meyer AE (1988) Future directions in surface preparation of dental implants. J Dent Educ 52(12):788–791
36. Vlacic-Zischke J, Hamlet SM, Friis T, Tonetti MS, Ivanovski S (2011) The influence of surface microroughness and hydrophilicity of titanium on the up-regulation of TGFbeta/BMP signalling in osteoblasts. Biomaterials 32(3):665–671
37. Olivares-Navarrete R, Hyzy SL, Hutton DL, Erdman CP, Wieland M, Boyan BD, Schwartz Z (2010) Direct and indirect effects of microstructured titanium substrates on the induction of mesenchymal stem cell differentiation towards the osteoblast lineage. Biomaterials 31 (10):2728–2735
38. Chakravorty N, Ivanovski S, Prasadam I, Crawford R, Oloyede A, Xiao Y (2012) The microRNA expression signature on modified titanium implant surfaces influences genetic mechanisms leading to osteogenic differentiation. Acta Biomater 8(9):3516–3523
39. Gittens RA, McLachlan T, Olivares-Navarrete R, Cai Y, Berner S, Tannenbaum R, Schwartz Z, Sandhage KH, Boyan BD (2011) The effects of combined micron-/submicron-

scale surface roughness and nanoscale features on cell proliferation and differentiation. Biomaterials 32(13):3395–3403
40. Brett PM, Harle J, Salih V, Mihoc R, Olsen I, Jones FH, Tonetti M (2004) Roughness response genes in osteoblasts. Bone 35(1):124–133
41. Zinelis S, Silikas N, Thomas A, Syres K, Eliades G (2012) Surface characterization of SLActive dental implants. Eur J Esthet Dent 7(1):72–92
42. Kuzyk PR, Schemitsch EH (2011) The basic science of peri-implant bone healing. Indian J Orthop 45(2):108–115
43. Spector M, Cease C, Xia TL (1989) The local tissue-response to biomaterials. Crit Rev Biocompat 5(3):269–295
44. Gilbert L, He X, Farmer P, Boden S, Kozlowski M, Rubin J, Nanes MS (2000) Inhibition of osteoblast differentiation by tumor necrosis factor-alpha. Endocrinology 141(11):3956–3964
45. Dimitriou R, Babis GC (2007) Biomaterial osseointegration enhancement with biophysical stimulation. J Musculoskelet Neuronal Interact 7(3):253–265
46. Muraglia A, Cancedda R, Quarto R (2000) Clonal mesenchymal progenitors from human bone marrow differentiate in vitro according to a hierarchical model. J Cell Sci 113(7):1161–1166
47. Erlebacher A, Filvaroff EH, Gitelman SE, Derynck R (1995) Toward a molecular understanding of skeletal development. Cell 80(3):371–378
48. Friedenstein AJ, Chailakhjan RK, Lalykina KS (1970) The development of fibroblast colonies in monolayer cultures of guinea pig bone marrow and spleen cells. Cell Prolif 3(4):393–403
49. Friedenstein AJ (1976) Precursor cells of mechanocytes. In: G.H. Bourne JFD, Jeon KW (eds) Int Rev Cytol, vol. 47. Academic Press, pp 327–359
50. Friedenstein AJ, Chailakhyan RK, Gerasimov UV (1987) Bone marrow osteogenic stem cells: in vitro cultivation and transplantation in diffusion chambers. Cell Tissue Kinet 20(3):263–272
51. Ehrlich PJ, Lanyon LE (2002) Mechanical strain and bone cell function: a review. Osteoporos Int 13(9):688–700
52. Schenk RK, Buser D (1998) Osseointegration: a reality. Periodontol 2000 17:22–35
53. Frost HM (1989) The biology of fracture healing. An overview for clinicians. Part II. Clin Orthop Relat Res 248:294–309
54. Frost HM (1989) The biology of fracture healing. An overview for clinicians. Part I. Clin Orthop Relat Res 248:283–293
55. Aubin JE, Liu F, Malaval L, Gupta AK (1995) Osteoblast and chondroblast differentiation. Bone 17(2 Suppl):77S–83S
56. Malaval L, Liu F, Roche P, Aubin JE (1999) Kinetics of osteoprogenitor proliferation and osteoblast differentiation in vitro. J Cell Biochem 74(4):616–627
57. Wall I, Donos N, Carlqvist K, Jones F, Brett P (2009) Modified titanium surfaces promote accelerated osteogenic differentiation of mesenchymal stromal cells in vitro. Bone 45 (1):17–26
58. Yamaguchi A, Komori T, Suda T (2000) Regulation of osteoblast differentiation mediated by bone morphogenetic proteins, hedgehogs, and Cbfa1. Endocr Rev 21(4):393–411
59. von Bubnoff A, Cho KWY (2001) Intracellular BMP signaling regulation in vertebrates: pathway or network? Dev Biol 239(1):1–14
60. Krishnan V, Bryant HU, MacDougald OA (2006) Regulation of bone mass by Wnt signaling. J Clin Invest 116(5):1202–1209
61. Gong Y, Slee RB, Fukai N, Rawadi G, Roman-Roman S, Reginato AM, Wang H, Cundy T, Glorieux FH, Lev D, Zacharin M, Oexle K, Marcelino J, Suwairi W, Heeger S, Sabatakos G, Apte S, Adkins WN, Allgrove J, Arslan-Kirchner M, Batch JA, Beighton P, Black GCM, Boles RG, Boon LM, Borrone C, Brunner HG, Carle GF, Dallapiccola B, De Paepe A, Floege B, Halfhide ML, Hall B, Hennekam RC, Hirose T, Jans A, Jüppner H, Kim CA, Keppler-Noreuil K, Kohlschuetter A, LaCombe D, Lambert M, Lemyre E, Letteboer T, Peltonen L, Ramesar RS, Romanengo M, Somer H, Steichen-Gersdorf E, Steinmann B, Sullivan B, Superti-Furga A, Swoboda W, van den Boogaard M-J, Van Hul W, Vikkula M, Votruba M,

Zabel B, Garcia T, Baron R, Olsen BR, Warman ML (2001) LDL Receptor-Related Protein 5 (LRP5) affects bone accrual and eye development. Cell 107(4):513–523

62. Tian E, Zhan F, Walker R, Rasmussen E, Ma Y, Barlogie B, Shaughnessy JD (2003) The role of the Wnt-signaling antagonist DKK1 in the development of osteolytic lesions in multiple myeloma. N Engl J Med 349(26):2483–2494
63. Olivares-Navarrete R, Hyzy SL, Hutton DL, Dunn GR, Appert C, Boyan BD, Schwartz Z (2011) Role of non-canonical Wnt signaling in osteoblast maturation on microstructured titanium surfaces. Acta Biomater 7(6):2740–2750
64. Olivares-Navarrete R, Hyzy SL, Park JH, Dunn GR, Haithcock DA, Wasilewski CE, Boyan BD, Schwartz Z (2011) Mediation of osteogenic differentiation of human mesenchymal stem cells on titanium surfaces by a Wnt-integrin feedback loop. Biomaterials 32(27):6399–6411
65. Laufer E, Nelson CE, Johnson RL, Morgan BA, Tabin C (1994) Sonic hedgehog and Fgf-4 act through a signaling cascade and feedback loop to integrate growth and patterning of the developing limb bud. Cell 79(6):993–1003
66. Xiao G, Jiang D, Gopalakrishnan R, Franceschi RT (2002) Fibroblast growth factor 2 induction of the osteocalcin gene requires MAPK activity and phosphorylation of the osteoblast transcription factor, Cbfa1/Runx2. J Biol Chem 277(39):36181–36187
67. Nobta M, Tsukazaki T, Shibata Y, Xin C, Moriishi T, Sakano S, Shindo H, Yamaguchi A (2005) Critical regulation of bone morphogenetic protein-induced osteoblastic differentiation by Delta1/Jagged1-activated Notch1 signaling. J Biol Chem 280(16):15842–15848
68. Raz P, Lohmann CH, Turner J, Wang L, Poythress N, Blanchard C, Boyan BD, Schwartz Z (2004) 1 alpha,25(OH)(2)D-3 regulation of integrin expression is substrate dependent. J Biomed Mater Res A 71A(2):217–225
69. Olivares-Navarrete R, Raz P, Zhao G, Chen J, Wieland M, Cochran DL, Chaudhri RA, Ornoy A, Boyan BD, Schwartz Z (2008) Integrin alpha2beta1 plays a critical role in osteoblast response to micron-scale surface structure and surface energy of titanium substrates. Proc Natl Acad Sci U S A 105(41):15767–15772
70. Olivares-Navarrete R, Hyzy S, Wieland M, Boyan BD, Schwartz Z (2010) The roles of Wnt signaling modulators Dickkopf-1 (Dkk1) and Dickkopf-2 (Dkk2) and cell maturation state in osteogenesis on microstructured titanium surfaces. Biomaterials 31(8):2015–2024
71. Zhao G, Schwartz Z, Wieland M, Rupp F, Geis-Gerstorfer J, Cochran DL, Boyan BD (2005) High surface energy enhances cell response to titanium substrate microstructure. J Biomed Mater Res A 74A(1):49–58
72. Klein MO, Bijelic A, Toyoshima T, Gotz H, von Koppenfels RL, Al-Nawas B, Duschner H (2010) Long-term response of osteogenic cells on micron and submicron-scale-structured hydrophilic titanium surfaces: sequence of cell proliferation and cell differentiation. Clin Oral Implants Res 21(6):642–649
73. Klein MO, Bijelic A, Ziebart T, Koch F, Kammerer PW, Wieland M, Konerding MA, Al-Nawas B (2013) Submicron scale-structured hydrophilic titanium surfaces promote early osteogenic gene response for cell adhesion and cell differentiation. Clin Implant Dent Relat Res 15(2):166–175

Chapter 5
Advances in Bioglass and Glass Ceramics for Biomedical Applications

Besim Ben-Nissan, Andy H. Choi, and Innocent Macha

Abstract Tissue engineering and advanced biomedical technologies have proved to be potential to improve the quality of human life. During the last four decades, the capability to engineer or repair new functional tissues has been a very effective approach to improve the quality of life of patients. Since its discovery by Hench and co-workers in the 1960s, bioglasses and glass ceramics have attracted considerable attention of many researchers because of their unique properties which can easily be tailored by manipulating its compositions and morphology. Over the years, many questions concerning its interactions with both hard and soft tissues have been answered with a multidisciplinary team of surgeons, scientists and engineers. Many clinical Bioglass® and other similar structures and compositions are being used for bone augmentation and restoration, in orthopaedic, dental and maxillofacial surgery and in general in the field of tissue engineering. They have proved to be efficient and effective, some with outperformance over other bioceramic and metal prostheses. It is our aim in this chapter to present the development of these important biomaterials focusing on the history, synthesis, properties, modern characterisation methods and the current development of nano- and biocomposite materials for clinical applications.

Keywords Bioglass • Glass ceramics • A-W glass • Osteosimulation • Sol–gel

5.1 Introduction

When a person suffers from a pain, the main concern for that individual is relieving the pain and returning to a healthy and functional lifestyle. Degeneration and diseases often result in the replacement of skeletal parts, such as the knees, hips, finger joints, elbows, vertebrae and teeth, and repair of the mandible surgically.

It is anticipated that the growth in these areas will continue due to a number of factors, for instance, the need due to the ageing population, improvements in

---

Dedicated to Prof Larry Hench who has given us the 'Bioglass' and beyond.

B. Ben-Nissan (✉) • A.H. Choi • I. Macha
Faculty of Science, University of Technology, Broadway, NSW 2007, Australia
e-mail: b.ben-nissan@uts.edu.au

Q. Li, Y.-W. Mai (eds.), *Biomaterials for Implants and Scaffolds*, Springer Series in Biomaterials Science and Engineering 8, DOI 10.1007/978-3-662-53574-5_5

technology and lifestyle, a better understanding of body functionality, an increasing preference by younger to middle-aged candidates for undergoing surgery, improved aesthetics and the need for better functions [1].

By definition, a biomaterial is a nondrug substance which is ideal to be placed in a system that can replace or enhance the roles of bodily organs or tissues. These materials are able to be in contact with bodily fluids and tissues while showing little or if any adverse reactions for prolonged periods of time.

The major key factors that are pertinent for the success of an implant are its biocompatibility and biofunctionality. Engineers and surgeons have identified, even at the initial stages of this field, the problems related to the design and materials selection that resulted in premature loss of implant function through mechanical failure, corrosion or inadequate biocompatibility of the component. Depending on the applications, bioactive glass and glass ceramics in addition to ceramic materials are ideal candidates with respect to the above functions, except for their brittle behaviour under functional loading.

In this chapter, our aim is to examine the general definitions of glass as well as the preparation methods, properties and applications of glass, glass ceramics and bioactive glasses currently available and in use. We will also introduce the development and progress of the commercially available and currently investigated bioglasses and glass ceramics. Furthermore, their chemistry, bioactivity and mechanisms of their bonding and interactions within a physiological environment, their preparation methods and their applications in the biomedical field will also be covered.

5.2 Glass and Glass Ceramics

Glass is an amorphous, hard and brittle material created from the molten product of oxides. The molten material is normally cooled rapidly in order to prevent crystallisation or devitrification.

For over thousands of years, glass has been known to mankind. A natural glass produced from silicate magna called obsidian was known to prehistoric people long before how to make glass was discovered. The Phoenicians are thought by many to have been the first people to make glass [1].

It is now possible from the means of how glass is manufactured to predict and control the properties. Much of this control derives from the purity and use of appropriate raw materials. The choice of raw materials is generally based on their glass-making properties, which will be discussed in the following sections.

5.2.1 *Raw Materials*

5.2.1.1 Glass Formers

In general, glass formers are oxides which can be turned into a glass without the need to use any other oxides. However, they require very high temperatures in order to melt initially. Silica (SiO_2) normally obtained from sand is the most common type of glass former. Other examples of glass formers include B_2O_3 and P_2O_5.

5.2.1.2 Modifiers

Modifiers, as their name suggests, are materials that may alter the properties of the glass-forming oxides. They are also the major groups of compounds typically added to silica. In addition, they may also be employed to avoid defects in the final glass products. Generally, two types of modifiers are added to glass-forming oxides: fluxes and stabilisers.

Fluxes

In chemical terms, fluxes are the components that change the underlying properties of the oxides when added to glass formers. For instance, the melting point of glass-forming oxides can be lowered by the addition of fluxes.

Some of the most common fluxes include oxides of sodium (NaO_2) and potassium (K_2O). In particular, the viscosity of the glass can be lowered through the addition of boric oxide (B_2O_3), which in turn increases the fluidity and thus permitting the compounds to move with a greater degree of freedom.

Stabilisers

Stabilisers can be used to improve the chemical durability of glass as well as prevent the crystallisation of oxides. In certain applications, crystallisation may be undesirable due to its effect on light scattering, hence a reduction in transparency. Stabilisers, similar to fluxes, may also affect the working temperature of glass formers. Examples of stabilisers include oxides of aluminium (Al_2O_3), calcium (CaO) and magnesium (MgO).

Refining and Melting Agents

During the conventional melt-based manufacturing of glass, small bubbles are detrimental as the properties of the glass are significantly affected by their presence.

To decrease the number of bubbles, compounds such as sodium nitrate, sodium sulphate, sodium chloride, calcium fluoride and carbon are added to the glass, and the glass is said to be refined. On the other hand, the purity and close control of additives are critically important during the synthesis of glasses for biomedical applications due to the issues of toxicity and biocompatibility.

5.3 Types of Glasses

The specific properties of glass can be obtained through its chemical composition. An indication of some types of glasses produced in this manner, together with the desired properties for a number of engineering applications, is given in Table 5.1.

5.3.1 *Aluminosilicate Glasses*

Aluminosilicate glasses are hard, usually have a good chemical resistance and do not devitrify readily. They also have high heat shock resistance and can withstand heat even better than borosilicate glasses. One specific type of aluminosilicate glass is used in the production of E-glass fibres (also contains CaO).

5.3.2 *Borosilicate Glasses*

Boron oxide (B_2O_3) serves as both a glass former and a modifier. Boron oxide also produces a glass with a low coefficient of thermal expansion, which results in a glass that is better equipped to deal with thermal shock. A common trade name for

Table 5.1 Types of glasses showing their chemical composition in weight percentage

Component	Soda–lime glass	Lead glass	Borosilicate glass	Aluminosilicate glass	High-silica glass Vycor®	45S5 Bioglass®
SiO_2	70–75	53–68	73–82	57	96	45
Na_2O	12–18	5–10	3–10	1.0	–	24.5
K_2O	0–1	1–10	0.4–1	–	–	–
CaO	5–14	0–6	0–1	5.5	–	24.5
PbO	–	15–40	0–10	–	–	–
B_2O_3	–	–	5–20	4.0	3	–
Al_2O_3	0.5–2.5	0–2	2–3	20.5	–	–
MgO	0–4	–	–	12.0	–	–
P_2O_5	–	–	–	–	–	6

borosilicate glasses is Pyrex, and they are often used in the areas where temperature differences are an issue. Crystallisation is prevented by the presence of alumina (Al_2O_3) in large quantities. They also improve the chemical durability and the hardness of the glass.

5.3.3 *Lead Glasses*

Lead glass is often referred to as crystal glass as a result of an improvement in machinability, thus permitting the glass to be more easily engraved. It also gives the glass a heaviness and blue appearance.

One of the most important properties of lead glass is its high refractive index, which gives brilliance when properly cut or graved. The melting point and hot working (shaping) temperature of the glass are lowered as the lead oxide (PbO) acts as a flux and a modifier to acceptable levels. Radiation shielding is another useful application for the lead glasses.

Flint and crown glasses are some of the older terms associated with glass. Flint glass was a term originally used to describe lead glass since flint was used as a source of good-quality silica free from colour. It is now more loosely used to describe glasses with good colour. Crown glasses are alkali–lime–silica based, such as soda–lime glass.

5.3.4 *Soda–Lime Glasses*

The presence of soda (Na_2O) in glass lowers the melting point of the glass, and the lime (CaO) keeps the glass from crystallising.

5.3.5 *Glass Ceramics*

By definition, a glass ceramic is essentially a glass in which the formation of nuclei is enhanced by using specific compositions, which are self-nucleating, or by adding an additional nucleating agent [2]. Very small crystals are contained inside the resultant material. A number of factors influence the glass ceramics' final properties: crystal orientation; intergranular bonding; percentage of crystallinity, of crystalline phase distribution and of any remaining glassy phase; and grain size. In the past, by controlling the base composition, the choice of nucleant (nucleating agent) and an appropriate heat treatment schedule, above-mentioned factors have been successfully controlled [2]. In the early days, work on glass ceramics was focused on the lithia–silica (Li_2O–Si_2O) system. Later on, alumina was presented to destabilise the basic composition (Li_2O–Si_2O–Al_2O_3). β-Spodumene, a polymorph of $LiAlSiO_4$, is precipitated to inhabit most of the volume of the glass ceramic, such as in a Pyroceram system. In this system, Si^{4+} is replaced by Al^{3+} in the network structure, and Li^+ is held in close proximity to maintain the charge balance. The preceding system was an $MgO–Al_2O_3–SiO_2$ system, in which the lithia is replaced completely by MgO. Nucleation is accomplished by TiO_2, ZrO_2 and SnO_2. In another composition, Na_2O is used to replace the lithia.

Extensive investigation has been carried out on glasses and glass ceramics and fabricated as bioactive or surface-active biomaterials with additions of CaO and P_2O_5 to their base compositions. A key advantage of phosphate-based materials is their chemical relationship with carbonated apatite which is one of the main constituents of bone and teeth. The structures of phosphate glasses and glass ceramics are based on the networks of corner-sharing phosphate tetrahedra. In addition, apatite–mullite glass ceramics based on $SiO_2–Al_2O_3–P_2O_5–CaO–CaF_2$ compositions have also been developed and observed to form fluorapatite and mullite with a specific heat treatment procedure.

5.3.6 *Machinable Glass Ceramics*

In order to improve the machinability of glass ceramics, the base composition ($MgO–Al_2O_3–SiO_2$) can be modified by replacing Li_2O with a mixture of MgF_2 and K_2O. By reheating these specific glasses in the temperature range of 650–1150 °C, machinable glass ceramics are produced with an emphasis of inducing a randomly oriented dispersion of tetra-silicic mica crystals. These crystals have the chemical formula of $KMg_{2.5}Si_4O_{10}F_2$ and a structure similar to the tri-silicic mica fluorophlogopite, $KMg_3AlSi_3O_{10}F_2$. Hence, the structure is analogous to the natural mica mineral phlogopite. It is relatively easy for rotation or cleavage to occur in the K^+ planes, and since the crystals in the glass ceramic are in random orientations, the propagating cracks are continuously deflected in different directions within the material which leads to a rapid absorption of the propagation energy. The fracture paths follow the mica–glass interfaces or mica cleavage planes, removing very small fragments during the process, so that a good machined finish is easily obtained [2].

5.3.7 *Bioglasses and Glass Ceramics*

Since the discovery by Hench and Wilson [3] of the bioglasses which bond to living tissue (Bioglass®), various types of bioactive glasses and glass ceramics with different functions such as high machinability, mechanical strength and fast setting ability have been developed.

Glasses that are primarily based on silica (SiO_2) which may also contain small amounts of other crystalline phases have been examined for implantation purposes.

The most successful and prominent application is Bioglass®, which is described in detail in various comprehensive reviews [4–6].

The first-generation bioactive glass compositions lie in the Na_2O–CaO–P_2O_5–SiO_2 system. In 1971, the first development of such a bioglass began when 45S5 Bioglass® with a composition of 45 % SiO_2, 24.5 % CaO, 24.5 % Na_2O and 6 % P_2O_5 by weight was proposed [7].

It was suggested by Hench [4] and Vrouwenvelder et al. [8] that when compared to hydroxyapatite (HAp), 45S5 Bioglass® has greater osteoblastic activity which is accredited to a rapid exchange of alkali ions with hydronium ions at the surface. This in turn led to the formation of a silica-rich layer over a period of time. The migration of Ca^{2+} and PO_4^{3+} is permitted on this layer to the silica-rich surface where they combine with soluble calcium and phosphate ions from the solution and the formation of an amorphous CaO–P_2O_5 layer takes place. Upon the interaction with OH, CO_3^{2+} and F from solution, this layer will then undergo crystallisation. Andersson and Kangasniemi [9] have also observed a similar phenomenon in bioglass with slightly modified compositions.

Glass ceramics from a similar composition with various degrees of crystallinity was prepared by Li et al. [10]. They discovered that the formation of an apatite layer was directly influenced by the amount of glassy phase that still remains, with total inhibition when the glassy phase constitutes less than about 5 weight percent (wt%). These specific glasses (for instance, Bioglass®) have been accepted as bioactive materials as a result of their surface activity; and they have been utilised for non-load-bearing applications. Bioglasses® have been used successfully in clinical applications as artificial middle ear bone implants and alveolar ridge maintenance implants [3] and recently as toothpaste additives.

A bioactive glass with precipitated crystalline apatite and reduced alkaline oxide content can be produced by using a specific heat treatment method. The resultant glass ceramic is referred to as Ceravitals, and it has been shown to have a higher mechanical strength but lower bioactivity compared to Bioglass®.

Kokubo et al. [11] produced a glass ceramic named A-W glass ceramic (Cerabone A-W) that contains oxyfluorapatite ($Ca_{10}(PO_4)_6(OH,F_2)$) and wollastonite ($CaO.SiO_2$) in an MgO–CaO–SiO_2 glassy matrix. It was reported in the early 1990s that the A-W glass ceramic spontaneously bonded to living bone without the formation of fibrous tissue around the glass. They have also developed a bioactive and machinable glass ceramic containing apatite and phlogopite ($(Na,K)Mg_3(Al\text{-}Si_3O_{10})(F)_2$) called Bioverits that were utilised in the past in such clinical applications as the artificial vertebra [11]. Currently the production and application of A-W glass are only restricted to research, whereas its commercial production has been discontinued.

5.4 Synthesis of Bioactive Glass

Bioactive glasses have been manufactured using conventional glass technology. The glass components of oxides or carbonates in the form of grains are mixed, melted and then homogenised at a temperature between 1250 and 1400 °C [12]. Bulk implants are produced when the molten glass is cast into steel or graphite moulds. It is often necessary for a final grind and polish to achieve the required tolerances. Even though this process has been changed in many ways in order to avoid grinding and polishing by producing different particle sizes directly, still the processes have many advantages.

Nanoparticles and nanofibres of bioactive glass have been made available several years ago, and they have been used either alone or combined with polymers in the form of a nanocomposite in the biomedical field. In the following section, various processing methods used to fabricate nanoscale bioactive glasses are presented.

5.4.1 Microemulsion Techniques

Microemulsions are thermodynamically stable dispersions of oil and water stabilised by a surfactant and, in many cases, a cosurfactant. The microemulsions can be of the droplet type, either with spherical oil droplets dispersed in a continuous medium of water or vice versa with spherical water droplets dispersed in a continuous medium of oil. Researchers have discovered that the key in controlling polydispersity and nanoparticle size is provided by adjusting the microemulsion and/or operation variables [13, 14]. It has been well known that this method is an ideal technique which is also capable of obtaining nanometre-sized inorganic particles with minimum agglomeration [15, 16].

On the other hand, the main disadvantages of the microemulsion techniques are the usage of a large quantity of oil and surfactant phases and the low yield in production [17]. Only a limited number of papers are currently available on the production of nanosized bioactive particles using this approach even though microemulsion technique provides an alternative means for synthesising several types of organic and inorganic nanometre-sized particles compared to other production methods [18, 19].

5.4.2 Laser Spinning Techniques

Extensive experimental work has been carried out over the past few years in the development of laser spinning techniques with definite control of the results to fabricate tailored products [20–22]. Recently, researchers have for the first time developed a novel technique for producing bioglass nanofibres, by using 'laser spinning' [23]. In this technique, a small quantity of precursor material is melted using a high-energy laser, to produce a superfine filament that is then lengthened and cooled by a powerful gas current.

The advantages of laser spinning technique include that the process is relatively fast and the nanofibres are produced within several microseconds. It is also able to produce glass nanofibres of compositions that would be difficult to obtain using other methods. The diameters of the fibres produced from laser spinning technique range from hundreds down to tenths of microns; in addition the types of products vary from disordered maths to continuous filaments [21]. On the other hand, the major drawback of laser spinning is that high energy is required during the production process, which consequently increases the production cost.

Laser spinning technique has been demonstrated to be an efficient approach for the production of nanofibres of bioactive glasses and new nanostructures with potential for tissue engineering scaffolds, as fillers in bone defects and as reinforcing agents in nanocomposites. The capability of the laser spinning technique to produce nanofibres with a wide range of compositions makes evident its potential to create nanofibres with different rates of bioresorption to control the release of active ions that have the potential to stimulate the gene expression and cellular response necessary for tissue regeneration [22, 23].

5.4.3 Gas Phase (Flame Spray) Synthesis

Flame spray technology has been used by ancient Chinese in Chinese ink artwork and with painting on cave walls [24]. Currently metal–organic precursor compounds are used by flame spray technology to generate nanoparticles at temperatures above 1000 °C. The formation of molecular nuclei is the basic principle of all gas phase synthesis methods. This is followed by condensation and coalescence that induce the subsequent growth of nanoparticles in high-temperature regions during the process [17, 25].

Numerous studies have been conducted in relations to the understanding of the dynamics and key variables of flame spray process as well as how they can be controlled in order to obtain nanoparticles of given size range and chemical compositions [26, 27]. Athanassiou et al. [27] discovered that the metal–carboxylate system is a very convenient precursor as it permits the synthesis of oxide nanoparticles of almost any composition. Furthermore, metal–organic salts are highly stable in air and tolerate humidity, and above all they are fully miscible among each other. Accordingly, the production of any type of nanoparticulate mixed oxides with high chemical homogeneity is allowed using this process.

Using the flame spray technique, bioactive glass nanoparticles in the 20–50-nm range were successfully produced by Vollenweider et al. [28], and they reported within the dentin samples a pronounced increase in mineral content which suggested rapid remineralisation. Mohn et al. [29] also demonstrated the ability of the flame spray technique to synthesise radio-opaque bioactive glass nanoparticles for potential root canal application.

Compared to other gas phase techniques, the advantage is the precursors do not require an additional energy despite the fact that the flame spray technique is an energy-intensive approach.

5.4.4 Sol–Gel Bioglass

The sol–gel processing of ceramics and glass materials began more than 150 years ago on silica gel [30, 31]. Preliminary studies on sol–gel indicated that under acidic conditions, the hydrolysis of $Si(OC_2H_5)_4$, tetraethyl orthosilicate (TEOS), resulted in SiO_2 in the form of a glass-like material [30] that could be drawn into fibres. In the early days, the silica gels were dried for more than a year in order to avoid the gel fracturing into a fine powder, and because of this, the whole process lost technological interest.

A considerable amount of attention has been attracted as the result of the formation of Liesegang rings [32] which led to numerous investigations carried out by researchers on the problem of the periodic precipitation phenomena which result in the formation of Liesegang rings and the growth of crystals from gels.

Using the sol–gel method, various types of coatings and films have also been developed. In particular are the antireflection coatings of indium tin oxide (ITO) and related compositions applied to glass window panes [33]. Compared with traditional glass melting or ceramic powder methods, the motivation for the sol–gel processing is first and foremost the potentially higher homogeneity and purity and the lower processing temperatures associated with the approach [33].

For the past two decades, the production of bioglass using the sol–gel process has become an interesting research field [33–38]. Sol–gel process involves the synthesis of an inorganic network by mixing the metal alkoxides in solution, followed by hydrolysis, gelation and low-temperature firing to produce a dense and stable glass powder. The network structure of the gel can be modified by controlling hydrolysis and polycondensation reactions during productions. Hence, structural variation can be produced without compositional changes (c.f. Fig. 5.1).

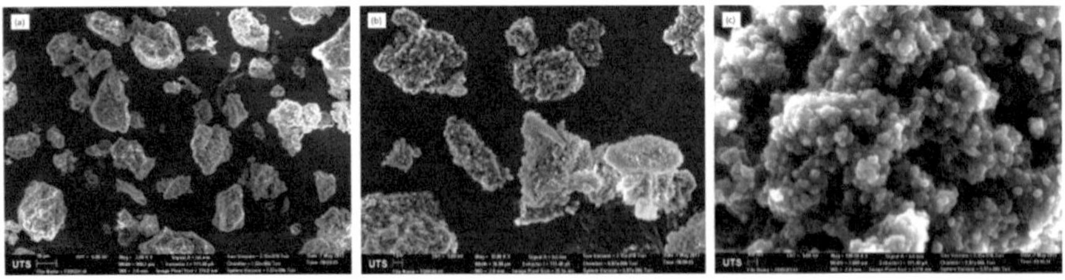

Fig. 5.1 SEM images of sol–gel-derived agglomerated 45S5 Bioglass® nanoparticles at (**a**) magnification *x*2, (**b**) magnification × 10 and (**c**) magnification × 100

Using gels, bioactive glasses can be prepared by sintering at temperatures between 600 and 700 °C, which reduces most of the disadvantages of high temperature processing with much better control over purity. Furthermore, by either modifying the microstructure or composition through processing parameters, a broader range as well as better control of bioactivity can be achieved [39].

Li et al. [12] reported that SiO_2–CaO–P_2O_5 powders produced by sol–gel are more bioactive than the melt-derived glasses of the same composition. In addition, Sepulveda et al. [40] examined the rates of dissolution and formations of surface layer on sol–gel and melt-derived bioglass, and they noticed the melt-derived 45S5 Bioglass® exhibited a lower rate than the 58S sol–gel bioglass powder. The high bioactivity of the sol–gel-derived materials is related to the microstructural features of the gels, i.e. grain and pore size associated with the large surface area, higher rate of dissolution and negative surface charge [41]. Furthermore, the sol–gel-derived bioactive glass has been proposed as alternative to glasses produced by melt and quenching methods, as they exhibit excellent degradation/resorption properties, more rapid bone bonding, improved homogeneity and purity and higher rate of apatite layer formation [12].

5.5 Biological and Adhesion Properties of Bioactive Glass

A certain compositional range of bioactive glasses containing SiO_2, Na_2O, CaO and P_2O_5 in specific proportions has demonstrated proper bonding of glass to bone. As mentioned earlier, there are three compositional changes separating them from soda–lime–silica glasses: high Na_2O and CaO content, less than 60 % SiO_2 and a high CaO/P_2O_5 ratio. Highly reactive surfaces are created from these compositional features when exposed to an aqueous medium. On the other hand, the amount of SiO_2 in bioactive glasses ranging between 45 and 60 % and as a result of repeated hot working can easily lead to problems in the formation of phase separation and crystallisation of the glassy material [7, 42]. Crystallisation of the material can cause a reduction in the rate of bioactivity of the glass [43], and a glassy phase of incontrollable composition is the result of partial crystallisation. Crystallisation of a bioactive glass can be controlled by its chemical composition [44, 45].

It has been reported that a new generation of bioactive glasses in the Na_2O–K_2O–MgO–CaO–B_2O_3–P_2O_5–SiO_2 system can be repeatedly heated without the risk of devitrification [46]. Hence, microspheres can be produced and sintered into porous implants of different shapes and sizes [47]. The porosity of a bioactive glass body does not only noticeably increase the total reacting surface of the glass but also allows a three-dimensional formation of the healing bony tissue. The mechanical strength and porosity of the bioactive glass implants can be controlled with different sintering times and temperatures [48]. To achieve the best mechanical strength of the sintered implant, the glass must retain its amorphous structure during the heat treatment.

5.5.1 *Bioactivity of the Glass*

As mentioned earlier the rates of osteostimulation of various types of bioactive particulates have been quantified by Oonishi et al. that provided the fundamental in vivo comparisons of Class A with Class B bioactive materials [49].

Bioactive glasses in Class A rapidly release soluble silicic acid and subsequently Ca^{2+}, leading to fast precipitation of calcium phosphate on the depleted Si-rich glass surface. On the other hand, bioactive glasses in Class B possess a low network dissolution rate [50, 51]. Glasses with a high rate of dissolution contain less than 55 wt% SiO_2 [51]. It has been shown that the higher the concentration of SiO_2 in the glass, the lower the rate of network dissolution and formation of a Si-rich layer. The rate of Si-rich gel formation on the glass surface is so low when the concentration of SiO_2 exceeds about 60 wt% that it has no practical significance on the bioactivity.

Strnad [52] and, later on, Karlsson and Ylänen [53] provided the reasonable explanations and revealed that the bioactivity of glass is based on the mean number of non-bridging oxygen ions in the silica tetrahedron. The charge of the oxygen ion in the corner is balanced by a network modifier anion which is Na^+, K^+ or Ca^{2+} instead of sharing a corner with another tetrahedron. Due to a rapid exchange of these anions for H^+ or H_3O^+ from the solution which occurs when exposed to body fluid, a hydration of the gel structure (=Si-(OH)) instead of (=Si-O Na^+, K^+) occurs.

Each silicon in silicate glasses is bonded to four oxygen atoms; hence the number of non-bridging oxygen ions in the tetrahedron can take any value between 0 and 4. When the number is 0, it represents a fully polymerised, three-dimensional network of silica tetrahedral. However, when the number is 4, it signifies a dissolved SiO_4 ion. The number must be greater than 2.6 in order to get bioactivity for a glass with the SiO_2 content of less than 60 wt% (c.f. Fig. 5.2).

Two to three non-bridging oxygen ions will result when the concentration of SiO_2 reaches between 50 and 55 wt% on the surfaces of glasses. This causes hydration of two or three oxygen ions with each silica tetrahedron, namely, forming ¼ $Si(OH)_2$ or -$Si(OH)_3$. Serra et al. [54, 55] examined the influence of non-bridging oxygen ions on the bioactivity of the glass. The number of non-bridging oxygen ions as a function of SiO_2 and Na_2O content in a glass is presented in Table 5.2.

The silica network is partially broken during the dissolution of the glass; and the SiOH and $Si(OH)_4$ groups are found on the uppermost layer of the glass. The higher the number of non-bridging oxygen ions in the gel, the higher the bioactivity of the glass. Finally, a totally dissolved monomeric SiO_4 ion is formed if none of the four oxygen ions is bridged. Yet, in this case the concentration of SiO_2 needs to be very low, i.e. less than 40 wt%, and it is questionable whether obtaining a glass phase of this composition is possible [56]. In summary, the crucial factor controlling the bioactivity of a glass is said to be the formation of the hydrated Si-rich gel on the glass surface for which the SiO_2 content should be 50–60 wt%.

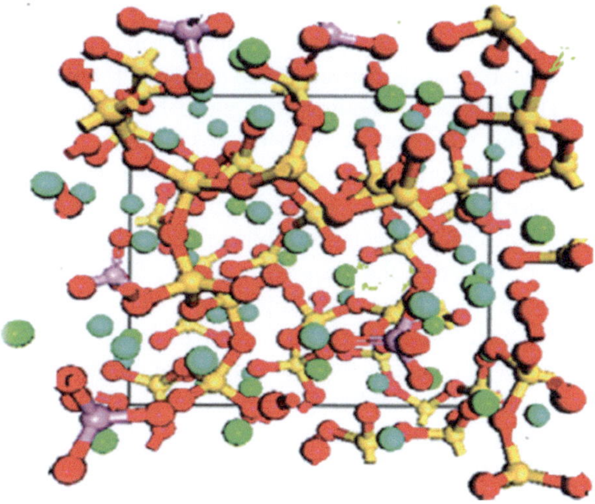

Fig. 5.2 Computational atomistic model of 45S5 Bioglass® compiled from a number of solid-state ^{17}O and ^{23}Na MQMAS, ^{29}Si, ^{31}P and ^{23}Na static and MAS NMR spectra simulation studies

Table 5.2 Number of non-bridging oxygen ions as a function of SiO_2 and Na_2O content in a glass (wt%)

Q^n	SiO_2	Na_2O	Non-bridging oxygen ions
4	100	0	0
3	66.6	33.3	1
2	50	50	2
1	40	60	3
0	33.3	66.6	4

5.5.2 *Interfacial Bond Strength of Bioactive Glass and Bone*

A number of investigations have reached a conclusion that the interfacial chemical reactions on the surface of bioactive glass result in a unique and firm bonding of bone to the glass implant. Mechanical testing has been used to emphasise the strength of the bonding in which the interfacial strengths of different biomaterials are compared with each other by determination of the push-out to failure forces.

Anderson et al. [57] revealed that true bioactive glasses bond to host bone through a firm layer of calcium phosphate. Nonetheless, glasses with SiO_2 amounts of approximately 60 wt% but containing 42.5 wt% of Al^{3+} showed only a low interfacial strength. Titanium cones were also used as reference, and they discovered the bonding strength of titanium implants was only about one-tenth of that of the bioactive glass implants. They also discovered the glass containing both SiO_2 and Al^{3+} greater than 60 wt% and 2.5 wt%, respectively, showed no bone contact at all.

Niki et al. [58] using the same method demonstrated the similar difference in bonding strength between titanium and bioactive glass implants. The bonding of bioactive glass to bone is based on the formation of a calcium phosphate layer connecting the bioglass implant to the host bone and an even dissolution of material. It can also be seen by comparing the bonding strength of HAp implants with those of bioactive glass, which depends on the difference in the type of the interfacial bonding between HAp and bone [58–60].

The interfacial bonding strength of bioactive glass to bone has been superior compared with that of HAp in most studies. The principle of categorising the bioactive materials in two distinct classes based on their bioactivity is supported by these findings. The silica-rich gel, in theory, is the weakest point of the interface between bioactive glass and bone. However, according to mechanical testing in most of the cases, the push-out failure by the maximum force occurs by fracture of the bone close to the glass implant [57, 61].

The valuable property of bioactive glasses being able to bond firmly to bone through chemical reactions and to ultimately be replaced by bone allows them to be used for medical applications. The constituents in bioactive glass are more importantly physiological chemicals or minerals found in the body: calcium, phosphorus, oxygen, silicon, sodium, potassium and magnesium. It has been reported that the concentration of the specific elements never increases to a level that could disturb the adjacent tissues during the bonding and formation of bone [60, 62]. On the other hand, the use of bioactive glass as an implant material or in manufacturing medical devices is limited by the mechanical properties of glass.

Consequently, the brittleness of glass implies that they cannot be used in the applications where load-bearing properties are required. Glass can be cast to plates, rods, etc., or it can be formed by sawing or grinding cast rods to rigid medical devices. Alternatively, glass can be used as a filler material in the form of particulate. The use of bioactive glass as a bioactive coating on mechanically stronger implant materials is also an option that has been widely studied.

5.6 Bioactive Glasses from Various Research Groups

In 1969, the concept of a strong bonding by chemical reactions between bone and glass-based synthetic materials occurring on a glass surface was first proposed by Hench et al. [63, 64]. The innovation concerned the chemical reactivity of the surface of a silica-based material, which had the amorphous structure of silicate glass. In the early 1970s, Hench appropriately named this Bioglass® [7]. In fact, bioactive glasses can be thought of as the precursors to all bioactive ceramics. The amorphous structure is a major characteristic of glasses. As stated earlier the structure of silicate glass in general is based on the SiO_4 tetrahedron. The tetrahedra are only linked to the oxygen ions at the corners. In crystalline silica, the tetrahedra are regularly arranged, which is characteristic of all crystalline materials. The tetrahedra in the structure of silica glass are present, but they are no longer regularly arranged; however, as in crystalline quartz, each of the oxygen ions still connects two tetrahedra.

Bioactive glasses bear a resemblance to ordinary soda–lime silica glass. Compared with ordinary glass, there is one main difference with the composition of bioactive glass. The amount of the network former SiO_2 in ordinary glass is 45 %, and the network modifier component consists mainly of approximately 14 % Na_2O and 10 % CaO, while bioactive glass consists of a significantly lower amount of network former that is replaced primarily by metal oxides or network modifiers. Usually in the bioglass compositions, the Na_2O (or K_2O) content and the ratio of Ca/P are relatively high [65].

Clinically bioactive glasses have been used successfully as bone-filling materials in orthopaedic and dental surgery [66–68]. This stimulates researchers to combine excellent mechanical properties of metals or polymers with a bioactive phase of either particles or fibres to produce a bioactive composite with optimised properties. For most of the bioactive glass compositions, the tensile bending strength is between 40 and 60 MPa with a low modulus of elasticity between 30 and 35 GPa.

5.6.1 Bioglass®: Hench and Co-workers

During the last five decades, bioglasses have attracted extensive attention of many researchers because of their unique properties which can easily be tailored by manipulating its compositions. The pioneering work of Hench [68] led to the first development of a bioactive silicate glass called 45S5 Bioglass® with a composition of 45 wt% SiO_2, 24.5 wt% Na_2O, 24.5 wt% CaO and 6 wt% P_2O_5. This is also commercially available as Bioglass® which provides an alternative interfacial bonding of an implant with host tissues.

This group of glasses has become known as bioactive glasses based on upon the following definition: a bioactive material is one that elicits a specific biological response at the interface of the material that results in the formation of bond between the host tissues and the material [69]. Many questions regarding its interactions with both soft and hard tissues have been answered over the years by a multidisciplinary team of materials scientists, orthopaedic surgeons, dental researchers, biomechanics experts and biologists. Many clinical Bioglass® devices, such as MEP®, ERMI®, HAPEX®, NovaBone®, NovaMin® and NovaThera®, are being utilised as substitute for bone augmentation and restoration, in orthopaedic, dental and maxillofacial surgery as well as in the field of tissue engineering [34]. They have proven to be efficient and some even outperformed other bioceramic and metal prostheses [66, 68].

Bioactive glasses are a class of biomaterials that bond to both soft and hard living tissues through the formation of a hydroxycarbonate apatite (HCA) layer on their surfaces [3, 7, 70]. Yet, it has been shown that controlled rates of release of ionic dissolution products from bioglass surface are the key phenomenon for bioactivity or bond formation, particularly critical concentrations of soluble silica and calcia ions [71, 72]. Reactions occurring on the surface of the glass lead to the formation of a silica gel layer and subsequent crystallisation of HCA. It was as assumption for many years that formation of biologically active HCA surface reaction layer was the critical requirement for bioactive behaviour [73–

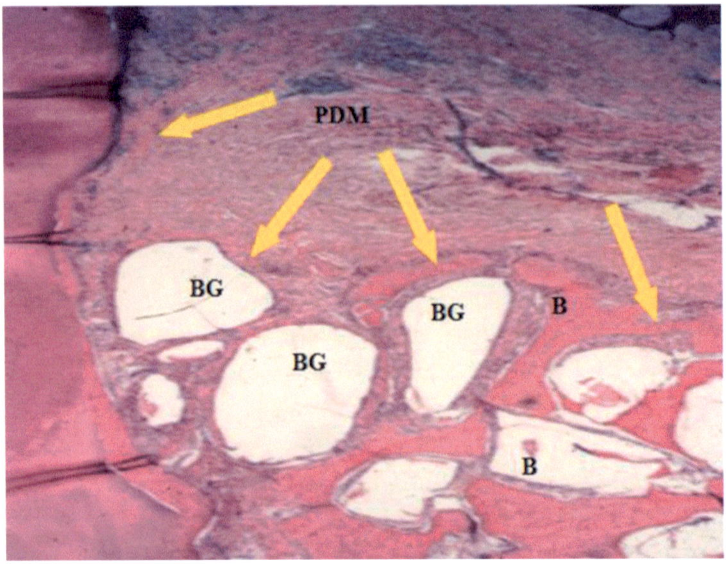

Fig. 5.3 Bioactive glass (BG) particulate used to enhance bone [B] formation around the tooth [T] and thereby restoring its function following treatment of periodontal, gum, disease in a Patas monkey periodontal defect model. The mineralised collagen is shown to surround the bioactive glass particles forming a regenerated bone structure. The periodontal ligament-labelled PDM that is stable above the regenerated bone. (Magnification 20×) (Photo courtesy of Dr. June Wilson [124])

75]. Numerous investigations have shown the formation of a surface HCA layer to be useful but not critical stage of reaction for bone regeneration [71, 76, 77]. As stated above, the key phenomenon is the controlled rates of release of ionic dissolution products, especially critical concentrations of soluble silica and calcia ions. Osteostimulation occurs only when the ions are at a particular ratio of ions and at a particular concentration range of 15–30 ppm Si and 60–90 ppm Ca.

The rate of bone bonding is dependent on the composition of the material. Compared with other glass compositions, a faster rate of bone bonding as well as bonding to soft tissues can be achieved when the SiO_2 content is less than 52 % by weight [60]. Rapid regeneration of trabecular bone with an amount, architecture and biomechanical quality of bone that matches that originally present in the site can be produced from compositions such as 45S5 Bioglass® with high rates of bioactivity [49, 51, 60, 65, 78]. The rapid regeneration of bone is the result of a combination of processes referred to as osteostimulation and osteoconduction (Fig. 5.3).

5.6.2 Åbo Akademi: Bioactive Glass from Finland

The research at the Åbo Akademi University initiated in the early 1980s when Yli-Urpo, Ylänen and Andersson et al. [9, 42] examined the glass transition temperature and biological behaviour of glasses in or near the bioactive compositional region in the system SiO_2–Na_2O–CaO–P_2O_5–Al_2O_3–B_2O_3. Later, an alumina-free bioactive glass was developed with a given composition of 53 % SiO_2, 23 % Na_2O, 20 % CaO and 4 % P_2O_5, and it is available as S53P4 [79].

Contributions of the group at the early stages were on the chemistry and viscosity relationship of a range of bioglasses. An extensive study was conducted by Brink [44, 80, 81] on the viscosity temperature dependence and biological activity of several different glass compositions in the SiO_2–Na_2O–CaO–P_2O_5–Al_2O_3–B_2O_3 system. She discovered that certain glass compositions possess a wider working range compared to conventional bioactive glasses. When the SiO_2 composition is too low, bioactivity can be obtained but the glass will crystallise, and this restricts their use only in the forms of crushed particles. On the other hand, when the SiO_2 content increases to 53–56 wt%, the working range is widened, and crystallisation of devitrification can be avoided [80]. The working range of the glasses examined was also influenced by the amounts of alkali and alkali earth oxides present. The larger working range allows the expanded medical use of the bioactive glasses due to the possibility, for instance, of fibre spinning and flame spraying into microspheres [44, 80].

The development of third generation of bioactive glasses denoted 13–93 has enabled spinning of high-quality thin bioactive glass fibres. From these fibres, a variety of bioactive glass fabrics can be manufactured. Furthermore, an impulse laser beam can be used to melt a fine powder made from the new bioactive glass. As a result, a glass coating on a titanium implant can be produced relatively easily. This coating consists of very small glass droplets firmly attached to the titanium. The glass shows excellent bioactivity in spite of the repeated high temperature procedures involved in the process [82, 83].

5.6.3 A-W Bioactive Glass from Japan

Various research groups in the 1980s and 1990s such as Gross et al., Bromer et al., Kitsugi et al., Nakamura and Yamamuro and Kokubo et al. [50, 84–93] introduced a range of phosphate-based glass and glass ceramics. Kokubo and Nakamura and their colleagues steadily heated glass powder in the MgO–CaO–P_2O_5–CaF_2–SiO_2 system up to 1050 °C. Consequently, a material consisting of crystalline wollastonite ($CaO.SiO_2$) and oxyfluorapatite ($Ca_{10}(PO_4)_6(O,F_2)$ within a homogenous glassy phase was produced [84, 85]. As mentioned earlier, this bioactive glass ceramic was referred to as A-W, derived from the names of the crystalline phases.

The bioactive A-W glass ceramic (A-W-GC) is a two-phase structure and reported to resemble the composite structure of bone, which can be machined into various shapes with diamond tools. The bending strength of the A-W-GC is almost double that of dense HAp and even higher than that of human cortical bone [86]. Other groups of researchers introduced different glass ceramics (Ceravitals, Bioverit I-IIIs, Ilmaplants, BAS-O) during the 1970s and 1980s [87–90]. All these glass ceramics consist of apatite crystals or apatite/wollastonite/phlogopite crystals within a homogenous glassy matrix. It was reported that A-W-GC elicits the highest mechanical strength and bioactivity (Class A) of all the glass ceramics [11, 50].

The dissolution of calcium from wollastonite or the glassy phase is believed to be the reason for the bioactivity of glass ceramic. The bonding between glass ceramic and bone is formed by the precipitation of the dissolved calcium from the material and phosphate originating from the body fluid [91, 92]. It was believed that the nucleation sites for the formation of calcium phosphate are provided by the silicate ions [85, 91]. Different calcium contents in the materials have an effect on the bioactivities of the glass ceramics. Rigid non-degradable bioactive glass ceramics can be produced with various methods for different applications [92]. Their applications include orthopaedics, odontology and in head and neck surgery as prostheses, spacers or granuled defect fillers.

Questions were raised regarding their appropriateness as a coating material with the development of next-generation bioactive glass ceramics. Using various techniques, the bioactive glass ceramics was fixed on load-bearing implants in early experiments [93, 94]. Takatsuka et al. [95] modified A-W-GC in 1993 and was successfully sintered on Ti-alloy due to their similar coefficients of thermal expansion. The bioactive coating showed the bonding strengths comparable with A-W-GC implants, which were used as the control. It has also been demonstrated that A-W-GC coatings have encouraging results in various other investigations [96–98]. It is believed that the glassy part of the material is mainly responsible for the ion dissolution from the material as stated earlier and, subsequently, the chemical reactions occurring on the material surface. Thus, one part of the coating substance is resorbed, and changes in the material's mechanical properties occur.

Investigation conducted by Kitsugi et al. [98] suggested that the use of A-W-GC-coated metal implants should be limited to short-term implantation only, due to the risk of fracture of the coating layer. Although successfully commercialised and clinically applied, currently no commercial production of A-W glass is available.

5.6.4 *Silicate Bioactive Glass*

One of the important trace elements in the human body is silicon (Si), and they are found at a level of 100 ppm in the bone and 200–550 ppm bound to extracellular matrix compounds [99]. The location of Si was reported to be at active calcification sites in the bones and directly involves in the mineralisation process of bone growth [100].

In the past decade, stimulated by the Si function in human body and the bioactive compositions of silicate-based bioglass, a new family of bioactive silicate ceramics has been developed with a wide range composition. It was discovered that bioactive silicate ceramics with specific compositions could significantly stimulate in vitro osteogenic differentiation for several stem cells and in vivo osteogenesis and angiogenesis. Bioactive silicate ceramics also possess distinct osteostimulation properties.

5.6.5 Bioactive Glass Composites

The purpose of bioactive glass composites is to combine and optimise the bioactive phase of either glass particles or fibres with the excellent mechanical properties of metals or polymers to improve properties such as flexibility and capacity to stand to deformation under loads. Numerous bioglass composites have been developed and tested for such biomedical applications as bone regeneration matrix and scaffolds [101–105], dental implant [106] and drug delivery systems [107–109].

An improvement in the bioactivity, degradation kinetics, mechanical properties and osteoblast responses has been reported by the presence of bioactive glasses in the composites compared to the pure bioglass or polymer [101, 110, 111]. For mechanical properties, such factors as the bioglass content and the dispersion of bioglass particles in the polymeric matrix are solely responsible for its improvement. As the amount of bioactive glass particles increases, the mechanical properties of the composites increase until the amount reaches 30 % where the mechanical properties begin to drop. Nonetheless, the optimal bioglass content in the composites is dependent on the applications of the composite materials [112].

5.7 Applications of Bioactive Glasses and Glass Ceramics

5.7.1 Ear, Nose, Throat and Maxillofacial Applications

Table 5.3 shows the compositions of the first bioactive glass, Bioglass®, and S53P4, both of which have been widely used for clinical applications. The glass can be cast into shaped implants for use as small medical devices in places subject to only minor mechanical loading. The glass is also relatively soft which makes it ideal for microsurgical drilling techniques [113].

Bioglass® has been used as cone-shaped implants to fill defects in the mandible and maxilla as well as to replace small bones in the middle ear. It also elicits a property of bonding to soft tissue, which has opened new possibilities for wider applications, such as, in ear, nose and throat surgery. Various electronic components are used within appropriate devices in the treatment of profound deafness.

Table 5.3 Compositions of Bioglass® and S53P4 (wt%)

Component	Bioglass®	S53P4
SiO_2	45	53
Na_2O	24.5	23
CaO	24.5	20
P_2O_5	6	4

Electrodes attached to the electronic devices outside and inside the middle ear are coated with Bioglass® [113]. The device is inserted so that a part is in contact with the bone, resulting in a firm anchoring. The other part of the bioactive glass-coated anchor passes through the eardrum and bonds to the soft tissue, thus providing a seal between the inner and outer ear.

The concept of filling a hole in the mandible after tooth extraction in an attempt to prevent resorption was introduced by Stanley et al. [114]. For this procedure, injection moulding was used to produce conical implants. A mating drill bit is used to prepare the bone for the implant to achieve the best possible fit of the conical implant.

Solid-shaped bioactive glass of a different composition (S53P4) has also been used in the treatment of facial injuries to replace the bone that supports the eye [115, 116]. The clinical results of Aitasalo et al. [116] suggested that thin, slowly resorbable bioactive glass provides a promising option for the reconstruction of orbital floor defects.

In odontology, bioactive glass particles are widely used to fill defects associated with periodontal disease, for instance, the loss of the bone surrounding teeth [75]. Some recent studies show promising results from using crushed bioactive glass or paste as obliteration material in frontal sinusitis and in special types of rhinitis [116–121].

The findings from Stoor et al. [120–122] suggested that the encouraging results of using bioactive glass crush in ear, nose and throat surgery are partially because of the antibacterial effects of bioactive glass paste on oral microorganisms and bacterial infections [122]. Sintering of bioactive glass microspheres enables the manufacture of rigid porous bioactive glass bodies. The rate of bone ingrowth into the three-dimensional porosity of the bioactive glass material is significantly higher compared with the similar porosity of porous titanium [123].

5.7.2 Treatment for Dentin Hypersensitivity

During the past decade, a number of consumer and professional products containing bioactive glass (45S5 Bioglass®) have been introduced into the market. The first product developed by NovaMin® Technologies was Oravive®, a daily use, fluoride-free dentifrice that contains 5 % of the bioactive glass ingredient NovaMin®. This product was cleared for use by FDA through a 510(k) product as a medical device for the rapid and continual reduction of tooth sensitivity through physical tubule occlusion. Today, CSPS has been formulated into over 15 products and is sold in over 20 countries, including the USA, Canada, India, China and a number of countries in Europe. These products have proven to be highly effective and the CSPS material has an unparalleled safety profile. Sensodyne Repair and Protect, manufactured by GlaxoSmithKline (GSK), is an over-the-counter dentifrice that provides NovaMin® technology to the consumer in many parts of the world [124].

5.7.3 Bone Graft Applications

Solid-shaped bioactive glass implants have been investigated using animal models for the reconstruction of deep osteochondral defects (joint surface defects, which penetrate the bone under the joint cartilage) [125–127]. Based on these studies, the bioactive glass implants bonded to the bone, but minimal, or at best moderate, rate of hyaline-like cartilage formation was observed. The use of porous bioactive glass implants resulted in more promising results [47].

Critical size defect can be defined as the smallest size defect that cannot heal spontaneously during the lifetime of a clinical subject. A number of clinical trials showed that an 8-mm diameter defect created in the calvaria of Sprague Dawley rats did not heal after a 12-week period. In contrast, many long bones contain a primary nutrient artery, whereas no primary nutrient artery exists in human calvaria.

The results of Lee et al. [128] have indicated that calcium phosphate glass (bioglass) can affect the differentiation and calcification of the pre-osteoblastic (MC3T3-E1) cells in vitro and promote new bone formation in the calvarial defects. Lim et al. [129] examined the osteoconductive effect of newly developed calcium phosphate glass cement (CPGC) in rabbit calvarial defects. They noticed bone formation rate of CPGC is initially slow, but increases at a specific time, showing the possibility of greater bone formation with time. The resorption rate of CPGC was greater than biphasic calcium phosphate.

It has been reported that by using bioactive glass as granules, bonding can be improved due to the factors such as the chemistry associated with the bioactivity, the reactivity caused by an increase in surface area and the method of application [51, 130–132]. They have also been documented to provide a promising option that can be utilised alone as a filler material to fill the gap around the implants or in bone defects [133–135]. However, according to Virolainen et al. [136], the bone-forming capacity of bioactive glass particulate seems to be lower compared with an autogenous bone graft.

Oonishi et al. used a critical-size defect model in a rabbit femoral condyle to quantify the histological sequence of osteostimulation by 45S5 Bioglass® particulate [49]. In comparison with synthetic HAp particles or bioactive A-W glass–ceramic particles, the studies on bioglass showed that there are both more rapid bone formation in the presence of the osteostimulation particles and regeneration of a more highly mineralised quality of bone in the defect. The rate of bone regeneration in the Oonishi model is related to the rate of release of the soluble Si and Ca ions from the particulates tested. A rapid rate of release is necessary for rapid bone regeneration and optimal fill of the defect by regenerated trabecular bone.

5.7.4 Bioglasses in In Situ Radiotherapy and Hyperthermia

In the treatment of cancer, one of the most common approaches is the removal of the diseased parts. However, recovery or return of full function is unfortunately seldom achieved. The mid-1980s saw the introduction of non-invasive treatment techniques in which only the cancer cells are destroyed.

In 1987, microspheres of $17Y_2O_3$–$19Al_2O_3$–$64SiO_2$ (mol%) glass with a diameter of 20–30 μm were shown to be effective for in situ radiotherapy of liver cancer [137, 138]. Using neutron bombardment, the nonradioactive ^{89}Yttrium in this glass can be activated to ^{90}Y, which is a β-emitter with a half- life of 64.1 h. The microspheres are usually injected into diseased liver through the hepatic artery and entrapped in small blood vessels, which block the blood supply to the cancer and directly irradiate the cancer with β-rays. As the β-ray transmits living tissue only 2.5 mm in diameter and the glass microspheres have high chemical durability, the surrounding normal tissue is hardly damaged by the β-rays.

These glass microspheres are commercially available and already used clinically in Australia, Canada and the USA. However, since they are produced by conventional glass melting techniques, the content of Y_2O_3 in the microsphere is limited to only 17 mole%. Pure Y_2O_3 polycrystalline microspheres with a diameter of 20–30 μm was successfully prepared by Kawashita et al. [138, 139] using a high-frequency induction thermal plasma melting technique. It was reported that they observed higher chemical durability than the Y_2O_3-containing glass microspheres. It was further reported that these ceramic microspheres are more effective for in situ radiotherapy of cancer.

Oxygen is known to be poorly supplied to cancerous cells to produce lactic acid and hence can be destroyed around 431 °C, whereas the normal living cells can be kept alive even around 481 °C. If ferri- or ferromagnetic materials are implanted around cancers and placed under an alternating magnetic field, it is expected that locally heated cancer cells can be destroyed by magnetic hysteresis loss of the ferri- or ferromagnetic materials.

Ferrimagnetic glass–ceramic compositions containing 36 wt% of magnetite (Fe_3O_4) nanoparticles (200 nm) within a CaO–SiO_2 matrix was prepared by Kawashita et al. [140, 141]. It was reported that cancerous cells in the medullary canal of a rabbit tibia were completely destroyed when this glass ceramic was inserted into the tibia and placed under an alternating magnetic field of 300 Oe with 100 kHz [140, 141]. Due to the size of the cancer cells, this kind of invasion treatment cannot be used on humans. In the case of humans, ferri- or ferromagnetic microspheres of 20–30 μm in diameter must be injected into the cancer through blood vessels similar to the radioactive microspheres. For this purpose, the heat-generating efficiency of the ferrimagnetic material must be further increased.

It has been reported that microspheres of 20–30 μm in diameter, in which the number of layers of magnetite particles is of 50 nm, were deposited on silica microspheres. The technique involved deposition of FeO(OH) from a solution and its subsequent transformation into Fe_3O_4 by a specific heat treatment at 600 °C under CO_2–H_2 gas atmosphere [140, 141]. The heat-generating efficiency of this material was reported to be about four times that of the glass ceramic described above.

5.8 Concluding Remarks

As discussed in this chapter, bioactive glasses and glass ceramics are strongly influenced by the synthesis methods employed, the chemistry and the compounds used and any other thermal processes used. All of these factors contribute to their final structure and hence to their long-term performance as bioactive materials. In the early 1970s, bioceramics were employed to perform biologically inert roles, such as providing parts for bone replacement. The realisation that cells and tissues in the body perform many other vital regulatory and metabolic roles has highlighted the limitations of inert synthetic materials as tissue substitutes. The demands placed on bioceramics have changed from maintaining an essentially physical function without eliciting a host response to providing a more integrated interaction with the host, which has been accompanied by increasing the demands on medical devices to improve the quality of life, as well as to extend its longevity.

Bioglasses can be employed as body-interactive materials, helping the body to heal or promoting regeneration of tissues, thus restoring physiological functions. This approach could be further explored in the development of next-generation bioglasses incorporating biogenic materials and specific drugs with a widened range of applications. Recently, the tissue engineering field has been directed to take advantage of the combined use of living cells and three-dimensional (3D) ceramic or bioglass structures to engineer neotissue to a patient's damaged site. Currently feasible and productive strategies have been aimed at combining a relatively traditional approach such as bioglass implants with the acquired knowledge applied to the field of cell growth and differentiation of osteogenic cells.

Bonding of glass ceramic to bone has been observed to occur between 2 weeks and 2 months after implantation. Clinical studies are promising and their use in the orthopaedic field is increasing. Glass ceramics are known to have high bending and compressive strength, and it has been reported that they could be used in the reconstruction of acetabular defects. Nevertheless, the challenge of providing safe and efficacious glass and glass ceramics with an acceptable biocompatibility level and the required properties remains. As the field of biomaterials finds increasing applications in cellular and tissue engineering, it will continue to be used in new ways as part of the most innovative therapeutic strategies.

References

1. Ben-Nissan B, Ylänen HO (2006) Bioactive glasses and glass ceramics, Wiley encyclopedia of biomedical engineering. Wiley, Hoboken
2. McMillan PW (1964) Glass ceramics. Academic, London
3. Hench LL, Wilson J (1984) Surface active materials. Science 226:630–636
4. Hench LL (1988) Bioactive ceramics. In: Ducheyne P, Lemons JE (eds) Bioceramics: materials characteristics vs. *in vivo* behavior. New York Academy of Science, New York
5. Kokubo T (1991) Recent progress in glass-based materials for biomedical applications. J Ceram Soc Japan 99:965–973
6. Kokubo T (1990) Novel biomaterials derived from glasses. In: Soga W, Kato A (eds) Ceramics: towards the 21st century. J Ceram Soc Japan, pp. 500–518.
7. Hench LL, Splinter RJ, Allen WC et al (1972) Bonding mechanisms at the interface of ceramic prosthetic materials. J Biomed Mater Res Symp 2:117–141
8. Vrouwenvelder WCA, Groot CG, de Groot K (1993) Histological and biochemical evaluation of osteoblasts cultured on bioactive glass, hydroxylapatite, titanium alloy, and stainless steel. J Biomed Mater Res 27:465–475
9. Andersson OH, Kangasniemi I (1991) Calcium phosphate formation at the surface of bioactive glass in vitro. J Biomed Mat Res 25:1019–1030
10. Li P, Yang Q, Zhang F et al (1992) The effect of residual glassy phase in a bioactive glass-ceramic on the formation of its surface apatite layer in vitro. J Mater Sci: Mater Med 3:452–456
11. Kokubo T, Shigematsu M, Nagashima Y et al (1982) Apatite-wollastonite containing glass-ceramic for prosthetic application. Bull Inst Chem Res 60:260–268
12. Li R, Clark AE, Hench LL (1991) An investigation of bioactive glass powders by sol-gel processing. J Appl Biomat 2:231–239
13. Arriagada FJ, Osseo-Asare K (1999) Synthesis of nanosize silica in a nonionic water-in-oil microemulsion: effects of the water/surfactant molar ratio and ammonia concentration. J Colloid Interf Sci 211:210–220
14. Singh S, Bhardwaj P, Singh V et al (2008) Synthesis of nanocrystalline calcium phosphate in microemulsion-effect of nature of surfactants. J Colloid Interf Sci 319:322–329
15. Karagiozov C, Momchilova D (2005) Synthesis of nano-sized particles from metal carbonates by the method of reversed mycelles. Chem Eng Process 44:115–119
16. Sun Y, Guo G, Tao D et al (2007) Reverse microemulsion-directed synthesis of hydroxyapatite nanoparticles under hydrothermal conditions. J Phys Chem Solids 68:373–377
17. Boccaccini AR, Erol M, Stark WJ et al (2010) Polymer/bioactive glass nanocomposites for biomedical applications: A review. Compos Sci Technol 70:1764–1776
18. Lim GK, Wang J, Ng SC et al (1996) Processing of fine hydroxyapatite powders via an inverse microemulsion route. Mater Lett 28:431–436
19. Lim GK, Wang J, Ng SC et al (1999) Formation of nanocrystalline hydroxyapatite in nonionic surfactant emulsions. Langmuir 15:7472–7477
20. Quintero F, Mann AB, Pou J et al (2007) Rapid production of ultralong amorphous ceramic nanofibers by laser spinning. Appl Phys Lett 90:153109–3
21. Quintero F, Pou J, Lusquiños F et al (2007) Experimental analysis of the production of micro- and nanofibres by Laser Spinning. Appl Surf Sci 254:1042–1047
22. Quintero F, Dieste O, Pou J et al (2009) On the conditions to produce micro- and nanofibres by laser spinning. J Phys D: Appl Phys 42:1–10
23. Quintero F, Pou J, Comesaña R et al (2009) Laser spinning of bioactive glass nanofibers. Adv Funct Mater 19:3084–3090
24. Pratsinis SE (1998) Flame aerosol synthesis of ceramic powders. Prog Energ Combust Sci 24:197–219
25. Stark WJ, Madler L, Maciejewski M et al (2003) Flame synthesis of nanocrystalline ceria-zirconia: effect of carrier liquid. Chem Comm 5:588–589

26. Madler L, Stark WJ, Pratsinis SE (2002) Flame-made ceria nanoparticles. J Mater Res 17:1356–1362
27. Athanassiou EK, Grass RN, Stark WJ (2010) Chemical aerosol engineering as a novel tool for material science: from oxides to salt and metal nanoparticles. Aerosol Sci Tech 44:161–172
28. Vollenweider M, Brunner TJ, Knecht S et al (2007) Remineralization of human dentin using ultrafine bioactive glass particles. Acta Biomater 3:936–943
29. Mohn D, Zehnder M, Imfeld T et al (2010) Radio-opaque nanosized bioactive glass for potential root canal application: evaluation of radiopacity, bioactivity and alkaline capacity. Int Endod J 43:210–217
30. Ebelmen M (1846) On the synthesis of silica gels from alkoxides. Annales de chimie et de physique 16:129
31. Graham T (1864) On the properties of silicic acid and other analogous colloidal substances. J Chem Soc 17:318–327
32. Liesegang RE (1896) Ueber einige Eigenschaften von Gallerten. Naturwissenschaftliche Wochenschrift 11:353–362
33. Hench LL, West JK (1990) The sol-gel process. Chem Rev 90:33–72
34. Cacciotti I, Lombardi M, Bianco A et al (2012) Sol-gel derived 45S5 bioglass: synthesis, microstructural evolution and thermal behaviour. J Mater Sci Mater Med 23:1849–1866
35. Chen QZ, Thouas GA (2011) Fabrication and characterization of sol-gel derived 45S5 Bioglass (R)-ceramic scaffolds. Acta Biomat 7:3616–3626
36. Saboori A, Rabiee M, Mutarzadeh F et al (2009) Synthesis, characterization and in vitro bioactivity of sol-gel-derived SiO_2-CaO-P_2O_5-MgO bioglass. Mat Sci Eng C-Bio S 29:335–340
37. Jie Q, Lin KL, Zhong JP et al (2004) Preparation of macroporous sol-gel bioglass using PVA particles as pore former. J Sol-Gel Sci Technol 30:49–61
38. Greenspan DC, Zhong JP, Chen XF et al (1997) The evaluation of degradability of melt and sol-gel derived Bioglass (R) in-vitro. Bioceramics 10:391–394
39. Sakka S (1985) Glasses and glass-ceramics from gels. J Non-Cryst Solids 73:651
40. Sepulveda P, Jones JR, Hench LL (2001) Characterization of melt-derived 45S5 and sol-gel-derived 58S bioactive glasses. J Biomed Mater Res 58:734–740
41. Pereira MM, Hench LL (1996) Mechanisms of hydroxyapatite formation on porous gel-silica substrates. J Sol-Gel Sci Technol 7:59–68
42. Andersson ÖH (1992) Glass transition temperature of glasses in the SiO_2-Na_2O-CaO-P_2O_5-Al_2O_3-B_2O_3 system. J Mat Sci Mat Med 3:326–328
43. Peitl Filho O, LaTorre GP, Hench LL (1996) Effect of crystallization on apatite-layer formation of bioactive glass 45S5. J Biomed Mater Res 30:509–514
44. Brink M (1997) Bioactive glasses with a large working range. Dissertation, Åbo Akademi University
45. Hayakawa S, Tsuru K, Ohtsuki C (1999) Mechanism of apatite formation on a sodium silicate class in a simulated body fluid. J Am Ceram Soc 82:2155–2160
46. Arstila HE, Vedel L, Hupa L et al (2004) Measuring the devitrification of bioactive glasses. Key Eng Mater 254–256:67–70
47. Ylänen HO, Helminen T, Helminen A et al (1999) Porous bioactive glass matrix in reconstruction of articular osteochondral defects. Ann Chir Gyn 83:237–245
48. Fröberg L, Hupa L, Hupa M (2004) Porous bioactive glasses with controlled mechanical strength. Key Eng Mater 254–256:973–976
49. Oonishi H, Hench LL, Wilson J et al (2000) Quantitative comparison of bone growth behaviour in granules in bioglass®, A-W glass-ceramic, and hydroxyapatite. J Biomed Mater Res 51:37–46
50. Hench LL (1997) Glass and genes: a forecast to future. Glastech Ber Glass Sci Technol 70:439–452
51. Hench LL (1998) Bioceramics. J Am Ceram Soc 81:1705–1727
52. Strnad Z (1992) Role of the glass phase in bioactive glass-ceramic. Biomaterials 13:317–321

53. Karlsson KH, Ylänen HO (1998) Porous bone implants. In: Vincenzini P (ed) Materials in clinical applications, advances in science and technology 28. 9th Cimtec-World Forum on New Materials, Florence
54. Serra J, González P, Liste S et al (2002) Influence of the non-bridging oxygen groups on the bioactivity of silicate glasses. J Mater Sci Mater Med 13:1221–1225
55. Serra J, González P, Liste S et al (2003) FTIR and XPS studies of bioactive silica based glasses. J Noncryst Solids 332:20–27
56. Ducheyne P, Brown S, Blumenthal N et al (1988) Bioactive glasses, aluminum oxide, and titanium. Ion transport phenomena and surface analysis. Ann NY Acad Sci 523:257–261
57. Andersson ÖH, Karlsson KH, Kangasniemi K (1990) Calcium-phosphate formation at the surface of bioactive glass in vivo. J. Non-Cryst Solids 119:290–296
58. Niki M, Ito G, Matsuda T et al (1991) Comparative push-out data of bioactive and non-bioactive materials of similar rugosity. In: Davies JE (ed) Bone-material interface. University of Toronto Press, Toronto
59. Fujiu T, Ogino M (1984) Difference of bone bonding behavior among surface active glasses and sintered apatite. J Biomed Mater Res 18:845–859
60. Wilson J, Pigott GH, Schoen FJ et al (1981) Toxicology and biocompatibility of bioglasses. J Biomed Mater Res 15:805–817
61. LeGeros RZ, LeGeros JP (1993) Dense hydroxyapatite. In: Hench LL, Wilson J (eds) An introduction to bioceramics, vol 1. World Scientific, Singapore
62. Lai W, Ducheyne P, Garino J (1998) Removal pathway of silicon released from bioactive glass granules in vivo. In: LeGeros RZ, LeGeros JP (eds) Bioceramics, vol 11. World Scientific, New York
63. Hench LL, West JK (1996) Biological applications of bioactive glasses. Life Chem Rep 13:187–241
64. Hench LL, Paschall HA (1973) Direct chemical bond of bioactive glass-ceramic materials to bone and muscle. J Biomed Mater Res 7:25–42
65. Hench LL (1991) Bioceramics: from concept to clinic. J Am Ceram Soc 74:1487–1510
66. Merwin GE (1990) Review of bioactive materials for otologic and maxillofacial applications. In: Yamamuro T, Hench LL, Wilson J (eds) Handbook of bioactive ceramics, vol 1. CRC Press, Florida
67. Cai YR, Zhou L (2005) Effect of thermal treatment on the microstructure and mechanical properties of gel-derived bioglasses. Mater Chem Phys 94:283–287
68. Hench LL (2006) The story of bioglass. J Mater Sci Mater Med 14:967–978
69. Hench LL, Andersson ÖH (1993) Bioactive glasses. In: Hench LL, Wilson J (eds) An introduction to bioceramics, vol 1. World Scientific, Singapore
70. Gross U, Kinne R, Schmitz HJ et al (1988) The response of bone to surface active glass/glass-ceramics. CRC Crit Rev Biocomput 4:2–15
71. Hench LL, Polak JM, Xynos ID et al (2000) Bioactive materials to control cell cycle. Mater Res Innov 3:313–323
72. Ylänen HO, Karlsson KH, Itälä A et al (2000) Effect of immersion in SBF on porous bioactive bodies made by sintering bioactive glass microspheres. J Noncryst Solids 275:107–115
73. Cao WP, Hench LL (1996) Bioactive materials. Ceram Int 22:493–507
74. Hench LL (1998) Bioactive materials: the potential for tissue regeneration. J Biomed Mater Res 41:511–518
75. Hench LL (1998) Bioceramics, a clinical success. Am Ceram Soc Bull 77:67–74
76. Loty C, Sautier J, Loty S et al (1998) Bioglass(R) promoted differentiation of cultured rat osteoblasts and created a template for bone formation. In: LeGeros RZ, LeGeros JP (eds) Bioceramics, vol 11. World Scientific, New York
77. Xynos ID, Hukkanen MVJ, Batten JJ et al (2000) Bioglass (R) 45S5 stimulates osteoblast turnover and enhances bone formation in vitro: Implications and applications for bone tissue engineering. Calcified Tissue Int 67:321–329

78. Hench LL, Hench JW, Greenspan DC (2004) Bioglass: a short history and bibliography. J Aust Ceram Soc 40:1–42
79. Andersson Ö (1990) The bioactivity of silicate glass. Dissertation. Åbo Akademi University
80. Niemelä T (2010) Self-reinforced bioceramic and polylactide based composites. Dissertation. Tampere University of Technology
81. Brink M (1997) The influence of alkali and alkaline earths on the working range for bioactive glasses. J Biomed Mater Res 36:109–117
82. Moritz N, Vedel E, Ylänen H et al (2003) Creation of bioactive glass coating on titanium by local laser irradiation, Part I: Optimisation of the processing parameters. Key Eng Mater 240–242:221–224
83. Vedel E, Moritz N, Ylänen H et al (2003) Creation of bioactive glass coating on titanium by local laser irradiation, Part II: Effect of the irradiation on the bioactivity of the glass. Key Eng Mater 240–242:225–228
84. Kokubo T, Ito S, Sakka S et al (1986) Formation of high-strength bioactive glass-ceramic in the system MgO-CaO-SiO_2-P_2O_5. J Mater Sci 21:536–540
85. Nakamura T, Yamamuro T (1993) Development of a bioactive ceramic, A/W glass-ceramic. In: Ducheyne P, Christiansen D (eds) Bioceramics, vol 6. Butterworth-Heinemann, Oxford
86. Kokubo T (1992) Bioactivity of glasses and glass-ceramics. In: Ducheyne P, Kokubo T, Van Blitterswijk CA (eds) Bone- bonding. Reed Healthcare Communications, Leiderdorp
87. Blencké BA, Brömer H, Deutscher KK (1978) Compatibility and long-term stability of glass-ceramic implants. J Biomed Mater Res 12:307–316
88. Vogel W, Höland W (1990) Development, structure, properties and application of glass-ceramics for medicine. J Non-Cryst Solids 123:349–353
89. Berger G, Sauer R, Steinborn G et al (1989) Clinical application of surface reactive apatite/wollastonite containing glass-ceramics. In: Mazurin OV (ed) Proceedings of XV international congress on glass. Leningrad, Nauka.
90. Pavek V, Novak Z, Strnad Z et al (1994) Clinical application of bioactive glass-ceramic BAS-O for filling cyst cavities in stomatology. Biomaterials 15:353–358
91. Kokubo T (1990) Surface chemistry of bioactive glass-ceramics. J Non-Cryst Solids 120:138–151
92. Kokubo T (1991) Bioactive glass-ceramics: properties and applications. Biomaterials 12:155–163
93. Strunz V, Bunte M, Gross UM et al (1978) Coating of metal implants with the bioactive glass-ceramics. Ceravital Dtsch Zahnarztl Z 33:862–865
94. Fuchs GA, Deutscher K (1981) Glass-ceramic coated implants. A simple model for a loaded hip prosthesis with a bioactive interface. Arch Orthop Trauma Surg 98:121–126
95. Takatsuka K, Yamamuro T, Kitsugi T et al (1993) A new bioactive glass-ceramic as a coating material on titanium alloy. J Appl Biomater 4:317–329
96. Ido K, Matsuda Y, Yamamuro T et al (1993) Cementless total hip replacement. Bioactive glass ceramic coating studied in dogs. Acta Orthop Scand 64:607–612
97. Li ZL, Kitsugi T, Yamamuro T et al (1995) Bone-bonding behavior under load-bearing conditions of an alumina ceramic implant incorporating beads coated with glass-ceramic containing apatite and wollastonite. J Biomed Mater Res 29:1081–1088
98. Kitsugi T, Nakamura T, Oka M et al (1996) Bone-bonding behavior of plasma-sprayed coatings of Bioglass®, AW-glass ceramic, and tricalcium phosphate on titanium alloy. J Biomed Mater Res 30:261–269
99. Schwarz K (1973) A bound form of silicon in glycosaminoglycans and polyuronides. Proc Natl Acad Sci USA 70:1608–1612
100. Carlisle EM (1970) Silicon: a possible factor in bone calcification. Science 167:279–280
101. Chen QZ, Boccaccini AR (2006) Poly(D, L-lactic acid) coated 45S5 Bioglass-based scaffolds: processing and characterization. J Biomed Mater Res A 77:445–457
102. Kim HW, Song JH, Kim HE (2006) Bioactive glass nanofiber-collagen nanocomposite as a novel bone regeneration matrix. J Biomed Mater Res A 79:698–705

103. Hong Z, Reis RL, Mano JF (2009) Preparation and in vitro characterization of novel bioactive glass ceramic nanoparticles. J Biomed Mater Res A 88:304–313
104. Hajiali H, Karbasi S, Hosseinalipour M et al (2010) Preparation of a novel biodegradable nanocomposite scaffold based on poly (3-hydroxybutyrate)/bioglass nanoparticles for bone tissue engineering. J Mater Sci Mater Med 21:2125–2132
105. Valenzuela F, Covarrubias C, Martinez C et al (2012) Preparation and bioactive properties of novel bone-repair bionanocomposites based on hydroxyapatite and bioactive glass nanoparticles. J Biomed Mater Res B Appl Biomater 100:1672–1682
106. Mehdikhani-Nahrkhalaji M, Fathi MH, Mortazavi V et al (2012) Novel nanocomposite coating for dental implant applications in vitro and in vivo evaluation. J Mater Sci Mater Med 23:485–495
107. Arcos D, Ragel CV, Vallet-Regi M (2001) Bioactivity in glass/PMMA composites used as drug delivery system. Biomaterials 22:701–708
108. Soundrapandian C, Datta S, Kundu B et al (2010) Porous bioactive glass scaffolds for local drug delivery in osteomyelitis: development and in vitro characterization. Aaps Pharmscitech 11:1675–1683
109. Zhu M, Wang H, Liu J et al (2011) A mesoporous silica nanoparticulate/beta-TCP/BG composite drug delivery system for osteoarticular tuberculosis therapy. Biomaterials 32:1986–1995
110. Kim HW, Lee HH, Chun GS (2008) Bioactivity and osteoblast responses of novel biomedical nanocomposites of bioactive glass nanofiber filled poly(lactic acid). J Biomed Mater Res A 85:651–663
111. Lee HH, Yu HS, Jang JH et al (2008) Bioactivity improvement of poly(epsilon-caprolactone) membrane with the addition of nanofibrous bioactive glass. Acta Biomater 4:622–629
112. Niemelä T, Niiranen H, Kellomäki M et al (2005) Self-reinforced composites of bioabsorbable polymer and bioactive glass with different bioactive glass contents. Part I: Initial mechanical properties and bioactivity. Acta Biomat 1:235–242
113. Wilson J, Yli-Urpo A, Happonen RP (1993) Bioactive glasses: clinical applications. In: Hench LL, Wilson J (eds) An introduction to bioceramics, vol 1. World Scientific, Singapore
114. Stanley HR, Hall MB, Clark AE et al (1997) Using 45S5 bioglass cones as endosseous ridge maintenance implants to prevent alveolar ridge resorption: a 5-year evaluation. Int J Oral Maxollofac Implants 12:95–105
115. Suominen E, Kinnunen J (1996) Bioactive glass granules and plates in the reconstruction of defects of the facial bones. Scand J Plast Reconstr Surg Hand Surg 30:281–289
116. Aitasalo K, Suonpää J, Kinnunen I et al (1999) Reconstruction of orbital floor fractures with bioactive glass (S53P4). In: Ohgushi H, Hastings GW, Yoshikawa T (eds) Bioceramics, vol 12. World Scientific, Singapore
117. Suonpää J, Sipilä J, Aitasalo K et al (1997) Operative treatment of frontal sinusitis. Acta Otolaryngol Suppl (Stockh) 529:181–183
118. Peltola M, Suonpää J, Aitasalo K et al (1998) Obliteration of the frontal sinus cavity with bioactive glass. Head Neck 20:315–318
119. Peltola M, Aitasalo K, Suonpää J et al (2006) Bioactive glass S53P4 in frontal sinus obliteration: A long-term clinical experience. Head Neck-J Sci Spec 28:834–841
120. Stoor P, Söderling E, Salonen JI (1998) Antibacterial effects of a bioactive glass paste on oral microorganisms. Acta Odontol Scand 56:161–165
121. Stoor P, Söderling E, Grenman R (1999) Interactions between the bioactive glass S53P4 and the atrophic rhinitis-associated microorganism Klebsiella ozaenae. J Biomed Mater Res 48:869–874
122. Stoor P, Pulkkinen J, Grenman R (2010) Bioactive glass s53p4 in the filling of cavities in the mastoid cell area in surgery for chronic otitis media. Ann Oto Rhinol Laryn 119:377–382
123. Ylänen HO (2000) Bone ingrowth into porous bodies made by sintering bioactive glass microspheres. Dissertation, Åbo Akademi University

124. Hench LL, Greenspan D (2013) Interactions between bioactive glass and collagen: a review and new perspectives. J Aust Ceram Soc 49:1–40
125. Heikkilä JT, Aho AJ, Yli-Urpo A et al (1993) Bioactive glass versus hydroxyapatite in reconstruction of osteochondral defects in the rabbit. Acta Orthop Scand 64:678–682
126. Suominen E, Aho AJ, Vedel E et al (1996) Subchondral bone and cartilage repair with bioactive glasses, hydroxyapatite, and hydroxyapatite-glass composite. J Biomed Mater Res 32:543–551
127. Aho AJ, Tirri T, Kukkonen J et al (2004) Injectable bioactive glass/biodegradable polymer composite for bone and cartilage reconstruction: Concept and experimental outcome with thermoplastic composites of poly(epsilon-caprolactone-CO-D, L-lactide) and bioactive glass S53P4. J Mater Sci Mater Med 15:1165–1173
128. Lee YK, Song J, Moon HJ et al (2004) In Vitro and in vivo evaluation of non-crystalline calcium phosphate glass as a bone substitute. Key Engineer Mater 254–256:185–188
129. Lim HC, Sohn JY, Park JC et al (2010) Osteoconductive effects of calcium phosphate glass cement grafts in rabbit calvarial defects. J Biomed Mater Res B 95B:47–52
130. Schepers E, De Clercq M, Ducheyne P et al (1991) Bioactive glass granulate material as a filler for bone lesions. J Oral Rehabil 18:439–452
131. Gatti AM, Zaffe D (1991) Long-term behavior of active glasses in sheep mandibular bone. Biomaterials 12:345–350
132. Garcia AJ, Ducheyne P (1994) Numerical analysis of extra- cellular fluid flow and chemical species transport around and within porous bioactive glass. J Biomed Mater Res 28:947–960
133. Gatti AM, Valdre G, Tombesi A (1996) Importance of micro-analysis in understanding mechanism of transformation in active glassy biomaterials. J Biomed Mater Res 31:475–480
134. Heikkilä JT, Aho HJ, Yli-Urpo A et al (1995) Bone formation in rabbit cancellous bone defects filled with bioactive glass granules. Acta Orthop Scand 66:463–467
135. Oonishi H, Hench LL, Wilson J et al (1999) Comparative bone growth behavior in granules of bioceramic materials of various sizes. J Biomed Mater Res 44:31–43
136. Virolainen P, Heikkilä J, Yli-Urpo A et al (1997) Histomorphometric and molecular biologic comparison of bioactive glass granules and autogenous bone grafts in augmentation of bone defect healing. J Biomed Mater Res 35:9–17
137. Kawashita M, Shineha R, Kim HM et al (2003) Preparation of ceramic microspheres for in situ radiotherapy of deep-seated cancer. Biomaterials 24:2955–2963
138. Kawashita M (2002) Ceramic microspheres for in situ radiotherapy of cancer. Mat Sci Eng C-Bio S 22:3–8
139. Kawashita M, Kokubo T, Inoue Y (1999) Preparation of Y_2O_3 microspheres for In Situ radiotherapy of cancer. In: Ohgushi H, Hastings GW, Yoshikawa T (eds) Bioceramics, vol 12. World Scientific, Singapore
140. Kawashita M, Tanaka M, Kokubo T et al (2002) Preparation of magnetite microspheres for hyperthermia of cancer. In: Brown S, Clarke I, Williams P (eds) Bioceramics, vol 14. Trans Tech Pub, Switzerland
141. Kawashita M, Tanaka M, Kokubo T et al (2005) Preparation of ferrimagnetic magnetite microspheres for in situ hyperthermic treatment of cancer. Biomaterials 26:2231–2238

Chapter 6
Clinical Resurfacing of Feldspar and Leucite Glass Ceramics Using Dental Handpieces and Burs

Ling Yin, Xiao-Fei Song, and Richard Stoll

Abstract This chapter summarises the resurfacing characteristics and material removal mechanisms of feldspar and leucite glass ceramics in simulated clinical resurfacing procedure by using air-turbine dental handpieces. It begins with description of feldspar and leucite glass ceramics as restorative and prosthetic materials in dentistry. A description of condition monitoring of simulated clinical resurfacing processes is provided, including in-process measurement of resurfacing forces, force ratios, torques and specific energy using force sensors and a high-speed data acquisition system. Information on surface roughness and surface morphology is also detailed. In particular, this chapter presents the studies on surface and subsurface damage mechanism using both finite element analysis (FEA) and experimental measurement. At the end of the chapter, potential future developments of dental ceramic resurfacing are given.

Keywords Dental ceramics • Resurfacing • Forces • Surface roughness • Brittle fracture • Ductile removal

6.1 Introduction

Ceramics are widely used as crown materials to replace missing teeth attributable to their excellent resemblance of tooth colours, chemical durability, wear resistance, biocompatibility and environmental friendliness [1–5]. Recent fast chair-side computer-aided design and computer-aided manufacturing (CAD/CAM) techniques performed in dental clinic have made them an even more attractive option

L. Yin (✉)
College of Science and Engineering, James Cook University, Townsville, QLD 4811, Australia
e-mail: ling.yin@jcu.edu.au

X.-F. Song
School of Mechanical Engineering, Tianjin University, Tianjin 300072, China

R. Stoll
College of Medicine and Dentistry, James Cook University, Cairns, QLD 4870, Australia

Q. Li, Y.-W. Mai (eds.), *Biomaterials for Implants and Scaffolds*, Springer Series in Biomaterials Science and Engineering 8, DOI 10.1007/978-3-662-53574-5_6

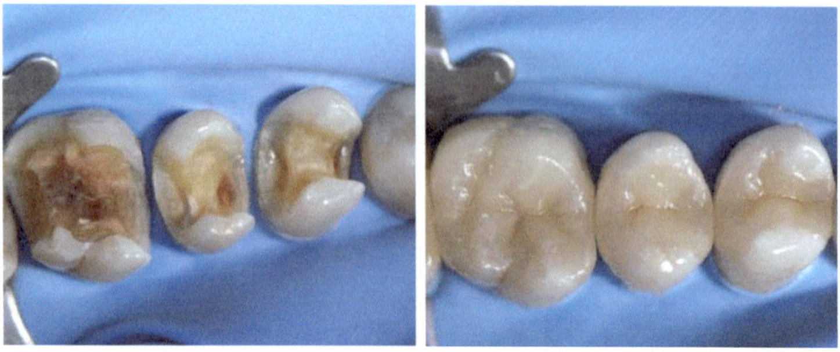

Fig. 6.1 Preparation for ceramic inlays 24–26 (*left*) and ceramic inlays made from leucite glass ceramic, IPS Empress (Ivoclar Vivadent), directly after cementation (*right*) (Clinical case: Prof. Dr. Richard Stoll, College of Medicine and Dentistry, James Cook University, Cairns, Australia)

[3, 6–8]. Ceramic crowns cost $2 billion annually worldwide [9]. Among many available dental ceramics, feldspar and leucite glass ceramics play an essential role in porcelain-fused metal (PFM) structures and all-ceramic restorations as veneers, inlays, onlays and single crowns [1, 10]. Conventionally, feldspar and leucite glass ceramic restorations are sintered and shaped using ceramic powder sintering and moulding techniques. Both materials in sintered states are machinable and can be directly fabricated to different shapes using chair-side dental CAD/CAM systems in dental offices [3, 8, 11]. Figure 6.1 shows a clinical case study conducted by the third author of this chapter, in which leucite glass ceramics were used as inlays for three crowns. In this case, the damaged enamel and dentin were removed. The teeth were prepared and three inlays created in one dental appointment using the chair-side dental CAD/CAM system. These inlays were then cemented directly to the prepared teeth. After occlusal and marginal adaptations, leucite glass ceramic inlays were polished to achieve aesthetic quality.

During the installation of ceramic restorations in the oral environment, they must be resurfaced and/or adjusted for occlusal and marginal adaptations (Fig. 6.2) using dental handpieces and diamond burs manipulated by dentists (Fig. 6.3). Such a resurfacing or adjusting process induces surface and subsurface damage in the ceramic prostheses, resulting in poor reliability of ceramic prostheses [3, 9–15]. This chapter presents our overview on resurfacing characteristics and material removal mechanisms of feldspar and leucite glass ceramics in simulated clinical conditions using air-turbine dental handpieces. It covers basic microstructures and properties of feldspar and leucite glass ceramics; in-process monitoring of speed, force, torque and energy involved in simulated clinical resurfacing; and surface quality such as roughness, surface morphology and phase transformation. In addition, recently findings related to surface and subsurface damage using both finite element analysis (FEA) and scanning electron microscopy (SEM) measurement are presented below.

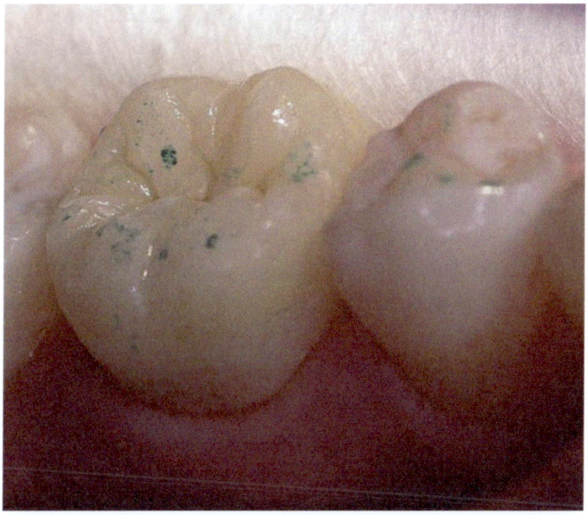

Fig. 6.2 Ceramic only after occlusal corrections. Resurfacing with diamond burs is necessary to adjust the occlusal contacts. Note that green spots represent undisturbed bites and free functional movements (Clinical case: Prof. Dr. Richard Stoll, College of Medicine and Dentistry, James Cook University, Cairns, Australia)

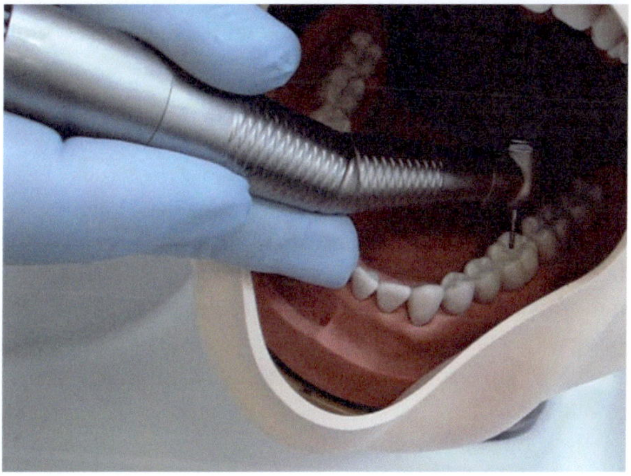

Fig. 6.3 Use of a dental handpiece for resurfacing of crowns on a manikin model. The handpiece is held with three fingers in a writing position (Clinical teaching case: Prof. Dr. Richard Stoll, College of Medicine and Dentistry, James Cook University, Cairns, Australia)

6.2 Feldspar and Leucite Glass Ceramics

6.2.1 Feldspar Porcelains

Porcelains have been used in dentistry to replace enamel and dentin since the eighteenth century. The first porcelains based on triaxial Chinese porcelain formulations have shown limited aesthetic results due to their white appearance and high opacity. Around 1830, Widman introduced feldspar porcelains, which rapidly became the preferred materials for dental restorations [16]. These porcelains were made of 78 % feldspar, kaolin, potash silicate and dehydrated borax [16]. Later, feldspar porcelains were made from potash feldspar ($K_2O \cdot Al_2O_3 \cdot 6SiO_2$) and quartz ($SiO_2$), which decompose to leucite crystals ($K_2O \cdot Al_2O_3 \cdot 4SiO_2$) and an amorphous glass phase at high temperatures [17]. The glass phase enhances translucency but is susceptible for crack propagation. The crystalline phases can function as a scaffold and increase mechanical strength by dispersion hardening. These components were then mixed with alkali metal carbonates as fluxes and metallic oxides for colouration in melting states at high temperatures. The melt porcelains were then rapidly quenched in cold water and finally ground to ceramic frits with average particle sizes of 20–30 μm [18].

In 1889, Land created the first dental crowns and patented them as "jacket crowns" using feldspar and aluminous ceramics baked on a thin platinum foil [19]. Unfortunately, due to the low mechanical strength and the lack of ideal cementation techniques, these jacket crowns were only used for low-load-bearing anterior teeth. In addition, fracture-induced high failure rates often occurred in these jacket crowns.

In 1925, Adriaansen invented a new layering and sintering process of porcelain in a special kiln [16]. This process enabled porcelain masses to be layered with different colours and translucencies for mimicking layered natural tooth substances by using slightly different sintering temperatures. Classic feldspathic porcelains are commonly used for veneering metal frameworks. Unfortunately, the thermal expansion behaviours of these porcelains were not ideal to match the thermal expansions of cast metal frameworks. Further, these porcelains lack desired strength, which are approximately 70–80 MPa [4], and are prone to brittle fracture under mechanical loading.

Porcelain-fused metal techniques were developed by Weinstein in the late 1950s as a solution to the high failure rate of feldspathic jacket crowns [19]. Cast frameworks are achieved with high accuracy for improved marginal fit. Adding nonprecious metal to the alloy formulation makes it possible to create an intentional oxide layer on the metal surface by controlled firing in a normal atmosphere with oxygen. This oxide layer forms the interface for the connection to the fired porcelain.

In 1965, higher-strength ceramics were developed by adding alumina crystals into the feldspathic glass matrix. Unfortunately, the aesthetic properties of these materials became inferior because the strengthened alumina scaffolds made the material opaque. To improve aesthetics, Mclean and Hughes developed the all-ceramic core–veneer structure using high-strength aluminous porcelain as a core framework veneered with a feldspathic porcelain with high translucency [19].

Modern feldspar porcelains are modified, containing sanidine, nepheline and anorthoclase crystals reinforced with glass matrix, as an example shown in X-ray diffraction spectra (Fig. 6.4) [20] for Cerec Vitablocs Mark II (VITA Zahnfabrik, Germany). These porcelain blocks contain fine-particle feldspar crystals with matching abrasion characteristics of natural tooth enamel. They have been used clinically with considerable success since 1991 [1] and are now widely used as inlays, onlays, veneers and anterior crowns for VITA Cerec Dental CAD/CAM systems [21–23]. The mechanical properties are reported with Vickers

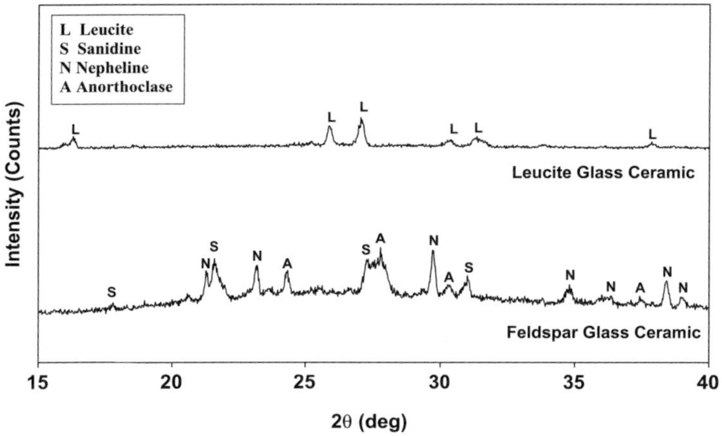

Fig. 6.4 X-ray diffraction pattern of the feldspar and leucite glass ceramics (Reprinted with permission from Ref. [20]. Copyright 2013 by Elsevier)

hardness = 6.2 GPa, Young's modulus = 68 GPa, fracture toughness = 0.9 MPa.m$^{1/2}$ and strength = 100 MPa [24, 25].

6.2.2 Leucite Glass Ceramics

Leucite glass ceramics are specially designed to fit the thermal expansion coefficients of different metal frameworks (gold alloys, cobalt chromium alloys, titanium alloys) and later the frameworks made of high-strength ceramics. Adding finely dispersed leucite grains ($K(AlSi_2O_6)$) results in increased flexural strength and improved wear patterns [26].

Typical ceramic masses for porcelain-fused metal techniques contain 15–25 % leucite crystals, which have a high thermal expansion coefficient (25×10^{-6}/°C) compared with the glass matrix (8×10^{-6}/°C) [4]. The difference in thermal expansion creates strong compressive stress around leucite crystals after cooling to reinforce the structure and improve the crack resistance. Special materials for all-ceramic crowns contain up to 45 % leucite crystals, which enhance the fracture strength to approximately 104 MPa in comparison to 70 MPa strength of classic feldspathic porcelains [4]. Porcelain-fused metal crowns and bridges have been used now for more than four decades and are still fairly popular, even if good aesthetics are difficult to achieve due to the necessity of an opaque layer. By 2005 more than 50 % of all dental restorations were based on porcelain-fused metal techniques [27].

Fine-structured leucite glass ceramics, ProCAD blocks (Ivoclar Vivadent), are widely used in dental CAD/CAM systems. The X-ray diffraction spectrum of this material is shown in Fig. 6.4 [20], indicating that it contains mainly leucite crystals in a glass matrix. The sizes of leucite crystals were measured to be approximately 5–10 μm [28] in a glass matrix. The mechanical properties of the material are Vickers hardness $H = 5.6$ GPa, Young's modulus $E = 70$ GPa, fracture toughness $K_c = 1.3$ MPa.m$^{1/2}$ and flexural strength $\sigma = 127$ MPa [29].

6.3 Simulated Clinical Resurfacing Using Dental Handpieces

6.3.1 Clinical Resurfacing Process

When installing dental restorations in the human mouth, clinical resurfacing of restorations is necessary to adjust the occlusal contacts and marginal fits [30, 31]. Figure 6.2 demonstrates a clinical case of a ceramic inlay after occlusal corrections. This process starts with the necessary reshaping followed by a finishing and polishing process using dental handpieces and abrasive tools in the oral environment as shown in Fig. 6.3. In order to reduce the surface roughness, abrasive tools with decreasing grit sizes are used for finishing. These tools include diamond burs, flexible discs and strips to adjust to the tooth morphology and the intraoral conditions. Polishing process is carried out with rubber polishing tips or polishing paste and brushes [32–34].

Usually a dental ceramic surface is covered with a layer of glaze. Dental glazes are made mainly of a glassy material and applied as the last firing step during the production of ceramic restorations. After clinical adjustments or reshaping, it is usually recommended to reglaze the surfaces in the laboratory. Because this would take another appointment, many dentists prefer to polish the surfaces intraorally through four to five finishing/polishing steps to reduce the surface roughness of the resurfaced areas. Intraoral resurfacing is controlled by manual operations of individual dentists and resurfacing quality determines the life and function of restorations. Therefore, it requires a fundamental understanding of material responses for avoiding adverse effects when carried out inadequately. In this regard, surface and subsurface damages have been particularly identified in resurfacing brittle materials like dental ceramics [35–38].

6.3.2 Dental Handpieces and Burs

Like human enamel, ceramic restorations are usually ground intraorally by dental diamond burs, which are single-layered diamond grinding wheels of 1-mm diameters manufactured by electroplating. The cutting portion of these burs consists of a single layer of synthetic or natural diamond held in place on the form or hub by an

(a)
(b)

Fig. 6.5 Scanning electron micrographs of a new coarse grit diamond bur (**a**) before cutting and (**b**) after cutting (Reprinted with permission from Ref. [41]. Copyright 2009 by Elsevier)

electroplated nickel or chromium binder [39, 40]. Figure 6.5 shows the surface of an electroplated diamond bur with abrasive grains tips protruded above the electroplated nickel [41]. Typically the nickel or chromium layer is equal to about 30 % the grain dimensions, although its thickness may be varied. Since these diamond burs contain only a single layer of superabrasive, they are generally less expensive than bonded types and widely used as disposable or single-patient-use burs to minimise the risk of cross-contamination of blood-borne pathogens

[42]. Diamond burs have ultrafine, fine, medium, coarse and supercoarse grit sizes ranging from 10 to 150 μm. Fine-particle diamonds are used for finishing (grit size 15–30 μm); coarse diameters (125–150 μm) are used for quick removal.

Diamond burs are usually rotating at high speed, which depending on their diameter and grit size ranges between 40,000 and 450,000 rpm driven by dental handpieces (usually angulated) either for lab work or for intraoral preparation and surface reduction. Traditionally, high speeds were achieved using the air turbine, invented by Borden in 1957 [43]. A handpiece with an air turbine is called a high-speed handpiece containing ball bearings and a tiny turbine wheel driven by a mixture of water and pressurised air. Wear of ball bearings can cause the diamond bur to oscillate, resulting in additional surface damage to the workpiece. High-speed handpieces have limited optimal torque–speed characteristics. Thus, it is very difficult to adjust the cutting speed to the needs through these diamond instruments. The cutting speed is reduced by reducing the handpiece air pressure, resulting in reduced torque applied in the cutting process. Typically, most dentists use high-speed handpieces at high speeds and do not adjust the rotational speed to the optimal work characteristics of the bur. As an alternative they use electric dental handpieces to have constant toques at a large range of rotational speeds of 100–40,000 rpm electronically driven by electrical motors. These motors can be operated at nearly constant torques under different loads and rotational speeds. The range of rotational speed can be extended by using speed-increasing handpieces which use cogwheel to raise the maximum speed of 40,000–200,000 rpm using a factor of 1:5. It has been demonstrated that electric handpieces are more efficient than air-turbine handpieces in cutting various materials used in dentistry, especially machinable glass ceramics [43].

Generally diamond instruments grind the surface by scratching dents into the surface, resulting in roughness. These rough surfaces have to be finished to create a smooth surface. For high gloss, a polishing process is necessary additionally. In finishing process, fine abrasives embedded in a metallic carrier or a rubber polishing instrument are used.

6.3.3 Testing Apparatus and Methodology for Simulation of Clinical Resurfacing

Although high-speed air turbines provide poor torque characteristics, they are commonly used in dental clinical cutting and finishing for proper occlusal contacts and removal of the damaged crowns/inlays/onlays and cementing media [44] due to their high-speed capabilities. In intraoral clinical adjusting, the performance of the dental handpieces and burs is essential to control adjusting quality which determines the function and life of a restoration. The quality measures in adjusting a restoration include material removal rate, surface roughness and degree of surface damage [39, 45–47]. However, reliable standardised testing of high-speed dental

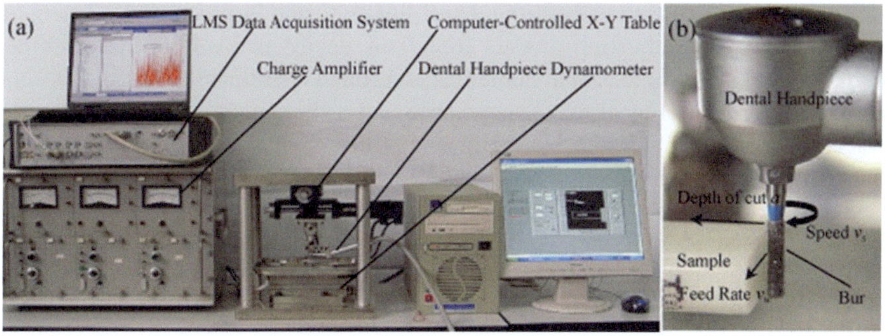

Fig. 6.6 Computer-assisted experimental setup for in-process assessment and monitoring of dental cutting (Reprinted with permission from Ref. [41]. Copyright 2009 by Elsevier)

handpieces is a challenge [48] because rotational speed, force, torque and finishing energy are very difficult to quantify precisely. Therefore, accurate measurement systems enabling quantitative assessment of these parameters for studies of intraoral adjusting process using dental handpieces are highly desirable [49, 50].

Early handpiece testing systems were mechanically controlled, enabling only force control [51, 52]. These apparatus were used in studying the effects of handpiece loads [51, 53], bur grit sizes [54], handpiece spray patterns [55], coolant flow rates [56], irrigation solutions and pressures [57] and chemomechanical influences [58, 59] on cutting efficiency of enamel and mica glass ceramics. Modified apparatus were developed adding air pressure regulators, displacement transducers, revolution counters and torque transducers for force, rotational and torque measurements [50, 52]. However, all these mechanically controlled apparatus cannot be used to simulate the handpiece movement in clinical adjusting with variable depths of cut and feed rates, which can cause the changes in cutting speeds.

Computer-assisted dental cutting systems were later developed [45, 48]. One apparatus consisted of a piezoelectric force dynamometer, a charge amplifier and a computer data acquisition system [45] for providing constant loads to the handpiece during cutting. With this apparatus, dental ceramics with a wide range of mechanical properties were studied with respect to material response to dental cutting, including mica-containing glass ceramics [45, 46], glass-infiltrated alumina [47], feldspathic porcelain and yttria-stabilised tetragonal zirconia [39]. Another apparatus comprised two platforms on precision microslides, a transducer for monitoring the dental handpiece rotations and a strain gauge for force measurement [48], with which the cutting performances of clinical and industrial handpieces against glass were evaluated. These computer-assisted cutting devices can only be used to cut grooves at the fixed loads due to the lack of two-degree-of-freedom (2-DOF) moving functionality. Meanwhile, the measurement of cutting speeds depended on a strobe-type tachometer [45], or a photodiode [52], or a fibre optic tachometer [60–62], resulting in instantaneous or discontinuing speed assessment. How the rotation speed varies with the depth of cut and feed rate remained immeasurable, which are constantly variable and virtually indefinable during the clinical dental finishing.

The recently developed computer-assisted 2-DOF apparatus shown in Fig. 4.6 enabled the simulation of the common clinical adjusting practice in which both feed rate and depth of cut can be controlled and measured and in-process assessment of in vitro handpiece adjusting process [63]. This device is a mini-CNC machine, consisting of a two-dimensional numerical controlled coordinate worktable serving as the carrier of a clinical dental handpiece and a three-component piezoelectric force dynamometer, an electric charge amplifier, and a high-speed LMS data acquisition system for in-process measurement. Details of this device can be found in Ref. [63]. With this device, both the tangential and normal cutting forces can be monitored and measured in both time and frequency domains. The handpiece rotational speeds can be subsequently obtained via fast Fourier transform (FFT) in the frequency domain. Further, cutting torque T and specific cutting energy U can be determined using the following equations:

$$T = F_t d_s/2 \tag{6.1}$$

$$U = F_t v_s/a v_w b \tag{6.2}$$

where F_t is the tangential force, d_s is the diameter of the diamond bur, v_s is the grinding speed, a is the depth of the cut, v_w is the feed rate and b is the thickness of the work sample.

6.4 Resurfacing Speeds, Forces, Torques and Energy

As coarse burs are often used to remove a large amount of materials, resulting in the poorest surface roughness and most surface and subsurface damage, it is important to understand the cutting characteristics of coarse diamond burs using high-speed dental handpieces. The average diameter of the diamond grits was estimated to be 106–125 μm from a series of micrographs obtained by scanning electron microscopy [64]. In this section, utilising some published data [65], the investigation attempted to compare the material responses of feldspar and leucite glass ceramics to resurfacing process.

6.4.1 Resurfacing Speeds

Resurfacing speeds for feldspar and leucite glass ceramics as the functions of depth of cut at the feed rates of 15 mm/min and 60 mm/min are shown in Fig. 6.7a. The results show that the resurfacing speeds for these two materials (feldspar and leucite) decreased with the depth of cut. Resurfacing speeds for feldspar and leucite glass ceramics as the functions of feed rate at the depths of cut of 10 μm and 50 μm are shown in Fig. 6.7b, showing that the resurfacing speeds for both materials decreased with the feed rate. In particular, cutting leucite at the high feed rate of 60 mm/min and the deep depth of cut of 50 μm caused the speed reduction by

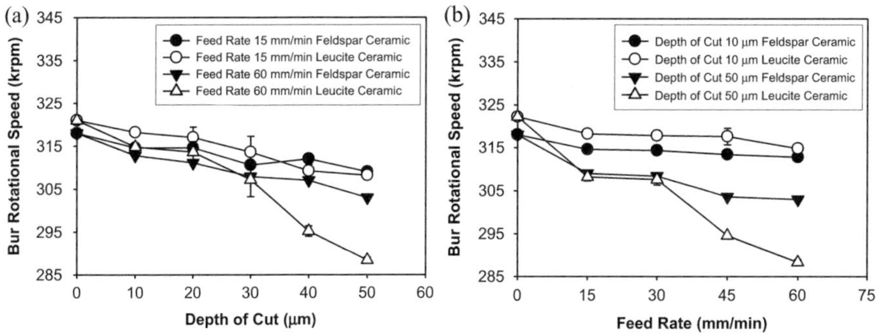

Fig. 6.7 Bur rotational speed versus (**a**) depth of cut and (**b**) feed rate

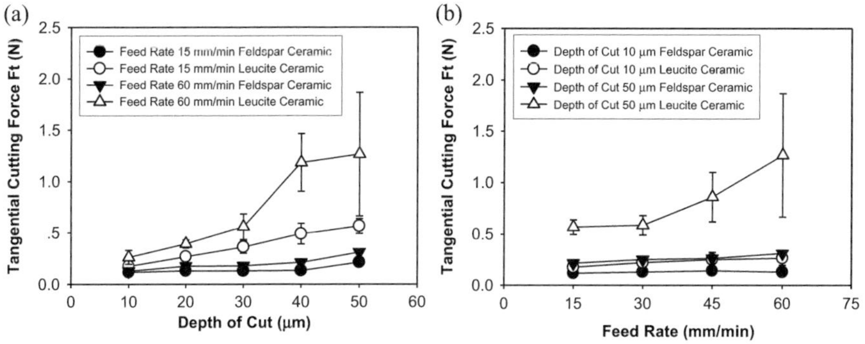

Fig. 6.8 Tangential cutting force *Ft* versus (**a**) depth of cut and (**b**) feed rate

approximately 10 % to 288 krpm from the average unloaded rotational speeds of approximately 320 krpm.

6.4.2 *Resurfacing Forces*

Tangential cutting forces for feldspar and leucite glass ceramics as the functions of depth of cut at the feed rates of 15 mm/min and 60 mm/min are shown in Fig. 6.8a. The tangential forces for both materials increased with the depth of cut at any feed rate. However, the tangential forces for leucite glass ceramic at both feed rates of 15 mm/min and 60 mm/min are significantly higher than those of the feldspar glass ceramic (ANOVA, $p < 0.05$). Tangential cutting forces for the two materials as the functions of feed rate at the depths of cut of 10 μm and 50 μm are shown in Fig. 6.8b. For the feldspar ceramic, the increased depth of cut only resulted in a slight increase in the tangential force. In comparison, the tangential forces for the leucite glass ceramic at the small depth of cut of 10 μm were similar to the force values for feldspar ceramic. However, at the deep depth of cut at 50 μm, the

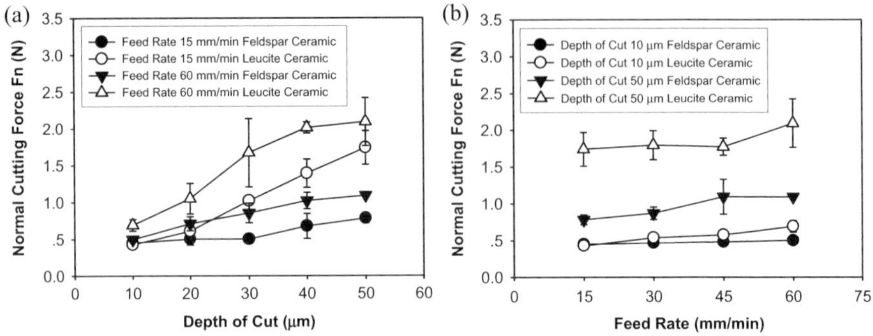

Fig. 6.9 Normal cutting force *Fn* versus (**a**) depth of cut and (**b**) feed rate

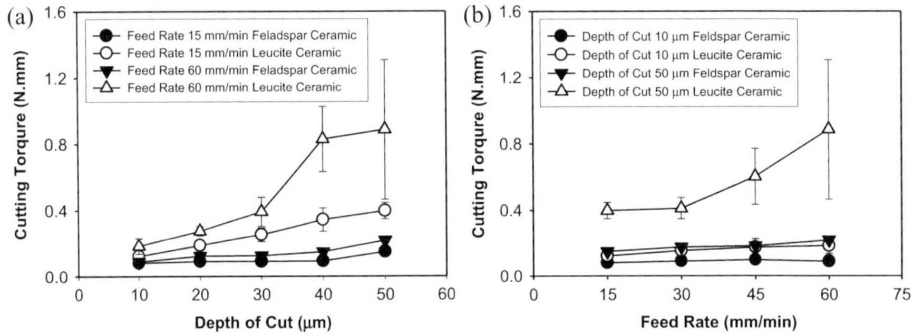

Fig. 6.10 Cutting torque versus (**a**) depth of cut and (**b**) feed rate

tangential forces for the leucite glass ceramic are 2–4 times higher than those for the feldspar glass ceramic.

Normal cutting forces for feldspar and leucite glass ceramics as the functions of depth of cut at the feed rates of 15 mm/min and 60 mm/min are shown in Fig. 6.9a. The normal forces for both materials also significantly increased with the depth of cut at any feed rate (ANOVA, $p < 0.05$). Also, the forces for the leucite glass ceramic are higher than those for the feldspar glass ceramic. In particular, at a higher feed rate and depth of cut, the normal forces for the leucite glass ceramic nearly doubled. Normal cutting forces for the two materials as the functions of feed rate at the depths of cut of 10 μm and 50 μm are shown in Fig. 6.9b. At the depth of cut of 10 μm, the normal forces for these two materials were very close, slightly increasing with the feed rate. At the depth of cut of 50 μm, the normal forces for the leucite glass ceramic were twice of the forces for the feldspar ceramic.

6.4.3 Resurfacing Torques

Cutting torques for the feldspar and leucite glass ceramics as the functions of depth of cut at the feed rates of 15 mm/min and 60 mm/min are shown in Fig. 6.10a. It shows the torques for leucite glass ceramic are higher than those for the feldspar ceramic. The torques for the feldspar ceramic did not change much with the feed rate and depth of cut, while cutting leucite glass ceramic, the torques increased significantly with the depth of cut (ANOVA, $p < 0.05$). Cutting torques for the feldspar and leucite glass ceramics as the functions of feed rate at the depths of cut of 10 μm and 50 μm are plotted in Fig. 6.10b. It shows that the torques for cutting the leucite glass ceramic at the depth of cut of 50 μm are at least 2–5 times higher than those for the two materials cut at the other conditions.

6.4.4 Resurfacing Energy

The specific cutting energy for feldspar and leucite glass ceramics as functions of the depth of cut at the feed rates of 15 mm/min and 60 mm/min is shown in Fig. 6.11a. Overall, the specific cutting energy for these two materials significantly decreased with the increase in depth of cut (ANOVA, $p < 0.05$). The specific cutting energy values for leucite glass ceramic were always higher than those of the feldspar glass ceramic. For instance, at the feed rate of 60 mm/min, the specific cutting energy for leucite ranged from 84 to 128 J/mm^3 in comparison with the specific energy at the level of 24–59 J/mm^3 for the feldspar ceramic. At the feed rate of 15 mm/min, the specific cutting energy for leucite ranged from 205 to 325 J/mm^3 in comparison with the specific energy at the level of 61–214 J/mm^3 for the feldspar ceramic. The specific cutting energy for these two materials as the function of feed rate at the depths of cut 10 μm and 50 μm is given in Fig. 6.11b. It demonstrates that the specific cutting energy decreased when increasing the feed rate at any depths of cut. At the depth of cut of 10 μm, the specific cutting energy for both materials was consumed at higher values than that at the larger depths of cut. Also it shows at any cutting conditions, the specific cutting energy for leucite glass ceramic was much higher than that of the feldspar ceramic.

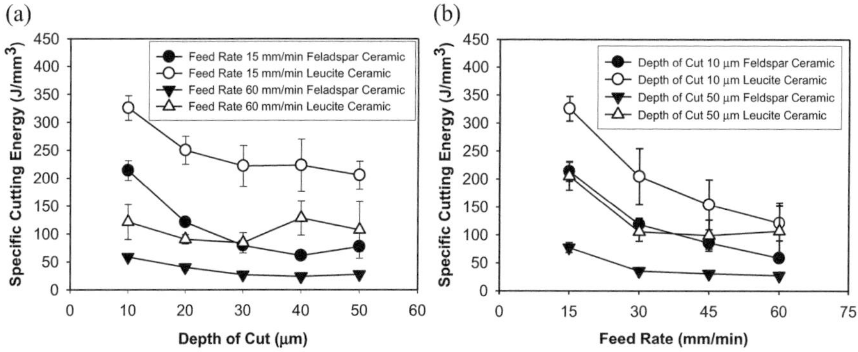

Fig. 6.11 Specific cutting energy versus (**a**) depth of cut and (**b**) feed rate

6.5 Surface Quality in Simulated Clinical Resurfacing

The reliability of dental ceramic restorations, especially for high-load-bearing posterior restorations, is often critically dependent upon the quality of the surface produced by dental resurfacing using diamond burs. Surface quality is considered to consist of two aspects: surface integrity and surface topography [66]. Surface integrity is associated with mechanical and microstructural alternations to the surface layer induced by machining. For brittle material machining, the most important aspects of surface integrity are associated with fracture, i.e., surface and subsurface damage, and thermal damage caused by excessive grinding temperatures, i.e., phase transformation. Surface topography refers to the geometry of machined surfaces, which is usually characterised by surface roughness.

The present section is mainly concerned with surface roughness in dental ceramic resurfacing using coarse diamond burs. We begin with measurement of surface roughness using stylus profilometry, followed by the distractive morphological features of machined surfaces for the feldspar and leucite glass ceramics. Quantitative characterisation of subsurface damage for both materials is carried out using non-destructive manner, namely, finite element analysis (FEA), and destructive measurement with SEM. The FEA model is then considered for describing the generation of subsurface stresses at the material–bur interfaces to theoretically predict subsurface damage of dental ceramic during resurfacing. This provides a certain degree of insight into how various cutting conditions might affect the resurfacing quality. Machining heat-induced phase transformation in resurfacing leucite glass ceramic is also described. Finally, material removal mechanisms in resurfacing of dental ceramics are discussed.

6.5.1 Surface Roughness

The arithmetic mean surface roughness R_a values as function of depth of cut at the feed rate of 15 mm/min and 60 mm/min are shown in Fig. 6.12a. The arithmetic mean surface roughness R_a values as a function of feed rate at the depths of cut of 10 μm and 50 μm are shown in Fig. 6.12b. These data show that the roughness values are in the range of 5–7 μm under the applied cutting conditions. The effects of depth of cut and feed rate on surface roughness are not significant (ANOVA, $p > 0.05$).

6.5.2 Surface Morphology

The SEM micrographs obtained from the feldspar ceramic surfaces through the coarse diamond burs at a depth of cut of 10 μm for a complete variation of the feed

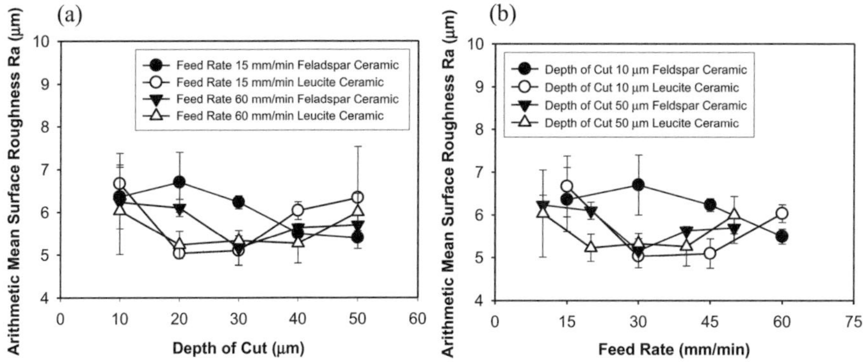

Fig. 6.12 Arithmetic mean surface roughness versus (**a**) depth of cut and (**b**) feed rate

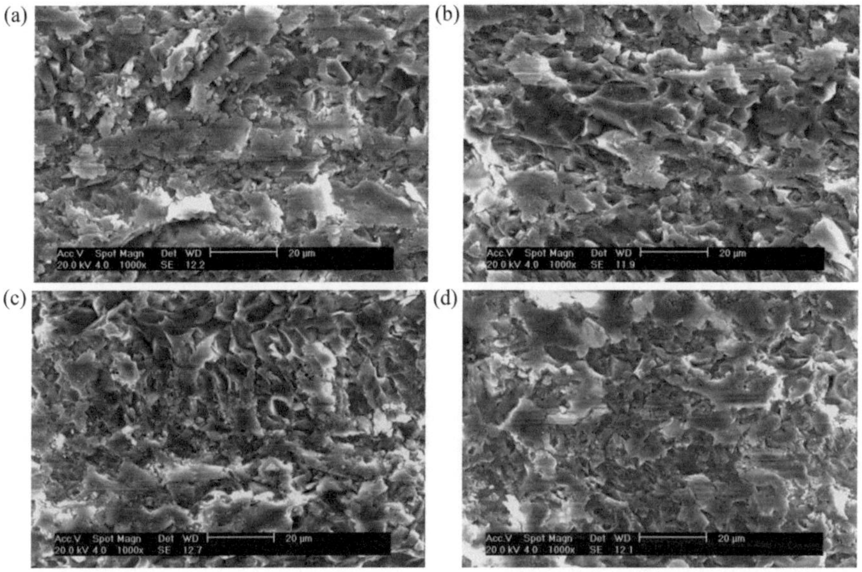

Fig. 6.13 SEM micrographs of the surfaces adjusted for the feldspar ceramic at depth of 10 μm with feed rates (**a**) 15 mm/min, (**b**) 30 mm/min, (**c**) 45 mm/min and (**d**) 60 mm/min (Reprinted with permission from Ref. [64]. Copyright 2006 by Wiley Periodicals, Inc.)

rates from 15 to 60 mm/min are shown in Fig. 6.13 [64]. No significant differences on the feldspar ceramic surfaces machined at the feed rates from 15 to 60 mm/min can be observed. The machined surfaces obtained at a much large depth of cut of 50 μm are shown in Fig. 6.14 [64]. The structures of the surfaces machined at different depths of cut of 10 and 50 μm looked similar, although it is expected to have larger machining grooves and coarser surfaces at the larger feed or depth of cut. All these feldspar ceramic surfaces featured with plastic deformation, microfracture, smeared areas and micro debris.

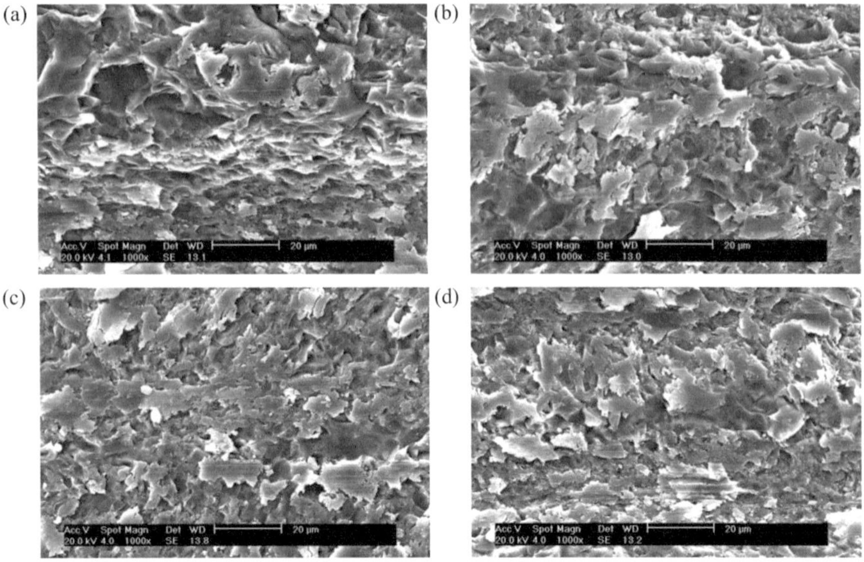

Fig. 6.14 SEM micrographs of the surfaces adjusted for feldspar ceramic at depth of 50 µm with feed rates (**a**) 15 mm/min, (**b**) 30 mm/min, (**c**) 45 mm/min and (**d**) 60 mm/min (Reprinted with permission from Ref. [64]. Copyright 2006 by Wiley Periodicals, Inc.)

The SEM micrographs obtained from the leucite glass ceramic surfaces from the coarse diamond burs at a depth of cut of 10 µm for a complete variation of the feed rates from 15 to 60 mm/min are shown in Fig. 6.15 [67]. Although these leucite ceramic surfaces featured with plastic deformation, microfracture, smeared areas and micro debris, the surface produced at the low feed rate of 15 mm/min shows more smoothness than the surface generated at the high feed rate of 60 mm/min. The surface morphologies obtained at a much large depth of cut of 50 µm are shown in Fig. 6.16 [67]. These surfaces also demonstrate similar characteristics, i.e., coexistence of plastic deformation and brittle fracture. It is also observed that at the great depth of cut of 50 µm and high feed rate, more microfracture occurred on the machined surface (Fig. 6.15d).

Comparing the feldspar and leucite surfaces in Figs. 6.13 and 6.15 at the depth of cut of 10 µm and in Figs. 6.14 and 6.16 at the depth of cut of 50 µm, both materials revealed the mixed mode of material removal characteristics, i.e., ductile removal and brittle fracture, as the dominant removal mechanisms. However, the leucite glass ceramic showed more plastic than feldspar ceramic with more plastically deformed regions generated in particular at the small depth of cut and feed rate (Fig. 6.15a versus Fig. 6.13a). Although both material surfaces contained cracks, chipping and brittle fracture, intergranular and transgranular fractures of the fine-grained feldspar and leucite crystals in the fractured regions were not easily identified. Irregular fracture without clear reinforced crystal–glass interfaces was the feature due to lateral/median cracks. In the plastically removed regions, the interactions of diamond grits produced similar machining traces of metallic

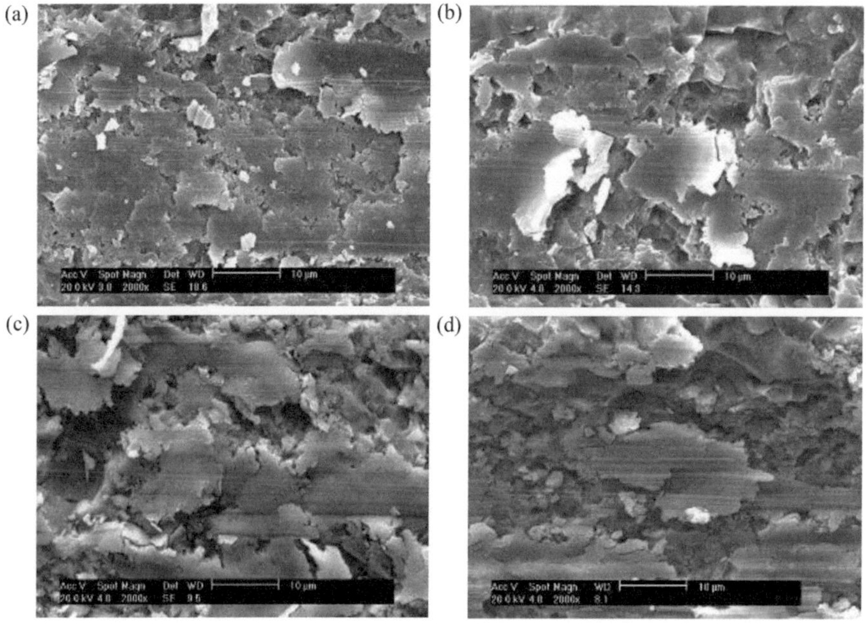

Fig. 6.15 SEM micrographs of the surfaces adjusted for leucite ceramic at depth of 10 μm with feed rates (**a**) 15 mm/min, (**b**) 30 mm/min, (**c**) 45 mm/min and (**d**) 60 mm/min (Reprinted with permission from Ref. [67]. Copyright 2012 by Elsevier)

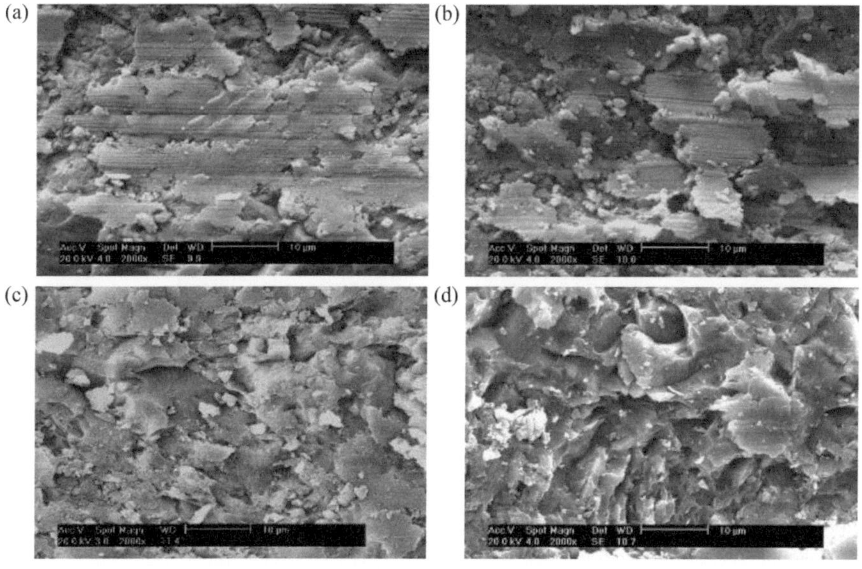

Fig. 6.16 SEM micrographs of the surfaces adjusted for leucite ceramic at depth of 50 μm with feed rates (**a**) 15 mm/min, (**b**) 30 mm/min, (**c**) 45 mm/min and (**d**) 60 mm/min (Reprinted with permission from Ref. [67]. Copyright 2012 by Elsevier)

materials on the feldspar and leucite glass ceramic surfaces companied with microcracks.

6.5.3 Subsurface Damage: FEA Modelling and Experimental Measurement

The FEA simulation was conducted to model the dental resurfacing process based on workpiece–bur contact mechanics described in Fig. 6.6b. A two-dimensional FEA was developed to predict tensile, shear, compressive and equivalent von Mises stresses. Details of the establishment of this model can be found in Ref. [68]. Surface and subsurface damage in the resurfacing process resulted from the severe tensile stresses exceeding the ultimate strength σ of the workpiece material underneath the workpiece–bur contact zone. Thus, the failure criterion was established based on the maximum normal stress σ_t (the first principal stress) criterion. For the given work materials, the ultimate strength σ values for the feldspar and leucite glass ceramics are 100 MPa [24] and 127 MPa [29], respectively. Subsequently, the depths of subsurface damage of the workpiece under the different resurfacing conditions were determined as functions of resurfacing operational parameters. To validate the FEA-predicted values, the destructively revealing subsurface damage measurement was applied to the work materials by manually polishing the cross-sections of the machined materials using progressively smaller alumina abrasives and diamond pastes of sizes down to 0.5 μm [68]. The subsurface damage depths were then measured under SEM [68].

Figure 6.17a demonstrates the contour plot of the maximum principal stress distribution for feldspar ceramic at the workpiece–bur contact zone at the depth of 10 μm and feed rate of 15 mm/min [69]. Figure 6.17b shows the detailed plot of the stress distribution in Fig. 6.17a [69]. The results show that the tensile stresses were distributed under the workpiece–bur contact zone and increased with the decrease in the distance to the resurfaced surface. The maximum tensile stress was estimated to be 875 MPa at the diamond grit exit point. Figure 6.17c demonstrates the contour plot of the maximum principal stress distribution for feldspar ceramic at the workpiece–bur contact zone at the depth of 50 μm and feed rate of 60 mm/min [69]. Figure 6.17d shows the detailed plot of the stress distribution in Fig. 6.17c [69]. The results also show similar stress distribution features, but the maximum tensile stress was estimated to be 1215 MPa at the diamond grit exit point, which is much higher than the maximum stress obtained at the depth of cut 10 μm and the feed rate of 15 mm/min.

Figure 6.18a displays the contour plot of the maximum principal stress distribution for leucite glass ceramic at the workpiece–bur contact zone at the depth of 10 μm and feed rate of 15 mm/min [70]. Figure 6.18b shows the detailed plot of the stress distribution in Fig. 6.18a [70]. The results exhibit the similar distributions for leucite glass ceramic to those for feldspar ceramic comparing Fig. 6.17a with 6.17b.

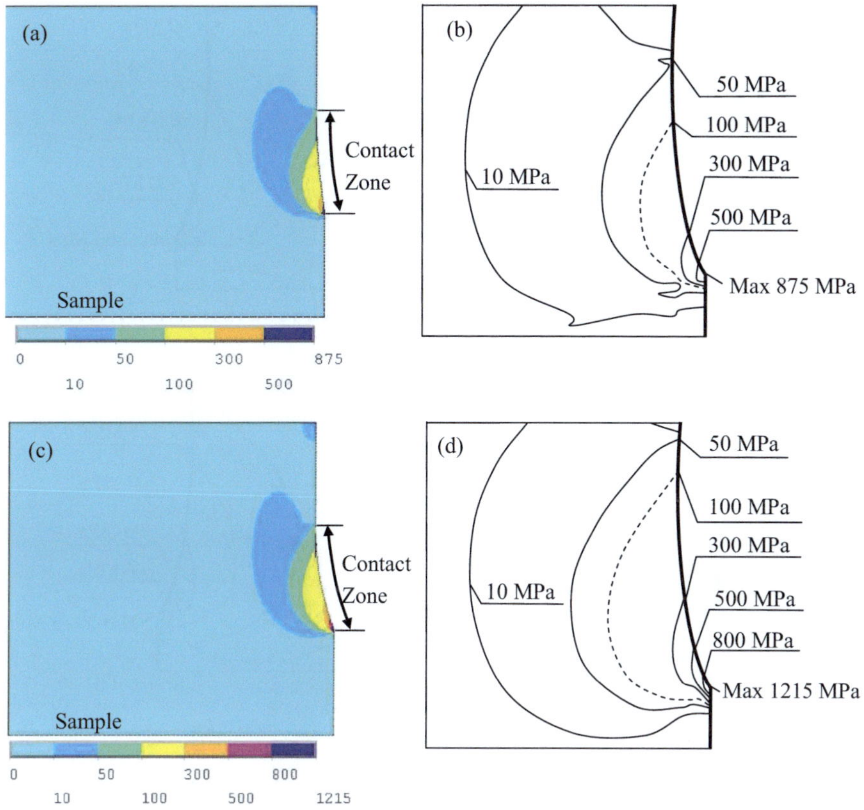

Fig. 6.17 (**a**) Contour plot of maximum principal stress distribution and (**b**) detailed plot of the stress distribution at the bur–prosthesis contact zone at the depth of cut of 10 μm and feed rate of 15 mm/min; (**c**) maximum principal stress distribution and (**d**) detailed plot of the stress distribution at the depth of cut of 50 μm and feed rate of 60 mm/min for feldspar ceramic (Reprinted with permission from Ref. [69]. Copyright 2009 by Elsevier)

However, the maximum principal stress of 866 MPa for the leucite glass ceramic is lower than the maximum stress of 875 MPa for the feldspar ceramic. Figure 6.18c demonstrates the contour plot of the maximum principal stress distribution for the leucite glass ceramic at the workpiece–bur contact zone at the depth of 50 μm and feed rate of 60 mm/min [70]. Figure 6.18d shows the detail plot of the stress distribution in Fig. 6.18c [70]. The maximum tensile stress was estimated to be 1203 MPa at the diamond grit exit point, which is much higher than the maximum stress obtained at the depth of cut 10 μm and the feed rate of 15 mm/min. This maximum stress for the leucite glass ceramic is lower than that for the feldspar ceramic at the same machining condition.

The SEM micrographs of the cross-sections of feldspar ceramic material machined at the depths of cut 10 μm and 50 μm and the feed rates of 15 mm/min and 60 mm/min are shown in Fig. 6.19 [69]. The maximum subsurface damage

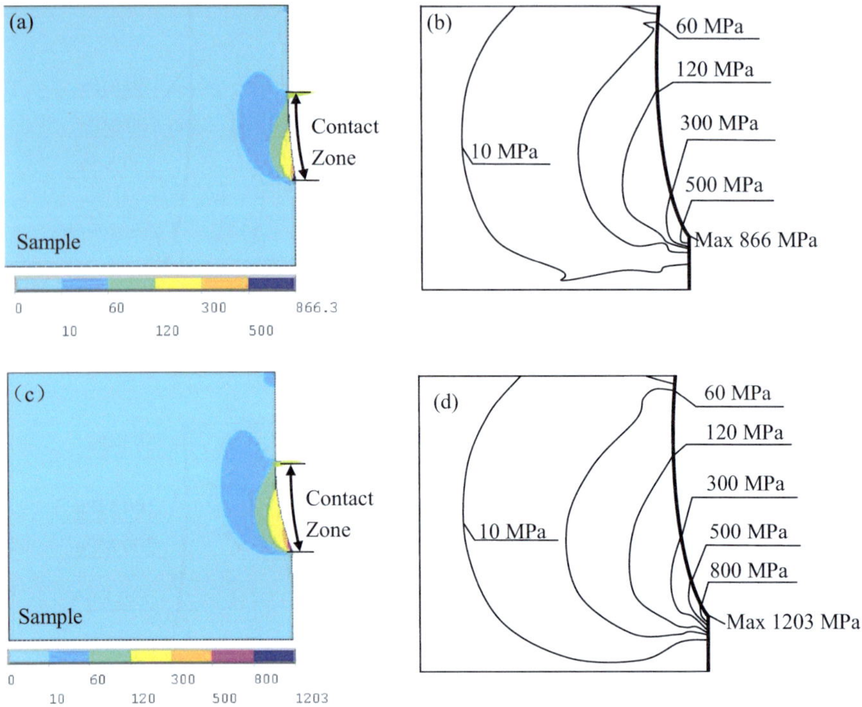

Fig. 6.18 (**a**) Contour plot of maximum principal stress distribution and (**b**) detailed plot of the stress distribution at the bur–prosthesis contact zone at the depth of cut of 10 μm and feed rate of 15 mm/min; (**c**) maximum principal stress distribution and (**d**) detailed plot of the stress distribution at the depth of cut of 50 μm and feed rate of 60 mm/min for leucite ceramic (Reprinted with permission from Ref. [70] 2010. Blackwell Publishing Ltd)

depth was estimated to be 74 μm (Fig. 6.19d) at the depth of 50 μm and the feed rate of 60 mm/min, which is about 2.6 times the minimum subsurface damage depth of 28 μm at the depth of cut of 10 μm and the feed rate of 15 mm/min (Fig. 6.19a).

The SEM micrographs of the cross-sections of leucite glass ceramic material machined at the depths of cut 10 μm and 50 μm and the feed rates of 15 mm/min and 60 mm/min are shown in Fig. 6.20 [70]. The maximum subsurface damage depth was estimated to be 65 μm (Fig. 6.20d) at the depth of 50 μm and the feed rate of 60 mm/min, which is about 3.4 times the minimum subsurface damage depth of 19 μm at the depth of cut of 10 μm and the feed rate of 15 mm/min.

Based on the FEA modelling and SEM measurement, it is found that the resurfacing process parameters, the depth of cut and the feed rate, greatly affected the degree of subsurface damage, which are associated with the diamond grit depth of cut. Figure 6.21 shows the maximum FEA-predicted and the average maximum SEM-measured depths of subsurface damage for the feldspar ceramic versus diamond grit depth of cut [69]. It is seen that the maximum FEA-predicted subsurface damage depths are in agreement with the average maximum

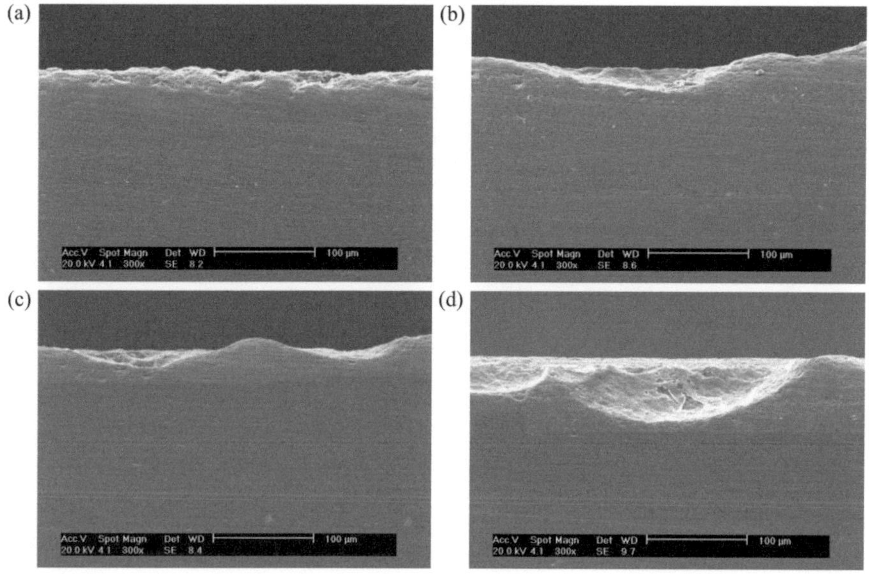

Fig. 6.19 SEM micrographs of the maximum depths of subsurface damage induced in the feldspar ceramics at the depth of cut of 10 μm and the feed rates of (**a**) 15, (**b**) 60 mm/min; at the depth of cut of 50 μm and the feed rates of (**c**) 15, (**d**) 60 mm/min (Reprinted with permission from Ref. [69]. Copyright 2009 by Elsevier)

SEM-measured values. Both predicted and measured subsurface damage depths approximately linearly increased with the diamond grit depth of cut with coefficients of determination of 0.92 and 0.89, respectively.

Figure 6.22 shows the maximum FEA-predicted and the average maximum SEM-measured depths of subsurface damage for the leucite glass ceramic versus diamond grit depth of cut [70]. A great validation of the maximum FEA-predicted subsurface damage depth in comparison with the average maximum SEM-measured values is also seen. Both predicted and measured subsurface damage depths in leucite glass ceramic also approximately linearly increased with the diamond grit depth of cut with coefficients of determination of 0.92 and 0.89, respectively.

6.5.4 *Surface Phase Transformation*

The dental resurfacing process requires extremely high-energy expenditure per unit volume of material removed. Virtually all of this energy is converted to heat which is concentrated within the workpiece–bur contact area. The high temperatures produced can cause various types of thermal damage to dental ceramics, in particular, phase transformation, thermal residual stresses, cracks and reduced fatigue

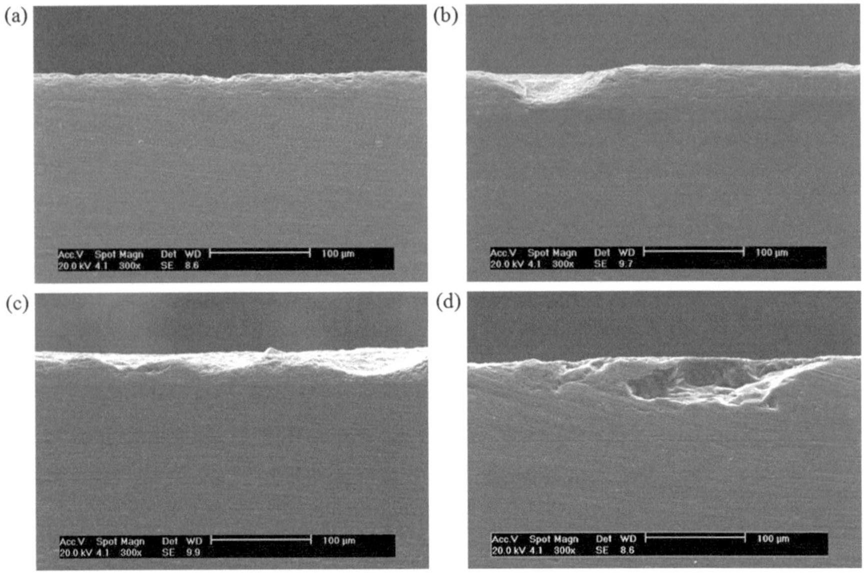

Fig. 6.20 SEM micrographs of the maximum depths of subsurface damage induced in the leucite ceramics at the depth of cut of 10 μm and the feed rates of (**a**) 15, (**b**) 60 mm/min; at the depth of cut of 50 μm and the feed rates of (**c**) 15, (**d**) 60 mm/min (Reprinted with permission from Ref. [70]. Copyright 2010 Blackwell Publishing Ltd)

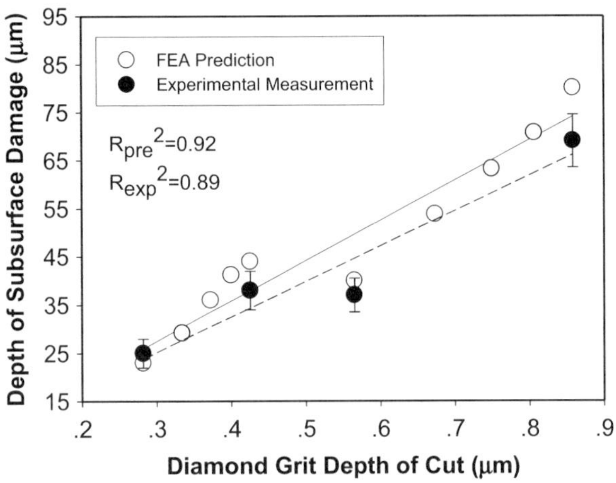

Fig. 6.21 Predicted and measured depths of subsurface damage versus diamond grit depth of cut for feldspar ceramic (Reprinted with permission from Ref. [69]. Copyright 2009 by Elsevier)

strength. Although thermal aspects in engineering grinding have been extensively studied [66], thermal-related issues in dental resurfacing largely remain mysteries.

Abrasive machining occurs by the interaction of discrete diamond abrasive grains on the bur surface with the ceramic workpiece. In dental resurfacing of

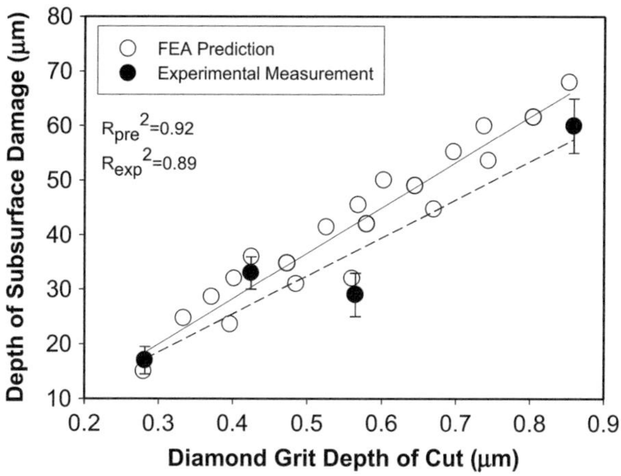

Fig. 6.22 Predicted and measured depths of subsurface damage versus diamond grit depth of cut for leucite ceramic (Reprinted with permission from Ref. [70]. Copyright 2010 by Blackwell Publishing)

dental ceramics using high-speed handpieces and diamond abrasives, the workpiece materials undergo both mechanical and thermal impacts due to resurfacing forces and heat. The resurfacing energy can induce crack initiation and propagation, debris generation and plastic deformation. In this process, the maximum temperature rise T_m in the cutting zone can be estimated as a band source of heat, which moves along the surface to the part being cut at the workpiece velocity, and expressed [71] as

$$T_m = \frac{1.13RUV_w{}^{1/2}a^{3/4}}{(k\rho c)^{1/2}d_s{}^{1/4}} \tag{6.3}$$

where R = the fraction of the grinding energy heating the workpiece, k = thermal conductivity, ρ = density, c = the specific heat of the workpiece material, V_w = workpiece feed rate, a = depth of cut and d_s = diameter of wheel.

In dental resurfacing of ceramics discussed in this chapter, the resurfacing conditions are as follows: V_w = 15–60 mm/min, a = 10–50 μm and d_s = 1.4 mm. For the leucite glass ceramic, the specific cutting energy U spanned 107–326 J/mm^3 [41]. R was selected to be 25 % based on the general observation of approximately 25 % of the machining energy transported as heat to the workpiece in ceramic machining [72, 73]. The physical properties of leucite glass ceramic are ρ = 2.47 g/cm^3, k = 1 (W/m-K) [74] and c = 0.9 J/g−K [75]. Adding an ambient temperature of 25 °C, the estimated maximum resurfacing temperatures in machined leucite glass ceramic surfaces were estimated to be 651–1727 °C [67]. These high resurfacing temperatures provided the external driving conditions for the phase transformations of leucite crystals in the glass ceramic.

There are several methods which can be used to measure phase transformation in machined surfaces, including X-ray diffraction, transmission electron microscopy and Raman spectroscopy. To provide the evidence of phase transformation in dental ceramic resurfacing, laser micro-Raman spectroscopy was applied to the control

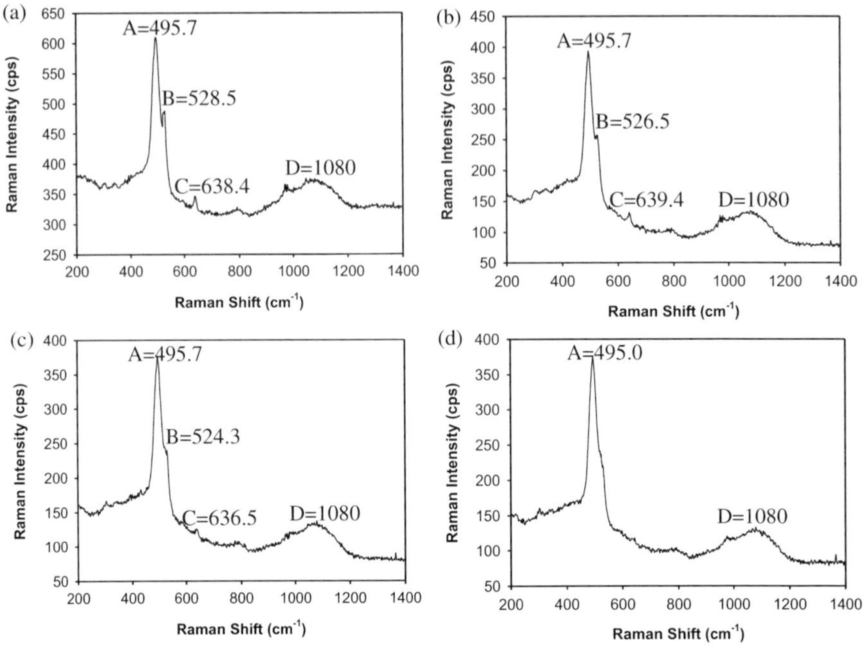

Fig. 6.23 Raman spectra of (**a**) the unadjusted leucite glass ceramic surface, (**b**) the leucite glass ceramic surface adjusted at 10 μm depth of cut and 15 mm/min feed rate, (**c**) the leucite glass ceramic surface adjusted at 30 μm depth of cut and 15 mm/min and (**d**) 500 μm depth of cut and 60 mm/min feed rate (Reprinted with permission from Ref. [67]. Copyright 2013 by Elsevier)

and machined leucite glass ceramic surfaces. Figure 6.23 shows the Raman spectra of the control and resurfaced leucite glass ceramic surfaces at different resurfacing conditions [67]. Figure 6.23a shows the Raman spectrum for the control surface which was in sintered state. Figure 6.23b–d is the Raman spectra of the adjusted surfaces at 10 μm depth of cut and 15 mm/min feed rate, 30 μm depth of cut and 15 mm/min feed rate and 50 μm-depth of cut and 60 mm/min feed rate, respectively. Compared to the control surface in Fig. 6.23a, intensities for peak A at 495 cm^{-1} Raman line frequency gradually weakened on the machined surfaces shown in Fig. 6.23b–d. Peak B at 529 cm^{-1} wave number was shifted to lower wave numbers of 526 cm^{-1} and 524 cm^{-1} on the machined surfaces and finally merged with peak A at 495 cm^{-1} wave number. Peak C at 638 cm^{-1} wave number in the control surface was also shifted and finally disappeared on the machined surfaces. The intensity of peak D at 1080 cm^{-1} wave number was noticeably stronger in the control surface than those in the machined surfaces. The Raman shifts shown in Fig. 6.23 evidently indicate that phase transformations occurred in the resurfacing process.

In the leucite crystals, the phase transformation from a tetragonal to a cubic polymorph occurs at 625 °C [76, 77]. The high temperatures during resurfacing leucite glass ceramic provided the phase transformation temperature conditions. In dental resurfacing process, coolant was also applied to the resurfacing area, resulting in a complex cooling and heating condition where more complicated phase transformations of leucite crystals from tetragonal–cubic–tetragonal transformations might have occurred. Phase transformations in machined leucite glass ceramic can cause volume contraction. From cubic to tetragonal structures, leucite crystals have approximately 1.2 % volume contraction [78], leading to the microcrack initiation and propagation in and around the crystals [78]. Thus, resurfacing-induced phase transformations promoted crack generation and fracture in resurfaced ceramic surfaces.

6.5.5 Material Removal Mechanisms

The mechanisms of material removal in abrasive machining of ceramics are often explored using indentation and scratching mechanics because the types of damage produced in these two processes are alike. Therefore, indentation mechanics can predict machining performance with reasonably good accuracy [79–81] although the thermal effect in indentation and scratching is generally neglected but it plays an important role in machining.

Resurfacing with a diamond bur containing multiple abrasive grits is a much more complex process than indentation [82–85]. For the feldspar and leucite glass ceramics, material removal mechanisms in resurfacing include fracture and plastic deformation (Figs. 6.13, 6.14, 6.15 and 6.16). Although the measured tangential and normal cutting forces are all less than 3 N (Figs. 6.8 and 6.9), the fundamental removal processes are controlled by the single-diamond abrasives of the two materials and their forces. Thus, the estimation of the cutting forces per grit, particularly, the normal cutting forces per grit, is essential in understanding the material removal mechanisms. The cutting force per grit is defined as a ratio of the measured cutting force against the active diamond abrasive particles involved in cutting. Thus, the average normal force per grit F_n' can be expressed as [79]

$$F_n' = F_n / l_c b N \tag{6.4}$$

where F_n = measured normal cutting force, l_c = contact length between the bur and the workpiece, b = width of contact and N = total number of active grits per unit area.

The density of diamond abrasives can be determined from the SEM imaging of diamond bur surfaces (Fig. 6.8). However, not all the abrasives on the bur surfaces were involved in cutting. It is generally accepted that the fraction of active abrasive grits on fixed abrasive tools, such as single-layered diamond burs, engaging in cutting process, is approximately 1–10 % [86].

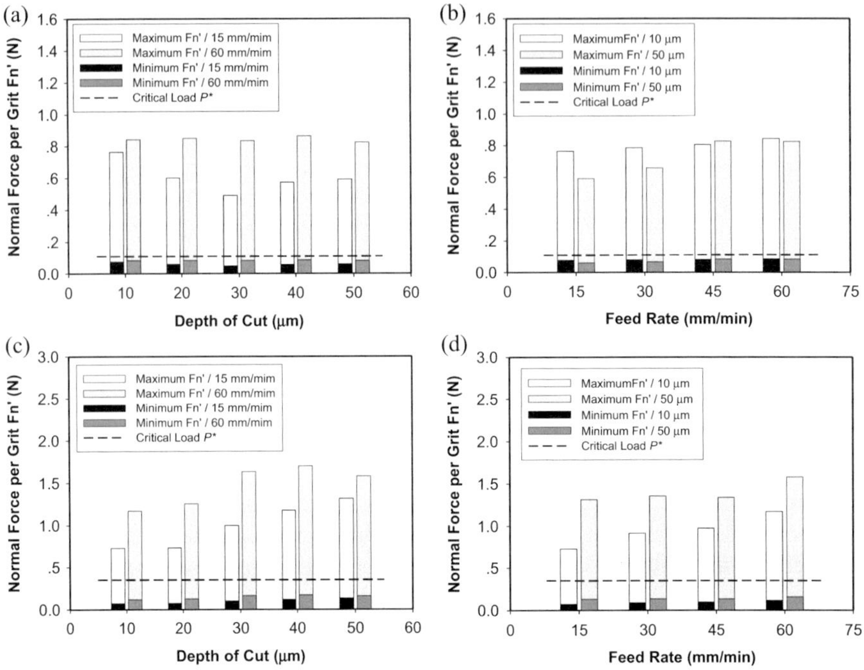

Fig. 6.24 Maximum and minimum normal forces per grit versus (**a**) depth of cut and (**b**) feed rate for the feldspar ceramic; maximum and minimum normal forces per grit versus (**c**) depth of cut and (**d**) feed rate for the leucite ceramic. Fig. 6.24c, d (Reprinted with permission from Ref. [67]. Copyright 2012 Elsevier)

For the feldspar ceramic, the maximum and minimum normal forces per grit versus depth of cut and feed rate are plotted in Fig. 6.24a, b, respectively. At the 15 mm/min feed rate, the maximum normal forces per grit range from 0.59 to 0.76 N when increasing the depth of cut from 10 to 50 μm. Accordingly, the minimum normal forces per grit are in the range of 0.059–0.076 N. At 60 mm/min, the maximum normal forces per grit are in the range of 0.82–0.86 N for 10–50 μm depth of cut, while the minimum normal forces per grit scale are between 0.082 and 0.086 N. For the leucite glass ceramic, the maximum and minimum normal forces per grit versus feed rate and depth of cut are plotted in Fig. 6.24c, d, respectively [67]. At the 15 mm/min feed rate, the maximum normal forces per grit range from 0.73 to 1.32 N when increasing the depth of cut from 10 to 50 μm. Accordingly, the minimum normal forces per grit are in the range of 0.073–0.13 N. At the 60 mm/min, the maximum normal forces per grit are in the range of 1.17–1.58 N for 10–50 μm depth of cut, while the minimum normal forces per grit scale are between 0.12 and 0.16 N.

Both fracture and plastic deformation were observed in dental surfacing of feldspar and leucite glass ceramics. It is of interest to compare the estimated normal cutting forces per grit with the force thresholds for brittle–ductile fracture transitions, P^*, which is expressed as [87]

$$P^* = \left(54.47\alpha/\eta^2\theta^4\right)\left(K_c/H\right)^3 K_c \tag{6.5}$$

where $\alpha = 2/\pi$, $\theta = 0.2$ and $\eta = 1$ for the typical intensity and extent of tensile field, K_c = toughness and H = Vickers hardness. For the feldspar and leucite glass ceramics, the force thresholds P^* are determined to be 0.11 N and 0.35 N.

Under the applied dental resurfacing conditions, the minimum normal forces per grits for feldspar and leucite glass ceramics are lower than their critical thresholds, while the maximum normal forces per grits for the two materials are higher than their critical thresholds. This explains the reason why both fracture and plastic deformation occurred in the resurfacing processes for the two materials. Attributed to the nature of the mixed brittle and ductile mode in dental resurfacing, the changes in depth of cut or feed rate did not significantly influence surface roughness for both materials (Fig. 6.12). However, the increase in diamond grit depth of cut produced the much deeper subsurface damage in both materials (Figs. 6.21 and 6.22). Further, the resurfacing conditions profoundly affected the specific cutting energy and created the thermal impact to dental ceramics, resulting in complex phase transformations (Fig. 6.23). The resurfacing temperature and machining temperature-induced phase transformations also contributed to crack initiation and propagation in the resurfacing process.

Dentists usually use coarse diamond grit burs in highly efficient gross material reduction for both enamel and ceramic restorative materials. In restorative dentistry, feldspar and leucite glass ceramics for veneers, onlays and inlays are required to obtain precise marginal and occluding fits with neighbouring and mating enamel or prosthetic teeth. The final adjustment with diamond burs must achieve good surface integrity with minimum resurfacing-induced damage in ceramic restorations. Clinical failure rates in multilayer ceramic restorations, especially in external ceramic veneers, are found to be high [88–90]. Therefore, for high reliability of ceramic restorations, resurfacing brittle feldspar porcelains and leucite glass ceramics with coarse diamond burs must be carefully conducted.

6.6 Concluding Remarks

Dental resurfacing using handpieces and diamond burs is a manual cutting process in which the resurfacing quality depends on manual skills of individual dentists. Dental care costs associated with ceramic restorations are very expensive, and the use of diamond burs for resurfacing often imparts resurfacing-induced damage with a concomitantly negative impact on reliability of ceramic restorations. A great amount of work has been performed in order to understand the dental resurfacing of feldspar and leucite glass ceramics. Understanding of the fundamental of the mechanics of material deformation and removal is becoming clearer. This will generate information that can be used by dentists to optimise the resurfacing process in clinical process selection and by engineers to develop new dental handpieces and dental materials for durable ceramic restorations.

The research results presented in this chapter confirmed that the response of dental ceramics to the resurfacing process greatly depends on the microstructure that controls the material removal mechanisms. In resurfacing feldspar and leucite ceramics, both the tangential and normal forces for the two materials were measured to increase with either the depth of cut or the feed rate. An increase in either depth of cut or feed rate did not affect the surface roughness and morphology. The resurfaced surfaces for the two materials consist of microfracture and chipping, ductile removal traces, smeared areas and debris. The mixed microfracture and ductile removal mode was the primary mechanism for resurfacing both materials. Subsurface stresses beneath the two resurfaced materials varied with the resurfacing conditions. Subsurface damage was found to be the linear consequence of the penetration of the diamond grit depth of cut for both feldspar and leucite glass ceramics. Thermal-related phase transformations were discussed towards resurfacing leucite glass ceramic. However, further studies are needed to understand the thermal modelling of fracture and plastic mixed mode in dental ceramic removal. The results presented can be used as a qualitative guidance to clinical dental practice on cutting mechanisms of material removal using dental handpieces with diamond burs.

Acknowledgements This chapter represents an extensive and still ongoing work supported by the National Science Foundation of China via NSFC Project Grant Nos. 50475115 and 51375335; the Australian Research Council via ARC LE110100016; the Department of Industry, Innovation, Science, Research and Tertiary Education, Australia, via ACSRF GMB12029; and the James Cook University Collaboration Grants and Incentive Schemes.

References

1. Kelly JR (2004) Dental ceramics: current thinking and trends. Dent Clin N Am 48:513–530
2. Thompson JY, Stoner BR, Piascik JR (2007) Ceramics for restorative dentistry: critical aspects for fracture and fatigue resistance. Mater Sci Eng C 27:565–569
3. Rekow ED, Silva NRFA, Coelho PG, Zhang Y, Guess P, Thompson VP (2011) Performance of dental ceramics: challenges for improvements. J Dent Res 90:937–952
4. Denry I, Holloway JA (2010) Ceramics for dental applications: a review. Materials 3:351–368
5. van Noort R (2002) Introduction to dental materials, 2nd edn. Elsevier, Oxford
6. Miyazaki T, Hotta Y, Kunii J, Kuriyama S, Tamaki Y (2009) A review of dental CAD/CAM: current status and future perspectives form 20 years of experience. Dent Mater J 28:44–56
7. Mörmann WH (2006) The evolution of the CEREC system. JADA 137:75–135
8. Kelly JR (2007) Development of a meaningful systematic review of CAD/CAM reconstructions and fiber-reinforced composites. Clin Oral Implants Res 18(Suppl 3):205–217
9. Rekow D, Thompson VP (2007) Engineering long-term clinical success of advanced ceramic prostheses. J Mater Sci Mater Med 18:47–56

10. Pjetursson BE, Sailer I, Zwahlen M, Hämmerie CH (2007) A systematic review of the survival and complication rates of all-ceramic and metal-ceramic reconstructions after an observation period of at least 3 years. Clin Oral Implants Res 18(suppl 3):73–85
11. Otto T, De Nisco S (2002) Computer-aided direct ceramic restorations: a 10-year prospective clinical study of Cerec CAD/CAM inlays and onlays. Int J Prosthodont 15:122–128
12. Rekow D, Thompson VP (2005) Near-surface damage–a persistent problem in crowns obtained by computer-aided design and manufacturing. Proc Inst Mech Eng H J Eng Med 219:233–243
13. Chang CW, Waddell JN, Lyons KM, Swain MV (2011) Cracking of porcelain surface arising from abrasive grinding with a dental air turbine. J Prosthodont 20:613–620
14. Yin L, Song XF, Song YL, Huang T, Li J (2006) An overview of in vitro abrasive finishing & CAD/CAM of bioceramics in restorative dentistry. Int J Mech Tools Manufact 46:1013–1026
15. Guazzato M, Albakry M, Quada L, Swain MV (2004) Influence of grinding, sandblasting, polishing and heat treatment on the flexural strength of a glass-infiltrated alumina-reinforced dental ceramic. Biomaterials 25:2153–2160
16. Al-Wahadni A (1999) The roots of dental porcelain: a brief historical perspective. Dent News 2:43–44
17. Darvell BW (2009) Materials sciences for dentistry, 9th edn. Woodhead Publishing Limited, Cambridge
18. Rasmussen ST, Nagaji-Okumu W, Boenke K, O´Brien WJ (1997) Optimum particle size distribution for reduced sintering shrinkage of a dental porcelain. Dent Mater 13:43–50
19. Helvey G (2010) A history of dental ceramics. Compt Rendus Geosci 31:309–311
20. Song XF, Yin L, Peng JH, Lin B (2013) Cutting characteristics of dental glass ceramics during in vitro dental abrasive adjusting using a high-speed electric handpiece. Ceram Int 39:6237–6249
21. Nakamura T, Dei N, Kojima T, Wakabayashi K (2003) Marginal and internal fit of Cerec 3 CAD/CAM all-ceramic crowns. Int J Prosthodont 16:244–248
22. Hansen S (2000) Preparations for Cerec 3: where are the limits. Int J Comput Dent 3:197–205
23. Giordano RA (1996) Dental ceramic restorative systems. Compend Contin Educ Dent 17:779–794
24. Deng Y, Lawn BR, Lloyd IK (2002) Characterization of damage modes in dental ceramic bilayer structures. J Biomed Mater Res Part B 63:137–145
25. Kim HW, Dent Y, Miranda P, Pajares A, Kim HE, Lawn BR (2001) Effect of flaw state on the strength of brittle coatings on soft substrates. J Am Ceram Soc 84:2377–2384
26. Ironside JG, Swain MV (1998) Ceramics in dental restorations: a review and critical issues. J Aust Ceram Soc 34:78–91
27. Höland W, Schweiger M, Rheinberger VM, Kappert H (2009) Bioceramics and their application for dental restorations. Adv Appl Ceram 108:373–380
28. Giordano R (2006) Materials for chairside CAD/CAM-produced restorations. JADA 137:14S–21S
29. Bindl A, Mormann WH (2002) An up to 5-year clinical evaluation of posterior in-ceram CAD/CAM core crowns. Int J Prosthodont 15:451–456
30. Curtis AR, Wright AJ, Fleming GJP (2006) The influence of surface modification techniques on the performance of a Y-TZP dental ceramic. J Dent 34:195–206
31. Stuedevant C, Roberson T, Heymann H, Sturdevant J (1995) The art and science of operative dentistry, 3rd edn. Moshy, St. Louis
32. De Jager N, Feilizer AJ, Davidson CL (2000) The influence of surface roughness on porcelain strength. Dent Mater 16:381–388
33. Finger WJ, Noack MD (2000) Postadjustment polishing of CAD/CAM ceramic with luminescence diamond gel. Am J Dent 13:8–12
34. Wright MD, Masri R, Driscoll CF, Romberg E, Thompson GA, Runyan DA (2004) Comparison of three systems for the polishing of an ultra-low fusing dental porcelain. J Prosthet Dent 92:486–490

35. Song XF, Yin L, Han YG, Wang H (2008) In vitro rapid adjustment of porcelain prostheses using a high-speed dental handpiece. Acta Biomater 4:414–424
36. Song XF, Yin L, Han YG, Wang H (2008) Micro fine finishing of a feldspar porcelain for dental prostheses. Med Eng Phys 30:856–864
37. Song XF, Yin L (2010) Quantitative effect of diamond grit size on subsurface damage induced in dental adjusting of porcelain surfaces. Proc Inst Mech Eng H J Eng Med 224:1185–1193
38. Xu HHK, Kelley RJ, Jahanmir S, Thompson V, Rekow ED (1997) Enamel subsurface damage due to tooth preparation with diamonds. J Dent Res 76:1698–1706
39. Yin L, Jahanmir S, Ives LK (2003) Abrasive machining of porcelain and zirconia with a dental handpiece. Wear 255:975–989
40. Yin L, Han YG, Song XF, Wang H (2007) Effect of diamond burs on process and damage involving in vitro dental resurfacing of a restorative porcelain. J Phys D Appl Phys 40:5291–5300
41. Song XF, Yin L, Han YG (2009) In-process assessment of dental cutting of a leucite-reinforced glass-ceramic. Med Eng Phys 31:214–220
42. Christensen HJ, Christensen RP (1991) Single patient-use diamond rotary instruments. CRA Newsl 15:1–2
43. Choi C, Driscoll CF, Romberg E (2010) Comparison of cutting efficiencies between electrical and air-turbine dental handpieces. J Prosthet Dent 103:101–107
44. Dyson JE, Darvell BW (1993) The development of the dental high-speed air turbine handpiece. Part 1. Aust Dent J 38:49–58
45. Dong X, Yin L, Jahanmir S, Ives LK, Rekow ED (2000) Abrasive machining of glass-ceramics with a dental handpiece. Mach Sci Technol 4:209–233
46. Yin L, Ives LK, Jahanmir S (2004) Effects of fluids on the simulated clinical dental machining of a glass ceramic. J Am Ceram Soc 87:173–175
47. Yin L, Ives LK, Jahanmir S, Rekow ED, Romberg E (2001) Abrasive machining of glass-infiltrated alumina with diamond burs. Mach Sci Technol 5:43–61
48. Gegauff AG, Rosenstiel SF, Johnston WM, Gangji RK (1998) Handpiece degradation associated with performance testing of diamond rotary cutting instruments. Aust Dent J 43:342–348
49. Dyson JE, Darvell BW (1995) Dental air turbine handpiece performance testing. Aust Dent J 40:330–338
50. Norling BK, Stanford JW (1976) Evaluation performance of dental rotary cutting instruments. In: The cutting edge: interfacial dynamics of cutting and grinding, US Department of Health, Education, and Welfare, DHEW Publication No. (NIH) 76–670, Washington, DC
51. Siegel SC, von Fraunhofer JA (1997) Effect of handpiece load on the cutting efficiency. Mach Sci Technol 1:1–13
52. Westland IAN (1980) The energy requirement of the dental cutting process. J Oral Rehabil 7:51–63
53. Siegel SC, von Fraunhofer JA (1999) Dental cutting with diamond burs: heavy-handed or light-touch? J Prosthodont 8:3–9
54. Siegel SC, von Fraunhofer JA (2000) Cutting efficiency of three diamond bur grit sizes. JADA 131:1706–1710
55. Siegel SC, von Fraunhofer JA (2002) The effect of handpiece spray patterns on cutting efficiency. JADA 133:184–188
56. von Fraunhofer JA, Siegel SC (2000) Handpiece coolant flow rates and dental cutting. Oper Dent 25:544–548
57. Siegel SC, von Fraunhofer JA (1999) Irrigation solution and pressure effects on tooth sectioning with surgical burs. Oral Surg Oral Med Oral Pathol Oral Radiol Endod 87:552–556
58. von Fraunhofer JA, Siegel SC (2003) Using chemomechanical assisted diamond bur cutting for improved efficiency. JADA 134:53–58
59. von Fraunhofer JA, Siegel SC (2000) Enhanced dental cutting through chemomechanical effects. JADA 131:1465–1469

60. Dyson JE, Darvell BW (1997) A laboratory evaluation of two brands of disposable air turbine handpiece. Br Dent J 182:15–21
61. Dyson JE, Darvell BW (1999) Torque, power and efficiency characterization of dental air turbine handpieces. J Dent 27:573–586
62. Dyson JE, Darvell BW (1999) Flow and free running speed characterization of dental air turbine handpieces. J Dent 27:465–477
63. Yin L, Song XF, Qu SF, Huang T, Mei JP, Yang ZY, Li J (2006) Performance evaluation of a dental handpiece in simulation of clinical finishing using a novel 2-DOF in vitro apparatus. Proc Inst Mech Eng H J Eng Med 220:929–938
64. Yin L, Song XF, Qu SF, Han YG, Wang H (2006) Surface integrity and removal mechanism in simulated dental finishing of a feldspathic porcelain. J Biomed Mater Res B Appl Mater 79B:365–378
65. Yin L, Song XF (2011) Grindability of dental ceramics in the in vitro oral regime. Int J Abrasive Technol 4:204–222
66. Malkin S, Guo C (2008) Grinding Technology: theory & Application of Machining with Abrasives, 2nd edn. Industrial Press, New York
67. Song XF, Yin L (2012) Surface morphology and fracture in handpiece adjusting of a leucite-reinforced glass ceramics with coarse diamond burs. Mater Sci Eng A 534:193–202
68. Song XF, Yin L, Han YG, Li J (2008) Finite element analysis of subsurface damage of ceramic prostheses in simulated intraoral dental resurfacing. J Biomed Mater Res B Appl Mater 85B:50–59
69. Song XF, Yin L (2009) Subsurface damage induced in dental resurfacing of a feldspar porcelain with coarse diamond burs. J Biomechanics 42:355–360
70. Song XF, Yin L (2010) Stress and damage at the bur-prosthesis interface in dental adjustments of a leucite-reinforced glass ceramic. J Oral Rehabil 37:680–691
71. Malkin S, Ritter JE (1989) Grinding mechanisms and strength degradation for ceramics. ASME J Eng Ind 111:167–174
72. Zhu B, Guo C, Sundenland JE, Malkin S (1995) Energy partition to the workpiece for grinding of ceramics. Ann CIRP 44:1267–1271
73. Brinksmeier E, Aurich JC, Govekar E, Heinzel C, Hoffmeister HW, Klocke F, Peters J, Rentsch R, Stephenson DJ, Uhlmann E, Weinert K, Wittmann M (2006) Advances in modeling and simulation of grinding processes. Ann CIRP 55:667–696
74. Ashby MF (2005) Materials selection in mechanical design, 3rd edn. Butterworth-Heinemann, Oxford
75. Newton H, Hayward SA, Redfern SAT (2008) Order parameter coupling in leucite: a calorimetric study. Phys Chem Miner 35:11–16
76. Heaney PJ, Veblen DR (1990) A high-temperature study of the low-high leucite phase transition using the transmission electron microscope. Am Mineral 75:464–476
77. Wyckoff RWC (1963) Crystal structure. Wiley, New York
78. Denry IL, Mackert JR Jr, Holloway JA, Rosenstiel SF (1996) Effect of cubic leucite stabilization on the flexural strength of feldspathic dental porcelain. J Dent Res 75:1928–1935
79. Jahanmir S, Xu HHK, Ives LK (1999) Mechanism of materials removal in abrasive machining of ceramics. In: Jahanmir S, Ramulu M, Koshy P (eds) Machining of ceramics and composites. Marcel Dekker, New York
80. Marinescu I, Rowe B, Yin L, Wobker HG (2000) Abrasive processes. In: Marinescu I, Tonshoff HK, Inasaki I (eds) Handbook of ceramic grinding and polishing. Noyes Publications/William Andrew Publishing, New York
81. Xu HHK, Smith DT, Jahanmir S (1996) Influence of microstructure on indentation and machining of dental glass-ceramics. J Mater Res 11:2325–2337
82. Song XF, Yin L (2010) Induced damage zone in micro fine dental finishing of a feldspar porcelain. Med Eng Phys 32:417–422

83. Song XF, Peng JH, Yin L, Lin B (2013) A machining science approach to dental cutting of glass ceramics using an electric handpiece and diamond burs. ASME J Manufact Eng 135:011014-1–6
84. Yin L, Han YG, Song XF, Li J, Wang H (2007) In vitro study on high rotation deep removal of ceramic prostheses in dental surgery. J Biomed Mater Res B Appl Biomater 82B:334–345
85. Yin L (2012) Property-process relations in clinical abrasive adjusting of dental ceramics. J Mech Behav Biomed Mater 16:55–65
86. Stephenson DJ, Vesalovac D, Manley S, Corbett J (2001) Ultra-precision grinding of hard steels. Precis Eng 25:336–345
87. Lawn BR, Evans AG (1977) A model for crack initiation in elastic/plastic indentation fields. J Mater Sci 12:2195–2199
88. Lawn BR, Deng Y, Miranda P, Pajares A, Chai H, Kim DK (2002) Overview: damage in brittle layer structures from concentrated loads. J Mater Res 17:3019–3036
89. Lawn BR, Deng Y, Lloyd IK, Janal MN, Rekow ED, Thompson VP (2002) Materials design of ceramic-based layer structures for crowns. J Dent Res 81:433–438
90. Swain MV (2009) Unstable cracking (chipping) of veneering porcelain on all-ceramic dental crowns and fixed partial dentures. Acta Biomater 5:1668–1677

Chapter 7
Polymer Blends and Composites for Biomedical Applications

S.T. Lin, L. Kimble, and D. Bhattacharyya

Abstract The versatility of polymers has enabled to implement many new ideas in the biomedical field and continues to play a significant role in finding new and improved solutions in the exciting multidisciplinary fields of implants and scaffold tissue engineering. Polymers are rapidly replacing other traditional biomaterials such as metals and ceramics attributable to their versatility. Material properties of polymers will be discussed in a context specific to biomedical engineering here, which includes biocompatibility, biodegradation, biochemical and biomechanical behaviours. Biopolymers have been used as implantable materials for a broad range of biomedical applications, such as cardiology, cartilage, vasculature, bone, wound healing, drug delivery and prosthetic dentistry. Also biopolymers have become a primary material used for fabricating scaffolds in tissue engineering, a fast emerging area for tackling a critical issue in tissue and organ shortage. To address these two above-mentioned application areas, this chapter is divided into two sections: The first focuses on tissue scaffolds, including the design requirements, fabrication methods and cellular testing. The second discusses coronary stents and their development, investigating into the potential of biopolymer blends as a candidate for biodegradable coronary stents.

Keywords Polymer blends • Scaffold tissue engineering • Implant • Coronary stent • Composites

7.1 General Introduction

Biomaterial research has proposed a wide variety of applications in the field of tissue engineering and regenerative medicine, ranging from metals and ceramics to polymers, both naturally derived and synthetic materials. Among these, polymers have played a significant role and hold importance mainly due to their flexible and adjustable chemical and physical designs, being able to improve their performance

S.T. Lin • L. Kimble • D. Bhattacharyya (✉)
Centre for Advanced Composite Materials, The University of Auckland, Auckland, New Zealand
e-mail: s.lin@auckland.ac.nz; d.bhattacharyya@auckland.ac.nz

Q. Li, Y.-W. Mai (eds.), *Biomaterials for Implants and Scaffolds*, Springer Series in Biomaterials Science and Engineering 8, DOI 10.1007/978-3-662-53574-5_7

through easily adaptable production techniques and the possibility of being tailored to suit the requirements of the application.

The versatility of polymers has inspired many new ideas in the biomedical field and continues to play a significant role in finding new and improved solutions in the exciting multidisciplinary field of implants and tissue engineering. Due to the interdisciplinary nature of this field, to develop and enhance further research, the combined knowledge from biological sciences, chemistry and engineering must be utilised to construct indispensable innovations for improving human health.

The term *biomaterials* was defined in the second consensus conference on definitions in biomaterials science, of the European Society for Biomaterials [1], as 'a material intended to interface with biological systems to evaluate, treat, augment or replace any tissue, organ, or function of the body'. The use of biomaterials dates back to more than 2000 years ago, when gold was extensively used in dentistry [2]. Other applications of biomaterials were used by the old civilisations of Romans, Egyptians, Indians and Chinese people for thousands of years for artificial eyes, ears, teeth and noses for aesthetic purposes or reconstruction of missing or defective parts of the body [3].

Since the middle of the last century, advancements allowed the first biodegradable polymeric sutures to be approved in the 1960s [4]. Another application of biomaterials using poly(2-hydroxyethyl methacrylate) (polyHEMA) was developed by Wichterle, also in the 1960s, for contact lens applications [5].

Advancements over the centuries have improved surgical techniques, sterilisation methods and biomaterials knowledge, which have enabled the development of new methods and devices to improve human health. Biomaterials have been used for implants such as sutures, bone and joint replacements, vascular grafts, heart valves and dental implants and also for medical devices such as pacemakers, biosensors, artificial hearts and tubes [3]. Significant developments in other areas of regenerative medicine has also extensively used biomaterials for repairing damaged tissue such as cartilage, bone, muscle, skin and blood vessels [6].

Polymers are rapidly replacing other traditional material choices such as metals and ceramics in biomedical applications due to their versatility. Applications for biopolymers include neural, cartilage, vascular, bone, wound dressing, drug delivery systems and dental applications. Also biopolymers have been the primary materials used for scaffold fabrication in tissue engineering applications [7]. Polymers can be classified into natural and synthetic polymers. Natural polymers are often considered to be biocompatible due to their natural compositions, and it is no surprise that they were the first used in clinical applications [8]. Natural polymers include collagen, gelatin, elastin, actin, keratin, chitosan, chitin, cellulose, silk and hyaluronic acid. Synthetic polymers include polyethylene, polypropylene, polyvinylchloride, polyurethanes, silicone, rubbers, hydrogels and polytetrafluoroethylene (PTFE).

Armentano et al. [9] has classified biopolymers into two main groups comprising of biodegradable polymers and biosourced polymers. Biodegradable polymers have been used extensively in medical applications and are defined as being capable of breaking down into molecules found in the environment such as carbon dioxide, carbon and methane, under the enzymatic action of microorganisms, in a defined period of time (European standard EN 13432).

Biodegradable polymers can be further classified into two major groups: (1) naturally derived materials and (2) synthetic materials. Favourable characteristics of naturally derived materials include their biological compatibility which supports cell adhesion and function. However, the drawbacks of poor mechanical properties and their limited supply leading to costly factors encourage alterations or other alternatives to be found. On the other hand, synthetic materials possess hydrophobic surfaces and low cell-recognition signals, whereas their mechanical strength, manufacturing versatility and overall controllable characteristics have encouraged more research to focus on the many new possibilities of synthetic materials to be used [7]. Apart from reconstruction of tissue, polymeric biomaterials are also important in the applications such as bone cement, degradable sutures, bone screws and dental devices.

Biocompatibility is a primary requirement for biomaterials and is a critical characteristic that must be satisfied before it can be used in the body. Cell–material interactions are also crucial when biomaterials are applied clinically. Major factors including surface topography, surface chemistry, mechanical properties and biological cues can all influence cell behaviour and end response to their interactions with biomaterials. Careful design of biomaterials for specific applications can control and modulate the cell adhesion, proliferation, migration and differentiation. By using polymeric biomaterials, it is now possible to adjust the material properties, by modifying chemical composition, varying the fabrication method and altering the physical structure. While many other biomaterials have also been studied intensively and can also be adjusted and designed for different applications, they may not possess as much flexibility as polymeric materials offer.

For a material to be qualified as a biomaterial, it must first satisfy the primary requirement of being biocompatible, which is the ability of a material to perform with an appropriate host response in a specific application, or the quality of not having toxic or injurious effects on biological systems [1]. The host response to a biomaterial implant can depend on a multitude of factors ranging from the chemical, physical, biological, biomechanical and degradation properties to the structure, dimensions and shape of the implant [8].

Another important factor of biomaterials is the biodegradability in numerous applications. Current trends predict that many permanent prostheses and related devices used for temporary biomedical applications will soon be replaced by biodegradable substitutes [8]. Biodegradable materials have become more and more popular with keen interest developing further to solve current challenges such as long-term biocompatibility issues as well as the technical and ethical issues associated with revision surgeries [8]. Both natural and synthetic polymers can be biodegradable. Although degradable natural polymers such as collagen have been used for thousands of years for biomedical applications, synthetic polymers have started to gain popularity over the years since the latter half of the 1960s [10].

Note that while there are advantages of biological materials over synthetic materials such as biodegradability, favourable cell adhesion properties and having similar mechanical properties to that of natural tissue, there are several major deficiencies of using natural biological materials such as viral infections, antigenicity, unstable material supply and batch inconsistency [10]. These unfavourable deficiencies have led to the decrease in the demand of biological materials and instead have increased the need for synthetic materials with improved properties and flexibility.

Other advantages of synthetic polymers include their uniformity and their predictability, which can be tailored and used to design specific products to fulfil specific applications. The properties of polymers affect the physical structure and thermal and chemical characteristics [11]. The majority of biodegradable polymers available on the market for regenerative medicine and tissue engineering applications are based on collagen or polyester materials. By combining different materials physically or chemically and using appropriate processing methods, many desired characteristics can be created to produce biocompatible products for biomedical applications.

Biodegradation of polymeric biomaterials works by allowing polymer erosion to occur. The mode of degradation can either involve the material degrading hydrolytically or enzymatically [10]. The majority of natural biological polymers rely on enzymatic degradation. However, hydrolytically degradable polymers are preferred for use in implants due to minimal variations compared to enzymatically degradable polymers [12]. Some of the most promising hydrolytically sensitive synthetic polymers developed for biomedical applications include poly(α-esters), polyurethanes, polyanhydrides and poly(ester amide)[8]. The earliest and most extensively studied class of biodegradable polymers is the poly(α-esters) group, and, among this group, the most extensively investigated polymers are the poly(α-hydroxy acid)s, which include poly(glycolic acid) and poly(lactic acid) [8]. Polyglycolide is highly crystalline (45–55 %) and thus possesses a high tensile modulus. It has been processed in a variety of methods including extrusion, injection and compression moulding, particulate leaching and solvent casting, to produce desirable structures for biomedical applications [13]. The first biodegradable synthetic suture called DEXON® was approved by the Food and Drug Administration (FDA) in 1969 and was based on polyglycolide. The degradation product of polyglycolide in the body is glycine, which can be excreted in the urine or converted into carbon dioxide and water via the citric acid cycle [14]. Polylactides exist in two different forms, poly (L-lactic acid) (PLLA) and poly(D-lactic acid) (PDLA), which are formed from L-lactide and D-lactide stereoisomers, respectively. Additionally, copolymers can be produced from L-lactide and D-lactide and are abbreviated PDLLA. PLLA has a crystallinity of approximately 37 %, a glass transition temperature of 60–65 °C and a melting temperature of approximately 175 °C [15]. PLLA is semi-crystalline, while PDLLA copolymers tend to be amorphous [16]. PLLA has a high elastic modulus of 3.2–3.7 GPa and strength of 55–60 MPa, while an equimolar PDLLA copolymer has an elastic modulus of 0.9 GPa and strength of 41 MPa[17]. Orthopaedic products such as BioScrew®, Bio-Anchor® and Phantom Suture Anchor® have been produced based on PLLA. PDLLA is preferred for developing drug delivery systems compared to PLLA, due to its lower strength and subsequent faster degradation rate.

Polylactides degrade into lactic acid, a normal human metabolic by-product which can be broken down into water and carbon dioxide via the citric acid cycle [14].

A range of poly(lactide-co-glycolide) (PLGA) polymers has also been developed and studied for a wide range of biomedical applications. Different ratios of glycolic acid and L-lactic acid can be used to obtain different characteristics. PLGA has been commercially used as meshes (Vicryl Mesh®), suture reinforcements, skin replacement materials and tissue scaffolding structures. Degradation rates of PLGA depend on such chemical parameters as glycolic acid and L-lactic acid ratios and molecular weight. PLGA has been FDA approved for use in humans, and its versatile processibility enables controllable shapes, structures and degradation rates to be formed.

Poly(caprolactone) (PCL) is a semi-crystalline polyester and is highly processible due to its solubility in a wide range of solvents. PCL has a melting temperature of 55–60 °C and has the ability to form miscible blends with a wide range of polymers. PCL has a relatively low tensile strength of 23 MPa but an extremely high elongation over 700 % [13]. The rate of degradation of PCL is much lower than PLA and needs approximately 2–3 years, making it suitable for longer-term drug delivery systems.

Polyurethanes possess excellent mechanical properties with good biocompatibility and structural versatility. This has attracted interest in their usage for biomedical applications which have been used as cardiac pace makers and vascular grafts. Polyanhydrides degrade by surface erosion due to their hydrophobic nature, which makes them suitable for controlled-release applications [13].

Poly(ester amide) has been developed to combine the excellent mechanical properties of polyamides and the biodegradability of polyesters [18]. Poly(ester amide) has been investigated as potential suture materials. CAMEO® is based on a poly(ester amide) blend which has been developed for site-specific delivery of small hydrophobic drug and peptides.

With the few examples given for the types of polymers and their versatility in terms of production method and overall properties, many possibilities can arise by combining the different polymers and other biomaterials available, to create endless innovations for biomedical applications.

The flourishing and rapidly advancing field of tissue engineering aims to replace, regenerate or improve damaged tissues and organs that have lost their functions. The three general strategies that have been adopted by tissue engineering include (1) implantation of isolated cells or cell substitutes; (2) delivery of tissue-inducing substances, such as growth factors, and placing cells onto or within matrices [19]; and (3) the use of tissue scaffolds, where cells are seeded onto the substrate to create implantable tissue constructs.

Tissue scaffolds are porous structures which provide mechanical support for cells, which play an important role in the regeneration of neotissue. Scaffolds mimic the natural extracellular matrix (ECM) and create an environment similar to that of the ECM in our bodies. The ECM is a noncellular component that exists within all tissues and organs. Each type of tissue has its own ECM composition and structure which are generated during tissue development through dynamic and mutual conversations between the various cellular components. Scaffolds facilitate the regeneration of tissue by acting as a temporary ECM for cell attachment, proliferation, differentiation and subsequent growth until the tissue is completely restored.

Scaffolds have been researched and used in a number of areas such as bone, cartilage, skin, vascular tissues, neural tissues and vehicles for controlled drug delivery. The design and fabrication of tissue scaffolds are of vital importance to the tissue engineering and have become a major focus of biomaterial research recently. The most often used synthetic biopolymers for 3D scaffolds are saturated poly(α-hydroxy esters) which include PLA, PGA, PLGA and PCL. The mechanical properties and cellular adhesion and proliferation are enhanced through incorporation of nanoparticles into the synthetic particles [20].

Another important area of biomaterials is to make the implantable devices for restoring malfunction of the body. A typical example is the use of stents to mechanically support blood vessels inside the human body. Coronary arteries are the vessels commonly treated by stenting strategy due to the prevalence of coronary artery disease (CAD). CAD has become very widespread within developed regions of the world and is the leading cause of death in the US and Europe [21]. CAD is basically the build-up of plaque within the coronary arteries. Excessive plaque build-up leads to constriction of flow through the vessel, in which case the implantable stents need to be deployed to restore normal flow.

To address these two above-mentioned application areas, this chapter is divided into two major sections: The first will focus on tissue scaffolds, including the design requirements, fabrication methods and cellular testing. The second will discuss coronary stents and their development, investigating into the potential of PLLA/PBS blend as a candidate for biodegradable coronary stents.

7.2 Tissue Scaffolds

Tissue engineering and regenerative medicine combines the knowledge and advancements from multiple disciplines with the ultimate goal to create biological substitutes and replacements that can immensely improve the lives of human beings who suffer from loss or damage of body parts due to accidents and diseases. This field has grown to see the many potential applications that the fruits of research can be used for and has recognised the huge international interest that has contributed to this exciting area of improving the quality of lives for mankind.

There are nevertheless many challenges seen in the field of tissue engineering. Nerem [22] pointed out that the challenge of imitating nature to potentially solve tissue engineering issues in terms of donor tissue and organ shortages has three different categories that need to be addressed: *cell technology*, *construct technology* and integration of these into the living system. In summary, Nerem refers to *cell technology* as involving cell sourcing, manipulation of cell function and the effective use of stem cell technology. C*onstruct technology* includes engineered three-

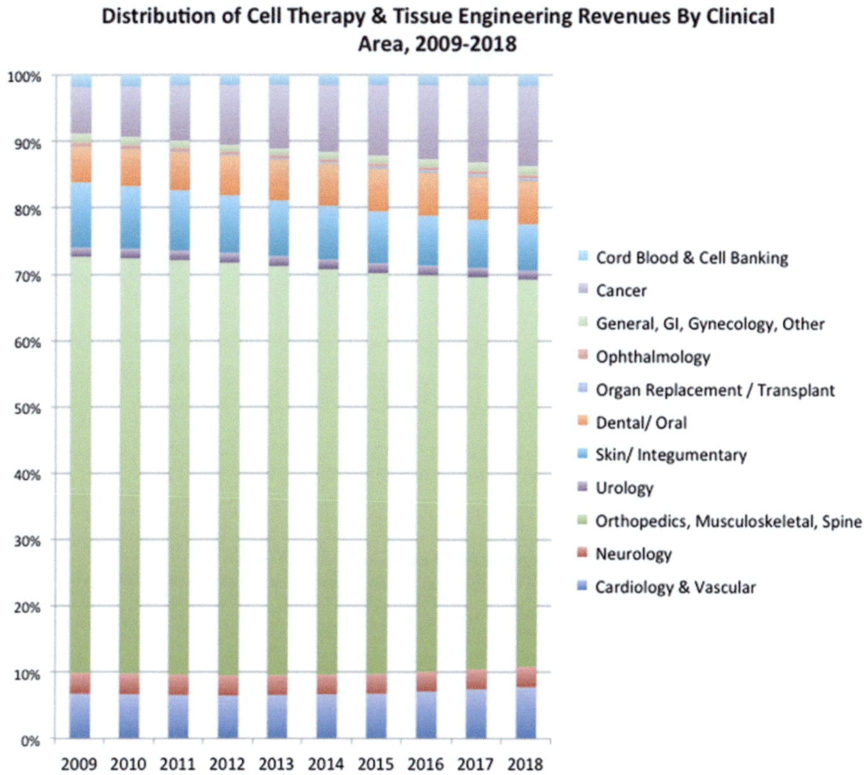

Fig. 7.1 'Distribution of cell therapy and tissue engineering revenues by clinical area, 2009–2018' (Report #S520) (Reprinted from Ref. [23], Copyright 2011, with permission from MedMarket Diligence, LLC)

dimensional architectures which either mimic a specific tissue or provide a delivery vehicle for cells.

Figure 7.1 shows the global market of tissue engineering, cell therapy and transplantation by clinical areas from 2009 to 2018. The orthopaedics, musculoskeletal and spine sector clearly dominates the market and has been predicted to continue to dominate the market right through to 2018.

Figure 7.2 shows the increase of global solid organ transplantations from 2009 to 2012 based on the Global Observatory on Donation and Transplantation (GODT) data, produced by the WHO-ONT collaboration [24]. Based on the GODT organisation, there was a 9.59 % increase in global organ transplantation activity from 2009 to 2012. Although the global activity of organ transplantation increases annually, the statistics for 2012 showed that only less than 10 % of global needs were satisfied. Kidneys are the most commonly transplanted organs worldwide, followed closely by the liver, heart, lung, pancreas and then small bowel among

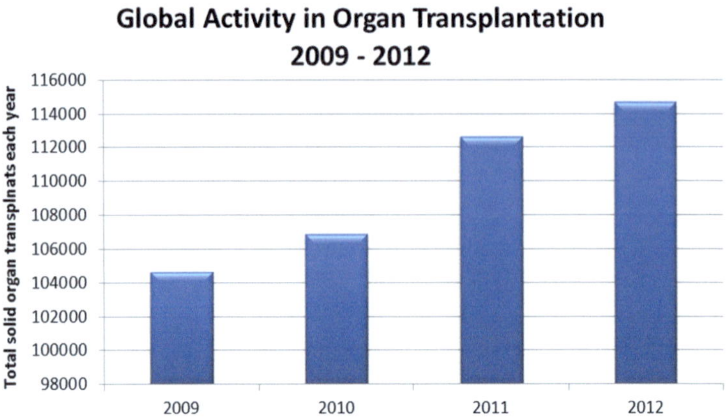

Fig. 7.2 Global activity in solid organ transplantation from 2009–2012. (Plotted based on data from the WHO-ONT Global Observatory on Donation and Transplantation) [24]

Table 7.1 Global activity in solid organ transplantation from 2009–2012

	Kidney	Liver	Heart	Lung	Pancreas	Small bowel	Total
2009	72,100	21,175	5405	3650	2320	–	104,650
2010	73,179	21,602	5582	3927	2362	227	106,879
2011	76,118	23,721	5741	4278	2564	209	112,631
2012	77,818	23,986	5935	4359	2423	169	114,690

Data from the WHO-ONT Global Observatory on Donation and Transplantation [24]

other organs and tissues. The major problem is to access enough donations of tissues and organs for all the patients who need them.

Table 7.1 summarises global activity in solid organ transplantation from 2009 to 2012. Based on the incredible numbers of transplantations annually, even though it is only a small fraction of the amount that is actually required, the field of tissue engineering will continue to motivate researchers worldwide to engage in and be part of the ever increasing health demands of humanity and to constantly improve and develop existing technologies even further.

Another report on the tissue engineering and stem cell technologies by Jaklenec et al. [25] shows that the orthopaedic industry also lead the field in terms of sales for commercial products or services in 2011, taking up 50 % of sales.

As the largest sector of commercial product sales in the tissue engineering and stem cell being taken up by the orthopaedic and wound healing industry, it makes sense to explore more options in construct technology used in this area. An approach to designing tissue-like substitutes pioneered by Langer and Vacanti [19] is the cell-seeded polymeric scaffolds. The challenge here is to design a scaffold that will allow cells to create their own matrix. The structure and morphology of the scaffold is what determines the 'environment' that the cells are living in. Hence, it is a great design challenge to create the perfect suitable environment to stimulate cell matrix deposition and subsequently proliferation, migration and differentiation. Research of suitable scaffolds is one thing; development of cost-effective manufacturing processes to produce these scaffolds is another aspect which many can often overlook. Ultimately, these engineered products will need to be conveniently and readily available to industry and clinicians. Hence, when designing tissue scaffolds, the ease of manufacture and increase of availability of manufactured devices are the important aspects to consider.

What is needed in the development of tissue scaffolds is an understanding of the environment in which specific cells are able to survive, and then recreate the environment using biocompatible and/or biodegradable materials for some specific applications. This has now drawn attention on finding the most suitable material for the specific requirements.

Different materials have different properties that may be better suited for use in specific applications. For example, the skin is a relatively soft tissue and therefore would not require a stiff material to support, whereas bone, on the other hand, needs to withstand much higher compressive stresses and would therefore require a much stiffer scaffold that is able to provide similar mechanical properties to the tissue which we are aiming to regenerate.

Each material would contain more favourable properties suited for specific applications compared to other materials. Since each tissue in the body has its particular role and therefore a specific set of favourable characteristics, it seems illogical to design just one super material that will cater to different purposes in tissue engineering [26]. By recognising that there are multiple aspects that need careful consideration to complete the process of designing a suitable scaffold, one should better understand the things required at each stage of research and development for delivering a product, thereby contributing to the field of tissue engineering. With this in mind, we will now focus on the topic of tissue scaffolds, as it is one of the major components required to regenerate a three-dimensional functional tissue.

7.2.1 Tissue Scaffold Materials

One of the major considerations of tissue scaffolds is the choice of material. The minimum requirement for any material is biocompatibility, both before and after degradation if the material is biodegradable. Biomaterials have recently had an impact on scaffold tissue engineering [27]. For example, by combining scaffolds with cells, the skin can be made and used for patients with burns. Various other applications involving a combination of polymers and cells such as corneas, cartilage, bone and liver have been in clinical trials [27, 28].

Many naturally occurring biological scaffolds that have great biocompatibility are available. However, one of the disadvantages of using these scaffolds is their poor mechanical properties. For this reason, synthetic polymers have emerged to solve this problem. Mechanical properties do play an important role especially for load-bearing applications. Polymers can be chosen based on the mechanical properties required. They can also be processed in a way that may increase their mechanical properties. In addition to the favourable mechanical properties of polymers, their processing ability is another advantageous aspect, hence drawing popular demands of polymeric research in the biomedical field.

The question is which manufacturing method or process will allow the chosen bulk material to be processed into a structure suitable for the biological application that the scaffold is intended to be used for. Depending on the end application of scaffolds, different mechanical and chemical properties may be required. With so many aspects to consider, designing a scaffold with optimal characteristics such as desired strength, degradation, porosity, structure and surface, shapes and sizes is more manufacturable when using polymers [29].

7.2.2 Scaffold Design

7.2.2.1 General Structural and Morphology Requirements

Scaffolds are typically three-dimensional structures that mimic and promote an in vivo environment to support and enhance cell viability for regenerating tissues [30]. Scaffolds need to mimic the architecture of the natural extracellular matrix (ECM) environment to assist the body to heal [31]. When designing scaffolds, the following requirements are often considered:

1. Biomaterials of choice should take into account the physical and chemical properties required for the end application [32].
2. Structure and morphology of biomaterials should mimic the host tissue's structure and biological functions [33].
3. Scaffold must be biocompatible, both before and after degradation [34].
4. Scaffold must possess a porous, interconnected architecture which enables transportation of cells and cell nutrients as well as provides mechanical support during neotissue regeneration [35].
5. Scaffold surface should support cell adhesion, proliferation, migration and differentiation [36].
6. Interconnected pores with appropriate pore size to allow cell infiltration and vascularisation [37, 38].
7. Controlled biodegradability to support growth of new tissue [39, 40].

Cells need a structure to provide mechanical support while regenerating tissue. In the natural human body, the extracellular matrix (ECM) is what provides this support. The goal to imitate nature means that the natural extracellular matrix that is a composite of proteins, glycoproteins and proteoglycans is an important model that researchers are mimicking when designing scaffolds [41]. Collagen is a protein and a major component in the ECM which arranges into a fibrous network with diameters ranging from 50 to 500 nm [42, 43]. With the fibrous property that collagen possesses, ECMs have a porous structure which allows the cells to proliferate and migrate into the ECM structure thereby differentiating into the required tissue. The architecture of ECM provides the environment that the cells grow in, which strongly influences the behaviour of the cells and the type of tissue it will differentiate into [15, 44, 45]. Generally, scaffolds must have a porous structure with sizes similar to that of the cells to be used for the particular application. By creating an imitation of the ECM using synthetic and artificial materials, limitations such as batch-to-batch variation and disease transmission associated with the materials from mammalian sources when using naturally derived biological materials can be avoided [27].

Porosity

Porosity is one of the most important aspects of a tissue scaffold as mentioned previously and is necessary in bone regeneration as shown by Kuboki et al. where direct osteogenesis occurred on the porous scaffolds [46]. Without these pores, the transport and migration of the cells and nutrients would simply be impossible and would not be assisting the cells to produce their own ECM. It is still a challenge to accurately characterise the porosity of scaffolds as there are many different types of nanostructures created from various manufacturing methods, which lead to very distinctive pore structures.

Different techniques to test and characterise the porosity may be required for different scaffolds fabricated. Some porosity characterisation techniques include mercury porosimetry [47], image analysis [48], gravimetry [49] and liquid displacement [50] methods based upon density and volume. Porosity looks at pore size, pore distribution and interconnectivity of the pores. All of these factors play their part in determining and characterising the porosity of the scaffold. In effect, a change in one could affect the other, so to study the porosity and alter the morphology and dimension, one needs to look at all the aspects that contribute to the porosity of the scaffold as a whole.

Pore Size

Pore size can directly influence the porosity of the scaffold, and in turn, affect the behaviour of the cells. Lower porosity stimulates osteogenesis, as the cell is forced to aggregate due to suppression of cell proliferation, while higher porosity allows the cells to infiltrate into the scaffold, creating more ingrowth [37]. There is, however, a compromise that has to be made for the latter, where mechanical properties maybe sacrificed if a higher porosity needs to be achieved. There is thus a limit to which this balance of porosity and functionality can be achieved, which also depends on the rate of tissue growth and the rate of scaffold degradation. It has also been shown in the previous work [51] that although specific surface area provided by scaffolds with small pores allows better initial cell adhesion, the effect of larger pores which provide better cell and nutrient infiltration is more important as it better promotes cell proliferation and migration into the centre of the scaffold.

Interconnectivity

Depending on the type of scaffold and how it is produced, the interconnectivity of the material used for producing the porous scaffold can differ vastly. MFC scaffolds are a great example of how the interconnectivity of the structure can vary just by controlling the type of polymer used. In the MFC scaffolds, the fibrils can create an interconnected 3D network or create a fibrillar network by controlling the type of polymers used. Electrospun scaffolds, on the other hand, have a different type of connectivity mechanism, where the individual fibres intertwine and tangle with each other to create the nanofibrillar network. This kind of structure will undoubtedly allow the scaffold to have more elongation as the fibres will be allowed to stretch alongside each other. With this type of structure, the compressive strength may not be as high as that for the MFC scaffolds, where the fibrils are interconnected, forming a more rigid structure. From these examples, it can be seen that although the same type of material is used to create nanofibrous networks, the mechanism for which the nanofibres integrate to form a network is an important factor in determining and characterising the properties of the scaffold.

7.2.2.2 Cell–Scaffold Interactions

The ECM provides a structure which holds cells together to form tissues and organs. It provides anchorage and mechanical support for the cells and is also responsible for controlling and regulation of cell adhesion, spreading, proliferation, migration, differentiation and apoptosis by mechanical and biochemical communications with cells [52]. This bidirectional communication between cell and ECM influences the behaviour of each other and is important in determining how much ECM is synthesised or degraded and subsequently the fate of the cell. The realm of tissue engineering involves the use of biomaterials that can mimic the natural ECM to facilitate in cell proliferation and differentiation for the specific tissue requirements.

Cell adhesion is one of the first interactions that occur between the cell and the ECM followed by cell spreading onto the ECM. Migration of the cells is also an important aspect, especially during development and regeneration of tissues. Cell migration is encouraged by breaking the existing cell from the ECM bonds and formation of new bonds in other areas of the ECM. Cell proliferation and differentiation are also affected by the cell–ECM interaction, even though the precise mechanism for how they cooperate is still unknown. The current understanding of the behaviour of cells, proteins and other key biological factors will no doubt facilitate the amalgamation of cells and constructs to form and recreate new tissues that can be incorporated into the body.

7.2.2.3 Design Requirements for Orthopaedic Applications

Osteoinduction is part of the normal bone healing and formation of bone process, and for it to take place, osteoconduction, the growth of bone on a surface, does not just depend on biological factors but also the response of cells to implants. Successful osseointegration is achieved when there is a stable bone to implant contact where the anchorage will remain over a long period [53], enough to support the formation of new tissue. The four main components required for successful bone regeneration includes osteogenic cells, osteoconductive scaffolds, growth factors and the mechanical environment, which is referred to as the diamond concept [54, 55]. This shows that the development of osteoconductive scaffolds is a significant aspect, in which the synthesis of suitable tissue scaffolds is essential to accomplishing the regeneration of bone tissue.

It is important to be able to control the pore sizes as studies have shown that pore sizes affects cell behaviour and bone formation [37, 56]. The minimum pore size required for bone scaffolds is considered to be 100 μm due to cell size, migration requirements and biotransport [37]. However, pore sizes larger than 300 μm have been recommended to support formation of capillaries and new bone. This is important as vascularised tissue such as bone requires pores that are large enough for cell migration as well as vascular ingrowth [57]. Pore sizes around 1000 μm favour osteoblast phenotype expression, and pores around 500 μm allow more bone formation, so Sicchieri [56] has concluded that the ideal scaffold for bone tissue engineering should present pores in both sizes within the same scaffold.

7.2.3 Fabrication of Scaffolds and Assessment of Cell Viability

7.2.3.1 Scaffold Fabrication

Some common techniques as shown in Fig. 7.3 used to fabricate scaffolds include electrospinning, gas foaming [58], rapid prototyping [59], thermally induced phase separation (TIPS) [60], NFC, freeze drying [61], self-assembly [62] and solvent casting/particulate leaching [63].

One of the most important features that a tissue scaffold must possess is porosity. There are many different techniques for synthesising porous structures such as electrospinning, thermally induced phase separation, solvent casting and particulate leaching, porogen leaching, gas foaming and emulsification/freeze drying. Currently, the two main fabrication techniques used in bone tissue engineering are electrospinning and thermally induced phase separation [57]. These will be discussed further later. Recently, there has been research on a novel manufacturing method which uses a basic manufacturing process, extrusion, and further post-processing to fabricate porous scaffolds which have the potential to be completely solvent-free. This technique will also be discussed in more detail later.

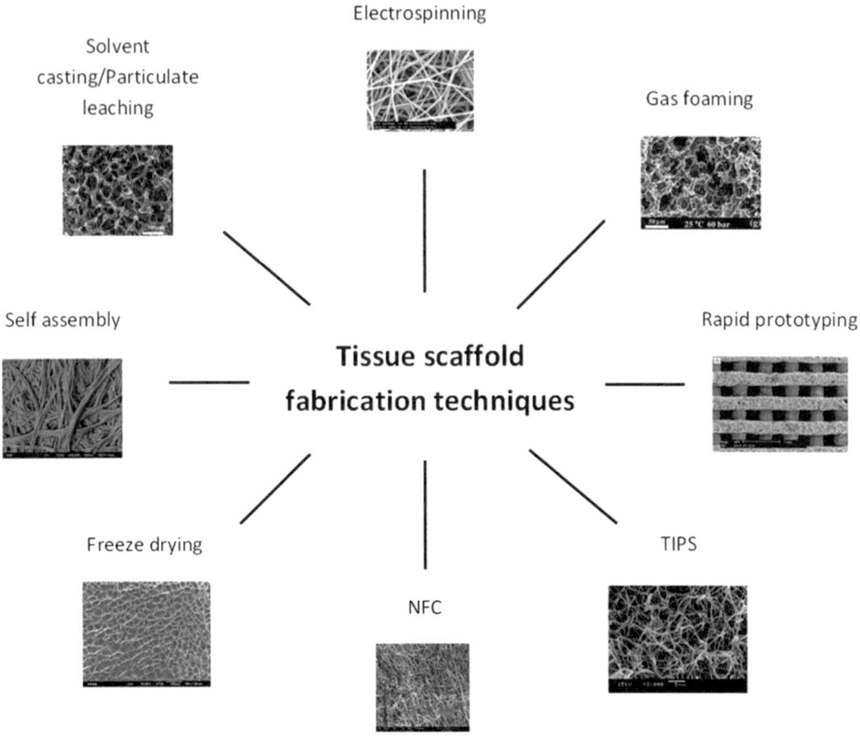

Fig. 7.3 Fabrication techniques for tissue scaffold: electrospinning, gas foaming (Reprinted from Ref. [58], Copyright 2011), rapid prototyping (Reprinted from Ref. [59], Copyright 2005), TIPS (Reprinted from Ref. [60], Copyright 2009), NFC, freeze drying (Reprinted from Ref. [61], Copyright 2009), self-assembly (Reprinted from Ref. [62], Copyright 2011), solvent casting or particulate leaching (Reprinted from Ref. [63], Copyright 2009). All with permission from Elsevier

Electrospinning

Electrospinning has received tremendous interest and been extensively researched in the past decade [64–66]. It has been recognised as a technique to produce nanofibres that have been widely studied for applications in the biomedical field [67–69]. Due to the similarity of the electrospun fibres to natural ECM, electrospinning has gained huge popularity, especially in the field of bone tissue engineering [70, 71]. Figure 7.4 shows a typical electrospun network which is composed of nanofibres overlapping and intertwined to form a fibrillar network with a very porous structure. A major drawback of electrospinning is the use of organic solvents, most of which are toxic to cells. A study by Lederer [72] showed that although the organic solvent content decreases after vacuum treatment of fibrillar scaffolds, there may still be traces that are undetectable, enough to negatively affect cell growth on the scaffolds. For this reason, there is a need for the scaffolds to be produced completely free of organic solvents.

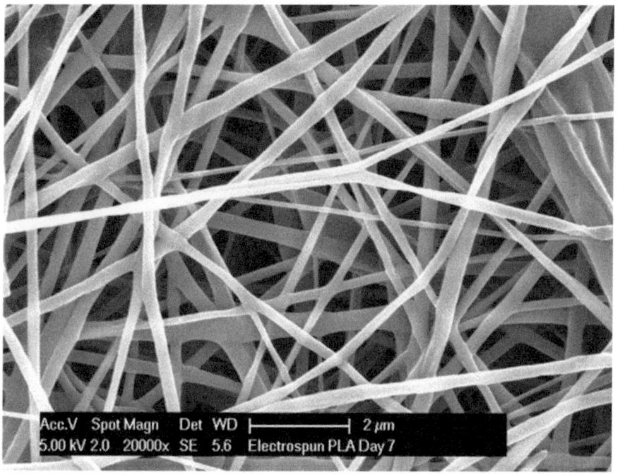

Fig. 7.4 Electrospun PLA scaffold

Thermally Induced Phase Separation (TIPS)

The TIPS technique produces a 3D nanofibrous scaffold by taking advantage of the thermodynamic instability of polymer solutions under certain conditions [33]. As described by Holzwarth [57], the TIPS process involves five steps: polymer dissolution, phase separation and gelatin, solvent extraction, freezing and freeze drying. When phase separation occurs, a polymer-rich phase with a higher concentration of polymer and a polymer lean phase with a lower concentration of polymer are formed. When the solvent is extracted and removed, the polymer-rich phase solidifies; different morphologies will form depending on the conditions of the system [33, 73]. Nanofibrous, synthetic biodegradable scaffolds have been fabricated using this method for use in tissue scaffold applications [74].

Nanofibrillar Composite Technique (NFC)

The nanofibrillar composite (NFC) technique utilises common engineering and commodity polymers to create nanofibrils of high strength and stiffness dispersed in an isotropic matrix. This technique is an emerging concept that employs melt blending of polymers to create an even distribution of insitu reinforcing nanofibrils through simple extrusion, drawing and post-processing [75, 76]. The NFC manufacturing method uses two thermodynamically immiscible polymers to create a fibrillar composite network. The polymers must have sufficient drawability to allow the formation of reinforcing fibrils and must be processed at a single temperature without the degradation of either polymer [75, 76]. One of the main advantages of this technique is that there is the opportunity for creating scaffolds which are completely free of organic solvents, by suitably selecting the isotropic matrix such that only water is required in the matrix removal process. Figure 7.5

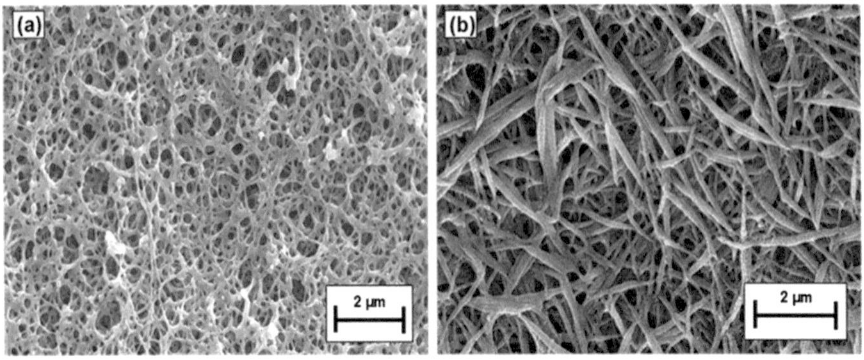

Fig. 7.5 Scaffolds manufactured using the NFC concept produced from (**a**) PLA and (**b**) PETG

shows the typical morphology of scaffolds manufactured using the MFC technique from (a) PLA and (b) PETG.

Natural and synthetic polymers have the advantages of processability, decent mechanical properties, immunological stability, manufacturability and the ease of being able to design the shape and architectures for accommodating the host tissues requirements. Where biodegradability is required, the type of polymer used can be chosen to fit the required degradation rate. This can be attributed to the large and diverse polymeric materials that have been available. Not only are they widely available, they are also simple to modify and can also be processed using a large variety of manufacturing techniques that are currently very well known and have been used for many different polymer processing. Some of the most common industrial manufacturing processes include injection moulding, blow moulding and extrusion.

Using extrusion as the main manufacturing process, polymers can be processed to produce nanoscale architectures. With the formation of nanofibres and nanopores, one of the applications which would welcome these nano-features is in the biomedical field. Tissue scaffolds require that the matrix should be highly porous to enable the cells to migrate and infiltrate the structure, transport of cell nutrients and removal of waste products and at the same time to maintain the overall mechanical properties of the synthetic ECM matrix to support cell growth.

The process of extrusion starts off with blending a mixture of polymer pellets which are thermodynamically immiscible so that the polymers will stay separate and preserve their individual properties. The polymers are melted inside a barrel which has either a single or twin screw to further blend the melted polymers. Once the blended polymers leave the die, the blended yarn is drawn by pulling and elongating the extrudate onto a winding drum which continuously rotates and pulls on the blended yarn. The final product produced from this extrusion process is a yarn of thread-like blended polymer composite.

To achieve nanoporous networks using extrusion as the main manufacturing process requires various steps in the post-extrusion section. Once a yarn of blended polymer composite is produced from the extrusion process, this yarn is transferred to a frame which is in the shape of interest, in this case, a rectangular stainless steel frame. The transfer of the yarn can be done in various ways such as winding manually onto the frame or by using winders or lathes.

To create the porous structure that is required in tissue scaffolds, one of the components of the composite blend will need to be removed. When one component of the composite blend is removed, the remaining structure will be composed of the matrix that was not removed and the porous holes that were once filled up by the polymer that has been removed. There can be a wide variety of polymer blends which can be chosen depending on the type of properties needed. When a polymer which is water soluble is chosen as the polymer that will be removed to form the porosity of the network, then only water is required in the removal process.

7.2.3.2 Assessment of Cell Viability

To assess the cytocompatibility of cells on the scaffold material produced, mouse osteoblasts (bone-forming cells) were used in cell culture techniques to grow the cells on the materials over a period of time. Tenocytes were also used to try different cell types on the same scaffolds. Qualitative analysis was achieved by conducting live/dead staining of cells that have grown on the scaffold up to a total of 20 days and 14 days for osteoblasts and tenocytes, respectively.

One of the most important steps in the cell culture is sterilisation. A common problem with polymers is their sensitivity to heat. The method of sterilisation in most labs is autoclaving which uses pressurised steam to heat the material being sterilised. This is obviously a concern for polymers as the temperature at which lab equipment are sterilised at is typically 121 °C for 15–20 min depending on the size of the load. Polymers are sensitive to heat and typically have low glass transition temperatures. PLLA which is used in the NFC manufacturing process has a glass transition temperature of 55–60 °C. Glass transition temperatures for polyethylene terephthalate and polyvinyl alcohol are 70 °C and 85 °C, respectively. All polymers used in this project have glass transition temperatures below 100 °C.

For the purpose of cell culture, ethanol has been chosen to sterilise the materials which will be used to assess cell growth. Although ethanol technically does not sterilise, it does disinfect by killing microbial cells, but has no effect on spores. Ethanol works by denaturing proteins through a process that requires water; hence, ethanol must be diluted to 60–90 % to work effectively in disinfection of the materials. The manufactured NFC scaffolds were soaked in 70 % ethanol for a minimum of 30 min and left to dry at room temperature under sterile conditions.

UV radiation has damaging effects on cells and also makes a great tool for sterilisation. To further ensure the materials are sterile, they were exposed to UV radiation for 30 min each side. UV radiation was chosen partly due to its convenience and safety of use as it does not have high penetration so is safe to use in small areas such as laminar flow hoods.

In preparation for seeding cells onto the sterilised scaffolds, the materials were soaked overnight in the culture media used for maintenance of the cells. Tenocytes

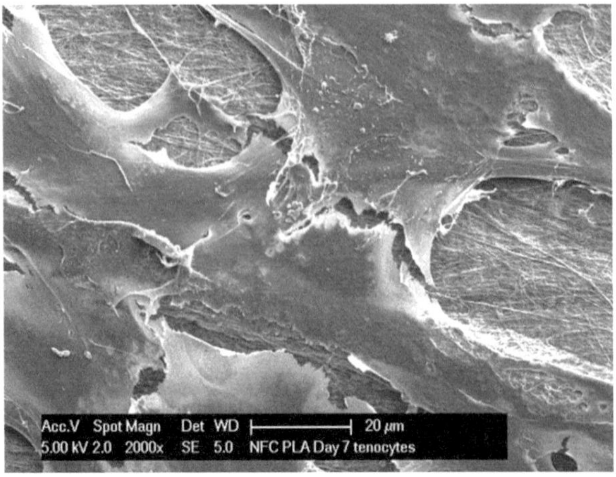

Fig. 7.6 Tenocytes grown for 7 days on PLA scaffold fabricated using the NFC technique

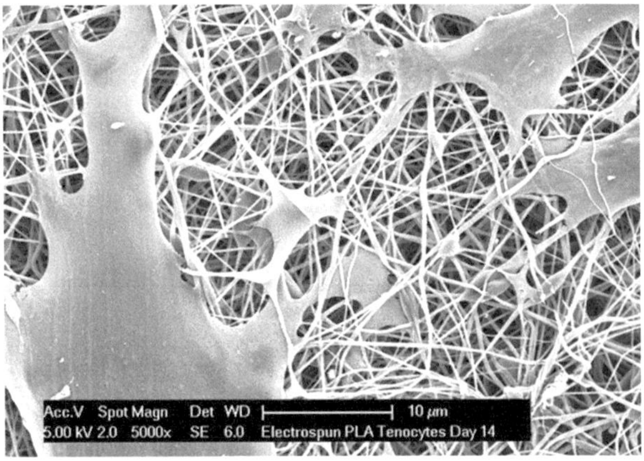

Fig. 7.7 Tenocytes grown on the electrospun scaffold for 14 days

were used to study the cytocompatability on the scaffolds. Figure 7.6 shows the tenocytes have spread across the surface of the PLA scaffold after 7 days of cell culture. The limited penetration of cells into the scaffold can be improved by increasing the porosity of the scaffold. Cell attachment on the surface of the scaffold demonstrates that the NFC fabrication technique has potential to produce scaffolds which can be completely solvent-free.

Figure 7.7 illustrates how the tenocytes have migrated beneath the top surface of the electrospun network on day 14 of cell culture. This shows the importance of having a porous interconnected structure, creating a three-dimensional space that allows cells to embed themselves within the scaffold. Traditional cell culture practice often uses 2D cell culture plates to study cells. As tissues are 3D structures, the significance of 3D cell culture studies have become paramount in mimicking the natural environment of host cells more closely. Being able to alter the pore size and porosity of the scaffold through controlling manufacturing process is an important step in mimicking the ECM of the natural host tissue.

7.2.4 Other Porous Scaffolds and Surface Modification Methods

Several porous scaffolds using polymeric materials such as PLGA and PLLA and collagen have been developed and studied by the researchers from the National Institute for Materials Science (NIMS). They have developed funnel-like scaffolds using ice particulates, collagen scaffolds with micro-patterned biological molecules, ECM scaffolds derived from MSCs (chondrocytes and fibroblasts) and hybrid porous scaffolds (synthetic and natural). The surface of scaffolds can be modified to promote cell growth and can be designed to accommodate particular desired characteristics. One example of surface modification of scaffolds can be referred to the work of Lu et al. [77], where funnel-like PLGA–collagen hybrid scaffolds have demonstrated to facilitate cell seeding and homogeneous cell distribution, ECM production and chondrogenesis. These funnel-like collagen sponges were produced by using embossing ice particulates as a template. A diverse range of surface patterns can be formed on the scaffold surfaces by creating and adjusting the pattern of the ice particulates formed.

Cell functions such as angiogenesis have been manipulated by incorporating biological micro-patterned surfaces onto scaffolds. Guided blood vessel formation was achieved by preparing collagen sponges with micro-patterned vascular endothelial growth factor (VEGF). VEGF was micro-patterned in the 3D collagen sponges using micro-patterned collagen/VEGF ice lines, prepared by a dispersing machine [78]. VEGF–micro-patterned collagen sponges have demonstrated blood vessel regeneration after 6 weeks of implantation [78].

Porous ECM scaffolds have also been derived from mesenchymal stem cells (MSCs), chondrocytes and fibroblasts [81, 80]. Cells were initially cultured on poly (lactic-co-glycolic acid) (PLGA) templates until ECM was generated by the cells. The construct was then decellularised and the PLGA mesh was removed, leaving an ECM scaffold (Fig. 7.8). Using this method, three types of ECM scaffolds were produced using MSCs, chondrocytes and fibroblasts. MSCs and fibroblasts were cultured in these cell-derived ECM scaffolds to examine their potential as scaffolds for cartilage and skin tissue engineering. The MSC- and chondrocyte-derived ECM scaffolds supported cell adhesion, promoted cell proliferation and the production of ECM and demonstrated stronger stimulatory effects on the chondrogenesis of MSC. The fibroblast-derived ECM scaffolds were shown to help with fibroblast proliferation and production of ECM.

Hybrid scaffolds have also been developed to create an improved structure that combines the superior qualities of both scaffold materials. He et al. [81] developed a hybrid poly(L-lactic acid) (PLLA)-collagen hybrid sponge in the shape of a cup

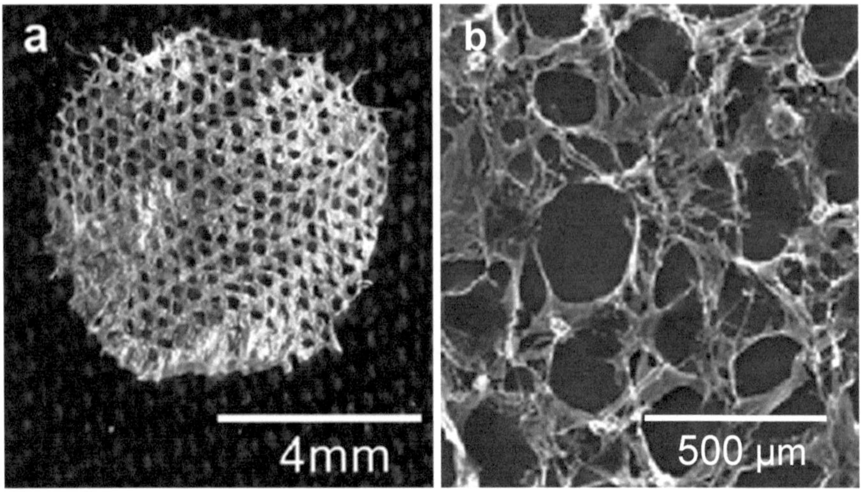

Fig. 7.8 Gross appearance of ECM scaffolds derived from MSCs (**a**) and SEM image of the scaffold (**b**). Reprinted from Ref. [80], Copyright 2010, with permission from Elsevier

with the PLLA sponge enclosing a collagen sponge in the centre. The cup-shaped PLLA sponge skeleton provided the hybrid sponge with high mechanical strength, high porosity and high cell retention and protection against cell leakage during cell seeding, while the collagen sponge in the centre contributed to high porosity and facilitated cell adhesion and distribution. Cartilage-like tissue has also been shown to form on the hybrid sponge when cultured with chondrocytes.

Another example of a hybrid scaffold was developed by Dai et al. [82], where the hybrid structure of the 3D scaffold combined the advantages of type I collagen and PLGA-knitted mesh, as shown in Fig. 7.9. The mesh provided the skeleton, while the collagen micro-sponges facilitated cell seeding and tissue formation. Bovine chondrocytes were cultured on these scaffolds and transplanted into mice for up to 8 weeks. The transplants showed homogeneous cell distribution, natural chondrocyte morphology and abundant cartilaginous ECM deposition. The mechanical strength of the engineered cartilage when compared to native articular cartilage reached up to at least 49 % in Young's modulus and 62 % in stiffness.

From these examples, it can be seen that not only is there a wide and varied choice of materials and processing methods available, but also there are many more possibilities by creating different combinations using different materials and processing methods available. There is also the biological aspect that will create even more possibilities, which needs to be taken into account. The inclusion of the biological aspects into the scaffolds, such as bioactive growth factors, will also open up another area to study which includes a large variety of incorporation methods into the scaffolds.

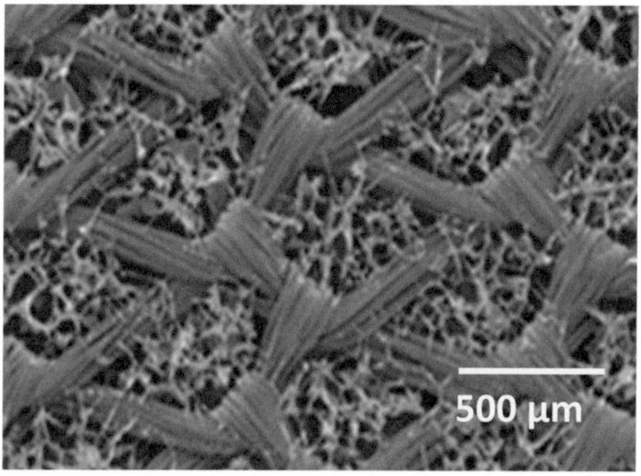

Fig. 7.9 Hybrid PLGA and type I collagen scaffold (Reprinted from Ref. [82], Copyright 2009, with permission from Elsevier)

7.2.5 Commercial and Industry Perspective

The interdisciplinary nature of the tissue engineering is one of the most exciting research areas that have led to rapid advancements as innovations in the related fields have emerged and expanded, while obstacles are being overcome. Tissue scaffold materials and fabrication techniques play a crucial role where significant progress has been achieved to provide structural support for successful tissue regeneration. Nature has provided brilliant examples to mimic, and together with technology, the society is on its way to recreating tissues and organs, with the hope of improving the quality of human lives.

It is no surprise that one of the fastest growing markets for tissue engineering and regenerative medicine products is to improve human health and longevity. To support this, the market has been creating new products based on biomaterial technologies, including both synthetic and naturally derived materials. Other technologies that have developed include genetically engineered materials, stem cell technology and cell culture technology, enabling development of even more innovative devices to enhance this interdisciplinary field of tissue engineering.

The end goal for research and development of tissue scaffolds is to improve the quality of life of humans in need of a tissue or organ replacement. One of the main methods in achieving this which has been discussed in this chapter involves creating scaffolds which mimic the ECM to provide structural support for cells to produce the required tissue naturally. For all the extensive research going on to be fully utilised, there must be a product that is produced for the patient to be able to receive the benefits that the innovations of science and engineering has created. There are numerous companies working to translate and commercialise the research, to create a product or service that can be of use for society. Commercial polymeric scaffolds that are available is summarised in Table 7.2, which has been extracted from [83].

Table 7.2 Commercial polymeric scaffolds extracted from Ref. [83]

Polymer	Biomedical application	Trade name
PGA	First biodegradable synthetic suture in 1969	DEXON
	Bone internal fixation devices	Biofix
PLLA	Orthopaedic fixation devices	Bio-Anchor, Meniscal Stinger
		The Clearfix Meniscal Dart
	High-strength fibres (FDA approved in 1971)	DEXON
	Ligament replacement of augmentation devices	Dacron
	Blood vessel conduits	
	Human immunodeficiency virus or correction of facial fat loss	
PLDLA	Bioresorbable implant material	Resomer
PLGA	Multifilament suture	Vicryl, Vicryl Rapide and CRVL
	Skin graft	Vicryl Mesh
PLGA collagen	Tissue regeneration membrane	Cytoplast Resorb
PLGA	Drug delivery vehicle	Lupron Depot
	First commercially developed monofilament suture (1980)	PDS
PDA	Orthopaedic applications	Pins
PCL	Long-term contraceptive device	Capronor
PDLLA-CL	Monofilament suture	MONOCRYL
PGCL, PLCL, PETG	Drug delivery	SynBioSys
PCLTMC &PGCL	Flexible suture materials	Maxon
	Orthopaedic tacks and screws	Acufex
PHBHV	Bone pins, plates, drug delivery	
PEU	Tissue engineering application	DegraPol
LDI-based PU	Orthopaedic applications and bone cement	Polynova
PEAs	Site-specific delivery of small hydrophobic drugs & peptides	CAMEO
POE	Tissue adhesives	Dermabond
	Bilayer skin substitute	INTEGRA Dermal
		Regeneration Template
	Wound dressings	Biobrane and AlloDerm
Collagen	Bioengineered skin equivalents	TransCyte
HA	Wound dressing application	HYAFF
	Synthetic bone graft	Ossigel
HMW viscous HA	Corneal transplantation and glaucoma surgery	Amvisc and Amvisc Plus
Viscous HA	Relieve pain and improve joint mobility for osteoarthritis	Synvisc, Orthovisc

With the promising products that are currently in use on the market as well as many other companies investing in this area of research [25], the growth of the tissue engineering field will continue to flourish in the hopes of creating even more life-saving technologies.

7.2.6 Summary

The interdisciplinary nature of the tissue engineering is one of the most exciting research areas that have led to rapid advancements as innovations in the related fields have emerged and expanded, while obstacles are being overcome. Tissue scaffold materials and fabrication techniques play a crucial role where significant progress has been achieved to provide structural support for successful tissue regeneration. Nature has provided brilliant examples for us to mimic, and together with technology, we are on the way to recreating tissues and organs, with the hope of improving the quality of lives for humans.

7.3 Stents

The human body is an extraordinarily complex system comprised of many parts and systems all working in unison to maintain and sustain health. Being mostly fluid, it is not surprising that there are various tubes within the body with functions ranging from delivery of nutrients to transmission of chemical signals and removal of metabolic waste. Sometimes these vessels may become compromised, thus losing their ability to perform their roles. In such cases, medical intervention can help to restore function by providing the vessels or tubes with support via the use of stents. In general, a stent is *a splint placed temporarily inside a duct, canal or blood vessel to aid healing or relieve an obstruction*, according to the Oxford English Dictionary [84]. The practice of implanting or deploying a stent into a vessel or tube is referred to as ‘stenting’.

Coronary arteries are the vessels commonly treated by stenting because of the prevalence of coronary artery disease (CAD). CAD has become very widespread within developed regions of the world and is the leading cause of death in the US and Europe [21]. From here onwards, ‘stents’ and ‘stenting’ refer to coronary artery stents and the implantation of stents into coronary arteries, respectively. CAD is basically the build-up of plaque within the coronary arteries, as shown in Fig. 7.10. Excessive plaque build-up leads to obstruction of flow through the vessel, in which case the vessel must be treated to restore normal flow.

CAD may be treated in several ways, namely bypass surgery, angioplasty or stenting. Bypass surgery was first introduced in 1968, before angioplasty and stenting were developed [4]. During bypass surgery, a section of healthy artery is extracted from one of the legs of the patient and is used to bypass the blocked

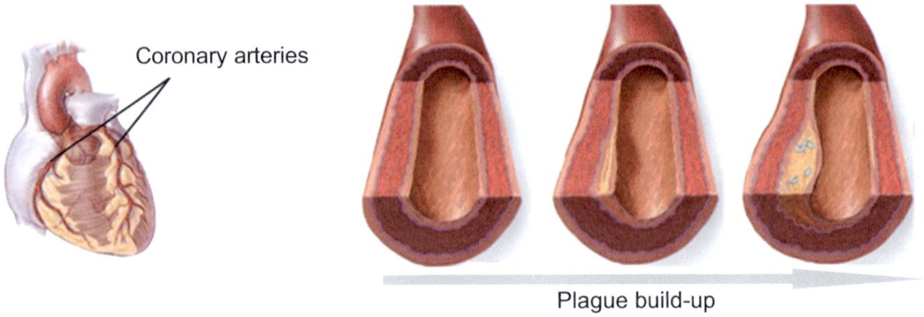

Fig. 7.10 Position of coronary arteries (*left*) and progression of plaque build-up within a coronary artery (*right*). Images adapted from www.medmovies.com

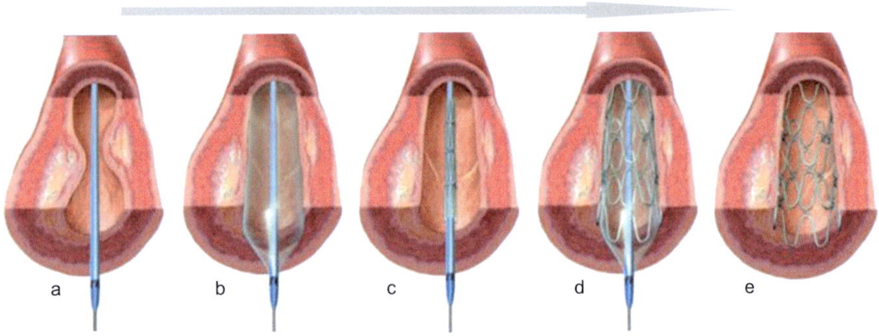

Fig. 7.11 Stenting procedure: (**a**) catheter insertion, (**b**) balloon expansion, (**c**) insertion of catheter with stent mounted on the end after removal of the balloon catheter, (**d**) stent deployment, (**e**) stented vessel. Images adapted from www.medmovies.com

section of a coronary artery, hence named bypass surgery (also known as coronary artery bypass grafting, CABG). In 1977, percutaneous transluminal coronary angioplasty (PTCA) was introduced. PTCA is a less invasive technique than CABG and begins with insertion of a catheter into the target vessel. Once the catheter is in position, a balloon on the end of it is expanded to open the blockage caused by the plaque (illustrated by a–b of Fig. 7.11), then the balloon is deflated and the catheter is removed. Unfortunately, the rate of restenosis (re-narrowing of the vessel) after PTCA is high; thus, stenting of coronary arteries after PTCA was introduced. The use of stenting began in 1986, and the procedure begins with PTCA, and then a second catheter, with a stent mounted over the end, is inserted into the vessel. Once the end of the catheter is located at the target region, the stent is deployed by balloon expansion, as shown in c–d of Fig. 7.11. The balloon is then deflated and the catheter is removed, leaving the stent in place to provide support to the vessel (Fig. 7.11e).

7.3.1 Introduction to Coronary Stents

7.3.1.1 Bare Metal Stents

The first stents were relatively simple in nature when compared with stents of today and were primarily made of medical-grade stainless steel [85] (316 L stainless steel) and less commonly of cobalt–chromium or nickel–titanium alloys. Stents of this nature fit into the category of 'bare metal stents' (BMSs). Although stainless steel has excellent mechanical properties, it contains small amounts of nickel, molybdenum and manganese to which some people are allergic [86], thus heightening the risk of restenosis (i.e. re-narrowing of the vessel) in some patients [87]. Restenosis occurs via an inflammatory reaction at the stented site of the vessel which causes smooth muscle cells to migrate to the surface of the inner wall of the vessel and proliferate. This proliferation (i.e. multiplication and spreading) of the cells is what causes the vessel to re-narrow [88]. Furthermore, blood platelets (also known as thrombocytes) have a tendency to stick to BMSs which can cause a clot, or thrombus, to form at the stented site, a phenomenon called thrombosis. This is extremely dangerous since a thrombus may break away from the stent and cause a heart attack [89, 90]. Stent thrombosis occurring soon (within 30 days) after implantation is common in the case of BMSs, although the introduction of anti-platelet therapy for patients who received BMS implantations greatly reduced occurrence rates [90].

7.3.1.2 Coated Metal Stents

Due to the common occurrence of restenosis and thrombosis after BMS implantation [91], a need was seen to alter the surface characteristics of BMSs without changing their mechanical properties, since it seemed that restenosis resulted mainly from the body's chemical interaction with BMSs. Experimentation with coating BMSs began, and a new category of stents was formed called 'coated metal stents' (CMSs). Several different coatings have been applied to stents, including platinum, carbon, gold, silicon carbide, phosphorylcholine, polymers and titanium–nitride–oxide [89, 92], in an attempt to lower the restenosis and thrombosis rates. The results of coating stents were mixed, and in some cases, such as in the case of gold-coated stents, restenosis rates were even higher than those of uncoated stents [93].

7.3.1.3 Drug-Eluting Stents

The first stent coatings were passive, and the train of thought was to make stents as benign and stable as possible to prevent undesirable responses within patents' vessels. Coated stents eventually evolved by way of a new train of thought: what if the coating could play an active role in preventing the body's responses responsible for complications after stent implantation? Thus this strategy began the era of drug-eluting stents (DESs), which are metal stents loaded with drugs which are gradually released to provide local treatment to prevent restenosis. DESs are a significant improvement over BMSs and CMSs, but a problem which persists is the presence of a permanent, foreign object in the body. Furthermore, studies on the outcomes of treatment with DESs have revealed that late stent thrombosis rates are sometimes even higher than those of BMSs [94], and the cause may be that endothelialisation of the stent struts is delayed by drug elution [95].

7.3.1.4 Recap and the Next Phase of Stent Evolution: Biodegradable Stents

Taking a step back and considering the challenges faced by stent technology throughout its evolution from BMSs to DESs, it is noted that the initial complications faced after BMS implantation were acute, occurring soon after implantation, and were addressed as stents evolved to DESs. However, complications still persist but tend to occur later after implantation, for example, late stent thrombosis. Naturally, it is expected that the next evolutionary step is able to address this. It is recognised that stented vessels need support for only up to 6 months while they heal [96], so development of stents which degrade and essentially disappear after their jobs are done began; these stents are known as biodegradable or bioabsorbable stents. Biodegradable stents offer the advantage of completely disappearing after their service, making any future intervention less complicated. Furthermore, there is no need for rest-of-life pharmaceutical treatment as is the case for permanent stents in which case aspirin is taken indefinitely after treatment [93, 97].

Figure 7.12 shows a summary of the evolution of CAD treatment and highlights the key issues addressed and remaining with each evolutionary step. Before biodegradable stent development is discussed from a materials perspective, let us lay the foundation for this by looking at stents from an engineering point of view.

7.3.2 Stents: An Engineering Point of View

In order to better understand the challenges of biodegradable stent development, it is useful to first think about what a stent must endure during its lifetime.

7.3.2.1 Stent Deployment: The Need for Ductility

As a starting point to describe what is required of stent materials, imagine that a stent has been navigated to the target site of a vessel needing support. Now, the stent is deployed via balloon expansion in which the stent is mounted is inflated, as shown in Fig. 7.13a, b. Keep in mind that the stent is expanded to a diameter greater than the desired final diameter. Once expansion of the stent is complete, the balloon

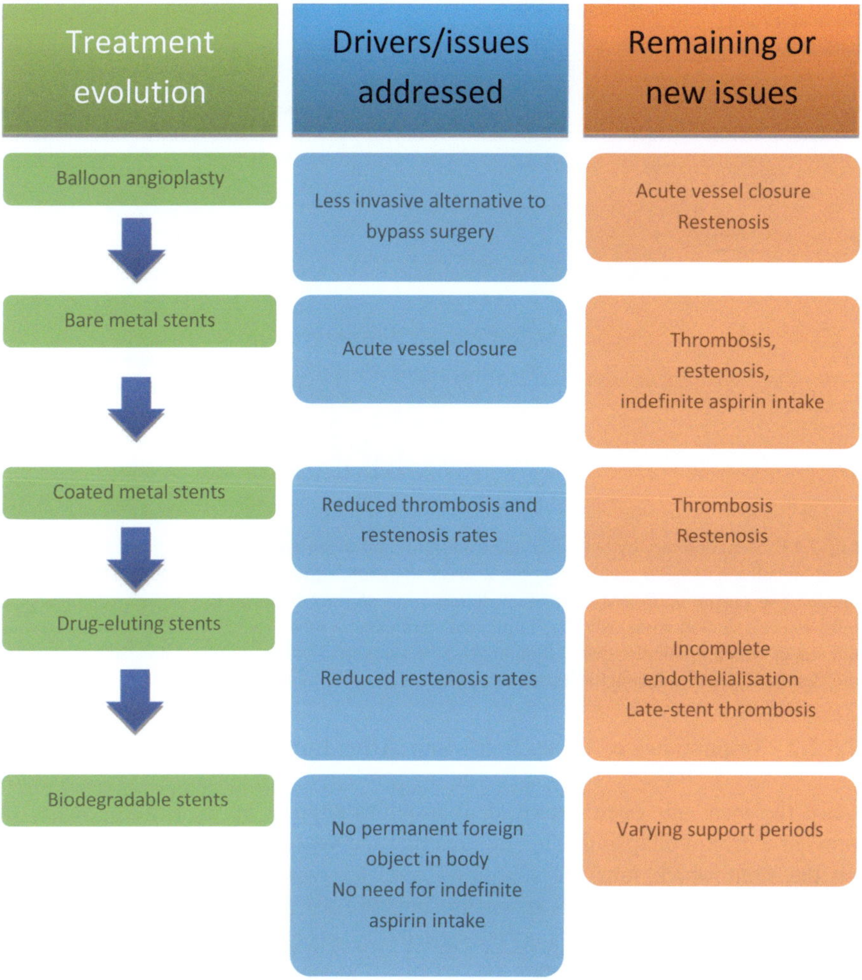

Fig. 7.12 The evolution of stents and the issues addressed with each step in progress as well as issues which remained or new issues which arose

is deflated and withdrawn as shown in Fig. 7.13c. While the balloon is deflated, the stent diameter reduces somewhat because the elastic strains within the stent material are recovered, which is why the stent had to be expanded beyond the desired final diameter. Once the balloon has been deflated and withdrawn, the stent remains in place to support the vessel, Fig. 7.13d.

From a material point of view, the important fact to note is that the stent has to undergo permanent deformation during the deployment process. This permanent deformation leads to the first of many material requirements: ductility. Ductile materials can be subjected to large strains before breaking, while brittle materials fracture instead of deforming and stretching.

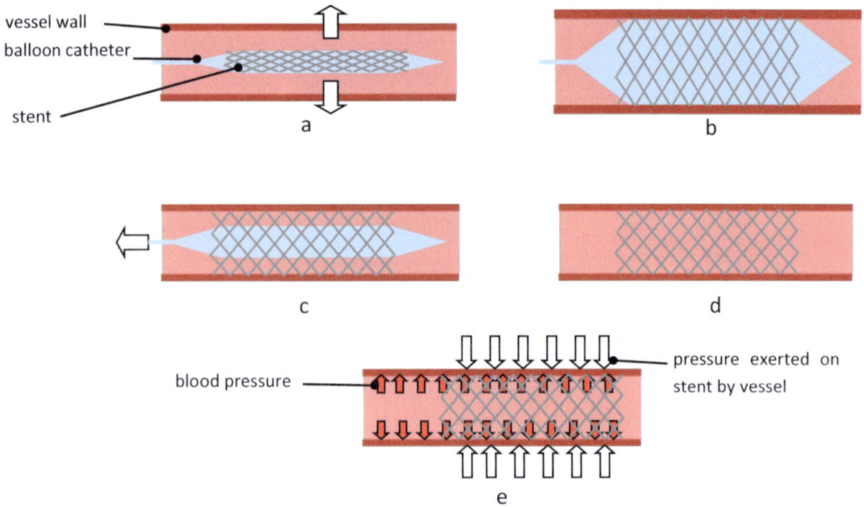

Fig. 7.13 Stent delivery by balloon expansion (**a**–**d**) and schematic of stent loading conditions (**e**). Stent on balloon catheter reaches target site and expansion begins (**a**), stent expanded beyond final diameter to ensure sufficient permanent deformation of stent material (**b**), balloon deflated and removed (**c**), stented vessel (**d**). The implanted stent experiences a radial crushing load exerted by the vessel which fluctuates since blood pressure in the vessel (which opposes pressure exerted by the vessel) fluctuates during each cardiac cycle

7.3.2.2 Importance of Creep Behaviour After Implantation

Once the stent has been deployed, it provides support to the healing vessel to prevent it from collapsing. This implies that the vessel exerts an inward pressure on the stent which must be supported until the vessel has healed sufficiently, meaning that the stent needs to endure pressure for an extended period of time. With long-term loading comes the possibility of creep, which is the gradual deformation of a material under load even if the stresses caused by this load are well below the maximum load the material can handle. In the case of a stent, creep would cause a gradual collapse, resulting in re-narrowing of the vessel. Creep is an especially important consideration for biodegradable stents for two main reasons, the first being that the majority of biodegradable stents are made of thermoplastic polymers which are prone to creep deformation and the second being the effect of degradation on material performance.

It is fairly challenging to design a stent with creep because of the numerous variables involved. For example, if a stent collapses slightly through creep deformation and the vessel experiences a corresponding narrowing, the pressure exerted on the stent decreases because the vessel is now less 'stretched' than it was immediately after stent implantation. Therefore the creep rate would slow down since the lower the stresses in a material, the lower the creep rate.

Furthermore, as a vessel heals, we should expect that the pressure it exerts on a stent decreases as it gradually regains the ability to support itself. This implies that

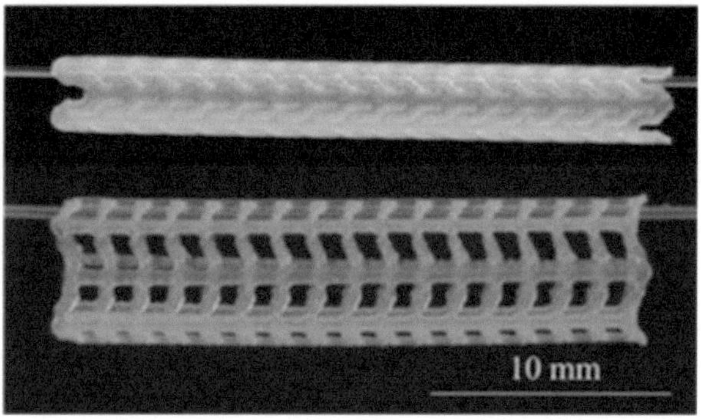

Fig. 7.14 A stent prototype made of a PLLA/P4HB blend. The stent is shown before (*top*) and after (*bottom*) balloon expansion [98]. The stent diameter remains enlarged because of permanent deformation of the PLLA/P4HB during balloon expansion

resistance to creep deformation is most critical in the early stages after stent implantation, but there seems to be a gap in the knowledge of the healing profile of a stented vessel, from an engineering point of view at least (Fig. 7.14).

7.3.2.3 Material Fatigue Considerations

With every heartbeat, blood pressure in coronary arteries fluctuates [99], and some branches also experience significant curvature changes as they bend and unbend during the cardiac cycle [100]. Blood pressure fluctuations result in subsequent vessel diameter fluctuations which would, in turn, cause the pressure exerted on an implanted stent to fluctuate. Furthermore, a stent implanted in a region where the vessel's curvature changes significantly would be forced to bend and unbend with each heartbeat. Both of these phenomena result in the presence of cyclic stresses in the stent, which raises the concern of fatigue failure. In the case of biodegradable stents, fatigue failure is destined to occur at some point when the stent material integrity has diminished enough, but care must be taken to prevent premature fatigue failures.

7.3.2.4 Material Degradation: A Critical Variable

The material considerations discussed so far apply to both permanent stents and biodegradable stents, but a consideration unique to biodegradable stents is the effect of degradation on the mechanical characteristics of the material. In order to design a biodegradable stent, we first need to understand how the properties of a potential stent material will change with time as it degrades. It is a complex process because there is still much to be learned about the rate at which support required by a healing vessel decreases, whether or not it is linear and how much it varies from patient to patient depending on age, medical conditions, etc. Perhaps when there is more knowledge in this area, biodegradable stents could be tailored to meet the needs of specific patients.

7.3.2.5 Engineering Solutions vs. Clinical Implications

At first glance, some of the challenges of stent design seem trivial to solve in engineering, but these trivial solutions may have negative clinical implications. For example, making stent struts thicker and wider enhances the support provided to the vessel but results in more restriction of blood flow as well as increased risk of small side branches of the vessel being blocked. Furthermore, endothelialisation would be more difficult in the case of thicker struts. To enhance stent performance while minimising negative impacts on clinical outcomes, stent materials must be developed to have desirable mechanical properties. The next section will outline progress of biodegradable stent material development and compare the various materials which have been on, or are currently under, investigation for biodegradable stents.

7.3.3 Materials Under Investigation for Biodegradable Stents

The engineering point of view provides insights into the mechanical requirements of biodegradable stent materials, and some of the medical requirements were discussed under stent evolution. With these in mind, the challenge of developing materials with suitable properties for the application may be getting clearer. Table 7.3 summarises some of the requirements of stents and stent materials.

Because of the array of demands of biodegradable stent materials, it is not surprising that researchers are experimenting with a wide range of materials with a broad spectrum of properties. To illustrate this, a selection of biodegradable stents is shown in Table 7.4. Note that these stents in Table 7.4 have been through clinical trials. The radial support period of these stents varies from days (in the case of a magnesium stent) through to 6 months for a poly(L-lactic acid) (PLLA) stent.

As an example of the pros and cons of different materials, the magnesium and polymer stents can be compared further. The magnesium stent has the distinct

Table 7.3 Stent and stent material requirements

Requirement	References
Biocompatibility of stent material and its degradation products	[101–103]
Low thrombogenicity to prevent stent thrombosis	[85]
The material must retain enough strength for the stent to provide sufficient support for 6 months	[103–105]
Fragments of material must not be released into the bloodstream during degradation	[103]
Radio-opaque for tracking during delivery	[85,103]
Stent must be able to withstand a minimum crush pressure of 100 kPa	[103]
The material must have sufficient flexibility to withstand being bent to get through tortuous vessels during delivery	[85,101]
The material must deform plastically upon balloon expansion to avoid recoil	[103]

Table 7.4 Comparison of biodegradable stents [104]

Stent	Material	Drug eluting?	Drug eluted	Radial support period	Absorption time
Igaki-Tamai	PLLA	No	–	6 months	2 years
BVS	PLLA	Yes	Everolimus	Cohort A – weeks	2 years
				Cohort B – 3 months	
REVA	Tyrosine-derived polycarbonate	No	–	3–6 months	2 years
Magnesium stent	Magnesium alloy	No	–	Days or weeks	4 months
BTI	Salicylate linker	Yes	Sirolimus and salicylic acid	3 months	6 months

disadvantage of a short period of vessel support because it degrades fairly quickly. However, an advantage over the polymeric stents is that magnesium has far superior elastic modulus, so it can be designed to have thinner, narrower struts than polymeric stents while still offering good vessel support. Another advantage of magnesium is the short time for total absorption – just 4 months versus 2 years for a PLLA stent – but, again, this comes at the cost of a short vessel support period.

Magnesium is not the only metal which has been considered. Iron stents have been under investigation too. Iron takes longer to degrade in the body than magnesium, and it has superior mechanical properties to polymers, but it seems that researchers have steered away from it because of toxicity concerns [106].

7.3.3.1 Prominence of PLLA

PLLA is a very prominent material in biodegradable stent material research, both in the case of medical device companies and university research groups. Abbott Vascular (USA), Igaki Medical Planning Company (Japan), Elixir Medical Corporation (USA), ART (France) and possibly others have developed PLLA-based stents, some of which have been through clinical trials. In fact, in the first clinical trial a biodegradable stent in humans was done with Igaki-Tamai stents, which are made of PLLA.

PLLA is attractive because of its relatively high strength and stiffness when compared with other biodegradable polymers. Furthermore, it has a low enough degradation rate that stents made of PLLA can provide support for 6 months. However, PLLA suffers from brittleness which heightens the risk of stent strut fracture during deployment. For this reason, researchers have been investigating ways of modifying PLLA to be more ductile.

7.3.3.2 Modification of PLLA

There are various means of modifying polymers to alter the properties and to enhance ductility, methods such as plasticiser addition, blending with rubbery polymers and copolymerisation.

Attempts at modifying PLLA were made by Grabow et al., who blended PLLA with poly(4-hydroxybutyrate) (P4HB), as well as poly(caprolactone) (PCL), and attempted to produce biodegradable stents from these blends [36, 37]. The ductility of the blends was far greater than that of PLLA, but there were significant reductions in other mechanical properties. In the case of the PLLA/P4HB blend, tensile strength was reduced by 20 %, while stiffness was reduced by 50 %, which is undesirable since sufficient stiffness is a high priority for stenting applications. The PLLA/PCL blend exhibited an increase in strength but also a 50 % decrease in stiffness, as well as a major loss of creep resistance when compared with neat PLLA. Thus the PLLA/PCL blend was found to be unsuitable for application in biodegradable stents because stents made from this blend would possibly collapse prematurely due to low stiffness and insufficient resistance to creep.

Other work done on enhancing the ductility of PLLA involved blending with either poly(butylene succinate) (PBS) or poly(butylene succinate-co-L-lactate) (PBSL). While the work was a general study not aimed at application for biodegradable stents, the results were indicative and promising. In this study, Shibata et al. showed that the tensile elongation at break of PLLA is significantly enhanced by blending it with PBS or PBSL [107]. Furthermore, the losses of strength and stiffness were not as extreme as those exhibited by the PLLA/P4HB and PLLA/PCL blends investigated by Grabow et al. [36, 37]. For this reason, these blends are of considerable interest to the manufacturers of biodegradable stents, but there is still a lot which is unknown about them; for example, how does PBS addition influence the creep resistance of PLLA and how will degradation affect the blends' strength, stiffness and creep resistance?

7.3.3.3 PLLA/PBS: A Potential Candidate for Biodegradable Stents

The ductility of PLLA/PBS blends makes them promising candidates for the manufacture of biodegradable stents. This is the motivation for recent work which has focussed on characterising the changes in material behaviour of PLLA/PBS blends as they degrade.

Specimen Preparation PLLA and PBS were melt-blended in various ratios with up to 25 % PBS using a twin screw extruder. The blends were subsequently used to produce dog bone-type specimens via injection moulding.

Degradation Specimens were submerged in phosphate-buffered saline, with a pH of 7.4, in a temperature-controlled water bath which was used to maintain a temperature of 37 °C. The degradation period spanned 24 weeks, and specimens were removed at intervals between 0 and 24 weeks for testing.

Tensile and Creep Tests Tensile and constant-load creep tests were performed on non-degraded and degraded specimens. Tensile tests were performed in an Instron universal testing machine at a crosshead extension rate of 50 mm/min, while loads for creep tests were applied by dead weights hanging from the specimen being tested. All tests were performed in an environmental chamber at 37 °C, and degraded specimens were tested immediately after removal from the degradation medium to ensure that they were tested in a saturated state to obtain relevant results.

Results of Tensile Tests Four different PLLA/PBS blends, as well as neat PLLA and neat PBS, were compared to determine the effects of degradation and PBS content on the changes in mechanical characteristics of PLLA/PBS blends. The changes in Young's moduli of the blend specimens as they degrade are of interest. As can be seen in Fig. 7.15, the moduli of the blends decrease gradually from 0 to 24 weeks of degradation, while those of neat PLLA and neat PBS actually increase slightly during the first 8 weeks and then stabilise.

The implications of the gradual decreases in moduli of PLLA/PBS blends during degradation could be positive if we consider that as a stented vessel heals, the amount of support it requires should decrease gradually. Figure 7.16 shows the microstructures of the PLLA/PBS specimens before degrading and after degrading. The latter becomes more porous structurally, lowering its mechanical properties.

Results of Creep Tests Creep tests were done on the specimens of one blend – 75/25 PLLA/PBS and neat PLLA, for comparison. The results of creep tests at different stresses on non-degraded specimens revealed that the initial creep rates of

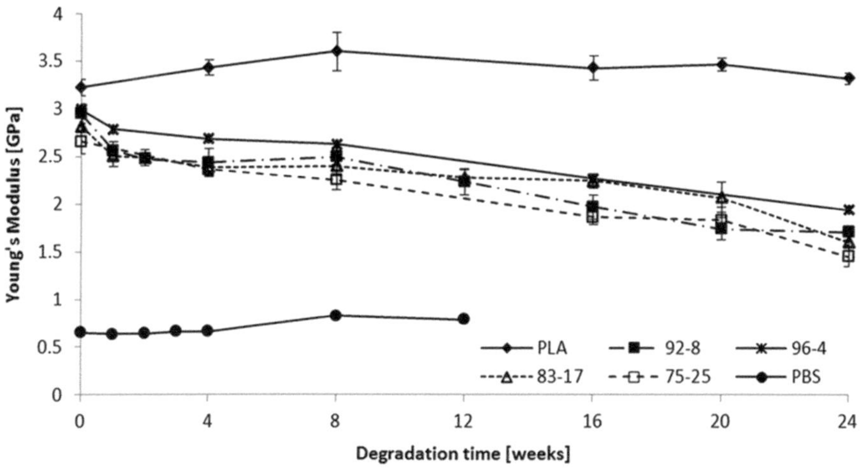

Fig. 7.15 Young's moduli of samples of PLLA/PBS, PLLA and PBS degraded for various periods of time. Error bars represent standard deviations of samples of five specimens each

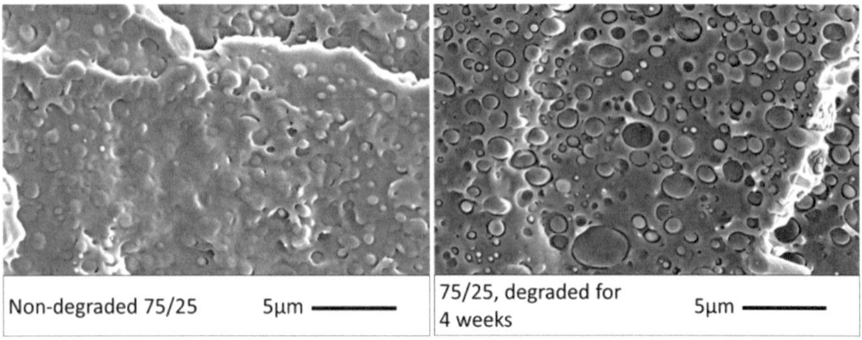

Fig. 7.16 Scanning electron microscope images of cryo-fractured 75/25 PLLA/PBS specimens: non-degraded (*left*) and degraded for 4 weeks (*right*) [108]

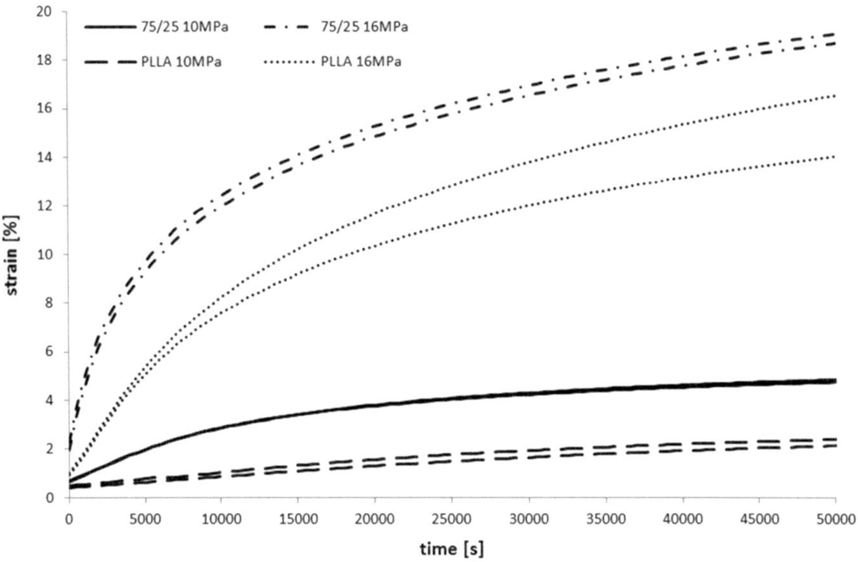

Fig. 7.17 Strain–time plot showing the first 50,000 s of constant-load creep tests performed on PLLA and 75/25 specimens. Results of two specimens from each material type are shown for each load. Stresses indicated are based on initial cross-sectional area (i.e. engineering stresses). All tests were performed at 37 °C

the 75/25 specimens were 3–4 times higher than those of neat PLLA, but physical ageing which occurred during creep tests slowed the creep rates significantly. Once creep rates stabilised after decreasing with physical ageing, the creep rates of the 75/25 blend and neat PLLA were almost the same for a given stress, as shown in Fig. 7.17.

The higher creep rates of the PLLA/PBS blend are not favourable for the application but are an expected result stemming from ductility enhancement.

Annealing was considered as a means of enhancing creep resistance, and the results from creep tests on 75/25 blend specimens annealed for 1 week at 45 °C are compared with the results of as-moulded specimens in Fig. 7.18. It is clear that annealing significantly enhances creep resistance, where the annealed 75/25 specimens exhibit the creep rates well below those of the neat PLLA. However, tensile testing of specimens annealed under the same conditions showed that the ductility enhancement from PBS addition is lost. Shorter annealing time retain some ductility but will result in a less significant boost in creep resistance, so further experiments can be done to find a balance between ductility and creep resistance.

The results of creep tests of non-degraded specimens provide important insights into the behaviour of PLLA/PBS blends, but critical to the application as biodegradable stent materials is understanding of how the creep resistance changes as the material degrades. Thus creep tests were also performed on degraded specimens. Again, a 75/25 PLLA/PBS blend was compared with neat PLLA. All the tests were done at a constant load equivalent to an engineering stress of ~10 MPa. Interestingly, the neat PLLA shows increases in creep resistance up until 8 weeks of degradation and then decreases in creep resistance from 8 to 16 weeks of degradation, as can be seen in Fig. 7.19 (left). The increase in creep resistance during the first 8 weeks of degradation can be attributed to physical ageing.

The 75/25 blend shows a trend of decreasing creep resistance with increasing degradation time. This may, at first, seem like a definite disadvantage, but it must be kept in mind that while a stented vessel heals, it will gradually exert less and less

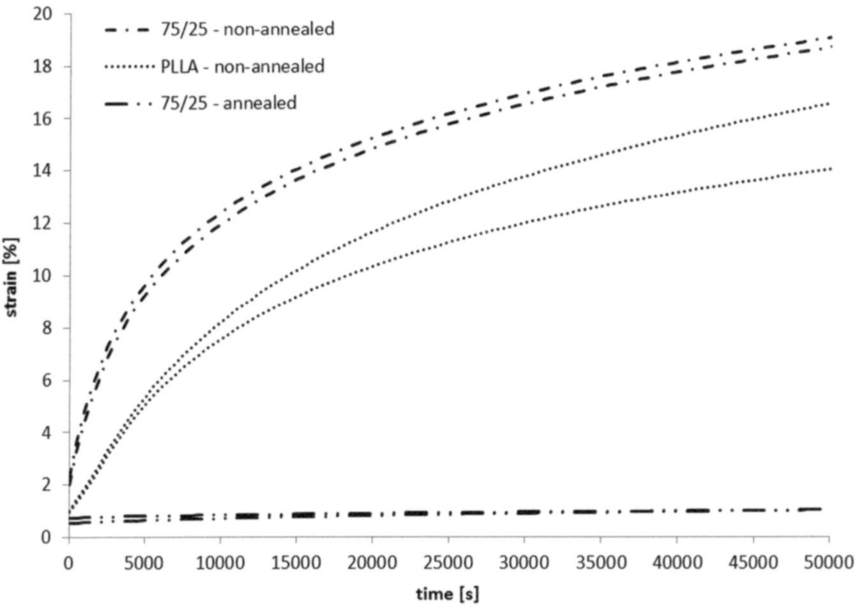

Fig. 7.18 Strain–time plots of 16 MPa creep tests of annealed 75/25 and as-moulded 75/25 and PLLA specimens. Each curve represents the results of an individual specimen

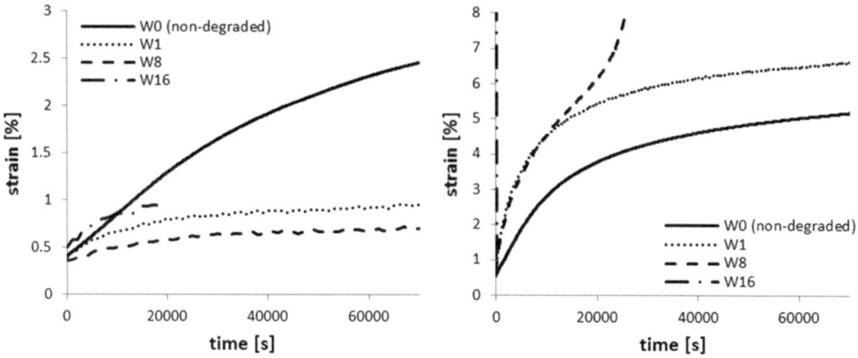

Fig. 7.19 Strain–time plots from constant-load creep tests (engineering stress ~10 MPa) of non-degraded and degraded PLLA (*left*) and 75/25 PLLA/PBS (*right*). All tests were performed at 37 °C

pressure on the stent, so a gradual decrease in the stent's ability to support the vessel is not necessarily disadvantageous. The ideal rate of decrease in support provided by a stent is not well understood, as far as the authors are aware.

7.3.4 Summary

Blending PLLA with PBS greatly enhances ductility, which is attractive for application as a biodegradable stent material. This work serves to elucidate the effects of degradation on the mechanical performance of PLLA/PBS blends in order to better understand how biodegradable stents made of these blends would perform. Results show that PLLA/PBS blends exhibit gradual decreases in their moduli as degradation progresses, while neat PLLA showed no loss over the same 24 week period. A 75/25 blend showed a gradual decrease in creep resistance with increasing degradation time, while PLLA exhibited increasing creep resistance during the first 8 weeks of degradation and a decrease from 8 to 16 weeks. The implications of the results are that a stent made of a PLLA/PBS blend would lose its ability to provide support to a healing vessel at a higher rate than a neat PLLA stent, but this may not necessarily be a negative implication since a stented vessel should require a decreasing level of support as it heals.

References

1. The Williams dictionary of biomaterials (1999) Liverpool, Liverpool University Press
2. Ratner BD, Hoffman AS, Schoen FJ, Lemons JE (2004) Biomaterials science: an introduction to materials in medicine. Academic Press, Orlando

3. Ramakrishna S, Mayer J, Wintermantel E, Leong KW (2001) Biomedical applications of polymer-composite materials: a review. Compos Sci Technol 61(9):1189–1224
4. Majumdar J, Edmond L (2006) Polymers in biomedical applications. Australas Biotechnol 16 (2):14–15
5. Wichterle O, Lím D (1960) Hydrophilic gels for biological use. Nature 185:117–118
6. Tang X, Thankappan SK, Lee P, Fard SE, Harmon MD, Tran K et al (2014) Chapter 21 – polymeric biomaterials in tissue engineering and regenerative medicine. In: Kumbar SG, Laurencin CT, Deng M (eds) Natural and synthetic biomedical polymers. Elsevier, Oxford, pp 351–371
7. Armentano I, Dottori M, Fortunati E, Mattioli S, Kenny JM (2010) Biodegradable polymer matrix nanocomposites for tissue engineering: a review. Polym Degrad Stab 95 (11):2126–2146
8. Nair LS, Laurencin CT (2007) Biodegradable polymers as biomaterials. Prog Polym Sci 32 (8–9):762–798
9. Armentano I, Bitinis N, Fortunati E, Mattioli S, Rescignano N, Verdejo R et al (2013) Multifunctional nanostructured PLA materials for packaging and tissue engineering. Prog Polym Sci 38(10–11):1720–1747
10. Barbucci R (2002) Integrated biomaterials science. Springer, New York
11. Odian G (2004) Principles of polymerization. Wiley, Inc., New Jersy
12. Katti DS, Lakshmi S, Langer R, Laurencin CT (2002) Toxicity, biodegradation and elimination of polyanhydrides. Adv Drug Deliv Rev 54(7):933–961
13. Gunatillake P, Mayadunne R, Adhikari R (2006) Recent developments in biodegradable synthetic polymers. In: El-Gewely MR (ed) Biotechnology Annual Review, vol 12. Elsevier, New York, pp 301–347
14. Maurus PB, Kaeding CC (2004) Bioabsorbable implant material review. Oper Tech Sports Med 12(3):158–160
15. Middleton JC, Tipton AJ (2000) Synthetic biodegradable polymers as orthopedic devices. Biomaterials 21(23):2335–2346
16. Letchford K, Sodegraad A, Plackett D, Gilchrist S, Burt H (2011) Lactide and glycolide polymers. Chapter 9. In: Domb A, Kumar N, Azra A (eds) Biodegradable polymers in clinical use and clinical development. Chichester/West Sussex, Wiley
17. Harte I, Birkinshaw C, Jones E, Kennedy J, DeBarra E (2013) The effect of citrate ester plasticizers on the thermal and mechanical properties of poly(DL-lactide). J Appl Polym Sci 127(3):1997–2003
18. Okada M (2002) Chemical syntheses of biodegradable polymers. Prog Polym Sci 27 (1):87–133
19. Langer R, Vacanti JP (1993) Tissue engineering. Science 260(5110):920–926
20. Okamoto M, John B (2013) Synthetic biopolymer nanocomposites for tissue engineering scaffolds. Prog Polym Sci 38(10–11):1487–1503
21. Murray CJ, Lopez AD (1997) Mortality by cause for eight regions of the world: global burden of disease study. Lancet 349:1269–1276
22. Nerem RM (2007) Chapter two – the challenge of imitating nature. In: Lanza RP, Langer RS, Joseph V (eds) Principles of Tissue Engineering, 3rd edn. Academic Press, Burlington, pp 7–14
23. Tissue engineering, cell therapy and transplantation: products, technologies & market opportunities, worldwide, 2009–2018. 2011
24. Organ Donation and Transplantation Activities 2012: GLOBAL OBSERVATORY ON DONATION AND TRANSPLANTATION; 2012 [cited 2013]. Available from: http://www.transplant-observatory.org/Pages/Data-Reports.aspx
25. Ana J, Andrea S, Elizabeth D, Angela S, Robert L (2012) Progress in the tissue engineering and stem cell industry "Are we there yet?". Tissue Eng Part B 18(3):155–166
26. Seal BL, Otero TC, Panitch A (2001) Polymeric biomaterials for tissue and organ regeneration. Mat Sci Eng R Rep 34(4–5):147–230

27. Langer R, Tirrell DA (2004) Designing materials for biology and medicine. Nature 428 (6982):487–492
28. Vacanti JP, Langer R (1999) Tissue engineering: the design and fabrication of living replacement devices for surgical reconstruction and transplantation. Lancet 354 Suppl 1(0): S32–S4.
29. Fuchs JR, Nasseri BA, Vacanti JP (2001) Tissue engineering: a 21st century solution to surgical reconstruction. Ann Thorac Surg 72(2):577–591
30. Fakirov S, Bhattacharyya D, Hutmacher D (eds) (2009) Applications of microfibrillar polymer-polymer composites for biomedical purposes. In: Processing and fabrication of advanced materials XVII, New Delhi, India.
31. Barnes CP, Sell SA, Boland ED, Simpson DG, Bowlin GL (2007) Nanofiber technology: designing the next generation of tissue engineering scaffolds. Adv Drug Deliv Rev 59 (14):1413–1433
32. Shoichet MS (2009) Polymer scaffolds for biomaterials applications. Macromolecules 43 (2):581–591
33. Ma PX (2008) Biomimetic materials for tissue engineering. Adv Drug Deliv Rev 60 (2):184–198
34. Tuzlakoglu K, Bolgen N, Salgado AJ, Gomes ME, Piskin E, Reis RL (2005) Nano- and micro-fiber combined scaffolds: a new architecture for bone tissue engineering. J Mater Sci Mater Med 16(12):1099–1104
35. Vacanti JP (2003) Tissue and organ engineering: can we build intestine and vital organs? J Gastrointest Surg 7(7):831–835
36. Liu C, Xia Z, Czernuszka JT (2007) Design and development of three-dimensional scaffolds for tissue engineering. Chem Eng Res Des 85(7):1051–1064
37. Karageorgiou V, Kaplan D (2005) Porosity of 3D biomaterial scaffolds and osteogenesis. Biomaterials 26(27):5474–5491
38. Hutmacher DW (2001) Scaffold design and fabrication technologies for engineering tissues – state of the art and future perspectives. J Biomater Sci Polym Ed 12(1):107–124
39. Cima LG, Vacanti JP, Vacanti C, Ingber D, Mooney D, Langer R (1991) Tissue engineering by cell transplantation using degradable polymer substrates. J Biomech Eng 113(2):143–151
40. Kweon H, Yoo MK, Park IK, Kim TH, Lee HC, Lee H-S et al (2003) A novel degradable polycaprolactone networks for tissue engineering. Biomaterials 24(5):801–808
41. Yurchenco PD, Birk DE, Mecham RP (1994) Collagen fibril assembly, deposition, and organization into tissue-specific matrices. In: Yurchenco PD, Birk DE, Mecham RP (eds) Extracellular matrix assembly and structure. Academic Press, San Diego
42. Elsdale T, Bard J (1972) Collagen substrata for studies on cell behavior. J Cell Biol 54 (3):626–637
43. Venugopal J, Prabhakaran MP, Zhang Y, Low S, Choon AT, Ramakrishna S (2010) Biomimetic hydroxyapatite-containing composite nanofibrous substrates for bone tissue engineering. Philos Trans R Soc A Math Phys Eng Sci 368(1917):2065–2081
44. U.S. Markets for Orthopedic Biomaterials for Viscosupplementation and Cartilage, Ligament/Tendon, and Meniscal Repair and Regeneration. CA, USA: 2013a
45. U.S. Markets for Orthopedic Biomaterials for Bone Repair and Regeneration. CA, USA: 2013b
46. Lin ST, Bhattacharyya D, Fakirov S, Matthews B, Cornish J (2013) A novel microfibrillar composite approach towards manufacturing nanoporous tissue scaffolds. Mech Adv Mater Struct 21(3):237–243
47. Giesche H (2006) Mercury porosimetry: a general (practical) overview. Part Part Syst Charact 23(1):9–19
48. Ghasemi-Mobarakeh L, Semnani D, Morshed M (2007) A novel method for porosity measurement of various surface layers of nanofibers mat using image analysis for tissue engineering applications. J Appl Polym Sci 106(4):2536–2542

49. Intelligent Hydrogel (2012) Handbook of intelligent scaffold for tissue engineering and regenerative medicine. Pan Stanford Publishing, p 97
50. Nazarov R, Jin H-J, Kaplan DL (2004) Porous 3-D scaffolds from regenerated silk fibroin. Biomacromolecules 5(3):718–726
51. Murphy CM, Haugh MG, O'Brien FJ (2009) The effect of mean pore size on cell attachment, proliferation and migration in collagen–glycosaminoglycan scaffolds for bone tissue engineering. Biomaterials 31(3):461–466
52. Nori A, Yim EKF, Chen S, Leong KW (2008) Cell-substrate interactions, Principles of Regenerative Medicine. Academic Press, San Diego, pp 666–685
53. Albrektsson T, Johansson C (2001) Osteoinduction, osteoconduction and osseointegration. Eur Spine J 10:S96–S101
54. Billström GH, Blom AW, Larsson S, Beswick AD (2013) Application of scaffolds for bone regeneration strategies: current trends and future directions. Injury 44 Suppl 1(0):S28–S33
55. Giannoudis PV, Einhorn TA, Marsh D (2007) Fracture healing: the diamond concept. Injury 38 Suppl 4(0):S3–S6
56. Sicchieri LG, Crippa GE, de Oliveira PT, Beloti MM, Rosa AL (2012) Pore size regulates cell and tissue interactions with PLGA–CaP scaffolds used for bone engineering. J Tissue Eng Regen Med 6(2):155–162
57. Holzwarth JM, Ma PX (2011) Biomimetic nanofibrous scaffolds for bone tissue engineering. Biomaterials 32(36):9622–9629
58. Ji C, Annabi N, Hosseinkhani M, Sivaloganathan S, Dehghani F (2012) Fabrication of poly-DL-lactide/polyethylene glycol scaffolds using the gas foaming technique. Acta Biomater 8 (2):570–578
59. Li JP, de Wijn JR, Van Blitterswijk CA, de Groot K (2006) Porous Ti6Al4V scaffold directly fabricating by rapid prototyping: preparation and in vitro experiment. Biomaterials 27 (8):1223–1235
60. Beachley V, Wen X (2010) Polymer nanofibrous structures: fabrication, biofunctionalization, and cell interactions. Prog Polym Sci 35(7):868–892
61. Wu X, Liu Y, Li X, Wen P, Zhang Y, Long Y et al (2010) Preparation of aligned porous gelatin scaffolds by unidirectional freeze-drying method. Acta Biomater 6(3):1167–1177
62. Mishra A, Loo Y, Deng R, Chuah YJ, Hee HT, Ying JY et al (2011) Ultrasmall natural peptides self-assemble to strong temperature-resistant helical fibers in scaffolds suitable for tissue engineering. Nano Today 6(3):232–239
63. Sin DC, Miao X, Liu G, Wei F, Chadwick G, Yan C et al (2010) Polyurethane (PU) scaffolds prepared by solvent casting/particulate leaching (SCPL) combined with centrifugation. Mater Sci Eng C 30(1):78–85
64. Ahn YC, Park SK, Kim GT, Hwang YJ, Lee CG, Shin HS et al (2006) Development of high efficiency nanofilters made of nanofibers. Curr Appl Phys 6(6):1030–1035
65. Lannutti J, Reneker D, Ma T, Tomasko D, Farson D (2007) Electrospinning for tissue engineering scaffolds. Mater Sci Eng C 27(3):504–509
66. Reneker DH, Yarin AL (2008) Electrospinning jets and polymer nanofibers. Polymer 49 (10):2387–2425
67. Agarwal S, Wendorff JH, Greiner A (2008) Use of electrospinning technique for biomedical applications. Polymer 49(26):5603–5621
68. Bhattarai SR, Bhattarai N, Yi HK, Hwang PH, Cha DI, Kim HY (2004) Novel biodegradable electrospun membrane: scaffold for tissue engineering. Biomaterials 25(13):2595–2602
69. Kumbar SG, James R, Nukavarapu SP, Laurencin CT (2008) Electrospun nanofiber scaffolds: engineering soft tissues. Biomed Mater 3(3):034002
70. Zhang Y, Reddy V, Wong S, Li X, Su B, Ramakrishna S et al (2010) Enhanced biomineralization in osteoblasts on a novel electrospun biocomposite Nanofibrous substrate of hydroxyapatite/collagen/chitosan. Tissue Eng A 16(6):1949–1960
71. Shao S, Zhou S, Li L, Li J, Luo C, Wang J et al (2011) Osteoblast function on electrically conductive electrospun PLA/MWCNTs nanofibers. Biomaterials 32(11):2821–2833

72. Lederer A, Harnisch C, Bhattacharyya D, Fakirov S (2010) Organic solvent traces in fibrillar scaffolds for tissue engineering. J Biomim Biomater Tissue Eng 7:1–6
73. Martínez-Pérez CA, Olivas-Armendariz I, Castro-Carmona JS, García-Casillas PE (2011) Scaffolds for tissue engineering via thermally induced phase separation, advances in regenerative medicine. In: Wislet-Gendebien S (ed) InTech. doi:10.5772/25476. Available from: http://www.intechopen.com/books/advances-in-regenerative-medicine/scaffolds-for-tissue-engineering-via-thermally-induced-phase-separation
74. Ma PX, Zhang R (1999) Synthetic nano-scale fibrous extracellular matrix. J Biomed Mater Res 46(1):60–72
75. Fuchs C, Bhattacharyya D, Fakirov S (2006) Microfibril reinforced polymer–polymer composites: application of Tsai-Hill equation to PP/PET composites. Compos Sci Technol 66 (16):3161–3171
76. Fakirov S, Kamo H, Evstatiev M, Friedrich K (2004) Microfibrillar reinforced composites from PET/LDPE blends: morphology and mechanical properties. J Macromol Sci Phys 43 (4):775–789
77. Lu H, Ko Y-G, Kawazoe N, Chen G (2011) Culture of bovine articular chondrocytes in funnel-like collagen-PLGA hybrid sponges. Biomed Mater 6(4):045011
78. Oh HH, Lu H, Kawazoe N, Chen G (2012) Spatially guided angiogenesis by three-dimensional collagen scaffolds micropatterned with vascular endothelial growth factor. J Biomater Sci Polym Ed 23(17):2185–2195
79. Lu H, Hoshiba T, Kawazoe N, Koda I, Song M, Chen G (2011) Cultured cell-derived extracellular matrix scaffolds for tissue engineering. Biomaterials 32(36):9658–9666
80. Lu H, Hoshiba T, Kawazoe N, Chen G (2011) Autologous extracellular matrix scaffolds for tissue engineering. Biomaterials 32(10):2489–2499
81. He X, Lu H, Kawazoe N, Tateishi T, Chen G (2010) A novel cylinder-type poly(L-lactic acid)-collagen hybrid sponge for cartilage tissue engineering. Tissue Eng Part C Methods 16 (3):329–338
82. Dai W, Kawazoe N, Lin X, Dong J, Chen G (2010) The influence of structural design of PLGA/collagen hybrid scaffolds in cartilage tissue engineering. Biomaterials 31 (8):2141–2152
83. Dhandayuthapani B, Yoshida Y, Maekawa T, Sakthi Kumar D (2011) Polymeric scaffolds in tissue engineering application: a review. Int J Polym Sci 2011
84. Dictionaries O. “stent”. Oxford Dictionaries: Oxford University Press
85. Mani G, Feldman MD, Patel D, Agrawal CM (2007) Coronary stents: a materials perspective. Biomaterials 28:1689–1710
86. Hillen U, Haude M, Erbel R, Goos M (2002) Evaluation of metal allergies in patients with coronary stents. Contact Dermatitis 47(6):353–356
87. Köster R, Vieluf D, Kiehn M, Sommerauer M, Kahler J, Baldus S et al (2000) Nickel and molybdenum contact allergies in patients with coronary in-stent restenosis. Lancet 356 (9245):1895–1897
88. Kraitzer A, Kloog Y, Zilberman M (2008) Approaches for prevention of restenosis. J Biomed Mat Res Part B Appl Biomater 85(2):583–603
89. Serruys PW, Kutryk MJB, Ong ATL (2006) Coronary-artery stents. N Engl J Med 354 (5):483–495
90. Lemesle G, Delhaye C, Bonello L, de Labriolle A, Waksman R, Pichard A (2008) Stent thrombosis in 2008: definition, predictors, prognosis and treatment. Arch Cardiovasc Dis 101 (11–12):769–777
91. Van Der Giessen WJ, Serruys PW, Van Woerkens LJ, Beatt KJ, Visser WJ, Jongkind JF et al (1990) Arterial stenting with self-expandable and balloon-expandable endoprostheses. Int J Card Imaging 5(2–3):163–171
92. O’Brien B, Carroll W (2009) The evolution of cardiovascular stent materials and surfaces in response to clinical drivers: a review. Acta Biomater 5:945–958

93. Kastrati A, Schomig A, Dirschinger J, Mehilli J, von Welser N, Pache J et al (2000) Increased risk of restenosis after placement of gold-coated stents: results of a randomized trial comparing gold-coated with uncoated steel stents in patients with coronary artery disease. Circulation 101(21):2478–2483
94. Webster MW, Ormiston JA (2007) Drug-eluting stents and late stent thrombosis. Lancet 370 (9591):914–915
95. Finn AV, Joner M, Nakazawa G, Kolodgie F, Newell J, John MC et al (2007) Pathological correlates of late drug-eluting stent thrombosis: strut coverage as a marker of endothelialization. Circulation 115(18):2435–2441
96. Ormiston J, Webster M (2007) Absorbable coronary stents. Lancet 369(9576):1839–1840
97. Ferrari E, Benhamou M, Cerboni P, Marcel B (2005) Coronary syndromes following aspirin withdrawal: a special risk for late stent thrombosis. J Am Coll Cardiol 45(3):456–459
98. Grabow N, Bünger CM, Schultze C, Schmohl K, Martin DP, Williams SF et al (2007) A biodegradable slotted tube stent based on poly(l-lactide) and poly(4-hydroxybutyrate) for rapid balloon-expansion. Ann Biomed Eng 35(12):2031–2038
99. Tverdal A (1987) Systolic and diastolic blood pressures as predictors of coronary heart disease in middle aged Norwegian men. Br Med J 294(6573):671–673
100. Gross MF, Friedman MH (1998) Dynamics of coronary artery curvature obtained from biplane cineangiograms. J Biomech 31(5):479–484
101. Peng T, Gibula P, Yao KD, Goosen MFA (1996) Role of polymers in improving the results of stenting in coronary arteries. Biomaterials 17(7):685–694
102. Bertrand OF, Sipehia R, Mongrain R, Rodés J, Tardif JC, Bilodeau L et al (1998) Biocompatibility aspects of new stent technology. J Am Coll Cardiol 32(3):562–571
103. Venkatraman S, Boey F, Lao LL (2008) Implanted cardiovascular polymers: natural, synthetic and bio-inspired. Prog Polym Sci 33:853–874
104. Ormiston JA, Serruys PWS (2009) Bioabsorbable coronary stents. Circ Cardiovasc Interv 2 (3):255–260
105. Colombo A, Karvouni E (2000) Biodegradable stents:"Fulfilling the mission and stepping away". Circulation 102:371
106. Ramcharitar S, Serruys PW (2008) Fully biodegradable coronary stents: progress to date. Am J Cardiovasc Drugs 8(5):305–314
107. Shibata M, Inoue Y, Miyoshi M (2006) Mechanical properties, morphology, and crystallization behavior of blends of poly(l-lactide) with poly(butylene succinate-co-l-lactate) and poly (butylene succinate). Polymer 47:3557–3564
108. Kimble LD, Bhattacharyya D, Easteal AJ (2011) Degradation characteristics and its effects on mechanical characteristics of a biodegradable polymer composite of PLLA and PBS for use as a stent material. In: Processing and fabrication of advanced materials, Auckland 2011

Chapter 8
Electrospun Polymer Scaffolds: Their Biomedical and Mechanical Properties

Gui-Ying Liao, Xing-Ping Zhou, Xiao-Lin Xie, and Yiu-Wing Mai

Abstract In recent years, electrospun polymer scaffolds have shown great promise and potential for biomedical applications. Besides, copolymers and polymer blends, polymer composites with inorganic particles, such as HA and CNT, are widely used. And the alignment of reinforced fibres is beneficial to improve the mechanical properties and biological response of scaffolds. Further, the physical and chemical surface modifications for electrospun fibres are commonly applied to promote the interaction between the scaffold and cells in tissue engineering applications. In this chapter, we reviewed recent advances in electrospun polymer scaffolds with special emphasis on their biomedical and mechanical properties and the effects of the surface modifications.

Keywords Electrospinning • Scaffolds • Modification • Mechanical properties • Biomedical applications

8.1 Introduction

Electrospinning is a simple, relatively efficient technique to fabricate polymer fibrous scaffolds with diameters ranging from several nanometres to several micrometres [1, 2]. The electrospun fibrous scaffolds have extraordinary high surface area-to-volume ratio and high porosity with excellent pore interconnection and have been widely used in a range of hi-tech fields, such as filtration [3], sensors [4, 5], protective clothes and biomaterial applications [6–9].

G.-Y. Liao
Faculty of Material Science and Chemistry, China University of Geosciences, Wuhan 430074, China

X.-P. Zhou • X.-L. Xie (✉)
School of Chemistry and Chemical Engineering, Huazhong University of Science and Technology, Wuhan 430074, China
e-mail: xlxie@hust.edu.cn

Y.-W. Mai
School of Aerospace, Mechanical & Mechatronic Engineering, The University of Sydney, Sydney, NSW 2006, Australia

Q. Li, Y.-W. Mai (eds.), *Biomaterials for Implants and Scaffolds*, Springer Series in Biomaterials Science and Engineering 8, DOI 10.1007/978-3-662-53574-5_8

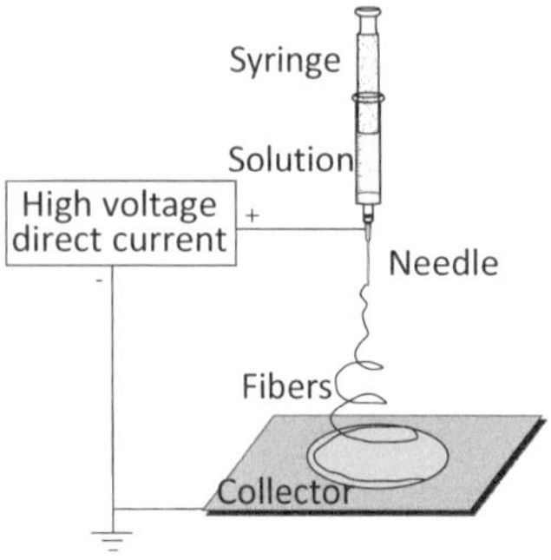

Fig. 8.1 Scheme for electrospinning apparatus

Electrospinning was first introduced by Formhals in 1934 as a patent [10] and later revived by Reneker's groups [11–16]. They studied the electrospinning process for a series of different polymers and demonstrated the mechanism for the formation of electrospun polymer fibres. A basic theory of electrospinning is utilising electrostatic forces of highly charged polymer jets to produce continuous fibres after solvent evaporation in spinning process. A typical electrospinning set-up, as shown in Fig. 8.1, usually consists of three major components: a high-voltage power supply, a nozzle and a grounded collecting plate (usually a metal screen, plate or rotating mandrel). Upon applying an electric field, the polymer solution with a moderate viscosity forms the Taylor cone at the tip of an injecting device. When the electric voltage applied between the injector and the collector exceeds the surface tension force of the Taylor cone, the charged jets are eventually drawn towards the collecting plate. During the travel of the fibrous jets, the solvent in the jet stream gradually evaporates, generating a solidified non-woven fibrous scaffold. The morphological structure and surface properties of electrospun fibres depend on the physical parameters of the polymer solution (e.g. concentration, viscosity, conductivity and surface tension) as well as the spinning process conditions (e.g. applied voltage, distance between capillary tip and collection screen, temperature and humidity of the ambient environment) [14, 17, 18].

In order to meet the demands in biomedical applications, it is essential to control the chemical composition to endow the electrospun fibrous scaffold with desired properties, such as hydrophilicity, mechanical modulus and strength, biocompatibility, biodegradability and cell interactions. Additionally, the fibre diameter, morphology and porosity of the electrospun fibrous scaffolds can be manipulated by the fabrication process, and these structural factors also have important effects on the properties and functionalities of scaffolds. For example, the drugs or biopolymers are incorporated inside the fibre core by two-phase electrospinning process; the electrospun fibrous scaffolds are suitable for the controlled release over a prolonged time [19]. Also, blending modifications with bioactive molecules, such as gelatin, proteins, nucleic acids and carbohydrates, have been employed to enhance the aqueous solubility, biocompatibility and bio-recognition of electrospun fibrous scaffolds [20], which subsequently provides bio-modulating or biomimetic microenvironments for the contacting cells and tissues.

Generally, tissue engineering is a multidisciplinary field that has evolved in parallel with recent advances of materials and biotechnology. The usage of electrospun fibrous scaffolds for tissue engineering has drawn a great deal of attention in the past several years. For examples, the fibrous scaffolds have been demonstrated as suitable substrates for tissue engineering [8, 9, 21, 22], wound dressing [23], artificial blood vessels [24, 25] and vehicles for controlled drug delivery [26]. Furthermore, the electrospun scaffold should physically resemble the nanofibrous features of extracellular matrix (ECM) with suitable mechanical properties, which is beneficial for promoting the adhesion, spreading and proliferation of cells in tissue engineering.

This chapter focused on the recent advances in the use of electrospun polymer scaffolds for biomedical applications, with emphasis on polymer materials, technology, surface modification and biomedical and mechanical properties of the electrospun polymer scaffolds.

8.2 Polymer Materials as Electrospun Scaffolds

There are a wide range of polymer materials that can be electrospun. However, for the applications of fibrous scaffolds, the chosen polymer materials must meet some special requirements, such as biocompatibility and biodegradation.

8.2.1 Natural, Synthetic Polymers and Copolymers

Typical natural polymers include collagen, casein, chitosan, chitin, cellulose acetate, gelatin, silk protein, fibrinogen, etc. Scaffolds fabricated from natural polymers promise better clinical functionality. Natural polymers normally exhibit better biocompatibility, low immunogenicity and better inherent capacity for binding cells compared with synthetic polymers. Collagen, the principal structural element of the ECM in tissues, has been fabricated into fibrous scaffolds for cell growth and penetration [21]. Pawlowski et al. [27] reported that collagen is considered as ‘ideal’ scaffold material in tissue engineering, which provides structural support for the tissue. How et al. [28] for the first time reported that type I collagen fibres were successfully electrospun and characterised with scanning electron microscopy (SEM) and transmission electron microscopy (TEM). Afterwards, many researchers studied the electrospun collagen scaffolds, and these fibrous collagen scaffolds can closely mimic the native collagen network and apply for wound dressings and preliminary vascular tissue engineering [29–34].

Gelatin derived from collagen by controlled hydrolysis is also commonly used for biomedical applications due to its biodegradability and biocompatibility [35–40]. However, gelatin fibres are difficult to be fabricated by the conventional wet/dry spinning because of the polyelectrolytic nature and strong hydrogen bonding of gelatin [33, 41–43]. So gelatin has been electrospun for tissue engineering scaffolds by blending with other polymers [22, 44].

Attributable to the good biocompatibility, biodegradability, minimal inflammatory reaction and excellent mechanical properties, silk fibroin (SF) protein has been extensively studied for biomedical applications [45–50]. Recently, many research groups found SF protein can be easily electrospun; and the effect of electrospinning parameters on the morphology and the diameter of such fibres were systematically studied [51–55]. Wang et al. [56, 57] electrospun silk fibroin using an aqueous solution from *B. mori* in order to solve the potential concerns of chemical residuals from solvents, and they found that the concentrated silk aqueous solution was needed for increasing the solution spinnability. When the aqueous silk solution was up to 28 % (w/v), silk fibres with circular cross sections and smooth exterior surfaces were formed, and their diameters were 400–800 nm. Zhu et al. [58, 59] investigated the effects of solution pH on morphology and properties of the electrospun silk fibres. They found that reduction of solution pH decreases the concentration of aqueous silk fibroin solutions that could be electrospun. Subsequently, the average diameter and diameter distributions of the electrospun silk fibres became smaller and narrower. Further, the morphology of the electrospun silk fibres changed from ribbon-like to a uniform cylinder with the combined reduction in pH and concentration.

Compared with natural polymers, synthetic polymers have many advantages, such as cheaper cost, predictable uniformity, desired degradation rate and higher mechanical properties. Recently, the synthetic polymers, such as poly(lactic acid) (PLA) [60, 61], poly(glycolic acid) (PGA) [12, 62, 63], polyurethane (PU) [64], PEO [65], poly(vinylalcohol) [66, 67], poly(ε-caprolactone) (PCL) and polydioxanone [68] have been electrospun into fibrous scaffolds for biomedical applications thanks to their distinctive degradation and excellent biocompatibility.

It is well known that the morphology, pore size, biodegradability, mechanical and other physical properties of the electrospun scaffolds can be tailored by using copolymers. Generally, the biodegradable hydrophobic polyesters, such as PLA and PCL, lack cell affinity for tissue engineering, but the incorporation of a proper hydrophilic polymer segment efficiently solves the problem. Recently, the PLLA–PEG block copolymers were successfully synthesised and electrospun into fibres for sustained release of hydrophilic antibiotics [69], DNA delivery [70], fibroblast cell attachment and proliferation [71]. Kim et al. [72] reported that the electrospun PLA–PEG block copolymer fibres present appropriate characteristics to be considered as a new kind of biodegradable scaffolds. Also, P(LA-*b*-CL) block copolymers are electrospun to non-woven fibrous mats as scaffolds for the culture of somatic cells, such as smooth muscle cells (SMCs) and endothelial cells (ECs) [73–75]. The results showed that these cells could adhere and proliferate well on P(LA-*b*-CL) fibrous scaffolds. Know et al. [76] synthesised the biodegradable high-molecular-mass poly(L-lactide-co-ε-caprolactone) (PLCL) by ring-opening copolymerisation and electrospinning the nano- and microstructured PLCL fibres, and they found that human umbilical vein endothelial cells (HUVECs) were well adhered and proliferated on these fibrous scaffolds.

PLGA is the copolymer of glycolide (G) and lactide (L) and has been electrospun as fibrous scaffolds. Katti et al. [26] studied the potential use of PLGA fibrous scaffolds as an antibiotic delivery vehicle for the treatment of wounds. Zong et al. [77] found that the PLGA fibrous scaffolds degrade faster than the casting film with the same composition due to the high surface area-to-volume ratio and the high water adsorption ability.

Poly(3-hydroxybutyrate-co-3-hydroxyvalerate) (PHBV) is another biodegradable and biocompatible copolymer derived from microbial polyesters. Lee et al. [78] found that the electrospun PHBV nanofibrous scaffolds provided a much more suitable environment for the attachment and growth of chondrocytes derived from rabbit ears, compared to the PHBV cast films. Choi et al. [79] studied the diameter and degradation rate of PHBV fibre and found that addition of a small amount of benzyl trialkyl ammonium chlorides in the electrospinning solution decreased the fibre diameter and accelerated the degradation rate of PHBV fibre.

8.2.2 Polymer Blends

Copolymerisation and polymer blending are two effective means to combine different polymers for yielding new materials properties. In comparison with the copolymerisation, polymer blending is a simpler and more effective method for tissue engineering applications. Thus, properties of electrospun scaffolds can be tailored with desired new functions by selecting a combination of proper components and adjusting the component ratio. For example, PLA is most promising and widely used as the candidate scaffolds for tissue engineering. However, its brittleness has limited its wider biomedical applications. PCL is a biodegradable, semicrystalline and rubbery polymer owing to its low glass transition (~−50°C) and melting temperatures (~60°C) [80]. It has been often utilised to improve the elasticity of PLA via blending with PCL, and PLA/PCL blend cast films were previously prepared as engineered tissue implants [81–83].

Our group studied the electrospinning of PLLA/PCL blends, especially focused on optimising the process conditions [84]. The PLLA/PCL blend fibres with defect-free morphology and uniform diameter could be electrospun by PLLA/PCL (1/1) blend with a solution concentration of 10 wt. %, applied voltage 20 kV and TCD 15 cm. For the first time, we explored the response of adipose-derived stem cells (ADSCs) on PLLA/PCL blend fibrous scaffold. The morphology and interactions between ADSCs and PLLA/PCL blend fibrous scaffolds were examined by using inverted phase contrast microscopy (IPCM) and SEM.

Figure 8.2 shows ADSCs attachment and growth on the PLLA/PCL fibrous scaffolds. After being seeded on the PLLA/PCL fibrous scaffolds for 1 day, most ADSCs do not adhere to the fibres, but they grow to typical elongated morphology (Fig. 8.2a, b). At 3 days, the ADSCs expand on the fibrous scaffolds with a pattern of pseudopods as shown in Fig. 8.2c, d. After 7 days, an increasing number of cells grow along the fibre orientation direction, forming a three-dimensional network

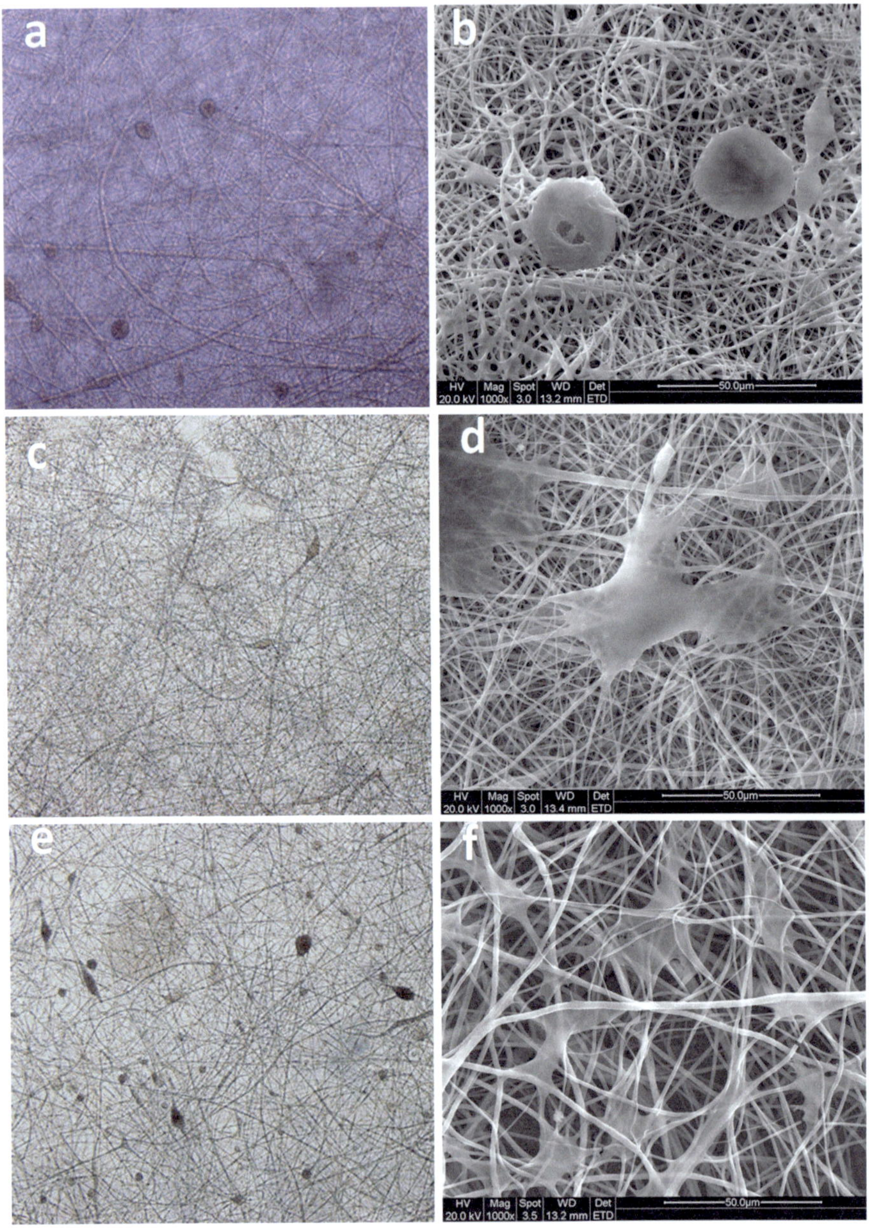

Fig. 8.2 Morphology ADSCs on scaffolds after seeding for 1 day [(**a**) by IPCM, (**b**) by SEM], 3 days [(**c**) by IPCM, (**d**) by SEM] and 7 days [(**e**) by IPCM, (**f**) by SEM] (Magnification: IPCM 100×; SEM 1000×) (Reproduced from Ref. [84] by permission of John Wiley & Sons Ltd)

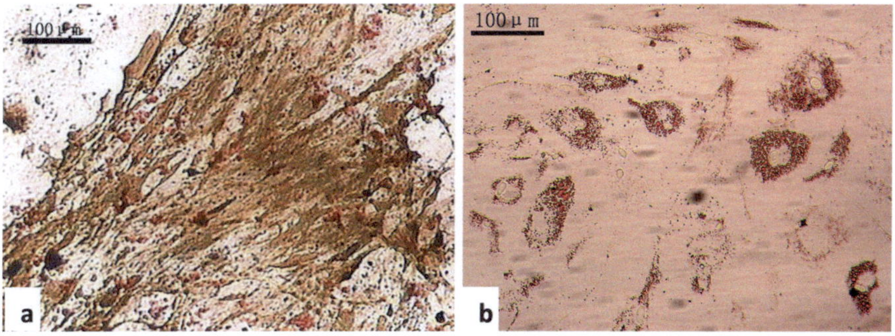

Fig. 8.3 Immunohistochemistry staining for characterisation of osteogenesis and adipogenesis: (**a**) von Kossa staining for osteogenic differentiation. The mineralised ECM was stained *brown*; (**b**) oil *red* O staining for adipogenic differentiation. The accumulated lipid was stained *red* (Magnification 200×) (Reproduced from Ref. [84] by permission of John Wiley & Sons Ltd)

with a fibrous pattern (Fig. 8.2e, f). These observations indicate that the PLLA/PCL blend fibres are biocompatible with ADSCs and are a good candidate for scaffold tissue engineering. The pluripotency of ADSCs on scaffolds was assessed by immunohistochemistry. The positive expression in Fig. 8.3 confirms the multilineage differentiation of ADSCs on scaffolds. In Fig. 8.3a, von Kossa staining shows calcium deposition in the ECM, which indicates osteogenesis. In Fig. 8.3b, oil red O staining shows the lipid accumulation in the ECM, which indicates adipogenesis.

In tissue engineering field, a biocompatible scaffold should meet various requirements to support the stem cell to differentiate into desired cell lineage. Similar to the pluripotency of ADSCs in conventional culture and expansion [85–88], the multilineage differentiation of ADSCs on such scaffold indicate the prospect to replace the native ECM for tissue engineering. Our group also compared the electrospun fibrous membrane with cast film of PLLA/PCL blend. The XRD patterns (Fig. 8.4) revealed that the crystallinity of electrospun PLLA/PCL blend fibres is significantly lower than that in the PLLA/PCL blend cast film, which is due to the rapid solidification of the polymer solution during electrospinning which hinders proper crystallisation.

Many other biocompatible polymers have been blended with PLA to electrospin the fibrous scaffolds. For example, PEG is often introduced into PLA because of its hydrophilicity and non-toxicity to modify the bulk properties of PLA. Spasova et al. [89] electrospun the nano- and microstructured PLLA/PEG blend fabrics with different compositions. They investigated the effect of the concentration of the mixed solutions and the ratio of PLLA/PEG on the fibre diameter and morphology. Wang et al. [90] also fabricated the PLA/PEG blend fibrous membranes. They found that the surface wettability of all membranes was influenced by PEG concentration, and the NIH3T3 cells could attach and spread on all samples. The blend of type I collagen and PEO could provide a convenient, non-toxic and non-denaturing way to generate fibrous scaffolds containing collagen [91].

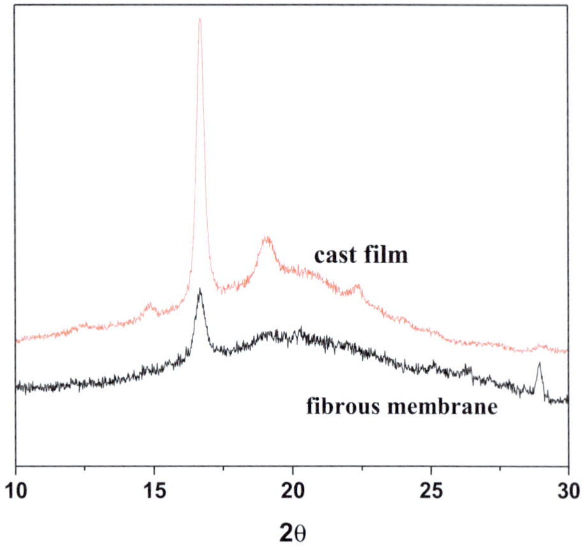

Fig. 8.4 XRD patterns of electrospun fibrous membrane and cast film of PLLA/PCL (1/1) blend (Reproduced from Ref. [84] by permission of John Wiley & Sons Ltd)

Gelatin and PCL in 2,2,2-trifluoroethanol (TFE) at a ratio of 50:50 to produce a gelatin/PCL blend fibrous scaffold by electrospinning [43]. The scaffold showed enhanced mechanical properties and more favourable wettability than those obtained from either PCL or gelatin scaffolds alone. Bone marrow stromal cells (BMSCs) were found to attach and grow well on the surface of the blend fibrous scaffold, suggesting the potential use of gelatin/PCL blend fibrous scaffolds for preparation of the three-dimensional tissue construct.

8.2.3 Polymer Composites

The idea of incorporating nanoscale fillers into polymer matrix has been extended to prepare polymer composites for electrospun fibrous scaffolds. A number of research groups have tried to electrospin such polymer composites with silver particles [92, 93], calcium carbonate [94], calcium phosphate [95] and hydroxyapatite (HA)[96, 97]; the fabricated nanofibrous scaffolds were found to be useful in biomedical applications. Especially, carbon nanotubes (CNTs) have been compounded to impart more functions in polymeric materials, such as thermal, electrical, magnetic, optical and increased mechanical properties [98].

Till now, researchers have electrospun a number of polymer/CNT nanocomposites with different matrices, such as polyethylene oxide (PEO) [99–101], poly(methyl methacrylate) (PMMA) [102–104], poly(acrylonitrile) (PAN) [105, 106], epoxy [107], nylon [108], polycarbonate [109], polyurethane (PU) [110], polystyrene (PS) [110, 111] and polyimide (PI) [112]. Liu et al. [104] fabricated the high-strength and high-modulus PMMA/multiwalled carbon nanotube (MWNT) composite nanofibres by electrospinning. Compared to the pure PMMA nanofibres, composite fibres with 5 wt. % MWNTs showed ~157 % increase in tensile strength and 260 % improvement in elastic modulus. Similarly, Chen et al. [112] electrospun PI/MWNT nanocomposite fibres with high strength and high toughness. Also, the 5 % weight loss temperature of the electrospun PI fibrous membranes was significantly improved by ~20 °C with the incorporation of only 3.5 wt. % MWNTs. Baji et al. [113] aligned and dispersed MWCNTs in PA6,6 successfully to fabricate self-assembled CNT-based nanofibres by electrospinning PA6,6/MWCNT/formic acid/dichloromethane solution. The addition of MWCNTs increased significantly both modulus and strength of the electrospun fibres. Saeed et al. [114] attempted to electrospin PCL/MWNT nanocomposite fibres and found that the PCL/*p*-amino benzoic acid functionalised-MWNT nanocomposite fibres had better thermal stability than PCL and PCL/pristine-MWNT nanocomposite fibres. The functionalised nanocomposite nanofibres showed a relatively larger diameter than the pure PCL nanofibres and formed fewer beads than the PCL/pristine-MWNT nanocomposite fibres. As the content of functionalised-MWNTs exceeded 2 wt. %, the nanocomposites could not be electrospun. Mei et al. [115] successfully electrospun PLLA/MWNT/HA composite fibrous membrane. They found that the membrane promoted the adhesion and proliferation of human periodontal ligament cells but inhibited those of gingival epithelial cells.

There are some basic requirements for designing polymer scaffolds [116]. First, the materials are biocompatible, and the biodegradability is required. In some cases, the degradation rate should match the rate of neotissue formation. Second, the scaffold must possess the required structural integrity with the appropriate mechanical properties to prevent the pores of the scaffold from collapsing during neotissue formation. Third, the scaffold should be non-toxic to cells, positively interacting with the cells to promote cell adhesion, proliferation, migration and differentiated cell function. So, the polymeric material selection plays a key role in the fabrication of scaffolds. Additionally, new innovations in electrospinning, such as the scaffolds with oriented fibre alignment, and physical and chemical modifications of the scaffolds after electrospinning are able to render the scaffolds with enhanced properties and suitable functionality.

8.3 Scaffolds with Oriented Fibre Alignment for Tissue Engineering

The possibility of controlling fibre deposition pattern makes electrospinning a powerful approach for fabricating scaffolds with a defined architecture in terms of fibre orientation. The fibres could be aligned through collecting substrate and applying electric or magnetic fields [117–122]. One of the most alignment techniques is to use a rotating drum collector instead of grounded collecting plate, and the diameter of the fibres can be controlled and tailored through adjusting the rotational speed of the drum [117, 121, 123, 124]. At rotational speeds slower than the fibre take-up speed, random fibres are obtained on the drum. At higher speeds, a centrifugal force is developed near the vicinity of the circumference of the rotating drum, which elongates the fibres before being collected on the drum [124]. However, at much higher speeds, the take-up velocity breaks the depositing fibre jet, and continuous fibres are not collected. Besides, in tissue engineering, the alignment is important for the applications of electrospun fibres in sensors, filters and electronic devices. Ghasemi-Mobarakeh et al. [125] fabricated both random and aligned electrospun PCL/gelatin composite nanofibrous scaffolds, and they found that the aligned nanofibres strongly supported the nerve stem cells and enhanced the neurite outgrowth and cell differentiation.

Also, previous studies demonstrated that aligned electrospun nanofibres could control the orientation of neurons caused by the contact guidance [9, 125–127]. For example, the cells cultured on the aligned nanofibres exhibited an alignment factor of 0.74, much higher than 0.19 on the randomly orientated scaffold [128]. Schnell et al. [127] examined the ability of aligned nanofibrous scaffolds to direct axonal outgrowth and glial cell migration in peripheral nerve regeneration. Both PCL and collagen/PCL nanofibrous scaffolds were found to support oriented outgrowth of axons and glial cell migration, the collagen/PCL blend was found to give superior guidance of axons. These experiments demonstrate the potential applications in which it is desirable to develop a nanofibrous scaffold containing aligned fibres.

Our group also fabricated aligned PLLA/PCL/F-MWNT composite membranes by electrospinning [129]. Firstly, MWNTs were functionalised with strong acid oxidation (denoted hereafter by F-MWNT) to improve their dispersion in PLLA/PCL (1/1) blends. Owing to the high rotation speed of the drum collector at 3000 rpm, the electrospun fibres are highly aligned. However, higher rotation speed also more possibly leads to breakage of the fibres. From Fig. 8.5, F-MWNTs are well dispersed in the electrospun composite fibres with 1.25 wt. % nano-filler and aligned along the fibre axis, leading to the smooth surface of electrospun fibres. However, when F-MWNTs are increased to 3.75 wt. %, MWNTs tend to aggregate in the spun fibres, and some protruded parts of F-MWNTs existed on the fibre surface, yielding the beaded structure and a wider fibre diameter distribution. Figure 8.6 shows the morphological changes of the PLLA/PCL blend and PLLA/PCL/F-MWNT composite fibrous membranes as they are degraded in PBS. At 1 week, all samples almost retain their smooth surface, swell and conglutinate with the adjacent fibres. And the increased porosity and lower crystallinity of the PLLA/PCL/F-MWNT composite fibrous membranes allow water molecules to diffuse into the fibre more easily, leading to further swelling and conglutination. At 5 weeks, the electrospun PLLA/PCL blend fibres become thinner due to biodegradation, and the electrospun composite fibres with 1.25 and 3.75 wt. % F-MWNTs become rougher and thinner. Furthermore, the fibrous membrane loses its original structure; and the disintegration of the fibres occurs in the composite membranes because of hydrolysis of PLLA and PCL.

As shown in Fig. 8.7, the cells attach and spread along the scaffolds. Typically, the ADSCs rearrange themselves in parallel to the aligned fibrous membranes with

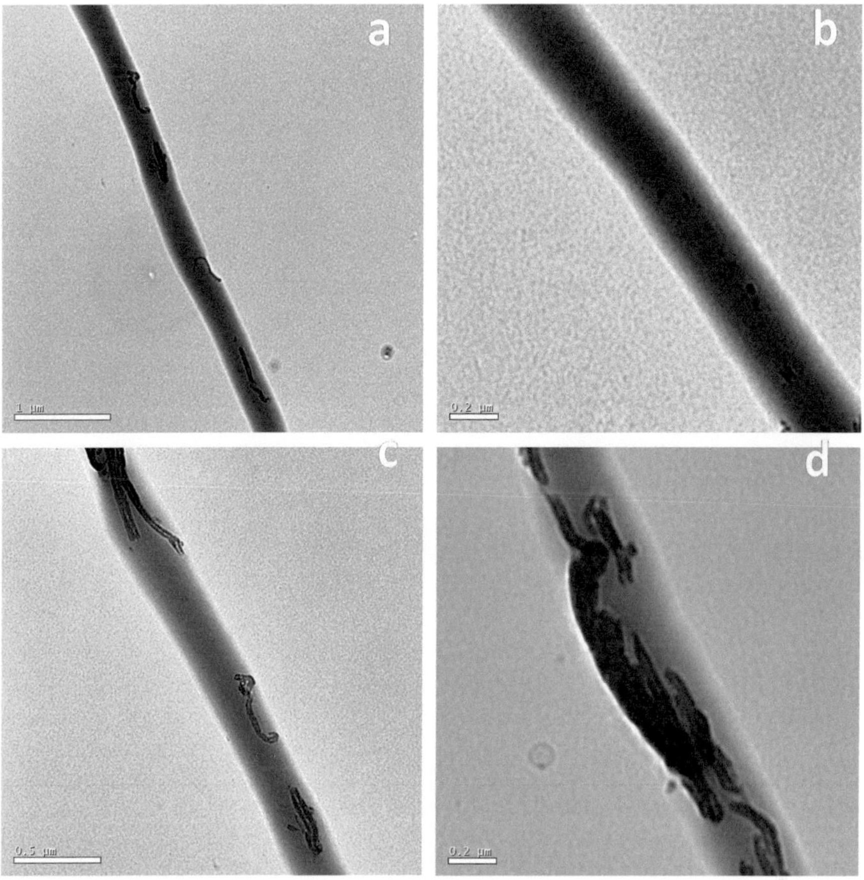

Fig. 8.5 TEM images of PLLA/PCL/F-MWNT composite fibres with 1.25 wt. % (**a** and **b**) and 3.75 wt. % (**c** and **d**) of F-MWNTs (Reprinted from Ref. [129], Copyright 2012, with permission from Elsevier)

0 wt. %, 1.25 wt. % and 3.75 wt. % of F-MWNTs. This phenomenon of reorientation, which is called contact guidance [9, 125–127], indicates the fibrous alignment induces the long axis of the cells to be in the same direction as the linear fibre by cytoskeletal remodelling. The results implied that controlled cellular orientation can be obtained by controlling the aligned fibres. This is important for the engineering of those tissues whose function comes from their oriented architecture, such as nerve, bone and smooth muscle.

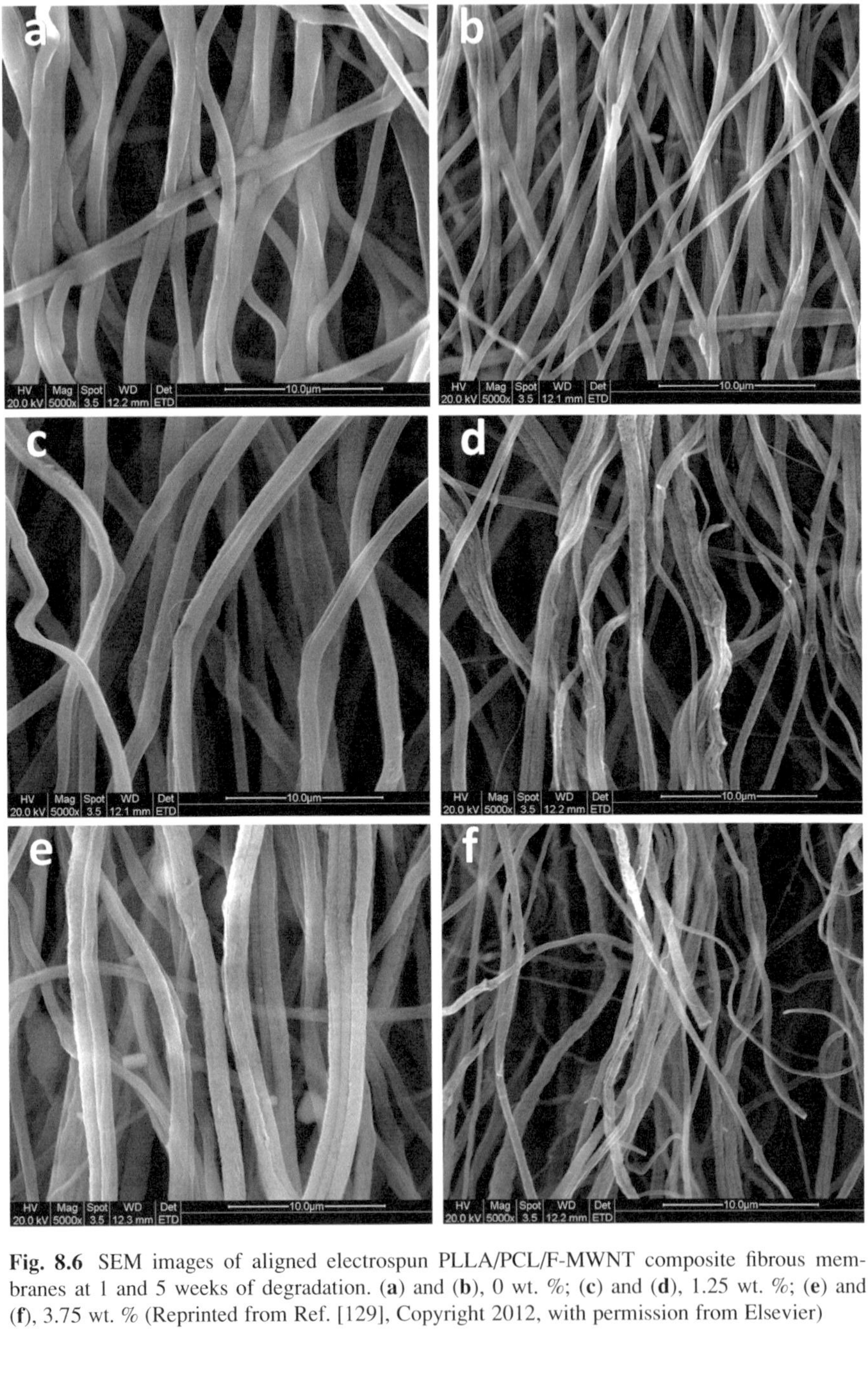

Fig. 8.6 SEM images of aligned electrospun PLLA/PCL/F-MWNT composite fibrous membranes at 1 and 5 weeks of degradation. (**a**) and (**b**), 0 wt. %; (**c**) and (**d**), 1.25 wt. %; (**e**) and (**f**), 3.75 wt. % (Reprinted from Ref. [129], Copyright 2012, with permission from Elsevier)

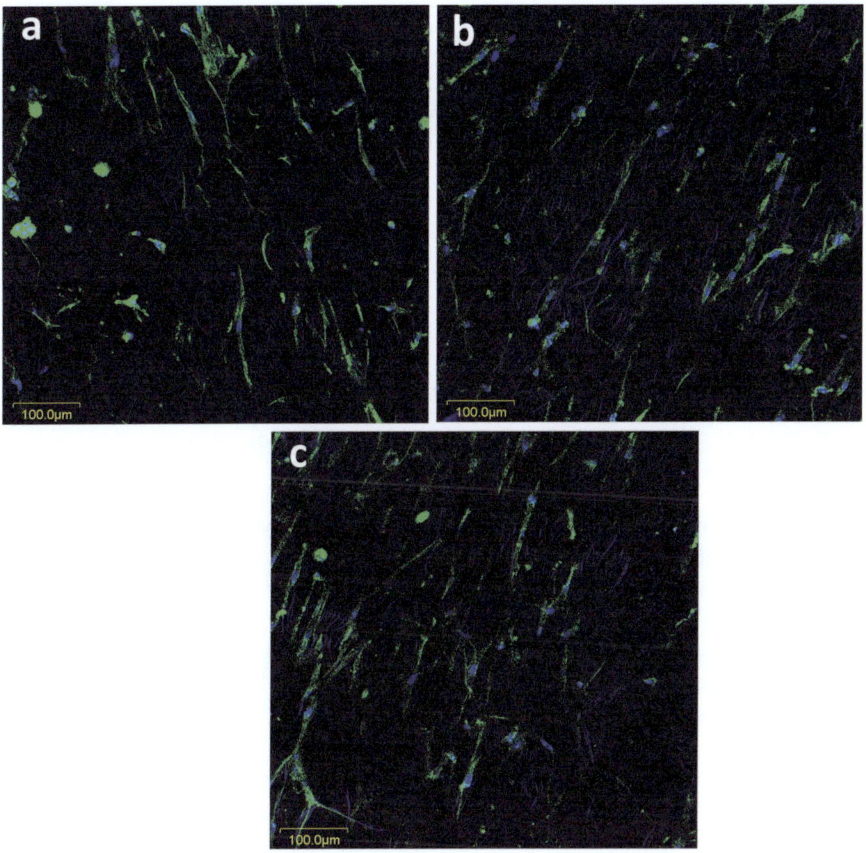

Fig. 8.7 Cell reorientation on the aligned PLLA/PCL/F-MWNT composite fibrous membranes with different content of F-MWNTs. (**a**) 0 wt. %, (**b**) 1.25 wt. % and (**c**) 3.75 wt. % (Reprinted from Ref. [129], Copyright 2012, with permission from Elsevier)

8.4 Mechanical Properties of Electrospun Polymer Scaffolds

The mechanical properties of the electrospun scaffolds must be matched to those of the native tissue. Thus the design of the scaffolds should mimic the architecture of natural tissues. Ideally, cells are contained in a 'microenvironment' that achieves a distribution of forces which encourages native tissue regeneration and maintenance while avoiding a cellular hypotrophic or hypertrophic response. Moreover, the flexibility of seeding stem cells and human cells on the electrospun fibrous scaffolds makes materials most suitable for tissue engineering applications [130, 131]. Besides, mimicking the structure of ECM, the fibrous scaffolds should be designed to possess its properties including high elasticity and stiffness [132–136]. This suggests a thorough understanding of the mechanical behaviours of

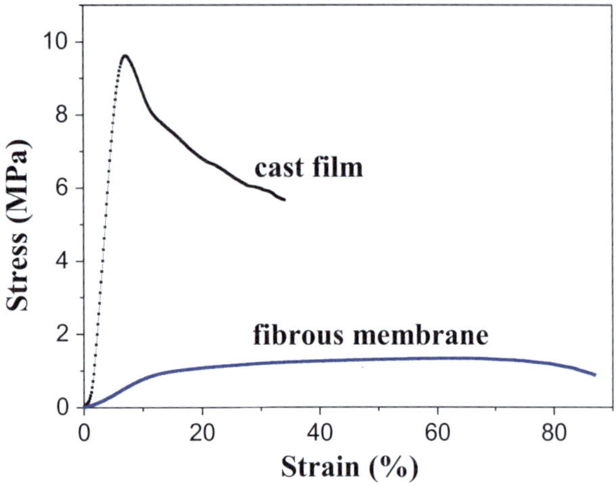

Fig. 8.8 Tensile stress–strain curves of the electrospun fibrous membrane and cast film of PLLA/PCL (1/1) blend (Reproduced from Ref. [84] by permission of John Wiley & Sons Ltd)

electrospun scaffolds is essential. For performance analysis, Young's modulus of elasticity, tensile strength and strain at break were investigated since these values are commonly reported for tissue engineering applications.

Electrospinning is different to other moulding processes and provides electrospun fibres with different mechanical properties. In our previous study [84], we evaluated mechanical properties of the PLLA/PCL blend fibrous membrane and cast film (Fig. 8.8). Since the electrospun PLLA/PCL (1/1) blend fibrous membrane has a higher porosity and lower crystallinity, its Young's modulus and tensile strength are expected to decrease to 6.46 MPa and 1.21 MPa from 89.0 MPa and 9.4 MPa of the PLLA/PCL (1/1) blend cast film, but its elongation at break increases to 85.6 % from 32.4 % of the cast film. The high porosity and ductility provide the electrospun PLLA/PCL (1/1) blend fibrous membrane with a potential as tissue scaffold. Chen et al. [112] also reported that the tensile strength and elongation at break (or toughness) of electrospun membrane are much higher than those of the cast film, due to the high orientation of the electrospun nanofibres in the membranes.

Shields et al. [31] reported that electrospun collagen fibres with a diameter of about 100 nm intended for articular cartilage repair have Young's modulus of 170 MPa and maximum stress of 3.3 MPa. These values closely match the cartilage mechanical properties of Young's modulus of 130 MPa and maximum stress of 20 MPa [137]. Soffer et al. [138] successfully electrospun silk into tubular structures with an inner diameter of ~3 mm and an average wall thickness of 0.15 mm. An average tensile strength of 2.42 ± 0.48 MPa and a linear modulus of 2.45 ± 0.47 MPa were obtained. Recently, inorganic particles, such as HA and CNTs, have been widely co-electrospun into polymer nanofibres for enhanced mechanical properties.

8.4.1 CNT-Reinforced Electrospun Fibrous Scaffolds

Many studies showed that the incorporation of CNTs reinforces the mechanical properties of electrospun fibres [139–142]. In our previous study [129], we evaluated mechanical properties of the aligned PLLA/PCL/F-MWNT fibrous scaffold. Figure 8.9 shows the stress–strain curves of PLLA/PCL blend and PLLA/PCL/F-MWNT composite fibrous membranes. Both tensile strength and Young's modulus became substantially higher with increase of the F-MWNTs. At 1.25 wt. % F-MWNTs, the composite fibrous membrane shows improvements of 39.9 % in modulus and 76.2 % in tensile strength. And at 3.75 wt. % F-MWNTs, the Young's modulus and tensile strength of the composite fibrous membrane further increase by 101.8 % and 134.6 %, respectively. Thus, the aligned F-MWNTs reinforce the electrospun PLLA/PCL blend fibrous membrane. The results have been observed in the electrospun PA6/MWNT, silk/MWNT and PAN/MWNT composite fibrous membranes [140–142]. As expected, the interfacial adhesion ensures the efficient load transfer from polymer matrix to F-MWNTs, which leads to high mechanical properties. Moreover, the ductility, as revealed by the elongation at break, shows to increase by 58.6 % and 34 % at 1.25 and 3.75 wt. % F-MWNTs, respectively, for the composite fibrous membrane in comparison with the PLLA/PCL blend membrane [129]. The poorer ductility of the composite membrane at the higher content of F-MWNT is largely due to the aggregation of the nano-fillers [140, 142].

Sen et al. [110] fabricated SWCNT-reinforced polystyrene (PS) and PU fibrous membranes using electrospinning method. They found that the SWCNT bundles are oriented parallel to the PS/SWCNT nanofibre axis. The tensile strength and the Young's modulus of PU/ester-functionalised SWCNT composite membranes are enhanced by 104 and 250 % as compared to the electrospun pure PU membranes. They have also developed a flexible approach to the alignment of SWNT that allows their hierarchical assembly, and orientation of SWNT is directionally controllable [143]. Aligned nanofibrous nanocomposites of nylon 6 and surface-

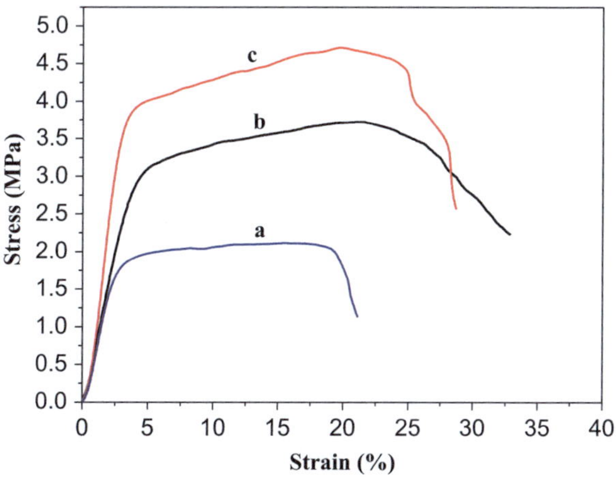

Fig. 8.9 Tensile stress–strain curves of aligned electrospun PLLA/PCL/F-MWNT composite fibrous membranes with different contents of F-MWNTs. (**a**) 0 wt. %, (**b**) 1.25 wt. % and (**c**) 3.75 wt. % (Reprinted from Ref. [129], Copyright 2012, with permission from Elsevier)

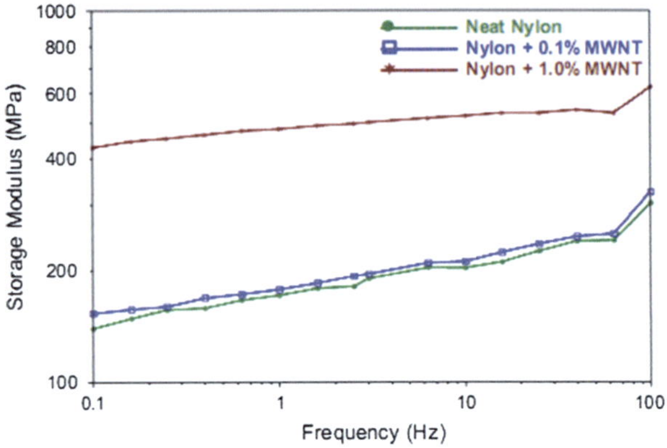

Fig. 8.10 Effect of MWNT on storage modulus of the non-woven aligned fibre mat at 6000 rpm (Reprinted from Ref. [108], Copyright 2007, with permission from Elsevier)

modified MWNTs were successfully prepared via electrospinning, using a rotating mandrel [108], which showed that the effects of nylon fibre alignment and MWNT orientation on the mechanical properties were manifested, which increased with high take-up speed and MWNT concentration. A twofold modulus increase is also observed for the neat nylon 6 as the speed increases from 3000 to 4500 rpm, but with little increase at 6000 rpm. The aligned fibres exhibited a much higher stiffness than the randomly aligned mat. At a given collector speed (6000 rpm), Fig. 8.10 shows an increase in modulus with MWNT loading. The largest increase in the modulus is the 1 wt. % MWNTs loading. Such factors as MWNTs and high take-up speed resulted in formation of aligned nanofibrous scaffolds with MWNTs alignment and mechanical stiffness. Ge et al. [105] reported highly oriented, large area continuous composite nanofibre sheets made from surface-oxidised MWNTs and poly(acrylonitrile) (PAN). They found that the tensile modulus values of the compressed composite nanofibre sheets were improved significantly to 10.9 and 14.5 GPa along the fibre winding direction at the MWNT loading of 10 and 20 wt. %, respectively.

It has been known that polyimide (PI) is among the ultrastrong polymers but usually possesses low toughness or elongation at break. High performance PI nanocomposites fibrous membranes were successfully fabricated with high toughness and enhanced overall mechanical properties by incorporation of CNTs [112]. Adding 1 wt. % CNTs can dramatically improve the overall tensile properties of PI membranes. With increasing the CNT content, the modulus of the membranes increases evidently. For example, the PI/CNT composite membrane with 10 wt. % CNTs possesses the highest tensile modulus, and the optimised tensile or yield strength is observed for the membrane containing 3.5 wt. % F-MWNTs, whose elongation at break can reach nearly 100 %. When the CNT content is further increased from 3.5 to 10 wt. %, all the values of the tensile or yield strength and elongation at break gradually decrease. For the membrane containing 10 wt. % MWNTs, its tensile strength is even lower than that of the neat PI membrane. Therefore, the tensile results may indicate that CNT agglomerations are probably formed to certain extent when the CNT content is above 3.5 wt. %.

8.4.2 HA-Reinforced Electrospun Fibrous Scaffolds

The development of scaffolds mimicking the composition, structure and mechanical properties of human bone matrix has become one of the major goals in the bone regeneration and tissue engineering fields. Human bone is a ceramic/biopolymer hybrid with a three-dimensional woven structure made up of 65–70 wt. % HA ($Ca_{10}(PO_4)_6(OH)_2$) crystals and 30–35 wt. % type I collagen fibres. In bone, the HA crystals mainly contribute to its compressive strength and stiffness, while collagen fibres provide the corresponding tensile properties.

To mimic the human bone matrix, Kim et al. [96] fabricated a HA/gelation fibrous scaffold by electrospinning. The HA/gelatin mixture was lyophilised and dissolved in the organic solvent HFP and then electrospun under controlled conditions. With this method, the HA nanocrystals are well distributed within the gelatin fibres. Compared with pure gelatin, the nanocomposite fibres significantly improve the bone-derived cellular activity, thus signifying good potential in the application of guided tissue (bone) regeneration. Stanishevsky et al. [144] also electrospun the HA/collagen composites for hard tissue scaffold applications and demonstrated that the strength of the fibres can be controlled by loading HA fillers. The properties of the electrospun material can be easily controlled by the HA content in the fibres.

Collagen fibres are self-assembled in an orderly fashion and generate channels or grooves. Mineral particles originate and develop at the grooves that can grow in length and width as the sheets of mineral platelets. The mineral platelets are placed parallel to each other and provide strength to the composite. Thus, the arrangement of collagen and bone crystals at the structural level can critically affect the mechanical integrity of the whole system [145, 146]. The strength of the tissue scaffolds processed by the conventional methods lacks the architecture of the natural composites, and hence their mechanical properties are drastically different from natural bone composites. However, the electrospinning technique is capable of mimicking the protein-guided mechanism and aligns the HA particles along the fibre axis direction.

Fibrous PCL/HA nanohybrids were fabricated by Bianco et al. [147], in which the HA content ranged from 2 to 55 wt. %. Electrospun mats showed a non-woven architecture; their average fibre size was 1.5 ± 0.5 μm and porosity 80–90 %. Up to 6.4 wt. % HA, the nanohybrids displayed enhanced mechanical and dynamo-mechanical properties. However, for nanohybrids with 25–55 wt. % HA, the yielding stress, ultimate tensile strength and strain at failure decreased due to the increased micrometric HA clusters.

HA and PLA were fabricated into composite fibrous scaffolds by electrospinning [97]. A surfactant, hydroxysteric acid (HSA), was used to effectively disperse hydrophilic HA particles in chloroform solutions of PLA. Cellular assay experiments indicated that the electrospun scaffolds have excellent cell attachment and proliferation properties as well as an enhanced expression of alkaline phosphatase at 7 days of culturing. Peng et al. [148] also attempted to improve the mechanical strength, modulus and toughness of the PLLA/HA electrospun scaffolds by aligning the needle-shaped HA particles within PLLA nanofibres.

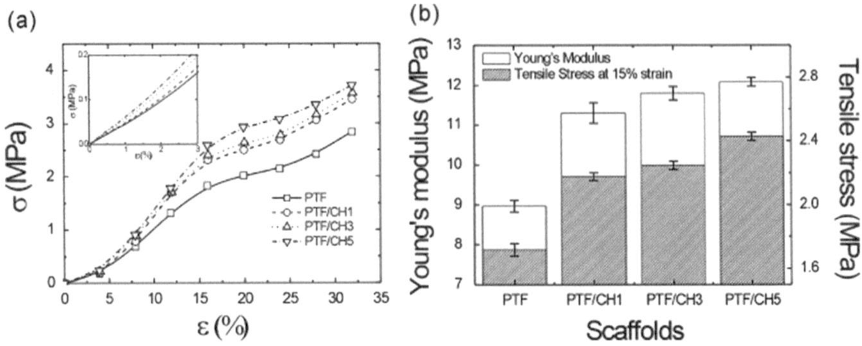

Fig. 8.11 (**a**) Stress–strain curves for the scaffolds and (**b**) comparisons of Young's modulus and tensile stress at 15 % strain between PTF and PTF/CH scaffolds (n = 5). PTF refers the PCL nanofibres-embedded PCL/β-TCP as a scaffold, where the symbols 'P', 'T' and 'F' denote PCL strut, β-tricalcium phosphate and PCL fibres, respectively. CH1, CH3 and CH5 refer to the collagen/HA with 1, 3 and 5wt. % of HA, respectively (Reprinted with the permission from Ref. [149], Copyright 2012 American Chemical Society)

For bone tissue regeneration, a porous scaffold must provide sufficient temporary mechanical support to withstand in vivo stresses and avoid excessive new tissue deformation. Bioceramics have been applied widely for bone tissue regeneration, attributable to their excellent biochemical cues for the cells. However, the major shortcoming of these materials is their brittleness compared to native bone. Recently, a simple coating technique with bioceramic has been developed to reinforce the scaffolds. For example, Yeo and Kim [149] fabricated the PCL nanofibres-embedded PCL/β-tricalcium phosphate (β-TCP) composite scaffolds and used a simple coating process to reinforce the scaffolds with collagen/HA mixture. The stress–strain curves of the composite scaffolds as a function of the HA concentration in the coating solution (Fig. 8.11a) reveal a typical curve for porous materials. As shown in Fig. 8.11b, the Young's modulus of the composite scaffolds increases with the HA concentration in the collagen coating solution. As coated by 5 wt. % collagen/HA mixture, the Young's modulus and tensile stress at 15 % strain of surface-reinforced scaffolds increase from 8.9 MPa and 1.8 MPa of the untreated scaffolds to 12.1 MPa and 2.6 MPa, respectively. The reason may be the reinforcing effect of the coated nanosised HA particles and the slightly reduced porosity of the scaffolds [150]. From these results, we can infer that the simple coating process with bioceramics is beneficial to reinforcement of the electrospun fibrous scaffolds.

8.5 Surface Modification of Electrospun Scaffold for Biomedical Applications

As discussed above, the modifications of copolymerisation, blending, composition and alignment significantly improve physical and biological properties of electrospun fibrous scaffolds. Further, surface chemical or physical modifications with bioactive molecules or cell-recognisable ligands are often essential to render the electrospun fibrous scaffolds with bio-modulating or biomimetic microenvironments for cells and tissues.

8.5.1 Chemical Immobilisation and Surface Graft Polymerisation

Chemical immobilisation and surface graft polymerisation have been introduced not only to confer surface hydrophilicity but also to introduce multifunctional groups on the surface of electrospun fibrous scaffolds for enhancing the adhesion, proliferation and differentiation of cells [25, 151–155]. Primary amine and carboxylate groups are most extensively employed to immobilise bioactive molecules. As reported by Kim and Yoo [156], biomolecules are covalently immobilised via peptide bond through amino groups, and then a matrix metalloproteinase (MMP)-cleavable linker is introduced between gene–vector complex and the electrospun scaffolds, so that gene release can be controlled by external MMP cleavage. Also, carboxylic groups on the surface of polymeric fibres with different amounts of polyacrylic acid are employed for conjugation with collagen [157]. Similarly, acrylic acid-immobilised fibres were conjugated to amine groups to prepare aminated fibres [158]. These fibres are further employed for in vitro cultivation of umbilical cord blood cells. For example, poly(acrylonitrile-co-maleic acid) (PANMA) is electrospun, and then lipase is immobilised onto the fibrous surface through the reaction between carboxylic groups of PANMA and the amine groups of lipase [159, 160]. Hydroxyl groups were also employed for the chemical immobilisation of bioactive molecules. For example, Jia et al. [161] synthesised hydroxyl-terminated PS (PS-OH) with initiator containing hydroxyl, and then alpha-chymotrypsin is covalently attached on the surface of the electrospun PS-OH fibres.

Ma et al. [25] reported a chemical approach for modification of the electrospun polyethylene terephthalate (PET) nanofibre surface by grafting gelatin to overcome the chemical and biological inertness of the PET surface. The electrospun PET scaffolds were treated with formaldehyde to generate hydroxyl groups. After methacrylic acids were polymerised on the modified electrospun fibre surface with Ce (IV) as the initiator, gelatins were conjugated to immobilise on the nanofibrous scaffolds. They also tested the bioactivity of the gelation-modified electrospun PET scaffold by using endothelial cells (ECs). The gelatin-modified PET scaffold showed an obvious improvement in cell adhesion, spreading and proliferation compared with the unmodified PET scaffold. The electrospun cellulose acetate fibrous scaffold was hydrolysed and followed by grafting of PEG diacylchloride, and lipase enzyme was then attached to the scaffold surface through the coupling with PEG spacers [153]. The results showed that the bound lipase exhibited much better retention ability of catalytic activity after exposure to cyclohexane (81 %), toluene (62 %) and hexane (34 %) than the activity of the free lipase (25 %). Similarly, Aznar-Cervantes et al. [162] successfully modified the silk fibroin nano- and micromeshes through surface graft polymerisation of pyrrole. Both of silk fibroin and polypyrrole-coated silk fibroin meshes show quite similar bioactivity for human fibroblast's (hFb) attachment and growth. Similar results are obtained by seeding adult human mesenchymal stem cells (ahMSCs) on the above two meshes. But, mechanical properties of the meshes are greatly improved. After surface graft polymerisation of pyrrole, the Young's modulus of the modified meshes increases to 310.5 MPa from 266.7 MPa of the uncoated meshes. Furthermore, the modified meshes have higher electroactivity allowing anion storage and delivery during oxidation/reduction reactions in aqueous solutions. For hepatocyte culture, Chua et al. [163] grafted a hepatocyte-specified galactose ligand onto electrospun poly(ε-caprolactone-co-ethyl ethane phosphate) (PCLEEP) nanofibres. As shown in Fig. 8.12, the electrospun PCLEEP nanofibres are first cleaned by ethanol and grafted with poly(acrylic acid) (PAA) by photo-induced polymerisation. Then, 1-*O*-(6′-aminohexyl)-D-galacto-pyranoside (AHG) is conjugated to the PAA chains in a sodium phosphate buffer containing N-hydroxysulfosuccinimide (NHS) and 1-ethyl-3-(3-dimethylaminopropyl) carbodiimide hydrochloride (EDC). During cell culture, hepatocytes adhere to the surface through the galactose-asialoglycoprotein receptor (ASGPR). The results showed that hepatocytes are cultured on electrospun galactosylated scaffolds with superior biological properties such as cell attachment, albumin synthesis and 3-methylcholanthrene-induced cytochrome P450 function.

Except for the electrospun nanofibrous scaffolds, the spin-coating films are fabricated with the same materials and modified with the same procedure for comparison. After 8 days, hepatocytes cultured on modified electrospun scaffolds form spheroids that engulfed the galactosylated nanofibres (Fig. 8.13d–f). Compared with the modified cast films (Fig. 8.13a–c), the spheroids are immobilised on the scaffold and would not detach from the scaffold upon agitation. The results showed that hepatocyte spheroid immobilisation and stabilisation strategy through the use of galactosylated nanofibrous scaffolds would be advantageous in the design of a bioartificial liver assist device.

8.5.2 Surface Physical Adsorption and Assembly

For the above surface chemical modification, the immobilised molecules are not easily leached out from the surface-modified fibres when incubated over an extended period due to covalent immobilisation. But surface physical modifications, such as surface physical adsorption and assembly, are much simpler to load biomolecules onto electrospun scaffolds, which is to dip the scaffolds into an aqueous phase containing biomolecules.

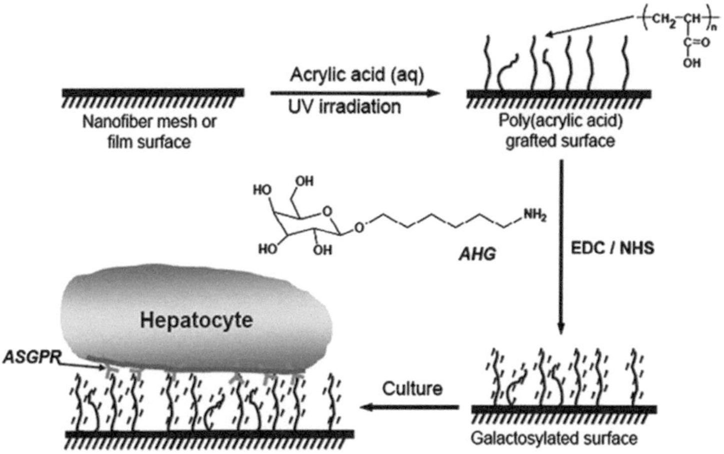

Fig. 8.12 Surface modification scheme for galactose conjugation to PCLEEP nanofibre mesh and spin-cast film (Reprinted from Ref. [163], Copyright 2005, with permission from Elsevier)

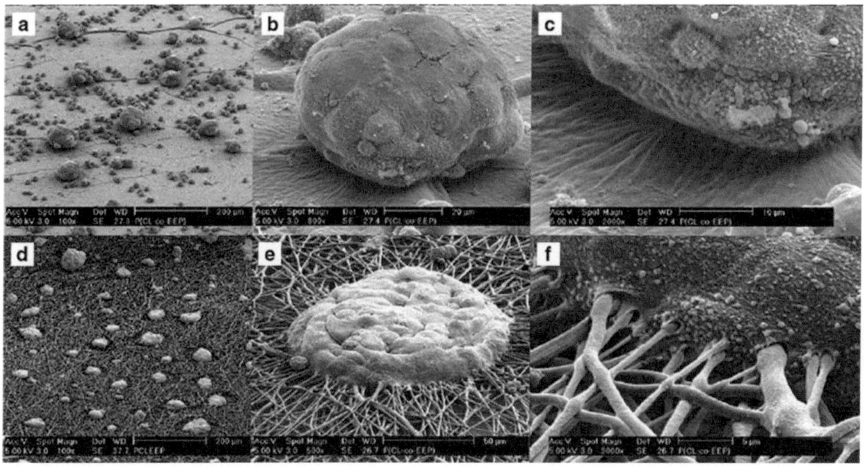

Fig. 8.13 SEM images of hepatocytes after 8 days of culture: (**a–c**) hepatocytes cultured on galactosylated spin-cast film formed around spheroids; (**d–f**) in contrast, hepatocytes cultured on galactosylated electrospun scaffold showed aggregates that engulfed the functional nanofibres (Reprinted from Ref. [163], Copyright 2005, with permission from Elsevier)

On the principle of physical interaction, biomolecules in the form of solutions or emulsions attach to the surface of scaffolds via electrostatic forces, hydrogen bonding, hydrophobic interaction and van der Waals interaction [164–167]. Heparin, a highly sulphated glycosaminoglycan, has strong binding affinity with various growth factors such as fibroblast growth factor (FGF), vascular endothelial growth factor (VEGF), heparin-binding epidermal growth factor (HBEGF) and transforming growth factor-β (TGF-β). Firstly, heparin is immobilised on the surface of electrospun fibrous scaffolds, and growth factors are attached for local delivery of growth factors and consequent mitogenic induction [168]. Loading drug is a very straightforward and effective method due to the unique morphological feature of electrospun fibres. For example, to load a commercial antibiotic drug, Biteral®, the drug solution is simply dropped on PCL non-woven sheets for adsorption [169]. From the in vitro release data, nearly 80 % of the initial burst is observed within 3 h and the release ends after almost 18 h. A rapid drug release profile is highly desirable for preventing infections at an early stage.

The assembly of target molecules or functional nanoparticles such as silver or HA on the surface of electrospun fibres has been attempted for biomedical applications [170–173]. Seyedjafari et al. [174] reported that nano-HA (n-HA) was coated on the plasma-treated surface of electrospun PLLA nanofibres. They used human cord blood-derived unrestricted somatic stem cells (USSC) under osteogenic induction to investigate the capacity of the scaffolds for bone formation. During osteogenic differentiation, significantly higher values of ALP activity, biomineralisation and bone-related gene expression were observed on n-HA/PLLA compared to PLLA scaffolds. The results showed that surface-coated n-HA stimulates the effect of fibres on the orientation of USSC towards osteolineage.

A versatile surface modification method is layer-by-layer (LbL) multilayer assembly that allows surface of fibres to be precisely coated, and synthetic polyions, biopolymers such as DNA and enzymes, viruses, dendrimers, colloids, inorganic particles and dyes are easily incorporated into the multilayers [175]. Many groups have realised the potential of multilayers for biomedical applications [176–183]. Ge et al. [184] used electrospinning and LbL assembly to fabricate the hollow multilayered PE nanofibres by selectively removing the fibre templates. The PS/MWCNT nanofibres were employed as templates to self-assembly multilayered polyelectrolytes by LbL assembly; thus, hollow PE/MWCNT composite nanofibres were obtained by selectively removing part of the template [185]. Müller et al. [186] reported that the polyelectrolyte multilayer was deposited on the surface of electrospun fibres. The PS fibre surface was endowed with negative charges by sulphonation of phenyl groups, and then poly(allylamine hydrochloride) (PAH) and poly(styrene sulphonate) (PSS) was conducted on the PS fibre surface via LbL assembly, followed by the dissolution of PS core fibres, resulting in hollow polyelectrolyte complex tubes. Di-block oligonucleotides (polyA15G15 and polyT15C15) multilayers were also built-up based on the DNA hybridisation mechanism by LbL assembly. Upon build-up cycles, the DNA multilayer grew in a linear manner, showing a smoother surface compared to the PAH/PSS multilayer surface. It indicates that this facile surface modification of electrospun fibres with synthetic polymers and biopolymers could provide an opportunity for creating a variety of drug-releasing surfaces.

Our group also fabricated chondroitin sulphate (CS)/chitosan (CHS) multilayer-modified PLLA/PCL blend fibres with the goal of combining the good biocompatibility of the natural extracellular matrix-like molecules. Firstly, 1,6-hexanediamine is dissolved in isopropyl alcohol; and hydrochloric acid solution is used to activate the PLLA/PCL blend substrate in order to obtain a stable positively charged surface that can be further used to deposit biomacromolecule polyelectrolytes by LbL assembly. The CS/CHS multilayer modified PLLA/PCL fibrous scaffolds were investigated by X-ray photoelectron spectroscopy (XPS) and contact angle. From Fig. 8.14, the unmodified PLLA/PCL blend fibrous surface generates the three expected peaks, indicating that this surface contains three carbon regions, i.e. the binding energies of 284.5 eV for $C_{C\text{-}H}$, 286.7 eV for $C_{C\text{-}O}$ and 289.0 eV for $C_{C=O}$, respectively. After amination treated by 1,6-hexanediamine, the intensity of $C_{C\text{-}H}$ peak increases notably, and there appears a new carbon peak at 287.2 eV, indicating the existence of an amide bond on the surface of PLLA/PCL fibres. For the CS/CHS multilayer assembled PLLA/PCL blend fibrous surface, the carbon peak of amide indicates that the CS/CHS multilayers cover the fibrous surface. Besides, there are obvious nitrogen peaks (400.1 eV) on both aminated and CS/CHS multilayer assembled PLLA/PCL fibres (Fig. 8.14c, e), while there is no detectable nitrogen on the electrospun PLLA/PCL blend fibres (Fig. 8.14a). Furthermore, Fig. 8.15 shows that the hydrophilicity of PLLA/PCL blend fibrous surface is evidently enhanced after the amination treatment and LbL assembly of CS and CHS layers. Compared with conventional coatings, polyelectrolyte LbL multilayers are stable and easy to process, indicating that the LbL assembly may be a good choice for modifying 3D scaffolds for drug delivery and tissue engineering.

8.6 Conclusion

Electrospun polymer fibrous scaffolds have held great promise and been of considerable potential for biomedical applications in the recent years. A successful fabrication of fibrous scaffolds must start with the proper polymeric materials, a judicious fabrication pathway and possible postmodification with functional reagent. Tremendous efforts have been made to search for suitable scaffold materials. An ideal scaffold should have similar biochemical and biomechanical properties to the ECM. The desirable properties of the electrospun fibrous scaffolds can be achieved by copolymerisation, blending and composition. Especially, inorganic particles, such as HA and CNTs, have been widely co-electrospun into polymer nanofibres for reinforcing the fibres. Besides, the oriented fibre alignment also significantly improves the physical and biological properties of fibrous scaffolds, which can be used to control the mechanical properties as well as the biological response. Furthermore, the surface physical and chemical modifications of electrospun fibres are often conducted to obtain the desired scaffold properties and enhance the interaction between cells and scaffolds in tissue engineering applications. Notably, LbL assembly is widely used attributable to the precise control on coating thickness and composition. As an advanced polymer processing

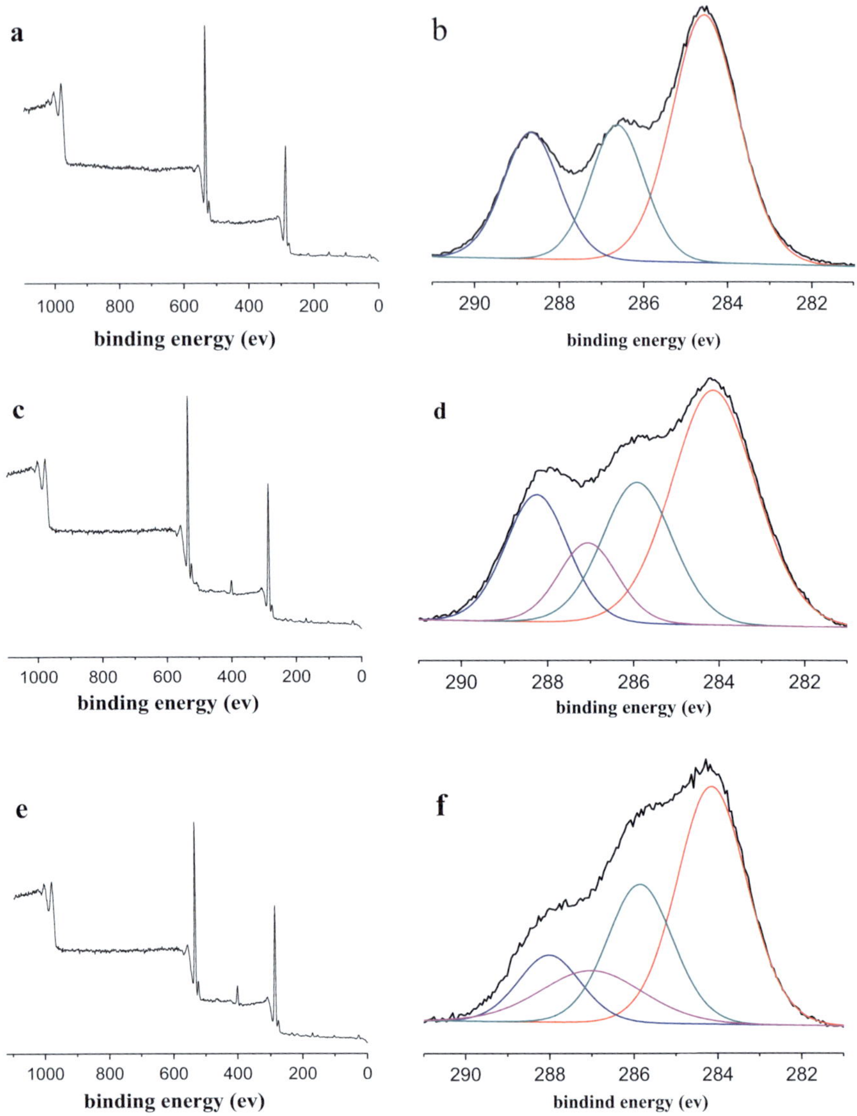

Fig. 8.14 XPS spectra of different PLLA/PCL fibrous membranes: (**a**) and (**b**) the unmodified PLLA/PCL, (**c**) and (**d**) aminated PLLA/PCL, and (**e**) and (**f**) CS/CHS assembled PLLA/PCL

technique, electrospinning has emerged for extensive applications in biomedical engineering, whereas its true potential has yet to be fully realised. It is expected to gain a better fundamental understanding of the electrospinning, develop the innovative electrospinning techniques and expand more applications in biomedical engineering in the future.

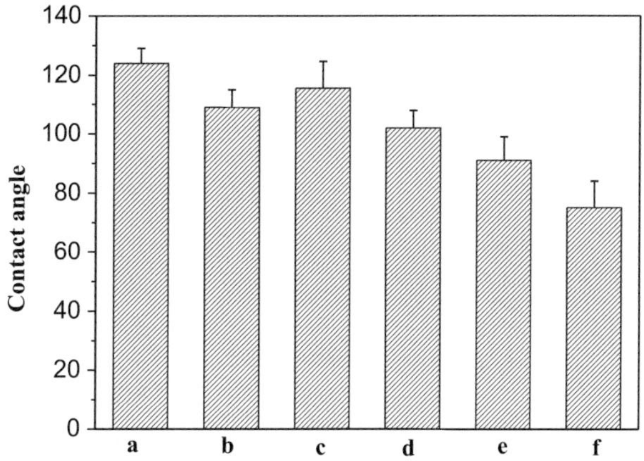

Fig. 8.15 Contact angle data of PLLA/PCL fibrous membranes with amination and different assembled layers. (**a**) The unmodified PLLA/PCL virgin, (**b**) amination, (**c**) one layer (**d**) two layers, (**e**) three layers and (**f**) five layers

Acknowledgement The authors sincerely thank the National Natural Science Foundation of China (21477118) and National Basic Research Program of China (973 Program) (2011CB606002) for support of this work.

References

1. Doshi J, Reneker DH (1995) Electrospinning process and applications of electrospun fibers. J Electrostat 35:151–160
2. Reneker DH, Chun I (1996) Nanometer diameter fibers of polymers, produced by electrospinning. Nanotechnology 7:216–223
3. Schreuder-Gibson H, Gibson P, Wadsworth L, Hemphil SL, Vontorcik J (2002) Effect of filter deformation on the filtration and air flow for elastomeric nonwoven media. Adv Filtr Sep Technol 15:525–537
4. Wang B, Luo L, Ding Y, Zhao D, Zhang Q (2012) Synthesis of hollow copper oxide by electrospinning and its application as a nonenzymatic hydrogen peroxide sensor. Colloid Surf B Biointerfaces 97:51–56
5. Wang XY, Kim YG, Drew C, Ku BC, Kumar J, Samuelson LA (2004) Electrostatic assembly of conjugated polymer thin layers on electrospun nanofibrous membranes for biosensors. Nano Lett 4:331–334
6. Gorji M, Jeddi AAA, Gharehaghaji AA (2012) Fabrication and characterization of polyurethane electrospun nanofiber membranes for protective clothing applications. J Appl Polym Sci 125(5):4135–4141
7. Liu HQ, Kameoka J, Czaplewski DA, Craighead HG (2004) Polymeric nanowire chemical sensor. Nano Lett 4:671–675
8. Riboldi SA, Sampaolesi M, Neuenschwander P, Cossu G, Mantero S (2005) Electrospun degradable polyesterurethane membranes: potential scaffolds for skeletal muscle tissue engineering. Biomaterials 26:4606–4615
9. Yang F, Murugan R, Wang S, Ramakrishna S (2005) Electrospinning of nano/micro scale poly(L-lactic acid) aligned fibers and their potential in neural tissue engineering. Biomaterials 26:2603–2610
10. Formhals A (1934) Apparatus for producing artificial filaments from material such as cellulose acetate. US patent no. 1975504

11. Zachariades AE, Porter RS, Doshi J, Srinivasan G, Reneker D (1995) High modulus polymers. A novel electrospinning process. Polym News 20:206–207
12. Fang X, Reneker DH (1997) DNA fibers by electrospinning. J Macromol Sci B 36:169–173
13. Srinivasan G, Reneker DH (1995) Structure and morphology of small diameter electrospun aramid fibers. Polym Int 36:195–201
14. Fong H, Reneker DH (1999) Elastomeric nanofibers of styrene-butadiene-styrene triblock copolymer. J Polym Sci B Polym Phys 37:3488–3493
15. Yarin AL, Koombhongse S, Reneker DH (2001) Taylor cone and jetting from liquid droplets in electrospinning of nanofibers. J Appl Phys 90:4836–4846
16. Yarin AL, Koombhongse S, Reneker DH (2001) Bending instability in electrospinning of nanofibers. J Appl Phys 89:3018–3026
17. Desai K, Kit K, Li JJ, Zivanovic S (2008) Morphological and surface properties of electrospun chitosan nanofibers. Biomacromolecules 9:1000–1006
18. Aluigi A, Vineis C, Varesano A, Mazzuchetti G, Ferrero F, Tonin C (2008) Structure and properties of keratin/PEO blend nanofibres. Eur Polym J 44:2465–2475
19. Sanders EH, Kloefkorn R, Bowlin GL, Simpson DG, Wnek GE (2003) Two-phase electrospinning from a single electrified jet: microencapsulation of aqueous reservoirs in poly(ethylene-co-vinyl acetate) fibers. Macromolecules 36:3803–3805
20. Pham QP, Sharma U, Mikos AG (2006) Electrospinning of polymeric nanofibers for tissue engineering applications: a review. Tissue Eng 12:1197–1211
21. Ferreira AM, Gentile P, Chiono V, Ciardelli G (2012) Collagen for bone tissue regeneration. Acta Biomater 8:3191–3200
22. Ma Z, Kotaki M, Inai R, Ramakrishna S (2005) Potential of nanofiber matrix as tissue engineering scaffolds. Tissue Eng 11:101–109
23. Khil MS, Cha DI, Kim HY, Kim IS, Bhattarai N (2003) Electrospun nanofibrous polyurethane membrane as wound dressing. J Biomed Mater Res B Appl Biomater 67B:675–679
24. Buttafoco L, Kolkman NG, Poot AA, Dijkstra PJ, Vermes I, Feijen J (2005) Electrospinning collagen and elastin for tissue engineering small diameter blood vessels. J Control Release 101:322–324
25. Ma Z, Kotaki M, Yong T, He W, Ramakrishna S (2005) Surface engineering of electrospun polyethylene terephthalate (PET) nanofibers towards development of a new material for blood vessel engineering. Biomaterials 26:2527–2536
26. Katti DS, Robinson KW, Ko FK, Laurencin CT (2004) Bio-resorbable nanofiber-based systems for wound healing and drug delivery: optimization of fabrication parameters. J Biomed Mater Res B Appl Biomater 70B:286–296
27. Pawlowski KJ, Barnes CP, Boland ED, Wnek GE, Bowlin GL (2004) Biomedical nanoscience: electrospinning basic concepts, applications, and classroom demonstration. Mater Res Soc Symp Proc 827:17–28
28. How TV, Guidoin R, Young SK, Part H (1992) Engineering design of vascular prostheses, proceedings of the institution of mechanical engineers. J Eng Med 206:61–72
29. Matthews JA, Wnek GE, Simpson DG, Bowlin GL (2002) Electrospinning of collagen nanofibers. Biomacromolecules 3:232–238
30. Matthews JA, Boland ED, Wnek GE, Simpson DG, Bowlin GL (2003) Electrospinning of collagen type II: a feasibility study. J Bioact Compat Polym 18:125–134
31. Shields KJ, Beckman MJ, Bowlin GL, Wayne JS (2004) Mechanical properties and cellular proliferation of electrospun collagen type II. Tissue Eng 10:1510–1517
32. Boland ED, Matthews JA, Pawlowski KJ, Simpson DG, Wnek GE, Bowlin GL (2004) Electrospinning collagen and elastin: preliminary vascular tissue engineering. Front Biosci 9:1422–1432
33. Telemeco TA, Ayres C, Bowlin GL, Wnek GE, Boland ED, Cohen N (2005) Regulation of cellular infiltration into tissue engineering scaffolds composed of submicron diameter fibrils produced by electrospinning. Acta Biomater 1:377–385

34. Rho KS, Jeong L, Lee G, Seo BM, Park YJ, Hong SD (2006) Electrospinning of collagen nanofibers: effects on the behavior of normal human keratinocytes and early-stage wound healing. Biomaterials 27:1452–1461
35. Ikada Y, Tabata Y (1998) Protein release from gelatin matrices. Adv Drug Deliv Rev 31:287–301
36. Kuijpers AJ, Engbers GH, Krijgsveld J, Zaat SA, Dankert J, Feijen J (2000) Cross-linking and characterisation of gelatin matrices for biomedical applications. J Biomater Sci Polym Ed 11:225–243
37. Kuijpers AJ, van Wachem PB, van Luyn MJ, Plantinga JA, Engbers GH, Krijgsveld J, Zaat SA, Dankert J, Feijen J (2000) In vivo compatibility and degradation of crosslinked gelatin gels incorporated in knitted Dacron. J Biomed Mater Res 51:136–145
38. Yamamoto M, Ikada Y, Tabata Y (2001) Controlled release of growth factors based on biodegradation of gelatin hydrogel. J Biomater Sci Polym Ed 12:77–88
39. Yao CH, Liu BS, Hsu SH, Chen YS, Tsai CC (2004) Biocompatibility and biodegradation of a bone composite containing tricalcium phosphate and genipin crosslinked gelatin. J Biomed Mater Res 69A:709–717
40. Balakrishnan B, Jayakrishnan A (2005) Self-cross-linking biopolymers as injectable in situ forming biodegradable scaffolds. Biomaterials 26:3941–3951
41. Nagura M, Yokota H, Ikeura M, Gotoh Y, Ohkoshi Y (2002) Structures and physical properties of cross-linked gelatin fibers. Polym J 34:761–766
42. Kidoaki S, Kwon IK, Matsuda T (2005) Mesoscopic spatial designs of nano and microfiber meshes for tissue-engineering matrix and scaffold based on newly devised multilayering andmixing electrospinning techniques. Biomaterials 26:37–46
43. Zhang Y, Ouyang H, Lim CT, Ramakrishna S, Huang ZM (2005) Electrospinning of gelatin fibers and gelatin/PCL composite fibrous scaffolds. J Biomed Mater Res B Appl Biomater 72:156–165
44. Ma Z, He W, Yong T, Ramakrishna S (2005) Grafting of gelatin on electrospun poly (caprolactone) nanofibers to improve endothelial cell spreading and proliferation and to control cell orientation. Tissue Eng 11:1149–1158
45. Gosline JM, Demont ME, Denny MW (1986) The structure and properties of spider silk. Endeavour 10:37–43
46. Altman GH, Diaz F, Jakuba C, Calabro T, Horan RL, Chen J (2003) Silk-based biomaterials. Biomaterials 24:401–416
47. Park WH, Jeong L, Yoo DI, Hudson S (2004) Effect of chitosan on morphology and conformation of electrospun silk fibroin nanofibers. Polymer 45:7151–7157
48. Meinel L, Hofmann S, Karageorgiou V, Kirker-Head C, McCool J, Gronowicz G (2005) The inflammatory responses to silk films in vitro and in vivo. Biomaterials 26:147–155
49. Dal Pra I, Freddi G, Minic J, Chiarini A, Armato U (2005) De novo engineering of reticular connective tissue in vivo by silk fibroin nonwoven materials. Biomaterials 26:1987–1999
50. Horan RL, Antle K, Collette AL, Wang Y, Huang J, Moreau JE, Volloch V, Kaplan DL, Altman GH (2005) In vitro degradation of silk fibroin. Biomaterials 26:3385–3393
51. Min BM, Lee G, Kim SH, Nam YS, Lee TS, Park WH (2004) Electrospinning of silk fibroin nanofibers and its effect on the adhesion and spreading of normal by human keratinocytes and fibroblasts in vitro. Biomaterials 25:1289–1297
52. Min BM, Jeong L, Nam YS, Kim JM, Kim JY, Park WH (2004) Formation of silk fibroin matrices with different texture and its cellular response to normal human keratinocytes. Int J Biol Macromol 34:223–230
53. Jin HJ, Chen J, Karageorgiou V, Altman GH, Kaplan DL (2004) Human bone marrow stromal cell responses to electrospun silk fibroin mats. Biomaterials 25:1039–1047
54. Sukigara S, Gandhi M, Ayutsede J, Micklus M, Ko F (2003) Regeneration of Bombyx mori silk by electrospinning—part 1: processing parameters and geometric properties. Polymer 44:5721–5727

55. Sukigara S, Gandhi M, Ayutsede J, Micklus M, Ko F (2004) Regeneration of Bombyx mori silk by electrospinning. Part 2. Process optimization and empirical modeling using response surface methodology. Polymer 45:3701–3708
56. Wang H, Zhang Y, Shao H, Hu X (2005) Electrospun ultra-fine silk fibroin fiber from aqueous solutions. J Mater Sci 40:5359–5363
57. Wang H, Shao H, Hu X (2006) Structure of silk fibroin fibers made by an electrospun process from a silk fibroin aqueous solution. J Appl Polym Sci 101:961–968
58. Zhu J, Shao H, Hu X (2007) Morphology and structure of electrospun mats from regenerated silk fibroin aqueous solutions with adjusting pH. Int J Biol Macromol 41:469–474
59. Zhu J, Zhang Y, Shao H, Hu X (2008) Electorspinning and rheology of regenerated Bombyx mori silk fibroin aqueous solutions: the effects of pH and concentration. Polymer 49:2880–2885
60. Yang F, Xu CY, Kotaki M, Wang S, Ramakrishna S (2004) Characterization of neural stem cells on electrospun poly(L-lactic acid) nanofibrous scaffold. J Biomater Sci Polym Ed 15:1483–1497
61. Jing Z, Xu XY, Chen XS, Liang QZ, Bian XC, Yang LX, Jing XB (2003) Biodegradable electrospun fibers for drug delivery. J Control Release 92:227–231
62. Boland ED, Wnek GE, Simpson DG, Pawlowski KJ, Bowlin GL (2001) Tailoring tissue engineering scaffolds using electrostatic processing techniques: a study of poly(glycolic acid) electrospinning. J Macromol Sci A 38:1231–1243
63. Boland ED, Telemeco TA, Simpson DG, Wnek GE, Bowlin GL (2004) Utilizing acid pretreatment and electrospinning to improve biocompatibility of poly(glycolic acid) for tissue engineering. J Biomed Mater Res B Appl Biomater 71B:144–152
64. Verreck G, Chun I, Rosenblatt J, Peeters J, Van Dijck A, Mensch J, Noppe M, Brewster ME (2003) Incorporation of drugs in an amorphous state into electrospun nanofibers composed of a water-insoluble, nonbiodegradable polymer. J Control Release 92:349–360
65. Son WK, Youk JH, Lee TS, Park WH (2004) The effects of solution properties and polyelectrolyte on electrospinning of ultrafine poly (ethylene oxide) fibers. Polymer 45:2959–2966
66. Ding B, Kim HY, Lee SC, Shao CL, Lee DR, Park SJ, Kwag GB, Choi KJ (2002) Preparation and characterization of a nanoscale poly(vinyl alcohol) fiber aggregate produced by an electrospinning method. J Polym Sci B Polym Phys 40:1261–1268
67. Yao L, Haas TW, Guiseppi-Elie A, Bowlin GL, Simpson DG, Wnek GE (2003) Electrospinning and stabilization of fully hydrolyzed poly(vinyl alcohol) fibers. Chem Mater 15:1860–1864
68. Boland ED, Coleman BD, Barnes CP, Simpson DG, Wnek GE, Bowlin GL (2005) Electrospinning polydioxanone for biomedical applications. Acta Biomater 1:115–123
69. Xu XL, Zhong W, Zhou SF, Trajtman A, Alfa M (2010) Electrospun PEG-PLA nanofibrous membrane for sustained release of hydrophilic antibiotics. J Appl Polym Sci 118:588–595
70. Luu YK, Kim K, Hsiao BS, Chu B, Hadjiargyrou M (2003) Development of a nanostructured DNA delivery scaffold via electrospinning of PLGA and PLA-PEG block copolymers. J Control Release 89:341–353
71. Bhattarai SR, Bhattarai N, Yi HK, Hwang PH, Cha DI, Kim HY (2004) Novel biodegradable electrospun membrane: scaffold for tissue engineering. Biomaterials 25:2595–2602
72. Kim K, Yu M, Zong X, Chiu J, Fang D, Seo YS, Hsiao BS, Chu B (2003) Control of degradation rate and hydrophilicity in electrospun non-woven poly(d, l-lactide) nanofiber scaffolds for biomedical applications. Biomaterials 24:4977–4985
73. Mo XM, Xu CY, Kotaki M, Ramakrishna S (2004) Electrospun P(LLA-CL) nanofiber: a biomimetic extracellular matrix for smooth muscle cell and endothelial cell proliferation. Biomaterials 25:1883–1890
74. Xu CY, Inai R, Kotaki M, Ramakrishna S (2004) Aligned biodegradable nanofibrous structure: a potential scaffold for blood vessel engineering. Biomaterials 25:877–886

75. Xu CY, Inai R, Kotaki M, Ramakrishna S (2004) Electrospun nanofiber fabrication as synthetic extracellular matrix and its potential for vascular tissue engineering. Tissue Eng 10:1160–1168
76. Kwon IK, Kidoaki S, Matsuda T (2005) Electrospun nano- to microfiber fabrics made of biodegradable copolyesters: structural characteristics, mechanical properties and cell adhesion potential. Biomaterials 26:3929–3939
77. Zong X, Fang D, Kim K, Ran S, Hsiao BS, Chu B, Brathwaite C, Li S, Chen E (2002) Nonwoven nanofiber membranes of poly(lactide) and poly (glycolide-co-lactide) via electrospinning and application for antiadhesions. Polym Prepr (Am Chem Soc Div Polym Chem) 43:659–660
78. Lee IS, Kwon OH, Meng W, Kang IK (2004) Nanofabrication of microbial polyester by electrospinning promotes cell attachment. Macromol Res 12:374–378
79. Choi JS, Lee SW, Jeong L, Bae SH, Min BC, Youk JH, Park WH (2004) Effect of organosoluble salts on the nanofibrous structure of electrospun poly(3-hydroxybutyrate-co-3- hydroxyvalerate). Int J Biol Macromol 34:249–256
80. Lee KH, Kim HY, Khil MS, Ra YM, Lee DR (2003) Characterization of nano-structured poly (ε-caprolactone) nonwoven mats via electrospinning. Polymer 44:1287–1294
81. Na YH, He Y, Shuai X, Kikkawa Y, Doi Y, Inoue Y (2002) Compatibilization effect of poly (ε-caprolactone)-b-poly(ethylene glycol) block copolymers and phase morphology analysis in immiscible poly(lactide)/poly(ε-caprolactone) blends. Biomacromolecules 3:1179–1186
82. Ajami-Henriquez D, Rodríguez M, Sabino M, Castillo RV, Müller AJ, Boschetti-de-Fierro A, Abetz C, Abetz V, Dubois P (2008) Evaluation of cell affinity on poly(L-lactide) and poly(ε-caprolactone) blends and on PLLA-b-PCL diblock copolymer surfaces. J Biomed Mater Res A 87:405–417
83. Calandrelli L, Calarco A, Laurienzo P, Malinconico M, Petillo O, Peluso G (2008) Compatibilized polymer blends based on PDLLA and PCL for application in bioartificial liver. Biomacromolecules 9:1527–1534
84. Liao GY, Chen L, Zeng XY, Zhou XP, Xie XL, Peng EJ, Ye ZQ, Mai YW (2011) Electrospun PLLA/PCL blend fibers and their cellular response to adipose-derived stem cells. J Appl Polym Sci 120:2154–2165
85. Gimble JM, Katz AJ, Bunnell BA (2007) Adipose-derived stem cells for regenerative medicine. Circ Res 100:1249–1260
86. Zuk PA, Zhu M, Mizuno H, Huang J, Futrell JW, Katz AJ, Benhaim P, Lorenz HP, Hedrick MH (2001) Multilineage cells from human adipose tissue: implications for cell-based therapies. Tissue Eng 7:211–228
87. Zuk PA, Zhu M, Ashjian P, De Ugarte DA, Huang JI, Mizuno H, Alfonso ZC, Fraser JK, Benhaim P, Hedrick MH (2002) Human adipose tissue is a source of multipotent stem cells. Mol Biol Cell 13:4279–4295
88. Rodríguez LV, Alfonso Z, Zhang R, Leung J, Wu B, Ignarro LJ (2006) Clonogenic multipotent stem cells in human adipose tissue differentiate into functional smooth muscle cells. Proc Natl Acad Sci 103:12167–12172
89. Spasova M, Stoilova O, Manolova N, Altankov G, Rashkov I (2007) Preparation of PLLA/PEG nanofibers by electrospinning and potential applications. J Bioact Compat Polym 22:62–76
90. Wang BY, Fu SZ, Ni PY, Peng JR, Zheng L, Luo F, Liu H, Qian ZY (2012) Electrospun polylactide/poly(ethylene glycol) hybrid fibrous scaffolds for tissue engineering. J Biomed Mater Res Part A 100A:441–449
91. Huang L, Nagapudi K, Apkarian RP, Chaikof EL (2001) Engineered collagen-PEO nanofibers and fabrics. J Biomater Sci Polym Ed 12:979–993
92. Son WK, Youk JH, Lee TS, Park WH (2004) Preparation of antimicrobial ultrafine cellulose acetate fibers with silver nanoparticles. Macromol Rapid Commun 25:1632–1637
93. Melaiye A, Sun ZH, Hindi K, Milsted A, Ely D, Reneker DH, Tessier CA, Youngs WJ (2005) Silver(I)-imidazole cyclophane gem-diol complexes encapsulated by electrospun tecophilic

nanofibers: formation of nanosilver particles and antimicrobial activity. J Am Chem Soc 127:2285–2291
94. Fujihara K, Kotaki M, Ramakrishna S (2005) Guided bone regeneration membrane made of polycaprolactone/calcium carbonate composite nanofibers. Biomaterials 26:4139–4147
95. Fan HS, Wen XT, Tan YF, Wang R, Cao HD, Zhang XD (2005) Compare of electrospinning PLA and PLA/b-TCP scaffold in vitro. Mater Sci Forum 475–479:2379–2382
96. Kim HW, Song JH, Kim HE (2005) Nanofiber generation of gelatin-hydroxyapatite biomimetics for guided tissue regeneration. Adv Funct Mater 15:1988–1994
97. Kim HW, Lee HH, Knowles JC (2006) Electrospinning biomedical nanocomposite fibers of hydroxyapatite/poly(lactic acid) for bone regeneration. J Biomed Mater Res A 79A:643–649
98. Xie XL, Mai YW, Zhou XP (2005) Dispersion and alignment of carbon nanotubes in polymer matrix: a review. Mater Sci Eng R 49:89–112
99. Zhou W, Wu Y, Wei F, Luo G, Qian W (2005) Elastic deformation of multiwalled carbon nanotubes in electrospun MWCNTs-PEO and MWCNTs-PVA nanofibers. Polymer 46:12689–12695
100. Salalha W, Dror Y, Khalfin RL, Cohen Y, Yarin AL, Zussman E (2004) Single-walled carbon nanotubes embedded in oriented polymeric nanofibers by electrospinning. Langmuir 20:9852–9855
101. Dror Y, Salalha W, Khalfin RL, Cohen Y, Yarin AL, Zussman E (2003) Carbon nanotubes embedded in oriented polymer nanofibers by electrospinning. Langmuir 19:7012–7020
102. Sung JH, Kim HS, Jin HJ, Choi HJ, Chin IJ (2004) Nanofibrous membranes prepared by multiwalled carbon nanotube/poly(methyl methacrylate) composites. Macromolecules 37:9899–9902
103. Sundaray B, Subramanian V, Natarajan TS, Krishnamurthy K (2006) Electrical conductivity of a single electrospun fiber of poly(methyl methacrylate) and multiwalled carbon nanotube nanocomposite. Appl Phys Lett 88:143114–143116
104. Liu LQ, Tasis D, Prato M, Wagner HD (2007) Tensile mechanics of electrospun multiwalled nanotube/poly(methyl methacrylate) nanofibers. Adv Mater 19:1228–1233
105. Ge JJ, Hou HQ, Li Q, Graham MJ, Greiner A, Reneker DH, Harris FW, Cheng SZD (2004) Assembly of well-aligned, multiwalled carbon nanotubes in confined polyacrylonitrile environments: electrospun composite nanofiber sheets. J Am Chem Soc 126:15754–15761
106. Ra EJ, An KH, Kim KK, Jeong SY, Lee YH (2005) Anisotropic electrical conductivity of MWCNT/PAN nanofiber paper. Chem Phys Lett 413:188–193
107. Allaoui A, Bai S, Cheng HM, Bai JB (2002) Mechanical and electrical properties of a MWNT/epoxy composite. Compos Sci Technol 62:1993–1998
108. Jose MV, Steinert BW, Thomas V, Dean DR, Abdalla MA, Price G, Janowski GM (2007) Morphology and mechanical properties of nylon 6/MWNT nanofibers. Polymer 48:1096–1104
109. Kim GM, Michler GH, Potschk P (2005) Deformation processes of ultrahigh porous multiwalled carbon nanotubes/polycarbonate composite fibers prepared by electrospinning. Polymer 46:7346–7351
110. Sen R, Zhao B, Perea D, Itkis ME, Hu H, Love J, Bekyarova E, Haddo RC (2004) Preparation of single-walled carbon nanotube reinforced polystyrene and polyurethane nanofibers and membranes by electrospinning. Nano Lett 4:459–464
111. Mazinani S, Ajji A, Dubois C (2009) Polystyrene-carbon nanotubes electrospun fibers: process. Struct Prop Polym 50:3329–3342
112. Chen D, Liu TX, Zhou XP, Tjiu WC, Hou HQ (2009) Electrospinning fabrication of high strength and toughness polyimide nanofiber membranes containing multiwalled carbon nanotubes. J Phys Chem B 113:9741–9748
113. Baji A, Mai YW, Wong SC, Abtahi M, Du X (2010) Mechanical behavior of self-assembled carbon nanotube reinforced nylon6, 6 fibers. Compos Sci Technol 70:1401–1409
114. Saeed K, Park SY, Lee HJ, Baek JB, Huh WS (2006) Preparation of electrospun nanofibers of carbon nanotube/polycaprolactone nanocomposite. Polymer 47:8019–8025

115. Mei F, Zhong JS, Yang XP, Ouyang XY, Zhang S, Hu XY, Ma Q, Lu JG, Ryu SK, Deng XL (2007) Improved biological characteristics of poly (1-Laclic Acid) electrospun membrane by incorporation of multiwallad carbon nanotubes/hydroxyapatite nanoparticles. Biomacromolecules 8:3729–3735
116. Fang J, Niu HT, Lin T, Wang XG (2008) Applications of electrospun nanofibers. Chin Sci Bull 53:2265–2286
117. Sundaray B, Subramanian V, Natarajan TS, Xiang RZ, Chang CC, Fann WS (2004) Electrospinning of continuous aligned polymer fibers. Appl Phys Lett 84:1222–1224
118. Pan H, Li L, Hu L, Cui X (2006) Continuous aligned polymer fibers produced by a modified electrospinning method. Polymer 47:4901–4904
119. Li D, Wang Y, Xia Y (2003) Electrospinning of polymeric and ceramic nanofibers as uniaxially aligned arrays. Nano Lett 3:1167–1171
120. Li D, Wang Y, Xia Y (2004) Electrospinning nanofibers as uniaxially aligned arrays and layer-by-layer stacked films. Adv Mater 16:361–366
121. Theron A, Zussman E, Yarin AL (2001) Electrostatic field-assisted alignment of electrospun nanofibres. Nanotechnology 12:384–390
122. Yang D, Lu B, Zhao Y, Jiang X (2007) Fabrication of aligned fibrous arrays by magnetic electrospinning. Adv Mater 19:3702–3706
123. Katta P, Alessandro M, Ramsier RD, Chase GG (2004) Continuous electrospinning of aligned polymer nanofibers onto a wire drum collector. Nano Lett 4:2215–2218
124. Fennessey SF, Farris RJ (2008) Fabrication of aligned and molecularly oriented electrospun polyacrylonitrile nanofibers and the mechanical behavior of their twisted yarns. Polymer 45:4217–4225
125. Ghasemi-Mobarakeh L, Prabhakaran MP, Morshed M, Nasr-Esfahani MH, Ramakrishna S (2008) Electrospun poly(ε-caprolactone)/gelatin nanofibrous scaffolds for nerve tissue engineering. Biomaterials 29:4532–4539
126. Bini TB, Gao S, Wang S, Ramakrishna S (2006) Poly(l-lactide-co-glycolide) biodegradable microfibers and electrospun nanofibers for nerve tissue engineering: an in vitro study. J Mater Sci 41:6453–6459
127. Schnell E, Klinkhammer K, Balzer S, Brook G, Kleeb D, Dalton P (2007) Guidance of glial cell migrtion and axonal growth on electrospun nanofibers of poly-ε-caprolactone and a collagen/poly-ε-caprolactone blend. Biomaterials 28:3012–3025
128. Baker SC, Atkin N, Gunning PA (2006) Characterisation of electrospun polystyrene scaffolds for three-dimensional in vitro biological studies. Biomaterials 27(16):3136
129. Liao GY, Zhou XP, Chen L, Zeng XY, Xie XL, Mai YW (2012) Electrospun aligned PLLA/PCL/functionalised multiwalled carbon nanotube composite fibrous membranes and their bio/mechanical properties. Compos Sci Technol 72:248–255
130. Wang YZ, Blasioli DJ, Kim HJ, Kim HS, Kaplan DL (2006) Cartilage tissue engineering with silk scaffolds and human articular chondrocytes. Biomaterials 27:4434–4442
131. Moroni L, Licht R, de Boer J, de Wijn JR, van Blitterswijk CA (2006) Fiber diameter and texture of electrospun PEOT/PBT scaffolds influence human mesenchymal stem cell proliferation and morphology, and the release of incorporated compounds. Biomaterials 27:4911–4922
132. Li WJ, Laurencin CT, Caterson EJ, Tuan RS, Ko FK (2002) Electrospun nanofibrous structure: a novel scaffold for tissue engineering. J Biomed Mater Res 60:613–621
133. Yoshimoto H, Shin YM, Terai H, Vacanti JP (2003) A biodegradable nanofiber scaffold by electrospinning and its potential for bone tissue engineering. Biomaterials 24:2077–2082
134. Powell HM, Supp DM, Boyce ST (2008) Influence of electrospun collagen on wound contraction of engineered skin substitutes. Biomaterials 29:834–843
135. Kenawy ER, Bowlin GL, Mansfield K, Layman J, Simpson DG, Sanders EH (2002) Release of tetracycline hydrochloride from electrospun poly(ethylene-co-vinylacetate), poly(lactic acid), and a blend. J Control Release 81:57–64

136. Goldberg M, Langer R, Jia XQ (2007) Nanostructured materials for applications in drug delivery and tissue engineering. J Biomat Sci Polym Ed 18:241–268
137. Zhang XH, Reagan MR, Kaplan DL (2009) Electrospun silk biomaterial scaffolds for regenerative medicine. Adv Drug Deliv Rev 61:988–1006
138. Soffer L, Wang X, Zhang X, Kluge J, Dorfmann L, Kaplan DL, Leisk G (2008) Silk-based electrospun tubular scaffolds for tissue-engineered vascular grafts. J Biomater Sci Polym Ed 19:653–664
139. Mathew G, Hong JP, Rhee JM, Lee HS, Nah C (2005) Preparation and characterization of properties of electrospun poly(butylene terephthalate) nanofibers filled with carbon nanotubes. Polym Test 24:712–717
140. Lee BS, Yu WR (2010) PA6/MWNT nanocomposites fabricated using electrospun nanofibers containing MWNT. Macromol Res 18:162–169
141. Wei K, Xia JH, Kim BS, Kim IS (2011) Multiwalled carbon nanotubes incorporated bombyx mori silk nanofibers by electrospinning. J Polym Res 18:579–585
142. Saeed K, Park SY (2010) Preparation and characterization of multiwalled carbon nanotubes/polyacrylonitrile nanofibers. J Polym Res 17:535–540
143. Gao JB, Yu AP, Itkis ME, Bekyarova E, Zhao B, Niyogi S, Haddon RC (2004) Large-scale fabrication of aligned single-walled carbon nanotube array and hierarchical single-walled carbon nanotube assembly. J Am Chem Soc 126:16698–16699
144. Stanishevsky A, Chowdhury S, Chinoda P, Thomas V (2008) Hydroxyapatite nanoparticle loaded collagen fiber composites: microarchitecture and nanoindentation study. J Biomed Mater Res 86:873–882
145. Stupp SI, Brawn PV (1997) Molecular manipulation of microstructures: biomaterials, ceramics, and semiconductors. Science 277:1242–1248
146. Stupp SI, LeBonheur V, Walker K, Li LS, Huggins KE, Keser M (1997) Supramolecular materials: self-organized nanostructures. Science 276:384–389
147. Bianco A, Federico ED, Moscatelli I, Camaioni A, Armentano I, Campagnolo L, Dottori M, Kenny JM, Siracusa G, Gusmano G (2009) Electrospun poly(ε-caprolactone)/Ca-deficient hydroxyapatite nanohybrids: microstructure, mechanical properties and cell response by murine embryonic stem cells. Mater Sci Eng C 29:2063–2071
148. Peng F, Shaw MT, Olson JR, Wei M (2011) Hydroxyapatite needle-shaped particles/poly (L-lactic acid) electrospun scaffolds with perfect particle-along-nanofiber orientation and significantly enhanced mechanical properties. J Phys Chem C 115:15743–15751
149. Yeo MG, Kim GH (2012) Preparation and characterization of 3D composite scaffolds based on rapid-prototyped PCL/β-TCP struts and electrospun PCL coated with collagen and HA for bone regeneration. Chem Mater 24:903–913
150. Shor L, Guceri S, Wen X, Gandhi M, Sun W (2007) Fabrication of three-dimensional polycaprolactone/hydroxyapatite tissue scaffolds and osteoblast-scaffold interactions in vitro. Biomaterials 28:5291–5297
151. Turmanova S, Minchev M, Vassilev K, Danev G (2008) Surface grafting polymerization of vinyl monomers on poly(tetrafluoroethylene) films by plasma treatment. J Polym Res 15:309–318
152. Mori M, Uyama Y, Ikada Y (1994) Surface modification of polyethylene fiber by graft-polymerization. J Polym Sci Polym Chem 32:1683–1690
153. Kou RQ, Xu ZK, Deng HT, Liu ZM, Seta P, Xu YY (2003) Surface modification of microporous polypropylene membranes by plasma-induced graft polymerization of alpha-allyl glucoside. Langmuir 19:6869–6875
154. Liu ZM, Xu ZK, Wang JQ, Wu J, Fu JJ (2004) Surface modification of polypropylene microfiltration membranes by graft polymerization of N-vinyl-2-pyrrolidone. Eur Polym J 40:2077–2087
155. Yao C, Li XS, Neoh KG, Shi ZL, Kang ET (2008) Surface modification and antibacterial activity of electrospun polyurethane fibrous membranes with quaternary ammonium moieties. J Membr Sci 320:259–267

156. Kim HS, Yoo HS (2010) MMPs-responsive release of DNA from electrospun nanofibrous matrix for local gene therapy: in vitro and in vivo evaluation. J Control Release 145 (3):264–271
157. Park K, Ju YM, Son JS, Ahn KD, Han DK (2007) Surface modification of biodegradable electrospun nanofiber scaffolds and their interaction with fibroblasts. J Biomater Sci Polym Ed 18:369–382
158. Chua KN, Chai C, Lee PC, Tang YN, Ramakrishna S, Leong KW, Mao HQ (2006) Surface-aminated electrospun nanofibers enhance adhesion and expansion of human umbilical cord blood hematopoietic stem/progenitor cells. Biomaterials 27:6043–6051
159. Ye P, Xu ZK, Wu J, Innocent C, Seta P (2006) Nanofibrous membranes containing reactive groups: electrospinning from poly(acrylonitrile-co-maleic acid) for lipase immobilization. Macromolecules 39:1041–1045
160. Li SF, Chen JP, Wu WT (2007) Electrospun polyacrylonitrile nanofibrous membranes for lipase immobilization. J Mol Catal B Enzym 47:117–124
161. Jia HF, Zhu GY, Vugrinovich B, Kataphinan W, Reneker DH, Wang P (2002) Enzyme carrying polymeric nanofibers prepared via electrospinning for use as unique biocatalysts. Biotechnol Prog 18:1027–1032
162. Aznar-Cervantes S, Roca MI, Martinez JG, Meseguer-Olmo L, Cenis JL, Moraleda JM, Otero TF (2012) Fabrication of conductive electrospun silk fibroin scaffolds by coating with polypyrrole for biomedical applications. Bioelectrochemistry 85:36–43
163. Chua KN, Lim WS, Zhang P, Lu H, Wen J, Ramakrishna S, Leong KW, Mao HQ (2005) Stable immobilization of rat hepatocyte spheroids on galactosylated nanofiber scaffold. Biomaterials 26:2537–2547
164. Yoon JJ, Chung HJ, Park TG (2007) Photo-crosslinkable and biodegradable pluronic/heparin hydrogels for local and sustained delivery of angiogenic growth factor. J Biomed Mater Res A 83A:597–605
165. Lode A, Reinstorf A, Bernhardt A, Wolf-Brandstetter C, Konig U, Gelinsky M (2008) Heparin modification of calcium phosphate bone cements for VEGF functionalization. J Biomed Mater Res A 86A:749–759
166. McGonigle JS, Tae G, Stayton PS, Hoffman AS, Scatena M (2008) Heparin-regulated delivery of osteoprotegerin promotes vascularization of implanted hydrogels. J Biomater Sci Polym Ed 19:1021–1034
167. Stendahl JC, Wang LJ, Chow LW, Kaufman DB, Stupp SI (2008) Growth factor delivery from self-assembling nanofibers to facilitate islet transplantation. Transplantation 86:478–481
168. Joung YK, Bae JW, Park KD (2008) Controlled release of heparin-binding growth factors using heparin-containing particulate systems for tissue regeneration. Expert Opin Drug Deliv 5:1173–1184
169. Bolgen N, Vargel I, Korkusuz P, Menceloglu YZ, Piskin E (2007) In vivo performance of antibiotic embedded electrospun PCL membranes for prevention of abdominal adhesions. J Biomed Mater Res B Appl Biomater 81B:530–543
170. Li LS, Stupp SI (2005) One-dimensional assembly of lipophilic inorganic nanoparticles templated by peptide-based nanofibers with binding functionalities. Angew Chem Int Ed 44:1833–1836
171. Kalra V, Lee J, Lee JH, Lee SG, Marquez M, Wiesner U, Joo YL (2008) Controlling nanoparticle location via confined assembly in electrospun block copolymer nanofibers. Small 4:2067–2073
172. Dong H, Wang D, Sun G, Hinestroza JP (2008) Assembly of metal nanoparticles on electrospun nylon 6 nanofibers by control of interfacial hydrogen-bonding interactions. Chem Mater 20:6627–6632
173. Rujitanaroj PO, Pimpha N, Supaphol P (2008) Wound-dressing materials with antibacterial activity from electrospun gelatin fiber mats containing silver nanoparticles. Polymer 49:4723–4732

174. Seyedjafari E, Soleimani M, Ghaemi N, Shabani I (2010) Nanohydroxyapatite-coated electrospun poly(L-lactide) nanofibers enhance osteogenic differentiation of stem cells and induce ectopic bone formation. Biomacromolecules 11:3118–3125
175. Decher G (1997) Fuzzy nanoassemblies: toward layered polymeric multicomposites. Science 277:1232–1237
176. Delcorte A, Bertrand P, Wischerhoff E, Laschewsky A (1997) Adsorption of polyelectrolyte multilayers on polymer surfaces. Langmuir 13:5125–5136
177. Picart C, Mutterer J, Richert L, Luo Y, Prestwich GD, Schaaf P, Voegel JC, Lavalle P (2002) Molecular basis for the explanation of the exponential growth of polyelectrolyte multilayers. Proc Natl Acad Sci U S A 99:12531–12535
178. Thierry B, Winnik FM, Merhi Y, Silver J, Tabrizian M (2003) Bioactive coatings of endovascular stents based on polyelectrolyte multilayers. Biomacromolecules 4:1564–1571
179. Thierry B, Kujawa P, Tkaczyk C, Winnik FM, Bilodeau L, Tabrizian M (2005) Delivery platform for hydrophobic drugs: prodrug approach combined with selfassembled multilayers. J Am Chem Soc 127:1626–1627
180. Zhang J, Senger B, Vautier D, Picart C, Schaaf P, Voegel JC, Lavalle P (2005) Natural polyelectrolyte films based on layer-by layer deposition of collagen and hyaluronic acid. Biomaterials 26:3353–3361
181. Tang ZY, Wang Y, Podsiadlo P, Kotov NA (2006) Biomedical applications of layer-by-layer assembly: from biomimetics to tissue engineering. Adv Mater 18:3203–3224
182. Kim BS, Park SW, Hammond PT (2008) Hydrogen-bonding layer-by-layer assembled biodegradable polymeric micelles as drug delivery vehicles from surfaces. ACS Nano 2:386–392
183. Quinn A, Such GK, Quinn JF, Caruso F (2008) Polyelectrolyte blend multilayers: a versatile route to engineering interfaces and films. Adv Funct Mater 18:17–26
184. Ge LQ, Pan C, Chen HH, Wang X, Wang C, Gu ZZ (2007) The fabrication of hollow multilayered polyelectrolyte fibrous mats and its morphology study. Colloids Surf A 293:272–277
185. Pan C, Ge LQ, Gu ZZ (2007) Fabrication of multi-walled carbon nanotube reinforced polyelectrolyte hollow nanofibers by electrospinning. Compos Sci Technol 67:3271–3277
186. Müller K, Quinn JF, Johnston AP, Becker RM, Greiner A, Caruso F (2006) Polyelectrolyte functionalization of electrospun fibers. Chem Mater 18:2397–2403

Chapter 9
Electrospun Nanofibrous Scaffolds for Soft Tissue Regeneration

Dave Wei-Chih Chen and Shih-Jung Liu

Abstract This chapter aims to provide a general overview on the applications of electrospun biodegradable nanofibrous scaffolds for soft tissue regeneration. The soft tissue and extracellular matrix is first introduced. The tissue or cellar host responses to injury, including inflammation, wound healing and foreign-body reaction, is outlined. The fabrication of nanofibrous scaffold made of biodegradable polymers via electrospinning is then presented. The properties of the fabricated scaffolds, including morphology, mechanical strength and biodegradability, are discussed in detail. The development of electrospun scaffolds for soft tissue regeneration in various clinical applications is also reviewed. Finally, the future trend for electrospun nanofibrous scaffolds is addressed.

Keywords Soft tissue regeneration • Inflammation • Wound healing • Foreign-body reaction • Electrospun nanofibrous scaffolds • Tissue engineering

9.1 Introduction

Technological improvement in biology, medicine, chemistry, engineering and material science have allowed deeper insights into the microstructural and molecular levels of organisation in tissues and biomaterials, providing innovative approaches and tools for medical treatments. The replacement of damaged or failed tissues/organs by natural tissue instead of adopting artificial implants has become an emerging strategy in tissue engineering. Scaffold tissue engineering is generally defined as engineering a suitably structured and biocompatible scaffold that is seeded with cells and other growth factors, allowing the tissues to be regenerated

D.W.-C. Chen
Chang Gung Memorial Hospital, Keelung Branch, F7, No 222 Mai-King Road, Keelung, Taiwan
e-mail: achih121@ms75.hinet.net

S.-J. Liu (✉)
Mechanical Engineering, Chang Gung University, 259, Wen-Hwa 1st Road, Kwei-Shan, Tao-Yuan 333, Taiwan
e-mail: shihjung@mail.cgu.edu.tw

Q. Li, Y.-W. Mai (eds.), *Biomaterials for Implants and Scaffolds*, Springer Series in Biomaterials Science and Engineering 8, DOI 10.1007/978-3-662-53574-5_9

in vitro and to partially develop the host tissue extracorporeally before implantation. To achieve the goal of tissue reconstruction, the scaffold should be of a porous, interconnected and permeable structure to permit the infiltration of cells and nutrients. It should also exhibit the appropriate surface morphology and chemistry for cell adhesion and proliferation. In addition, the scaffold also needs to exhibit mechanical properties comparable with the native tissue being engineered and the right degree of biodegradability, such that it degrades to form soluble non-toxic products when the tissue is fully formed. An ideal scaffold should therefore (1) allow cell attachment and migration, (2) deliver and retain cells and biochemical factors, (3) enable diffusion of vital cell nutrients and expressed products and (4) exert certain mechanical and biological influences to modify the behaviour of the cell phase.

Nanofibres prepared via electrospinning offer several advantages such as an extremely high surface-to-volume ratio, tunable porosity, flexibility with respect to scaffold size and shape and the ability to control the composition to achieve the desired results from its properties and functionality. Furthermore, the nanofibrous network is capable of creating a dynamic, three-dimensional (3D) microenvironment mimicking the native extracellular matrix (ECM) in which cells are maintained [1].

This chapter provides some general overview regarding the applications of electrospun biodegradable nanofibrous scaffolds for soft tissue regeneration. The soft tissue and extracellular matrix is introduced first. The tissue or cellar host responses to injury, including inflammation, wound healing and foreign-body reaction, is addressed. The fabrication of nanofibrous scaffold made of biodegradable polymers via electrospinning is then presented. The properties of the fabricated scaffolds, including morphology, mechanical strength and biodegradability, etc., are discussed in detail. The development of electrospun scaffolds for soft tissue regeneration in various clinical applications is also reviewed. Finally the future trend for electrospun nanofibrous scaffolds is addressed.

9.2 Soft Tissue and Extracellular Matrix

9.2.1 Soft Tissue

Soft biological tissues exist in many forms, each with a unique microstructure specialised for a specific function. Nonetheless, soft tissues are composed of the same basic constituents: cells and extracellular matrix (ECM) as shown in Fig. 9.1. The main functions of the soft tissue include tissue production, regeneration and remodelling of the ECM. The composition, structure and functions of ECM vary greatly in different tissues. In general, cellular material occupies approximately 20 % of the total tissue volume, whereas the ECM accounts for the remaining 80 % [2].

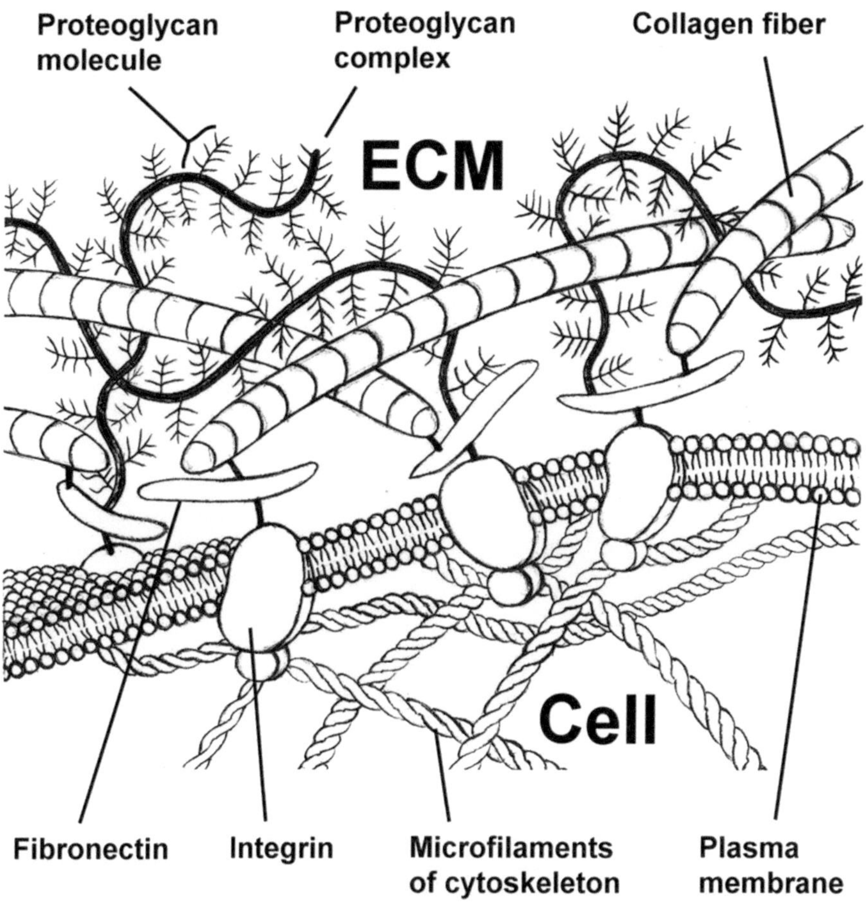

Fig. 9.1 Cell and extracellular matrix (ECM)

Cells are the fundamental structural and functional units of tissues and organs. In all tissues, cells are assembled during embryonic development into coherent groups through specific cell–cell and cell–matrix interactions. Each type of tissue has a distinctive pattern of structural organisation adapted to its particular function, which is strongly influenced by metabolic [3] or mechanical factors [4, 5].

Conversely, the ECM serves many functions such as [6]:

- It endows a tissue with strength and resilience and thereby maintains its shape.
- It serves as a biologically active scaffold on which cells can migrate or adhere.
- It helps regulate the phenotype of cells.
- It anchors many substances, including growth factors, proteases and their inhibitors.
- It provides an aqueous environment for the diffusion of nutrients, ions, hormones and metabolites between cells and the capillary network.

During normal development and as a component of tissue response to injury, adhesive interactions coordinate with cell surface receptors and, subsequently, with the cytoskeleton and the nucleus [7]. The resulting intracellular signaling affects a variety of events, including gene expression and cell proliferation, mobility and differentiation.

In many respects, therefore, the ECM regulates cell shape, orientation, movement and overall function; however, cells (e.g. fibroblasts) fashion and maintain the ECM. As such, a strong symbiotic relationship exists between these two components.

9.2.2 Extracellular Matrix

The ECM consists of two main components: protein fibres (collagen and elastin), which include elastic fibres that are extremely flexible and behave like rubber, and collagen fibres that are stiff and form the main tensile load-bearing components in tissues. The amorphous matrix or ground substance in which fibres are embedded is a viscous gel composed of water, proteoglycans (PGs) and other glycoproteins [8–10].

Matrix components and the mechanical forces that cells experience markedly influence the maintenance of cellular phenotype and affect cell shape, polarity and differentiated function through receptors for specific ECM molecules (such as integrins) on cell surfaces. The resulting changes in cytoskeletal organisation and the production of second messengers can modify gene expression. ECM plays a critical role in cytodifferentiation and organogenesis, and it is a scaffold that allows orderly repair after injury. The flow of information between cells and ECM is called dynamic reciprocity.

Therefore, from a mechanical point of view, soft connective tissue must be considered and analysed as a fibre-reinforced composite material [8, 11]. Fibrous proteins, particularly collagen, are the reinforcing fibres of the ground substance. The mechanical behaviour of the tissue is determined by the properties and quantity of the components and their interactions. Furthermore, the specific orientation of collagen fibres determines the anisotropic response of soft tissues. Because collagen elements are characterised by a stiffness that is significantly higher than that of the ground substance, they are largely responsible for the tensile behaviour of soft connective tissue. By contrast, because of the high length-thickness ratio of collagen elements, the compression behaviour of the tissue is mainly determined by the ground substance and its interaction with the fibrous network. The microstructural phenomena that develop within soft tissue during loading take time to develop completely in both compressive and tensile mechanical states. With regard to the latter, time dependence is less evident because microstructural rearrangements within collagen fibres take place more quickly.

9.2.2.1 Protein Fibres (Collagens and Elastin)

Collagen is characterised by a strongly hierarchical organisation. Small tropocollagen molecules link together to form fibrils, which in turn give rise to fibres and fibre bundles. Within soft tissue, collagen fibrils show a typical wavy configuration in the unstrained state, referred to as crimped, which is characterised by a helical nature with a periodicity between 10 and 100 μm, depending on tissue type [12]. Collagens are composed of a triple helix of three polypeptide α-chains; approximately 30 α-chains form nearly 20 distinct collagen types. Types I, II and III are interstitial or fibrillar collagens and are the most abundant. Types IV, V and VI are nonfibrillar (or amorphous) and are present in interstitial tissue and basement membranes.

PGs, most often decorin- [13, 14] and fibril-associated collagens with interrupted triple helix filaments [15], form interfibrillar bonds, which tie adjoining fibrils together to form fibres and seem to have a definite role in guaranteeing their mechanical coupling. Owing to their hierarchical organisation, collagen-reinforcing elements have a complex mechanical response that can be evaluated by analysing the mechanical behaviour of the components and the interactions that occur when a tensile load is applied.

Elastic fibres confer passive recoil to various tissues and are critical components of heart valves and the aorta, in which repeated pulsatile flow would cause unacceptable shear on noncompliant tissue, and of intervertebral discs, in which the repetitive forces of ambulation along the spine are dissipated. Elastin also forms the layers called laminae in the walls of arteries. Unlike collagen, elastin can be stretched. The stretching of an artery every time when the heart pumps blood is followed by the recoil of elastin, which restores the diameter of the artery between heartbeats.

9.2.2.2 Amorphous Matrix or Ground Substance

Amorphous matrix or ground substance is a viscous gel that is mainly composed of an electrolytic water solution containing positive sodium ions and highly negatively charged PGs. The PGs are long, molecular structures that develop along an axis of hyaluronic acid.

Hyaluronic acid consists of many repeats of a simple disaccharide which is stretched end to end. It binds a large amount of water, forming a viscous hydrate gel, which gives connective tissue turgor pressure and the capability to resist compression. This ECM component helps provide both resilience and a lubricating feature to many types of connective tissue, particularly those found in the cartilage of joints.

Other proteins are laterally attached to hyaluronan axis and structured around their own axis. Threads of amino acids called glycosaminoglycans (GAGs) are in turn attached along this last axis. All GAGs are covalently attached to a protein backbone to form PGs, which has a structure that schematically resembles a bottlebrush.

The time-dependent mechanical properties of soft biological tissue are strongly influenced by the fluid fluxes that the amorphous matrix or ground substance undergoes when external loads are applied. Fluid flux phenomena depend on the rheological behaviour of the amorphous matrix or ground substance itself [16]. This behaviour is determined by the combined action of GAGs and hyaluronic acid [17]. Two main phenomena occur when compressive loads are applied to a tissue: the ground substance undergoes fluid fluxes within the solid skeleton, and the space between GAGs is reduced. Tissue compressive stiffness is, therefore, determined by ions. The movement of liquid phases within the porous solid structures of the tissue is a time-dependent phenomenon, which explains that the compressive stiffness of the tissue is correlated with the rate of the loading applied. In fact, high-strain rate conditions prevent ground substance flux from flowing, resulting in high compression stiffness owing to the incompressible nature of the gel. Reduction of the strain rate causes major fluid flux and in turn decreases the compression stiffness.

9.2.2.3 Cell–Matrix Interactions

Like cell–cell interactions, cell–matrix interactions have a high degree of specificity, requiring initial recognition, physical adhesion, electrical and chemical communication, cytoskeletal reorganisation and cell migration. Moreover, adhesion receptors may also act as transmembrane signaling molecules that transmit information about the environment to the inside of cells and mediate the effects of signals initiated by growth factors or compounds controlling tissue differentiation. Moreover, the ECM components (e.g. ligands) with which cells interact are immobilised and not in solution. However, soluble (secreted) factors also modulate cell–cell communication in the normal and pathologic regulation of tissue growth and maturation. Cell surface adhesion molecules that interact with ECM include the integrin adhesion receptors and the vascular selectins.

The integrins are cell receptors with diverse specificity that bind ECM proteins, other cell surface proteins and plasma proteins and control cell growth, differentiation, gene expression and motility [7]. Some integrins bind only a single component of the ECM, e.g. fibronectin, collagen or laminin. Other integrins interact with several of these polypeptides. In contrast to hormone receptors, which have high affinity and low abundance, integrins exhibit low affinity and high abundance and bind weakly to several different but related matrix molecules. This property allows integrins to promote cell–cell interactions as well as cell–matrix binding.

9.3 Inflammation, Wound Healing and Foreign-Body Reaction

Implant-induced tissue reactions are gaining increasing importance with the emergence of novel materials and devices. In-depth understanding of foreign-body and inflammatory responses is a prerequisite to solve biological problems that currently exist with some artificial implants.

Placement of a biomaterial in an in vivo environment requires injection, insertion or surgical implantation, all of which injure the tissues or organs involved. [18] Inflammation, wound healing and foreign-body reaction are generally considered components of the host tissue or cellular responses to an injury or implantation procedure.

The sequence of responses following an injury (Fig. 9.2) includes blood/material interactions, provisional matrix formation, acute inflammation, chronic inflammation, granulation tissue development, foreign-body reaction and fibrosis/fibrous capsule development. The overlap and simultaneous occurrence of these events should be considered; for example, the foreign-body reaction at the implant interface may be initiated with the onset of acute and chronic inflammation.

In the very early stage of the implantation process, blood/material interactions occur as proteins adsorb to the biomaterial surface, and a blood-based provisional matrix develops on and around the biomaterial. The provisional matrix forms the initial thrombus (blood clot) at the interface between the tissue and the biomaterial. Protein adsorption and formation of the fibrin-rich provisional matrix are closely linked in their mechanistic responses. Injury to the vascularised connective tissue

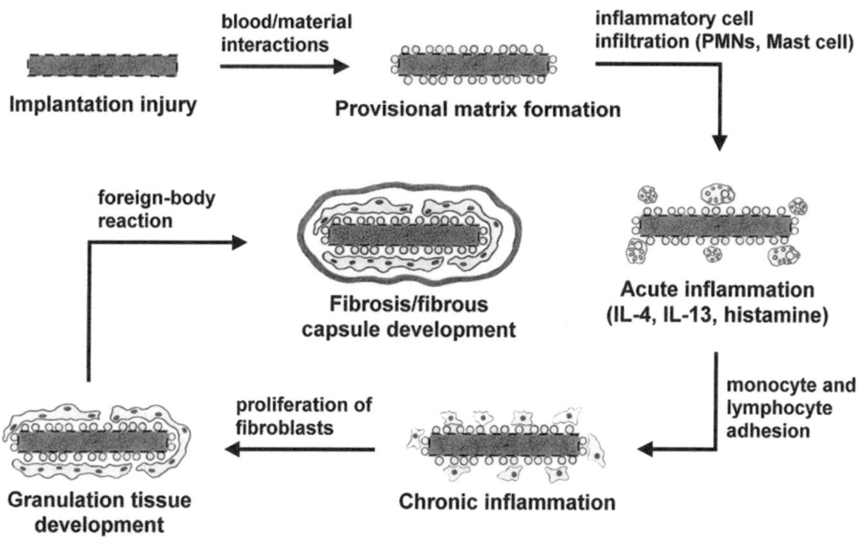

Fig. 9.2 The sequence of responses following an implant-induced tissue reaction

not only initiates the inflammatory responses (innate immunity) but also leads to thrombus formation, which involves activation of the extrinsic and intrinsic coagulation systems, the complement system, fibrinolytic system, kinin-generating system and platelets.

9.3.1 *Inflammation*

9.3.1.1 Acute Inflammation

Acute inflammation is an almost immediate response to injury and is non-specific; it may occur as a result of any injury short of one that is immediately fatal. The inflammatory response is usually of a short duration and typically occurs before the immune response is established. The primary purpose of inflammation is to remove the injurious agent and limit the extent of tissue damage.

Neutrophils (polymorphonuclear leukocytes [PMNs]) characterise the acute inflammatory response. In addition, mast cell degranulation with histamine release and fibrinogen adsorption is known to mediate acute inflammatory responses to implanted biomaterials [19, 20]. Interleukin-4 (IL-4) and interleukin-13 (IL-13) are also released from mast cells in the degranulation process and can play significant roles in determining the extent of the subsequent foreign-body reaction [21, 22].

Biomaterial-induced inflammatory responses may be modulated by histamine-mediated phagocyte recruitment and phagocyte adhesion to implant surfaces, which is facilitated by the adsorbed host fibrinogen. Both H1 and H2 histamine receptor antagonists greatly reduce the recruitment of monocytes/macrophages and neutrophils to implant surfaces. Protein adsorption and monocyte/macrophage adhesion are the significant elements of foreign-body reaction. The acute inflammatory response to biomaterials usually resolves quickly, often within 1 week, depending on the extent of injury at the implant site.

9.3.1.2 Chronic Inflammation

Acute infections are usually self-limiting and are rapidly controlled by the host defences. In contrast, chronic inflammation is self-perpetuating and may last for weeks, months or even years. The development of chronic inflammation may result from a recurrent or progressive acute inflammatory process or from low-grade responses that fail to generate an acute reaction.

Following acute inflammation, chronic inflammation is identified by the presence of mononuclear cells (e.g. monocytes and lymphocytes) at the implant site. Chronic inflammation is less uniform histologically than acute inflammation; thus, this term has been used diagnostically to identify a wide range of cellular responses. The presence of mononuclear cells, including lymphocytes and plasma cells, is considered chronic inflammation. This chronic inflammatory response to biomaterials is usually of a short duration and is confined to the implant site.

Chronic inflammation also involves the proliferation of fibroblasts instead of formation and release of exudates. As a result, the risk of scarring and deformity is usually considered greater in chronic inflammation than in acute inflammation. Agents that induce chronic inflammation are typically low-grade, persistent irritants that are unable to penetrate deeply or spread rapidly.

Chronic inflammation has also been used to describe the foreign-body reaction, in which monocytes, macrophages and foreign-body giant cells are present at the biomaterial interface. With biocompatible materials, an early resolution of the acute and chronic inflammatory responses occurs; the chronic inflammatory response involving mononuclear cells usually lasts no longer than 2 weeks. The persistence of the acute and/or chronic inflammatory responses beyond a 3-week period usually indicates an infection.

9.3.2 Wound Healing

Following resolution of the acute and chronic inflammatory responses, granulation tissue develops and is identified by the presence of macrophages, infiltration of fibroblasts and neovascularisation of the healing tissue. Granulation tissue is the precursor to fibrous capsule formation and is separated from the implant or biomaterial by the cellular components of the foreign-body reaction, i.e. monocytes in a single or double layer, macrophages and foreign-body giant cells.

After fibrous encapsulation occurs, the lesion is generally referred to as a granuloma. A foreign-body granuloma is thus composed of the foreign body surrounded by giant cells within a zone of macrophages, lymphocytes and granulocytes and, finally, an encapsulating membrane of fibrous tissue.

The result of the inflammatory process is wound healing. Tissue injury, no matter how minute, disrupts tissue continuity (both structure and composition) and often causes a loss of function in the injured area. Ideally, restoration of the injured tissue would generate a new tissue that was identical to the pre-injury tissue. However, complete regeneration and restoration of continuity and function is an exception rather than the rule. Generally, as cells become more specialised, they lose their ability to proliferate and show poor regenerative potential. The healing of specialised tissue involves repair by fibrous tissue substitution (i.e. scar tissue); thus, tissue continuity is restored, but the original function of the injured tissue may be partially or completely lost.

In addition to the degree of specialisation, many factors may influence wound healing, and all of these variables should be considered when designing an implantation protocol. Florey [23] describes these factors in more detail than can be covered in this chapter. Briefly, some of the more important factors that directly affect wound healing are as follows: (1) the position of the wound in the body, (2) the interference of blood supply to the surrounding tissue, (3) the apposition and immobilisation of cut surfaces and (4) the general health and nutritional status of the experimental subjects.

9.3.3 Foreign-Body Reaction

The foreign-body reaction (Fig. 9.3), comprising mainly macrophages and/or foreign-body giant cells, may persist at the tissue-implant interface for the lifetime of the implant. Generally, fibrosis (i.e. fibrous encapsulation) surrounds the biomaterial or implant with its interfacial foreign-body reaction, thereby isolating the implant and foreign-body reaction from the local tissue environment. Early in the inflammatory and wound healing responses, macrophages are activated upon adherence to the material surface.

The form and topography of the biomaterial surface determine the composition of the foreign-body reaction. With biocompatible materials, the composition of the foreign-body reaction in the implant site may be controlled by the surface properties of the biomaterial, the form of the implant and the ratio of the biomaterial surface area to the implant volume. For example, high surface-to-volume implants such as fabrics, porous materials, particulates or microspheres will have higher proportions of macrophages and foreign-body giant cells at the implant site than smooth-surface implants, in which fibrosis will play a more significant role.

Davila [24, 25] suggests that large implants impair the nutrient supply to the surrounding tissue. Studies on tumour production by implanted polymers suggest a similar situation [26, 27]. Thin fibres (30–50 microns in diameter) of most materials are well tolerated in tissue and have a thin fibrous capsule, a good blood supply and good cellularity. Davila has shown [25] that for a variety of inert materials, the diameter of the fibre has a greater influence on the foreign-body reaction than the type of material does. Davila's work establishes an explanation for the success of velours, felts, weaves, knits and other textile structures in implant applications.

The development of novel biomaterials, biomedical devices and tissue-engineered constructs necessitates thorough understanding of the biological responses to implanted materials. Once a biomaterial is introduced into the body, a sequence of events occurs in the surrounding tissue, ultimately ending in the formation of foreign-body giant cells at the tissue–material interface. The consequences of the reaction to the material surface can be devastating.

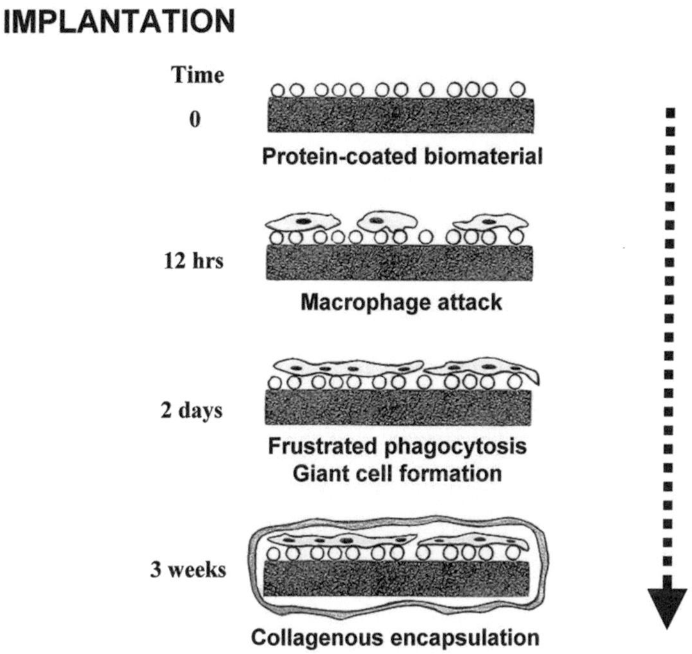

Fig. 9.3 Foreign-body reaction

9.4 Electrospinning of Nanofibrous Scaffold

9.4.1 Biomaterials for Scaffolds

The first issue with regard to tissue engineering is the choice of suitable material. Many different materials (natural and synthetic, biodegradable and permanent) have been investigated for use of scaffolds. Most of these materials have been known in the medical field before the advent of tissue engineering as a research topic. When choosing a material for a tissue engineering application, it needs to meet a number of requirements. Most importantly, the material must be biocompatible and induce minimum toxicity as well as inflammatory and possibly immune responses. An ideal material for the scaffolds should therefore have the following properties: (1) does not induce an inflammatory/toxic response, disproportionate to its beneficial effect, (2) is metabolised in the body after fulfilling its purpose leaving no trace, (3) can be easily processed into the final product form, (4) has acceptable shelf life and (5) can be easily sterilised. For scaffolds in tissue engineering, a high porosity and an adequate pore size are required to facilitate cell seeding and diffusion throughout the whole structure of both cells and nutrients.

Biodegradability is often an essential factor since scaffolds should preferably be absorbed by the surrounding tissues without the necessity of a surgical removal. The rate at which degradation occurs has to coincide as much as possible with the rate of tissue formation: this means that while cells are fabricating their own natural matrix structure around themselves, the scaffold is able to provide structural integrity within the body and eventually it will break down leaving the neotissue, newly formed tissue which will take over the mechanical load.

A range of novel materials has been developed to enhance the bioactive or therapeutic properties of these nanofibrous scaffold via surface modifications, including the immobilisation of functional cell-adhesive ligands and bioactive molecules such as drugs, enzymes and cytokines [28]. In addition, scaffolds that are intended for tissue regeneration need to have the mechanical strength needed for the creation of a macroporous scaffold that will retain its structure after implantation, particularly in the reconstruction of hard, load-bearing tissues, such as bones and cartilages. Table 9.1 lists the mechanical properties of human tissue [29]. The biostability of many implants depends on such factors as strength, elasticity, absorption at the material interface and chemical degradation.

Potential materials with these characteristics include natural polymers, synthetic polymers, ceramics, metals and combinations of these materials. Despite biocompatible materials such as metals and ceramics have been used extensively for surgical implantations, they have two major disadvantages for tissue engineering applications. First, they are mostly not biodegradable, and, second, their processability is limited. For these reasons, polymeric materials have received increasing attentions from the scientific and medical communities.

Natural polymers, such as collagens, glycosaminoglycan, starch, chitin and chitosan, have been used to repair nerves, skin, cartilage and bone [29]. While naturally occurring biomaterials may most closely simulate the native cellular milieu, large batch-to-batch variations upon isolation from biological tissues is the main limitation for their wide applications. Poor mechanical performance is also a drawback for transplantation scaffolds made from natural polymers.

Within the subdivision of synthetic materials, one can further delineate between biodegradable and non-degradable materials. Biodegradable materials have been the more popular choice due to the elimination of a second surgery to remove the implanted scaffold [30]. Additionally, the rate of degradation can be controlled to some extent to coincide with the rate of new tissue formation, by altering parameters such as polymer blends, and ratio of amorphous to crystalline segments. Among the synthetic polymers, the aliphatic polyesters including polylactide (PLA), poly (glycolide), poly(lactic-*co*-glycolic acid) (PLGA) and poly(ε-caprolactone) (PCL) have been extensively investigated and have been approved by the Food and Drug

Table 9.1 Mechanical properties of human tissues [29]

Tissue	Tensile strength (Mpa)	Compressive strength (Mpa)	Modulus (MPa)
Cancellous bone	N/A	4–12	20–500
Cortical bond	60–160	130–180	3000–30,000
Cartilage	3.7–10.5	N/A	0.7–15.3
Ligament	13–46	N/A	65–541
Tendon	24–112	N/A	143–2310

Table 9.2 Characteristics of typical biodegradable polymers [30]

Polymer[a]	Melting point (°C)	Glass transition temperature (°C)	Modulus[b] (GPa)	Elongation (%)	Degradation time [c] (months)
PGA	225–230	35–40	7.0	15–20	6–12
PLLA	173–178	60–65	2.7	5–10	>24
PDLLA	Amorphous	55–60	1.9	3–10	12–16
PCL	58–63	−65–60	0.4	300–500	>24
PDS	N/A	−10–0	1.5	N/A	6–12
PGA–TMC	N/A	N/A	2.4	N/A	6–12
PLGA 85/15	Amorphous	50–55	2.0	3–10	5–6
75/25	Amorphous	50–55	2.0	3–10	4–5
65/35	Amorphous	45–50	2.0	3–10	3–4
50/50	Amorphous	45–50	2.0	3–10	1–2
Bone			10–20		
Steel			210		

[a]*PGA* poly(glycolide), *PLLA* poly(L-lactide), *PDLLA* poly(DL-lactide), *PCL* poly(-ε-caprolactone), *PDS* polydioxanone, *PGA–TMC* poly(glycolide)–trimethylene carbonate, *PLGA* poly(lactide-co-glycolide)

[b]Tensile or flexural modulus

[c]Time to complete resorption

Administration (FDA) for the manufacture of various medical devices [31]. These polymers have been approved for, and have a history of safe use in, humans. After being introduced into the body, the polymeric materials induce only a minimal inflammatory response and biodegrade through the hydrolysis of its ester linkages. Table 9.2 summarises the characteristics of these biodegradable polymers.

There are, however, some limitations associated with these biodegradable polymers. All polyesters release acidic degradation products that can adversely affect biocompatibility. These polyesters tend to be relatively stiff materials. While this may be an advantage in load-bearing applications, it becomes a disadvantage when mechanical compliance with soft tissue or blood vessels is required. Furthermore, none of these polyesters provide a chemically reactive pendent chain for the easy attachment of drugs, crosslinkers or biologically active moieties. Thus, simple poly (α-hydroxy ester)s have performed well in establishing the foundation and feasibility of tissue engineering; it may not be optimally suited for the construction of polymeric cell scaffolds serving a variety of applications.

Despite the popularity and apparent benefits of using biodegradable materials, the use of toxic organic solvents for the fabrication of micro- and nanofibres is a major limitation of fibres obtained from synthetic polymers, which would require thorough washing or solvent evaporation treatment prior to use with cells. Natural polymers act as alternatives to synthetic polymers and offer a few advantages such as solubility in aqueous media due to their hydrophilic nature in addition to limited or nonexistent immunogenicity and cytotoxicity.

In order to more accurately mimic the natural ECM, research has also examined the electrospinning of natural materials such as collagen, chitosan, gelatin, fibrinogen, chitin and hyaluronic acid [29, 32]. However, these materials often lack the desired physical properties or are difficult to electrospin on their own, which has led to the development of hybrid materials, which consist of a blend of synthetic and natural materials.

9.4.2 Electrospinning Process

Currently, there are three techniques available for the synthesis of nanofibres, namely, electrospinning, self-assembly and phase separation. Among these techniques, electrospinning is the most widely studied technique and has also demonstrated the most promising results in terms of tissue engineering applications [32]. Despite its long history, the electrospinning technique has not gained too much attention as a potential polymer processing method for applications in tissue engineering and drug delivery until the recent 10 years.

Electrospinning is a simple and effective nanofabrication method and affords an opportunity to engineer the scaffolds with micro-to-nanoscale topography and high porosity similar to the natural extracellular matrix (ECM) [1]. It can be used to prepare nanofibrous membranes with diameters ranging from 5 to 500 nm, which are 10^2 to 10^4 times smaller than those prepared by the traditional method of solution or melt spinning. The high surface-to-volume ratio of electrospun scaffolds can enhance cell, drug loading and mass transfer properties. Electrospun fibres can be randomly distributed and highly oriented, allowing the control of the bulk mechanical properties as well as the biological response to the scaffolds. Furthermore, various pharmaceuticals and biomolecules including antibiotics and anticancer agents, proteins, living cells, DNA, RNA, etc., can be incorporated into electrospun scaffolds.

In an electrospinning process, a polymer solution placed inside a syringe is driven out from a melt capillary that is connected to high-voltage power supply (Fig. 9.4a). As the electrostatic attraction between the oppositely charged solution and collecting plate and the electrostatic repulsions between alike charges in the solution become stronger, the leading edge of the solution changes from a rounded meniscus to a cone (so-called Taylor cone, which was first proposed by G. Taylor in 1969 [33]). A fibre jet is thus ejected from the Taylor cone as the electric field strength exceeds the surface tension of the polymer solution. The fibre jet travels through the air allowing the solvent to evaporate. Nanofibres are collected in the form of non-woven membranes on a grounded collector after solvent evaporation. Electrospinning also provides the advantages of fabricating nanofibres from a huge range of materials. Of the major classes of materials, electrospinning is able to produce nanofibres of polymers, composites, semiconductors and ceramics [34].

Typically, the use of stationary collector will result in the formation of a randomly oriented fibre mat. By changing the collector geometry, nanofibres with

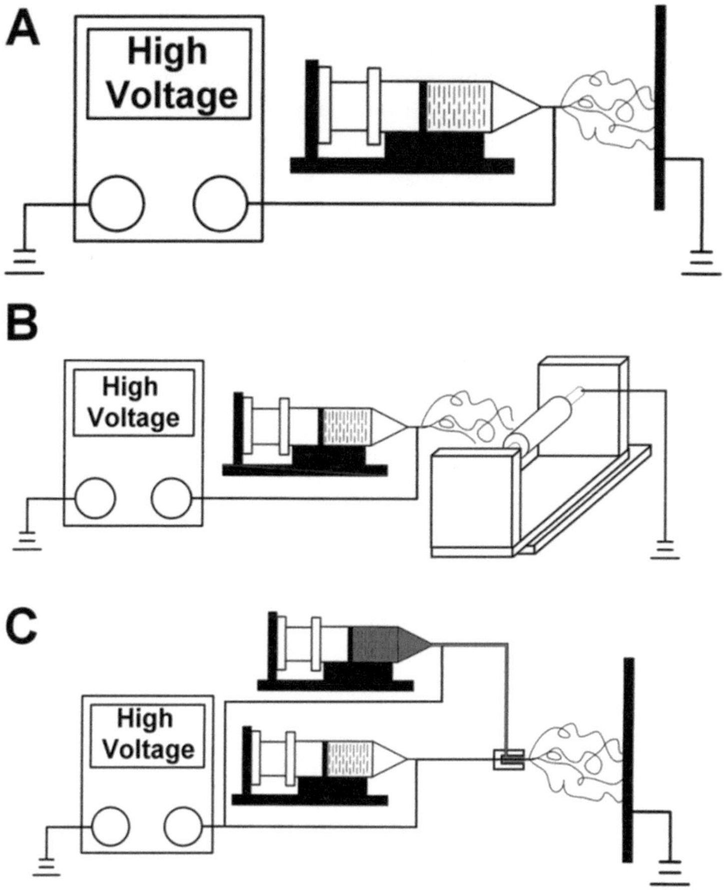

Fig. 9.4 Schematic for (**a**) the regular electrospinning setup, (**b**) employment of a rotating collector, (**c**) assembly for electrospinning of core–sheath nanofibres

various morphologies can be obtained. As an example, the assembly in Fig. 9.4b allows one to prepare nanofibrous membranes with high fibre orientations by employing a rotating collector, while a rotating mandrel can be used to form a tubular scaffold. In addition, the use of multi-nozzles for simultaneous spinning to form multiscale (mixed micro and nanoscale) or multi-materials fibrous scaffolds is also feasible (Fig. 9.4c). Other collector assemblies for preparing nanofibres of various morphologies can be found in the review paper by Teo and Ramakrishna in 2006 [35].

The fibre diameters and morphologies of electrospun nanofibrous membrane are strongly influenced by the processing parameters used in the electrospinning process. Among various parameters such as solvent, polymer concentration, applied voltage, flow rate, etc., the polymer concentration is most important which determines the spinnability of a solution. The solution must have a sufficiently high polymer concentration for chain entanglements to occur. The polymer concentration influences both the viscosity and the surface tension of the solution, both of which are very important parameters in the electrospinning process. If the solution is too dilute, the polymer fibre will break up into droplets before reaching the collector (Fig. 9.5a) due to the effects of surface tension. Fibres gradually form with the increase in the concentration (Fig. 9.5b), and fibrous mat can be obtained with the increase in the polymer concentration (Fig. 9.5c). The nanofibrous membranes, prepared from polymer solution using the electrospinning technique, possess unique microporous structures which are formed by a stack of fibrous layers and interstices between the fibres. Nevertheless, if the solution is too concentrated, the fibres cannot be formed due to the high viscosity, which makes it difficult to control the solution flow rate through the capillary. Thus, an optimum range of polymer concentrations exists in which nanofibres can be electrospun when all other parameters are held constant.

Depending on electrospinning assemblies and materials/solvents used, the exact influence of the processing parameters on the morphologies of electrospun fibres may be varied. By adjusting the processing parameters such as solvent, applied voltage, flow rate, etc., nanofibrous membranes with various fibre diameters and morphologies can be obtained. A number of general relationships between processing parameters and fibre morphology reviewed and summarised by Sill and von Recum [1] are listed in Table 9.3.

9.4.3 Electrospun Nanofibrous Scaffolds

There are several requirements in the design of scaffolds for tissue engineering. Many of these requirements are complex and not yet fully understood. In addition to being biocompatible both in bulk and degraded form, these scaffolds should possess appropriate material properties to provide an ideal biomechanical environment for the neotissues. The scaffolds should also be porous and permeable to permit the ingress of cells and nutrients and should exhibit the appropriate surface structure and chemistry for cell attachment.

The use of electrospun fibres and fibre meshes in tissue engineering applications often involves several considerations, including choice of material, fibre orientation, porosity, surface modification and tissue application. Choices in materials include both natural and synthetic (biodegradable and non-degradable) materials, as well as hybrid blends of these two, which can provide an optimal combination of mechanical and biomimetic properties. By varying the processing and solution parameters, the fibre orientation (aligned vs. random) and porosity/pore size (cell infiltration) of the electrospun scaffold can be controlled and optimised for each individual application. Srinivasan et al. [36] showed that multiscale architectures (Fig. 9.6) have been found favourable not only in bone regeneration but also in the regeneration of soft tissues including cardiovascular tissue, neural tissue, cartilage, and skin. The unique properties of multiscale scaffolds have been pivotal in better

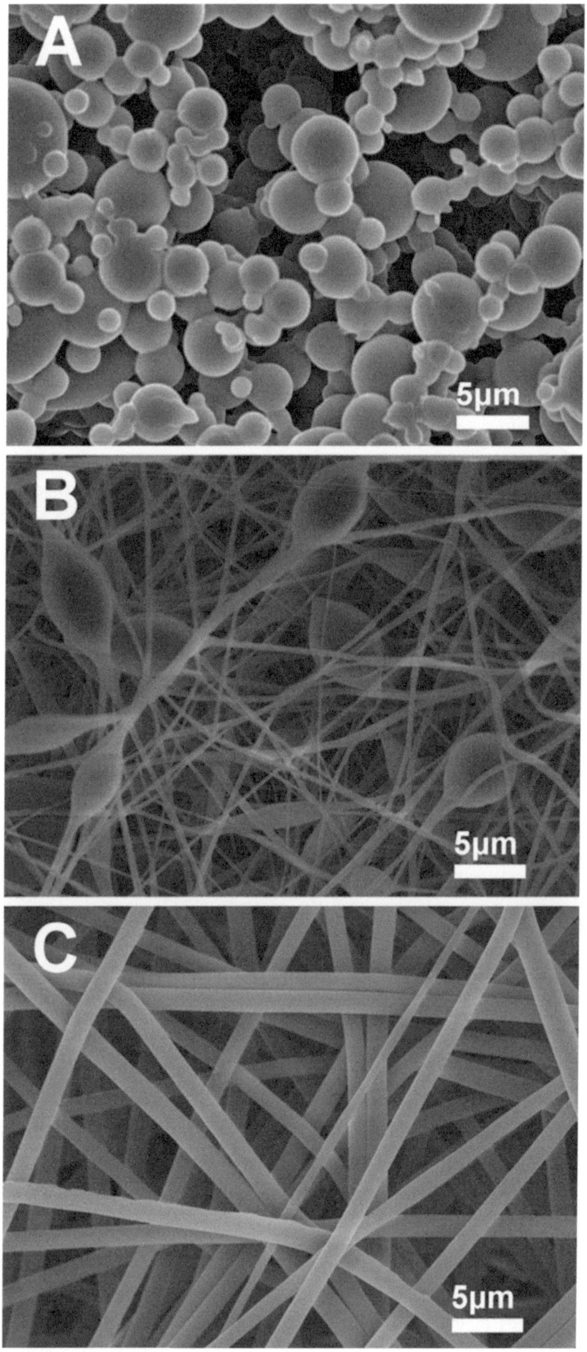

Fig. 9.5 SEM images of electrospun nanofibres (**a**) if the solution is too dilute, the polymer fibre will break up into droplets, (**b**) fibres gradually form with the increase in the concentration, (**c**) fibrous mat can be obtained with the increase in the polymer concentration

Table 9.3 Effects of processing parameters on fibre morphology [1]

Parameter	Fibre morphology
Applied voltage ↑	Fibre diameter initially ↓, then ↑ (not monotonic)
Flow rate ↑	Fibre diameter ↑ (beaded morphologies occur if the flow rate is too high)
Distance between capillary and collector ↑	Fibre diameter ↓ (beaded morphologies occur if the distance between the capillary and collector is too short)
Polymer concentration (viscosity) ↑	Fibre diameter ↑ (within optimal range)
Solution conductivity ↑	Fibre diameter ↓
Solvent volatility ↑	Fibres exhibit microtexture (pores on their surface, which increase surface area)

mimicking the ECM and promoting vascularisation. After fabrication, the surface of the scaffold can be modified with a high density of bioactive molecules due to the relatively high scaffold surface area. Due to the flexibility in material selection as well as the ability to control the scaffold properties, electrospun scaffolds have been employed in a number of different tissue applications including vascular, bone, neural and tendon/ligament.

Depending on the envisioned applications, pore size must be carefully controlled. The effect of implant pore size on tissue regeneration has been emphasised by experiments demonstrating optimum pore size of 5 μm for neovascularisation, 5–15 μm for fibroblast ingrowth, close to 20 μm for the ingrowth of hepatocytes, 20–125 μm for regeneration of adult mammalian skin, 40–100 μm for osteoid ingrowth and 100–350 μm for regeneration of bone. Fibrovascular tissues appear to require pores sizes greater than 500 μm for rapid vascularisation and for the survival of transplanted cells [29]. In addition to pore size and porosity, the shape and tortuosity can affect tissue ingrowth. Strong cell adhesion and spreading often favour proliferation, while rounded cell morphology is required for cell-specific function. Thus, a polymer scaffold must act as a suitable substrate to maintain differentiated functions without hindering proliferation.

Despite it has been reported that the electrospinning process may denaturalise the biological and structure properties of a natural protein such as collagen [37], the experimental result by Liu et al. [38] suggested that the PLGA/collagen nanofibrous matrix remains intact during the processing procedure and can act as an excellent scaffold for cell adhesion and growth. Presently, nanofibrous materials that mimic the native extracellular matrix and promote the adhesion of various cells are being developed as tissue-engineered scaffolds for the skin, cartilage, liver, kidney, heart, tendon/ligament, nerve, cornea, etc., which will be reviewed as follows.

Skin

Skin is a barrier which protects injured tissues, and the regeneration of skin is one of many important medical issues. When the skin is seriously damaged through disease or trauma, artificial skin using synthetic or natural polymer is essential due to limitation of self-repair and donor-site morbidity. Up to the present, skin is one of

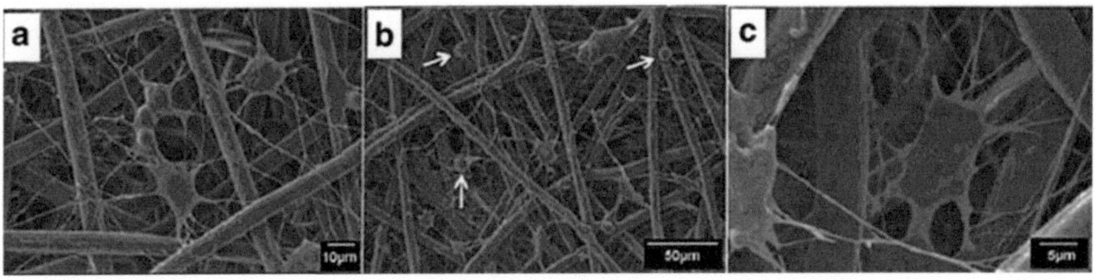

Fig. 9.6 SEM images of cell attachment after 12 h of incubation. (**a**) Cell attachment on multiscale scaffold. (**b**) Cell growth into the multiscale scaffold; *arrows* indicate spherical morphology of cells attached to microfibres. (**c**) Cell access to the interior of the multiscale scaffold through the pores in the microfibres (Reprinted from Ref. [36], with kind permission from Springer Science + Business Media)

the most investigated organs for tissue engineering. Electrospun scaffolds made of various materials, including collagen followed by crosslinking [39]; PCL [40]; PCL/collagen [41, 42] and PCL/gelatin [43]; PLA [44]; chitosan-grafted PCL [45]; poly(glycerol sebacate) [46]; hydrogel comprising poly(ethylene glycol) (PEG), poly(propylene glycol) (PPG) and PCL [47]; silk fibroin treated with plasma [48]; chitosan, gelatin and their blends [49]; polyvinyl alcohol (PVA), polyhydroxybutyrate (PHB) and their blends [50]; chitosan–PLGA–poly(ethylene oxide) (PEO) [51]; poly(vinyl alcohol) (PVA)/gelatin [52]; PLA/chitosan blends [53]; and PVA coated with chitosan, hyaluronic acid, collagen or silk fibroin [54], have been developed for the in vitro cultivation of fibroblasts. Good cell adhesion, growth and proliferation have been observed on these scaffolds in vitro. In vivo, several researchers applied the electrospun scaffolds as wound dressings [37, 38, 55–60] on animal models. It was found that nanofibrous membranes were functionally active in responses to fibroblasts and were very effective as wound healing accelerators in early-stage wound healing. These empirical results demonstrate that electrospun nanofibres may be a good candidate as a wound dressing for skin regeneration.

Cartilage

Articular cartilage has a limited capacity for self-repair. Untreated injuries of cartilage may lead to osteoarthritis. Articular cartilage repair remains a significant and growing clinical challenge with the ageing population. The ECM of articular cartilage is a 3D structure comprised of proteinaceous fibres and a hydrogel ground substance that together provides the physical and biological cues to instruct cell behaviour. Mass transport is one of the most significant challenges in tissue engineering. Large-scale cell transplantation in open structures is presently limited by inadequate nutrient delivery. Cells more than approximately 200 μm from a blood supply are either metabolically inactive or necrotic due to low oxygen tension [29]. It is for this reason that cartilage, with its very low metabolic activity, has been one of the few cell types successfully engineered into large tissue structures. In vitro studies of chondrocyte cultivation on electrospun nanofibrous scaffolds made of various materials, including PCL [61] and starch-compounded PCL [62], chitosan

[63], collagen-coated carboxymethyl chitosan [64] and double-layered nano-/microfibrous chitosan membranes [65], PLGA [66], alginate [67], PLLA [68] and PCL nanofibres/PLA microfibres [69], have been successfully conducted. Other scaffolds have also been developed for growth and differentiation of mesenchymal stem cells (MSCs) for chondrogenesis [70–73]. All these fabricated scaffolds showed promising results for cell proliferation.

In the in vivo aspect, Casper et al. [74] implanted PCL nanofibre scaffolds, with or without chitosan coating, under the periosteum in 6-month-old rabbits. Transforming growth factor-beta 1 (TGF-beta 1) or vehicle was injected into each implant site. Cell infiltration was observed in these scaffolds. They observed that the cartilage yielded from the periosteum significantly increased by subperiosteal TFG-beta 1 injection. Abedi et al. [75] studied the autologous effects of transplantation of mesenchymal stem cells (MSCs) with a collagen-poly(vinyl alcohol) (PVA) scaffold. The histological observations showed that the MSCs/collagen–PVA repair group exhibited better chondrocyte morphology, continuous subchondral bone and much thicker newly formed cartilage compared with the control group at 12 weeks post operation. Cobrun et al. [76] developed fibrous scaffolds composed of poly(vinyl alcohol) and the biological cue chondroitin sulphate with fibre dimension on the nanoscale for application to articular cartilage repair. Their result showed that the nanofibrous scaffolds enhance chondrogenic differentiation of mesenchymal stems cells as indicated by increased ECM production and cartilage-specific gene expression while also permitting cell proliferation. When implanted it into rat osteochondral defects, acellular nanofibrous scaffolds supported enhanced chondrogenesis marked by proteoglycan production minimally apparent in defects left empty.

Liver

The emerging fields of tissue engineering and biomaterials might have begun to provide potential treatment options for liver failure. Freshly isolated porcine hepatocytes are a very attractive cell source in the cell-based therapies to treat liver failure because of unlimited availability. However, due to the loss of hepatocyte functions in vitro, there is a need to develop a functional culture system to keep the cells metabolically active. Several research groups developed nanofibrous scaffolds using self-assembling peptides for culturing hepatocyte [77–81]. Other than the peptide-based scaffolds, Hashemi et al. [82] tested the ability of electrospun PCL nanofibre scaffold to support and maintain hepatic differentiation of human cord blood-derived unrestricted somatic stem cells in vitro. They showed that hepatocyte-like cells differentiation on the PCL scaffold can be a candidate for tissue engineering and cell therapy of hepatic tissues. Furthermore, electrospun scaffolds of other materials including cellulose hydrogels [83], PLLA and collagen [84] have also been developed for hepatic differentiation studies. The research group of Chu et al. [85–87] has also developed bioartificial liver support system using electrospun chitosan nanofibres. They demonstrated that no infective porcine endogenous retroviruses were detected in canine models and the developed support system has a reliable microbiological safety profile.

Kidney

Relatively less work has been done on the tissue engineering of the kidney. Schindler et al. [88] proposed a nanofibrillar matrices prepared by electrospinning a polymer solution of polyamide onto glass coverslips. When the normal rat kidney cells were grown on nanofibres in the presence of serum, they displayed the morphology and characteristics of their counterparts in vivo. Zhang et al. [89] explored the substrate-mediated gene delivery by employing a DNA immobilised electrospun nanofibres. Their nanofibre-based gene delivery system exhibited high transfection efficiency, in which >65 % of human embryonic kidney 293 cells and >40 % of mesenchymal stem cells were transfected with green fluorescent protein gene. Bakota et al. [90] proposed an injectable multidomain peptide nanofibre hydrogel as a delivery agent for stem cell secretome. In vitro experiments demonstrated that release of stem cell secretome from the hydrogels in the presence of glomerular epithelial cells treated with high glucose significantly reduced protein permeability in a model of diabetes-induced kidney injury.

Tendon/Ligament

Interfacial tissues such as tendon and ligament are specialised and ubiquitous tissues in human body, which integrate soft and hard tissue, and are characterised by their complex and heterogeneous biochemical and structural properties. The repair of interfacial tissues after injuries remains challenging; current clinical methods of fixation and tissue regeneration have not resulted in full recovery of damaged tissues. An ideal graft such as tendon graft requires it to not only exhibit physiologically relevant mechanical properties but also be able to facilitate functional graft integration by promoting the regeneration of the native tendon-to-bone interface. Various efforts have been made in preparing different nanofibrous scaffolds for tissue engineering of tendon/ligament; some of them used the self-assembling peptide-based scaffolds [91], hybrid silk-based scaffolds covered with self-assembling nanofibres [92] and scaffolds prepared by the partial dissolution method [93]. As far as the electrospinning technique is used, Inanc et al. [94] used an electrospun PLGA nanofibre membrane scaffolds for the engineering of human periodontal ligament cells. Their results demonstrated the feasibility of periodontal ligament cell-containing, tissue-like and osteogenic differentiation properties of cells. Moffat et al. [95] designed a PLGA nanofibre-based scaffold for engineering rotator cuff tendon. It was observed that rotator cuff fibroblasts cultured on the aligned scaffolds attached along the nanofibres long axis, whereas the cells on the unaligned scaffold were polygonal and randomly oriented. Furthermore, mechanical properties of the aligned nanofibre scaffolds were significantly higher than those of the unaligned. Li et al. [96] developed a continuously graded, bone-like calcium phosphate coating on a non-woven mat of electrospun nanofibres, and they found that the gradient in mineral content resulted in a gradient stiffness of the scaffold, which further influenced the activity of mouse pre-osteoblast MC3T3 cells. Since tendon is a specific connective tissue composed of parallel collagen fibres, Yin et al. [97] demonstrated that the aligned electrospun nanofibre structure provides an instructive microenvironment for hTSPC differentiation and may lead to the development of desirable engineered tendons. In addition, to improve the mechanical properties of engineered scaffolds, Sahoo et al. [98] and Teh et al. [99] adopted kitted silk as the scaffold materials for ligament tissue engineering applications. Meanwhile, scaffolds of other materials, including PCL/collagen and PLA/collagen [100], collagen–glycosaminoglycan [101], hydroxyapatite-coated PLGA [102], cellulose [93], hydrogel [103], etc., have been developed aiming for tendon repair applications. All these scaffolds exhibited enhancing capability for cell proliferation and differentiation. Recently, Erisken et al. [104] found that controlling the scaffold fibre diameter is critical in the design of scaffolds for functional and guided connective tissue repair. This provides some new insights into the role of matrix parameters in guiding soft tissue healing.

Cornea

The cornea is the transparent front part of the eye that covers the iris, pupil and anterior chamber. Only limited works have been conducted on the engineering of corneal replacement and for promoting regenerative healing of the cornea after disease and/or injury. English et al. [105] developed anisotropically aligned collagen nanofibres via electrospinning and solvent casting and successfully evaluated the response of corneal fibroblasts to the nanofibrous scaffold. They observed that the corneal fibroblasts aligned parallel to the direction of the aligned oriented electrospun mats. Muthusubramaniam et al. [106] grew the corneal fibroblasts isolated from bovine corneas on collagen nanofibrous scaffolds and found that matrix nanotopography downregulates the fibrotic phenotype, promotes formation of the quiescent keratocyte phenotype and influences matrix synthesis. Gao et al. [107] investigated the contribution of fibre arrangement to guiding the aligned growth of corneal stroma cells. They found that corneal stroma cells grew highly orderly on the aligned scaffold, while the cells grow disordered on the randomly oriented scaffold. In addition, the cells exhibited higher viability in aligned scaffold than that in randomly oriented scaffold.

Heart

The in vitro generation of a three-dimensional myocardial tissue-like construct that employs cells, biomaterials and biomolecules can be a promising strategy in cardiac tissue regeneration. Compared to the in vitro [108–110] and in vivo [111–113] progress made in the engineering of cardiovascular tissue using self-assembling peptides, the development of electrospun scaffolds is relatively limited. Heydarkhan-Hagvall et al. [114] developed three-dimensional electrospun ECM-based hybrid scaffolds, namely, gelatin/PCL and collagen/elastin/PCL scaffolds, for cardiovascular tissue engineering. Scanning electron microscopy and nuclei staining of cell-seeded scaffolds demonstrated the complete cell attachment to the surfaces of both hybrid scaffolds, while cell migration into the scaffold was predominantly seen in the gelatin/PCL hybrid. Balguid et al. [115] seeded human venous myofibroblasts in electrospun PCL scaffolds and found that cell penetration increased proportionally with increasing fibre diameter. They concluded that fibre diameter is a crucial parameter to allow for homogeneous cell delivery in electrospun scaffolds. Chung et al. [116] developed small diameter tubes fabricated from poly(L-lactide-co-ε-caprolactone) copolymers via melt spinning and electrospinning for vascular tissue engineering scaffolds. They demonstrated that the mechanical properties of the prototype tubes exceeded the transverse tensile value of natural arteries of similar calibre. Stout et al. [117] investigated cardiac tissue cell functions on PLGA filled with carbon nanofibres that have a higher conductivity. Their results showed that cardiomyocyte density increases with greater amounts of carbon nanofibres in PLGA for up to 5 days. This indicates the conductive materials promoted the adhesion and proliferation of the cells. Courtney et al. [118] fabricated poly(ester urethane) urea scaffold via electrospinning and demonstrated that the high-velocity spun scaffolds exhibited highly native anisotropic mechanical properties closely resembling the native pulmonary heat valve leaflet. Li et al. [119] co-electrospun fibrous scaffolds from the blend of PLGA and two natural proteins, gelatin and elastin. They cultured H9c2 rat cardiac myoblasts on the scaffolds and found that myoblasts grew equally as well or slightly better on the scaffolds than on tissue-culture plastic. Recently, Hussain et al. [120] developed fibronectin-coated chitosan nanofibre scaffolds for cardiovascular tissue engineering. The experimental results demonstrated that the chitosan nanofibres retained their cylindrical morphology in long-term culture of ventricular cardiomyocytes and exhibited good cellular attachment and spreading in the presence of fibronectin.

Nerve

Despite many nerve prostheses have been proposed in recent years, in the case of consistent loss of nervous tissue, peripheral nerve injury is still a traumatic pathology that impairs patient's movements by interrupting his/her motor–sensory pathways. During the past few decades, tissue engineering has opened the door to new approaches. Bridging larger nerve gaps between proximal and distal ends requires exogenous tubular constructs with uniaxially aligned topographical cues to promote the axonal regrowth due to the lack of fibrin cable formation. An ideal scaffold for neural regeneration would be both fibrous and electrically conductive. It has been generally accepted that aligned nanofibre scaffolds enhance growth and proliferation of neural cells such as Schwann cells, dorsal root ganglion neurons, etc. Electrospinning technique may thus provide a potential alternative to engineering of nervous tissues. To date, various successes have been achieved to partially construct neural system function in rat models by employing the self-assembling peptide-based hydrogels [121–126]. Relatively, the progress in the engineering of neural prostheses using electrospun scaffolds of different materials mainly remains in the in vitro stage [127]. Only few in vivo studies have been reported. Panseri et al. [128] used the electrospun tubes made of PLGA/PCL blends to regenerate a 10-mm nerve gap in a rat sciatic nerve. Their results showed that in most of the treated animals, the electrospun tubes induced nervous regeneration and functional reconnection of the two severed sciatic nerve tracts. This indicates that electrospun tubes, even with no additional biological coating or drug loading treatment, are promising scaffolds for functional nervous regeneration. Clements et al. [129] developed nerve guidance channels containing stacked thin films of aligned poly (acrylonitrile-co-methylacrylate) fibres and implanted the channels into rats. Their results indicated that the channels supported the regeneration across the nerve gap, thereby resulting in functional muscular reinnervation. Wang et al. [130] constructed a chitosan non-woven nanofibre mesh tubes consisting of oriented fibres by the electrospinning method which were bridge-grafted into rat sciatic nerve defects. Functional recovery and electrophysiological recovery of rats were observed in time. Kim et al. [131] prepared muscle precursor cell-seeded PCL nanofibres and placed the fibres under the female rat's urethra after pudendal nerve denervation. Their experimental results indicated that the nanofibres have not only provided support to the deficient sphincter but also actively improved the sphincter's function.

9.5 Conclusion

The technological improvement in biology, medicine, chemistry, engineering and material science have allowed to gain deeper insights into the architectural and molecular organisation of tissues and materials, providing innovative approaches and tools for medical treatments. Developments in this multidisciplinary field of tissue engineering have yielded a novel set of tissue replacement parts and implementation strategies. Scientific advances in biomaterials, stem cells, growth and differentiation factors and biomimetic environments have created unique opportunities to fabricate tissues in vitro from combinations of engineered extracellular matrices, cells and biologically active molecules. The major challenge now facing tissue engineering is the need for more complex functionality, as well as both functional and biomechanical stability in in vitro grown tissues destined for transplantation. The continued success of tissue engineering will grow from the convergence of engineering and basic research advances in tissue, matrix, growth factor, stem cell and material science. Eventually, it is expected that the engineered tissues would be able to be used for the replacement of damaged or failed tissues/organs directly.

Acknowledgements The authors thank Ms. Yu-Chun Kao for her assistance in preparing the figures.

References

1. Sill TJ, von Recum HA (2008) Electrospinning: application in drug delivery and tissue engineering. Biomaterials 29:1989–2006

2. Frank CB, Shrive NG (1999) Biological materials. In: Biomechanics of the musculo-skeletal system. Wiley, Chichester/New York, pp 107–126
3. Carmeliet P (2000) Mechanisms of angiogenesis and arteriogenesis. Nat Med 6:389–395
4. Ingber DE (2002) Mechanical signaling and the cellular response to extracellular matrix in angiogenesis and cardiovascular physiology. Circ Res 91:877–887
5. Carter DR, van der Meulen MCH, Beaupré GS (1996) Mechanical factors in bone growth and development. Bone 18:5S–10S
6. Schoen FJ (1997) Aortic valve structure-function correlations: role of elastic fibers no longer a stretch of the imagination. J Heart Valve Dis 6:1–6
7. Bokel C, Brown NH (2002) Integrins in development: moving on, responding to, and sticking to the extracellular matrix. Dev Cell 3:311–321
8. Minns RJ, Soden PD, Jackson DS (1973) The role of the fibrous components and ground substance in the mechanical properties of biological tissues: a preliminary investigation. J Biomech 6:153–165
9. Fawcett DW (1986) Bloom and Fawcett: a textbook of histology, 11th edn. WB.Saunders Company, Philadelphia
10. Alberts B, Bray D, Lewis J, Raff M, Roberts K, Watson JD (1994) Molecular biology of the cell, 3rd edn. Garland Publishing, New York
11. Limbert G, Taylor M (2002) On the constitutive modelling of biological soft connective tissues. A general theoretical framework and explicit forms of the tensors of elasticity for strongly anisotropic continuum fiber-reinforced composites at finite strain. Int J Solid Struct 39(8):2343–2358
12. Freed AD, Doehring TC (2005) Elastic model for crimped collagen fibrils. J Biomech Eng 127(4):587–593
13. Redaelli A, Vesentini S, Soncini M, Vena P, Mantero S, Montevecchi FM (2003) Possible role of decorin glycosaminoglycans in fibril to fibril force transfer in relative mature tendons – a computational study from molecular to microstructural level. J Biomech 36 (10):1555–1569
14. Raspanti M, Alessandrini A, Ottani V, Ruggeri A (1997) Direct visualization of collagen-bound proteoglycans by tapping-mode atomic force microscopy. J Struct Biol 119:118–122
15. Eyre DR, Pietka T, Weis MA, Wu JJ (2004) Covalent cross-linking of the NC1 domain of collagen type IX to collagen type II in cartilage. J Biol Chem 279(4):2568–2574
16. Szwajczak E (2004) Dependence of hyaluronan aqueous solution viscosity on external fields, part II. Russ J Biomech 8(1):89–94
17. Nishimura M, Yan W, Mukudai Y, Nakamura S, Nakamasu K, Kawata M, Kawamoto T, Noshiro M, Hamada T, Kato Y (1998) Role of chondroitin sulphate-hyluronan interactions in the viscoelastic properties of extracellular matrices and fluids. Biochim Biophys Acta 1380 (1):1–9
18. Homsy CA (1970) Bio-compatibility in selection of materials for implantation. J Biomed Mater Res 4:341–356
19. Zdolsek J, Eaton JW, Tang L (2007) Histamine release and fibrinogen adsorption mediate acute inflammatory responses to biomaterial implants in humans. J Transl Med 5:31
20. Tang L, Jennings TA, Eaton JW (1998) Mast cells mediate acute inflammatory responses to implanted biomaterials. Proc Natl Acad Sci U S A 95(15):8841–8846
21. Keegan AD (2001) IL-4. In: Oppenheim JJ, Feldman M (eds) Cytokine reference. Academic, San Diego
22. McKenzie ANJ, Matthews DJ (2001) IL-13. In: Oppenheim JJ, Feldman M (eds) Cytokine reference. Academic, San Diego
23. Florey HW (1970) General pathology. Saunders, New York, pp 510–516
24. Davila JC (1966) Prosthesis and living tissue: conflict compatibility (editional). Ann Thorac Surg 2:126
25. Davila JC, Lautsch EV, Palmer TE (1968) Some physical factors affecting the acceptance of synthetic materials as tissue implants. Ann N Y Acad Sci 146:138–147

26. Oppenheimer BS, Oppenheimer ET, Stout AP, Danishefsky I (1953) Malignant tumors resulting from embedding plastics in rodents. Science 118:305–306
27. Stinson NE (1964) The tissue reaction induced in rats and guinea pigs by polymethyl methacrylate and stainless steel. Br J Exp Pathol 45:21–29
28. Kubinova S, Sykova E (2010) Nanotechnologies in regenerative medicine. Minim Invasive Ther Allied Technol 19:144–156
29. Yang S, Leong KF, Du Z, Chua CK (2001) The design of scaffolds for use in tissue engineering. Part I. Traditional factors. Tissue Eng 7(6):679–689
30. Middleton JC, Tipton AJ (2000) Synthetic biodegradable polymers as orthopedic devices. Biomaterials 21:2335–2346
31. Nair LS, Laurencin CT (2007) Biodegradable polymers as biomaterials. Prog Polym Sci 32:762–798
32. Vasita R, Katti DS (2006) Nanofibers and their applications in tissue engineering. Int J Nanomed 1(1):15–30
33. Taylor G (1969) Electrically driven jets. Proc Natl Acad Sci Lond A313(1515):53–475
34. Huang ZM, Zhang YZ, Kotaki M, Ramakrishna S (2003) A review on polymer nanofibers by electrospinning and their applications in nanocomposites. Compos Sci Technol 63:2223–2253
35. Teo WE, Ramakrishna S (2006) A review on electrospinning design and nanofibre assemblies. Nanotechnolgy 17:R89–R106
36. Srinivasan S, Jayakumar R, Chennazhi KP, Levorson EJ, Mikos AG, Nair SV (2011) Multiscale fibrous scaffolds in regenerative medicine. Adv Polym Sci 246:1–20
37. Rho KS, Jeong L, Lee G, Seo BM, Park YJ, Hong SD, Roh S, Cho JJ, Park WH, Min BM (2006) Electrospinning of collagen nanofibers: effects on the behaviour of normal human keratinocytes and early-stage wound healing. Biomaterials 27:1452–1461
38. Liu SJ, Kau YC, Chou CY, Chen JK, Wu RC, Yeh WL (2010) Electrospun PLGA/collagen nanofibrous membrane as early-stage wound dressing. J Membr Sci 355:53–59
39. Dong B, Arnoult O, Smith ME, Wnek GE (2009) Electrospinnign of collagen nanofibers scaffolds from benign solvents. Macromol Rapid Commun 30:539–542
40. Reed CR, Han L, Andrady A, Caballero M, Jack MC, Collins JB, Saba SC, Loboa EG, Cairns BA, van Aalst JA (2009) Composite tissue engineering on polycaprolactone nanofibers scaffolds. Ann Plast Surg 62:505–512
41. Venugopal J, Ramakrishna S (2005) Biocompatible nanofibers matrices for the engineering of a dermal substitute for skin regeneration. Tissue Eng 11:847–854
42. Yang XC, Shah JD, Wang HJ (2009) Nanofiber enabled layer-by-layer approach toward three-dimensional tissue formation. Tissue Eng Part A 15:945–956
43. Chong EJ, Phan TT, Lim IJ, Zhang YZ, Bay BH, Ramakrishna S (2007) Evaluation of electrospun PCL/gelatin nanofibrous scaffold for wound healing and layered dermal reconsititution. Acta Biomater 3:321–330
44. Leong MF, Rasheed MZ, Lim TC, Chian KS (2009) In vitro cell infiltration and in vivo cell infiltration and vascularization in a fibrous, highly porous poly(D, L-lactide) scaffold fabricated by cryogenic electrospinning technique. J Biomed Mater Res Part A 91A:231–240
45. Chen HL, Huang J, Yu JH, Liu SY, Gu P (2011) Electrospun chitosan-graft-poly(epsilon-caprolactone)/poly(epsilon-caprolactone) cationic nanofibrous mats as potential scaffolds for skin tissue engineering. Int J Biol Macromol 48:13–19
46. Yi F, Laven DA (2008) Poly(glycerol sebacate) nanofibers scaffolds by core/shell electrospinning. Macromol Biosci 8:803–806
47. Loh XJ, Peh P, Liao S, Sng C, Li J (2010) Controlled drug release from biodegradable thermoresponsive physical hydrogel nanofibers. J Control Release 143:175–182
48. Jeong L, Yeo IS, Kim HN, Yoon HI, Jang DH, Jung SY, Min BM, Park WH (2009) Plasma-treated silk fibroin nanofibers for skin regeneration. Int J Biol Macromol 44:222–228

49. Dhandayuthapani B, Krishnan UM, Sethuraman S (2010) Fabrication and characterization of chitosan-gelatin nanofibers for skin tissue engineering. J Biomed Mater Res Part B 94B:264–272
50. Asran AS, Razghandi K, Aggarwal N, Michler GH, Groth T (2010) Nanofibers from blends of polyvinyl alcohol and polyhydroxy butyrate as potential scaffold material for tissue engineering of skin. Biomacromolecules 11:3413–3421
51. Lim HJ, Kim CJ, Oh EJ, Kim TJ, Jung SY, Choi JH, Lee WJ, Kwon OH, Chung HY (2011) Hybrid scaffolds composed of chitosan-PLGA-PEO nanofibers and PLGA microfibers for artificial skin. Tissue Eng Regen Med 8:108–115
52. Yang C, Wu XM, Zhao YH, Xu L, Wei SC (2011) Nanofibrous scaffold prepared by electrospinning of poly(vinyl alcohol)/gelatin aqueous solutions. J Appl Polym Sci 121:3047–3055
53. Shalumon KT, Sathish D, Nair SV, Chennazhi KP, Tamura H, Jayakumar R (2012) Fabrication of aligned poly(lactic acid)-chitosan nanofibers by novel parallel blade collector method for skin tissue engineering. J Biomed Nanotechnol 8:405–416
54. Lee SY, Jang DH, Kang YO, Kim OB, Jeong L, Kang HK, Lee SJ, Lee CH, Park WH, Min BM (2012) Cellular response to poly(vinyl alcohol) nanofibers coated with biocompatible proteins and polysaccharides. Appl Surf Sci 258:6914–6922
55. Park SN, Lee HJ, Lee KH, Suh H (2003) Biological characterization of EDC-crosslinked collagen-hyaluronic acid matrix in dermal tissue restoration. Biomaterials 24:1631–1641
56. Chen JP, Chang GY, Chen JK (2008) Electrospun collagen/chitosan nanofibrous membrane as wound dressing. Colloids Surf A PhysioChem Eng Asp 313–314:183–188
57. Kumbar SG, Nukavarapu SP, James R, Nair LS, Laurencin CT (2008) Electrospun poly(lactic acid-co-glycolic acid) scaffolds for skin tissue engineering. Biomaterials 29:4100–4107
58. Yang Y, Zhu X, Cui W, Li X, Jin Y (2009) Electrospun composites mats of Poly[(D, L-ladctide)-co-glycolide] and collagen with high porosity as potential scaffolds for skin tissue engineering. Macromol Mater Eng 294:611–619
59. Kurpinsk KT, Stephenson JT, Janairo RRR, Lee HM, Li S (2010) The effect of fiber alignment and heparin coating on cell infiltration into nanofibrous PLLA scaffolds. Biomaterials 31:3536–3542
60. Chen DWC, Liao JY, Liu SJ, Chan EC (2012) Novel biodegradable sandwich-structured nanofibrous drug-eluting membranes for repair of infected wounds: an in vitro and in vivo study. Int J Nanomed 7:763–771
61. Li WJ, Danielson KG, Alexander PG, Tuan RS (2003) Biological response of chondrocytes cultured in three-dimensional nanofibrous poly(epsilon-caprolactone) scaffolds. J Biomed Mater Res Part A 67A:1105–1114
62. de Silva MA, Crawford A, Mundy J, Martins A, Araujo JV, Hatton PV, Reis RL, Neves NM (2009) Evaluation of extracellular matrix formation in polycaprolactone and starch-compounded polycaprolactone nanofibers meshes when seeded with bovine articular chondrocytes. Tissue Eng Part A 15:377–385
63. Subramanian A, Vu D, Larsen GF, Lin HY (2005) Preparation and evaluation of the electrospun chitosan/PEO fibers for potential applications in cartilage tissue engineering. J Biomater Sci Polym Ed 16:861–873
64. Lu GY, Sheng BY, Wei YJ, Wang G, Zhang LH, Ao Q, Gong YD, Zhang XF (2008) Collagen nanofibers-covered porous biodegradable carboxymthyl chitosan microcarriers for tissue engineering cartilage. Eur Polym J 44:2820–2829
65. Shim IK, Suh WH, Lee SY, Lee SH, Heo SJ, Lee MC, Lee SJ (2009) Chitosan nano-/microfibrous double-layered membrane with rolled-up three-dimensional structures for chondrocyte cultivation. J Biomed Mater Res Part A 90A:595–602
66. Shin HJ, Lee CH, Cho IH, Kim YJ, Lee JY, Kim IA, Park KD, Yui N, Shin JW (2006) Electrospun PLGA nanofibers scaffolds for articular cartilage reconstruction: mechanical stability, degradation and cellular responses under mechanical stimulation in vitro. J Biomater Sci Polym Ed 17:103–119

67. Bhattarai N, Li ZS, Edmondson D, Zhang MQ (2006) Alginate-based nanofibrous scaffolds: structural, mechanical, and biological properties. Adv Mater 18:1463–1467
68. Li WJ, Jiang YJ, Tuan RS (2006) Chondrocyte phenotype in engineered fibrous matrix is regulated by fiber size. Tissue Eng 12:1775–1785
69. Thorvaldsson A, Stenhamre H, Gaten holm P, Walkenstrom P (2008) Electrospinning of highly porous scaffolds for cartilage regeneration. Biomacromolecules 9:1044–1049
70. Xin XJ, Husaain M, Mao JJ (2007) Continuing differentiation of human mesenchymal stem cells and induced chondrogenic and osteogenic lineages in electrospun PLGA nanofibers scaffold. Biomaterials 28:316–325
71. Mohammadi Y, Soleimani M, Fallahi-Sichani M, Gazme A, Haddadi-Asl V, Arefian E, Kiani J, Moradi R, Atashi A, Ahmadbeigi N (2007) Nanofibrous poly(epsilon-caprolactone)/poly(vinyl alcohol)/chitosan hybrid scaffolds for bone tissue engineering using mesenchymal cells. Int J Artif Organ 30:204–211
72. Hu J, Feng K, Liu XH, Ma PX (2009) Chondrogenic and osteogenic differentiations of human bone marrow-derived mesenchymal stem cells on a nanofibrous scaffold with designed pore network. Biomaterials 30:5061–5067
73. Shafiee A, Soleimani M, Chamheidari GA, Shyedjafari E, Dodel M, Atashi A, Gheisari Y (2011) Electrospun nanofiber-based regeneration of cartilage enhanced by mesenchymal stem cells. J Biomed Mater Res Part A 99A:467–478
74. Casper ME, Fitzsimmons JS, Stone JJ, Meza AO, Huang Y, Ruesink TJ, O'Driscoll SW, Reinholz GG (2010) Tissue engineering of cartilage using poly-epsilon-caprolactone nanofibers scaffolds seeded in vivo with periosteal cells. Osteoarthr Cartil 18:981–991
75. Abedi G, Sotoudeh A, Soleymani M, Shafiee A, Mortazavi P, Afatoonian MR (2011) A collagen-poly(vinyl alcohol) nanofibers scaffold for cartilage repair. J Biomater Sci Polym Ed 22:2445–2455
76. Coburn JM, Gibson M, Monagles S, Patterson Z, Elisseeff JH (2012) Bioinspired nanofibers support chondrogenesis for articular cartilage repair. Proc Natl Acad Sci 109:10012–10017
77. Navarro-Alvarez N, Soto-Gutierrez A, Rivas-Carrillo JD, Chen Y, Yamamoto T, Yuasa T, Misawa H, Takei J, Tanake N, Kobayashi N (2006) Self-assembling peptide nanofibers as a novel culture system for isolated porcine hepatocytes. Cell Transplant 15:921–927
78. Wang S, Nagrath D, Chen PC, Berthiaume F, Yarmush ML (2008) Three-dimensional primary hepatocyte culture in synthetic self-assembling peptide hydrogel. Tissue Eng Part A 14:227–236
79. Mehta G, Williams CM, Alvarez L, Lesniewski M, Kamm RD, Griffith LG (2010) Synergistic effects of tethered growth factors and adhesion ligands on DNA synthesis and function of primary hepatocytes cultured on soft synthetic hydrogel. Biomaterials 31:4657–4671
80. Sun LJ, Zhao XJ (2012) A self-assembling peptide RADA 16-I integrated with spider fibroin uncrystalline motifs. Int J Nanomed 7:571–580
81. Malinen MM, Palokangas H, Yliperttula M, Urtti A (2012) Peptide nanofibers hydrogel induces formation of bile canaliculi structures in three-dimensional hepatic cell culture. Tissue Eng Part A 18:2418–2425
82. Hashemi SM, Soleimani M, Zargarian SS, Haddadi-Asl V, Ahmadbeigi N, Soudi S, Gheisari Y, Hajarizadeh A, Mohammadi Y (2009) In vitro differentiation of human cord blood-derived unrestricted somatic stem cells into hepatocyte-like cells on poly(epsilon-caprolactone) nanofibers scaffolds. Cell Tissue Organ 190:135–149
83. Bhattacharya M, Malinen MM, Lauren P, Lou YR, Kuisma SW, Kanninen L, Lille M, Corlu A, GuGuen-Guillouze C, Ikkala O, Laukkanen A, Urtti A, Yliperttula M (2012) Nanofibrillar cellulose hydrogel promotes three-dimensional liver cell culture. J Control Release 164:291–298
84. Ghaedi M, Soleimani M, Shabani I, Duan YY, Lotfi AS (2012) Hepatic differentiation from human mesenchymal stem cells on a novel nanofibers scaffold. Cell Mol Biol Lett 17:89–106

85. Chu XH, Shi XL, Feng ZQ, Gu JY, Xu HY, Zhang Y, Gu ZZ, Ding YT (2009) In vitro evalution of a multi-radial-flow bioreactor based on galactosylated chitosan nanofiber scaffolds. Biomaterials 30:4533–4538
86. Han B, Shi XL, Zhang Y, Chu XH, Gu JY, Xizo JQ, Ren HZ, Tan JJ, Gu ZZ, Ding YT (2012) Microgiological safety of a novel-artificial liver support system based on porcine hepatocytes: an experimental study. Eur J Med Res 17:13
87. Shi XL, Zhang Y, Chu XH, Han B, Gu JY, Xiao JQ, Tan JJ, Gu ZZ, Ren HZ, Yuan XW, Ding YT (2012) Evaluation of a novel hybrid bioartificial liver based on a multi-layer flat-plate bioreactor. World J Gastroenterol 18:3752–3760
88. Schindler M, Ahmed I, Kamal J, Nur-E-Kamal A, Grafe TH, Chung HY, Meiners S (2005) A synthetic nanofibrillar matrix promotes in vivo-like organization and morphogenesis for cells in culture. Biomaterials 26:5624–5631
89. Zhang J, Duan YJ, Wei D, Wang LY, Wang HJ, Gu ZW, Kong DL (2011) Co-electrospun fibrous scaffold-adsorbed DNA for substrate-mediated gene delivery. J Biomed Mater Res A 96A:212–220
90. Bakota EL, Wang Y, Danesh FR, Hartgerink JD (2011) Injectable multidomain peptide nanofibers hydrogel as a delivery agent for stem cell secretome. Biomacromolecules 12:1651–1657
91. Kumada Y, Zhang SG (2010) Significatn type I and type III collagen production from human periodontal ligment fibroblasts in 3D peptide scaffolds without extra growth factors. Plos One 5:e10305
92. Chen KL, Sahoo S, He PF, Ng KS, Toh SL, Goh JCH (2012) A hybrid silk/RADA-based fibrous scaffold with triple hierarchy for ligament regeneration. Tissue Eng Part A 18:1399–1409
93. Mathew AP, Oksman K, Pierron D, Harmand MF (2012) Fibrous cellulose nanocomposites scaffolds prepared by partial dissolutn for potential use as ligament or tendon substitutes. Carbohydr Polym 87:2291–2298
94. Inanc B, Arslan YE, Seker S, Elcin AE, Elcin YM (2009) Periodontal ligament cellular structures engineered with electrospun poly(DL-lactide-co-glycolide) nanofibrous membrane scaffold. J Biomed Mater Res A 90A:186–195
95. Moffat KL, Kwei ASP, Spalazzi JP, Doty SB, Levine WN, Lu HH (2009) Novel nanofibers-based scaffold for rotator cuff repair and augmentation. Tissue Eng Part A 15:115–126
96. Li XR, Xie JW, Lipner J, Yuan XY, Thomopoulos S, Xia YN (2009) Nanofiber scaffolds with gradations in mineral content for mimicking the tendon-to-bone insertion site. Nano Lett 9:2763–2768
97. Yin Z, Chen X, Chen JL, Shen WL, Gao L, Ouyang HW (2010) The regulation of tendon stem cell differentiation by the alignment of nanofibers. Biomaterials 31:2163–2175
98. Sahoo S, Toh SL, Goh JCH (2010) PLGA nanofibers-coated silk microfibrous scaffold for connective tissue engineering. J Biomed Mater Res B 95B:19–28
99. Teh TKH, Toh SL, Goh JCH (2011) Aligned hybrid silk scaffold for enhanced differentiation of mesenchymal stem cells into ligament fibroblasts. Tissue Eng Part C 17:687–703
100. Ladd MR, Lee SJ, Stitzel JD, Atala A, Yoo JJ (2011) Co-electrospun dual scaffolding system with potential for muscle-tendon junction tissue engineering. Biomaterials 32:1549–1559
101. Caliari SR, Harley BAC (2011) The effect of anisotropic collagen-GAG scaffolds and growth factor supplementation on tendon cell. Biomaterials 32:5330–5340
102. Liu WY, Yeh YC, Lipner J, Xie JW, Sung HW, Thomopoulos S, Xia YN (2011) Enhancing the stiffness of electrospun nanofibers scaffolds with a controlled surface coating and mineralization. Langmuir 27:9088–9093
103. Carr LR, Krause JE, Ella-Menye JR, Jiang SY (2011) Single nonfouling hydrogel with mechanical and chemical functionality gradients. Biomaterials 32:8456–8461
104. Erisken C, Zhang X, Moffat KL, Levine WN, Lu HH (2013) Scaffold fiber diameter regulates human tendon fibroblast growth and differentiation. Tissue Eng Part A 19:519–528

105. English A, Azeem A, Gaspar DA, Keane K, Kumar P, Keeney M, Rooney N, Pandit A, Zeugolis DI (2012) Preferential cell response to anisotropic electrospun fibrous scaffolds under tension-free conditions. J Mater Sci Mater Med 23:137–148
106. Muthusubramaniam L, Peng L, Zaitseva T, Paukshto M, Martin GR, Desai TA (2012) Collagen fibril diameter and alignment promote the quiescent keratocyte phenotype. J Biomed Mater Res A 100A:613–621
107. Gao Y, Yan J, Cut XJ, Wang HY, Wang Q (2012) Aligned fibrous scaffold induced aligned growth of corneal stroma cells in vitro culture. Chem Res Chin Univ 28:1022–1025
108. Davis ME, Motion JPM, Narmoneva DA, Takahashi T, Hakuno D, Kamm RD, Zhang SG, Lee RT (2005) Injectable self-assembling peptide nanofibers create intramyocardial micro-environments for endothelial cells. Circulation 111:442–450
109. Ceylan H, Tekinay AB, Guler MO (2011) Selective adhesion and growth of vascular endothelial cells on bioactive peptide nanofibers functionalized stainless steel surface. Biomaterials 32:8797–8805
110. Guo HD, Cui GH, Yang JJ, Wang C, Zhu J, Zhang LS, Jiang J, Shao SJ (2012) Sustained delivery of VEGF from designer self-assembling peptides improves cardiac function after myocardial infarction. Biochem Biophys Res Commun 424:105–111
111. Dubois G, Segers VFM, Bellamy V, Sabbah L, Peyrad S, Bruneval P, Hagege AA, Lee RT, Menasche P (2008) Self-assembling peptide nanofibers and skeletal myoblast transplantation in infracted myocardium. J Biomed Mater Res Part B 87B:222–228
112. Webber MJ, Tongers J, Renault MA, Roncalli JG, Losordo DW, Stupp SI (2010) Development of bioactive peptide amphiphiles for therapeutic cell delivery. Acta Biomater 6:3–11
113. Lin YD, Luo CY, Hu YN, Yeh ML, Hsueh YC, Chang MY, Tsai DC, Wang JN, Tang MJ, Wei EIH, Springer ML, Hsieh PCH (2012) Instructive nanofibers scaffolds with VEGF create a microenvironment for arteriogenesis and cardiac repair. Sci Transl Med 4:146ra109
114. Heydarkhan-Hagvall S, Schenke-Layland K, Dhanasopon AP, Rofail F, Smith H, Wu BM, Shemin R, Beygui RE, MacLellan WR (2008) Three-dimensional electrospun CCM-based hybrid scaffolds for cardiovascular tissue engineering. Biomaterials 29:2907–2914
115. Balguid A, Mol A, van Marion MH, Bank RA, Bouten CVC, Baaijens FPT (2009) Tailoring fiber diameter in electrospun poly(epsilon-caprolactone) scaffolds for optimal cellular infiltration in cardiovascular tissue engineering. Tissue Eng Part A 15:437–444
116. Chung SW, Ingle NP, Montero GA, Kim SH, King MW (2010) Bioresorbable elastomiric vascular tissue engineering scaffolds via melt spinning and electrospinning. Acta Biomater 6:1958–1967
117. Stout DA, Basu B, Webster TJ (2011) Poly(lactic-coglycolic acid): carbon nanofibers composites for myocardial tissue engineering applications. Acta Biomater 7:3101–3112
118. Courtney T, Sacks MS, Stankus J, Guan J, Wagner WR (2006) Design and analysis of tissue engineering scaffolds that mimic soft tissue mechanical anisotropy. Biomaterials 27:3631–3638
119. Li M, Mondrinos MJ, Chen X, Gandhi MR, Ko FK, Lelkes PI (2006) Co-electrospun poly (ladtide-co-glycolide), gelatin, and elastin blends for tissue engineering scaffolds. J Biomed Mater Res Part A 79A:963–973
120. Hussain A, Collins G, Yip D, Cho CH (2013) Functional 3-D co-culture model using bioactive chitosan nanofibers scaffolds. Biotechnol Bioeng 110:637–647
121. McGrath AM, Novikova LN, Novikova LN, Wiberg M (2010) BD PuraMatrix peptide hydrogel seeded with Schwann cells for peripheral nerve regeneration. Brain Res Bull 83:207–213
122. Gelain F, Panseri S, Antonini S, Cunha C, Donega M, Lowery J, Taraballi F, Cerri G, Montagna M, Baldissera F, Vescovi A (2011) Tranplantation of nanostructured composite scaffolds results in the regeneration of chronically injured spinal cords. ACS Nano 5:227–236
123. Zhang WW, Zhan XD, Gao MY, Hamilton AD, Liu ZY, Jiang YW, Su HX, Dai X, He B, Kang XN, Zeng YX, Wu WT, Guo JS (2012) Self-assembling peptide nanofibers scaffold enhanced with RhoA inhibitor CT04 improves axonal. J Nanomater 724857.

124. Meng H, Chen RY, Xu LN, Li WC, Chen LY, Zhao XJ (2012) Peripheral nerve regeneration in response to synthesized nanofibers scaffold hydrogel. Life Sci J Acta Zhengzhou Univ Oversea Ed 9:42–46
125. Moradi F, Bahktiari M, Hoghataei MT, Nobakht M, Soleimani M, Hasanzadeh G, Fallah A, Zarbakhsh S, Hejazian LB, Shirmohammadi M, Maleki F (2012) BD PuraMatrix peptide hydrogel as a culture system for human fetal Schwann cells in spinal cord. J Neurosci Res 90:2335–2348
126. Nayagam BA, Back house SS, Cimenkaya C, Shepherd RK (2012) Hydrogel limits stem cell dispersal in the deaf cochlea: implications for cochlear implants. J Neural Eng 9:065001
127. Saracino GAA, Cigognini D, Silva D, Caprini A, Gelain F (2013) Nanomaterials design and tests for neural tissue engineering. Chem Soc Rev 42:225–262
128. Panseri S, Cunha C, Lowery J, Del Carro U, Taraballi F, Amadio S, Vescovi A, Gelain F (2008) Electrospun micro- and nanofibers tubes for functional nervous regeneration in sciatic nerve transactions. BMC Biotechnol 8:39
129. Clements IP, Kim YT, English AW, Lu X, Chung A, Bellamkonda RV (2009) Thin-film enhanced nerve guidance channels for peripheral nerve repair. Biomaterials 30:3834–3846
130. Wang W, Itoh S, Konno K, Kikkawa T, Ichinose S, Sakai K, Ohkuma T, Watabe K (2009) Effects of Schwann cell alignment along the oriented electrospun chitosan nanofibers on nerve regeneration. J Biomed Mater Res Part A 91A:994–1005
131. Kim IG, Piao S, Hong SH, Kim SW, Hwang TK, Oh SH, Lee JH, Lee JY (2012) The effect of a bioactive tissue-engineered sling in a rat of stress incontinence model. J Biomed Mater Res Part A 100A:286–292

Chapter 10
Biomimic Design of Periosteum: Construction Strategies, Scaffold Design and Cell Sources

Yin Xiao, Wei Fan, Ross Crawford, and Dietmar W. Hutmacher

Abstract In terms of bone physiology, the periosteum plays critical roles in both bone formation and defect healing. Periosteum is a dual-layered soft tissue membrane that contains osteogenic progenitor cells in the cambial layer, as well as blood supply and supportive cells in the fibrous layer. Transplantation of autogenous or allogenous periosteum has been applied successfully in the repair of various-sized bone defects, especially in large bone defects. However, two major concerns exist in relation to the insufficient autologous donor tissues and donor site morbidity or immunological rejection related to allogeneic tissues. Periosteum tissue engineering is to mimic the natural structure of periosteum, which will guide bone formation in a physiological manner. This chapter provides current information about the construction strategies, scaffold design and cell sources for the periosteum tissue engineering based on the structure and functions of natural periosteum.

Keywords Scaffold • Periosteum • Tissue engineering • Stem cells • Bone • Biomaterials

10.1 Introduction

Restoring bone defects and its normal function has long since been the final ambition of orthopaedic surgeons regardless of the size of the defect. To realise this ambition, bone transplantation therapies, including autogenic, allogeneic and xenogeneic transplantations, have been attempted and studied [1]. However, these therapies are always faced difficulty with either insufficient supply of donor tissue

Y. Xiao (✉) • R. Crawford • D.W. Hutmacher
Institute of Health and Biomedical Innovation, Queensland University of Technology, Kelvin Grove, QLD 4059, Australia
e-mail: yin.xiao@qut.edu.au

W. Fan
School of Stomatology, Wuhan University, Hubei, China

Q. Li, Y.-W. Mai (eds.), *Biomaterials for Implants and Scaffolds*, Springer Series in Biomaterials Science and Engineering 8, DOI 10.1007/978-3-662-53574-5_10

or possible immune rejections after transplantation, which prevents the bone transplantation from large-scale clinical applications.

Bone tissue engineering is to construct an artificial bone substitute to restore bone defects and normal function. Various biomaterials, such as collagen, polymers and bioceramics are used as scaffold materials for bone tissue engineering [2, 3]. These materials play dual roles in the bone defect area: as templates to restore the bone tissues and scaffolds to deliver therapeutic cells and/or various related growth factors [4–6]. However, the bone defect healing via engineered bone substitute is very much different from the natural healing process which is normally induced and guided by periosteum. Bone healing induced by periosteum have many advantages over other methods, such as healing with natural bone structure, optimal implant/host integration, appropriate vascularisation and minimal ectopic ossification.

Transplantation of autogenous or allogenous periosteum has been applied successfully in the repair of various-sized bone defects, especially in large bone defects [7]. In spite of this, the supply of periosteum grafts always remains in shortage. To solve this problem, periosteum tissue engineering becomes one of the focused biomedical engineering areas. As recently pointed out in a review article by Zhang et el, periosteum tissue engineering could assist in structural de novo bone formation and is therefore a promising approach for bone defect restoration [8]. Since there have been many studies in this area, this chapter attempted to focus a brief review on the periosteum tissue engineering.

10.2 Structure and Functions of Periosteum

10.2.1 Structure of Periosteum

Periosteum is a dense connective tissue membrane covering the outer surface of most bones except the joint [9]. Histologically, the periosteum is thought to consist of two different layers (Fig. 10.1) [9–11]: the outer fibrous layer mainly contains fibroblast, blood vessel networks, collagen fibres and extracellular matrix [11, 12], and the inner layer, also referred to as the cambium layer, attaches directly to the bone surfaces and is highly cellular of mature osteoblasts and osteogenic progenitor cells [9, 11, 13–15]. Based upon these anatomical features, the periosteum can be described as a vascularised dual-layered 'osteogenic device' as it has both osteogenic cells and blood vessel networks [11, 16]. It supplies blood to bone, especially the cortical bone [17], and is regarded as the 'umbilical cord' of bone tissues [18].

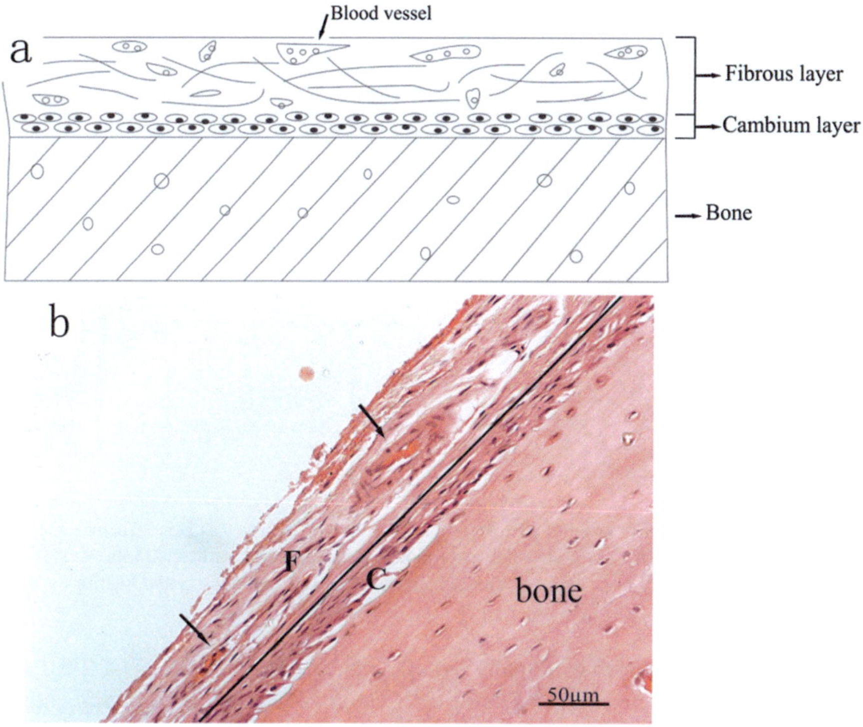

Fig. 10.1 Dual-layered structure of periosteum. (**a**) Schematic illustration of the two different layers of periosteum; (**b**) histological dual-layered structure of periosteum (*F* fibrous layer, *C* cambium layer, *arrows* blood vessels)

10.2.2 Function of Periosteum

Periosteum plays critical roles in both bone development and defect healing. There are two different patterns of in vivo bone development: intramembranous and endochondral ossifications, in both of which the periosteum plays critical roles [19]. For intramembranous ossification, the mesenchymal cells differentiate directly into osteogenic progenitor cells to form a primitive periosteum [20]. Then these progenitor cells in the periosteum differentiate into osteoblasts and bone formation process takes place. For the endochondral ossification, the perichondrium (cell layer surrounding cartilage) firstly develops from mesenchymal cells to form a cartilage template [11, 21]. Then the template develops into bone along with the perichondrium turning into the periosteum.

Periosteum also plays critical roles in bone fracture healing (Fig. 10.2). Without periosteum, many bone fractures would end up with non-union. The bone fracture healing process basically repeats the intramembranous and endochondral ossification processes as described above [22, 23]. Blood clots (haematoma) in the fracture area will trigger an acute inflammation, followed by blood vessel invasion and

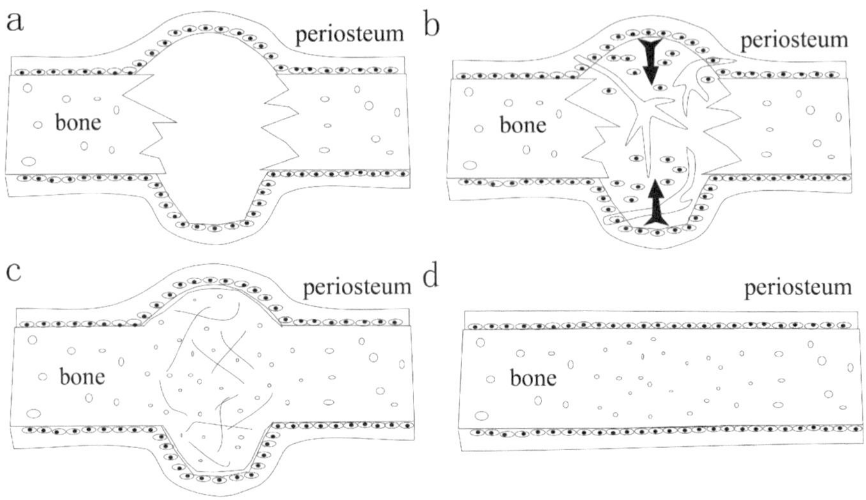

Fig. 10.2 Illustration of the role of periosteum in bone defect healing. (**a**) Bone fracture site and haematoma; (**b**) osteogenic progenitor cell migration and blood vessel infiltration into the fracture site from periosteum; (**c**) bone callus formation; (**d**) bone callus remodelling and healing

cartilage formation which will finally turn into bone callus (Fig. 10.2) [11, 23]. During this process, osteogenic progenitor cells could come from periosteum, endosteum, and bone marrow. Several studies had indicated that the progenitor cells from periosteum are most important to the healing response [9, 15, 24–28]. Uddstromer and colleagues had shown that periosteum plays the most important role in fracture healing [29, 30]. Oni and colleagues demonstrated that fracture healing was delayed when periosteum was removed [31, 32].

10.3 Construction Strategies for Periosteum Tissue Engineering

10.3.1 Bioartificial Periosteum

As mentioned above, periosteum could generally be described as a dual-functional organ: bone formation and blood supply. To engineer a functional periosteum, the following six strategies could be considered (Fig. 10.3): (1) acellular bioactive membrane [33, 34], (2) acellular bioactive membrane carrying growth factors [35, 36], (3) scaffold-free osteogenic cell sheet [37, 38], (4) membrane seeded with osteogenic cells [39, 40], (5) membrane seeded with osteogenic cells plus growth factors [41] and (6) membrane seeded with both osteogenic and angiogenic cells [42, 43].

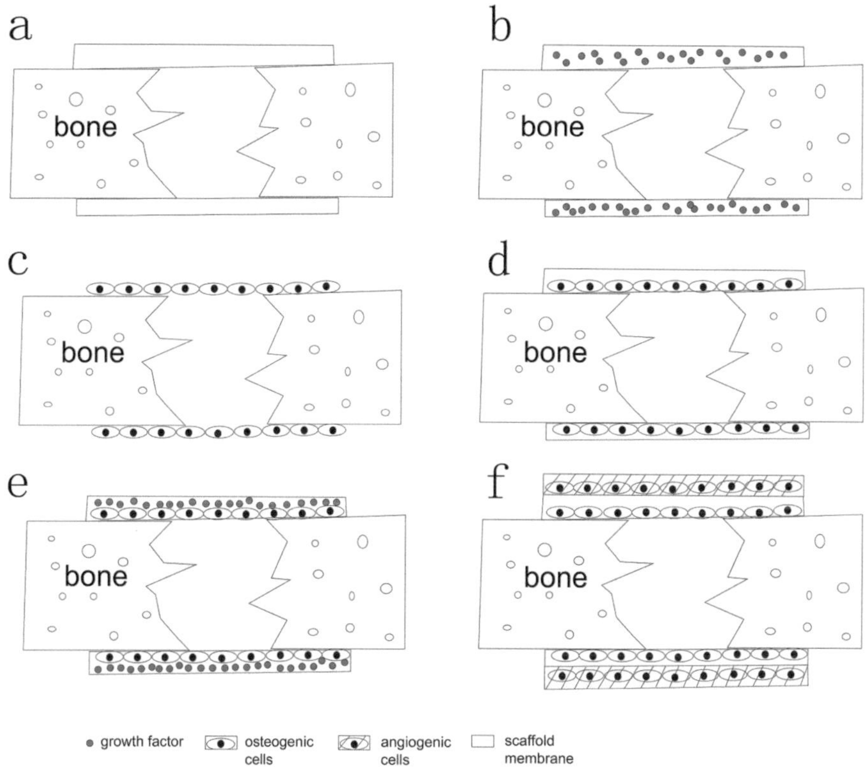

Fig. 10.3 Construction strategies for the periosteum tissue engineering. (**a**) Acellular membrane; (**b**) acellular membrane carrying growth factors; (**c**) osteogenic cell sheet; (**d**) membrane seeded with osteogenic cells; (**e**) membrane seeded with osteogenic cells and growth factors; (**f**) membrane seeded with osteogenic and angiogenic cells

The materials used to make the membrane scaffold could be fibrin, collagen, polymers or natural tissue membranes such as submucosa of intestines. Nevertheless, most studies published so far used acellular bioactive membranes, single osteogenic cell sheet or membranes carrying only osteogenic cells [33, 34, 37, 44]. For example, Neel et al. used an acellular periosteal replacement membrane for bone graft containment at the allograft-host junction [33]. Hattori [45] demonstrated the healing of a severe open fracture by applying a bioartificial periosteum made of collagen sponge carrying osteogenic cells. In another study, submucosa from the small intestine was used to mimic periosteum onto which bone marrow stromal cells (BMSCs) were seeded [46]. The obvious drawback of this approach is that scaffold materials have to be sourced from the small intestine, which means another surgical operation on the patient to harvest scaffold materials.

As these engineered periostea are either acellular or single cell based, which is different from the dual-layered structure of periosteum, it would be difficult for these constructs to carry out both 'bone formation' and 'blood supply' functions in vivo. Although much work has been done under the subject of periosteum tissue engineering [17, 47–49], very limited references could be found addressing dual-layered engineered periosteum that contains both osteogenic and angiogenic factors/cells, not to mention in vivo assessments of any such constructs. More importantly, a dual-layered membrane scaffold designed to accommodate osteogenic and angiogenic cells, respectively, should be developed to better mimic the real periosteum and achieve its full in vivo functions.

10.3.2 Dual-Layered Scaffold Design for Periosteum Tissue Engineering

In light of the limitations and obstacles of the current approaches towards engineering a periosteal replacement, significant improvements must be made in terms of design of scaffolds for such applications. Multifunctionalities of the periosteum as a tissue capable of initiating bone healing process, supplier of vascular networks to the underlying bone and a barrier membrane for soft tissue must be addressed. One approach to achieving this goal is to fabricate constructs using polymeric materials by mimicking the architecture and features of the periosteum. A potential design for a periosteum scaffold is shown in Fig. 10.4. Dual-layered scaffold mimicking both the fibrous and cambium layers of the native tissue would be appropriate (Fig. 10.4a).

Both layers of the envisioned scaffold could be fabricated using a modified electrospinning technique. Electrospinning is suitable due to its speed and versatility in generating polymeric fibres with diameters in the orders of tens to thousands of nanometres [50, 51]. Its enormous potential in the field of tissue engineering as a method of scaffold fabrication has been widely reported [52–54]. A modification of the electrospinning set-up allowed the fabrication of highly porous, cell-penetrable fibrous layer by simultaneous co-deposition of poly (β-caprolactone) (PCL)-based polymeric fibres with hyaluronic acid (HA) hydrogel

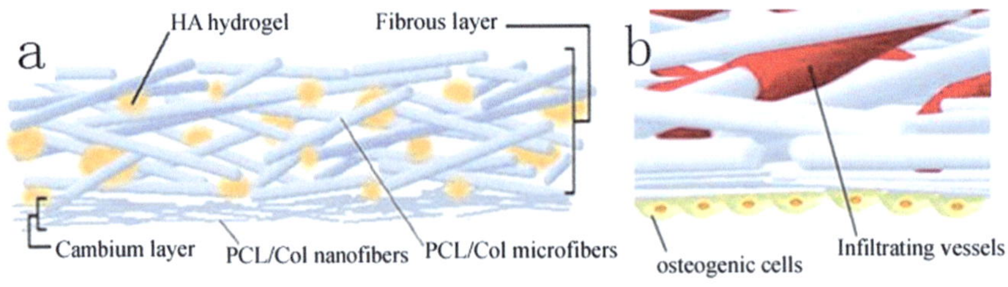

Fig. 10.4 Schematic representation of a dual-layered scaffold design for the application in periosteum tissue engineering

[55]. As the cambium layer, conventional electrospun submicron fibres (i.e. nanofibres) could be deposited on one side of the fibrous layer. The eventual goal is to allow infiltration of new capillaries and fibrous tissues into the constructs via the fibrous layer and delivery of osteogenic progenitor cells via the cambium layer's surface to aid in the repair of the underlying bone defect (Fig. 10.4b).

10.3.3 Electrospinning Process for the Fabrication of Periosteum

Prospective application of electrospun nanofibres shown in Fig. 10.5 as the cambium layer in the periosteum construct stems from widely reported studies pertaining to suitability of nanofibres as support structures for proliferation and differentiation of mesenchymal progenitor cells and scaffolds for new mesenchymal tissues. Li et al. reported a favourable response when mesenchymal stem cells were cultured on PCL nanofibres with specific expression of cartilage genes and deposition of cartilage-like matrix [56]. Yoshimoto et al. reported that a bone-like tissue rich in collagen type I and calcified minerals was obtained on the nanofibre scaffolds where mesenchymal stem cells of bone marrow origin were cultured in vitro [57]. Similar observations were made when a composite nanofibre formulation of PCL and collagen type I (PCL/Col) was used as scaffolds. The synthetic–natural polymeric composite fibres exhibited smooth morphology with a relatively uniform fibre diameter throughout the mesh. When the bone marrow mesenchymal cells were seeded and cultured on the surface of these nanofibre meshes, thick

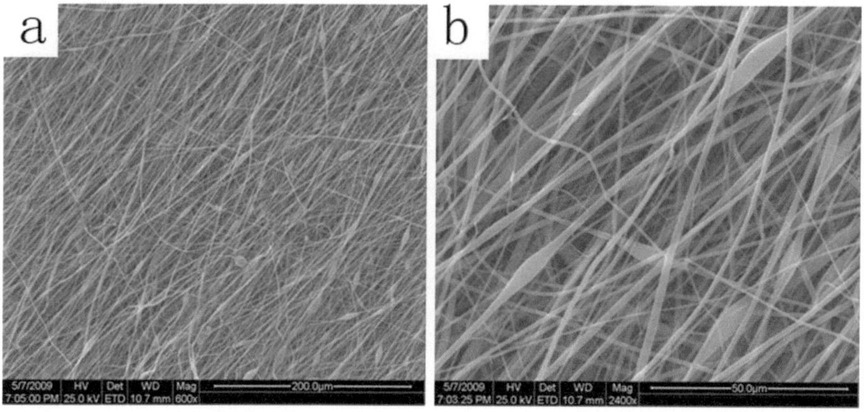

Fig. 10.5 Scanning electronic microscopy (SEM) images of electrospun nanofibres for the scaffold of periosteum cambium layer. Magnifications: (**a**) ×600, (**b**) ×2400

multilayering of cells and tissue was seen after 4 weeks of in vitro culture. This tissue demonstrated the deposition of collagen type I, osteocalcin proteins and heavy matrix mineralisation which suggested differentiation of the cells towards osteogenic lineage. The mesh's ability to support proliferation, differentiation and new bone-like tissue formation makes it a promising candidate as the cambium layer in the periosteum scaffold.

Engineering the fibrous layer required modifications to the electrospinning process to allow the fabrication of a phase which is porous enough to enable cellular infiltration. Furthermore, this layer must support endothelial cells and infiltrating capillaries. Conventional electrospinning often results in dense deposition of nanofibres not allowing cells to infiltrate into the structure [58–63]. Several approaches in attempts to tackle this problem have been reported with varying outcomes from direct blending of polymers with water-soluble gelatin [64], selective polymer leaching [65], salt leaching [66] and the use of micron-sized fibres [67]. Another plausible approach is the simultaneous deposition of electrospun micron-sized fibres with electrosprayed hydrogel (Fig. 10.6). In this approach, PCL/Col microfibres in the size range of 1–2 μm (Fig. 10.6a) were co-deposited with HA hydrogel via an electrospinning–electrospraying process [55]. Globules of the hydrogel were embedded throughout the fibrous structure of the resulting mesh (Fig. 10.6b – transverse view, 10.6c – planar view). A more open-pore structure was created by depositing slightly larger fibres using electrospinning [68], and the inclusion of the HA-based hydrogel would provide passages and compartments into which cells and tissues could migrate.

Rapid and extensive infiltration of osteoblasts was observed on these meshes after 10 days of in vitro culture (Fig. 10.7a). The cells could be seen in the interior of the fibrous matrix as pointed out by the arrow heads. Histological staining of the sections revealed cells populating the entire thickness of the mesh (Fig. 10.7b, arrow heads indicate cell nuclei). Monolayering of cells on the mesh's surface as traditionally seen on electrospun scaffolds was not observed. The suitability of this fibrous mesh as a periosteum scaffolding material was further investigated with a coculture system of endothelial cells and fibroblasts. It has been reported previously that coculturing endothelial cells with fibroblasts improved their viability, function and formation of tube-like structure in vitro [69–71]. Observations of the cocultured cells on the mesh revealed endothelial tube-like formations on the surface (Fig. 10.7c, arrow heads). These structures were similar to those previously reported when endothelial phenotype was preserved in vitro by coculturing with smooth muscle cells [72] or mesenchymal cells [73]. Furthermore, the assays performed on the section revealed that ingrowth of the endothelial networks occurred into the scaffolds' interior, i.e. subsurface migration (Fig. 10.7d). These results suggested that the fibrous meshes allowed the endothelial cell population to reorganise in vitro into tube-like structures often seen preceding the process of vasculogenesis. In addition, the architecture and pore geometry of the scaffold were sufficient in enabling migration of the endothelial capillary into the matrix.

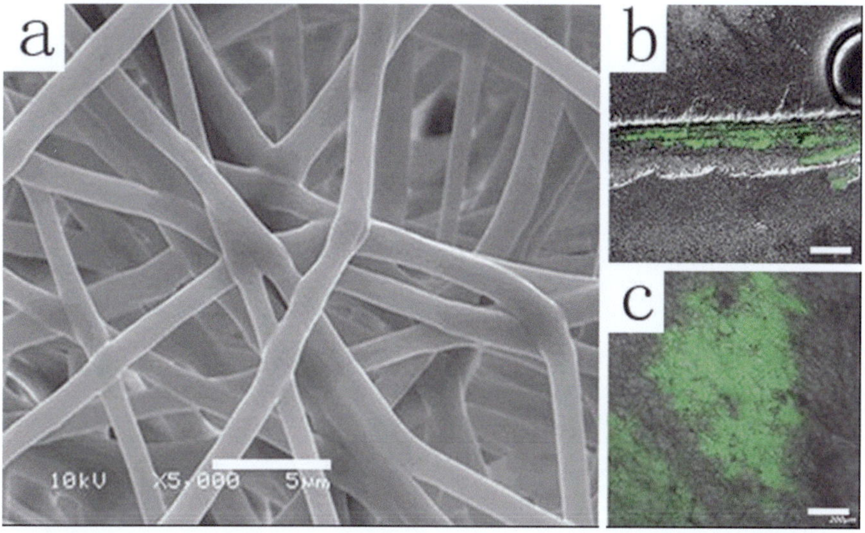

Fig. 10.6 Construction of fibrous layer for the periosteal tissue scaffolding. (**a**) PCL/Col scaffolds with microfibres were fabricated. (**b** and **c**) The co-deposited HA-based hydrogels (labelled with *green* fluorescence) were distributed throughout the fibrous interior. *Bar* represents 5 μm in (**a**) and 200 μm in (**b**, **c**)

10.4 Cell Sources for Periosteum Tissue Engineering

To engineer a fully functional periosteum, i.e. bone formation and blood supply, two kinds of cells are required: osteogenic and angiogenic cells. For the osteogenic cells, there are many different choices. It can be mature osteoblasts or osteogenic progenitor cells (or stem cells).

10.4.1 Osteogenic Cells

Osteoblasts can be separated directly from bone tissues, while the progenitor or stem cells can come from different origins. Most often used stem cell source for osteogenesis is the bone marrow stromal cells (BMSC). Bone marrow contains two types of stem or progenitor cell systems: the haematopoietic cell system and non-haematopoietic BMSCs [74, 75]. When cultured in vitro, BMSCs rapidly attach to the culture surfaces and can be easily separated from the non-adherent haematopoietic cells by repeatedly washing. BMSCs, when cultured in vitro, are negative for CD45, CD14, CD31 and CD34, but positive for CD105, CD44, CD73 and CD90 cell surface markers [76]. They are a mixture of progenitor cells which can be differentiated into various mesodermal cells, especially osteoblasts, chondrocytes, fibroblasts or adipocytes [77]. The osteogenic abilities of BMSCs

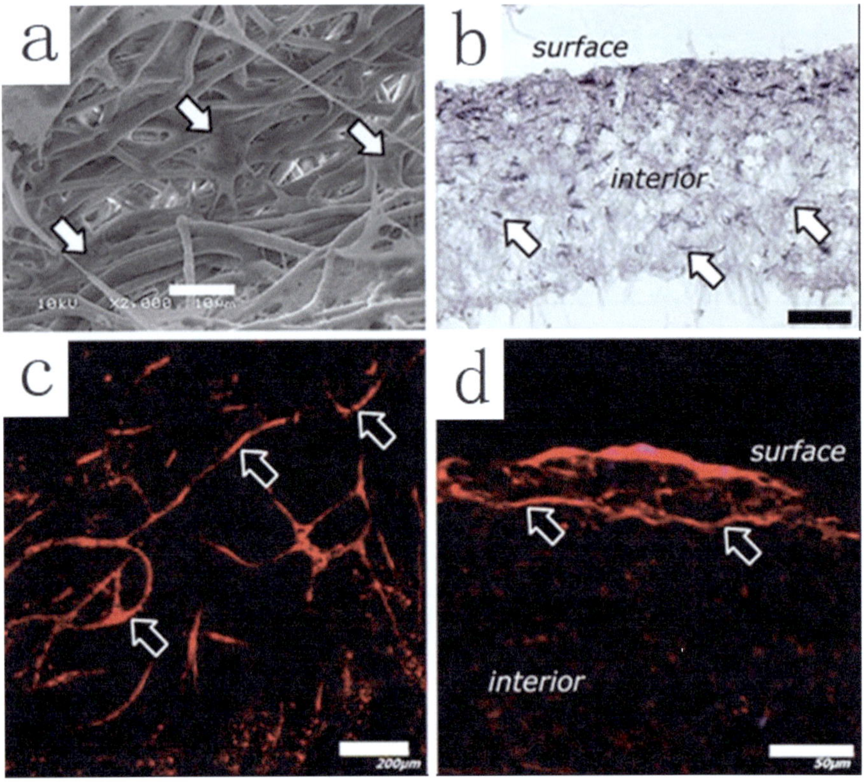

Fig. 10.7 Cellular infiltration into the fibrous matrix of the scaffolds. (**a**) SEM images showing the infiltration of human foetal osteoblasts (*arrows*) into the interior of the fibrous mesh. (**b**) Penetration of cells was uniform throughout the entire thickness of the scaffold (*arrows* indicating the cell nuclei). (**c** and **d**) Coculture of endothelial cells and fibroblasts on these meshes revealed self-assembly of ECs into capillary-like structures (*red* fluorescence) on the surface (**c**) as well as the interior of the mesh. (**d**) *Bar* represents 10 μm in (**a**), 50 μm in (**b**), 200 μm in (**c**), and 50 μm in (**d**)

have been well documented both in vitro and in vivo and have been applied to help bone defect restoration [78, 79]. Osteogenic progenitor cells can also be derived from fat tissues (adipocytes), dental tissue (such as dental pulp and periodontal ligament) or even the periosteum itself (from cambium layer), though the specific makers for these progenitor cells are still unclear [76, 80–82]. Osteogenic differentiation of these progenitor cells as well as their in vivo application for bone tissue engineering has been widely reported [80–82].

10.4.2 *Angiogenic Cells*

The other important cell type for functional periosteum tissue engineering is the angiogenic cells that can help in vivo vascularisation. For in vivo vasculogenesis and angiogenesis, there are several potential cell sources: mature endothelial cells (MECs or ECs) from vessels, such as cells from human umbilical vein (HUV), and endothelial progenitor cells (EPCs) from bone marrow or peripheral blood. MECs, especially those from the HUV, are often used as a cell source for in vitro and in vivo angiogenesis [83, 84]. A limiting factor with these cells is that allogeneic MECs may induce adverse immunological responses [85]. EPCs are actually a fraction of haematopoietic stem cells found in bone marrow and peripheral blood [86]; hence, bone marrow cells are a valuable source of autologous and immunologically neutral stem cells for vasculogenesis and angiogenesis [87]. Although the phenotype of EPC has not been completely clarified yet, they are now thought to be positive for CD133, CD34 and VEGFR2 but negative for CD45 and CD14 cell surface markers [88]. Based upon these markers, EPCs could be selected out from peripheral blood or bone marrow. Although the number of EPCs in bone marrow or peripheral blood is very low, when isolated and expanded in vitro, EPCs can proliferate and be expanded for at least twenty populations in comparison with MECs [86].

10.5 Conclusions

Periosteum tissue engineering is to mimic the natural structure of periosteum to guide bone formation in a physiological manner. This chapter tried to provide current information about the periosteum engineering with the emphasis on the construction strategies, scaffold design and cells sources based upon the structure and functions of periosteum in bone development and defect healing. An appropriate construction strategy that combines proper cell sources and scaffolds may help produce a fully functional engineered periosteum substitute.

References

1. Parikh SN (2002) Bone graft substitutes in modern orthopedics. Orthopedics 25 (11):1301–1309; quiz 10-1
2. Kim SS, Sun Park M, Jeon O, Yong Choi C, Kim BS (2006) Poly(lactide-co-glycolide)/hydroxyapatite composite scaffolds for bone tissue engineering. Biomaterials 27 (8):1399–1409
3. Niu X, Fan Y, Liu X, Li X, Li P, Wang J, Sha Z, Feng Q (2011) Repair of bone defect in femoral condyle using microencapsulated chitosan, nanohydroxyapatite/collagen and poly (l-lactide)-based microsphere-scaffold delivery system. Artif Organs 35(7):E119–E128

4. Nishikawa M, Myoui A, Ohgushi H, Ikeuchi M, Tamai N, Yoshikawa H (2004) Bone tissue engineering using novel interconnected porous hydroxyapatite ceramics combined with marrow mesenchymal cells: quantitative and three-dimensional image analysis. Cell Transplant 13 (4):367–376
5. Yoshikawa H, Myoui A (2005) Bone tissue engineering with porous hydroxyapatite ceramics. J Artif Organs 8(3):131–136
6. Premaraj S, Mundy B, Parker-Barnes J, Winnard PL, Moursi AM (2005) Collagen gel delivery of Tgf-beta3 non-viral plasmid DNA in rat osteoblast and calvarial culture. Orthod Craniofac Res 8(4):320–322
7. Knothe Tate ML, Ritzman TF, Schneider E, Knothe UR (2007) Testing of a new one-stage bone-transport surgical procedure exploiting the periosteum for the repair of long-bone defects. J Bone Joint Surg Am 89(2):307–316
8. Zhang X, Awad HA, O'Keefe RJ, Guldberg RE, Schwarz EM (2008) A perspective: engineering periosteum for structural bone graft healing. Clin Orthop Relat Res 466(8):1777–1787
9. Allen MR, Hock JM, Burr DB (2004) Periosteum: biology, regulation, and response to osteoporosis therapies. Bone 35(5):1003–1012
10. Squier CA, Ghoneim S, Kremenak CR (1990) Ultrastructure of the periosteum from membrane bone. J Anat 171:233–239
11. Malizos KN, Papatheodorou LK (2005) The healing potential of the periosteum molecular aspects. Injury 36(Suppl 3):S13–S19
12. Asaumi K, Nakanishi T, Asahara H, Inoue H, Takigawa M (2000) Expression of neurotrophins and their receptors (TRK) during fracture healing. Bone 26(6):625–633
13. Ito Y, Fitzsimmons JS, Sanyal A, Mello MA, Mukherjee N, O'Driscoll SW (2001) Localization of chondrocyte precursors in periosteum. Osteoarthr Cart 9(3):215–223
14. Nakahara H, Bruder SP, Haynesworth SE, Holecek JJ, Baber MA, Goldberg VM, Caplan AI (1990) Bone and cartilage formation in diffusion chambers by subcultured cells derived from the periosteum. Bone 11(3):181–188
15. Fang J, Hall BK (1997) Chondrogenic cell differentiation from membrane bone periostea. Anat Embryol (Berl) 196(5):349–362
16. Allen MR, Burr DB (2005) Human femoral neck has less cellular periosteum, and more mineralized periosteum, than femoral diaphyseal bone. Bone 36(2):311–316
17. Hutmacher DW, Sittinger M (2003) Periosteal cells in bone tissue engineering. Tissue Eng 9 (Suppl 1):S45–S64
18. Chanavaz M (1995) The periosteum: the "umbilical cord" of bone. Quantification of the blood supply of cortical bone of periosteal origin. Rev Stomatol Chir Maxillofac 96(4):262–267
19. Yang Y (2009) Skeletal morphogenesis during embryonic development. Crit Rev Eukaryot Gene Expr 19(3):197–218
20. Chung UI, Kawaguchi H, Takato T, Nakamura K (2004) Distinct osteogenic mechanisms of bones of distinct origins. J Orthop Sci 9(4):410–414
21. Shapiro F (2008) Bone development and its relation to fracture repair. The role of mesenchymal osteoblasts and surface osteoblasts. Eur Cell Mater 15:53–76
22. Peters A, Schell H, Bail HJ, Hannemann M, Schumann T, Duda GN, Lienau J (2010) Standard bone healing stages occur during delayed bone healing, albeit with a different temporal onset and spatial distribution of callus tissues. Histol Histopathol 25(9):1149–1162
23. Dimitriou R, Tsiridis E, Giannoudis PV (2005) Current concepts of molecular aspects of bone healing. Injury 36(12):1392–1404
24. Engdahl E, Ritsila V, Uddstromer L (1978) Growth potential of cranial suture bone autograft. II. An experimental microscopic investigation in young rabbits. Scand J Plast Reconstr Surg 12 (2):125–129
25. O'Driscoll SW, Fitzsimmons JS (2000) The importance of procedure specific training in harvesting periosteum for chondrogenesis. Clin Orthop Relat Res 380:269–278

26. O'Driscoll SW, Salter RB (1986) The repair of major osteochondral defects in joint surfaces by neochondrogenesis with autogenous osteoperiosteal grafts stimulated by continuous passive motion. An experimental investigation in the rabbit. Clin Orthop Relat Res 208:131–140
27. O'Driscoll SW, Marx RG, Fitzsimmons JS, Beaton DE (1999) Method for automated cartilage histomorphometry. Tissue Eng 5(1):13–23
28. Wakitani S, Yamamoto T (2002) Response of the donor and recipient cells in mesenchymal cell transplantation to cartilage defect. Microsc Res Tech 58(1):14–18
29. Uddstromer L (1978) The osteogenic capacity of tubular and membranous bone periosteum. A qualitative and quantitative experimental study in growing rabbits. Scand J Plast Reconstr Surg 12(3):195–205
30. Uddstromer L, Ritsila V (1979) Healing of membranous and long bone defects. An experimental study in growing rabbits. Scand J Plast Reconstr Surg 13(2):281–287
31. Oni OO, Gregg PJ (1991) An investigation of the contribution of the extraosseous tissues to the diaphyseal fracture callus using a rabbit tibial fracture model. J Orthop Trauma 5(4):480–484
32. Oni OO, Stafford H, Gregg PJ (1992) A study of diaphyseal fracture repair using tissue isolation techniques. Injury 23(7):467–470
33. Neel M (2003) The use of a periosteal replacement membrane for bone graft containment at allograft-host junctions after tumor resection and reconstruction with bulk allograft. Orthopedics 26(5 Suppl):s587–s589
34. Jegoux F, Goyenvalle E, Cognet R, Malard O, Moreau F, Daculsi G, Aguado E (2010) Mandibular segmental defect regenerated with macroporous biphasic calcium phosphate, collagen membrane, and bone marrow graft in dogs. Arch Otolaryngol Head Neck Surg 136 (10):971–978
35. Yonamine Y, Matsuyama T, Sonomura T, Takeuchi H, Furuichi Y, Uemura M, Izumi Y, Noguchi K (2010) Effectable application of vascular endothelial growth factor to critical sized rat calvaria defects. Oral Surg Oral Med Oral Pathol Oral Radiol Endod 109(2):225–231
36. Okafuji N, Shimizu T, Watanabe T, Kimura A, Kurihara S, Furusawa K, Hasegawa H, Kawakami T (2006) Tissue reaction to poly (lactic-co-glycolic acid) copolymer membrane in rhBMP used rabbit experimental mandibular reconstruction. Eur J Med Res 11(9):394–396
37. Ma D, Yao H, Tian W, Chen F, Liu Y, Mao T, Ren L (2011) Enhancing bone formation by transplantation of a scaffold-free tissue-engineered periosteum in a rabbit model. Clin Oral Implants Res 22:1193–1199
38. Ouyang HW, Cao T, Zou XH, Heng BC, Wang LL, Song XH, Huang HF (2006) Mesenchymal stem cell sheets revitalize nonviable dense grafts: implications for repair of large-bone and tendon defects. Transplantation 82(2):170–174
39. Warnke PH, Douglas T, Sivananthan S, Wiltfang J, Springer I, Becker ST (2009) Tissue engineering of periosteal cell membranes in vitro. Clin Oral Implants Res 20(8):761–766
40. Schonmeyr B, Clavin N, Avraham T, Longo V, Mehrara BJ (2009) Synthesis of a tissue-engineered periosteum with acellular dermal matrix and cultured mesenchymal stem cells. Tissue Eng Part A 15(7):1833–1841
41. Guo HG, Yao FL, Ma XL, Yao KD (2008) An experimental study on rabbit's radial bone defect healed by application of mimetic periosteum with tissue-engineered bone. Zhonghua Zheng Xing Wai Ke Za Zhi 24(1):63–67
42. Fan W, Crawford R, Xiao Y (2010) Enhancing in vivo vascularized bone formation by cobalt chloride-treated bone marrow stromal cells in a tissue engineered periosteum model. Biomaterials 31(13):3580–3589
43. Koob S, Torio-Padron N, Stark GB, Hannig C, Stankovic Z, Finkenzeller G (2011) Bone formation and neovascularization mediated by mesenchymal stem cells and endothelial cells in critical-sized calvarial defects. Tissue Eng Part A 17(3-4):311–321
44. Zhao L, Zhao J, Wang S, Xia Y, Liu J, He J, Wang X (2011) Evaluation of immunocompatibility of tissue-engineered periosteum. Biomed Mater 6(1):015005

45. Hattori K, Yoshikawa T, Takakura Y, Aoki H, Sonobe M, Tomita N (2005) Bio-artificial periosteum for severe open fracture—an experimental study of osteogenic cell/collagen sponge composite as a bio-artificial periosteum. Biomed Mater Eng 15(3):127–136
46. Zhang KG, Zeng BF, Zhang CQ (2005) Periosteum construction in vitro by small intestinal submucosa combined with bone marrow mesenchymal stem cell. Zhonghua Wai Ke Za Zhi 43 (24):1594–1597
47. Fan W, Crawford R, Xiao Y (2008) Structural and cellular differences between metaphyseal and diaphyseal periosteum in different aged rats. Bone 42(1):81–89
48. Seeman E (2003) Periosteal bone formation—a neglected determinant of bone strength. N Engl J Med 349(4):320–323
49. Augustin G, Antabak A, Davila S (2007) The periosteum. Part 1: anatomy, histology and molecular biology. Injury 38(10):1115–1130
50. Li D, Xia YN (2004) Electrospinning of nanofibers: reinventing the wheel? Adv Mater 16 (14):1151–1170
51. Reneker DH, Yarin AL, Fong H, Koombhongse S (2000) Bending instability of electrically charged liquid jets of polymer solutions in electrospinning. J Appl Phys 87(9):4531–4547
52. Pham QP, Sharma U, Mikos AG (2006) Electrospinning of polymeric nanofibers for tissue engineering applications: a review. Tissue Eng 12(5):1197–1211
53. Han D, Gouma PI (2006) Electrospun bioscaffolds that mimic the topology of extracellular matrix. Nanomedicine 2(1):37–41
54. Schindler M, Ahmed I, Kamal J, Nur-E-Kamal A, Grafe TH, Chung HY, Meiners S (2005) A synthetic nanofibrillar matrix promotes in vivo-like organization and morphogenesis for cells in culture. Biomaterials 26(28):5624–5631
55. Ekaputra AK, Prestwich GD, Cool SM, Hutmacher DW (2008) Combining electrospun scaffolds with electrosprayed hydrogels leads to three-dimensional cellularization of hybrid constructs. Biomacromolecules 9(8):2097–2103
56. Li WJ, Tuli R, Okafor C, Derfoul A, Danielson KG, Hall DJ, Tuan RS (2005) A three-dimensional nanofibrous scaffold for cartilage tissue engineering using human mesenchymal stem cells. Biomaterials 26(6):599–609
57. Yoshimoto H, Shin YM, Terai H, Vacanti JP (2003) A biodegradable nanofiber scaffold by electrospinning and its potential for bone tissue engineering. Biomaterials 24(12):2077–2082
58. He W, Ma Z, Yong T, Teo WE, Ramakrishna S (2005) Fabrication of collagen-coated biodegradable polymer nanofiber mesh and its potential for endothelial cells growth. Biomaterials 26(36):7606–7615
59. Jin HJ, Chen JS, Karageorgiou V, Altman GH, Kaplan DL (2004) Human bone marrow stromal cell responses on electrospun silk fibroin mats. Biomaterials 25(6):1039–1047
60. Min BM, Lee G, Kim SH, Nam YS, Lee TS, Park WH (2004) Electrospinning of silk fibroin nanofibers and its effect on the adhesion and spreading of normal human keratinocytes and fibroblasts in vitro. Biomaterials 25(7-8):1289–1297
61. Mo XM, Xu CY, Kotaki M, Ramakrishna S (2004) Electrospun P(LLA-CL) nanofiber: a biomimetic extracellular matrix for smooth muscle cell and endothelial cell proliferation. Biomaterials 25(10):1883–1890
62. Shin HJ, Lee CH, Cho IH, Kim YJ, Lee YJ, Kim IA, Park KD, Yui N, Shin JW (2006) Electrospun PLGA nanofiber scaffolds for articular cartilage reconstruction: mechanical stability, degradation and cellular responses under mechanical stimulation in vitro. J Biomater Sci Polym Ed 17(1-2):103–119
63. Venugopal JR, Zhang YZ, Ramakrishna S (2006) In vitro culture of human dermal fibroblasts on electrospun polycaprolactone collagen nanofibrous membrane. Artif Organs 30(6):440–446
64. Zhang Y, Ouyang H, Lim CT, Ramakrishna S, Huang ZM (2005) Electrospinning of gelatin fibers and gelatin/PCL composite fibrous scaffolds. J Biomed Mater Res B Appl Biomater 72 (1):156–165

65. Kidoaki S, Kwon IK, Matsuda T (2005) Mesoscopic spatial designs of nano- and microfiber meshes for tissue-engineering matrix and scaffold based on newly devised multilayering and mixing electrospinning techniques. Biomaterials 26(1):37–46
66. Nam J, Huang Y, Agarwal S, Lannutti J (2007) Improved cellular infiltration in electrospun fiber via engineered porosity. Tissue Eng 13(9):2249–2257
67. Pham QP, Sharma U, Mikos AG (2006) Electrospun poly(epsilon-caprolactone) microfiber and multilayer nanofiber/microfiber scaffolds: characterization of scaffolds and measurement of cellular infiltration. Biomacromolecules 7(10):2796–2805
68. Eichhorn SJ, Sampson WW (2005) Statistical geometry of pores and statistics of porous nanofibrous assemblies. J R Soc Interface 2(4):309–318
69. Sorrell JM, Baber MA, Caplan AI (2007) A self-assembled fibroblast-endothelial cell co-culture system that supports in vitro vasculogenesis by both human umbilical vein endothelial cells and human dermal microvascular endothelial cells. Cells Tissues Organs 186 (3):157–168
70. Oberringer M, Meins C, Bubel M, Pohlemann T (2007) A new in vitro wound model based on the co-culture of human dermal microvascular endothelial cells and human dermal fibroblasts. Biol Cell 99(4):197–207
71. Black AF, Berthod F, L'Heureux N, Germain L, Auger FA (1998) In vitro reconstruction of a human capillary-like network in a tissue-engineered skin equivalent. FASEB J 12 (13):1331–1340
72. Elbjeirami WM, West JL (2006) Angiogenesis-like activity of endothelial cells co-cultured with VEGF-producing smooth muscle cells. Tissue Eng 12(2):381–390
73. Rouwkema J, De Boer J, Van Blitterswijk CA (2006) Endothelial cells assemble into a 3-dimensional prevascular network in a bone tissue engineering construct. Tissue Eng 12 (9):2685–2693
74. Bianco P, Riminucci M, Gronthos S, Robey PG (2001) Bone marrow stromal stem cells: nature, biology, and potential applications. Stem Cells 19(3):180–192
75. Bianco P, Kuznetsov SA, Riminucci M, Gehron Robey P (2006) Postnatal skeletal stem cells. Methods Enzymol 419:117–148
76. Mosna F, Sensebe L, Krampera M (2010) Human bone marrow and adipose tissue mesenchymal stem cells: a user's guide. Stem Cells Dev 19(10):1449–1470
77. Reyes M, Lund T, Lenvik T, Aguiar D, Koodie L, Verfaillie CM (2001) Purification and ex vivo expansion of postnatal human marrow mesodermal progenitor cells. Blood 98 (9):2615–2625
78. Lucarelli E, Donati D, Cenacchi A, Fornasari PM (2004) Bone reconstruction of large defects using bone marrow derived autologous stem cells. Transfus Apher Sci 30(2):169–174
79. Mastrogiacomo M, Papadimitropoulos A, Cedola A, Peyrin F, Giannoni P, Pearce SG, Alini M, Giannini C, Guagliardi A, Cancedda R (2007) Engineering of bone using bone marrow stromal cells and a silicon-stabilized tricalcium phosphate bioceramic: evidence for a coupling between bone formation and scaffold resorption. Biomaterials 28(7):1376–1384
80. Estrela C, Alencar AH, Kitten GT, Vencio EF, Gava E (2011) Mesenchymal stem cells in the dental tissues: perspectives for tissue regeneration. Braz Dent J 22(2):91–98
81. Lin CS, Xin ZC, Deng CH, Ning H, Lin G, Lue TF (2010) Defining adipose tissue-derived stem cells in tissue and in culture. Histol Histopathol 25(6):807–815
82. Gassling V, Douglas T, Warnke PH, Acil Y, Wiltfang J, Becker ST (2010) Platelet-rich fibrin membranes as scaffolds for periosteal tissue engineering. Clin Oral Implants Res 21 (5):543–549
83. Koch S, Yao C, Grieb G, Prevel P, Noah EM, Steffens GC (2006) Enhancing angiogenesis in collagen matrices by covalent incorporation of VEGF. J Mater Sci Mater Med 17(8):735–741
84. Sarkar S, Lee GY, Wong JY, Desai TA (2006) Development and characterization of a porous micro-patterned scaffold for vascular tissue engineering applications. Biomaterials 27 (27):4775–4782

85. Shepherd BR, Enis DR, Wang F, Suarez Y, Pober JS, Schechner JS (2006) Vascularization and engraftment of a human skin substitute using circulating progenitor cell-derived endothelial cells. FASEB J 20(10):1739–1741
86. Reyes M, Dudek A, Jahagirdar B, Koodie L, Marker PH, Verfaillie CM (2002) Origin of endothelial progenitors in human postnatal bone marrow. J Clin Invest 109(3):337–346
87. Zisch AH (2004) Tissue engineering of angiogenesis with autologous endothelial progenitor cells. Curr Opin Biotechnol 15(5):424–429
88. Ahrens I, Domeij H, Topcic D, Haviv I, Merivirta RM, Agrotis A, Leitner E, Jowett JB, Bode C, Lappas M, Peter K (2011) Successful in vitro expansion and differentiation of cord blood derived CD34+ cells into early endothelial progenitor cells reveals highly differential gene expression. PLoS One 6(8):e23210

Chapter 11
Characterisation of Hydrogel Scaffolds Under Compression

J. Tong, Y.-H. Hsu, K. Madi, A. Cossey, and A. Au

Abstract Although a variety of scaffolds have been developed in recent years for a range of applications, the repair of load-bearing tissues, such as articular cartilage in the knee, is still in its infancy due to the exceptional demands on mechanical strength and stiffness. Unfortunately, rigorous in vitro mechanical characterisation has often been superseded by in vivo testing in animals, where the loading scenarios often bear little resemblance to those in human, which has significantly restricted the potential range of clinical applications. A comprehensive mechanical characterisation is essential if scaffolds are to be used for load-bearing applications. In this chapter, we report the characterisation of viscoelastic behaviour of hydrogel scaffolds. The key factors, including the effects of constraint, strain rate and sample microstructure, on the mechanical properties of a hydrogel scaffold will be investigated. Some of the latest techniques such as micro-CT imaging, in situ image-guided failure assessment and digital volume correlation (DVC) will be explored in the characterisation of the hydrogel scaffold under uniaxial compression.

Keywords Cartilage • Bone • Scaffold • Compression • Mechanical properties • μCT • DVC

11.1 Introduction

As surgical techniques and medical knowledge continue to advance, there is an increasing demand for engineered scaffolds that act as permanent or temporary support structures for the ingrowth of new tissues. Load-bearing applications, such

J. Tong (✉) • Y.-H. Hsu • K. Madi
School of Engineering, University of Portsmouth, Anglesea Building, Anglesea Road, Portsmouth PO1 3DJ, UK
e-mail: jie.tong@port.ac.uk

A. Cossey
Spire Portsmouth Hospital, Portsmouth PO9 5NP, UK

A. Au
Smith & Nephew, 150 Minuteman Rd, Andover, MA 01810, USA

Q. Li, Y.-W. Mai (eds.), *Biomaterials for Implants and Scaffolds*, Springer Series in Biomaterials Science and Engineering 8, DOI 10.1007/978-3-662-53574-5_11

as repair of articular cartilage in the knee, require that the scaffolds have the necessary mechanical strength and stiffness close to those of native tissues.

Articular cartilage is a smooth, shock-absorbent material on the surface of articular joints [1]. It is responsible for providing lubrication and compressive stiffness to the joint during articulation while responding viscoelastically to mechanical loading [2]. Articular cartilage is difficult to treat following injuries, as it neither expresses the typical wound-healing phenotype observed in many other tissues nor spontaneously regenerates [3, 4]. Unlike highly vascular tissues such as the skin and bone, articular cartilage has a low cell density, leading to a poor capacity for self repair [5].

The use of biodegradable scaffolds to repair articular cartilage has been studied by many [6, 7]. Polylactide-co-glycolides have frequently been used for tissue engineering applications attributable to their good biodegradability, reasonable biocompatibility, mechanical strength and easy producibility [8]. Repair of osteochondral defects involves two types of distinct tissues, articular cartilage and subchondral bone. One possible solution may be the development of engineered osteochondral constructs [9–13]. A synthetic scaffold is resorbable hydrophilic made of a patented composite material with polylactide-co-glycolide, calcium sulphate and poly(glycolide) fibres [14]and designed to replace worn-out cartilage surfaces in order to restore mobility and relieve joint pain. It is formulated to be porous and resorbable to allow ingrowth of new healing tissues and to be suitable for filling osteochondral defects in the form of cylindrical plugs. These scaffolds have two layers; the bottom layer is designed to imitate the morphology of trabecular bone and the top layer to simulate articular cartilage. Although some clinical applications have been reported [15–18], there is a lack of information on the mechanical performance of the implant under physiological loading conditions. Preclinical assessments based on in vitro experiments under simulated physiological loading conditions are the necessary first steps towards a successful clinical implementation of the implant for knee repair purposes.

In this chapter, the monotonic and fatigue behaviour of the scaffold is examined under compression. Novel experimental techniques such as micro-CT imaging, in situ loading and digital volume correlation (DVC) have been utilised in the characterisation of strain distribution of the samples under uniaxial compression [19]. The results will hopefully provide a basic framework on the in vitro characterisation of synthetic scaffolds for load-bearing applications.

11.2 Background

A variety of biological and synthetic scaffolds have been developed for repair of articular cartilage and the underlying subchondral bone [10, 12–14, 20–27]. Bone and cartilage tissues exhibit viscoelastic behaviour, and the replacement scaffolds should have similar properties in order to maintain mechanical integrity with the surrounding tissues during physiological loading conditions. Synthetic scaffolds often lack the physical and mechanical properties necessary to sustain long-term applications [2]. Although biocompatibility and bio-related issues have been studied widely, evaluation of mechanical properties has been an area of underdevelopment. Mechanical properties of scaffolds are often unreported; and for those reported, testing parameters and conditions vary greatly. Mechanical behaviour of cartilage/bone is known to vary with test conditions, such as strain rate, strain amplitudes and testing environment [28, 29]. This is a main challenge in the design of testing protocols of artificial scaffolds. Although a number of protocols have been used in the literature [12–14, 25, 30–40], a comparison between the results generated from different experimental procedures and protocols is difficult.

A range of strain rates has been used in the literature representative of the loading conditions experienced in the knee and hip. In compression tests, high strain rates have been shown to increase the measured elastic modulus [14, 30–37]. Lai et al. [34] reported an increase in compressive stiffness with strain rates from 3.3×10^{-5}/s to 3.3×10^{-4}/s. Radin et al. [35] demonstrated that articular cartilage stiffness increased with strain rate over the range from 2.7×10^{-3}/s to 0.124/s. Carter et al. [33] analysed the influence of strain rate from 0.001/s to 10/s on the strength and the stiffness of trabecular bone specimens and found that both strength and modulus were approximately proportional to strain rate raised to the power of 0.06. Silyn-Roberts and Broom [36] conducted impact testing on cartilage-on-bone samples at a strain rate of 2.4×10^{3}/s and showed that, at high strain rates, bone failures could occur without structural damage to the articular cartilage and that when failure did occur in the articular cartilage, the failure mode was more characteristic of a 'brittle' material.

A number of scaffolds and bones were tested in tension [26, 38, 39], which bears little resemblance to in vivo loading conditions experienced in the knee or hip. Most of compressive tests were carried out under unconfined loading conditions [12–14, 40], while confined configuration is more relevant to most in vivo loading conditions. In the confined tests reported, various clearances between the size of the specimen and the size of the confined chamber have been used, with some of them used smaller specimens [41], some used equal size [42, 43] and some used slightly larger specimens [44, 45]. Furthermore, the evaluation of the mechanical properties of scaffolds is rarely done under physiological conditions, i.e. in aqueous solution at 37 °C. Mechanical properties of hydrated scaffold samples are known to be much lower than those of dry samples [13, 14, 21, 40].

Compression testing of hydrogel scaffolds was performed by Slivka et al. [14] to investigate the influence of physiological testing conditions, manufacturing methods, anisotropic properties caused by predominant fibre orientation, amounts of fibre reinforcement and viscoelasticity at a range of strain rates. Using the same testing modality, the mechanical properties of the scaffolds in physiological conditions were compared with those of articular cartilage from pig and goat. Most of these compressive tests were carried out under unconfined conditions. Moreover, stress relaxation (or creep) properties were often overlooked, despite that these are responsible for the time-dependent behaviour of scaffolds, which are most relevant to clinical applications.

Furthermore, human bone is subject to a variety of loading patterns during daily routine activities. A typical loading condition is repeated or cyclic loading as experienced in walking or running in daily life. Bone response under such loading conditions may be referred to as fatigue behaviour [46, 47]. Fatigue damage is a process of gradual mechanical degradation caused by repeated loading at stress or strain much lower than those required to fracture in a single application of force. As a result, damage due to cyclic loading is of significant interest for design and application of synthetic scaffolds. In a conventional fatigue test, specimens are subjected to a constant amplitude load till failure to determine the number of cycle to failure at a given load range. A number of studies based on this method have been published on the fatigue behaviour of bones [39, 48–60]. Some studies have also been carried out on synthetic biopolymers [61, 62]. A great number of samples may be needed to obtain the fatigue behaviour under variable stress amplitudes. Step-wise testing has since been introduced which would allow the generation of fatigue data with only a small number of samples [63, 64].In stepwise tests, the samples are subject to loads with a range of amplitudes; in each, a number of cycles are allowed to elapse, thus providing an accelerated testing regime with increased volume of data at reduced test duration. One important parameter obtained from such tests is the evolution of secant modulus [51, 63, 65], which has been used as an indication to damage accumulation [60, 66].

Standard mechanical testing does not take into account the real morphology of the scaffold structure and complex physical phenomena such as strain localisation, which are important factors in dictating the mechanical response and damage evolution of the scaffold [67–70]. With the recent and rapid progress of microfocus computed tomography (μCT), combined with the development of in situ experiments [67, 71, 72], digital volume correlation (DVC) has become a powerful tool to quantify deformation and failure modes of cellular materials [73–77]. Analysis of continuum level strain maps allows critical local strains to be identified thereby providing valuable information on design of scaffold microstructures. Few studies, however, have used this technique to investigate the mechanical behaviour of multiphase osteochondral scaffolds. Micro-CT images of a dual-layer osteochondral scaffold were obtained under compressive loading by Harley et al. [21]. Although the internal microstructure of the cartilaginous, interfacial and osseous regions of the scaffold was characterised, deformation of each layer was only estimated qualitatively from visual observation. In a recent study, Malekipour and co-workers [78] calculated the deformation of subchondral bone and articular cartilage in native osteochondral plugs from the observation of real-time micro-CT images, prior to and post compression. They showed evidence that the subchondral trabecular bone can absorb deformation energy during failure, thus protecting the articular cartilage from damage. Strain localisation often occurs in the trabecular bone [68, 70] and is likely to be the mechanism by which the energy is dissipated in the subchondral bone. If the bone phase of dual-layer osteochondral scaffolds has a similar morphology to that of trabecular bone, similar behaviour may be expected.

In what follows, the viscoelastic behaviour of a hydrogel scaffold is presented. Monotonic stress–strain curves were obtained under compression under simulated typical physiological conditions to investigate the contribution of the bone layer on the overall viscoelastic behaviour, the effects of strain rate (walking/impact) and the effects of constraint (confined/unconfined). Preliminary multistep cyclic tests have been carried out on the bone samples to study the fatigue behaviour of the osteochondral scaffold under increasing compressive cyclic loading conditions. Damage development and failure modes of the scaffold were evaluated using image-guided failure analysis, together with the DVC method.

11.3 Mechanical Evaluation

11.3.1 Monotonic Testing

A hydrogel scaffold plug (Smith & Nephew), as shown in Fig. 11.1, was used for this study. The scaffold is made of a patented composite material with polylactide-co-glycolide, calcium sulphate and poly(glycolide) fibres [14]. The dual-layer design of the scaffold contains both cartilage (Scaffold C) and bone (Scaffold B) phases. The pores in the scaffold are interconnected to allow cell migration and

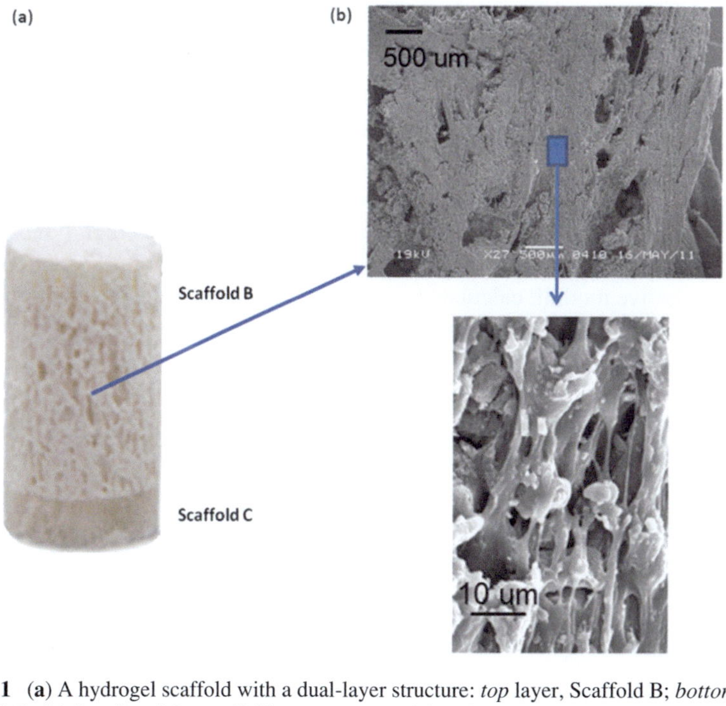

Fig. 11.1 (**a**) A hydrogel scaffold with a dual-layer structure: *top* layer, Scaffold B; *bottom* layer, Scaffold C. (**b**) Details of the scaffold structure containing fibres and calcium sulphate particles from SEM micrograph

extracellular matrix continuity. The diameter of the implant is about 11 mm, and the lengths of the cartilage and bone layers are 1.97 mm ± 0.22 mm and 16.7 mm ± 0.34 mm, respectively, the latter taken at a ratio of 0.86 length over diameter [28, 33].

Monotonic tests were carried out on a servohydraulic testing machine (MTS Landmark® Servohydraulic Test System) equipped with an environmental chamber to which phosphate-buffered saline (PBS) solution was filled and controlled at a temperature of 37 °C. The samples were soaked overnight prior to testing, and a cyclic preconditioning (ten cycles of compression at 0.008 strain, at a strain rate of 0.005/s, followed by unloading) was applied to eliminate residual stresses due to sample preparation and to achieve a steady-state mechanical response. The samples were loaded between two stainless steel loading platens. Smooth, impermeable platens were used in unconfined conditions, while a porous platen with a pore size of 300–600 μm (larger than the average pore size of the scaffolds ~300 μm [79]) was selected under confined condition, as shown in Fig. 11.2. The diameter of the scaffolds was about 10.75 ±0.15 mm. The confining chamber was chosen slightly larger (10.98 mm). This small gap has the advantage to eliminate a potential friction between the top platen and the confining chamber [80, 81].

Monotonic tests were performed on the scaffold (dual layer) and Scaffold B (bone phase) specimens in unconfined and confined compression at two representative strain rates: walking (0.002/s) and impact (0.1/s) [33]. Engineering stress values were computed by dividing the reaction force by the initial area of each specimen. The compressive modulus of each specimen was taken to be the slope of the stress–strain curve in the most linear part of the pre-yield loading region. With the modulus defined in this manner, the initial small nonlinear behaviour due to surface irregularities of the specimen during contact with the platens is disregarded [33]. The compressive strength is defined as the peak stress to failure.

Stress–strain curves of the scaffold and Scaffold B specimens are presented in Figs. 11.3 and 11.4 for the selected conditions. All the curves exhibit typical foam-type behaviour, with a linear elastic region followed by a nonlinear yield plateau. The compressive moduli, calculated in the linear portion, are depicted in Fig. 11.5. The contribution of the bone layer on the overall viscoelastic behaviour, the effects

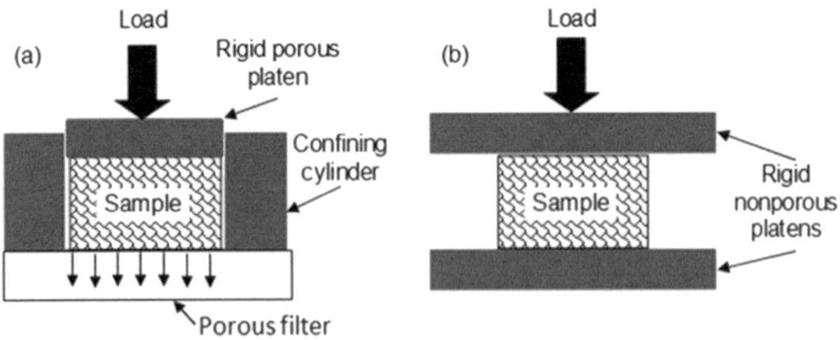

Fig. 11.2 Schematic of the experimental arrangements: (**a**) confined and (**b**) unconfined compression

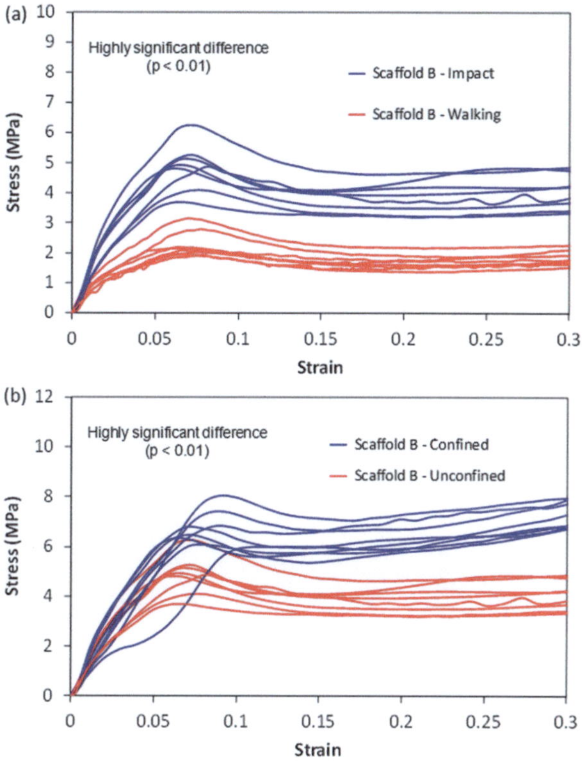

Fig. 11.3 Stress–strain curves of Scaffold B obtained in PBS at 37 °C: (**a**) unconfined compression (walking vs. impact), (**b**) impact (confined vs. unconfined)

of strain rate (walking/impact) and confinement have been statistically investigated through the Student's T-test of the compressive modulus, as shown in Table 11.1.

The effects of confinement and strain rate on compressive modulus are highlighted. Higher yield strength and compressive modulus are obtained for Scaffold B and scaffold specimens when the strain rate is increased from walking to impact or when testing in a confined condition (vs. unconfined condition, except in walking for Scaffold B). For example, the average yield strength and modulus of Scaffold B specimens tested in the confined conditions during impact are 6.74 ± 0.69 MPa and 94.11 ± 6.45 MPa, respectively, while those tested during walking are 3.10 ± 0.82 MPa and 38.66 ± 9.84 MPa, respectively. Whatever the condition, a highly significant difference is observed for the effect of strain rate, while the effect of confinement varies from possible to significant difference (except for impact). The gap between the specimens and the confining chamber can reach up to 0.38 mm, which might explain why less 'highly significant difference' is observed for the effect of confinement. As illustrated in Fig. 11.3b, the difference between the confined and the unconfined stress–strain responses becomes more visible after 5 % strain. The effect of confinement on the compressive modulus is likely to be less significant for smaller diameter specimens. Except for the impact confined condition, no significant difference is observed between the

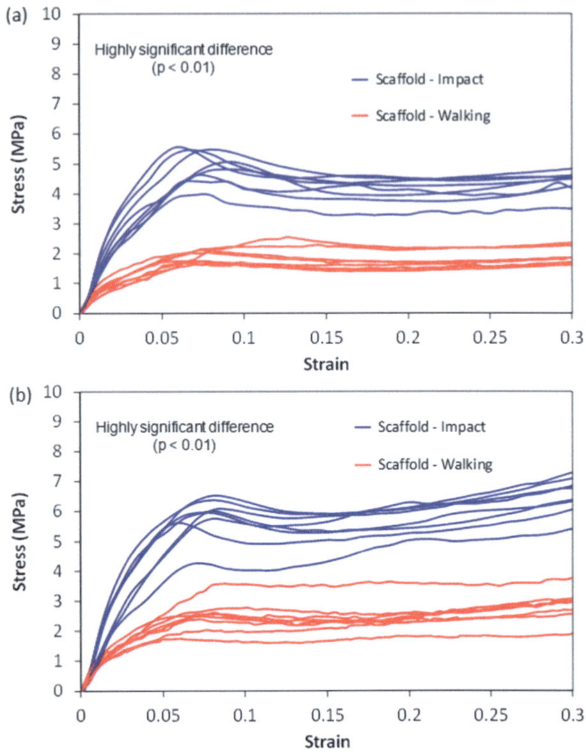

Fig. 11.4 Stress–strain curves of the scaffold obtained in PBS at 37 °C: (**a**) unconfined compression (impact vs. walking), (**b**) confined compression (impact vs. walking)

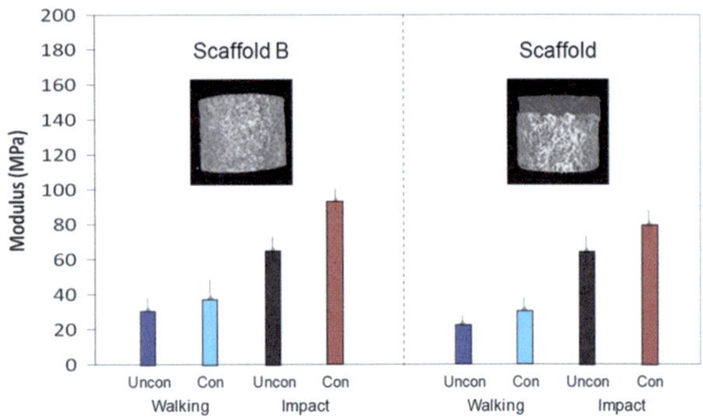

Fig. 11.5 Compressive moduli of Scaffold B and scaffold measured in PBS at 37 °C

stiffness of the bone layer (Scaffold B) and that of the dual layer (scaffold). Generally, the compressive moduli of Scaffold B are slightly higher (~20 %) than that of the scaffold.

Table 11.1 Student T-test results for compressive modulus of Scaffold B and scaffold measured under selected loading conditions

Confinement (uncon/con)	Scaffold B		Scaffold	
	Walking	Impact	Walking	Impact
	X	XXX	XX	XX
Strain rate (walking/impact)	TruFitB		TruFitB	
	Uncon	Con	Uncon	Con
	XXX	XXX	XXX	XXX
Scaffold B vs. scaffold	Walking		Impact	
	Uncon	Con	Uncon	Con
	X	X	O	XX

XXX highly significant difference ($P < 0.01$)
XX significant difference ($0.01 < P < 0.05$)
X highly significant difference ($0.05 < P < 0.1$)
O difference not established ($P > 0.1$)

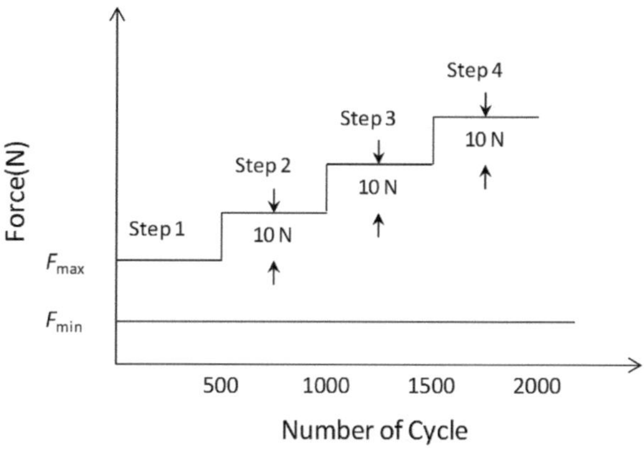

Fig. 11.6 The loading scheme of a stepwise fatigue test ($F_{max} = 10$ N; $F_{min} = F_{preload} = 5$ N), following the protocol of Topolinski et al., 2011 [63]

11.3.2 Fatigue Testing

Fatigue testing was carried out on a Bose ElectroForce 3200 Testing system equipped with an environmental chamber to which PBS solution was filled and controlled at a temperature of 37 °C. Each specimen was placed carefully at the centre of the platens inside the environmental chamber. During the testing, the specimens were unconstrained [63] between the platens of the testing machine as fixation of the specimen to the test platens may increase its stiffness [82]. Five specimens of Scaffold B (bone layer) were tested under load control [28, 48–50, 52, 53, 56, 57, 59, 63, 83–85] with a stepwise increase of maximum stress while keeping the minimum stress constant, following a testing protocol of Topolinski et al. [63].

A preload of 5 N was applied first to ensure good end contact, and this preload was subsequently kept constant as the minimum load throughout the test. The maximum load started from 10 N with a gain of 10 N at the successive steps, as shown in Fig. 11.6. The maximum load was kept constant during a period of

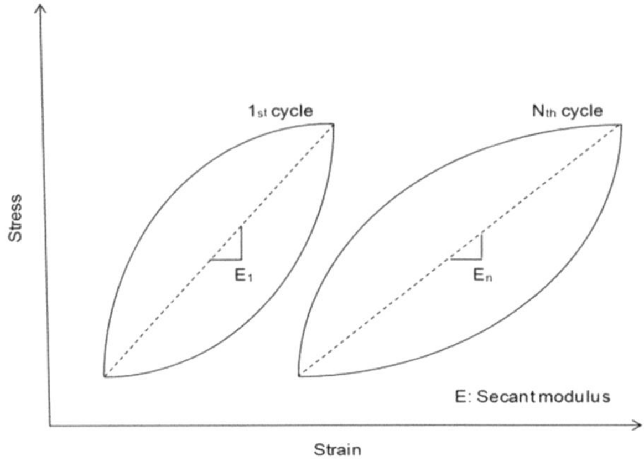

Fig. 11.7 Secant modulus (Ei) is defined as the stress range divided by the strain range at a given cycle i, which is determined by the slope of the line connecting the minimum and the maximum stress values of the cycle

500 cycles and increased to the next level thereafter. The loading scheme was adopted from Topolinski et al. [63] to allow easy comparison with the results from the human trabecular bone [63]. The loading waveform was sinusoidal at a frequency of 1 Hz.

Engineering stress and strain were calculated by using the applied load, displacement and the original dimension of the specimens, where lateral deformation under compression was not considered. The changes in the secant modulus and the maximum and minimum strains with fatigue loading were recorded. The change in the secant modulus is taken as indicative of damage accumulation in the specimen [60, 66] in the fatigue studies of bones from the literature [39, 48, 51, 53–59, 63–65, 84]. The secant modulus at a given cycle was defined as $\Delta\sigma/\Delta\varepsilon = (\sigma_{max} - \sigma_{min})/(\varepsilon_{max} - \varepsilon_{min})$, determined from the stress–strain curve. Figure 11.7 illustrates this as the slope of the line connecting the lowest and the highest point of a stress–strain loop. The secant modulus and strains were measured throughout the tests. The cyclic stress–strain curves were also compared with those obtained under the monotonic loading conditions.

The evolution of the secant modulus with cycles is shown in Fig. 11.8a for the five Scaffold B samples tested. In all the cases, it appears that an increase in secant modulus with cycle persisted for most of the loading steps, particularly the early ones. Only towards later at higher load levels, reductions in secant modulus become evident. The initial hardening seems to be somewhat unexpected, certainly in contrast to the continuing increase in the residual strain with cycle, as shown in Fig. 11.8b, where the maximum and the minimum compressive strains of the five samples are recorded. Interestingly, the samples with lower residual strains (B1, B2, B3) tend to have a higher secant modulus (Fig. 11.8a). Both maximum and minimum strains increased with the number of cycles during the entire test, and the gap between the maximum and the minimum strains is roughly constant for each sample, indicating that the strain range stays constant. In addition, the strain rate increases with the increase in the number of cycles. It is known that residual strain or cyclic creep plays an important role in material failure due to the

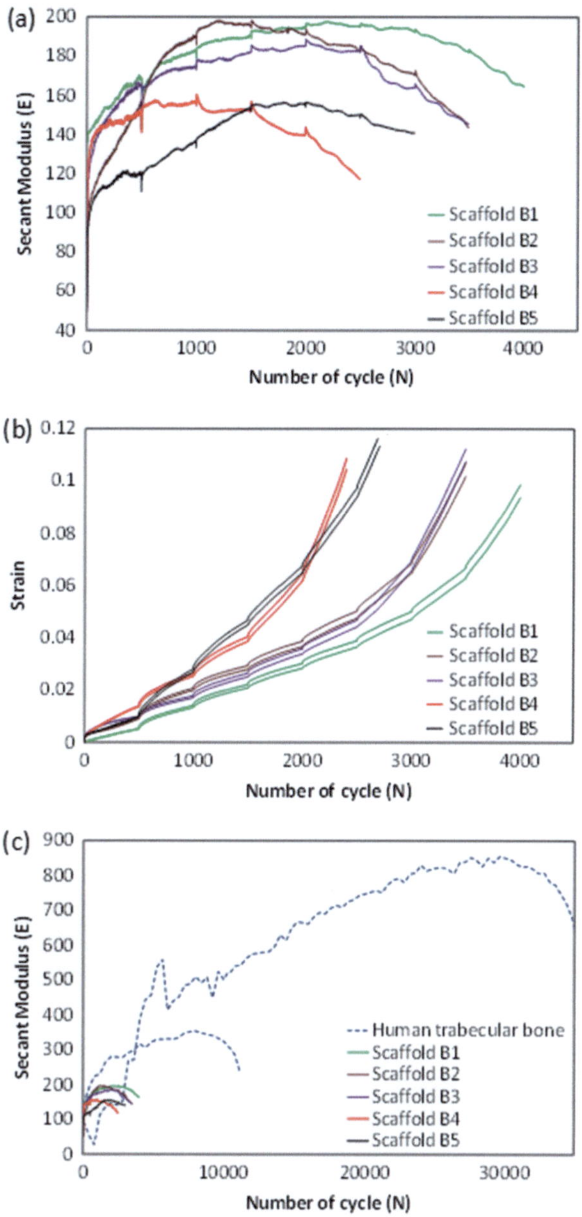

Fig. 11.8 (**a**) The evolution of secant modulus as a function of cycles for Scaffold B, (**b**) the development of the maximum and minimum strains with cycle and (**c**) the comparison of secant modulus of Scaffold B and human trabecular bone [63]

accumulated plastic deformation [60, 65]. Increase in strains with the number of cycles has been generally observed when testing bones under cyclic loading [57, 64], although increasing strain rate during the entire test was found in bovine trabecular bone [64]. Three stages of deformation during compressive fatigue tests have been reported for human trabecular bone [57], including a transient behaviour characterised by a rapid increase of strain within the initial load cycles, a saturation of strain and an acceleration towards final catastrophic failure.

When the secant modulus of the Scaffold B specimens is compared with those of human trabecular bones [63], as shown in Fig. 11.8c, much lower secant modulus and total number of cycles to failure were obtained for the scaffold, although the patterns of evolution with cycle appear to be similar between the two. An initial increase in modulus has been observed for Scaffold B at most of the loading levels except the highest, which appears to be consistent with the observation in some of the reports [65, 86].

The stress–strain loops of the first cycles at the beginning of each fatigue loading step are presented in Fig. 11.9a. Each centre of the loops was moved to the origin (0,0), and then the points at the top of each loop were linked to form the initial cyclic stress–strain curve. Figure 11.9b shows the final cyclic stress–strain curve which was obtained similarly using the loops of the final cycles at the end of each loading step. These cyclic stress–strain loops at the first and the final cycles do not appear to differ significantly (c.f. Fig. 11.10, CSS_1 and CSS_f), suggesting that the stress softening may not be significant. Figure 11.10 shows a comparison of cyclic and monotonic stress–strain curves for a typical specimen of Scaffold B. Here LS1_0 to LS5_0 are monotonic stress–strain curves, while CSS_1 and CSS_f are the first and the final cyclic stress–strain curves. The monotonic curves are the

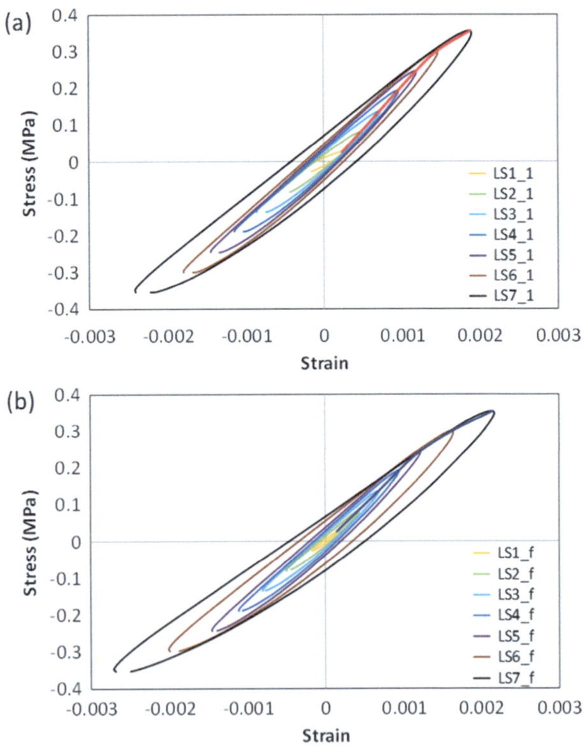

Fig. 11.9 Cyclic stress–strain responses: (**a**) loops of first cycles at the beginning of each loading step; (**b**) loops of the final cycles at the end of each loading step

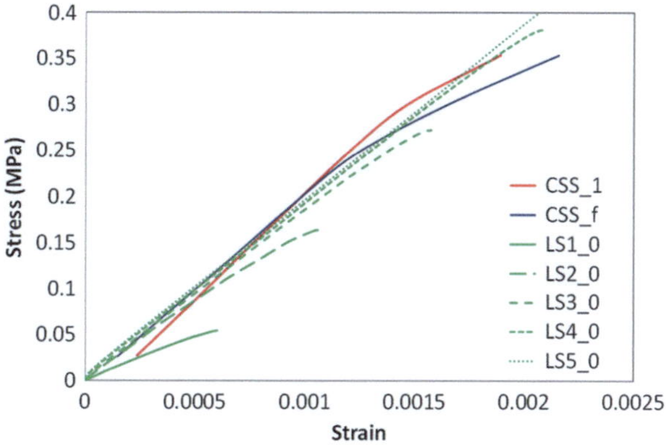

Fig. 11.10 Comparison of the cyclic and the monotonic stress–strain curves of a typical sample

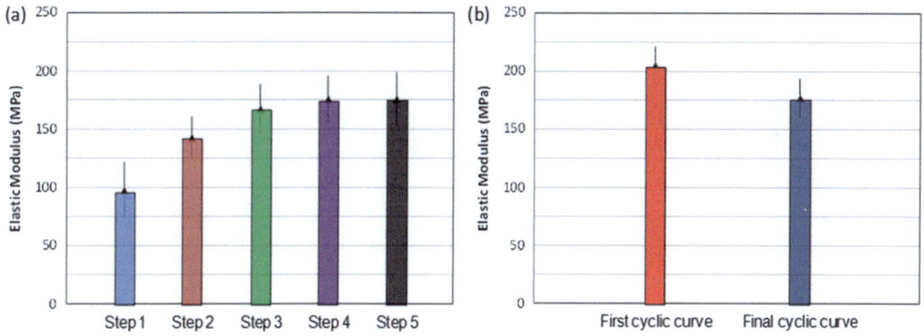

Fig. 11.11 The elastic modulus of (**a**) monotonic curves and (**b**) cyclic stress–strain curves

loading parts of a stress–strain curve at the beginning of each loading step. The slopes of these curves signify the modulus of elasticity.

A comparison of the mean elastic modulus of the stress–strain curves is shown in Fig. 11.11. The elastic modulus of monotonic stress–strain curves increases with the number of loading steps, and the moduli of the cyclic curves are generally higher than those of monotonic counterparts, suggesting stress hardening, consistent with the trend shown in Fig. 11.8a. However, the elastic modulus of first cyclic stress–strain curve is higher than that of final cyclic stress–strain curve, suggesting damage accumulation due to fatigue.

11.4 Damage Assessment

Studies on strain localisation and damage evolution of biological tissues and biomaterials are important to biomedical engineering applications of joint repair and replacement materials. With the recent and rapid progress of microfocus computed tomography (μCT, Fig. 11.12), combined with in situ experiments and digital volume correlation (DVC), powerful tools are available to investigate the

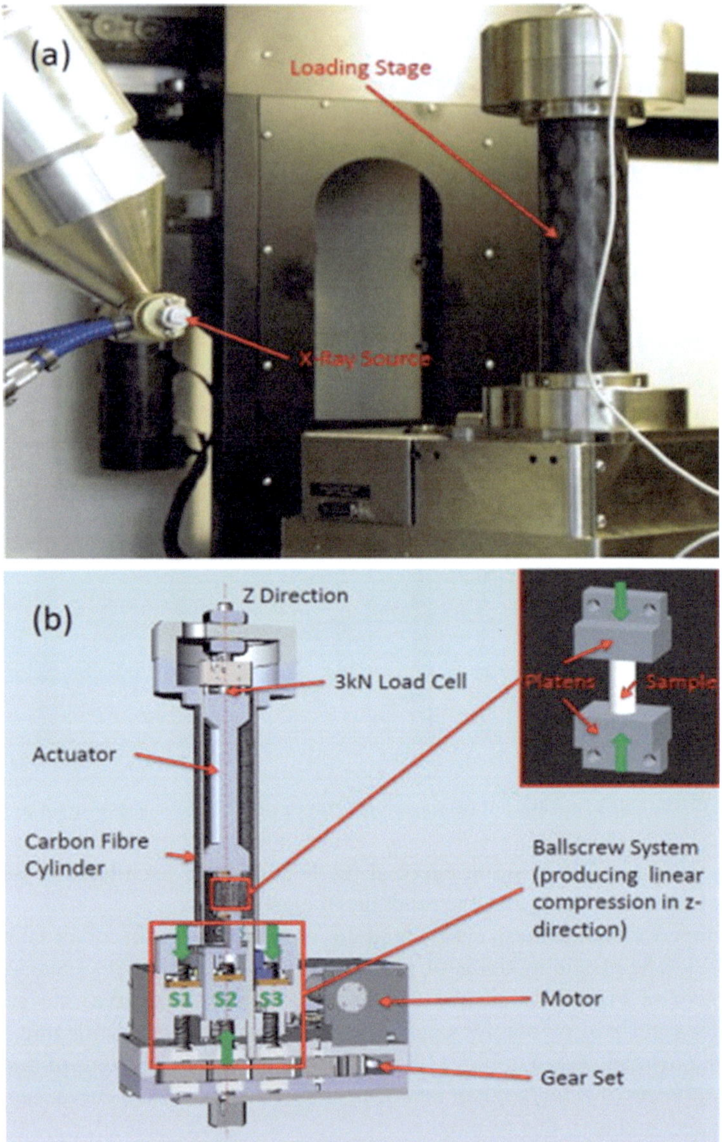

Fig. 11.12 (**a**) The micromechanical testing device is positioned in the micro-CT chamber, and (**b**) the linear compression applied to the sample is generated through a ball screw system that drives the jaws symmetrically in opposite directions (Reprinted with permission from Ref. [19]. Copyright © 2013 Elsevier)

deformation and failure modes of cellular materials. In this section, a 3D full-field study of strains and failure mechanisms are presented in the dual-layer scaffold (Fig. 11.1) under uniaxial compression.

11.4.1 Characterisation of 3D Morphology

The 3D morphology of the scaffold was characterised using micro-computed tomography (CT XRay101 Inspection System, Metris XTek Systems Ltd, Fig. 11.12a). The scanner was set to a voltage of 60 kV, a current of 51 μA and an isotropic voxel size of 23 μm. The volume images of the bone and the cartilage phases were cleaned by applying a 3D median filter and binarised to separate the pores from the struts. 3D morphometric indices were computed using the bone image analysis plug-in, BoneJ [87], as implemented in ImageJ. Morphological parameters of the scaffold (Fig. 11.1) were obtained and shown in Table 11.2. The mean strut thickness and mean strut spacing of the bone phase are about twice higher than those of the cartilage phase. A predominant plate-like structure is found for the bone phase (SMI~0.74–0.88), while a mixture of plate-like and rod-like structures is obtained for the cartilage phase (SMI~1.41–1.83). The morphometric indices of the bone phase compare well with those obtained from human bones extracted from proximal tibia [88] and distal femur [89].

11.4.2 In Situ Testing and Time-Lapsed Imaging

A novel customised micromechanical loading device (Deben Ltd., UK), equipped with a 3 kN miniature load cell, was used to load the sample in the micro-CT

Table 11.2 Morphometric values obtained from μCT images of the specimens. The results obtained on the bone phase are compared with the values obtained on human bones extracted from the proximal tibia [88] and distal femur [89]

	BV/TV	Tb.th (mm)	Tb.sp (mm)	SMI
Bone phase alone (sample 1)	0.33	0.2 ± 0.07	0.68 ± 0.53	0.82
Bone phase alone (sample 2)	0.33	0.17 ± 0.05	0.59 ± 43	0.88
Dual layer (model 1)				
Bone phase with the dual layer	0.34	0.17 ± 0.05	0.45 ± 0.24	0.86
Cartilage phase with the dual layer	0.42	0.13 ± 0.06	0.25 ± 0.13	1.83
Dual layer (model 2)				
Bone phase with the dual layer	0.41	0.19 ± 0.06	0.40 ± 0.22	0.74
Cartilage phase with the dual layer	0.40	0.12 ± 0.03	0.24 ± 0.12	1.41
Proximal tibia [88]	0.28 ± 0.03	0.22 ± 0.01	0.55 ± 0.05	0.70 ± 0.45
Distal femur [89]	0.33 ± 0.04	0.24 ± 0.02	0.48 ± 0.04	/

chamber (Nikon XTH-225 X-ray & CT Inspection System). The loading device is shown in Fig. 11.12b and it has been used in the previous studies [19, 90]. The loading stage uses an analogue resistive extensometer with a 16-bit AD converter for accurate elongation measurement, achieving a nominal strain resolution of 15 με.

The effect of bone thickness on the local strain fields was studied using material models with two thicknesses: 16.7 mm for model 1 and 8 mm for model 2. The lengths of the cartilage phase are similar in both models and measured as 1.97 mm and 2.19 mm, respectively. The local strain fields were also studied in the bone phase. The specimens were prepared by separating them manually from the cartilage phase using a circular saw. The lengths of the bone samples are 16.01 mm (sample 1) and 16.33 mm (sample 2). The diameter of all samples is 11 mm.

Before testing, the ends of the bone specimens were embedded about 1.5 mm into custom-made stainless steel end-caps using acrylic resin to minimise the end artefacts [67, 68]. The gauge length after the fixation was approximately 13 mm, thus achieving an aspect ratio of 1.18:1. For the dual-layer specimens, the end-caps were only glued to the edge of the bone phase due to the limited thickness of the cartilage phase. The lengths of the bone phase were about 15.2 mm and 6.5 mm, achieving an aspect ratio of 1.38:1 and 0.59:1, respectively.

In situ testing was carried out with a preload of 5 N applied, and a complete scan was performed using the scanner settings cited above. The specimens were then stepwise compressed along the longitudinal direction (OZ) to about 0.4 mm (yield) and about 1.1 mm (post-yield softening), at a constant displacement rate of 0.01 mm/s (see Figs. 11.13 and 11.14), representative of slow to normal walking loading conditions (0.001–0.002/s).

11.4.3 Digital Volume Correlation (DVC)

The DVC method was used to compute the 3D displacement and strain fields from a pair of images, namely, a reference reconstructed image obtained in the preloaded stage and a deformed image obtained after compressing the specimens to 0.4-mm displacement. The correlation algorithm, implemented into the LaVision DVC software (Davis, 8.0.1, LaVision GmbH, Goettingen, Germany), uses the fast Fourier transform (FFT) for computing cross-correlation of subvolumes.

Strain maps of the axial strain, ε_{zz}, and shear strain in the xz plane, ε_{xz}, in the bone phase alone the specimen are illustrated in Fig. 11.15a. Evident axial strain localisation occurred in the bands oriented horizontally and more preferentially along the 45 direction. Locally, the axial strains may reach up to 10 %, which are about 4–6 times the mean strains (Table 11.3). Elsewhere, the strains seem to be lower and more homogeneously distributed. Clockwise rotation (shear) is found precisely in these bands versus counterclockwise rotation elsewhere. These strain distributions are consistent with the failure mechanisms in the microstructure (Fig. 11.13a). At the specimen level, compression and rotation of the cells are

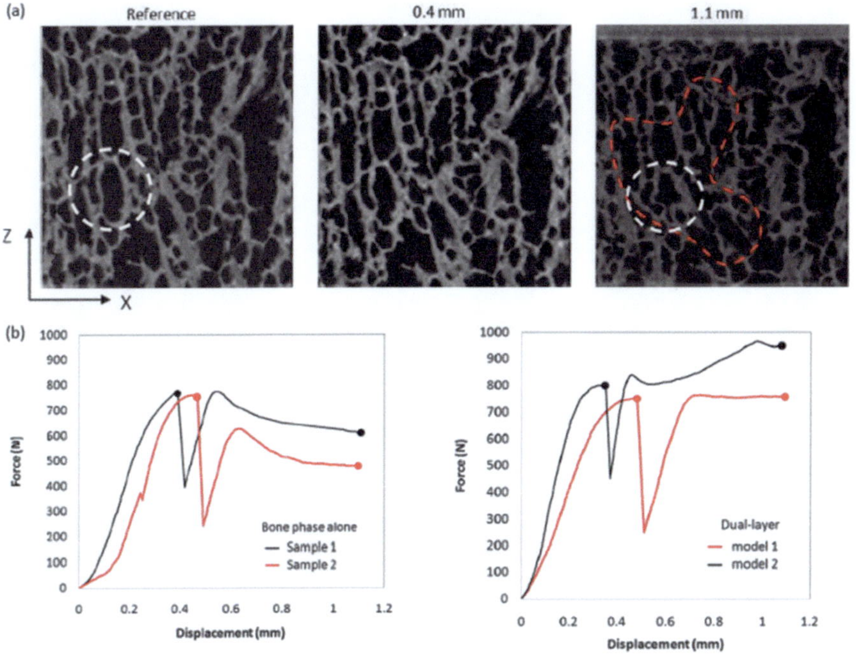

Fig. 11.13 (**a**) 2D sections extracted at the core of the bone phase representing the reference and the deformed morphologies (0.4- and 1.1-mm displacements) of the specimen. Bending of plate-like struts is evident after 1.1-mm displacement (marked in *white*); (**b**) force versus displacement curves for the bone and the dual-layer specimens

observed in the zones of high strains after compressing the sample to 1.1 mm (marked in red in Fig. 11.13a), while bending of plate-like struts occurred at the microstructural level (marked in white in Fig. 11.13a).

Strain fields in the dual layer are described as follows. The mean axial strain values are given in Table 11.3. It seems that the macroscopic bone strains are closer to the responses of the bone phase and the interface than that of the cartilage phase. The bone phase deforms about twice more than the cartilage phase (2.48 and 1.9 for models 1 and 2, respectively) and about 1.5 times more than the interface (1.46 and 1.24 for models 1 and 2, respectively). The strain of the bone phase within the dual layer is also very close to that of the bone phase. The analysis of the axial and the shear strain maps reveals the localised strain bands in the bone, similar to those obtained in the bone phase (see Figs. 11.15, 11.16 and 11.17). The histograms of the axial strain component look also similar (Fig. 11.15b). All the curves are bell-shaped and asymmetric with respect to the mean value, a consequence of strain localisation.

For model 1, the bands of high strain extend up to the upper interface without crossing the cartilage phase (Figs. 11.16 and 11.18a). The strains are heterogeneously distributed in the interface (Fig. 11.18a) with the maximal compressive strains of about 6–10 %. On the other hand, the strains in the cartilage phase are

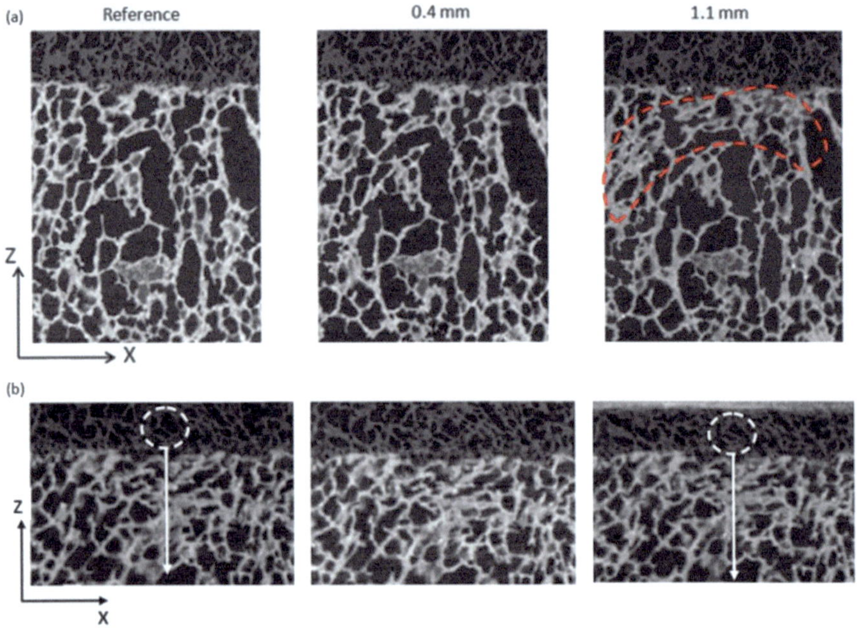

Fig. 11.14 2D sections extracted at the core of the dual-layer representing the reference and deformed morphologies (0.4- and 1.1-mm displacements) of the specimens: (**a**) model 1; (**b**) model 2. Buckling of rod-like struts is evident after 1.1-mm displacement (marked in *white*)

relatively homogeneously distributed (Fig. 11.16), with the maximal compressive strains of about 2 %. Reducing by half the bone phase thickness (model 2) leads to more localised strains in both the interface and the cartilage phase (Figs. 11.17 and 11.18b). Locally, the maximal compressive strains of about 7% are reached inside the cartilage phase and more than 10 % at the interface. At the microstructural level, buckling of rod-like struts was found in the cartilage phase (marked in white in Fig. 11.14b). In the interface, no apparent interfacial debonding was observed from the CT images, although the development of interfacial shear is evident from the shear strain maps (Fig. 11.18c and d).

11.5 Discussion

The mechanical behaviour of a polymer-based scaffold was characterised under uniaxial compression. Confining the scaffold or increasing the strain rate has been found to lead to higher compressive stresses, similar to the responses found in the human bone and articular cartilage [91, 92]. The compressive moduli of the dual-layer scaffold and Scaffold B (bone phase alone) are similar, as opposed to the wide range of compressive modulus of human trabecular bones (20–673 MPa) [33, 93–

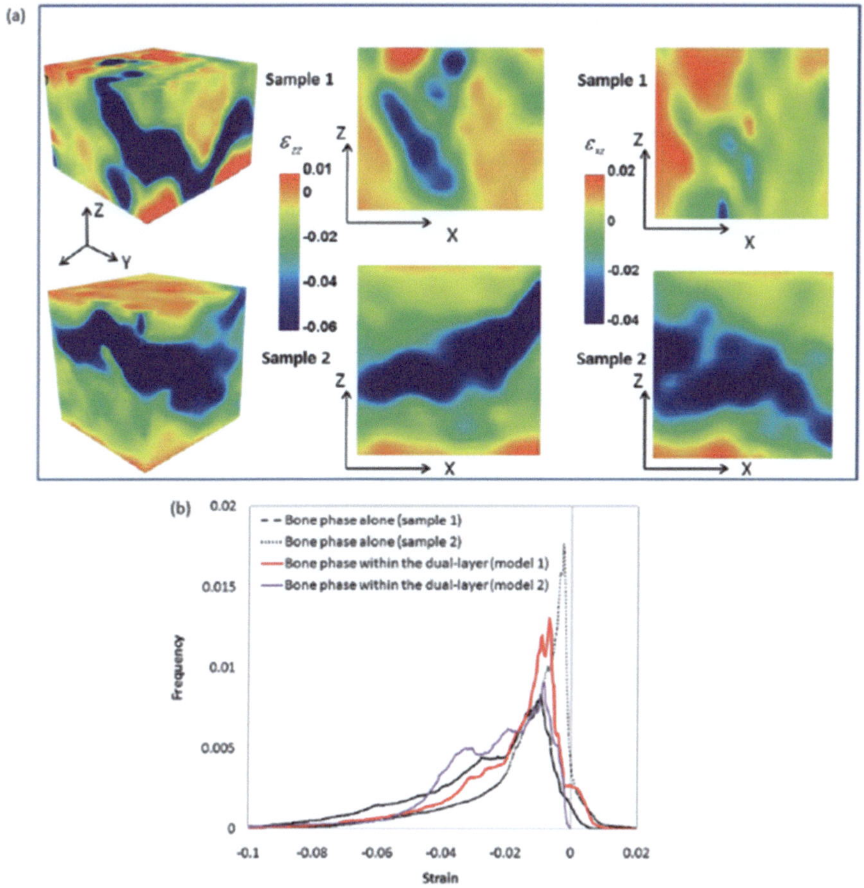

Fig. 11.15 (**a**) Visualisation of the axial strain, ε_{zz}, and shear strain, ε_{xz}, of the bone sample obtained with a subvolume size of 32 voxels (0.736 mm), overlapped by 50 %; (**b**) histograms of the axial strain, ε_{zz}, of the bone phase alone and the bone phase within the dual layer. The histograms were obtained with a class interval size of $\Delta\varepsilon = 0.0001$. Dimensions of the volumes are $313 \times 313 \times 227$ voxels^3 (i.e. $7.2 \times 7.2 \times 5.2$ mm^3)

99] and bovine trabecular bones (117–2990 MPa) [95, 99–101] reported in the literature.

The compressive modulus of Scaffold B in unconfined compression was compared with that of human femoral and tibial bones tested under the similar loading conditions [33, 102, 103]. Carter et al. [33] reported that the average compressive modulus of human trabecular tibial bones extracted from the plateau was 56.6 ±9.7 MPa during walking and 81.5 ± 8 MPa during impact. The mechanical properties of human tibial metaphysis trabecular bone was determined by Goldstein et al. [102] at a strain rate similar to that of walking, and the results are found to be site dependent. The compressive modulus was between 112 and 336 MPa in the medial side and between 52 and 251 MPa in the lateral side. There is a central

Table 11.3 Average axial strains values obtained by the DVC after compressing the bone phase and dual-layer specimens to 0.4-mm displacement

	Subvolume size (mm)	Average axial strain (%)	Standard deviation (%)
Bone phase alone (sample 1)	0.736	2.9	2.3
Bone phase alone (sample 2)	0.736	1.66	2.2
Dual layer (model 1)	0.736	1.78	1.71
Bone phase with the dual layer (77 %)	0.736	2.01	1.85
Cartilage phase with the dual layer (18 %)	0.736	0.81	0.35
Interface (5 %)	0.736	1.37	1.1
	0.253	1.24	1.56
Dual layer (model 2)	0.736	2.2	1.61
Bone phase with the dual layer (61 %)	0.736	2.54	1.81
Cartilage phase with the dual layer (30 %)	0.736	1.33	0.74
Interface (9 %)	0.736	2.04	1.1
	0.253	1.81	1.9

column of trabecular bone with extremely low modulus (between 21 and 105 MPa), which extends upwards from the intramedullary space towards the subchondral plate, possibly due to microstructural defects. Kuhn et al. [103] reported that the average compressive modulus of distal femoral metaphyseal trabecular bone was about 203 ±196 MPa in the medial–lateral width and 298 ± 224 MPa in the anterior–posterior length. The large standard deviations in the femoral modulus data seem to reflect the dependence of properties on metaphyseal location. The average compressive modulus of Scaffold B was found to be 32 ± 6 MPa (walking) and 68 ± 8 MPa (impact), which is close to the data reported by Carter et al. [33] (56.6 ± 9.7 MPa, walking; 81.5 ±8 MPa, impact). In addition, Harley et al. [13] suggested that target mechanical properties for a dry scaffold are defined by the Young's modulus of developing osteoid tissue (25–100 kPa) [104–106], rather than that of mature cortical or trabecular bone, as the scaffold is a site for induced regeneration of bone in an empty defect site rather than maintenance of an already mature bone.

Multistep fatigue tests have been carried out on Scaffold B under increasing compressive cyclic loading conditions. The modulus and the number of cycles to failure of the Scaffold B are, however, significantly lower than those of human trabecular bone [63] under the same testing protocol. The results of Scaffold B show an increase in the secant modulus and stress hardening during the initial steps of fatigue loading, consistent with that observed in human trabecular bone [63] under multistep fatigue testing. The initial hardening is also consistent with the results obtained under conventional constant amplitude fatigue testing. Linde and Hvid [86] reported that in human trabecular bones the stiffness increases until a

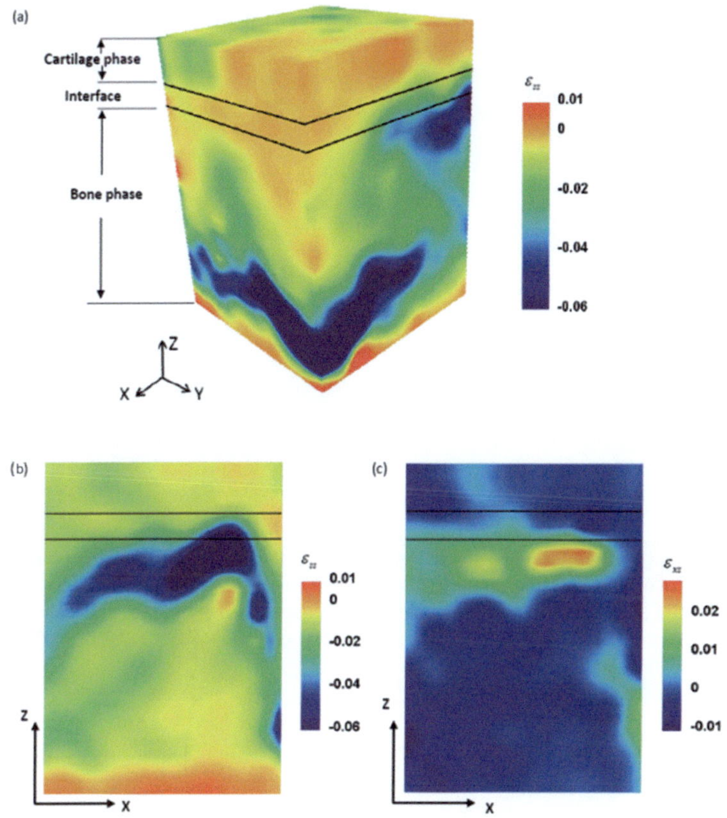

Fig. 11.16 (**a**) 3D visualisation of the axial strain, ε_{zz}, of the dual layer (model 1) obtained with a subvolume size of 32 voxels (0.736 mm), overlapped by 50 %. Visualisation of the axial and shear strains, ε_{zz} and ε_{xz}, in a 2D section extracted from the core of the volume, (**b**) and (**c**), respectively. Dimensions of the volume are $313 \times 313 \times 416$ voxels^3 (i.e. $7.2 \times 7.2 \times 9.6$ mm^3). The interface thickness is about 1 mm

stress level about 50% of ultimate stress is reached followed by decreasing stiffness, although others reported decreasing in modulus from the beginning to the end [48, 52, 54–57, 107, 108]. Michel et al. [65] studied the fatigue behaviour of bovine trabecular bones under load control using a sinusoidal compressive load profile at a frequency of 2 Hz. The results show that the pattern of modulus change with the number of cycles was associated with the loading level. At low cyclic load levels, the modulus increased initially followed by a rapid drop in the final stage. At high cyclic loads, a continuous decrease in modulus from the beginning was found. The authors [65] suggested that both creep and damage accumulation may be responsible for fatigue failure of trabecular bone, i.e. bone fails by creep under high cyclic loads while by microcrack damage accumulation at low cyclic loads. A more recent study suggested, however, that creep effects are negligible in fatigue loading cases for trabecular bone [109]. Further work may be required to confirm the role of creep

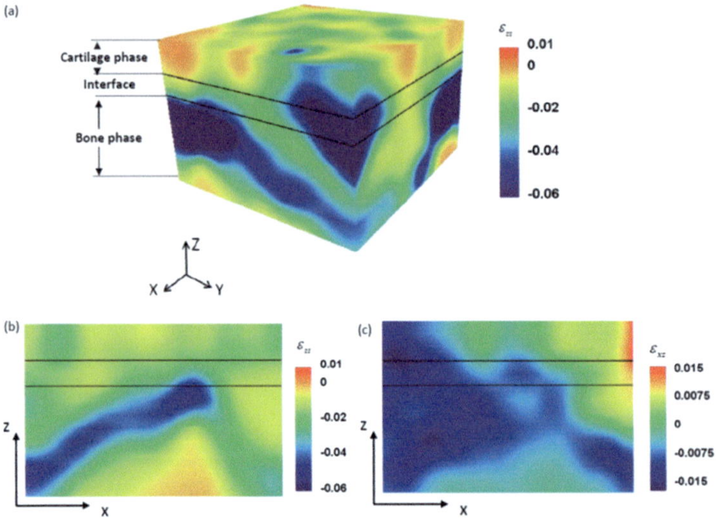

Fig. 11.17 (**a**) 3D visualisation of the axial strain, ε_{zz}, of the dual layer (model 2) obtained with a subvolume size of 32 voxels (0.736 mm), overlapped by 50 %. Visualisation of the axial and shear strains, ε_{zz} and ε_{xz}, in a 2D section extracted from the core of the volume, (**b**) and (**c**), respectively. Dimensions of the volume are $313 \times 313 \times 224$ voxels^3 (i.e. $7.2 \times 7.2 \times 5.2$ mm^3). The interface thickness is about 1 mm

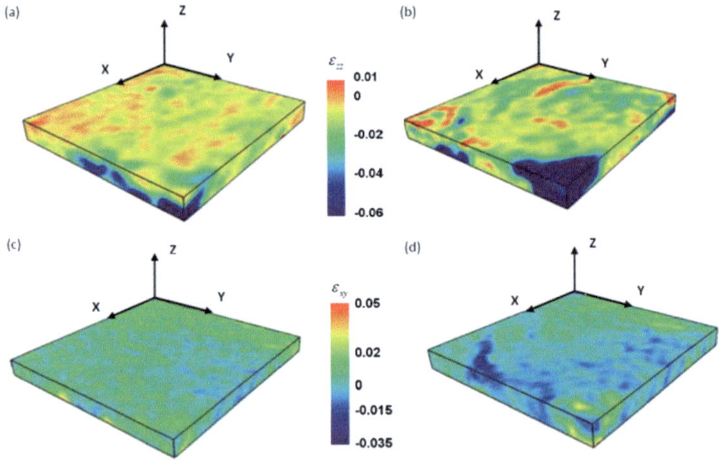

Fig. 11.18 3D visualisations of the axial and interfacial shear strain, ε_{zz} and ε_{xy}, of the interface, (**a**), (**c**) model 1; (**b**), (**d**) model 2. The results were obtained with a subvolume size of 11 voxels (0.253 mm), overlapped by 50 %. Dimensions of the volumes are $313 \times 313 \times 40$ voxels^3 (i.e. $7.2 \times 7.2 \times 0.92$ mm^3)

under cyclic loading conditions. Multistep tests seem to be useful in assessing the fatigue behaviour of scaffolds. These tests allow the reduced number of samples/ test duration for analysis of fatigue properties of biomaterials.

3D full-field strains in the dual-layer scaffold material were measured using the latest techniques, including micro-CT imaging, in situ loading and digital volume correlation, to gain new insights into the failure mechanisms in the bone, the cartilage and the transitional interface regions under compression. The analysis of the strain maps revealed large areas undergoing minimal deformation, whereas failure occurred preferentially in well-defined strain concentration bands. Compressive and shear failure modes were observed at the specimen level at a macroscopic strain of about 2 %. Similar failure modes were reported by Nazarian and co-workers on human trabecular bones compressed at an apparent strain of 1.8 % [68]. Thurner and co-workers [70] have also reported oblique failure bands in trabecular bone specimens compressed at around 2% strain. At microstructural level, bending of plate-like individual struts was observed in the regions of high strain, which seems to be the main mode of failure. Indeed, the bone phase of the scaffolds has a predominant plate-like structure, and bending is often observed to be the failure mode of choice for plate-like structures [68].

In the dual-layer specimens, the bone phase and the interface seem to play an important role in protecting the cartilage phase from excessive deformation. Designing a dual-layer scaffold with a reduced bone phase thickness would promote damage within the cartilage phase and increase the damage in the bone phase and at the interface. In the cartilage phase, buckling of rod-like struts was observed locally. So far, we have yet to be able to perform a detailed analysis of the distribution of failed plate versus rod-like struts, while it is likely that both bending of the plates and buckling of the rods are responsible for failure of cartilage [68].In the interface, high compressive strains combined with increased interfacial shear have been found, although no microcracking or interfacial debonding was observed from the CT images.

Some researchers [78, 110] have investigated the failure of osteochondral plugs in racehorse and bovine bone in simulated impact-induced trauma. In Malekipour et al. (2012) [78], plugs consisted of full cartilage and subchondral bones, thus achieving a lower aspect ratio for the bone phase (0.11 vs. 0.59 used herein for model 2). Microcracks extending from the calcified region down to the trabecular bone were observed as well as surface fissures in the cartilage. In Burgin and Aspden (2008) [110],however, the thickness of the bone phase was varied up to 12 mm to a maximum aspect ratio of1.33, close to that of model 1 (~1.38). The modulus of the bone-on-cartilage samples reached a constant value when the bone thickness exceeded about 10 times the cartilage thickness. Under these conditions, impacts produced damage in the bone rather than in the cartilage. These results are consistent with our findings. No damage was found in the cartilage phase when the bone phase thickness was about 8 times or higher than the cartilage phase thickness. When the bone thickness was reduced by half, damage develops in the cartilage phase, and even more damage is found in the bone phase and in the interface. In addition, Malekipour et al. [78] found high strains in bone and concluded that bone absorbs a relatively high level of energy, which may be protective to cartilage, consistent with our findings.

Some limitations in the study of strain distribution should be acknowledged. These include first-order shape functions that were used in the correlation algorithm to depict the shape change of the deformed subset. Future work will involve higher-order displacement gradients during the multipass approach, which will allow the localised effects to be measured more accurately [73]. The experiments should also be performed in an environment closer to in vivo conditions. Water acts as a plasticiser and tends to increase polymer flexibility and fluidity [111, 112], which might affect the results.

To summarise, the results from the characterisation of a hydrogel scaffold demonstrate that mechanical testing, image-guided failure analysis and digital volume correlation are valuable tools that may be applied to porous materials in general. The results and the methodologies used might be also of interest in the characterisation of other types of scaffolds for a range of applications in biomedical engineering.

Acknowledgements The authors would like to acknowledge Smith & Nephew for providing the samples and the University of Portsmouth for financial support.

References

1. Freeman MAR (1979) Adult articular cartilage. 2, Revised edn. Pitman Medical, Tunbridge Wells/GB
2. Suh J-K, Arøen A, Muzzonigro TS, Disilvestro M, Fu FH (1997) Injury and repair of articular cartilage: related scientific issues. Oper Tech Orthop 7(4):270–278
3. Yannas IV (2001) Tissue and organ regeneration in adults. Springer, New York
4. Spector M (2006) Biomaterials-based tissue engineering and regenerative medicine solutions to musculoskeletal problems. Swiss Med Wkly 136:293–301
5. Luyten FP, Dell'Accio F, De Bari C (2001) Skeletal tissue engineering: opportunities and challenges. Best Pract Res Clin Rheumatol 15(5):759–769
6. Freed LE, Vunjak-Novakovic G, Biron RJ, Eagles DB, Lesnoy DC, Barlow SK, Langer R (1994) Biodegradable polymer scaffolds for tissue engineering. Nat Biotechnol 12:689–693
7. Langer R, Vacanti JP, Vacanti CA, Atala A, Freed LE, Vunjak-Novakovic G (1995) Tissue engineering. Biomed Appl Tissue Eng 1(2):151–161
8. Seal BL, Otero TC, Panitch A (2001) Polymeric biomaterials for tissue and organ regeneration. Mater Sci Eng R Rep 34(4–5):147–230
9. Angele P, Kujat R, Nerlich M, Yoo J, Goldberg V, Johnstone B (1999) Engineering of osteochondral tissue with bone marrow mesenchymal progenitor cells in a derivatized hyaluronan-gelatin composite sponge. Tissue Eng 5(6):545–554
10. Hung CT, Lima EG, Mauck RL, Taki E, LeRoux MA, Lu HH, Stark RG, Guo XE, Ateshian GA (2003) Anatomically shaped osteochondral constructs for articular cartilage repair. J Biomech 36(12):1853–1864
11. Schaefer D, Martin I, Jundt G, Seidel J, Heberer M, Grodzinsky A, Bergin I, Vunjak-Novakovic G, Freed LE (2002) Tissue-engineered composites for the repair of large osteochondral defects. Arthritis Rheum 46(9):2524–2534

12. Sherwood JK, Riley SL, Palazzolo R, Brown SC, Monkhouse DC, Coates M, Griffith LG, Landeen LK, Ratcliffe A (2002) A three-dimensional osteochondral composite scaffold for articular cartilage repair. Biomaterials 23(24):4739–4751
13. Harley BA, Lynn AK, Wissner-Gross Z, Bonfield W, Yannas IV, Gibson LJ (2010) Design of a multiphase osteochondral scaffold. II Fabrication of a mineralized collagen–glycosaminoglycan scaffold. J Biomed Mater Res Part A 92(3):1066–1077
14. Slivka MA, Leatherbury NC, Kieswetter K, Niederauer GG (2001) Porous, resorbable, fiber-reinforced scaffolds tailored for articular cartilage repair. Tissue Eng 7(6):767–780
15. Carmont MR, Carey-Smith R, Saithna A, Dhillon M, Thompson P, Spalding T (2009) Delayed incorporation of a Trufit Plug: perseverance is recommended. Arthroscopy 25 (7):810–814
16. Melton JT, Wilson AJ, Chapman-Sheath P, Cossey AJ (2010) TruFit CB® bone plug: chondral repair, scaffold design, surgical technique and early experiences. Expert Rev Med Dev 7(3):333–341
17. Dhollander AAM, Liekens K, Almqvist KF, Verdonk R, Lambrecht S, Elewaut D, Verbruggen G, Verdonk PCM (2012) A pilot study of the use of an osteochondral scaffold plug for cartilage repair in the knee and how to deal with early clinical failures. Arthroscopy 28(2):225–233
18. Pearce CJ, Gartner LE, Mitchell A, Calder JD (2012) Synthetic osteochondral grafting of ankle osteochondral lesions. Foot Ankle Surg 18:114–118
19. Madi K, Tozzi G, Zhang QH, Tong J, Cossey A, Au A, Hollis D, Hild F (2013) Computation of full-field displacements in a scaffold implant using digital volume correlation and finite element analysis. Med Eng Phys 35(9):1298–1312
20. Hsu YH, Lupton C, Tong J, Cossey A, Au A (2014) Mechanical characterisation of a scaffold under monotonic and cyclic loading conditions. Int J Exp Comput Biomech 2(4):359–375
21. Harley BA, Lynn AK, Wissner-Gross Z, Bonfield W, Yannas IV, Gibson LJ (2010) Design of a multiphase osteochondral scaffold III: fabrication of layered scaffolds with continuous interfaces. J Biomed Mater Res A 92(3):1078–1093
22. Toolan BC, Frenkel SR, Pachence JM, Yalowitz L, Alexander H (1996) Effects of growth-factor-enhanced culture on a chondrocyte-collagen implant for cartilage repair. J Biomed Mater Res 31:273–280
23. Athanasiou K, Schmitz JP, Agrawal CM (1998) The effects of porosity on in vitro degradation of polylactic-acid-polyglycolic acid implants used in repair of articular cartilage. Tissue Eng 4(1):53–63
24. Lu L, Zhu X, Valenzuela RG, Currier BL, Yaszemski MJ (2001) Biodegradable polymer scaffolds for cartilage tissue engineering. Clin Orthop Relat Res 391:S251–S270
25. Oka M, Ushio K, Kumar P, Ikeuchi K, Hyon SH, Nakamura T, Fujita H (2000) Development of artificial articular cartilage. Proc Inst Mech Eng H J Eng Med 214:59–68
26. Bera B (2009) Development of artificial articular cartilage. Sadhana 34(5):823–831
27. Oka M, Noguchi T, Kumar P, Ikeuchi K, Yamamuro T, Hyon SH, Ikada Y (1990) Development of an artificial articular cartilage. Clin Mater 6:361–381
28. Park S, Hung CT, Ateshian GA (2004) Mechanical response of bovine articular cartilage under dynamic unconfined compression loading at physiological stress levels. OsteoArthritis Cartilage 12:65–73
29. Korhonen RK, Jurvelin JS (2010) Compressive and tensile properties of articular cartilage in axial loading are modulated differently by osmotic environment. Med Eng Phys 32:155–160
30. Wright TM, Hayes WC (1976) Tensile testing of bone over a wide range of strain rates: effects of strain rate, microstructure and density. Med Biol Eng Comput 14(6):671–680
31. Currey JD (1988) Strain rate and mineral content in fracture models of bone. J Orthop Res 6:32–38
32. Schaffler MB, Burr DB (1988) Stiffness of compact bone: effects of porosity and density. J Biomech 21(1):13–16

33. Carter DR, Hayes WC (1977) The compressive behavior of bone as a two-phase porous structure. J Bone Joint Surg (Am) 59(7):954–962
34. Lai WM, Mow VC, Roth V (1981) Effects of nonlinear strain-dependent permeability and rate of compression on the stress behavior of articular cartilage. J Biomech Eng 103(2):61–66
35. Radin EL, Paul IL, Lowy M (1970) A comparison of the dynamic force transmitting properties of subchondral bone and articular cartilage. J Bone Joint Surg (Am) 52:444–456
36. Silyn-Roberts H, Broom ND (1990) Fracture behaviour of cartilage-on-bone in response to repeated impact loading. Connect Tissue Res 24(143–156)
37. Race A, Broom ND, Robertson P (2000) Effect of loading rate and hydration on the mechanical properties of the disc. Spine 25(6):662–669
38. Messner K (1993) Hydroxylapatite supported Dacron plugs for repair of isolated full-thickness osteochondral defects of the rabbit femoral condyle: mechanical and histological evaluations from 6–48 weeks. J Biomed Mater Res 12:1527–1532
39. Zioupos P, Casinos A (1998) Cumulative damage and the response of human bone in two-step loading fatigue. J Biomech 31:825–833
40. Slivka MA, Leatherbury NC, Kieswetter K, Niederauer GG (2000) In vitro compression testing of fiber-reinforced, bioabsorbable, porous implants. In: Mauli Agrawal C, Parr JE, Lin ST (eds) Synthetic bioabsorbable polymers for implants. American Society for Testing and Materials, West Conshohocken, pp 124–135
41. Buschmann MD, Soulhat J, Shirazi-Adl A, Jurvelin JS, Hunziker EB (1998) Confined compression of articular cartilage: linearity in ramp and sinusoidal tests and the importance of interdigitation and incomplete confinement. J Biomech 31:171–178
42. Williamson AK, Chen AC, Sah RL (2001) Compressive properties and function-composition relationships of developing bovine articular cartilage. J Orthop Res 19:1113–1121
43. Korhonen RK, Laasanena MS, Toyras J, Rieppob J, Hirvonena J, Helminen HJ, Jurvelin JS (2002) Comparison of the equilibrium response of articular cartilage in unconfined compression, confined compression and indentation. J Biomech 35:903–909
44. Perie D, Korda D, Iatridis JC (2005) Confined compression experiments on bovine nucleus pulposus and annulus fibrosus: sensitivity of the experiment in the determination of compressive modulus and hydraulic permeability. J Biomech 38:2164–2171
45. Soltz MA, Ateshian GA (1998) Experimental verification and theoretical prediction of cartilage interstitial fluid pressurization at an impermeable contact interface in confined compression. J Biomech 31:927–934
46. Martin RB (2003) Fatigue microdamage as an essential element of bone mechanics and biology. Calcif Tissue Int 73:101–107
47. Taylor M, Tanner KE (1997) Fatigue failure of cancellous bone: a possible cause of implant migration and loosening. J Bone Joint Surg 79-B:181–182
48. Pattin CA, Calert WE, Carter DR (1996) Cyclic mechanical property degradation during fatigue loading of cortical bone. J Biomech 29(1):69–79
49. O'Brien FJ, Taylor D, Lee TC (2003) Microcrack accumulation at different intervals during fatigue testing of compact bone. J Biomech 36:973–980
50. Yeni YN, Fyhrie DP (2002) Fatigue damage-fracture mechanics interaction in cortical bone. Bone 30(3):509–514
51. Cotton JR, Winwood K, Zioupos P, Taylor M (2005) Damage rate is a predictor of fatigue life and creep strain rate in tensile fatigue of human cortical bone samples. J Biomech Eng 127:213–219
52. Fleck C, Eifler D (2003) Deformation behaviour and damage accumulation of cortical bone specimens from the equine tibia under cyclic loading. J Biomech 36:179–189
53. Yamamoto E, Crawford RP, Chan DD, Keaveny TM (2006) Development of residual strains in human vertebral trabecular bone after prolonged static and cyclic loading at low load levels. J Biomech 39:1812–1818
54. Zioupos P, Wang XT, Currey JD (1996) The accumulation of fatigue microdamage in human cortical bone of two different ages in vitro. Clin Biomech 11:365–375

55. Moore TLA, Gibson LJ (2003) Fatigue microdamage in bovine trabecular bone. J Biomech Eng 125:769–776
56. Moore TLA, Gibson LJ (2003) Fatigue of bovine trabecular bone. J Biomech Eng 125:761–768
57. Dendorfer S, Maier HJ, Taylor D, Hammer J (2008) Anisotropy of the fatigue behaviour of cancellous bone. J Biomech 41:636–641
58. Carter DR, Hayes WC (1977) Compact bone fatigue damage – I. Residual strength and stiffness. J Biomech 10:325–337
59. Rapillard L, Charlebois M, Zysset P (2006) Compressive fatigue behavior of human vertebral trabecular bone. J Biomech 39:2133–2139
60. Dendorfer S, Maier HJ, Hammer J (2009) Fatigue damage in cancellous bone: an experimental approach from continuum to micro scale. J Mech Behav Biomed Mater 2(1):113–119
61. Palissery V, Taylor M, Browne M (2004) Fatigue characterization of a polymer foam to use as a cancellous bone analog material in the assessment of orthopaedic devices. J Mater Sci Mater Med 15(1):61–67
62. Meyer RW, Pruitt LA (2001) The effect of cyclic true strain on the morphology, structure, and relaxation behavior of ultra high molecular weight polyethylene. Polymer 42:5293–5306
63. Topolinski T, Cichanski A, Mazurkiewicz A, Nowicki K (2011) Study of the behavior of the trabecular bone under cyclic compression with stepwise increasing amplitude. J Mech Behav Biomed Mater 4(8):1755–1763
64. Guillén T, Ohrndorf A, Tozzi G, Tong J, Christ H-J (2012) Compressive fatigue behavior of bovine cancellous bone and bone analogous materials under multi-step loading conditions. Adv Eng Mater 14(5):B199–B207
65. Michel MC, Guo X-DE, Gibson LJ, McMahon TA, Hayes WC (1993) Compressive fatigue behavior of bovine trabecular bone. J Biomech 26(4–5):453–463
66. Zioupos P, Gresle M, Winwood K (2008) Fatigue strength of human cortical bone: age, physical, and material heterogeneity effects. J Biomed Mater Res A 86A(3):627–636
67. Nazarian A, Muller R (2004) Time-lapsed microstructural imaging of bone failure behavior. J Biomech 37(1):55–65
68. Nazarian A, Stauber M, Zurakowski D, Snyder BD, Muller R (2006) The interaction of microstructure and volume fraction in predicting failure in cancellous bone. Bone 39 (6):1196–1202. doi:10.1016/j.bone.2006.06.013
69. Stops AJF, Harrison NM, Haugh MG, O'Brien FJ, McHugh PE (2010) Local and regional mechanical characterisation of a collagen-glycosaminoglycan scaffold using high-resolution finite element analysis. J Mech Behav Biomed Mater 3(4):292–302
70. Thurner PJ, Wyss P, Voide R, Stauber M, Stampanoni M, Sennhauser U, Müller R (2006) Time-lapsed investigation of three-dimensional failure and damage accumulation in trabecular bone using synchrotron light. Bone 39(2):289–299
71. Buffiere JY, Maire E, Adrien J, Masse JP, Boller E (2010) In situ experiments with X ray tomography: an attractive tool for experimental mechanics. Exp Mech 50(3):289–305
72. Youssef S, Maire E, Gaertner R (2005) Finite element modelling of the actual structure of cellular materials determined by X-ray tomography. Acta Mater 53(3):719–730
73. Bay BK, Smith TS, Fyrhie DP, Saad M (1999) Digital volume correlation: three-dimensional strain mapping using X-ray tomography. Exp Mech 39:217–226
74. Germaneau A, Doumalin P, Dupre JC (2007) 3D strain field measurement by correlation of volume images using scattered light: recording of images and choice of marks. Strain 43 (3):207–218
75. Liu L, Morgan EF (2007) Accuracy and precision of digital volume correlation in quantifying displacements and strains in trabecular bone. J Biomech 40(15):3516–3520
76. Roux S, Hild F, Viot P, Bernard D (2008) Three-dimensional image correlation from X-ray computed tomography of solid foam. Compos A: Appl Sci Manuf 39(8):1253–1265
77. Verhulp E, van Rietbergen B, Huiskes R (2004) A three-dimensional digital image correlation technique for strain measurements in microstructures. J Biomech 37(9):1313–1320

78. Malekipour F, Oetomo D, Vee Sin Lee P (2012) Osteochondral injury during simulated drop landing compression: pre and post impact micro-computed tomography. Paper presented at the 30th annual conference of biomechanics in sports, University of Melbourne, Australia
79. Madi K, Booker A, Tozzi G, Zhang Z-Y, Hsu Y-H, Lupton C, Tong J, Cossey A, Au A, N'Guyen F (2011) Viscoelastic modelling and full-field strain computation of biphasic scaffold for osteochondral defect repair. Paper presented at the ECCOMAS – international conference on tissue engineering, Lisbon, Portugal, June 2–4
80. Kalyanam S, Yapp RD, Insana MF (2009) Poro-viscoelastic behavior of gelatin hydrogels under compression-Implications for bioelasticity imaging. J Biomech Eng 131(8):1–13
81. DiSilvestro MR, Suh J-KF (2001) A cross-validation of the biphasic poroviscoelastic model of articular cartilage in unconfined compression, indentation, and confined compression. J Biomech 34:519–525
82. Linde F, Hvid I (1989) The effect of constraint on the mechanical behaviour of trabecular bone specimens. J Biomech 22(5):485–490
83. Caler WE, Carter DR (1989) Bone creep-fatigue damage accumulation. J Biomech 22:625–635
84. Haddock SM, Yeh OC, Mummaneni PV, Rosenberg WS, Keaveny TM (2004) Similarity in the fatigue behavior of trabecular bone across site and species. J Biomech 37:181–187
85. Fray ME, Altstadt V (2003) Fatigue behaviour of multiblock thermoplastic elastomers. 1. Stepwise increasing load testing of poly(aliphatic/aromatic-ester) copolymers. Polymer 44:4635–4642
86. Linde F, Hvid I (1987) Stiffness behaviour of trabecular bone specimens. J Biomech 20 (1):83–89
87. Doubea M, Kłosowskia MM, Arganda-Carrerasb I, Cordelièresc FP, Doughertyd RP, Jacksone JS, Schmidf B, Hutchinsong JR, Shefelbinea SJ (2010) BoneJ: free and extensible bone image analysis in ImageJ. Bone 47(6):1076–1079
88. Beuf O, Ghosh S, Newitt DC, Link TM, Steinbach L, Ries M, Lane N, Majumdar S (2002) Magnetic resonance imaging of normal and osteoarthritic trabecular bone structure in the human knee. Arthritis Rheum 46(2):385–393
89. Ding M, Hvid I (2000) Quantification of age-related changes in the structure model type and trabecular thickness of human tibial cancellous bone. Bone 26(3):291–295
90. Tozzi G, Zhang Q-H, Tong J (2012) 3D real-time micromechanical compressive behaviour of bone–cement interface: experimental and finite element studies. J Biomech 45(2):356–363
91. Bursac PM, Obitz TW, Eisenberg SR, Stamenovic D (1999) Confined and unconfined stress relaxation of cartilage: appropriateness of a transversely isotropic analysis. J Biomech 32:1125–1130
92. Kelly N, McGarry JP (2012) Experimental and numerical characterisation of the elasto-plastic properties of bovine trabecular bone and a trabecular bone analogue. J Mech Behav Biomed Mater 9:184–197
93. Yang S, Leong K-F, Du Z, Chua C-K (2001) Review: the design of scaffolds for use in tissue engineering. Part I Traditional factors. Tissue Eng 7(6):679–689
94. Augat P, Link T, Lang TF, Lin JC, Majumdar S, Genant HK (1998) Anisotropy of the elastic modulus of trabecular bone specimens from different anatomical locations. Med Eng Phys 20:124–131
95. Keaveny TM, Pinilla TP, Crawford RP, Kopperdahl DL, Lou A (1997) Systematic and random errors in compression testing of trabecular bone. J Orthop Res 15(1):101–110
96. Kopperdahl DL, Keaveny TM (1998) Yield strain behavior of trabecular bone. J Biomech 31 (7):601–608
97. Goulet RW, Goldstein SA, Ciarelli MJ, Kuhn JL, Brown MB, Feldkamp LA (1994) The relationship between the structural and orthogonal compressive properties of trabecular bone. J Biomech 27(4):375–389
98. Linde F, Hvid I, Madsen F (1992) The effect of specimen geometry on the mechanical behaviour of trabecular bone specimens. J Biomech 25(4):359–368

99. Poumarat G, Squire P (1993) Comparison of mechanical properties of human, bovine bone and a new processed bone xenograft. Biomaterials 14(5):337–340
100. Swartz DE, Wittenberg RH, Shea M, White AA III, Hayes WC (1991) Physical and mechanical properties of calf lumbosacral trabecular bone. J Biomech 24(11):1059–1068
101. Keaveny TM, Wachtel EF, Ford CM, Hayes WC (1994) Differences between the tensile and compressive strengths of bovine tibial trabecular bone depend on modulus. J Biomech 27 (9):1137–1146
102. Goldstein SA, Wilson DL, Sonstegard DA, Matthews LS (1983) The mechanical properties of human tibial trabecular bone as a function of metaphyseal location. J Biomech 16 (12):965–969
103. Kuhn JL, Goldstein SA, Ciarelli MJ, Matthews LS (1989) The limitations of canine trabecular bone as a model for human: a biomechanical study. J Biomech 22(2):95–107
104. Garcia AJ, Reyes CD (2005) Bio-adhesive surfaces to promote osteoblast differentiation and bone formation. J Dent Res 84(5):407–413
105. Kong HJ, Polte TR, Alsberg E, Mooney DJ (2005) FRET measurements of cell-traction forces and nano-scale clustering of adhesion ligands varied by substrate stiffness. Proc Natl Acad Sci U S A 102(12):4300–4305
106. Engler AJ, Sen S, Sweeney HL, Discher DE (2006) Matrix elasticity directs stem cell lineage specification. Cell 126:677–689
107. Schaffler MB, Radin EL, Burr DB (1989) Mechanical and morphological effects of strain rate on fatigue of compact bone. Bone 10:207–214
108. Zioupos P, Wang XT, Currey JD (1996) Experimental and theoretical quantification of the development of damage in fatigue tests of bone and antler. J Biomech 29:989–1002
109. Moore TLA, O'Brien FJ, Gibson LJ (2004) Creep does not contribute to fatigue in bovine trabecular bone. J Biomech Eng 126(3):321–329
110. Burgin LV, Aspden RM (2008) Impact testing to determine the mechanical properties of articular cartilage in isolation and on bone. J Mater Sci 19:703–711
111. Houchin ML, Neuenswander SA, Topp EM (2007) Effect of excipients on PLGA film degradation and the stability of an incorporated peptide. J Control Release 117(3):413–420
112. Kranz H, Ubrich N, Maincent P, Bodmeier R (2000) Physicomechanical properties of biodegradable poly(D, L-lactide) and poly(D, L-lactide-co-glycolide) films in the dry and wet states. J Pharm Sci 89(12):1558–1566

Chapter 12
Computational Design for Scaffold Tissue Engineering

Che-Cheng Chang, Yuhang Chen, Shiwei Zhou, Yiu-Wing Mai, and Qing Li

Abstract Structure of tissue scaffold plays a critical role in guiding and supporting cell proliferation and differentiation. One widely accepted way to create a desirable biomechanical environment is to have it match the mechanical and biological properties of native host tissue. However, conventional design process typically involves laborious trial and error, and it is sometimes very difficult to achieve the desired biomimeticity when multiple criteria are involved. This chapter aims to present a systematic methodology for the design of tissue scaffold structures, in which the stiffness and diffusivity criteria are taken into account to address various biomechanical requirements in tissue engineering. The scaffolds with periodic microstructures are considered herein, which can be fabricated using 3D printing or additive manufacturing technologies. In this design process, the finite element (FE)-based homogenisation technique is employed to characterise effective material properties, and topology optimisation is carried out using the inverse homogenisation technique, in which (1) bulk modulus, (2) diffusivity and (3) their combination are formulated as the design objectives. To assess the optimised design, we simulate and examine the bone tissue regeneration inside the scaffolds under certain biomechanical conditions in two different models, specifically Wolff's remodelling and the mechanobiology rules. The tissue regeneration results demonstrate how different design criteria lead to different outcomes, signifying the importance of scaffold design and the proposed methodology.

Keywords Scaffold • Tissue engineering • Topology optimisation • Homogenisation • Additive manufacturing • Diffusivity

---

C.-C. Chang • Y.-W. Mai • Q. Li (✉)
School of Aerospace, Mechanical & Mechatronic Engineering, The University of Sydney, Sydney, NSW 2006, Australia
e-mail: Qing.Li@Sydney.edu.au

Y. Chen
School of Engineering & Physical Sciences, Mechanical, Process & Energy Engineering, Heriot-Watt University, Edinburgh EH14 4AS, UK

S. Zhou
Centre for Innovative Structures and Materials (CISM), RMIT University, Melbourne, Australia

Q. Li, Y.-W. Mai (eds.), *Biomaterials for Implants and Scaffolds*, Springer Series in Biomaterials Science and Engineering 8, DOI 10.1007/978-3-662-53574-5_12

12.1 Introduction

A key to success in tissue engineering has been to develop sophisticated 3D porous scaffolds that provide appropriate biological and mechanical conditions for cells to generate desirable and functional tissues [1]. The complex roles of the microstructures of tissue scaffolds in the regulation of biomechanical environment are gradually recognised recently. However, the structural requirements can vary significantly from site to site and from tissue type to tissue type, making the design and fabrication highly case dependent and often involving laborious trial-and-error experimental processes. Furthermore, it can be difficult to assure a smooth biomechanical transition from empty scaffold to scaffold–tissue construct in the design stage given the random nature of traditional porous scaffold structure and neotissue ingrowth. To tackle this problem and better control the biomechanical outcomes of scaffolding, an inverse design procedure based on the periodic base cell has exhibited notable advantages [2–6]. Further, mathematical modelling is believed to be of significant potential in prediction of tissue growth, thereby helping design of more predictive scaffolds [7–9].

The development of various additive manufacturing and solid free-form fabrication (SFF) technologies is making the controllable base cell designs particularly attractive [10–14]. Exploitation of homogenisation [15] and its inverse form [2] offer a promising alternative to costly experimental characterisation and design of scaffolds. Biomimetic mechanical properties have become a possible design criterion since Hollister and his colleagues [2–4] introduced topology optimisation technique by matching the stiffness of designed scaffolds to that of trabecular bones. It would be interesting to study how different design criteria determine the performance of scaffolds. As such, a more suitable optimisation formulation can be established.

It is however unclear how tissue ingrowth gradually affects the biomechanical conditions that are obtained in an initial stage. It would be necessary to assess the fundamental hypothesis of whether a matching stiffness to host bone could best stimulate tissue generation in a timely fashion [16]. To investigate how scaffold interacts with tissue growth, Adachi et al. presented a computational model that transforms the remodelling algorithms of long bone to a base cell model [7–9]. Later, Byrne et al. [17] adopted the mechanobiological algorithm for remodelling simulation. Sanz-Herrera et al. [9] further explored the effect of tissue ingrowth on mechanical properties of constructs within a multiscale framework by accounting for host bone (macro) and scaffold pore (micro). Chen et al. incorporated degradation model of polymeric scaffolds [18] and tissue ingrowth model through mechanobiological simulation in the design analysis and optimisation; and they found that degradation and tissue regeneration may not necessarily take place in a harmonic way if no design optimisation is carried out [6]. These studies provided evidences how numerical remodelling could help better design scaffolds for more efficient in vivo and in vitro tests. To date, there is a growing need to consolidate different scaffold design processes for better correlating biomechanical criteria with the resultant tissue growth.

This chapter aims to first explore how different design criteria affect scaffold structures and then determine how the different designs of scaffold structures could affect tissue regeneration on a microscopic level. Specifically, the inverse homogenisation method is adopted to optimise base cell topologies for either matching host bone behaviours or maximising the overall properties. The optimised scaffolds are then assessed and compared in terms of the effectiveness of tissue generation through Wolff's remodelling [19] and mechanobiology [17] rules.

12.2 Materials and Methods

The rapid development of additive manufacturing (3D printing) and the solid freeform fabrication (SFF) technologies [20] has enabled various direct and indirect fabrication of a full range of biomaterials, with sophisticated configurations, adequate geometric accuracy and structural stability [13]. For this reason, periodic scaffold architectures comprising of identical base cells (also known as representative volume element, RVE) have drawn increasing attention recently, largely attributable to their more controllable and tailorable effective material properties [21]. In this chapter, we will present a systematic methodology suitable for the analysis and design of such periodic structures to attain desirable biomechanical properties for tissue engineering applications.

12.2.1 Characterisation of Effective Material Properties by Homogenisation

The first step of tissue scaffold design is the determination of biomechanical properties of scaffold, which is often required to assess its potential performance prior to tissue engineering experiments. In a periodically structured scaffold, the size of base cell (100 ~ 500μm) is considered much smaller than the bulk scaffold dimension (typically in cm scale). In this context, the asymptotic homogenisation technique [22–24] can be applied to unit cell models to characterise the effective (bulk) physical properties of a scaffold when compositional and microstructural configuration is given. In this chapter, the homogenised elasticity and diffusivity properties are derived as follows.

12.2.1.1 Elasticity Tensor

The homogenisation of the effective elasticity tensor $\mathbf{C}^H$ can be conducted within the finite element (FE) framework, as [24]

$$C_{ij}^H(\rho^e) = \frac{1}{|\Omega|}\sum_{e=1}^{NE}\left(\mathbf{I} - \frac{\partial \mathbf{u}_i}{\partial \mathbf{x}}\right)[\mathbf{K}^e(\rho^e)]\left(\mathbf{I} - \frac{\partial \mathbf{u}_j}{\partial \mathbf{x}}\right)|\Omega^e| \tag{12.1}$$

where C_{ij}^H denotes the homogenised paramaters of elasticity tensor; ρ^e denotes the density of element e, whose normalised form will be used as the design variable in the topology optimisation for inverse homogenisation; NE is the number of elements in the base cell model; $\mathbf{K}^e(\rho^e)$ is the elemental stiffness matrix; and $|\Omega|$ and $|\Omega^e|$ are the volumes of base cell (which is the volume of the entire base cell design domain) and e-th element, respectively. The homogenised stiffness tensor $\mathbf{C}^H$ is thus expressed in the following form:

$$\mathbf{C}^H = \begin{bmatrix} C_{11}^H & C_{12}^H & C_{13}^H & & & \\ C_{21}^H & C_{22}^H & C_{23}^H & & & \\ C_{31}^H & C_{32}^H & C_{33}^H & & & \\ & & & C_{44}^H & & \\ & & & & C_{55}^H & \\ & & & & & C_{66}^H \end{bmatrix} \tag{12.2}$$

For the finite element analysis, the displacement field $\boldsymbol{u}$ is obtained through solving the following equilibrium equation in the base cell model

$$\int_{\Omega}\frac{\partial}{\partial x}\mathbf{K}^e(\rho^e)\frac{\partial}{\partial \mathbf{x}}\mathbf{u}d\Omega = \int_{\Omega}\frac{\partial}{\partial \mathbf{x}}\mathbf{K}^e(\rho^e)d\Omega \tag{12.3}$$

where $\frac{\partial}{\partial \mathbf{x}}\mathbf{u}$ is also known as the characteristic strain of the base cell model. In a 3D case, there exist six unique characteristic strain fields, including three normal components and three shear components [25].

The elemental stiffness matrix $\mathbf{K}^e$ is a function of the material density, ρ^e. This is often defined as $\mathbf{K}^e = f(\rho^e)\mathbf{K}$, where $f(\rho^e)$ is a real function, usually formulated based on the power law and the solid isotropic material with penalisation (SIMP) principle widely adopted in topology optimisation [26]. $\mathbf{K}$ is the original stiffness matrix of the base material. Each element has a density between 0 (completely void) and 1 (completely solid) and a unique $\mathbf{K}^e$ value.

The right-hand side of Eq. (12.3) is the ideological unit test strain. From an FEA perspective ($\mathbf{Ku} = \mathbf{f}$), the right-hand side of the equilibrium equation represents the nodal force ($\mathbf{f}$, where $\mathbf{f} = \int_{\Omega}\frac{\partial}{\partial \mathbf{x}}\mathbf{K}^e(\rho^e)d\Omega$) that induces the characteristic strain response. The global stiffness matrix on the left-hand side of the equation is the standard stiffness matrix assembly ($\mathbf{K} = \int_{\Omega}\frac{\partial}{\partial \mathbf{f}}\mathbf{f}^e(\rho^e)\frac{\partial}{\partial \mathbf{f}}d\Omega$). Assembling the right-hand side of the equation over the discretised FE domain of base cell produces a force vector that can be applied on nodal level.

The periodic boundary condition is applied to all the nodal pairs on the opposite boundaries of the RVE model by means of coupling, i.e. the displacement of a node and its paired partner on the other side of RVE is made equal. For example, all nodes on the RVE boundary facing the negative-x direction are coupled to the nodes on the boundary facing the positive-x direction on the opposite face [16]. Thus the displacement field is continuous from one base cell to another. In normal strain scenarios, if symmetry is assumed, symmetry boundary condition can be applied: the nodal displacement on the boundaries facing the $x/y/z$ direction has zero $x/y/z$ displacement, respectively (otherwise it will penetrate the base cell right next to it). In the shear strain scenarios, on the other hand, the boundary nodes are not allowed to move in the non-shear directions. In the x–y shear strain case, for example, the nodes on all RVE boundaries are not allowed to move in the z direction, the nodes on the x boundary can only move in the x direction and the nodes on the y boundary can only move in the y direction. A summary of the prescribed boundary conditions is provided in Table 12.1 for clarification.

To reduce the computational cost of 3D FEA, geometric and kinematic symmetry conditions are applied whenever possible [27]. Specifically, the base cell centre is taken as the origin of a Cartesian coordinate system, and one-eighth of the cubic base cell is considered, whose six outer boundaries are located at x, y, $z=0$, 1, respectively. The cubic RVE domain is meshed with structured cubic hexahedral elements for simplicity of modelling.

12.2.1.2 Diffusivity Tensor

The homogenisation of the effective diffusivity is implemented in a similar fashion to that of the stiffness tensor. The effective diffusivity tensor D_{ij}^H is calculated as

$$\mathbf{D}_{ij}^H(\rho^e) = \frac{1}{|\Omega|}\sum_{e=1}^{NE}\mathbf{D}^e(\rho^e)\left(\mathbf{I} - \frac{\partial\varphi}{\partial\mathbf{x}}\right)|\Omega^e| \tag{12.4}$$

where $\mathbf{D}^e$ is the elemental diffusivity matrix of some chemical species across a given fluid. The homogenised diffusivity tensor can be expressed in the following form:

Table 12.1 Symmetry conditions for the different test strains [16]

Test strains	$x=0, 1$	$y=0, 1$	$z=0, 1$
$\hat{\varepsilon}_{ij},\ i=j$	$u_x^e=0$	$u_y^e=0$	$u_z^e=0$
$\hat{\varepsilon}_{12}$	$u_y^e=u_z^e=0$	$u_x^e=u_z^e=0$	$u_z^e=0$
$\hat{\varepsilon}_{23}$	$u_x^e=0$	$u_x^e=u_z^e=0$	$u_x^e=u_y^e=0$
$\hat{\varepsilon}_{13}$	$u_y^e=u_z^e=0$	$u_y^e=0$	$u_x^e=u_y^e=0$

$$\mathbf{D}^H = \begin{bmatrix} D_{11}^H & & \\ & D_{22}^H & \\ & & D_{33}^H \end{bmatrix} \tag{12.5}$$

The characteristic concentration field, φ, is obtained by solving the following equation:

$$\int_\Omega \frac{\partial}{\partial \mathbf{x}} \mathbf{D}^e(\rho^e) \frac{\partial}{\partial \mathbf{x}} \varphi d\Omega = \int_\Omega \frac{\partial}{\partial \mathbf{x}} \mathbf{D}^e(\rho^e) d\Omega \tag{12.6}$$

which is very similar to the equilibrium equation in the stiffness case. In 3D space, there exist three unique $\frac{\partial \varphi}{\partial \mathbf{x}}$ terms, corresponding to x, y and z directions. This equation can be solved as a standard thermal equation by first assembling the right-hand side of the equation to create the nodal force vector ($\mathbf{f} = \int_\Omega \frac{\partial}{\partial \mathbf{x}} \mathbf{D}^e(\rho^e) d\Omega$) and then the global diffusivity matrix ($\mathbf{K} = \int_\Omega \frac{\partial}{\partial \mathbf{x}} \mathbf{D}^e(\rho^e) \frac{\partial}{\partial \mathbf{x}} d\Omega$). The elemental diffusivity matrix, $\mathbf{D}^e$, is also a function of the density of individual element (ρ^e), i.e. $\mathbf{D}^e = f(\rho^e)\mathbf{D}$, where $\mathbf{D}$ is the nominal diffusivity in the pure fluid phase.

The periodic boundary conditions can be applied by pairing all concentration degree of freedom (DoF) on the opposite boundary surfaces of the RVE. If symmetry can be assumed, symmetric boundary conditions and degree of freedom (DoF) constraints can be applied instead. For example, in the x strain case, every node on the positive and negative x RVE boundaries is given a concentration of zero (DoF constraint), whereas all other boundaries are left unconstrained (symmetry). The characteristic concentration is allowed to have a negative value since it is only a relative term.

12.2.2 *Inverse Homogenisation and Topology Optimisation*

Following the characterisation directly using the homogenisation, topology optimisation is carried out to determine the optimal material distribution in a base cell form that yields either the maximum or desired material properties [28, 29]. Such a design process is known as the 'inverse homogenisation', in which the desired homogenised properties determine the porous microstructure of a scaffold inversely.

12.2.2.1 Targeted Stiffness Tensor

The stiffness properties of bone scaffolds should match those of host bone for functional reasons [3, 30]. In topology optimisation context, we can translate such requirement to a cost function in terms of the differences between the targeted stiffness $\mathbf{C}^*$ and actual effective (i.e. homogenised) stiffness $\mathbf{C}^H$, as follows:

$$\begin{cases} \min\limits_{\rho^e} J_S(\rho^e) = \sum\limits_{i,j=1}^{6} \left(C_{ij}^* - C_{ij}^H(\rho^e) \right)^2 \\ \text{subject to} : 0 < \rho_{\min} \le \rho^e \le 1 \\ \frac{1}{NE} \sum\limits_{e=1}^{NE} (1 - \rho^e) = V_0 \end{cases} \tag{12.7}$$

where $\rho_{\min}$ is the minimum density that a finite element can have and the superscript e denotes elemental property. A non-zero value for elemental density $\rho_{\min}$ is required to avoid singularity in the finite element calculation.

To prevent the formation of numerical artefacts such as checkerboard pattern, a nonlinear diffusion technique is adopted here [31, 32]. The method of moving asymptotes (MMA) algorithm [33] is employed to determine the topological evolution. The sensitivity function with respect to the design variable ρ^e can be determined by using the adjoint variable method and written as

$$\begin{aligned} \frac{\partial J_S}{\partial \rho^e} = & -2 \sum_{i,j=1}^{6} r_{ij} \left(C_{ij}^* - C_{ij}^H(\rho^e) \right) \frac{\partial C_{ij}^H(\rho^e)}{\partial \rho^e} \\ & - \tau^2 \mathrm{div} \left[\frac{\partial \varphi}{\partial (\|\nabla \rho^e\|)} \frac{1}{\|\nabla \rho^e\|} \nabla \rho^e \right] \end{aligned} \tag{12.8}$$

where div stands for the divergence operator and

$$\frac{\partial C_{ij}^H(\rho^e)}{\partial \rho^e} = \sum_{e=1}^{NE} \left(\widehat{\mathbf{u}}_i^* - \mathbf{u}_i^e \right)^T \frac{\partial \mathbf{K}^e(\rho^e)}{\partial \rho^e} \left(\widehat{\mathbf{u}}_j^* - \mathbf{u}_j^e \right) |\Omega^e| \tag{12.9}$$

12.2.2.2 Targeted Diffusivity

The porous phase of a bone scaffold must allow unhindered nutrient transport and mass movement. In cartilage tissue engineering, for example, the effective diffusivity is expected to match that of the native tissue to mimic the local diffusion environment [34]. To design a base cell with a diffusivity target, we formulate a cost function (J_D) based on the difference between the desired diffusivity $\mathbf{D}^*$ and the actual effective (homogenised) diffusivity $\mathbf{D}^{\mathrm{H}}$ of the model in a fashion similar to the stiffness topology optimisation formulation:

$$\begin{cases} \min_{\rho^e} J_D(\rho^e) = \sum_{i=1}^{3}\left(D_{ii}^{*} - D_{ii}^{H}(\rho^e)\right)^2 \\ \text{subject to}:\ 0 < \rho_{\min} \le \rho^e \le 1 \\ \frac{1}{NE}\sum_{e=1}^{NE}(1-\rho^e) = V_0 \end{cases} \tag{12.10}$$

The sensitivity of the effective diffusivity is also a function of the elemental density as follows:

$$\frac{\partial J_D}{\partial \rho^e} = 2\sum_{i=1}^{3}\left(D_{ii}^{*} - D_{ii}^{H}(\rho^e)\right)\frac{\partial D_{ii}^{H}(\rho^e)}{\partial \rho^e} \tag{12.11}$$

Note that the sensitivity function in this case has a positive sign since a change in elemental density has the opposite effect on the diffusivity. For the mathematical similarity between diffusion and conduction problems [35], the readers are recommended to refer to the detailed derivation and a MATLAB program for the inverse conductive homogenisation calculation provided by us [36].

12.2.2.3 Combined Stiffness and Diffusivity

Both stiffness and diffusivity of a tissue scaffold can be maximised or be matched to the host tissue properties simultaneously to achieve biomimeticity [37]. Such a design task can be accomplished using multiobjective topology optimisation techniques [38–42]. In the case of maximisation, the objective function is formulated as follows:

$$\begin{cases} \min_{\rho^e} J(\rho^e) = \sum_{e=1}^{NE}\left[w_C\frac{C^*}{\sum_{i,j}^{6}\delta_{ij}C_{ij}^{H}} + w_D\frac{D^*}{\sum_{i,j}^{3}\delta_{ij}D_{ij}^{H}}\right] \\ \text{subject to}:\ 0 < \rho_{\min} \le \rho^e \le 1 \\ \frac{1}{NE}\sum_{e=1}^{NE}(1-\rho^e) = V_0 \\ w_C + w_D = 1 \end{cases} \tag{12.12}$$

where w_C and w_D are the weight factors for the effective stiffness and effective diffusivity cost functions, respectively, C^* is the maximum stiffness, D^* is the maximum diffusivity and δ_{ij} is the Kronecker delta ($\delta_{ij} = 1$ when $i = j$, and $\delta_{ij} = 0$ when $i \neq j$). The cost functions $\frac{C^*}{\sum_{i,j}^{6}\delta_{ij}C_{ij}^{H}}$ and $\frac{D^*}{\sum_{i,j}^{3}\delta_{ij}D_{ij}^{H}}$ are the inverse of individual effective material properties and are normalised [39]. The weight factors indicate the relative importance of these two material properties in an individual design scenario ($w_C + w_D = 1$).

12.2.3 Computational Remodelling Simulation

In this chapter, we consider two different remodelling rules, namely, Wolff's rule [19] and mechanoregulatory [17] rules, as follows.

12.2.3.1 Modelling for Wolff's Rule

The tissue remodelling is a process of balancing bone apposition (osteoblastic process) and bone resorption (osteoclastic process) [43], which is driven by local mechanical stimuli. Mathematical models capable of simulating the remodelling process have been widely available on a macroscopic level [44–46], whereas relatively speaking, limited studies have been conducted on the microscopic level involving implanted scaffolds [7, 9, 17].

To describe how the load-bearing tissue grows within the scaffold pores, the remodelling rules established in long bone are considered phenomenologically applicable [7]. Following the typical remodelling rules in literature [45], tissue is regarded as 3D continuum media whose deformation is quasi-static and which is typically governed by linear elasticity theory. The apposition and resorption of tissue can be determined in terms of strain energy density (SED) as [19]

$$\psi^e = \frac{1}{2}\overline{\varepsilon}^e\overline{\sigma}^e \tag{12.13}$$

where $\overline{\varepsilon}^e$ and$\overline{\sigma}^e$ denote the elemental strain and stress, respectively. The change in elemental bone density ϑ^e is triggered when the elemental SED is higher or lower than the remodelling thresholds [44, 45], defined as

$$\gamma^e = \frac{\partial \vartheta^e}{\partial t} = \begin{cases} \alpha[\psi - (1+s)\psi_n], & \psi > (1+s)\psi_n \\ 0, & (1-s)\psi_n \le \psi \le (1-s)\psi_n \\ \alpha[\psi - (1+s)\psi_n], & \psi > (1+s)\psi_n \end{cases} \tag{12.14}$$

where ψ_n is a site-specific homeostatic equilibrium parameter and s the half-width of the 'lazy zone' [45]. As a constant, α reflects the bone remodelling rates for different tissues and sites. Thus $\vartheta^{e(n)}$ can be updated per time step Δt via a forward Euler algorithm, from time step n to time step $(n+1)$, as

$$\vartheta^{e(n+1)} = \vartheta^{e(n)} + \gamma^e \Delta t \tag{12.15}$$

The choice of time step Δt should be sufficiently small to ensure the stability of remodelling simulations.

It is noted that the scaffold and host tissue are more often than not subject to dynamic loading in vivo, in which the apposition and resorption of the bone are determined by the difference between the actual stimulus and local tissue mechanical stimulation as reported by [47]. However, a precise determination of such loading spectrum and many other relevant biological factors is by no means easy. For this reason, a static loading has been assumed in the remodelling studies in bone and scaffold [7–9]. We will explore the relative effects of different scaffold stiffness on tissue regeneration. As long as the same load (direction, magnitude and pattern) is applied, the remodelling results can be well differentiated from different scaffold stiffnesses; thus, their relative performance can be properly determined.

As described by Sanz-Herrera et al. [9] and Byrne et al. [17], mesenchymal stem cells (MSC) could be seeded or could migrate along scaffold pore surfaces to form a continuous cellular layer after implanted into host. Under certain biomechanical conditions, such cells differentiate and generate osteoblasts, forming immature bone substance in the cellular layer with extremely low modulus. The immature tissue will further remodel into mineralised mature bone inside the scaffold. In this study, it is assumed that the remodelling starts from such an immature tissue layer that is evenly distributed on the scaffold surfaces [7, 9, 17].

12.2.3.2 Modelling for Mechanoregulatory Rule

Scaffold strain can produce certain level of biophysical stimulus and promote mesenchymal stem cells (MSCs) differentiation and proliferation. To model how the biophysical stimuli determine tissue regeneration, the mechanoregulatory rule is employed herein. The mechanoregulatory model adopts mechanical strain and fluid flow to modulate cell differentiation. This algorithm has shown considerable implication to model the growth details of various cell phenotypes under different levels of biophysical stimuli [48].

In this model, the pore region of the scaffold is considered to be initially occupied by granulation tissue after a certain period of culturing in a bioreactor, in which the lattices are constructed within each granulation element as a cellular media, allowing various cell phenotypes to potentially occupy. The number of lattice points is determined by the size of element and average diameter of tissue cells [6]. In this model, we randomly seeded 5 % MSCs initially into each lattice which are allowed to further proliferate and differentiate. To account for the cell proliferation and migration, the random walk algorithm [17] is also implemented here.

Having defined the cell proliferation and migration in the *lattice scale*, the MSC differentiation stimulus S is defined in relation to local physical fields as [48]

$$S = \frac{\tau}{a} + \frac{v}{b} \begin{cases} S < 0.01 & \text{absorption} \\ 0.01 < S < 0.53 & \text{osteoblast} \rightarrow \text{mature bone} \\ 0.53 < S < 1 & \text{osteoblast} \rightarrow \text{immature bone} \\ 1 < S < 3 & \text{chondrocyte} \rightarrow \text{cartilage} \\ S > 3 & \text{fibroblast} \rightarrow \text{fibros tissue} \end{cases} \quad (12.16)$$

where τ and v are the octahedral shear strain and fluidic velocity within the base cell of tissue–scaffold construct, respectively. Following the literature, constants $a = 0.0375$ and $b=3$ μms^{-1} that were measured from experiments are adopted to generate biophysical stimulus S for differentiation [17].

It is assumed that each MSC stays for 7 days [17], after which it becomes mature to be able to proliferate or differentiate. Thus, different cell phenotypes would be differentiated from MSCs according to the calculated biophysical stimulus S in Eq. (12.16), where only a certain percentage of mature MSCs in each lattice, defined by a differentiation probability p_d, differentiates every day. To calculate material properties in each lattice, we adopted the material parameters of different cell phenotypes and the algorithm reported by Byrne et al. [17].

12.3 Results and Discussion

12.3.1 Example with the Targeted Stiffness Tensor

Although trabecular bone is generally orthotropic and has three symmetric planes and nine independent elasticity constants, the studies on scaffold design with the inverse homogenisation were usually simplified into six orthotropic elastic properties (i.e. three Young's moduli and three shear moduli) [2–4], making the objective function (Eq. (12.7)) more achievable.

Within the base cell model (40 × 40 × 40 8-node hex elements), the red, green and white colours are used to represent the neo-bony tissue, scaffold and connected voids in the results below, respectively (from dark to light in the greyscale copy of this chapter).

The elasticity tensor of mini-pig mandibular condyle trabecular bone with 50 % porosity [2, 4] is used as the target stiffness here. The base material used for the scaffold design is isotropic with a Poisson's ratio of ν=0.3 and a Young's modulus of 6 GPa, which is higher than that of mini-pig mandibular condyle trabecular bone (around 2.5 GPa), but matches common biomaterials used for fabricating tissue scaffolds [2, 4].

The elasticity tensor of such a trabecular bone $\mathbf{C}^0$ is weighted by a multiplier β, as $\mathbf{C}^* = \beta\mathbf{C}^0$, in order to study the effect of different levels of targets $\mathbf{C}^*$ on bone remodelling. The porosity of 50 % and original target elastic tensor $\mathbf{C}^0$ ($\beta = 1$) are based on in vitro tests and have been used in the previous studies [2, 4].

The figures in Table 12.2 display the optimised base cells of scaffold with prescribed (target) stiffness values. These designs exhibit a spatially bi-continuous architecture, whose formation is attributed to the anisotropy of the stiffness targets. A base cell with optimised stiffness [39] and optimised diffusivity or permeability [42, 49] would otherwise resemble the well-known tri-continuous Schwarz P architecture, which may be a more ideal structure for cell ingrowth.

Table 12.2 Results of scaffold designs (porosity = 50 %)

$\mathbf{C}^* = 0.80\mathbf{C}^0$	$\mathbf{C}^* = 0.85\mathbf{C}^0$	$\mathbf{C}^* = 0.90\mathbf{C}^0$
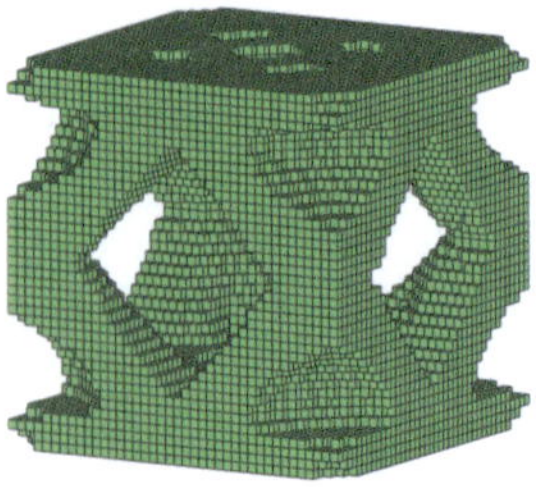	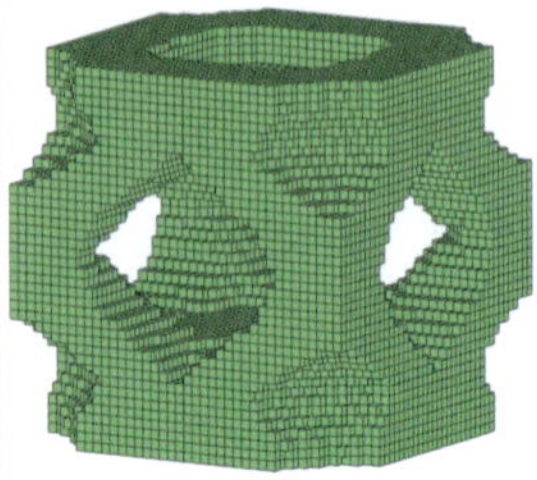	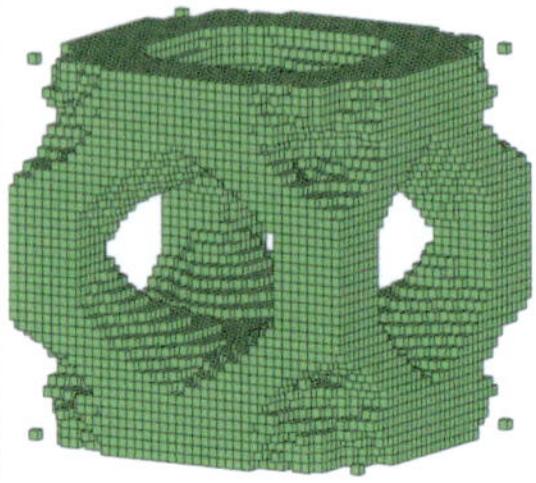
$\mathbf{C}^* = 0.95\mathbf{C}^0$	$\mathbf{C}^* = 1.00\mathbf{C}^0$	$\mathbf{C}^* = 1.05\mathbf{C}^0$
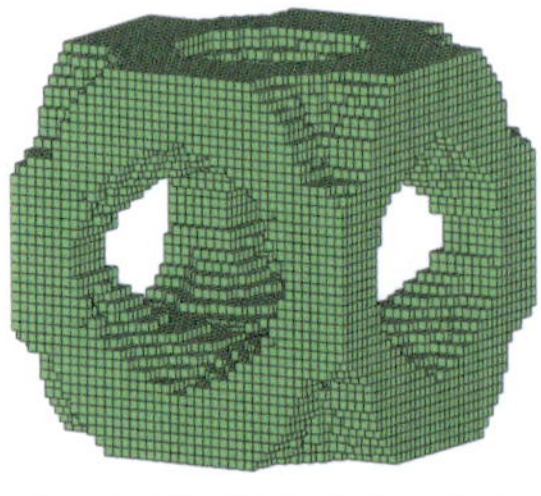	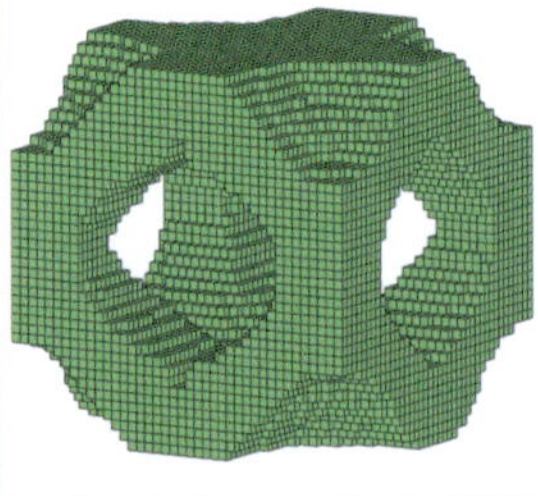	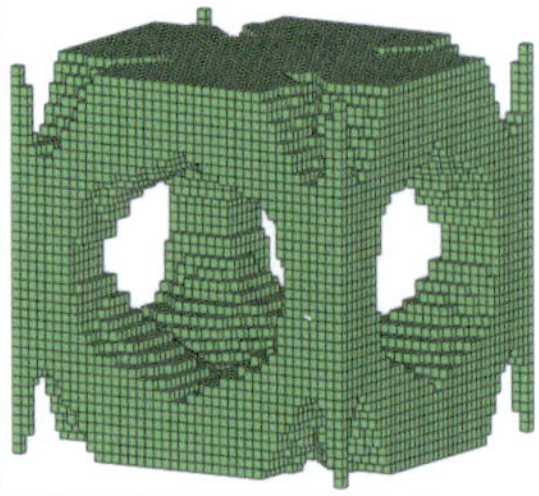
$\mathbf{C}^* = 1.10\mathbf{C}^0$	$\mathbf{C}^* = 1.15\mathbf{C}^0$	$\mathbf{C}^* = 1.20\mathbf{C}^0$
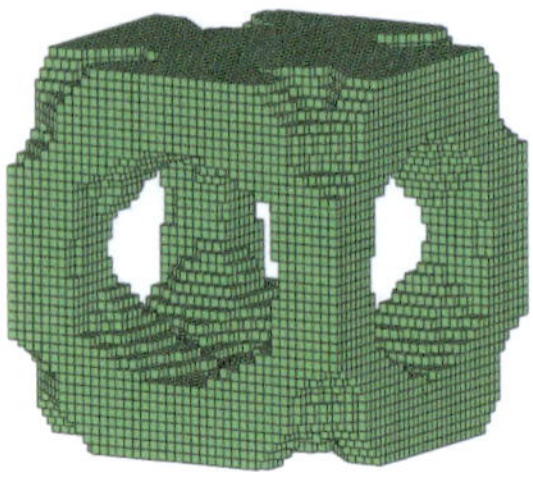	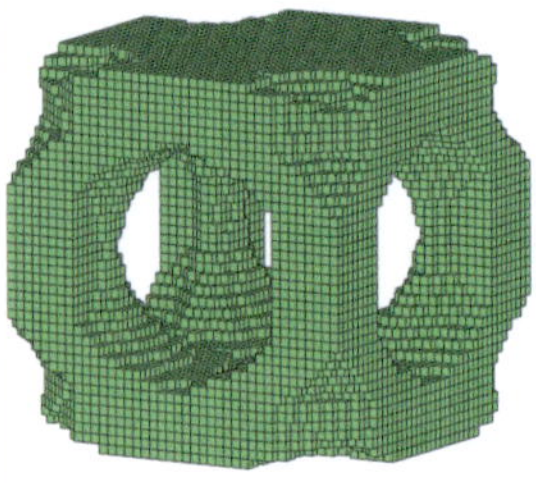	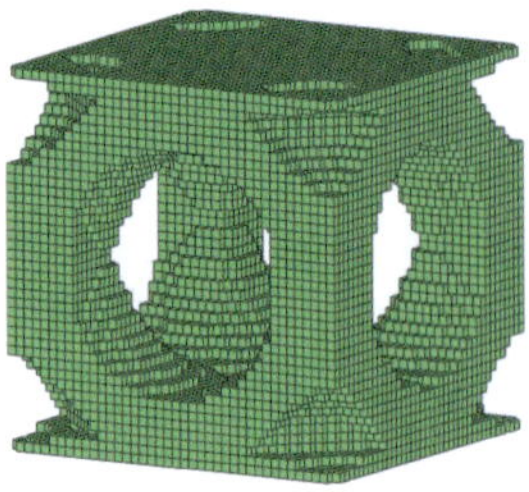

Following the design optimisation, the scaffolds are examined for their remodelling performance in terms of neotissue volume. Here, a remodelling rate constant $\alpha = 0.75$ is used; we keep the lazy zone ($2s$=4/3) and site-specific homeostatic equilibrium (ψ_n=0.03) unchanged in all the remodelling simulations for comparison. The remodelling results in scaffolds with different stiffness values are shown in Table 12.3. These neotissue elements indicate different distribution patterns in the different base cells. Note that the generation of neotissue affects the stiffness of the scaffold, which in turn affects the remodelling in the subsequent steps.

Figure 12.1 compares the remodelling results for different base cells of scaffold over a time frame of 20 steps. Obviously, the stiffness design with $\beta = 1.00$ generates the highest bone volume, indicating its clear merit in stimulating

Table 12.3 Results of remodelling in scaffolds with different stiffnesses ($\alpha = 0.75$)

$\mathbf{C}^* = 0.80\mathbf{C}^0$	$\mathbf{C}^* = 0.85\mathbf{C}^0$	$\mathbf{C}^* = 0.90\mathbf{C}^0$
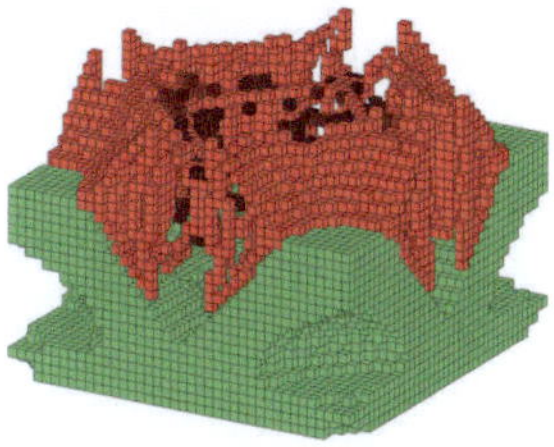	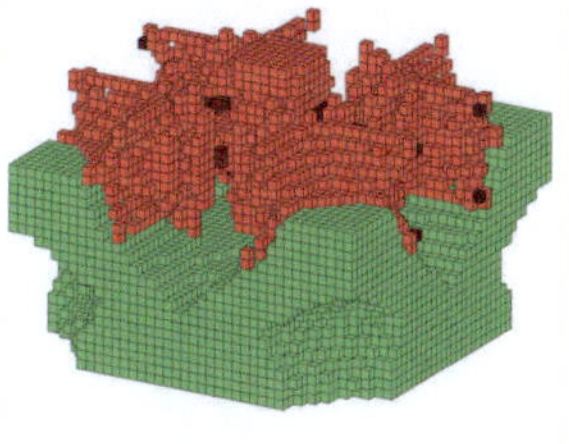	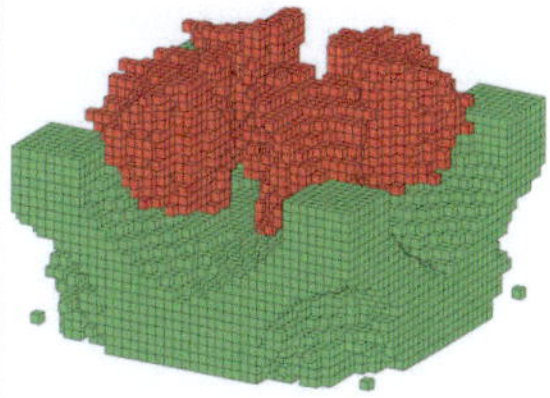
$\mathbf{C}^* = 0.95\mathbf{C}^0$	$\mathbf{C}^* = 1.00\mathbf{C}^0$	$\mathbf{C}^* = 1.05\mathbf{C}^0$
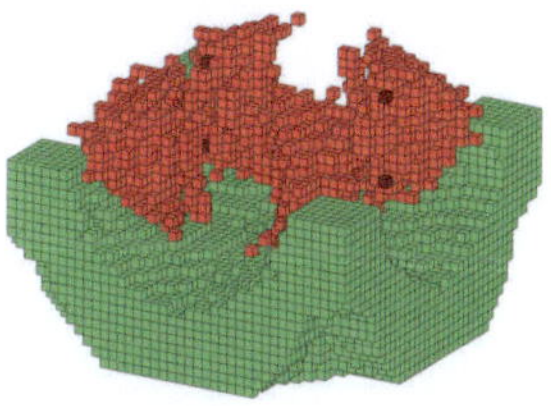	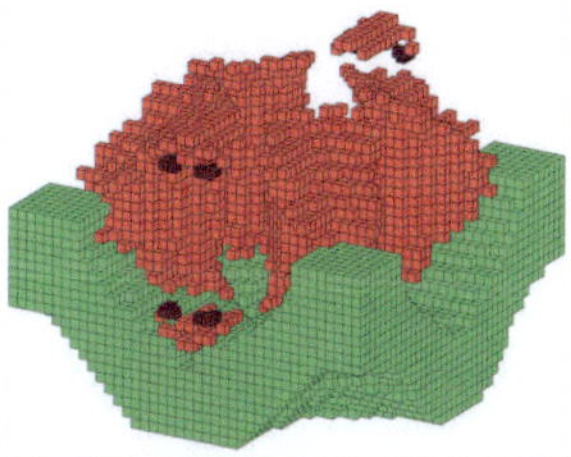	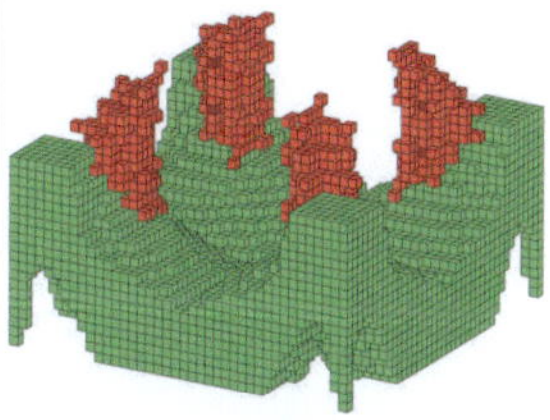
$\mathbf{C}^* = 1.10\mathbf{C}^0$	$\mathbf{C}^* = 1.15\mathbf{C}^0$	$\mathbf{C}^* = 1.20\mathbf{C}^0$
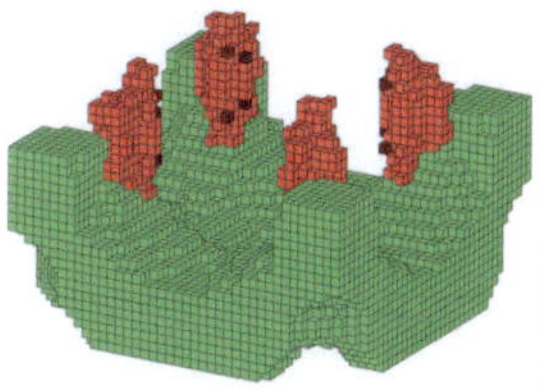	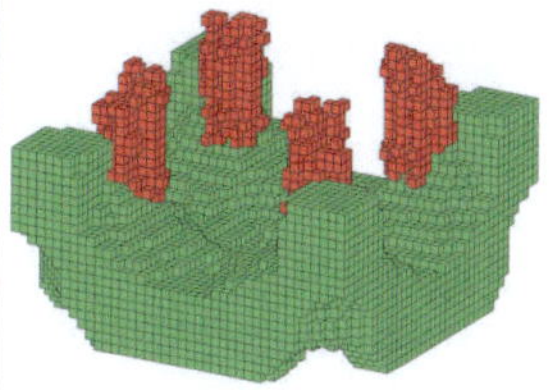	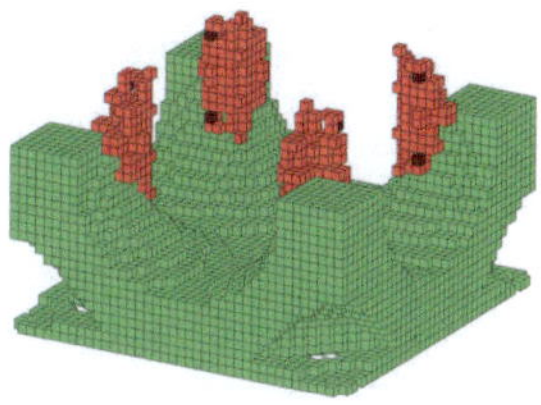

neotissue regeneration. Interestingly, although the tissue growth is not the fastest for $\beta = 1.00$ in the beginning, it exceeds all others after five time steps and maintains its leading position until reaching the state of equilibrium.

The reason why the scaffolds with lower β (e.g. $\beta = 0.80$) exhibits higher neotissue growth in the beginning is that their higher flexibility makes the high SED distribution spread out more evenly inside the scaffold structure. Nevertheless, this advantage quickly diminishes when neotissue stiffens the inner walls of the scaffolds.

In the bone remodelling simulations, the load is not applied directly onto the scaffolds but via a rigid plate on the top of the base cell. The remodelling parameters, ψ_n, s and the uniaxial loading are prescribed with the reasonable values to make tissue remodelling visible from an early stage and comparable in the final stage. It should be noted, however, that selection of the remodelling parameters does not influence the scaffold's relative performance in remodelling.

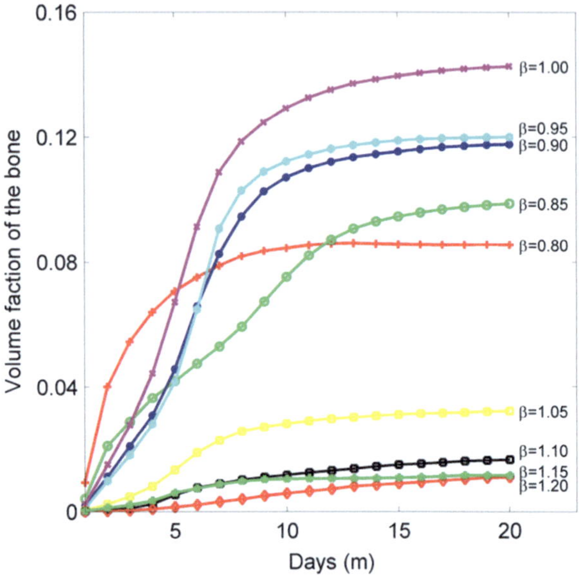

Fig. 12.1 Bone remodelling processes in scaffolds with different stiffness values over time ($\alpha = 0.75$) (Reprinted from Ref. [16], Copyright 2010, with permission from Elsevier)

12.3.2 Example for Target Diffusivity

As shown in Table 12.4, different designs of base cells have been obtained using the topology optimisation technique where each model has attained its prescribed effective diffusivity value. The porosity of the base cells were 50 % in all design scenarios. Here we have considered two diffusivity targets: one is 0.75 times the theoretical maximum value (i.e. $\mathbf{D}^H = 0.75\mathbf{D}^{\max}$) and the other is 0.5 times the theoretical maximum value (i.e. $\mathbf{D}^H = 0.5\mathbf{D}^{\max}$), where $\boldsymbol{D}^{\max}$ is 0.4 at a porosity of 50 %. Distinct structural features can be observed in these models with different diffusivity targets and among the models with the same diffusivity target but different initialisation settings (Table 12.4b–d).

The results show that for given a diffusivity target lower than the theoretical maximum ($D^{max} = 0.4$), topology optimisation process does not produce a unique solution. In fact, the resultant architecture of base cell is influenced by the choice of its initial model as well as optimisation parameters, as demonstrated by simulation results (b), (c) and (d) in Table 12.4. It is noted that although models (a) and (b) have different diffusivity targets, their structures are somehow similar, which is likely a result of using the same initial model. This reflects the nature of the inverse homogenisation where multiple design solutions may be found to be of a similar goal [50].

Table 12.4 Base cells of tissue scaffold with different diffusivity targets and different initialisation settings

Design target	Optimised base cell	Periodic structure $3 \times 3 \times 3$
(a) Initial design 1: $\mathbf{D}^* = 0.75\mathbf{D}^{max}_{50\%}$ $\mathbf{D}^H = \begin{bmatrix} 0.2995 & 0 & 0 \\ 0 & 0.2995 & 0 \\ 0 & 0 & 0.2995 \end{bmatrix}$	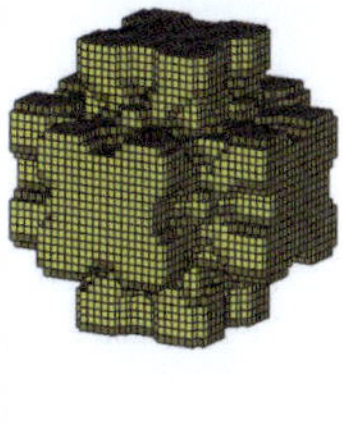	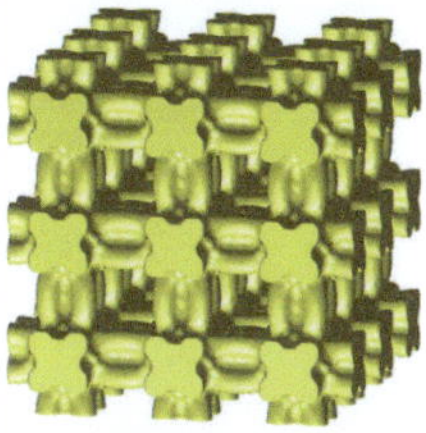
(b) Initial design 1: $\mathbf{D}^* = 0.50\mathbf{D}^{\mathrm{max}}_{50\,\%}$ $\mathbf{D}^H = \begin{bmatrix} 0.2020 & 0 & 0 \\ 0 & 0.2020 & 0 \\ 0 & 0 & 0.2020 \end{bmatrix}$	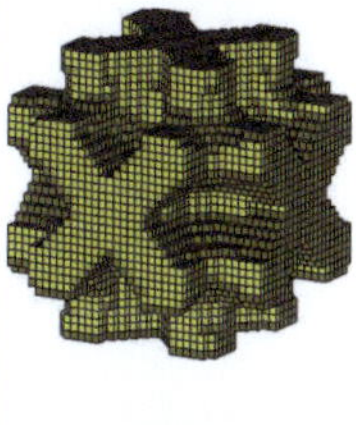	
(c) Initial design 2: $\mathbf{D}^* = 0.50\mathbf{D}^{\mathrm{max}}_{50\,\%}$ $\mathbf{D}^H = \begin{bmatrix} 0.2000 & 0 & 0 \\ 0 & 0.2000 & 0 \\ 0 & 0 & 0.2000 \end{bmatrix}$		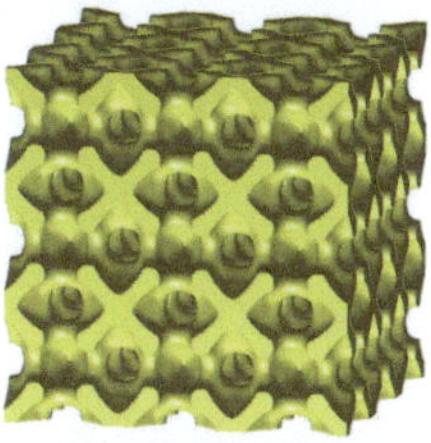
(d) Initial design 3: $\mathbf{D}^* = 0.50\mathbf{D}^{\mathrm{max}}_{50\,\%}$ $\mathbf{D}^H = \begin{bmatrix} 0.2006 & 0 & 0 \\ 0 & 0.2006 & 0 \\ 0 & 0 & 0.2006 \end{bmatrix}$	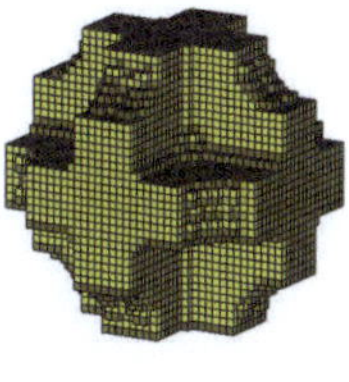	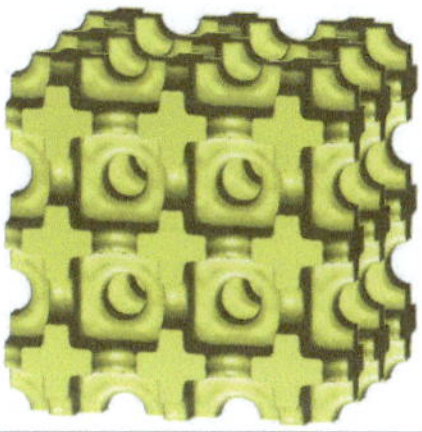

12.3.3 *Example for Combined Stiffness and Diffusivity*

We can also combine the stiffness and diffusivity criteria to create a multiobjective optimisation problem. In this chapter, we have formulated it as a maximisation problem of these two material properties as shown in Eq. (12.12). A full spectrum of base cell designs, each with a special weight factor from Eq. (12.12), has been obtained thereafter to construct the Pareto front (Fig. 12.2). The porosity of base cell remains to be 50 % in all these optimal designs.

Some resultant base cells are shown in Table 12.5, where yellow blocks represent solid and the rest of the domain is void. At $w_C = 0$ (indicating the diffusivity

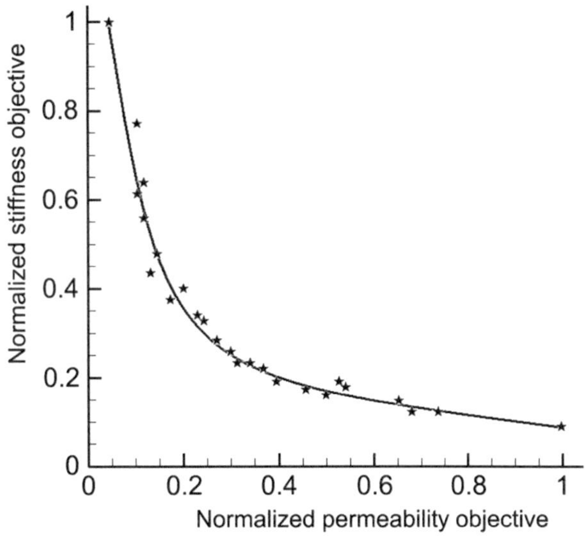

Fig. 12.2 Pareto front of the 3D multiobjective topology optimisation

maximisation only [49]), solid phase becomes discontinuous, and the design cannot be fabricated and utilised in reality. As w_C increases, the solid interconnection strengthens. The solid phase has a rounder shape at a low w_C value and acquires a more rigid shape as w_C approaches to 1. When w_C reaches 1, the porous phase becomes discontinuous, which prevents all biotransport in the scaffold.

Following the multiobjective topology optimisation, three representative base cell designs shown in Table 12.5b–d are further examined for polymeric degradation and mechanoregulatory tissue regeneration. Figure 12.3 shows the percentages of cell phenotypes in different design cases in the course of regeneration. It can be seen that, as the emphasis on the diffusivity increases (i.e. from Case (b) to Case (d)), the corresponding design has more osteoblasts (approximately 15 %) differentiated from MSCs.

Note that although Case (d) ($w_C = 0.48$) has a relatively lower stiffness in the initial design due to more emphasis on the diffusivity design ($w_D = 0.52$), it exhibits good connectivity of regenerated bony tissue structures, thereby presenting higher effective properties in both stiffness and permeability in the final tissue–scaffold construct. It also promotes effective tissue regeneration and results in more bone formation than the other two cases which have higher w_C. This may suggest that, as long as the scaffold stiffness meets the requirements for mechanical support, increasing the diffusivity of scaffold design can be more beneficial. In other words, the diffusivity criterion appears to play a more critical role than the stiffness criterion in the design of scaffold microarchitecture if enhancing tissue regeneration is the primary goal.

It must be pointed out that while the remodelling results shown in Table 12.3 and Fig. 12.3 provide important insights into the time-dependent outcomes of these several optimised scaffolds, the challenge remains how to optimise the scaffold for

Table 12.5 Optimised base cells with combined stiffness and diffusivity objective

Design with combined stiffness and diffusivity	Optimised base cell	Periodic structure $3 \times 3 \times 3$
(a) $w_C = 1.0$, $w_D = 0.0$ $C_{11}^H = C_{22}^H = C_{33}^H = 0.4412$ $C_{44}^H = C_{55}^H = C_{66}^H = 0.1006$ $D_{11}^H = D_{22}^H = D_{33}^H = 0$	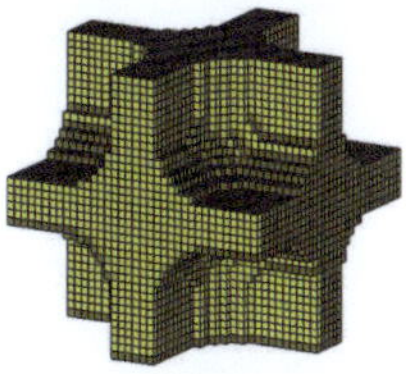	
(b) $w_C = 0.92$, $w_D = 0.08$ $C_{11}^H = C_{22}^H = C_{33}^H = 0.3861$ $C_{44}^H = C_{55}^H = C_{66}^H = 0.0880$ $D_{11}^H = D_{22}^H = D_{33}^H = 0.0269$	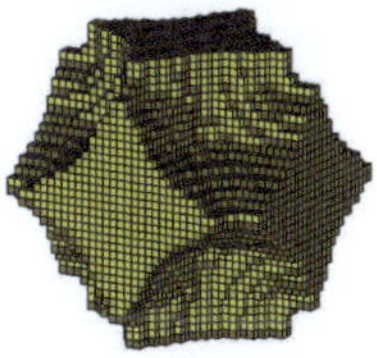	
(c) $w_C = 0.64$, $w_D = 0.36$ $C_{11}^H = C_{22}^H = C_{33}^H = 0.3443$ $C_{44}^H = C_{55}^H = C_{66}^H = 0.0744$ $D_{11}^H = D_{22}^H = D_{33}^H = 0.1538$	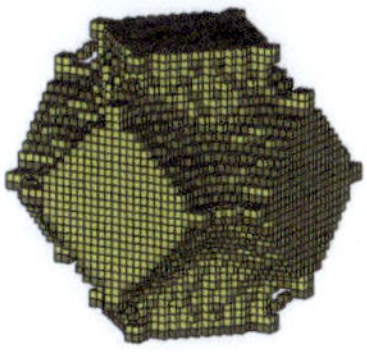	
(d) $w_C = 0.48$, $w_D = 0.52$ $C_{11}^H = C_{22}^H = C_{33}^H = 0.3336$ $C_{44}^H = C_{55}^H = C_{66}^H = 0.0714$ $D_{11}^H = D_{22}^H = D_{33}^H = 0.3237$		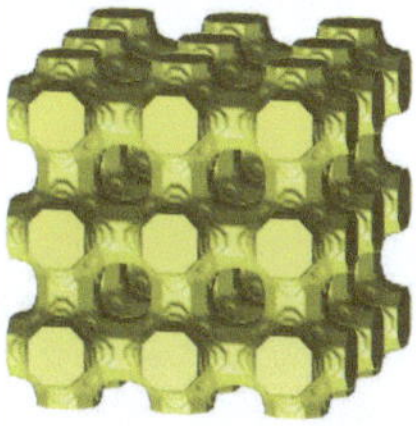
(e) $w_C = 0.0$, $w_D = 0.1$ $C_{11}^H = C_{22}^H = C_{33}^H = 0$ $C_{44}^H = C_{55}^H = C_{66}^H = 0$ $D_{11}^H = D_{22}^H = D_{33}^H = 0.3975$	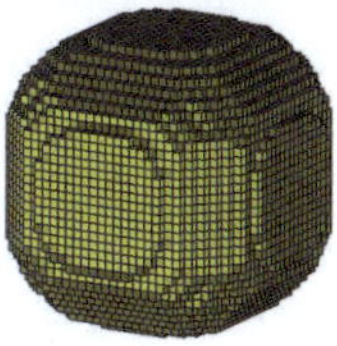	

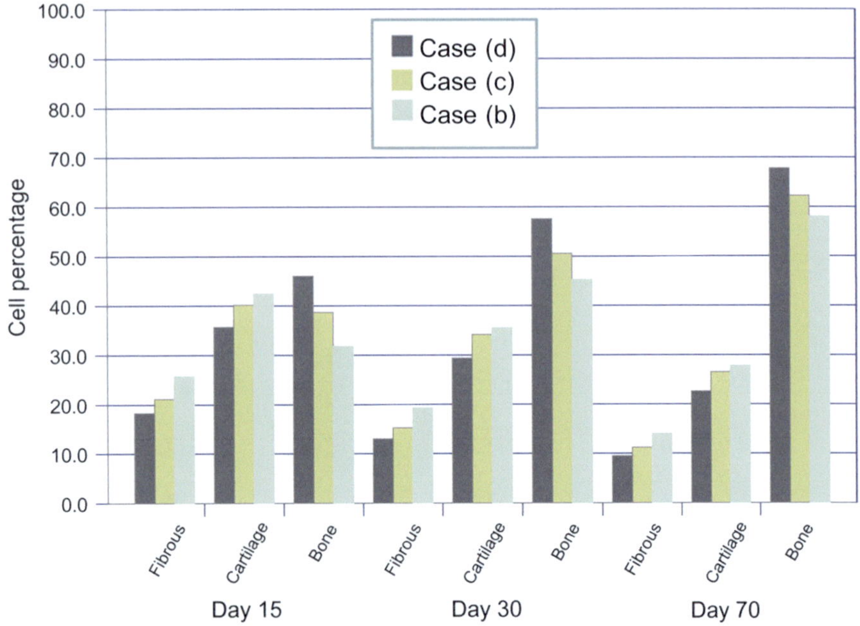

Fig. 12.3 Percentages of cell phenotypes during tissue regeneration within different scaffold architectures in the three representative cases (Reprinted from Ref. [6], Copyright 2011, with permission from Elsevier)

assuring an ongoing, rather than initial, performance. This implies that the remodelling-based design optimisation should be a topic for the futuristic studies.

12.4 Conclusion

This chapter developed a systematic methodology for structural design of periodic tissue scaffolds, in which the mechanical and biological requirements of scaffold were formulated as the stiffness and diffusivity criteria. In the periodic structures, base cell finite element (FE) models were created under periodic boundary conditions. To characterise the effective stiffness and effective diffusivity, the finite element-based homogenisation technique was employed. For any given base cell materials and configuration, the effective or homogenised properties can be obtained from the finite element analysis.

In order to attain desired effective material properties, an inverse homogenisation was formulated to seek possible base cell configuration. In this chapter, we considered three different design scenarios: (1) desired stiffness, (2) desired diffusivity and (3) combination of maximum stiffness and diffusivity. It was shown that these different criteria led to different base cell topologies.

To assess the performance of optimised scaffolds under different criteria, we also modelled the tissue regeneration in these scaffolds and examined their relative performances in terms of volume of functional tissues (e.g. bone). The remodelling calculation on these different scaffold structures provided some important insights into how to impose these design criteria for achieving certain tissue generation outcome.

It must be pointed out that the design optimisation presented in this chapter has restricted to two relatively simple criteria (elasticity and diffusivity) from a biomechanical perspective and topological variables from a structural perspective. As a matter of fact, tissue engineering is a highly complex process and involves a full range of multidisciplinary challenges and requirements. The future optimisation of scaffolds should therefore consider as many relevant factors as possible with other design variables, such as chemical composition and growth factor concentration, rather than structural topology.

Acknowledgement The financial supports from the Australian Research Council through the Future Fellowship and Discovery Scheme are greatly appreciated.

References

1. Langer R, Vacanti JP (1993) Tissue engineering. Science 260(5110):920–926
2. Lin CY, Kikuchi N, Hollister SJ (2004) A novel method for biomaterial scaffold internal architecture design to match bone elastic properties with desired porosity. J Biomech 37 (5):623–636
3. Hollister SJ (2005) Porous scaffold design for tissue engineering. Nat Mater 4(7):518–524
4. Lin CY et al (2005) Functional bone engineering using ex vivo gene therapy and topology-optimized, biodegradable polymer composite scaffolds. Tissue Eng 11(9–10):1589–1598
5. Hollister SJ, Maddoxa RD, Taboas JM (2002) Optimal design and fabrication of scaffolds. Biomaterials 23:4095–4103
6. Chen Y, Zhou S, Li Q (2011) Microstructure design of biodegradable scaffold and its effect on tissue regeneration. Biomaterials 32(22):5003–5014
7. Adachi T et al (2006) Framework for optimal design of porous scaffold microstructure by computational simulation of bone regeneration. Biomaterials 27(21):3964–3972
8. MacArthur BD, Oreffo ROC (2005) Bridging the gap. Nature 433(7021):19
9. Sanz-Herrera JA, Garcia-Aznar JM, Doblare M (2009) On scaffold designing for bone regeneration: a computational multiscale approach. ACTA Biomater 5:219–229
10. Sun W et al (2004) Computer-aided tissue engineering: application to biomimetic modelling and design of tissue scaffolds. Biotechnol Appl Biochem 39(1):49–58
11. Sun W et al (2005) Bio-CAD modeling and its applications in computer-aided tissue engineering. Comput Aided Des 37:1097–1114
12. Marga F et al (2012) Toward engineering functional organ modules by additive manufacturing. Biofabrication 4(2):12
13. Williams JM et al (2005) Bone tissue engineering using polycaprolactone scaffolds fabricated via selective laser sintering. Biomaterials 26(23):4817–4827
14. Hollister SJ (2009) Scaffold design and manufacturing: from concept to clinic. Adv Mater 21 (32–33):3330–3342

15. Fang Z, Starly B, Sun W (2005) Computer-aided characterization for effective mechanical properties of porous tissue scaffolds. CAD Comput Aid Des 31:65–72
16. Sturm S et al (2010) On stiffness of scaffolds for bone tissue engineering—a numerical study. J Biomech 43(9):1738–1744
17. Byrne DP et al (2007) Simulation of tissue differentiation in a scaffold as a function of porosity, Young's modulus and dissolution rate: application of mechanobiological models in tissue engineering. Biomaterials 28:5544–5554
18. Chen Y, Zhou S, Li Q (2011) Mathematical modeling of degradation for bulk-erosive polymers: applications in tissue engineering scaffolds and drug delivery systems. Acta Biomater 7 (3):1140–1149
19. Huiskes R et al (2000) Effects of mechanical forces on maintenance and adaptation of form in trabecular bone. Nature 405(6787):704–706
20. Sun W et al (2004) Computer-aided tissue engineering: overview, scope and challenges. Biotechnol Appl Biochem 39:29–47
21. Cadman JE et al (2013) On design of multi-functional microstructural materials. J Mater Sci 48 (1):51–66
22. Bensoussan A, Papanicolaou G, Lions JL (1978) Asymptotic analysis for periodic structures, vol 5, Studies in mathematics and its applications. North Holland Publishing Co., Amsterdam. xxiv, 700 23 cm
23. Sanchez-Palencia E (1980) Non-homogeneous media and vibration theory. Lecture Notes in Physics. Vol 127. Springer, Berlin
24. Guedes JM, Kikuchi N (1990) Preprocessing and postprocessing for materials based on the homogenization method with adaptive finite element methods. Comput Methods Appl Mech Eng 83:143–198
25. Hassani B, Hinton E (1998) A review of homogenization and topology optimization I – homogenization theory for media with periodic structure. Comput Struct 69(6):707–717
26. Bendsoe MP, Sigmund O (2013) Topology optimization: theory, methods, and applications. Springer Science & Business Media, Berlin
27. Silva ECN, Fonseca JSO, Kikuchi N (1998) Optimal design of periodic piezocomposites. Comput Methods Appl Mech Eng 159(1-2):49–77
28. Sigmund O (1994) Design of material structures using topology optimisation. Technical University of Denmark, Lyngby
29. Sigmund O (1994) Tailoring materials for specific needs. J Intell Mater Syst Struct 5 (6):736–742
30. Catledge SA et al (2007) An electrospun triphasic nanofibrous scaffold for bone tissue engineering. Biomed Mater 2:142–150
31. Aubert G, Kornprobst P (2006) Mathematical problems in image processing:partial differential equations and the calculus of variations. 2nd edn. Springer, New York, xxxi:377
32. Wang MY, Zhou S, Ding H (2004) Nonlinear diffusions in topology optimization. Struct Multidiscip Optim 28(4):262–276
33. Svanberg K (1987) The method of moving asymptotes – a new method for structural optimization. Int J Numer Methods Eng 24(2):359–373
34. Malda J et al (2004) Oxygen gradients in tissue – engineered Pegt/Pbt cartilaginous constructs: measurement and modeling. Biotechnol Bioeng 86(1):9–18
35. Steven G, Li Q, Xie Y (2000) Evolutionary topology and shape design for general physical field problems. Comput Mech 26(2):129–139
36. Zhou S et al (2012) Design and fabrication of biphasic cellular materials with transport properties–a modified bidirectional evolutionary structural optimization procedure and MATLAB program. Int J Heat Mass Transf 55(25):8149–8162
37. Kang H, Lin C-Y, Hollister SJ (2010) Topology optimization of three dimensional tissue engineering scaffold architectures for prescribed bulk modulus and diffusivity. Struct Multidiscip Optim 42(4):633–644

38. Guest JK, Prevost JH (2006) Optimizing multifunctional materials: design of microstructures for maximized stiffness and fluid permeability. Int J Solids Struct 43(22-23):7028–7047
39. de Kruijf N et al (2007) Topological design of structures and composite materials with multiobjectives. Int J Solids Struct 44(22):7092–7109
40. Chen Y, Zhou S, Li Q (2009) Computational design for multifunctional microstructural composites. Int J Mod Phys B 23(06n07):1345–1351
41. Chen Y, Zhou S, Li Q (2010) Multiobjective topology optimization for finite periodic structures. Comput Struct 88(11):806–811
42. Hollister SJ, Lin CY (2007) Computational design of tissue engineering scaffolds. Comput Methods Appl Mech Eng 196(31–32):2991–2998
43. Parfitt AM (1994) Osteonal and hemi-osteonal remodeling – the spatial and temporal framework for signal traffic in adult human bone. J Cell Biochem 55(3):273–286
44. Carter DR (1984) Mechanical loading histories and cortical bone remodeling. Calcif Tissue Int 36:S19–S24
45. Huiskes R et al (1987) Adaptive bone-remodeling theory applied to prosthetic-design analysis. J Biomech 20(11–12):1135–1150
46. Rice JC, Cowin SC, Bowman JA (1988) On the dependence of the elasticity and strength of cancellous bone on apparent density. J Biomech 21(2):155–168
47. Beaupré GS, Orr TE, Carter DR (1990) An approach for time-dependent bone modeling and remodeling – theoretical development. J Orthop Res 8:651–661
48. Prendergast PJ, Huiskes R, Soballe K (1997) Biophysical stimuli on cells during tissue differentiation at implant interfaces. J Biomech 30(6):539–548
49. Guest JK, Prevost JH (2007) Design of maximum permeability material structures. Comput Methods Appl Mech Eng 196(4–6):1006–1017
50. Zhou S, Li Q (2008) Computational design of multi-phase microstructural materials for extremal conductivity. Comput Mater Sci 43(3):549–564

Chapter 13
Bioactive Scaffolds with Multifunctional Properties for Hard Tissue Regenerations

Chengtie Wu, Jiang Chang, and Yin Xiao

Abstract The impact of bone/dental diseases and trauma in the whole world has increased significantly in the past decades. It is of great importance to develop bioactive scaffolds with multifunctional properties, such as osteogenesis, angiogenesis, cementogenesis, drug delivery and antibacterial property for hard tissue regeneration. Conventional bioactive scaffolds cannot efficiently combine these functions. A new class of bioactive glass, referred to as mesoporous bioactive glass (MBG), was developed several years ago, which possesses highly ordered mesoporous channel structure and high-specific surface area. Due to their special nanostructure, MBG scaffolds show multifunctional potential for hard tissue regeneration application. In this chapter, we review the recent research advances of multifunctional MBG scaffolds, including the preparation of different forms of MBG scaffolds, osteogenesis, angiogenesis, cementogenesis, drug delivery and antibacterial property. The future perspective of MBG scaffolds was further discussed for hard tissue regeneration application by harnessing their special multifunction.

Keywords Bioactive scaffolds • Mesoporous bioactive glass • Multifunction • Osteogenesis • Angiogenesis

13.1 Introduction

The treatment of hard tissue defects, especially large bone and periodontal defects resulting from trauma, infection, tumour or genetic malformation, represents a major challenge for clinicians [1]. To solve these problems, bioactive porous

C. Wu (✉) • J. Chang
State Key Laboratory of High Performance Ceramics and Superfine Microstructure, Shanghai Institute of Ceramics, Chinese Academy of Sciences, 200050 Shanghai, People's Republic of China
e-mail: chengtiewu@mail.sic.ac.cn

Y. Xiao
Institute of Health & Biomedical Innovation, Queensland University of Technology, 4059 Brisbane, QLD, Australia

Q. Li, Y.-W. Mai (eds.), *Biomaterials for Implants and Scaffolds*, Springer Series in Biomaterials Science and Engineering 8, DOI 10.1007/978-3-662-53574-5_13

scaffolds have been widely studied to regenerate the lost/damaged hard tissues [2]. For better regeneration of large hard tissue defects, bioactive scaffolds should possess not only osteoconductivity (for guidance of new bone growth) but also the ability to stimulate both osteogenesis (for promoting new bone formation) and angiogenesis (for inducing vascularisation) [1, 3–5]. In addition, in bone reconstruction surgery, osteomyelitis caused by bacterial infection is an ever-present and serious complication. Conventional treatments include systemic antibiotic administration, surgical debridement, wound drainage and implant removal [6]. These approaches, however, are rather inefficient and may result in additional surgical interventions for the patients.

A new approach for solving this problem is to introduce local drug release system into the implant site. The advantages of this treatment include high delivery efficiency, continuous action, reduced toxicity and convenience to the patients [6, 7]. For this reason, bioactive scaffolds with an in-built drug delivery and antibacterial property would be very useful for bone and periodontal tissue regeneration and could solve the risk of osteomyelitis incidences caused by infection of the bone. Therefore, ideal bioactive porous scaffolds for the treatment of large bone and periodontal defects should possess multiple functions by combining angiogenesis, osteostimulation and drug delivery with antibacterial properties. However, to our best knowledge, few bioactive porous scaffolds possess such 'real' multifunctional properties [8].

Conventional bioactive calcium phosphate (Ca-P)-based bioceramic scaffolds, such as hydroxyapatite (HAp) and β-tricalcium phosphate (β-TCP), possess osteoconductivity, but lack osteostimulation and drug delivery function due to few nanopores in the sintered scaffolds treated by high temperature. Recent study has shown that the sintered Ca-P-based bioceramics, especially HAp, lack full biodegradability after implantation [9, 10]. Although β-TCP ceramics have been regarded as biodegradable materials, their degradation kinetics tends to be slow [11].

Bioactive glasses have played an increasingly important role in bone tissue regeneration applications by virtue of their generally excellent osteoconductivity, osteostimulation and degradation rate [1, 12–16]. Typically, the melt bioactive glass, called 45S5 Bioglass®, was pioneered by Hench [17, 18] and was first developed using traditional melt method at high temperature (1300–1500 °C). The 45S5 Bioglass® has been regarded as bioactive bone regeneration materials which are able to bond closely with the host bone tissue [17]. Further studies have also showed that the Ca and Si containing ionic products released from the 45S5 contribute to its bioactivity, as both Ca and Si are found to stimulate osteoblast proliferation and differentiation [19–24]. Xynos et al. further found that 45S5 Bioglass® is able to enhance the expression of a potent osteoblast mitogenic growth factor, insulin-like growth factor-2 (IGF-2) [23, 25]. However, the 45S5 Bioglass® has a number of limitations [25]. One of them is the fact that it needs to be melted at a very high temperature (>1300 °C), and the other is its lack of microporous structure inside the materials with low specific surface area; therefore, the bioactivity of melt bioactive glasses will mainly depend on the contents of SiO_2

[25]. Generally, the bioactivity of melt bioactive glasses will decrease with the increase in the SiO_2 contents [1, 18, 26]. In the early 1990s, in an effort to overcome the limitation of melt bioactive glasses, Li et al. prepared sol–gel bioactive glasses [27]. Although sol–gel bioactive glasses have better compositional range and bioactivity than melt bioactive glasses, the micropore distribution is not uniform and inadequate for efficient drug loading and release [25, 28, 29].

To overcome the limitations of conventional bioactive glasses (without well-ordered mesopore structures for drug delivery), it is of great importance to design and develop a new class of biomaterials which combine multifunctional properties, such as osteogenesis, angiogenesis, drug delivery and antibacterial characteristics. Yu et al., for the first time, prepared the mesoporous bioactive glass (MBG) particles in 2004 by the combination of sol–gel method and supramolecular chemistry of surfactants [30, 31]. Their study has paved a new avenue for applying nanotechnology to regenerative medicine by coupling drug delivery with bioactive materials. Their materials are based on a CaO-SiO_2-P_2O_5 composition and have a highly ordered mesopore channel structure with a nanoscale pore size ranging from 5 to 20 nm. Compared to conventional non-mesopore bioactive glasses (NBG), the MBG possesses a more optimal surface area, pore volume, ability to induce in vitro apatite mineralisation in SBF and excellent cytocompatibility [31–35]. However, for bone and periodontal tissue regeneration, MBG particles are not always ideal. It is of great interest and importance to develop MBG scaffolds with multifunctional properties. Therefore, in this chapter, we review the recent advances of MBG scaffolds, as multifunctional materials for hard tissue regeneration.

13.2 Preparation and Characterisation of Multifunctional MBG Scaffolds

MBG scaffolds could be prepared by three approaches [35]. The first is the porogen method, in which Yun et al. applied methyl cellulose as the porogen to prepare porous MBG scaffolds with large pore size of 100 μm and mesopore size of around 5 nm; however, the prepared large pores are not fairly uniform and interconnective though the mesoporous channels are well ordered [36].

The second is the polymer template method, which has been widely used. We, for the first time, prepared the MBG scaffolds with a large pore size of 400 μm by using polyurethane sponge as a porous template [37]. At the same time, Li et al. also prepared the MBG scaffolds using the same technique [38]. After that, we have developed a series of MBG scaffolds with varying compositions for drug delivery and bone tissue engineering applications as shown in Fig. 13.1 [7, 39–41]. The advantages of the MBG scaffolds prepared by the polyurethane sponge template method are their highly interconnective pore structure and controllable pore size (porosity), while the disadvantage is the low mechanical strength of the material

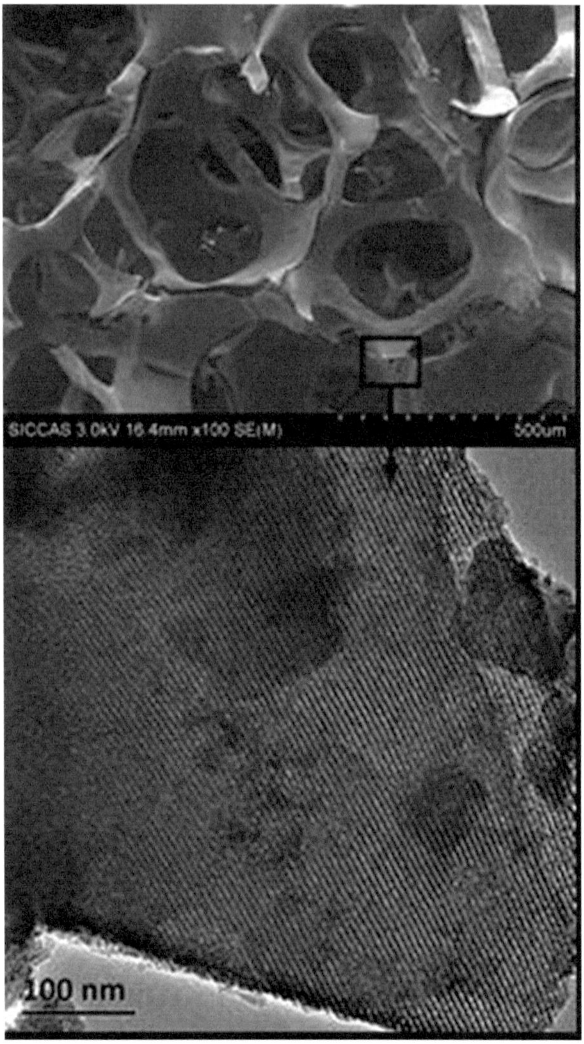

Fig. 13.1 SEM and TEM analysis for the MBG scaffolds prepared by spongy template method. SEM (*upper image*) showed highly interconnective porous scaffolds with large pore size of 300–500 μm; TEM (*lower image*) showed that the large pore walls of scaffolds had well-ordered mesoporous channel structure (around 5 nm)

[42]. The compressive strength of the MBG scaffolds prepared by the polymer template method is lower than 200 kPa.

To better control the pore morphology, pore size, porosity and mechanical strength, 3D plotting technique (also called additive fabrication, direct writing or printing) has been developed to prepare porous MBG scaffolds. The significant advantage of this technique is that the architectures of the scaffolds can be concisely controlled by layer-by-layer plotting under mild conditions [43–45]. Yun and Garcia, et al. prepared the hierarchical 3D porous MBG scaffolds using a combination of double polymer template and rapid prototyping techniques [46, 47]. In their study, they mixed the MBG gel with methylcellulose and then printed, sintered at 500–700 °C to remove polymer templates for obtaining the MBG scaffolds. The main limitation of their method for preparing MBG scaffolds is the need of methylcellulose and the additional sintering procedure. Although the obtained MBG scaffolds have uniform pore structure, their mechanical strength is compromised because of the incorporation of methylcellulose which results in some micropores. Recently, we reported a new facile method to prepare hierarchical and multifunctional MBG scaffolds with controllable pore architecture, excellent mechanical strength and mineralisation ability for bone regeneration application by a modified 3D printing technique using polyvinyl alcohol (PVA) as a binder as shown in Fig. 13.2. The 3D-printed MBG scaffolds obtained possess a high mechanical strength which is about 200 times of that of the MBG scaffolds prepared using traditional polyurethane foam as templates. The compressive strength could reach 16 MPa. Such scaffolds have highly controllable pore

Fig. 13.2 MBG scaffolds, pore morphology and microstructure. (**a**) MBG scaffolds, obtained by the 3D printing method with different sizes, shapes and morphologies. (**b**, **c** and **d**) MBG scaffolds with different pore sizes (varying from 1307 ± 40 μm (**b**) and 1001 ± 48 μm (**c**) to 624 ± 40 μm (**d**)). (**d**, **e** and **f**) MBG scaffolds with different pore morphologies. (**g**) Pore morphology of the bottom side for MBG scaffolds. The pores on the bottom side keep open. (**h**) SEM image of the microstructure of pore walls. (**i**) TEM micrographs demonstrating the well-ordered mesopore channel structure of the pore walls in scaffolds; the size of mesopore channel is about 5 nm (Reprinted with permission from Ref. [48] copyright 2011 by Elsevier)

Table 13.1 The mesoporous structure characteristics of MBG scaffolds

Scaffold compositions	Surface area (m^2/g)	Pore volume (cm^3/g)	Pore size (nm)	References
$CaO-P_2O_5-SiO_2$	350	0.33	4.8	[37]
$CuO-CaO-P_2O_5-SiO_2$	310–330	0.36–0.44	3.8–4.7	[8]
$CoO-CaO-P_2O_5-SiO_2$	127–180	0.15–0.19	4.1–4.5	[49]
$SrO-CaO-P_2O_5-SiO_2$	88–200	0.11–0.27	5.0	[50]
$MgO-CaO-P_2O_5-SiO_2$	269	0.34	3.6	[51]
$B_2O_3-CaO-P_2O_5-SiO_2$	194–234	0.21–0.24	5.1–5.3	[41]
$Fe_2O_3-CaO-P_2O_5-SiO_2$	268	–	4.5	[40]
$ZrO_2-CaO-P_2O_5-SiO_2$	227–287	0.27–0.32	3.4–4.1	[7]

architecture, excellent apatite mineralisation ability and sustained drug delivery property [35, 48].

Currently, the prepared MBG scaffolds are mainly based on the compositions of $CaO-P_2O_5-SiO_2-MxOy$ (M: Cu, Co, Zr, Zn, Sr and B) system. The incorporation of functional elements of Cu, Co, Zr, Zn, Sr or B decreased the surface area and mesopore volume of MBG scaffolds. However, they still maintain high mesoporous level, and their surface area and mesopore volume are generally in the range of 200–400 m^2/g and 0.2–0.4 cm^3/g, respectively. The well-ordered mesopore size of the prepared MBG scaffolds is in the range of 4–5.5 nm. The typical structural characteristics of the prepared MBG scaffolds with varied compositions are shown in Table 13.1.

13.3 The In Vitro and In Vivo Osteogenesis, Angiogenesis and Cementogenesis of Multifunctional MBG Scaffolds

In the past 5 years, we have systematically investigated the in vitro and in vivo osteogenesis, angiogenesis and cementogenesis of the MBG scaffolds incorporated with varied functional elements. It was found that these functional elements in the MBG scaffolds play an important role in improving their multifunctional properties. The functional effects of different elements in MBG scaffolds are summarised in Table 13.2.

13.3.1 The Osteogenesis of MBG Scaffolds

It was found that the MBG scaffolds possess excellent apatite mineralisation ability as shown in Fig. 13.3, which was regarded one of the critical factors to contribute to

Table 13.2 The multifunctional properties the MBG scaffolds with varied compositions

Scaffold compositions	Multifunctional properties
CaO-P_2O_5-SiO_2	Osteogenesis, drug delivery
MgO-CaO-P_2O_5-SiO_2	
B_2O_3-CaO-P_2O_5-SiO_2	
ZrO_2-CaO-P_2O_5-SiO_2	
CoO-CaO-P_2O_5-SiO_2	Osteogenesis, angiogenesis, drug delivery
CuO-CaO-P_2O_5-SiO_2	
Fe_2O_3-CaO-P_2O_5-SiO_2	Osteogenesis, hypothermia, drug delivery
SrO-CaO-P_2O_5-SiO_2	Osteogenesis, cementogenesis, drug delivery
Li_2O-CaO-P_2O_5-SiO_2	

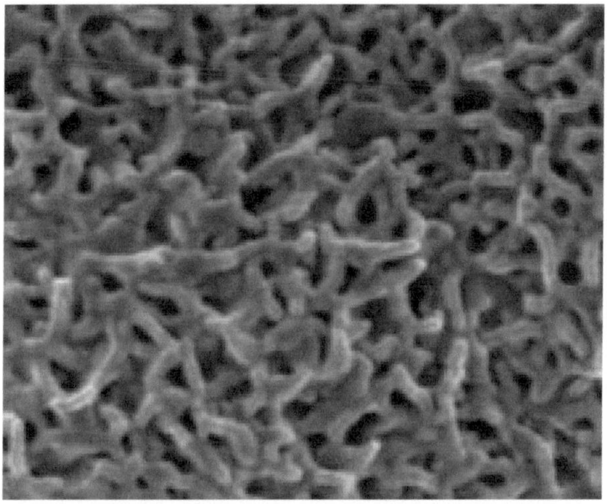

Fig. 13.3 The MBG scaffolds possess excellent apatite mineralisation ability in the simulated body fluids

the in vivo bioactivity of bone regeneration materials. Compared with non-mesoporous bioactive glass (NBG) scaffolds, the MBG scaffolds have significantly improved apatite mineralisation ability in simulated body fluids attributable to their high surface area and mesoporous volume [35]. In this regard, Garcia et al. studied the mechanism of apatite mineralisation of MBG by using nuclear magnetic resonance spectroscopy [52]. The significant difference of the apatite formation mechanism between MBG and conventional NBG is that MBG does not require the typical 'first three stages' [52], but conventional NBG does [26]. In the first three stages, conventional NBG releases M^+ ions and form Si-OH groups, and then Si-OH groups form networks by repolymerisation. However, the surface of MBG is already inherently 'prepared' to accelerate the first three stages of the conventional NBG [52].

In addition to the excellent apatite mineralisation ability in the simulated body fluids, the MBG scaffolds possess excellent in vitro osteogenesis, which is evidenced by the attachment, proliferation and differentiation of bone-forming cells in the scaffolds as shown in Fig. 13.4. The incorporation of Mg, Sr, B, Fe

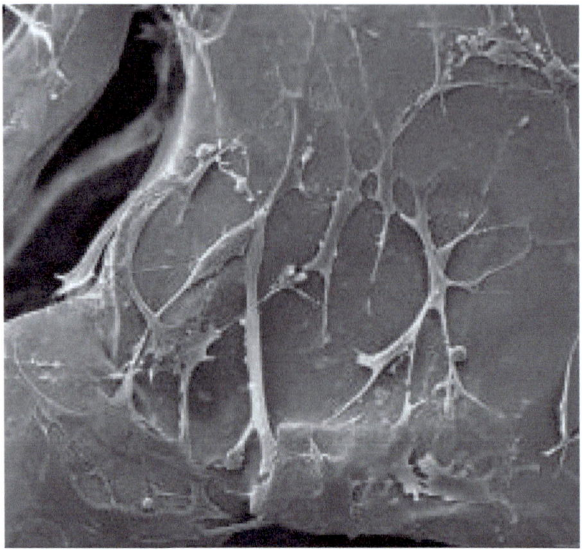

Fig. 13.4 BMSCs growing in MBG scaffolds

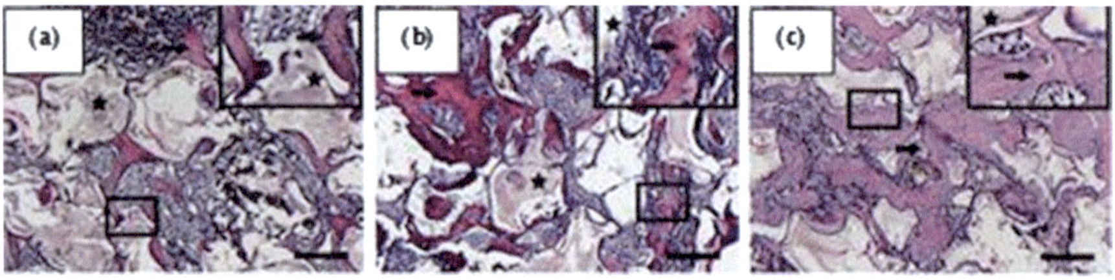

Fig. 13.5 The in vivo osteogenesis of the Sr-containing MBG scaffolds after implanted for 8 weeks. (**a**) MBG, (**b**) 2.5 % Sr-MBG and (**c**) 5 % Sr-MBG

and Zr significantly enhanced the cell proliferation and bone-related gene expression of osteoblasts or bone marrow stromal cells (BMSCs) [41, 42, 51].

Critical-sized femur defects in ovariectomised rats were created to simulate an osteoporotic phenotype. After implanted for 8 weeks, the results showed that the MBG scaffolds induced new bone formation in the osteoporotic bone defects, and the incorporation of Sr into the MBG scaffolds significantly stimulated new bone formation in the osteoporotic bone defects, indicating that the MBG scaffolds possess excellent in vivo osteogenesis (see Fig. 13.5).

13.3.2 The Angiogenesis of MBG Scaffolds

It is known that angiogenesis of porous scaffolds is of great importance to stimulate the tissue formation. Some studies have suggested that insufficient level of oxygen, a condition known as hypoxia, plays a critical role in cell recruitment, cell differentiation and vessel formation, linking osteogenesis closely to angiogenesis [53–56]. Hypoxia-inducible factor-1 (HIF-1), a transcriptional factor consisting of α- and β-subunits (HIF-1α and HIF-1β), has already been identified as one of the critical proteins directly reacting to hypoxia [57]. Under a hypoxic condition, HIF-1α binds to HIF-1β and initiates the transcription of hypoxia-sensitive genes that include vascular endothelial growth factor (VEGF) among others [58, 59]. Hypoxia can be artificially mimicked by stabilising HIF-1α expression and has been suggested as a potential strategy to promote neovascularisation [60–62].

To prepare the hypoxia-mimicking MBG scaffolds, we have incorporated Cu or Co into the MBG scaffolds to induce the pro-angiogenesis of BMSCs. The results showed that incorporation of chemical Cu (Fig. 13.6) and Co (Fig. 13.7) ions into MBG scaffolds is a viable way to inducing hypoxia effect on the BMSCs. Both Cu-MBG scaffolds and their ionic extracts could stimulate hypoxia-inducible factor (HIF)-1α and vascular endothelial growth factor (VEGF) expression in human bone marrow stromal cells (hBMSCs). In addition, both Cu-MBG scaffolds and their ionic extracts significantly promoted the osteogenic differentiation of hBMSCs by improving their bone-related gene expression (alkaline phosphatase (ALP), osteopontin (OPN) and osteocalcin (OCN)) [8]. Similarly, low amounts of Co ($<5\,\%$) incorporated into the MBG scaffolds had no significant cytotoxicity, and their incorporation significantly enhanced VEGF protein secretion, HIF-1α expression and bone-related gene expression in BMSCs, and also the Co-MBG scaffolds support BMSC attachment and proliferation [49]. The study suggested that parts of Cu or Co in MBG scaffolds significantly improved both the angiogenesis and osteogenesis of BMSCs with a multifunctional effect for bone tissue engineering.

13.3.3 The Cementogenesis of MBG Scaffolds

In addition to the osteogenesis and angiogenesis of MBG scaffolds in vitro and in vivo, Sr- or Li-containing MBG scaffolds significantly stimulated the proliferation and bone-/cementum-related gene expression of periodontal ligament cells. Sr plays an important role in influencing the mesoporous structure of MBG scaffolds in which high contents of Sr decreased the well-ordered mesopores as well as their surface area/pore volume. Sr^{2+} ions could be released from Sr-MBG scaffolds in a controlled way. The incorporation of Sr into MBG scaffolds has significantly stimulated alkaline phosphatase (ALP) activity and osteogenesis-/cementogenesis-related gene expression (ALP, Runx2, Col I, OPN and CEMP1) of PDLCs. Furthermore, the Sr-MBG scaffolds in simulated body fluid environment still maintain their excellent apatite mineralisation ability. The study suggested that the incorporation of Sr into MBG scaffolds is a viable way to stimulate the biological response of PDLCs [50].

The Li-MBG scaffolds with hierarchically large pores (300–500 μm) and well-ordered mesopores (5 nm) were also successfully prepared by incorporating Li^{+} ions into the scaffolds. We further investigated the cell proliferation and

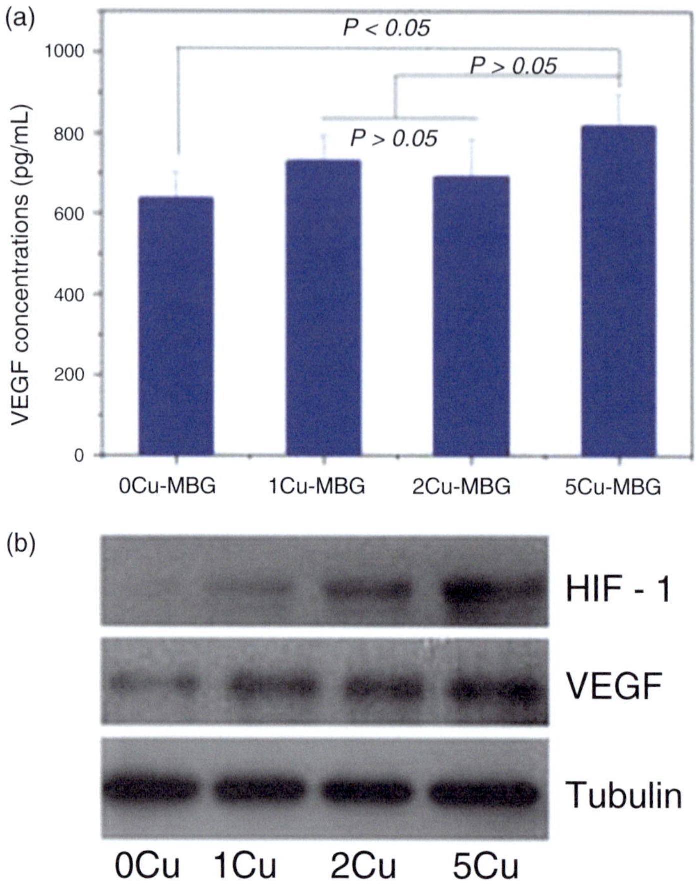

Fig. 13.6 VEGF secretion by ELISA (**a**) and HIF-1α and VEGF expression by western blotting (**b**) for hBMSCs on Cu-MBG scaffolds (Reprinted with permission from Ref. [8] copyright 2013 by Elsevier)

cementogenic differentiation, including Wnt- and Shh-related gene expression of hPDLCs cultured with the Li-MBG scaffolds and Li^+ ion-containing medium. It was found that the incorporation of 5% Li^+ into MBG scaffolds significantly enhanced cell proliferation and cementogenic differentiation, as well as activation of Wnt and Shh signaling pathways in hPDLCs (see Fig. 13.8). Li^+ by itself was sufficient to promote the cell proliferation, differentiation and cementogenic-related gene expression in hPDLCs. These results suggested that the Li^+ ions released from such bioactive MBG scaffolds play an important role in enhancing cementogenesis of PDLCs on bioactive scaffolds and this biological reaction may be via activation of Wnt and Shh signaling pathways [63].

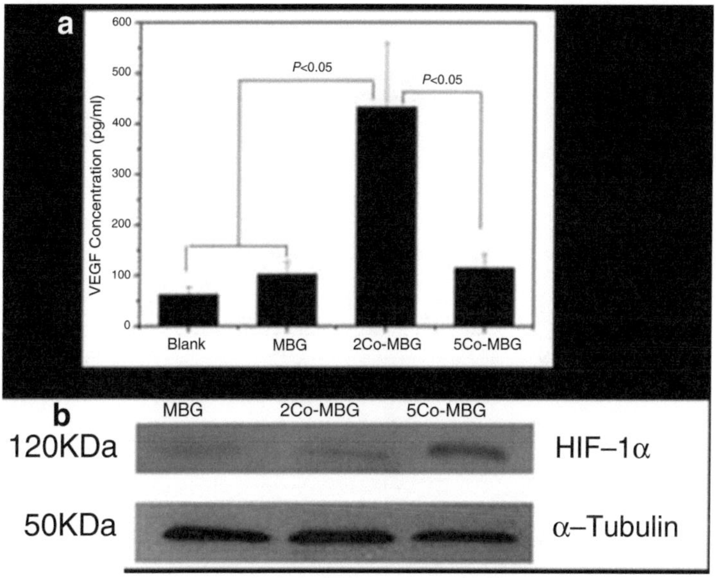

Fig. 13.7 VEGF secretion by ELISA (**a**) and HIF-1α expression by western blotting (**b**) for hBMSCs on Co-MBG scaffolds (Reprinted with permission from Ref. [49] copyright 2012 by Elsevier)

13.4 The Drug Delivery, Antibacterial Property and Tissue Stimulation of Multifunctional MBG Scaffolds

One of the significant advantages for MBG scaffolds is that they possess higher specific surface area and pore volume than conventional bioactive glasses. The loading efficiency of drug and growth factors in MBG is significantly higher than that in conventional bioactive glasses [64, 65]. The drug release kinetics in MBG is lower than that in conventional bioactive glasses. These characteristics make MBG useful for drug delivery. In the past 5 years, the MBG scaffolds with varied compositions have been used for the study of drug delivery [25, 35]. Up to now, the MBG scaffolds have been used for delivery of gentamicin [7, 51, 65], ampicillin [49], dexamethasone [41], dimethyloxallyl glycine (DMOG) and vascular endothelial growth factor (VEGF) [66]. The studies have indicated that the controllable delivery of ampicillin in the MBG scaffolds significantly inhibited the viability of bacteria (see Fig. 13.9).

Dexamethasone was loaded into MBG scaffolds, and it was found that the MBG scaffolds could efficiently load dexamethasone and release it in a controllable way. The sustained release of dexamethasone from the MBG scaffolds significantly enhanced alkaline phosphatase activity and gene expressions (Col I, Runx2, ALP and BSP) of osteoblasts in the scaffolds (see Fig. 13.10), suggesting that dexamethasone-loaded MBG scaffolds show great potential as a release system to

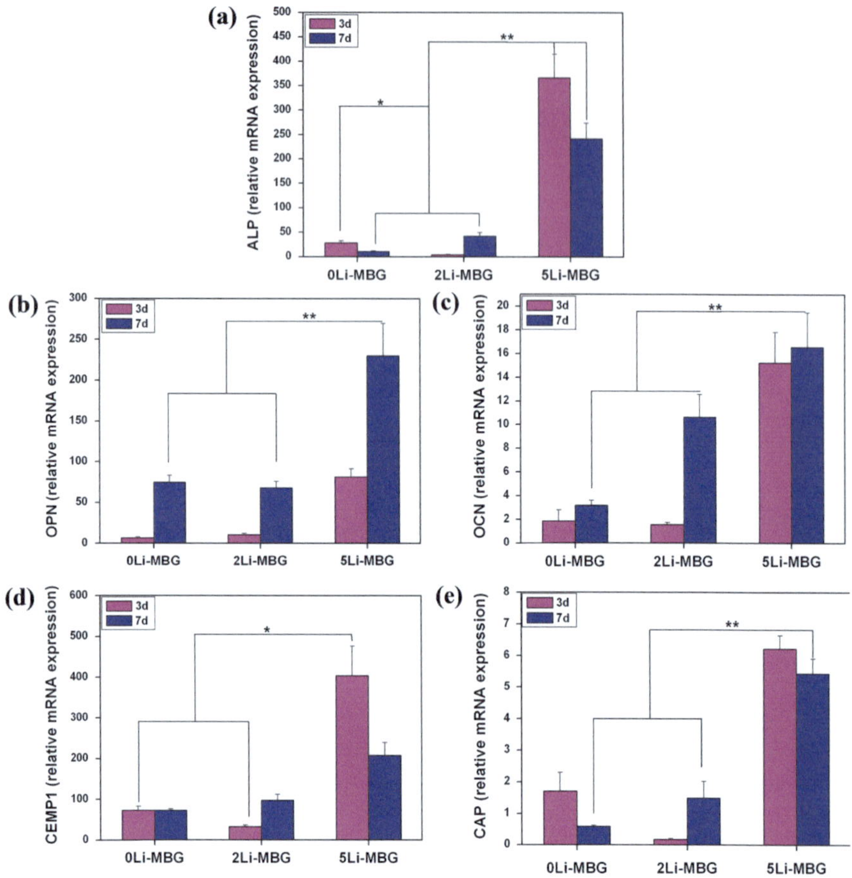

Fig. 13.8 The effect of Li contents in MBG scaffolds on bone-related gene expression of ALP (**a**), OPN (**b**), OCN (**c**) and cementum-specific markers of CEMP1 (**d**) and CAP (**e**) for hPDLCs (Reprinted with permission from Ref. [63] copyright 2012 by Elsevier)

enhance osteogenesis and may be used for bone tissue engineering applications in the future [35, 41].

Recently, we have loaded DMOG in MBG scaffolds. The results showed that the loading and release of DMOG in the MBG scaffolds can be efficiently controlled by regulating their mesoporous properties via the addition of different contents of mesopore-template agent. DMOG delivery in the MBG scaffolds had no cytotoxic effect on the viability of hBMSCs. DMOG delivery significantly induced HIF-1α stabilisation, VEGF secretion and bone-related gene expression of hBMSCs in the MBG scaffolds. Furthermore, it was found that the MBG scaffolds with slow DMOG release significantly enhanced the expression of bone-related genes than those with instant DMOG release. The results suggested that the controllable delivery of DMOG in the MBG scaffolds can mimic a hypoxic microenvironment,

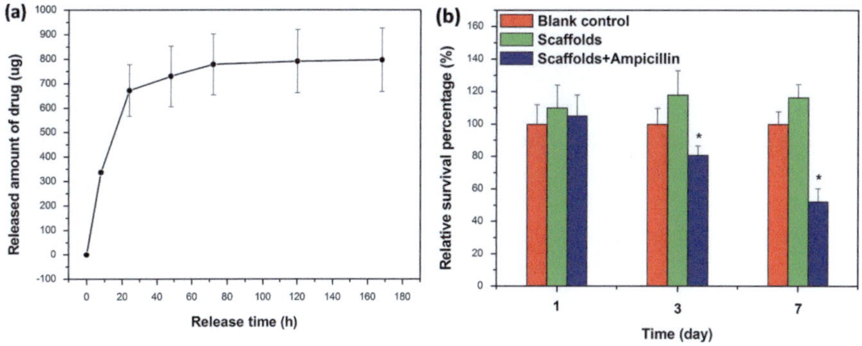

Fig. 13.9 Sustained release of ampicillin from the MBG scaffolds (**a**) and its antibacterial effect (**b**). *significant difference for the group of scaffolds loaded with ampicillin, compared to blank control and scaffolds groups not loaded with ampicillin ($P < 0.05$) (Reprinted with permission from Ref. [49] copyright 2012 by Elsevier)

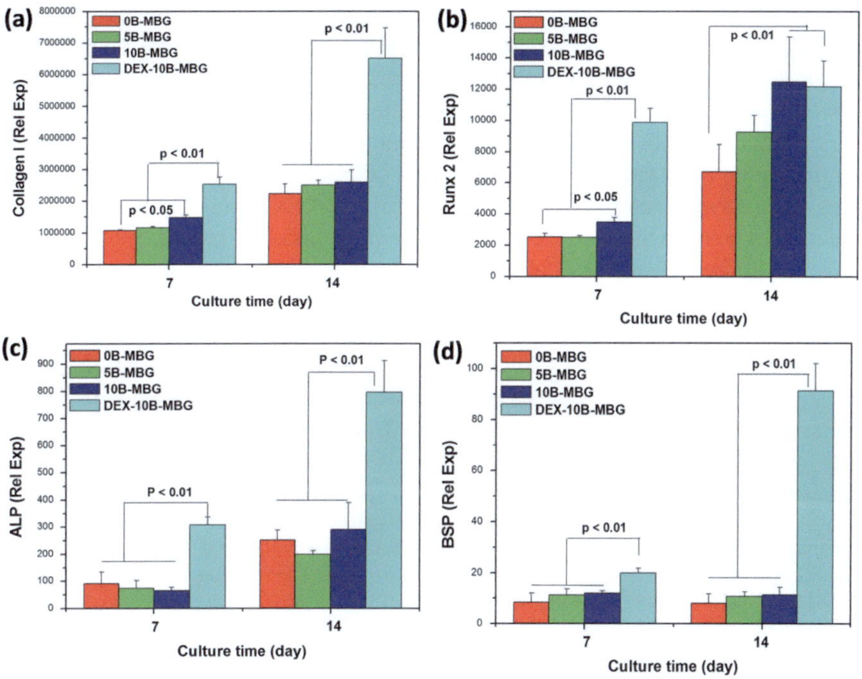

Fig. 13.10 The bone-relative gene expression of Collagen I (**a**), Runx 2 (**b**), ALP (**c**) and BSP (**d**) for osteoblasts by RT-qPCR. The incorporation of 10 % of B into MBG scaffolds enhanced the expression of Collagen I (at day 7) and Runx 2 (at day 7 and 14). DEX-loaded B-MBG scaffolds significantly enhanced the expression of Collagen I, Runx2, ALP and BSP of osteoblasts, compared to non-DEX-loaded B-MBG scaffolds (Reprinted with permission from Ref. [41] copyright 2011 by Elsevier)

which not only improves the angiogenic capacity of hBMSCs but also enhances their osteogenic differentiation.

In addition to the drug delivery, MBG scaffolds could be used for the delivery of vascular endothelial growth factor (VEGF). It was found that tMBG scaffolds have significantly higher loading efficiency and more sustained release of VEGF than non-mesoporous bioactive glass (NBG) scaffolds; and VEGF delivery from the MBG scaffolds improved the viability of endothelial cells. The study suggested that the mesopore structures in the MBG scaffolds play an important role in improving the loading efficiency, decrease the burst effect and maintain the bioactivity of VEGF, indicating that MBG scaffolds are an excellent carrier of VEGF for potential bone tissue engineering application [35, 66].

13.5 Conclusions and Perspective

In this chapter, we reviewed the recent research advances of multifunctional MBG scaffolds for hard tissue regeneration. Three preparation methods, characterisation, in vitro/in vivo osteogenesis, angiogenesis, cementogenesis, drug delivery and the corresponding functional effect on antibacterial, tissue stimulation have been reviewed. The MBG scaffolds allow combining the multifunctional properties as outlined above by varying their chemical compositions and delivering different drug and growth factors. The multifunctional properties were regarded to be of great importance to the improvement of the bone/periodontal regeneration and anti-infection ability. Therefore, multifunctional MBG scaffolds showed great potential for hard tissue regeneration. However, up to now, most of the studies have been focused on the in vitro experiments, and only few in vivo studies have been conducted to confirm their osteogenesis. Other functions of MBG scaffolds, such as angiogenesis, cementogenesis and antibacterial properties, should be further confirmed in vivo by using large animal models.

Acknowledgements Funding for related study was provided by the Recruitment Program of Global Young Talent, China (Dr Wu), the National High-Technology Research and Development Program of China (863 Program, SS2015AA020302), the National Natural Science Foundation of China (Grant 31370963), the Program of Shanghai Outstanding Academic Leaders (15XD1503900) and the Key Research Program of Chinese Academy of Sciences (Grant KGZD-EW-T06) and ARC Discovery (DP120103697).

References

1. Hench LL, Thompson I (2010) Twenty-first century challenges for biomaterials. J R Soc Interface 7(Suppl 4):S379–S391. doi:rsif.2010.0151.focus [pii] 10.1098/rsif.2010.0151.focus
2. Park JK, Shim JH, Kang KS, Yeom J, Jung HS, Kim JY, Lee KH, Kim TH, Kim SY, Cho DW, Hahn SK (2011) Solid free-form fabrication of tissue-engineering scaffolds with a poly(lactic-

co-glycolic acid) grafted hyaluronic acid conjugate encapsulating an intact bone morphogenetic protein-2/poly(ethylene glycol) complex. Adv Funct Mater 21(15):2906–2912
3. Kim TG, Shin H, Lim DW (2012) Biomimetic scaffolds for tissue engineering. Adv Funct Mater 22(12):2446–2468
4. Wang C, Xue Y, Lin K, Lu J, Chang J, Sun J (2012) The enhancement of bone regeneration by a combination of osteoconductivity and osteostimulation using beta-CaSiO3/beta-Ca3(PO4)2 composite bioceramics. Acta Biomater 8(1):350–360
5. Hu YC, Zhong JP (2009) Osteostimulation of bioglass. Chin Med J (Engl) 122(19):2386–2389
6. Zhao LZ, Yan XX, Zhou XF, Zhou L, Wang HN, Tang HW, Yu CZ (2008) Mesoporous bioactive glasses for controlled drug release. Microporous Mesoporous Mater 109 (1–3):210–215
7. Zhu Y, Zhang Y, Wu C, Fang Y, Wang J, Wang S (2011) The effect of zirconium incorporation on the physiochemical and biological properties of mesoporous bioactive glasses scaffolds. Microporous Mesoporous Mater 143:311–319
8. Wu C, Zhou Y, Xu M, Han P, Chen L, Chang J, Xiao Y (2013) Copper-containing mesoporous bioactive glass scaffolds with multifunctional properties of angiogenesis capacity, osteostimulation and antibacterial activity. Biomaterials 34(2):422–433
9. Lu JX, Descamps M, Dejou J, Koubi G, Hardouin P, Lemaitre J, Proust JP (2002) The biodegradation mechanism of calcium phosphate biomaterials in bone. J Biomed Mater Res 63(4):408–412
10. Ducheyne P, Radin S, King L (1993) The effect of calcium phosphate ceramic composition and structure on in vitro behavior. I Dissolution. J Biomed Mater Res 27(1):25–34
11. Xu S, Lin K, Wang Z, Chang J, Wang L, Lu J, Ning C (2008) Reconstruction of calvarial defect of rabbits using porous calcium silicate bioactive ceramics. Biomaterials 29 (17):2588–2596
12. Misra SK, Ansari T, Mohn D, Valappil SP, Brunner TJ, Stark WJ, Roy I, Knowles JC, Sibbons PD, Jones EV, Boccaccini AR, Salih V (2010) Effect of nanoparticulate bioactive glass particles on bioactivity and cytocompatibility of poly(3-hydroxybutyrate) composites. J R Soc Interface 7(44):453–465
13. Chen QZ, Thompson ID, Boccaccini AR (2006) 45S5 Bioglass-derived glass-ceramic scaffolds for bone tissue engineering. Biomaterials 27(11):2414–2425
14. Jones JR, Tsigkou O, Coates EE, Stevens MM, Polak JM, Hench LL (2007) Extracellular matrix formation and mineralization on a phosphate-free porous bioactive glass scaffold using primary human osteoblast (HOB) cells. Biomaterials 28(9):1653–1663
15. Jones JR, Ehrenfried LM, Hench LL (2006) Optimising bioactive glass scaffolds for bone tissue engineering. Biomaterials 27(7):964–973
16. Wu ZY, Hill RG, Yue S, Nightingale D, Lee PD, Jones JR (2011) Melt-derived bioactive glass scaffolds produced by a gel-cast foaming technique. Acta Biomater 7(4):1807–1816
17. Hench LL (1991) Bioceramics: from concept to clinic. J Am Ceram Soc 74:1487–1510
18. Hench LL (1998) Biomaterials: a forecast for the future. Biomaterials 19(16):1419–1423
19. Gough JE, Jones JR, Hench LL (2004) Nodule formation and mineralisation of human primary osteoblasts cultured on a porous bioactive glass scaffold. Biomaterials 25(11):2039–2046
20. Gough JE, Notingher I, Hench LL (2004) Osteoblast attachment and mineralized nodule formation on rough and smooth 45S5 bioactive glass monoliths. J Biomed Mater Res A 68 (4):640–650
21. Valerio P, Pereira MM, Goes AM, Leite MF (2004) The effect of ionic products from bioactive glass dissolution on osteoblast proliferation and collagen production. Biomaterials 25 (15):2941–2948
22. Xynos ID, Edgar AJ, Buttery LD, Hench LL, Polak JM (2001) Gene-expression profiling of human osteoblasts following treatment with the ionic products of Bioglass 45S5 dissolution. J Biomed Mater Res 55(2):151–157

23. Xynos ID, Edgar AJ, Buttery LD, Hench LL, Polak JM (2000) Ionic products of bioactive glass dissolution increase proliferation of human osteoblasts and induce insulin-like growth factor II mRNA expression and protein synthesis. Biochem Biophys Res Commun 276(2):461–465
24. Hoppe A, Guldal NS, Boccaccini AR (2011) A review of the biological response to ionic dissolution products from bioactive glasses and glass-ceramics. Biomaterials 32 (11):2757–2774
25. Wu C, Chang J, Xiao Y (2011) Mesoporous bioactive glasses as drug delivery and bone tissue engineering platforms. Ther Deliv 2(9):1189–1198
26. Hench LL, Polak JM (2002) Third-generation biomedical materials. Science 295 (5557):1014–1017
27. Li R, Clark AE, Hench LL (1991) An investigation of bioactive glass powders by sol-gel processing. J Appl Biomater 2(4):231–239
28. Arcos D, Lopez-Noriega A, Ruiz-Hernandez E, Terasaki O, Vallet-Regi M (2009) Ordered mesoporous microspheres for bone grafting and drug delivery. Chem Mater 21(6):1000–1009. doi:10.1021/Cm801649z
29. Wu C, Chang J (2013) Silicate bioceramics for bone tissue regeneration. J Inorg Mater 28 (1):29–39
30. Yan X, Yu C, Zhou X, Tang J, Zhao D (2004) Highly ordered mesoporous bioactive glasses with superior in vitro bone-forming bioactivities. Angew Chem Int Ed Engl 43(44):5980–5984
31. Yan X, Huang X, Yu C, Deng H, Wang Y, Zhang Z, Qiao S, Lu G, Zhao D (2006) The in-vitro bioactivity of mesoporous bioactive glasses. Biomaterials 27(18):3396–3403
32. Leonova E, Izquierdo-Barba I, Arcos D, Lopez-Noriega A, Hedin N, Vallet-Regi M, Eden M (2008) Multinuclear solid-state NMR studies of ordered mesoporous bioactive glasses. J Phys Chem C 112(14):5552–5562
33. Garcia A, Cicuendez M, Izquierdo-Barba I, Arcos D, Vallet-Regi M (2009) Essential role of calcium phosphate heterogeneities in 2D-hexagonal and 3D-cubic SiO_2-CaO-P_2O_5 mesoporous bioactive glasses. Chem Mater 21(22):5474–5484
34. Alcaide M, Portoles P, Lopez-Noriega A, Arcos D, Vallet-Regi M, Portoles MT (2010) Interaction of an ordered mesoporous bioactive glass with osteoblasts, fibroblasts and lymphocytes, demonstrating its biocompatibility as a potential bone graft material. Acta Biomater 6(3):892–899. doi:S1742-7061(09)00401-2 [pii] 10.1016/j.actbio.2009.09.008
35. Wu C, Chang J (2012) Mesoporous bioactive glasses: structure characteristics, drug/growth factor delivery and bone regeneration application. Interface Focus 2:292–306
36. Yun H, Kim SE, Hyun YT, Heo S, Shin J (2008) Hierarchically mesoporous-macroporous bioactive glasses scaffolds for bone tissue regeneration. J Biomed Mater Res B Appl Biomater 87:374–380
37. Zhu Y, Wu C, Ramaswamy Y, Kockrick E, Simon P, Kaskel S, Zreiqat H (2008) Preparation, characterization and in vitro bioactivity of mesoporous bioactive glasses (MBGs) scaffolds for bone tissue engineering. Microporous Mesoporous Mater 112(1–3):494–503
38. Li X, Wang XP, Chen HR, Jiang P, Dong XP, Shi JL (2007) Hierarchically porous bioactive glass scaffolds synthesized with a PUF and P123 cotemplated approach. Chem Mater 19 (17):4322–4326. doi:10.1021/Cm0708564
39. Wu C, Fan W, Gelinsky M, Xiao Y, Simon P, Schulze R, Doert T, Luo Y, Cuniberti G (2011) Bioactive SrO-SiO(2) glass with well-ordered mesopores: characterization, physiochemistry and biological properties. Acta Biomater 7(4):1797–1806
40. Wu C, Fan W, Zhu Y, Gelinsky M, Chang J, Cuniberti G, Albrecht V, Friis T, Xiao Y (2011) Multifunctional magnetic mesoporous bioactive glass scaffolds with a hierarchical pore structure. Acta Biomater 7(10):3563–3572
41. Wu C, Miron R, Sculeaan A, Kaskel S, Doert T, Schulze R, Zhang Y (2011) Proliferation, differentiation and gene expression of osteoblasts in boron-containing associated with dexamethasone deliver from mesoporous bioactive glass scaffolds. Biomaterials 32(29):7068–7078
42. Wu C, Zhang Y, Zhu Y, Friis T, Xiao Y (2010) Structure-property relationships of silk-modified mesoporous bioglass scaffolds. Biomaterials 31(13):3429–3438

43. Franco J, Hunger P, Launey ME, Tomsia AP, Saiz E (2010) Direct write assembly of calcium phosphate scaffolds using a water-based hydrogel. Acta Biomater 6(1):218–228. doi:S1742-7061(09)00283-9 [pii] 10.1016/j.actbio.2009.06.031
44. Miranda P, Pajares A, Saiz E, Tomsia AP, Guiberteau F (2008) Mechanical properties of calcium phosphate scaffolds fabricated by robocasting. J Biomed Mater Res A 85(1):218–227. doi:10.1002/jbm.a.31587
45. Miranda P, Saiz E, Gryn K, Tomsia AP (2006) Sintering and robocasting of beta-tricalcium phosphate scaffolds for orthopaedic applications. Acta Biomater 2(4):457–466. doi:S1742-7061(06)00022-5 [pii] 10.1016/j.actbio.2006.02.004
46. Yun HS, Kim SE, Hyeon YT (2007) Design and preparation of bioactive glasses with hierarchical pore networks. Chem Commun 21:2139–2141. doi:10.1039/B702103h
47. Garcia A, Izquierdo-Barba I, Colilla M, de Laorden CL, Vallet-Regi M (2011) Preparation of 3-D scaffolds in the SiO_2-P_2O_5 system with tailored hierarchical meso-macroporosity. Acta Biomater 7(3):1265–1273
48. Wu C, Luo Y, Cuniberti G, Xiao Y, Gelinsky M (2011) Three-dimensional printing of hierarchical and tough mesoporous bioactive glass scaffolds with a controllable pore architecture, excellent mechanical strength and mineralization ability. Acta Biomater 7 (6):2644–2650
49. Wu C, Zhou Y, Fan W, Han P, Chang J, Yuen J, Zhang M, Xiao Y (2012) Hypoxia-mimicking mesoporous bioactive glass scaffolds with controllable cobalt ion release for bone tissue engineering. Biomaterials 33(7):2076–2085
50. Wu C, Zhou Y, Lin C, Chang J, Xiao Y (2012) Strontium-containing mesoporous bioactive glass scaffolds with improved osteogenic/cementogenic differentiation of periodontal ligament cells for periodontal tissue engineering. Acta Biomater 8:3805–3815
51. Zhu Y, Li X, Yang J, Wang S, Gao H, Hanagata N (2011) Composition-structure-property relationship of the CaO-MxOy-SiO_2-P_2O_5 (M = Zr, Mg, Sr) mesoporous bioactive glass (MBG) scaffolds. J Mater Chem 21:9208–9218
52. Eden M, Gunawidjaja PN, Lo AYH, Izquierdo-Barba I, Garcia A, Arcos D, Stevensson B, Grins J, Vallet-Regi M (2010) Biomimetic apatite mineralization mechanisms of mesoporous bioactive glasses as probed by multinuclear (31)P, (29)Si, (23)Na and (13)C solid-state NMR. J Phys Chem C 114(45):19345–19356
53. Fan W, Crawford R, Xiao Y (2010) Enhancing in vivo vascularized bone formation by cobalt chloride-treated bone marrow stromal cells in a tissue engineered periosteum model. Biomaterials 31(13):3580–3589
54. Fu OY, Hou MF, Yang SF, Huang SC, Lee WY (2009) Cobalt chloride-induced hypoxia modulates the invasive potential and matrix metalloproteinases of primary and metastatic breast cancer cells. Anticancer Res 29(8):3131–3138
55. Basini G, Grasselli F, Bussolati S, Baioni L, Bianchi F, Musci M, Careri M, Mangia A (2011) Hypoxia stimulates the production of the angiogenesis inhibitor 2-methoxyestradiol by swine granulosa cells. Steroids 76:1433–1436
56. Oladipupo S, Hu S, Kovalski J, Yao J, Santeford A, Sohn RE, Shohet R, Maslov K, Wang LV, Arbeit JM (2011) VEGF is essential for hypoxia-inducible factor-mediated neovascularization but dispensable for endothelial sprouting. Proc Natl Acad Sci U S A 108(32):13264–13269
57. Semenza GL (2009) Regulation of oxygen homeostasis by hypoxia-inducible factor 1. Physiology (Bethesda) 24:97–106
58. Liu W, Shen SM, Zhao XY, Chen GQ (2012) Targeted genes and interacting proteins of hypoxia inducible factor-1. Int J Biochem Mol Biol 3(2):165–178
59. Ahluwalia A, Tarnawski AS (2012) Critical role of hypoxia sensor—HIF-1alpha in VEGF gene activation. Implications for angiogenesis and tissue injury healing. Curr Med Chem 19 (1):90–97
60. Finney L, Vogt S, Fukai T, Glesne D (2009) Copper and angiogenesis: unravelling a relationship key to cancer progression. Clin Exp Pharmacol Physiol 36(1):88–94

61. Gerard C, Bordeleau LJ, Barralet J, Doillon CJ (2010) The stimulation of angiogenesis and collagen deposition by copper. Biomaterials 31(5):824–831
62. Hu GF (1998) Copper stimulates proliferation of human endothelial cells under culture. J Cell Biochem 69(3):326–335
63. Han P, Wu C, Chang J, Xiao Y (2012) The cementogenic differentiation of periodontal ligament cells via the activation of Wnt/beta-catenin signalling pathway by Li(+) ions released from bioactive scaffolds. Biomaterials 33(27):6370–6379
64. Xia W, Chang J (2006) Well-ordered mesoporous bioactive glasses (MBG): a promising bioactive drug delivery system. J Control Release 110(3):522–530
65. Zhu YF, Kaskel S (2009) Comparison of the in vitro bioactivity and drug release property of mesoporous bioactive glasses (MBGs) and bioactive glasses (BGs) scaffolds. Microporous Mesoporous Mater 118(1–3):176–182. doi:10.1016/j.micromeso.2008.08.046
66. Wu C, Fan W, Chang J, Xiao Y (2013) Mesoporous bioactive glass scaffolds for efficient delivery of vascular endothelial growth factor. J Biomater Appl 28(3):367–374

Chapter 14
Challenges for Cartilage Regeneration

Fariba Dehghani and Ali Fathi

Abstract Articular cartilage is a resilient connective tissue, which covers the surface of bones to facilitate their movements against each other. Due to unique mechanical properties, cartilage has a prominent role in locomotion and mobility of the human body. This tissue however has limited capability of regeneration and repair due to its low metabolism and avascular structure. Trauma, degenerative conditions and inflammatory arthritis lead to lifetime disability states and pain. The scope of this chapter is to first provide an overview of mechanical, biological and micro-architectural properties of articular cartilage and the effect of aging on these characteristics. Then the cartilage treatment techniques that have been proposed for different types of cartilage defects are discussed. Cell-based therapies, such as autologous chondrocyte implantation (ACI) technique, have been developed to achieve reproducible results regardless of patients' age, gender and physical conditions. The second generation of ACI is a tissue engineering-based technique, which includes the use of appropriate cell type, bioactive molecules such as growth factors and proper scaffold to regenerate cartilage. The favourable types of cells, biological compounds and properties of biomaterials for cartilage regeneration have also been discussed in this chapter. Finally, the biomaterial products that have been examined in clinical trial for cartilage repair are outlined, and their properties and clinical results are discussed.

Keywords Articular cartilage • Tissue engineering • Scaffold • Tissue regeneration • Biopolymer

14.1 Articular Cartilage Properties and Aging

Hyaline articular cartilage covers the ends of articulating bones [1]. It is a resilient connective tissue with low friction and high load-bearing capacity. Cartilage serves a critical role in mobility of one bone against another. Chondrocyte is the main cell

---

F. Dehghani (✉) • A. Fathi
School of Chemical and Biomolecular Engineering, The University of Sydney, Sydney, NSW 2006, Australia
e-mail: Fariba.Dehghani@Sydney.edu.au

Q. Li, Y.-W. Mai (eds.), *Biomaterials for Implants and Scaffolds*, Springer Series in Biomaterials Science and Engineering 8, DOI 10.1007/978-3-662-53574-5_14

type scattered within an extracellular matrix (ECM) of cartilage [2]. Breakdown or any degree of damage in this tissue leads to substantial reduction in mobility of the human body and pain and subsequently has negative impact on patients' lifestyle. Cartilage has limited capability of regeneration and repair due to its low metabolism and the absence of vascularisation in its structure [3, 4]. To design and engineer a cartilage, it is essential to have better understanding over the mechanical and biological properties of this tissue. Mechanical, physiochemical and biological properties of articular cartilage are mainly affected by its biochemical composition as well as its structural properties that are reviewed in this section.

14.1.1 Biochemical Composition

The composition of articular cartilage varies during the tissue development. In a mature cartilage, 70–80 % of its content is water. The solid fraction of articular cartilage is mainly collagen (50–75 %), proteoglycan (15–30 %) and other protein molecules [5, 6]. The collagen network provides shear and tensile stiffness, whereas proteoglycan molecules bring about compressive stiffness to cartilage ECM. The collagen network also suppresses the high swelling tendency of the proteoglycan molecule and preserves the functional integrity of cartilage [7]. The mixture of collagen and proteoglycan, therefore, forms an integrated mesh-like network with superior mechanical properties. Concentration of collagenous proteins and proteoglycan along with non-collagenous proteins in the structure of articular cartilage substantially affects the mechanical properties and functionality of articular cartilage.

Collagen has a primary role in the function and structure of all connective tissues throughout the human body. Collagen is composed of repeating amino acid sequences (mainly glycine, proline and hydroxyproline) and possesses a triple helix structure. In articular cartilage, collagen type II is predominant [8], which provides shear and tensile stiffness to cartilage ECM. In addition to collagen type II, cartilage ECM is composed of other types of collagen.

Other fibrillar and globular collagen types, such as types V, VI and IX, also exist in cartilage ECM [9]. The roles of these types of collagen are still unknown, but it is believed that they support the integration of cartilage structure by affecting the intermolecular interaction in collagen type II [5, 6].

Proteoglycans are large macromolecules consisted of a protein segment in core, covered with polysaccharide chain, known as glycosaminoglycan. The molecular weight of proteoglycans varies in the range of 50,000 kDa to 100 kDa [10, 11]. Proteoglycan networks function as a mesh, which covers the organised collagen network. Majority of this biopolymer is one of the factors that provide structural integrity to cartilage. The primary proteoglycan in articular cartilage network is aggrecan. This proteoglycan consists of a hyaluronan core with chondroitin and keratin sulphate in side chains. The presence of these two carboxyl and sulphate groups gives articular cartilage network a negative charge (known as a fixed charge density) [12]. This overall negative charge leads to hydrophilic and high swelling properties to cartilage network [7, 13]. The mechanical functionality of cartilage on the other hand is highly dependent on the fluid pressurisation within the tissue. Loss of proteoglycan can, therefore, decrease water intake capacity and thus fluid pressure within the cartilage network. Lack of fluid pressure in cartilage substantially decreases the mechanical strength of this tissue [13].

Cartilage ECM also contains a small fraction of non-collagenous proteins and other matrix constituents. Non-collagenous proteins include cartilage oligomeric proteins, fibronectin, thrombospondin, matrix glycine–leucine–alanine, chondrocalcin, superficial proteins and elastin [14]. Other matrix constituents of cartilage ECM are lipids, phospholipids and inorganic crystal compounds [15, 16]. The role of each of these molecules in the function of articular cartilage is still not clear. Collagen and proteoglycan are the two predominant compounds that affect the cartilage functionality. In this chapter, therefore, the main focus is on collagen type II and proteoglycan rather than other minor compounds [7]. In addition to biochemical composition, the microstructures and micro-layouts of articular cartilage affect the biomechanical and biological properties of cartilage.

14.1.2 Cartilage Microstructure

The structure of articular cartilage substantially varies from the surface of articular cartilage to bone [17, 18]. The biochemistry, cell morphology and cell arrangement vary in different regions within articular cartilage. The schematic overview of articular cartilage is shown in Fig. 14.1. The tissue can be divided into superficial, middle, deep and calcified regions.

The top surface of articular cartilage is covered with very thin proteinaceous layer, termed as lamina splendens [18]. The zonal region right beside the lamina splendens is a superficial zone, which has a thickness within the range of 4 to 8 mm for the healthy cartilage of a man [17]. The cells in this region are densely packed with discoidal shapes that are oriented along with the collagen fibres [19]. The middle or transitional layer zone occupies 40–60 % of the total articular cartilage thickness (equivalent to 16–22 mm in healthy male cartilage) [17]. The deep zone is the last region of purely hyaline tissue. The thin layer, which separates the deep zone from calcified region of articular cartilage, is called tidemark. The calcified region is the transitional zone between elastic cartilage and rigid bone tissues [20].

14.1.3 Cartilage Mechanical Function

The main role of articular cartilage is to act as low-friction, load-bearing, wear-resistant surface for mobility of bones over decades of continuous use. The force applied on cartilage depends on the location of the joint. The forces exerted on the

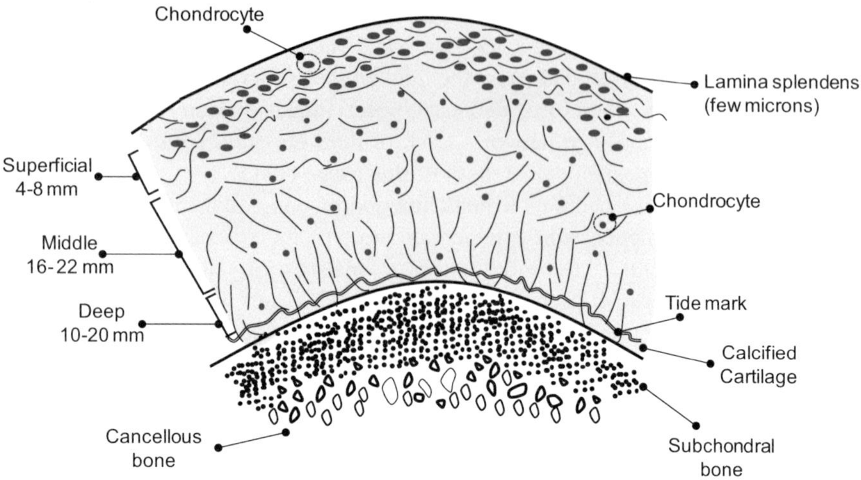

Fig. 14.1 Schematic layout of articular cartilage and thickness of different zones of articular cartilage in a healthy knee joint (The image is generated by accumulating data from different sources [18, 21–23])

shoulder, ankle, heap and knee are 1.5, 2.5, 3.3 and 3.5 times of the human body weight, respectively [24]. The biochemical characteristics of articular cartilage directly affect the performance of the tissue in the joint and its mechanical functionality. Any change in mechanical and biochemical properties of articular cartilage might dramatically alter the loading profile exerted on the joint, which may degrade tissue and eventually lead to loss of articular cartilage [3, 4].

The deformation of cartilage plays an important role in its mechanical functionality, which is governed by the rate of absorbance or release of fluid, mainly water, through its solid structure [25, 26]. For example, sudden loading on cartilage releases water from its structure; this subsequently absorbs the impact of stress and covers the tissue. In addition, release of water leads to expansion of cartilage which in turn increases the surface area of contact (between cartilage and the bone) and thus decreases the impact of stress on skeleton [25, 26].

Loading and deformation of articular cartilage generate a combination of compressive, tensile and shear stresses along with friction throughout the tissue [27]. Some of the important mechanical behaviour of articular cartilage is summarised in Table 14.1 and are discussed in this section. It is important to note that all mechanical properties of cartilage are continuously changed during human growth and affected due to health condition [28–32].

14.1.3.1 Compression Behaviour

Compressive loading is one of the primary types of mechanical stress exerted on articular cartilage. The confined compressive modulus experienced by articular

Table 14.1 Important mechanical properties of native cartilage

Mechanical properties		Refs
Compression modulus (MPa)	0.08–2.1	[31, 33, 34]
Tensile modulus (MPa)	4.8–25	[25]
Strain at failure (mm/mm)	30 %	[35]
Practical strain rate	0–1 mm/s	[33]
Shear modulus (MPa)	0.07–0.65	[36, 37]
Coefficient of friction	0.001	[38]

cartilage varies in the range of 0.08 to 2.1 MPa from superficial to deep layers of adult bovine cartilage, respectively [31, 32, 39]. The mechanism of cartilage to cope with high compressive stresses is predominantly described by permeability of cartilage structure.

Cartilage structure has a low liquid permeability, leading to high resistance of tissue against fluid flow within its structure. Under compression, therefore interstitial fluid is subjected to very high pressure. After unloading, the fluid is redistributed (from high pressure to low pressure spots) within the tissue and imparts viscoelastic properties to the cartilage [26, 40, 41]. Volumetric changes and viscoelastic properties of articular cartilage are, therefore, the two predominant factors affecting the compressive behaviours of articular cartilage.

Volumetric changes occur as fluid moves out from the structure of articular cartilage under compression. Upon the unloading of the tissue from compression stress, cartilage recovers its initial dimension and absorbs the lost fluid. In this cycle hence, the solid structure exhibits both high viscoelasticity and water uptake properties to be able to cope with compression stresses and also keep its original shape [38]. Over a course of a day, however, the bulk of cartilage is compressed in the range of 15–20 % of its initial volume, which can be fully recovered within a period of inactivity (e.g. sleeping period) [42].

14.1.3.2 Tensile Properties

Tension in cartilage occurs either when two cartilages slide against each other and pull towards a single direction or when a cartilage is compressed, pulling the surrounding tissue towards the loading region. As cartilage is subjected to tension, collagen fibres within the tissue structure align and stretch along the loading axis. As the strain is in the range of 0–15 %, the crosslinked collagen network starts stretching, and thus the cartilage exhibits linear response [43]. As the strain increases, the crosslinked collagen fibres themselves start stretching. In higher range of strain (above 15 %) therefore, cartilage exhibits higher stiffness [44, 45]. The structural and physical properties of articular cartilage therefore affect the behaviour of this tissue under tension condition. These include collagen fibre density, their length and degree of crosslinking and strength of ionic bonds between collagen and proteoglycan networks [46, 47].

The tensile modulus of mature articular cartilage is significantly higher than its compression modulus, and it varies in the range of 4.8–25 MPa from deep to the superficial layers, respectively [25]. The tensile modulus of articular cartilage increases by maturation [29, 48].

14.1.3.3 Shear Stress

Articular cartilage is subjected to shear stress in its deep tissue when the joint undergoes rotational or translational movement. In theory, pure shear just causes stretching of tissue (it causes no compressive stress on the tissue). The shear stress on cartilage is independent on the fluid pressure within its structure, and thus it can be used to characterise the solid fraction of cartilage regardless of fluid dynamics in it [49]. The equilibrium shear stress in cartilage varies in the range of 0.05–0.7 MPa [36, 37].

14.1.3.4 Friction Behaviour

Friction quantifies the resistive force between two subjects as they are in contact with each other and move laterally relative to each other. Native cartilage gives mobility to the bone by its lubrication properties. Under high dynamic and static load conditions, the coefficient of friction for human cartilage is very low, and it is in the order of 0.001 [38]. Several theories have been proposed to explain low friction force between cartilage surfaces. These include but not necessarily limited to elasto-hydrodynamic lubrication [50, 51] and fluid pressurisation theories [52, 53]. It shows that the synovial fluid becomes thicker due to the deformation of applied compression on cartilage, which gives superior lubrication properties to articular cartilage. Compression and lubrication properties of cartilage therefore are closely correlated.

14.1.4 Articular Cartilage Aging and Pathology

Articular cartilage is a highly resilient connective tissue with very important biomechanical role in the human body. Cartilage has an essential function in the movement of the human body and mobility of bones against each other. Any breakdown in this tissue results in substantial reduction in standards of living and substantial level of pain. Cartilage from skeletally immature, mature and older patients exhibits very different biomechanical and biological properties. As cartilage ages, it becomes more prone to injuries [54, 55]. The damage to this tissue might result from torsional loading, joint misalignment, foreign bodies in the joint and osteoarthritis. It is critical to first understand the aging process of cartilage and then the factors that lead to cartilage damage to be able to develop an effective treatment strategy for articular cartilage defects.

Similar to many organs, aging has significant impact on the characteristics of cartilage. Skeletally mature, immature and old cartilages are different in respect to their thickness [54, 55], vascularisation, chondrocyte population [56] and chondrocyte regeneration quality [57, 58]. Immature cartilage contains blood vessels as it is still undergoing tissue formation (endochondral ossification). It is also thicker than mature cartilage and its thickness decreases by aging [54, 55]. The population of chondrocyte cells also decreases overtime by aging [56]. In addition to chondrocytes' cell reduction in mature cartilage, aging also brings lower metabolic activity, increases apoptosis (a process of programmed cell death) and elevates passive responses of cells to growth factors [57, 58].

Biomechanical properties of cartilage change by aging. For example, the degree of crosslinking in collagen increases [59] as protein and lipids are covalently bonded with sugars (i.e. glycation). The length and molecular weight of proteoglycan also decrease as its protein content decreases [60]. These variations reduce the stiffness/strength of cartilage and induce the risk of tissue failure [61]. Studies showed that generally a cartilage approaches its peak in elasticity in 40 years of age, while the viscoelastic energy reaches its maximum value earlier within 16–29 years old. Both elasticity and viscoelasticity decline at a steady rate [62]. Collagen alignment also decreases in the middle and deep zone of cartilage by age which in turn decreases the tensile properties of cartilage [63].

Both biological and biomechanical properties of articular cartilage decrease by time. The problematic issues are, therefore, the lack of healing responses and also the decrease in the initial mechanical properties of cartilage. The overall changes in the biochemical properties of articular cartilage are schematically shown in Fig. 14.2.

Repeated non-physiological loading on tissue over the years and biological, biomechanical and other systematic changes on articular cartilage are the factors that make the tissue vulnerable to damage. Cartilage damages are either due to injuries or osteoarthritis. In addition to the impact of aging on the nature of articular cartilage, other factors such as hormonal therapy and diseases play a role in properties of cartilage. For instance, oestrogen replacement in ovariectomised sheep leads to substantial changes in the structure and mechanical properties of articular cartilage, which is relevant to menopausal women [64]. In addition, anti-inflammatory treatments such as intra-articular administration of methylprednisolone diversely affect the properties of articular cartilage [65]. Some diseases such as diabetes also have negative impact on cartilage properties [66].

14.1.4.1 Cartilage Injuries

Sudden impact, repeating loads, damage in other connective tissue and also foreign bodies affect the loading profile on cartilage and, therefore, result in cartilage damage as shown schematically in Fig. 14.3. The effect of load and stress on

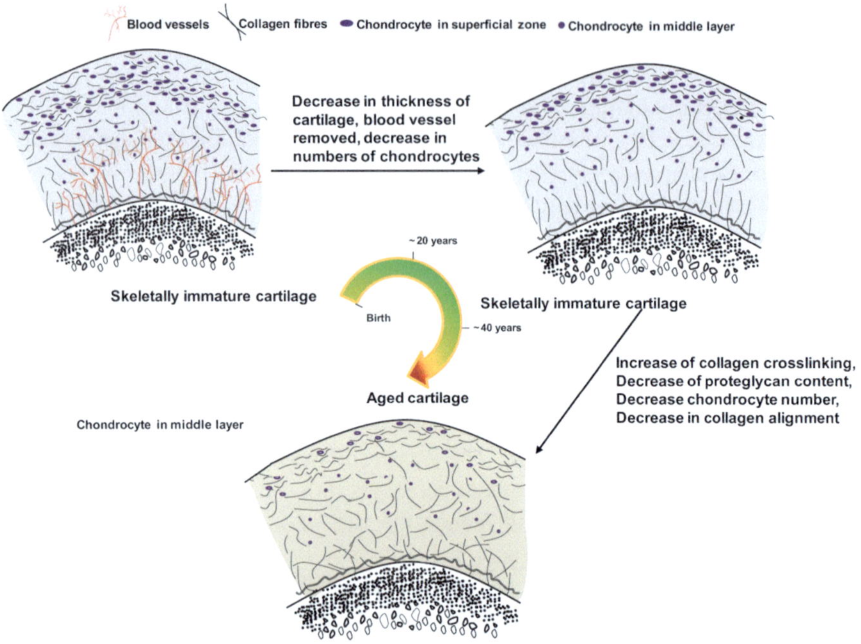

Fig. 14.2 Biochemical changes in the structure of cartilage from skeletally immature cartilage to mature and aged cartilage (The image is regenerated by accumulating data from different references [54, 55, 60–63])

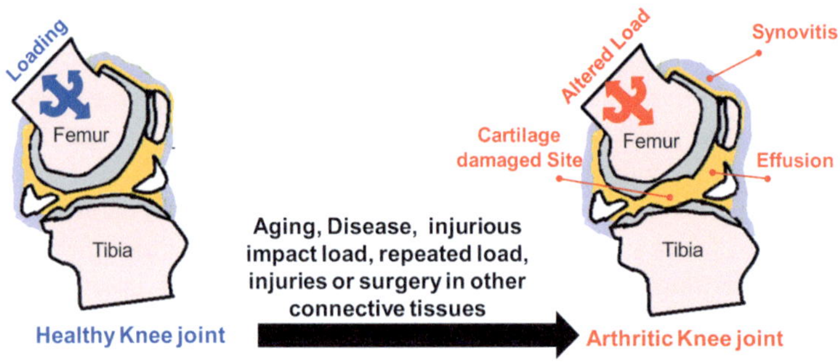

Fig. 14.3 Cartilage injuries, causes and their effect on loading profile in connective tissue

cartilage is a function of frequency of loading and their period of exposure. Due to the viscoelastic nature of articular cartilage and based on the theory of confined compression moduli, both load and strain rates significantly affect cartilage stiffness which should be taken into account for determining the load of injury. For instance, during the normal physical activity, the knee cartilage is subjected to 3.5 times the body weight [24]. Therefore, for a male with an average weight of 70 Kg, the force on his joint is subject to around 1.5 MPa stress by assuming the surface area of tibial plateau of 1670 mm^2 [67]. During running, this load approaches to 50 $MPa.s^{-1}$ and 100 $MPa.s^{-1}$ that depends on the stress rate. However, the impact of loading from injury on cartilage is any load with time between two peak loads in the order of milliseconds (e.g. <30 ms) along with at least one of the following criteria: (i) stress rate greater than 1000 $MPa.s^{-1}$, (ii) loading rate above 100 $kN.s^{-1}$ or (iii) strain rate in excess of 500 $mm.mm^{-1}.s^{1}$[68]. It is important to note that these criteria are only applied to healthy cartilage; aging and other systematic changes in cartilage make cartilage more vulnerable to damage.

14.1.4.2 Osteoarthritis

Osteoarthritis (OA) is one of the major health issues worldwide and it is a burden for elderly population. Symptomatic OA manifests itself with severe pain in the joint and lack or even loss of mobility in the defected joint [69, 70]. The cost of treatment and healthcare for promoting the lifestyle of patients who suffered from OA is enormous. The Australian Institute of Health and Welfare reported that OA affects more than 1.3 million Australians in 2007 [71]. The existing trend suggests that in 2050, more than seven million Australians will be affected by OA [72].

The OA mostly caused by biochemical and biomechanical changes that systematically occur in articular cartilage. It might also be attributed to traumatic joint injuries such as accident and sport. It is estimated that approximately 11 % of Australian working force (young and middle-aged population) suffers from arthritis (mainly OA) [72].

14.1.5 Natural Articular Cartilage Repairing Process

There are two types of cartilage damages: partial- and full-thickness defects [73]. Partial-thickness damage is limited to the cartilage, and the subchondral bone is not violated in this type of damages. The site of defect has, therefore, no access to bone marrow-derived stem cells [3]; the cartilage thus lacks in intrinsic capability to heal the defected site [3, 74]. The defected site in this case might significantly expand by time since there is no healing process naturally commenced by the tissue [74]. This damage eventually leads to OA by aging. On the other hand, in full-thickness cartilage defect, the lesion has access to bone marrow-derived stem cells which allows the cartilage to undergo some spontaneous healing process [75].

In the full-thickness damage, also called osteochondral defect, the healing process extends greatly after 2 weeks. The subchondral blood vessels bring progenitor cells (mainly mesenchymal stem cells) into the defected site. These cells are more bioactive in generating cartilage ECM compared to natural chondrocytes. The migration, differentiation and proliferation of mesenchymal stem cells (MSC) at the defected site take place 2 weeks post injury. The blood from subchondral bone forms a fibrin clot, which contains platelets. These can secrete biofactors to recruit mesenchymal stem cells to form cartilage. MSCs produce collagen type II and collagen type I to fill the defected site. After approximately 6–8 weeks, the defected site is filled with collagen type I and type II [76–78]. From this point onwards, the production of collagen type II is completely switched to collagen type I. After 1 year the repaired cartilage consists of hyaline and fibrocartilage tissue [75, 79]. Fibrocartilage tissue suffers from lack of mechanical strength and physical stability [80]. These lead to cartilage matrix degeneration through fibrillation [81], chondrocyte loss and dedifferentiation and GAG loss [82]. Subsequently, deep cracks appear within the structure of cartilage after the first year, and subsequently complete failure of cartilage occurs [76–78].

Lack of chondrogenesis cell in partial- and also formation of fibrocartilage in full-thickness articular cartilage damages might lead to the OA occurrence in a patient. Therefore, articular cartilage damage must be treated with therapeutic strategies at very early stages.

14.2 Therapies for Articular Cartilage Damages

Several cartilage repair techniques have been proposed to treat different types of cartilage defects. Conventional therapeutic strategies are classified in two groups, therapeutic intervention without biological compounds or with active biologics. In this section an overview of these two groups of therapies is provided.

14.2.1 Therapeutic Intervention without Active Compounds

No biological compound is used in this group of therapeutic interventions. The efficiency of these treatment techniques relies on their stimulation impact on chondral or subchondral tissue for cartilage regeneration. The main techniques in this category are lavage, chondral shaving, debridement, Pridie drilling and microfracture that are described briefly in this section.

14.2.1.1 Lavage and Arthroscopy

Lavage or irrigation of the defected site with solution of sodium chloride, Ringer or Ringer and lactate has been practised for treatment of OA of the knee. The defected site in this technique is rinsed, using closed-needle hole or arthroscopic techniques [83]. It is claimed that thorough rinsing of tissue removes intra-articularly active pain signaling molecules from the defected site, thus leading to the relief of pain in patients. The irrigation of cartilage surface might also lead to extraction of proteoglycan and aggrecans from the superficial surface of articular cartilage, which might temporarily improve the adhesion of repaired cells at the defected site

[84, 85]. In clinical studies, however, lavage (irrespective of whether it is performed with closed-needle hole or arthroscopic techniques) appears to resolve the issue for a short period of time [86, 87]. This approach is more effective for the patients with history of trauma (such as sports injury, tearing of the ligament or meniscus or traumatic structural lesions) compared to the cases with other types of OA [84, 88].

14.2.1.2 Chondral Shaving

Chondral shaving is conducted with arthroscopic techniques to mechanically remove the defected site, using appropriate surgical instrument. In recent years, it is only performed for treatment of chondromalacia patellae pain. The results of in vivo studies suggest that this procedure does not have any impact on cartilage regeneration in mature rabbits after 12 weeks. The remaining cartilage also underwent degeneration due to apoptotic cell loss [89–91].

14.2.1.3 Debridement

This approach involves meniscectomy process in which the chondral defected site is mechanically isolated, the lesion site underwent lavage process and all free bodies are removed from the joint [92]. The removal of chondral defect tissues leads to cell apoptosis and thus cartilage degeneration at the surrounding tissue. In addition, the meniscectomy process leads to skeletal malalignment and significant changes in the loading profile at the joint. The results of in vitro, in vivo and clinical studies demonstrated that debridement alone exacerbates the osteoarthritic conditions [93, 94].

14.2.1.4 Pridie Drilling

In this technique, therapeutic holes at the defected site are drilled from the articular cartilage surface into the subchondral bone marrow. The drilling is performed close to the defected articular cartilage sites. This stimulates the spontaneous repair reaction at the defected site [95–97]. The intervention to drill the holes (2 mm–2.5 mm in diameter) includes such methods as osteochondritis dissecans, which is a painful process. It is claimed that this technique is beneficial for OA patients by promoting the migration of chondrogenesis cells to the surface of the defected site [95, 98, 99]. In vitro and in vivo studies showed that Pridie drilling on rabbit resulted in formation of fibrocartilage tissue. This method may be accompanied with inflammation at the defected joint [100]. Clinical studies, however, showed that Pridie drilling is a safe treatment for cartilage repair for a short period only [101].

14.2.1.5 Microfracture

The biological basis of this technique is the same as Pridie drilling. The only differences between Pridie drilling and microfracture techniques are the size and numbers of holes [102]. In microfracture technique, micro-sized pores (from 500 μm to 1 mm in diameter) are generated within the entire articular cartilage lesion site. This technique is efficient for lesions with average size of less than 2.3 cm^2. The depth of holes is approximately 4 mm and 3–4 holes are generated per cm^2 of the cartilage defected site. The smaller diameter of holes in this technique, compared to Pridie technique, leads to less adverse impact on biomechanical properties of the subchondral bone [103]. Animal studies confirmed the regeneration of tissue by using this method. In clinic, the microfracture technique is mainly applied for articular cartilage damages in young athletes [102]. Positive results are reported for cartilage treatments by microfracture; in 75 % of cases, pain relief and improvement in joint functionality are reported. However, application of this method for the patients with OA with lack of adequate number of bone marrow-derived mesenchymal stem cells is not promising [88, 104].

14.2.2 Allogeneic Osteochondral and Chondral Grafting (Full Osteochondral Allograft)

In this technique, allogeneic osteochondral or chondral graft is used to fill the articular cartilage defected site, which has no intention to stimulate cartilage repair responses. It relies on replacing the defected tissue with healthy cartilage that is usually derived from cadavers [105, 106]. Patients with substantial osteochondral defects such as tumour reaction, osteonecrosis, broad OA, osteochondritis dissecans and extensive trauma have benefited from this treatment technique. However, there are immunological problems associated with this technique which might lead to complete rejection of the grafted tissue. Animal studies showed that allogeneic grafts survived under immunosuppressive conditions. In addition, matching the histocompatibility between the grafted and native tissue is required to reduce cell-mediated cytotoxicity and antibody titre [107, 108]. Clinical studies with this treatment technique revealed that the immunoresponses in the human body are less than those in animals [109–111]. In addition, the osteochondral transplant grafts survive for a longer period of time even after freezing and lyophilisation [109–111]. The success rates of 65–85 % are reported for this treatment technique even after follow-up period of 10 years [112, 113]. The application of this method, however, is limited due to scarcity of fresh donor and problems associated with the handling and storage of frozen allograft tissues. It is also critical to contemplate the risk of disease transmission for allogeneic osteochondral and chondral grafting [88].

Table 14.2 Results from clinical studies of MF and FOA techniques for articular cartilage defect treatment

Treatment technique	No. of joint	Average age (yrs.)	Lesion size (cm^2)	Results, year (successful cases %)[1]	Refs.
MF	11	38.5	2	1 (100), 1.5 (0)	[114]
FOA	20	42	NR	2(90), 5 (35), 10 (15)	[115]
	14	37	NR	2(57), 5(43), 10 (29)	[116]

[1]For example 2 (90) represented: after 2 years of follow-up time, there are 90 % of successful cases

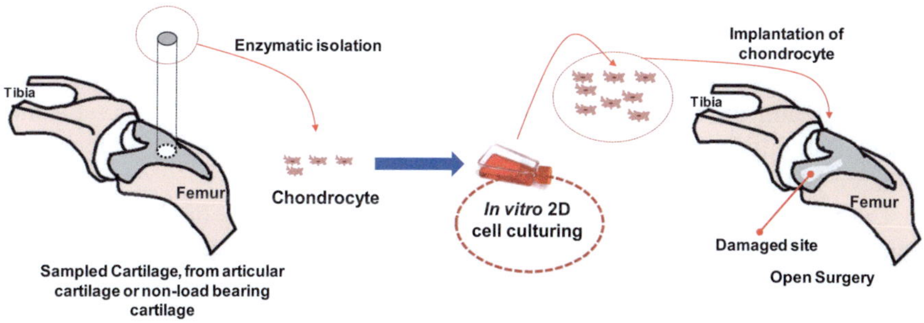

Fig. 14.4 Schematic overview of classical ACI technique for articular cartilage treatment

Among all the previously mentioned techniques for cartilage repair, microfracture (MF) and fresh osteochondral allograft (FOA) are the only methods with acceptable biological basis. Different human studies investigated the efficacy of these techniques for treatment of articular cartilage defect. The results from the clinical studies on efficacy of MF and FOA techniques are summarised in Table 14.2.

14.2.3 Autologous Implantation Technique

Different cell-based therapies have been proposed such as autologous chondrocyte implementation (ACI) technique for treatment of cartilage defects [117]. ACI is established in 1994 [117] and thereafter fully approved by the US Food and Drug Administration (FDA) in 1997 [118]. This treatment technique is schematically shown in Fig. 14.4. The first generation of ACI technique provided significant and long-term benefits for patients as per providing tissue functionality and pain relief with better lifestyle. The major problematic issues in this method are the serious damage that imposed at the donor collection site [88]; monolayer in vitro culture of chondrocyte, which leads to the formation of fibrocartilage [119]; and also hypertrophy or ossification of the patched periosteum [120].

14.2.4 Motivation for Tissue Engineering

A demand for tissue engineering of cartilage arises from two perspectives, the high risk of failure in using traditional treatment techniques and the large numbers of patients suffering from articular cartilage defects. Articular cartilage damages can occur during childhood, in young adults and also in elderly people. Osteochondrosis and osteochondritis are joint defects that occur mainly in children due to the lower capacity of skeletally immature cartilage to high range of stresses. The rate of knee cartilage injuries is more than 25 % of participants in any sport activity. In addition, articular cartilage damage in elbow and shoulder joints commonly occurs in athletes who play baseball and cricket, for example [121–123]. It is estimated that one out of three children suffers from severe cartilage damage requiring medical treatment. The cost of treatment for articular cartilage damage is estimated to be $ 1.8 billion per annum considering that more than 30 million school-aged children just in the USA participate in sport activities [124].

During the last decade, the first generation of ACI technique has been the major approach for the treatment of cartilage defects [118]. Cartilage tissue engineering is considered as a second generation of ACI and has been proposed to address the issues with current cartilage treatments to improve autologous chondrocyte implementation techniques [125–129]. Tissue engineering involves using suitable type of cells, scaffolds and bioactive molecules such as growth factors [130]. Tissue engineering approaches will be discussed comprehensively in the next section.

14.3 Tissue Engineering of Cartilage

Tissue engineering is the modern approach in treatment of articular cartilage defects using suitable types of cells, biomaterials and bioactive molecules such as growth factors [130]. The schematic overview of tissue engineering approaches for treatment of damaged cartilage is shown in Fig. 14.5. Briefly, suitable cell types such as chondrocyte and stem cell (e.g. from autologous sources) are harvested from patients, and then the cells are cultured in vitro. Chondrogenesis biofactors may be used to promote the capacity of cells for cartilage regeneration. A biomaterial matrix is required for 3D cell growth, which is comprised of scaffolds for in vitro cell growth or a cell carrier system for in vivo applications. For cartilage tissue engineering, there are two approaches, namely, in vitro and in vivo cartilage regeneration. In the former, cells are seeded on the scaffolds and the construct is cultured for a specific period of time. The resulted autologous tissue is then transplanted into the patient via arthrotomy (open surgery) or arthroscopy. In the latter, the suspension of cells in bioengineered matrix is injected into the articular cartilage damaged site. Selection of proper cells and incorporation of chondrogenesis biofactors and the bioengineered matrix have pivotal role in

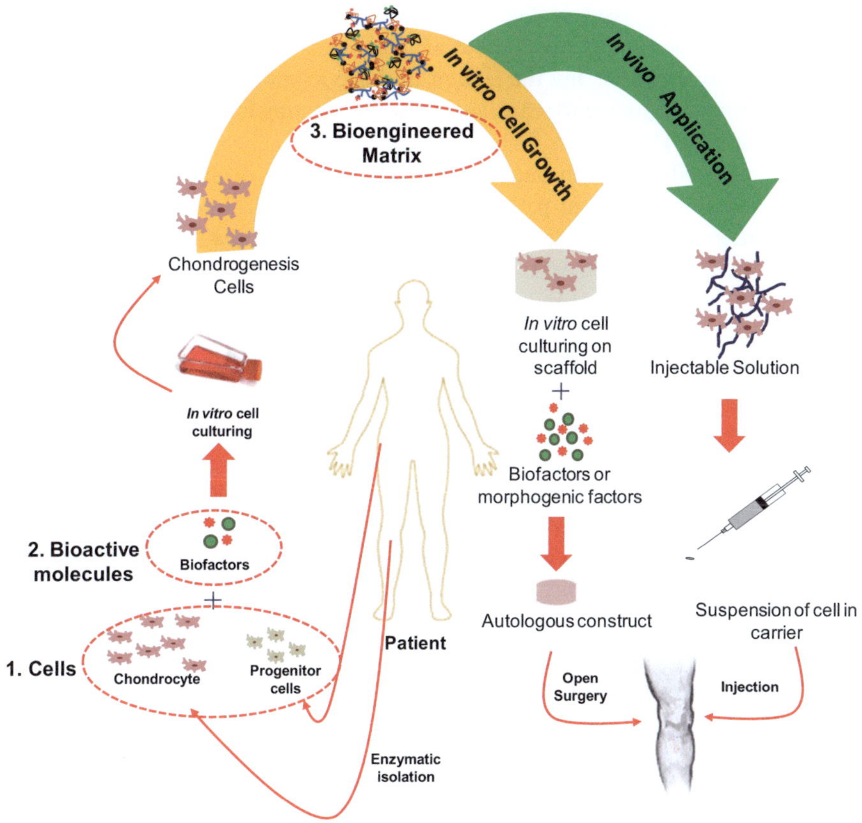

Fig. 14.5 Modern ACI treatment technique for articular cartilage repair

modern ACI technique [131]. Suitable cell types, bioactive compounds and characteristics of biomaterials for cartilage tissue engineering are discussed below.

14.3.1 Cells

Several different cell sources are proposed for cartilage tissue engineering. Autologous chondrocyte, isolated from hyaline or articular cartilage, however is regarded as the most common cell type. By extracting cells from patient's own body, the issue of any immune response can be avoided. In addition, chondrocyte is already differentiated into target cartilage phenotype and can secrete cartilage ECM, such as collagen and proteoglycan [132]. For the cases with extensive cartilage damage or disease, procurement of autologous chondrocyte is not possible. An alternative method is to use allogeneic chondrocyte from a donor tissue. This approach, however, is limited by disease transmission and also host body immune response.

In general, the major issue in the application of both allogeneic and autologous chondrocytes is the limited numbers of available cells, the instability of chondrocyte in monolayer culture and the lack of intrinsic repair capacity [131]. A promising alternative cell source for cartilage tissue engineering is autologous progenitor cells or stem cells [133].

Adult stem cells reside throughout the different parts of the body and can be differentiated along different pathways such as chondrogenesis and osteogenesis lineages. Stem cells from fat tissue (adipose) and bone marrow mesenchymal stem cells (BM-MSC) have been extensively used for different tissue engineering applications [133]. Stem cells exhibit multipotent differentiation capacity which can be used to improve clinical treatment techniques in various locomotion tissues [134], including the bone [135], fat [136], ligament [137, 138] and articular cartilage [136, 139].

Stem cells exhibit high proliferation and growth rate, and thus for cell procurement, little sampling from donor site is required. The sampling process for adipose stem cells is also straightforward and less invasive compared to chondrocyte procurement. The process therefore is advantaged by minimal donor site morbidity and pain level. For a direct comparison between the efficacy of chondrocyte and stem cells for cartilage repair, two populations of patients are treated with either chondrocyte or stem cells [140]. The results from this study showed that articular cartilage defect treatment with autologous stem cells is as successful as the one using chondrocyte. By considering the limited number and low quality of chondrocyte in the defected tissues, treatment with stem cells has more potential for ACI applications.

The use of BM-MSC also enables simultaneous repair of the bone and cartilage, which ultimately results in promoting remodelling and integration of the regenerated cartilage with the host tissue [141, 142]. However, the monolayer culture of both stem cells and chondrocytes possesses the issue of telomere shortening,[1] loss of proliferative rate and multipotency [143–145]. An alternative source for stem cell is embryonic stem cell that has unlimited capacity for proliferation in monolayer culturing and is promising for a broad range of tissue engineering applications [133]; however, commercialisation of embryonic stem cell-based discoveries is banned in many countries, such as European countries.

14.3.2 Bioactive Factors

Regeneration and growth of cartilage and its integration with the surrounding tissues rely on the biochemical signaling of cells within the regenerating tissue. Bioactive factors include small drug-like molecules, growth factors or any other

[1]Human (and other) somatic cells without telomerase gradually lose telomeric sequences as a result of incomplete replication.

molecule that has cell motif sites and can bond with cells to create biological responses. The intensity, duration and sequence of stimulation factors affect the metabolic activity of cells and their ECM exertion.

14.3.2.1 Chondrogenesis Small Drug-Like Molecules

Small drug-like molecules have developed to selectively regulate transcriptional factors of subcellular localisations and activities [146, 147]. For cartilage tissue engineering, kartogenin is identified as a small molecule which can promote chondrogenesis and chondrocyte differentiation of MSC by disrupting interaction of filamin-A with transcription factor CBFβ. This regulates the CBFβ-RUNX1 transcriptional program, which ultimately induces chondrogenesis. The positive effect of this molecule on chondrogenesis has been studied and proved by in vitro and two animal model studies that were subjected to osteoarthritis disease. Application of drug-like selective regulator molecules for transcriptional subcellular factors is limited for their intrinsic complexity. Chondrogenesis of BM-MSC is, therefore, mostly promoted by using exogenous anabolic factors, loaded within the network of scaffold.

14.3.2.2 Growth Factors

Chondrogenesis can be promoted by using exogenous anabolic factors [148]. The growth factors include but not limited to TGF-β [148, 149] and BMP family [150–152] that have been used to promote chondrogenesis. Most commonly used growth factors for articular cartilage applications and their in vitro and in vivo effects are summarised in Table 14.3.

TGF-β superfamily is involved in tissue repair and inflammation responses following a cartilage injury [153, 154]. Controversy results are obtained for the effect of TGF-β superfamily for cartilage tissue engineering. For therapeutic application, TGF-β superfamily can prolong cartilage life by minimising or even eliciting the biological and biomechanical changes in cartilage over the years. For tissue engineering applications, some studies confirmed the positive effect of TGF-β1 in chondrogenesis proliferation and growth. The positive effect of TGF-β1 in cartilage tissue engineering, however, depends on the differentiation state of cells; for freshly isolated chondrocytes, addition of TGF-β1 had no significant effect on cell growth. The incorporation of growth factor, however, significantly affects the proliferation and proteoglycan synthesis of chondrocyte, cultured in vitro after 1 week of isolation [155]. TGF-β1 had negative impact for cartilage repair. For instance, it is observed that the synthesis of proteoglycan by arthritic chondrocytes is decreased when adding TGF-β1 to the media [156]. This reduction may result in formation of articular cartilage with unfavourable properties.

Bone morphogenetic protein (BMP) superfamily also plays an important role in endochondral bone and cartilage formations. More than 20 types of BMP have been

Table 14.3 Different growth factors, used for articular cartilage tissue engineering, and results achieved in vitro and in vivo

Growth factor	Results	Refs.
TGF-β1	No significant effect on freshly isolated cells	[153–158]
	Improve proteoglycan synthesis on chondrocytes after 1 week of post-isolation	
	Proteoglycan synthesis decreased by arthritic chondrocytes	
BMP-1	Promotes the expression of proteoglycan and collagen more than TGF-β1	[154, 159, 160]
BMP-2	Regulates proteoglycan and collagen production and helps to adjust the biomechanical and biochemical properties of regenerated tissue	[159, 160]
BMP-4	Increases cell proliferation, proteoglycan formation as well as bone formation	[160, 161]
BMP-7	Decreases collagen type I expression, increases proteoglycan and ECM production and cellular proliferation	[162, 163]
BMP-12 and BMP-13	Promotes synthesis of GAG, less significant effect compared to BMP-2	[164]

identified. In tissue engineering applications, BMPs are commonly used for bone repair and regeneration. For cartilage tissue engineering, BMPs also enhance the osteochondral integration of the defected cartilage by promoting osteogenesis and chondrogenesis at the defected site. It is shown that BMP-1 has more stimulation effect on cells to express proteoglycan and collagen compared to TGF-β1 [165]. BMP-2 also regulates the formation of collagen and proteoglycan from chondrocytes [159, 160]. In addition it promotes the healing process of cartilage defects in vivo [154]. BMP-4 stimulates proteoglycan expression and osteochondral tissue formation and also enhances cellular proliferation for articular cartilage regeneration [160, 161]. Addition of such BMP growth factors as BMP-7, BMP-12 and BMP-13, particularly BMP-2, enhances ECM formation [160] and cell proliferation [162]. In addition, BMP-7 suppresses expression of collagen type I and differentiation of fibroblast in vivo [163], which inhibits the formation of fibrocartilage at the defected site [164].

14.3.3 Biomaterials for Cartilage Regeneration

In a tissue engineering approach, biomaterials are used either for fabrication of 3D scaffolds for in vitro tissue regeneration or synthesis of an injectable vehicle to deliver cells/drugs to the defected site of cartilage for in vivo cartilage regeneration. In both techniques, biomaterials play a critical role in cellular growth and tissue regeneration. The physicochemical and biological properties of biomaterials substantially affect the functionality of repaired cartilage [166].

14.3.4 Properties for Biomaterials

Biomaterials are used as physical supports for cell growth and to avoid spillover and asymmetric distribution of cells. This is important to promote synthesis of cartilage ECM and to regenerate functional tissues. In case of cartilage tissue engineering, the biomaterials support the newly formed tissues to promote the integration of repaired cartilage with host tissue. The physical and biological properties of biomaterial used for scaffold fabrication play important roles in cell responses, adhesion and infiltration to form functional 3D structure cartilage [166]. Biomaterials must be biocompatible and exhibit cell adhesive surface properties with suitable microstructure for 3D cell proliferation. They also must be mechanically strong to support the newly regenerated tissue in vivo.

14.3.4.1 Biocompatibility and Surface Properties

Particular attention has been paid on the biocompatibility of biomaterials. Biocompatibility is predominantly affected by the chemical and biological properties of biomaterials used for cartilage repair. A biomaterial is biocompatible when it elicits neither cytotoxic effects nor inflammatory responses within the surrounding tissue [167].

Surface properties of biomaterials affect in vitro cellular adhesion, phenotype maintenance, intracellular signaling and in vivo cell recruitment, healing and osteochondral integrations [168–170]. Cell responses to the ECM matrix and the new regenerated tissues are mediated through an interfacial layer formed on the surface of scaffold or biomaterial. This layer is formed by non-specific absorption (not chemical conjugation) of ECM proteins with a biomaterial when it is in a proper physiological environment. As an example, hydrophilic properties of a polymer such as gelatine and poly(vinyl alcohol) promote the formation of interfacial layer and thus enhance the adhesion of cells [171]. The incorporation of peptides in the form of long chain of ECM proteins (such as fibronectin, laminin, elastin and collagen) or short peptide sequences, derived from ECM proteins (such as arginine–glycine–aspartic acid), provides cell binding sites on scaffold to mediate cell responses, thereby enhancing tissue regeneration [172, 173].

14.3.4.2 Microstructural and Mechanical Properties

The microstructure, porosity and pore interconnectivity are critical factors for biomaterials that are used for tissue engineering. Porosity allows the cell migration into the 3D structure of scaffold, and pore interconnectivity is a key factor for nutrient, oxygen and waste transfer into and from the cells in scaffolds [174–178]. For each cell type a range of pore sizes is required to mimic the innate tissue and allow the cells' adhesion and regeneration [179]. For in vitro cartilage tissue engineering, the average pore size in the range of 250–500 μm is recommended [180]. Small pore size resulted in occlusion and obstruction of pores, which then prevents cellular penetration within the 3D structure of scaffolds. Pores in the range of 75–100 μm can result in growth of un-mineralised osteoid tissues [181]. Additionally, only fibrous tissues penetrate within a scaffold with an average pores size of 10 μm or less. Low average pore size, therefore, leads to the formation of fibrocartilage rather than cartilage. Meanwhile, the mechanical strength of physical supports decreases by increasing the average pore size. Therefore, it is important to tune the void volume (or average pore size) in scaffolds for cartilage tissue engineering to both enable the migration of chondrogenic cells and maintain the required structural strength [178].

For in vivo cartilage tissue engineering, chondrogenic cells are suspended within the polymeric matrix, and the suspension is gelled in situ. There is no need for cells to immigrate through pores, and thus large pores from 250 to 500 μm are not necessary anymore. It is shown that small pores that are less than 100 μm in biomaterials induce osteochondral formation in vivo, while a larger pore size leads to osteogenesis before cartilage formation [182]. As an example, chondrocyte maintains its phenotype, and cartilage ECM is produced by encapsulating cells within an injectable chitosan/starch/β-glycerol hydrogel with average pore size in the range of 19.8–26.4 μm [183].

The biomaterials provide a temporary mechanical support to bearing in vivo loadings and stresses during the tissue regeneration. One of the key factors in successful tissue engineering is to develop a mechanically strong scaffold that its degradation rate corresponds to the rate of regeneration of ECM. External loads and stresses stimulate cell proliferation, remodelling and tissue regeneration [184–186]. It is essential that loads gradually transfer from the biomaterials (supporting cell growth and tissue regeneration) to the regenerated cartilage to promote tissue remodelling. It is therefore, critical to control the degradation rate and mechanical strength of scaffold to ensure sufficient structural integrity of matrix is retained during the regeneration of cartilage [187]. The rapid degradation of biomaterials is not desirable as it provokes excessive stresses and impact loads to the developed tissues prior to sufficient growth and remodelling cartilage. This effect might result in complete failure of regenerated tissue construct. On the other hand, the slow degradation of biomaterials may shield the cells against external stimulating stresses, which can decrease the proliferation and growth rate of chondrogenesis cells. It is important to design scaffolds with the mechanical properties that mimic cartilage tissues for in vitro and in vivo applications. The compressive modulus of native cartilage varies from 0.08 to 2.1 MPa [31, 32, 39] and its tensile modulus in between 4.8 and 25 MPa [25]. It might be possible to use biomaterials that may not fully meet these mechanical properties, as the newly formed cartilage might provide extra structural integrity after implantation.

14.3.5 *Scaffold for In Vitro Tissue Engineering*

Tissue engineering techniques have been proposed for the treatment of articular cartilage defects. In modern ACI, 3D scaffolds are used to address the issues associated with monolayer culture of chondrogenesis cells in vitro such as dedifferentiation and ossification of chondrogenesis cells [126]. In vitro cell studies showed that chondrocyte phenotype can be maintained up to 8 months of post seeding in 3D scaffold [188]. In the clinical approach for the treatment of cartilage defect, chondrogenesis cells (chondrocytes or stem cells) are seeded on a biodegradable scaffold and cultured in vitro. The construct is harvested in vitro, and cell viability and chondrogenesis of cultured cells are continually tested for a period of 6 weeks. Subsequently, the regenerated tissue, formed within the scaffold, is transplanted at the defected site (most commonly with open surgery). The efficacy of this technique for the treatment of articular cartilage defect is substantially affected by the characteristics of scaffolds used for in vitro cell growth [188]. Different biomaterials are attempted for the fabrication of scaffolds for cartilage regenerations. These include biodegradable synthetic and natural polymers that are either hydrophobic or hydrophilic.

14.3.5.1 Synthetic Polymers

Synthetic polymers exhibit reproducible and predictable physicochemical, mechanical and degradation properties, all of which can be closely tuned to fulfil the requirements. In addition, the risk of toxicity, immunogenicity and infections is low in the application of synthetic polymers for different biomedical applications since they constituted of well-known molecular structure. Poly(α-hydroxy esters) are widely used for cartilage tissue engineering, and they are often processed to form 3D porous structures with hydrophobic properties. Meanwhile, poly(vinyl alcohol) (PVA), poly(ethylene glycol) and polyacrylates (PEs) formed hydrophilic structures with high water content, called hydrogel. Hydrogels are a class of biomaterials, composed of natural or synthetic polymer chains with very high water content (above 30 wt%) [189]. Hydrogels become the material of choice as scaffold for cartilage tissue engineering applications attributable to their hydrophilic properties, high water content, superior permeability of nutrients, long chain molecules, proteins and oxygen [174, 179, 190–193]. Some of the in vitro and in vivo outcomes, from the applications of main synthetic polymers as scaffold for tissue growth, are summarised in Table 14.4 and comprehensively discussed in the following sections.

Table 14.4 The pros and cons observed from in vivo and in vitro applications of synthetic polymers for cartilage repair

Biomaterial	Positive outcomes	Negative outcomes	Refs.
PGA	Maintenance of chondrocyte phenotype in vitro and in vivo	Initial in vitro cell culturing is necessary to initiate ECM formation in vitro	[194–197]
PLGA	Can maintain the chondrocyte phenotype in 2 weeks of in vitro	Initial in vitro culturing is necessary prior to in vivo implantation	[194–197]
PLA	Minimising release of acid as the result of degradation	Biochemical properties inferior to native tissue	[198, 199]
	Maintaining structural mechanical support for a long time	Low cell adhesive surface properties	
	Cartilaginous appearance		
PCL	High structural integrity in in vitro culturing	Very low chondrocyte adhesion and proliferation	[200–202]
PVA	Similar water content as natural cartilage	Dedifferentiate chondrocyte due to very low mechanical properties	[203–207]
	Has high growth factor loading capacity		
	Osteochondral		
PEG-ma	Photo-crosslinkable, suitable for cell encapsulation	Lack of mechanical strength for load-bearing cartilage	[208–210]
	Chondrogenesis cells induced cartilage ECM formation by the addition of required growth factors		
PEG-da	Photo-crosslinkable and suitable for cartilage regeneration	Lack of cell motif sites	[211–215]
	Tuneable mechanical and physical properties to match the requisites for cartilage repair		
	Can act as a crosslinking agent for different PEG-based polymers		
OPF	Formation of cartilage-like tissue by using OPF hydrogel for cartilage regeneration both in vitro and in vivo	The lack of cell motif sites might lead to low chondrogenesis cell proliferation and growth	[216–218]
		Non-biodegradable properties of this hydrogel might lead to unpredictable problems and unreproducible results	

Poly(α-Hydroxy Esters)

Poly(α-hydroxy esters) (PHEs) is a class of synthetic biodegradable polymers that have been used for the preparation of scaffolds for cartilage tissue engineering.

They include poly(lactic acid) (PLA), poly(glycolic acid) (PGA), poly(lactic-*co*-glycolic acid) (PLGA) and poly(ε-caprolactone) (PCL). Based on the position of methyl group in the lactic acid monomer, there are three stereoisomers of PLA (D (−), L(+) and D,L). The degree of crystallinity in PLLA is higher than those of PDLA and PDLLA. All PHE polymers have had the FDA approval for different biomedical applications [219].

PHEs can be easily processed, and their degradation and mechanical and physical properties are tuneable over a wide range by changing their molecular weight, crystallinity and copolymer composition. Their degradation process via a random, bulk hydrolysis of ester bonds in the polymer chain, however, might induce premature bulk failure of scaffolds. In addition, the release of acidic degradation products can cause strong inflammatory responses [220, 221]. These synthetic polymers degrade to monomeric acids and thereafter to carbon dioxide and water through de-esterification phase. PGA molecules are degraded to glycine and PLA to lactic acid. In vivo, polymeric degradation products are exerted by natural pathways via respiratory routes and renal filtration [222].

The kinetics of degradation in PHEs are affected by different factors, including (i) copolymer composition, (ii) molecular weight, (iii) degree of crystallinity, (iv) polydispersity index, (v) structural morphology (pore size and porosity) and (vi) distribution of chemically active compounds such as proteins in their structures [223, 224]. In PLGA scaffolds, for example, the degradation rate strongly depends on lactic/glycolic monomer ratio and crystallinity of lactic monomer [223]. PHE scaffolds exhibit two profiles of degradation, surface and bulk degradation. Surface degradation presents easier diffusion of soluble oligomer and neutralisation of the carboxylic end groups by surrounding buffer solution in vitro or in vivo. Conversely, the degradation rate in bulk is promoted by autocatalysis [225]. Therefore, PLA with a methyl pending group degrades slower compared to PGA without any pending group. In addition, the hydrolysis of amorphous polymers such as PDLLA is faster due to lack of crystalline regions [225].

The mechanical properties of PHEs depend on the molecular weight, microstructure and crystallinity of polymers. In general, PGA is more hydrophilic and rigid, whereas PLA is more flexible (higher elastic modulus) with low degradation rate. Copolymerisation of these two polymers in different ratios can be used to form PLGA polymer with optimised mechanical, degradation and water uptake properties. PLGA has amorphous structure because PLA and PGA are not tightly coupled and, therefore, it exhibits higher degradation rate compared to both PGA and PLA [226].

PLA, PLGA and PGA are used for cartilage tissue engineering in the forms of fibres (electrospun as discussed in Chap. 8) or foamed scaffolds. In vitro and in vivo studies showed the maintenance of chondrocyte phenotype on PLGA and PGA scaffolds [194, 197]. But functional cartilage could only be achieved by short-term in vitro chondrocyte culturing on the scaffolds and then in vivo implantation of constructs [195, 196]. Electrospun PLA scaffolds have been used for in vitro cartilage tissue engineering. Chondrocyte maintains its chondrogenic phenotype after 7 days of culturing on PLA [199]. One-year animal studies using allogeneic perichondrial cells [227] and autogenous perichondrial cells [198] on PLA scaffold showed inconsistent subchondral bone regeneration.

In addition, regenerated tissues have been disadvantaged by inferior biochemical properties compared to natural cartilage [198]. The limited application of these types of polymers for cartilage tissue regeneration is due to the poor cell adhesion to their surface. PLA has been conjugated with monomethoxy poly(ethylene glycol) (mPEG) to increase its hydrophilicity and cellular adhesive properties [228]. The compressive modulus of PLA/mPEG polymer, however, decreased significantly compared to PLA [228].

Poly(ε-caprolactone) or PCL is aliphatic linear polyester, which undergoes autocatalysed bulk hydrolysis. The degradation process of this biomaterial is slow due to its semi-crystalline nature and hydrophobicity [229, 230]. The packed macromolecular arrays retard fluid diffusion into the bulk of hydrophobic PCL. This polymer is, therefore, used as a long-term implant (e.g. for years) in different biomedical applications. To increase the degradation rate of this polymer and also its processability, PCL is copolymerised with different PHEs [229, 230]. The copolymerisation, however, substantially decreases the mechanical strength of PCL copolymer and thus limited their applications for cartilage tissue engineering. In addition, the hydrophobic surface of this synthetic polymer might adversely affect the cell adhesion and proliferation. To achieve PCL-based scaffolds with more favourable biological properties, composite scaffolds of PCL and naturally derived polymers such as PCL with chitosan [231], hyaluronan, fibrin [232] and elastin [200, 201] have been prepared. In one study PCL porous scaffold has been fabricated using gas foaming by high pressure CO_2 and salt leaching techniques. Then elastin is impregnated into these pore structures. The in vitro study demonstrated that chondrocyte cell adhesion and proliferation within the 3D structure of this PCL/elastin composite scaffold are substantially enhanced compared to neat PCL [201].

Acidic degradation products of PHEs can cause adverse tissue reactions and might induce immunoresponsive reactions. To counteract the acidic degradation process for some of PHEs and also to stabilise the pH of the surrounding environment, these polymers are combined with basic compounds [223, 224]. Calcium phosphate compounds and bioactive glasses are the two main additives used for this purpose. The addition of bioactive glass might also modify the mechanical properties of scaffolds and promote osteoconductivity of biomaterial. Bioactive glasses are thus used for bone tissue engineering rather than cartilage regeneration.

One of the major drawbacks of PHEs is their hydrophobicity, which can adversely affect the cell phenotype, cellular growth and proliferation. Different techniques, such as surface modification [200, 201], NaOH surface treatment [233] and ammonia plasma treatment [234], have been attempted to promote chondrogenesis cell adhesion on the surface of PHE. For instance, coating the surface of PLLA with chitosan and collagen enhances the cellular adhesion. However, cell proliferation and differentiation in PLA/collagen scaffold is inhibited due to blockage of pores.

Poly(vinyl Alcohol) (PVA)

PVA is hydrophilic biocompatible polymer that can be crosslinked to form hydrogel. It is historically used for cartilage regeneration applications [235] and can be engineered to have similar water uptake properties as native cartilage [203]. PVA hydrogel can be cut into the required shapes and then transplant into the patient's body through an open surgery process. In vitro cell studies on pure PVA hydrogel showed that low mechanical strength of the construct might lead to dedifferentiation of seeded chondrocyte, and hence further processing is required to increase its mechanical strength. Poly(lactic-co-glycolic acid) microparticles have been embedded within PVA hydrogel network, and insulin-like growth factor-1 (IGF-1) has been loaded in the hydrogel, which showed that the sustained release of IGF-1 can enhance cartilage formation which might lead to effective integration of the construct with the surrounding tissue [207].

Poly(ethylene Glycol)-Based Polymers

Poly(ethylene glycol) (PEG), also known as poly(oxyethylene) or poly(ethylene oxide), is one of the most extensively investigated non-biodegradable, synthetic, hydrophilic polymers for different cartilage tissue engineering applications [236]. This is due to its hydrophilicity, acceptable cell compatibility and non-cytotoxicity. PEG can also be easily functionalised with different reactive end groups. Copolymer of hydrophilic poly(ethylene glycol) (PEG) and different biodegradable and biocompatible polyesters, such as polylactide (PLA), poly(-ε-caprolactone) and poly(glycolide) (PGA), have drawn great attention for their tuneable characteristic parameters [237].

PEG macromer is functionalised with methacrylate (ma) groups to form a photo-crosslinkable hydrogel, suitable for cartilage tissue engineering [208]. Different chondrogenesis cell types, including chondrocytes, embryonic stem cells and MSCs, are encapsulated with PEG-ma hydrogels and induced to form cartilage tissue in the presence of growth factor [208–210]. Diacrylate (da)-functionalised macromers of PEG have also been developed for different cartilage tissue engineering applications [211–215]. The lack of cell motif sites within its structure is the main drawback of this polymer. Due to high activity of PEG-da macromer, it can be used as a chemical crosslinking agent for different PEG-based macromers [212].

More biomimetic derivative macromers of PEG have been synthesised by conjugating collagen-mimetic peptide –(Pro-Hyp-Gly)$_x$– with PEG macromers. In vitro cell study showed that MSC proliferates and both collagen and proteoglycan are produced within this hydrogel [238]. In addition, the incorporation of PEG to chondroitin sulphate-based hydrogels increases the production of cartilage ECM proteins from MSCs seeded within this hydrogel [239]. PEG can also be functionalised by the addition of fumarate groups to the macromer using fumaric acid. Oligo(poly(ethylene glycol) fumarate) (OPF) is the fumarate-functionalised, photo-crosslinkable PEG macromer. In a rabbit model with osteochondral defects, acellular OPF hydrogel has been used, and it is observed that native MSCs migrate within the 3D structure of these hydrogels to form fibrocartilage at the lesion site. Encapsulation of external MSCs within the OPF hydrogel structure results in regeneration of cartilage [218]. Different in vitro and in vivo studies have been conducted to investigate the capability of OPF hydrogels to deliver different growth factors to the defected site to promote natural process of cartilage tissue regeneration. These studies showed the potential of OPF hydrogels for encapsulation of different growth factors for cartilage tissue engineering [216, 217]. Tuneable properties, easy to process and functionalised, hydrophilic and biocompatible properties of PEG-based hydrogels are the main advantages of this group of biomaterials for cartilage tissue engineering.

Polyacrylates (PEs)

Poly(2-hydroxyethyl methacrylate) (PHEMA), poly(methyl methacrylate), poly (ethyl methacrylate) and poly(tetrahydrofurfuryl methacrylate) are the main polyacrylate-based hydrogels used for cartilage tissue engineering. It has been attempted to use PHEMA/MMA hydrogel for articular cartilage repair. However, the regenerated tissue exhibited lower mechanical strength compared to the surrounding native cartilage. Compliance of the fabricated PHEMA/poly(methyl methacrylate) hydrogel might lead to the formation of fibrocartilage as a result of implantation of construct in vivo [240]. Sawtell et al. also reported the cartilage inductive properties of PEMA/poly(tetrahydrofurfuryl methacrylate) hydrogel. In vitro studies showed the expression of GAG from seeded chondrocytes on this hydrogel. This results indicated the potential of PEMA/poly(tetrahydrofurfuryl methacrylate) hydrogel for cartilage repair [241]. Animal studies on this hydrogel showed the regeneration of hyaline cartilage at the subchondral defected site in rabbits [242]. The non-biodegradation properties of this group of biomaterials might lead to some noncontrollable biological behaviour by the cartilaginous construct after in vivo implantation. This is the main drawback in the application of these polyacrylate biomaterials for cartilage repair.

14.3.5.2 Naturally Derived Hydrogels

The feasibility of using biopolymers such as protein and polysaccharides for cartilage tissue engineering has been examined [5, 6]. The presence of cell motif sites in naturally derived polymer promotes their cellular adhesive properties. Protein-based hydrogels that have been attempted for cartilage tissue engineering include collagen, fibrin, silk and elastin-like polypeptides (ELPs). Commonly used polysaccharides are hyaluronic acid, agarose, alginate and chitosan. The common methods used for crosslinking these polymers and a summary of their properties are listed in Table 14.5, while more details are provided in the following discussion.

Table 14.5 Natural hydrogels for in vitro cartilage tissue engineering

Biomaterial	Crosslinking method	Comments	Refs.
Collagen types I and II	Physical/chemical (mixed with alginate) glutaraldehyde)	Bioactive, but poor mechanical properties	[243–249]
		Chondrogenesis after 3 days when mixed with alginate	
		No cell degeneration after 24 weeks	
		For physical crosslinking, possible to incorporate cells and chondrogenesis biofactors	
		Chemical crosslinking slightly increases the mechanical properties, but there is a risk of cytotoxicity	
		In vivo cell study with chemically crosslinked collagen in rabbit model	
		Might be immunogenic	
Fibrin	Physical	Poor mechanical properties	[88, 250–252]
		Immunoresponsive effect	
		Promote natural healing process at the defected site	
		Chondrocyte and biofactors can be incorporated	
Silk	Physical	High mechanical strength, risk of immunoresponses	[253–256]
		Tedious purification required to minimise this risk	
		Stem cells and chondrocyte maintained chondrogenic phenotype	
		Might initiate adverse immunoresponses	
		Required complicated purification process	
Alginate	Chemical (ion induced)	Easy to produce, cost-effective	[176, 243, 257–259]
		Chondrocytes and biofactors can be incorporated within its structure	
		Low bioactivity, slow and inconsistent degradation rate	
		Low cell adhesive properties	
Chitosan	Physical/chemical (genipin and glutaraldehyde)	Easy to process and functionalised	[260–263]
		Chondrocyte maintains its phenotype in this hydrogel	
		Good cell adhesion and proliferation	
		Possess low mechanical properties	
Chondroitin sulphate	Physical	Inhibit GAG production	[259, 264–268]
		High cost	

(continued)

Table 14.5 (continued)

Biomaterial	Crosslinking method	Comments	Refs.
Elastin-like polypeptides	Physical/chemical (glutaraldehyde)	Maintain chondrocyte phenotype	[201, 269–272]
		Functionalised to form covalent bonding and crosslinking	
		Tuneable chemical structure to promote chondrogenesis	
		Lack of mechanical strength	
		High cost	

Collagen

Collagen type II and type I are used for cartilage repair as these are the key types of collagens that exist in this organ [243, 273]. Chondrogenesis cells bind to collagen hydrogel via integrins, which induces chondrogenesis signaling that promotes cartilage formation. Collagen type II initiates and maintains chondrogenesis phenotype of mesenchymal stem cells enhancing the effect of TGF-β1 on cartilage formation [243]. The main advantage associated with collagen type I is its potential to spontaneously form hydrogel at physiological temperature and pH. Despite the fact that collagen type I is only found in the structure of diseased or damaged cartilage, the studies showed that the articular chondrocyte maintains its phenotype in collagen type I. Chondrocytes synthesised cartilage ECM component (e.g. collagen type II and proteoglycan) when using hydrogels fabricated from collagen type I [248]. Chondrocytes embedded within a collagen type I hydrogel are used for the treatment of full-thickness articular cartilage defect in small animals. Moderate regeneration of articular cartilage surface is reported [248]. In another study, however, it is shown that after 2 weeks of in vitro culture, only 30 % of chondrocytes on collagen type I hydrogel maintained their chondrocytic phenotype (spherical shape) [249]. Nevertheless, when using hydrogels from collagen type II, more than 60 % of chondrocytes maintained their spherical shape [249]. Buma et al. developed a composite hydrogel of collagen types I and II to further mimic the biochemical properties of natural cartilage. In this approach deep layer of hydrogel is formed from collagen type I for subchondral recruitment of stem cells. The more superficial layers of hydrogel, however, are composed of collagen type II that maintains chondrogenesis phenotype of cells [274]. Results from the application of collagen type II hydrogels for treatment of osteochondral defect in rabbit model showed the formation of both hyaline cartilage and the bone at the defected site. However, the mechanical properties of regenerated tissues are significantly lower than native tissues [244].

Several strategies have been undertaken to enhance the mechanical strength of collagen-based hydrogels such as crosslinking [243], mixing collagen with a synthetic polymer such as PLGA [275], bioactive glass [275] and hydroxyapatite [276]. For chemical crosslinking of collagen, the amine side group of lysine and hydroxylysine is chemically bonded with a crosslinking agent. Glutaraldehyde

[245], hexamethylene diisocyanate [277] and 1-ethyl-3-(3-dimethylaminopropyl) carbodiimide [246] are the examples of crosslinkers [247]. However, the effect of chemical crosslinking on mechanical properties and degradation of collagen hydrogel is trivial [243, 278].

Elastin and Elastin-Like Polypeptides (ELPs)

Elastin is 68 kDa protein comprised of approximately 800 amino acid residues [279]. It has elasticity and mechanical strength that mimic native cartilage and ligament tissues [280]. Elastin contains hydrophobic and hydrophilic domains, which provides crosslinking sites with neighbouring molecules [281]. Application of elastin in tissue engineering, however, is limited for many years by its extreme water insolubility [282]. This has been improved by increasing availability of animal-derived soluble elastin through acidic (α-elastin) [283, 284], alkaline (k-elastin) [284] and enzymatic hydrolysis of elastin [285, 286]. In addition, a recently developed recombinant full-length elastin precursor, known as recombinant tropoelastin (rhTE), has been developed suitable for biomedical applications [285]. It is viable to synthesise elastin-like polypeptides (ELPs) by polymerisation of pentapeptide motif VPGVG and control physical and functional properties at the generic or chemical level [279].

Early studies showed the positive effect of elastin in promoting production of chondrocyte ECM such as collagen type II and proteoglycan in long-term monolayer culture of chondrocyte without dedifferentiation [269]. After 10 days of culturing chondrocyte in thermosensitive ELP solution, its phenotype is maintained and both collagen type II and GAG are produced [269]. Primary chondrocyte [287] and adult stem cell [288] have been cultured using coacervated ELP structure for cartilage tissue engineering. It has been demonstrated that ELP promotes the differentiation of stem cell that has undergone chondrocytic pathway even in the absence of any specific chondrocyte growth factor [288]. Elimination of growth factor significantly reduces the cost of differentiation and cartilage regeneration [285]. However, the shear moduli of ELP are fourfold lower than that of articular cartilage. The addition of crosslinking agent is one option to enhance the mechanical strength of ELP [37, 287]. For instance ELP is functionalised with glutamine to fabricate an enzymatic crosslinking site and create hydrogel [270]. This ELP-based hydrogel exhibits chondrogenesis behaviour and produces cartilage ECM proteins [270].

ELP-based biomaterials are chemically crosslinked from their active lysine group to increase their mechanical properties [289–291]. Lim et al. fabricated ELP hydrogel by reacting lysine containing ELPs with an organophosphorus crosslinker, β-[tris(hydroxymethyl)phosphino]propionic acid (THPP) in less than 5 min [289]. Both in vitro and in vivo cell studies confirmed the formation of cartilage ECM with these hydrogels [289, 290]. The mechanical strength of elastin-based hydrogel can be enhanced by synthesising this class of molecules with more crosslinking sites. It is also feasible to use naturally derived elastin and mix it with mechanically stronger tropoelastin to enhance their mechanical properties [292].

Level of crosslinking, formulation, molecular weight and concentration of ELPs are the important factors that may affect the properties of ELP hydrogel and its performance for cartilage repair [271]. It is found that the molecular weight of ELPs has negligible effect on the physiochemical and biological properties of regenerated cartilage [293]. However, the crosslinking and also mechanical properties of ELP have significant impact on cartilage regeneration. The human tropoelastin has been crosslinked with genipin and created a hydrogel with compressive modulus in the range reported for articular cartilage [272]. This sample is then press-fitted into osteochondral defect site in a knee joint of rabbit for in vivo studies. Preliminary results showed no significant inflammation and high level of hyaline articular cartilage formation.

The high cost of producing elastin by recombinant technology or protein synthesis, immunogenicity of naturally derived elastin and low mechanical properties are the hurdles for application of elastin for cartilage repair despite its excellent biological properties.

Fibrin

Fibrin, which is produced by enzymatic cleavage of fibrinogen, is used for cartilage tissue engineering due to its role in natural wound healing [88, 250]. It promotes healing process within the extravascular space. Similar to other natural polymers, products of fibrin degradation are not toxic [250]. Fibrin has been used as a scaffold to deliver chondrocyte [294], mesenchymal stem cell [295] or growth factors [296] for cartilage tissue engineering applications. The natural healing process is optimised by implanting fibrin clot at the defected site [297, 298]. It can, therefore, promote spreading of endogenous blood over the large volume of the lesion site, which otherwise would be occupied with a developing haematoma. Chondrogenesis cells have been incorporated within the network of fibrin hydrogel to further enhance the healing process [251]. Both in vitro and in vivo results confirmed the positive impact of incorporated chondrogenesis cells with fibrin clot for cartilage regeneration [299, 300]. Despite these positive results, due to the low mechanical strengths and immunoresponsive effect of fibrin, this protein has minimal potential to be used directly for cartilage tissue engineering [252, 301, 302].

Silk

Silk fibroin is a typical protein that forms the filament of native silkworm. It has a broad range of applications due to its unique physicochemical properties. Silk mimics many characteristic properties of cartilage extracellular metrics and has potential for cartilage repair. These properties include high mechanical strength, flexibility, low degradation rate and water permeability [254, 303–305]. The physically crosslinked silk hydrogel is used for chondrogenesis of bone marrow-derived mesenchymal stem cells, in which chondrogenic growth factors are used in culture media [306]. The chondrogenesis of MSCs is further increased by the incorporation of IGF-1 growth factor to silk hydrogel [307]. In vitro cell study on silk hydrogel showed great promise for the application of this type of hydrogel for full-thickness cartilage repair using both chondrocytes and stem cells [308, 309]. A structural protein blend system based on silkworm, silk fibroin and recombinant human tropoelastin has also been developed to form a scaffold with high mechanical strength, controllable degradation behaviour and elasticity [310, 311]. These studies showed human mesenchymal stem cell adhered and proliferated on this scaffold, exhibiting high potential of this protein blend for cartilage repair.

Care must be taken in purification of silk to remove sericin from fibroin silk to inhibit adverse immune response at the host tissue. In vivo studies demonstrated that pure fibroin silk has low immunogenicity and elicits foreign body response. Limited studies claimed that granuloma might form due to abandoned phagocytic response to silk by giant body cells and macrophages [256]. Compared with other biopolymer, however, silk is a desirable natural polymer for cartilage repair.

Chitosan

Chitosan, a positively charged polymer, is a linear polysaccharide that consists of randomly distributed N-acetyl-D-glucosamine and β-(1,4)-linked-D-glucosamine units [312]. It has been broadly used for biomedical applications for the low cost, low toxicity and immunostimulatory effects [260]. Molecular structure of chitosan resembles glycosaminoglycan, which also presents in the molecular structure of GAG. It thus interacts with different articular cartilage growth factors, adhesion proteins and receptors; hence chitosan can stimulate chondrogenesis of cells. In addition, physicochemical and biological properties of chitosan rely on the activity of glucosamine residues from acetylation [313], alkylation [314], carboxymethylation [315] and conjugation of chitosan with methacrylic acid and lactic acid [316, 317]. These techniques have been used to fulfil the characteristics of chitosan-based hydrogels for cartilage repair. The mechanical properties of these chitosan-based hydrogels are increased. Chitosan has been crosslinked with different reagents such as glutaraldehyde [318, 319], 1-ethyl-3-(3-dimethylaminopropyl) carbodiimide hydrochloride [320] and genipin [321–323] to increase its mechanical properties.

Porous chitosan hydrogel has been produced by gas foaming and lyophilisation techniques to create porosity in 3D structure and enhance cell proliferation [261, 321, 324]. For example, Ji et al. simultaneously used gas-foamed and crosslinked chitosan (using either genipin or glutaraldehyde) under higher pressure CO_2 [321, 326]. These pores allowed the nutrient and oxygen transfer, hence the proliferation of fibroblast cells in 3D structure of chitosan hydrogel. In another study, it is demonstrated that chitosan enhances the natural regeneration process of articular cartilage in the rat joint [325]. Polyelectrolytic complex of chondroitin sulphate and chitosan also provides a good mechanical structure for the adhesion and attachment of chondrocytes and MSC [162, 262]. Chondrocyte cells maintained their round or polygonal morphology and had undergone modest degree of mitosis [326]. Chitosan is used to promote cartilage wound healing as an injectable formulation. As an example, BST-CarGel, a chitosan-based biomaterial, is commercially available for cartilage regeneration [327, 328]. However, due to low mechanical strength, neat chitosan cannot be used for the fabrication of 3D hydrogels for regeneration of full cartilage.

Chondroitin Sulphate

Chondroitin sulphate (CS) is a GAG-based biomaterial composed of a chain of *N*-acetylgalactosamine and glucuronic acid [329]. It has been initially used in articular cartilage repair as a preventive and healing compound [330]. The in vitro [264, 265] and in vivo [266] studies demonstrated that CS promotes the metabolic activity of cartilage, preventing cartilage from degeneration in osteoarthritis.

Controversy results nevertheless reported in the literature for the application of CS hydrogel for cartilage repair. Many studies provided evidence that CS hydrogel inhibits the secretion of cartilage ECM such as collagen precursors [331]. In vitro studies showed that the addition of CS (with concentration of 100 mg/ml) also reduced GAG content in cartilage ECM in long-term culture despite chondrocyte viability [332]. In addition, photo-crosslinkable methacrylate derivative of CS inhibits the synthesis of cartilage ECM compounds [239]. This effect might be due to the presence of negative charge on the CS hydrogel, which attracts free cations within the culture medium. This effect increases the osmolarity within the hydrogel, which has an adverse impact on cell growth within the hydrogel [259].

This issue associated with CS is resolved by using a combination of CS with other hydrogels. For instance, it is found that chondrocyte maintained its phenotype and GAG production was not interfered in the mixture of chitosan with CS [267]. In addition, proteoglycan (related to GAG) production increased in CS-based hydrogel that covalently bonded with collagen type I [268]. Chondrocyte proliferated within this hydrogel and produced proteoglycan. Addition of CS in PEG hydrogel also improved the expression of chondrogenic gene from chondrocytes, enhancing the production of cartilage ECM compared to pure PEG hydrogel [333]. Compared with other biopolymers, CS production cost is high. In addition, its applications may have negative impact on ECM generation for cartilage repair. These data illuminate the limited applications of CS and low potential of using this compound for cartilage repair to date [259].

Hyaluronan (Hyaluronic Acid)

Hyaluronan (hyaluronic acid, HA) is the primary physiological component of the articular cartilage matrix [334]. The physical interaction between the molecule networks of hyaluronan can form extensively long, biodegradable and biocompatible molecules [335]. Theoretically, HA is superior for cartilage repair if it can be implanted in an unmodified form [336]. However, high degradation rate and poor mechanical strength are the major hurdles for its direct application in cartilage repair. The degradation of hyaluronan might lead to chondrolysis under certain conditions [337]. Different approaches, such as esterification [338] and crosslinking [335, 339], have been undertaken to improve its properties. However, these methods showed adverse effect on HA biocompatibility [340].

HA has been used for chondrocyte and stem cell encapsulations to regenerate cartilage. The in vitro and in vivo studies underlined the feasibility of cell proliferation and synthesis of cartilage ECM in a modified form of HA [341, 342] and as a cell carrier for chondrocytes [343, 344] or bone marrow-derived stems cells [345, 346]. Despite all biological and physiochemical issues associated with hyaluronan, Hyalograft C, a hyaluronic acid-based biomaterial, has been commercialised for cartilage repair, and it is in clinical trial phase.

Alginate

Alginate is a binary copolymer of $(1 \rightarrow 4)$-linked β-D-mannuronic acid-*co*-α-L-guluronic acid. It can readily form bonds with different divalent metal ions, including calcium, magnesium and barium. This chemical bonding can be used to form alginate hydrogels for different biomedical applications, such as cartilage repair. Superior biological properties, high cell response and low cost are the main advantages of alginate hydrogels. Alginate is used for different cartilage tissue engineering applications such as preserving chondrocyte phenotype, organisation and turnover and differentiation of adipose-derived adult stem cells and bone marrow-derived stem cells for 3D cell growth [176, 243, 257, 258]. In vitro studies showed that chondrocytes, seeded within an alginate hydrogel, synthesised high level of cartilage ECM protein (i.e. collagen type II). The chondrogenesis of cells can be further promoted by the addition of BMP-2 in the structure of alginate hydrogel [347].

The effect of alginate hydrogel on chondrogenesis of chondrocytes has also been studied by comparing the in vitro results from 3D growth in alginate with conventional 2D culture in flask [347], which showed higher expression of collagen type II from chondrocytes seeded within alginate hydrogel compared to control normal 2D growth in the presence of IGF-1 and BMP-1 growth factors. Cai et al. showed that bone marrow-derived mesenchymal stem cells can be well distributed within an alginate hydrogel [348]. After 2 weeks of in vitro culturing that hydrogel is implanted into nude mice, the encapsulated bone marrow-derived mesenchymal stem cells exhibited continued process of induced chondrogenesis in vivo. High expression of cartilage extracellular matrix proteins (such as collagen type II and aggrecan) confirmed that the alginate-based cartilaginous implants are actively chondrogenic during bone marrow-derived mesenchymal stem cell terminal differentiation.

The main drawbacks in application of alginate for cartilage repair are lack of cell motif sites within its structure and also low and unpredictable degradation behaviour [259]. The former might lead to a low level of chondrogenesis cell adhesion that prevents cell proliferation within the 3D structure. In addition, alginate is negatively charged that inhibits the absorption of proteins to its structure and interferes with the diffusion of biofactors and proteins. Low cell adhesion and protein absorption both might lead to decreasing chondrogenesis cell proliferation within the alginate hydrogels. Previous studies showed that functionalisation of alginate with arginine–glycine–aspartic acid (RGD) sequence enhances the chondrocyte adhesion [349] and thus can address low cell adhesive properties of this biomaterial.

The slow degradation rate of alginate and its unpredictable profile might have adverse effect on the application of this polymer for cartilage repair. Bouhadir et al. addressed this issue by preparing a biodegradable alginate hydrogel using periodate-oxidised alginate. This polymer is crosslinked with calcium ions and the hydrogel degraded within 9 days in PBS solution [350]. In vivo application of this alginate-based hydrogel showed that chondrocyte encapsulated initiated native cartilage formation at the defected site after 7 days of implantation [350]. The most challenging issue in application of alginate for cartilage repair is the extraction of this material from different sources that might have different physicochemical properties, mechanical strengths and degradation rates [259].

14.3.6 Injectable Hydrogels for In Vivo Cartilage Formation

Injectable hydrogels have been used to deliver chondrogenesis cells or drugs to the defected site in a minimally invasive manner to decrease patient morbidity upon the treatment procedure. As shown schematically in Fig. 14.6, a solution that contains a polymer, cells, drug or any combination of these three is injected to the lesion site. The polymeric solution is then crosslinked in situ to form a solid structure at the site. The cells along with the polymeric matrix are surrounded with chondrogenic biological and mechanical signaling that enhances cartilage regeneration. The polymeric matrices are usually degraded gradually, while cartilage ECM is synthesised by chondrogenic cells that are either externally provided or migrated from subchondral regions. Cartilaginous physiochemical environment and delivery of chondrogenic cell/drugs in minimally invasive manner are the main advantages of this technique.

The favourable polymers for injection are those that possess the following characteristics:

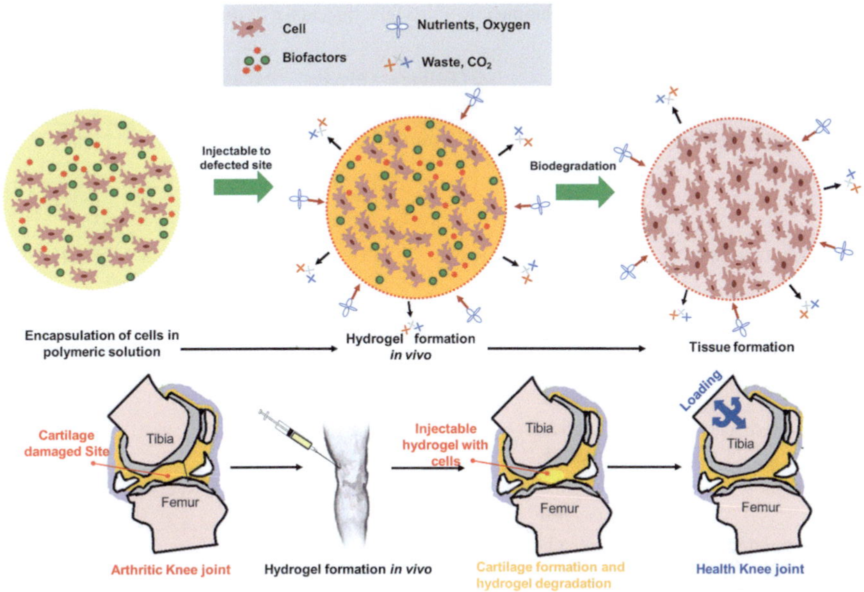

Fig. 14.6 Schematic overview of cartilage tissue engineering, using injectable hydrogels as cell carrier

- Cell adhesive property, biofactor loading capacity and sufficient mechanical strength
- Adjustable gelation properties to facilitate injectability during surgical operation and rapid hydrogel formation in the body to inhibit transfer of formulation to surrounding tissues
- Biocompatibility without toxic chemicals and severe conditions for gelation to promote cell viability

Different strategies have been attempted for in situ gelation such as redox polymerisation, photo-polymerisation, Michael addition, Schiff and enzymatic reactions and physical approaches such as pH induction and thermogelation. The following sections provide an insight into each of these methods.

14.3.6.1 Chemical Reaction

Chemical stimulus induces in situ gelation of polymeric solution by forming chemical changes in the molecular structure of precursors or by formation of covalent bond in polymeric system. The chemical reactions include redox and photo-polymerisation of acrylate-functionalised macromers, Michael addition, Schiff reaction scheme and enzymatic reactions. It is critical to select the conditions that precursors, initiators and catalysts are soluble in aqueous media to develop a biocompatible formulation [351]. A brief summary of injectable chemical stimuli

Table 14.6 Different gelation techniques to crosslink injectable hydrogels for cartilage tissue engineering

Polymer	Gelling strategy	Gelling time	Mechanical/degradation behaviour	Refs.
KGM/collagen–PLA[a]	Redox APS/TEMED	15 min	G' = 0.87–2.15 MPa	[352]
OPF/gelatin[b]	Redox APS/TEMED	8 min	NR	[353]
Chitosan (acrylated)[a]	Redox APS/TEMED	NR	Degrade in 18 days in PBS	[354]
PEG-da/HA[b]	UV photo-crosslink	NR	NR	[355]
PEG-dimethacrylate[a]	UV photo-crosslink	NR	60–590 kPa	[356, 357]
PEG-dimethacrylate/ PDS[a]	UV photo-crosslink	NR	40–70 kPa	[358]
PLA–PEG–PLA/AES[a]	UV photo-crosslink	NR	7 kPa–97 kPa by 6 weeks of culture	[359]
Methacrylated hyaluronic acid[ab]	Laser photo-crosslink	NR	5kPa–120 kPa by 6 weeks of culture	[360, 361]
Methacrylated alginate[a]	UV photo-crosslink	NR	NR	[362]
Gelatin-methacrylate[a]	UV photo-crosslink	30 s	0.5 kPa–10 kPa	[363, 364]
Col-PEG with thiolated PEG[b]	Michael addition	30 min	15 kPa–18 kPa	[238]
Chitosan–hyaluronic acid[c]	Schiff reaction	1–4 min	10 kPa–30 kPa	[365]
Hyaluronic acid//H_2O_2[a]	Enzymatic reaction	10–20 s	0.1 kPa–2 kPa	[366]
Tyramine chitosan/ HRP/H2O2[a]	Enzymatic reaction	NR	1 kPa–5 kPa, 40 % mass loss in 3 weeks	[367]

NR not reported in the reference
[a]chondrocyte
[b]MSC cell growth
[c]acellular

systems, used for cartilage tissue engineering, is presented in Table 14.6. This section is focused on the properties, type of cell, gelation and degradation behaviour and mechanical properties of this class of hydrogels for cartilage repair.

Redox Polymerisation and Photo-Crosslinking

Acrylate- or methacrylate-functionalised macromers are crosslinked by free radicals, produced from redox reaction in an aqueous solution. Two systems have been used to initiate these reactions that include ammonium persulphate/N,N,

N'N'-tetramethylethylenediamine (APS/TEMED) or APS/L-ascorbic acid (AA) [352, 368]. APS/TEMED redox initiation system is used to crosslink collagen-coated PLA micro-carriers in hydrogel precursor of konjac glucomannan (KGM) for cartilage repair. The composite collagen–PLA/KGM precursor formed hydrogel at 37 °C in 15 min [352]. In vitro studies showed proliferation of chondrocyte cells on this in situ formed hydrogel, demonstrating the potential of this hydrogel for cartilage repair.

In addition, OPF macromer is crosslinked with redox initiation system to form injectable hydrogels for cartilage regeneration [217, 353]. Park et al. loaded TGF-β1 growth factor into the structure of OPF hydrogel crosslinked with PEG-da using redox initiation system of APS/TEMED [353]. In their study the biological properties of injectable hydrogel were enhanced by addition of gelatin microspheres that were crosslinked with GA. It is observed that MSCs that are encapsulated within OPF/gelatin maintained viable and synthesised cartilaginous ECM proteins [353]. In another study, injectable OPF/gelatin hydrogel is used for coculture of osteogenic and chondrogenic cells to adjacent subchondral bone condition [217]. In vitro studies showed the synthesis of GAG, collagen type II and aggrecan by encapsulated MSC in OPF/gelatin hydrogel. These data suggested that OPF/gelatin and the developed crosslinking strategy may have potential for cartilage tissue engineering [217, 353].

In addition to synthetic polymers, such as OPF, naturally derived polymers such as chitosan are also crosslinked with redox initiation system. Acrylate-functionalised chitosan hydrogel is crosslinked with redox initiation system of APS/TEMED and used for cartilage repair [354]. Encapsulated chondrocytes within this hydrogel maintained their spherical phenotype. The hydrogel is completely degraded in 8 days, using lysozyme to mimic physiological environment [354].

Redox polymerisation is considered as a biologically benign process. The generation of free radical ions, however, might have negative impact on cells, biofactors and surrounding tissues. The biological consequences of releasing free radicals are a major concern of using this strategy. Further research is required to be conducted to fully understand their effects prior to broad applications in cartilage and other tissue engineering [369].

Different biomaterials are photo-crosslinked under ultraviolet (UV), visible and laser light sources. Photo-initiators are used to release free radicals to initiate the crosslinking. Irgacure 2959 and eosin/triethanolamine are the most widely used photo-initiator in biomedical applications which are FDA approved and commercially available. Both synthetic and naturally derived polymers can be photo-crosslinked to form hydrogel. Synthetic macromers, such as PEG-da, PEG-dimethacrylate/star-shaped poly(dimethylsiloxane) methacrylate, methacrylate end-capped PLA–PEG–PLA, mono-2-(acryloyloxy)-ethyl succinate grafter poly(vinyl alcohol) and OPF/PEG diacrylate, are photo-crosslinked for biomedical applications. In addition, naturally derived copolymers, including methacrylated chondroitin sulphate, methacrylated HA, PLA methacrylated HA, methacrylated glycol chitosan, heparin methacrylamide, methacrylated alginate and methacrylated alginate, are photo-crosslinked to form in situ injectable hydrogels.

PEG is functionalised with methacrylate groups to form photo-crosslinkable hydrogel, suitable for cartilage tissue engineering. Chondrocyte embedded within the 3D structure of this hydrogel induces chondrogenic ECM production. Mesenchymal stem cell [355] and also embryonic cell [210] are encapsulated in this photo-crosslinkable hydrogel. By using growth factor (β-TGF), cartilage is formed in both of these two studies [210, 355, 370]. A solution of PEG-da and HA with TGF-β3 and Irgacure 2959 is used to deliver MSC in vivo [355]. After subcutaneous injection, the skin of mice is exposed to UV light. PEG-da macromers are photo-crosslinked, leading to formation of in situ hydrogel. The encapsulated MSC synthesised collagen type II and proteoglycan. This result showed the chondrogenesis properties of PEG-da/HA injectable hydrogel that can be used for cartilage regeneration [355]. PEG-dimethacrylate is also photo-crosslinked by UV radiation [356, 357]. Chondrocyte is encapsulated within this injectable hydrogel, and upon in situ gelation, GAG and collagen type II are produced.

The compressive modulus of this hydrogel is varied in the range of 60–590 kPa by changing the concentration of macromer in injectable precursor [356, 357]. The modulus of hydrogels affects both anabolic and catabolic activity of encapsulated cells [356, 357]. For instance, GAG is synthesised in softer hydrogel fabricated from PEG-dimethacrylate, while in hydrogels with a higher mechanical strength, collagen type II is mainly produced by encapsulated chondrocyte cells. RGD is incorporated into the 3D structures of PEG-dimethacrylate-based hydrogels to enhance cell proliferation. PEG-dimethacrylate and star-shaped poly (dimethylsiloxane) (PDS) methacrylate are crosslinked with acryloyl-PEG-RGD by photo-polymerisation. The compressive modulus of this hydrogel varies in a range of 40–70 kPa, depending on the composition of injectable precursor. Despite favourable biological performance of PEG-based hydrogels,application in cartilage repair is limited due to the lack of biodegradability [358].

Methacrylated end-capped PLA–PEG–PLA can be photo-crosslinked by forming IPN hydrogel with mono-2-(acryloyloxy)-ethyl succinate (AES)-grafted PVA. This IPN hydrogel is fabricated to achieve desirable mechanical, biological and gelation properties for cartilage tissue engineering [359]. This study showed that when chondrocytes are encapsulated in this hydrogel, cartilage ECM is formed within 6-week culture. The entanglement of cartilage ECM within the structure of hydrogel dramatically enhanced the compressive modulus of construct from 7 to 97 kPa [359].

Naturally derived macromer of chondroitin sulphate, functionalised with methacrylate groups, is synthesised to form hydrogel with UV, using Irgacure 2959 as photo-initiator [371]. High cell viability is detected for encapsulated chondrocytes during the in situ gelation. In the presence of suitable enzyme (chondroitinase with concentration of 0.8 mg/ml), the hydrogel is degraded within 24 h, whereas in the absence of this enzyme, the hydrogel retains its structure up to 7 days [371]. IPN hydrogel of methacrylated chondroitin sulphate and PEG-dimethacrylate is also formed for cartilage regeneration [239]. The compressive modulus of this hydrogel is controlled by changing the concentration of polymers [239].

Methacrylated hyaluronic acid is crosslinked using eosin/triethanolamine as photo-initiator [360]. The crosslinking process is activated using argon laser at 514 nm. Eosin is excited by laser to the triplet state, and then triethanolamine releases an electron to produce the free radical anion of eosin and radical cation of ethanolamine. This free radical cation can polymerise methacrylated HA. Laser beam can reach deep tissue; therefore, it could have more applications for cartilage tissue engineering compared to visible light and UV [360]. In vitro and in vivo study confirmed that chondrocyte maintains its spherical phenotype when encapsulated within this system [360], and chondrogenic proteins, such as collagen type II, are synthesised [361]. In vitro studies showed that in 6 weeks, chondrogenesis is induced in the presence of TGF-β3 using this hydrogel with encapsulated MSC cells. The formation of cartilage ECM and synthesis of GAG and collagen type II by MSCs resulted in an increased compressive modulus from 5 kPa to 120 kPa [361].

Alginate is functionalised with methacrylate groups to form photo-crosslinkable biopolymer. The effect of concentration of Irgacure 2595, the photo-crosslinker reagent, on the physical properties of this hydrogel is examined, which included swelling behaviour, compressive modulus and degradation behaviour. After 3 weeks, chondrocyte maintained its spherical phenotype [362]. In addition to alginate and hyaluronic acid, gelatin-methacrylate (Gel-ma) that creates hydrogel under UV within 30 s has been attempted for cartilage repair [363]. The compressive modulus of this hydrogel varied from 0.5 to 10 kPa based on the concentration of polymer [364]. Although adverse biological effect has not been observed in using the hydrogel formation strategy, the impact of UV radiation for in situ delivery for non-invasive operation and surrounding tissues is still questionable due to free radical formation [369].

Michael Addition

Michael addition is the 1,4-addition of nucleophiles to α,β-unsaturated ketones or esters (electrophiles) [369]. Amine- and thiol-functionalised macromers are the main nucleophiles, whereas acrylate-, methacrylate- and methacrylamide-functionalised macromers are the main electrophiles in Michael addition. The combination of these two in polymer solution is required for in situ gelation [369]. This reaction scheme is favourable for biomedical applications such as cartilage repair due to its high gelation efficiency in physiological condition without any side products. Different combinations of synthetic and naturally derived polymers are used to form in situ gelled systems for cartilage repair, using Michael addition.

Thiolated hyaluronic acid and PEG vinylsulfone (PEG-VS) macromers are in situ crosslinked within 14 min, using Michael addition scheme. Encapsulated chondrocyte maintained their phenotype after 21 days, while this hydrogel is degraded within this period. GAG and collagen type II are produced when using these cell-laden hydrogel underlining their high potential for cartilage repair [372]. To accelerate the in situ gelation of hyaluronic acid-based hydrogels, poly (ethylene glycol)-bis-maleimide (PEG-BM) is used. This system exhibited in situ gelation within approximately 1 min through Michael addition scheme.

Heparin-based hydrogels are formed, using thiolated heparin and Michael addition scheme [373]. Thiolated heparin and PEG-da are in situ gelled at physiological condition using Michael addition. This hydrogel promotes the in vitro re-differentiation of encapsulated dedifferentiated rabbit chondrocytes. In vivo studies are conducted by transplanting the hydrogel in the subcutaneous dorsum of mice, which showed the proliferation of chondrocyte in vivo and formation of cartilage without using any biofactors [373].

Semi-interpenetrated network (SIPN) scaffold is also fabricated by incorporating in situ gelled heparin-based precursors (thiolated heparin–PEG-da system) and poly(L-lactide-*co*-ε-caprolactone) (PLCSL) scaffold. BMP-2 and chondrocytes are encapsulated within this system and is locally delivered to the defected cartilage site to promote the formation of calcified fibrocartilaginous transition region. This hydrogel enhanced the integrity of regenerated cartilage and secured its attachment to the surrounding tissue [374]. In addition, thiolated gelatin is crosslinked using PEG-da through Michael addition scheme. The gelation time is in between 3 and 5 min depending on the concentration of macromers in the precursor system. Bone marrow-derived MSCs are encapsulated within this hydrogel and exhibited a high level of viability. This system has been used for different cartilage regeneration applications [375]. More complicated systems are designed by conjugation of synthetic and naturally derived copolymers to closely tune the gelation, degradation and mechanical properties of this group of hydrogels.

Collagen-mimetic peptide (Col-P), which contains a GFOGER sequence (responsible to maintain chondrocyte phenotype), is conjugated with poly(ethylene glycol) tetraacrylate to form Col-P-*co*-PEG macromer. This macromer could form gel in 30 min upon mixing with thiolated PEG in physiological environment (37 °C and 7.4 pH) [238]. The encapsulated MSCs showed a higher degree of chondrogenesis compared with the thiolated PEG hydrogel without the addition of peptide sequence (no conjugation of Col-P). The compressive modulus of hydrogels is tuned from 15 to 18 kPa by changing the concentration of macromers within the precursor solution. The softer gel induced a higher degree of chondrogenesis differentiation of MSCs compared to the stiffer gel [238], due to a lower mass transfer rate in the latter system.

Schiff Reaction

Schiff-based reaction schemes are based on the chemical reactions between an amine and aldehyde groups. It is one of the promising schemes in the formation of in situ gelled hydrogels due to high yield in physiological condition [365]. *N*-Succinyl-chitosan and aldehyde hyaluronic acid macromers are synthesised and chemically conjugated to form an injectable precursor. The in situ gelation time of this system in physiological environment varied from 1 to 4 min [365]. The crosslinking density within the macromers affects the mechanical properties within 10 kPa to 30 kPa, and the degradation time varies between 1 and 30 days. In vitro studies showed that the encapsulated chondrocytes retained their phenotype, when encapsulated in this hydrogel [365]. Most of the injectable hydrogels, formed with this reaction scheme, suffered from low mechanical properties. This class of hydrogels, therefore, is not widely used for cartilage tissue engineering.

Enzymatic Reaction

Enzymes can form new bonds or can cleave specific bonds in a polymer to induce gelation. Due to the specificity of enzymatic reactions, the other chemical moieties in polymers are not interfered. Therefore, enzymatic gelation is a rational platform with low risk of side products. Enzymes such as horseradish peroxidase (HRP) [376], phosphatase [377], tyrosinase [378], thermolysin [379], α-galactosidase [380] and esterase [381] have been used to prepare hydrogels through enzymatic reactions. The gelation occurred by crosslinking polymer networks or by decreasing the solubility of polymer in aqueous solution[2].

HRP is the most widely used enzyme for the preparation of hydrogel for cartilage tissue regeneration. Tyramine-*co*-hyaluronic acid (THA) macromer is synthesised which undergoes instant gelation in the presence of HRP. For in vivo studies, THA is dissolved in H_2O_2 and subcutaneously injected into rats, followed by separate injection of HRP [366]. This polymer instantly formed hydrogel after the addition of HRP. The gelation time and the mechanical strength of the resulted hydrogel are controlled by changing the concentration of HRP. The gelation time is less than 10 s when HRP concentration is from 1.3 to 2.2 unit/ml. This hydrogel exhibited compressive modulus of 0.1–2 kPa [366].

Chitosan is also functionalised with tyramine groups [367], which are crosslinked with HRP/H_2O_2 system to form hydrogel. The compressive modulus of this hydrogel varies in the range of 1–5 kPa by changing the concentration of functionalised chitosan from 1 to 2 wt%. In the presence of lysozyme, chitosan hydrogel is rapidly degraded and loses 60 % of its weight after 3 weeks. The chondrocyte viability in this hydrogel is high and their phenotype is maintained after 2 weeks of encapsulation [367].

Enzymes are involved in the gelation process. After the formation of gels, the enzymes act as impurities that might have biological impact on encapsulated cells and also the host tissue. Additionally, the denaturation of an enzyme in the body may induce immunogenicity. Due to these reasons, the application of this group of in situ gelled precursors for cartilage tissue engineering is limited [369].

---

[2]Hydrogel is formed through condensation process upon decrease of solubility of polymer in aqueous solution.

14.3.6.2 Physically Induced Gelation

Hydrogel can be formed via physical stimulation of polymers to create interaction between molecules. Thermo- and pH-responsive stimulators are the most common approach for the fabrication of hydrogels. In physical stimuli, intermolecular interactions such as van der Waals, hydrogen and covalent bonding result in phase transition behaviour. Physically induced gelation scheme, therefore, provides a mild condition for delivery of chondrogenesis cells to the defected site, which might exhibit low cytotoxicity and enhance cell viability and regenerate cartilage at the defected site. This section provides an overview for different types of physically induced gelation systems (pH and thermoresponsive) that have been attempted for cartilage repair.

pH-Induced Gelation

Changes in pH can induce in situ gelation of polymers. Different synthetic and naturally derived polymers can be functionalised with carboxylic acid-derived monomers, such as methacrylic acid (MAA [382, 383] and AA [384–386]), to synthesise copolymers that can undergo gelation by variation of pH [387]. The functionalised polymer with MAA and AA exhibited pKa value of approximately 5 and 4.8, respectively [387]. It is, therefore, feasible to incorporate the cells into the solution, when the pH is below the pKa. The hydrogel is formed by increasing the pH above this value. However, cells and growth factors tolerate physiological pH (6–7.5) and cannot maintain viable out of this range for a long period. Care must be taken in using pH-sensitive hydrogels to ensure having less impact on cell viability. For this reason, pH-sensitive hydrogels have not been used broadly for tissue engineering of cartilage.

Thermogelation

Temperature variation has an impact on the molecular conformation of thermoresponsive polymers. Two types of these polymers are identified, (i) lower critical solution temperature (LCST) and (ii) upper critical solution temperature (UCST), shown schematically in Fig. 14.7. In the former, the polymer maintains miscible only at any temperature below the LCST. In the latter, however, the opposite phenomenon occurs, in which the polymer is only miscible above the UCST. Thermogelation is a promising and clean approach for hydrogel formation and development of an injectable formulation due to the absence of any chemical, reagent and enzyme that might exhibit an adverse effect on cell viability and performance. Table 14.7 summarises different thermoresponsive injectable hydrogels that are synthesised for cartilage regeneration. These injectable systems are discussed more in depth in this section.

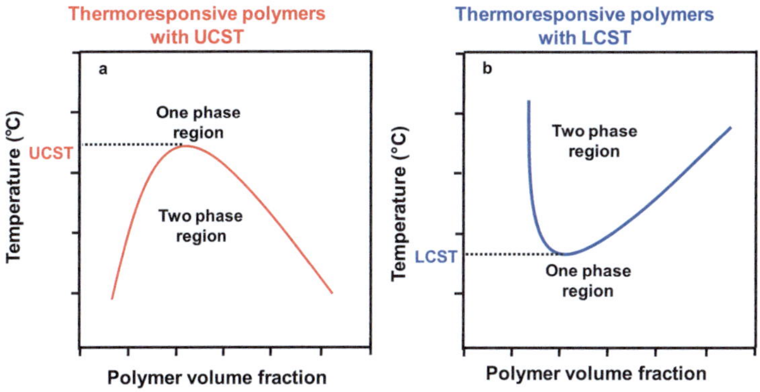

Fig. 14.7 Schematic illustration of phase transition behaviour for thermosensitive polymers with upper critical solution temperature (UCST) (**a**) and lower critical solution temperature (LCST) (**b**)

The polymers that possess LCST below the body fluid are favourable for tissue engineering. In this case, the biofactors and cells are incorporated into the solution at low temperature with low risk of denaturation and minimal impact on cell viability. Poly(N-isopropylacrylamide) (PNIPAAm), Pluronic®, elastin-like polypeptides (ELPs), chitosan-derived polymers, functionalised hyaluronic acid and heparin are the main synthetic and naturally derived polymers used to form thermoresponsive precursor for cartilage tissue engineering.

The LCST of PNIPAAm (32 °C) is close to physiological temperature (37 °C), and it can be readily tuned by adding hydrophilic and hydrophobic side chains to its molecular structure. PNIPAAm is a biocompatible polymer with very high rate of phase transition behaviour. Therefore, PNIPAAm is the most commonly used thermoresponsive polymer for tissue engineering applications. PNIPAAm-based copolymers form gel through coil-to-globe phase transition process [403]. Hydrogel formations are initiated by increasing the temperature above the LCST of copolymer [404]. For fabrication of biodegradable PNIPAAm-based hydrogels, it is critical to conjugate hydrophilic moieties, such as acrylic acid or PEG, and a hydrophobic segment to PNIPAAm-based macromers [387, 388]. The mechanical properties of PNIPAAm-based copolymers are increased by conjugating hydrophobic moieties such as n-alkyl acrylate and poly(lactide) macromers [387]. The incorporation of hydrophobic macromer resulted in increasing compressive modulus [387].

Yun et al. synthesised more biocompatible PNIPAAm-based copolymer by the incorporation of acrylic acid (AAc) segments to PNIPAAm molecule to form P (NIPAAm-*co*-AAc). TGF-β3 growth factor is encapsulated within this hydrogel to promote cartilage formation. In vitro cell study showed that chondrocytes retained their phenotype after 8 weeks. A solution of precursor, chondrocyte and TGF-β3 growth factor is injected subcutaneously into nude mice and formed gel at the injected location. After 8 weeks, the regenerated cartilage acquired normal histological and physiochemical properties [389].

Table 14.7 Different thermoresponsive hydrogels for cartilage regeneration

Polymer precursor	Gelling temperature	Degradation behaviour	Mechanical properties	Refs.
P(NIPAAm-*co*-propylacrylic acid)[a]	37 °C	NR	1 kPa (Comp Mod)	[387, 388]
P(NIPAAm-propylacrylic acid-butyl acrylate)[a]	>37 °C	NR	2 kPa (Comp Mod)	[387, 388]
P(NIPAAm-*co*-acrylic acid)[+]	~37 °C	Retain for 8 weeks	NR	[389]
P(NIPAAm-PLDLA-dextran)[+]	32 °C	Retain for 4 weeks	NR	[390]
PNIPAAm-g-methylcellulose[+]	~32 °C	Retain for 4 weeks	NR	[391, 392]
DNA-modified ELP[+]	~35 °C	NR	$G^d = 80$ pa	[287, 393]
P(NIPAAm-AAc-NAS-HEMAPLA)[b]	18 °C–26 °C	85 wt% in 21 days	~0.5 MPa (Tensile Mod)	[394]
Chitosan/GP[+]	37 °C	Retain in 3 weeks	NR	[395, 396]
Chitosan/GP/starch[+]	37 ± 2 °C	67 % loss in 56 days	NR	[183]
Chitosan/PPO–PEO[+]	25 °C	Retained in 28 days	NR	[397]
Chitosan/PNIPAAm[d]	<37 °C	NR	NR	[398]
Chitosan/PNIPAAm/HA[+]	30 °C	NR	NR	[399]
PEO–PPO–PEO[+]	37 °C	Fast dissolution rate	Very weak	[400–402]

NR not reported in the study
[a]Acellular matrix
[b]chondrocyte
[c]smooth muscle cells
[d]MSCs

A porous structure of poly(NIPAAm)-based hydrogel is formed by the incorporation of PLDLA and dextran (conjugation via chemical bonding) to form a copolymer with LCST at32 °C. The chondrogenic ECM protein, such as collagen type II, is formed after 4 weeks of encapsulation of chondrocyte within this hydrogel. To assess the phenotype of chondrocyte after culturing within this hydrogel, they are detached from the surface by decreasing the temperature from 37 °C to below 32 °C (LCST of hydrogel). The detached chondrocyte exhibited a round shape which confirmed that its phenotype is maintained during this period.

Poly(NIPAAm)-*g*-methylcellulose copolymer is also synthesised to form hydrogel at 32 °C [391, 392]. ATDC5, a chondrogenic cell line, is encapsulated in this hydrogel to assess its chondrogenesis properties. The in vitro studies confirmed the high potential of this injectable hydrogel for cartilage tissue engineering due to the low degree of cytotoxicity and high cell proliferation within this hydrogel [391, 392].

Another thermoresponsive hydrogel is produced by the conjugation of chitosan with PNIPAAm. This copolymer is water soluble with the LCST less than 37 °C [398]. MSCs are mixed with this copolymer solution and injected for assessing the application of hydrogel for cartilage tissue engineering. The hydrogel is formed in the body temperature and promising results were acquired; chondrocytic markers were produced including GAGs and collagen type II at the injected site [398].

HA is also conjugated with PNIPAAm to form thermoresponsive poly (NIPAAm-co-HA) hydrogel. Preliminary studies on this hydrogel showed continuous and sustained release of fluorescein isothiocyanate (FITC)-labelled bovine serum albumin up to 60 h by in vivo subcutaneous injection on the dorsal surface of rabbit. These data demonstrated the potential of thermosensitive hydrogel for cartilage tissue engineering [405].

Chitosan/PNIPAAm copolymer is grafted with hyaluronic acid (HA) to further mimic the properties of natural cartilage ECM. Chitosan/PNIPAAm/HA hydrogel formed injectable hydrogel above 5 wt% at 30 °C. In vitro cell study with this hydrogel showed that chondrocyte maintains its morphology and posed a high degree of proliferation and differentiation [399].

These studies underlined that most of PNIPAAm copolymers conjugated with natural or synthetic polymers are suitable for chondrogenesis cells to produce cartilage ECM. They might be favourable systems for developing an injectable formulation; however, it is still in its infancy, and further research is required to select a polymer with desirable injection properties, stability, degradation rate and mechanical strength for regenerating cartilage.

Synthetic and naturally derived polymers, such as block copolymers of ethylene oxide (PEO) and propylene oxide (PPO), elastin-like polypeptides (ELPs) and chitosan with thermoresponsive properties, were used to form injectable hydrogels for cartilage tissue engineering. Block copolymer of silk and elastin peptide sequence (SELP) were used as acellular therapy for cartilage tissue repair in a rabbit model of an osteochondral defect [406, 407]. In this study SELP was injected into the osteochondral defect site on the femoral condyles of rabbit knee and crosslinked in vivo [407]. SELP hydrogels were also used for cartilage tissue engineering, using mesenchymal stem cell (MSC). Molecular structure of SELP copolymer is changed to achieve a thermosensitive copolymer, named SELP-47 K. This copolymer undergoes gelation at 37 °C. MSCs are encapsulated within SELP-47 K hydrogel in the presence and absence of chondrogenic TGF-β3 growth factor. After 28 days, cartilaginous matrix components (sGAG and collagen type II) are formed by MSC encapsulated in SEL-47 K hydrogel in both cases (in the presence and absence of TGF-β3) [393]. This result showed that ELP can act as an engineered bioactive molecule to stimulate chondrogenesis pathway in MSC.

A thermosensitive chitosan-based hydrogel was fabricated, using β-glycerol phosphate disodium salt (GP) as sol–gel initiator at physiological pH and temperature [395]. GP showed an osteogenic effect when added to bone marrow stromal cells. In vitro study of chitosan/GP hydrogel showed its capability to deliver an osteogenic mixture of β-transforming growth factor (β-TGF) and encapsulated chondrocyte over 3 weeks [396]. The use of chitosan as a cationic polysaccharide in this mixture led to the adhesion of hydrogel to tissue surface which normally bear net anionic characteristic. In addition, chitosan/GP mixed with chondrocyte is used as cytocompatible space filler [408]. BioSyntech Inc. (Laval, Quebec, Canada) developed the thermoresponsive (chitosan/GP) solution, which is in clinical trial for cartilage tissue engineering [409].

The properties of chitosan/GP hydrogel were further improved by the incorporation of starch to the thermoresponsive mixture [183]. The injectable chitosan/GP/starch mixture had a gelation temperature of $37 \pm 2\ ^\circ C$. The hydrogel also exhibited microporous structure with 67 % of degradation within 56 days in PBS solution containing 0.02 mg/ml of lysozyme. Chondrocyte remained its phenotype after 14 days of culturing within this hydrogel [183].

In addition, injectable chitosan-based hydrogel was developed by fabricating interpenetrating polymeric network of chitosan with other natural polymers such as alginate and hyaluronate, hyaluronic acid and heparin, which enhanced the production of collagen type II and increased the rate of cellular proliferation after 2 weeks of cell growth [410, 411]. Combining chitosan with other biomaterials, however, does not necessarily result in favourable effects. For example, the combination of chitosan with chondroitin sulphate and dermatan sulphates showed adverse effect on production of collagen type II and morphology of chondrocyte cells [412].

Alternatively, chitosan-based thermosensitive hydrogel is prepared by graft copolymerisation with Pluronic® (block copolymer based on ethylene oxide and propylene oxide) (PPO–PEO). This thermosensitive hydrogel (chitosan/PPO–PEO) is used for cartilage tissue engineering and had sol–gel transition temperature of 25 °C. Chondrocyte proliferation and GAG production are significantly increased after 28 days by using chitosan/PPO–PEO in situ gelled precursor [397].

Copolymer of hyaluronic acid conjugated with heparin and Pluronic® (block copolymer based on ethylene oxide and propylene oxide) (PPO–PEO) is synthesised to form in situ gelled at 37 °C in less than 10 min. TGF-β3 is successfully loaded within the structure of hydrogel and continuously released from hydrogel for 20 days. This resulted in formation of cartilage ECM at full-thickness cartilage defect of rabbit knee [413].

HA is also conjugated with PNIPAAm to form thermosensitive hydrogel p (NIPAAm-*co*-HA). Preliminary studies on this hydrogel showed continuous and sustained release of FITC-labelled bovine serum albumin up to 60 h by in vivo subcutaneous injection on the dorsal surface of rabbit. This demonstrated the potential of this thermosensitive hydrogel for cartilage tissue engineering [405].

Therapeutic agents such cartilaginous bioactive compounds as BMP-2 were also delivered to the cartilage lesion site with a HA-based injectable hydrogels to control the release of bioactive compounds [414]. These HA-based hydrogels are conjugated with a heparin sulphate proteoglycan and are used to deliver BMP-2. The controlled and slow release of BMP-2 and the presence of proteoglycan within the structure of this hydrogel had an anabolic influence on articular cartilage in an osteoarthritis model. The synthesis of proteoglycans and other cartilaginous ECMs is stimulated upon the injection of this hydrogel at the lesion site [414].

14.3.7 Products Approached Clinical Trial for Cartilage Repair

Current cell-based therapies for cartilage repair fall into three categories: (1) cell or tissue implementation [415–418], (2) cartilage or bone grafts [419, 420] and (3) bone marrow stimulation through either abrasion, arthroplasty, Pridie drilling or microfracture [96, 421, 422]. Promising clinical results have been reported for most of these treatments [327]. Based on the preferred treatment by the surgeon, different classes of biomaterials can be selected. The major available products for cartilage repair are BST-CarGel (e.g. filler in bone marrow stimulation) and Hyalograft C, CaReS, TruFit, NeoCart, Pluronic and PEG-da-based injectable hydrogel. A brief summary of these treatments is provided in Table 14.8. This section aims to provide insight about the properties, type of cell and results of animal and clinical studies.

14.3.7.1 BST-CarGel

BST-CarGel is developed to stabilise blood clot at the defected site by dispersing biological adhesive solution at the wound site. This technique involves the use of an aqueous solution of chitosan in glycerol phosphate buffer at pH 7 [396]. Intrinsic biocompatible and biodegradable properties of components and neutral pH of this solution make it biocompatible, biodegradable and adhesive to native tissue. In surgical applications, BST-CarGel is mixed with blood with a ratio of 1:3 to generate normal clot with reinforced properties and impede clot retraction. BST-CarGel is injected (normally with 18-G needle) at the lesion site in liquid form and solidifies in 10 min [423, 424]. The cationic nature of chitosan increases the adhesive property of the mixture to cartilage lesion and thus ensures longer clot residency at the cartilage defected site. This method provides critical blood components, red cells and nutrients above the bone marrow wound site (holes or microfracture) to ensure initiation and activation of tissue regeneration and repair [327].

Animal studies have been conducted using BST-CarGel [424, 440, 441]. Skeletally mature rabbit (8–15 months old) are used to assess the characteristics of regenerated cartilage after implementation of BST-CarGel. It is observed that BST-CarGel stimulates the proliferation of stromal cells through the gel towards the lesion site. Vascularisation within the subchondral bone is also significantly increased which indicates positive impact for cartilage regeneration. The BST-CarGel, which is mainly chitosan, is degraded via neutrophil phagocytosis after approximately 1 month [440].

In another animal study, 3–6-year-old sheep models are used, in which BST-CarGel is injected in a surgically prepared 1-cm^2 condylar and trochlear defects. The cartilage regeneration in this defected side is compared with a negative control (microfracture only without any filler) after 6 months of implantation. It is

Table 14.8 General information of commercial scaffolds/hydrogels for cartilage tissue engineering applications

Commercial product	Application/method of delivery	Mechanical/gelling properties	Rehabilitation program	Opinion	Ref.
Chitosan (BST-CarGel)	Blood clot formation, 10 s of mixing and then injection with 18-G needle	Solidifies in 10 min	The knee is immobilised for 24 h with soft braces. Soft braces are recommended for the first 2 weeks. The joint is non-load bearing for at least 6 weeks post surgery by using crutches. It is possible to have a full load bearing in 9–11 weeks after the surgery. The patients are not allowed to participate in any intense sport activity within the first year after the surgery	Safe, no unpredicted effect based on blood analysis and physical examination and better level of pain, stiffness and function based on WOMAC questionnaires	[327, 328, 396, 423, 424]
Benzilic acid of hyaluronic acid (Hyalograft C)	Full articular cartilage replacement, arthroscopic and mini-arthrotomy implantation	Degrades in 4 months, insoluble in water	Immobilised for 24 h after surgery with braces and non-load bearing for 4 weeks. Gradually proceed to full load bearing within 10–12 weeks. No intense sport activity at least in the first year of surgery	It can provide excellent outcome for the active and young only	[342, 425–430]
Collagen type I (CaReS)	Full articular cartilage replacement, open surgical process to fill the cartilage defected site	Not reported	Knee joint immobilises for 48 h (<10 ° of flexion). From the third day after surgery, knee flexion is limited to 30 ° for 21 days and thereafter to 60 ° for another 21 days Bicycle training after 6 weeks from surgery and muscle enhancement training after	IKDC score in all patients significantly increased; pain significantly is decreased. Surgeons rated 61 % of the outcomes as very good	[[165], [431, 432]]

			12 weeks. No intense sport or physical activity for 1 year		
PLGA/calcium sulphate (TruFit)	The defected site is drilled, and the plugs are inserted at the defected site to promote cancellous bone and cartilage formation	Degradation in 9 months	No braces are used as support, 0–60 ° of passive flexion, for the first 4 weeks after operation, partial load bearing, between 4 and 6 complete range of movement and cycling and swimming to strengthen the joint	80 % improvement in KOOS score after 12 months; after this time, the patients' conditions are worsening because of pain and joint functionality. Repeated operation is required in 70 % of cases after 18 months	[73, 389, 433–437]
Collagen type I (NeoCart)	Full articular cartilage replacement, open surgical process to fill the cartilage defected site	Not very robust, might damage before implantation	For approximately 10 days, the joint is immobilised; for 6 weeks after surgery, non-load bearing on the surgical knee; for 12 weeks muscle enhancement training. Within the first year after surgery, no intense sport physical activity	Improvement based on VAS scale and level of pain, approximately 85 % success rate in increasing knee function	[438, 439]

Therapeutic strategies include (1) cell or tissue implementation, (2) cartilage or bone grafts and (3) bone marrow stimulation observed that there is a high level of adhesion between the BST-CarGel/blood clot, bone and cartilage. The volume and quality of hyaline cartilage regenerated at the defected site are also increased. In addition, relatively mature articular cartilage is observed in the sheep model [424, 441].

Depending on the size and the location of the lesion, there are two approaches that surgeons can use to implant BST-CarGel: (1) mini-open and (2) arthroscopic approaches [327] in clinical applications. In the former a mini-arthrotomy is used to facilitate visualisation of the lesion and delivery of BST-CarGel. Arthroscopic method is feasible only when the entire lesion site is within arthroscopic field of view. It is critical to deliver the mixture of BST-CarGel and blood over individual bone marrow stimulation channels (holes or microfractures) and then over the remaining lesion. In most of the cases, therefore, incision is required to implant BST-CarGel at the exact lesion site.

In 2003–2004 Health Canada's Special Access Program for medical device assessed the BST-CarGel for cartilage repair in human cases. In this study, 33 patients (22 males and 11 females) are treated with BST-CarGel. The treatment is carried out on a case-by-case basis, and it is not legally contemplated as a clinical trial due to the absence of negative control. The outcomes of this study are not reliable as there is no control on the examination of patients and lesion [327]. For example, the size of the lesion ranged from 0.5 cm^2 to 12 cm^2; BST-CarGel is delivered for 22 patients by arthroscopy and for 11 patients by mini-arthrotomy. Nevertheless, the treated patients suffered from both traumatic and degenerative lesions.

It is concluded that BST-CarGel treatment is safe as no complication is observed from physical examination of 33 patients and their blood tests. The Western Ontario and McMaster (WOMAC) Universities Osteoarthritis Index [328] questionnaires are administrated preoperatively and postoperatively after 3, 6 and 12 months. After 12 months postoperatively, pain, stiffness and function index value (based on WOMAC questionnaires) are significantly decreased underlining clinical benefit of using BST-CarGel [327].

The lesion grade (depth), location, size and status of the opposing chondral surface are factors that play a critical role in selecting BST-CarGel for cartilage repair. BST-CarGel has not yet been approved for sale in any country, and further investigations and clinical trials are still required.

14.3.7.2 Hyalograft C

Hyaluronic acid (HA)-based scaffolds such as Hyaff 11 have been used for cartilage tissue engineering applications. Hyaff 11 is made of linear derivative of HA modified by complete esterification of the carboxyl functions of glucuronic acid with benzyl group [338]. HA-containing scaffolds are biocompatible and support cell–cell interaction, cluster formation and extracellular matrix production for cartilage tissue engineering [442]. Hyaff 11 is a 3D fibrous scaffold that is fabricated from 20-μm thick fibres that are insoluble in water [338, 443]. This scaffold undergoes a hydrolysis process, releasing benzyl alcohol and hyaluronan [427].

Hyalograft C is a tissue engineering graft, comprised of autologous chondrocyte, grown on Hyaff 11 scaffolds. This product was attempted for treatment of knee cartilage defects caused by either trauma or osteochondritis diseases in 1999 [429, 444]. In most cases arthroscopic techniques have been used for implantation of Hyalograft C due to the easy handling properties of Hyaff 11 [445]. Hyalograft C has been approved by the Food and Drug Administration (FDA) and is successfully used for the treatment of different articular cartilage defects in more than 3600 patients [428–430].

Several clinical studies are conducted to assess the therapeutic effect of Hyalograft C for articular cartilage treatment [425, 429, 444]. In one clinical study, 53 patients (31 males and 22 females) with mean age of 32 ± 12 years are contemplated for the treatment with Hyalograft C. The average size of cartilage defect is $4.4 \pm 1.9\ \text{cm}^2$ in these patients who are examined for 7 years. Based on the cartilage lesion site, either arthroscopic or mini-arthrotomy (medial or lateral parapatellar arthrotomy) techniques have been used to access the lesion site of patients. The procedure for the preparation of implant involves several steps. For enzymatic isolation of autologous chondrocytes, articular cartilage is harvested from non-weight-bearing area of the knee joint. The chondrocytes are expanded on conventional monolayer cell culture flasks for 2 weeks and then seeded on Hyaff 11 and cultured for another 2 weeks in vitro. Before the implantation of construct, the lesion site is debrided, and cartilage defect site is prepared by complete excision of all nonviable tissues [446]. The defected cartilage site is cleaned to the depth of 2 mm to avoid disrupting the subchondral plate. Subsequently, the knee joint is drained of fluid to assist graft delivery and visualisation. Afterwards, the implant with the required size and shape is delivered either with arthroscopic or mini-arthrotomy implantation. In most of the cases, except for patellar and selected trochlear lesions, there is no need for open surgery, and the Hyalograft C implant can be delivered with arthroscopy [425, 428]. Due to the intrinsic adhesive properties of Hyaff 11, there is no need to use additional fixation devices such as tissue glues. This approach eradicates the use of inorganic chemicals in implantation, which promotes the biocompatibility of implants [425]. Hyalograft C provides required support for in vivo cartilage growth during the rehabilitation procedure, and it is completely dissolved and degraded after 4 months post implantation [426].

Based on different clinical tests, Hyalograft C autograft can provide excellent outcome for the repair of deep articular cartilage defects for young and active patients who suffered from singular defects, with good knee alignment and stable joint [444, 447–449]. The effect for other patients is questionable, and it appears that the patients with secondary indications may require further surgeries due to the continuation of pain and swelling after 6-month to 5-year implantation of Hyalograft C [444]. Therefore, further follow-up studies are required to determine the long-term effect of cartilage defect treatment with Hyalograft C.

14.3.7.3 CaReS

Cartilage Regeneration System (CaReS) is a collagen type I hydrogel, prepared from rat tail tendon [432]. In this process, chondrocytes are isolated from the autologous cartilage biopsy specimen. Subsequently, the isolated cells are suspended in a double-buffered 4-(2-hydroxyethyl)-1-piperazineethanesulfonic acid (HEPES)[3] solution and gently mixed with type I collagen with the volume ratio of 1:1 (HEPES to collagen). The final mixture (chondrocyte and collagen type I) is then allowed to form hydrogel when they are incubated at 37 °C. Generally, the cell-seeded implants are cultured in autologous serum for a period of 10–13 days [431]. Quality control analysis is conducted to determine cell viability of higher than 80 % and expression of collagen type II for ensuring chondrogenesis from the seeded cells [431, 432].

The therapeutic effect of clinical treatment with CaReS is studied from 2003 to 2008 on 116 patients (67 males and 49 females) with average age of 32.5 ± 8.9 years. The patients suffered from cartilage defects as the result of either trauma degeneration (84 patients) or osteochondritis dissecans (32 patients) with an average defected size of 5.37 ± 2.7 cm^2 (35 patients with lesion size less than 4 cm^2 and 81 above this value) [431]. Chondral defect site is at femoral condyle, patella/trochlea or tibial plateau sites.

Depending on the cartilage defected site, medial or lateral parapatellar arthrotomy has been used to access the lesion site [431]. The defected cartilage site is debrided down to the subchondral bone. The base of the cartilage defect site is then coated with fibrin glue. After which the CaReS implants (with 1-mm wider diameter than the defected site) are push-fitted into the trimmed chondral defected site. Generally, a hydrogel is fabricated with twice the height of the defected cartilage. It is then fitted into the defected site by squeezing the hydrogels and removing 50 % of its water content.

The functional outcomes of the treatment procedure with CaReS are evaluated using the International Cartilage Repair Society (ICRS) and the International Knee Documentation Committee (IKDC) scales. ICRS is a four-level scale, used to categorise functionality and status of cartilage and pain level, while IKDC is a subjective knee assessment questionnaire. At mean follow-up time (30.2 months), IKDC score is significantly ($p < 0.001$) improved compared to preoperative condition (from 42.2 ± 13.8 to 70.5 ± 18.7). The pain level is also significantly decreased ($p < 0.001$) from 6.7 ± 2.2 to 3.2 ± 3.1 from preoperative condition to latest follow-up time. The IKDC results and pain comprehensive reduction level in patients demonstrated the benefit of CaReS for the treatments of traumatic or degenerative articular cartilage defects. During the surgery and in particular the debridement of the subchondral bone, bone marrow space is opened, which provides access for chondroprogenitor cells to CaReS hydrogel (culture with autologous chondrocyte). Therefore, cells can migrate to the defected site and produce

[3]HEPES is a buffer solution, widely used in vitro cell culturing to maintain neutral pH in media.

cartilage extracellular matrix. It is suggested that autologous chondrocytes cultured on CaReS hydrogel are not the exclusive cell source for cartilage formation [431].

14.3.7.4 TruFit

TruFit bone (or cartilage) substitute plugs (Smith & Nephew, Andover, MA) are cylindrical-shaped scaffolds comprised of PLGA and calcium sulphate that are mechanically stable [433]. These scaffolds are commercially available with deferent diameters (7, 9 and 11 mm) [434] and are clinically used to promote cartilage and bone regeneration to restore osteochondral defects [435]. The scaffolds are designed to degrade within a year after implantation (approximately 9 months) [73]. They are used for back filling femoral donor site during mosaicplasty or for primary repair of full-thickness articular cartilage of the femoral condyle lesions [436]. During the operation, the defected sites are drilled and the plugs (TruFit scaffolds) inserted into the drilled site. TruFit scaffolds promote cancellous bone formation due to the presence of osteoinductive calcium sulphate components in its structure with regeneration of fibrocartilage on the surface [450]. It is claimed that this material promotes the regeneration of articular cartilage in full-thickness chondral defect by supporting chondrogenesis cell migration from the surrounding tissue to the defected site [433]. Different in vitro animal and human studies support the positive impact of using TruFit plugs for cartilage regeneration.

TruFit implants can be bioabsorbed in vivo within 1 year after implantation to create space for further regeneration of cartilage ECM [73]. A mini-open surgery at the defected site is performed to deliver the implant TruFit plugs to the osteochondral lesion site. The defected site is then shaved, and the edges of the damaged cartilage are trimmed back to stable healthy location. The scaffolds are then inserted into the defected site to promote osteochondral tissue regeneration [433]. Single or multiple holes (based on the decision made by the surgeon to use single plug or multiple plugs) are drilled with the depth from 8 to 12 mm [437]. It is critical that the diameter of drilled holes and plugs is matched with the size of the lesion site. The plug is then filled with implant and surface of implant is adjusted with healthy cartilage. It is reported that this tamping process might deform the implant; therefore, a bridge distance of 1–2 mm is contemplated while using multiple plugs [437]. It is important that the edges of implants are in direct contact with the surrounding chondral surface to induce normal cartilage regeneration. This strategy enables natural migration of chondrogenesis cells to the site and thereafter regeneration of articular cartilage [437].

The functional outcome of treatment with TruFit is assessed with clinical outcome score (KOOS). The study is conducted on 10 patients (15–50 years old) with 20 % grade III and 80 % grade IV cartilage defect and an average lesion size of 2.65 cm^2. After 1 year, 80 % of patients (8 out of 10) had improvement based on clinical outcome score (KOOS). The clinical outcomes of the operation for the other two patients are poor according to the implemented clinical outcome score. Subsequent monitoring (in 18 months and 24 months) revealed that the clinical outcome score of patients is reduced significantly. Pain and inflammation are increased in patients and joint functionality is significantly decreased. The implants are removed from 7 patients (7 out of 8). Histological analysis showed the formation of hyaline cartilage on the implants, but a bony cyst is also formed within the regenerated cartilage rather than bony restoration [437].

In a recent clinical study, 15 patients with almost similar lesion grade and an average size of 2 cm^2 are treated with TruFit plugs. After 1 year, same as the previous clinical study, 80 % of patients are improved. Three patients out of 15 have undergone reoperation in less than 1 year. The study is undergoing to evaluate the efficacy of TruFit in the long term [450].

14.3.7.5 NeoCart

NeoCart implant (Histogenics Corporation, Waltham, Massachusetts) is a 3D biodegradable bovine collagen type I scaffold. For cartilage tissue engineering application, NeoCart is seeded with autologous chondrocytes followed by in vitro cultured in bioreactor to promote cartilage regeneration. The resulting product is a chondrogenic active implant, which is rich in proteoglycan and glycosaminoglycan compounds. Preclinical trials and in vitro studies demonstrated that NeoCart implantation at lesion site leads to hyaline cartilage repair at full-thickness defect sites. It is proposed that NeoCart can be used for the treatment of full-thickness (grade III) cartilage lesion of femoral condyle. The treatment process comprised of five main steps, namely, biopsy, cell isolation, cell expansion, 3D culture in bioreactor and implantation [438].

Different in vitro and animal studies are performed to investigate the efficacy of this method for articular cartilage treatment [438]. The development process of NeoCart commenced from the isolation of chondrocyte cells from biopsy specimen taken from the patient. For harvesting cells, approximately 200–400 mg of tissue is taken from non-weight-bearing portion of femoral condyle or from the femoral notch of the lateral knee. During this process, the subchondral bone is not interfered. The biopsy specimen is then processed in laboratory to isolate chondrocyte cells. The cells are then seeded on 3D collagen type I hydrogel and culture in bioreactor. The operation condition, such as hydrostatic pressure, inside the bioreactor is tuned to stimulate chondrocytes to synthesise cartilage glycoprotein [439, 451]. After the levels of produced glycosaminoglycan and proteoglycan approached to a defined value, the scaffolds are removed from the bioreactor and further cultured in static condition. The average culture time (i.e. dynamic and static) is 67 ± 18 days. The cartilage lesion site is then shaved and trimmed before the implantation of the NeoCart. After this step the implant is cut to fit in the defected site and implanted by an open surgery. The surgical knee is then immobilised for 10 ± 2 days after the surgery [438] followed by a passive range of motion to strengthen the joint and surrounding muscles. For 6 weeks after implantation, the surgical knee is non-load bearing with restriction only to rehabilitation similar to femoral condyle microstructure and ACI-type protocols.

The efficacy of NeoCart for the treatment of full-thickness articular cartilage defect is studied on ten patients with grade III cartilage lesion of femoral condyle with an average defected size of 2.2 cm^2. The patients are in the range of 18–55 years old. In two cases, the implants are damaged due to intraoperative motion testings and the procedure is not preceded. The other patients had an isolated grade III chondral injury to the weight-bearing region either in the medial or lateral condyle. Based on visual analogue scale and pain scores, there are significant improvements in all 8 patients. The results of average range of motion evaluation and also knee function assessment with IKDC scale, however, indicated that 7 out of 8 patients had improvement after operation using this implant [438].

14.3.7.6 Pluronic and PEG-da Systems

Pluronic®[4] is a commercially available polymeric system that undergoes physical crosslinking at physiological temperature (37 °C). This biomaterial is used as an injectable system for cartilage regeneration. Chondrocyte suspended in pluronic solution is used for mandibular condylar reconstruction [452]. Pluronic® solution is advantaged by its mild gelation and favourable biocompatibility properties. However, the application of pluronic solution in cartilage tissue engineering is limited due to its very poor mechanical strength, quick dissolution and high permeability [400]. A combination of Pluronic® with other injectable polymers has been used. These formulations include Pluronic®/PEG/NIPAAm, Pluronic®/poly(lactic acid/glycolic acid) (PLGA)[401, 402], Pluronic®/chitosan and Pluronic®/HAPromising [397].

Pluronic®/HA known as a X-HA is used at articular defect model of full-thickness defect of rabbit [413]. Adipose-derived stem cells are stimulated to undergo chondrogenic differentiation, using X-HA hydrogel, loaded with TGF-β. Copolymer of hyaluronic acid conjugated with heparin and Pluronic ® is synthesised to form the hydrogel at 37 °C in less than 10 min. TGF-β3 is successfully loaded within the structure of this hydrogel and could be released continuously in 20 days, which promoted cartilage ECM formation at full-thickness cartilage defect of rabbit knee [413]. Due to superior biological properties of naturally derived polymers, different protein-based polymers such as elastin-like polypeptides are also used for fabrication of hydrogel.

A PEG-da-based injectable hydrogel achieved clinical trial for the treatment of cartilage defects [453]. This PEG-da-based hydrogel is designed to support cartilage matrix production with easy surgical applications. In this approach, to bond the PEG-da-based hydrogel with the cartilage, chondroitin sulphate adhesive is first applied to the lesion site, and the joint is filled with polymer solution. The polymer solution contains 100 mg/ml PEG-da, 5 mg/ml hyaluronic acid and 0.5 mg/ml of Irgacure as photo-initiator in PBS [453]. A specially designed cone is used to apply

[4]Pluronic® is triblock copolymer of PEO–PPO–PEO.

light to the polymer solution to induce the gelation at a constant rate. Fifteen patients with symptomatic cartilage defects are treated with this injectable hydrogel after microfracture, and three patients are treated just with microfracture as control. After 6 months of surgery, no adverse effect is reported and the use of adhesive photo-crosslinked polymer allowed for greater filling of the defected site [453]. In addition, the patients who are treated with the injectable hydrogels reported a decrease in overall pain severity overtime

14.4 Conclusion

Articular cartilage is highly resilient connective tissue with unique mechanical properties which facilitate the mobility of the human body. The avascular structure and low metabolic activity of this tissue resulted in limited capability of this tissue for self-regeneration and repair. Early treatment approaches lead to unpredictable outcomes which are substantially interrelated with age, gender and physical conditions of patients. Tissue engineering approaches are therefore deemed to be more efficient for in vitro or in vivo regeneration of cartilage. Clinical studies on the commercially available biomaterials for cartilage tissue engineering showed that in the most of cases, the long-term final outcomes are unpredictable. The success rate in the best cases based on current results is 80 % for TruFit and 85 % for NeoCart. Many available treatments involve open surgery for transplantation of implant. The massive invasion in the joint has adverse impacts on the healing process of surgical knees. As a result, complicated rehabilitation protocols are generally recommended to patients after surgeries. The side effects of open surgeries and also not fully satisfied rehabilitation process in patients result in the failure of many treatment cases. Additionally, the defected cartilage may include an irregular shape that cannot be repaired by standard-sized scaffolds. Therefore, less invasive approaches such as injectable systems for delivery of cartilaginous construct to the defected site are favoured to tackle the current problems in cartilage tissue engineering. Injectable hydrogels have been contemplated as a non-invasive means for cartilage tissue engineering applicable for regular and irregular shaped cartilage lesions.

References

1. Simon TM, Jackson DW (2006) Articular cartilage: injury pathways and treatment options. Sports Med Arthrosc 14:146–154
2. Mankin HJ (1982) The response of articular cartilage to mechanical injury. J Bone Joint Surg Am 64:460–466
3. LaPorta TF, Richter A, Sgaglione NA, Grande DA (2012) Clinical relevance of scaffolds for cartilage engineering. Orthop Clin N Am 43:245–254

4. Brittberg M (2010) Cell carriers as the next generation of cell therapy for cartilage repair: a review of the matrix-induced autologous chondrocyte implantation procedure. Am J Sports Med 38:1259–1271
5. Poole CA (1993) The structure and function of articular cartilage matrixes. Inflamm Dis Ther 12:1–35
6. Wu W, Billinghurst RC, Pidoux I, Antoniou J, Zukor D, Tanzer M et al (2002) Sites of collagenase cleavage and denaturation of type II collagen in aging and osteoarthritic articular cartilage and their relationship to the distribution of matrix metalloproteinase 1 and matrix metalloproteinase 13. Arthritis Rheum 46:2087–2094
7. McCarty WJ, Nguyen QT, Hui AY, Chen AC, Sah RL (2011) Comprehensive biomaterials. Elsevier, London
8. Deshmukh K, Nimni ME (1973) Isolation and characterization of cyanogen bromide peptides from the collagen of bovine articular cartilage. Biochem J 133:615–622
9. Eyre DR, Wu J-J (1995) Collagen structure and cartilage matrix integrity. J Rheumatol Suppl 43:82–85
10. Roughley PJ, Lee ER (1994) Cartilage proteoglycans: structure and potential functions. Microsc Res Tech 28:385–397
11. Watanabe H, Yamada Y, Kimata K (1998) Roles of aggrecan, a large chondroitin sulfate proteoglycan, in cartilage structure and function. J Biochem 124:687–693
12. Maroudas A, Muir H, Wingham J (1969) Correlation of fixed negative charge with glycosaminoglycan content of human articular cartilage. Biochim Biophys Acta Gen Subj 177:492–500
13. Ateshian GA, Lai WM, Zhu WB, Mow VC (1994) An asymptotic solution for the contact of two biphasic cartilage layers. J Biomech 27:1347–1360
14. Broom ND (1984) Further insights into the structural principles governing the function of articular cartilage. J Anat 139(Pt 2):275–294
15. Boskey AL (1981) Current concepts of the physiology and biochemistry of calcification. Clin Orthop Relat Res 157:225–257
16. Poole AR, Matsui Y, Hinek A, Lee ER (1989) Cartilage macromolecules and the calcification of cartilage matrix. Anat Rec 224:167–179
17. Hall FM, Wyshak G (1980) Thickness of articular cartilage in the normal knee. J Bone Joint Surg Am 62:408–413
18. MacConaill MA (1951) The movements of bones and joints; the mechanical structure of articulating cartilage. J Bone Joint Surg (Br) 33B:251–257
19. Stockwell RA (1971) The interrelationship of cell density and cartilage thickness in mammalian articular cartilage. J Anat 109:411–421
20. Radin EL, Rose RM (1986) Role of subchondral bone in the initiation and progression of cartilage damage. Clin Orthop Relat Res 213:34–40
21. Hunziker EB, Herrmann W, Schenk RK (1983) Ruthenium hexammine trichloride (RHT)-mediated interaction between plasmalemmal components and pericellular matrix proteoglycans is responsible for the preservation of chondrocytic plasma membranes in situ during cartilage fixation. J Histochem Cytochem 31:717–727
22. Kumar P, Oka M, Toguchida J, Kobayashi M, Uchida E, Nakamura T et al (2001) Role of uppermost superficial surface layer of articular cartilage in the lubrication mechanism of joints. J Anat 199:241–250
23. Wu JP, Kirk TB, Zheng MH (2008) Study of the collagen structure in the superficial zone and physiological state of articular cartilage using a 3D confocal imaging technique. J Orthop Surg Res 3:29
24. Mathew G, Hanson BP (2009) Global burden of trauma: need for effective fracture therapies. Indian J Orthop 43:111–116
25. Temple MM, Bae WC, Chen MQ, Lotz M, Amiel D, Coutts RD et al (2007) Age- and site-associated biomechanical weakening of human articular cartilage of the femoral condyle. Osteoarthr Cartil 15:1042–1052

26. Mansour JM, Mow VC (1976) The permeability of articular cartilage under compressive strain and at high pressures. J Bone Joint Surg Am 58:509–516
27. Freeman MAR (1979) Adult articular cartilage. Pitman Medical, Tunbridge Wells
28. Chen AC, Bae WC, Schinagl RM, Sah RL (2001) Depth- and strain-dependent mechanical and electromechanical properties of full-thickness bovine articular cartilage in confined compression. J Biomech 34:1–12
29. Williamson AK, Chen AC, Masuda K, Thonar EJMA, Sah RL (2003) Tensile mechanical properties of bovine articular cartilage: variations with growth and relationships to collagen network components. J Orthop Res 21:872–880
30. Johannessen W, Elliott DM (2005) Effects of degeneration on the biphasic material properties of human nucleus pulposus in confined compression. Spine (Phila Pa 1976) 30:E724–E729
31. Schinagl RM, Gurskis D, Chen AC, Sah RL (1997) Depth-dependent confined compression modulus of full-thickness bovine articular cartilage. J Orthop Res 15:499–506
32. Athanasiou KA, Agarwal A, Dzida FJ (1994) Comparative study of the intrinsic mechanical properties of the human acetabular and femoral head cartilage. J Orthop Res 12:340–349
33. Katakai D, Imura M, Ando W, Tateishi K, Yoshikawa H, Nakamura N et al (2009) Compressive properties of cartilage-like tissues repaired in vivo with scaffold-free, tissue engineered constructs. Clin Biomech 24:110–116
34. Changoor A, Fereydoonzad L, Yaroshinsky A, Buschmann MD (2010) Effects of refrigeration and freezing on the electromechanical and biomechanical properties of articular cartilage. J Biomech Eng 132:064502
35. Bray JC, Merrill EW (1973) Poly(vinyl alcohol) hydrogels for synthetic articular cartilage material. J Biomed Mater Res 7:431–443
36. Buckley MR, Gleghorn JP, Bonassar LJ, Cohen I (2008) Mapping the depth dependence of shear properties in articular cartilage. J Biomech 41:2430–2437
37. Setton LA, Mow VC, Howell DS (1995) Mechanical behavior of articular cartilage in shear is altered by transection of the anterior cruciate ligament. J Orthop Res 13:473–482
38. Linn FC (1967) Lubrication of animal joints. I. The arthrotripsometer. J Bone Joint Surg Am 49:1079–1098
39. Athanasiou KA, Rosenwasser MP, Buckwalter JA, Malinin TI, Mow VC (1991) Interspecies comparisons of in situ intrinsic mechanical properties of distal femoral cartilage. J Orthop Res 9:330–340
40. Maroudas A, Bullough P (1968) Permeability of articular cartilage. Nature 219:1260–1261
41. Basalo IM, Mauck RL, Kelly T-AN, Nicoll SB, Chen FH, Hung CT et al (2004) Cartilage interstitial fluid load support in unconfined compression following enzymatic digestion. J Biomech Eng 126:779–786
42. Armstrong CG, Bahrani AS, Gardner DL (1979) In vitro measurement of articular cartilage deformations in the intact human hip joint under load. J Bone Joint Surg Am 61:744–755
43. Akizuki S, Mow VC, Muller F, Pita JC, Howell DS, Manicourt DH (1986) Tensile properties of human knee joint cartilage: I. Influence of ionic conditions, weight bearing, and fibrillation on the tensile modulus. J Orthop Res 4:379–392
44. Freeman MA (1969) Tensile properties of articular cartilage. Nature 220:1127–1128
45. Roth V, Mow VC (1980) The intrinsic tensile behavior of the matrix of bovine articular cartilage and its variation with age. J Bone Joint Surg Am 62:1102–1117
46. Kempson GE, Muir H, Pollard C, Tuke M (1973) Tensile properties of the cartilage of human femoral condyles related to the content of collagen and glycosaminoglycans. Biochim Biophys Acta Gen Subj 297:456–472
47. Schmidt MB, Mow VC, Chun LE, Eyre DR (1990) Effects of proteoglycan extraction on the tensile behavior of articular cartilage. J Orthop Res 8:353–363
48. Williamson AK, Chen AC, Sah RL (2001) Compressive properties and function—composition relationships of developing bovine articular cartilage. J Orthop Res 19:1113–1121

49. Hayes WC, Mockros LF (1971) Viscoelastic properties of human articular cartilage. J Appl Physiol 31:562–568
50. Belyi VA, Kupchinov BI, Ermakov SF, Rodnenkov VG, Bobrysheva SN (1988) Lubricants to recover tribological properties of human joints. Int SAMPE Symp Exhib 33:645–651
51. Dowson D, Jin ZM (1986) Micro-elastohydrodynamic lubrication of synovial joints. Eng Med 15:63–65
52. Krishnan R, Kopacz M, Ateshian GA (2004) Experimental verification of the role of interstitial fluid pressurization in cartilage lubrication. J Orthop Res 22:565–570
53. Kupchinov BI (1989) Tribological aspects of the functioning of joints. Trenie Iznos 10:1013–1018
54. Armstrong CG, Gardner DL (1977) Thickness and distribution of human femoral head articular cartilage. Changes with age. Ann Rheum Dis 36:407–412
55. Meachim G (1971) Effect of age on the thickness of adult articular cartilage at the shoulder joint. Ann Rheum Dis 30:43–46
56. Vignon E, Arlot M, Vignon G (1977) The cellularity of fibrillated articular cartilage. A comparative study of age-related and osteoarthrotic cartilage lesions from the human femoral head. Pathol Biol 25:29–32
57. Adams CS, Horton WE Jr (1998) Chondrocyte apoptosis increases with age in the articular cartilage of adult animals. Anat Rec 250:418–425
58. Barbero A, Grogan S, Schafer D, Heberer M, Mainil-Varlet P, Martin I (2004) Age related changes in human articular chondrocyte yield, proliferation and post-expansion chondrogenic capacity. Osteoarthr Cartil 12:476–484
59. Eyre DR, Dickson IR, Van NK (1988) Collagen cross-linking in human bone and articular cartilage. Age-related changes in the content of mature hydroxypyridinium residues. Biochem J 252:495–500
60. Axelsson I, Bjelle A (1979) Proteoglycan structure of bovine articular cartilage. Variation with age and in osteoarthrosis. Scand J Rheumatol 8:217–221
61. Bank RA, Bayliss MT, Lafeber FPJG, Maroudas A, Tekoppele JM (1998) Osteochondral resurfacing of the knee joint with allograft. Clinical analysis of 33 cases. Biochem J 330:345–351
62. Ding M (2000) Age variations in the properties of human tibial trabecular bone and cartilage. Acta Orthop Scand Suppl 292:1–45
63. Hyttinen MM, Arokoski JP, Parkkinen JJ, Lammi MJ, Lapvetelainen T, Mauranen K et al (2001) Age matters: collagen birefringence of superficial articular cartilage is increased in young guinea-pigs but decreased in older animals after identical physiological type of joint loading. Osteoarthr Cartil 9:694–701
64. Turner AS, Athanasiou KA, Zhu CF, Alvis MR, Bryant HU (1997) Biochemical effects of estrogen on articular cartilage in ovariectomized sheep. Osteoarthr Cartil 5:63–69
65. Murray RC, DeBowes RM, Gaughan EM, Zhu CF, Athanasiou KA (1998) The effects of intra-articular methylprednisolone and exercise on the mechanical properties of articular cartilage in the horse. Osteoarthr Cartil 6:106–114
66. Athanasiou KA, Fleischli JG, Bosma J, Laughlin TJ, Zhu CF, Agrawal CM et al (1999) Effects of diabetes mellitus on the biomechanical properties of human ankle cartilage. Clin Orthop Relat Res 182–9
67. Wluka AE, Wang Y, Davis SR, Cicuttini FM (2005) Tibial plateau size is related to grade of joint space narrowing and osteophytes in healthy women and in women with osteoarthritis. Ann Rheum Dis 64:1033–1037
68. Aspden RM, Jeffrey JE, Burgin LV (2002) Impact loading of articular cartilage. Osteoarthr Cartil 10:588–589; author reply 90.
69. Lohmander LS, Ostenberg A, Englund M, Roos H (2004) High prevalence of knee osteoarthritis, pain, and functional limitations in female soccer players twelve years after anterior cruciate ligament injury. Arthritis Rheum 50:3145–3152

70. Roos H, Adalberth T, Dahlberg L, Lohmander LS (1995) Osteoarthritis of the knee after injury to the anterior cruciate ligament or meniscus: the influence of time and age. Osteoarthr Cartil 3:261–267
71. A picture of osteoarthritis in Australia. Australian Institute of Health and Welfare; 2007 series no. 5, Cat. no. PHE 93, Canberra: AIHW
72. Painful realities: The economic impact of arthritis in Australia. Canberra: Arthritis Australia 2012
73. Ahmed TAE, Hincke MT (2010) Strategies for articular cartilage lesion repair and functional restoration. Tissue Eng Part B 16:305–329
74. Goldberg VM, Caplan AI, Barry FP, Fink DJ, Marshak DR, Burns JS (2002) Osteoarthritis cartilage regeneration. Osiris Therapeutics, Inc., Columbia
75. McCormick F, Yanke A, Provencher MT, Cole BJ (2008) Minced articular cartilage – basic science, surgical technique, and clinical application. Sports Med Arthrosc 16:217–220
76. Furukawa T, Eyre DR, Koide S, Glimcher MJ (1980) Biochemical studies on repair cartilage resurfacing experimental defects in the rabbit knee. J Bone Joint Surg Am 62(A):79–89
77. Shapiro F, Koide S, Glimcher MJ (1993) Cell origin and differentiation in the repair of full-thickness defects of articular cartilage. J Bone Joint Surg Am 75:532–553
78. Hjertquist SO, Lemperg R (1971) Histological, autoradiographic, and microchemical studies of spontaneously healing osteochondral articular defects in adult rabbits. Calcif Tissue Res 8:54–72
79. Temenoff JS, Mikos AG (2000) Review: tissue engineering for regeneration of articular cartilage. Biomaterials 21:431–440
80. Adachi N, Ishikawa M, Sera S, Ochi M (2007) Articular cartilage regeneration (Knee joint). Bone 21:473–476
81. Ghadially JA, Ghadially R, Ghadially FN (1977) Long-term results of deep defects in articular cartilage. A scanning electron microscope study. Virchows Arch B Cell Pathol 25:125–136
82. Squires GR, Okouneff S, Ionescu M, Poole AR (2003) The pathobiology of focal lesion development in aging human articular cartilage and molecular matrix changes characteristic of osteoarthritis. Arthritis Rheum 48:1261–1270
83. Chang RW, Falconer J, Stulberg SD, Arnold WJ, Manheim LM, Dyer AR (1993) A randomized, controlled trial of arthroscopic surgery versus closed- needle joint lavage for patients with osteoarthritis of the knee. Arthritis Rheum 36:289–296
84. Ike RW, Arnold WJ (1992) Arthroscopic lavage of osteoarthritic knees. J Bone Joint Surg – B 74:788–789
85. Hunziker EB, Kapfinger E (1998) Removal of proteoglycans from the surface of defects in articular cartilage transiently enhances coverage by repair cells. J Bone Joint Surg – B 80:144–150
86. Felson DT (2010) Arthroscopy as a treatment for knee osteoarthritis. Best Pract Res Clin Rheumatol 24:47–50
87. Anderson MA, Payne JT, Kreeger JM, Wagner-Mann CC, Schmidt DA, Mann FA (1993) Effects of intra-articular chlorhexidine diacetate lavage on the stifle in healthy dogs. Am J Vet Res 54:1784–1789
88. Hunziker EB (2002) Articular cartilage repair: Basic science and clinical progress. A review of the current status and prospects. Osteoarthr Cartil 10:432–463
89. Tew SR, Kwan APL, Hann A, Thomson BM, Archer CW (2000) The reactions of articular cartilage to experimental wounding: Role of apoptosis. Arthritis Rheum 43:215–225
90. Mitchell N, Shepard N (1987) Effect of Patellar Shaving in the Rabbit. J Orthop Res 5:388–392
91. Hunziker EB, Quinn TM (2003) Surgical removal of articular cartilage leads to loss of chondrocytes from cartilage bordering the wound edge. J Bone Joint Surg – A 85:85–92
92. McLaren AC, Blokker CP, Fowler PJ, Roth JN, Rock MG (1991) Arthroscopic debridement of the knee for osteoarthrosis. Can J Surg 34:595–598

93. Messner K, Fahlgren A, Ross I, Andersson B (2000) Simultaneous changes in bone mineral density and articular cartilage in a rabbit meniscectomy model of knee osteoarthrosis. Osteoarthr Cartil 8:197–206
94. Messner K, Fahlgren A, Persliden J, Andersson BM (2001) Radiographic joint space narrowing and histologic changes in a rabbit meniscectomy model of early knee osteoarthrosis. Am J Sports Med 29:151–160
95. Müller B, Kohn D (1999) Indication for and performance of articular cartilage drilling using the Pridie method. Orthopade 28:4–10
96. Insall JN (1967) Intra-articular surgery for degenerative arthritis of the knee. A report of the work of the late K. H. Pridie. J Bone Joint Surg (Br) 49:211–228
97. Insall J (1974) The Pridie debridement operation for osteoarthritis of the knee. Clin Orthop Relat Res 101:61–67
98. Goldman RT, Scuderi GR, Kelly MA (1997) Arthroscopic treatment of the degenerative knee in older athletes. Clin Sports Med 16:51–68
99. Beiser IH, Kanat IO (1990) Subchondral bone drilling: a treatment for cartilage defect. J Foot Surg 29:595–601
100. Hice G, Freedman D, Lemont H, Khoury S (1990) Scanning and light microscopic study of irrigated and nonirrigated joints following burr surgery performed through a small incision. J Foot Surg 29:337–344
101. Schmidt H, Schulze KJ, Cyffka R (1988) Results of treatment of cartilage damage by Pridie drilling of the knee joint. Ergebnisse der Behandlung von Knorpelschäden durch PRIDIE-Bohrung am Kniegelen 35:117–122
102. Breinan HA, Martin SD, Hsu HP, Spector M (2000) Healing of canine articular cartilage defects treated with microfracture, a type-II collagen matrix, or cultured autologous chondrocytes. J Orthop Res 18:781–789
103. Sledge SL (2001) Microfracture techniques in the treatment of osteochondral injuries. Clin Sports Med 20:365–378
104. Pittenger MF, Mosca JD, McIntosh KR (2000) Human mesenchymal stem cells: progenitor cells for cartilage, bone, fat and stroma. 3–11.
105. Paccola CAJ, Xavier CAM, Goncalves RP (1979) Fresh immature articular cartilage allografts. A study on the integration of chondral and osteochondral grafts both in normal and in papain-treated knee joints of rabbits. Arch Orthop Trauma Surg 93:253–259
106. Lee TQ, Shrader TA, Wang YP, Glaser FE, Kim WC, McMahon PJ (1999) The use of entire fresh patellar allograft for articular cartilage replacement in rabbits: a long-term interdisciplinary study. J Musculoskelet Res 3:305–316
107. Stevenson S (1987) The immune response to osteochondral allografts in dogs. J Bone Joint Surg Am 69:573–582
108. Hickey MJ, Ohta I, Shigetomi M, Hurley JV, Kuwata N, O'Brien BM (1994) Vascularized heterotopic osteochondral allografts in a rat model following long-term immunosuppression. J Reconstr Microsurg 10:255–260
109. Bakay A, Csonge L, Papp G, Fekete L (1998) Osteochondral resurfacing of the knee joint with allograft. Clinical analysis of 33 cases. Int Orthop 22:277–281
110. Bell RS, Davis A, Allan DG, Langer F, Czitrom AA, Gross AE (1994) Fresh osteochondral allografts for advanced giant cell tumors at the knee. J Arthroplasty 9:603–609
111. Marco F, Lopez-Oliva F, Fernandez F-AJM, de Pedro JA, Perez AJ, Leon C et al (1993) Osteochondral allografts for osteochondritis dissecans and osteonecrosis of the femoral condyles. Int Orthop 17:104–108
112. McDermott AG, Langer F, Pritzker KP, Gross AE (1985) Fresh small-fragment osteochondral allografts. Long-term follow-up study on first 100 cases. Clin Orthop Relat Res 197:96–102
113. Mahomed MN, Beaver RJ, Gross AE (1992) The long-term success of fresh, small fragment osteochondral allografts used for intraarticular post-traumatic defects in the knee joint. Orthopedics 15:1191–1199

114. Kreuz PC, Steinwachs MR, Erggelet C, Krause SJ, Konrad G, Uhl M et al (2006) Results after microfracture of full-thickness chondral defects in different compartments in the knee. Osteoarthr Cartil 14:1119–1125
115. Jamali AA, Emmerson BC, Chung C, Convery FR, Bugbee WD (2005) Fresh osteochondral allografts: results in the patellofemoral joint. Clin Orthop Relat Res 437:176–185
116. Torga SR, Teitge RA (2006) Fresh osteochondral allografts for patellofemoral arthritis: long-term follow up. Clin Orthop Relat Res 444:193–200
117. Brittberg M, Lindahl A, Nilsson A, Ohlsson C, Isaksson O, Peterson L (1994) Treatment of deep cartilage defects in the knee with autologous chondrocyte transplantation. N Engl J Med 331:889–895
118. Trattnig S, Millington SA, Marlovits S (2007) MR imaging of osteochondral grafts and autologous chondrocyte implantation. Eur Radiol 17:103–118
119. Schnabel M, Marlovits S, Eckhoff G, Fichtel I, Gotzen L, Vecsei V et al (2002) Dedifferentiation-associated changes in morphology and gene expression in primary human articular chondrocytes in cell culture. Osteoarthr Cartil 10:62–70
120. Kuroda T, Matsumoto T, Mifune Y, Fukui T, Kubo S, Matsushita T et al (2011) Therapeutic strategy of third-generation autologous chondrocyte implantation for osteoarthritis. Ups J Med Sci 116:107–114
121. Tandogan NR, Karaeminogullari O, Ozyurek A, Ersozlu S (2004) Periarticular fractures of the knee in child and adolescent athletes. Acta Orthop Traumatol Turc 38(Suppl 1):93–100
122. Parkkari J, Pasanen K, Mattila VM, Kannus P, Rimpela A (2008) The risk for a cruciate ligament injury of the knee in adolescents and young adults: a population-based cohort study of 46 500 people with a 9 year follow-up. Br J Sports Med 42:422–426
123. Hickey GJ, Fricker PA, McDonald WA (1997) Injuries of young elite female basketball players over a six-year period. Clin J Sport Med 7:252–256
124. Adirim TA, Cheng TL (2003) Overview of injuries in the young athlete. Sports Med 33:75–81
125. Tuli R, Li W-J, Tuan RS (2003) Current state of cartilage tissue engineering. Arthritis Res Ther 5:235–238
126. Iwasa J, Engebretsen L, Shima Y, Ochi M (2009) Clinical application of scaffolds for cartilage tissue engineering. Knee Surg Sports Traumatol Arthrosc 17:561–577
127. Le DC, Guery J, Laulan J (2004) Results of a five-year series of 44 trapeziectomies associated with ligamentoplasty and interposition arthroplasty. Chir Main 23:149–152
128. Bruns J, Kersten P, Lierse W, Silbermann M (1993) Autologous transplantation of rib perichondrium in treatment of deep cartilage defects of the knee joint of sheep. Morphologic comparison of two resorbable fixation methods. Unfallchirurg 96:462–467
129. Getgood A, Brooks R, Fortier L, Rushton N (2009) Articular cartilage tissue engineering: today's research, tomorrow's practice? J Bone Joint Surg (Br) 91:565–576
130. Langer RS, Vacanti JP (1993) Tissue engineering. Science 260:920–926
131. Park I-K, Cho C-S (2010) Stem cell-assisted approaches for cartilage tissue engineering. Int J Stem Cells 3:96–102
132. Kim IL, Mauck RL, Burdick JA (2011) Hydrogel design for cartilage tissue engineering: a case study with hyaluronic acid. Biomaterials 32:8771–8782
133. Hwang NS, Elisseeff J (2009) Application of stem cells for articular cartilage regeneration. J Knee Surg 22:60–71
134. Pittenger MF, Mackay AM, Beck SC, Jaiswal RK, Douglas R, Mosca JD et al (1999) Multilineage potential of adult human mesenchymal stem cells. Science 284:143–147
135. Noël D, Djouad FCJ (2002) Regenerative medicine through mesenchymal stem cells for bone and cartilage repair. Curr Opin Investig Drugs 3:1000–1004
136. Barry FPMJ (2004) Mesenchymal stem cells: clinical applications and biological characterization. Int J Biochem Cell Biol 36:568–584

137. Trubiani ODPR, Traini T, Pizzicannella J, Scarano A, Piattelli A, Caputi S (2005) Morphological and cytofluorimetric analysis of adult mesenchymal stem cells expanded ex vivo from periodontal ligament. Int J Immunopathol Pharmacol 18:213–221
138. Trubiani OOG, Caputi S, Piatelli A (2006) Adult mesenchymal stem cells in dental research: a new approach for tissue engineering. Int J Immunopathol Pharmacol 19:451–460
139. Caplan AI (2007) Adult mesenchymal stem cells for tissue engineering versus regenerative medicine. J Cell Physiol 213:341–347
140. Nejadnik H, Hui JH, Feng Choong EP, Tai BC, Lee EH (2010) Autologous bone marrow-derived mesenchymal stem cells versus autologous chondrocyte implantation: an observational cohort study. Am J Sports Med 6:1110–1116
141. Fan HHY, Zhang C, Li X, Lv R, Qin L, Zhu R (2006) Cartilage regeneration using mesenchymal stem cells and a PLGA-gelatin/chondroitin/hyaluronate hybrid scaffold. Biomaterials 27:4573–4580
142. Uematsu K, Hattori K, Ishimoto Y, Yamauchi J, Habata T, Takakura Y et al (2005) Cartilage regeneration using mesenchymal stem cells and a three-dimensional poly-lactic-glycolic acid (PLGA) scaffold. Biomaterials 26:4273–4279
143. Banfi A, Bianchi G, Notaro R, Luzzatto L, Cancedda R, Quarto R (2002) Replicative aging and gene expression in long-term cultures of human bone marrow stromal cells. Tissue Eng 8:901–910
144. Parsch D, Fellenberg J, Bruemmendorf TH, Eschlbeck A-M, Richter W (2004) Telomere length and telomerase activity during expansion and differentiation of human mesenchymal stem cells and chondrocytes. J Mol Med 82:49–55
145. Vacanti V, Kong E, Suzuki G, Sato K, Canty JM, Lee T (2005) Phenotypic changes of adult porcine mesenchymal stem cells induced by prolonged passaging in culture. J Cell Physiol 205:194–201
146. Zhu S, Wurdak H, Wang J, Lyssiotis CA, Peters EC, Cho CY et al (2009) A small molecule primes embryonic stem cells for differentiation. Cell Stem Cell 4:416–426
147. Wurdaka H, Zhua S, Mina KH, Aimoneb L, Lairsona LL, Watsonb J et al (2010) A small molecule accelerates neuronal differentiation in the adult rat. PNAS 107:16542–16547
148. Richardson SM, Hoyland JA, Mobasheri R, Csaki C, Shakibaei MAM (2010) Mesenchymal stem cells in regenerative medicine: opportunities and challenges for articular cartilage and intervertebral disc tissue engineering. J Cell Physiol 222:23–32
149. Johnstone B, Hering TM, Caplan AI, Goldberg VM, Yoo JU (1998) In vitro chondrogenesis of bone marrow-derived mesenchymal progenitor cells. Exp Cell Res 238:265–272
150. Chiou MXY, Longaker MT (2006) Mitogenic and chondrogenic effects of fibroblast growth factor-2 in adipose-derived mesenchymal cells. Biochem Biophys Res Commun 343:644–652
151. Longobardi LORL, Aakula S, Johnstone B, Shimer K, Chytil A, Horton WA, Moses HL, Spagnoli A (2006) Effect of IGF-I in the chondrogenesis of bone marrow mesenchymal stem cells in the presence or absence of TGF-beta signaling. J Bone Miner Res 21:626–636
152. LA Solchaga PK, Porter JD, Goldberg VM, Caplan AI, Welter JF (2005) FGF-2 enhances the mitotic and chondrogenic potentials of human adult bone marrow-derived mesenchymal stem cells. J Cell Physiol 203:398–409
153. Frenkel SR, Saadeh PB, Mehrara BJ, Steinbrech DS, Cocker RS, McCormick SA et al (1998) Transforming growth factor beta superfamily members: role in cartilage modeling. Surg Forum 49:516–518
154. Frenkel SR, Saadeh PB, Mehrara BJ, Chin GS, Steinbrech DS, Brent B et al (2000) Transforming growth factor beta superfamily members: role in cartilage modeling. Plast Reconstr Surg 105:980–990
155. Van der Kan P, Vitters E, van der Berg W (1992) Differential effect of transforming growth factor beta on freshly isolated and cultured articular chondrocytes. J Rheumatol 19:140–145

156. Verschure PJ, Joosten LAB, Van der Kraan PM, Van der Berg WB (1994) Responsiveness of articular cartilage from normal and inflamed mouse knee joints to various growth factors. Ann Rheum Dis 53:455–460
157. Blunk T, Sieminski AL, Gooch KJ, Courter DL, Hollander AP, Nahir M et al (2002) Differential effects of growth factors on tissue-engineered cartilage. Tissue Eng 8:73–84
158. Sporn MB, Roberts AB, Wakefield LM, Assoian RK (1986) Transforming growth factor-β: biological function and chemical structure. Science (Washington, D C, 1883-) 233:532–534
159. Valcourt U, Gouttenoire J, Moustakas A, Herbage D, Mallein-Gerin F (2002) Functions of transforming growth factor-β family type I receptors and smad proteins in the hypertrophic maturation and osteoblastic differentiation of chondrocytes. J Biol Chem 277:33545–33558
160. Pecina M, Jelic M, Martinovic S, Haspl M, Vukicevic S (2002) Articular cartilage repair: the role of bone morphogenetic proteins. Int Orthop 26:131–136
161. Luyten FP, Yu YM, Yanagishita M, Vukicevic S, Hammonds RG, Reddi AH (1992) Natural bovine osteogenin and recombinant human bone morphogenetic protein-2B are equipotent in the maintenance of proteoglycans in bovine articular cartilage explant cultures. J Biol Chem 267:3691–3695
162. Mattioli-Belmonte M, Gigante A, Muzzarelli RA, Politano R, De BA, Specchia N et al (1999) N, N-dicarboxymethyl chitosan as delivery agent for bone morphogenetic protein in the repair of articular cartilage. Med Biol Eng Comput 37:130–134
163. Kaps C, Bramlage C, Smolian H, Haisch A, Ungethum U, Burmester G-R et al (2002) Bone morphogenetic proteins promote cartilage differentiation and protect engineered artificial cartilage from fibroblast invasion and destruction. Arthritis Rheum 46:149–162
164. Gooch KJ, Blunk T, Courter DL, Sieminski AL, Vunjak-Novakovic G, Freed LE (2002) Bone morphogenetic proteins-2, −12, and −13 modulate in vitro development of engineered cartilage. Tissue Eng 8:591–601
165. O'Connor WJ, Botti T, Khan SN, Lane JM (2000) The use of growth factors in cartilage repair. Orthop Clin North Am 31:399–410
166. Hunziker EB (1999) Biologic repair of articular cartilage. Defect models in experimental animals and matrix requirements. Clin Orthop Relat Res 367:S135–S146
167. Risbud M, Endres M, Ringe J, Bhonde R, Sittinger M (2001) Biocompatible hydrogel supports the growth of respiratory epithelial cells: possibilities in tracheal tissue engineering. J Biomed Mater Res 56:120–127
168. Boyan BD, Hummert TW, Dean DD, Schwartz Z (1996) Role of material surfaces in regulating bone and cartilage cell response. Biomaterials 17:137–146
169. McClary KB, Ugarova T, Grainger DW (2000) Modulating fibroblast adhesion, spreading, and proliferation using self-assembled monolayer films of alkylthiolates on gold. J Biomed Mater Res 50:428–439
170. Quirk RA, Chan WC, Davies MC, Tendler SJB, Shakesheff KM (2001) Poly(L-lysine)-GRGDS as a biomimetic surface modifier for poly(lactic acid). Biomaterials 22:865–872
171. Chu PK, Chen JY, Wang LP, Huang N (2002) Plasma-surface modification of biomaterials. Mater Sci Eng R R36:143–206
172. Humphries MJ, Akiyama SK, Komoriya A, Olden K, Yamada KM (1986) Identification of an alternatively spliced site in human plasma fibronectin that mediates cell type-specific adhesion. J Cell Biol 103:2637–2647
173. Shin H, Jo S, Mikos AG (2003) Biomimetic materials for tissue engineering. Biomaterials 24:4353–4364
174. Peppas NA, Hilt JZ, Khademhosseini A, Langer R (2006) Hydrogels in biology and medicine: from molecular principles to bionanotechnology. Adv Mater 18:1345–1360
175. Khademhosseini A, Langer R (2007) Microengineered hydrogels for tissue engineering. Biomaterials 28:5087
176. Nichol JW, Khademhosseini A (2009) Modular tissue engineering: engineering biological tissue from the bottom up. Soft Matter 5:1312–1319

177. Vacanti JP, Morse MA, Saltzman WM, Domb AJ, Perez-Atayde A, Langer R (1988) Selective cell transplantation using bioabsorbable artificial polymers as matrices. J Pediatr Surg 23:3–9
178. Mikos AG, Sarakinos G, Lyman MD, Ingber DE, Vacanti JP, Langer R (1993) Prevascularization of porous biodegradable polymers. Biotechnol Bioeng 42:716–723
179. Annabi N, Nichol JW, Zhong X, Ji C, Koshy S, Khademhosseini A et al (2010) Controlling the porosity and microarchitecture of hydrogels for tissue engineering. Tissue Eng Part B 16:371–380
180. Di Maio E, Mensitieri G, Iannace S, Nicolais L, Li W, Flumerfelt RW (2005) Structure optimization of polycaprolactone foams by using mixtures of CO2 and N2 as blowing agents. Polym Eng Sci 45:432–441
181. Zhang Y, Fan W, Ma Z, Wu C, Fang W, Liu G et al (2010) The effects of pore architecture in silk fibroin scaffolds on the growth and differentiation of mesenchymal stem cells expressing BMP7. Acta Biomater 6:3021–3028
182. Karageorgiou V, Kaplan D (2005) Porosity of 3D biomaterial scaffolds and osteogenesis. Biomaterials 26:5474–5491
183. Ngoenkam J, Faikrua A, Yasothornsrikul S, Viyoch J (2010) Potential of an injectable chitosan/starch/β-glycerol phosphate hydrogel for sustaining normal chondrocyte function. Int J Pharm 391:115–124
184. Duncan RL, Turner CH (1995) Mechanotransduction and the functional response of bone to mechanical strain. Calcif Tissue Int 57:344–358
185. Carter DR, Blenman PR, Beaupre GS (1988) Correlations between mechanical stress history and tissue differentiation in initial fracture healing. J Orthop Res 6:736–748
186. Jin M, Emkey GR, Siparsky P, Trippel SB, Grodzinsky AJ (2003) Combined effects of dynamic tissue shear deformation and insulin-like growth factor I on chondrocyte biosynthesis in cartilage explants. Arch Biochem Biophys 414:223–231
187. Hutmacher DW (2000) Scaffolds in tissue engineering bone and cartilage. Biomaterials 21:2529–2543
188. Gerard C, Catuogno C, Amargier-Huin C, Grossin L, Hubert P, Gillet P et al (2005) The effect of alginate, hyaluronate and hyaluronate derivatives biomaterials on synthesis of non-articular chondrocyte extracellular matrix. J Mater Sci Mater Med 16:541–551
189. Lee KY, Mooney DJ (2001) Hydrogels for tissue engineering. Chem Rev 101:1869–1879
190. Slaughter BV, Khurshid SS, Fisher OZ, Khademhosseini A, Peppas NA (2009) Hydrogels in regenerative medicine. Adv Mater 21:3307–3329
191. Peppas NA (1987) Hydrogels in medicine and pharmacy. CRC Press, Florida
192. Jabbari E (2006) Biomimetic hydrogel/apatite nanocomposite scaffolds for bone regeneration. Mater Res Soc Symp Proc 897E
193. Jabbari E, Nozari S (2000) Swelling behavior of acrylic acid hydrogels prepared by g-radiation crosslinking of polyacrylic acid in aqueous solution. Eur Polym J 36:2685–2692
194. Freed LE, Marquis JC, Nohria A, Emmanual J, Mikos AG, Langer R (1993) Neocartilage formation in vitro and in vivo using cells cultured on synthetic biodegradable polymers. J Biomed Mater Res 27:11–23
195. Liu Y, Chen F, Liu W, Cui L, Shang Q, Xia W et al (2002) Repairing large porcine full-thickness defects of articular cartilage using autologous chondrocyte-engineered cartilage. Tissue Eng 8:709–721
196. Chu CR, Coutts RD, Yoshioka M, Harwood FL, Monosov AZ, Amiel D (1995) Articular cartilage repair using allogeneic perichondrocyte-seeded biodegradable porous polylactic acid (PLA): a tissue-engineering study. J Biomed Mater Res 29:1147–1154
197. Vacanti CA, Langer R, Schloo B, Vacanti JP (1991) Synthetic polymers seeded with chondrocytes provide a template for new cartilage formation. Plast Reconstr Surg 88:753–759
198. Dounchis JS, Bae WC, Chen AC, Sah RL, Coutts RD, Amiel D (2000) Cartilage repair with autogenic perichondrium cell and polylactic acid grafts. Clin Orthop Relat Res 377:248–264

199. W-j L, Danielson KG, Alexander PG, Tuan RS (2003) Biological response of chondrocytes cultured in three-dimensional nanofibrous poly(e-caprolactone) scaffolds. J Biomed Mater Res A 67A:1105–1114
200. Annabi N, Fathi A, Mithieux SM, Weiss AS, Dehghani F (2011) Fabrication of porous PCL/elastin composite scaffolds for tissue engineering applications. J Supercrit Fluids 59:157–167
201. Annabi N, Fathi A, Mithieux SM, Martens P, Weiss AS, Dehghani F (2011) The effect of elastin on chondrocyte adhesion and proliferation on poly ([var epsilon]-caprolactone)/elastin composites. Biomaterials 32:1517–1525
202. W-j L, Danielson KG, Alexander PG, Tuan RS (2003) Biological response of chondrocytes cultured in three-dimensional nanofibrous poly(ε-caprolactone) scaffolds. J Biomed Mater Res Part A 67A:1105–1114
203. Ushio K, Oka M, Hyon S-H, Hayami T, Yura S, Matsumura K et al (2003) Attachment of artificial cartilage to underlying bone. J Biomed Mater Res Part B 68B:59–68
204. Gu Z, Xiao J, Zhang X (1999) Development of artificial articular cartilage-PVA-hydrogel. Beijing Keji Daxue Xuebao 21:40–43
205. Oka M (2001) Biomechanics and repair of articular cartilage. J Orthop Sci 6:448–456
206. Guo T, Yang T, Xiao J, Long H, Chen Y, Pei F et al (2009) Repair of articular cartilage defect in rabbits by novel biomimetic composite material of polyvinyl alcohol hydrogel/nano-hydroxyapatite + polyamide 66. Zhonghua Chuangshang Zazhi 25:748–750
207. Spiller KL, Liu Y, Holloway JL, Maher SA, Cao Y, Liu W et al (2012) A novel method for the direct fabrication of growth factor-loaded microspheres within porous nondegradable hydrogels: Controlled release for cartilage tissue engineering. J Control Release 157:39–45
208. Elisseeff J, Anseth K, Sims D, McIntosh W, Randolph M, Yaremchuk M et al (1999) Transdermal photopolymerization of poly(ethylene oxide)-based injectable hydrogels for tissue-engineered cartilage. Plast Reconstr Surg 104:1014–1022
209. Sharma B, Williams CG, Khan M, Manson P, Elisseeff JH (2006) In vivo chondrogenesis of mesenchymal stem cells in a photopolymerized hydrogel. Plast Reconstr Surg 119:112–120
210. Hwang NS, Varghese S, Theprungsirikul P, Canver A, Elisseeff J (2006) Enhanced chondrogenic differentiation of murine embryonic stem cells in hydrogels with glucosamine. Biomaterials 27:6015–6023
211. Nguyen QT, Hwang Y, Chen AC, Varghese S, Sah RL (2012) Cartilage-like mechanical properties of poly(ethylene glycol)-diacrylate hydrogels. Biomaterials 33:6682–6690
212. Shung AK, Behravesh E, Jo S, Mikos AG (2003) Crosslinking characteristics of and cell adhesion to an injectable poly(propylene fumarate-co-ethylene glycol) hydrogel using a water-soluble crosslinking system. Tissue Eng 9:243–254
213. Park H, Temenoff JS, Holland TA, Tabata Y, Mikos AG (2005) Delivery of TGF-β1 and chondrocytes via injectable, biodegradable hydrogels for cartilage tissue engineering applications. Biomaterials 26:7095–7103
214. Sokmen N, Ayhan F, Ayhan H (2008) Gelatine containing photopolymerized poly(ethylene glycol) diacrylate hydrogels for drug delivery. Polym Prepr (Am Chem Soc, Div Polym Chem) 49:1054–1055
215. Drapala PW, Brey EM, Mieler WF, Venerus DC, Kang DJJ, Perez-Luna VH (2011) Role of thermo-responsiveness and poly(ethylene glycol) diacrylate cross-link density on protein release from poly(N-isopropylacrylamide) hydrogels. J Biomater Sci Polym Ed 22:59–75
216. Holland TA, Bodde EWH, Cuijpers VMJI, Baggett LS, Tabata Y, Mikos AG et al (2007) Degradable hydrogel scaffolds for in vivo delivery of single and dual growth factors in cartilage repair. Osteoarthr Cartil 15:187–197
217. Guo X, Park H, Liu G, Liu W, Cao Y, Tabata Y et al (2009) In vitro generation of an osteochondral construct using injectable hydrogel composites encapsulating rabbit marrow mesenchymal stem cells. Biomaterials 30:2741–2752

218. Guo X, Park H, Young S, Kretlow JD, Van den Beucken JJ, Baggett LS et al (2010) Repair of osteochondral defects with biodegradable hydrogel composites encapsulating marrow mesenchymal stem cells in a rabbit model. Acta Biomater 6:39–47
219. Stoltz JF, Magdalou J, Netter P, Pinzano A, Zille H, Paquet J et al (2010) Evaluation of intra-articular delivery of hyaluronic acid functionalized biopolymeric nanoparticles in healthy rat knees. Biomed Mater Eng 20:235–242
220. Bergsma EJ, Rozema FR, Bos RR, de Bruijn WC (1993) Foreign body reactions to resorbable poly(L-lactide) bone plates and screws used for the fixation of unstable zygomatic fractures. J Oral Maxillofac Surg 51:666–670
221. Martin C, Winet H, Bao JY (1996) Acidity near eroding polylactide-polyglycolide in vitro and in vivo in rabbit tibial bone chambers. Biomaterials 17:2373–2380
222. An YH, Woolf SK, Friedman RJ (2000) Pre-clinical in vivo evaluation of orthopaedic bioabsorbable devices. Biomaterials 21:2635–2652
223. Dunn AS, Campbell PG, Marra KG (2001) The influence of polymer blend composition on the degradation of polymer/hydroxyapatite biomaterials. J Mater Sci Mater Med 12:673–677
224. Heidemann W, Jeschkeit S, Ruffieux K, Fischer JH, Wagner M, Kruger G et al (2001) Degradation of poly(D, L)lactide implants with or without addition of calciumphosphates in vivo. Biomaterials 22:2371–2381
225. Rezwan K, Chen QZ, Blaker JJ, Boccaccini AR (2006) Biodegradable and bioactive porous polymer/inorganic composite scaffolds for bone tissue engineering. Biomaterials 27:3413–3431
226. Bazile DV, Ropert C, Huve P, Verrecchia T, Marland M, Frydman A et al (1992) Body distribution of fully biodegradable [14C]-poly(lactic acid) nanoparticles coated with albumin after parenteral administration to rats. Biomaterials 13:1093–1102
227. Chu CR, Dounchis JS, Yoshioka M, Sah RL, Coutts RD, Amiel D (1997) Osteochondral repair using perichondrial cells. A 1-year study in rabbits. Clin Orthop Relat Res 340:220–229
228. Xiong L, He Z (2011) Synthesis and application for porous scaffold materials of mono-methoxy polyethylene glycol/polylactide diblock copolymer. J Macromol Sci Part B Phys 50:1226–1233
229. Pitt CG, Jeffcoat AR, Zweidinger RA, Schindler A (1979) Sustained drug delivery systems. I. The permeability of poly(ε-caprolactone), poly(DL-lactic acid), and their copolymers. J Biomed Mater Res 13:497–507
230. Ye WP, Du FS, Jin WH, Yang JY, Xu Y (1997) In vitro degradation of poly(caprolactone), poly(lactide) and their block copolymers: influence of composition, temperature and morphology. React Funct Polym 32:161–168
231. Coombes AGA, Verderio E, Shaw B, Li X, Griffin M, Downes S (2002) Biocomposites of non-crosslinked natural and synthetic polymers. Biomaterials 23:2113–2118
232. Schagemann JC, Kurz H, Casper ME, Stone JS, Dadsetan M, Sun Y-L et al (2010) The effect of scaffold composition on the early structural characteristics of chondrocytes and expression of adhesion molecules. Biomaterials 31:2798–2805
233. Park GE, Webster TJ (2005) Mechanisms of increased chondrocyte adhesion on nanometer surface featured NaOH-treated PLGA. J Biomed Nanotechnol 1:306–312
234. Thissen H, Chang KY, Tebb TA, Tsai WB, Glattauer V, Ramshaw JAM et al (2006) Synthetic biodegradable microparticles for articular cartilage tissue engineering. J Biomed Mater Res Part A 77A:590–598
235. Peppas NA, Merrill EW (1977) Crosslinked poly(vinyl alcohol) hydrogels as swollen elastic networks. J Appl Polym Sci Symp 21:1763–1770
236. Amini AA, Nair LS (2012) Injectable hydrogels for bone and cartilage. Biomed Mater 7:(13pp)
237. Nguyen MK, Lee DS (2010) Injectable biodegradable hydrogels. Macromol Biosci 10:563–579

238. Liu SQ, Tian Q, Hedrick JL, Hui JHP, Ee PLR, Yang YY (2010) Biomimetic hydrogels for chondrogenic differentiation of human mesenchymal stem cells to neocartilage. Biomaterials 31:7298–7307
239. Bryant SJ, Arthur JA, Anseth KS (2005) Incorporation of tissue-specific molecules alters chondrocyte metabolism and gene expression in photocrosslinked hydrogels. Acta Biomater 1:243–252
240. Malmonge SM, Zavaglia CA, Belangero WD (2000) Biomechanical and histological evaluation of hydrogel implants in articular cartilage. Braz J Med Biol Res 33:307–312
241. Sawtell RM, Downes S, Kayser MV (1995) An in vitro investigation of the PEMA/THFMA system using chondrocyte culture. J Mater Sci Mater Med 6:676–679
242. Reissis N, Kayser M, Bentley G, Downes S (1995) A hydrophylic polymer system enhanced articular cartilage regeneration in vivo. J Mater Sci Mater Med 6:768–772
243. Bosnakovski D, Mizuno M, Kim G, Takagi S, Okumura M, Fujinaga T (2006) Chondrogenic differentiation of bovine bone marrow mesenchymal stem cells (MSCs) in different hydrogels: influence of collagen type II extracellular matrix on MSC chondrogenesis. Biotechnol Bioeng 93:1152–1163
244. Wakitani S, Goto T, Pineda SJ, Young RG, Mansour JM, Caplan AI et al (1994) Mesenchymal cell-based repair of large, full-thickness defects of articular cartilage. J Bone Joint Surg Am 76:579–592
245. Harriger MD, Supp AP, Warden GD, Boyce ST (1997) Glutaraldehyde crosslinking of collagen substrates inhibits degradation in skin substitutes grafted to athymic mice. J Biomed Mater Res 35:137–145
246. Wissink MJB, Beernink R, Poot AA, Engbers GHM, Beugeling T, Van Aken WG et al (2001) Relation between cell density and the secretion of von Willebrand factor and prostacyclin by human umbilical vein endothelial cells. Biomaterials 22:2283–2290
247. Van LMJA, Van WPB, Olde DLHH, Dijkstra PJ, Feijen J, Nieuwenhuis P (1992) Secondary cytotoxicity of crosslinked dermal sheep collagens during repeated exposure to human fibroblasts. Biomaterials 13:1017–1024
248. Nehrer S, Breinan HA, Ramappa A, Hsu HP, Minas T, Shortkroff S et al (1998) Chondrocyte-seeded collagen matrices implanted in a chondral defect in a canine model. Biomaterials 19:2313–2328
249. Kon E, Delcogliano M, Filardo G, Altadonna G, Marcacci M (2009) Novel nano-composite multi-layered biomaterial for the treatment of multifocal degenerative cartilage lesions. Knee Surg Sports Traumatol Arthrosc 17:1312–1315
250. Haisch A, Loch A, David J, Pruss A, Hansen R, Sittinger M (2000) Preparation of a pure autologous biodegradable fibrin matrix for tissue engineering. Med Biol Eng Comput 38:686–689
251. Fortier LA, Nixon AJ, Mohammed HO, Lust G (1997) Altered biological activity of equine chondrocytes cultured in a three-dimensional fibrin matrix and supplemented with transforming growth factor β-1. Am J Vet Res 58:66–70
252. Li W-J, Tuan RS (2005) Polymeric scaffolds for cartilage tissue engineering. Macromol Symp 227:65–75
253. Horan RL, Antle K, Collette AL, Wang Y, Huang J, Moreau JE et al (2005) In vitro degradation of silk fibroin. Biomaterials 26:3385–3393
254. Qin G, Kaplan DL (2012) Silk-based biomaterials: biology, properties, and clinical applications. CRC Press, Boca Raton, pp 421–31.
255. Dal Pra I, Freddi G, Minic J, Chiarini A, Armato U (2005) De novo engineering of reticular connective tissue in vivo by silk fibroin nonwoven materials. Biomaterials 26:1987–1999
256. Altman GH, Diaz F, Jakuba C, Calabro T, Horan RL, Chen J et al (2002) Silk-based biomaterials. Biomaterials 26:401–416
257. Mehlhorn AT, Schmal H, Kaiser S, Lepski G, Finkenzeller G, Stark GB et al (2006) Mesenchymal stem cells maintain TGF-β-mediated chondrogenic phenotype in alginate bead culture. Tissue Eng 12:1393–1403

258. Cheng N-C, Estes BT, Awad HA, Guilak F (2009) Chondrogenic differentiation of adipose-derived adult stem cells by a porous scaffold derived from native articular cartilage extracellular matrix. Tissue Eng Part A 15:231–241
259. Balakrishnan B, Banerjee R (2011) Biopolymer-based hydrogels for cartilage tissue engineering. Chem Rev 111:4453–4474
260. De Souza R, Zahedi P, Allen CJ, Piquette-Miller M (2009) Biocompatibility of injectable chitosan–phospholipid implant systems. Biomaterials 30:3818–3824
261. Jancar J, Slovikova A, Amler E, Krupa P, Kecova H, Planka L, et al (2007) Mechanical response of porous scaffolds for cartilage engineering. Physiol Res 56:S17–S25
262. Medrado GCB, Machado CB, Valerio P, Sanches MD, Goes AM (2006) The effect of a chitosan-gelatin matrix and dexamethasone on the behavior of rabbit mesenchymal stem cells. Biomed Mater 1:155–161
263. Sa-Lima H, Caridade SG, Mano JF, Reis RL (2010) Stimuli-responsive chitosan-starch injectable hydrogels combined with encapsulated adipose-derived stromal cells for articular cartilage regeneration. Soft Matter 6:5184–5195
264. Lippiello L (2003) Glucosamine and chondroitin sulfate: biological response modifiers of chondrocytes under simulated conditions of joint stress. Osteoarthr Cartil 11:335–342
265. Chan PS, Caron JP, Rosa GJM, Orth MW (2005) Glucosamine and chondroitin sulfate regulate gene expression and synthesis of nitric oxide and prostaglandin E(2) in articular cartilage explants. Osteoarthr Cartil 13:387–394
266. Uebelhart D, Thonar EJ, Delmas PD, Chantraine A, Vignon E (1998) Effects of oral chondroitin sulfate on the progression of knee osteoarthritis: a pilot study. Osteoarthr Cartil 6(Suppl A):39–46
267. Sechriest VF, Miao YJ, Niyibizi C, Westerhausen-Larson A, Matthew HW, Evans CH et al (2000) GAG-augmented polysaccharide hydrogel: a novel biocompatible and biodegradable material to support chondrogenesis. J Biomed Mater Res 49:534–541
268. van Susante JLC, Pieper J, Buma P, van Kuppevelt TH, van Beuningen H, van der Kraan PM et al (2001) Linkage of chondroitin-sulfate to type I collagen scaffolds stimulates the bioactivity of seeded chondrocytes in vitro. Biomaterials 22:2359–2369
269. Betre H, Chilkoti A, Setton L. A (2002) A two step recovery system based on thermally sensitive elastin-like polypeptide scaffolds for cartilage tissue engineering. Proceedings of the Second Joint EBMS/BMES Conference pp 829–30
270. McHale MK, Setton LA, Chilkoti A (2006) Synthesis and in vitro evaluation of enzymatically cross-linked elastin-like polypeptide gels for cartilaginous tissue repair. Tissue Eng 11:1768–1779
271. Ong SR, Trabbic-Carlson KA, Nettles DL, Lim DW, Chilkoti A, Setton LA (2006) Epitope tagging for tracking elastin-like polypeptides. Biomaterials 27:1930–1935
272. Hrabchak C, Rouleau J, Moss I, Woodhouse K, Akens M, Bellingham C et al (2010) Assessment of biocompatibility and initial evaluation of genipin cross-linked elastin-like polypeptides in the treatment of an osteochondral knee defect in rabbits. Acta Biomater 6:2108–2115
273. Stark Y, Suck K, Kasper C, Wieland M, van Griensven M, Scheper T (2006) Application of collagen matrices for cartilage tissue engineering. Exp Toxicol Pathol 57:305–311
274. Pieper JS, van Tienen T, van Susante JLC, van der Kraan PM, Veerkamp JH et al (2003) Cross-linked type I and type II collagenous matrices for the repair of full-thickness articular cartilage defects – a study in rabbits. Biomaterials 24:3255–3263
275. Lu HH, El-Amin SF, Scott KD, Laurencin CT (2003) Three-dimensional, bioactive, biodegradable, polymer-bioactive glass composite scaffolds with improved mechanical properties support collagen synthesis and mineralization of human osteoblast-like cells in vitro. J Biomed Mater Res A 64:465–474
276. Nandakumar A, Fernandes H, de Boer J, Moroni L, Habibovic P, van Blitterswijk CA (2010) Fabrication of bioactive composite scaffolds by electrospinning for bone regeneration. Macromol Biosci 10:1365–1373

277. Nowatzki PJ, Tirrell DA (2003) Physical properties of artificial extracellular matrix protein films prepared by isocyanate crosslinking. Biomaterials 25:1261–1267
278. Nimni ME, Cheung D, Strates B, Kodama M, Sheikh K (1987) Chemically modified collagen: a natural biomaterial for tissue replacement. J Biomed Mater Res 21:741–771
279. Sandberg LB, Soskel NT, Leslie JG (1981) Elastin structure, biosynthesis, and relation to disease states. N Engl J Med 304:566–579
280. Nettles DL, Chilkoti A, Setton LA (2010) Applications of elastin-like polypeptides in tissue engineering. Adv Drug Deliv Rev 62:1479–1485
281. Alberts B, Johnson A, Lewis J, Raff M, Roberts K, Walter P (2002) Cell junctions, cell adhesion, and the extracellular matrix. Garland Science, New York
282. Daamen WF, Hafmans T, Veerkamp JH, van Kuppevelt TH (2001) Comparison of five procedures for the purification of insoluble elastin. Biomaterials 22
283. Partridge SM, Davis HF, Adair GS (1955) Connective tissue. II. Soluble proteins derived from partial hydrolysis of elastin. Biochem J 61:11–21
284. Mandli I, Kellers SML (1970) Chemistry and molecular biology of the intercellular matrix. In: Balzas EA (ed) New York. Academic Press, p 665
285. Rnjak-Kovacina J, Daamen WF, Pierna M, Rodrı´guez-Cabello JC, Weiss AS (2011) Elastin biopolymers. In: Ducheyne P (ed) Comprehensive biomaterials. Elsevier Science, Amsterdam, pp 329–346
286. Antonicelli F, Bellon G, Debelle L, Hornebeck W (2007) Elastin-elastases and inflamm-aging. Curr Top Dev Biol 79:99–155
287. Betre H, Setton LA, Meyer DE, Chilkoti A (2002) Characterization of a genetically engineered elastin-like polypeptide for cartilaginous tissue repair. Biomacromolecules 3:910–916
288. Betre H, Ong SR, Guilak F, Chilkoti A, Fermor B, Setton LA (2006) Chondrocytic differentiation of human adipose-derived adult stem cells in elastin-like polypeptide. Biomaterials 27:91–99
289. Lim DW, Nettles DL, Setton LA, Chilkoti A (2007) Rapid cross-linking of elastin-like polypeptides with (Hydroxymethyl)phosphines in aqueous solution. Biomacromolecules 8:1463–1470
290. Trabbic-Carlson K, Setton LA, Chilkoti A (2003) Swelling and mechanical behaviors of chemically cross-linked hydrogels of elastin-like polypeptides. Biomacromolecules 4:572–580
291. Lim DW, Nettles DL, Setton LA, Chilkoti A (2008) In situ cross-linking of elastin-like polypeptide block copolymers for tissue repair. Biomacromolecules 9:222–230
292. Annabi N, Mithieux SM, Weiss AS, Dehghani F (2010) Cross-linked open-pore elastic hydrogels based on tropoelastin, elastin and high pressure CO_2. Biomaterials 31:1655–1665
293. Nettles DL, Haider MA, Chilkoti A, Setton LA (2009) Neural network analysis identifies scaffold properties necessary for in vitro chondrogenesis in elastin-like polypeptide biopolymer scaffolds. Tissue Eng Part A 16:11–20
294. Silverman RP, Passaretti D, Huang W, Randolph MA, Yaremchuk MJ (1999) Injectable tissue-engineered cartilage using a fibrin glue polymer. Plast Reconstr Surg 103:1809–1818
295. Worster AA, Brower-Toland BD, Fortier LA, Bent SJ, Williams J, Nixon AJ (2001) Chondrocytic differentiation of mesenchymal stem cells sequentially exposed to transforming growth factor-β1 in monolayer and insulin-like growth factor-I in a three-dimensional matrix. J Orthop Res 19:738–749
296. Nixon AJ, Fortier LA, Williams J, Mohammed H (1999) Enhanced repair of extensive articular defects by insulin-like growth factor-I-laden fibrin composites. J Orthop Res 17:475–487
297. Whatley JS, Dejardin LM, Arnoczky SP (2000) The effect of an exogenous fibrin clot on the regeneration of the triangular fibrocartilage complex: an in vivo experimental study in dogs. Arthroscopy 16:127–136

298. Paletta GA, Arnoczky SP, Warren RF (1992) The repair of osteochondral defects using an exogenous fibrin clot. An experimental study in dogs. Am J Sports Med 20:725–731
299. van Susante JL, Buma P, Schuman L, Homminga GN, van den Berg WB, Veth RPH (1999) Resurfacing potential of heterologous chondrocytes suspended in fibrin glue in large full-thickness defects of femoral articular cartilage: an experimental study in the goat. Biomaterials 20:1167–1175
300. Hendrickson DA, Nixon AJ, Grande DA, Todhunter RJ, Minor RM, Erb H et al (1994) Chondrocyte-fibrin matrix transplants for resurfacing extensive articular cartilage defects. J Orthop Res 12:485–497
301. Kawabe N, Yoshinao M (1991) The repair of full-thickness articular cartilage defects. Immune responses to reparative tissue formed by allogeneic growth plate chondrocyte implants. Clin Orthop Relat Res 268:279–293
302. Henning CE, Lynch MA, Yearout KM, Vequist SW, Stallbaumer RJ, Decker KA (1990) Arthroscopic meniscal repair using an exogenous fibrin clot. Clin Orthop Relat Res 252:64–72
303. Gobin AS, Froude VE, Mathur AB (2005) Structural and mechanical characteristics of silk fibroin and chitosan blend scaffolds for tissue regeneration. J Biomed Mater Res Part A 74A:465–473
304. Scheibel T (2006) Silk-a biomaterial with several facets. Appl Phys A Mater Sci Process 82:191–192
305. Vepari C, Kaplan DL (2007) Silk as a biomaterial. Prog Polym Sci 32:991–1007
306. Meinel L, Hofmann S, Karageorgiou V, Zichner L, Langer R, Kaplan D et al (2004) Engineering cartilage-like tissue using human mesenchymal stem cells and silk protein scaffolds. Biotechnol Bioeng 88:379–391
307. Uebersax L, Merkle HP, Meinel L (2008) Insulin-like growth factor I releasing silk fibroin scaffolds induce chondrogenic differentiation of human mesenchymal stem cells. J Control Release 127:12–21
308. Wang Y, Blasioli DJ, Kim H-J, Kim HS, Kaplan DL (2006) Cartilage tissue engineering with silk scaffolds and human articular chondrocytes. Biomaterials 27:4434–4442
309. Wang Y, Kim U-J, Blasioli DJ, Kim H-J, Kaplan DL (2005) In vitro cartilage tissue engineering with 3D porous aqueous-derived silk scaffolds and mesenchymal stem cells. Biomaterials 26:7082–7094
310. Hu X, Wang X, Rnjak J, Weiss AS, Kaplan DL (2010) Biomaterials derived from silk-tropoelastin protein systems. Biomaterials 31:8121–8131
311. Hu X, Park S-H, Gil ES, Xia X-X, Weiss AS, Kaplan DL (2011) The influence of elasticity and surface roughness on myogenic and osteogenic-differentiation of cells on silk-elastin biomaterials. Biomaterials 32:8979–8989
312. Dash M, Chiellini F, Ottenbrite RM, Chiellini E (2011) Chitosan—A versatile semi-synthetic polymer in biomedical applications. Prog Polym Sci 36:981–1014
313. Kubota N, Tatsumoto N, Sano T, Toya K (2000) A simple preparation of half N-acetylated chitosan highly soluble in water and aqueous organic solvents. Carbohydr Res 324:268–274
314. Lin H-Y, Chou C-C (2004) Antioxidative activities of water-soluble disaccharide chitosan derivatives. Food Res Int 37:883–889
315. Bedekar AN, Pise AC, Thatte CS, Rathnam MV (2010) Study on optimization of carboxymethylation of chitosan obtained from squilla chitin. Asian J Chem 22:7675–7682
316. Gong Y, Zhu Y, Liu Y, Ma Z, Gao C, Shen J (2007) Layer-by-layer assembly of chondroitin sulfate and collagen on aminolyzed poly(L-lactic acid) porous scaffolds to enhance their chondrogenesis. Acta Biomater 3:677–685
317. Milosavljevic NB, Milasinovic NZ, Popovic IG, Filipovic JM, Kalagasidis KMT (2011) Preparation and characterization of pH-sensitive hydrogels based on chitosan, itaconic acid and methacrylic acid. Polym Int 60:443–452
318. Ma L, Gao C, Mao Z, Zhou J, Shen J, Hu X et al (2003) Collagen/chitosan porous scaffolds with improved biostability for skin tissue engineering. Biomaterials 24:4833–4841

319. Shanmugasundaram N, Ravichandran P, Neelakanta RP, Ramamurty N, Pal S, Panduranga RK (2001) Collagen-chitosan polymeric scaffolds for the in vitro culture of human epidermoid carcinoma cells. Biomaterials 22:1943–1951
320. Lu G, Kong L, Sheng B, Wang G, Gong Y, Zhang X (2007) Degradation of covalently cross-linked carboxymethyl chitosan and its potential application for peripheral nerve regeneration. Eur Polym J 43:3807–3818
321. Ji C, Annabi N, Khademhosseini A, Dehghani F (2011) Fabrication of porous chitosan scaffolds for soft tissue engineering using dense gas CO2. Acta Biomater 7:1653–1664
322. Ji C, Annabi N, Hosseinkhani M, Sivaloganathan S, Dehghani F (2012) Fabrication of poly-DL-lactide/polyethylene glycol scaffolds using the gas foaming technique. Acta Biomater 8:570–578
323. Mwale F, Iordanova M, Demers CN, Steffen T, Roughley P, Antoniou J (2005) Biological evaluation of chitosan salts cross-linked to genipin as a cell scaffold for disk tissue engineering. Tissue Eng 11:130–140
324. Ji C, Khademhosseini A, Dehghani F (2011) Enhancing cell penetration and proliferation in chitosan hydrogels for tissue engineering applications. Biomaterials 32:9719–9729
325. Lu JX, Prudhommeaux F, Meunier A, Sedel L, Guillemin G (1999) Effects of chitosan on rat knee cartilages. Biomaterials 20:1937–1944
326. Suh JK, Matthew HW (2000) Application of chitosan-based polysaccharide biomaterials in cartilage tissue engineering: a review. Biomaterials 21:2589–2598
327. Shive MS, Hoemann CD, Restrepo A, Hurtig M, Duval N, Ranger P et al (2006) BST-CarGel: in situ chondroInduction for cartilage repair. Oper Tech Orthop 16:271–278
328. Bellamy N, Buchanan WW, Goldsmith CH, Campbell J, Stitt LW (1988) Validation study of WOMAC: a health status instrument for measuring clinically important patient relevant outcomes to antirheumatic drug therapy in patients with osteoarthritis of the hip or knee. J Rheumatol 15:1833–1840
329. Seyrek E, Dubin P (2010) Glycosaminoglycans as polyelectrolytes. Adv Colloid Interface Sci 158:119–129
330. Uebelhart D, Thonar EJ, Zhang J, Williams JM (1998) Protective effect of exogenous chondroitin 4,6-sulfate in the acute degradation of articular cartilage in the rabbit. Osteoarthr Cartil 6(Suppl A):6–13
331. Handley CJ, Brooks P, Lowther DA (1980) Suppression of collagen synthesis by chondrocytes by exogenous concentrations of proteoglycan subunit. Biochem Int 1:270–276
332. Bian L, Kaplun M, Williams DY, Xu D, Ateshian GA, Hung CT (2009) Influence of chondroitin sulfate on the biochemical, mechanical and frictional properties of cartilage explants in long-term culture. J Biomech 42:286–290
333. Varghese S, Hwang NS, Canver AC, Theprungsirikul P, Lin DW, Elisseeff J (2008) Chondroitin sulfate based niches for chondrogenic differentiation of mesenchymal stem cells. Matrix Biol 27:12–21
334. Akmal M, Singh A, Anand A, Kesani A, Aslam N, Goodship A et al (2005) The effects of hyaluronic acid on articular chondrocytes. J Bone Joint Surg (Br) 87:1143–1149
335. Goa KL, Benfield P (1994) Hyaluronic acid. A review of its pharmacology and use as a surgical aid in ophthalmology, and its therapeutic potential in joint disease and wound healing. Drugs 47:536–566
336. Responte DJ, Natoli RM, Athanasiou KA (2012) Identification of potential biophysical and molecular signalling mechanisms underlying hyaluronic acid enhancement of cartilage formation. J R Soc Interface 9:3564–3573
337. Bulpitt P, Aeschlimann D (1999) New strategy for chemical modification of hyaluronic acid: preparation of functionalized derivatives and their use in the formation of novel biocompatible hydrogels. J Biomed Mater Res 47:152–169
338. Campoccia D, Doherty P, Radice M, Brun P, Abatangelo G, Williams DF (1998) Semisynthetic resorbable materials from hyaluronan esterification. Biomaterials 19:2101–2127

339. Vercruysse KP, Marecak DM, Marecek JF, Prestwich GD (1997) Synthesis and in vitro degradation of new polyvalent hydrazide cross-linked hydrogels of hyaluronic acid. Bioconjug Chem 8:686–694
340. Barbucci R, Magnani A, Rappuoli R, Lamponi S, Consumi M (2000) Immobilisation of sulphated hyaluronan for improved biocompatibility. J Inorg Biochem 79:119–125
341. Aigner J, Tegeler J, Hutzler P, Campoccia D, Pavesio A, Hammer C et al (1998) Cartilage tissue engineering with novel nonwoven structured biomaterial based on hyaluronic acid benzyl ester. J Biomed Mater Res 42:172–181
342. Grigolo B, Lisignoli G, Piacentini A, Fiorini M, Gobbi P, Mazzotti G et al (2001) Evidence for redifferentiation of human chondrocytes grown on a hyaluronan-based biomaterial (HYAFF11): molecular, immunohistochemical and ultrastructural analysis. Biomaterials 23:1187–1195
343. Knudson CB (1993) Hyaluronan receptor-directed assembly of chondrocyte pericellular matrix. J Cell Biol 120:825–834
344. Brun P, Abatangelo G, Radice M, Zacchi V, Guidolin D, Gordini DD et al (1999) Chondrocyte aggregation and reorganization into three-dimensional scaffolds. J Biomed Mater Res 46:337–346
345. Radice M, Brun P, Cortivo R, Scapinelli R, Battaliard C, Abatangelo G (2000) Hyaluronan-based biopolymers as delivery vehicles for bone-marrow-derived mesenchymal progenitors. J Biomed Mater Res 50:101–109
346. Solchaga LA, Dennis JE, Goldberg VM, Caplan AI (1999) Hyaluronic acid-based polymers as cell carriers for tissue-engineered repair of bone and cartilage. J Orthop Res 17:205–213
347. Grunder T, Gaissmaier C, Fritz J, Stoop R, Hortschansky P, Mollenhauer J et al (2004) Bone morphogenetic protein (BMP)-2 enhances the expression of type II collagen and aggrecan in chondrocytes embedded in alginate beads. Osteoarthr Cartil 12:559–567
348. Cai X, Lin Y, Ou G, Luo E, Man Y, Yuan Q et al (2007) Ectopic osteogenesis and chondrogenesis of bone marrow stromal stem cells in alginate system. Cell Biol Int 31:776–783
349. Genes NG, Rowley JA, Mooney DJ, Bonassar LJ (2004) Effect of substrate mechanics on chondrocyte adhesion to modified alginate surfaces. Arch Biochem Biophys 422:161–167
350. Bouhadir KH, Lee KY, Alsberg E, Damm KL, Anderson KW, Mooney DJ (2001) Degradation of partially oxidized alginate and its potential application for tissue engineering. Biotechnol Prog 17:945–950
351. Li Y, Rodrigues J, Tomas H (2012) Injectable and biodegradable hydrogels: gelation, biodegradation and biomedical applications. Chem Soc Rev 41:2193–2221
352. Hong Y, Gong Y, Gao C, Shen J (2008) Collagen-coated polylactide microcarriers/chitosan hydrogel composite: injectable scaffold for cartilage regeneration. J Biomed Mater Res Part A 85A:628–637
353. Park H, Guo X, Temenoff JS, Tabata Y, Caplan AI, Kasper FK et al (2009) Effect of swelling ratio of injectable hydrogel composites on chondrogenic differentiation of encapsulated rabbit marrow mesenchymal stem cells in vitro. Biomacromolecules 10:541–546
354. Hong Y, Song H, Gong Y, Mao Z, Gao C, Shen J (2007) Covalently crosslinked chitosan hydrogel: Properties of in vitro degradation and chondrocyte encapsulation. Acta Biomater 3:23–31
355. Sharma B, Williams CG, Khan M, Manson P, Elisseeff JH (2007) In vivo chondrogenesis of mesenchymal stem cells in a photopolymerized hydrogel. Plast Reconstr Surg 199:112–120
356. Villanueva I, Hauschulz DS, Mejic D, Bryant SJ (2008) Static and dynamic compressive strains influence nitric oxide production and chondrocyte bioactivity when encapsulated in PEG hydrogels of different crosslinking densities. Osteoarthr Cartil 16:909–918
357. Nicodemus GD, Skaalure SC, Bryant SJ (2011) Gel structure has an impact on pericellular and extracellular matrix deposition, which subsequently alters metabolic activities in chondrocyte-laden PEG hydrogels. Acta Biomater 7:492–504

358. Hou Y, Schoener CA, Regan KR, Munoz Pinto D, Hahn MS, Grunlan MA (2010) Photo-cross-linked PDMSstar-PEG hydrogels: synthesis, characterization, and potential application for tissue engineering scaffolds. Biomacromolecules 1:648–656
359. Martens PJ, Bryant SJ, Anseth KS (2003) Tailoring the degradation of hydrogels formed from multivinyl poly(ethylene glycol) and poly(vinyl alcohol) macromers for cartilage tissue engineering. Biomacromolecules 4:283–292
360. Nettles DL, Vail TP, Morgan MT, Grinstaff MW, Setton LA (2004) Photocrosslinkable hyaluronan as a scaffold for articular cartilage repair. Ann Biomed Eng 32:391–397
361. Erickson IE, Huang AH, Sengupta S, Kestle S, Burdick JA, Mauck RL (2009) Macromer density influences mesenchymal stem cell chondrogenesis and maturation in photocrosslinked hyaluronic acid hydrogels. Osteoarthr Cartil 17:1639–1648
362. Jeon O, Bouhadir KH, Mansour JM, Alsberg E (2009) Photocrosslinked alginate hydrogels with tunable biodegradation rates and mechanical properties. Biomaterials 30:2724–2734
363. Nichol JW, Koshy ST, Bae H, Hwang CM, Yamanlar S, Khademhosseini A (2010) Cell-laden microengineered gelatin methacrylate hydrogels. Biomaterials 31:5536–5544
364. Hu X, Ma L, Wang C, Gao C (2009) Gelatin hydrogel prepared by photo-initiated polymerization and loaded with TGF-β1 for cartilage tissue engineering. Macromol Biosci 9:1194–1201
365. Tan H, Rubin JP, Marra KG (2010) Injectable in situ forming biodegradable chitosan-hyaluronic acid based hydrogels for adipose tissue regeneration. Organogenesis 6:173–180
366. Jin R, Moreira TLS, Dijkstra PJ, van Blitterswijk CA, Karperien M, Feijen J (2010) Enzymatically-crosslinked injectable hydrogels based on biomimetic dextran-hyaluronic acid conjugates for cartilage tissue engineering. Biomaterials 31:3103–3113
367. Tran NQ, Joung YK, Lih E, Park KM, Park KD (2010) Supramolecular hydrogels exhibiting fast in situ gel forming and adjustable degradation properties. Biomacromolecules 11:617–625
368. Hu P, Xu B (2003) Injectable hydrogel scaffold for cartilage tissue engineering. Tsinghua University, People's Republic of China, p 6
369. Ko DY, Shinde UP, Yeon B, Jeong B (2010) Recent progress on in situ formed gels for biomedical applications. Prog Polym Sci
370. Sharma D, George P, Button PD, May BK, Kasapis S (2011) Thermomechanical study of the phase behaviour of agarose/gelatin mixtures in the presence of glucose syrup as co-solute. Food Chem 127:1784–1791
371. Li Q, Williams CG, Sun DDN, Wang J, Leong K, Elisseeff JH (2003) Photocrosslinkable polysaccharides based on chondroitin sulfate. J Biomed Mater Res Part A 68A:28–33
372. Habibovic P, Juhl MV, Clyens S, Martinetti R, Dolcini L, Theilgaard N et al (2010) Comparison of two carbonated apatite ceramics in vivo. Acta Biomater 6:2219–2226
373. Kim M, Kim SE, Kang SS, Kim YH, Tae G (2011) The use of de-differentiated chondrocytes delivered by a heparin-based hydrogel to regenerate cartilage in partial-thickness defects. Biomaterials 32:7883–7896
374. Lee J, Choi WI, Tae G, Kim YH, Kang SS, Kim SE et al (2011) Enhanced regeneration of the ligament–bone interface using a poly(l-lactide–co-ε-caprolactone) scaffold with local delivery of cells/BMP-2 using a heparin-based hydrogel. Acta Biomater 7:244–257
375. Zhang J, Skardal A, Prestwich GD (2008) Engineered extracellular matrices with cleavable crosslinkers for cell expansion and easy cell recovery. Biomaterials 29:4521–4531
376. Davis NE, Ding S, Forster RE, Pinkas DM, Barron AE (2010) Modular enzymatically crosslinked protein polymer hydrogels for in situ gelation. Biomaterials 31:7288–7297
377. Yang Z, Liang G, Xu B (2007) Enzymatic control of the self-assembly of small molecules: a new way to generate supramolecular hydrogels. Soft Matter 3:515–520
378. Chen T, Embree HD, Brown EM, Taylor MM, Payne GF (2003) Enzyme-catalyzed gel formation of gelatin and chitosan: potential for in situ applications. Biomaterials 24:2831–2841

379. Toledano S, Williams RJ, Jayawarna V, Ulijn RV (2006) Enzyme-triggered self-assembly of peptide hydrogels via reversed hydrolysis. J Am Chem Soc 128:1070–1071
380. Burke MD, Park JO, Srinivasarao M, Khan SA (2005) A novel enzymatic technique for limiting drug mobility in a hydrogel matrix. J Control Release 104:141–153
381. Hughes M, Xu H, Frederix PWJM, Smith AM, Hunt NT, Tuttle T et al (2011) Biocatalytic self-assembly of 2D peptide-based nanostructures. Soft Matter 7:10032–10038
382. Hoare T, Pelton R (2004) Functional group distributions in carboxylic acid containing poly (N-isopropylacrylamide) microgels. Langmuir 20:2123–2133
383. Jones JA, Novo N, Flagler K, Pagnucco CD, Carew S, Cheong C et al (2005) Thermoresponsive copolymers of methacrylic acid and poly(ethylene glycol) methyl ether methacrylate. J Polym Sci A Polym Chem 43:6095–6104
384. Han CK, Bae YH (1998) Inverse thermally-reversible gelation of aqueous N-isopropylacrylamide copolymer solutions. Polymer 39:2809–2814
385. Chen G, Hoffman AS (1995) Graft copolymers that exhibit temperature-induced phase transitions over a wide range of pH. Nature 373:49–52
386. Schilli CM, Zhang M, Rizzardo E, Thang SH, Chong YK, Edwards K et al (2004) A new double-responsive block copolymer synthesized via RAFT polymerization: poly (N-isopropylacrylamide)-block-poly(acrylic acid). Macromolecules 37:7861–7866
387. Garbern JC, Hoffman AS, Stayton PS (2010) Injectable pH- and temperature-responsive poly (N-isopropylacrylamide-co-propylacrylic acid) copolymers for delivery of angiogenic growth factors. Biomacromolecules 11:1833–1839
388. Pollock JF, Healy KE (2010) Mechanical and swelling characterization of poly(N-isopropyl acrylamide-comethoxy poly(ethylene glycol) methacrylate) sol-gels. Acta Biomater 6:1307–1318
389. Yun K, Moon HT (2008) Inducing chondrogenic differentiation in injectable hydrogels embedded with rabbit chondrocytes and growth factor for neocartilage formation. J Biosci Bioeng 105:122–126
390. Huang X, Zhang Y, Donahue HJ, Lowe TL (2007) Porous thermoresponsive-co-biodegradable hydrogels as tissue-engineering scaffolds for 3-dimensional in vitro culture of chondrocytes. Tissue Eng 13:2645–2652
391. Sa-Lima H, Tuzlakoglu K, Mano JF, Reis RL (2011) Thermoresponsive poly (N-isopropylacrylamide)-g-methylcellulose hydrogel as a three-dimensional extracellular matrix for cartilage-engineered applications. J Biomed Mater Res Part A 98A:596–603
392. Lue S, Liu M, Ni B (2011) Degradable, injectable poly(N-isopropylacrylamide)-based hydrogels with low gelation concentrations for protein delivery application. Chem Eng J 173:241–250
393. Haider M, Cappello J, Ghandehari H, Leong K (2008) In vitro chondrogenesis of mesenchymal stem cells in recombinant silk-elastinlike hydrogels. Pharm Res 25:692–699
394. Guan J, Hong Y, Ma Z, Wagner WR (2008) Protein-reactive, thermoresponsive copolymers with high flexibility and biodegradability. Biomacromolecules 9:1283–1292
395. Cho J, Heuzey MC, Bégin A, Carreau PJ (2005) Physical gelation of chitosan in the presence of beta-glycerophosphate: the effect of temperature. Biomacromolecules 6:3267–3275
396. Chenite A, Chaput C, Wang D, Combes C, Buschmann MD, Hoemann CD et al (2000) Novel injectable neutral solutions of chitosan form biodegradable gels in situ. Biomaterials 21:2155–2161
397. Park KM, Lee SY, Joung YK, Na JS, Lee MC, Park KD (2009) Thermosensitive chitosan-pluronic hydrogel as an injectable cell delivery carrier for cartilage regeneration. Acta Biomater 5:1956–1965
398. Abe M, Takahashi M, Tokura S, Tamura H, Nagano A (2004) Cartilage-scaffold composites produced by bioresorbable beta-chitin sponge with cultured rabbit chondrocytes. Tissue Eng 10:585–594

399. Iwasaki N, Kasahara Y, Yamane S, Igarashi T, Minami A, Nisimura S-i (2011) Chitosan-based hyaluronic acid hybrid polymer fibers as a scaffold biomaterial for cartilage tissue engineering. Polymers 3:100–113
400. Liu Y, Lu W-L, Wang J-C, Zhang X, Zhang H, Wang X-Q et al (2007) Controlled delivery of recombinant hirudin based on thermo-sensitive Pluronic F127 hydrogel for subcutaneous administration: in vitro and in vivo characterization. J Control Release 117:387–395
401. Cohn D, Lando G, Sosnik A, Garty S, Levi A (2006) PEO-PPO-PEO-based poly(ether ester urethane)s as degradable reverse thermo-responsive multiblock copolymers. Biomaterials 27:1718–1727
402. Jeong B, Bae YH, Kim SW (2000) In situ gelation of PEG-PLGA-PEG triblock copolymer aqueous solutions and degradation thereof. J Biomed Mater Res 50:171–177
403. de las Alarcon CH, Pennadam S, Alexander C (2005) Stimuli responsive polymers for biomedical applications. Chem Soc Rev 34:276–285
404. Heskins M, Guillet JE (1968) Solution properties of poly(*N*-isopropylacrylamide). J Macromol Sci Chem A2:1441
405. Ha DI, Lee SB, Chong MS, Lee YM (2006) Preparation of thermo-responsive and injectable hydrogels based on hyaluronic acid and poly(N-isopropylacrylamide) and their drug release behaviors. Macromol Res 14:87–93
406. Cappello JCJ, Dorman M, Mikolajczak M, Textor G, Marquet M, Ferrari F (1990) Genetic engineering of structural protein polymers. Biotechnol Prog 6:198–202
407. Nettles DL, Vali TP, Flahiff CM, Walkenhorst J, Carter AJ, Setton LA (2005) Injectable silk-elastin for articular cartilage defect repair. Trans of the ORS Washington, DC, p 1366
408. Hoemann CD, Sun J, Légaré A, McKee MD, Buschmann MD (2005) Tissue engineering of cartilage using an injectable and adhesive chitosan-based cell-delivery vehicle. Osteoarthr Cartil 13:318–329
409. Ruel-Gariépy E, Shive M, Bichara A, Berrada M, Le Garrec D, Chenite A et al (2004) A thermosensitive chitosan-based hydrogel for the local delivery of paclitaxel. Eur J Pharm Biopharm 57:53–63
410. Li Z, Zhang M (2005) Chitosan–alginate as scaffolding material for cartilage tissue engineering. J Biomed Mater Res A 75A:485–493
411. Yamane S, Iwasaki N, Majima T, Funakoshi T, Masuko T, Harada K et al (2005) Feasibility of chitosan-based hyaluronic acid hybrid biomaterial for a novel scaffold in cartilage tissue engineering. Biomaterials 26:611–619
412. Chen Y-L, Lee H-P, Chan H-Y, Sung L-Y, Chen H-C, Hu Y-C (2007) Composite chondroitin-6-sulfate/dermatan sulfate/chitosan scaffolds for cartilage tissue engineering. Biomaterials 28:2294–2305
413. Jung HH, Park K, Han DK (2010) Preparation of TGF-β1-conjugated biodegradable pluronic F127 hydrogel and its application with adipose-derived stem cells. J Control Release 147:84–91
414. Safran CB, Farach-Carson MC, Jia X, Srinivasan PP, Jha A (2012) Injectable delivery system for heparan sulfate-binding growth factors. University of Delaware, USA, p 30
415. Dell'Accio F, Vanlauwe J, Bellemans J, Neys J, de Bari C, Luyten FP (2003) Expanded phenotypically stable chondrocytes persist in the repair tissue and contribute to cartilage matrix formation and structural integration in a goat model of autologous chondrocyte implantation. J Orthop Res 21:123–131
416. Grande DA, Pitman MI, Peterson L, Menche D, Klein M (1989) The repair of experimentally produced defects in rabbit articular cartilage by autologous chondrocyte transplantation. J Orthop Res 7:208–218
417. Miot S, de Freitas PS, Wirz D, Daniels AU, Sims TJ, Hollander AP, Mainil-Varlet P et al (2006) Cartilage tissue engineering by expanded goat articular chondrocytes. J Orthop Res 24 (5):1078–1085
418. Martin I, Obradovic B, Treppo S, Grodzinsky AJ, Langer R, Freed LE et al (2000) Modulation of the mechanical properties of tissue engineered cartilage. Biorheology 31:1–2

419. Bugbee WD, Convery FR (1999) Osteochondral allograft transplantation. Clin Sports Med 18:67–75
420. Hangody L, Feczkó P, Bartha L, Bodó G, Kish G (2001) Mosaicplasty for the treatment of articular defects of the knee and ankle. Clin Orthop Relat Res 391:S328–S336
421. Steadman JR, Rodkey WG, Singleton SB, Briggs KK (1997) Microfracture technique for full-thickness chondral defects: technique and clinical results. Oper Tech Orthop 7:300–304
422. Johnson LL (2001) Arthroscopic abrasion arthroplasty: a review. Clin Orthop Relat Res 391: S306–S317
423. Hoemann C, Sun J, McKee M, Hurtig M, Rivard GE, Rossomacha E, et al (2005) Rabbit hyaline cartilage repair after marrow stimulation depends on the surgical approach together with an in situ stabilized chitosan-GP blood clot. Transactions 11th Canadian connective tissue conference, 1372
424. Hoemann CD, Hurtig M, Rossomacha E, Sun J, Chevrier A, Shive MS et al (2005) Chitosan-glycerol phosphate/blood implants improve hyaline cartilage repair in ovine microfracture defects. J Bone Joint Surg Am 87:2671–2686
425. Gobbi A, Kon E, Berruto M, Francisco R, Filardo G, Marcacci M (2006) Patellofemoral full-thickness chondral defects treated with Hyalograft-C: a clinical, arthroscopic, and histologic review. Am J Sports Med 34:1763–1773
426. Benedetti L, Cortivo R, Berti T, Berti A, Pea F, Mazzo M et al (1993) Biocompatibility and biodegradation of different hyaluronan derivatives (Hyaff) implanted in rats. Biomaterials 14:1154–1160
427. Girotto D, Urbani S, Brun P, Renier D, Barbucci R, Abatangelo G (2003) Tissue-specific gene expression in chondrocytes grown on three-dimensional hyaluronic acid scaffolds. Biomaterials 24:3265–3275
428. Marcacci M, Berruto M, Brocchetta D, Delcogliano A, Ghinelli D, Gobbi A et al (2005) Articular cartilage engineering with Hyalograft C: 3-year clinical results. Clin Orthop Relat Res 435:96–105
429. Nehrer S, Domayer S, Dorotka R, Schatz K, Bindreiter U, Kotz R (2006) Three-year clinical outcome after chondrocyte transplantation using a hyaluronan matrix for cartilage repair. Eur J Radiol 57:3–8
430. Weidenbecher M, Henderson JH, Tucker HM, Baskin JZ, Awadallah A, Dennis JE (2007) Hyaluronan-based scaffolds to tissue-engineer cartilage implants for laryngotracheal reconstruction. Laryngoscope 117:1745–1749
431. Schneider U, Rackwitz L, Andereya S, Siebenlist S, Fensky F, Reichert J et al (2011) A prospective multicenter study on the outcome of type I collagen hydrogel-based autologous chondrocyte implantation (CaReS) for the repair of articular cartilage defects in the knee. Am J Sports Med 39:2558–2565
432. Welsch GH, Mamisch TC, Zak L, Blanke M, Olk A, Marlovits S et al (2010) Evaluation of cartilage repair tissue after matrix-associated autologous chondrocyte transplantation using a hyaluronic-based or a collagen-based scaffold with morphological MOCART scoring and biochemical T2 mapping: preliminary results. Am J Sports Med 38:934–942
433. Carmont MR, Carey-Smith R, Saithna A, Dhillon M, Thompson P, Spalding T (2009) Delayed incorporation of a TruFit plug: perseverance is recommended. Arthroscopy 25:810–814
434. Melton JTK, Wilson AJ, Chapman-Sheath P, Cossey AJ (2010) TruFit CB bone plug: chondral repair, scaffold design, surgical technique and early experiences. Expert Rev Med Devices 7:333–341
435. Kerker JT, Leo AJ, Sgaglione NA (2008) Cartilage repair: synthetics and scaffolds: basic science, surgical techniques, and clinical outcomes. Sports Med Arthrosc 16:208–216
436. McNickle AG, Provencher MT, Cole BJ (2008) Overview of existing cartilage repair technology. Sports Med Arthrosc 16:196–201
437. Joshi N, Reverte-Vinaixa M, Diaz-Ferreiro EW, Dominguez-Oronoz R (2012) Synthetic resorbable scaffolds for the treatment of isolated patellofemoral cartilage defects in young

patients: magnetic resonance imaging and clinical evaluation. Am J Sports Med 40:1289–1295
438. Crawford DC, Heveran CM, Cannon WD Jr, Foo LF, Potter HG (2009) An autologous cartilage tissue implant NeoCart for treatment of grade III chondral injury to the distal femur: prospective clinical safety trial at 2 years. Am J Sports Med 37:1334–1343
439. Kim HT, Zaffagnini S, Mizuno S, Abelow S, Safran MR (2006) A peek into the possible future of management of articular cartilage injuries: gene therapy and scaffolds for cartilage repair. J Orthop Sports Phys Ther 36:765–773
440. Hoemann CD, Sun J, McKee MD, Chevrier A, Rossomacha E, Rivard GE et al (2006) Chitosan-glycerol phosphate/blood implants elicit hyaline cartilage repair integrated with porous subchondral bone in microdrilled rabbit defects. Osteoarthr Cartil 15:78–89(Epub 2006 Aug 8)
441. Buschmann MD, Hoemann CD, Hurtig MB (2006) Cartilage repair: analysis and strategies. In: William RJ (ed) Cartilage repair with chitosan/glycerol-phosphate stabilised blood clots. Totowa Human Press, Totowa, pp 83–106
442. Grigolo B, Lisignoli G, Piacentini A, Fiorini M, Gobbi P, Mazzotti G et al (2002) Evidence for redifferentiation of human chondrocytes grown on a hyaluronan-based biomaterial (HYAff 11): molecular, immunohistochemical and ultrastructural analysis. Biomaterials 23:1187–1195
443. Pavesio A, Abatangelo G, Borrione A, Brocchetta D, Hollander AP, Kon E et al (2003) Hyaluronan-based scaffolds (Hyalograft C) in the treatment of knee cartilage defects: preliminary clinical findings. Novartis Found Symp 249:203–17; discussion 29–33, 34–8, 39–41
444. Nehrer S, Dorotka R, Domayer S, Stelzeneder D, Kotz R (2009) Treatment of full-thickness chondral defects with hyalograft C in the knee: a prospective clinical case series with 2 to 7 years' follow-up. Am J Sports Med 37(Suppl 1):81S–87S
445. Kon E, Di MA, Filardo G, Tetta C, Busacca M, Iacono F et al (2011) Second-generation autologous chondrocyte transplantation: MRI findings and clinical correlations at a minimum 5-year follow-up. Eur J Radiol 79:382–388
446. Marcacci M, Zaffagnini S, Kon E, Visani A, Iacono F, Loreti I (2002) Arthroscopic autologous chondrocyte transplantation: technical note. Knee Surg Sports Traumatol Arthrosc 10:154–159
447. Henderson I, Lavigne P, Valenzuela H, Oakes B (2007) Autologous chondrocyte implantation: superior biologic properties of hyaline cartilage repairs. Clin Orthop Relat Res 455:253–261
448. Knutsen G, Drogset JO, Engebretsen L, Grontvedt T, Isaksen V, Ludvigsen TC et al (2007) A randomized trial comparing autologous chondrocyte implantation with microfracture. Findings at five years. J Bone Joint Surg Am 89:2105–2112
449. Cole BJ (2008) A randomized trial comparing autologous chondrocyte implantation with microfracture. J Bone Joint Surg Am 90:1165; author reply –6
450. Dhollander AAM, Liekens K, Almqvist KF, Verdonk R, Lambrecht S, Elewaut D et al (2012) A pilot study of the use of an osteochondral scaffold plug for cartilage repair in the knee and how to deal with early clinical failures. Arthroscopy 28:225–233
451. Safran MR, Kim H, Zaffagnini S (2008) The use of scaffolds in the management of articular cartilage injury. J Am Acad Orthop Surg 16:306–311
452. Weng Y, Cao Y, Silva CA, Vacanti MP, Vacanti CA (2001) Tissue-engineered composites of bone and cartilage for mandible condylar reconstruction. J Oral Maxillofac Surg 59:185–190
453. Sharma B, Fermanian S, Gibson M, Unterman S, Herzka DA, Cascio B et al (2013) Human cartilage repair with a photoreactive adhesive-hydrogel composite. Sci Transl Med 5:167ra6, 10 pp

To the loving memory of my father:

Elder James Ofiri Arimoro, who passed on to glory on 5th January 2020. May his gentle soul continue to rest in peace with the Lord. Amen.

And to my mother:

Mrs Rose Arimoro

Contents

Abbreviations

ADR	Alternative Dispute Resolution
AfDB	African Development Bank
ALSCON	Aluminium Company of Nigeria
BBO	Buy-Build-Operate
BCASL	Bi-Courtney Aviation Services Limited
BCHSL	Bi-Courtney Highway Services Limited
BEE	Black Economic Empowerment
BLOT	Build-Lease-Operate-Transfer
BLTM	Build-Lease-Transfer-Maintain
BOOT	Build-Own-Operate-Transfer
BOT	Build-Operate-Transfer
BPP	Bureau of Public Procurement
CoI	Committee on Infrastructure
CPI	Consumer Price Index
CSFs	Critical Success Factors
D&B	Design and Build
DBFO	Design-Build-Finance-Operate
DEA	Department of Economic Affairs
DFI	Development Finance Institution
ECA	Export Credit Agencies
FAAN	Federal Airports Authority of Nigeria
FDI	Foreign Direct Investment
FGN	Federal Government of Nigeria
GDP	Gross Domestic Product
GoI	Government of India
ICRC	Infrastructure Concession Regulatory Commission
IFC	International Finance Corporation
IPO	Initial Public Offering
JVA	Joint Venture Agreement
LDO	Lease-Develop-Operate
LMICs	Low- and Middle-Income Countries
MAGA	Material Adverse Government Action
MCT	Model Contract Terms

MDAs	Ministries, Departments and Agencies
MF	Ministry of Finance
MLIs	Multilateral Lending Institutions
NCAA	National Civil Aviation Agency
NCP	National Council on Privatisation
NEPA	National Electric Power Authority
NGOs	Non-Governmental Organisations
NHAI	National Highways Authority of India
OECD	Organisation for Economic Cooperation and Development
OM	Operation and Maintenance
OP	Offtake Purchaser
PFI	Private Finance Initiative
PPP	Public-Private Partnership
PPPAC	Public-Private Partnership Appraisal Committee
RFP	Request for Proposal
RoI	Return on Investment
ROT	Rehabilitate-Operate-Transfer
SDGs	Sustainable Development Goals
SHA	Shareholders' Agreement
SPV	Special Purpose Vehicle
SSA	Sub-Saharan Africa
TA	Treasury Approval
UK	United Kingdom
UN	United Nations
UNCITRAL	United Nations Commission on International Trade Law
UNECE	United Nations Economic Commission for Europe
US	United States
VfM	Value for Money
VGF	Viability Fund Gap
WBG	World Bank Group

Statutes

Brazilian Civil Code Law 2002
Brazilian Decree No. 8,420/2015
Brazilian Federal Law 8,666/1999
Brazilian PPP Law 11,079/2004
Brazilian PPP Law for the State of Minas Gerais No. 14,868/2003
Constitution of the Federal Republic of Nigeria 1999 (as amended)
Constitution of the Republic of South Africa 1996
Cross Rivers Public-Private Partnership Law 2010
Debt Management Office Establishment Act of 2003
Ekiti State Public-Private Partnership Law 2011
Foreign Exchange (Monitoring and Miscellaneous) Provisions Act of 1995
Indian Contracts Act 1872
Infrastructure Concession Regulatory Commission Establishment (Etc.) Act of 2005
Lagos State Public-Private Partnership Law 2011
National Inland Waterways Act of 1997
Nigerian Investment Promotion Commission Act of 1998
Public Finance Management Act of 1999
Public-Private Participation in Infrastructure Development Law 2009
Rivers State Public Private Initiative Law 2009
The Brazilian Constitution 1988
The Constitution of India
The Highways Act of 1971
The Municipal Finance Management Act of 2003
The Public Enterprises and Commercialisation Act of 1999
Treasury Regulation 16, 2004
Utilities Charges Commission Act of 1992

Cases

Aguas de Tunari v Bolivia ICSID Case No ARB/o2/03
Amadi v Pool House Group Co (1966) 2 All NLR
Arjay Ltd & Ors v Airline Management Support Ltd (2003) LPELR 555 (SC)
Attorney General Nasarawa State v Attorney General Plateau State [2012] 10 NWLR (Pt 1309)
BFI Group Corporation v Bureau of Public Enterprises (2012) All FWLR 672
Bredenkamp & Ors v Standard Bank of SA Ltd 2020 ZASCA 75
Brisley v Drotsky 2002 (4) SA 1 (SCA)
Doherty v Balewa (1961) 1 All NLR 604
Everfresh Market Virginia (Pty) Ltd v Shoprite Checkers (Pty) Ltd 2012 (1) SA 256 (CC)
L Schuler AG v Wickman Machine Tool Sales Ltd [1974] AC 235
Mohammed's Leisure Holdings (Pty) Ltd v Southern Sun Hotel (Pty) Ltd (183/17) [2017] ZASCA 1
Olu Adegboruwa v Attorney General of the Federation and three Ors (Unreported) FHC/L/CS/1405/12
Perry v United States 294 US 330 (1934)

Preface

Given the wide deficit in infrastructure in emerging economies around the globe, the need to involve the private sector in financing infrastructure through public-private partnership (PPP) is gaining popularity. This book comparatively examines PPP in emerging economies and particularly investigates how the model is administered in some selected countries, including Brazil, India, South Africa and Nigeria.

The book reviews the literature and discusses the concept of PPP itself as distinct from other forms of public procurement, the legal frameworks in the selected countries, general policy issues which arise in administering PPP, and it also evaluates some PPP projects in the selected jurisdictions. The common problems with PPP in emerging economies are identified and solutions are provided. The book is a reviewed version of the author's PhD thesis and a reflection of the author's practical experience in the private sector. This book will serve as an introduction for those who desire to gain insight into the subject of PPP, and it can serve as resource material for policymakers, lawyers, the academia, investment managers and project managers. The book is divided into three sections and nine chapters.

Section one: introduction to public-private partnership

Chapter 1 introduces and reviews the PPP model of infrastructure procurement to set the tone for the discussion in subsequent chapters of the book. It discusses the main features as well as the appropriate reasons for a government to adopt the PPP model. Further, the chapter examines the advantages of PPP over the traditional public procurement model. This chapter also reviews important PPP concepts, such as critical success factors (CSFs), project life cycle, value for money, bankability and greenfield and brownfield projects. The aim of Chapter 1 is to introduce the reader to PPP, to underline the gains and the various types of PPPs as well as to highlight the need to identify projects that may be successfully developed using the PPP model.

The second chapter discusses the existence of an appropriate framework as a prerequisite to creating an environment that fosters private investment in infrastructure, especially in emerging economies. In this chapter, the issues, challenges and strategies that policymakers need to consider before designing or reforming the legal framework for emerging markets are discussed. The aim of this chapter is to highlight the need for countries to learn from the successes achieved using PPPs in jurisdictions similar to their own. At the core of the discussion is the fact that countries must determine how legislation should identify in which sectors to use PPP, how tariffs are to be set and adjusted, the role to be played by different institutions, how PPPs should be procured, methods for dispute resolution and the protection of PPP assets.

The third chapter focuses on PPP contracts. A contract is a legally binding agreement that recognises and governs the rights and duties of the parties in the agreement. The PPP contract is a highly complex form of contract. In a PPP, there is usually a main contract (i.e. the concession itself) and other subcontracts. In this chapter, the discussion focuses on the structure of the PPP contract, the various types of agreements required to be signed in pursuit of a PPP project and other key contractual issues. Also for consideration in this chapter is a discussion on the procurement process and the elements and contents of a PPP contract. The aim of Chapter 3 is to introduce PPP contracts to the reader and to emphasise the need for governments in emerging economies to respect PPP contractual agreements in order to sustain the interests of private-sector partners in financing public facilities.

Section two: public-private partnership in Brazil, India, Nigeria and South Africa

Chapter 4 discusses PPP in Brazil. It focuses on the regime created in the country to enable the private sector to participate in the design, funding, maintenance and operation of public facilities. A key feature of PPP in Brazil is the impact of the government guarantees that have been introduced. Similarly, there is an arrangement that allows the public sector to own shares in a project company. Worthy of note is that Brazil has implemented a sophisticated legal framework for PPP. This is, however, not without challenges when it comes to the regulation and administration of PPP in the country.

The focus of Chapter 5 is on India. The study of India's PPP framework is relevant given the fact that India, with a population of over 1 billion people, is the largest PPP market in the world. A number of key innovations have been introduced in India to make PPP suitable to the local environment. For example, employing annuity payments for PPP projects and the use of PPP to provide projects that bring the government closer to the governed has been the hallmark of PPP arrangements in India. This chapter examines the framework and practice of PPP in India and highlights practices in the country that can be replicated in other emerging economies, especially as regards PPP projects that directly connect with the local people.

In Chapter 6, the discussion is on Nigeria and the legal environment for the arrangement and practice of PPP in that country. Nigeria has turned to PPP as an alternative to traditional procurement in order to bridge the country's wide infrastructure deficit, which is estimated to be in the region of about US$8 billion per annum. Further, the Nigerian framework for PPP is not clearly defined, leading to gaps in policy and overlapping laws that make PPP implementation challenging. Unsurprisingly, PPP in Nigeria has thus far produced mixed results, thereby raising a need for clear policy guidelines.

The seventh chapter examines PPP in South Africa. Unlike the other countries dealt with in the previous chapters, South Africa operates a hybrid legal system. The legal system in South Africa is a mix of distinct legal traditions that include a civil-law system inherited from the Dutch, the English common law and African customary law. As a general rule, South Africa follows the principles of English common law in both criminal and civil procedure, company law, constitutional law and the law of evidence, whereas Roman-Dutch common law applies in the South African law of contract, tort and private law. It is important to bear this in mind in a legal analysis dealing with PPP in South Africa. The country demonstrated its commitment to PPP in April 1997 when the Cabinet commissioned the then Minister of Finance to develop a comprehensive PPP framework for the country. Due to its well-developed financial market, South Africa is well ahead of its benchmark peers because of its relative ease to private capital. This chapter examines, among others, South Africa's administrative and legal framework for arranging and executing PPP, the fundamentals for PPP in the country and, importantly, the protection of PPP assets in the country.

Section three: current practice and the future of public-private partnership in emerging economies

Chapter 8 presents a comparative overview of the regulatory environments for PPP practice in emerging economies using Brazil, India, Nigeria and South Africa as case studies. The aim of the chapter is to show how the various countries have developed their various frameworks to cater to their local situations and what lessons other countries may learn from the approaches that have so far been adopted. The discussion focuses on a range of themes to consider what policies or strategies enhanced PPP success and what might be done to improve in other areas. The chapter also highlights areas of similarities and divergence in the selected countries. Success of the PPP model in any of these jurisdictions depends on the enabling environment and the structures put in place to attract both local and foreign private investment.

The ninth chapter is the conclusion and discusses the future of PPP in emerging economies. PPP offers opportunities for governments around the world to leverage private-sector expertise and funds. For emerging economies, the need to ensure that PPP arrangements are successful is even more expedient due to huge infrastructure deficits that affect the general standard of living in these countries. In this chapter, an attempt is made to review the literature and to provide measures that should be put in place to attract investors, unlock domestic finance for PPP and ensure that there is smooth and efficient administration of PPP relationships. This final chapter is prescriptive and provides recommendations.

Acknowledgements

Let me begin by appreciating the Lord Almighty for His mercy and grace to begin and complete this work.

I would like to thank Professor Ada Ordor of the Centre for Comparative Law, University of Cape Town, South Africa, for her research guidance in my doctoral journey and for being an excellent mentor to me. In the same vein, I wish to appreciate Professor Andrew Hutchison for his invaluable contributions to the research. I am also very thankful to Dr Peter Orji, Dr Dorothy Kwagala-Igaga and Dr Phil Harris for their unflinching support and invaluable contributions.

I found immense support while preparing this book from the resources at St Mary's University Twickenham, London. I am particularly grateful to Dr Judith Bourne, the Law Programme Leader at the university, for her mentorship. I am also indebted to Neena Samota for her professional guidance and to other colleagues at St Mary's University for their support.

To my mother who has always been a pillar of support, I say a big thank you. My siblings, Dr Theodora Odagwe, Professor Francis Arimoro, Rev Samuel Arimoro, Mrs Mercy Obasohan and Mrs Susan Moore, have always been there for me. May God bless you all. My wife, Joke, and my son, Jathniel, both deserve special mention for the huge sacrifices they made while I embarked on this research.

Finally, I celebrate Dr Duke Imajemite of the Eternal Life Ministries International London for being a wonderful father to me.

1 Introduction to public-private partnerships

1.1 Background

In contemporary times, it is unfeasible for the government of any country to supply public infrastructure to match the demand by its citizens. Over the years, a shortage of funds has resulted in a huge deficit in government budgets for infrastructure, especially in emerging economies. As a result of the massive costs involved in infrastructure procurement, as well as other competing demands for public-sector spending, governments can no longer bear the entire burden of funding public infrastructure. It, therefore, behoves governments to develop and implement policies and strategies that would facilitate public-infrastructure procurement and funding to improve the lives of the population. Investment in public infrastructure plays a part in economic growth in any given country. Poor infrastructure can impede the growth and competitiveness of any economy.[1] Consequent upon the foregoing, a collaboration with the private sector to fund infrastructure procurement could be relied on as an alternative to traditional public procurement. The public-private partnership (PPP) model allows for a collaboration between the public sector/government and the private sector for the latter to design, fund, manage and operate public facilities for a term in exchange for the payment of tolls or charges by end users or the government. The main objective of PPPs all over the world is basically to 'ensure the delivery of well maintained, cost-effective public infrastructure . . . by leveraging private sector expertise and transferring risk to the private sector.'[2]

PPPs are now emerging as a viable alternative source of infrastructure investment in emerging economies.[3] This is because a successful PPP arrangement can provide a better and more cost-effective public service and speed up the

1 Jeffrey Delmon, *Public-Private Partnership Projects in Infrastructure: An Essential Guide for Policy Makers* (Cambridge: Cambridge University Press, 2011) 1.

2 National Treasury PPP Unit, *Introducing Public Private Partnerships in South Africa* (Pretoria: National Treasury Unit, 2007) 4.

3 ER Yescombe, *Public-Private Partnerships in Sub-Saharan Africa: Case Studies for Policymakers* (Dar es Salaam: Uongozi Institute, 2017) 3.

level of its implementation. In addition to benefiting from private-sector expertise, the public sector is also able to concentrate on policymaking when PPPs are in place. Given that governments in emerging markets cannot raise the huge funds required for large-scale infrastructure projects to reduce the wide deficit, collaborating with the private sector can help to mitigate the government's financial burden.[4] PPPs represents a solution for governments to be able to meet the infrastructure needs of the public with the participation of the private sector.[5]

1.2 What is PPP?

There has not been, and it is difficult to imagine that there would one day be, a universal definition of what PPP is. Even though there is a consensus that PPP is a collaboration between the public and private sectors for the procurement of public infrastructure,[6] that alone does not clearly show what a PPP is. It is important that, in defining the term PPP, one does not confuse it with other similar arrangements between the public and private sectors. For example, a PPP is not the same thing as privatisation. In a privatisation arrangement, the public authority divests all or some of its shares in a public enterprise to a private-sector entity. Privatisation, simply put, is the transfer of ownership rights in a state-owned enterprise to the private sector.[7] Here, there is an arrangement which involves a collaboration between the public authority and the private sector but which is not a PPP. An arrangement which involves the private sector managing a public facility is a management contract and not the same as a PPP, as this does not involve the construction of a new facility or the rehabilitation of an existing one. Similarly, a service arrangement between a public authority and a private-sector entity which involves the provision of a service, for example, the daily cleaning of a public facility, is not a PPP, even though there is an arrangement between the public sector and a private-sector interest. It is important to state that a PPP is not the outsourcing of functions or a donation by a private party for the public good.[8]

What then is a PPP? Pierson and McBride have provided a guide for distinguishing and identifying a PPP.[9] These elements can help delineate whether a

4 Shakil S Malek and PV Akalkotar, 'Driving Forces Leading to the Adoption of PPP – Perspectives from Gujarat (India), Hong Kong and Australian Practitioners' (2016) 2(9) *International Journal for Innovative Research and Technology* 6.

5 Valentina Estrada, *Comparative Study of the Implementation of Public-Private Partnership* (Bogota: Funación Ambiente Y Recursos Naturales, 2017) 3.

6 George Nwangwu, *Public Private Partnerships in Nigeria* (Basingstoke: Palgrave Macmillan, 2016) 2.

7 Sinclair Davidson, 'Why Is Privatisation So Controversial?' (2014) 30 *Policy* 19 available at <www.cis.org.au/app/uploads/2015/04/images/stories/policy-magaize/2014-autumn/30-1-14-davidson-sinclair.pdf >accessed 24 March 2018.

8 National Treasury PPP Unit, *op cit* (note 2) 7.

9 G Pierson and P MacBride, 'Public/Private Sector Infrastructure Arrangements' (1996) 73 *CPA Communique* 1–4.

partnership between the public sector and a private-sector entity is a PPP or not. They argue as follows: first, there has to be a transfer of land, property or facility by the government to a private-sector entity; second, the private-sector entity builds or renovates a facility; third, the public-sector entity specifies the operating services for the facility; fourth, services are provided by the private-sector entity for a defined period and fifth, the private sector agrees to transfer the facility to the public sector at the end of the arrangement. It follows that where any of these elements is missing, the arrangement is not a PPP.[10] Perhaps the view by Pierson and McBride expressed previously influenced the definition offered by Yescombe. Yescombe defines PPP thus:

- A long-term contract between a public-sector entity (the 'public authority') and a private-sector entity ('the project company') involving significant risk transfer to the private sector.
- Under this contract, the project company is responsible for the design, building (or upgrading), finance, operation and maintenance of public infrastructure (the 'asset').
- The private sector financial investment is repaid from revenues generated by the asset under the terms of the PPP contract, payable either by users of the asset (e.g. a toll-road concession) or by the public authority (e.g. government accommodation) or a combination of the two.
- At the end of the PPP contract, the asset usually remains in, or reverts to, public-sector ownership. (Thus, a PPP is not the same thing as privatisation.)[11]

PPP has also been defined as follows:

> A commercial transaction between a government institution and a private partner in which the private party either performs an institutional function on behalf of the institution for a specified or indefinite period or acquires the use of state property for its own commercial purposes for a specified or indefinite period. The private party receives a benefit for performing the function or by utilising state property, either by way of compensation from a revenue fund, charges or fees collected by the private party from users or customers of a service provided to them, or a combination of such compensation and such charges or fees.[12]

A PPP is, therefore, a long-term binding contract between the public sector and a private-sector consortium for the design, financing, construction

10 Augustine Arimoro, 'An Appraisal of the Framework for Public Private Partnership in South Africa' (2018) 13(3) *European Procurement and Public Private Partnership Law Review* 215.

11 ER Yescombe, *op cit* (note 3) 7.

12 Vanessa Vallée, *Public-Private Partnerships in the Middle East and North Africa* (Paris: OECD, 2014) 19.

and management of public assets for a fixed term of usually between 20 and 30 years within which period risk is transferred to the private sector and at the termination of which the asset or assets are transferred back to the public sector. Typically, the main features of PPPs are that they are cooperative and contractual relationships with shared responsibilities.

1.3 Definitions of other terms

Because of the technical nature of the subject, it is not out of place to clearly define other terms related to PPP. The aim is to provide a background to assist the reader in getting a good grasp of the PPP process, administration and regulation.

1.3.1 Infrastructure

This term goes hand in glove with the concept of PPP, and it is difficult or even impossible to explain what PPP is without mentioning 'infrastructure.' Infrastructure refers to 'the essential facilities and services that the economic productivity of a community or organisation depends on. As a real return asset class, infrastructure includes those assets that are involved in the movement of goods, people, water, and energy.'[13] In the words of Chambers, 'Infrastructure assets are the physical structures, facilities, and networks that provide essential services to the public. These assets include transport structures (roads, bridges, tunnels, railways, airports, and seaports), energy and utility companies, communication entities, and social services such as educational facilities and hospitals.'[14] Some authors writing about PPP have distinguished between 'economic' infrastructure and 'social' infrastructure. One such writer is Yescombe, who says, 'public infrastructures are facilities that are necessary for the functioning of the economy and society.'[15] He further subdivides public infrastructure into two categories:

- 'Economic' Infrastructure, such as transportation facilities and utility networks (for water, sewage, electricity, etc.), i.e. infrastructure considered essential for day-to-day economic activity; and
- 'Social' Infrastructure includes schools, hospitals, libraries, prisons, etc.[16]

13 Jeffrey E Fulmer, 'What in the World is Infrastructure' (Infrastructure Investor, July/August 2009) available at <www.corridortrust.com/uploads/Infrastructure_Investor.pdf> accessed 23 November 2015.
14 Judy Chambers, *Infrastructure Research Report* (San Francisco: Pension Consulting Alliance Inc., 2007) 1.
15 ER Yescombe, *op cit* (note 3) 1.
16 Ibid.

1.3.2 Public sector

The public sector is defined as an economic activity that is owned, controlled and financed by the state on behalf of the population.[17] In Nigeria, the public sector can be further categorised into three divisions, namely, the federal, state and local government authorities. Ministries, departments or agencies (MDAs) at any of the tiers of government may represent the government at that tier.[18] The public sector is ultimately responsible for determining the objectives for any PPP project as well as ensuring that the delivery outcomes are met. Specifically, as far as a PPP project is concerned, the public sector is responsible for defining the business and the services required and the public-sector resources available to pay for them; managing the expectations of the local community; ensuring that the enabling environment is provided; specifying the priorities, targets and output to be met and taking steps to ensure adherence to pre-defined objectives.[19] Again, public-sector regulatory bodies are responsible for issuing permits and licenses, and designing the regulatory framework.[20] Governments may also take up equity in the special purpose vehicle (SPV) to reduce the private sponsors' risk perceptions or to provide some sort of assurance to the public that the asset is not meant to benefit the private sector to the detriment of the ordinary citizen.

1.3.3 Private sector

The private sector may be described as the economic activity that is owned, controlled and financed by private individuals to make profits.[21] Put simply, the private sector refers to business interests or enterprises not owned by the government or any of its MDAs. The private-sector partner in a PPP arrangement is usually referred to as the private consortium or concessionaire, the project company or the SPV.[22] The private-sector party is responsible for focusing on the project objectives laid down by the government, producing and delivering the project following the standards set out by the government, raising funds for the needs of the project and returning to the government the facility/asset in the order set out in the PPP contract upon its termination. The concept of ownership is fundamental in drawing a line between the public and private

17 Ibid.

18 Nigeria is a federation of 36 states and a federal capital territory and has three different tiers of government.

19 Darrin Grimsey and Mervyn K Lewis, *Public Private Partnerships* (Cheltenham: Edward Elgar, 2004) 111.

20 Ibid 112.

21 ER Yescombe, *Public-Private Partnerships: Principles of Policy and Finance* (Amsterdam, Netherlands: Elsevier, 2007) 1.

22 The four terms are used interchangeably in this study to refer to the private sector entity that partners with the government for the procurement of a PPP infrastructure.

sectors. Ownership refers to the possession of property, whereby the owner exercises rights and control over it. The property may be land, intellectual property or other assets, either financial or non-financial. Ownership implies responsibility for actions regarding the property, whose rights are usually protected by law.[23] Lienart posits that the private sector is those entities of the economy not owned by the government or agencies of the government.[24] He further avers that such entities (other than those limited by guarantee) are established for making profit (or even privately owned, not-for-profit organisations). Another distinguishing factor is the trite principle that public corporations are the creation of government legislation. For example, the federal government of Nigeria establishes universities[25] and other institutions of higher learning, public-utility[26] companies and agencies[27] by Acts of the National Assembly. Similarly, at the state level, the government may create public corporations through laws enacted by the various state houses of assembly.[28]

1.3.4 *Greenfield and brownfield PPPs*

A greenfield project involves building a new facility,[29] for example, the Murtala Mohammed Airport Terminal 2 Building in Ikeja, Lagos State, Nigeria. On the other hand, a brownfield project involves the reconstruction or rehabilitation of an existing facility[30]. The Lagos-Ibadan Expressway Concession is an example of a brownfield project.

1.3.5 *Terms used in place of PPP in some jurisdictions*

In practice, other terms are being used in different jurisdictions in place of the term PPP. The choice of terminology is dependent on what suits the policy drafters in that jurisdiction. For example, in Canada and the United States, PPPs are simply referred to as 'P3s.' The United Kingdom, Japan and Malaysia use the term 'Private Finance Initiative' in place of PPP. In Australia, PPPs are called Privately Financed Projects.

23 Ian Lienart, 'Where Does the Public-Sector End and the Private Sector Begin'? (2009) *International Monetary Fund Working Paper*, 4.
24 Ibid.
25 For example, the University of Maiduguri, a tertiary institution owned by the federal government of Nigeria was established vide the University of Maiduguri Act of 1975.
26 The Power Holding Company of Nigeria (now defunct) was a public electricity distribution company that was created by the Electric Power Sector Reform (EPSRA) Act 2005.
27 For example, the Federal Road Safety Commission in Nigeria body vested with the mandate to ensure safety on roads is a creation of the Federal Road Safety Act 1998.
28 For example, the Road Traffic Management Agency of Rivers State (TIMARIV) established by the Traffic Management Law of Rivers State 2009.
29 Baruch Feigenbaum, 'Risk and Rewards of Public-Private Partnerships for Highways' (2011) *Reason Foundation Policy Brief* No. 98, 3 available at <http://reason.org/files/public_private_partnerships_for_highways.pdf> accessed 1 July 2017.
30 Ibid.

Table 1.1 Other terms for PPP

Terminology in use	*Jurisdiction(s)*
P3	- Canada and the United States
Private Finance Initiative	- United Kingdom, Japan, Malaysia
Privately Financed Projects	- Australia

Having discussed the definition of PPP and other terms earlier, an analysis of the reasons why countries adopt the model is considered next.

1.4 The rationale for adopting PPPs

The growth of any economy will be truncated without the availability of infrastructure and services. Unfortunately, due to budget constraints, countries can no longer cope with the demand for the provision of infrastructure. There is no doubt that infrastructure shortage in emerging economies is a major obstacle to 'improved living standards, enterprise and development.'[31] There are several reasons why emerging economies across the globe are adopting the PPP model of infrastructure procurement. PPPs offer a good opportunity for governments everywhere to embark on core social and economic programmes while relying on a structured partnership with the private sector to provide for the infrastructure needs of the populace. With regards to emerging economies, the impact and potential of PPPs in their development cannot be overstressed. For example, the effect of the global financial crisis between 2007 and 2010 was a shortfall of capital inflows into emerging economies.[32] Notwithstanding current global recovery, the cost of foreign loans and the effect of the loans on a nation's economy make PPPs a better option for the government.

The massive costs involved in infrastructure procurement and huge infrastructure deficit necessitates the adoption of PPP as an alternative to traditional public procurement. It has been argued that new infrastructure could cost low- and middle-income countries (LMICs) anywhere between 2 per cent and 8 per cent of gross domestic product (GDP) per year to 2030 to reach an infrastructure-efficiency goal.[33] Further, the world needs to invest US$57 trillion in infrastructure through 2030 just to keep pace with anticipated growth.[34]

31 Ibid 2. The above definition is the South African definition of the term PPP.

32 Tony Dolphin and Laura Chappell, 'The Effect of the Global Financial Crisis on Emerging and Developing Economies' (2010) *Report of the Institute for Public Policy and Research*, 8.

33 Marianne Fay and Julie Rozenberg, *Beyond the Gap* (Washington, DC: World Bank Group, 2019) 1.

34 McKinsey Global Institute, 'Infrastructure Productivity: How to Save $1 Trillion a Year' (2013) available at <www.mckinsey.com/~/media/McKinsey/Industries/Capital%20Projects%20and%20Infrastructure/Our%20Insights/Infrastructure%20productivity/MGI%20Infrastructure_Full%20report_Jan%202013.ashx> accessed 24 October 2019.

Inadequate infrastructure adds significant costs to doing business, especially in emerging markets. Infrastructure like roads, ports, railways, airports, telecoms and power supply enables the economy to run efficiently.[35] It is therefore pertinent that in the face of scarce resources the public sector should consider PPP as an alternative to traditional procurement. The goals are as follows: Goals 1 (no poverty), 3 (good health and wellbeing), 6 (clean water and sanitation), 7 (affordable and clean energy) and 11 (sustainable cities and communities) of the United Nations (UN) Sustainable Development Goals (SDGs).[36] To realise these goals, the public sector needs to partner with the private sector.

Unlike a traditional procurement where the government pays for 'capital and operating costs and carries the risk associated with cost overruns and late delivery,'[37] in a PPP, the expertise and years of experience of a private entity may be procured for the design, construction, maintenance and operation of a public facility.[38] This means that the public authority can then concentrate on policymaking. PPP saves governments the trouble of being responsible for the staffing, maintenance and operation of public facilities. Since state-owned enterprises are generally considered inefficient in emerging markets,[39] engaging the private sector through PPP is potentially advantageous to those economies.

PPPs are a good vehicle for achieving other objectives of the government as well. For example, in South Africa, PPP has been deployed as a strategy for achieving Black Economic Empowerment (BEE). The government of South Africa has structured the PPP process in that country beginning from the appointment of the transaction advisor to the final procurement of the project company to meet with specific targets aimed at ensuring that the blacks in the country are empowered.[40] For each PPP project in South Africa, a BEE scorecard with targets for the project company has to be satisfied. These include:

1 Equity: to achieve meaningful and beneficial direct ownership of substantial equity interests by black people, black women and black enterprises;
2 Management and employment: to achieve effective participation in the management control of the private party and its subcontractors by black people and black women;

35 Sarah Boumphrey, 'Dealing with Infrastructure Deficit in Emerging Markets' (2014) *Market Research Blog* <https://blog.euromonitor.com/dealing-with-the-infrastructure-deficit-in-emerging-markets/> accessed 24 October 2019.

36 United Nations, 'Sustainable Development Goals' (2015) <https://sustainabledevelopment.un.org/sdgs> accessed 24 October 2019 – the 2030 Agenda for Sustainable Development, adopted by the UN member states in 2015, provides a shared blueprint for peace and prosperity for people and the planet, now and into the future.

37 National Treasury PPP Unit, *op cit* (note 2) 4.

38 Ibid.

39 Mark Mobius, 'South Africa; Key Issues and Challengers' (2017) <http://emergingmarkets.blog.franklintempleton.com/2017/03/16/south-africa-key-issues-and-challenges/> accessed 25 October 2019.

40 National Treasury PPP Unit, *op cit* (note 2) 15.

3 Subcontracting: to ensure that the private party contracts to a significant proportion of its subcontracting and procurement to black people, black women and black enterprises; and
4 Local socio-economic impact: to promote positive local socio-economic impact from the project to the benefit of small, medium and micro enterprises (SMMEs), the disabled, the youth and non-governmental organisations (NGOs) within a targeted area of the project's operations.[41]

The Government of India (GoI) has utilised, and continues to deploy, PPP as a tool for the delivery of high-priority public utilities and infrastructure.[42] By so doing, the GoI is close to achieving 1,500 PPP projects in various stages of implementation, making India one of the leading PPP markets in the world.[43] The main reason for the adoption of PPP in Brazil is to ensure that there is more investment in infrastructure, given that an adequate supply of infrastructure services is critical to sustainable economic development. Former President of Brazil Ms Dilma Rousseff once stated, and rightly so, that 'without the private sector involvement, the infrastructure Brazil needs will never be built.'[44]

The high incidence of cases of corruption in the public sector in emerging economies make the choice of PPPs expedient. For example, before Nigeria embarked on a privatisation and commercialisation regime during President Olusegun Obasanjo's Peoples' Democratic Party–led administration, nearly all public-utility companies in the country were operating at a loss, even though taxpayers paid for the use of such facilities. Bad management and outright thievery continued to drain the Nigerian economy. The corrupt practices of public-sector officials negatively affected the fortunes of the National Electric Power Authority (NEPA),[45] the Nigerian Telecommunications (NITEL)[46] and a host of other public-sector corporations, causing a situation of chaos and despair.[47] Utilities under the management of the public sector in Nigeria have failed over the years and have been a subject of research.[48] The provision of uninterrupted supply of power, efficient telephony services, potable water

41 Ibid.
42 Department of Economic Affairs, 'Public Private Partnerships in India' (2018) available at <www.pppinindia.gov.in/overview> accessed 25 October 2019.
43 Ibid.
44 The World Bank, 'Brazil Overview' (2013) available at <www.worldbank.org/en/country/brazil/overview> accessed 15 January 2015.
45 NEPA used to be the Nigeria's sole power generating and distribution corporation. It was renamed Power Holding Corporation of Nigeria (PHCN) before it was unbundled to give rise to an era of multiple power generating and distribution companies with private sector participation.
46 NITEL used to be Nigeria's sole telecom firm with a monopoly on fixed telecom services.
47 Asaju Kayode, Sunday O Adagba and Felix Anyio, 'Corruption and Service Delivery: The Case of Nigerian Public Service' (2013) 1(1) *Wudpecker Journal of Public Administration* 3.
48 Ademola Ariyo and Afeikhena Jerome, 'Utility Privatisation and the Poor: Nigeria in Focus' (2004) (12) *Global Issue Papers* 15.

supply and air, road and rail transport services have been elusive in the Nigerian setting, despite the country's oil wealth.[49]

The use of PPPs encourages the injection of private-sector capital. The effect of this is that the lenders and promoters of PPP projects will put rigorous measures in place to ensure that a project is viable and stays on track. Some of the measures include due diligence, thorough monitoring and control mechanisms throughout the duration of the project.[50]

1.5 Types of PPPs

There are use different types of PPP models that have been adopted across the globe. The choice of model depends on its suitability in the context of the country where it is adopted. According to Yescombe, PPPs can be classified by the legal nature of private-sector involvement in the facility using such expressions as Build-Operate-Transfer (BOT), Design-Build-Finance-Operate (DBFO), Operation and Maintenance (OM),[51] etc.[52] However, it needs to be stated that whichever type of model is adopted, they fall into two broad categories depending on whether it is the end user that is paying for the service (concession) or the public sector (private finance initiative).

1.5.1 Concession

This is a contractual agreement whereby a facility is given to the private sector, which then operates the facility for a certain period. In most cases, this also includes building and designing the facility as well. With regard to concessions, it has been observed that they have the longest history of public-private financing.[53] Specifically, a concession is a contractual arrangement whereby the project component or contractor undertakes the construction and financing of any infrastructure or facility, as well as the operation and maintenance thereof, and includes the supply of equipment and machinery for any infrastructure and the provision of any services.[54]

In most cases, the concession model is used to provide for financing, design, construction, management and maintenance of facilities often borne by user fees. Examples include the provision of pipe-borne water, gas, electricity and public transport. Concessions are usually not ideal for social programmes like

49 Ibid.

50 National Treasury PPP Unit, *op cit* (note 2) 12.

51 This author does not view this type of arrangement as a proper PPP.

52 ER Yescombe, *op cit* (note 21) 13.

53 United Nations Economic Commission for Europe (2008) cited in Augustine E Arimoro, 'An Evaluation of the Legal Framework for Public-Private Partnerships in Nigeria' (Unpublished LLM Dissertation, University of Derby, Derby, 2014).

54 Section 36 ICRC Act, 2005.

health services, prisons, courts and education. According to Yescombe, the typical elements of a concession are:[55]

1 A project company, owned by private investors;
2 Financing for the project's capital cost ('capex') through shareholder equity and project-finance debt;
3 A Design and Build (D&B) contract, under which the contractor agrees to design and construct the completed road and related works (e.g. toll booths) to the required specification, at a fixed price and schedule;
4 An operating contract, under which a maintenance company provides road maintenance services;
5 A concession agreement (a standard name for this type of PPP contract) with the public authority;
6 Cash flow after operating costs ('opex') (i.e. mainly payments on the operating and maintenance contracts) being used, firstly, for debt service and then to pay distributions to the investors.[56]

1.5.2 The Private Finance Initiative (PFI)

Under PFI schemes, privately financed contracts for public facilities and public works are paid for by a public authority and not by the end users. Yescombe identifies the following as the key elements of the PFI model:

1 A project company, owned by private investors;
2 Financing of the project's capex through shareholder equity and project-finance debt;
3 A D&B contract, under which the contractor agrees to construct the facility to the required specification, at fixed price and schedule;
4 A soft facility-maintenance (FM) contract, under which a service company provides services such as cleaning, security and catering, etc.;
5 A hard FM contract under which a maintenance company or original D&B provides building-maintenance services;
6 Cash flow after opex – mainly payments on the FM contracts is used firstly for debt service and then to pay distributions to investors.[57]

The PFI model was developed in the UK in 1992 and has been adopted by some countries, including parts of Canada, France, Australia, Singapore and the US.[58] The PFI is a PPP type in which the public sector does not own the asset

55 ER Yescombe, *op cit* (note 21) 8.
56 Ibid 8.
57 Ibid 10.
58 JR Barlow and S Wright, 'De Facto Privatisation of a Renewed Role for the EU? Paying for Europe's Healthcare Infrastructure in a Recession' (2010) *Journal of the Royal Society of Medicine* 51.

but pays the PFI contractor a stream of committed revenue payments for the use of the facilities during the contract period. Once the contract is concluded, ownership of the facility ether remains with the private-sector company or is returned to the public sector as per the terms of the contract.[59]

The distinction between concession and PFI could be very thin in the sense that, in a PFI, it is possible for members of the public to pay 'shadow tolls' with the government subsidising the costs.[60]

Following the two major divisions mentioned previously, there are other sub-divisions of PPP models flowing from the first two categories (i.e. concession and PFI). The gist behind the distinction is based on the allocation of responsibilities as well as the risk borne by the public-sector and private-sector partners to the contract.[61] Worthy of note is that ownership of the facility has little or nothing to do with the PPP model applied, and, hence, the concession or PFI model can be used with the following PPP types:

1. **Build-Operate-Transfer (BOT)** – The BOT is a contractual arrangement whereby the private sector undertakes to finance, design, construct under a turnkey risk basis, operate and maintain an infrastructure project for a specified period, after which the project facilities are transferred to the granting authority, usually without any payment of compensation.[62]
2. **Buy-Build-Operate (BBO)** – This partnership involves the transfer of a public asset to a private or quasi-public entity, usually under a contract that the assets are to be upgraded and operated for a specified period. Public control is exercised through the contract at the time of transfer.[63]
3. **Build-Own-Operate-Transfer (BOOT)** – In this form of partnership, the private sector finances, builds, owns and operates a facility and charges user fees for a specified period, after which ownership is transferred back to the public sector if not already transferred upon the completion of the facility.[64]
4. **Build-Lease-Operate-Transfer (BLOT)** – In a BLOT partnership, a private-sector entity receives a franchise to finance, design, build and operate a leased facility and to charge user fees for the lease period against payment of rent.[65]

59 HK Yong, *Public-Private Partnerships Policy and Practice: A Reference Guide* (Commonwealth Secretariat, 2010) 10.

60 ER Yescombe, *op cit* (note 21) 13.

61 H Brooks, L Liebman and C Shelling, *Public-Private Partnerships: New Opportunities for Meeting Social Needs* (Cambridge, MA: Ballinger. 1996) 16.

62 Belarus Draft PPP Law available at <www.economy.gov.by/dadvfiles/002076_1973331_engexpertiza.pdf> accessed 28 October 2014.

63 Richard G Little, 'Public Private Partnerships: An Informational Summary Prepared for the IEL Business Committee on Infrastructure' (2010) *North Carolina University* 15.

64 Ibid.

65 Ibid.

5 **Design-Build-Finance-Operate (DBFO)** – Under DBFO, the government retains the title to the land and leases it to the private-sector consortium over the lifespan of the concessionary agreement.[66]
6 **Build-Lease-Transfer-Maintain (BLTM)** – Here, the private-sector consortium uses its finances to build the facility and then leases it from the public-sector entity before transferring the facility back to the public sector at the termination of the arrangement. There is, however, an obligation on the part of the private-sector consortium to maintain the facility after the transfer of the asset to the public sector.
7 **Lease-Develop-Operate (LDO)** – Under this arrangement, the private-sector consortium leases the infrastructure asset, usually an empty piece of land, from the public-sector entity and finances the development of the facility before operating it as an asset.
8 **Rehabilitate-Operate-Transfer (ROT)** – In ROT, the private-sector entity is to refurbish an existing facility and operate it under the contract for a given term, after which the facility is transferred back to the public sector.[67]

1.6 PPP distinguished from other similar types of procurement

To grasp what a PPP is, it is important to distinguish between PPP and other forms of public procurement.

1.6.1 PPPs vs public-sector procurement

PPP is an alternative approach to public-sector procurement of public infrastructure. On the other hand, conventional public-sector procurement is the use of public revenue or funds borrowed by the public authority to finance infrastructure. This is the traditional means for providing public infrastructure. In a typical public-sector procurement (Design-Bid-Build), the public authority sets out the specifications and the design of the facility, calls for bids based on the details and pays for the construction of the facility.[68] Here, the public authority funds the entire cost of the project and remains in charge of the maintenance and operation of the facility. In a PPP, on the other hand, the public authority specifies the requirement in terms of final output, but it is left for the private sector to design, finance, build and operate the facility, usually for a long term.

66 SM Levy, *Build, Operate, Transfer: Paving the Way for Tomorrow's Infrastructure* (Hoboken, NJ: John Willey & Sons, 1996) 34.
67 See Section 28 Ekiti State Public-Private Partnership Law No.12, 2011. See also Section 35 Lagos State Public-Private Partnership Law 2011.
68 ER Yescombe, *op cit* (note 21) 4.

Table 1.2 Differences between public procurement and public-private partnership

Public procurement	*PPP*
Each phase may be awarded to different contractors	All phases are awarded to the same contractor
Budgetary allocation is required on the part of the government	PPPs are off budget as the private sector provides the finance required
Project lifespan is often short- to medium-term	Project lifespan is often long-term

According to Yescombe, the PPP approach as it relates to risk, ensures the following are transferred from the public authority to the project company:

1 The cost of the design and construction of the facility
2 Market demand for the facility (usage)
3 Service provided by the facility (including its availability for use)
4 The facility's operation and maintenance costs[69]

1.6.2 PPPs vs privatisation

Privatisation may be considered as any quantifiable transaction by which the state's ultimate ownership of corporate entities is reduced.[70] According to Abiola and Abiola, privatisation involves the divesture of government interest in companies in which it has a substantial shareholding.[71] Nigeria used to be a country with many state-owned enterprises prior to the advent of civilian rule in 1999. Shortly after assuming power via the electoral ballot, the administration of President Olusegun Obasanjo initiated the creation of the Bureau for Public Enterprises to ensure the smooth sale of several government-owned entities. The chief reason for the divestitures was that state-owned corporations had been poorly managed and had become drainpipes for government resources.[72]

The Organisation for Economic Cooperation and Development (OECD) has identified four methods of privatisation. The first is *trade sales*, which can be undertaken by private placement or by trade-sale auctions. A second method is by *share offerings*. This can be done by either an initial public offering (IPO) of all or a tranche of the corporation's shares on a stock exchange, secondary

69 Ibid.

70 OECD, *Privatisation in the 21st Century: Recent Experiences of OECD Countries Report of Good Practices* (Paris: OECD, 2006) 13.

71 Alimi M Abiola and RO Abiola, 'Impact of Privatisation on the Growth of Nigerian Public Enterprises: A Case Study of Selected Enterprises in Nigeria' available at <http://dspace.futa.edu.ng/jspul/handle> accessed 10 April 2015.

72 *This Day*, 'Privatisation in Nigeria' available at <www.thisdaylive.com/articles/privatisation-in-nigeria-the-promise-the-peril/126714/> accessed 10 April 2015.

Table 1.3 Differences between privatisation and PPP

Privatisation	*PPP*
As soon as an enterprise is sold, the government's involvement is reduced to a regulatory role	The flexibility of the agreement may provide a role for the government to play
Ownership of the asset is transferred to the private sector.	Ownership of the asset is retained with the government as assets are transferred at the end of the contract
Private entity bears all the risk	Risk is shared between the partners

public offering or offering by means of book building when the government charges a few investment banks with placing tranches of shares of already listed government corporations with institutional investors. The third method that can be adopted is the *management or employee buy-out*. Where this is applicable, corporations can be sold to legal entities controlled by the incumbent staff or management. A fourth method can be done through *capital increases*, by issuing additional stock and thus diluting the government's ownership.[73] The method that is adopted for privatisation is usually dependent on local circumstances. Thus, in countries where, for instance, the capital market is underdeveloped, IPOs could be challenging, and thus trade sales to foreign firms in similar industries are preferred.[74]

While there is a consensus that the sale of government shareholdings in public corporations in whole or in part to private owners is privatisation, there appears to be a controversy regarding the sale of other government assets, such as land or buildings. In a country like the United States (US), with few state-owned enterprises, the term 'privatisation' is commonly applied to the act of contracting for public services. In the commercial space, privatisation could mean the transformation of a company previously quoted on the stock exchange to one no longer quoted. For this study, however, it will suffice to say that privatisation is the sale of a government's shareholding in state-owned enterprises, whether as an outright sale or a reduction in shareholding. On the other hand, a PPP, as has been noted earlier, is a contractual arrangement between the government and a private consortium to jointly provide public amenities.

1.6.3 Outsourcing vs PPP

Outsourcing is the mere hiring of a service (such as a cleaning service or a security guard service). It is a form of partnership between the public and private sectors without risk transfer. In a PPP, the private sector assumes substantial

73 OECD, *op cit* (note 70) 13.

74 S Estrin, J Hanousek, E Kocenda and J Svejnar, 'The Effects of Privatisation and Ownership in Transition Economies' (2009) 47(3) *Journal of Economic Literature* 699–728.

risk for financing a project's capital and operating costs as well as the design and building of the facility, managing its operations to some specified standards, normally over an agreed-upon time.[75]

1.7 Advantages and disadvantages of PPPs

Like any other form of procurement for public infrastructure, PPPs have their share of merits and demerits. Both the public and private sectors can derive benefits from using PPP as a tool for the provision of infrastructure assets and services for the populace. While the private sector enjoys new business activity, better margins and gets long-term revenues, the public partner also benefits from the expertise and efficiency that the private sector provides, especially in a market economy where stiff competition exists.

Several researchers have discussed the advantages of PPP.[76] This section examines some of them.

Strategic Partnering identified the following five key advantages for adopting PPP:[77]

1 Access to finance: PPPs can offer access to private capital when governments have limited cash;
2 Access to technology, people and skills: For the public sector, PPP affords the opportunity to access the latest technology, management and people skills from the private sector. This also provides an opportunity for innovation on the part of the public sector;
3 Transfer of risk: The public sector avoids bearing risk inherent in the ownership of physical assets, which is wholly borne by the private-sector partner;
4 Investment opportunities: Without PPPs, few private-sector companies would have the chance to work and gain experience on major infrastructure projects; and
5 Business development: Private-sector companies that work with the public sector can build on the gains of the business and grow.

Koveous and Yourougou distinguished between public-sector and private-sector partners and indicated the specific benefits that each sector accrues when PPPs are adopted.[78]

75 Public Private Partnership Commission Malawi, 'PPP' available at <www.pppc.mw/faq.html> accessed 12 April 2015.

76 Strategic Partnering, 'The Five Key Advantages of Public-Private Partnerships' (2015) available at <http://strategic-partnering.net/the-five-key-advantages-of-public-private-partnerships/> accessed 23 March 2017.

77 Ibid.

78 Peter Koveous and Pierre Yourougou, 'Public-Private Partnerships in Emerging Markets' (2005) available at <www.financepractitioner.com/contentFiles/QF01/hmz2o7ek/11/0/publicprivate-partnerships-in-emerging-markets.pdf> accessed 28 March 2015.

They list the specific benefits for the public sector as follows:

1 Reduces project costs and time while enhancing its overall efficiency and effectiveness;
2 Enables access to learning from private-sector resources, technology and managerial skills;
3 Enhances credit and, consequently, access to long-term financing;
4 Pursues an integrated approach to project completion; and
5 Involves participation from various partners and may legitimise the project in the eyes of the citizenry and other stakeholders.[79]

For the private sector, they opine that the analysis is based on the profitability of the project in terms of dollars and cents and is more objective than conducted by the public sector.[80]

According to Walker et al., the following are the benefits of PPPs:

1 Relief of financial burden on the part of the government and the public;
2 Relief of administrative burden;
3 Reduction in the size of (inefficient) bureaucracy;
4 Better services to the public;
5 Encouragement of growth; and
6 The government can better focus and fund social issues, such as health, education, pension and the arts.[81]

Governments are inclined towards PPP based on the following reasons:

1 The ability to develop new infrastructure services, despite short-term fiscal constraints;
2 Value for money through efficiencies in procurement, construction and operation; and
3 Improved service quality and innovation using private-sector expertise and performance incentives.

The private sector is considered to bring better expertise and efficiency to the table when it comes to matters of business. It is noteworthy that PPP comes as a relief to the government, as raising capital from loans becomes a burden on the economy. Again, the private sector can offer value for money (VfM), as it is better suited to drive costs to the lowest-possible level. This is especially vital in developing economies where government contracts are usually seen as a means of rewarding those who supported politicaloffice holders into positions of authority with such contracts always overpriced.

79 Ibid 3.
80 Ibid 4.
81 C Walker, J Mulchahy, A Smith, PTI Lam and R Cochrane, *Privatised Infrastructure* (London: Thomas Telford, 1995) 10.

Some demerits of the PPP model of procurement have also been identified.[82] A study of these demerits is important in order to guard against them and to ensure an efficient PPP framework that is attractive to both local and foreign investors. The disadvantages that could arise with PPP projects when not efficiently managed include the following:

1 A lengthy bidding process that takes a long time from the initial phase of public-sector assessment to the signing of the contract. The process of inviting, preparing, assessing and fine-tuning bids is complex and laborious;[83]
2 The number of parties involved in a PPP, the complex negotiations and high transaction and legal costs;
3 The public authority may obtain cheaper loans than the private sector consortium can obtain;
4 The cost attached to debt;
5 Possibility of loss of jobs or transfer from being a public-sector staff to a private-sector staff because of project hand-overs;
6 Currency risk. In this case, it is important to bear in mind that payment for use of the facility would be local, and where loans are foreign, there is the attendant foreign currency risk involved. The important question is what happens if the local currency is devalued?
7 The private sector may only be interested in making profits and not concerned about the welfare of citizens.
8 PPP projects tend to fail, especially due to a lack of adequate skill on the part of the private-sector partners who may have no prior experience. This could mar whatever gains could result from adopting the PPP option in the first place.

1.8 The critical success factors for PPPs

There are some essential characteristics required to have successful PPP projects. These fundamentals have been referred to as critical success factors (CSFs). CSFs are the key areas of activity in which favourable results are absolutely necessary for a manager to achieve set goals.[84] According to Babatunde et al. the CSFs for successful PPP projects are a competitive procurement process, a thorough and realistic assessment of the cost and benefits, a favourable framework, an appropriate risk allocation and risk sharing, government involvement by providing a guarantee, political support, stable macroeconomic policy and

82 Esther Cheung, 'Developing a Best Practice Framework for Implementing Public Private Partnerships (PPP) in Hong Kong' (Unpublished PhD Thesis, Queensland University of Technology, Queensland, 2009) 55.

83 Ibid.

84 Solomon Olusola Babatunde, Akintayo Opawole and Olusegun E Akinsiku, 'Critical Success Factors in Public-Private Partnership on Infrastructure Delivery in Nigeria' (2012) 10(3) *Journal of Facilities Management* 215.

the availability of the financial market.[85] They posit that the parties to the PPP arrangement to ensure successful implementation of infrastructural projects using PPP and to achieve optimum objectives of the contractual agreement should give these identified CSFs due consideration.[86] To elaborate further, it is pertinent to state that the elements discussed in this section are essential for successful PPP projects.

1.8.1 A favourable framework for PPP

There must be an enabling structure in place prior to initiating PPPs in the first instance. An enabling framework must include a legal framework. There must be legislation or a body of legislation that backs PPP. Certain other legislation must be amended or repealed to make PPPs practicable. It may even require constitutional amendments in some cases. For example, in Nigeria, there are some items in the Exclusive Legislative List in the Second Schedule to the 1999 Constitution of the Federal Republic of Nigeria (as amended), that fall within the purview of the federal government, and no matter how needful a project is, a state government may not initiate a PPP project as touching any of the items on that list.

In a similar vein, there must be a regulatory framework to monitor PPP projects. For example, the ICRC Act of 2005, apart from serving as the primary law for PPP projects involving the federal government of Nigeria and any of its MDAs, established a regulatory commission to superintend over PPP projects as well as take into its custody all signed PPP agreements. Following this, it is fundamental that the framework must be clear and devoid of ambiguities. It is essential for the success of PPPs that the parties (i.e. the public sector and the private party) understand what their role is and what part the other party should play.

1.8.2 Transparency and anticorruption

One of the challenges of development in emerging economies is the vexed issue of corruption. It is fundamental that if a government must adopt PPP that the transactions must be free of corrupt practices. Good governance advocates transparency, equal treatment and open competition. The lack of these is a source of worry to potential investors, whether foreign or local. It is no doubt that corruption increases the cost of doing business as well as poor output. To curb corrupt practices in PPP procurement, Delmon recommends the following:

1 The use of financial and fiduciary management, ring-fencing revenue and subsidy flows from the government to demonstrate project viability and attract investment;[87]

85 Ibid 223.

86 Ibid.

87 Jeffrey Delmon, *op cit* (note 1) 16.

2 Improved access to information about the project and the procurement process, for example, through a dedicated project website with all the relevant information for contract bidding and award, which will attract bidders and improve competition;[88] and
3 The project procurement must be transparent and competitive.[89]

It is imperative, therefore, that for PPPs to succeed in emerging economies, the government must commit to the fight against corruption. In this regard, the efforts by the Nigerian government to fight corruption is well noted, especially with the passing into law of the Corrupt Practices and Other Related Offences Act No. 6 of 2003 to underscore this commitment. Specifically, Section 14 of the Act provides as follows:

> Any person who –
>
> a asks for, receives or obtains property or benefits of any kind for himself or any other person; or agrees or attempts to receive or obtain any property or benefit of any kind for himself or any other person, on account of –
>
> i anything already done or omitted to be done, or any favour or disfavour already shown to any person by a public officer in the discharge of his official duties or in relation to any matter connected with the functions, affairs or business of a government department, public body or other organisation or institution in which the public officer is serving as such or
>
> ii anything to be afterwards done or omitted, or any favour or disfavour to be afterwards shown to any person, by a public officer in the discharge of his official duties or in relation to any such matter as aforesaid,
>
> is guilty of an offence of official corruption and on conviction be liable to imprisonment for seven (7) years.

1.8.3 Ensuring a healthy investment environment for PPPs

In so far as a healthy investment climate is delivered and the proper practice is put in place to ease doing business in any given economy, investments in infrastructure can become an alternative asset class for private investors, provided an acceptable risk/return profile is offered.[90] It is essential that there is political

88 Ibid.
89 Ibid.
90 OECD, *Private Financing and Government Support to Promote Long-Term Investments in Infrastructure* (Paris: OECD, 2014) 5.

will on the part of the public authority to pursue PPP and the legal and regulatory regime appropriate to ensure PPP success. The three elements mentioned earlier are vital, and the lack of any of them will certainly discourage potential investors.

1.9 The PPP project cycle

PPPs are considered by their nature very complex arrangements. A typical PPP would involve a range of players and stakeholders, including public officials, private entities and persons representing a variety of interests. From the period in which the project is conceived to its execution and operation, the partnership needs to be organised in a systematic and transparent fashion.

The starting point of a PPP project is usually when the project is conceived based on a need for it and the satisfaction that the PPP model is the appropriate procurement method for the project. The government ministry, department or agency identifies the need for the project and, after getting the requisite approval, calls for bids from private-sector consortiums. It is also possible that a private-sector body may make an unsolicited[91] bid for a project. Once a suitable bidder is chosen, the project is implemented. The project cycle varies depending on the jurisdiction. In South Africa, for instance, at the inception of a project, the procuring institution registers the project with the National Treasury's PPP Unit.[92] Thereafter, advisors appointed from the private sector undertake a feasibility study. If the feasibility study shows that a PPP is a viable option, the government body moves forward with the bidding process.

1.10 Selecting the right projects for PPPs

It is not feasible that all public infrastructure projects are structured or procured using the PPP model. Besides, potential investors are also concerned about their return on investment (RoI). At the project selection phase, it is important for the public authority to conduct a high- level review of the service need (i.e. the justification of the project and its prospects for delivery as a PPP).[93] This step is referred to as the 'strategic business case' phase. At this stage, it is necessary for the public sector to acquire the services of experts before arriving at a decision about a project's suitability. More so, projects that are not viable or bankable in terms of investments or that do not align with government policy requirements may be eliminated at this stage.[94]

91 Private companies often approach governments directly with new project ideas, typically referred to as unsolicited proposals.

92 National Treasury Unit, *op cit* (note 2) 19.

93 The World Bank, *Attracting Investors to African Public-Private Partnerships* (Washington, DC: The World Bank, 2009) 19.

94 Ibid.

According to the World Bank,[95] the project-selecting stage poses the following three questions that would determine whether a project is suitable for PPP:

1 What are the project's scope and requirements?
2 Can the project be delivered as a PPP?
3 Should the project be delivered as a PPP?

1.10.1 The scope of the project and requirements

The reasons for initiating a project may be obvious; for example, city decongestion may require road expansion or the need to upgrade power facilities due to an increase in the population. The decision to address the need may have been discussed at the policy level, but there is a need at this point for an investment plan. It is strategic to consider which solution is the best approach to the public need. For example, where there is city congestion, would a road expansion be the solution, or would a rail network expansion or implementation be the right option? One of the challenges of government procurement over time has been a rush into providing solutions which have not been clearly thought out in the first place. For example, the Rivers Monorail, a project initiated by the Rivers State government of Nigeria. The idea behind the project was to help ease congestion within the Port Harcourt main town and surrounding areas and to link up with the new Greater Port Harcourt town. Unfortunately, the private sector pulled out of the arrangement, and the administration of Governor Rotimi Amaechi continued with the project. The question is, would a rail project not have been the better option for such a venture given the high cost involved in monorail projects? Similarly, it is important to establish the business need of the PPP project and assess the costs and benefits of different options available, irrespective of whether they are procured as a PPP or traditional government procurement.

1.10.2 Is the project PPP viable?

According to the World Bank,[96] there are three questions that need to be answered to determine the viability of a project for PPP. First, who will pay for the project (affordability)? Secondly, what are the risks inherent in the project, and how should they be dealt with (risk allocation)? And thirdly, is the resulting project capable of raising the required debt financing (bankability) and attract contractors and other equity investors? There is a need to involve experts in assisting the public authority to provide answers to these questions that must be addressed before arriving at the PPP option for any public project.

The argument here is vital as it relates to emerging economies. For example, politics plays a key factor in project location and implementation in Nigeria.

95 Ibid 20.
96 Ibid 23.

Sometimes, the motivation behind the initiation of a project may not be for the need or profitability of the project but mainly for winning the support of the electorate or to reward a geographical area for support. For example, the leadership of the People's Democratic Party (PDP), which is now the main opposition party in Nigeria, criticised President Muhammadu Buhari over statements he made thousands of miles away in the United States indicating that Nigerians who gave him 97 per cent of their votes will be treated better than those who gave him 5 per cent.[97] The president and commander-in-chief of the federal republic was referring to projects that would be embarked upon by his government. It follows that if this is the approach of the Buhari administration to governance, projects may be in areas where they may not be required merely as a form of a political reward.

In South Africa, all prospective PPP projects are subjected to three basic tests. Where the answers to the tests are in the affirmative, a PPP is considered the appropriate vehicle for procuring that public asset.[98] The tests are:

1 Can substantial *risk* be transferred to the private sector?
2 Is the project *affordable* to the procuring government ministry, department or agency?
3 Does a PPP procurement option show *value for money*?

1.11 Affordability, risk allocation, bankability and value for money

These four concepts are very important factors in determining whether a project should be undertaken as a PPP. With regard to affordability, it is important to build up an expected flow of the operating cost and maintenance costs for projects at the selection phase. Loans as well as investor returns are to be paid from the cash flow. Thus, a project finance model is required to assess this. The assessment carried out by the experts must show that the project is affordable. In addition to assessing the sources of revenue linked with the affordability of the project, it is essential to establish a complete picture of the risks that flow from the project.[99]

The subject of risk and PPP is one that is crucial for a discussion on successful PPP projects. A successful project must benefit from workable, commercially viable, and cost-effective risk sharing.[100] It is fundamental that risk must

97 Henry Umoru, 'PDP Blasts Buhari, Accuses Him of Planning to Run a Discriminatory, Vindictive, Divisive Government' *The Vanguard*, 26 July 2015. See the video on Youtube where Buhari made the statement in an interview at <www.youtube.com/watch?v=ZYUBTU2ZgFY> accessed 29 March 2017.

98 National Treasury Unit, *op cit* (note 2) 5.

99 Ibid 24.

100 Jeffrey Delmon, *op cit* (note 1) 95.

be allocated before a conclusion is reached about whether a given project is suitable for PPP. Usually, for finance projects, certain risks (such as market risk, political risk and completion risk) will be allocated by the grantor to the SPV in relation to the role the latter plays in the project. Thus, for bearing such risks, the SPV is compensated by higher returns on its investment. However, Delmon notes that project financing is obtained primarily through the lenders rather than the investment or liability of shareholders.[101] In turn, the lenders will attempt to limit their own assumption of risk by requiring the SPV to allocate as much of its risk as possible to the different counterparties, for example, the offtake purchaser, the construction contractor and the OM contractor. This effort to transfer the project risk to these subcontractors is known as 'back-to-back' risk allocation. It is, however, rare to achieve back-to-back risk transfer where the SPV will completely transfer all the risk to other parties.[102]

Value for money (VfM) is not a new concept. It is about maximising the impact of each dollar spent to improve the lives of the ordinary citizen. The achievement of VfM outcome in the use of public funds is considered vital in the procurement and delivery of each public investment project. VfM is a consideration for the sponsoring agency throughout the process of procurement. The UK Treasury defines VfM as 'the optimum combination of whole-life costs and quality (or fitness for purpose) of the good or service to meet the user's requirement.'[103]

Governments around the world are gradually shifting towards PPPs to deliver infrastructure to pursue VfM. VfM is not necessarily the choice of goods or services based on the lowest bid price but is, rather, a choice based on the whole-life costs of the project or service.[104] The VfM test is necessary to determine the suitability of a project to be executed as a PPP. Basically, a PPP may provide VfM compared to traditional procurement if the advantages of risk transfer combined with private-sector incentives, experience and innovation – in improved service delivery or efficiencies over the project lifetime – outweigh the increased costs of contract and financing.[105] It follows that the granting authority (public sector) must determine the VfM for both traditional procurement and PPP before a choice is made about whether the project is PPP viable. Simply put, the purpose for VfM analysis is to indicate whether to implement proposed projects as PPPs or to use other forms of traditional public procurement to execute a given project.

101 Ibid 97.
102 Ibid 98.
103 The World Bank, *Value-For-Money Analysis – Practices and Challenges* (Washington, DC: The World Bank, 2013) 10.
104 D Morrallos and A Amekudzi, 'The State of the Practice of Value for Money Analysis in Comparing Public Private Partnerships to Traditional Procurements' (2008) 13(2) *Public Works Management and Policy* 114.
105 The World Bank, *op cit* (note 103) 10.

1.12 Conclusion

This preliminary chapter provides a background to the theory of PPP. The introduction in this first chapter sets the tone for appreciating the discussion on the practice of PPP in at least four different emerging economies in subsequent chapters. This chapter introduces the reader to the PPP phenomenon and the rationale for its adoption by countries around the globe, including in emerging markets. It highlights the merits and demerits of adopting the PPP model of procurement and differentiates PPP from other similar forms of public procurement.

The chapter covers key topics in current PPP discourse, such as the critical success factors for PPP arrangements, the need to ensure a healthy investment environment for PPPs, the project cycle for PPPs, the need to select the right projects for PPP arrangements and very key PPP concepts like affordability, risks, bankability and VfM. This chapter, therefore, provides a foundation for the discussion of the practice of PPP in the selected emerging markets covered in this book.

The focus of the next chapter is a discussion on the importance of creating a legal framework for administering and regulating PPPs in emerging economies. Chapter 2 will, among other things, evaluate key issues that may impact on PPP arrangements in a country and the need to find solutions to legal challenges surrounding the implementation of successful PPP regimes in emerging markets.

References

Abiola, A.M., & Abiola, R.O. (2015). Impact of Privatisation on the Growth of Nigerian Public Enterprises: A Case Study of Selected Enterprises in Nigeria. Retrieved from dspace.futa.edu.ng/jspul/handle.

Arimoro, A.E. (2014). *An Evaluation of the Legal Framework for Public-Private Partnerships in Nigeria* (Unpublished master's thesis). University of Derby, Derby.

Arimoro, A. E. (2018). An Appraisal of the Framework for Public Private Partnership in South Africa. *European Procurement and Public Private Partnership Law Review, 13*(3), 215.

Ariyo, A., & Jerome, A. (2004). *Utility Privatisation and the Poor: Nigeria in Focus*. Global Issue Papers.

Barlow, J., Roehrich, J.K., & Wright, S. (2010). De Facto Privatization or a Renewed Role for the EU? Paying for Europe's Healthcare Infrastructure in a Recession. *Journal of the Royal Society of Medicine, 103*(2), 51–55. doi:10.1258/jrsm.2009.090296.

Boumphrey, S. (2018, February 22). Dealing with the Infrastructure Deficit in Emerging Markets. Retrieved from https://blog.euromonitor.com/dealing-with-the-infrastructure-deficit-in-emerging-markets/.

Brooks, H., Liebman, L., & Shelling, C. (1996). *Public-Private Partnerships: New Opportunities for Meeting Social Needs*. Cambridge, MA: Ballinger.

Chambers, J. (2007). *Infrastructure Research Report*. San Francisco: Pension Consulting Alliance Inc.

Cheung, E. (2009). *Developing a Best Practice Framework for Implementing Public Private Partnerships (PPP) in Hong Kong* (Unpublished doctoral dissertation). Queensland University of Technology, Australia.

Davidson, S. (2014). Why Is Privatisation So Controversial. Retrieved from www.cis.org.au/app/uploads/2015/04/images/stories/policy-magaize/2014-autumn/30-1-14-davidson-sinclair.pdf.

Delmon, J. (2011). *Public-Private Partnership Projects in Infrastructure: An Essential Guide for Policy Makers*. Cambridge: Cambridge University Press.

Department of Economic Affairs. (2018). Public Private Partnership in India. Retrieved from www.pppinindia.gov.in/overview.

Dolphin, T., & Chappell, L. (2010). *The Effect of the Global Financial Crisis on Emerging and Developing Economies*. London: Institute for Public Policy and Research.

Estrin, S., Hanousek, J., Kocenda, E., & Syejnar, J. (2009). The Effects of Privatisation and Ownership in Transition Economies. *Journal of Economic Literature, 47*(3), 699–728.

Feigenbaum, B. (2011). Risk and Rewards of Public-Private Partnerships for Highways. Retrieved from http://reason.org/files/public_private_partnerships_for_highways.pdf.

Fulmer, J.E. (2009). What in the World Is Infrastructure? Retrieved from www.corridortrust.com/uploads/Infrastructure_Investor.pdf.

Government of Belarus. (2014). Страница не найдена |. Retrieved from www.economy.gov.by/dadvfiles/002076_1973331_engexpertiza.pd.

Grimsey, D., & Lewis, M.K. (2004). *Public Private Partnerships*. Cheltenham: Edward Elgar Publishing Ltd.

Kayode, A., Adagba, S.O., & Anyio, F. (2013). Corruption and Service Delivery: The Case of Nigerian Public Service. *Wudpecker Journal of Public Administration, 1*(1), 3.

Koveous, P., & Yourougou, P. (2005). Public-Private Partnerships in Emerging Markets. Retrieved from www.financepractitioner.com/contentFiles/QF01/hmz2o7ek/11/0/publicprivate-partnerships-in-emerging-markets.pdf.

Levy, S.M. (1996). *Build, Operate, Transfer: Paving the Way for Tomorrow's Infrastructure*. Hoboken, NJ: John Wiley & Sons.

Lienart, I. (2009). *Where Does the Public-Sector End and the Private Sector Begin?* Vol. 4. Washington, DC: International Monetary Fund.

Little, R.G. (2010). *Public Private Partnerships: An Informational Summary Prepared for the IEL Business Committee on Infrastructure*. Chapel Hill, NC: North Carolina University.

Malek, S.S., & Akalkotar, P.V. (2016). Driving Forces Leading to the Adoption of PPP – Perspectives from Gujarat (India), Hong Kong and Australian Practitioners. *International Journal for Innovative Research and Technology, 2*(9), 6.

McKinsey Global Institute. (2013). Infrastructure Productivity: How to Save $1 Trillion a Year. Retrieved from www.mckinsey.com/~/media/McKinsey/Industries/Capital%20Projects%20and%20Infrastructure/Our%20Insights/Infrastructure%20productivity/MGI%20Infrastructure_Full%20report_Jan%202013.ashx.

Mobious, M. (2017, June 8). South Africa: Key Issues and Challenges. Retrieved from http://emergingmarkets.blog.franklintempleton.com/2017/03/16/south-africa-key-issues-and-challenges/.

Morallos, D., & Amekudzi, A. (2008). The State of the Practice of Value for Money Analysis in Comparing Public Private Partnerships to Traditional Procurements. *Public Works Management & Policy, 13*(2), 114–125. doi:10.1177/1087724x08326176.

National Treasury Unit. (2007). *Introducing Public Private Partnerships in South Africa*. Pretoria: Author.

Nwangwu, G. (2016). *Public Private Partnerships in Nigeria*. Basingstoke: Springer.

OECD. (2006). *Privatisation in the 21st Century: Recent Experiences of OECD Countries Report of Good Practices*. Paris: Author.

OECD. (2014). *Private Financing and Government Support to Promote Long-Term Investments in Infrastructure*. Paris: Author.

Olusola Babatunde, S., Opawole, A., & Emmanuel Akinsiku, O. (2012). Critical Success Factors in Public-Private Partnership (PPP) on Infrastructure Delivery in Nigeria. *Journal of Facilities Management, 10*(3), 212–225. doi:10.1108/14725961211246018.

Onyejiuwa, C. (2015, July 23). *Muhammadu Buhari Says He Will Treat Nigerians Who Did Not Vote for Him Unequally* [Video file]. Retrieved from www.youtube.com/watch?v=ZYUBTU2ZgFY.

Pierson, G., & MacBride, P. (1996). Public/Private Sector Infrastructure Arrangements. *CPA Communique, 73*, 1–4.

Public Private Partnership Commission Malawi. (2015). PPP. Retrieved from www.pppc.mw/faq.html.

Strategic Partnering. (2015, March 23). The Five Key Advantages of Public Private Partnerships. Retrieved from http://strategic-partnering.net/the-five-key-advantages-of-public-private-partnerships/.

Thisday. (2015). Privatisation in Nigeria. Retrieved from www.thisdaylive.com/articles/privatisation-in-nigeria-the-promise-the-peril/126714/.

Umoru, H. (2015, July 26). PDP Blasts Buhari, Accuses Him of Planning to Run a Discriminatory, Vindictive, Divisive Government. *Vanguard*.

The United Nations. (2015). SDGs: Sustainable Development Knowledge Platform. Retrieved from https://sustainabledevelopment.un.org/sdgs.

Vallée, V. (2014). *Public-Private Partnerships in the Middle East and North Africa*. Paris: OECD.

Walker, C.T. (1995). *Privatized Infrastructure: The Build Operate Transfer Approach*. London: Thomas Telford.

The World Bank. (2009). *Attracting Investors to African Public-Private Partnerships: A Project Preparation Guide*. Washington, DC: World Bank Publications.

The World Bank. (2013a). Brazil Overview. Retrieved from www.worldbank.org/en/country/brazil/overview.

The World Bank. (2013b). *Value-for-Money Analysis – Practices and Challenges: How Governments Choose When to Use PPP to Deliver Public Infrastructure and Services*. Washington, DC: Author.

Yescombe, E.R. (2007). *Public-Private Partnerships: Principles of Policy and Finance*. Amsterdam, Netherlands: Elsevier.

Yescombe, E.R. (2017). *Public-Private Partnerships in Sub-Saharan Africa: Case Studies for Policymakers, 2017*. DareSalam: Uongozi.

Yong, H.K. (2010). *Public-Private Partnerships Policy and Practice: A Reference Guide*. London: Commonwealth Secretariat.

2 The framework for public-private partnerships

2.1 Introduction

Public-private partnerships are, by their nature, very complex arrangements. They represent a radically different approach to public procurement than the traditional method. Unlike traditional procurement, where the public authority engages a private company as a supplier of assets or services, in a PPP, the relationship moves beyond that of a client-supplier to a partnership between the public authority and a private consortium. The mandate of the private consortium is to deliver an infrastructure project over a long term in return for a reward in the form of tolls or charges. It is important that there is clarity in the manner in which projects are initiated, arranged, procured and managed during the tenure of the PPP contract. This is the very reason why governments that desire to adopt PPP to procure public infrastructure must establish a framework that defines the rules and provide a guide for all stakeholders, including public officials, private sector participants and other stakeholders, such as the community where the PPP project is to be located. A comprehensive approach to PPP administration is made up of policy, law, regulations and procedures setting down what should be done by different agencies of the government and how the responsibilities of the different parts of the government throughout the PPP project cycle knit together.

This chapter deals with the policy, legal and regulatory frameworks for the efficient running of a PPP regime, especially in emerging economies. Before deciding on implementing PPPs as a solution to a country's infrastructure deficit, it is vital that the public authority establishes a clear policy for using the PPP model. When a government adopts a PPP policy, the next step is to put in place a legal and regulatory framework to serve as a guide and to provide investors and promoters the confidence that the process is clear and predictable.

This chapter discusses the need for a framework, state policies for PPPs, the legal framework and the institutional framework. Dispute resolution is also a very important focus in the chapter, given the fact that PPPs are complex, and disputes are bound to arise. The need to determine how disputes arising from a PPP arrangement are to be resolved usually determines whether investors, lenders or promoters would be interested in participating in a PPP arrangement, especially in developing markets.

2.2 The need for a framework

According to the World Bank, the PPP framework refers to 'the policy procedures, institutions, and rules that together define how PPPs will be implemented – that is, how they will be identified, assessed, selected, budgeted for, procured, monitored and accounted for.'[1] In a similar vein, the UNCITRAL *Legislative Guide on Privately Financed Infrastructure Projects* states that the existence 'of an appropriate legal framework' is a prerequisite to creating an environment that fosters private investment in infrastructure.[2] More importantly, the UNCITRAL document stipulates the need to ensure that PPP laws remain 'sufficiently flexible and responsive to keep pace with the developments in various infrastructure sectors in the economy.'[3] Even though it is possible to implement PPPs on a one-off basis without a supporting framework, it is worthy to note that most countries with a successful PPP programme have built that programme on a viable PPP framework.[4]

The establishment of a clear framework for PPPs in any jurisdiction restates the government's commitment to ensuring that PPPs succeed.[5] It outlines how projects are to be procured, implemented, managed and operated. Without a doubt, investors or promoters are more likely to show interest in jurisdictions where the framework for PPPs is clear, rather than in a jurisdiction where there is lack of clarity in the process. A clear framework for PPPs is essential for promoting governance within them. For example, the United Nations Economic Commission for Europe (UNECE) has defined governance as 'the process in government actions and how things are done, not just what is done.'[6] The importance of a well-thought-out policy and legal and regulatory framework for PPPs cannot be overstressed, especially because PPPs are complex long-term transactions that are affected by many areas of law.[7] Delmon notes that a conducive PPP framework must aim to achieve the following:[8]

- the political will to pursue PPP, and the legal and regulatory regime appropriate to enable and encourage PPP

1 The World Bank, *Public-Private Partnerships Reference Guide Version 2.0* (Washington, DC: The World Bank Group, 2014) 65.

2 UNCITRAL Legislative Guide on Privately Financed Infrastructure Projects UN 2001 A/CN.9/SER.B/B/4 23.

3 Ibid.

4 The World Bank, *op cit* (note 1) 65.

5 Ibid.

6 The United Nations Economic Commission for Europe, *Guidebook on Promoting Good Governance in PPPs* (New York, NY: UNECC, 2008) 13–14.

7 Esther Cheung, Albert PC Chan, Patrick TI Lam et al, 'A Comparative Study of the Critical Success Factors for Public Private Partnerships (PPP) Between Mainland China and the Hong Kong Special Administrative Region' (2012) 30(13/14) *Facility Management Development* 653.

8 Jeffrey Delmon, *Creating a Framework for Public-Private Partnership (PPP) Programs: A Practical Guide for Decision Makers* (Washington, DC: The World Bank, 2014) 2.

- selection, design and development of "good" projects – the most appropriate and feasible projects for PPP
- allocating risk to the private sector while insulating investors from those risks best borne by the contracting agency or the Government
- ensuring that the financial markets are in a position (legally, financially and practically) to provide the project with the investment it needs (debt, equity and otherwise), including by providing Government support.[9]

Furthermore, Delmon argues that a simpler framework is better.[10] This is because, in the early days of implementing a PPP regime, it is usually a learning process, especially for everyone involved in procuring PPPs in that jurisdiction. As such, it is generally ideal to make the process as simple as possible. This is to enable key stakeholders to understand the framework and interact more easily.

The essence of having a PPP framework, among other things, is so that the government can establish what the PPP policy is, pass the necessary laws and regulation, establish a PPP unit and other institutions to administer the process, select and develop a pipeline of projects to be executed using the PPP model and monitor the PPP process and projects. In this chapter, the PPP framework refers to the following:

1 The policy: this refers to the plan and action taken by the government to address public issues.[11]
2 The legal framework: this refers to how laws and regulatory structures can be used to encourage PPP and support and regulate the institutions implementing PPP.[12]
3 The institutional framework: this includes the persons who are involved and have the decision-making power and how they perform their functions.
4 The dispute-resolution process: this refers to the process of resolving conflicts that arise during the PPP process.

2.3 Policy and PPP

In simple terms, a policy refers to the principles by which a government is guided. A public policy is a 'deliberate and (usually) careful decision that provides a guidance for addressing selected public concerns.'[13] The formulation of policy involves the identification and analysis of a range of actions to respond

9 Ibid.
10 Ibid.
11 Richa Singh, *Civil Society and Policymaking in India: In Search of Democratic Spaces* (Oxfam India, 2014) 1 available at <www.oxfamindia.org/sites/default/files/WP7-Civil-Scty-n-plcy-mkg-in-India.pdf> accessed 16 November 2019.
12 Ibid.
13 Sherri Torjman, *What Is Policy?* (Ottawa: The Caledon Institute of Social Policy, 2005) 4.

to public concerns.[14] Public policies are typically 'designed to achieve defined goals and present solutions to societal problems.'[15] Determining the best design to achieve the goal(s) stated in the policy are crucial to policymaking. Often, governments design policies to provide both short-term and long-term solutions to identified challenges.

The problem of huge infrastructure deficits and the impact they can have on the economy is one that should be of concern to any government around the world. The case of emerging economies is even more critical, as the supply of infrastructure needs to improve to match increasing demand. There are huge concerns that factors such as rural-urban drift and growing population can significantly impact on the economy and well-being of citizens of countries in emerging economies, such as India and Nigeria. According to the United Nations, from 2017 to 2050, 'it is expected that half of the world's population growth will be concentrated in just nine countries: India, Nigeria, the Democratic Republic of the Congo, Pakistan, Ethiopia, the United Republic of Tanzania, the United States, Uganda and Indonesia.'[16] It is therefore critical that countries make plans to provide for their infrastructure needs. Often, those plans are designed as policies. The question that follows is how do countries make their policies? A discussion on policymaking in the selected countries (i.e. Brazil, India, Nigeria and South Africa) follows.

2.3.1 Policymaking in Brazil, India, Nigeria and South Africa

The concept of public policy is crucial to emerging economies. This is because it is a tool that can be used to drive development and provide solutions to societal problems. Policymaking is central to governments, as they commit significant time, energy and resources towards developing policies.[17] A good policy initiated by a government should aim to provide solutions and drive economic growth. The problem with developing economies, however, is the lack of willpower to follow through with a holistic implementation of the developmental plans usually encapsulated in such policies.

The Brazilian Constitution of 1988 (as amended) defines the political institutions and the powers of the political actors in the policymaking process in the country. In Brazil, strong presidential powers drive the policymaking process

14 Ibid.

15 Christopher Knill and Jale Tosun, 'Policy Making' in Daniele Caramani (ed.), *Comparative Politics* (New York: Oxford University Press, 2008) 495.

16 The United Nations, 'World Population Projected to Reach 9.8 Billion in 2050, and 11.2 Billion in 2100' *UN News* 21 June 2017 available at <www.un.org/development/desa/en/news/population/world-population-prospects-2017.html> accessed 5 November 2019.

17 Dahida Deewua Philip, 'Public Policy Making and Implementation in Nigeria: Connecting the Nexus' (2013) 3(6) *Public Policy and Administration Research* 56.

which is subject to democratic checks and balances.[18] Thus, as far as the federation is concerned, the president of the country determines what the policy objectives of the state will be. The problem with this is that the concentration of the policymaking powers on the president may not yield the desired results without a supportive institutional framework. This contrasts with India, where both the government and the civil service play a part in the policymaking process. However, it is worth noting that Brazil has recognised that infrastructure investments should be considered a policy priority. As such, the implementation of recent infrastructure policies, such as the Growth Acceleration Programme (or PAC, to use the Portuguese acronym), shows the government's commitment to spur economic growth through the development of infrastructure.[19] During the Rouseff administration, the Brazilian government involved the private sector in the construction and maintenance of infrastructure through PPP arrangements and concessions.[20]

In India, the government, with its civil-service machinery, is responsible for policymaking decisions.[21] The criticism against the policymaking process in India is based on a lack of public consultation before policy decisions are made.[22] It has been suggested that public participation needs to occur with four different audiences before policy decisions are reached (i.e. the public, the relevant stakeholders, inter-ministerial and inter-departmental bodies and experts and activists).[23]

The dominant feature of the policymaking process in Nigeria is the principle of federal supremacy.[24] The Nigerian Constitution gives so much power to the central government. Thus, the federal government is mandated to provide the overall direction and leadership in the planning process, from the formulation stage to implementation.[25] The weakness in the Nigerian situation is the lack of initiative on the part of subnational governments.[26] One of the challenges with policymaking in Nigeria is the multiplication of agencies involved in policy implementation. For example, the multiple institutions

18 Lee J Alston, Marcus André Melo, Bernardo Mueller and Carlos Pereira, *Political Institutions, Policymaking Processes and Policy Outcomes in Brazil* (Washington, DC: Inter-American Development Bank, 2006) 5.

19 Edmund Amman, Werner Baer, Thomas Trebat and Juan Villa Lora, 'Infrastructure and Its Role in Brazil's Development Process' (2016) 62 *The Quarterly Review of Economics and Finance* 66–73.

20 Ibid 68.

21 Archit Puri, 'Policy Making in India: Who's Behind It?' *Indian National Interest*, 26 August 2017 available at <https://nationalinterest.in/policy-making-in-india-whos-behind-it-4fd2f6255714> accessed 16 November 2019.

22 Aditi Agrawal, 'Policy Next: How to Improve India's Policymaking Processes' *Medianama*, 5 July 2019 available at <www.medianama.com/2019/07/223-policynext-how-to-improve-indias-policy-making-processes/> accessed 16 November 2019.

23 Ibid.

24 Dahida Deewua Philip, *op cit* (note 17) 60.

25 Ibid.

26 Nigeria is a federation of 36 states and a federal capital territory.

involved in regulating PPP in Nigeria further complex the PPP process in the country.[27]

The case of South Africa, as far as policymaking is concerned, is unique. This is because there is a deliberate intention to right the wrongs of the past.[28] Due to the country's history, which is dominated by colonialism, racism and apartheid, post-apartheid policymaking in that country aims to redress the economic imbalances and inequalities that characterised the apartheid era and which are still a source of concern. To its credit, the South African government uses PPP as policy tool to address inequality through the implementation of the Black Economic Empowerment (BEE) policy. For example, the South African government formalised the Code of Good Practice in 2004 for BEE in PPP. As a result, each PPP project in South Africa has a set of targets for the private party in relation to participation of black South Africans in the PPP process.[29]

The problem with this policy is that it puts a burden on private businesses that consider investing in PPP projects in South Africa. First, why should the government transfer its duty to redress inequality by mandating private entities to ensure that black people, black women and black enterprises own substantial shares in the project companies? Secondly, what is the guarantee that this would not be abused by promoters who would merely name black people as shareholders just to fulfil the requirement?

It is important to state that a good PPP regime that will ensure successful arrangements, implementation and operation of PPP projects begins with a government policy adopting PPP and setting in motion the necessary modalities for the implementation of a PPP framework. As such, it behoves the public authority to ensure that the right policy is put in place. In addition, the political actors must have the political will to ensure that PPPs succeed. Whether it is in Brazil, where the president has wide powers in terms of policymaking, in India, where there is a growing call for more stakeholder participation, in Nigeria, where the federal government leads and the subnational government follows, or in South Africa, where policies are directed at creating a balance in the society, it is important that the right policy is implemented with a view to develop the economy and address social problems.

A good policy for PPP should address the following important aspects of a PPP regime:

1 The purpose of the policy – its vision and goals
2 Identification of the responsibilities for public entities
3 The types of projects to be executed using the PPP model
4 Government support for PPP projects

27 Augustine Edobor Arimoro, 'Institutional Framework for Public-Private Partnerships in Nigeria: Is It a Case of Too Many Cooks for One Pot of Broth?' (2019) 40(2) *Business Law Review* 73–79.

28 Vusi Gumede, 'Public Policy Making in a Post-Apartheid South Africa: A Preliminary Perspective' (2008) 38(2) *Africanus* 7–23.

29 National Treasury PPP Unit, *Introducing Public Private Partnerships in South Africa* (Pretoria: National Treasury PPP Unit, 2007) 15.

2.4 Legal framework for PPP

The legal framework for PPP refers to the laws and regulations that underpin the PPP programme in any jurisdiction.[30] The legal framework usually enables the government to enter into PPP contracts, setting the rules and limits for how PPPs are to be arranged, regulated, managed and operated. In most cases, the law establishing the legal framework also creates a PPP unit or a government regulatory body tasked with the mandate to regulate and administer PPPs in that jurisdiction. The legal framework is often anchored on a legal instrument that implements the PPP policy.[31]

There is no doubt that an 'independent, fair and efficient legal framework is a key factor for successful PPP project implementation.'[32] Cheung et al. argue that a transparent and stable legal framework should help make the contracts and agreements bankable and should entail adequate dispute resolution mechanisms to ensure stability in PPP arrangements.[33]

The need for a specific PPP law often depends on the country's legal system. The case of Nigeria is noteworthy. While an Act that would establish PPP in the country was pending before the country's legislature, some PPPs were procured under extant procurement laws. Whereas some developed common law countries (e.g. the UK) do not have a specific PPP law, it is important for emerging economies to have one for the purpose of clarity and because they do not have very strong institutions compared to developed economies. The case of India is also unique. Even though there is no specific PPP law in that country, there are institutions that have been created to ensure PPP success. In any case, what suits the economic development of any given country should be adopted. This author, however, favours the creation of PPP-specific or secondary legislation to provide clarity to investors and promoters.

2.4.1 Key issues for a PPP legal framework

Under this subheading, it is important to consider the problems that may arise when a legal framework for PPP is established. Delmon has identified some of these issues.[34] Addressing these key issues can go a long way in providing domestic and foreign investors assurance that the government intends to be bound by PPP contracts and arrangements. This is a major source of worry in emerging markets. These issues are as follows:

30 The World Bank, *op cit* (note 1) 65.

31 Jeffrey Delmon, *op cit* (note 8) 5.

32 Esther Cheung, Albert PC Chan, Patrick TI Lam, Daniel WM Chan and Yongjian Ke, *op cit* (note 7).

33 Ibid.

34 Jeffrey Delmon, *op cit* (note 8) 7.

Vires

It is important that the legal framework describes which government entities have the power to perform which functions associated with a PPP project. Where a party performs an act outside of that party's legal rights, it would be judged to be ultra vires and would be void under the law. An example is the case of state governments in Nigeria that have no power to enter into contracts dealing with inland waterways, federal roads or aviation, among other items listed in the Exclusive Legislative List contained in Schedule II of the 1999 Constitution of the Federal Republic of Nigeria. Even though some state governments, like Akwa Ibom and Delta, have constructed airports within their localities, a prospective investor should be concerned about the legality of such a contract if it were to be procured as a PPP.

Procurement

The procurement process must be clear to all involved in the PPP process. The importance of public consultation in the build-up to the signing of a PPP contract cannot be overemphasised. There has been a trail of criticisms by stakeholders of people being alienated from the decision-making process in the award of PPP concessions to winning consortiums. For example, it has been argued that the PPP procurement process in South Africa is 'riddled with corrupt practices in what has become known as *tenderpreneurship*.'[35]

The selection process must be specified in clear terms and must be seen to be fair by all parties involved. Delmon also suggests an applicable regime for challenging the award of projects to winning consortiums.[36]

Land rights and acquisitions

This should be of serious concern to PPP promoters and investors. Whereas land can be acquired for public use in Nigeria by the authorities subject to the payment of adequate compensation to the landowner(s), it is not that simple in a place like India. Land acquisition has been identified as one of the bottlenecks militating against the execution of PPP projects in a country that is the largest PPP market in the world.[37] Government of India's (GoI) attempts at forcible land acquisition for private industry under a colonial-era law have

35 Madeleine C Fombad, 'Accountability Challenges in Public-Private Partnerships from a South African Perspective' (2013) 7(1) *African Journal of Business Ethics* 11–25, 11.

36 Jeffrey Delmon, *op cit* (note 8) 7.

37 The Economic Times, 'Land Acquisition, Lack of Fund Among Bottlenecks for PPP Projects' *The Economic Times*, 7 August 2014 available at <https://economictimes.indiatimes.com/news/economy/infrastructure/land-acquisition-lack-of-fund-among-bottlenecks-for-ppp-projects/articleshow/39822989.cms> accessed 16 November 2019.

led to violence and resistance by the Indian people.[38] A new law that sought to provide a solution to this problem in 2013 did not achieve the desired results. After coming into power in May 2014, the administration of Narenda Modi introduced nine key amendments to the 2013 law. This move notwithstanding, land acquisition for PPP is quite challenging in India.

To make PPPs successful, it is vital that the legal system and framework for PPP make the acquisition of land for PPP as well as the compensation for landowners as smooth as possible to encourage private-sector interests in PPPs.

Tariff collections

It is common knowledge that private entities that enter into PPP relationships do so for the expected return on investment (RoI). End users of PPP facilities are expected to make toll payments or pay charges for the use of those facilities. It is important that the legal framework defines how the charges or tolls will be set and how they can be adjusted over time. Furthermore, the legal framework should state the extent to which the project company can enforce its rights to collect tariffs through penalties or disconnections.[39]

Dispute resolutions

PPPs are complex contracts. Because of this, conflicts are inevitable. Failure to address such disputes early and cheaply may negatively impact on the PPP regime in any given jurisdiction.

Generally, parties to a PPP project would prefer to submit any disputes that may arise in the course of the PPP contract to arbitration. This is because it is cheap, flexible and offers ease of award execution. International arbitration benefits from the experience of sophisticated arbitrators as well as from the speed of the process. This is in addition to being backed up by the New York Convention.[40]

Security rights over PPP assets

Given the fact that lenders recourse in the event of a PPP failure lies in the project company, it is not uncommon for lenders to want to exercise a right of control over the project company's assets in order to protect the lenders' assets. It is therefore significant to include rules that deal with the taking of security over different projects.

38 Shivam Vij, 'India's Land Acquisition Bill Passes: A Win for the Economy?' *The Christian Science Monitor*, 30 August 2013 available at <www.csmonitor.com/World/Asia-Pacific/2013/0830/India-s-land-acquisition-bill-passes-A-win-for-the-economy> accessed 16 November 2019.

39 Jeffrey Delmon, *op cit* (note 8) 8.

40 The United Nations Convention on the Recognition and Enforcement of Foreign Arbitral Awards (1958).

2.5 The institutional framework

A good PPP framework must spell out a well-designed institutional framework with clear and strong political support.[41] Although PPP offers an opportunity for a government to tap into private-sector skill, capacity and finance in order to reduce public-infrastructure deficit, it is essential for the government to ensure coordination of the process to implement PPP successfully.[42] Therefore, the setting up of an institutional framework to effectively administer PPPs in any jurisdiction is a success driver. Thus, while the private-sector consortium is expected to provide the design, source the financing, then build or rehabilitate the facility as well as maintain the infrastructure and provide services, the onus is on the public authority to ensure there is a structure to guarantee successful PPP outcomes.[43] The difference between the legal framework for PPPs and the institutional framework for PPPs is that the former provides the substructure for the process, and the latter is the design for its success. The institutional framework for PPP is therefore those organs, agencies or state structures put in place by law to ensure that PPPs are successfully administered.[44] These agencies or entities are either created by legislation or as units within government departments.[45]

The institutional framework provides the responsibilities of the agencies of the state in the PPP process. It defines which institution plays what role at every point.[46] A government's institutional set up for PPP should include provision for a PPP unit,[47] standard procedures, and guideline tools to identify, structure, evaluate, award and monitor PPP projects.[48] The institutional framework for PPP in any jurisdiction, therefore, is made up of the specialised unit(s) or programmes structured to develop and supervise PPP projects. They play a pivotal role in the promotion of PPP solutions.[49] On the other hand, it should be noted that the PPP unit, which in most cases is the main institutional actor in the regulation

41 Jeffrey Delmon, *op cit* (note 8) 11.

42 The World Bank, *op cit* (note 1) 1.

43 Augustine Edobor Arimoro, *op cit* (note 27).

44 Tesborne Tafesse Beyene, 'Policy, Legal, and Institutional Frameworks for PPP Implementation in Development Process: Stakeholders' Perspective' (2015) 14(3) *China-USA Business Review* 155.

45 The Institute for Public-Private Partnerships Inc (IP3), *Development of Policy, Legal, and Institutional Framework for the Public-Private Partnership Program in Malawi* (Washington, DC: The Institute for Public-Private Partnerships Inc., 2007) 38.

46 Ibid 82.

47 This may be known by another nomenclature. For example, Nigeria's national PPP unit is referred to as the ICRC while that of South Africa is named the National Treasury PPP Unit.

48 The Institute for Public-Private Partnerships, 'Development of Policy, Legal, and Institutional Framework for the Public-Private Partnership Programme in Malawi -Final Report' (2007) available at <www.sadcpppnetwork.org/wp-content/uploads/2015/02/MalawiFinalReport.pdf> accessed 20 March 2018.

49 Economic and Social Commission for Asia and the Pacific, 'PPP Policy, Legal and Institutional Frameworks in Asia and the Pacific' (2017) 7 available at <www.unescap.org/sites/default/files/S4_PPP-Policy-Legal-Institutional-Frameworks_0.pdf> accessed 21 March 2018.

and administration of PPP, does not initiate projects. The responsibility for initiating projects is the task of the line ministry, department or agency (MDA) that has direct oversight of the proposed facility. In the same vein, the guidelines for the operation of the institutions regulating PPP must be clear 'to ensure a fair, transparent, and competitive bidding process. Dispute resolution mechanisms should also be in place to deal with differences that will inevitably arise between the public and private partners during the life of a long-term PPP contract.'[50]

Furthermore, it is imperative that the institutional framework for PPP in any given jurisdiction is made simple without the complexity of multiple actors.[51] Where there have been complexities, it has been noted, there are high incidences of PPP governance issues which, in turn, result in project failures.[52] There are at least two options in providing such clarity. The government may choose to enact a dedicated law or adopt a policy document. While a law provides a stronger basis, policy documents, on the other hand, are more easily modified to suit-changing circumstances, especially in the early phase of a PPP regime. More importantly, using old structures to regulate PPP may be an invitation for failure since that type of PPP was not envisaged at the time when some of the structures were set up.[53] It will amount to the proverbial 'putting new wine in old wine bottles.'

2.5.1 A role for state institutions

The institutional theory has been used to explain both individual and organisational actions.[54] The theory attends to the deeper and more resilient aspects of social behaviour and culture.[55] It considers the processes by which structures, including schemas, rules, norms and routines, become established as authoritative guidelines for social behaviour.[56] Thoenig asserts that public agencies as organisations are considered as institutional actors in as far as their field units appropriate and promote values and interests that are embedded in the local communities in which they operate and not just as machines implementing goals and values defined by a principal.[57]

50 Ibid 6.

51 Martin van den Hurk and Koen Verhoest, 'The Governance of Public-Private Partnerships in Sports Infrastructure: Interfering Complexities in Belgium' (2015) 33 *International Journal of Project Management* 201–211, 201.

52 Ibid.

53 Jeffrey Delmon, *op cit* (note 8) 27.

54 Jerry Goodstein and W Richard Scott, 'Institutional Theory and Institutional Change: Introduction to the Special Research Forum' (2002) 45(1) *Academy of Management Journal* 45.

55 W Richard Scott, 'Institutional Theory' in George Ritzer (ed.), *Encyclopedia of Social Theory* (Vol. 1) (London: Sage Publications Inc., 1995) 408–114.

56 Ibid 408.

57 Jean-Claude Thoenig, 'Institutional Theories and Public Institutions: New Agendas and Appropriateness' in BG Peters and J Pieerre (eds.), *The Handbook of Public Administration* (London: Sage Publications Ltd, 2011) 3.

A study of behaviour of state institutions, especially in developing economies, is important. This is because no matter how good laws and developmental plans are, the responsibility to see to their successful implementation or otherwise is a function of state institutions. Weingast asserts, and rightly so, that the problem with developing countries is not the institutional technologies for providing the rule of law, such as property rights, civil rights, personal liberties, incorporation laws, corporate governance structures, contract law and judicial systems, but failure of state institutions to perform their roles effectively.[58] It follows, therefore, that a government can conceive a good approach to providing solutions to societal problems, develop a policy and pass laws to implement the policy and still fail to achieve its goals, not necessarily because the laws were defective but for the ineffectiveness of state machinery to implement the laws.

Schmidt posits that there are four types of institutional approaches.[59] These are the rational choice theory, the historical theory, the sociological theory and the discursive institutionalism theory.[60] The rational choice theory states that actors have fixed preferences and act rationally to maximise their preferences.[61] The sociological approach examines how actors follow rules and norms, assuming their identities and cultures are the sources of interest for individuals.[62] This looks at how human institutions shape actors and not how actors shape institutions.[63] Thus, every fresh individual that joins the institution with a different mindset and objectives soon begins to act like others in that institution. The sociological approach clearly explains the situation in developing countries, as there remains no change in attitude to work. The historical theory states that institutions are sets of regularised practices built over time. For its part, the discursive institutionalism construct examines how actors generate and legitimise ideas through a logic of communication, focusing on the interactive process through which ideas are generated.[64]

If a government must transform its governance to meet the aspirations of the people, it is imperative that the institutions of state play a pivotal role. This is because the institutions of state are the arena within which policymaking takes place, and policymaking is contingent upon cooperation among the gladiators.[65] In the same vein, it is noted that the 'most daunting frontier still

58 Barry R Weingast, 'Why Developing Countries Prove So Resistant to the Rule of Law' (2008) available at <http://jenni.uchicago.edu/WJP/Vienna_2008/Weingast_ROL_MS_2%2000_08-0519.pdf> accessed 21 March 2018.

59 V Schmidt, 'Give Peace a Chance: Reconciling Four (Not Three) "New Institutionalisms"' in D Beland and R Cox (eds.), *Ideas and Politics in Social Science Research* (Oxford: Oxford University Press, 2010).

60 Ibid.

61 Daniel Friel, 'Understanding Institutions: Different Paradigms, Different Conclusions' (2017) 52 *Revista de Administração* 212–214, 213.

62 Ibid.

63 Ibid.

64 Ibid.

65 Peter John, *Analysing Public Policy* (London: A & C Black, 1998) 38.

to be crossed in most of postcolonial Africa is the creation and maintenance of institutions that will uphold transparency and the rule of law.'[66] Therefore, for the state to provide good governance, there is a corresponding requirement that the institutions of state must embrace best practices, have regard for the rule of law and ensure transparency and fairness to all, irrespective of affiliation or persuasion.

While it is important that institutions of state live up to their role of evolving sustainable and people-oriented governance,[67] it is important that the institutions are not created in such a way that they play overlapping roles or where gaps are created as to which institution is to act in any given circumstance.

2.5.2 How the institutional framework can be designed to support PPPs

Every successful PPP programme requires the setting up of strong 'PPP institutions' to administer and regulate PPP transactions. For example, countries like India, South Africa and Nigeria have established PPP units or agencies of government created directly by primary or subsidiary legislation. In South Africa, a PPP unit has been created under the National Treasury, whilst in Nigeria, the Infrastructure Concession Regulatory Commission (ICRC) was established by the federal government in 2005 to oversee PPP at the national level. A good institutional framework to support the PPP regime in any jurisdiction should adequately mobilise significant expertise and effort from dedicated team members.[68]

There is an emerging trend with regard to what it should take for a project to be approved as a PPP. For example, India and South Africa have 'multi-stage approvals for their PPP projects and all relate to the commitment of public funds or contingent support'[69] The countries have ministries of finance leading on approvals based on the economic viability of the project. This is in addition to value for money (VfM) and risk assessments that are prerequisites for qualifying a project to be procured as a PPP. In South Africa, for instance, there are three standard tests applied to determine whether a project should be procured as a PPP.[70] The answer to these three questions determines whether PPP or the traditional form of procurement should be adopted:

1 Can substantial *risk* be transferred to the private sector?
2 Is the project *affordable* to the procuring institution?
3 Does a PPP procurement option show *value for money*?

66 R Joseph, 'Challenges of a Frontier Region' in L Diamond and MF Plattner (eds.), *Democratisation in Africa: Progress and Retreat* (Baltimore, MD: JHU Press, 2010) 11.

67 Hakeeem Olatunji Tijani, 'Globalisation, Institution and Public Private Partnership: The Nigerian Experience' (2015) 43 *Journal of Law, Policy and Globalisation* 4.

68 Jeffrey Delmon, *op cit* (note 8) 12.

69 Ibid.

70 National Treasury PPP Unit, *op cit* (note 29) 5.

It is through the institutional framework for PPP set in place that South Africa can determine and assess whether a project meets the requirements of these basic tests.

Furthermore, the PPP institutional framework must outline the procurement stages for PPP projects and how they would be coordinated. A steering committee may be created to ensure that there is coordination amongst the different government agencies involved. India provides a good case study in this regard. For example, the Government of India (GoI) aims to ensure better coordination of projects by putting in place a mechanism that includes the public authority, developer and other agencies to facilitate efficient communication and implementation.

In this author's view, it is more appropriate to establish a single PPP unit that is charged with the responsibility of coordinating and regulating PPP in any given jurisdiction.[71] The rationale for this is that it reduces state bureaucracy and provides clarity. The case in Nigeria, where there are several agencies of government involved in the administration of PPP transactions, creates a lot of overlap and could potentially give room to muscle flexing by government institutions and could negatively affect the country's PPP regime.[72]

It is essential that the institutional framework for PPP in emerging economies is designed to efficiently identify which projects are suitable for PPP. In Nigeria, for instance, projects are sometimes initiated for political reasons, for example, to 'reward' a region for voting massively for that government. It is important that before a project is procured as a PPP, it should be viable in the long run. For example, an airport procured as a PPP in a northeast state in Nigeria may not be profitable for a PPP investor as there is not enough air traffic in that region of the country.

In sum, the PPP institutional framework must be designed to ensure a smooth and efficient project-selection process, a well-coordinated project-approval process and a robust and corruption-free bidding process; the framework should also give room for an excellent regulatory procedure for PPP projects. This should be the standard to ensure a successful PPP regime, especially in emerging economies where the institutions of state are still developing.

2.6 Creation of a PPP law

As stated previously, a comprehensive approach to PPP involves identifying the policy and then crystallising it into a PPP law to serve as framework for PPP. For emerging economies, it is appropriate to have a PPP law in place to show investors that the government is committed to a successful PPP regime.

In a bid to update the United Nations Commission on International Trade Law (UNCITRAL) Guidelines and Model Legislative Provisions in 2014,

71 Augustine Edobor Arimoro, *op cit* (note 27).
72 Ibid.

UNCITRAL's Secretariat and advisers identified that the legislative text on PPPs should include those based on the minimum features of a PPP and should also address whether the payment for the services would be derived from the public authority, from end users or from a combination of both.[73] This is important to avoid confusion. For example, the Nigerian PPP law is the Infrastructure Concession Regulatory Commission (Establishment, etc.) Act of 2005. The law makes mention only of concessions[74] without mentioning the project finance initiative (PFI).[75] The assumption, therefore, is that, as far as PPP in Nigeria is concerned, PFI is not envisaged. The South African regulations provide a clearer picture.

In 2014, the UNCITRAL Colloquium found that there is an evolving trend in law and practice and that countries respond in different ways to PPP practice. Evidence also shows that as a country gains experience with successful PPP, more opportunities emerge for wider PPP application.[76] Even though the UNCITRAL guidelines comprehensively spell out the items that a PPP law should address and cover, this author is of the view that PPP practice in any given jurisdiction should determine what the law should cover. The PPP law should be designed to meet the socio-cultural and economic life of the people concerned and allow for amendments to ensure that the aim of adopting it in that jurisdiction is achieved. At the minimum, a PPP law should aim to address the following:

1 The definition of what PPP is. This should be clear and certain but not overly restrictive;[77]
2 The general purpose and scope of the law (geographical, national, subnational etc.);
3 The forms of PPP;
4 The government entities responsible for the implementation of PPP programmes at the national and subnational levels, the development of a pipeline of PPP projects and the authority to enter PPP agreements. Identify persons that are eligible or ineligible to be a partner;
5 The roles of different government entities at the national and subnational levels;
6 Administrative coordination, approvals and the decision-making process;
7 The regulation of PPP through PPP agreement or through an independent regulator under sector law;

73 United Nations General Assembly A/CN.9/821 UNCITRAL. Forty-seventh Session. New York, 7–18 July 2014 and; 'Possible Future Work on PPPs Report' *UNCITRAL Colloquium on PPPs* 3–4 March 2014 Vienna, Austria.

74 In a concession, end-users pay for using the PPP facility.

75 In a PFI the government pays the project company for the use of the facility by members of the public.

76 Philip Kelly, *Preparing a Public-Private Partnership Law: Observations from the International Experience* (Manila: Asian Development Bank, 2016) 12–13.

77 Ibid 53.

8 The funds for project preparation;
9 The power to appoint PPP advisers and the process of appointment;
10 Public investment management and project selection – VfM and whole-of-life cost;
11 Public financial management – affordability and fiscal risk assessment of actual, hidden, implicit and contingent liabilities;
12 Procurement principles and purposes;
13 Government financial accounts and national income accounting for PPPs;
14 Unsolicited proposals;
15 The selection of a partner and the methods of selection;
16 The settlement of disputes;
17 The sources of finances; and
18 Government step-in rights.

The PPP law of any jurisdiction is a matter of style, and there is no standard about how much detail a PPP law must contain. In principle, however, a PPP law should aim to address broad principles with a degree of certainty.[78]

2.7 Setting up the PPP unit

To have a successful PPP regime, the creation of a dedicated PPP unit cannot be overemphasised. A dedicated PPP unit refers to any 'organisation set up with full or partial aid of the government to ensure that necessary capacity to create, support and evaluate multiple public-private partnership agreements are made available and reside in government.'[79] Put in simple terms, 'government teams concentrating skills in PPPs with the public administration are often called PPP units.'[80]

These dedicated units are entrusted with specific functions in PPP administration and regulation. They define PPP policies and processes and build the capacity of implementing agencies to follow the outlined processes. It is the responsibility of the PPP unit to prepare guidance documents and standard operating documents for PPPs within their jurisdiction. The PPP unit is responsible for promoting PPP both within the government and to members of the public. The staff are experts trained to provide technical support in implementing PPP projects. In addition, the PPP unit is charged with the task of gatekeeping, or reviewing and overseeing, the management of PPP projects to ensure efficiency and affordability. They play a role in the approval or non-approval of PPP projects and give advice on the approval process. It is possible to have more than one PPP unit performing different roles. This is, however,

78 Ibid 24.
79 OECD, *Dedicated Public-Private Partnership Units: A Survey of Institutional and Governance Structures* (Paris, France: OECD Publishing, 2010) 11.
80 PPP Knowledge Lab, 'Dedicated PPP Units' (2019) available at <https://pppknowledgelab.org/guide/sections/32-dedicated-ppp-units> accessed 18 November 2019.

not advisable, as multiple agencies do not only increase administrative costs but also upsurge the chance of having several government agencies playing overlapping roles.

In some countries, the PPP unit is a creation of law, and it does not matter what name it is known by. For example, in Nigeria, the Infrastructure Concession Regulatory Commission (Establishment Etc.) Act of 2005 created the Infrastructure Concession Regulatory Commission (ICRC), which is the country's PPP unit. In South Africa, the PPP Unit was established under the country's National Treasury in 2000. It is the lead agency for PPP in the country, and, apart from its regulatory function, the unit plays an important role in the development of the PPP market in South Africa. In India, the PPP unit is referred to as the PPP Cell in the Department of Economic Affairs (DEA). The PPP Cell was set up in 2006 and acts as the Secretariat for the PPP Appraisal Committee (PPPAC), Empowered Committee (EC), and Empowered Institution (EI) for the projects proposed for financial support through the Indian Viability Gap Fund (VGF). The PPP Cell is also responsible for policy-level matters concerning PPPs, including schemes, programmes, model concession agreements and capacity building.[81] In Brazil, the Federal PPP Project Unit is responsible for outlining the technical, economic and financial aspects of federal projects. The unit also performs feasibility studies and is a part of the Ministry of Planning.[82]

A review of international practice reveals that PPP units may sometimes be an independent government agency, like Nigeria's ICRC, or be part of a line ministry in the government, like the South African PPP Unit[83], the Indian PPP Cell[84] and the Brazilian PPP Project Unit.[85] What is important is that the units, by whatever name they are called, are to be regarded not just as regulators but also be PPP champions within their various jurisdictions. What remains to be stated is what role these units should play in PPPs arranged at the subnational levels. In Nigeria, Brazil and India, it is clear enough since these three are federations. Subnational governments have to create their distinct PPP units. In South Africa, however, the PPP Unit in the National Treasury performs the same functions for PPPs arranged at the provinces.[86]

81 Department of Economic Affairs, 'PPP Cell, Infrastructure Division' (2019) available at <www.pppinindia.gov.in/overview> accessed 18 November 2019.

82 Thiago Fernandes Moreira and Thiago Luís Sombra, 'Brazil' (2019) *The Public-Private Partnership Law Review – Edition 5* available at <https://thelawreviews.co.uk/edition/the-public-private-partnership-law-review-edition-5/1189691/brazil> accessed 18 November 2019.

83 Housed in the National Treasury.

84 Housed in the Department of Economic Affairs.

85 Housed in the Ministry of Planning.

86 Mark Dutz, Clive Harris, Inderbir Dhingra and Chris Shugart, 'Public-Private Partnership Units' (2006) *Public Policy for the Private Sector* available at <http://siteresources.worldbank.org/EXTFINANCIALSECTOR/Resources/282884-1303327122200/311Dutz_Harris_Dhingra_Shugart.pdf> accessed 18 November 2019.

2.8 Regulation of PPP contracts

In this subsection, the discussion focuses on the regulation of PPP contracts by an agency of government. Usually, this task is undertaken by the PPP unit in the jurisdiction concerned. Regulation is important for several reasons. First, it provides certainty. Secondly, it helps to sustain the PPP system and provides direction for all stakeholders involved.[87] It is worthy to note that PPPs may be regulated by contract without the need for a separate regulatory agency.[88] This approach is not suitable for emerging markets due to the fact that public-authority agencies that contract with the private sector are known to wield too much power. For example, the Federal Airports Authority of Nigeria (FAAN)[89] and Bi-Courtney Aviation Services Limited (BCASL), the concessionaire for the Murtala Mohammed Terminal II concession, have not had a smooth relationship due to the excessive powers that the governmental department exercises. Therefore, an independent regulator would be beneficial to assure investors that the government has the political will to ensure PPP success.

Another term for PPP regulation is PPP governance. This involves the establishment of a clear, predictable institutional framework that is supported by competent and well-resourced officials.[90] PPP regulation, or governance, must ensure that the process for awarding PPP contracts is transparent. Furthermore, the institutions of government in a PPP transaction should aim to achieve success. The authorities must be adequately prepared and ensure that PPP projects meet the VfM requirements and that the tender process is competitive. In line with a government's fiscal policy, it is vital that the central budget authority ensure that the project is affordable.[91]

Given the complex nature of PPP transactions, the public authorities in emerging economies need to ensure that their PPP units have the requisite in-depth financial, legal, economic and project-management skills to ensure that PPP deals are not only closed but also monitored to ensure performance.[92]

2.9 Resolution of PPP disputes

Due to the complex nature of PPP transactions, it is not uncommon for the parties to have disputes. The disputes may involve parties from a variety of legal,

87 Gonzalo Ruiz Diaz, 'The Contractual and Administrative Regulation of Public-Private Partnership' (2017) 48 *Utilities Policy* 109–121.

88 The World Bank Group, 'Regulation by Contract' (2016) available at <https://ppp.worldbank.org/public-private-partnership/regulation-contract> accessed 19 November 2019.

89 Which is the public authority responsible for the concession.

90 OECD, 'Recommendation of the Council on Principles for Public-Private Partnerships' (2012) available at <www.oecd.org/governance/budgeting/PPP-Recommendation.pdf> accessed 16 November 2019.

91 Ibid.

92 Ibid.

social and cultural backgrounds.[93] If a PPP is to succeed, it is paramount that dispute-resolution measures be put in place. In most cases, the private-sector partner will feel safer if an alternative dispute resolution (ADR) mechanism is put in place[94]. The legal basis for the settlement of disputes is an important consideration for PPP arrangements as well as for the implementation of PPP projects. Private parties (concessionaires, financiers and contractors) feel encouraged to participate in PPP projects when they have the assurance that the disputes between themselves and the governmental agency or other parties (for example, the service users of the facility) can be resolved fairly, efficiently and in a timely manner.[95]

It is vital for the legal system in an emerging economy to define a clear-cut policy framework for the resolution of PPP disputes. The framework must be such that it assures a fair return to investors and protects the interest of the users of the facilities, especially the poor. This is a prerequisite for a sound PPP regime.[96] Resorting to arbitration to resolve PPP disputes is ideal in the event of a misunderstanding or a conflict because of its flexibility and greater ease of award execution.[97] Generally, the cost of arbitration is cheaper than court proceedings. The proceedings in an arbitration are held in private, and the public, including rival companies, do not get access to potentially sensitive information. As a result, parties in an arbitration do not run the risk of any damaging publicity arising out of the proceedings.[98]

Furthermore, international arbitration awards can be enforced as if they were domestic awards under the New York Convention.[99] Even though a resort to litigation may occur, it is not recommendable because of the high cost involved and the long-term nature of PPPs. Litigation may also result in hostility and may smear the image of the parties. Other commonly used methods for dispute resolution include facilitated negotiation, where a facilitator is appointed by the parties in a contract to provide an opinion; conciliation and mediation, whereby a person or panel is appointed by the parties to provide independent and impartial assistance to help them resolve the dispute; adjudication by regulatory body, whereby matters of dispute may be referred to the regulatory authority if a statutory authority with powers to adjudicate upon disputes between the contracting government agency and the concessionaire exists.

93 Jeffrey Delmon, *op cit* (note 8) 8.
94 United Nations ESCAP, *A Guidebook on Public-Private Partnership in Infrastructure* (Bangkok: United Nations, 2011) 74.
95 Ibid.
96 KS Harisanker and G Sreeparvathy, 'Rethinking Dispute Resolution in Public-Private Partnerships for Infrastructure Development in India' (2013) 5(1) *Journal of Infrastructure Development* 21.
97 Jeffrey Delmon, *op cit* (note 8) 8.
98 Lucy Jones, *Introduction to Business Law* (Oxford: Oxford University Press, 2011) 36.
99 This is provided for by the United Nations Convention on the Enforcement of Arbitral Awards (1958) otherwise referred to as the "New York Convention."

2.9.1 The challenge with PPP disputes

PPPs involve large infrastructure projects with parties sometimes cutting across transnational boundaries. A failure to address issues arising from disputes can be counterproductive as well as devastating. Again, the question of jurisdiction poses a hard nut to crack. It is for this reason that the parties generally prefer to submit to arbitration considering its flexibility and ease of award execution. The parties may choose to instead refer disputes initially to mediation or negotiation.

2.9.2 The choice of law

It is noted that the governing law of contract will, to some extent, define the obligations of the parties and provide the basis for interpretation of their intent expressed in the contract.[100] However, the parties may, in the project agreements, define the laws that will be applicable in the event of a dispute. It may not be wise to subject the contract to multiple legal systems in order not to create a conflict-of-laws situation.

2.10 Protection for PPP assets

Investments in infrastructure assets provide a means of diversification for investors, especially given the volatility of equity investments.[101] It follows, therefore, that a system that makes comprehensive provision for the protection of invested assets, especially with regard to infrastructure market space, would attract the attention of investors. Again, since infrastructure assets are less liquid than traditional assets, and given the long duration of the investment, investors need to be reassured that they can recoup their investments and make a profit.

One of the ways to ensure investors' assets in PPPs are protected is to ensure that good governance measures are adopted. Governance in this sense relates to exercising political, economic and administrative authority to properly guide a nation's socio-economy.[102] Good governance as it relates to PPP connotes the sustenance of a healthy relationship between the public-sector institutions and the private sector, and between public institutions *inter se* in the administration and regulation of PPP. To achieve this, certain drivers have been identified, such as accountability and transparency on the part of public officials, political stability, the competence and effectiveness of public officials, the quality of regulation provided by the regulatory bodies, respect for the rule of law and the

100 Ibid 154.

101 Oluwaseun Oluwasanmi, 'Public Private Partnership and Nigerian Economic Growth: Problems and Prospects' (2014) 5(11) *International Journal of Business and Social Science* 139.

102 United Nations Economic Commission for Europe (UNECE), *Governance in Public Private Partnerships for Infrastructure Development* (Geneva: UNECE, 2004) 4.

sanctity of contract and control of corruption.[103] Promoting good governance will therefore provide prospective investors with the assurance that their assets are protected.

Furthermore, the government must be willing to provide guarantees for projects to give lenders the confidence they need. For example, Bi-Courtney Highway Services Limited, a company that won a Nigerian bid to rehabilitate the Lagos-Ibadan Expressway, failed to convince any lender to fund the project in the absence of a guarantee from the federal government of Nigeria.

2.11 Conclusion

Although it is possible to arrange PPPs independent of a formal PPP framework, i.e. before the formal PPP framework has been established, the formation of a dedicated PPP framework indicates that the government is committed to PPP success. As discussed in this chapter, a PPP framework must provide clarity and uniformity in the PPP process. The framework includes the policy, the legal framework, the institutional framework and the regulatory mechanism put in place to ensure that there is a successful PPP regime.

Furthermore, it is important for emerging economies to put in place a legal framework for PPP. The fundamental requirements for the establishment of an efficient PPP framework must be assured. First, the government must articulate its intent to utilise PPP in the procurement of infrastructure in the form of a policy. Second, there is a need to ensure that the legal framework enables the government to enter PPPs. The laws must set out how a PPP is to be undertaken. Third, there must be in place an institutional framework for the administration and regulation of PPP. In most cases, a PPP unit must be created.

The chapter highlighted the need to ensure regulation of PPP by setting up an independent entity rather than by the sole regulation of contracts. The advantages of using an independent public agency as a regulator include the ability to wane the powers of the public institution, thereby creating a level playing field for the contracting institution and the private-sector partners.

Dispute resolution was another important aspect considered in this chapter. The lack of a clear-cut dispute resolution mechanism for PPP transactions in any jurisdiction is akin to planning to fail from the start. The reason is because PPPs are highly complex infrastructure transactions and are susceptible to conflicts. The parties also need to be assured that conflicts will be resolved as inexpensively as possible.

A discussion on the need to provide protection for investors' assets in PPPs rounds off the discussion on PPP framework. The next chapter will examine the PPP contract from needs assessment to tendering and contract award.

103 Ibid.

References

Agrawal, A. (2019, July 12). PolicyNext: How to Improve India's Policy-Making Processes. Retrieved from www.medianama.com/2019/07/223-policynext-how-to-improve-indias-policy-making-processes/.

Amann, E., Baer, W., Trebat, T., & Lora, J. V. (2016). Infrastructure and Its Role in Brazil's Development Process. *The Quarterly Review of Economics and Finance, 62*, 66–73. doi:10.1016/j.qref.2016.07.007.

Arimoro, A. E. (2019). Institutional Framework for Public-Private Partnerships in Nigeria: Is It a Case of Too Many Cooks for One Pot of Broth? *Business Law Review, 40*(2), 73–79.

Beyene, T. T. (2015). Policy, Legal, and Institutional Frameworks for PPP Implementation in Development Process: Stakeholders' Perspective. *China-USA Business Review, 14*(3). doi:10.17265/1537–1514/2015.03.003.

Cheung, E., Chan, A. P., Lam, P. T., Chan, D. W., & Ke, Y. (2012). A Comparative Study of Critical Success Factors for Public Private Partnerships (PPP) Between Mainland China and the Hong Kong Special Administrative Region. *Facilities, 30*(13/14), 647–666. doi:10.1108/02632771211273132.

Delmon, J. (2014). *Creating a Framework for Public-Private Partnership (PPP) Programs: A Practical Guide for Decision Makers*. Washington, DC: The World Bank.

Department of Economic Affairs. (2019). PPP Cell. Retrieved from www.pppinindia.gov.in/overview.

Dutz, M., Harris, C., Dhingra, I., & Shugart, C. (2019). Brazil – The Public-Private Partnership Law Review – Edition 5 – TLR. Retrieved from https://thelawreviews.co.uk/edition/the-public-private-partnership-law-review-edition-5/1189691/brazil.

Economic and Social Commission for Asia and the Pacific. (2017). PPP Policy, Legal and Institutional Frameworks in Asia and the Pacific. Retrieved from https://www.unescap.org/sites/default/files/PPP%20Policy-Legal-Institutional%20Frameworks_2017.pdf.

Fombad, M. (2013). Accountability Challenges in Public-Private Partnerships from a South African Perspective. *African Journal of Business Ethics*, 7(1), 11. doi:10.4103/1817-7417.119954.

Friel, D. (2017). Understanding Institutions: Different Paradigms, Different Conclusions. *Revista de Administração, 52*(2), 212–214. doi:10.1016/j.rausp.2016.12.001.

Gumede, V. (2008). Public Policy Making in a Post-Apartheid South Africa: A Preliminary Perspective. *Africanus, 38*(2), 7–23.

The Institute for Public-Private Partnerships Inc. (2007). *Development of Policy, Legal, and Institutional Framework for the Public-Private Partnership Program in Malawi*. Washington, DC: The Institute for Public-Private Partnerships.

John, P. (1998). *Analysing Public Policy*. London: A&C Black.

Jones, L. (2011). *Introduction to Business Law*. Oxford: Oxford University Press.

Joseph, R. (2010). Challenges of a Frontier Region. In L. Diamond & M. F. Plattner (Eds.), *Democratization in Africa: Progress and Retreat*. Baltimore, MD: JHU Press.

Kelly, P. (2016). *Preparing a Public-Private Partnership Law: Observations from the International Experience*. Manila: Asian Development Bank.

Knill, C., & Tosun, J. (2008). Policy Making. In *Comparative Politics*. New York, NY: Oxford University Press.

National Treasury PPP Unit. (2007). *Introducing Public Private Partnerships in South Africa*. Pretoria: National Treasury PPP Unit.

OECD. (2010). *Dedicated Public-Private Partnership Units A Survey of Institutional and Governance Structures: A Survey of Institutional and Governance Structures*. Paris, France: OECD Publishing.

Oluwasanmi, O. (2014). Public Private Partnership and Nigerian Economic Growth: Problems and Prospects. *International Journal of Business and Social Science, 5*(11), 139.

Philip, D.D. (n.d.). Public Policy Making and Implementation in Nigeria: Connecting the Nexus. *Public Policy and Administration Research, 3*(6), 56.

Policy, C.I., & Torjman, S. (2005). *What Is Policy? [Electronic Resource].* Ottawa: Caledon Institute of Social Policy.

PPP Knowledge Lab. (2019). Dedicated PPP Units. Retrieved from https://pppknowledgelab.org/guide/sections/32-dedicated-ppp-units.

Puri, A. (2017, August 29). Policy Making in India: Who's Behind It? Retrieved from https://nationalinterest.in/policy-making-in-india-whos-behind-it-4fd2f6255714.

Ruiz Diaz, G. (2017). The Contractual and Administrative Regulation of Public-Private Partnership. *Utilities Policy, 48*, 109–121. doi:10.1016/j.jup.2016.04.011.

Schmidt, V. (2010). Give Peace a Chance: Reconciling Four (Not Three) "New Institutionalisms". In D. Beland & R.H. Cox (Eds.), *Ideas and Politics in Social Science Research.* New York, NY: Oxford University Press.

Singh, R. (2014). Civil Society and Policymaking in India: In Search of Democratic Spaces. Retrieved from www.oxfamindia.org/sites/default/files/WP7-Civil-Scty-n-plcy-mkg-in-India.pdf.

Tijani, H.O. (n.d.). Globalisation, Institution and Public Private Partnership: The Nigerian Experience. *Journal of Law, Policy and Globalisation, 43*, 4.

Tina Dacin, M., Goodstein, J., & Richard Scott, W. (2002). Institutional Theory and Institutional Change: Introduction to the Special Research Forum. *Academy of Management Journal, 45*(1), 45–56. doi:10.5465/amj.2002.6283388.

The United Nations. (2017, October 23). World Population Projected to Reach 9.8 Billion in 2050, and 11.2 Billion in 2100. Retrieved from www.un.org/development/desa/en/news/population/world-population-prospects-2017.html.

United Nations Commission on International Trade Law. (2001). *UNCITRAL Legislative Guide on Privately Financed Infrastructure Projects.* New York, NY: United Nations Publications.

United Nations Economic Commission for Europe. (2004). *Governance in Public Private Partnerships for Infrastructure Development.* UNECE.

United Nations. Economic Commission for Europe. (2008). *Guidebook on Promoting Good Governance in Public-Private Partnerships.* New York, NY: United Nations Publications.

United Nations ESCAP. (n.d.). *A Guidebook on Public-Private Partnership in Infrastructure.* United Nations.

Van den Hurk, M., & Verhoest, K. (2015). The Governance of Public – Private Partnerships in Sports Infrastructure: Interfering Complexities in Belgium. *International Journal of Project Management, 33*(1), 201–211. doi:10.1016/j.ijproman.2014.05.005.

Vji, S. (2014, August 7). Land Acquisition, Lack of Fund Among Bottlenecks for PPP Projects. Retrieved from https://economictimes.indiatimes.com/news/economy/infrastructure/land-acquisition-lack-of-fund-among-bottlenecks-for-ppp-projects/articleshow/39822989.cms.

Weingast, B.R. (2008). Why Developing Countries Prove So Resistant to the Rule of Law. Retrieved from http://jenni.uchicago.edu/WJP/Vienna_2008/Weingast_ROL_MS_2%2000_08-0519.pdf.

The World Bank. (2014). *Public-Private Partnerships Reference Guide Version 2.0.* Washington, DC: Author.

The World Bank. (2016). Regulation by Contract. Retrieved from https://ppp.worldbank.org/public-private-partnership/regulation-contract.

3 The public-private partnership contract

3.1 Introduction

The PPP contract is a specialised form of contract, as it is made up of not just the main 'concession' or 'PFI' but also includes other sub-contracts, including engineering, procurement and construction, supplies, operation/management services and repairs.[1] PPP contracts are complex and usually long term. The main contract is usually signed between the public authority and the concessionaire or project company. For the project company to execute the project, other sub-contracts are necessary, for example, a contract between the project company and another party for the supply of materials or a contract between the concessionaire and a management company to manage and operate the completed facility.

For the purpose of clarity, it needs to be emphasised here that the term 'partnership' used in a PPP does not mean that the arrangement works like a typical business partnership since the parties have different interests.[2] The interest of the public sector is to provide infrastructure for its citizens, whereas that of the private-sector consortium is to make a profit. PPP contracts, therefore, codify the business relationship by defining the roles and responsibilities of the partners, including risk sharing and rewards.[3] Drafting a PPP contract to be signed by the government and a private-sector consortium is a challenging task that requires legal and technical expertise.[4]

In this chapter, to clearly understand how the PPP contract operates, the discussion begins with the procurement phase of a PPP project. This starts the moment the project is conceived by the public authority. The assumption here

1 ER Yescombe, *Public-Private Partnerships: Principles of Policy and Finance* (Amsterdam, Netherlands: Elsevier, 2007) 7.

2 G Noble, 'The Role of Contracts in Public Private Partnership' (2006) *University of Wollongong Research Online* available at <http://ro.uow.edu.au/cgi/viewcontent.cgi?article=1599&context=commpapers> accessed 18 March 2018.

3 Ibid.

4 Rui Cunha Marques, 'Public-Private Partnership Contracts: A Tale of Two Cities with Different Contractual Arrangements' (2010) available at <http://bear.warrington.ufl.edu/centers/purc/docs/papers/0915_Marques_Public_Private_Partnership.pdf> accessed 15 March 2018.

is that the project in question has passed the three viability tests mentioned in the previous chapter. These are the affordability of the project, the project satisfies the VfM requirements and the appropriate risks can be transferred. When these requirements are satisfactorily met, then depending on the legal framework applicable in the jurisdiction in question, approvals may be sought for the project. Following the approval, the procuring agency may then advertise for bids. When the right bid is chosen and a consortium is selected, a PPP contract is signed. This is the focus of the discussion in this chapter. The chapter then concludes with a discussion on the sanctity of PPP contracts and the need for all parties to be bound by the agreements that have been reached.

3.2 The PPP procurement process

Starting off a discussion on PPP contracts with the procurement process provides a background to the way a PPP contract is structured. The aim here is to draw the reader's attention to the preliminary processes involved in structuring PPP contracts.

Cheung has identified four key parties to every PPP contractual arrangement.[5] They include:

- The public sector authority;
- The consortium, that is, the private-sector partner(s) of the project;
- The staff employed by the project; and
- The public, or the end users of the facility.

In a traditional PPP setting, the government is usually more concerned with transferring the risk associated with the design, construction, management and operation to the private sector and satisfying the needs of the public.[6] The consortium, for its part, is usually motivated by profits and hence will be willing to accept some risk.[7] It is submitted, however, that project failures can occur where the intention of the government is merely to transfer risk and utterly neglect its responsibility to the public simply because it considers PPP a one-stop solution or, on the other hand, when the private-sector consortium is only driven by the need to increase profit margins. It is understandable that the private sector is in business to make profits in the first place and would not commit funds or source for finance for an unprofitable venture. It is imperative that both the private sector and the public sector must be 'partners' in a PPP arrangement to ensure successful outcomes. The employees of the project are those who work for the consortium. The success of the project ensures that they remain employed, and their commitment to the work ensures that the project is carried

5 Esther Cheung, 'Developing a Best Practice Framework for Implementing Public Private Partnerships (PPP) in Hong Kong' (Unpublished PhD Thesis, Queensland University of Technology, 2009) 46.

6 Ibid.

7 Ibid.

out on schedule. Thus, they are important stakeholders in any PPP project. The end users are members of the public who benefit from the project. Their opinion and buy-in is crucial to the success of any project. It is important that they also be considered as stakeholders, even at the initiation phase.

Delmon[8] names the key parties to a PPP contract as the following:

1 The grantor: the public authority (national or local government, agency or some regulatory authority);
2 The project company: the sponsors who identify a project. The private investors typically set up a new company (project company), which is usually a limited-liability special purpose vehicle (SPV);
3 The lenders: usually a group of commercial banks, development banks or even infrastructure funds;
4 Multilateral agencies, such as the World Bank or other international organisations;
5 Export Credit Agencies (ECAs): entities set up by countries to encourage the export of goods and services by their nationals;
6 Offtake Purchaser (OP): guarantees to purchase the use of the project at take-off. This may be the government or an agency of the government;
7 Input Supplier (IS): assumes supply risk for the input necessary for the operation of the project;
8 The construction contractor: designs, builds, tests and commissions the project. It is not the SPV. The responsibility of the construction contractor is similar to that of a private contractor in a traditional public-procurement contract; and
9 The operator: operates and maintains the project over an extended period. It is responsible for the day-to-day running and management of the facility in the operational phase of the PPP contract.

The parties mentioned here are among the wide variety of stakeholders in any given PPP arrangement. In addition, state policymakers, legislators who create the legal environment and equity investors or institutional investors that provide pension and infrastructure funds are important players in successful PPP projects.[9]

3.2.1 The stages of a PPP project

Generally, PPP projects evolve through a series of stages, culminating in the operation and service phase. The various stages include:

8 Jeffrey Delmon, *Public-Private Partnership Projects in Infrastructure: An Essential Guide for Policy Makers* (Cambridge: Cambridge University Press, 2011) 23.

9 Baruch Feigenbaum, 'Risk and Rewards of Public-Private Partnerships for Highways' (2011) (98) *Reason Foundation Policy Brief* 3 available at <http://reason.org/files/public_private_partnerships_for_highways.pdf> accessed 1 July 2017.

Needs assessment/analysis

At the initial stage, the public sector identifies the need for an infrastructure facility. This is usually done in the form of a cost-benefit analysis. At this point, the public sector considers what means it has for financing the project and whether or not it is affordable and viable. It is important at this stage to analyse the political, legal and social factors that affect the project.[10]

Preparation and conception

If the analysis confirms the requirement of the PPP option as more suitable than traditional procurement for the provision of the project, preparations are then carried out to enable the take-off of a PPP.[11]

Tendering process and contract award

Upon confirmation of the suitability of PPP for a project, the government decides what procurement procedure to follow based on extant applicable laws. Typically, the government will employ competitive tendering, which would include output specifications as to the infrastructure facility and the length and terms of the PPP contract in the invitation to tender. Prospective sponsors, normally acting as a consortium, carry out feasibility studies and prepare their bids. It is the public sector's responsibility to evaluate the bids and then compile a list of final bidders for negotiation, during which further terms are discussed and after which the bidder that best conforms to the award criteria is selected.[12]

Implementation and contract management

Under this stage, the PPP contract is implemented. The facility is completed and becomes operational. Usually, the project company engages a service company to manage the day-to-day operations of the facility. Upon the award of the contract and the financial close of the PPP project, contract management can be of two types:[13]

1 Ensuring the project company is in line with the regulatory and legal provisions of the sector and the country; and
2 Technical monitoring of the project to ensure that key terms and performance indicators are met.

10 Hans Wilheim Alfen (ed.), *Public-Private Partnership in Infrastructure Development* (Weimar: Bauhaus-Universitat, 2009) 19.

11 Ibid.

12 Ibid.

13 HK Yong, *Public-Private Partnerships Policy and Practice: A Reference Guide* (London: Commonwealth Secretariat, 2010) 48.

It is also possible that the contract may be renegotiated because of a lack of compliance with the agreed-upon terms and/or a deviation from the expected promises of sector improvements, for example, where a government or the private-sector consortium fails to honour contractual terms, or in a case where there is a need to alter the design of the project.[14] Therefore, PPP plans must be well thought-out, and the advice of experts should be sought before contracts are concluded to avoid the inconvenience of having to renegotiate contracts and the delays this may cause to the project.

Contract termination

The final stage of any PPP project is the contract termination phase. At termination, the facility is to be transferred to the government, usually for nil or nominal consideration, in accordance with the terms of the agreement.[15] The transfer is an important element in a PPP because, even though the government transfers the ownership in the facility to the consortium during the lifetime of the PPP contract, it is not a divesture of the interest of the government in the facility, as is the case with privatisation.

3.3 The elements of a PPP contract

Under the concession/PFI agreement, the grantor gives a series of rights to the project company to build and operate a unit or feature of government infrastructure for a determined tenure. The main issues to be addressed in a PPP contract are the start and completion dates for the project. Governments, particularly in emerging economies, are often motivated by political interest associated with the completion of the project during that government's term of office.

It is important that the concession/PFI contract itself makes provisions for elements such as the obligations of each party; the tenure of the contract; the ownership of the land and facility; the allocation of risks and consequences; the construction, commissioning, operation and maintenance of the facility; performance requirements; payments and other financial matters; price review adjustments; amendments and variations of the agreement; monitoring and review; dispute resolution; termination of the contract; end-of-term arrangements; service delivery management; contract compliance and management renegotiation.[16]

Following a request from member countries of the Group of 20 (G20),[17] staff at the World Bank were mandated to prepare a report recommending a model

14 Ibid 50.

15 Ibid 19.

16 Economic and Social Commission for Asia and the Pacific, 'Main Contents of a Contract Agreement' (2008) available at <www.unescap.org/ttdw/ppp/ppp_primer/711_main_contents_of_a_contract_agreement.html> accessed 18 March 2018.

17 A group consisting of 19 countries plus the European Union (EU). South Africa is a member of the group.

language for PPP contracts.[18] The outcome of the exercise was a number of key 'Model Contract Terms' (MCTs), set out under eight headings, namely, force majeure, Material Adverse Government Action, change in law, termination payments, refinancing, lenders' step-in rights, confidentiality and transparency and dispute resolution.[19] These new or 're-modelled' terms introduced in the report by Shrybman and Sinclair are discussed next.

Where there are circumstances beyond the control of the parties to the PPP contract, making it impossible for the contract to be executed or for the parties to fulfil their obligations under the PPP contract – for example, political events such as war, acts of terror, nuclear explosions and natural disasters (such as earthquakes, floods, landlines), strikes and protests – a *force majeure* occurs. In the World Bank Group's (WBG) recommendation, general labour disturbances, such as boycotts and strikes, which are unique to the private-sector partner or sub-contractors and occur outside the country do not constitute a *force majeure* but a default by the private partner.[20] The implication of this is that if there is a failure on the part of the private sector to fulfil its obligation(s) as a result of strike action outside the host country of the PPP project, the private partner bears the risk and will be considered in default of the contractual agreement. This is a departure from the conventional norm and ought not to be the case. Implementing such a proposal will stifle private-sector interest in PPPs, especially in countries that do not have a significant market advantage.

The WBG's proposal identifies what is referred to as a *Material Adverse Government Action* (MAGA).[21] A MAGA event occurs when there is an act or omission by the contracting authority, or any relevant public authority, which occurs during the term of the contract and which renders the private partner incapable of complying with the terms of the agreement. In a MAGA event, the private-sector partner shall be excused from the performance of the PPP contract to the extent that it is prevented, hindered or delayed in the performance of its obligations by reason of the MAGA and shall be entitled to compensation under the PPP contract. This new proposed term is commendable, but the question of what should constitute adequate compensation needs to be carefully considered. It is better that the public authority refrain from committing any MAGA, unless it is necessary and in the interest of public policy. The reason is that one failed PPP project is a message to PPP investors and promoters that any future dealings with the public authority concerned is vulnerable to cancellation.

Based on the recommendations by the WBG, a *change in law* that can affect a PPP contract occurs when any new applicable law is enacted; an existing

18 Steven Shrybman and Scott Sinclair, *A Standard Contract for PPPs the World Over: Recommended PPP Contractual Provisions Submitted to G20* (Washington, DC: The World Bank, 2016) 7.

19 Ibid 10.

20 Ibid 14.

21 Report 2.2(3).

applicable law is repealed, modified or re-enacted; any government entity imposes any material condition in connection with the issuance, renewal, modification, revocation or non-renewal (other than in accordance with the existing applicable law) of any approval; and/or taxes, which were not foreseeable at the time the successful bidder submitted its bid and which have a material adverse effect on the ability of a party in a PPP contract to fulfil its obligations, are levied. The WBG recommends that the public sector should bear a change in law risk only when it is the author of discriminatory reforms, in which case the private sector should be compensated to leave the latter in no better nor worse position than it would have been had such a law not been made.

This recommendation is also flawed. It seems that the WBG has not considered the nature of developing and emerging economies before making this recommendation. The situation that the proposal enables may just afford the public authority the room to cleverly absolve itself of its obligations by passing a new law that affects the project while claiming that it is not discriminatory.

With reference to *termination payments*, the WBG recommendation is in line with conventional norms. Thus, when the public authority voluntarily terminates the PPP contract, for reasons of public policy, for example, the private-sector party is to be compensated. Also, where the public authority, by way of default, makes it impracticable for the private-sector party to perform its obligation(s), the public authority is to pay the private party compensation to ensure that the latter is left in no better nor worse condition than it would have been had the early termination not occurred. While this insertion in the proposals is commendable and ensures the protection of the assets of the investors/lenders, it is important to state that a private-sector investor will appreciate and derive more satisfaction from a completed project executed from a business point of view than from receiving compensation for default by the contracting authority. No matter the amount paid out as compensation, it cannot compare with successfully completing a project and receiving what is due.[22] Therefore, the fact that compensation can be paid or that a buy-back can be structured should not constitute sufficient reason to cancel a project.

With regard to *dispute resolution*, the WBG proposes a reliance on the World Bank's Investor-State Dispute Settlement (ISDS) procedure.[23] The report proposes the following steps for the resolution of PPP disputes: first, a mutual commitment to try to resolve the disagreement promptly and amicably; second,

22 The buy-back of Lekki-Epe Toll Road Concession by the Lagos State Government of NIgeria, is a good example.

23 In accordance with the Proposed Dispute Settlement Provision. The ISDS system itself relies on the ratification of treaties. Many developing countries consider that the ISDS is biased in favour of investors, especially from developed countries, at the expense of public policy and democratic governance. This situation has led many developing countries to limit their exposure to ISDS. For example, Brazil has never ratified any treaty that included ISDS. South Africa also, intends to end the use of ISDS in its trade and investments treaties. See Steven Shrybman and Scott Sinclair, *op cit* (note 18) 21.

an agreement that technical disputes be referred to an expert to recommend solution; and third, that more intractable issues be brought before a dispute board comprised of representatives of both parties, which may be empowered to reach a binding resolution through consensus. The proposal notes that, given 'the time and the cost of international arbitration, serious consideration should be given to the use of mandatory alternative dispute resolution mechanisms (such as the dispute boards).'[24] The report proposes further that, if the board fails to resolve the dispute within 30 days, the dispute shall be referred to and finally settled by international arbitration.[25] Unfortunately, this recommendation clearly seeks to sideline the domestic courts of emerging and developing countries.[26] One of the first investor-state disputes that attracted global interest was that of *Aguas del Tunari v Bolivia*.[27] In that case, the government of Bolivia cancelled a water-services concession on the grounds of price hikes that triggered public protests. The concessionaire subsequently sued under a Bolivia-Netherlands investment treaty.[28] In its defence, the Bolivian government argued that the concession agreement provided for disputes between public authorities and the concessionaire to be resolved 'in Bolivian courts in accordance with Bolivian laws.'[29] The tribunal rejected this defence and ruled that the 'forum selection' clause in the concession agreement was unclear and, in its place, asserted that it had jurisdiction over the claim. Clearly, there needs to be a balance between the protection of investors' assets and the public policy of a state. Furthermore, if emerging and developing economies can improve on their rule-of-law index, investors will gain confidence that domestic courts can be objective and fair in their decisions.

3.3.1 The concession agreement

Under this agreement, the public-sector authority (grantor) grants a concession to the project company or SPV to build and operate a public infrastructure for a predetermined (concession) period. The agreement should also set out the legal and tax regimes applicable to the project. To enter this agreement, the grantor must have the backing of the law to do so. The grantor's act must thus be *intra vires*. Where the granting authority acts without a legal right to do so

24 Proposed Dispute Settlement Provision S. 8.2, Article 23, 52.

25 Ibid.

26 Steven Shrybman and Scott Sinclair, *op cit* (note 18) 23.

27 *Aguas del Tunari SA, Claimant/Investor v Republic of Bolivia* ICSID Case No ARB/02/3 available at <www.iiapp.org/media/uploads/aguas_del_tunari_v_bolivia.rev.pdf> accessed 18 March 2018.

28 It emerged during arbitration that, prior to bringing its claim as public opposition was developing, the foreign investor 'migrated' corporate ownership of the privatised assets from the Cayman Islands to the Netherlands to have access to the Netherlands-Bolivia BIT International Investment Arbitration and Public Policy. *Aguas del Tunari v Bolivia* supra. Case summary available at <www.iiapp.org/media/uploads/aguas_del_tunari_v_bolivia.rev.pdf> accessed 18 March 2018.

29 *Aguas del Tunari v Bolivia* supra. 'Decision on Respondent's Objections to Jurisdiction' 21.

(*ultra vires*), the agreement may not be enforceable on grounds of illegality. In current practice, the concession agreement, the offtake purchase agreement, and/or the input supply can be combined in one agreement.[30]

The contents of the concession agreement would generally contain the following elements[31]:

1 Completion date: the public authority's need for the facility is usually immediate because of political factors;
2 Condition of assets: if there are existing assets being transferred, their condition should be stated;
3 Construction and operation: the project company must meet up with certain minimum standards;
4 Government guarantees: the government may give guarantees to public-sector bodies taking part in the concession;
5 Performance of the project: this should cover maintenance needs and costs, operation, health and safety and environmental issues;
6 Maintenance regime: this is to ensure that the facility is efficiently maintained during the concession; and
7 Exclusivity: the project company may want to maintain some exclusive rights.

3.3.2 Sub-contracts

As mentioned earlier, apart from the concession or PFI agreement between the public authority and the private project company, there are a number of other sub-contracts that must be entered into for a PPP project to be concluded.

Offtake purchase agreement

This element of the PPP contract allocates the market risk of demand and the price for project output to the offtake purchaser(s), usually one or more public-service providers. This agreement defines and delimits the revenue stream to be received by the SPV.[32]

The input supply agreement

It may be that the PPP project requires some form of input for its operation, for example, power supply, fuel or water. The SPV may not want to bear the risk of the unavailability of the input when required and at the appropriate

30 Jeffrey Delmon, *op cit* (note 8) 119.
31 Ibid.
32 Ibid 123.

price. Therefore, the SPV will often enter a contract with an input supplier to provide the necessary input. Key highlights in the agreement would include elements such as price; quality, quantity and timing; duration; transport; testing and inspection.

The construction contract

In practice, the SPV will allocate the task of designing and building the project to a construction contractor. The construction contract would define the responsibilities of the construction contractor and the SPV vis-à-vis the PPP project. The construction stage of the project is usually regulated by a turnkey (meaning that, upon completion, one only needs to 'turn the key' to commence operation of the facility) construction contract, referred to as the D&B (Design and Build). It may also be possible to have several turnkey contracts for the same PPP project, depending on the nature of the project itself. The key elements in the construction contract should include the following: time for completion, construction price, performance risk, site conditions and defects liability.

The operation and maintenance agreement

Upon the completion of the construction, the SPV will be required to maintain the facility during the tenure of the concession. This function will involve managing the operation of the facility, providing maintenance and developing a relationship with the offtake purchaser where necessary. The key elements of the O&M agreement include: performance risk, operating cost and public face of services (i.e. the relationship between the operator, its employees and the end users).

The financing agreement

This agreement details the terms and conditions pursuant to which the lenders accept to lend funds to the SPV set up for the project. The lenders may include commercial banks,[33] export credit agencies (ECAs), bondholders, multilateral lending institutions (MLIs) and bilateral lending institutions. The lenders are responsible for the financing of a substantial portion of the project and are therefore very influential in the drafting of such agreements involved in the BOT project to ensure the project's bankability.

The Shareholders Agreement

The Shareholders' Agreement (SHA) contains the terms binding the SPV and its shareholders. It involves several documents, for example, a sponsor's

33 For example, StanbicIBTC and First Bank of Nigeria Plc are among the lenders to the Lekki Concession Company (LCC), the SPV set up for the Lekki-Epe Toll Road Concession Project.

agreement for the pre-financial close, joint venture agreement (JVA), memorandum and articles of association (MEMAT), shareholder loan, standby equity and other similar documentation. The SHA would usually contain the terms regarding the business of the SPV, the conditions precedent to its creation, the procedure for issuing new shares, the allocation of project costs and the management of the project company, including decision-making and voting. The agreement may as well include non-competition clauses to preclude shareholders from entering activities of the same kind either directly or indirectly that are in competition with the SPV.

Hedging arrangements

It is possible to share some financial risk through instruments such as derivatives, swaps, future contracts or hedging. These arrangements, complex as they are, require a party to compensate the other in the event of a specified risk in exchange for a fee. It is also possible for the parties to swap risk with each party compensating the other. An example is the exposure to foreign-exchange risk. This can be mitigated by swapping currency requirements with another market participant or by an agreement to buy one currency at a fixed price in another currency at a future date. Derivatives could then be used to manage interest rates.[34]

Insurance arrangements

All parties involved in the project are required in practice to provide insurance for the project. More importantly, the SPV needs to ensure comprehensive insurance coverage for the entire project itself. This is to avoid a gap in insurance coverage.[35] The following insurance coverage would be ideal for a PPP project:

1 Materials and equipment required for the project during transportation from the manufacturer to the site;
2 All operations and assets on the site;
3 Professional indemnity for the design;
4 All operational damage risk;
5 Third-party liability risk for a claim made by a third party for the acts or omissions of the SPV or any of the contractors or subcontractors to the project;
6 Consequential losses emanating from delayed start-up, loss of profit and business-interruption insurance;
7 Automobile policy for all operational vehicles;
8 Workers' compensation/employer's insurance; and
9 Directors' and officers' liability.[36]

34 Jeffrey Delmon, *op cit* (note 8) 144.
35 Ibid.
36 Ibid 147.

3.4 Designing the main concession or PFI contract

The main concession or PFI contract defines the relationship between the parties and describes their rights and responsibilities, allocating risk and providing mechanisms for dealing with any change that may be required.[37] It is important in determining the tenure of the contract that recourse is had regarding the need for the private consortium to adopt a whole-life costing approach to the project design, service management and guaranteeing service performance at the lowest cost. Usually, a PPP project's contractual term is around 20 to 30 years, depending on the nature of the project.

The key commercial terms to be included in the contract must be clear for all the parties involved. A good draft should define the following:

1 The performance requirements;
2 The payment mechanisms;
3 How tolls and charges can be adjusted;
4 Provisions for a dispute resolution mechanism in the event of a conflict; and
5 The terminal date of the contract.

The need for the PPP contract to be as clear as possible cannot be overemphasised, as this would save all parties from making assumptions regarding their respective roles. For example, a PPP contract between the federal government of Nigeria and Bi-Courtney Highway Services Limited failed to explicitly define the role of the concessionaire and that of the grantor, which ultimately contributed to the failure of the project. In the end, while Bi-Courtney Highway Services Limited considered itself merely as a facilitator with regard to project finance, the federal government expected Bi-Courtney to provide funding for the project.[38]

It is key that the contract enumerates the very important parts that will make the PPP project successful. First, the performance requirements (i.e. the required quality and quantity of assets and services in addition to monitoring and enforcement mechanisms) must be stated. This may include penalties. Second, the payment mechanism must be defined. How will the project company recoup its investments? This may be through the payment of tolls or charges. It must also be stated whether the end users or the government are responsible for the payments. It may be possible to have a combination of both.[39] Third, the method for resolving disputes and, finally, the procedure for termination of the contract, including handover provisions for the facility. It is noteworthy that some countries have made efforts to design standard PPP contract templates to have some degree of uniformity.

37 PPP Knowledge Lab, 'Designing PPP Contracts' (2019) available at <https://pppknowledgelab.org/guide/sections/61-designing-ppp-contracts> accessed 18 November 2019.
38 Further discussion on this is contained in the Chapter Six on Nigeria.
39 PPP Knowledge Lab, *op cit* (note 37).

It is advisable to consider including clauses dealing with the following in a PPP contract:[40]

1 Performance requirements and performance-management issues;
2 Contract breaches, a penalty system and default events;
3 Events that give rise to compensation and balancing regulations;
4 Financially related provisions, such as financial structure, minimum/maximum equity and leverage, refinancing, ownership, insurance requirements and early termination; and
5 Hand-back provisions.

As much as possible, it is better for the concession contract to cover as much ground as possible in a manner devoid of ambiguity. The items listed by the Economic and Social Commission for Asia and the Pacific may serve as a guide for emerging markets. They list the following items to be included in a PPP contract:[41]

- Obligations of parties to the agreement (the private party, the contract awarding agency and the government)
- Tenure of contract and access rights to the project site
- Ownership of land and facility
- Sector specific special issues
- Allocation of risks (and consequences)
- Construction, commissioning, operation and maintenance of the facility
- Performance requirements (service delivery and other technical, quality and safety standards)
- Availability of contracted services and procedures for variations of service scope
- Payment and other financial matters (including penalties for failure to meet performance requirements)
- Price review and adjustments
- Step-in rights (of the government, financiers)
- Insurance
- Change in service requirements
- Upgrading and technological obsolescence
- Amendment and variation of agreement
- Monitoring and review (including data collection, compilation and reporting)

40 APMG International, 'Main Contents of the Contract: Rights, Obligations and Framework to Govern Changes and Risk' (2019) available at <https://ppp-certification.com/ppp-certification-guide/91-main-contents-contract-rights-obligations-and-framework-govern-changes> accessed 18 November 2019.

41 Economic and Social Commission for Asia and the Pacific (ESCAP), 'Main Contents of a Contract Agreement' (2008) available at <www.unescap.org/ttdw/ppp/ppp_primer/711_main_contents_of_a_contract_agreement.html> accessed 18 November 2019.

- Contingency planning
- Dispute resolution
- Termination of the contract
- End of term arrangements
- Service delivery management
- Contract compliance and management
- Renegotiation

A key purpose of a PPP contract is to use it to identify and allocate the risks involved with the delivery of the facility for use by the public. The clauses will address how such risks are to be managed between the grantor and the project company.[42]

3.5 PPP arrangements and sanctity of contract

A PPP is unique in the sense that it represents a contract between a private party and the public authority. Given that the government or public agencies are always the dominant partners in PPP arrangements, a discussion on the concept of sanctity of contract as it relates to PPP is important. This is more so as governments in emerging markets struggle to submit to the rule of law and the need to respect agreements. In Anglo-American common law, like in India and Nigeria, formation of a contract generally requires an offer, acceptance, consideration and mutual intent for the parties to enter legal relations and be bound thereby. In civil law jurisdictions, such as in Brazil and South Africa, contract law is a branch of the law of obligations.

In the first place, a contract is 'an agreement made between two or more parties which is legally binding on them.'[43] It is an agreement enforceable by the law, between two or more parties, to do or to abstain from doing some act or acts, their intention being to create legal relations and not merely to exchange mutual promises.[44] The law expects that the parties are competent to enter into a legally binding agreement. According to Black's Law Dictionary, a contract is:

> A deliberate engagement between competent parties, upon a legal consideration, to do, or abstain from doing some act. . . . It is an agreement creating obligation, in which there must be competent parties, subject-matter, legal consideration, mutuality of agreement, and mutuality of

42 European PPP Expertise Centre, 'A Guide to the Main Provisions of an Availability-based PPP Contract' (2018) available at <www.wbif.eu/storage/app/media/Library/8.%20Public%20Private%20Partnership/5.%205-Main-Provisions-of-an-Availability-based-PPP-Contract-FINAL-310818.pdf> accessed 19 November 2019.

43 Lucy Jones, *Introduction to Business Law* (Oxford: Oxford University Press, 2011) 83.

44 Agbonika John Alewo, 'The Principle and Nature of Law of Contract in Nigeria: Formation of Binding Contract' (2012) 5(4) *Journal of Politics and Law* 123.

> obligation, and agreement must not be so vague or uncertain that terms are not ascertainable.[45]

Such agreements are considered fundamental to business.[46] An agreement is not a contract unless there is an intention for the parties be bound thereby.[47] It follows that if parties willingly enter into a contract, the terms of that contract are to prevail except if they are illegal or impossible to perform. Thus, not all promises should be legally enforceable.[48] For example, an agreement between friends to meet at the cinema by 4:00 P.M. on Saturday must be assumed to be an agreement of a social nature and not meant to be binding on the parties. Generally, the setting in which the agreement is made can help to determine the intention of the parties. If the agreement was made in a social or domestic setting, the courts would view it as a social or domestic agreement. On the other hand, if the agreement was made in a *commercial setting*, it is to be assumed, unless proven otherwise, that there was an intention on the part of the parties to the agreement that legal obligations were created.[49] In the Nigerian case of *Amadi v Pool House Group Co*,[50] the plaintiff was a stacker who claimed to have won a lump sum. The defendant successfully denied any liability by relying on an honour clause that the contract was not intended to be binding.

It is a truism that the commercial and economic lives of people in society are woven around agreements. It follows that commerce and trade would become chaotic if the law allowed a promisor to break his or her promises without, at least, placing him or her under the obligation to pay a compensation to their promisee for the loss caused by their default. This is because the law generally regards contracts as sacrosanct – the principle of sanctity of contract. Thus, where parties duly enter a contract, they must honour their obligations under that contract.

The law of contract is concerned with determining whether there is a legally binding agreement between the parties and ensuring that there is a remedy in a situation where a party fails to perform an obligation in accordance with the terms of the agreement. It becomes clearer where there is some form of exchange between the parties based on their agreement.[51] The standard for determining whether the parties intended to create a legally binding agreement is that of a reasonable man. In common law, the question is will a reasonable person, observing the words and the conduct of the parties objectively and considering the nature and context of the agreement, consider that there was

45 Henry Campbell Black, *Black's Law Dictionary* 4 ed (St Paul, MN: West Group, 1968) 394.

46 Lucy Jones, *op cit* (note 43) 119.

47 The parties maybe natural or artificial, a private or government body.

48 Brian Coote, 'The Essence of Contract: Part II' (1988) 1 *The Journal of Commonwealth Literature* 183, 192.

49 Lucy Jones, *op cit* (note 43) 119.

50 (1966) 2 All NLR.

51 Ibid 117.

an intention to create legal relations? If the answer is yes, then the court would order the party in breach to compensate the injured party.[52]

For an agreement to be considered a contract, a promise to undertake or assume an obligation must be communicated.[53] The law, therefore, should recognise a promise as a contract when a reasonable person in the promisee's position would expect performance or equivalent compensation.[54] A valid contract is binding upon the parties. It can only be modified or terminated by the consent of the parties or if provided for by the law. The parties to a contract must, unless legally excused from performance, perform their respective duties under the contract.[55]

The principle of the sanctity of contract has, in the context addressed by this study, become more compelling due to the emergence of private-sector participation in the provision of infrastructural services, with far-reaching effects.[56] The consequences of the failure of the government to adhere to the principle of sanctity of contract are severe, shaking the confidence of prospective investors in taking an investment decision.[57] Sanctity of contract entails that obligations in a contract must be honoured because the contract was entered into willingly.[58] Contracts freely entered into must be honoured and, where necessary, enforced by the courts.[59] The doctrine of sanctity of contract, also known as *pacta sunt servanda* came into question in the South African case of *Everfresh Market Virginia (Pty) Ltd v Shoprite Checkers (Pty) Ltd*,[60] where the court invoked 'the age-old contractual doctrine that agreements solemnly made should be honoured and enforced (*pacta sunt servanda*).'[61] The decision of the Supreme Court of South Africa in *Mohammed's Leisure Holdings (Pty) Ltd v Southern Sun Hotel (Pty) Ltd*[62] reinforces the need to ensure that contractual agreements are respected, especially when the terms of the contract are not against public policy. Hence, the principle of *pacta sunt servanda* should be applied. The case before the Supreme Court was an appeal against the decision of the Gauteng Local Division of the High Court. The court entered judgement in favour of the plaintiff (Southern Sun Hotels Interest (Pty) Ltd) on the grounds that an eviction of the plaintiff based on their breach of Clause 20 of the lease

52 Ibid 118.

53 Stephen A Smith, *Contract Theory* (Oxford: Oxford University Press, 2004) 57.

54 Dena Valente, 'Enforcing Promises: Consideration and Intention in the Law of Contract' (Unpublished Thesis, University of Otago, Otago, 2010) 4.

55 Kla P Berger, 'Sanctity of Contracts' (2009) available at <www.trans-lex.org/919000/_/sanctity-of-contracts/> accessed 17 November 2019.

56 Olatunde Ayeni, 'The Need for Sanctity of Contracts for the Success of the Power Sector Reform: An Investor's Experience' *The Lawyer* (2016), a *This Day* weekly Pull-out 24 April, 8–10.

57 Ibid.

58 Dale Hutchison, Chris-James Pretorius and JE du Plessis, *The Law of Contract in South Africa* (Oxford: Oxford University Press, 2012) 21.

59 Luanda Hawthorne, *Contract Law: A Casebook for Students* (Cape Town: Juta and Company, 1994) 173.

60 2012 (1) SA 256 (CC).

61 Supra para 70.

62 (183/17) [2017] ZASCA 1.

agreement for failing to pay rent to the defendant on the due date was manifestly unreasonable, unfair and offended public policy. The Supreme Court held that 'it was a material term of the agreement that should the respondent fail to pay the rental on due date, then the appellant would be entitled to cancel the lease and retake possession.'[63] It therefore follows that, in so far as enforcing a contract will not lead to an illegality or where doing so does not offend public policy, the parties must respect the terms of the agreement.[64]

In South Africa, the principle of sanctity of contract is applied in line with the 1996 Constitution of the Republic of South Africa,[65] which promotes the principles of dignity, equality and justice.[66] In the case of *Brisley v Drotsky*,[67] Cameron JA used section 39(2) of the Constitution to connect the common law of contract with these constitutional values. Similarly, in *Bredenkamp & Ors v Standard Bank of SA Ltd*,[68] the court *inter alia* held that contractual promises should be kept and that the exercise of a contractual right, which does not involve public policy considerations or constitutional values, does not have to be fair to warrant being set aside when it is not in breach of the constitutional values of equality and justice.

The Supreme Court of Nigeria was firm in upholding the duty to honour binding agreements involving the public sector or governments in their sovereign might, as illustrated in *Attorney General Nasarawa State v Attorney General Plateau State*.[69] At the creation of Nasarawa State out of the former Plateau State, the military administrators had a meeting with General Abacha, the then Head of State, during which some areas of Plateau State were, by agreement, allocated to Nasarawa State. Later, the government of Plateau State failed to abide by the agreement, and the Nasarawa State government instituted action to enforce the agreement. The Supreme Court noted:

> If mutual agreement entered by parties to it shall be treated lavishly and that any party shall be allowed to unilaterally resile from the commitment both parties have signed to bind themselves, then the essence of any agreement or mutual contract is woefully defeated.[70]

Further deprecating the attitude of the Plateau State government in seeking to unilaterally resile from its agreement with the Nasarawa State government, Peter-Odili JSC said:

> This attempt by the defendant is reckless with capacity to encourage lawlessness and disobedience to constituted authority and the Rule of Law

63 Supra para 5.
64 See also *Roazar CC v The Falls Supermarket CC* 2017 ZASCA, 166.
65 *Barkhuizen v Napier* 2007 (7) BCLR 691 (CC).
66 Supra.
67 2002 (4) SA 1 (SCA) para 88–95.
68 2010 ZASCA, 75.
69 [2012] 10 NWLR (Pt 1309) 419.
70 *Attorney General Nasarawa State v Attorney General Plateau State* supra 458C per Muhammad JSC.

> which outcome would not rule out chaos. People or those in charge of institutions or government at every level should be cautious and wary of taking steps that are definitely not in keeping with the peace and order of this nation. The defendants are bound and stopped from going against that Agreement.[71]

It has been noted that for a prospective investor who wishes to enter into a contract with the public sector in a developing economy, the following questions may arise: first, would such a contract in writing be respected? Second, can the investor enforce the terms in case of default? Third, would an investor have a remedy? And where there is a remedy, would the government honour the remedial measures? Fourth, if there is a change in government, would a previous administration's commitments be respected by the succeeding administration? Fifth, would the government as a party honour its own obligations under the contract?[72]

The importance of respect for contracts by the government came into question in the United States[73] in *Perry v United States*,[74] when the court, per Chief Justice Hughes, held as follows:

> The United States are as much bound by their contracts as are individuals. . . . When the United States, with constitutional authority, makes contracts, it has similar rights and incurs responsibilities similar to those of individuals who are parties to such instruments. . . . The [contrary] argument . . . is in substance that Government cannot by contract restrict the exercise of a sovereign power. But the right to make binding obligations is a competence attaching to sovereignty. . . . The binding quality of the promise of the United States is of the essence of the credit which is . . . pledged. The fact that the United States may not be sued without its consent is a matter of procedure which does not affect the legal and biding character of its contracts.[75]

It is pertinent to note that sanctity of contract is enshrined in the Constitution of the United States under Article I, Section 10. It provides, in the relevant part, that 'No state shall . . . pass any Bill of Attainder, ex post facto Law, or Law impairing the obligation of contracts.' What this means is that the US government is prohibited by the Constitution from taking any action that may retroactively alter the terms of a contract.

71 Supra 489.
72 Olatunde Ayeni, *op cit* (note 57) 9.
73 This is of persuasive authority in Nigeria.
74 294 U.S. 330 (1934).
75 Ibid 551–554. The case of the *Attorney General of Nasarawa State v the Attorney General Plateau State* cited Supra.

When a private entity deals with the government, certain questions arise. First, can the investor enforce the terms of the agreement where the government defaults? Second, where the investor obtains remedy against the government, will such a remedy be honoured? And third, what happens if there is a change in government? Will the new government honour the agreements of its predecessor in office? The answers to these questions is hinged on sanctity of contract, and therefore investors consider whether a country's legal and regulatory environment favours cross-border projects.[76] In a contractual relationship between the state and a private-sector entity, both parties are bound by their agreement. In *BFI Group Corporation v Bureau of Public Enterprises*,[77] the respondent advertised for expression of interest by interested bidders for the privatisation of the Aluminium Company of Nigeria. The appellant completed the request for proposals (RFP) issued by the National Council on Privatisation (NCP). The RFP contained the term that a bidder would be selected on the basis of approval by the NCP. The relevant clause in the RFP stipulated that bid proposals would remain valid for 60 days after the submission date and that proposals were binding offers acceptable by the Bureau of Public Enterprises (BPE) to form a binding contract between the parties during the validity period. Undertakings and agreement signed by the appellants also contained a clause that 10 per cent of the acceptable bid price would be paid within 15 working days of the signing of the share purchase agreement, and that the outstanding 90 per cent would be paid within 90 calendar days. The appellant was successful in his bid of US$410 million for the 77.5 per cent shares of the federal government in the Aluminium Smelter Company of Nigeria (ALSCON). By a letter dated 17 June 2006, the respondent, in confirming the appellant's success, unilaterally introduced a term stipulating that 10 per cent of the bid price must be paid within 15 days of the appellant's receipt of the letter. The appellant fulfilled all conditions for the validation of its bid, including the procurement of a bid bond. The respondent, however, repudiated the agreement on the basis that the 10 per cent of the bid price was not paid within 15 days of the receipt of its letter. The appellant instituted a suit at the Federal High Court, claiming various declaratory and injunctive reliefs. The trial court dismissed the claims. The appeal to the Court of Appeal was also dismissed. Aggrieved still, the appellant appealed to the Supreme Court. The Supreme Court, in a decision in favour of the respondents, held *inter alia* that the court must treat as sacrosanct the terms of an agreement freely entered by the parties.

The doctrine of sanctity of contract was greatly influenced by the Ecclesiastical Courts in England as well as by the Court of Chancery. These courts

76 Paul Obo Idornigie, 'Towards Adopting an Appropriate Dispute Resolution Mechanism to Promote Investments to Enhance Energy Access in Africa' in Yinka Omorogbe and Ada Ordor (eds.), *Ending Africa's Energy Deficit: Achieving Sustainable Energy for All in Africa* (Oxford: Oxford University, 2018) 164.

77 (2012) All FWLR 676.

sought to provide a remedy by filling the wide gap in law left under the common law. Thus, where a promisor had made a pledge and failed to perform his agreement, his failure constituted at that time an ecclesiastical offence for which he was answerable in church courts as a sinner in need of correction. This was because the King's courts only ratified or enforced contracts made under a pledge of faith and the Constitutions of Clarendon issued in 1164.

In Brazil, the general position of the law is that contracting parties are authorised to determine the specific terms and conditions that will be applicable to their contractual relationship, to the extent that the terms in the contract are not illegal or against public order.[78] Under Article 422 of the Brazilian Civil Code, the parties must act in accordance with the principles of probity and good faith, which are tightly connected with the *pacta sunt servanda* principle. The case of Brazil is unique as there are specific laws which make PPP contracts binding on the government. These include Federal Law 11,079/2004, which introduced PPP, and Federal Law 12,462/2011, which created the Differentiated Government Procurement Regime.[79]

In accordance with Section 10 of the Indian Contracts Act of 1872, all agreements are contracts if they are made by the free consent of parties competent to contract for a lawful consideration and with a lawful object and are not expressly declared to be void. With regard to PPP in India, it has been argued as follows:

> PPPs are specified to constitute legally bound and rigid contractual agreements, as one party is the government and for it only formally signed understandings (legal contracts) are necessary. These also become essential as the public agent has adhered to the needs of maintaining transparency, accountability, equity, and consistency. Signed and legally enforceable contracts are argued to be necessary to protect the public and private interests in the projects.[80]

It is therefore vital that governments in emerging markets identify the problems that give rise to contractual difficulties and seek a holistic strategy to ensure these difficulties do not occur in new agreements with the private sector as far as PPP is concerned.

78 Leonardo Padilha de Lima Cosa and Bruno Triani Belchior, 'Enforceability of the JOA Forfeiture Mechanism Under Brazilian Law' (2014) available at <www.mayerbrown.com/files/uploads/Documents/PDFs/2014/May/140527-Newsletter-Energy-Review.PDF#page=22> accessed 19 November 2019.

79 Mauro Moura, Filipe Scherer Oliveira and Veirano Advogados, 'Brazil' (2019) available at <https://thelawreviews.co.uk/edition/the-government-procurement-review-edition-7/1193590/brazil> accessed 19 November 2019.

80 Swapnil Garg and Sachin Garg, 'Rethinking Public-Private Partnerships: An Unbundling Approach' (2017) 25 *Transportation Research Procedia* 3789–3807, 3796.

3.5.1 The classical approach to sanctity of contract

The doctrine of sanctity of contract had a primary role in securing a transactional framework in classical law. It prevented contractors from avoiding some or all of their obligations in a contract by raising excuses as to why they could not perform. However, contractors could be released from the terms of the contract through interpretation of the doctrines of frustration and mistake.[81]

3.5.2 A modern approach to sanctity of contract

In modern times, the approach is more an interventionist one. This is quite different from the classical model, as the core question in the modern approach centres on whether is it reasonable to hold a contractor to an apparent bargain.[82] The difference in the two views is illustrated in the English case of *L Schuler AG v Wickman Machine Tool Sales Ltd*.[83] In that case, 'L' and 'M' entered an agreement which stipulated as a condition that 'W' must visit the named manufacturers under Clause 7(b) of the agreement. The majority decision of the House of Lords was that Clause 7(b) was not a condition in the strict sense (i.e. 'L' had no right to withdraw when 'W' breached the term). However, it was the dissenting opinion that highlights the principle of sanctity of contract. Per Lord Wilberforce:

> To call the clause arbitrary, capricious or fantastic, or to introduce as a test of its validity the ubiquitous reasonable man, is to assume, contrary to the evidence, that both parties to the contract adopted a standard of easy-going tolerance rather than one of aggressive, insistent punctuality and efficiency. This is not an assumption I am prepared to make, nor do I think myself entitled to impose the former standard upon the parties if their words indicate, as they plainly do, the latter.[84]

Following this, it can be deduced that Lord Wilberforce's judgement was that the agreement between the parties should be respected and that sanctity of contract be upheld. That view represents the classical view that a contract must be respected in its entirety. However, the modern approach to sanctity of contract is represented by the majority House of Lords judgement, which considered that the obligation to visit a named manufacturer does not go to the

81 Husam MS Botosh, 'Striking the Balance Between the Boundaries of Certainty and Fairness in the Law Governing Letters of Credit' (Unpublished PhD Thesis, University of Sheffield, Sheffield, 2000) 60.

82 JN Adams and R Brownsword, *Key Issues in Contract* (London: Lexis Law Publishing, 1995) 52.

83 [1974] AC 235.

84 [1974] AC 235, 263.

root of the contract and warrant its termination; rather, the parties should read the contract through the lens of reasonableness.

It remains to be stated by way of conclusion that the doctrine of sanctity of contract cannot be convincing without genuine freedom of contract. Even though in the modern era, courts tend to consider whether it is reasonable for the parties to perform the terms of a contract, it is sacrosanct that parties who, of their own volition, enter contractual obligations respect the terms of their agreement. As pointed out in *Perry v United States* earlier, nation states that enter into contractual obligations with private parties must be held accountable like individuals.

3.6 Conclusion

Contracts are agreements into which the parties involved voluntarily enter. The intention of the parties is that they will be bound by their promises and that the promises should be enforced in the event of a breach. A PPP contract is a specialised form of contract that is usually long-term and complex. The discussion in this chapter on PPP contracts relates more with the fact that the parties to a PPP contract are usually a public authority and the private sector. Even though one of the parties in a PPP contract is the government, the law imposes a requirement for all parties to be bound by their promise.

Worthy of mention is the fact that every contract must not breach the provision of the law. This is because a breach of the law in the first place makes the contract *ipso facto* void. This is another reason why the services of experts are required in handling PPP agreements. Where, for instance, a subnational government is, under the Constitution of the country, precluded from contracting in any area that is reserved for the national government, a PPP contract in that area may be declared void. For example, the Exclusive Legislative List in the 1999 Constitution of Nigeria (as amended) lists items such as aviation, airports, federal roads, inland waterways, among others to be matters under the exclusive purview of the federal government of Nigeria. As such, a PPP contract between any subnational government in the country and a private-sector consortium for the construction or rehabilitation of an airport or federal highway is unconstitutional, and any such agreement is void in the first place. Therefore, prospective investors, lenders and promoters of PPP projects must seek expert opinion before making any agreements.

Given the highly complex nature of PPP contracts, it is advisable to develop a standard PPP contract template to serve as a guide and to provide uniformity, such as South Africa has done. Furthermore, this chapter pointed out the need to include specified items in the contract to ensure clarity. Apart from the main PPP contract itself, it is worthy of note that there are other sub-contracts that must be negotiated and agreed upon by the project company to ensure successful delivery of the PPP project. These include supply contracts, lending agreements, shareholding agreements, engineering contracts, construction contracts, operation and maintenance contracts, among others.

The subsequent chapters will deal with the legal framework and practice of PPP in selected emerging economies, including Brazil, India, Nigeria and South Africa. The next chapter discusses PPP in Brazil.

References

Adams, J.N., & Brownsword, R. (1995). *Key Issues in Contract*. London: Lexis Law Publishing (Va).

APMG International. (2019). Main Contents of the Contract: Rights, Obligations and Framework to Govern Changes and Risks. Retrieved from https://ppp-certification.com/ppp-certification-guide/91-main-contents-contract-rights-obligations-and-framework-govern-changes.

Ayeni, O. (2016, April 24). The Need for Sanctity of Contracts for the Success of the Power Sector Reform: An Investor's Experience. *This Day*, pp. 8–10.

Berger, K.P. (2016, March 1). Sanctity of Contracts. Retrieved from www.trans-lex.org/919000/_/sanctity-of-contracts/.

Black, H.C., & Garner, B.A. (1968). *Black's Law Dictionary*. St Paul, MN: West Group.

Botosh, H.M. (n.d.). *Striking the Balance Between the Boundaries of Certainty and Fairness in the Law Governing Letters of Credit* (Unpublished doctoral dissertation). University of Sheffield, Sheffield.

Cheung, E. (2009). *Developing a Best Practice Framework for Implementing Public Private Partnerships (PPP) in Hong Kong* (Unpublished doctoral dissertation). Queensland University of Technology, Australia.

Coote, B. (1988). The Essence of Contract: Part I. *The Journal of Commonwealth Literature*, 192.

De Lima Cosa, L.P., & Belchior, B.T. (2014). Enforceability of the JOA Forfeiture Mechanism Under Brazilian Law. Retrieved from www.mayerbrown.com/files/uploads/Documents/PDFs/2014/May/140527-Newsletter-Energy-Review.PDF#page=22.

Delmon, J. (2011). *Public-Private Partnership Projects in Infrastructure: An Essential Guide for Policy Makers*. Cambridge: Cambridge University Press.

Economic and Social Commission for Asia and the Pacific (ESCAP). (2008). Main Contents of a Contract Agreement. Retrieved from www.unescap.org/ttdw/ppp/ppp_primer/711_main_contents_of_a_contract_agreement.html.

European PPP Expertise Centre. (2018). A Guide to the Main Provisions of an Availability-Based PPP Contract. Retrieved from www.wbif.eu/storage/app/media/Library/8.%20Public%20Private%20Partnership/5.%205-Main-Provisions-of-an-Availabili.

Feigenbaum, B. (2011). Retrieved from http://reason.org/files/public_private_partnerships_for_highways.pdf.

Garg, S., & Garg, S. (2017). Rethinking Public-Private Partnerships: An Unbundling Approach. *Transportation Research Procedia, 25*, 3789–3807. doi:10.1016/j.trpro.2017.05.241.

Hawthorne, L., & Lotz, J.G. (1995). *Contract Law: Case Book for Students*. Cape Town: Juta and Company.

Hutchison, D., & Pretorius, C. (2012). *The Law of Contract in South Africa*. Oxford: Oxford University Press.

Idornigie, P.O. (2018). Towards Adopting an Appropriate Dispute Resolution Mechanism to Promote Investments to Enhance Energy Access in Africa. In Y. Omorogbe & A. Ordor (Eds.), *Ending Africa's Energy Deficit and the Law: Achieving Sustainable Energy for All in Africa*. New York, NY: Oxford University Press.

Jones, L. (2011). *Introduction to Business Law*. Oxford: Oxford University Press.

Marques, R.C. (2010). Public-Private Partnership Contracts: A Tale of Two Cities with Different Contractual Arrangements. Retrieved March 15, 2018, from http://bear.warrington.ufl.edu/centers/purc/docs/papers/0915_Marques_Public_Private_Partnership.pdf.

Moura, M. (2019). Brazil – The Government Procurement Review – Edition 7 – TLR. Retrieved from https://thelawreviews.co.uk/edition/the-government-procurement-review-edition-7/1193590/brazil.

Noble, G. (2006). The Role of Contracts in Public Private Partnership. Retrieved from http://ro.uow.edu.au/cgi/viewcontent.cgi?article=1599&context=commpaper.

PPP Knowledge Lab. (2019). Designing PPP Contracts. Retrieved from https://pppknowledgelab.org/guide/sections/61-designing-ppp-contracts.

Shrybman, S., & Sinclair, S. (2016). *A Standard Contract for PPPs the World Over: Recommended PPP Contractual Provisions Submitted to G20*. Washington, DC: The World Bank.

Smith, S.A. (2004). *Contract Theory*. Oxford: Oxford University Press.

Valente, D. (2010). *Enforcing Promises: Consideration and Intention in the Law of Contract* (Unpublished doctoral dissertation). University of Otago, Otago.

Wilheim Alfen, H. (Ed.). (2009). *Public-Private Partnership in Infrastructure Development*. Weimar: Bauhaus-Universitat.

Yescombe, E.R. (2007). *Public-Private Partnerships: Principles of Policy and Finance*. Amsterdam, Netherlands: Elsevier.

Yong, H.K. (2010). *Public-Private Partnerships Policy and Practice: A Reference Guide*. London: Commonwealth Secretariat.

4 Brazil

4.1 Introduction

This chapter addresses the lessons that might be learnt from Brazil in the successful administration of PPP. Brazil provides a good case study because of its role as a leading emerging economy in South America and the size of its PPP market. This chapter examines the framework for PPP in Brazil along the themes of critical success factors (CSFs) and PPP governance. While CSFs consist of the fundamentals required to create a successful PPP regime, PPP governance describes the mechanisms that make an environment conducive for PPP investments. Under CSFs, sub-themes, such as legal and policy framework, stable political environment and government agencies, are discussed. Sub-themes for PPP governance include, among others, a coherent policy, anti-corruption, competitive bidding, rule of law and efficient risk sharing.

The chapter begins with an introduction to Brazil, its socio-economic and political background and the potential for doing business in that country. The discussion then shifts to the nation's laws and the practice of PPP. To conclude, several examples of PPP projects in Brazil are discussed to show how the law is put in practice.

4.2 Introducing Brazil

Brazil is officially referred to as the Federative Republic of Brazil. It is the largest country in South America. At 8.5 million square kilometres and with a population size that is estimated to be over 208 million people, the country is the fifth-largest in terms of area and population.[1] The capital of the country is Brasília, but São Paulo is the country's most populous city. Brazil is a federation (or union) of 26 states,[2] the Federal District and 5,570 municipalities. It is the largest country with Portuguese as the official language and, incidentally, the

1 Instituto Brasileiro de Geografia e Estatística, 'Area Territorial Brasileira' (2015) available at <www.webcitation.org/64i0P2Lb0?url=www.ibge.gov.br/home/geociencias/cartografia/default_territ_area.shtm%20> accessed 15 November 2019.

2 The states are Acre, Algoas, Amapa, Amazonas, Bahia, Ceara, Distrito Federal, Espirito Santos, Goias, Maranhao, Mato Grosso do Sul, Minas Gerais, Para, Paraiba, Parana, Pernambuco, Piaui, Rio de Janeiro, Rio Grande do Sui, Rondonia, Roraima, Santa Catarina, Sao Paulo, Sergipe and Tocantins.

only Portuguese-speaking country in the Americas.[3] Brazil is regarded as one of the most multicultural and ethnically diverse nations on earth.[4] It lies on the Atlantic Ocean to the east and shares common boundaries with other countries in South America, except for Ecuador and Chile. It thus has 10 neighbours, namely: French Guiana, Suriname, Guyana, Venezuela and Colombia on the north; Uruguay and Argentina to the south and Paraguay, Bolivia and Peru on the west. It covers about 47.3 per cent of the South American continent.[5]

The Brazilian economy is relatively large. However, in contrast to the previous decade wherein Brazil was lauded alongside other peers, such as Russia, India, China and South Africa, as one of the BRICS powers (i.e. emerging economies with high growth rates that could potentially outperform developed economies by 2050), the current outlook seems to suggest that Brazil does not belong in that league.[6] Since the election of the current president, Jair Bolsonaro, there has not been improvements in unemployment levels. Economic recovery has been sluggish, the currency and the stock market have not faired any better.[7] This gloomy picture notwithstanding, Brazil is one of the largest PPP markets in the world due to its population size. Furthermore, a successful PPP regime in that country could potentially impact on economic growth and lead to the revival of the Brazilian economy. Brazil is very rich in biodiversity; it has abundant agricultural, mineral and energy potential. However, Brazil is challenged by high rates of social inequality, corruption and extensive bureaucracy.[8] Brazil's GDP per capita is US$16,068, and it was ranked 109 out of 190 countries in the Ease of Doing Business Rankings in 2018.[9]

Brazil is a civil law country. It enacted a 2002 Civil Law Code to replace the previous 1916 Civil Law Code. The latest constitution was ratified in 1988. Mr Jair Bolsonaro assumed the office of chief of state and head of government on 1 January 2019 and appointed his cabinet. The term of office for the president and his deputy is a single four-year term (with eligibility for a second term). The last elections were held in October 2018; the next scheduled presidential election will take place in October 2022. The legislative branch is a National Congress made up of the Senate, with 81 seats, and a Chamber of Deputies, with 513 seats.[10]

3 S George Philander, *Encyclopedia of Global Warming and Climate Change* (Thousand Oaks, CA: Sage Publications, 2012) 148.
4 BBC Brasil, 'Mundo Movimento' available at <www.bbc.com/portuguese/especial/migrantes/migrantes.shtml> accessed 19 November 2019.
5 United Nations, 'Brazil – The Land' (2014) available at <https://web.archive.org/web/20141023154830/www.un.int/brazil/brasil/brazil-land.htm> accessed 19 November 2019.
6 Daniel Gallas and Daniele Palumbo, 'What's Gone Wrong with Brazil's Economy' (2019) *BBC News* available at <www.bbc.co.uk/news/business-48386415> accessed 19 November 2019.
7 Ibid.
8 PWC, *Doing Business and Investing in Brazil* (Sao Paulo: PWC, 2013) 11.
9 Global Edge, 'Brazil: Introduction' (2019) available at <https://globaledge.msu.edu/countries/brazil> accessed 19 November 2019.
10 Central Intelligence Agency, 'Brazil' (2019) available at <www.cia.gov/library/publications/the-world-factbook/geos/br.html> accessed 19 November 2019.

4.3 PPP in Brazil

The PPP model as a form of procurement in Brazil was created in 2003.[11] This was made vide the PPP Law for the State of Minas Gerais (State Law No. 14,868/2003), and later on, in 2004, PPP was introduced to the state of São Paulo vide State Law No. 11, 6888. A federal law for PPP was passed in the same year (i.e. Federal Law No. 11,070, which is known as the Federal PPP Law). The law was signed by former President Luiz Inácio Lula da Silva on 30 December 2004 and took immediate effect. Of interest is the fact tht the federal statute in Brazil also applies to federal, state and local government agencies; special funds; public foundations and state-owned or partially owned companies.[12] It is noted that the PPP law in Brazil was passed with the intent to 'attract private investment in infrastructure projects in Brazil in the following areas: water and sewage, health and hospitals . . . roads, urban mobility, underground transportation and transportation in general.'[13]

A total of about 951 PPP projects have reached financial closure in Brazil since 1990. The total investment in PPP is over US$3.6 billion.[14] The government department responsible for regulating and monitoring PPP projects is the Parcerias Público-Privadas (PPP Unit) housed in the Ministry of Planning.[15] It is worth noting that there are also sub-national PPP frameworks at the state level in the country.

The rationale for the introduction of PPP in Brazil is to provide a solution to the infrastructure deficit that is taking a toll on the country's economy.[16] The Brazilian PPP Law established several broad guidelines for the PPP programme in the country.[17] These include:

1 The efficient implementation of governmental programmes and the use of public resources;
2 Respect for the rights of private firms contracted to provide services andthe end users of the services;
3 Non-delegability of the government's regulatory powers;
4 Fiscal responsibility;
5 Transparency in decision-making procedures;

11 Thiago Fernades Moeriera and Thiago Luís Sombra, 'Brazil' (2019) available at <https://thelawreviews.co.uk/edition/the-public-private-partnership-law-review-edition-5/1189691/brazil> accessed 19 November 2019.

12 See the PPP Law of 2004 Art 1.

13 Ibid at para 1.

14 PPP Knowledge Lab, 'Brazil' (2019) available at <https://pppknowledgelab.org/countries/brazil> accessed 19 November 2019.

15 Ibid.

16 Welber Barral and Adam Haas, 'Public-Private Partnership in Brazil' (2007) 41(3) *The International Lawyer* 957–973, 957.

17 Andrew J Dell'Olio, 'Public-Private Partnerships in Brazil: Opportunities and Risks for Investors' (2005) *Migalhas* available at <www.migalhas.com.br/dePeso/16,MI16861,11049-PublicPrivate+Partnerships+in+Brazil+Opportunities+and+Risks+for> accessed 19 November 2019.

6 The fair allocation of risk between the parties; and
7 The financial sustainability of specific projects.

Brazil operates both the concession and private finance initiative (PFI) types of PPP.[18] In a concession, the end users of the facility pay for its use. On the other hand, in the PFI type of PPP, the public authority pays the project company for the use of the facility by members of the public.[19]

4.4 The framework for PPP in Brazil

In Chapter 2, the importance of a legal framework for PPP is discussed extensively. There is no doubt that, 'an independent, fair and efficient legal framework is a key factor for successful PPP project implementation.'[20] Cheung *et al.* argue that a transparent and stable legal framework should help make the contracts and agreements bankable and should entail adequate dispute resolution mechanisms to ensure stability in PPP arrangements.[21] Having introduced the importance of a legal framework for PPP earlier, this chapter examines the legal framework for private-sector participation in infrastructure in Brazil.

Fahye Andrade de Alencar Loiola has argued that 'Considering the need for additional sources to complement the gap for investment in economic and social infrastructure, Brazilian governments at federal, state and municipal levels have acknowledged that immediate private funding for long-term projects is an important investment alternative.'[22] It follows, therefore, that the public sector in Brazil has identified the need to resort to PPP as a tool to deal with the country's infrastructure deficit. Going about it the right way to achieve this objective requires setting up and implementing a framework that will enable successful outcomes. It needs to be stated as well that one of the most important steps for the implementation of PPP in any jurisdiction is the design of an appropriate legal framework that is attractive to both domestic and foreign investors.

To begin with, it is noteworthy that the Constitution of Brazil does not expressly make mention of the regulation of PPPs. It does, however, mention the general rules and principles dealing with concessions that affect the bidding

18 Mattos Filho, 'An Introduction to Public-Private Partnerships in Brazil' *Lexology*, 5 April 2019 available at <www.lexology.com/library/detail.aspx?g=485048ca-79be-40a3-8b51-84d727eb5d20> accessed 9 December 2019.

19 ER Yescombe, *Public-Private Partnerships: Principles of Policy and Finance* (Amsterdam, Netherlands: Butterworth-Heinemann, 2007) 8.

20 Esther Cheung, Albert PC Chan, Patrick TI Lam, Daniel WM Chan and Yongjian Ke, 'A Comparative Study of Critical Success Factors for Public Private Partnerships (PPP) Between Mainland China and the Hong Kong Special Administrative Region' (2012) 30(13/14) *Facility Management Development* 647–666.

21 Ibid 648.

22 Fahye Andrade de Alencar Loiola, 'The Formulation of Public-Private Partnership Projects for Infrastructure Development in Brazil: An Institutional Analysis of the Municipality of Fortaleza' (Unpublished PhD Thesis, University of Sheffield, Sheffield, 2013) 20.

process where the public sector is involved.[23] Article 175 of the Federal Constitution of Brazil provides as follows:

> The Government is responsible for providing public utility services, either directly or under regimes of concessions or permits, always through public bidding as provided by law.
>
> The law shall provide for:
>
> I the regime for companies that have concession or permits to provide public utility services, the special character of their contracts and the extension thereof and conditions for lapse, supervision and termination of concessions or permits;
> II rights of users;
> III rate policy;
> IV obligation to maintain adequate service.

The importance of this is that the government is responsible for providing public services, whether directly or indirectly, in Brazil.[24] Furthermore, the Constitution gives the government the power to enter into concession agreements with the private sector for the provision of public-infrastructure facilities. It is noteworthy, however, that at the federal level, two types of services are exclusively to be provided by the government: the postal service and the air postal service.[25]

The 11.079/04 Act (the PPP Law) established a PPP regime at the federal level in Brazil. The same procedure also applies for the federating states.[26] The law on PPP provides that it applies to government entities, special funds, semi-autonomous agencies, public foundations, government-controlled companies, mixed public-private corporations and all other entities that are directly or indirectly controlled by the federal government, the states, the Federal District of Brasilia or its municipalities.[27] Queiroz et al. note that, based on federal law, the states and municipalities in Brazil can enact their own PPP laws. They cite the example of the states of Minas Gerais and São Paulo,[28] which have implemented projects in tandem with local laws that have been found compatible with the federal law.[29]

23 Art 23 (xi) Federal Constitution of Brazil 1988.
24 Welber Barral and Adam Haas, *op cit* (note 16) 960.
25 Art 21 Federal Constitution of Brazil 1988.
26 Welber Barral and Adam Haas, *op cit* (note 16) 960.
27 Article 1 Brazil Public-Private Partnership Law.
28 Cesar Queiroz, Gaston Astensiano and Tomas Serebrisky, 'An Overview of the Brazilian PPP Experience form a Stakeholders' Viewpoint (2014) Inter-American Development Bank available at <https://publications.iadb.org/bitstream/handle/11319/6399/An%20Overview%20of%20the%20Brazilian%20PPP%20Experience%20from%20a%20Stakeholders%C2%BF%20Viewpoint%20final.pdf?sequence=1> accessed 5 July 2017.
29 This is quite like the situation in Nigeria where some states have also enacted their own PPP laws like the Infrastructure Concession and Regulatory C omission (Establishment Etc) Act2005 except for Rivers State that has a much broader PPP law.

Brazilian PPP law emphasises on the binding nature of PPP arrangements in the following words:[30]

> For the purposes of this law, public-private partnership contracts are deemed to be agreements entered into between government or public sector entities and private sector entities that establish a legally binding obligation to establish or manage, in whole or in part, services, undertakings and activities in the public interest, in which the private sector partner is responsible for the financing, investment and management, pursuant to the following guidelines:
>
> I Effectiveness in fulfilling the missions of the State and in using society's resources;
> II Respect for the rights and interests of those who should receive services, as well as the private entities responsible for providing those services;
> III There shall be no delegation of functions that are regulatory, jurisdictional or involve exercising police powers;
> IV Fiscal responsibility in entering into and executing partnerships;
> V Transparency in decision-making and other procedures;
> VI Distribution of risks in accordance with the contracting parties' risk management capabilities; and
> VII Financial sustainability and social and economic advantages of the partnership project.

These provisions indicate that the public authority will not unilaterally cancel contracts without recourse to the law. This position is good for business, especially as it supports the safety of the invested assets. The PPP law in Brazil identifies several categories of transactions that can be classified under PPP, including:[31]

1 Service contracts which may or may not be preceded by a public-works project;
2 The performance of an activity within the jurisdiction of the government or a public-sector entity, which may or may not be preceded by a public-works project;
3 Carrying out a public-works project for the government or public-sector entity; and
4 Carrying out a public-works project for sale, rental or lease to the government or to a public-sector entity.

30 Article 2 Brazil PPP Law.
31 Article 3 Brazil PPP Law.

PPP is thus a much wider concept in Brazil than, say, Nigeria, which limits PPPs to the concession type. Every PPP contract in Brazil must contain some clauses that have been stipulated by the law. These clauses are:[32]

1 A period of validity compatible with the amortisation of the investments made, with a limit of 30 years;
2 Penalties to be applied to government and public-sector entities, and to the private-sector partner, in the event of a failure to fulfil the contractual obligations;
3 Possible circumstances for contract termination prior to the end of the contract's term, as well as criteria for calculating the required compensation payments owed; and
4 Sharing with the government or public-sector entity the economic gains arising from a change in financing conditions, pursuant to the terms stipulated in the contract.

It remains to be stated that the provisions of Article 4 of the Brazilian PPP law further strengthen the PPP regime in the country. This is because the combined effect of Articles 2 and 4 gives and reinforces the binding effect of PPP contracts and provides for the insertion of penalties in the contract document in the event of a failure by the public sector or the private sector to deliver on the terms of the agreement. The law also is not skewed in favour of the public authorities. The effect is that it further makes PPP investment in the country attractive, especially to foreign investors.

An important insertion in the PPP law of Brazil can be found under Articles 6, 7, 8 and 9 dealing with guarantees. This feature permits that the obligation of the public authority to pay a concessionaire be guaranteed by, among other instruments backed by law, a pledge of revenues, creation or use of special funds, purchase of a guarantee from insurance companies that are not under public control, guarantees by international organisations or financial institutions not controlled by any government authority or guarantees by guarantor funds or state-owned companies created for that purpose.[33] This well-thought-out aspect of the law in Brazil is a stimulant for private-sector investors. The failure to provide or a lack of guarantees could result in failure to attract funding for projects. Under the law in Brazil, the public authority is authorised to provide guarantees for meeting obligations assumed by the private-sector partners because of PPP contracts.[34]

Furthermore, PPP contracts may stipulate that commitments related to counterpart instalment payments owed by the government or a public-sector

32 Article 4 Brazil PPP Law.
33 Bruno Werneck and Mário Saadi, *The Public-Private Partnership Law Review*, 3rd Ed. (London: Law Business Research, 2016) vi.
34 Article 6 Brazil PPP Law 2004.

entity may be paid off on behalf of the institution that financed the partnership project, as a guaranty for meeting financing conditions.[35]

Articles 10, 11 and 12 of the law regulates the bidding process for PPP contracts in Brazil. The law stipulates that the contracting of PPPs shall be preceded by a bidding process, which takes part in stages:

1 **Pre-qualification**. Under this stage, there will be a public notice of the request for bid proposals. The public authority may:

   a) Require guaranties of the bid proposals and of the execution of the contract that are greater than those established in the legislation in force, if they are consistent with the financial or other burden(s) resulting from failure to comply with the terms of contract;
   b) Require that the bidder present a financing pledge made by companies or financial institutions that meet the requirements of strength and safety established in the public notice;
   c) Require that the winning party must set up a company for the specific purpose of managing the partnership activities and must adopt standardised accounting practices and financial statements;
   d) Allow the winning bidder to be put in charge of preparing the project plan for achieving the purpose of the partnership activity that was the subject of the bidding process or allow an alternative project plan to be presented in the bidding process;
   e) Allow the possibility of adopting arbitration for the resolution of disputes arising from the execution of the contract.

2 **The Bidding Stage**. Under Article 11, after the pre-qualification stage and if it was stipulated in the public notice, the bidding process shall comply with the following procedures:

   a) The public authority shall receive technical bid proposals from the bidders and may request that changes it decides are suitable to serve the public interest be made until the bid proposals are satisfactory;
   b) A reasonable and sufficient time shall be established for satisfying the requests made by the public authority;
   c) Once the stage for improving the technical bid proposals is completed, the public authority shall receive the price proposals from the bidders;
   d) The bidders may present new and successive price proposals until one is declared to be the winner under the terms and conditions stipulated in the public notice;
   e) The public notice may limit the right to present new and successive price proposals to bidders that are included in a specific range established in the public notice; those who present the three best proposals may present new and successive price proposals.

35 Article 7 Brazil PPP Law 2004.

3 **The Selection Stage**. Here, to judge the bid proposals, the following criteria may be adopted:

a) The lowest rate;
b) The best techniques;
c) The lowest counterpart instalment payments for the public authority;
d) The judging criteria provided for in this article may be combined;
e) The public authority may require, as a means of breaking ties, that bidders provide evidence of social responsibility.

4.5 Stable political and social environment

It is clear that successful PPP implementation in an given jurisdiction requires a stable political and social environment.[36] Furthermore, PPP success is hugely reliant on the stability and capability of the host government.[37] Cheung et al. note, and rightly so, that political and social issues that go beyond the private sector's domain should be handled by the government.[38] The way the country handles regime changes vis-à-vis projects procured via PPP and the ease of investors investing in the country's market space is the subject of focus under this heading. Again, 'if unduly victimised, it is legitimate that the private sector participants should be adequately compensated.'[39] A brief examination of the socio-political environment in Brazil is undertaken next.

4.5.1 The socio-political environment and PPP in Brazil

Brazil is the fifth-largest country on the globe with an estimated population of 208 million people[40] and ranks after China, India, the United States and Indonesia in that order. There is thus a large market for investment. It should be added that Brazil has the largest economy in Latin America. Like Nigeria, Brazil has experienced several years of military rule. It returned to civilian rule in 1985 after two decades of military dictatorship. Brazil experienced a quantum economic growth between 2003 and 2014. The period witnessed about 29 million people coming out of poverty and inequality, which resulted in the income level of the poorest 40 per cent of the population rising on an average of 7.1 per cent within the period. The World Bank notes, however, that the rate of reduction in poverty and inequality in Brazil appears to have stagnated since 2015.[41] In a report carried out by Price Waterhouse Coopers (PWC), the country was described as a considerably closed economy in the 1970s and

36 Esther Cheung *et al*, *op cit* (note 20) 6.
37 Ibid.
38 Ibid.
39 Ibid.
40 See Instituto Brasileiro de Geografia e Estatística, *op cit* (note 1) above.
41 The World Bank, 'Brazil' (2016) available at <www.worldbank.org/en/country/brazil/overview> accessed 2 October 2016.

1980s with trade liberalisation taking effect in the 1990s. This culminated in the lifting of trade barriers and protective practices.[42]

Unlike the United States and Canada, where federalism was a method for uniting states and provinces that had been previously autonomous political entities, federalism as it is in Brazil is a technique to dividing what had always been a unitary system of government.[43] It is a three-tiered federation of 24 states, 2 federal territories, a federal district and 4,300 municipalities.[44] The Brazilian federation has three independent branches, namely, executive, legislative and judicial. The president of the Republic heads the executive branch and superintends over several executive departments, the heads of which are appointed and are known as the Cabinet. Cabinet members answer to the president but need not be legislators.[45] The country's legislative body is made up of a Senate[46] and a House of Representatives.[47] The country's judicial branch is made up of federal, state and local courts with the Supreme Court of Brazil being the court of last resort.[48] The main source of Brazilian civil law is the Civil Code of 2002 and subsequent legislations. The country's legal system has been described as slow and laborious.[49]

Democracy in Brazil only commenced in the 1980s. Between 1980 and 2020, several coalition parties have been in power. These include the Party of Brazilian Social Democracy (PSDB), the Liberal Front Party (PFL), and the Party of the Brazilian Democratic Movement (PMDB).[50] Whereas the PFL represents the country's conservative front, the Communist Party of Brazil (PC) is the main opposition to the present-day government in the country.[51]

It is of significance that the government of Brazil plays a vital role in controlling a few sectors of the nation's economy. This is because of the perceived value of those sectors to the economy. For example, power generation and telecommunications are considered very strategic. However, the country plans to water down state monopolies via privatisation and divestiture.[52] This is where PPP can also take the front stage.

The Brazilian economy fell into a deep recession in 2016. The World Bank notes that the country's growth rate has decelerated steadily since the beginning

42 PWC, *op cit* (note 8) 25.

43 Keith S Rosenn, 'Federalism in Brazil' (2005) 43 *Duquesne Law Review* 577.

44 Anwar Shah, 'The New Fiscal Federalism in Brazil' (2010) available at <http://documents.worldbank.org/curated/en/480641468743787324/The-new-fiscal-federalism-in-Brazil> accessed 11 May 2018.

45 Ibid 12.

46 There are 81 senators, three from each of the 26 states and from the Federal District of Brasilia.

47 A total of 513 representatives make up the House of Representatives. The number of representatives is determined by population size of the various states that make up the federation.

48 PWC, *op cit* (note 8) 25.

49 Ibid 13.

50 Amelia Meyer, 'Brazil Politics – Intro' (2010) available at <www.brazil.org.za/politics-intro.html> accessed 4 October 2016.

51 Ibid.

52 Ibid.

of this decade, from an average annual growth of 4.5 per cent between 2006 and 2010 to 2.1 per cent between 2011 and 2014. In 2015, the country's GDP contracted by 3.8 per cent and was expected to further fall by at least 3 per cent in 2016.[53] This situation may not encourage positive investor sentiments towards the country in addition to the current political crisis that Brazil is facing. However, economic recovery seems to be on track after growth accelerated in the last quarter of 2017.[54]

On 31 August 2016, the Brazilian Senate impeached President Dilma Rousseff, the country's first female president, and removed her from office on allegations of manipulating the country's budget. That impeachment put an end to 13 years of rule by the Leftist Workers' Party, an era that witnessed the country's economic boom and the lifting of millions into the middle class, thus raising the country's global economic profile.[55]

President Michel Tremer,[56] who succeeded President Roussef, announced that his government aimed to pursue several 'fiscal adjustment measures and a reform agenda to re-establish confidence and to restore a favourable investment environment.'[57] It is important to note that the measures, if implemented to the letter, are essential in gaining the confidence of the private sector in investing, especially in the infrastructural development of the country. On 1 January 2019, Mr Jair Bolsonaro was sworn in as the 38th president of Brazil following the 2018 presidential election.

In Brazil, presidents have significant powers, including law-making powers usually exercised either by proposing laws to the National Congress or by using *Medidas Provisórias* (provisional measures), an instrument with the force of law that a sitting president can enact in situations of emergency and necessity with the exception of making changes to areas such as criminal or electoral laws. Under Article 84 of the Federal Constitution, the president has the powers to do any or all of the following, among other things:

1 appoint and dismiss ministers of the Federal Government;
2 exercise, with assistance of the ministers of the Federal Government, the upper management of the federal administration;
3 initiate legislation, in the manner and cases provided for in the Constitution;
4 approve, promulgate and order publication of laws, as well as issue decrees and regulations for their faithful execution;
5 veto bills, either in whole or in part;

53 The World Bank, *op cit* (note 41).

54 Focus Economics, 'Brazil Economic Outlook – GDP, Inflation, CPI and Interest Rate' (2018) available at <www.focus-economics.com/countries/brazil> accessed 11 May 2018.

55 Simon Romero, 'Dilma Rouseff Is Ousted as Brazil's President in Impeachment Vote' *The New York Times* available at <www.nytimes.com/2016/09/01/world/americas/brazil-dilma-rousseff-impeached-removed-president.html?_r=0> accessed 4 October 2016.

56 He was the former vice president under Rousseff.

57 The World Bank, *op cit* (note 41).

6 to provide for by decree with respect to:

a) organisation and functioning of the federal administration, when this does not imply an increase in expense nor the creation or abolition of public agencies;
b) the abolition of public positions or offices, when occupied;

7 maintain relations with foreign states and accredit their diplomatic representatives;
8 conclude international treaties, conventions and acts, subject to the approval of the National Congress;
9 decree a state of defense or a state of siege;

- send a governmental message and plan the National Congress at the opening of the legislative session, describing the country's situation and requesting actions he deems necessary; and
- grant pardons and commute sentences, after hearing, if necessary, from the agencies instituted by law.

It is, therefore, without doubt that the President of Brazil has enormous powers and can, to a large extent, impact on lawmaking, including making key decisions that affect the success of the country's PPP regime. Furthermore, since the success or otherwise of a PPP regime is also dependent on the exercise of the political willpower to ensure that PPP projects succeed, the president can use his powers effectively to ensure that PPP arrangements and projects, especially at the federal level, are successfully executed.

4.5.2 Public agencies administering PPP in Brazil

In Brazil, there is no dedicated single agency that administers PPP at the federal level. Instead, there are several agencies tasked with administering different aspects of the country's PPP programme. These agencies include the Ministry of Finance; the Ministry of Planning, Budget and Management; the National Treasury Secretariat and the Partnership Steering Committee.

Specifically, the Ministry of Planning, Budget and Management (MPOG) is responsible for assessing, modelling and monitoring potential PPP projects which have been designated as priorities by the Partnership Steering Committee (CGP).[58]

On its part, the Ministry of Finance (MF) appraises any proposed PPP project and makes sure that the program is within the maximum allowable allocation for PPP projects. The limit is set at 3 per cent of the net current revenues as stipulated in Articles 195 and 239 of the Brazilian Constitution.[59]

58 Cesar Queiroz, Gaston Astensiano and Tomas Serebrisky, *op cit* (note 28) 14.
59 Ibid.

It is the responsibility of the CGP[60] to do the following:[61]

1. Approve the projects and PPP contracts;
2. Authorise the opening of the bidding process;
3. Define the priority services to be provided under PPP arrangements;
4. Define the criteria for analysing the appropriateness and timing of contracts;
5. Set up the procedures for contract award;
6. Authorise the launching of the bidding and approving the bidding documents;
7. Approve the PPP plan and monitor and evaluate its implementation;
8. Review the contract-monitoring reports;
9. Develop standard bidding documents and sample PPP contracts; and
10. Authorise the use of resources of the PPP Guarantee Fund to guarantee the government's financial obligations.

4.6 Sponsored and common concessions

In Brazil, a PPP is created when the public authority delegates a project or service's operation to a private party. As previously noted, a PPP project may be structured in such a way that government pays the project company for the use of the facility by citizens, or citizens are required to pay the project company for their use of the public facility. The PPP model referred to as 'sponsored concession' deals with the management of a public service, which may or may not be preceded by the construction of a public facility.[62] Sponsored concessions are different from 'common concessions.' In the latter case, this applies where the government delegates a public service preceded by the construction of a public facility but does not pay; therefore, the remuneration to the project company is paid only by the end users of the facility.[63] These type of concessions are regulated by the 8.987/95 Act and the 9.074 Act.[64]

Administrative concessions are different from general building contracts; in general contracts, the administration contracts with a private person to execute a project, whereas in an administrative concession, the contractual object is to provide a service to the administration, even in cases where the execution of a project is involved.[65] In Brazil, PPPs cannot be used to execute projects that are under US$9 million or services that will continue for fewer than five years or where the aim of the contract is to supply handwork or goods.[66]

60 Established by Presidential Decree No. 5385/05 and modified by Decree No 6.037/07.
61 Cesar Queiroz, Gaston Astensiano and Tomas Serebrisky, *op cit* (note 28) 15.
62 Welber Barral and Adam Haas, *op cit* (note 16) 961.
63 Ibid.
64 Ibid.
65 Ibid.
66 Art 10 of the 11.079/04 Act.

4.7 The parties to a Brazilian PPP contract

A regular PPP contract in Brazil involves at least four different categories of stakeholders. These include the public authority, the project company, the guarantor and the investor. Brazilian PPP law specifically mentions the specific requirements and limitations for all parties involved in a PPP transaction.

4.7.1 The public authority

The public authority here refers to the government and its agencies, including special funds, semi-autonomous agencies, public foundations, government-owned companies and other entities owned directly or indirectly by the government at different levels.[67]

4.7.2 The project company

The project company, sometimes referred to as the private partner or the Special Purpose Company, which is a distinct personality from the consortium that bids for the contract, will be legally responsible for the execution of the PPP project. The project company is often a creation of the bidding consortium as soon as a bid is won and the project needs to be executed. It is essential that prior to the signing of the PPP contract, the winning consortium creates a project company to manage in the project. Furthermore, the company must comply with all Brazilian accounting rules and use corporate management patterns.[68]

4.7.3 The guarantor

One of the high points of the PPP regime in Brazil is the provision for state guarantees.[69] This is an innovation in agreements with the public authority. The aim is to ensure that the private party is assured of payments in the event of claims against the public authority.[70] In Brazil, payment obligations undertaken by the public authority in PPP arrangements may be guaranteed by:

1 pledge of revenues;
2 creation or use of special funds contemplated by law;
3 purchase of guarantees from insurance companies that are not under public control;
4 guarantees by international organisations or financial institutions not controlled by any government authority; or
5 guarantees put by guarantor funds or state-owned companies created especially for that purpose.

67 Including the federal, states, municipalities and the Federal District of Brasília.
68 Art 10.
69 Thiago Fernades Moeriera and Thiago Luís Sombra, *op cit* (note 11).
70 Ibid.

It needs to be pointed out that the guarantor may or may not be a state-owned entity. The guarantor may well be an international agency. The law encourages the participation of third parties as guarantors.[71] The law in Brazil authorises a list of possible guarantors that is not closed, for example, special funds and private financial institutions. In Brazil, the PPP Guarantee Fund (FGP) to guarantee government payments to private corporations.[72]

4.7.4 The investor

Brazilian law grants financial institutions the power to provide tax incentives to private investors who invest in PPP projects[73] The country's National Monetary Council is responsible for setting the guidelines for tax incentives linked to PPPs, as well the role of pension funds in funding PPP contracts.[74] In the same vein, the public financial institutions in Brazil can play the role of investors.[75] Credit transactions made by these financial institutions may not exceed 70 per cent of the private partner's total resources. This percentage may rise in certain areas, depending on the level of development in those parts of the country.

4.8 Scorecard for PPP projects in Brazil

Like most developing economies, and despite being the sixth-largest economy in the world, Brazil has a substantial infrastructure gap to deal with. This is more evident in the transport sector. The country lacks a viable railroad network and must find the means to deal with many stretches of unpaved roads. In response, the Brazilian Development Bank (BNDES), the Inter-American Development Bank (IDB) and IFC collaborated to create the Private Sector Participation Programme (PSP Brazil) in 2008 to form the Brazilian alliance to implement innovative PPPs and to foster best practices through making available consulting services to regional and municipal governments.[76] In order to ensure a smooth take off of a PPP regime in that country, the PPP programme empowers the federal government of Brazil to issue completion guarantees and to allow private-sector participants to pledge their revenue streams to lenders and permit arbitration to resolve disputes. The programme in that country also sets up a fiduciary fund to hold assets contributed by the public authority to support payment obligations of the government. Where there is a default in payment by the public sector, the funds held in trust would pay out to the

71 Welber Barral and Adam Haas, *op cit* (note 16) 964.
72 Ibid.
73 Lei No. 11.079 Art 23.
74 Lei No. 11.079 Art 24.
75 Welber Barral and Adam Haas, *op cit* (note 16) 966.
76 World Bank Group for the G20 Investment and Infrastructure and Working Group, *Overcoming Constraints to the Financing of Infrastructure* (Washington, DC: The World Bank, 2014) 6.

private investor from quotas based on the aggregate value of the assets held by the fund[77].

The pilot PPP project was the concession to expand, rehabilitate, operate and maintain 667 kilometres of federal roads in the state of Bahia. The concession reached a close in October 2009. Notably, this project introduced a new structure that serves as a model for the development or similar federal and road projects.[78] This road concession led to new innovations to the PPP concept itself. Because the quality of the service on the concession could not be maintained in the long term without increases in fees or tariffs paid by end users, some changes were made to the Brazilian road concession model. The changes can be described as the 'three-fold innovations.' First, is the introduction of the *focus on performance parameters,*[79] the second is *the concept of the traffic trigger*[80] and the third is the *re-equilibrium discount.*[81]

The World Bank Group for the G20 Investment and Infrastructure notes that the evolution of the road concession model and the efforts by the government of Brazil have in no small measure improved the country's perception of international investors, thus making the country attractive to foreign direct investment to the country's road concession projects.[82]

This thesis next appraises a few PPP deals closed between the government of Brazil and the private sector with the aim of deducing lessons that can be applied in Nigeria.

The Rio de Janeiro/Galeão-Antonio Carlos Jobim International Airport, which was previously known as the Galeão International Airport, is Brazil's largest and was previously managed by the state-owned company Empresa Brasileira de Infra-Estrututra Aeroportuaria (Infraero). It was concessioned to Aeroporto Rio de JaneiroS/A after the signing of a concession contract between the National Civil Aviation Agency (NCAA) and the concessionaire in April 2014. The concessionaire is made up of Odebrecht Transport (60 per cent stake) and Singapore's Changi (40 per cent stake). The concessionaire formed a consortium with the Brazilian government–owned Infraero (49 per cent).[83] It is submitted that the ownership structure of the consortium in charge

77 Cythian Urda Kassis and Anthony Girolami, 'Brazil's Challenge' (2004) *Latin Finance Reprints* available at <www.shearman.com/~/media/Files/NdewsInsights/Publications/2004/10/Brazils-Challenge/Files/Download-PDF-Brazils-Challenge/FileAttachment/PDF_1004.pdf> accessed 11 May 2018.

78 World Bank Group for the G20 Investment and Infrastructure and Working Group, *op cit* (note 81) 6.

79 This refers to performance parameters which are the outcomes required of the operator who has a freedom to employ appropriate innovative technology, construction and methods in such a way that it can be effectively measured.

80 The 'traffic trigger' concept in a contract serves to obligate the concessionaire to increase roadway capacity to maintain a minimum level of service to the end-users. This means that the contract would not need a schedule of pre-determined investments as was in the case of the earlier concession.

81 This is the index used to reduce tariff when performance parameters ae not being met.

82 World Bank Group for the G20 Investment and Infrastructure and Working Group, *op cit* (note 81) 8.

83 Infrastructure Management Programme, 'Public-Private Partnership (PPP)-Case Study' (2015) available at <www.icao.int/sustainability/PPP%20Case%20Studies/PPP_Airport_Brazil.pdf>> accessed 5 December 2016.

of the Rio de Janeiro International Airport is a perfect example of how to calm the nerves of members of the public who are anti-PPPs on the basis that PPP is another form of transferring public assets to the private sector to further impoverish the poor. The government can still own companies that can be competitive and run like private-sector entities.

Brazil has maintained consistency in improving on its infrastructure fortunes as a means of sustaining a vibrant economy. It is noteworthy that despite GDP declines in 2014 and 2015, the country auctioned the concession of 16 toll roads in 2016, and there are plans to concession 4 federal airports, including those of Salvador, Fortaleza, Florianopolis and Porte Alegre. It is submitted that the country's consistency in the use of PPP as a model of infrastructure procurement sends positive signals to investors.

With regard to financing PPP, 'Brazil offers deep capital markets, domestic players with infrastructure experience and local-currency financing options. BNDES is the primary source of funding for infrastructure projects.'[84] It is the submission of this thesis that countries must seek ways of offering long-term finance, especially for projects that do not pass the currency exchange risk test. Other sources of finance for PPP infrastructure in Brazil include multilateral and development banks, export credit institutions, institutional investors, such as pension funds, private banks and other government-controlled banks. There are also infrastructure funds and other development conglomerates. Vittor and Samples also note that Chinese investment in Brazil has grown rapidly, reaching about US$17 billion in 2010.

4.9 Brief case studies of PPP projects in Brazil

This section appraises some selected PPP projects arranged and executed in Brazil to examine the law and practice of PPP in the country. The selected projects cut across the hydro energy, healthcare and education sectors.

4.9.1 PCH Figueirópolis and PCH Ludesa

While the PCH Figueirópolis is a 20 MW small hydroelectric plant, the PCH Ludesa is a 30 MW small hydroelectric plant. The PPP partners for the project are Electrobrás, a major Brazilian electric utility company. It is also Latin America's largest electric utility company and the tenth-largest in the world, with the Brazilian government as the public sector owning 52 per cent of its shares[85] on the one hand and Companhia Hidroelétria Figueirópolis SA and Ludesa Energética SA as private-sector participants on the other hand.[86]

84 Jose Luis Vittor and Tim R Samples, 'PPPs and Latin America Infrastructure Markets: Brazil and Chile' (2011) 19(7) *Latin American Law and Business Report* 3.

85 It is worth noting that public-sector entities in Brazil are part owned by the private sector. The semi-privatisation of these entities helps to instil private-sector commitment to business while not entirely giving up government interest.

86 Global Sustainable Electricity Partnership, 'Brazil: PCH Figueirópolis and PCH Ludesa' (2017) available at <www.gsep-ppp.org/case-studies/pch-figueiropolis-and-ludesa/> accessed 7 July 2017.

The financing for the project is structured as a long-term loan from Banco do Brasil by means of the Mid-West Constitutional Financing Fund (FCO). The FCO is a vital instrument used to assist businesses within the Midwest region of the country to generate social and economic development. The PPP partners provided the financing entity with energy purchase guarantees under the Brazilian government's Programme of Incentives for Alternative sources.[87] The successful funding of the projects is likely because of the guaranteed purchase of energy to be provided by both plants. The reason is that lenders and investors are primarily concerned about how the funds lent or invested can be recouped in addition to interests derived or profit margin, as the case may be.

4.9.2 Hospital do Subúrbio

The Hospital do Subúrbio is in the city of Salvador in the Brazilian state of Bahia. It is the first PPP in health care to be structured in Brazil. In a bid to improve health care to the citizens and to make the population derive high-quality emergency health services, the state of Bahia opted to contract out, on a PPP basis, the rehabilitation of the hospital. The state government sought the assistance of the International Financial Corporation (IFC) to provide consulting services on PPPs in health care.[88] According to the IFC, a consortium composed by leading Brazilian regional healthcare company Promedia and French facilities management and non-medical services company Dalkia won the bid. The role of the concessionaire was to equip, maintain and operate both clinical and non-clinical services at the hospital for a period of ten years with an option to renew for another ten-year period.[89]

Under the agreement, payment to the concessionaire was tied to key performance targets, thereby creating incentives for high levels of performance. The agreement also required the auditing of the performance criteria by a third-party company. The project has turned out to be a success; in the hospital's first year of operation, it outperformed expectations by more than 50 per cent as far as emergency demand was concerned. It was also ranked by Klynveld Peat Marwick Goerdeler (KPMG) as one of the world's most innovative projects in its '100 Infrastructure: World Cities Edition' report.[90] It is submitted that the success of the Hospital do Subúrbio is attributable to the way it is structured, tying remuneration of the concessionaire to outlined performance indices under the PPP contract as well as the appointment of a qualified third-party auditor to monitor the concessionaire's adherence to the agreed-upon performance indicators.

87 Ibid.

88 International Financial Corporation, 'Public-Private Partnership Stories, Brazil: Hospital do Subúbio' (2013) available at <www.ifc.org/wps/wcm/connect/b4450500498391bf85dcd7336b93d75f/PPPStories_Brazil_HospitalDoSuburbio.pdf?MOD=AJPERES> accessed 10 May 2018.

89 Ibid 2.

90 Ibid.

4.9.3 Belo Horizonte schools

Belo Horizonte is the third-largest city in Brazil. The city has made education one of its priorities in a bid to improve the competitiveness of its workforce in the long-term as well as to support the national government's policy objectives. Notably, the city gained the IFC's support to structure a model for the private sector to fund preschool and primary schools in the city. This led to Brazil's first PPP initiative in the educational sector, with a concession awarded in July 2012. As per the IFC, the Educar Consortium, led by Brazilian construction company Odebrecht, won the 20-year concession for the construction of primary schools and preschool facilities in Belo Horizonte.[91]

The concession contract required the concessionaire to build 32 new preschools and 5 primary schools to be delivered within a space of 2 years and with primary schools becoming operational within 1 year. This was a record time compared with other public-sector procured projects in Brazil. The terms of the contract required the city to provide sites for the facilities while the concessionaire was responsible for the construction and operation of non-pedagogical services, such as cleaning, surveillance, laundry, maintenance and utilities management. This enabled the directors of the schools to concentrate on teaching rather than managing multiple vendors.[92] The adoption of PPP to provide early-school facilities is a novel idea in an emerging economy. Furthermore, streamlining the functions of the concessionaire and the school directorship as far as management is concerned is commendable. There is no point saddling the concessionaire with the responsibility of managing teachers, a task which the consortium is not skilled in, or, as previously noted, diverting the attention of the schools' directorship to a relationship with vendors. The author of this work believes that this will bring out the best from all the parties involved.

4.10 Good governance and PPP in Brazil

Here, the discussion centres on the concept of good governance in the administration and regulation of PPP in Brazil. As an introduction, it has been argued that 'despite the hurdles associated with PPP projects in that country, Brazil's dynamism and forward-thinking characteristics have consistently provided investors with new opportunities to do business.'[93] Since good governance is key to PPP success, an analysis of the mechanism put in place to ensure that

91 International Financial Corporation, 'Public-Private Partnership Stories, Brazil: Belo Horizonte Schools' (2012) available at <www.ifc.org/wps/wcm/connect/b81888004c410f909f12dff12db12449/PPPStories_Brazil_BeloHorizonteSchools.pdf?MOD=AJPERES> accessed 10 May 2018.

92 Ibid.

93 World Finance, 'Navigating Public Private Partnerships in Brazil' (2014) available at <www.worldfinance.com/infrastructure-investment/project-finance/navigating-public-private-partnerships-in-brazil> accessed 4 July 2017.

PPPs are effectively administered and managed in Brazil will serve as a guide for other developing economies.

Brazil's policy on PPP states that the objective of the programme is to 'promote, co-ordinate, regulate, and audit the activities of the private sector agents who, as collaborators, participate in the implementation of public policies aimed at the development of the state and the collective wellbeing.'[94] This leads to the question, what does Brazil seek to achieve with a PPP regime in place? According to Amann et al.:

> Well before the emergence of its current political and economic crisis, Brazil's once favorable track record on inclusive growth masked serious structural deficiencies. One of the most important of these centered – and continues to center – on the quality and quantity of its infrastructure. The infrastructural challenges facing Brazil are epitomized in the well documented difficulties that surrounded the construction of facilities for the 2016 Rio Olympics. However, the infrastructural issue runs far deeper than this heavily publicized case, extending across transportation, energy, telecommunications, sanitation and housing.[95]

The issues noted here have given rise to infrastructure moving to the heart of the country's policy agenda, and since 2007, the Brazilian government has been attempting to engineer a step change in the scale and quality of infrastructure across considered sectors.[96] During the Lula and Rousseff administrations, the government made efforts to raise investments in highways, railways, energy, air transportation, telecommunications, housing, water supply and sanitation. The thrust of the state's agenda to improve on the country's infrastructure and to tackle the country's ingrained underspending on infrastructure, it was decided to turn to PPP with injection of public resources to support private-investment activity.[97] Furthermore, since the global economic slowdown in 2009, the government of Brazil has further prioritised infrastructure investment as well as private participation in infrastructure procurement.[98] Thus, considering the need to bridge its infrastructure deficit in economic and social infrastructure, the governments at the federal, state and municipal levels in Brazil have acknowledge that private funding for long-term projects is a vital investment

94 See Legislative assembly of the State of São Paulo, Brazil (2204) Law 11688 ("PPP Law"). São Paulo, Article 1. See also APMG International, 'Objectives of the PPP Framework' available at <https://ppp-certification.com/ppp-certification-guide/13-objectives-ppp-framework> accessed 3 July 2017.

95 Edmund Amman, Werner Baer, Thomas Trebat and Juan Villa Lora, 'Infrastructure and Its Role in Brazil's Development Process' (2016) 60 *The Quarterly Review of Economics and Finance* 66–73, 66.

96 Ibid.

97 Ibid 72.

98 The World Bank, 'Brazil' (2018) *PPP Knowledge Lab* available at <https://pppknowledgelab.org/countries/brazil> accessed 28 May 2018.

alternative to traditional public-sector procurement. It is in this context that PPP has become a policy tool in that country.

In Brazil, PPPs are conducted in the frame of a PPP programme facilitated by a specialised government agency. At the federal level, the Federal Public-Private Partnership Steering Committee (Comitê Gestor de PPP Federal; CGP) is responsible for administering the PPP programme.[99] A similar institution is in place in some of the states and municipalities. For example, in the state of São Paulo, the regulatory body is the Steering Counsel of Public-Private Partnership (Conselho Gestor de Parcerias Público Privadas).[100]

Therefore, the important question is, how coherent is PPP policy in Brazil? This writer believes that, for a prospective investor seeking to participate in infrastructure procurement in Brazil, the regulatory framework in that country allows for procuring PPPs in the first place. Second, the policy and legal framework regulating PPPs in Brazil has delineated the three tiers of government. Thus, the investor must determine whether in any case the public partner is the federal, state or municipal government. In the case of the federal government of Brazil, the launching of any PPP project requires the analysis and formal approval of the Ministry of Finance.[101] Third, the approval of a PPP project must be based on a study showing *inter alia* 'the convenience and the opportunity of procuring a PPP by identifying the reasons justifying the choice of the form of public-private partnership.'[102] Fourth, Brazilian PPP law requires the procuring authority to include a draft of the contract in the request for proposals.[103] It is submitted that this makes the arrangement clearer for the parties right from the start and allows only parties who have the capacity for such projects to participate in the bidding process, unlike a situation where a party realises after winning the bid that it does not have the wherewithal to execute such a project. It is also submitted that as far as clarity of purpose is concern, by adopting the PPP model of infrastructure procurement, the government of Brazil seeks to improve its infrastructure delivery potential and stimulate economic growth. Again, the government has put in place the necessary machinery to allow for private participation in infrastructure procurement.

To ensure a successful PPP regime, the institutions with the responsibility of approving, monitoring and regulating PPPs must be above board, consistent and empowered to make decisions. Any sign of weakness on the part of the regulatory bodies is an indication that there may be conflicts in the future that could lead to protracted disputes. It is important that the regulatory bodies

99 The CGP was created by Article 14 of the PPP Law and is further regulated by Federal Decree No. 5,585 of 2005.

100 The World Bank, 'Benchmarking PPP Procurement 2017 in Brazil' (2017) available at <http://bpp.worldbank.org/data/exploreeconomies/brazil/~/media/WBG/BPP/Documents/PPP2017-CountryFiles/Brazil-PPP.pdf> accessed 5 July 2017.

101 Article 10 PPP Law 2004.

102 See Article 10.I of the PPP Law 2004.

103 Article 11 PPP Law 2004.

must not be subservient to public-sector agencies. A robust and efficient institutional framework is critical in attracting private investment for infrastructure projects.[104] In the case of Brazil, at the federal level, the institutions charged with the responsibility of approving, monitoring and regulating PPPs are the Ministry of Planning, Budget and Management (MPOG); the Ministry of Finance (MF) and the Partnership Steering Committee (CGP). In Brazil, the challenge has been with regulation at the sub-national level, as the sub-national governments lack experience in structuring PPPs.[105] To solve this, the federal government of Brazil is continuously assisting with the training and advising of institutions at the sub-national level.[106]

Investors require an effective and transparent judicial system to carry out their contracts and settle any disputes that may arise while doing business.[107] Importantly, the World Bank considers the rule of law one important dimension of governance in the control of corruption.[108] Notably, the Constitution of the Federative Republic of Brazil provides that the law shall regulate, based on national interests, the foreign capital investments, shall encourage reinvestments and shall regulate the remittance of profits.[109] With respect, this writer submits that investors may be wary of this provision of the Brazilian Constitution, given the fact that the term 'national interest' is subject to different interpretations. Nevertheless, the Brazilian government has shown that it is supportive of FDI and all other forms of investments, provided they do not contravene local policy regarding foreign investment and national security.[110] As far as enforcing contracts is concerned, the World Bank ranked Brazil as number 37 in the world in 2017.[111]

Article 1 of the Constitution of 1988 states that the Federative Republic of Brazil is a democratic state founded on the rule of law. The principles of legality and separation of powers are well entrenched in that country. However,

104 The World Bank, *The State of PPPs: Infrastructure Public-Private Partnerships in Emerging Markets and Developing Economies* (Washington, DC: The World Bank, 2016) 26.

105 Richard Cabello, 'Challenges for Sub-national Governments to Implement PPPs: The Brazilian Experience' (2011) a presentation at the Public Private Partnership Conference in Lagos, Nigeria, 14–15 November available at <www.ifc.org/wps/wcm/connect/369873004956be7c91afbd849537832d/4.2_PPPs+and+Sub-Nationals+Lessons+from+Around+the+World+-+Challenges+for+Sub-national+Governments+to+Implement+PPPs+-+Richa.pdf?MOD=AJPERES> accessed 5 July 2017.

106 Ibid.

107 OECD, 'Protecting Investment: Legal Frameworks for Infrastructure Investment in Egypt, Jordan, Morocco and Tunisia' (2014) available at <www.oecd.org/globalrelations/Legal%20Study_EN.pdf> accessed 5 July 2017.

108 Helder Ferreira de Mendonça and Andrè Oliveira da Fonseca, 'Corruption, Income, and Rule of Law: Empirical Evidence from Developing and Developed Economies' (2012) 32(2) *Brazilian Journal of Political Economy* 305–314, 310.

109 Article 172 Constitution of Brazil 1988 (as amended).

110 PWC, *op cit* (note 8).

111 The World Bank, 'Doing Business Data' (2017) available at <www.doingbusiness.org/data/exploreeconomies/brazil> accessed 5 July 2017.

Brazil passed through a phase of dictatorship when the executive power was strengthened above other political branches.[112] It has been argued that judges in Brazil are now seen by society as being completely devoid of any accountability because of the judicial independence provided for in the 1988 Constitution.[113] Zimmermann believes that the limited number of judges, corruption, nepotism and politicisation in Brazil are canker worms eating into the fabric of the country's judiciary system. With respect, this writer differs from Zimmermann's view that the independence of the judiciary is responsible for the ills mentioned previously. While conceding that judges have abused that independence and put the judiciary in bad light, this writer believes this is a common problem with developing economies. This is an area where Brazil needs to improve on to encourage investors to do business in that country.

In certain countries, it has been noted, the privatisation process and the shift to PPP was intended to reduce corruption by removing certain assets from the control of the public sector. Despite good intentions, PPPs have not been corruption-proof.[114] One of the main causes of corruption in PPPs is the lack of a tendering process or even the absence of transparency in that process. Again, corruption is the main reason why there is a widespread use of post-contractual renegotiations in Latin-American concessions.[115] It must be noted that the main legal developments in relation to doing business in Brazil is the adoption of anti-corruption laws and regulations, in response to anti-corruption protests.[116] Decree No. 8,420 of 18 March 2015 was adopted as the implementing regulation of the Anti-Corruption Law No. 12 of 1 August 2013. The new legal framework provided for the strict liability of companies for acts of corruption of local and foreign government officials.[117]

The bidding process involves a series of steps, including procurement notice, prequalification and shortlisting, invitation to tender, interaction with bidder and evaluation of tenders, leading to the contract award. A competitive bidding process is required to precede the execution of any PPP project.

112 Ana Paula Barbosa-Fohrmann and Aline da Cruz de Moura, 'The Rule of Law in Brazil' (2011) *Understandings of the Rule of Law in Various Legal Orders in the World Lecture Series* 3.

113 Augusto Zimmermann, 'How Brazilian Judges Undermine the Rule of Law: A Critical Appraisal' (2008) 11 *International Trade and Business Law Review* 179–217.

114 The World Bank, 'Corruption and PPPs: Challenges and Solutions' (2013) available at <http://siteresources.worldbank.org/INTDOII/Resources/Corruption_and_PPPs_backgrounder.pdf> accessed 10 May 2018.

115 Elisabeth Iossa and David Martimort, 'Corruption in Public-Private Partnerships, Incentives and Contract Incompleteness' (2014) *CESifo DICE Report* 3, 16.

116 See British Broadcasting Corporation, 'Hundreds of Thousands Rally Against Corruption in Brazil' (2015) available at <www.bbc.co.uk/news/world-latin-america-32280674> accessed 5 July 2017.

117 Alice Dourado, Cristiana Borja, Leonardo Canabrava, Lucas Spadano, Patricia Salles and Campos Fialho Canabrva Borja Andrade Salles Advogados, 'Doing Business in Brazil' (2016) available at <https://uk.practicallaw.thomsonreuters.com/0-503-8385?transitionType=Default&contextData=(sc.Default)&firstPage=true&bhcp=1> accessed 2 July 2017.

In Brazil, before the bidding commences, drafts of the invitation to bid and the agreement to public consultation must be published in the press. The notice must stipulate the purpose for the bidding process and identify the scope of the project, the length of the contract and its estimated value.[118] Pursuant to Law No. 11,079/2004, Article 12, Item II, the evaluation committee shall establish the evaluation criteria as price, technical or both. The general principle that has been adopted in the country is that the bidding documents are not to be changed during the bidding process, and that provision includes the contract and its economic terms since they are part of the bidding documents. That principle is enunciated in Articles 3 and 41 of the Federal Law No. 8,666/199. In cases where there are unsolicited proposals, such a proposal must contain an explanation of how the proposed project meets public needs.[119] Afterwards, the public authority shall publish a public notice inviting third parties to offer contributions to the project, defining its scope and criteria and how the project will meet public interest. Once the unsolicited proposal is filed, the procuring authority has an obligation to issue a public call for proposals, to verify if there are other private parties interested in the project. Thus, unsolicited proposals eventually lead to competitive bidding as well.

4.11 Conclusion

Whereas some authors have mixed feelings as to whether the PPP model of procurement is a solution to the problem of poor infrastructure in emerging economies, the practice of PPP in Brazil, for instance, shows that with political will and the right environment PPP projects can thrive.

Brazil is a good example for other emerging economies. The PPP framework in Brazil may well serve as a template for other emerging economies, especially in Latin America. Being conscious of the importance of foreign direct investment, Brazil has fine-tuned its PPP laws to capture the fancy of potential foreign investors. For example, the Brazilian PPP laws emphasise that the PPP agreement between the public authority and the private-sector entity shall be legally binding. This provision of the law gives confidence to the would-be investor. The introduction of guarantees also strengthens confidence in the Brazilian PPP framework. Furthermore, the innovation that allows the public authority to own shares in project companies in order to assure the public that PPP is not a ploy to transfer public interest to the private sector helps to boost confidence in the people that PPP is not another means of exploiting the ordinary people.

The next chapter examines PPP law, framework and practice in India.

118 Bruno Werneck and Mário Saadi, *op cit* (note 33).
119 Article 3 of the Decree No. 8,428/2015.

References

Amann, E., Baer, W., Trebat, T., & Lora, J.V. (2016). Infrastructure and Its Role in Brazil's Development Process. *The Quarterly Review of Economics and Finance*, *62*, 66–73. doi:10.1016/j.qref.2016.07.007.

APMG International. (2017). Objectives of the PPP Framework. Retrieved from https://ppp-certification.com/ppp-certification-guide/13-objectives-ppp-framework.

Barbosa-Fohrmann, A.P., & Da Cruz de Moura, A. (2011). The Rule of Law in Brazil. *Understandings of the Rule of Law in Various Legal Orders in the World Lecture Series 3*, 3.

Barral, W., & Haas, A. (2007). Public-Private Partnership in Brazil. *The International Lawyer*, *41*(3), 957–973.

BBC. (2015). Hundreds of Thousands Rally Against Corruption in Brazil. Retrieved from BBC website: <=““ p=““>.

BBC Brazil. (2019). Mundo Movimento. Retrieved from www.bbc.com/portuguese/especial/migrantes/migrantes.shtml.

Cabello, R. (2011, November). *Challenges for Sub-national Governments to Implement PPPs: The Brazilian Experience*. Paper Presented at Public Private Partnership Conference, Lagos.

Central Intelligence Agency. (2019). South America: Brazil – The World Factbook. Retrieved from www.cia.gov/library/publications/the-world-factbook/geos/br.html.

Cheung, E., Chan, A.P., Lam, P.T., Chan, D.W., & Ke, Y. (2012). A Comparative Study of Critical Success Factors for Public Private Partnerships Partnerships (PPP) Between Mainland China and the Hong Kong Special Administrative Region. *Facility Management Development*, *30*(13–14), 647–666.

Corruption, I. (n.d.). Rule of Law: Empirical Evidence from Developing and Developed Economies. *Brazilian Journal of Political Economy*, *32*(2), 305–314.

De Alencar Loiola, F.A. (2013). *The Formulation of Public-Private Partnership Projects for Infrastructure Development in Brazil: An Institutional Analysis of the Municipality of Fortaleza* (Unpublished doctoral dissertation). University of Sheffield, Sheffield.

Dell'Olio, A.J. (2005, October 5). Public-Private Partnerships in Brazil: Opportunities and Risks for Investors. Retrieved from www.migalhas.com.br/dePeso/16,MI16861,11049-PublicPrivate+Partnerships+in+Brazil+Opportunities+and+Risks+for.

Dourado, A., Borja, C., Canabrava, L., Spadano, L., Salles, P., Falho, C., & Advogados, C.B. (2016). Doing Business in Brazil. Retrieved from https://uk.practicallaw.thomsonreuters.com/0-503-8385?transitionType=Default&contextData=(sc.Default)&firstPage=true&bhcp=1.

Filho, M. (2019, April 5). An Introduction to Public-Private Partnerships in Brazil. Retrieved from www.lexology.com/library/detail.aspx?g=485048ca-79be-40a3-8b51-84d727eb5d20.

Focus Economics. (2018). Brazil Economy – GDP, Inflation, CPI and Interest Rate. Retrieved from www.focus-economics.com/countries/brazil.

Gallas, D., & Palumbo, D. (2019, May 27). What's Gone Wrong with Brazil's Economy? Retrieved from www.bbc.co.uk/news/business-48386415.

Global Edge. (2019). Brazil: Introduction. Retrieved from https://globaledge.msu.edu/countries/brazil.

Global Sustainable Electricity Partnership. (2017). Brazil: PCH Figueirópolis and PCH Ludesa. Retrieved from <=““ p=““>.

Infrastructure Management Programme. (2015). Public-Private Partnership (PPP)-Case Study. Retrieved from www.icao.int/sustainability/PPP%20Case%20Studies/PPP_Airport_Brazil.pdf.

Instituto Brasileiro de Geografia e Estatística. (2015). Area Territorial Brasileira. Retrieved from www.webcitation.org/64i0P2Lb0?url=www.ibge.gov.br/home/geociencias/cartografia/default_territ_area.shtm%20.

International Financial Corporation. (2012). *Public-Private Partnership Stories*. Brazil: Belo Horizonte Schools.

International Financial Corporation. (2013). *Public-Private Partnership Stories*. Brazil: Hospital do Subúbio. Retrieved from www.ifc.org/wps/wcm/connect/b4450500498391bf85dcd7336b93d75f/PPPStories_Brazil_HospitalDoSuburbio.pdf?MOD=AJPERES.

Iossa, E., & Martimort, D. (2014). *Corruption in Public-Private Partnerships, Incentives and Contract Incompleteness* (3). CESifo DICE Report.

Kassis, C. U., & Girolami, A. (2004). Brazil's Challenge. Retrieved from www.shearman.com/~/media/Files/NdewsInsights/Publications/2004/10/Brazils-Challenge/Files/Download-PDF-Brazils-Challenge/FileAttachment/PDF_1004.pdf.

Meyer, A. (2010). Brazil Politics – Intro. Retrieved from www.brazil.org.za/politics-intro.html.

Moeriera, T. F., & Sombra, T. L. (2019). Brazil – The Public-Private Partnership Law Review – Edition 5 – TLR. Retrieved from https://thelawreviews.co.uk/edition/the-public-private-partnership-law-review-edition-5/1189691/brazil.

OECD. (2014). *Protecting Investment: Legal Frameworks for Infrastructure Investment in Egypt*. Jordan: Morocco and Tunisia. Retrieved from www.oecd.org/globalrelations/Legal%20Study_EN.pdf.

Philander, S. G. (2012). *Encyclopedia of Global Warming and Climate Change, Second Edition*. Thousand Oaks, CA: Sage Publications.

PPP Knowledge Lab. (2019, December 9). Brazil. Retrieved from https://pppknowledgelab.org/countries/brazil.

Price Water House Coopers. (2013). *Doing Business in Brazil*. Sao Paulo: Price Water House Coopers.

Queiroz, C., Astensiano, G., & Serebrisky, T. (2014). An Overview of the Brazilian PPP Experience form a Stakeholders' Viewpoint. Retrieved from https://publications.iadb.org/bitstream/handle/11319/6399/An%20Overview%20of%20the%20Brazilian%20PPP%20Experience%20from%20a%20Stakeholders%C2%BF%20Viewpoint%20final.pdf?sequence=1.

Romero, S. (2016, August 31). Dilma Rousseff Is Ousted as Brazil's President in Impeachment Vote. Retrieved from www.nytimes.com/2016/09/01/world/americas/brazil-dilma-rousseff-impeached-removed-president.html?_r=.

Rosenn, K. S. (2005). Federalism in Brazil. *Duquesne Law Review*, *43*, 577.

Shah, A. (2010). The New Fiscal Federalism in Brazil (English). Retrieved from http://documents.worldbank.org/curated/en/480641468743787324/The-new-fiscal-federalism-in-Brazil.

United Nations. (2014). Brazil – The Land. Retrieved from https://web.archive.org/web/20141023154830/www.un.int/brazil/brasil/brazil-land.htm.

Vittor, J. L., & Samples, T. R. (2011). PPPs and Latin America Infrastructure Markets: Brazil and Chile. *Latin American Law and Business Report*, *19*(7), 3.

Werneck, B., & Saadi, M. (2016). *The Public-Private Partnership Law Review*. London: Law Business Research.

The World Bank. (2013). Corruption and PPPs: Challenges and Solutions. Retrieved from http://siteresources.worldbank.org/INTDOII/Resources/Corruption_and_PPPs_backgrounder.pdf.

The World Bank. (2014). *Overcoming Constraints to the Financing of Infrastructure*. Washington, DC: Author.

The World Bank. (2016). Brazil. Retrieved from www.worldbank.org/en/country/brazil/overview.

The World Bank. (2017). Doing Business Data. Retrieved from www.doingbusiness.org/data/exploreeconomies/brazil.

The World Bank. (2019, December 11). Brazil. Retrieved from https://pppknowledgelab.org/countries/brazil.

World Finance. (2014). Navigating Public Private Partnerships in Brazil. Retrieved from www.worldfinance.com/infrastructure-investment/project-finance/navigating-public-private-partnerships-in-brazil.

Yescombe, E.R. (2007). *Public-Private Partnerships: Principles of Policy and Finance*. Amsterdam, Netherlands: Butterwirth-Heinemann.

Zimmermann, A. (2008). How Brazilian Judges Undermine the Rule of Law: A Critical Appraisal. *International Trade and Business Law Review, 11*, 179–217.

5 India

5.1 Introduction

Even though India's massive PPP programme has faced challenges in recent years,[1] in this chapter, India is presented as a PPP market that can serve as a model for other emerging economies in the successful administration of PPP. The choice of India is based on its role as a leading emerging economy in Asia as well as the size of the PPP market in that country. Furthermore, India is regarded as a country with massive growth potential. Under the right circumstances, India could become a global leader by 2041.[2] The approach in this chapter, as with the previous chapter, is to examine the framework for PPP in India along the themes of critical success factors (CSFs) and PPP governance. While CSFs consist of the fundamentals required to create a successful PPP regime, PPP governance describes the mechanisms that make an environment conducive for PPP investments. Under CSFs, sub-themes, such as legal and policy framework, stable political environment and government agencies are discussed. Sub-themes for PPP governance include, among other things, a coherent policy, anti-corruption, competitive bidding, rule of law and efficient risk sharing. The chapter begins with an introduction to India and its socio-economic and political background and the potential for doing business there. The discussion then shifts to the law and practice of PPP in the country with several case studies discussed to show how the law is put in practice.

5.2 Introducing India

The nation of India is located in the continent of Asia and occupies the greater part of South Asia. India is a constitutional republic made up of 28 states and eight union territories, with each state having a substantial amount of control over its affairs, 8 less fully empowered union territories and the nation's capital

1 Deblina Saha, 'PPPs in India – Will They Retain Their Former Glory?' (2017) available at <http://blogs.worldbank.org/ppps/ppps-india-will-they-regain-their-former-glory> accessed 13 December 2019.

2 Rameez Raja Shaik and Niketa Narain, 'Comparative Analysis of Infrastructure PPP in BRICS Nations' (2011) 20 *International Conference on Advancement in Information Technology with Workshop of ICBMG IPCSIT* 283.

territory Delhi, which includes the Indian capital of New Delhi.[3] India's population is one-sixth of the world's population and is second only to China in terms of population size.[4] Present-day India has about 3.2 million square kilometres and stretches from Cape Comorin, 8 degrees north of the equator, to its border with the disputed Kashmir region. India shares a border with Pakistan to the west and Bangladesh, China and Myanmar to the east. The country encounters challenges such as 'environmental degradation, extensive poverty, and widespread corruption; however, economic growth following the launch of economic reforms in 1991, a massive youthful population, and a strategic geographic location are contributing to India's emergence as a regional and global power.'[5] There is thus a very huge potential for India to develop rapidly with the right infrastructure in place, and an appropriate PPP strategy can play a huge role in that direction.

India was the world's seventh-largest economy as of April 2018.[6] The state of India, like Brazil, is also a federation with the Constitution of India being the *suprema lex*.[7] The Constitution enshrines the principle of division of powers amongst the different tiers of government (i.e. the central government, the state government and the local government).

The Republic of India operates a common-law system based on the English model.[8] The country's diverse economy is largely made up of traditional village farming, modern agriculture and a range of industries and services.[9]

India rolled out a PPP programme for the delivery of high-priority public facilities over the last decade in what has been regarded as the largest PPP programme in the world.[10] In the same vein, India ranks first in 'operational maturity' for PPP projects and third for sub-national PPP activity in the world.[11] The Government of India (GoI) aims to use PPP as a tool for 'improving the level and the quality of economic and social infrastructure services across the country.'[12] In this regard, the government considers PPP as a means for 'harnessing private sector investment and operational efficiencies in the provision of public assets and services.'[13]

3 AL Srivatava, YG Percival Spear, Romila Thapar and R Champakalashmi, 'India' *Britannica* available at <www.britannica.com/place/India> accessed 12 December 2019.

4 Ibid.

5 Central Intelligence Agency, 'India' (2019) available at <www.cia.gov/library/publications/the-world-factbook/geos/in.html> accessed 13 December 2019.

6 Research Republic, *Developing India's Infrastructure Through Public Private Partnerships: A Resource Guide* (London: City of London, 2008) 36.

7 Sunil Seth and Vasanth Rajasekaran, 'India' in Bruno Werneck and Mário Saadi (eds.), *The Public-Private Partnership Law Review* (London: Law Business Research Ltd, 2017) 110.

8 Central Intelligence Agency, *op cit* (note 5).

9 Ibid.

10 Department of Economic Affairs, 'PPP in India' (2019) available at <www.pppinindia.gov.in/overview> accessed 13 December 2019.

11 Ibid.

12 Department of Economic Affairs, *National Public Private Partnership Policy* (New Delhi: Department of Economic Affairs, 2011) 2.

13 Ibid.

5.3 Legal framework for PPP in India

PPP in India is defined as follows:

> Public Private Partnership means an arrangement between a government / statutory entity / government owned entity on one side and a private sector entity on the other, for the provision of public assets and/or public services, through investments being made and/or management being undertaken by the private sector entity, for a specified period of time, where there is well defined allocation of risk between the private sector and the public entity and the private entity receives performance linked payments that conform (or are benchmarked) to specified and predetermined performance standards, measurable by the public entity or its representative.[14]

It is clear from this definition that PPP in India includes the provision of services for members of the public by a private-sector entity. This is in contradistinction with, for example, Nigeria or South Africa, where a PPP is distinct from a service contract between the public authority and a private-sector entity.

It is interesting to note that 'there is no overarching legal framework for PPPs at the national level' in India.[15] In its place, however, the Government of India (GoI) has a number of guidelines and frameworks as well as an appraisal and approval committee to see to it that there is adequate commitment towards infrastructure PPP.[16] The absence of a standard law regulating PPPs may be an albatross for PPP in India, except there is a continuous record of PPP successes to give private-sector investors the confidence that the process is effective and efficient.

Again, the GoI has launched many institutional initiatives for PPPs as follows:[17]

1 The setting up of a Committee on Infrastructure (CoI) chaired by the Prime Minister of India. The primary purpose of the committee is to formulate and implement policies that enable the development of a world-class infrastructure in the country in addition to promoting the delivery of high-standard public services that match international best practice;
2 The creation of a Viability Gap Fund (VGF) for making infrastructure projects commercially viable. This, in addition to the India Infrastructure Finance Company Limited (IIFCL), provide log-term capital to aid

14 Ibid 4.
15 Research Republic, *Developing India's Infrastructure Through Public Private Partnerships: A Resource Guide* (London: City of London, 2008) 36.
16 Sunil Seth and Vansanth Rajasekaran, *op cit* (note 7) 10.
17 Research Republic, *op cit* (note 15) 42.

finance PPPs. The funding usually comes in the form of a capital grant during the construction phase;
3 The creation of the PPP Appraisal Committee (PPPAC) to structure the project appraisal process to effectively eliminate administrative hurdles; and
4 The standardisation of bidding and contractual documents, such as request for qualification (RFQ), request for proposal (RFP) and model concession agreements (MCA) for making the procurement process rapid.

A potential PPP investor in India is saddled with the task of looking up a few guidelines and studying the roles of different bodies in order to grasp the country's PPP process. Thus, while the process is a lot clearer in Brazil, the guidelines method used by India requires a more detailed study of the procedure.

In India, based on the guidelines, a bidder submits two separate bids for a PPP project: a technical bid and a financial bid. The process commences with an RFQ or, better still, Expression of Interest (EoI). Here, experienced bidders (i.e. those with the technical and financial capacity to undertake the project) are identified. The prospective bidders are then shortlisted for the RFP stage. At the RFP stage, the pre-qualified bidders are required to submit their financial offers. The stage that follows is the evaluation and grant stage. This involves evaluating the various bids to determine which bidder wins. In India, the standard for determining which bidder should be preferred is based on the bidder's experience in building infrastructure projects and its technical capacity. The parameters for measuring technical capacity are based on project and construction experience with PPP projects in the specified and core sectors.[18] This is entirely different from the Brazilian method of considering lowest counterpart funding on the part of the public authority and previous experience of social responsibility on the part of the bidders.

5.4 Land acquisition for PPP purposes

The acquisition of land for infrastructure purposes is one that has been challenging, especially in developing economies. In some climes, governments have been known to compulsorily acquire private land from their private owners, even without their willing consent. According to Jonathan Lindsay, the power to do this is known by a variety of names depending on a country's legal traditions, including eminent domain, expropriation, takings and compulsory purchase.[19] National Constitutions and laws are known to typically refer to

18 Ibid 114.
19 Jonathan Mills Lindsay, 'Compulsory Acquisition of Land and Compensation in Infrastructure Projects' (2012) 1(3) *PPP Insights: An Explanatory Note on Issues Relevant to Public-Private Partnerships* 1.

compulsory acquisition being used for 'public purposes,' for 'public use' and/or in 'the public interest.'[20]

Land acquisition in India is described as the most challenging aspect for pre-development activity in the country.[21] In the same vein, delay in land acquisition owing to native encumbrances is also considered as a risk factor in undertaking PPPs in the country.[22] In 2015, the GoI attempted a land law reform and sought to introduce a bill that would allow for the acquisition of land and payment of compensation with the consent of 70 per cent of the landowners. This bill did not see the light of day because of opposition by the people of India. Land acquisition thus continues to remain a major challenge for the nation.

5.5 Stable political and social environment

In the words of Cheung et al., 'successful PPP implementation requires stable political and social environment, which in turn relies on the stability and capability of the host government.'[23] They note, and rightly so, that political and social issues that go beyond the private sector's domain should be handled by the government. The way the country handles regime changes vis-à-vis projects procured via PPP and the ease of investors investing in the country's market space is the subject of focus under this heading. Again, 'if unduly victimised, it is legitimate that the private sector participants should be adequately compensated.'[24]

India is the largest country in Asia; it has 28 states and 8 union territories. It is also a culturally diverse country. India is a secular state and is considered the largest democracy in the world with a parliamentary form of government.[25] The country's population is expected to surpass that of China's in 2028 to become the most populous nation on earth.[26] As an economic powerhouse and nuclear-armed state, India occupies the position of an important power in Asia.[27] The Union Government of India is divided into the legislative, executive and judicial arms.

20 Ibid 2.

21 Ministry of Finance, Government of India, 'Tools and Resources' (2016) available at <http://toolkit.pppinindia.com/ports/module3-roiewp-learnings-development.php?links=roiewp1&links1=roiewp3&links2=roiewp3c> accessed 20 September 2016.

22 Ibid.

23 Esther Cheung, Albert PC Chan, Patrick TI Lam, Daniel WM Chan and Yongjian Ke, 'A Comparative Study of Critical Success Factors for Public Private Partnerships (PPP) Between Mainland China and the Hong Kong Special Administrative Region' (2012) 30(13–14) *Facility Management Development* 647–666.

24 Ibid.

25 Riad Josep, Jitesh Bansai, Puja Singhvi and Diana Dsouza (eds.), *Doing Business in India* (Ernst & Young, 2013) available at <www.ey.com/Publication/vwLUAssets/EY-doing-business-in-India-2013/$FILE/EY-Doing-business-in-India.pdf> accessed 7 July 2017.

26 This is according to UN estimates.

27 British Broadcasting Corporation, 'India Country Profile' available at <www.bbc.co.uk/news/world-south-asia-12557384> accessed 5 October 2016.

India voted for a new government in 2014 amidst a heightened anti-incumbency sentiment and voter restlessness. This was because of a perceived inability of the previous government to tackle corruption and deal with rising inflation. Mr Narendra Modi of the opposing Bharatiya Janata Party (BJP) won a landslide mandate to become the Prime Minister of India.[28]

It is noteworthy that, for the first time in India, in a span of 30 years, a single party attained absolute majority in the Lower House (the Lok Sabha)[29] and thereby eliminated any need for a coalition to form the government.[30] The ruling party is thus free from the whims and blackmail of smaller allies. This situation allowed the BJP to deliver on its manifesto without having to lobby the other parties, which often takes time and gives rise to delays in the implementation of state policies.

To stimulate private-sector participation in the funding of infrastructure in India, the GoI has two types of infrastructure debt fund (IDF) structures aimed at attracting new investment into the sector. There are challenges, however, that pertain to stretching the domestic banks as they approach their debt limits and the withdrawal of international banking institutions due to the global financial crisis. Thus, the new policy model by the GoI is to seek new types of investors 'who are well capitalised and seeking longer-term returns.' It is argued that the Indian model, if successful, can be a prototype for other developing countries.[31]

5.6 Well-organised and committed public agencies

The agency of government charged with the responsibility of overseeing PPP agreements from the bidding stage to the operation phase must essentially be effective and committed to ensuring PPP success. Because these agencies are public-sector oriented, the possibility of administrative bureaucracies that characterise the public sector in the developing world may hamper efficiency, thereby creating bottlenecks that will result in unnecessary delays. How well these agencies are structured is critical if PPPs must succeed.

In India, PPPs are administered by the PPP Cell, Infrastructure Division of the Department of Economic Affairs (DEA) alongside the following bodies, namely, the Public Private Partnership Appraisal Committee (PPPAC), the Empowered Committee and the Empowered Institution for the projects proposed for financial support through the Viability Gap Fund. The PPP Cell was established in 2006 in the DEA[32] and is responsible for policy schemes,

28 FTI Consulting, 'India's Investment Climate Under the New Government' (2014) *Global Risk and Investigations* available at <www.fticonsulting.com/~/media/Files/us-files/insights/white-papers/indias-investment-climate-under-the-new-government.pdf> accessed 5 October 2016.

29 The *Lok Sabha* is one of the two houses of parliament. It is the more powerful of the two houses.

30 Ibid.

31 The World Bank, 'Overcoming Constraints to the Financing of Infrastructure' (2014) *World Bank Report* 8.

32 Government of India, 'Public Private Partnerships in India' (2018) available at <www.pppinindia.gov.in/overview> accessed 11 May 2018.

programmes, capacity building and other ancillary matters that pertain to mainstreaming PPPs. The functions of the PPP Cell include the following:[33]

1 Exercising the administration and approval of central-sector PPP projects in all sectors costing more than Rs. 100 crore or more but less than Rs. 5,000 crore;
2 Matters and proposals relating to clearance by the PPPAC;
3 Matters and proposals relating to the VGF scheme for financial support to PPPs in infrastructure;
4 Matters and proposals relating to the scheme for the India Infrastructure Project Development Fund;
5 Developing multi-pronged and innovative interventions and support mechanisms for facilitating PPPs in the country, including technical-assistance programmes from bilateral and multilateral agencies on mainstreaming PPPs and support to state and local governments;
6 Managing training programmes, strategies, exposures for capacity building for PPPs and other matters relating to institution building for mainstreaming PPPs;
7 All international interfaces on PPPs and other matters concerning PPPs;
8 Matters relating to the management of PPP-related information; and
9 The toolkit for use by PPP practitioners across India in both the public and private sectors.

5.7 Scorecard for PPP in India

There is a huge record of PPP success in India despite the challenges associated with land acquisition and other associated factors in that country.[34] As per the GoI,[35] in 2006 there were over 500 PPP projects totalling about Rs. 340 billion.[36] Notably, India is the world's largest PPP market[37] due to recent significant growth in the number of PPPs there, according to a report by Ernst

33 Department of Economic Affairs, 'Infrastructure and Energy Division' (2016) available at <http://finmin.nic.in/the_ministry/dept_eco_affairs/infrastrucure_div/I&I_index.asp?pageid=2#PPP Cell> accessed 11 May 2016.

34 Although there have been some failures in PPPs in some power and metro rail projects as noted by Manish Agarwal in his article 'India's PPP Story: A Glass Half-Full' published in the *Financial Express* of 17 October 2015, considering the number of successful projects closed and executed, PPP in India is more of a success story.

35 Department of Economic Affairs (DEA), Ministry of Finance, Government of India and Asian Development Bank (ADB), *Facilitating Public-Private Partnership for Accelerated Infrastructure Development in India* (Manila: Asian Development Bank, 2006).

36 TI-UP Resource Centre, 'Public Private Partnerships in India' (2006) A Report by WSP International Management Consulting and Total Synergy Consulting 10.

37 Department of Economic Affairs (DEA) (2015), Report of the Committee on Revisiting and Revitalising Public Private Partnership Model of Infrastructure, ix.

and Young.[38] Thus, over time, a PPP system comprising institutions, developers, financiers, equity providers, policies and procedures has been developed in that country.[39] It is submitted that a consistent and seamless PPP framework would lead to a trust in the system by all stakeholders.

There is a significant contribution by multilateral agencies[40] to the PPP regime in India. This has in turn led to improving the investment climate in the country. Notably, the private-sector financing arm of the World Bank did set up an Indian Infrastructure Fund with a mandate to invest in a diversified portfolio of project-equity investments.[41] It is submitted that emerging economies need to make their processes clear and work on their institutions to reduce the bureaucracy often noted in government establishments to get the support of multilateral agencies.

There is a wide sectoral spread of PPP projects in India. This results in a broader impact of PPP being felt in the economy of that country. Mahapatra notes that Indian PPP diversity includes transport projects (roads, airports and ports), which are considered more successful. Indeed, 'the new airports at Delhi, Mumbai, Bangalore and Hyderabad and a large volume of highway projects taken up on BOT showcase the pragmatic success of PPPs in the country.'[42]

Another factor responsible for PPP successes in India as per Mahapatra is the 'streamlining of procedures for systematic and speedy appraisal and approval of projects.'[43] It is submitted that the regulators of PPP in any given jurisdiction must seek ways of organising the process that are devoid of bottlenecks and unnecessary delays. There is no point in having a 12-stage process if the job can effectively be done in 6 stages.

To incentivise private-sector participation in the country, the GoI has developed model concession agreements (MCAs) for PPPs, especially in the road sector, such as the MCAs for major road projects valued at more than Rs. 1 billion or minor projects costing less than Rs. 1 billion undertaken on a BOT (toll) basis and the MCAs for road projects structured as BOT (annuity).[44]

38 Ernst and Young, 'Public Private Partnership: The Next Continuum' (2013) a Report by Ernst and Young available at <www.ey.com/publication/vwluassets/ey-public-private-partnership-the-next-continuum/$file/ey-public-private-partnership-the-next-continuum.pdf> accessed 5 May 2018.

39 Ibid 6.

40 Such as the World bank, Asian Development bank (ADB) and Department for International Development (DFID).

41 Ernst and Young, *op cit* (note 38) 9.

42 Abhilasha Mahapatra, 'Sharing India's PPP Experience' (2015) a presentation at the UNESCAP Policy Dialogue on PPPs in Infrastructure held in Kathmandu on 22 September 2015, 5 available at <www.unescap.org/sites/default/files/Day%201%20-%20Session%202.2%20-%20India%20PPP.pdf> accessed 28 May 2018.

43 Ibid 8.

44 Satyanaryana N Kalidindi and L Boeing Singh, 'Financing Road Projects in India Using PPP Scheme' (2009) *Proceedings of the 2009 Mid-Continent Transportation Research Symposium*, Ames, Iowa, August 2009 at the Iowa State University 6.

These standard agreements are meant to provide uniformity in road PPP projects. In this regard, this researcher submits that a PPP structure must allow for the development of a uniform procedure, as this will give potential investors clarity of the process beforehand.

Since PPPs usually require long-term funding (equity or debt), it is noteworthy that the GoI has taken steps in this regard. There is now in place a scheme for financing commercially viable infrastructure projects in sectors, such as roads, power, solid waste management and water supply through an SPV called the India Infrastructure Finance Company Limited (IIFCL). In the same vein, a fund known as the India Infrastructure Project Development Fund (IIPD), with a take-off grant of Rs. 1 billion has been set up to provide financial assistance to state and central ministries for quality project development. This is in addition to the Viability Gap Funding Scheme launched in 2004 to meet the need of economically essential projects and make it commercially viable for private-sector partners.[45]

Structuring a PPP to benefit the locals in any given community other than them just being end users of the facility can help gain their support in no small measure. The state of Gujurat in India has adopted this strategy. In 2010, Gujurat's government sought the IFC's assistance to develop an innovative Mega Watts rooftop solar PPP project in the state capital of Gandhinagar by outfitting government buildings with solar panels. The execution of that project proved the potential of rooftop solar power in the country. Following this, the state government opted to replicate the same project but this time with the participation of the locals. The new project was to be built in the city of Vadodara with the panels on the rooftops of private houses. To execute this project, Madhav Solar (Vadodara Rooftop) Private Limited (the 'concessionaire') won the 25-year concession for a 5 MW rooftop solar project. Under the concession, Madhav Solar would instal solar photovoltaic panels on the rooftops of private properties and sell the energy generated to the local community. Madhav Solar would also offer a lease rental to the owners of the private properties for accessing and using their roofs. Apart from the sum of US$8 million in private investment, it was expected that the project would see 9,000 people receiving increased access to power supply. The IFC was to serve as the lead transaction advisor and manage the tender process, among other things.[46] It is submitted that such projects that have a way of benefitting locals will get their support. Adopting similar strategies in places where the local community opposes PPP projects can help to get their acceptance and support.

45 Ibid.

46 International Finance Corporation, 'Public-Private Partnership Stories, India: Vadodara Solar' (2015) available at <www.ifc.org/wps/wcm/connect/458a22804528ba90bc2dbcc66d9c728b/PPP stories_India_Vadodara+Solar.pdf?MOD=AJPERES> accessed 11 May 2018.

Following this, the author of this work agrees and adopts the position of the African Development Bank Group (AfDB) with regard to the success of PPP in India. As per the AfDB:

> India's story of success in implementing the Private-Public Partnership (PPP) model makes it an important partner in facilitating the adoption of this model in Africa. India is one of the developing countries to have successfully received large-scale investment to the tune of US $300 billion in infrastructure under the PPP model. In line with this, the Government of India has signed a Memorandum of Understanding with the African Development Bank Group to share the model agreements and legal documents associated with PPPs to facilitate implementation of this model in African countries.[47]

5.8 Brief case studies of flagship PPP projects in India

Under this section, some selected PPP projects executed in different sectors in India will be examined to have an insight into PPP practice in the country. The sectors covered are power, waste management and road transport.

5.8.1 Bhubaneswar street lighting

Bhubaneswar is the capital of the Indian state of Odisha. In the past, the city suffered from poor, outdated and inefficient street lighting, which was considered too expensive to improve. On that note, the city sought the IFC's assistance to structure a PPP transaction and a process for identifying a qualified private-sector partner. Consequent upon this, Shah Investments, Financials, Developments and Consultants Private Limited, an Indian energy services company, was awarded the PPP tender. The project was designed to ensure that the facilities would be paid for through energy savings realised form Bhubaneswar Municipal Corporation. The post-tender results showed that the project was expected to generate annual savings to the government of US$100,000, with a potential for replication throughout India.[48] The IFC noted that there was a series of consultations with private investors to identify potential deal-breakers. The result was the mitigation of risks, such as project viability, lack of payment security and ineffective monitoring and verification. The innovation advised by IFC is the use of advance payments via escrow accounts and the

47 African Development Bank Group, 'Lessons in Private-Public Partnership (PPP) from India' (2014) available at <www.afdb.org/en/news-and-events/article/lessons-in-private-public-partnership-ppp-from-india-13226/> accessed 11 May 2018.

48 International Finance Corporation, 'Public-Private Partnership Stories, India: Bhubaneswar Street Lighting' (2013) available at <http://ppp.worldbank.org/public-private-partnership/sites/ppp.worldbank.org/files/documents/PPP_Stories_India_Bhubaneswar_Street_Lighting_EN_2013.pdf> accessed 7 July 2017.

automatic approval of 75 per cent of operator invoices.[49] The project structure is a reflection that ideas relating to how a project can succeed can be obtained from the private sector.

5.8.2 Berhampur solid-waste management

Berhampur is another city in the state of Odisha. The city had a challenge with its solid waste-management system. Apart from this system being inadequate, it was not in compliance with national regulations. The Department of Housing and Urban Development of the Government of Odisha as well as the Berhampur Municipal Corporation sought an affordable solution for the procurement of an improved waste-management service to the locals. The IFC structured a PPP transaction on behalf of the public authority in both Odisha and Berhampur to attract a private operator to improve the efficiency and management of the system.[50]

According to the IFC, eight companies expressed interest in the project, and two eventually submitted bids. The winning bidder was a consortium led by UPL Environmental Engineers Limited, a large Indian environmental engineering construction firm with 15 years of experience in solid and hazardous waste management, waste-water treatment, recycling and other environmental projects. The concession agreement was signed on 30 August 2013, and the post-tender results showed that the private operator would manage a composting facility with a capacity of 150 tons per day. Of significance to this study is the fact that over 350,000 residents, one-third of whom live in low-income areas of Berhampur, are to benefit from daily door-to-door waste pick-up services without increasing costs to the municipality.[51] It is submitted that PPP projects should be structured in such a way so as not to increase the costs that the municipality should bear in line with the VfM concept and at the same time not over-pricing the service out of the reach of the ordinary end users of the facility.

5.8.3 The Tuni Anakapalli Annuity Road Project[52]

As per the Indian DEA[53], the Tuni Anakapalli Annuity Road Project is a road-expansion project undertaken by the National Highways Authority of India (NHAI) as one out of many other projects under the country's Golden Quadrilateral programme. The purpose of the project was to widen National Highway

49 Ibid.

50 International Financial Corporation, 'Public-Private Partnership Stories, India: Berhampur Solid Waste Management' (2013) available at <www.ifc.org/wps/wcm/connect/31b05382-bfae-48f7-9310-e32f53f44c36/PPPStories_India_BerhampurSolidWaste.pdf?MOD=AJPERES> accessed 6 December 2016.

51 Ibid.

52 The analysis in this section is based on the report by the Indian Department of Economic Affairs, *Public Private Partnership Projects in India: A Compendium of Case Studies* (New Delhi: Ministry of Finance, 2015) 22–28.

53 Ibid.

5 to accommodate a 4-lane dual carriageway for approximately 59 kilometres between Tuni and Anakapalli in the state of Andhra Pradesh on a PPP basis. The reason for adopting an annuity-styled PPP structure was based on the lack of attractiveness in tolling the road. The arrangement was that the NHAI would pay the concessionaire a fixed annuity sum of Rs. 29.48 crore semi-annually.

The GMR Group, in consortium with United Engineers Malaysia (UEM) and Berhad Group, was awarded the contract. The consortium thereupon set up an SPV by the name of GMR Tuni Anakapalli Expressways Private Limited (GTAEPL) to execute the project. Construction on the road commenced in May 2002 and ended in December 2004 after delays in the handing over of land by the NHAI caused the work to run a month longer than expected. Being awarded on a BOT (annuity) basis, the NHAI paid the concessionaire a fixed sum twice a year during the concession period to compensate for the capital cost and operational and maintenance expenses of the project along with a certain percentage of returns on investment. By the terms of the contract, if the concessionaire failed to make the carriageway available within the agreed-upon timeline, the annuity to be paid to the concessionaire would be proportionately reduced. The NHAI secured the annuity payment by the provision of a revolving letter of credit from a schedule bank in India throughout the period of operation.

It is noteworthy that GTAEPL was precluded from tolling or levying charges other than for advertisements on the road. Annuity was thus the only revenue for the concessionaire handling the project. Furthermore, GTAEPL entered an operations and maintenance agreement with UEM Limited (the O&M contractor) to operate and maintain the project facilities and to take full risk in their care. Under the terms of the agreement, at the end of the concession period in November 2019, the concessionaire would hand over the project assets free of cost to the NHAI.

GTAEPL secured funding for the project at low interest rates by securitising annuity payments receivable from NHAI, thus allowing the concessionaire to repay the debt and access funds at a lower cost. The project agreement also provided for the developer to receive an incentive fee for early completion, which attracted a bonus payment and, in the same vein, a penalty for delayed delivery. An earlier completion also meant that the concessionaire would earn annuities early. It is submitted that the annuity model of PPP concession structured for the Tuni Anakapalli Annuity Road Project can provide a solution to the problem of community resistance to the payment of tolls.

5.9 Good governance and PPP

Good governance is a prerequisite for PPP success. On the other hand, corruption in government is a serious obstacle to successful PPPs.[54] The United

54 R Hemming and International Monetary Fund, *Public-Private Partnerships, Government Guarantees, and Fiscal Risk* (Washington, DC: International Monetary Fund, 2006) 15.

Nations Development Programme (UNDP) views governance as the 'exercise of political, economic and administrative authority in the management of a country's affairs at all levels. It comprises mechanisms, process and institutions through which citizen and groups articulate their interests, exercise their legal rights, meet their obligations and mediate their differences.'[55] The World Bank defines governance as 'the exercise of political authority and the use of institutional resources to manage society's problems and affairs.'[56] Governance failure jeopardises public goods and business market value. Therefore, transparency as far as PPP is concerned is necessary. In the absence of accountability, the choice of the PPP pathway in the first place may be of no value. It is therefore important that beginning with the bidding process, no decision by the public authority must paint a picture of unfairness. According to Queiroz, 'at their best, PPPs can provide rapid injections of cash from private financiers, delivery of quality services, and overall cost-effectiveness the public sector cannot achieve on its own.'[57] He notes further that 'at their worst, PPPs can also drive up costs, under-deliver services, harm the public interest, and introduce new opportunities for fraud, collusion, and corruption.'[58] It is worth noting that high-value transactions are prone to attract the risk of corruption as private players may attempt to improperly influence transactions in their favour, and public officials may seek to extract private profit from public office. Therefore, good governance in PPP management is essential to ensure that the involvement of the private sector produces maximum benefits for the public. If PPPs are to bring the requisite benefits to the public, they need to first take place in a well-developed and regulated economic system and, second, in a context of 'good governance' in which the challenges entailed are managed sensitively so that both stakeholders' needs and underlying objectives are met.[59] The challenges to good governance and public acceptability of PPP are a vicious circle of weak institutions, lack of transparency in deals, conflicts of interest, corruption, distrust of the private sector enriching itself at the expense of the end user and the government losing the political will to promote PPP.[60]

55 Cited in Planning Commission: National Human Development Report 2001 New Delhi (Oxford: Oxford University Press, 1997) 4–15.

56 The World Bank, *Managing Development: The Governance Dimension* (Washington, DC: The World Bank, 1991).

57 Cesar Queiroz, 'The Essential Need for Good Governance in Public-Private Partnerships' (2013) available at <https://ptfund.org/the-essential-need-for-good-governance-in-public-private-partnerships/> accessed 5 July 2017.

58 Ibid.

59 Mark Richard Hayllar, 'Public-Private Partnerships in Hong Kong: Good Governance: The Essential Missing Ingredient'? (2010) 69 *Australian Journal of Public Administration* 101.

60 Geoffrey Hamilton, 'Role of Good Governance in Establishing Successful Public-Private Partnerships' (2011) available at <www.aik-invest.hr/wp-content/uploads/2015/11/geoffrey-hamilton_2.pdf> accessed 5 July 2017.

The key components for assessing good governance in PPP projects include, and are not limited to, a coherent PPP policy; strong enabling institutions; rule of law, including protecting property rights; the enforcement of contracts; bureaucratic efficiency; control of corruption; competitive bidding; disclosure of relevant information to the public and long-term monitoring by a regulatory body. Good governance in PPP is examined next.

In the case of India, there are at least six key factors identified here as the drivers for good PPP governance. These are a strong public-sector capacity to identify, structure and monitor PPP projects; community involvement; adequate funding; efficient risk sharing and sustainability.[61] These factors, including competitive bidding, are vital in ensuring the effective management and regulation of PPP projects in India. The GoI has issued a series of guidance papers and a PPP toolkit for the purpose of supporting preparation and the decision-making process for all PPP projects. The documents provide sector-specific instructions and can be used throughout all the stages of any project, from identification to feasibility studies to procurement to operation.[62]

5.9.1 Strong public-sector capacity

Taking into consideration the emergence of a strong private sector in India, there is a corresponding need on the part of the public sector to strengthen its governance capabilities. There must be a sustained political and bureaucratic commitment to ensure that projects are not only thought through but implemented so that such projects are not put at risk.[63] A case in point is the project for the modernisation of the Delhi International Airport in 2003. After the Airport Authority of India (AAI) board approved the transaction, it took three years for the final approval from the Empowered Group of Ministers to sanction the transaction. The delay, caused by a change in the central government, could have jeopardised the project. It is submitted that, like most developing countries, India must strengthen the capacity of its public sector to meet the demands of business in the modern era. Similarly, for effective governance, the regulators in India need to be empowered to not only determine tariff rates but also set and enforce performance standards or other measures to protect the private-sector partner from the might of the government agency sponsoring the project.

61 See generally, Public Policy Team and Athena Infonomics, 'Public Private Partnerships in India: Lessons from Experiences' (2012) available at <www.gov.uk/government/uploads/system/uploads/attachment_data/file/186989/Report-PPPLessonsFromExperiences270812.pdf> accessed 6 July 2017.

62 The World Bank, 'India' (2017) available at <https://pppknowledgelab.org/countries/india> accessed 10 July 2017.

63 Ibid.

5.9.2 Community involvement

The members of the community where the project is located are important stakeholders in any PPP project. The need to involve representatives of the local community at all stages cannot be overemphasised. It is argued that current efforts in this direction in India have not been satisfactory.[64] The non-involvement of community stakeholders led to residents of the coastal states of eastern India resisting the siting of large plants in densely populated and ecologically sensitive agricultural districts. Similarly, the 2,640 MW Sompeta plant proposed by Nagarjuna Construction Company and the 2,640 MW Bhavanapadu plant proposed by East Coast Energy led to protests that ended in police attacks and the deaths of locals. Regrettably, following coverage of the police action on television, it was revealed that a pattern of 'crony capitalism' was going on among the permitting agencies and corporate sponsors.[65]

5.9.3 Adequate funding

Investors are primarily concerned about return on investment (RoI). Because of this, it is vital that projects offer attractive enough returns to the private sector. In India, the support of the government in the form of VGF helps to make many commercially unviable projects feasible.[66] India has witnessed rapid growth in recent years as far as PPP is concerned, which is not unconnected to the fact that the local financial market there is vibrant.[67] However, there is concern that the local financial market would be unable to support continued mega growth in investment in PPPs.[68] Thus, for India, there is a need to ensure participation by foreign players, particularly strategic investors. It is submitted, therefore, that India should encourage pure-equity providers from abroad with incentives.

5.9.4 Efficient risk sharing

Because of the long gestation period for PPP projects, it becomes even more challenging to allocate risk than, say, in a project executed by traditional government procurement. Transfer of Risk to the private sector is what makes it attractive for the public sector. Notwithstanding, the focus should be on

64 Ibid.

65 Ted Nace, 'Down with Coal! The Grassroots Anti-Coal Movement Goes Global' (2011) *Grist* available at <http://grist.org/coal/2011-05-27-down-with-coal-the-grassroots-anti-coal-movement-goes-global/> accessed 6 July 2017.

66 Department of Economic Affairs, 'Schemes for Financial Support to Public Private Partnerships in Infrastructure (Viability Gap Funding Scheme)' (2017) available at <www.pppinindia.gov.in/schemes-for-financial-support> accessed 1 July 2017.

67 Clive Harris and Sri Kumar Tadimalla, 'Financing the Boom in Public Private Partnerships in Indian Infrastructure: Trends and Policy Implications' (2008) *Gridlines* 1.

68 Ibid.

risk sharing, not just risk transfer.[69] It is vital that all risks associated with the projects are thoroughly identified or else a project may eventually be disrupted because of unexpected glitches. Two Indian cases are worth citing here. The Hyderabad Outer Ring Road Project faced delays because the private-sector consortium had challenges acquiring land due to locals, especially farmers, objecting to the development. The Dhamra Port Project located at the north of the Gahimatha Marine Sanctuary was a worry to environmentalists as regular dredging affects fauna in the area. These are examples of stakeholders failing to identify the potential risks associated with the projects. In some cases, risk-mitigation measures should also be identified. It is worthy to note that, in India, attempts have been made to implement risk-sharing mechanisms by the instrumentality of law. For example, the Andhra Pradesh Infrastructure Development Enabling Act of 2001 required the disclosure of generic risk and allocation to be provided in the concession agreement.

5.9.5 Sustainability

It is important that the environment is not compromised, even as provision is being made to bridge the infrastructure gap. While it is given that infrastructure is key to economic growth, it needs to be stated on the other hand that there has to be a check to ensure the drive for infrastructure does not put undue pressure on the environment.[70] In 1994, the Environment Impact Assessment (EIA) notification required that restrictions be imposed on the expansion and modernisation of any activity or new projects being undertaken in any part of India, unless environmental clearance has been received.

5.10 Conclusion

India has made significant progress in facilitating private-sector participation in infrastructure procurement via the PPP model. As discussed in this chapter, the PPP market in India is unarguably the largest PPP market in the world. Furthermore, the experience of arranging PPPs in India has moved on from merely enabling the use of private-sector funds for infrastructure financing to a more sophisticated method of employing private-sector capacity and skills to deliver high-quality service.

There have been arguments about the results of the PPP programme in India. While conceding that PPP has not been without challenges there, it may suffice to say that India has shown that PPP can be developed in such a way that it addresses the infrastructure of a given environment taking local circumstances into consideration. For example, the use of annuity payments for PPP projects indicates that the GoI does not intend to put undue burden on the ordinary

69 Public Policy Team and Athena Infonomics, *op cit* (note 61).
70 Ibid.

citizens by making them pay directly for the use of the facilities, especially for certain road projects. Again, the identification and selection of PPP projects show a sense of commitment by the public authority to directly touch the lives of the citizens, for example, with sewage and electrification projects. One area of concern for India, however, is with regard to finding a solution to the challenge of acquiring communal land for PPP projects.

References

African Development Bank Group. (2014). Lessons in Private-Public Partnership (PPP) from India. Retrieved from www.afdb.org/en/news-and-events/article/lessons-in-private-public-partnership-ppp-from-india-13226/.

Agarwal, M. (2015, October 17). India's PPP Story: A Glass Half-Full. *Financial Express*.

British Broadcasting Corporation. (2019, February 18). India Country Profile. Retrieved from www.bbc.co.uk/news/world-south-asia-12557384.

Central Intelligence Agency. (2019). South Asia: India – The World Factbook. Retrieved from www.cia.gov/library/publications/the-world-factbook/geos/in.html.

Cheung, E., Chan, A. P., Lam, P. T., Chan, D. W., & Ke, Y. (2012). A Comparative Study of Critical Success Factors for Public Private Partnerships (PPP) Between Mainland China and the Hong Kong Special Administrative Region. *Facilities*, *30*(13/14), 647–666. doi:10.1108/02632771211273132.

Department of Economic Affairs (DEA), Ministry of Finance, Government of India, & Asian Development Bank (ADB). (2006). *Facilitating Public-Private Partnership for Accelerated Infrastructure Development in India*. New Delhi: Asian Development Bank.

Department of Economic Affairs (DEA). (2015a). *Public Private Partnership Projects in India: A Compendium of Case Studies*. New Delhi, Ministry of Finance.

Department of Economic Affairs (DEA). (2015b). *Report of the Committee on Revisiting and Revitalising Public Private Partnership Model of Infrastructure*. New Delhi: Author.

Department of Economic Affairs (DEA). (2016). Infrastructure and Energy Division. Retrieved from http://finmin.nic.in/the_ministry/dept_eco_affairs/infrastrucure_div/I&I_index.asp?pageid=2#PPPCell.

Department of Economic Affairs (DEA). (2017). Schemes for Financial Support to Public Private Partnerships in Infrastructure (Viability Gap Funding Scheme). Retrieved from www.pppinindia.gov.in/schemes-for-financial-support.

Department of Economic Affairs (DEA). (2019). Overview PPP in India. Retrieved from www.pppinindia.gov.in/overview.

Ernst and Young. (2013). Public Private Partnership: The Next Continuum. Retrieved from www.ey.com/publication/vwluassets/ey-public-private-partnership-the-next-continuum/$file/ey-public-private-partnership-the-next-continuum.pdf.

FTI Consulting. (2014). Investment Climate Under the New Government. Retrieved from www.fticonsulting.com/~/media/Files/us-files/insights/white-papers/indias-investment-climate-under-the-new-government.pdf.

Government of India. (2018). Public Private Partnerships in India. Retrieved from www.pppinindia.gov.in/overview.

Hamilton, G. (2011). Role of Good Governance in Establishing Successful Public-Private Partnerships. Retrieved from www.aik-invest.hr/wp-content/uploads/2015/11/geoffrey-hamilton_2.pdf.

Harris, C., & Tadimalla, S.K. (2008). Financing the Boom in Public Private Partnerships in Indian Infrastructure: Trends and Policy Implications. *Gridlines*, 1.

Hayllar, M.R. (2010). Public-Private Partnerships in Hong Kong: Good Governance – The Essential Missing Ingredient? *Australian Journal of Public Administration*, *69*, S99–S119. doi:10.1111/j.1467-8500.2010.00675.x.

Hemming, R., Anderson, B., Alier, M., Petrie, M., & Cangiano, M. (2006). *Public-Private Partnerships, Government Guarantees, and Fiscal Risk*. Washington, DC: International Monetary Fund.

International Financial Corporation. (2013). Public-Private Partnership Stories, India: Berhampur Solid Waste Management. Retrieved from www.ifc.org/wps/wcm/connect/31b05382-bfae-48f7-9310-e32f53f44c36/PPPStories_India_BerhampurSolid-Waste.pdf?MOD=AJPERES.

International Finance Corporation. (2013). Public-Private Partnership Stories, India: Bhubaneswar Street Lighting. Retrieved from http://ppp.worldbank.org/public-private-partnership/sites/ppp.worldbank.org/files/documents/PPP_Stories_India_Bhubaneswar_Street_Lighting_EN_2013.pdf.

International Finance Corporation. (2015). Public-Private Partnership Stories, India: Vadodara Solar. Retrieved from www.ifc.org/wps/wcm/connect/458a22804528ba90bc2dbcc66d9c728b/PPPstories_India_Vadodara+Solar.pdf?MOD=AJPERES.

Josep, R., Bansai, J., Singhyi, P., & Dsouza, D. (2013). Doing Business in India. Retrieved from www.ey.com/Publication/vwLUAssets/EY-doing-business-in-India-2013/$FILE/EY-Doing-business-in-India.pdf.

Kalidindi, S.N., & Singh, L.B. (2009). *Financing Road Projects in India Using PPP Scheme.* Paper Presented at Proceedings of the 2009 Mid-Continent Transportation Research Symposium, Ames, Iowa.

Lindsay, J.M. (2012). Compulsory Acquisition of Land and Compensation in Infrastructure Projects. *PPP Insights: An Explanatory Note on Issues Relevant to Public-Private Partnerships, 1*(3), 1.

Mahapatra, A. (2015). Sharing India's PPP Experience. Retrieved from www.unescap.org/sites/default/files/Day%201%20-%20Session%202.2%20-%20India%20PPP.pdf.

Ministry of Finance, Government of India. (2016). Tools and Resources. Retrieved from toolkit.pppinindia.com/ports/module3-roiewp-learnings-development.php?links=roiewp1&links1=roiewp3&links2=roiewp3c.

Nace, T. (2011, May 28). Down with Coal! The Grassroots anti-coal Movement Goes Global. Retrieved from http://grist.org/coal/2011-05-27-down-with-coal-the-grassroots-anti-coal-movement-goes-global.

Public Policy Team, & Athena Infonomics. (2012). Public Private Partnerships in India: Lessons from Experiences. Retrieved from www.gov.uk/government/uploads/system/uploads/attachment_data/file/186989/Report-PPPLessonsFromExperiences270812.pdf.

Queiroz, C. (2013). The Essential Need for Good Governance in Public-Private Partnerships. Retrieved from https://ptfund.org/the-essential-need-for-good-governance-in-public-private-partnerships/.

Research Republic. (2008). *Developing India's Infrastructure Through Public Private Partnerships: A Resource Guide*. London: City of London.

Saha, D. (2017). PPPs in India? Will They Regain Their Former Glory? Retrieved from http://blogs.worldbank.org/ppps/ppps-india-will-they-regain-their-former-glory.

Seth, S., & Rajasekaran, V. (2017). India. In B. Werneck & M. Saadi (Eds.), *The Public-Private Partnership Law Review*. London: Law Business Research Ltd.

Shaik, R. R., & Narain, N. (2011). Comparative Analysis of Infrastructure PPP in BRICS Nations. In *International Conference on Advancement in Information Technology with Workshop of ICBMG IPCSIT* (p. 283).

Srivatava, A., Thapar, R., & Champakalashmi, R. (2019). India. Retrieved from www.britannica.com/place/India.

The World Bank. (1991). *Managing Development: The Governance Dimension, a Discussion Paper.* Washington, DC: The World Bank.

The World Bank. (2017). India. Retrieved from https://pppknowledgelab.org/countries/india.

6 Nigeria

6.1 Introduction

One of the critical factors for a successful regime of private-sector participation in the provision of public infrastructure in any given jurisdiction is a legal, regulatory and administrative structure for PPP governance. First, no matter how well couched a PPP agreement is, it may be void or voidable if it is inconsistent with the country's laws. Second, the law may prohibit certain genres of projects within a locality, and third, in a constitutional federation like Nigeria, an act of the National Assembly[1] or a law of a State Assembly[2] is required to set up any regulatory body and provide legitimacy for any transaction involving the private and public sectors. To give legal backing to PPP policy in the country, the federal government of Nigeria and some Nigerian states have passed laws entrenching their respective PPP frameworks. The laws also establish administrative units for the regulation of PPPs at the national and sub-national levels.

For a potential investor in Nigerian infrastructure, it is expedient to understand the federal structure of the country. The current structure specifically delineates what projects the federal and state governments may execute, whether exclusively or concurrently, within their powers. It is therefore imperative to analyse the laws in order to avoid entering into an agreement that is *ipso facto* void.

This chapter focuses on the legal, institutional and regulatory framework for private-sector participation in infrastructure provision in Nigeria. The study takes on a descriptive view of the body of laws, the institutions established by the law to regulate PPPs and the political and social climate of the country. In doing so, this chapter demonstrates that some of the laws have been enacted based on international best practice. However, considering the number of failed PPP projects across the country, the chapter aims to analyse the laws based on some common themes to consider loopholes, overlaps and inconsistencies in them and to identify areas where changes should be made to enhance an effective PPP environment.

1 Where it concerns the federation itself.

2 If it relates to one of the states of the federation.

6.2 Introducing Nigeria

Nigeria is the most populous country in Africa. It was inhabited by about 184 million people in 2016, according to World Bank data.[3] The country accounts for 47 per cent of West Africa's population and has one of the largest youth populations in the world.[4] It is the continent's third-largest military power and the tenth-largest oil producer in the world.[5] Nigeria borders the Gulf of Guinea between Benin and Cameroon in West Africa and covers about 923,770 square kilometres, making it the 32nd largest country in the world, comparable in size to Venezuela and about twice the size of the U.S. state of California.[6] The territory comprising present-day Nigeria[7] was formerly made up of several kingdoms, emirates, clans, communities, villages and hamlets that were connected by trade, rivers, a common language or shared common boundaries. The British, upon colonising the territory, amalgamated both the Northern and Southern protectorates in 1914, under the administration of Lord Lugard, to form the geographical entity now referred to as Nigeria.[8]

Nigeria is one of the most urbanised countries in Africa, with at least 24 cities of over 100,000 residents. The country is highly diverse, with many ethnic, cultural and religious groups, which often leads to inter-ethnic and/or religious tensions sometimes resulting in outbreaks of violence. Nigeria is relatively low on human development indices when compared with other benchmark countries, such as South Africa and Egypt. As of 2007, half of the population was living below the poverty line on an estimated US$1.25 per day.[9] More so, the country fell behind schedule for the Millennium Development Goal attainment, including the goal of halving poverty by 2015.[10]

Nigeria plays a key role in the sub-region of West Africa and, as such, a large part of the economic activity in the sub-region is concentrated in the country.[11] Cross-border activities closely link southern Niger to the Hausa economy of northern Nigeria; similarly, Benin and Togo benefit from the

3 The World Bank, 'Nigeria' (2018) available at <www.worldbank.org/en/country/nigeria/overview> accessed 3 May 2018.

4 Ibid.

5 Organisation for Economic Cooperation and Development, 'Nigeria' (2018) available at <www.oecd.org/swac/publications/Nigeria_e-version_en_light.pdf> accessed 3 May 2018.

6 Central Intelligence Agency, *The World Fact Book*, 17 May 2015. Interestingly, Nigeria is one of the few countries in the world with significant oil resources to have a budget deficit. It is unfortunately well-known for increases in corruption, with an estimated US$300 billion worth of crude oil missing. General Sani Abacha, who was a former military leader of the country, is suspected to have embezzled more than US$4 billion in public funds between 1993 and his demise in 1998.

7 Nigeria is a federation of 36 states with a federal capital territory, Abuja.

8 Dapo Fafowora, 'Lord Lugard and the 1914 Amalgamation of Nigeria' *The Nation*, 14 Febraury 2013 available at <http://thenationonlineng.net/lord-lugard-and-the-1914-amalgamation-of-nigeria/> accessed 15 July 2018.

9 Inter Reseaux, 'Facts on Nigeria' (2010) available at <www.inter-reseaux.org/IMG/pdf/p4-7_Benchmarks.pdf> accessed 3 May 2018.

10 Ibid.

11 Organisation for Economic Cooperation and Development, *op cit* (note 5).

economic activity between Lagos and Ibadan. As the largest military power in the region, Nigeria was a major player towards restoring peace after the tragic civil wars in both Liberia and Sierra Leone.

Seven out of the 36 states in Nigeria are in the northwest zone, there are six states in the southwest zone, six in the south-south zone, six in the north-central, five in the southeast and six in the northeast zone. The country operates a presidential form of government with a president who is also the commander-in-chief of the armed forces and the head of state. At the sub-national level, the governors are the leaders and chief security officers of their respective states. Nigeria operates a bicameral legislature, consisting of the Senate and the House of Representatives, at the federal level. At the state level, members of the House of Assembly make laws for the good governance of their respective states. Nigeria attained self-rule on 1 October 1960 but has, at various times, experienced the incursion of the military into politics. Because of several years of military dictatorship, the country suffered from the militarisation of the civilian population, culminating in the disregard of due process by civilian rulers and public servants in positions of authority. On 29 May 1999, the military administration of General Abdulsalami Abubakar handed over power to a democratically elected government headed by President Olusegun Obasanjo, a former military head of state. There have not been any further military coups in the country. The fifth consecutive national elections were held in March and April 2015, and for the first time an opposition party, the All Progressive Congress (APC), won the majority of the votes and defeated the incumbent, Dr Goodluck Jonathan of the Peoples' Democratic Party (PDP). The administration of President Muhammadu Buhari took office on 29 May 2015, amid a severely weakened economy and large gaps in infrastructure.[12]

Despite its abundant natural resources and landmass, Nigeria is only 42nd among the 60 largest economies in the world.[13] This author believes this can be improved if the country can bridge its wide infrastructure gap to stimulate long-term economic growth.[14] In 2016, the Nigerian economy slipped into recession for the first time in more than 20 years. The result reflected adverse economic shocks, inconsistent economic policies and security challenges in the Northeast and Delta regions.[15] The country was ranked 169 out of 190 countries in the World Bank's *Doing Business Report* for 2017.[16]

12 The World Bank, *op cit* (note 3).

13 GTI Research, 'Infrastructure: The Key to Nigeria's Economic Diversification' available at <www.proshareng.com/admin/upload/reports/GTIResearchInfrastructur.pdf > accessed 30 June 2017.

14 Ibid.

15 Barbara Barungi, Ojijo Odhiambo and Robert Asogwa, 'Nigeria 2017' (2017) a report by African Economic Outlook available at <www.africaneconomicoutlook.org/en/country-notes/nigeria> accessed 30 June 2017.

16 In 2016, the federal government of Nigeria set up a presidential council on the Ease of Doing Business to improve the country's ranking by 20 places in the medium term. The measures put in place include the fast tracking of acquiring land titles, visa applications and issuance processes. The measures also aim at attracting foreign direct investment through the harmonised incentives and diaspora remittances and investments made available.

In 2010, the World Bank's diagnostic study of infrastructure in Africa estimated that Sub-Saharan Africa (SSA) needed to spend US$93 billion annually on infrastructure; however, the region was only spending US$45 billion, leaving a gap of US$48 billion every year.[17] Interestingly, the World Bank's Private Participation in Infrastructure Project database suggests that Africa's infrastructure development has been slow compared to other developing regions. Africa (and particularly Nigeria) has shown great potential for private investment in infrastructure, if the growth in mobile telephony is taken into consideration.[18] The gains recorded in that sector alone attracted about 23.9 per cent of foreign direct investment (FDI) into the Nigerian economy in 2014.[19] Furthermore, the sheer size of the Nigerian market, with an estimated projected population of 200 million people in the year 2020, is encouraging enough to sway investor-interest towards the country if the right investment framework/environment is implemented and maintained.[20]

Dr Ngozi Okonjo-Iweala, who served as the minister of finance and co-ordinating minister for the economy under the administration of Dr Goodluck Jonathan, asserted that Nigeria requires about US$14 billion per annum to bridge its infrastructure deficit but can only afford to spend about US$6 billion annually.[21] In simple arithmetic, there is an annual deficit of US$8 billion. The Vice President of Nigeria, Professor Yemi Osinbajo, stated in an address delivered at the knowledge-sharing forum organised by the African Development Bank (AfDB) in collaboration with the country's Federal Ministry of Finance, that the low level of completed PPP projects in the country is due to the trend on encumbrances arising from approval processes and unwieldy project appraisal.[22] This shows that there is an urgent need to ensure that PPP projects succeed as an alternative to the traditional form of infrastructure procurement. The current situation is exacerbated by a poor maintenance culture, the aging and overuse of existing facilities caused by growing populations in urban communities.

To buttress the poor state of infrastructure in Nigeria, it is not out of place to consider some data. Only about 39,500 kilometres of the country's 193,000

17 The World Bank, *Public Private Partnerships Reference Guide Version 2* (Washington, DC: The World Bank, 2014).

18 The World Bank, *Attracting Investors to African Public-Private Partnerships: A Preparation Guide* (Washington, DC: The World Bank, 2009) 3.

19 Ibid.

20 African Development Bank, *An Infrastructure Action Plan for Nigeria: Closing the Infrastructure Gap and Accelerating Economic Transformation* (Washington, DC: African Development Bank, 2014) 14.

21 Dr Okonjo-Iweala made the assertion while addressing a PPP stakeholders' workshop organised by the African Development Bank (AfDB) in Abuja. This occasioned the 12 November 2014 article in the *Daily Independent* 'Nigeria's $8 billion Infrastructure Deficit.'

22 Ndubuisi Francis, 'Osinbajo Laments Low Delivery of PPP Projects' *This Day*, 3 November 2016 available at <www.thisdaylive.com/index.php/2016/11/03/osinbajo-laments-low-delivery-of-ppp-projects/> accessed 10 July 2017.

kilometres of road network are paved.[23] While the country requires 8,000 megawatts of power supply, less than 3,000 is being generated despite the government's direct investment and several attempts to revamp the power sector.[24] As a result, the majority of the population resort to purchasing power-generating plants to provide for their power needs. In most parts of the country, including urban communities, the people lack access to pipe-borne water.[25] The available waterworks are mostly owned by the public sector with access to sanitation facilities put at 41 per cent in 2013.[26] The country's rail network, consisting of only 4,332 kilometres of railroad track, is grossly insufficient for a country of its size.[27] Additionally, more than 75 per cent of the locomotives managed by the Nigerian Railway Corporation (NRC) was not in use, according to a 2009 report.[28] Nigeria's infrastructure has long been a bottleneck for economic growth. According to the National Planning Commission:

> Road density in Nigeria, for example, is only about a fifth of that of India. The effect of weak infrastructure is most striking in the energy sector – Nigeria's per capita power consumption of 136 kWh p.a. is less than 3% of South Africa's 4,803 kWh.
>
> In order to close its current infrastructure gap and reach desired total stock required, Nigeria must aggressively increase infrastructure spending. The investments over the next 30 years total USD 3.0 trillion (constant 2010 prices), including investments needed for maintenance. Spending would need to ramp up fairly quickly, from the current 2–3% of rebased GDP to an average of around 7% over the 30 years. Given Nigeria's high GDP growth projected for the period, such a ramp-up is particularly challenging.[29]

It follows that the country must aggressively pursue an infrastructure master plan and ensure that specific targets are met to bridge the wide infrastructure

23 YA Abdulkareem and KA Adeoti, 'Road Maintenance and National Development' (2005) available at <http://ilorin.info/papers/publications/ROAD%20MAINTENANCE%20AND%20NATIONAL%20DEVELOPMENT.pdf> accessed 13 June 2017.

24 British Broadcasting Corporation, 'Power Cuts Embarrassing Nigeria' (2008) available at <http://news.bbc.co.uk/1/hi/world/africa/7252777.stm> accessed 14 June 2017.

25 AA Akinwale, 'The Menace of Inadequate Infrastructure in Nigeria' (2010) 2(3) *African Journal of Science, Technology, Innovation and Development* 214.

26 World Health Organisation, 'Nigeria' (2014) available at <www.who.int/water_sanitation_health/monitoring/investments/nigeria-10-nov.pdf?ua=1> accessed 17 June 2017.

27 C Kessides, 'The Contributions of Infrastructure to Economic Development: A Review of Experience and Policy Implications' (1993) *World Bank Discussion Papers* No. 213. World Bank, Washington, DC.

28 Ibid.

29 National Planning Commission, *Nigeria's National Integrated Infrastructure Master Plan* (Abuja: National Planning Commission, 2015) 15.

margin. See Appendix III for specific targets set out across all infrastructure sectors of the economy. Significantly, shortly after the US investment bank Goldman Sachs stated that Nigeria could possibly grow to become one of the top 20 economies in the world, the federal government of Nigeria in 2008 estimated that the country would need at least US$510 billion for investments in various infrastructure sectors up to 2018 if the country were to break into the top 20 world economies by 2020.[30]

Taking this into consideration, this chapter examines the legal, policy, administrative and regulatory framework for PPP (including its practice) in Nigeria to determine whether there are deficiencies that need to be addressed to improve their performance. Faced by budget constraints and a growing appetite for better service quality, several developed and developing countries have adopted the PPP model of infrastructure procurement and financing, which essentially involves private-sector participation in what was traditionally the preoccupation of the public sector. Following what was discussed previously, infrastructure development is a key area of interest for the government of Nigeria.

6.3 Nigeria's federal system and PPP

Alkali et al. note that Nigeria became a federation in 1954 vide the introduction of a federal constitution by the Nigerian (Constitution) Order in Council 1954.[31] The federation at present is made up of 36 states and a federal capital territory (Abuja).[32] Although Nigeria is considered a federation, the governance structure of the country is excessively centralised.[33] Due to prolonged periods of military incursion into politics in the country, the Nigerian state operates more like a unitary state than a federal one. There is a great deal of power concentrated in the federal government; for example, the federating states rely on the federal government for monthly fiscal allocations. As a result, the states remain subservient to the federal authority. Although the governor of a state is the chief security officer of that state, the governor has no control over the police. There have been cases where the security details of a state governor are withdrawn based on orders 'from above' (a term used in Nigeria to describe directives issued by the federal authority). For example, due to a conflict between the administration of Dr Goodluck Jonathan and Governor Rotimi Amaechi of Rivers State, the Inspector General of Police withdrew the

30 Business Monitor International, *Nigeria Infrastructure Report Q1: 2010: Including a Five-Year Industry Forecast to 2014* (Abuja: Business Monitor International, 2009) 5.

31 Alhaji Umar Alkali, US Abbo Jimeta, Awwal Ilyas Magashi and Tijanni, 'Nature and Sources of Nigerian Legal System: An Exorcism of a Wrong Notion' (2014) 5(4) *International Journal of Business, Economics and Law* 3.

32 Section 3 of the 1999 Constitution of the Federal Republic of Nigeria (as amended).

33 Aderonke Majekodunmi, 'Federalism in Nigeria: The Past, Current Peril and Future Hopes' (2015) 9(2) *Journal of Policy and Development Studies* 112.

security details of the Rivers State governor.[34] Unlike the position in the US federation, states in Nigeria do not have their own appeal courts or supreme courts. Appeals from State High Courts go to a centralised Court of Appeal,[35] and further appeals go to a single Supreme Court domiciled at the federal capital territory.[36] The current federal framework in Nigeria has been described as a bad marriage that all dislike but dare not leave.[37] Under the 1999 Constitution of the Federal Republic of Nigeria (as amended), the National Assembly (made up of the Senate and the House of Representatives)[38] has exclusive jurisdiction to legislate matters prescribed in the Exclusive Legislative List contained in the Second Schedule to the Constitution,[39] whereas the respective State Houses of Assembly have the power to make laws on any matter not included on the Exclusive Legislative List and matters on the Concurrent Legislative List.[40] It is important to note, however, that both the federal government and the states have powers to make laws regarding matters that are prescribed under the Concurrent Legislative List.

6.3.1 The Exclusive Legislative List vs necessity

Based on the doctrine of the supremacy of the constitution, the 1999 Constitution of the Federal Republic of Nigeria (as amended) is supreme, and any Law or Act by the Federal Government of Nigeria or any of the federating states that is inconsistent with the provisions of the Constitution is void *ab initio* to the degree of the inconsistency with the provisions of the Constitution.[41] The question of the supremacy of the Constitution was settled in the case of *Doherty v Balewa*.[42] In that case, the Supreme Court of Nigeria was called upon to determine whether, under the Commissions and Tribunals of Inquiry Act of 1961, the federal government had the power to set up bodies under Section 3(1) of the Act to deal with 'any matter or thing within federal competence anywhere within the federation?' It was held that since the Tribunals of Inquiry Act of 1961 purported to have power throughout the federation,

34 Stanley Azuakola, 'Just in: Police IG Withdraws Security Details of Gov. Amaechi, Sen. Saraki and Alhaji Baraje' *The Scoop*, 7 September 2013 available at <www.thescoopng.com/2013/09/07/just-in-police-ig-withdraws-security-details-of-gov-amaechi-sen-saraki-and-alhaji-baraje/> accessed 8 May 2018.

35 The Court of Appeal is divided into different judicial divisions and sits in certain states in the country. See section 237 of the 1999 Constitution of the Federal Republic of Nigeria (as amended).

36 Section 230 of the 1999 Constitution of the Federal Republic of Nigeria (as amended).

37 Aderonke Majekodunmi, *op cit* (note 33) 114.

38 Nigeria has a bicameral legislative structure at the federal level made up of the Senate and the House of Representatives. This is, however, not applicable at the state level.

39 Section 4 of the 1999 Constitution of the Federal Republic of Nigeria (as amended).

40 Ibid.

41 See Section 1(3) of the 1999 Constitution of the Federal Republic of Nigeria (as amended).

42 (1961) 1 All NLR 604.

the general power given to the Prime Minister under Section 3(1) of the Act and Section 3(4), which provided that neither the Commission nor any action of the Prime Minister in relation to the Act would be enquired into by any court of law, were contrary to the provisions of the Constitution. The Supreme Court declared Section 3(4) of the Act unconstitutional as it purported to limit the jurisdiction of the courts.

As such, a potential PPP investor needs to determine what level of government is being dealt with[43] (e.g. where the public partner is the federal government itself or any of its MDAs, the project may cover any or more of the items on the Exclusive Legislative List. If, on the other hand, the public partner is a state government or any of its ministries, departments or MDAs, any project that falls within the Exclusive Legislative List is a no-go).

It is assumed that the spirit behind the demarcation along the lines of the Exclusive and Concurrent Legislative Lists[44] – which indicate areas where both the states and the federal government can exercise powers – is to clearly distinguish between the functions of government at each level to avoid confusion. This notwithstanding, a situation where a state government identifies a need and such a government has the capacity to develop a project to cater to that need, depriving the people of the state such a project, even when the federal government is reluctant to embark on such a project, is certainly not in the intention of the drafters of the Constitution. The question remains, should certain items not be removed from the Exclusive Legislative List and moved to the Concurrent Legislative List in the interest of necessity? This is analysed next.

6.3.2 Items in the Exclusive Legislative List

As noted previously, the items contained in the list are exclusively reserved for the federal government. Notably, aviation, including airports, safety or aircraft; borrowing of moneys within or outside the country for the federation or any state;[45] banks, banking and bills of exchange; maritime, inland waterways; ports; mining; nuclear energy; prisons; railways and traffic on federal trunk roads, among other things.[46] It therefore follows that none of the federating state governments have the power to enter an arrangement for the provision of

43 This author has deliberately omitted the third level of government in the country due to the obvious lack of capacity on the part of government at that level to embark on such projects.

44 Discussed in section 6.3.3.

45 For example, a state within the country seeking a loan for any project must obtain permission from the federal government to do so. A case in point was the Rivers State application to the World Bank for a US$280 million loan to improve the state's water supply. The federal government under President Goodluck Jonathan was not forthcoming with the approval, which led to Governor Rotimi Amaechi accusing the federal government of political persecution. See <http://nationalmirroronline.net/new/280m-world-bank-loan-generates-controversy-in-rivers-state/> accessed 30 June 2016.

46 Second Schedule, Part I: Exclusive Legislative List 1999 CFRN (as amended).

any facility that touches on the Exclusive Legislative List, no matter how beneficial it may be. Doing so would amount to acting beyond the constitutional powers of the federating state in question. Strictly, only the federal government or any of its MDAs may deliver any project that is listed under the Exclusive Legislative List. This position of the Constitution came into focus in *The Registered Trustees of Licensed Telecommunication Operators of Nigeria v Lagos State Government.*[47] In a landmark ruling, Justice Auta of the Federal High Court in Lagos ruled that the Lagos State Government (LASG) had no right to impose the Lagos State Infrastructure Maintenance and Regulatory Agency Law of 2004 on telecom operators in the state. The law was enacted to empower the Lagos State Infrastructure Maintenance and Regulatory Agency (LASIMRA) to inspect and demolish or dismantle masts, towers or antennas of telecommunication operators. Again, the court ruled that it had jurisdiction to entertain the suit since telecommunication operations is under the Exclusive Legislative List.

Whether the LASG had acted beyond its powers as it relates to a PPP transaction was the subject of contention in *Olu Adegboruwa v Attorney General of the Federation and Three others.*[48] On 26 November 2012, Mr. Ebun-Olu Adegboruwa, a Lagos-based civil rights activist, filed a suit before the Federal High Court against four defendants, namely: the Attorney General of the Federation, the Nigerian Inland Waterways Authority, the Attorney General of Lagos State and the Lagos State Government. Mr Adegboruwa sought a declaration that the LASG's act of erecting a bridge on the Lagos Lagoon was illegal and unconstitutional as the waterways upon which the bridge was constructed are federal navigable waterways, and as such do not belong to the LASG. Mr Adegboruwa also sought an order restraining the LASG from further collection of tolls forthwith. The Federal High Court, presided over by Justice Saliu Saidu, in an erudite judgement delivered on 28 March 2014, held that the power of control of certain navigable waterways in Nigeria, including the instant waterway accommodating the Lekki-Ikoyi Bridge, falls within the matters listed in the Exclusive Legislative List of the 1999 Constitution of the Federal Republic of Nigeria (as amended), thus falling under the exclusive legislative purview of the FGN. Based on the foregoing, it is not within the powers of any state government in Nigeria to embark on any project that relates to navigable

47 Balancing Act Africa, 'Lagos State Loses Case Against Telecom Operators' available at <www.balancingact-africa.com/news/en/issue-no-345/telecoms/lagos-state-loses-ca/en> accessed 8 March 2016.

48 Unreported Suit No: FHC/L/CS/1405/12 see Ben Ezeamalu, 'Lagos Laws Do Not Cover Toll Collection on Lekki-Ikoyi Bridge, Court Rules' *Premium Times*, 27 March 2014 (Lagos) available at <www.premiumtimesng.com/news/157525-lagos-laws-cover-toll-collection-lekki-ikoyi-bridge-court-rules.html> accessed 8 March 2016. See also Kayode Oladipo and Chinedu Ihentu-Geoffrey, 'Bridging the Infrastructure Gap: The Lekki-Ikoyi Tolling Debate' available at <www.kwm.com/en/uk/knowledge/insights/bridging-the-infrastructure-gap-the-lekki-ikoyi-tolling-debate-20140723> accessed 8 March 2016.

waterways, even where the waterway is located within the territorial jurisdiction of that state.

The vexed question begging for answers remains, should state governments remain laid back even when they have the capacity to provide facilities because they are precluded from doing so on the basis that the project comes within the scope of the Exclusive Legislative List? This thesis argues that the law, as it is, is anti-developmental because state governments are much closer to the people than the central government, and items such as railways, inland waterways, airports and roads in general, whether federal trunk roads or not, must not be exclusively reserved for the federal government.

A few states in the country justifying the need for the location of airports within their localities have embarked on, and in some cases completed, the building of airports with a few already in operation.[49] The legality or otherwise of these airports is open for debate since aviation is a matter within the scope of the Exclusive Legislative List. Similarly, the reconstruction and rehabilitation of federal trunk roads under the past administration of Governor Rotimi Amaechi of Rivers State, with the expectation of a refund of expenses by the federal government, is itself illegal in the first place.[50] The current position of the law in Nigeria that limits states from providing infrastructure on the basis that such projects are under the Exclusive Legislative List is not good for the polity. There are instances where a state governor may be having differences with the federal government; in such situations, the federal government may choose to 'punish' the governor by denying the state any federally sponsored projects.[51]

6.3.3 Items in the Concurrent Legislative List

Both the federal and state governments may legislate on items under the Concurrent Legislative List. It has been described as a list of legislative agenda with 12 main subject areas prescribed in the Second Schedule of the Constitution.[52] These 12 items include: allocation of revenue; antiquities and monuments; archives; collection of taxes; electoral laws; electric power; exhibition of cinematograph films; industrial, commercial or agricultural development; scientific and technological research; statistics; trigonometry, cadastral and topographical

49 For example, the Asaba Airport and the Uyo Airport were built and are owned by the Delta and Akwa Ibom States, respectively.

50 Several states, including Anambra, seek a refund of moneys spent on the rehabilitation of federal roads. See Nwabueze Okonkwo, 'Obiano to FG: Refund Anambra's N25bn Spent on Federal Roads' *Vanguard*, 3 October 2015 (Lagos) available at <www.vanguardngr.com/2015/10/obiano-to-fg-refund-anambras-n25bn-spent-on-federal-roads/> accessed 30 June 2016.

51 Rivers State, under Governor Rotimi Amaechi, was completely neglected by President Goodluck Jonathan's administration based on the conflict between the state and the federal government, even though both were under the control of the same People's Democratic Party (PDP).

52 Charles Mwalimu, *The Nigerian Legal System* (New York: Peter Lang Publishing, 2009) 16.

surveys and university, technological and post-primary education. These are essentially matters that both the federal government and any of the federating states may act on, as the powers and jurisdiction can be shared.[53] The importance of having two separate lists delineating the powers of both the federal government and the states is thoughtfully to avoid confusion as well as to protect the federal structure that the country operates. However, there is a need to allow states to embark on developmental projects, especially when they have the necessary capacity. For example, a state like Lagos should be empowered by law to embark on projects like bridges over federal inland waterways or rehabilitating roads designated as federal trunk roads, even based on a PPP.

6.4 The essence of a framework

One of the critical success factors (CSFs) for PPPs is a healthy framework. According to the World Bank, the PPP framework refers to 'the policy procedures, institutions, and rules that together define how PPPs will be implemented – that is, how they will be identified, assessed, selected, budgeted for, procured, monitored and accounted for.'[54] In a similar vein, the UNCITRAL *Legislative Guide on Privately Financed Infrastructure Projects* states that the existence 'of an appropriate legal framework' is a prerequisite to creating an environment that fosters private investment in infrastructure.[55] More importantly, the UNCITRAL document stipulates the need to ensure that PPP laws remain 'sufficiently flexible and responsive to keep pace with the developments in various infrastructure sectors in the economy.'[56]

The need for 'a clear and stable legal environment for PPP projects, to reduce the perception of risk, attract more competition for projects, attract more lending and therefore reduce project costs'[57] cannot be overstressed. A government agency must have the necessary powers laid down by statute to enter into an agreement with a private consortium to undertake the obligations of that agreement. It is important that the framework should be clear, predictable and stable as well as commercially oriented. However, it must be noted that in the UK and some other common-law countries, 'PFI-Model PPPs are treated as a variety of government procurement, for which no special legal arrangements are needed.'[58] This approach is considered as mainly contractual. Yescombe

53 Note that in the event of a confusion between the federal government and states with regard to items in the Concurrent Legislative List, the federal government will override any of the states.

54 The World Bank, *op cit (*Note 17) 65.

55 UNCITRAL Legislative Guide on Privately Financed Infrastructure Projects UN 2001 A/CN.9/SER.B/B/4 23.

56 Ibid.

57 Jeffrey Delmon, *Public-Private Partnership Projects in Infrastructure: An Essential Guide for Policy Makers* (Cambridge: Cambridge University Press, 2011) 5.

58 ER Yescombe, *Public-Private Partnerships: Principles of Policy and Finance* (Amsterdam, Netherlands: Elsevier 2007), 31.

asserts that the advantage of the contractual approach is that there is greater flexibility to make changes to the PPP programme.[59] It is important, however, that there is a legal framework, as it is an opportunity for the government to:[60]

1 Confirm its political commitment through explicit legislation;
2 Set out the roles of the different arms of the government, including the control and approval of individual PPP projects;
3 Set out the basis on which a public authority may provide support for various risk (e.g. revenue guarantees);
4 Provide a procedure for the public authority to make changes in the project's specifications and a method of compensating the project company for resulting extra costs;
5 Provide clarity on investors' rights if the PPP contract is terminated early, whether because of default by the project company or because the public authority wants to take the facility back under public-sector control;
6 Give lenders the ability to take security over the PPP contract; and
7 If appropriate, allow for the provision of investment incentives, such as special tax treatment etc.

No doubt, the passing into law of the Nigerian ICRC Act of 2005, the setting up of the ICRC to administer federal PPP transactions across the country as well as similar laws enacted by some of the states in the federation are intended to serve as a palpable political will to entrench a successful PPP regime in the country with the main aims *inter alia* being to:

1 Bridge the infrastructure gap;
2 Create job opportunities;
3 Stimulate foreign direct investment into the economy;
4 Facilitate economic growth and development;
5 Enable the government at all tiers to concentrate on policymaking and social-development programmes; and
6 To save scarce government resources.

Simply put, within the context of this research, the legal framework refers to 'how laws and regulatory structures can be used to encourage PPP, support the institutions implementing PPP and regulate them.'[61] On the other hand, the institutional framework deals with the persons involved, the powers they possess to make decisions and the functions they are permitted by law to perform. It remains to be stated that the absence of a legal framework would lead to uncertainty and chaos. Investors usually consider the legal framework and the process for relief in the event of a dispute or a cancellation as very important.

59 Ibid 32.
60 Ibid.
61 Jeffrey Delmon, *op cit* (note 57) 3.

Where these are not clearly defined, it is always regarded as a sign not to do business, no matter the prospect of the investment and the expected RoI. As such, the law ought to be used as a tool to drive infrastructural development in the country in light of this. It follows that the legal framework must be clearly defined, holistic and demystified. A situation where there are various laws regulating the same process, with many of the laws overlapping each other, breeds confusion and could give rise to disputes, which could work against a successful PPP regime.

6.5 How PPP is administered in Nigeria

The principal Act that governs PPP in Nigeria is the Infrastructure Concession Regulatory Commission Establishment (Etc.) Act of 2005 (ICRCA 2005). This law provides the primary framework for private-sector participation in infrastructure development in Nigeria.[62] It also established the Infrastructure Concession Regulatory Commission (ICRC) to:[63]

1 Take custody of every concession agreement made under the Act and monitor compliance with the terms and conditions of such an agreement;
2 Ensure the efficient execution of any concession agreement or contract entered by the government;
3 Ensure compliance with the provisions of the Act; and
4 Perform other such duties as may be directed by the president, from time to time, and as are necessary or expedient to ensure the efficient performance of the functions of the commission under the Act.

Essentially, the ICRCA of 2005 is divided into seven parts. It needs to be stated for the sake of emphasis that the Act basically regulates PPPs that involve the federal government or any of its MDAs for the financing, construction, operation and maintenance of infrastructure. The states that desire to adopt a PPP policy are required to provide their own regulatory framework.[64]

6.5.1 Regulations under the Infrastructure Concession Regulatory Commission Establishment (Etc.) Act of 2005

The Act stipulates that for a private-sector consortium to undertake a PPP concession with the FGN or any of its MDAs, it must possess the financial capacity, relevant expertise and experience in undertaking such infrastructure development or maintenance.[65] Given that PPP is a recent phenomenon in Nigeria, it raises the question of whether local consortiums may be disadvantaged when

62 The Act was signed into law and came into force on 10 November 2005.
63 Sections 14 and 20 of the ICRCA of 2005.
64 S. 1(1) of the ICRCA of 2005. See also S. 2(1) of the ICRCA of 2005.
65 S. 2(3) of the ICRCA of 2005.

bidding for PPP projects with the more experienced foreign consortiums. Again, the Act requires that the consortium to win the bid for a project must be 'the one that submits the most technically and economically responsive bid.'[66]

To offer some assurances of stability to private investors, the Act provides that no agreement reached in respect of the Act shall be arbitrarily suspended, stopped, cancelled or changed, except in accordance with the provisions of the Act.[67]

Sections 14 and 15 of the Act establish the ICRC and provide for a Governing Board for the Commission, respectively. However, the Act is silent with regard to the funding process for PPP projects. The Act does not provide for detailed rules on how the procurement of PPP contracts should be carried out. The lacuna leaves the ICRC with wide powers to make regulations through policy statements. Furthermore, the Act lacks clarity in the following areas:

1 The approval process for PPP projects and the granting of a concession;
2 The scale of projects to be considered for private-sector participation and the mechanism for dealing with unsolicited proposals;
3 A dispute-resolution process in the event of a conflict arising from a PPP arrangement; and
4 The legality or otherwise of a PPP project not in consonance with the provisions of the Act.

Furthermore, the neglect to make a provision within the Act that deals with the funding of PPP projects is less than desired. This lacuna perhaps gave rise to the failure of the Lagos-Ibadan Expressway Concession awarded to Bi-Courtney Limited.[68]

6.5.2 Conventional public procurement vs PPP

Public procurement is not the same thing as PPP. However, it is important to note that there is an overlap of the Public Procurement Act (PPA) of 2007 into the administration of PPP in the country. The Act came into force on 4 June 2007 under the administration of the late President Umaru Musa Yar'Adua. As the country's first public-procurement law, the purpose of the Act was to ensure transparency, competitiveness, VfM and professionalism in the public-sector procurement system. The PPA established the National Council on Public Procurement (NCPP)[69] and the Bureau of Public Procurement (BPP).[70] These bodies regulate and monitor public procurement, harmonising

66 S. 2(2) of the ICRCA of 2005.
67 S.11 of the ICRCA of 2005.
68 The Concession did not consider funding as well. Whereas the federal government expected the concessionaire to fund the project, the latter felt that its position was that of a middleman mandated to search for an investor.
69 Section 1(1) of the PPA 2007.
70 Section 3(1) of the PPA 2007.

the existing government policies and setting standards for developing the legal framework and professional capacity for public procurement in the country.[71] While the BPP performs regulatory and administrative functions, the NCPP exerts control over the administration of the BPP to ensure that the objectives of the Act are realised.

The PPA is applicable to all forms of procurement, works and services undertaken by:

1 The FGN and all 'procuring agencies'; and
2 All other entities, which derive at least 35 per cent of the funds, appropriated or proposed to be appropriated, for any type of procurement from the federation's share of the budget.[72]

Under the PPA, the main method of procurement is by open competitive bidding referred to as 'Sealed Bidding.'[73] Under this method, the procuring authority, based on a defined criterion, effects public procurements by offering every interested bidder equal simultaneous information and opportunity to offer goods and works needed.[74] The aim is to make public procurement transparent as well as to put corruption in check. However, it has been noted that the main challenge to the Act is the reluctance on the part of the FGN to embrace in totality the full implementation of the Act, as public contract is a tool to reward political loyalists.[75]

It remains to be stated, however, that the Act does not clearly refer to PPP projects. It is safe to therefore assume that the PPA of 2007 applies specifically to traditional procurement by the public sector. The silence of the ICRCA with regard to the procurement process itself for concessions could lead to confusion. The PPA should have taken the ICRCA into consideration. While it has been assumed that the PPA should apply to make for the deficiency or the silence of the ICRCA of 2005, this researcher is of the firm opinion that the Act should not apply, as it was strictly intended for conventional public-procurement purposes.

6.6 Other laws to be considered

For anyone seeking to understand the administrative and regulatory process for PPP in Nigeria, it is necessary to reckon with other laws that overlap the ICRCA of 2005. These include the following:

71 See the Explanatory Memorandum and the Schedule to the PPA of 2007.

72 Section 15 of the PPA of 2007.

73 Section 16(1) (c) of the PPA of 2007.

74 OA Jacob, 'Procurement Law in Nigeria: Challenge for Attainment of Its Objectives' (2010) *University of Botswana Law Journal* 139.

75 Ibid 146.

6.6.1 The Public Enterprises and Commercialisation Act (PECA) of 1999

This Act lays down the framework for the privatisation and commercialisation of public assets in Nigeria. It established the National Council on Privatisation (NCP)[76] and the Bureau of Public Enterprises (BPE).[77] While the former is charged with the responsibility of setting and administering the FGN's policies and objectives on privatisation and approving transactions, the latter is responsible for the actual day-to-day privatisation activities. Several concessions, including the 26 seaports, the trade fair complex, Tafawa Balewa Square, the National Theatre and the hydroelectric power plants have all been consummated under the law by the BPE. The transactions still listed under the schedule to the PECA, including the concessions of the airports and the railways, could lead to conflicts between the BPE and the ICRC.

6.6.2 The Utilities Charges Commission Act (UCCA) of 1992

This Act established the Utilities Charges Commission.[78] The functions *inter alia* are as follows:[79]

1 To evaluate on a continuous basis, trends in tariffs charged by any of the public utilities listed in the Second Schedule to the Act;
2 To advise the FGN on guidelines within which increases in tariffs should be confined by scheduled utilities;
3 To design and develop an adequate information system relating to the Scheduled Utilities;
4 To keep charges and tariffs under constant surveillance and propose measures to regulate tariff charges; and
5 To prevent the undue exploitation of consumers.

The effect of the provisions of the UCCA of 1992 is that the Commission must approve the tariffs to be agreed between the concessionaire and the public sector. The Act specifies the utilities to include electricity, seaport, railways, postal services, airports and several others.

6.6.3 The Environmental Impact Assessment Act (EIAA) of 1992

The EIAA of 1992 was enacted to set out the general principles, procedures and methods to enable the prior consideration of environmental-impact assessment

76 Section 9 of the PECA of 1999.
77 Section 12 of the PECA of 1999.
78 Section 1(1) of the UCCA of 1992.
79 Section 6 of the UCCA of 1992.

on certain public or private projects. The Act specifically restricts any public or private project without prior consideration of the environmental impact.[80]

6.6.4 The Debt Management Office Establishment (Etc.) Act (DMOA) of 2003

This Act established the Debt Management Office (DMO).[81] The functions of the DMO include the following:[82]

1 Maintain a reliable database of all loans taken or guaranteed by the federal or state governments or any of their agencies;
2 Prepare and submit to the federal government a forecast of loan service obligations for each financial year;
3 Prepare and implement a plan for the efficient management of Nigeria's external and domestic debt obligations at sustainable levels compatible with the desired economic activities for growth and development and participate in negotiations aimed at realising those objectives;
4 Verify and service external debts guaranteed or directly taken by the federal government;
5 On an agency basis, service external debts taken by state governments and any of their agencies where the federal government guarantees such debts; and
6 Set guidelines for managing Federal Government financial risks and currency exposure with respect to all loans;

In sum, the DMO is saddled with the responsibility of maintaining a reliable database for all loans or guarantees taken by the FGN or any of the 36 states or their agencies, especially as they relate to financing infrastructure contracts or concessions.

6.6.5 The National Inland Waterways Act (NIWA) of 1997

This Act established the National Inland Waterways Authority[83] and provided that all navigable waterways, inland waterways, river-ports and internal waters of Nigeria, excluding all direct approaches to the ports listed in the Third Schedule to the Act and all other waters declared to be approaches to ports under or pursuant to the Nigerian Ports Authority Act, up to 250 metres beyond the upstream edge of the quay of such ports, would be under the exclusive management,

80 Section 2 of the EIAA of 1992.
81 Section 4(1) of the DMOA of 2003.
82 Section 6 of the DMOA of 2003.
83 Section 1(1) of the NIWA of 1997.

direction and control of the Authority.[84] A combined reading of the Second Schedule to the 1999 Constitution of the Federal Republic of Nigeria and the provisions of the NIWA of 1997 is to the effect that states are precluded from entering into concession agreements that involve inland waterways.

6.6.6 The Highways Act (Laws of the Federal Republic of Nigeria No. 35) (HA) of 1971

Under the HA of 1971, the Minister charged with the responsibility for roads is empowered to control federal highways.[85] The Minister's responsibilitiesinclude:[86]

1 Planning (including the research and designing of) federal highways;
2 Construction and maintenance;
3 Supervision of the road users; and
4 The regulation of traffic.

It is worthy to note that the Act empowers the Minister to erect, equip and maintain tollgates on any federal highway as when required with the approval of the President.[87] When there is a concession of any federal road in the country and there is a need for tolling, the authority lies with the Minister in charge of roads. Regrettably, the ICRCA of 2005 does not refer to the HA of 1971.

6.6.7 The Fiscal Responsibility Act No. 31 (FRA) of 2007

The FRA of 2007 provided for the prudent management of Nigeria's resources in order to ensure long-term macro-economic stability of the national economy, secured greater accountability and transparency in fiscal operations within the medium-term fiscal policy framework and established the Fiscal Responsibility Commission[88] (FRC) to ensure the promotion and enforcement of Nigeria's economic objectives and related matters.[89] The FRC is empowered to compel any person or government institution to disclose information relating to public revenues and expenditure and to carry out an investigation as to whether any person has violated any provision of the FRA.[90]

There ought to be a coordination between the ICRC, which is the primary body charged with PPP transactions in Nigeria, and the FRC where there is

84 Section 11 of the NIWA of 1997.
85 Section 1(1) of the HA of 1971.
86 Section 1(2) of the HA of 1971.
87 Section 2(1) of the HA of 1971.
88 Section 1(1) of the FRA of 2007.
89 See the main title to the Act.
90 Section 2(1) of the FRA of 2007.

any kind of borrowing or spending on infrastructure. More so, the FRC is supposed to sanction any such transaction. As such, potential investors run the risk of being stuck in the middle of their projects if the FRC ever decides to exercise its powers under Section 2 of the FRA.

6.7 Regulations at the sub-national level

As already noted, a potential PPP investor in Nigeria must primarily determine what level of government is being dealt with before agreeing to transact any business.[91] Furthermore, it is noteworthy that state laws apply at the sub-national level. A few proactive states in the federation have passed their own PPP laws and have established PPP units to administer PPP transactions within their various jurisdictions. Some of the states that have done so include the following:

6.7.1 Lagos State

The Lagos State Government (LASG) is one of the leading governments in the country as far as PPP is concerned. To demonstrate its commitment to delivering infrastructure to the people of the state, the LASG enacted and signed into law the Lagos State Public Private Partnership Law (LSPPPL) in June 2011.[92] The law repealed the previous Lagos State Roads (Private Participation) Authority Law of 2007. The LSPPPL 2011 established a PPP office in the state.

The LSPPL 2011 also provided for the following:

1 A requirement for the ratification of concession agreements by the State House of Assembly before implementation;
2 State House of Assembly approval of sums to be charged as toll or user fees;
3 Appeal against the decision of the Office to the Lagos State Public Procurement Agency;
4 State House of Assembly approval of the concession agreement; and
5 The increase of fines payable upon conviction for the refusal to pay service charges or tolls to ₦100,000 or six months of imprisonment.

6.7.2 Rivers State

The Rivers State Government (RVSG) has also made a proactive commitment to a PPP regime by enacting a PPP law and setting up a PPP office known as

91 At the federal level, the government may be represented by any of its MDAs, whereas at the sub-national level, a state government may also be represented by any of its MDAs.

92 Olaniwun Ajayi, 'Lagos State PPP Law' (2011) available at <www.olaniwunajayi.net/clientalert/PPP%20Newsletter%20Final%2011%2008%202011.pdf> accessed 11 April 2016.

the Bureau of Public-Private Partnerships.[93] PPP is referred to as the Public-Private Initiative in the state.[94] The RVSG signed into law the Public-Private Participation in Infrastructure Development Law in 2009.

In Rivers State, the following areas are clearly marked as 'no-go areas' for PPP:[95]

1 Defence;
2 Security of the State;
3 Urgent public need or emergency; and
4 Items under close bid as provided for in Section 21(4) of the Rivers State Public Procurement Law No. 4 of 2008.

The law also established an Infrastructure Development Finance Unit (IDFU) under the Ministry of Finance.[96] The main responsibility of the IDFU is to ensure VfM for the state by applying commercial standards in evaluating financial risks and costs.[97] Of significance is a provision for infrastructure credit guarantee (ICG). The RIVSG may upon the recommendation of the IDFU guarantee the credit of a private party who intends to obtain a loan from a financial institution for the execution of a PPP project for:[98]

1 Stimulating private-sector participation; and
2 Encouraging the participation of companies and businesses indigenous to Rivers State.

It is submitted that the ICG provision included in the Rivers State law is an incentive for private participation in infrastructure development.

Unlike the ICRCA of 2005 that is less comprehensive as far as the regulation of PPP in the country is concerned, the Rivers State law is more encompassing. However, limiting PPPs to a 20-year term as provided for under Section 62 of the law will remain a challenge for the private sector as well as the representing public-sector authority. This is so because infrastructure projects often suffer from long gestation periods up to the stage of execution and service delivery.

6.7.3 Ekiti State

The Ekiti State Government (EKSG) enacted the Ekiti State Public Private Partnership Law on 26 July 2011. The law established the Office of Public Private Partnership under Section 1 and permits state MDAs to enter PPP arrangements with qualified private project proponents. One important inclusion

93 Section 13 of the Public-Private Participation in Infrastructure Development Law of 2009.
94 Section 1 of the Public-Private Participation in Infrastructure Development Law of 2009.
95 Section 3(2) of the Public-Private Participation in Infrastructure Development Law of 2009.
96 Section 27 of the Public-Private Participation in Infrastructure Development Law of 2009.
97 Section 30(1) of the Public-Private Participation in Infrastructure Development Law of 2009.
98 Section 35 of the Public-Private Participation in Infrastructure Development Law of 2009.

in Ekiti State's PPP law is the provision for guarantees, letters of comfort or undertakings,[99] which gives some level of assurance to prospective investors. It is suggested that the federal government and other states of the federation should consider including guarantees in their main PPP laws to assure investors of the government's commitment as exemplified by Ekiti State.

6.7.4 Cross River State

The Cross River State Government (CRSG) enacted the Cross River Public Private Partnership Law in 2010.[100] In addition, the state enacted the Cross River State Process Intelligence Bureau for Public Procurement Law No. 15 on 30 December 2011 to ensure that due process was followed in PPP arrangements. The law provided *inter alia*:

> Subject to any exemption allowed by this law, public procurements shall be conducted by open competitive bidding in a manner which is transparent, timely, equitable for ensuring accountability and in conformity with this law and regulations.[101]

The other states that have set up a framework for private-sector participation in infrastructure delivery include Bayelsa, Delta, Akwa Ibom, Abia, Edo, Benue, Sokoto, Zamfara, Benue, Bauchi, Kaduna and Yobe.[102] It remains to be noted that an enabling environment for successful private-sector participation in infrastructure provision essentially entails the following:[103]

1 The existence of a private-sector participation in infrastructure law;
2 The establishment of a PPP office or unit in the state; and
3 The undertaking of projects.

6.8 Laws regulating Foreign Direct Investments (FDI) for infrastructure

To attract FDI into the Nigerian economy in general, the FGN has enacted laws to facilitate the importation of foreign capital for the purposes of investments in

99 S.9 of the Ekiti State Public Private Partnership Law of 2011.

100 John Ighodaro, 'C-River Govt Signs PPP Bill into Law' *Vanguard*, 4 August 2010 (Lagos) available at <www.vanguardngr.com/2010/08/c-river-govt-signs-ppp-bill-into-law/> accessed 29 May 2018.

101 African Gong, 'Cross River Highway Project; Buhari Tasked for Answers' (2015) available at <http://africangong.com/2015/11/08/cross-river-highway-project-citizen-demand-answers/> accessed 14 April 2016.

102 Martin O Dada and Olukayode S Oyediran, 'The State of Public Private Partnership in Nigeria' in Akintola Akintoye, Mathias Beck and Mohan Kumaraswamy (eds.), *Public Private Partnerships: A Global Review* (London: Routledge, 2015) 20.

103 Ibid.

the country. These laws also apply where there are foreign participants investing in the provision of infrastructure within the country.

6.8.1 *The Nigerian Investment Promotion Commission Act (NIPCA) of 1998*

The NIPCA of 1998 is the country's principal investment law and regulates the entry of FDI into the country. The Act established the Nigerian Investment Promotion Commission (NIPC).[104] The functions of the NIPC are to:[105]

1 Be the agency of the FGN to co-ordinate and monitor all investment promotion activities to which the NIPCA applies;
2 Initiate and support measures which shall enhance the investment climate in Nigeria for both Nigerian and non-Nigerian investors;
3 Promote investments in and outside Nigeria through effective promotional means;
4 Collect, collate, analyse and disseminate information about investment opportunities and sources of investment capital and advise, on request, the availability, choice or suitability of partners in joint-venture projects;
5 Register and keep records of enterprises to which the Act applies;
6 Identify specific projects and invite interested investors for participation in those projects;
7 Initiate, organise and participate in promotional activities, such as exhibitions, conferences and seminars, for the stimulation of investments;
8 Maintain a liaison between investors and MDAs, institutional lenders and other authorities concerned with investments;
9 Provide and disseminate up-to-date information on incentives available to investors;
10 Assist incoming and existing investors by providing support services;
11 Evaluate the impact of the NIPC in investments in Nigeria and make appropriate recommendations;
12 Advise the FGN on policy matters, including fiscal measures designed to promote the industrialisation of Nigeria or the general development of the economy;
13 Participate in the negotiation of investment promotion and protection agreements (IPPA); and
14 Other functions as are supplementary or incidental to the attainment of the objectives of the NIPCA.

104 Section 1(1) of the NIPCA of 1998.
105 Section 4 of the NIPCA of 1998.

6.8.2 Provisions relating to investments

The NIPCA has effectively abolished any restrictions, in respect to foreign shareholding in Nigeria, registered/domiciled enterprises with certain exemptions with regard to the production of arms and ammunition; the production of narcotics, drugs and psychotropic substances; the manufacture of military/paramilitary wears and accoutrements and participation in coastal and inland shipping.

Some of the notable provisions relating to investments include the following:

1. Non-Nigerians may invest and participate in the operation of any enterprise in Nigeria;[106]
2. Any enterprise with permitted foreign participation shall be registered, after incorporation with the NIPC;
3. A foreign enterprise may buy shares of any Nigerian enterprise in any convertible foreign currency;
4. A foreign investor in an approved enterprise is guaranteed unconditional transferability of funds through an authorised dealer, in freely convertible currency, be it:
    a) Dividends or profits (net of taxes) attributable to the investment or
    b) Payments in respect of loan servicing where a foreign loan has been obtained;
5. The remittance of proceeds (net of all taxes) and other obligations in the event of the sale or liquidation of the enterprise or any interest attributable to the investment; and
6. Total repatriation of capital, should the investor choose to relocate elsewhere.

6.8.3 Protection for FDI under the Foreign Exchange (Monitoring and Miscellaneous) Provisions Act (FEMMA) of 1995

The FEMMA of 1995 provides that no enterprise shall be nationalised or expropriated by any government of the federation, and no person who owns, whether wholly or in part, the capital of any enterprise shall be compelled by law to surrender his or her interest in the capital to any other persons. There would be no acquisition of an enterprise by the FGN unless the acquisition is in the national interest or for a public purpose under a law, which made provision for:

1. Payment of fair and adequate compensation, and
2. A right of access to the courts for the determination of the investor's interest of right and the amount of compensation to which the investor is entitled.

106 Except for the items listed in the preceding paragraph.

Again, the law provides for the payment of compensation without undue delay, and authorization given for its repatriation in convertible currency where applicable.[107]

6.9 Case studies of PPP projects in Nigeria

Under this section, some PPP projects that have been arranged in Nigeria are examined. The focus here is on projects that have passed the 'pipeline phase' and have moved on to the stage of execution and/or operation or that have been closed and are awaiting implementation. The method adopted for the analysis is the review of past studies, contract documents, reports and relevant policy documents. The projects under examination cut across various classes of infrastructure assets, namely, transport, health care and tourism. It is important to note that the PPP projects in focus include arrangements of both the federal government and state authorities with the private sector. This chapter addresses the question of how PPP projects have fared so far in Nigeria since the passing into law of the ICRCA of 2005 by the FGN at the national level and the passing of similar laws by states at the sub-national level. Thus, the cases discussed herein indicate the extent of compliance to the legal, policy and administrative framework that was the focus in Chapter 4.

The cases that have been reviewed in this chapter indicate that partnerships that go through the rigour of thorough planning, political commitment on the part of government, effective monitoring and management by experienced private partners are usually successful. It is important that political leaders involve community stakeholders right from the initiation phase of any project to gain their trust. Furthermore, it is important that the public sector undertake thorough feasibility studies that would address the questions of affordability, VfM and risk transfer. No less important also is the need to ensure a transparent bidding process before a preferred project company is selected. Finally, the importance of the skill of experts, including legal consultants, to draft the contract as well as the opinion of technical persons, such as engineers, project managers, surveyors and environmental specialists, to ensure that any given project is successful cannot be overemphasised.

6.9.1 The Lagos Ibadan Expressway project

The Lagos-Ibadan Expressway in Southwest Nigeria was conceived and constructed by the Federal Military Government under three different contracts between 1974 and 1978. The first section of the expressway from Lagos to Sagamu was constructed by Julius Berger Nigeria, the second section[108] from the Sagamu interchange to Alapako was constructed by Dumez (Nigeria) and

107 See the Rivers State PPP Handbook available at <http://riversbppp.gov.ng/images/pdf/rivers%20ppp%20handbook.pdf> accessed 23 April 2016.

108 A 45-kilometre stretch.

the third section from Alapako to Ojoo, including the Ibadan Bypass, was built by Strabag Nigeria. It is a 127.6-kilometre road connecting the industrial, financial and commercial hub of Lagos to Ibadan, the capital of Oyo State. The road is reputed to be one of Africa's busiest highways.[109] Over the years, however, the expressway has suffered from overuse without adequate maintenance.

To address the deplorable conditions of the expressway, the Federal Ministry of Works (FMoW) awarded a 25-year concession[110] for its rehabilitation to Bi-Courtney Highway Services Limited (BCHSL).[111] Consequent upon this, BCHSL engaged the services of local consultants to commence the design for the rehabilitation.[112] Furthermore, Project Management International was commissioned to manage a multi-disciplinary team made up of members of BCHSL, Group Five and Rand Merchant Bank, with Vela/VKE of South Africa providing technical support.[113]

Under the PPP arrangement, work on the expressway under consideration was to commence at the Ojota Interchange in Lagos and terminate at the Challenge Interchange in Ibadan, approximately 105 kilometres.

In their analysis, Babatunde et al.,[114] argue that the Federal Government of Nigeria and the concessionaire failed to consider several factors necessary for the project to succeed, hence the failure of the project to take off years after the concession agreement was signed. They also point out that the government officials did not have the requisite knowledge about PPP projects and failed to engage the services of experienced legal/transaction consultants/technical advisers.[115]

In November 2012, the administration of President Goodluck Jonathan revoked the concession that was awarded to BCHSL in 2009. The federal government of Nigeria cited a violation of the contract terms, particularly, the failure on the part of the concessionaire to secure the needed funds for the project. The then Minister for Works, Architect Mike Onolememen, who made the announcement, went further to indicate that the road would now be constructed by Julius Berger and RCC.[116]

109 The Punch Newspaper, 'Editorial' *The Punch*, 27 April 2016 (Lagos).

110 BCHLS was commissioned under a BOT arrangement to reconstruct the 105-kilometre Expressway with 100 per cent funding from the concessionaire.

111 The concession agreement entitled the concessionaire to revenue recoup rights, including charging vendors on the road and toll collections.

112 Project Management International, 'Lagos-Ibadan Expressway, Nigeria' available at <http://pmi-ltd.co.za/projects/66_BCHS-2011-Lagos_Ibadan_Expressway-Nigeria.pdf> accessed 12 August 2016.

113 Ibid.

114 Solomon Babatunde, Srinath Perera, Chika Udeaja and Lei Zhou, 'Challenges in Implementing Public Private Partnership Strategy for Infrastructure Delivery in Nigeria' available at <http://nrl.northumbria.ac.uk/17191/1/babatunde_et_al_ppp_conference_paper_(1).doc> accessed 20 August 2016.

115 Ibid.

116 Ini Ekott, 'At Last, FG Revokes Lagos-Ibadan Expressway Bi-Courtney Concession' *Premium Times*, 19 November 2012 (Lagos) available at <www.premiumtimesng.com/news/107689-at-last-fg-revokes-lagos-ibadan-expressway-bi-courtney-concession.html> accessed 21 August 2016.

As part of the terms of the concession, the concessionaire was supposed to pay fines in the event of a delay in the execution of the project,[117] and if there was a delay on the part of the Nigerian government, the concessionaire would receive commensurate extensions, alongside a defraying inflationary cost on the initially agreed-upon construction cost. However, the federal government of Nigeria did not make any claims for BCHSL to pay fines, which could amount to over ₦30 billion on account of the three-year delay in the execution of the project.[118] Following the revocation of the concession, BCHSL wrote to Onolememen on 29 January 2013 expressing a desire for arbitration, an offer to which the government did not respond.[119]

Subsequently, BCHSL approached the Federal High Court for an order to restrain the federal government of Nigeria from re-awarding a concession of the Lagos-Ibadan Expressway to any other construction company, arguing that any re-concession would amount to a breach of the contract between it and the FMoW.[120] The defendants in the suit were the Federal Minister of Works, the Attorney General of the federation and three companies. In a ruling on 25 April 2016, the Federal High Court, while not agreeing with the defendants that the suit was an abuse of court process, nevertheless held that the matter was brought outside the time limited by the Public Officers' Protection Act[121] and therefore dismissed the action in its entirety. This is because once a suit against a public officer is commenced more than three months after the cause of action arose, such a case should be held to be statute-barred and the court should decline jurisdiction.[122] The court further set aside its earlier mandatory injunction setting aside the Concession Agreement entered between the FGN

117 Which was agreed to be ₦100,000 per kilometre for a square metre of an unconstructed bridge along the route.

118 Ini Ekott, *op cit* (note 116).

119 Vanguard Newspapers, 'N167bN Lagos-Ibadan Expressway: How FG Ignored Arbitration Offer by Bi-Courtney' *The Vanguard*, 26 January 2016 (Lagos) available at <www.vanguardngr.com/2016/01/n167bn-lagos-ibadan-expressway-how-fg-ignored-arbitration-offer-by-bi-courtney/> accessed 29 May 2018.

120 The suit by BCHSL was instituted primarily to challenge the re-concession of the expressway rehabilitation to Motorways Asset Limited (an SPV set up by Infrastructure Bank Plc for the executors of the project – Julius Berger Nigeria Ltd and RCC Nigeria Ltd.)

121 See S. 2(a) of the Public Officers' Protection Act, which provides that 'where any action, prosecution, or other proceeding is commenced against any person for any act done in pursuance or execution or intended execution of any Act or Law or of any public duty or authority, or in respect of any alleged neglect or default in the execution of any such Act, Law, duty or authority, the following provisions shall have effect – Limitation of time – the action, prosecution, or proceeding shall not lie or be instituted unless it is commenced within three months next after the act, neglect or default complained of, or in case of continuance of damage or injury, within three months next after the ceasing thereof'

122 The Paradigm, 'Lagos-Ibadan Expressway: Bi-Courtney Highway Services Limited Loses Case Against the Federal Government' (2012) available at <www.theparadigmng.com/2016/04/26/lagos-ibadan-expressway-bi-courtney-highway-services-limited-loses-case-against-the-federal-government/> accessed 7 July 2017.

and Motorways Asset Limited, which the same court had earlier made on 11 December 2015.[123] It is evident that the lack of experience on the part of the private-sector consortium (i.e. BCHSL) as well as the lack of political will on the part of the federal government of Nigeria led to the failure of the Lagos-Ibadan Expressway Bi-Courtney Concession project. Therefore, it behoves the public sector to ensure that projects succeed in order to avoid sending the wrong signals to prospective private investors in the future. This is because investors who study the Bi-Courtney case will be concerned about the refusal of the Nigerian federal government to submit to arbitration more than the apparent lack of experience of the BCHSL.

In summary, the Lagos-Ibadan Expressway Bi-Courtney Concession project is considered a failure. The core reasons for this were that both parties lacked a proper understanding of how PPPs work and the federal government refused to provide a guarantee for the project company, which resulted in the reluctance of financial partners to be involved in the project. Other reasons include the failure of the concessionaire to source the needed funds required to finance the project; a poorly drafted concession agreement; no room given for arbitration by the Nigerian government, resulting in endless/multiple litigation; uncompetitive and non-transparent procurement, which led to the choosing of an inexperienced project company; poor project-development skills and the grantor's failure to conduct due diligence.

6.9.2 Lekki-Epe Concession Toll Road Project

The Lekki-Epe Concession Toll Road Project was conceived as a PPP scheme under a BOT model of infrastructure delivery. It was initially arranged to last for a 30-year period, following which the assets would be transferred to the Lagos State Government. It is important to state that this project was arranged pursuant to the Lagos State PPP law. It is thus an example of a PPP project at the sub-national level. As the flagship road concession project to be executed in the country, it was expected that the project would have set the ball rolling for many such projects around the country because of the international recognition the concession got. The awards the concession received included the *Africa Investors' Magazine* Award for the Transport Deal of the Year 2008; the Euromoney International 2007 Africa PPP of the Year; Reuters 2008 Africa Infrastructure Deal of the Year and the *IFC/Infrastructure Journal* Top 40 Emerging Market Award in 2013.[124]

123 Luminary Nigeria, 'Court Dismisses Bi-Courtney's Suit Seeking Termination of Lagos-Ibadan Expressway Concession' (2016) available at <www.luminaryng.com/court-dismisses-bi-courtneys-suit-seeking-termination-of-lagos-ibadan-expressway-concession/> accessed 21 August 2016.

124 Augustine Edobor Arimoro, 'Impact of Community Stakeholders on Public-Private Partnerships: Lessons from the Lekki-Epe Concession Toll Road' (2015) 3(7) *International Journal of Law and legal Studies* 165–167 165.

The justification for the project was the fact that Lagos experiences a continuous influx of population, which exerts significant pressure on the state's road infrastructure. The congestion on the road linking mainland Lagos to the central business district on the island is, considerably, very problematic. This is made worse by a lack of adequate public transport systems in the state. Thus, the main drive for the project was the intent to decongest the roads in the central business districts of Victoria Island and Ikoyi to make the areas more 'business-friendly.'[125]

Essentially, the project comprised 'the upgrading of approximately 49.5 km of the existing Epe Expressway linking Lekki to Epe on Victoria Island. Among others, street lightings will be provided, the four-lane dual carriageway will be expanded to six-lanes in some places, and toll plazas will be constructed, along with other administrative structures.'[126] The project was to last about 30 months, with the early phase (Falomo Bridge to Mobil House) planned to last for the first 9 months.

There have been allegations that the process leading to the award of the concession (i.e. bidding and selection) was 'shady,' with the ownership of the LCC coming into question when some alleged complicity on the part of government officials.[127] Some believed a former governor of Lagos State and a chieftain of the ruling party in the state had substantial interest in the project company that won the bid for the concession. Thus, Ayodele and Sotola identified a lack of transparency and openness as one of the issues that was skewed against the concession of the Lekki toll road. Again, the non-involvement of the community stakeholders in the period leading to the award of the concession proved costly.[128] To underscore the relevance of community stakeholder involvement in PPPs, Yescombe posits that, due to the public-service nature of PPPs, it is inevitable that they are subject to heavy political debate. As such, he recommends that there must be a 'political will on the public-sector side of the table, and the ability to communicate the case for pursuing PPP clearly and fairly.'[129]

Upon the commencement of the project, the LCC set up three toll gates, even before executing a substantial part of the project. The negative effect of that action at the time affected property values around the corridor with a depreciation of about 30 per cent, according to Uroko.[130] There were agitations

125 Africa Development Bank, 'Summary of Environmental and Social Impact Assessment for the Lekki Toll Road Project' (2007) available at <www.afdb.org/fileadmin/uploads/afdb/Documents/Environmental-and-Social-Assessments/ADB-BD-IF-2007-170-EN-NIGERIA-LEKKI-TOLL-ROAD-PROJECT-ESIA.PDF> accessed 21 August 2016.

126 Ibid.

127 Solomon Olusola Babatunde, Akintayo Opawole and Olusegun E Akinsiku, *op cit* (note 84).

128 AE Arimoro, *op cit* (note 124) 166.

129 ER Yescombe, *op cit* (note 58).

130 C Uroko, 'Multiple Tolls on Lekki-Epe Expressway Bring Down Property Value by 30 Percent' *Business Day*, 19 September 2013 (Lagos).

on the part of the residents along the corridor who contended that paying ₦250, ₦150 and ₦120 tolls on each of the three toll gates on a single journey was absurd. Their argument was that tolling should only commence upon the completion of the entire 49-kilometre stretch of the road. On the other hand, the concessionaire argued that under the concession agreement, they were empowered to commence the collection of tolls, even though less than 10 per cent of the road had been completed.

The question of whether an alternative road should have been available before tolls could be charged on the expressway was brought to bear by the Stakeholders Forum on the Lekki-Epe Expansion Project.[131] The group argued that there was a need for an alternative route in the first place for those who do not wish to ply the expressway and pay tolls.[132] However, in addressing the question of whether there is an obligation on either the concessionaire or the public authority to provide an alternative road for users who are unable or unwilling to pay tolls, it has been posited that the assertion that an alternative road must be provided before tolls can be charged has no basis in Nigerian law.[133]

It is worth mentioning that the Lekki-Epe toll road was the first PPP deal to achieve financial closure in the roads sub-sector in Nigeria. In addition, apart from attracting the sum of US$290 million of private investment from local and foreign investors, the project did obtain a 12-year loan from a consortium of local commercial banks. Before then, other infrastructure projects could only obtain a maximum of a seven-year loan period.[134]

The Lekki-Epe Concession Toll Road was meant to have a 30-year duration. It was financed by a consortium of Nigerian and foreign banks as well as by the LASG in the following order: US$42.5 million in mezzanine funding from the state government; US$85 million in debt from the African Development Bank; and US$109.7 million in funding from local commercial banks, including Zenith, First Bank, Fidelity Bank, Diamond Bank and United Bank for Africa (12-year note issuance facility). The sum of ₦6.93 billion was held as equity by a consortium consisting of Asset and Resource Management Company Limited (ARM), Africa Infrastructure Investment Fund (AIIF), Laure Projects and Hi-Tech Construction. The holder of the remaining US$8.3 million in equity

131 This is a group made up of residents of housing estates and owners of commercial interests in Lekki, opposed to aspects of the concession agreement between LCC and the Lagos State Government.

132 Dominis Nwelih, 'Why We Want Lekki-Epe Expressway Concession Deal Reviewed' *Sahara Reporters*, 1 September 2010 available at <http://saharareporters.com/2010/09/01/%E2%80%98%E2%80%99why-we-want-lekki-epe-expressway-concession-deal-reviewed%E2%80%99%E2%80%99> accessed 21 August 2016.

133 See Detail Solicitors, 'Nigeria PPP Review' (2012) 3 available at <www.detailsolicitors.com/media/archive2/articles/PPPreview.pdf> accessed 21 August 2016.

134 Cambridge Economic Policy Associates Ltd, 'Mobilising Finance for Infrastructure: A Study for the UK Department for International' available at <https://assets.publishing.service.gov.uk/media/57a08979ed915d622c00022b/61319-DfID_3_Three_page_summary.pdf > accessed 26 May 2018.

is unknown. The buy-back of the project by the LASG makes it a failure, as the project did not see out the entire tenure of the PPP arrangement. It is submitted that the reasons for the failure include the non-involvement of community stakeholders in the initiation phase; the perceived lack of transparency in the award of the concession; political opposition and rising costs not envisaged at the conception of the project, in addition to currency risk.

6.9.3 Murtala Mohammed Airport Terminal 2

The FGN, through its agency the Federal Airports Authority of Nigeria (FAAN), entered three different agreements with Bi-Courtney Aviation Services Limited (BCASL) within a space of four years. Nwangwu notes that the first BOT agreement was signed in April 2003 for a period of 12 years. A second agreement was signed in June 2004 to allow for an increase in the construction period from 18 to 33 months because of the concessionaire's slow pace of work. A third agreement, which extended the concession period from 12 to 36 years, was signed in February 2007.[135]

The concessionaire invested about US$250 million on the construction of the MMA2, with the bulk of the funding sourced from a consortium of six local banks, namely, Zenith, Oceanic,[136] GTBank, First City Monument Bank, Access and First Bank of Nigeria.[137] The construction work was completed and commissioned on 7 April 2007, with flight operations commencing on 7 May 2007.

Even though the project was successfully executed, the concession has not been without challenges. Essia and Yusuf[138] note that the project encountered 'challenges in securing long term financing agreement, and unwillingness of FAAN to support the project enforcing use of MMA2 by airlines as required in the PPP agreement.' They also note that the absence of a sustainable long-term financing model for PPP in the country was a challenge for the MMA2 concession. In addition, BCASL's shortcomings could have been avoided with better foresight, planning and realistic goal settings and timelines for delivery. More worrisome is the absence of a dispute-resolution mechanism other than having to resort to litigation compounded by FAAN's several refusals to obey court orders as well as a weak ICRC that has not been properly empowered to defend PPP projects or protect private investors.[139]

The court cases so far involving the concession 'either directly question the legality of the concession, duration of the concession or for breach of the

135 Ibid.
136 Now a part of Ecobank.
137 Solomon O Babatunde, Srinath Perera, Chika Udeaja and Lei Zhou, *op cit* (note 84).
138 Uwem Essia and Abubakar Yusuf, 'Public-Private Partnership and Sustainable Infrastructure in Nigeria' (2013) 3 *Advances in Management & Applied Economics* 15.
139 Ibid.

concession contract.'[140] There have been suits filed by either the public sector (the Ministry of Aviation) and the concessionaire against each other or by the FAAN against the concessionaire. The users (airlines) of the airport as well as the workers' union have at various times brought action against the concessionaire. The public sector claimed that BCASL had not paid ground rent for the use of MMA2[141] and that the concession was for 12 years and not 36 years, as claimed by the concessionaire.[142] On the other hand, the concessionaire claimed that the concession bars the FAAN from renovating or operating any other terminal within Lagos State and that this included the General Aviation Terminal (GAT),[143] which was the second terminal located a few metres from the MMA2 terminal under concession.[144] Because of this, the concessionaire contended that the government owed it proceeds from the operation of the GAT.[145] Court judgements 'confirming the owner of GAT as Bi-Courtney include the 2009 ruling of Justice J. Chikere of the Abuja Federal High Court.'[146] The same judgement was affirmed in a ruling on 13 February 2013 by Justice AR Mohammed of the same court in a suit filed by FAAN and the Ministry of Aviation asking the court to declare that they were not bound by the ruling of Justice Chikere. In his ruling, Justice Mohammed stated categorically that by suing the Attorney-General of the federation, Bi-Courtney's suit was binding on all agencies of the federal government.[147] It is

140 George Nwangwu, 'A Risk Approach to Enhancing Public-Private Partnership Projects in Nigeria' (Unpublished PhD Thesis, University of Hull, Hull, 2014) 278.

141 The ground rent is set at 5 per cent of the concessionaire's turnover, as stipulated in the concession agreement.

142 The government's case is that the Addendum Agreement between FAAN and BCASL, which increases the duration of the concession from 12 years to 36 years, was not approved by the Federal Executive Council (FEC) in line with the mandatory provisions of the ICRCA of 2005.

143 FAAN awarded the construction of GAT to rival MMA2 and contravened parts of the BASL/FAAN Agreement, especially the monopoly clause. See Wole Oyebade, 'How Not to Privatise Nigerian Airports, By Stakeholders' *Daily Nigerian News*, 29 July 2016 available at <www.dailynigerianews.com/2016/07/29/how-not-to-privatise-nigerian-airports-by-stakeholders/> accessed 25 August 2016.

144 Under Article 2.2 of the concession agreement, the grantor guarantees and assures that it will not build any new domestic terminal in Lagos State and that no existing domestic terminal will be materially improved throughout the concession period that would compete with the concessionaire for the same passenger tariff, provided the concessionaire shall have the right of first refusal if the passenger traffic during the concession period necessitates an expansion of the terminal and the first consideration if the grantor elects to build a new domestic terminal in Lagos State. The grantor further guarantees and assures that all scheduled flights in and out of FAAN's airport in Lagos State shall during the concession period operate from the terminal. FAAN further assures and guarantees that it shall not during the concession period cause or authorise the erection or development of a shopping mall or any facilities within 200 metres from the perimeter of the site capable of impeding and/or threatening the concessionaire's revenue generation.

145 Arik Air, one of the country's airlines, currently operates from the old domestic local airport, also referred to as the GAT.

146 Suit No. FHC/ABJ/CJ/50/2009.

147 Chinedu Eze, 'Bi-Courtney Claims Arik Owes it N12.5bn' *This Day*, 2 May 2016 (Lagos).

noteworthy that FAAN's appeals against court rulings against it have all been dismissed, yet FAAN maintains an 'above-the-law' posture.[148]

It is submitted that in a situation where an agency of the government which is a party to a concession, violates the agreement and at the same time refuses to obey court rulings is inimical to the essence of PPP in the first place. Since PPP is a new phenomenon in Nigeria, both local and foreign investors watch to see the performance of existing concessions before taking decisions in any future concession, and considering that PPPs are often long-term investments, a violation of the terms of such a contract just a few years into it does not augur well for the government.

Although the project is completed and operational, this writer, with respect, considers it a failure because the operation of the airport is marred by controversies. There is no clear-cut arbitration route to follow to resolve the myriad conflicts bedeviling the concession. The regulatory body (i.e. the ICRC) appears so weak that it cannot exercise any power to protect the investor from the might of the agency of the federal government. More worrying is the refusal of the FAAN to obey court rulings.

6.9.4 Cross River State Hospital

Given the deteriorating state of hospital infrastructure in Cross River State, in addition to a shortage of personnel, the people in the state started losing confidence in the facilities available, which in turn led to high incidences of self-medication and medical evacuation. The situation caused concern as there were only 36 hospitals and 938 doctors covering all the state's secondary health facilities, representing a doctor-population ratio of 0.21 doctors per 10,000 patients – one-fifth of the Sub-Saharan Africa (SSA) average.[149] The state, with just over 0.5 hospital beds per thousand people, had the lowest hospital density in the entirety of south-south Nigeria.[150]

As a part of Cross River State Government strategy aimed at reforming the health sector to enable the delivery of effective, efficient, qualitative and affordable healthcare services, it retained the International Finance Corporation (IFC) to provide advisory support towards the setting up of a hospital in Calabar using the PPP model.

Fifteen international firms responded to an invitation for expression of interest issued by the Cross River State Government in April 2012. Four of the

148 The Nation, 'FAAN, Bi-Courtney Bicker Over N1.2b Debt' *The Nation*, 1 April 2013 (Lagos) available at <http://thenationonlineng.net/faan-bi-courtney-bicker-over-n1-2b-debt/> accessed 25 August 2016.

149 International Finance Corporation, 'Cross River State Hospital PPP Project' presentation delivered by Bayo Oyewole at the Corporate Council for Africa Health and Infrastructure Working Group Breakfast Meeting, April 2014.

150 International Finance Corporation, 'Nigeria: Cross River State Hospital' (2013) available at <www.ifc.org/wps/wcm/connect/5668b20040c913338d3b9d5d948a4a50/PPPStories_Nigeria_CrossRiverHospital.pdf?MOD=AJPERES> accessed 1 September 2016.

bidders were prequalified. A ten-year concession was awarded to UCL Healthcare Services Limited,[151] an international consortium comprising Utopian Healthcare Consulting (US), Cure Hospital Management Services (US), Cunningham Group (US), Consultants Collaborative Partnership (Nigeria), ITB Nigeria Limited, Healthfore Technologies (India), Simed International (The Netherlands) and Cure Hospital Management Services, a US-based firm that was to provide clinical services. The Cconsortium was to bear some project development costs, deliver a turnkey hospital, and would operate the hospital under the terms defined in the PPP agreement.[152]

The transaction structure was for a Design-Build-Operate-Transfer (DBOT) PPP model to last for ten years. The construction cost, totalling about US$37 million, was to be financed by the Cross River State Government, the consortium was to bear some project costs, deliver a turnkey hospital and then be responsible for the day-to-day management of the hospital. The project was a 105-bed (80 beds reserved for public patients, 20 beds for private VIP treatment at commercial tariffs and 5 beds for ICU) referral hospital to serve the capital city of Calabar and its environs. The hospital was expected to have 6,000 admissions and 60,000 out-patient visits per year.[153] The transaction structure was designed as a ten-year project term expected to be operational in 2015. The private operator was responsible for the operations. The financial structure was CAPEX (approximately US$37 million) and OPEX (approximately US$2.4 million). The executional timeframe was put at two years to build and eight years to operate (with an option to exercise an additional two years). Out of the CAPEX, the Cross River State Government would fund 49 per cent, and the private consortium would fund 51 per cent.

Some of the lessons learnt from the project are as follows: political factors like election time table, high-level government commitment and a strong champion with the governor's ear are important, and a dearth of experience in healthcare PPPs can be a setback in such transactions. Another challenge was that there were only a few experienced bidders.

6.9.5 Tinapa project

The Tinapa project is a business and leisure resort located in Calabar, Cross River State, south-south Nigeria. It was conceived during the administration of Mr Donald Duke, who served as governor of the state between 1999 and 2007. The arrangement for the project between the Cross River State (grantor)

151 Incidentally UCL Healthcare Services Ltd had the lowest financial bid.

152 World Finance, 'Bridging the Healthcare Gap: The Calabar Specialist Hospital Aims to Improve National Access to Quality Healthcare in Nigeria' (2014) available at <www.worldfinance.com/infrastructure-investment/project-finance/the-calabar-specialist-hospital> accessed 1 September 2016.

153 Utopian, 'Calabar Specialist Hospital' (2014) available at <www.estateintel.com/wp-content/uploads/2014/10/Calabar-Specialist-Hospital-Intro.pdf> accessed 2 September 2016.

and Tinapa Business Resort Limited (concessionaire) has been considered successful in terms of the arrangement and construction of the project. The completion of the project also opened the tourism potential of the state.[154] The first phase of the project gulped US$350 million,[155] and the estimated cost for the entire project was US$125 billion.[156] The first phase of the project included the shopping complex; a cluster of warehouses and an entertainment strip consisting of a cinema complex, casino, restaurants, fisherman's village, arcade, internet café and a children's play area. The second phase included a hotel and conference building, the expansion of the leisure and entertainment facilities and the expansion of the cultural and education components. Under Phases Three and Four, the design included accommodation, agrotourism, ecotourism and a primate rehabilitation centre.

The major stakeholders for the project were the Cross River State Government, a consortium of local banks and the federal government of Nigeria (through the provision of permits and guarantees for the financing of the project). Standard Trust Bank (now a part of UBA Plc) provided ₦5 billion as a bridge financial facility to ensure the steady progression of construction work at the site.[157]

The resort was opened for business on 2 April 2007, barely a month before the expiration of Mr Donald Duke's tenure. It is located in Adiabo, by the River Calabar on the outskirts of the city of Calabar. The resort occupies 80,000 square metres.[158] However, since the commission of the resort by then president Olusegun Obasanjo in 2007, business activities have remained extremely low.[159] Notwithstanding, the project's financial viability is driven by expectations of import, export and trading activities, as well as services to be offered by the leisure and tourism components of the resort.[160]

Tinapa, which is modelled after similar resorts in Hong Kong, Singapore, Dubai and Bombay, was granted Free Trade Zone (FTZ) status.[161] Unfortunately, however, under the initial management of the project, it turned out to be

154 Murtala S Sagagi, 'Public-Private Dialogue as a Panacea to Poor Governance and low Public-Private Partnerships in Nigeria' in G Ramesh, V Nagadevara, G Naik and AB Suraj (eds.), *Public Private Partnerships* (London: Routledge, 2010) 92.

155 Anietie Akpan, 'TINAPA: A Dream . . . Still So Far Away' *The Guardian*, 11 May 2014 (Lagos) available at <http://barasolutions.com/mainGuardian/sunday-magazine-sp-509870158/161098-tinapa-a-dream-still-so-faraway> accessed 3 September 2016.

156 Iby Jerry W Bird, 'The Devil's Elbow at Obudu Ranch, Nigeria' (2010) *Africa Travel Magazine* available at <www.africa-ata.org/obudu_spd.htm> accessed 3 September 2016.

157 Ibid.

158 To be included in the resort are wholesale and retail trade centres and four emporiums of 10,000 square metres each.

159 Anietie Akpan, *op cit* (note 155).

160 Tinapa Calabar, 'Investment Opportunity in Tinapa' (2009) a presentation to investors available at <http://tinapa.com.ng/downloads/TINAPA_PRESENTATION.pdf> accessed 3 September 2016.

161 The implication for which includes exemption from all federal, state and local government taxes, levies and rates and entitlement to approved enterprises to import free of custom duty any capital goods, consumer goods, raw materials, components and articles intended to be used with an approved activity.

unprofitable. This led to the CRSG reaching an understanding with the Asset Management Corporation of Nigeria (AMCON) for the takeover of the management of the resort. The memorandum of understanding (MoU) stipulated that 'AMCON is to buy back Tinapa's debts totalling ₦18,509,744.797.05 and provide the sum of ₦26 billion for the revitalisation and resuscitation of the resort to reposition it as a private sector driven enterprise.'[162]

Even though a project may be successful in terms of arrangement and construction, the management of the project when it comes to the operation phase must be clearly thought out, otherwise a project considered successful may also fail, bringing into question whether PPPs can be relied upon as an alternative to traditional procurement. Despite the expertise available at the conception of the Tinapa project, the choice of the managers for the project was wrong in the final analysis. Thus, the successful execution of a project alone is not the only criterion to determine whether a PPP project is a success in its entirety. In this regard, the Tinapa project is not rated a success, as the element of 'good management,' which is one of the advantages of PPP, is so far lacking. The arrangement and construction of Phase One of Tinapa was, however, a success. The factors that gave rise to the success of that phase of the project were: the government's commitment to the success of the project, a successful financial arrangement, the federal government's provision of financial guarantee, the involvement of an experienced team of professionals and the state government's assurance that the project would outlive the administration that initiated it.[163]

6.10 Conclusion

Enterprises and persons with interest in participating with the FGN or any of the country's federating states in the provision of infrastructure would like to see a predictable and well-defined environment for PPP. Significantly, the regulatory environment for private-sector participation in infrastructure development in the country involves a body of complex laws. From the Constitution that limits the powers of states from entering into transactions that have been listed in the Exclusive Legislative List contained in the Second Schedule to the Constitution to the various state PPP laws and other laws requiring compliance, there is a need to make the PPP environment in Nigeria conducive for both domestic and foreign investors. Again, there is a shift from the indigenisation era, where foreigners were restricted under the Nigerian Enterprises Promotion Act of 1977, to the current era in which foreign investors can invest up to 100 per cent in a business enterprise in the country.

Since the passing into law of the Infrastructure Concession and Regulatory Commission Act of 2005 by the FGN at the national level and the implementation of the PPP policy introduced in 2008, there have been mixed results

162 Eyo Charles, 'AMCON Buys Over Tinapa Debt Burden' *Daily Trust*, 16 October 2013 (Kaduna) available at <www.dailytrust.com.ng/daily/business/7732-amcon-buys-over-tinapa-debt-burden> accessed 3 September 2016.

163 This was a core value upon which then governor Donald Duke hinged the project.

for PPP in Nigeria. In this chapter, the study examined some projects that have gone beyond the 'pipeline' phase and into execution (with some already in the operational phase). The projects selected for the study cut across the transport, health care and tourism sectors. While projects like the MMA2 Airport Concession, the Lekki-Epe Express Toll Road and the Tinapa Resort passed through the construction phase and into the operational phase, they all faced enormous challenges. The MMA2 project was marred by controversies between the grantor and the concessionaire, and the Lekki-Epe Toll Road project faced stiff opposition from residents along the road corridor, culminating in the buy-back of the concession by the Lagos State Government. The Tinapa Resort suffered from management issues and was considered not profitable before AMCON was engaged in the buy-back of the project's debts. However, the success of the Lagos BRT project is commendable, and the model should be an example for future projects.

The total failure of the Lagos-Ibadan Expressway Bi-Courtney Project is an example of how not to arrange a PPP project. The lack of experience on the part of the grantor and the concessionaire was evident. Granting the concession to Bi-Courtney was perhaps motivated by Bi-Courtney's successful completion of the MMA2 project. It turned out to be that Bi-Courtney's experience in aviation concession was not enough for the road project.

In the next chapter of this book, the discussion focuses on the legal framework and practice of PPP in South Africa.

References

Abdulkareem, Y.A., & Adeoti, K.A. (2005). Road Maintenance and National Development. Retrieved from http://ilorin.info/papers/publications/ROAD%20MAINTENANCE%20AND%20NATIONAL%20DEVELOPMENT.pdf.

African Development Bank. (2014). *An Infrastructure Action Plan for Nigeria: Closing the Infrastructure Gap and Accelerating Economic Transformation*. Washington, DC: Author.

African Gong. (2015, November 8). Cross River Highway Project; Buhari Tasked for Answers. Retrieved from http://africangong.com/2015/11/08/cross-river-highway-project-citizen-demand-answers.

Ajayi, O. (2011). Lagos State PPP Law. Retrieved from www.olaniwunajayi.net/clientalert/PPP%20Newsletter%20Final%2011%2008%202011.pdf.

Akinwale, A.A. (2010). The Menace of Inadequate Infrastructure in Nigeria. *African Journal of Science, Technology, Innovation and Development*, *2*(3), 214.

Akpan, A. (2014). TINAPA: A Dream . . . Still So Far Away. Retrieved September 3, 2016, from http://barasolutions.com/mainGuardian/sunday-magazine-sp-509870158/161098-tinapa-a-dream-still-so-faraway.

Alkali, A.U., Abbo-Jimeta, U.S., & Magashi, A.I. (2014). Nature and Sources of Nigerian Legal System: An Exorcism of a Wrong Notion. *International Journal of Business, Economics and Law*, *5*(4), 3.

Arimoro, A.E. (2015.). Impact of Community Stakeholders on Public-Private Partnerships: Lessons from the Lekki-Epe Concession Toll Road. *International Journal of Law and Legal Studies*, *3*(7), 165–167. Retrieved from http://internationalscholarsjournals.org/download.php?id=525664682036516910.pdf&type=application/pdf&op=1.

Azuakola, S. (2013, September 7). Just in: Police IG Withdraws Security Details of Gov. Amaechi, Sen. Saraki and Alhaji Baraje. Retrieved from www.thescoopng.com/2013/09/07/just-in-police-ig-withdraws-security-details-of-gov-amaechi-sen-saraki-and-alhaji-baraje/.

Babatunde, S., Perera, S., Udeaja, C., & Zhou, L. (2016). Challenges in Implementing Public Private Partnership Strategy for Infrastructure Delivery in Nigeria. Retrieved from http://nrl.northumbria.ac.uk/17191/1/babatunde_et_al_ppp_conference_paper_(1).doc.

Balancing Act Africa. (2016). Lagos State Loses Case Against Telecom Operators. Retrieved from www.balancingact-africa.com/news/en/issue-no-345/telecoms/lagos-state-loses-ca/en.

Barungi, B., Odhiambo, O., & Asogwa, R. (2017). Nigeria 2017. Retrieved from www.africaneconomicoutlook.org/en/country-notes/nigeria.

Bird, J.J. (2010). 'The Devil's Elbow at Obudu Ranch, Nigeria. Retrieved September 3, 2016, from www.africa-ata.org/obudu_spd.htm.

British Broadcasting Corporation. (2008). Power Cuts 'Embarrassing' Nigeria. Retrieved from http://news.bbc.co.uk/1/hi/world/africa/7252777.stm.

Business Monitor International. (2009). *Nigeria Infrastructure Report Q1: 2010: Including a Five-Year Industry Forecast to 2014*. Abuja: Author.

Cambridge Economic Policy Associates Ltd. (2015). Mobilising Finance for Infrastructure: A Study for the UK Department for International. Retrieved May 26, 2018, from https://assets.publishing.service.gov.uk/media/57a08979ed915d622c00022b/61319-DfID_3_Three_page_summary.pdf.

Central Intelligence Agency. (2015). *The World Factbook 2015*. Washington, DC: Author.

Charles, E. (2013, October 16). AMCON Buys Over Tinapa Debt Burden. Retrieved September 3, 2016, from www.dailytrust.com.ng/daily/business/7732-amcon-buys-over-tinapa-debt-burden.

Dada, M.O., & Oyediran, O.S. (2015). The State of Public Private Partnership in Nigeria. In A. Akintoye, M. Beck, & M. Kumaraswamy (Eds.), *Public Private Partnerships: A Global Review*. London: Routledge.

Daily Independent. (2016, November 12). Nigeria's $8 Billion Infrastructure Deficit. *The Daily Independent* [Lagos].

Delmon, J. (2011). *Public-Private Partnership Projects in Infrastructure: An Essential Guide for Policy Makers*. Cambridge: Cambridge University Press.

Detail Solicitors. (2016). Nigeria PPP Review. Retrieved from www.detailsolicitors.com/media/archive2/articles/PPPreview.pdf.

Ekott, I. (2012, November 20). At Last, FG Revokes Lagos-Ibadan Expressway Bi-Courtney Concession. Retrieved from www.premiumtimesng.com/news/107689-at-last-fg-revokes-lagos-ibadan-expressway-bi-courtney-concession.html.

Essia, U., & Yusuf, A. (2013). Public-Private Partnership and Sustainable Infrastructure in Nigeria. *Advances in Management & Applied Economics*, *3*, 15.

Eze, C. (2016, May 2). Bi-Courtney Claims Arik Owes it N12.5bn. *This Day* [Abuja].

Fafowora, D. (2013, February 13). Lord Lugard and the 1914 Amalgamation of Nigeria. Retrieved from http://thenationonlineng.net/lord-lugard-and-the-1914-amalgamation-of-nigeria.

Francis, N. (2016, November 3). Osinbajo Laments Low Delivery of PPP Projects. Retrieved from www.thisdaylive.com/index.php/2016/11/03/osinbajo-laments-low-delivery-of-ppp-projects/.

GTI Research. (2017). Infrastructure: The Key to Nigeria's Economic Diversification. Retrieved from www.proshareng.com/admin/upload/reports/GTIResearchInfrastructur.pdf.

Ighodaro, J. (2010, August 4). C-River Govt Signs PPP Bill into Law. Retrieved from www.vanguardngr.com/2010/08/c-river-govt-signs-ppp-bill-into-law.

Inter Reseaux. (2010). Facts About Nigeria. Retrieved from www.inter-reseaux.org/IMG/pdf/p4-7_Benchmarks.pdf.

International Finance Corporation. (2013). Nigeria: Cross River State Hospital. Retrieved September 1, 2016, from www.ifc.org/wps/wcm/connect/5668b20040c913338d3b9d5d948a4a50/PPPStories_Nigeria_CrossRiverHospital.pdf?MOD=AJPERES.

Jacob, O. A. (2010). Procurement Law in Nigeria: Challenge for Attainment of Its Objectives. *University of Botswana Law Journal*, 139.

Kessides, C. (1993). The Contributions of Infrastructure to Economic Development: A Review of Experience and Policy Implications. *World Bank Discussion Papers* No. 213. World Bank, Washington, DC.

KWMInsights. (2019, November 26). Retrieved from www.kwm.com/en/uk/knowledge/insights/bridging-the-infrastructure-gap-the-lekki-ikoyi-tolling-debate-20140723.

Luminary Nigeria. (2016, April 25). Court Dismisses Bi-Courtney's Suit Seeking Termination of Lagos-Ibadan Expressway Concession. Retrieved from www.luminaryng.com/court-dismisses-bi-courtneys-suit-seeking-termination-of-lagos-ibadan-expressway-concession/.

Majekodunmi, A. (2015). Federalism in Nigeria: The Past, Current Peril and Future Hopes. *Journal of Policy and Development Studies*, *9*(2), 112.

The Nation. (2013, March 31). FAAN, Bi-Courtney Bicker Over N1.2b debt. Retrieved August 25, 2016, from http://thenationonlineng.net/faan-bi-courtney-bicker-over-n1-2b-debt/.

National Planning Commission. (2015). *Nigeria's National Integrated Infrastructure Master Plan*. Abuja: Author.

Nwangwu, G. (2014). *A Risk Approach to Enhancing Public-Private Partnership Projects in Nigeria* (Unpublished doctoral dissertation). University of Hull, Hull.

Nwelih, D. (2010, September 1). Why We Want Lekki-Epe Expressway Concession Deal Reviewed. Retrieved from http://saharareporters.com/2010/09/01/%E2%80%98%E2%80%99why-we-want-lekki-epe-expressway-concession-deal-reviewed%E2%80%99%E2%80%99.

Okonkwo, N. (2015, October 3). Obiano to FG: Refund Anambra's N25bn Spent on Federal Roads. Retrieved from www.vanguardngr.com/2015/10/obiano-to-fg-refund-anambras-n25bn-spent-on-federal-roads.

Organisation for Economic Cooperation and Development. (2018). Nigeria. Retrieved from www.oecd.org/swac/publications/Nigeria_e-version_en_light.pdf.

Oyebade, W. (2016, July 29). How Not to Privatise Nigerian Airports, By Stakeholders. Retrieved August 25, 2016, from www.dailynigerianews.com/2016/07/29/how-not-to-privatise-nigerian-airports-by-stakeholders.

Oyewole, B. (2014). *Cross River State Hospital PPP Project*. Paper Presented at Corporate Council for Africa Health and Infrastructure Working Group Breakfast Meeting.

The Paradigm. (2016, April 26). Lagos-Ibadan Expressway: Bi-Courtney Highway Services Limited Loses Case Against the Federal Government. Retrieved from www.theparadigmng.com/2016/04/26/lagos-ibadan-expressway-bi-courtney-highway-services-limited-loses-case-against-the-federal-government/.

Premium Times. (2014, March 27). Lagos Laws Do Not Cover Toll Collection on Lekki-Ikoyi Bridge, Court Rules. Retrieved from www.premiumtimesng.com/news/157525-lagos-laws-cover-toll-collection-lekki-ikoyi-bridge-court-rules.html.

Project Management International. (2016). Lagos-Ibadan Expressway, Nigeria. Retrieved from http://pmi-ltd.co.za/projects/66_BCHS-2011-Lagos_Ibadan_Expressway-Nigeria.pdf.

Punch Newspaper. (2016, April 27). Editorial. *The Punch*.

Sagagi, M.S. (2010). Public-Private Dialogue as a Panacea to Poor Governance and low Public-Private Partnerships in Nigeria. In G. Ramesh, G. Naik, & A.B. Suraj (Eds.), *Public Private Partnerships* (p. 92). London: Routledge.

Techbuddie, P. (2016). World Bank Loan Generates Controversy in Rivers. Retrieved from http://nationalmirroronline.net/new/280m-world-bank-loan-generates-controversy-in-rivers-state/.

Tinapa Calabar. (2009). Investment Opportunity in Calabar. Retrieved September 3, 2009, from http://tinapa.com.ng/downloads/TINAPA_PRESENTATION.pdf.

Uroko, C. (2013, September 19). Multiple Tolls on Lekki-Epe Expressway Bring Down Property Value by 30 Percent. *Business Day* [Lagos].

Utopian. (2014). Calabar Specialist Hospital. Retrieved September 2, 2016, from www.estateintel.com/wp-content/uploads/2014/10/Calabar-Specialist-Hospital-Intro.pdf.

Vanguard Newspaper. (2016, January 26). N167bN Lagos-Ibadan Expressway: How FG Ignored Arbitration Offer by Bi-Courtney. Retrieved from www.vanguardngr.com/2016/01/n167bn-lagos-ibadan-expressway-how-fg-ignored-arbitration-offer-by-bi-courtney/.

The World Bank. (2009). *Attracting Investors to African Public-Private Partnerships: A Project Preparation Guide*. Washington, DC: World Bank Publications.

The World Bank. (2014). *Public Private Partnerships Reference Guide Version 2*. Washington, DC: Author.

The World Bank. (2018). Nigeria Overview. Retrieved from www.worldbank.org/en/country/nigeria/overview.

World Finance. (2014). Bridging the Healthcare Gap: The Calabar Specialist Hospital Aims to Improve National Access to Quality Healthcare in Nigeria. Retrieved September 1, 2016, from www.worldfinance.com/infrastructure-investment/project-finance/the-calabar-specialist-hospital.

World Health Organisation. (2014). Nigeria. Retrieved from www.who.int/water_sanitation_health/monitoring/investments/nigeria-10-nov.pdf?ua=.

Yescombe, E.R. (2007). *Public-Private Partnerships: Principles of Policy and Finance*. Amsterdam, Netherlands: Elsevier.

7 South Africa

7.1 Introduction

The sources of South African law include statutory law made by parliament, the common law (this includes the old Roman-Dutch authorities and judicial precedents derived from case law), African customary law and international law.[1] The Constitution of the Republic of South Africa is the supreme law of the Republic; any law or conduct inconsistent with it is invalid.[2] South Africa is the only African member of the Group of 20 (G20) countries.[3] It is ranked fifth overall in the 2014 Mo Ibrahim Index,[4] which measures the quality of governance in African countries. Of note, Mauritius, Botswana, Cape Verde and Seychelles occupy the first 4 places out of 52, compared to Nigeria's position at number 37.[5] The Republic of South Africa[6] is believed to have the most comprehensive experience of PPP in all of Africa.[7] The country has developed a unique PPP programme that showcases how developing countries that have an enhanced investment and financial sector can achieve milestones

1 E Davies, 'Foundations of Law' (2016) *Lecture Notes Rhodes University* 2 available at <www.ru.ac.za/media/rhodesuniversity/content/law/documents/courseoutlines2016/Foundations%20of%20Law%20Course%20Outline%202016.pdf> accessed 17 November 2018.

2 Section 2 of the Constitution of the Republic of South Africa No. 108 of 1996.

3 The G20 is a forum for international co-operation that brings together leaders, finance ministers and central bank governors of 20 countries, including the United States, Canada, Brazil, Argentina, Spain, Germany, France, Italy, Saudi Arabia, Turkey, Russia, China, Australia, the United Kingdom, South Korea, India, Japan, Indonesia, South Africa and the European Union. See OECD, 'G20 Members' available at <www.oecd.org/g20/g20-members.htm> accessed 17 February 2018.

4 Department of Trade and Industry, 'South Africa: Investor's Handbook 2014/15' (2014) available at <https://www2.deloitte.com/content/dam/Deloitte/za/Documents/tax/ZA_DTI-InvestinginSA_2014-15.pdf >accessed 11 May 2017.

5 Ibid.

6 South Africa, a multiparty, constitutional democracy, is situated on the southernmost tip of the African continent. It has a population of approximately 54 million people. It is considered a young and stable democracy.

7 Peter Farlam, 'Working Together: Assessing Public-Private Partnerships in Africa' (2005) 1 available at <www.oecd.org/investment/investmentfordevelopment/34867724.pdf> accessed 29 December 2019.

with a PPP programme. PPPs started in South Africa around the mid-1990s on an ad hoc basis. The National Roads Agency, which had already tolled parts of the major national roads, developed a framework for concessions to cope with budgetary constraints on the rehabilitation of parts of the network.[8] Due to its well-developed financial market, South Africa is well ahead of its benchmark peers because of the relative ease of access to private capital.[9]

The government of South Africa demonstrated its commitment to a PPP policy thrust in the delivery of quality infrastructure when the Cabinet commissioned the Minister of Finance to take steps to develop a comprehensive PPP framework for the country.[10] In April 1997, a team was set up to put together this legislative and institutional framework.[11] Several projects have since been completed, some of which will be reviewed later in this chapter.

South Africa's first PPP project was organised in 1996. It was the R2.6 billion N4 toll road that connects South Africa and the Port of Maputo in Mozambique. The debt on the transaction was guaranteed by the governments of South Africa and Mozambique.[12] This was followed by the rehabilitation and tolling of the N3 between Pretoria and Durban, for which the private-sector investors and lenders bore the full traffic risk.[13] Several other PPP projects have since followed, with many lessons learnt.

The discussion in this chapter focuses on the applicable legal framework, policy and institutional framework. Given that the country has a better record of managing PPPs than anywhere else in Africa, lessons learnt from the management of such projects in South Africa will be highlighted with a view to developing better PPP practice in other African countries, especially Nigeria. It is pertinent to point out that, as was the case with the previous chapter on Nigeria, this chapter is descriptive and offers insight into the practice of PPP in South Africa.

7.2 Legislative framework for PPP in South Africa

Following the mandate given to the Minister of Finance (noted in section 5.1), a holistic legislative and regulatory framework for PPP was put in place in the country at the national level. The Constitution of the Republic of South Africa also contains some important provisions with respect to the management and

8 Ibid 63.

9 Estian Calitz and Johan Fourie, 'Infrastructure in South Africa: Who is to Finance and Who is to Pay?' (2010) 27(2) *Development Southern Africa* 186.

10 National Treasury PPP Unit, *Introducing Public Private Partnerships in South Africa* (Pretoria: National Treasury, 2007) 7.

11 Ibid.

12 ER Yescombe, *Public-Private Partnerships: Principles of Policy and Finance* (Amsterdam, Netherlands: Elsevier, 2007) 47.

13 Ibid.

regulation of public contracts. These provisions have implications for PPP management as well. The body of laws regulating PPP in South Africa include the Constitution, the Public Finance Management Act of 1999, Treasury Regulation 16, the Municipal Finance Management Act of 2003 and the Municipal Systems Act of 2003.[14] These laws are examined in the sections that follow.

7.2.1 The Constitution of the Republic of South Africa

Although the Constitution of the Republic of South Africa does not specifically mention the term 'public-private partnership,' Section 217(1) stipulates that contracts involving the state of South Africa must be transparent. It provides as follows:

> When an organ of state contracts for goods or services, it must do so in accordance with a system which is fair, equitable, transparent, competitive and cost-effective (Introductory Statement, Section 217(1) of the Constitution of Republic of South Africa).

Since PPPs are a form of procurement contract involving the state, it follows that the provision of Section 217(1) will apply in all such arrangements in the country. Given South Africa's long history of inequality, entrenched during the apartheid era,[15] the post-1994 government of South Africa sought to provide common ground for all and promote equality. This provision of the Constitution represents one of the deliberate attempts to use the law to promote equality in the country.

The South African Constitution gives power to the country's parliament to make laws on matters listed in Schedules 4 and 5 of the Constitution.[16] The items listed include airports, housing, public transport and public works. Similarly, the Constitution grants powers to provinces with respect to certain matters upon which they can legislate. These matters include, among others, provincial roads, provincial parks, and facilities for accommodation and public transport.[17] It follows that there are limits on their powers to arrange PPPs, but where there are concurrent powers to legislate, both the national and provincial authorities may make PPP arrangements touching any item on the list. It should be noted that the preamble to the South African Constitution emphasises that it is the responsibility of the state to improve the quality of life of all its citizens. The public authority is therefore mandated to seek avenues to provide access to amenities, such as potable water, power, roads, ports and hospitals, to ensure the economic and social development of the people of South Africa.

14 National Treasury PPP Unit, *op cit* (note 10) 8.

15 During that period, it was not uncommon to see public procurement done in a manner that favoured the white minority to the detriment of others. There was discrimination against small and emerging firms. More details on this are provided in the section on South Africa's PPP policy.

16 Section 44 of the Constitution of South Africa.

17 Section 104 of the Constitution of South Africa.

7.2.2 The Public Finance Management Act of 1999

The Public Finance Management Act of 1999[18] is one of South Africa's main pieces of legislation governing PPP, the other being the Treasury Regulation 16. The Act was assented to on 2 March 1999 and came into operation on 1 April 2000.[19] It established the National Treasury, consisting of the Minister as head of the Treasury and the national department or departments responsible for financial and fiscal matters.[20] The focus of this piece of legislation is the improvement of financial management in the public sector.[21] The Act makes the heads of departments (the accounting officers) of national and provincial departments and the chief executive officers (CEOs) or boards of schedule three public entities (the accounting authorities) responsible for its implementation. These accounting officers or authorities are directly responsible to parliament or the provincial legislature for the effective management of their budgets to achieve public mandates.

The National Treasury in South Africa may issue instructions to institutions to which the Public Finance Management Act applies to facilitate the application of the Act and the regulations made under it.[22] It is on this basis that the National Treasury under the powers derived from the Act promulgated Treasury Regulation 16 on Public-Private Partnerships in 2004.[23] The Public Finance Management Act is not in itself a PPP law, and while it provides for financial accountability in government spending that includes PPP transactions, it largely delegates the power to regulate and administer PPPs to the National Treasury. The key legislation that sets out the procedure for the approval and management of PPPs is therefore Treasury Regulation 16. In addition to this, the National Treasury has issued PPP Practice Notes relying on powers derived from the Act.[24] These and other PPP regulations are examined in the sections below.

7.2.3 Treasury Regulation 16 (2004) to the Public Finance Management Act (Act No. 1 of 1999)

Treasury Regulation 16 is the central legislation governing PPPs for the national and provincial governments.[25] It defines PPP and sets out the standards to be met for a project to be so described. Under the Regulation, a

18 Act No. 1 of 1999.

19 See Government Gazette 33059 of 1 April 2010.

20 Section 5(1) of the Public Finance Management Act 1999.

21 National Treasury PPP Unit, *op cit* (note 10) 2.

22 Section 76(4) (g) of the Public Finance Management Act 1999.

23 HK Yong, *Public-Private Partnerships Policy and Practice: A Reference Guide* (London: Commonwealth Secretariat, 2010) 100.

24 Ibid.

25 PPPs for municipal government are governed by the Municipal Systems Act of 2000 and the Municipal Finance Management Act of 2003. Municipalities are therefore not subject to the Public Finance Management Act or to Treasury Regulation 16.

'public-private partnership means a commercial transaction between an institution and a private party in terms of which a private party – (a) performs an institutional function on behalf of the institution; and/or (b) acquires the use of state property for its own commercial purposes; and (c) assumes substantial financial, technical and operational risks in connection with the performance of the institutional function and/or use of state property; and (d) receives a benefit for performing the institutional function or from utilising the state property.'[26] For the sake of clarity, the Regulation defines an institution as 'a department, constitutional institution, a public entity listed, or acquired to be listed in schedules 3A, 3B, 3C and 3D to the Act, or any subsidiary of any such public entity.'[27] Under the Regulation, a 'private party' in relation to a PPP agreement means 'a party to a PPP agreement other than (a) an institution to which the Act applies; (b) a municipality or an enterprise or other entity controlled by one or more municipalities; or (c) the accounting officer, accounting authority or other person or body acting on behalf of an institution, municipality, enterprise or entity referred to in paragraph (a) or (b).' It is submitted that this is a rather vague way to define a party to a PPP transaction.

The Treasury Regulation 16 provides precise and detailed instructions for PPPs and has been amended since it was first issued in May 2000.[28] The Regulation envisages two types of PPPs, namely, where the private party performs an institutional function and where the private party acquires the use of state property for its own commercial purposes. There is also the possibility of a hybrid of these types.[29] By allowing for payments to involve a situation where the institution pays for the use of the facility or the private party collects tolls or fees from end users for the use of the facility or a combination of these,[30] it can be inferred that both concessions and private finance initiative (PFI) PPP types can be contracted in South Africa, depending on the nature of the need for the project.

Under the Regulation, only an accounting officer or an accounting authority may enter into a PPP agreement on behalf of the institution.[31] Furthermore, the accounting officer may not proceed with the procurement of a PPP agreement without the prior written approval of either the National Treasury or – if it is a provincial institution and the National Treasury has, in terms of section 10(1) (b) of the Act, delegated the appropriate powers to the provincial treasury[32] – the relevant provincial treasury. These provisions stress the value placed on financial prudence and accountability in PPP

26 National Treasury Unit, *Public Private Partnership Manual* available at <accessed>www.gtac.gov.za/Publications/PPP%20Manual.pdf>accessed 1 May 2017.

27 Ibid.

28 Ibid.

29 National Treasury PPP Unit, *op cit* (note 10) 8.

30 Ibid.

31 Treasury Regulation 16.2.1.

32 Treasury Regulation 16.3.1.

transactions in South Africa. Thus, the relevant treasury may only give such approval if satisfied that the proposed PPP will provide VfM; is affordable for the institution and will offer the appropriate technical, operational and financial risk to the private party.[33] This is considered the tripartite test for PPP in South Africa.[34]

Under the regulations in South Africa, a PPP does not involve the outsourcing of functions where substantial financial, technical and operational risk is retained by the institution; it is not a donation by a private party for a public good; it is not the privatisation of state assets and it does not constitute borrowing by the state.[35]

7.2.4 The Municipal Finance Management Act (Act No. 56 of 2003)

This Act[36] was enacted to ensure financial accountability and elimination of waste at the municipal level. The Act seeks to secure sound and sustainable management of the financial affairs of municipalities and other institutions in the local sphere of government by establishing treasury norms and standards for the local sphere of government.[37] Like the Public Finance Management Act, this Act lays down a tripartite test for PPP comprising affordability, VfM and risk transfer. The Act provides that a municipal authority can enter into a PPP agreement if these requirements are met.[38] It is worth noting that, like the Public Finance Management Act, the Municipal Finance Act is not an Act dedicated to PPP but one which provides general regulations on government spending that constitute a core element in PPP arrangements.

7.2.5 Municipal Systems Act (Act No. 32 of 2003)

This Act applies when a municipality reviews the options and decides on an appropriate mechanism to provide a municipal service. The Act lists the criteria and procedure for deciding on municipal-service provision, including cost-benefit analysis, a full assessment of the private party and the likely impact on municipal employment patterns.[39] The Act establishes clear guidelines on the involvement of the community in the procurement process.[40]

33 Treasury Regulation 16.3.2.

34 National Treasury PPP Unit, *op cit* (note 10) 5.

35 Ibid.

36 Act No. 176 of 13 February 2004.

37 See the Long Title to the Act.

38 Section 120 of the Municipality Financial Management Act of 2003.

39 Dominic Mitchell and Fakisandla Consulting, 'Capacity Development for Partnerships in South Africa: Increasing Service Delivery Through Partnerships Between Private and Public Sector' (2007) available at <https://thepartneringinitiative.org/wp-content/uploads/2014/08/PPP-overview-and-needs-assessment.pdf> accessed 30 December 2019.

40 Ibid.

7.2.6 The PPP manual and the standardised PPP provisions

Pursuant to the powers derived from the Public Finance Management Act, the National Treasury has issued nine different modules which make up the country's PPP manual.[41] These modules are regarded as practice notes and apply to departments, constitutional institutions and public entities as well as their subsidiaries.[42] The first module comprises the regulations for South African PPPs, the second is the Code for Black Economic Empowerment (BEE) in PPPs, the third provides for PPP inception and the fourth highlights the PPP feasibility study. To continue, the fifth module discusses PPP procurement in the country, the sixth regards managing PPP agreements, the seventh relates to auditing PPPs, the eighth regulates the accounting treatment of PPPs and the ninth is an introduction to project finance.

This manual and the Standardised Public-Private Partnership Provisions, developed after years of PPP practice, provide a standard structure for PPP in South Africa. Read together, the documents define a mechanism for the funding process for PPP transactions in the country.[43] Specifically, the Standardised PPP Provisions describe key issues that are likely to arise in PPP projects as regulated by the provisions of Treasury Regulation 16 and how these key issues must be dealt with in a PPP agreement so as to meet the requirements of 'substantial risk transfer,' 'value for money,' and 'affordability.'[44]

7.3 South Africa's PPP policy

Generally, PPP policies serve to define PPPs as distinct from other forms of procurement. The policies describe the reasons and/or goals for choosing PPP schemes while also providing general guidance for the implementation of PPP in any given jurisdiction. These policies may not carry the force of the law, but they clearly indicate the government's intentions.[45] The South African government's strategy in respect to PPP is thus laid out in various documents.[46]

The adoption of PPP by the government of South Africa is based on the cardinal premise that it can deliver better VfM than traditional procurement.[47] Other key factors include ensuring that project planning takes place within an enabling environment, which includes political support and buy-in from key

41 Section 76(4) (g) of the Public Finance Management Act 1999.

42 National Treasury *PPP Manual Module 1: South African Regulations for PPP* Number 2 of 2004.

43 National Treasury PPP Unit, *op cit* (note 10) 9.

44 National Treasury *Standardised PPP Provisions* First Issue, 11 March 2004 1.

45 European Investment Bank, 'Study on PPP Legal and Financial Frameworks in the Mediterranean Partner Countries: Volume 1- A Regional Approach' (2002) 61 available at <www.eib.org/attachments/med/ppp-study-volume-1.pdf> accessed 1 May 2017.

46 Axis Consulting, 'PPP Country Paper: South Africa' (2013) 11 available at <www.sadcpppnetwork.org/wp-content/uploads/2015/02/south_africa_27012014.pdf> accessed 2 May 2017.

47 National Treasury PPP Unit, *op cit* (note 10) 10.

stakeholders. In South Africa, all PPPs governed under Treasury Regulation 16 are subjected to this strict three-point test:[48]

1 Is substantial technical, operational and financial risk transferred to the private party?
2 Can the institution afford the envisaged fee?
3 Is it a value-for-money solution?

Based on the foregoing, a private consortium bidding for a PPP project in the country must clearly demonstrate that it possesses the capacity, skills and capability to deliver the project and that it can do so more efficiently than other parties. This is necessary to ensure that a project is not abandoned because a private-sector consortium lacks the ability to continue with it. Second, the public entity sponsoring the project must have the budget required for that entity to fulfil its requirements under the agreement, and third, it would not make any sense to adopt a PPP for a project if it would be cheaper to go the route of traditional procurement.

In South Africa, Black Economic Empowerment (BEE) is a national policy objective, and PPPs are regarded as a means of promoting it. This policy has been formalised in the Code of Good Practice for Black Economic Empowerment in Public-Private Partnerships, which was issued pursuant to the Public Finance Management Act.[49] The guiding purpose of the Code as stated in the Preamble is 'to redress the stifling economic effects of apartheid.'[50]

BEE is a key constituent of South African PPP projects, each of which is structured on a careful combination of financial, technical and BEE components to achieve VfM in the state's delivery of infrastructure.[51] Based on the Code, in the entire PPP process, from the appointment of the transaction advisor to the final procurement of the private party, certain BEE targets must be met. A scorecard for BEE has been formulated with targets that a private-sector consortium must meet for any PPP transaction.[52] These four targets are, first, that substantial direct ownership must be held by black people, black women and black enterprises. Second, black people must be involved in the management and employment of the private partner and its subcontractors. Third, a significant proportion of the subcontracting to be done by the private party must involve black people, black women and black enterprises; and fourth, the project must benefit the lives of the people within the area where the project is located, including small and medium enterprises, the disabled, the

48 Ibid 13.
49 Ibid 15.
50 See the Preamble to the *Code of Good Practice for Black Economic Empowerment in Public Private Partnerships* issued in 2004 by the National Treasury.
51 See Part 1: Policy on BEEE in PPPs of the Code of Good Practice for BEE.
52 National Treasury PPP Unit, *op cit* (note 10) 15.

youth, and non-governmental organisations (NGOs) within the target area.[53] It is worth noting that because of the commitment to BEE in PPP procurement, the National Treasury of South Africa has worked with the Development Bank of Southern Africa (DBSA) to create a facility to fund BEE equity in PPP transactions.[54]

Furthermore, South Africa has taken a bold initiative to curb corrupt practices in PPP procurement by the adoption of a Public Service Anti-Corruption Strategy, launched to fight bribery, embezzlement, fraud, extortion, the abuse of power, conflicts of interest, insider trading, favouritism and nepotism in the public service. This culminated in the passing of the Combating of Corrupt Activities Act of 2004.[55] The Act provides, among other things, for the establishment of a register of persons and companies convicted for corruption, thereby preventing them from taking part in public-sector procurement. It follows therefore that any person or entity whose name is included in the registered list of corrupt persons is disqualified from engaging in any PPP activity.

7.4 Institutional framework for PPP in South Africa

South Africa's institutional framework for PPP is made up of the agencies of the government that are tasked with the responsibility of monitoring and regulating the award of PPP projects in the country.[56] It is significant that there are only a few such institutions in the country, which means that a prospective PPP investor in South Africa is assured a minimum of bureaucracy to deal with. The institutions that regulate PPP in the country are discussed next.

7.4.1 The National Treasury's PPP Unit

Generally speaking, a PPP unit is responsible for policymaking, project identification, programme planning and general guidance, serving as a central repository of knowledge in any given jurisdiction. Based on these fundamentals, the National Treasury's PPP Unit was set up in the mid-2000s with technical assistance funding from USAID, the Deutsche Gesellschaft für Internationale Zusammenarbeit (GIZ), GmbH (GTZ) and the Department for International Development (DFID),[57] and was initially made up of five professional staff

53 Ibid.

54 Ibid 17.

55 Act No. 12 of 2004, vide the Government Gazette 26311, 28 April 2004.

56 The Institute for Public-Private Partnerships, *Development of Policy, Legal, and Institutional Framework for the Public-Private Partnership Programme in Malawi: Final Report* (Washington, DC: The Institute for Public-Private Partnerships, 2007) 38.

57 These foreign governmental agencies represent the United States (USAID), Germany (GTZ) and the United Kingdom (DFID). See Ryo Sasaki 'An in-depth International Comparison of Major Donor Agencies: How do they Systematically Conduct Country Program Evaluation?' (2011) 8(18) *Journal of MultiDisciplinary Evaluation* 29–45.

drawn from both public and private sectors.[58] It is the lead government agency for PPPs in South Africa. The main functions of the Unit are to ensure affordability, VfM and sufficient risk transfer in line with international best practice.[59] In doing so, the PPP Unit assumes responsibility for two broad tasks: providing technical assistance to government, departments, provinces and municipalities and providing treasury approvals during the pre-contract phases.[60]

The National Treasury is required by law to ensure accountability, transparency and sound financial control in the management of public finances in the country.[61] The National Treasury is also mandated to make regulations for issues pertaining to the effective management and efficient use of public finance. It is pursuant to this that the National Treasury issued Treasury Regulation 16.[62]

In fulfilling its mandate through its PPP Unit, the National Treasury develops, formulates and promotes the country's PPP policy; develops systems and documentation to formalise and standardise the PPP process; provides direct technical assistance to national and provincial departments and municipalities in preparing and procuring VfM PPPs; provides quarterly PPP training for both the public and private sectors; produces and distributes the PPP Quarterly and is the PPP knowledge management centre for the country; is in touch with international PPP bodies; ensures that international best practice for PPPs is followed in the South African context and works with provincial treasuries to oversee provincial PPPs.[63] To promote an enabling environment for PPPs, the PPP Unit seeks to facilitate certainty in the regulatory framework as well as drive Black Economic Empowerment.[64]

The National Treasury PPP Unit supports the procurement process for PPP at the three Treasury Approval stages. The aims are to ensure that affordability is demonstrated and to achieve financial closure.[65]

As of 30 April 2017, the National Treasury's PPP Unit in South Africa is made up of 17 professionals who are allocated projects depending on individual sector expertise and interest. The list of sectors[66] includes health, accommodation, energy, education, water, budget support, transport, contract

58 National Treasury, 'Public Private Partnership' available at <www.ppp.gov.za/Pages/About.aspx> accessed 30 April 2017.

59 Philippe Burger, 'The Dedicated PPP Unit of the South African National Treasury' available at <www.oecd.org/mena/governance/37146964.pdf> accessed 30 April 2017.

60 Ibid.

61 Section 215 of the South African Constitution.

62 Section 76 of the Public Finance Management Act.

63 National Treasury PPP Unit, *op cit* (note 10) 20.

64 National Treasury, *op cit* (note 58).

65 Axis Consulting, *op cit* (note 46) 14.

66 This reflects current government priorities, which may change from time to time. However, overarching considerations include BEE and the essential elements of a PPP: Affordability, value-for-money and transfer of significant financial, design, technical and operational risks to the private sector.

management, information and communication technology (ICT), project development facilities, tourism, business development, waste and international relations.[67]

7.4.2 Institutions of government

Treasury Regulation 16 defines institution as 'a department, a constitutional institution, a public entity listed or required to be listed in Schedules 3A, 3B, 3C and 3D to the Act, or any subsidiary of any such public entity.'[68] It follows that all line departments, provincial entities, public sector–owned bodies and other government enterprises listed in Schedules 3A, 3B, 3C and 3D of the Public Finance Management Act form a part of the institutional framework for PPP in the country, having statutory powers to engage in PPP negotiations and arrangements.

Apart from government institutions, there are other players involved in PPPs in South Africa. They include environmental organisations, trade unions and community-based organisations. It is usual to consult these stakeholders to provide input at various stages in the PPP cycle to promote transparency and community buy-in.[69]

7.5 PPP practice in South Africa

The National Treasury's PPP Unit has formulated a generic PPP project cycle for the country to ensure uniformity and consistency in PPP practice in South Africa.[70] Thus, by issuing the PPP manual and standardised process for PPP, the Unit has designed a comprehensive PPP programme for the country. But because of the complex nature of PPPs, the Unit makes provisions for a reasonable degree of flexibility where appropriate.[71]

The National Treasury's PPP manual methodically guides both public and private bodies through the various phases of the regulated PPP project cycle for national and provincial governments. The manual draws particularly on PPP experience in the country as well as international best practice to provide clarity.[72]

The initiative to identify and set up a PPP project rests with the relevant state or provincial institution and not with the PPP Unit.[73] The PPP Unit recommends a project it deems suitable, but only the National Treasury can grant

67 Ibid.
68 Act in this definition refers to the Public Finance Management Act.
69 National Treasury, *op cit* (note 58) 21.
70 Ibid 18.
71 Ibid.
72 National Treasury Unit, *op cit* (note 26).
73 Treasury Regulation 16.

approval. The initiative for and daily management of the PPP project remains with the relevant institutions, government departments and provinces.[74] The National Treasury's PPP manual describes the project preparation phase, during which Treasury Approvals I, IIA, IIB and III are granted. The manual indicates which module is relevant for each of these stages of approval.[75] Furthermore, the manual gives guidance on the management of PPP agreements, the audit and accounting treatment of PPPs and project finance.[76] Thus, Treasury Approval I or (TA I), marks the National Treasury's approval of the feasibility study, preparing the way for the actual tendering/procurement process for private-party consortia to deliver on the project. TA IIA, TA IIB and TA III, are the three further steps put in place to ensure that the project is properly designed, tendered and awarded. When TA III is granted by the Treasury, the project is considered 'closed.'[77]

The PPP project cycle[78] in South Africa consists of four phases: the inception phase, the feasibility study phase, the procurement phase and the implementation phase,[79] which are discussed in detail next.

7.5.1 Inception phase

All PPP projects in South Africa start off with an inception phase in accordance with the provisions of Regulation 16.3, pursuant to the Public Finance Management Act of 1999. A project is registered with National Treasury PPP Unit when the accounting officer of the procuring institution applies for its approval. The PPP Unit will then give approval if satisfied that the proposed PPP arrangement will provide VfM, is affordable and transfers appropriate technical, operational and financial risk to the private party. If the institution lacks the expertise to proceed with the procurement of a PPP agreement, the accounting officer of the institution is required by the Regulation to inform the relevant treasury, and, where necessary, a specialist consultant will be appointed for the purpose.

7.5.2 Feasibility study phase

The second phase in the PPP cycle in South Africa is the feasibility studies phase, during which the procuring institution appoints private-sector advisors

74 Philip Burger, *op cit* (note 59) 1.

75 Axis Consulting, *op cit* (note 46).

76 Ibid 16.

77 Ibid.

78 This refers to the processes, procedures, procurement methods and approvals that a PPP project must go through, commencing with the inception phase of the contract and continuing through to its termination phase.

79 Treasury Regulation 16 in terms of the Public Finance Management Act of 1999.

to conduct a study on the most appropriate mechanism for procuring the project.[80] The purpose of the feasibility study is to determine whether a proposed PPP agreement is in the best interests of an institution.[81] Thus, first, the feasibility study must be undertaken to explain the strategic and operational benefits of the PPP agreement in terms of the institution's objectives and government policy. Second, the study must specify the nature of the institutional function concerned, the form of PPP agreement contemplated and the basis for the selection of that form. Third, the study must show whether the agreement will provide VfM, is affordable for the institution and will transfer the appropriate technical, operational and financial risk to the private party. Fourth, the study must include any relevant information, figures and economic criteria used to justify the assessment. Finally, the study must explain the capacity of the institution to effectively enforce the agreement, including monitoring and regulating implementation and performance in terms of the agreement.

The feasibility study for a project is required to contain three parts in the following format:[82]

1 Sector needs analysis;
2 Affordability, risk transfer and how VfM can be realised; and
3 Institutional arrangements for monitoring the implementation of the PPP agreement.

The report of the study is to be submitted to the Natonal Treasury for approval in line with clause 16.3 of the Treasury Regulation.

7.5.3 Procurement phase

When a PPP option has been approved by the Treasury and a feasibility study shows that it is viable, the procuring institution invites the market to submit bids for the infrastructure and/or service-provision project.[83] The procurement procedure must be open, transparent and competitive and allow for the evaluation of the bids to determine which represents the best VfM. It is submitted that the Regulation ought to indicate the importance of the experience and competence of the private consortia that are bidding. This is because the party offering the cheapest cost of procurement may not have the requisite competence or experience.

During procurement, there are five stages that must be complied with: prequalification; request for proposals; best and final offer, where appropriate; negotiations and final closure. The process begins with the preparation of bid

80 National Treasury PPP Unit, *op cit* (note 10) 19.
81 Treasury Regulation 16.4.
82 Treasury Regulation 16.5.
83 National Treasury PPP Unit, *op cit* (note 10) 19.

documents and a draft PPP agreement in accordance with the provisions of the Public Finance Management Act. The accounting officer is responsible for designing and managing the procurement process to ensure that it conforms with Regulation 16.

The aim of pre-qualification is to reduce the total number of consortia in the PPP procurement process by selecting a limited number of bidders who are qualified financially and technically, possessing the skills and commitment required to execute the project. As already noted, there is also an obligation to meet the government's BEE policy. Prequalification affords the bidders the opportunity to ascertain the rules in place for the procurement process, and at this stage, all vital information about the project cycle is made available. Finally, prequalification enables the PPP Unit to gather information from the private consortia, which can be used in the future.

After pre-qualification, successful bidders may enter the request for proposal (RFP) stage. The RFP must provide information about the project's background, expected outcome and projected timeframe. Other relevant information to be contained in the RFP includes the laws, rules and regulations governing the procurement of PPPs[84]as well as the procedure for securing approval from the National Treasury.

7.5.4 Implementation phase

The project is deemed implemented once a suitable bidder has been chosen.[85] Upon submission, the bids are evaluated to select a preferred and reserve bidder. The evaluation procedure must comply with laid-down regulations that involve the appointment of an evaluation team as well as committees who must ensure that all declarations and codes are signed. It is instructive to note that the provisions of the Promotion of Administrative Justice Act and the BEE Code must be complied with to determine the best and final offer (BFO).

Subsequently, with the preferred bidder and reserve bidder already chosen, negotiation commences, which helps to eliminate gaps and provide clarity for the contract. It affords the parties an opportunity to structure a sound and durable agreement. When negotiation is successful, the result is the award of a PPP contract. As noted in Chapter 3, since PPPs involve a main contract and several ancillary agreements, negotiation should also provide clarity about other contracts that will follow from the main PPP agreement.

In summary, during the inception phase, the procuring institution registers the project with the PPP Unit. A feasibility study is then carried out by the procuring institution to determine the appropriate mechanism for procuring the project. The next phase is to invite the market to submit bids for the

84 The term 'procurement' here is used in a general sense and does not refer to traditional public procurement.

85 National Treasury PPP Unit, *op cit* (note 10) 19.

project, and this is followed by implementation (i.e. when a suitable bidder is chosen to execute the project).

7.5.5 Dispute resolution

South Africa's Arbitration Act No. 42 of 1965, Module 6 of the National Treasury PPP manual, and the Standardised PPP Provisions set out the procedure for dealing with disputes arising from PPP agreements.[86] A vital component of the PPP agreement is a provision for dispute resolution during the tenure of the PPP contract. The first step is for all disputes to be referred to the respective liaison or project officers to reach an amicable resolution. When this fails, the dispute should be referred to both the accounting officer of the institution and the CEO of the private consortium. If the dispute is not resolved at this stage, an independent mediator is to be appointed by the parties.[87] Where the dispute is still not amicably resolved, it is then referred to the courts for settlement.

7.5.6 Funding of PPPs in South Africa

Compared to those of its peers[88] in Sub-Saharan Africa (SSA), the financial market in South Africa is relatively well developed.[89] Most PPP funding comes from within the country and from institutional investors (banks, pension funds etc.).[90] It is important to note that when foreign money is involved, a hedge is generally used to protect the investors against currency fluctuations.[91] The financial market in South Africa contributes nearly 25 per cent of private-equity funds to the entire continent, second only to a nearly 50 per cent contribution from investors in the United States.[92] Furthermore, South Africa's private-equity market compares favourably with those in developed economies.[93] The country also dominates the African equity market, with a share of 80 per cent of SSA's private capital compared to Nigeria's 10 per cent.[94] It has been asserted that in the entire continent, 'only South Africa has domestic banks and a local capital market capable of consistently providing local currency financing for its infrastructure

86 Part 86 of the Standardised Public-Private Partnership Provisions.

87 Section 11(1) of the Arbitration Act as amended by Act No. 49 of 1996.

88 Other big emerging economies, such as Nigeria and Kenya.

89 The World Bank, *Establishing Public Private Partnerships: Lessons Learned from the Global South* (2015) 12 available at <https://openknowledge.worldbank.org/bitstream/handle/10986/21309/936290WP0Box380ion000for0disclosure.pdf?sequence=1&isAllowed=y> accessed 17 February 2018.

90 Ibid.

91 Ibid.

92 Mihasonirina Andrianaivo and Charles Amo Yartey, 'Understanding the Growth of African Financial Markets' (2009) *IMF Working Paper* WP/09/182, 9 available at <www.imf.org/external/pubs/ft/wp/2009/wp09182.pdf> accessed 6 May 2017.

93 Ibid 9.

94 Ibid.

projects on suitable terms and in significant amounts.'[95] The other economies in Africa have under-developed financial markets that oblige them to rely on short-term financial instruments. Given that foreign currency fluctuations (especially where there is devaluation) can negatively impact on debt funding, South Africa presents a good case study for other emerging economies on the continent on how an emerging economy can develop its market to suit its needs.

It is worthy of note that Treasury Regulation 16 is not prescriptive about the funding structure for PPPs in the country.[96] As a result, funding for any deal is dependent on the project and its sponsors. It is possible to have projects that do not involve any debt finance at all, as they can be funded directly and in their entirety by the sponsors through private equity and a contribution from the government's budget.[97] However, a generic project finance structure is in place.[98] Financing options available for PPP projects in South Africa are discussed next.

Bonds

Bond financing for PPP projects has been in use in private infrastructure financing in South Africa.[99] In a bond-financed deal, investors usually provide funds via a deal made by a bond arranger who is responsible for selling the bonds into the capital markets. The risk posed by the uncertainty of sufficient purchase of the bond is undertaken by an underwriter. In simple terms, bonds are loans made to large organisations, including corporations, cities and national governments. The size of these entities requires them to borrow the money from more than one source.[100] Bonds are usually interest-bearing loans that pay a coupon during the term of the loan and the principal at the maturity of the bond. The capital and interest payments on these bonds have been benchmarked by an inflation index, for example, the Consumer Price Index (CPI).[101] CPI-linked bonds have been used in toll-road financing in South Africa.[102]

95 Robert Sheppard, Stephen Von Klaudy and Geeta Kumar, 'Financing Infrastructure in Africa: How the Region Can Attract More Project Finance' (2006) (13) *Gridlines* 2 available at <https://openknowledge.worldbank.org/bitstream/handle/10986/10724/375490AFR0Grid1rastructure01PUBLIC1.pdf?sequence=1&isAllowed=y> accessed 6 May 2017.

96 National Treasury, *op cit* (note 42) 5.

97 Ibid.

98 National Treasury PPP Unit, 'South African Public Private Partnership Unit' (2009) a presentation at the OECD Conference held in Paris 5 and 6 March 2009 available at <www.oecd.org/gov/budgeting/42344511.pdf> accessed 9 May 2017.

99 Ibid.

100 Kinberly Amadeo, 'What Are Bonds, and How Do They Work?' (2016) available at <www.thebalance.com/what-are-bonds-and-how-do-they-work-3306235> accessed 6 May 2017.

101 Ibid.

102 Helge Switala, 'Project Finance and Obtaining Sufficient Funding for the Successful Completion of your Project' a presentation by the Project Manager, Development Bank of South Africa available at <www.dbsa.org/EN/About-Us/Publications/Documents/Project%20finance%20and%20obtaining%20sufficient%20funding%20for%20the%20successful%20completion%20of%20your%20project.pdf> accessed 9 May 2017.

Interestingly, despite a 2018 downgrading of South Africa's credit rating to a below-average rating by a major credit agency,[103] the bond market continues to thrive with foreign investors participating.[104] This may be attributed to the fact that the country's financial market is well developed, with investors continuing to evince confidence in the South African market. This writer believes that much more gain in terms of the performance of the market will be recorded following the swearing in of Mr Cyril Ramaphosa as president of South Africa in the wake of Mr Jacob Zuma's forced resignation from office.[105]

Equity

Equity refers to the funds contributed by the sponsors of the project and the other shareholders.[106] It represents the risk capital for the project and gives the shareholders of the SPV certain rights, including the right to returns subject to the performance of the project.[107] This usually occurs after the debt funders have been paid. Investors are attracted by the upside potential of the investment in relation to the risk involved. This aspect of the funding of a PPP project is very important as it relates to the capacity of the initiators of the project. In South Africa, as pointed out previously in 5.5.3, one of the factors in determining the best bid is the capacity of the bidding consortium and its ability to raise sufficient capital in the form of equity.

Debt

A large share of the financing of PPP projects is usually raised through debt.[108] As will be discussed in the case studies of PPP projects in South Africa, debt holders are concerned about the cash flow of the project to ensure consistent debt service (i.e. the payment of the principal amount/capital sum and the interest accruing).[109] Project debts are usually sourced as loans from commercial banks,[110] multilateral agencies (MAs), development finance institutions (DFIs) and export credit agencies (ECAs).

103 Fitch, a majority credit rating agency, cut South Africa's foreign and local currency ratings to junk status.

104 Nicholas Megaw, 'Foreign Investors Pile into South African Bonds Despite Fears' (2017) *Financial Times* available at <www.ft.com/content/dc920b6e-064d-3bef-b374-352c52d29367> accessed 6 May 2017.

105 The financial market is often influenced by political outcomes in the economy, especially when a new government is rated to outperform the previous one.

106 Helge Switala, *op cit* (note 102) 3.

107 Ibid.

108 The term 'debt' is preferred to the word 'credit.' The reason is because the investments in a PPP are treated as assets. What the SPV incurs for sourcing finance is a debt. Replacing 'debt' with 'credit' would mean the lender is an investor in the project, which is not usually the case.

109 Helge Switala, *op cit* (note 102) 3.

110 Webber Wentzel, 'Investing in South Africa: Charting the Legal Landscape with Webber Wentzel' (2015) available at <www.investinginsouthafrica.co.za/downloads/en/Webber_Wentzel_Investing_in_South_Africa_complete. pdf> accessed 11 May 2017.

7.5.7 *Protecting funds invested in PPP projects*

A commitment to protecting investors' and lenders' funds is at the core of South Africa's PPP framework. A watertight project preparation process is therefore required to prove the merits of the project to potential funders.[111] Other critical components of the feasibility study under Module 4 of the PPP manual include project due diligence, value assessment, economic valuation and a procurement plan. The procedure involves the engagement of advisors on behalf of the sponsors and the lenders to provide advice on technical, market, financial, legal and incidental matters.[112] This is fundamental to achieving financial closure[113] for the project. It should be noted that South Africa is globally ranked 10th out of 189 countries for good practice in protecting investors in business.[114]

The funding of specific projects in the South African currency offers protection against currency fluctuation risk. For example, the Sasol Natural Gas Project is an R8.6 billion project aimed at developing the gas fields and processing facility in Mozambique and operating a gas pipeline from the processing plant to facilities in South Africa.[115] Even though the project will produce both rand and dollar revenues, the bulk of the debt is ZAR denominated.[116]

The 1996 Constitution of the Republic of South Africa states that when an organ of state in the national, provincial or local sphere of government or other institution identified in the national legislation contracts for goods or services, it must do so in accordance with a system that is fair, equitable, transparent and cost-effective.[117] It follows that South African law emphasises transparency and accountability, which are key to ensuring that funds are protected and not wasted. This philosophy is the driving force behind the Public Finance Management Act and the Municipal Finance Management Act.

Examples abound in South Africa of projects structured in such a way as to ensure that there are sufficient revenue streams accruing in the short to long term. The aim is to optimise the performance of the PPP and encourage private participation. Two examples are worth mentioning here. The city of Johannesburg contracted with a consortium of international operators led by Suez. The project was structured in such a way that Johannesburg Water purchased some biogas-fuelled generators, and the contractor invested in other required capital infrastructure. The contract recovered its cost from the sale of bio-gas generated from the operations.[118] A second example is the city of Tshwane's PPP

111 See National Treasury PPP Unit, *PPP Project Cycle: Reflecting Treasury Regulation 16 to the Public Finance Management Act, 1999 National Treasury PPP Manual: Module 1* (Pretoria: Nation Treasury PPP Unit, 1999).

112 Helge Switala, *op cit* (note 102) 3.

113 Financial closure refers to the milestone in the project cycle that is reached when funds are secured.

114 World Bank, *Doing Business Report* (Washington DC, The World Bank 2014).

115 Helge Switala, *op cit* (note 102) 3.

116 Ibid.

117 Section 217(1).

118 Cornelius Ruiters and Maselaganye P Matji, 'Public Private Partnership Conceptual Framework and Models for the Funding and Financing of Water Services Infrastructure in Municipalities from Selected Provinces in South Africa' (2016) 42(2) *Water SA*.

with Magalies Water Board, ABSA Bank and Bigen Africa. The arrangement was structured to ensure sustainable revenue flows to Tshwane as it was the main beneficiary of the R500 million project.[119]

The protection of investments is vital to the sustainability of PPP arrangements in any economy. This is the spirit behind the passing into law of the Protection of Investment Act 22 of 2015.[120] The Act was passed to replace the bilateral investment treaties (BITs) with European countries and to make direct investment in the country attractive to foreign investors.[121] Historically, developing economies entered BITs to provide comfort to investors that their investments would be safe and protected. However, BITs have been criticised for creating unequal rights and obligations between developed and developing economies and for interfering with the developing countries' sovereignty.[122] Key provisions of the Protection of Investment Act are discussed next.

7.5.8 The Protection of Investment Act No. 22 of 2015

The Act defines an investor as 'an enterprise making an investment in the Republic regardless of nationality.'[123] It follows that the protection afforded indigenous investors applies to foreign investors as well. The purpose of the Act is threefold: first, to protect investment in accordance with and subject to the Constitution; second, to affirm the Republic's sovereign right to regulate investments in the public interest; and third, to confirm the Bill of Rights in the Constitution and the laws that apply to all investors and their investments in the Republic.[124] The Act applies to all investments in the Republic that are made in accordance with Section 2 of the Act.[125]

The Act stipulates that foreign investors must not be discriminated against.[126] The Republic must accord foreign investors and their investments a level of physical security equivalent to that enjoyed by domestic investors, in accordance

119 Ibid.

120 Gazette No. 39514 of 15 December 2015.

121 In 2012, South Africa terminated its BITs with European countries such as Denmark, Spain, Germany, Belgium, Luxembourg, Switzerland and Holland. It maintained the BITs with Russia and China.

122 Dentons, 'South Africa's Protection of Investment Act' (2017) available at <www.dentons.com/en/insights/newsletters/2017/january/26/south-africa-newsletter/south-africa-newsletter-january-edition/south-africas-protection-of-investment-act> accessed 9 May 2017.

123 Section 1 of the Protection of Investment Act of 2015.

124 Section 4 of the Protection of Investment Act of 2015.

125 Section 5 of the Protection of Investment Act of 2015. Section 2 of the Act defines 'investment' in the following terms: 'an enterprise may possess assets such as shares, stocks, debentures, securities as defined in the Financial Markets Act, 2012; a debt; loans to an enterprise; moveable or immovable property or other property rights such as mortgages, liens or pledges; claims to money or to any performance under contract having a financial value; copyrights, knowhow, goodwill, or intellectual property rights such as patents, trademarks, industrial designs and trade names to the extent that they are recognised under the law of South Africa; returns such as profits, dividends, royalties or income yielded by an investment; or rights or concessions conferred by law or under contract including licenses to cultivate, extract or exploit natural resources.'

126 Section 8 of the Protection of Investment Act of 2015.

with the minimum standards of customary international law.[127] Investors have the right to property in consonance with Section 25 of the Constitution of South Africa.[128] Furthermore, the Act provides that a foreign investor may, in respect of an investment, repatriate funds subject to taxation and other applicable legislation.[129]

Regarding disputes, when an investor has a dispute in respect to action taken by the government, the action having affected an investment of said investor, the investor may within six months of becoming aware of the dispute request the Department to facilitate its resolution by appointing a mediator.[130] A foreign investor is not precluded from approaching any competent court, independent tribunal or statutory body within South Africa for the resolution of the dispute.[131] When all domestic remedies have been exhausted and the dispute persists, the South African government may consent to international arbitration, with such arbitration conducted between South Africa and the home state of the foreign investor.[132] Thus, an investor who feels wronged by an action of the South African government or any of its agencies is clearly empowered by the law to seek redress. It is submitted, however, that what the South African government is giving with the right hand, it seeks to take away with the left, through the provision that the state must only consent to arbitration when domestic remedies have been exhausted and international arbitration becomes the option.

On 30 December 2016, the South African Department of Trade and Industry (DTI) issued Draft Regulations on Mediation Rules, which would apply to investment disputes between the government and investors.[133] Under the Rules, among other things, an aggrieved investor must declare a dispute within six months of becoming aware of the dispute, the investor and the DTI must agree on a mediator and the rules of the DTI must be complied with in the mediation.[134] It is submitted that only a foreign investor with confidence in the South African market will be satisfied with the Rules as couched, especially as the remedies available to the investor are not clearly specified.

7.6 Case studies of PPP projects in South Africa

The choice of projects selected as case studies is motivated by their status as flagship projects in their respective sectors of the economy. Furthermore, given

127 Section 9 of the Protection of Investment Act of 2015.

128 Section 10 of the Protection of Investment Act of 2015.

129 Section 11 of the Protection of Investment Act of 2015.

130 Section 13 of the Protection of Investment Act of 2015.

131 Dentons, *op cit* (note 122).

132 Ibid.

133 Annet van Hooft, 'South Africa: Draft Regulations on Mediation Rules for Investor-State Disputes' (2017) available at <www.twobirds.com/en/news/articles/2017/global/africa-newsletter-feb/south-africa-draft-regulations-on-mediation-rules-for-investor-state-disputes> accessed 11 May 2017.

134 Ibid.

the long-term nature of PPP contracts, these projects remain relevant as they are currently in operation, and the lessons learnt from them can serve as eye openers for prospective investors in South African PPPs.

7.6.1 The N4 from South Africa to Mozambique

In 1996, the governments of South Africa and Mozambique jointly signed a R3-billion[135] 30-year concession with a private consortium to build and operate the N4 toll road from Witbank (in South Africa) to Maputo (in Mozambique).[136] Even though the project was privately financed, the debt on the transaction was guaranteed by both the South African and Mozambican governments.[137] The concession was awarded to Trans African Concessions (TRAC), which became responsible for the financing, design, construction, rehabilitation, operation and maintenance of the toll road. The contract was signed with the South African National Roads Agency (SANRAL) and the Mozambique Roads Agency (ANE) and was set to end in 2027. The concessionaire now manages 630 kilometres of toll road, most of which is in South Africa, with only about 50 kilometres in Mozambique.[138]

The N4 financing was structured according to a 20:80 ratio.[139] The three construction companies involved in the project[140] contributed R331 million worth of equity,[141] with the rest of the capital coming from the SA Infrastructure Fund, Rand Merchant Bank Asset Management and five other investors. The debt investors included a consortium of four South African banks – ABSA, Nedcor, Standard Bank and First National Bank. Other investors included the Development Bank of Southern Africa and the Mine Employees and Officials Pension Funds.

One of the challenges the N4 project faced at its inception was its demand risk, given the volume of finance required for the construction work. The main question posed to the project's sponsors was whether there would be enough traffic using and paying for the road to generate sufficient income, given that there were other well-maintained free alternative routes.[142] Similarly, the project faced considerable payment risk along the Mozambican axis as the poor communities there were unable and unwilling to pay high toll fees. As a result, Trans African Concessions (TRAC) cross-subsidised the Mozambican portion of the road with higher revenues from the South African axis. There are currently eight toll points on the road with significant adjustments

135 By 1996 estimates.
136 Peter Farlam, *op cit* (note 7) 9.
137 ER Yescombe, *op cit* (note 12) 47.
138 PPIAF, *N4 Toll Road from South Africa to Mozambique* (Washington, DC: PPIAF, 2009) Toolkit for Public-Private Partnerships in Roads and Highways 92.
139 Financing of the project was split between 20 per cent equity and 80 per cent debt.
140 Stocks and Stocks, Bouygues, and Basil Road.
141 Which formed 20 per cent of the financing of the project.
142 Peter Farlam, *op cit* (note 7) 10.

for the Maputo corridor.[143] Four types of vehicles were considered for toll purposes (light, medium-heavy, large-heavy and extra-heavy). Tolls are collected at six main line toll plazas and at two ramp plazas. Only two toll plazas are in Mozambique.[144] The road is partly four-lane separated carriageways and partly two lanes with widening to accommodate large hauling vehicles, with a one-stop border facility developed at Komatiport/Ressano Garcia to reduce cross-border bottlenecks between the countries.[145]

The significant lessons to be learned from the N4 toll road are, first, that cross-subsidisation from more affluent South African users and substantial discounts for the regular Mozambican users helped reduce the user payment risk.[146] Second, the road has shortened the travel time from Pretoria to Maputo by at least three hours,[147] which makes it attractive to road users. Third, the road facilitated further private-sector investment in Mozambique, resulting in raised traffic volumes.[148] Fourth, the risk associated with the financing of the project was borne entirely by the TRAC consortium without government subsidies, although the governments of South Africa and Mozambique guaranteed the debt.

The success of the N4 toll road is an indicator of the viability of PPPs in the road sector when users are willing to pay. It is important to mention that initial traffic volumes were less than the financers of the project had envisaged. However, they regarded the traffic growth as acceptable, at rates of between 5 per cent and 7 per cent annually.[149]

Despite the success of the N4 toll road, some of the problems encountered during its implementation included complaints by users and commuters that a road that was used free of charge had become a toll road and higher-than-expected damage to the road caused by the overloading of trucks. These issues have been addressed by introducing much lower toll fees for commuters and locals and by implementing an efficient axle load–control system along the corridor.[150]

7.6.2 The Pelonomi and Universitas Hospital Co-location, Bloemfontein

This project is structured as a co-location PPP, which occurs when the public and private sectors operate a similar service and collaborate rather than compete, resulting in the public sector receiving revenue while the private sector generates profits.[151]

143 See current toll fees at <www.tracn4.co.za/toll-fees.html> accessed 24 May 2017.
144 PPIAF, *op cit* (note 138) 92.
145 Ibid.
146 Peter Farlam, *op cit* (note 7) 11.
147 TRAC, 'Toll Fees' <www.tracn4.co.za/> accessed 24 May 2017.
148 Peter Farlam, *op cit* (note 7) 11.
149 PPIAF, *op cit* (note 138) 93.
150 Ibid 95.
151 Shadrack Shuping and Sipho Kabane, 'Public-Private Partnerships: A Case Study of the Pelonomi and Universitas Hospital Co-location Project' available at <www.hst.org.za/uploads/files/chap10_07.pdf> accessed 24 May 2017.

The project was arranged in 2000 at the provincial level, with the aim of providing a better level of health care for South Africans, especially those living in the Free State. An agreement was eventually signed as a 16-and-a-half-year contract on 25 November 2002.[152] The PPP for the hospital co-location project was made up of three partners. The public agency in the partnership was the Free State Health Department (FSHD).[153] The FSHD selected its partner after conducting a competitive tendering process: having obtained the requisite permission from the Treasury to proceed, it invited interested parties to submit registrations of capability (ROC) and held informational meetings with 30 private parties indicating interest.[154] After studying a blueprint from Australia, the FSHD accepted three of the ROC bids, but only two responded to the request for proposals (RFP). A consortium of two healthcare companies was selected, the first a South African black empowerment company[155] and the other a healthcare company[156] with branches in South Africa and the United Kingdom.[157] The consortium held a 65 per cent stake in the concession and the remaining 35 per cent was offered to investors, doctors and, later, the state.[158]

Under the arrangement, the FSHD received monthly concession fees from the private partner for the bed and operating theatre space that it used in both hospitals. In addition, the private partner paid variable fees representing 2 per cent of patient turnover.[159] The inclusion of variable payments in the arrangement means that some operational risk is transferred to the FSHD because a portion of the revenue received is dependent on the success of the private partner.[160] However, the private partner retains the risk associated with the construction as it is responsible for all construction, renovations and upgrades.[161]

While the FSHD's role is to provide patient care in both hospitals, the private partner is responsible for all renovations and upgrades.[162] The upgrades at Pelonomi and Universitas Hospitals were completed on shared facilities and facilities for the use of the public hospital.[163] Apart from this, the private partner

152 The United Nations Office for South-South Cooperation, 'Hospital Co-location, Bloemfontein, South Africa' available at <http://academy.ssc.undp.org/GSSDAcademy/SIE/VOL15.aspx> accessed 24 May 2017.

153 The FSHD is the branch of the provincial government of the Free State in South Africa that oversees health-related issues and all the public health facilities, including hospitals.

154 The United Nations Office for South-South Cooperation, *op cit* (note 152).

155 With a 40 per cent stake in the consortium.

156 With a 25 per cent stake.

157 The United Nations Office for South-South Cooperation, *op cit* (note 152).

158 Ibid.

159 According to the contract, the private partners were expected to pay a fixed monthly rental fee of R40,000 per month for the use of the co-located facilities within the first five years and R60,000 per month subsequently. In addition, 1.32 per cent of the annual turnover before profit was to be paid back to the public sector.

160 The United Nations Office for South-South Cooperation, *op cit* (note 152).

161 Ibid.

162 Shadrack Shuping and Sipho Kabane, *op cit* (note 151).

163 The United Nations Office for South-South Cooperation, *op cit* (note 152).

upgraded the facilities that were for its own private patients, and in doing so, the private partner hired local construction companies. At one point, 26 Bloemfontein companies were subcontracted for a period of 8 months. The result was an injection of over R10 million into the local economy.[164]

The PPP for Pelonomi and Universitas Hospitals was 'considered extremely successful.'[165] Both hospitals have facilities that are presently functional, with the healthcare needs of the population (whether insured or uninsured) being met daily. Running costs have been reduced and the quality of care has been increased because of the PPP arrangement. Furthermore, the PPP has ensured reduced costs for both the FSHD and the private partner, especially as there was no need to build a new hospital.[166] Again, commitment on the part of the stakeholders contributed immensely to the success of this PPP arrangement.[167]

7.6.3 The prison contracts

Because of a significant shortage of prison space, the Departments of Correctional Services (DCS) and Public Works introduced a concept for the operation of private prisons in the country modelled after private prisons in the United Kingdom.[168] The government of South Africa subsequently signed two 25-year PPP contracts for maximum-security prisons in Bloemfontein and Louis Trichardt as part of its Department of Public Works' Asset Procurement and Operating Partnership Systems (APOPS) in 2000.[169]

Initially, the DCS called for bids from the private sector for the design and construction of 11 maximum-security prisons. This was later reduced to four, then again to two, after it was realised that costs had been vastly underestimated.[170] The two winning consortia, both of whom had more than 50 per cent black shareholding and included foreign-based prison management companies among their shareholders, acquired responsibility for designing, building, financing, operating and transferring the prisons.[171] The facilities hold an estimated 3,000 inmates each and became fully operational in less than

164 Ibid.

165 Ibid.

166 It is significant that both hospitals can attend to all citizens without any form of discrimination based on race.

167 National Treasury PPP Unit, 'Case Studies on the Public Private Partnerships at Humansdorp District Hospital, Universitas and Pelonomi Hospitals and Inkosi Albert Luthuli Central Hospital: Overall Findings and Recommendations' (2007) available at <www.ppp.gov.za/Legal%20Aspects/Case%20Studies/Humansdorp%20Overall%20findings.pdf> accessed 29 May 2017.

168 Peter Farlam, *op cit* (note 7) 15.

169 South African Institute of International Affairs, 'Case study: Private Prisons' (2005) available at <www.saiia.org.za/newsletters/case-study-private-prisons> accessed 29 May 2017.

170 Linda Mti, 'Review of Public Private Partnership Prison Contracts' a summary of a hearing before the Correctional Services Portfolio Committee, South African Parliament, 12 November 2002 available at <https://pmg.org.za/committee-meeting/2259/> accessed 29 May 2017.

171 Peter Farlam, *op cit* (note 7) 15.

two years after the close of the contract in 2002, at a cost of about R1.7 billion for the Bloemfontein prison and R1.8 billion for the one in Louis Trichardt.[172]

A review undertaken jointly by the DCS, National Treasury and the Department of Public Works (DPW) found that the Bloemfontein and Louis Trichardt PPP Prisons achieved lofty goals, including but not limited to competitive construction costs (R270 million for Bloemfontein's 2,928 inmates, and R303 million for Louis Trichardt's 3,024 inmates); construction completed on time and on budget; fast track delivery: less than two years from contract close to full operating capacity accommodating some 6,000 maximum-security prisoners; operating costs per inmate per day were broadly comparable with the public sector's operating costs; significantly higher-quality facilities and levels of service than in public prisons; a high level of black equity in the contractors (60 per cent Bloemfontein, 50 per cent Louis Trichardt) and significant black sub-contracting in the construction and operation of both prisons and, finally, the appropriate assumption of financial, technical and operational risk by the parties.[173]

This notwithstanding, the review also identified some low points in both projects. These were[174] that the Department for Correctional Services' (DCS) design and operating specifications were too high, based on ideal prison conditions, though the prisons remained driven by high DCS input specs; suitable feasibility work by the government should have established DCS' affordability limits prior to procurement; the relatively high cost of debt due to high base interest rates prevailing at the time of the deals (14.58 per cent Bloemfontein, 15 per cent Louis Trichardt); higher-than-normal margins charged by lenders, reflecting the perceived risk of early deals; higher-than-normal returns on equities, again reflecting perceived risk of early deals and the inability to increase populations in the PPP prisons, despite severe overcrowding in the DCS system.

Farlam[175] argues that 'a thorough feasibility study would have clarified the affordability limits of the Department of Correctional Services at the start of the process.' He also notes that 'experienced private sector operators can provide a better-quality service at comparable rates to the public sector.'[176]

7.6.4 *South Africa's Gautrain*

This modern rapid train link was conceived to provide a solution to South Africa's infrastructure problems in the rail sector.[177] The rail links the nation's

172 Ibid.

173 National Treasury PPP Unit, 'PPP Prisons Are Good Deals' (2002) 9(2) *PPP Quarterly* 25.

174 Ibid 17.

175 Peter Farlam, *op cit* (note 7) 17.

176 Ibid.

177 Centre for Public Impact, 'South Africa's Gautrain: Rail travel from Pretoria to Johannesburg' (2015) available at <www.centreforpublicimpact.org/case-study/gautrain-in-south-africa/ > accessed 19 February 2018.

capital, commercial centre and main airport. It is considered central to South Africa's national transport strategy. Consequently, from the 1998 feasibility study to the year 2012, when it came into operation, it has offered a huge learning opportunity to PPP stakeholders in South Africa.

The project was initiated in February 2000 by Mr Mghazima Shilowa, the premier of Gauteng Province, as one of the ten Spatial Development Initiatives (SDIs) of the Gauteng government to promote tourism, move towards an integrated transport system and help alleviate congestion on the roads, particularly along the Pretoria to Johannesburg International Airport (JIA) corridor. The project was also intended to stimulate economic growth, development and job creation.

Notably, being a PPP, the Gautrain involved relations with the private investors aiding in the funding and the external stakeholders engaged in the construction.[178] The Bombela Concession Company (Pty) Limited won the bid for the construction, operation and maintenance of the Gautrain until 2020.[179] Funding for the project was sourced from federal and provincial institutions, institutional investors (especially pension funds), the World Bank, the African Development Bank (AfDB), infrastructure funds and banks via the capital markets and debt markets. The project is a classic example of a PPP in the sense that it showcases the use of various instruments available in the financial market for the funding of PPPs. Significantly, the project received strong political support from the national government, which committed as much as R7.1 billion to it.

Despite initial public scepticism about the project,[180] its clear policy objectives and strong management on the part of the concessionaire and other public-sector agencies were factors that made a strong contribution towards its success.

7.7 Challenges to the implementation of PPP in South Africa

Despite South Africa's leading position in the commissioning of PPP projects in Africa, the implementation of PPP policy in the country has not been without challenges and criticism. In 2007, the Office of the Presidency of South Africa and the Business Trust commissioned the Castalia Consortium[181] to identify challenges facing PPPs in infrastructure in South Africa.[182] After conducting a series of interviews, the Castalia consortium reported the

178 Ibid.

179 Ibid.

180 Ibid.

181 Comprising Castalia Ltd and Ukhamba Advisory Services.

182 Castalia Strategic Advisors and Ukhamba Advisory Services, 'Key Challenges to Public Private Partnerships in South Africa: Summary of Interview Findings' (2007) available at <www.castalia-advisors.com/files/12345.pdf> accessed 29 May 2017.

following as potential bottlenecks in the successful implementation of PPP policy in the country:[183]

1 A lack of policy direction from the highest level of government, or at least a lack of clarity in the minds of implementing agencies and the private sector, on why South Africa should enter PPPs, what PPPs are and what is or should be the role of the PPP Unit;
2 Inconsistent commitment to PPPs in different parts and at different levels of the government;
3 A general mistrust among the implementing agencies of private-sector involvement in the provision of infrastructure services;
4 A lack of time, resources, know-how and authority among the staff of the agencies developing and implementing PPPs;
5 A policy bias towards traditional procurement and against PPPs;
6 A lack of fiscal imperative to use PPPs;
7 A completely different market and legal environment for PPPs in the municipalities, where all the noted problems are much more severe and infrastructure needs are much greater.

In a recent study, poor stakeholder consultation has been identified as one of the issues that needs to be addressed in South Africa.[184] On a similar note, Fombad[185] identifies accountability generally as a serious challenge for PPPs in South Africa and claims that such issues involve a lack of public consultation on the part of the public sector, a lack of transparency, corruption, a lack of competition, ineffective contract management and a failure to monitor performance. In this author's mind, where there is a lack of accountability, a project – no matter how well designed and structured – is doomed to fail from the start. The reason is that members of the public are very sceptical about PPP arrangements. If one considers that the procurement of infrastructure has been the sole responsibility of the public sector, a transaction with the private sector that lacks accountability will always be regarded as dubious.

Sanni and Hashim also note that inconsistency in the commitment of government agencies in South Africa affects PPP projects, and since PPP projects require a longer time for delivery, frequent changes in plans or policies may hamper their success.[186] Seeletse has argued that the deployment of unqualified personnel to handle PPP transactions has been a drawback for PPP in South

183 Ibid 35.

184 ER Yescombe, *Public-Private Partnerships in Sub-Saharan Africa* (Dar es Salaam: Uongozi Institute, 2017) 96.

185 Madeleine C Fombad, 'Accountability Challenges in Public-Private Partnerships from a South African Perspective' (2013) 7(1) *African Journal of Business Ethics* 11–25.

186 Afeez Olalekan Sanni and Maizon Hashim, 'Building Infrastructure Through Public Private Partnerships in Sub-Saharan Africa: Lessons from South Africa' (2014) 143 *Procedia: Social and Behavioural Sciences* 133–138.

Africa.[187] Yet, this author does not agree with his submission that there is a need for the establishment of a regulatory body for PPP in South Africa, if what he means by that is a body separate from the PPP Unit.[188] This author's view is that multiple bodies regulating PPP will only end up causing confusion and result in the unnecessary flexing of muscle by different government agencies.

7.8 Conclusion

In this chapter, the legal, policy, institutional and administrative framework for PPP in South Africa was analysed. The practice of PPP in the country in relation to this framework has formed part of the discussion; and to examine the law and policy in action, a few brief case studies of projects were presented. It seems that despite the relatively slow development of PPPs in Sub-Saharan Africa (SSA), when compared to other benchmark (middle-income) countries, South Africa has outperformed the others in using the PPP model for infrastructure procurement. Two reasons for this easily come to mind. The first is that compared to other SSA countries, such as Nigeria, institutions in South Africa are better structured. Institutional actors in PPP regulation must be guided by the need to respect contractual agreements and to abide by the rule of law in the discharge of their responsibilities. Secondly, the local financial market in South Africa is arguably the only developed one in SSA.

This is not to say that the framework and practice of PPP in South Africa is perfect. Indeed, as is the case with other strong PPP countries, like the UK, Canada, Australia and Hong Kong, PPP is evolving in South Africa, and there is always room for improvement.

References

Amadeo, K. (2006, November 29). What Bonds Are, How They Work and Can Protect You from Recession. Retrieved from www.thebalance.com/what-are-bonds-and-how-do-they-work-3306235.

Andrianaivo, M., & Yartey, C. O. (2009). Understanding the Growth of African Financial Markets' (2009) IMF Working Paper WP/09/182. Retrieved December 30, 2019, from www.imf.org/external/pubs/ft/wp/2009/wp09182.pdf.

Axis Consulting. (2013). PPP Country Paper: South Africa. Retrieved from www.sadcppp network.org/uploads/2015/02/south_africa_27012014.pdf.

Burger, P. (2017). The Dedicated PPP Unit of the South African National Treasury. Retrieved April 30, 2017, from www.oecd.org/mena/governance/37146964.pdf.

Calitz, E., & Fourie, J. (2010). Infrastructure in South Africa: Who Is to Finance and Who Is to Pay? *Development Southern Africa*, 27(2), 177–191. doi:10.1080/03768351003740449.

187 Solly Matshonisa Seeletse, 'Performance of South African Public-Private Partnerships' (2016) 14(2) *Problems and Perspectives in Management* 19.

188 Ibid 24.

Castalia Strategic Advisors, & Ukhamba Advisory Services. (2007). Key Challenges to Public Private Partnerships in South Africa: Summary of Interview Findings. Retrieved May 29, 2017, from https://castalia-advisors.com/files/12345.pdf.

Centre for Public Impact. (2015). South Africa's Gautrain: Rail Travel from Pretoria to Johannesburg. Retrieved February 19, 2018, from www.centreforpublicimpact.org/case-study/gautrain-in-south-africa/.

Davies, E. (2016). Foundations of Law. Retrieved November 17, 2018, from www.ru.ac.za/media/rhodesuniversity/content/law/documents/courseoutlines2016/Foundations%20of%20Law%20Course%20Outline%202016.pdf.

Dentons. (2017). South Africa's Protection of Investment Act. Retrieved December 30, 2019, from www.dentons.com/en/insights/newsletters/2017/january/26/south-africa-newsletter/south-africa-newsletter-january-edition/south-africas-protection-of-invest ment-act.

Department of Trade and Industry. (2014). South Africa: Investor's Handbook 2014/15. Retrieved May 11, 2017, from https://www2.deloitte.com/content/dam/Deloitte/za/Documents/tax/ZA_DTI-InvestinginSA_2014-15.pdf.

Development of Policy, Legal, and Institutional Framework for the Public-Private Partnership Programme in Malawi: Final Report. (2007). The Institute for Public-Private Partnerships.

European Investment Bank. (2002). Study on PPP Legal and Financial Frameworks in the Mediterranean Partner Countries: Volume 1- A Regional Approach. Retrieved May 1, 2017, from www.eib.org/attachments/med/ppp-study-volume-1.pdf.

Farlam, P. (2005). Working Together: Assessing Public-Private Partnerships in Africa. *Nepad Policy Focus* Report No.2. Retrieved from www.oecd.org/investment/investmentfor development/34867724.pdf.

Fombad, M.C. (2014). Accountability Challenges in Public – Private Partnerships from a South African Perspective. *African Journal of Business Ethics*, 7(1). doi:10.15249/7-1-33.

Matshonisa Seeletse, S. (2016). Performance of South African Private-Public Partnerships. *Problems and Perspectives in Management*, *14*(2), 19–26. doi:10.21511/ppm.14(2).2016.02.

Megaw, N. (2017, April 10). Foreign Investors Pile into South African Bonds Despite Fears. Retrieved from www.ft.com/content/dc920b6e-064d-3bef-b374-352c52d29367.

Mitchell, D., & Fakisandla Consulting. (2007). Capacity Development for Partnerships in South Africa: Increasing Service Delivery Through Partnerships Between Private and Public Secto. Retrieved December 30, 2019, from https://thepartneringinitiative.org/wp-content/uploads/2014/08/PPP-overview-and-needs-assessment.pdf.

Mti, L. (2003, March 17). Public Private Partnership Prison Contracts: Briefing. Retrieved May 29, 2017, from https://pmg.org.za/committee-meeting/2259/.

National Treasury. (2017). Public Private Partnerships. Retrieved April 30, 2017, from www.ppp.gov.za/Pages/About.aspx.

National Treasury PPP Unit. (2002). PPP Prisons Are Good Deals. *PPP Quarterly*, *9*(2).

National Treasury PPP Unit. (2007). *Introducing Public Private Partnerships in South Africa*. Pretoria: National Treasury Unit.

National Treasury PPP Unit. (2009). *South African Public Private Partnership Unit*. Retrieved May 9, 2017, from www.oecd.org/gov/budgeting/42344511.pdf.

National Treasury Unit. (2007). Case Studies on the Public Private Partnerships at Humansdorp District Hospital, Universitas and Pelonomi Hospitals and Inkosi Albert Luthuli Central Hospital: Overall Findings and Recommendations. Retrieved May 29, 2017, from www.ppp.gov.za/Legal%20Aspects/Case%20Studies/Humansdorp%20Overall%20findings.pdf.

OECD. (2018). G 20 Members. Retrieved February 17, 2018, from www.oecd.org/g20/g20-members.htm.

PPIAF. (2009). *N4 Toll Road from South Africa to Mozambique*. Washington, DC: Author.

Ruiters, C., & Matji, M.P. (2016). Public – Private Partnership Conceptual Framework and Models for the Funding and Financing of Water Services Infrastructure in Municipalities from Selected Provinces in South Africa. *Water SA*, *42*(2), 291. doi:10.4314/wsa.v42i2.13.

Sanni, A.O., & Hashim, M. (2014). a*Building Infrastructure Through Public Private Partnerships in sub-Saharan Africa: Lessons from South Africa. *Procedia – Social and Behavioral Sciences*, *143*, 133–138. doi:10.1016/j.sbspro.2014.07.374.

Sasaki, R. (2011). An in-depth International Comparison of Major Donor Agencies: How Do They Systematically Conduct Country Program Evaluation? *Journal of MultiDisciplinary Evaluation*, *8*(18), 29–45.

Sheppard, R., Von Klaudy, S., & Kumar, G. (2006). Financing Infrastructure in Africa: How the Region Can Attract More Project Finance. Retrieved May 6, 2017, from https://openknowledge.worldbank.org/bitstream/handle/10986/10724/375490AFR0Grid1rastructure01PUBLIC1.pdf?sequence=1&isAllowed=y.

Shuping, S., & Kabane, S. (2017). Public-Private Partnerships: A Case Study of the Pelonomi and Universitas Hospital Co-location Project. Retrieved May 24, 2017, from www.hst.org.za/uploads/files/chap10_07.pdf.

South Africa Institute of International Affairs. (2008, April 24). Case Study: Private Prisons. Retrieved May 29, 2017, from https://saiia.org.za/news/case-study-private-prisons/.

Switala, H. (2017). Project Finance and Obtaining Sufficient Funding for the Successful Completion of Your Project. Retrieved May 9, 2017, from www.dbsa.org/EN/About-Us/Publications/Documents/Project%20finance%20and%20obtaining%20sufficient%20funding%20for%20the%20successful%20completion%20of%20your%20project.pdf.

The United Nations. (2017). Hospital Co-location, Bloemfontein, South Africa. Retrieved May 24, 2017, from http://academy.ssc.undp.org/GSSDAcademy/SIE/VOL15.aspx.

Van Hooft, A. (2017). South Africa: Draft Regulations on Mediation Rules for Investor-State Disputes. Retrieved May 11, 2017, from www.twobirds.com/en/news/articles/2017/global/africa-newsletter-feb/south-africa-draft-regulations-on-mediation-rules-for-investor-state-disputes.

Wentzel, W. (2015). Investing in South Africa: Charting the Legal Landscape with Webber Wentzel. Retrieved May 11, 2017, from www.investinginsouthafrica.co.za/downloads/en/Webber_Wentzel_Investing_in_South_Africa_complete.%20pdf.

The World Bank. (2015). Establishing Public Private Partnerships: Lessons Learned from the Global South. Retrieved from https://openknowledge.worldbank.org/bitstream/handle/10986/21309/936290WP0Box380ion000for0disclosure.pdf?sequence=1&isAllowed=y.

Yescombe, E.R. (2007). *Public-Private Partnerships: Principles of Policy and Finance*. Amsterdam, Netherlands: Elsevier.

Yescombe, E.R. (2017). *Public-Private Partnerships in Sub-Saharan Africa: Case Studies for Policymakers*. Dar es Salaam: Uongozi Institute.

Yong, H.K. (2010). *Public-Private Partnerships Policy and Practice: A Reference Guide*. London: Commonwealth Secretariat.

8 A comparative examination of the regulatory environment for public-private partnership for Brazil, India, Nigeria and South Africa

8.1 Introduction

The frameworks for the regulation and administration of PPP in Brazil, India, Nigeria and South Africa have been discussed in Chapters 4, 5, 6 and 7, respectively. In those chapters, this writer provides a descriptive analysis of the law and practice of PPP in the selected countries. The approach in this chapter is analytical, critical and prescriptive.

PPP in emerging economies like Brazil, India, Nigeria and South Africa is at an earlier stage of the PPP market maturity curve, compared to the more developed PPP markets of the United Kingdom, Australia and Canada.[1] In this early stage, countries establish a framework, set up institutions to oversee PPP administration and commence projects. The more-developed PPP markets have moved on to an advanced stage where they continue to develop hybrid models.[2] While there is a lot to learn from the more-developed PPP markets, the position of this author is that emerging economies can learn better by re-evaluating their own frameworks and practices as well as the experiences of their peers.

In the preceding chapters, it was established that the introduction of the PPP model of infrastructure delivery in Brazil, India, Nigeria and South Africa has created an opportunity for the private sector to participate not just in the funding of projects but also in the design, building, rehabilitating, management and operation of public facilities. This is not unconnected to the recognition that utilising the PPP model as a means of delivering various types of asset-based public services and infrastructure has become a global public management reform trend.[3] For the sake of emphasis, and as noted previously, even though the distinction appears to be marginal, service contracts entered into by the

1 Alpana Kateja, 'Building Infrastructure: Private Participation in Emerging Economies' (2012) 37 *Procedia – Social and Behavioural Sciences* 368–378, 371.

2 Ibid.

3 Ole Helby Petersen, 'Public-Private Partnerships as Converging or Diverging Trends in Public Management? A Comparative Analysis of PPP Policy and Regulation in Denmark and Ireland' (2011) 12(2) *International Management Review* 1.

private sector and the government pre-date PPP and must be clearly distinguished from the latter form of infrastructure procurement. PPP provides the option of the private sector taking charge and playing the lead role in a function that was traditionally undertaken by the government.

Brazil, India, Nigeria and South Africa present very interesting case studies as far as emerging economies are concerned. While Brazil is a leading economy in South America, India is the largest PPP market in the globe, Nigeria is the most populous country in Africa and South Africa has one of the most developed PPP markets in the world. A study of the impact PPP has had on these economies is therefore important. The success and advantages of adopting PPP in these four countries could be beneficial to other emerging economies. Worthy of note is that the PPP experience in all four countries is not the same. India has achieved good success in using PPP to bring home projects that will make lives easier for the local populace. Brazil has shown that PPP is not all about handing over public resources to the private sector without some form of public ownership. South Africa has shown that PPP can succeed with an enabled local financial market to support project companies. In Nigeria, while PPP has been used to achieve significant results, there is still a lot to learn.

In this chapter, indicators and drivers of success for PPP arrangement and execution are examined in the four jurisdictions. These indicators are referred to as critical success factors (CSFs) for PPPs. Since these parameters determine whether PPPs will succeed, it is important to analyse the structures in the four countries to determine how policymakers can best design a successful PPP regime in an emerging economy. As a corollary, this chapter examines the four jurisdictions for areas of similarity and divergence.

8.2 The establishment of an adequate legal framework

An independent, fair and efficient legal framework is a key to successful PPP project implementation. Due to the very complicated nature of PPP, it is important that the branch of the law that regulates it is clear to investors and practitioners.[4] Brazil, India, Nigeria and South Africa all operate with three different levels of governance, with different sets of laws, in many cases, operating at the national and sub-national levels. It is therefore important for investors or interested stakeholders to know which laws apply at each level.

In this section, the legal frameworks for the implementation of a PPP regime in the selected countries are briefly examined. Also highlighted are the similarities between the selected countries in relation to the establishment and administration of a PPP regime. To begin, this author believes that the best way to implement a PPP regime in any given jurisdiction is to take into consideration

4 Anthony Smith, 'Policy, Legal and Regulatory Frameworks for Successful PPPs' (2012) available at <www.unescap.org/sites/default/files/4a-Policy-legal-regulatory-frameworks.pdf> accessed 5 October 2017.

the administrative and legal traditions of that jurisdiction as well as the policy-maker's objective(s). There is thus no single best way of giving force to a PPP framework. This notwithstanding, countries with greater levels of PPP success can serve as examples for others. Conversely, even those with good results have lessons to be learned from their peers with less impressive records. While it is clear that the enabling of fair and transparent PPP legislation is a fundamental requirement for PPP success, common law countries like the United Kingdom and Australia have established their PPP regimes through policy statements and administrative documents without enacting a PPP law.[5] Yet, in other common-law countries, PPP laws have been passed, especially where they were required to override existing laws that would have restricted the implementation of PPP projects.[6] This author agrees with the position that in developing or emerging common-law economies, such as Nigeria, a PPP law is important to provide 'greater force, stability, transparency, and accountability.'[7]

8.2.1 Brazil's PPP framework

PPP was introduced to Brazil vide the passing of Law No. 11,097/2004, which essentially provided for the involvement of private investors in the management of public interest and services.[8] The aim of establishing the framework was so PPPs could be well structured with special guarantees granted by the public authority to the private sector.[9] This was so that the infrastructure deficit in the country could be bridged and for economic growth.[10] The 2004 PPP law set up a new type of arrangement that allowed for both sponsored and administrative PPPs as well as the construction, maintenance and running of public utilities and infrastructure services.[11]

The 11,079/2004 Act (the PPP law) established the procedure for the federal government, states, the Federal District of Brasilia and local municipalities.[12] It is worth noting that the framework in Brazil provides for means of dispute

5 APMG International, 'Establishing a PPP Framework' available at <https://ppp-certification.com/ppp-certification-guide/152-legal-and-administrative-approaches-establishing-ppp-frameworks> accessed 12 October 2017.

6 Ibid.

7 Ibid.

8 American Chamber of Commerce for Brazil, 'How to Understand Public-Private Partnership in Brazil' (2016) available at <https://ticaret.gov.tr/data/5b8a43345c7495406a226f96/9da1bbb8390e8484fe4aa7ae0167c027.pdf> accessed 31 December 2019.

9 Ibid.

10 IDB Invest, 'Brazil's Challenges and Opportunities inn Infrastructure: A Public-Private Perspective' (2019) 6.

11 BRICS, 'Good Practices on Public-Private Partnership Frameworks (2018 Update)' (2018) available at <www.treasury.gov.za/comm_media/press/2018/2018113001%202nd%20Publication%20of%20BRICS%20PPP%20Frameworks.pdf> accessed 31 December 2019.

12 Welber Barral and Adam Haas, 'Public-Private Partnership in Brazil' (2007) 41(3) *The International Lawyer* 960.

settlement other than by way of litigation. The Accounting Court in Brazil, which exists within the scope of the federal and state governments, is tasked with the function of reviewing public balances from the financial and budgetary perspective.[13] This includes PPP contracts.[14] The Accounting Court is not a part of the judiciary but is a bureau of legislative power.[15]

8.2.2 India's PPP framework

The Constitution of India divides legislative responsibility between the National Parliament and the State Legislatures. The 7th Schedule of the Constitution contains a Union List, a State List and a Concurrent List. While the National Parliament of India is competent to make laws on matters listed in the Union List, State Legislatures may make laws on matters enumerated in the State List. Both the National and State Legislatures are competent to make laws on matters in the Concurrent List.[16] The key areas included in the Union List are ports, airports, railways, national highways, inland water transport, telecommunications, oilfields and mineral resources.

In India, there is sectoral legislation at the national level that provides for a legal framework for infrastructure projects, including PPP. Similarly, at the subnational level, some states in the union, like Gujarat, Punjab, Karnataka and Andhra Pradesh, have developed a legal framework for private-sector participation in infrastructure in areas where the states have competent jurisdiction in accordance with the Concurrent Legislative List.[17]

While there is no specific law setting up PPP in India, there have been policies and directives put in place to ensure that there is an enabling environment for PPP practice in the country. In India, PPPs are considered contractual arrangements, and as such, existing legislation and other legal requirements must not prohibit the use of PPPs.[18] The general legal enablement for PPP cut across a wide range of areas, including:

1 The regulation of tariffs
2 Awarding the PPP
3 Dispute resolution
4 Rights to exclusive service
5 The protection of foreign-exchange convertibility, to enable the repatriation of proceeds from the project (in the case of foreign investment).

13 The Constitution of Brazil Art. 70, 71, II.
14 Ibid.
15 Welber Barral and Adam Haas, *op cit* (note 12) 970.
16 Ministry of Finance, Government of India, 'Overview of PPP in India' (2020) available at <www.pppinindia.gov.in/toolkit/ports/module1-oopi-india-lffpii.php?links=tables1> accessed 2 January 2020.
17 Ibid.
18 Ibid.

It is pertinent to note, however, that some states[19] in India have chosen to create their own specific PPP laws to allow for clarity and to provide investors some level of assurance.[20]

8.2.3 Nigeria's PPP framework

Before discussing the framework for PPP in Nigeria, it is important to describe its legislative structure. While the federal legislators make laws at the national level, state lawmakers exercise a similar function at the state level. The Federal Republic of Nigeria consists of a central federal government, a federal capital territory, 36 states and 768 local governments.[21] The 1999 Constitution of the Federal Republic of Nigeria (as amended) assigns responsibility (with certain restrictions) to each tier of government for infrastructural development within the territory over which it exercises control.[22] Following from this, there could be as many PPP laws and frameworks as there are different units of government. Indeed, some states – including Lagos, Rivers, Cross River, Niger, Ekiti and Ogun – have established PPP frameworks with PPP units to oversee the administration of PPP projects in those states.

The basis for the establishment of a PPP framework in Nigeria was the policy of the Nigerian government to shed some of its responsibility for infrastructure development by increasing private-sector participation in critical sectors of the Nigerian economy. This was to be done through the privatisation and commercialisation of previously state-owned monopolies, especially in the telecommunications and power sectors.[23] Prior to the passing of the Infrastructure Concession and Regulatory Commission Establishment (Etc.) Act (ICRCA) of 2005, the federal government of Nigeria pursued a privatisation programme through which some state-owned enterprises were privatised. This process, which involved numerous transactions, including concessions, was conducted through the Bureau of Public Enterprises (BPE) under the Public Enterprises (Privatisation and Commercialisation) Act No. 28 of 1999. It is important to note that public enterprises were privatised by the Nigerian government in order to advance development and consumer access in those sectors: the mismanagement and under-utilisation that had characterised those

19 Including Gujarat, Punjab and Andhra Pradesh.

20 Without a strong legal framework in place, investors either will not be interested in PPP projects or may elect to demand for government guarantees or other compensations for the perceived legal and regulatory risks.

21 It is important to note that under the ICRCA of 2005, any arm of the government, with the exclusion of local government, can initiate and manage PPPs. Each state exercises relative autonomy in the implementation of PPP projects, and, as such, each makes and enforces its own laws and regulations.

22 Sections 4, 5 and 8 of the 1999 Constitution of the Federal Republic of Nigeria (as amended). Also, Schedules 2 and 4 of the Constitution.

23 Fred Onuobia, Okechukwu J Okoro and Bibitayo Mimiko, 'Nigeria' in Bruno Werneck and Mário Saadi (eds.), *The Public-Private Partnership Law Review* (London: Business Law Research, 2017) 157.

establishments had resulted in a huge waste of material and human resources. Regrettably, however, the privatisation programme in Nigeria left much to be desired. The programme was marred by a number of things, including the limited technical and financial capacity of some of the private companies and allegations of corrupt practices.[24] Furthermore, some of the enterprises sold to the private sector have performed more poorly in the hands of the new managers than they did when they operated as government-owned enterprises.[25] For example, the Nigerian Telecommunications Limited (NITEL) performed poorly under new management before it became moribund. Onuoha, Okoro and Mimiko observe that the late 1990s and beyond witnessed the federal government of Nigeria allocating some of its responsibilities for infrastructural development to the private sector[26] but point out that in more recent years there has been a shift towards PPPs.[27] It is pertinent to note that a number of concessions were put in place under the Privatisation Act, even after the ICRCA had been passed.[28] Indeed, for a long time it appeared as if the federal government of Nigeria 'could choose randomly between either of the two laws setting up PPP transactions as public authorities vacillated between either of the laws for different transactions.'[29]

With endemic budget deficits, the inefficient management of large infrastructure projects and services by the public sector, and the apparent failure of the privatisation programme, the Nigerian government's desire for a dynamic partnership with the private sector necessitated a policy shift towards a PPP regime for the procurement of infrastructure.[30] In sum, the establishment of a legal framework for the administration of PPP in Nigeria is, first, not unconnected with the failure of the privatisation initiative. Second, it is driven by the need to make the process for PPP procurement uniform and clear; and third, it is occasioned by the necessity of providing some form of assurance to private-sector investors that PPP contracts are binding.

8.2.4 South Africa's PPP framework

The involvement of the private sector in the procurement of public infrastructure in South Africa was based on the recognition that the private sector is better suited to provide effective services and the opportunity to introduce private capital and expertise into state enterprises.[31] The introduction of a PPP legal

24 Ibid 792.
25 Ibid.
26 Ibid.
27 Ibid 157.
28 George Nwangwu, *Public Private Partnership in Nigeria* (London: Palgrave Macmillan, 2016) 28.
29 Ibid.
30 Fred Onuoha, Okechukwu J Okoroand Bibitayo Mimiko, *op cit* (note 23) 157.
31 Axis Consulting, 'PPP Country Paper: South Africa' (2013) 11 available at <www.sadcpppnetwork.org/wp-content/uploads/2015/02/south_africa_27012014.pdf> accessed 13 October 2017.

framework hinged on the need to create an environment conducive to PPP success in the country.

Having established the feasibility of the PPP model of procurement, in April 1997, the South African Cabinet approved the appointment of an inter-departmental taskforce to advance both legislation and policy to facilitate the adoption of a PPP framework. Subsequently, a PPP Unit was set up under the National Treasury. Following this, a strategic framework for PPPs was endorsed in December 1999, while the National Treasury issued regulations for PPPs in April 2000.[32]

Given South Africa's history and the importance of public procurement to the economic well-being of its citizens, all forms of procurement in the Republic, including PPP, are required to conform with accepted principles of fairness.[33] This principle of fairness is boldly encapsulated in the preamble to the 1996 Constitution of the Republic of South Africa. While there is undoubtedly a need to heal the injustices of the past, it is the respectful opinion of this writer that the procurement of infrastructure by the private sector should not be considered an area where there should be questions as to whether certain groups in the community are represented. Such considerations must only apply when they relate to traditional public procurement. The reason for this submission is that the requirement to be fair to all communities has the tendency to stifle private-sector competition. Again, private-sector consortia that feel obliged to meet such targets often resort to malpractices to conform to their burdensome requirements.

8.2.5 Similarities in the frameworks of the selected countries

In this subsection, the focus is on the similarities in the PPP frameworks of the selected countries. The key points for discussion are the tiers of government, the establishment of regulatory units for PPP, the standards required for PPP procurement, the emphasis on value for money as a key driver for PPP and advancing PPP as a tool for development.

Brazil, India, Nigeria and South Africa all have governments constituted at the national, provincial and local spheres that are distinctive yet interdependent and interrelated. Brazil is made up of the union, states, the Federal District and counties.[34] India is made up of the union, the territories of the states and union territories specified in the First Schedule.[35] Nigeria is made up of the

32 Ibid.

33 S. 217(1) of the Constitution of the Republic of South Africa states that 'When an organ of state contracts for goods or services, it must do so in accordance with a system which is fair, equitable, transparent, competitive and cost-effective.'

34 Art. 20 of the Constitution of Brazil.

35 S. 1(1) of the Constitution of India.

federal government, the states and 774 local government areas.[36] The Republic of South Africa is made up of nine provinces,[37] but the local sphere of government in South Africa is the municipal government.[38]

In the selected countries for this study, value for money (VfM) is regarded as a key driver to support the PPP initiative of the public sector and has been introduced as follows:

> Value for Money is defined as the optimum combination of whole-of -life costs and quality (or fitness for purpose) of the goods or services to meet the user's requirement. VfM is not the choice of goods and services based on the lowest cost bid. To undertake a well-managed procurement, it is necessary to consider upfront, and at the earliest stage of procurement, what the key drivers of VfM in the procurement process will be.[39]

The gist of this definition is that in determining the value pursuing a PPP project, the public sector must make sure to consider the costs and savings over the life of the project. Although many PPP projects are successful, there are some unsatisfying results that have been shown to result from a lack of understanding of the mechanisms to achieve VfM.[40] In simple terms, VfM may be explained as follows:

> To decide whether or not to procure infrastructure through a normal tender process or through a PPP, a value-for-money test needs to be applied. How much will it cost for the institution to provide infrastructure and services itself compared to the costs of providing the same infrastructure and services through a PPP? If the comparison shows that a PPP is more cost-effective, the difference in cost between the two scenarios is known as value for money. If the value-for-money test shows that the traditional procurement method is more cost-effective, the PPP option will be pursued.[41]

Following this, the main rationale for using PPP as a procurement model is that they can deliver better VfM than traditional procurement. In Brazil, the execution of a PPP agreement must be preceded by a competitive bidding

36 S. 2(2) and S. 3 of the Constitution of Nigeria.

37 S. 103(1) of the 1996 Constitution of the Republic of South Africa (as amended). The provinces are Eastern Cape Free State, Gauteng, KwaZulu-Natal, Limpopo, Mpumalanga, Northern Cape, North West and Western Cape.

38 S. 151(1) of the 1996 Constitution of the Republic of South Africa (as amended).

39 HM Treasury, *Value for Money Assessment Guidance* (London: HM Treasury, 2006).

40 Nannan Wang, Xiaoyan Chen and Guobin Wu, 'Public Private Partnership, a Value for Money Solution for Clean Coal District Heating Operations' (2019) *Sustainability*. DOI: 10.3390su11082386.

41 National Treasury PPP Unit, *Introducing Public Private Partnerships in South Africa* (Pretoria: National Treasury, 2007) 6.

process and the VfM test is critical in determining the choice of PPP model for the procurement of any given project.[42] Under the Indian framework, the government seeks to increase VfM through mandatory requirements on environmental and social safeguards.[43] It is safe to say therefore that the VfM standards are taken to a higher level to ensure that the effect of using the PPP model is considered alongside other factors besides the monetary valuation. In the PPP life cycle for Nigeria, it is critical at the development phase of any project to determine that PPP is the right approach to be adopted in place of traditional procurement. Thus, a VfM analysis is usually undertaken at that stage.[44] In South Africa, there is a tripartite test for determining whether a project should be executed using the PPP model. The tests are:

1 Is substantial technical, operational and financial risk transferred to the private party?
2 Can the institution afford the envisaged fee?
3 Is it a VfM solution?[45]

It follows therefore that VfM considerations are key for determining the choice of PPP for the procurement of public-infrastructure projects in the selected countries. The vexed question, however, is how can the governments of these countries accurately and effectively determine that a project has passed the VfM test? It is important that emerging markets critically examine their methodologies for determining VfM, as there may be costs associated with a project that are not covered by the PPP process in itself[46] – for example, the cost of land – but which will ultimately contribute to the overall cost of the project. In this sense, it is appropriate to consider, first, the overall VfM of the project and, second, the VfM of the PPP contract itself.[47]

In the four different jurisdictions studied in this book, there are similar arguments in support for the use of the PPP model of procurement. Generally, governments all over the world, and especially in emerging economies, are

42 Thiago Fernandes Moreira and Thiago Luís Sombra, 'Brazil' (2019) available at <https://thelawreviews.co.uk/edition/the-public-private-partnership-law-review-edition-5/1189691/brazil> accessed 28 March 2020.

43 IISD, *Value for Money in Infrastructure Procurement: The Cost and Benefits of Environmental and Social Safeguards in India* (Manitoba: The International Institute for Sustainable Development, 2014) 5.

44 Chidi Izuwah, 'Financing Nigeria's Infrastructure: The PPP Imperative' (2017) available at <www.globalinfrafacility.org/sites/gif/files/GIF%20AC%20Meeting%20-%20Big%20Movers%20Panel%20-%20Nigeria.pdf> accessed 28 March 2020.

45 National Treasury PPP Unit, *op cit* (note 42) 13.

46 PPIAF, 'Public Private Partnership: Value for Money and the Public Private Partnership Procurement Process' (2007) available at <https://ppiaf.org/sites/ppiaf.org/files/documents/toolkits/highwaystoolkit/6/bibliography/pdf/value_for_money_and_the_public_private_partnership_procurement_process.pdf> accessed 28 March 2020.

47 Ibid.

increasingly adopting the PPP model of infrastructure procurement.[48] In Brazil, the choice of PPP as an alternative to traditional procurement is occasioned by the need to 'attract private investment in infrastructure projects . . . in the following areas: water and sewage, health and hospitals, administrative facilities and logistics, including roads, urban mobility, [and] underground transportation'[49] The Indian government adopted PPP in order to address the shortage in public infrastructure as well as the need for private investment to 'bolster the economy.'[50] PPP in Nigeria is the result of a need to ensure the participation of the private sector in financing the construction, development, operation, or maintenance of infrastructure development projects of the federal government through concession or contractual arrangements.[51] The South African authorities adopted the PPP method in order to facilitate rapid infrastructure delivery, leverage on private-sector skills and to encourage the injection of private-sector capital, among others.[52]

8.2.6 Dissimilarities in the frameworks of the selected countries

Even though the governments of the selected countries intend to achieve similar objectives using the PPP model of procurement for public-infrastructure needs, there are marked differences in the way that the governments of the various countries have set about to achieve their similar objective. The aim of this analysis is to look at these differences and consider how best emerging economies can learn from one another as opposed to the practice of 'borrowing' laws and practices from developed economies, which has been the bane of developing economies in the past. Furthermore, while successes in other jurisdictions can serve as a guide, the wholesale 'importation' of a highly successful framework without adjusting it to the local situation courts failure from the start.[53] For example, as Lee notes, several developing countries, including Vietnam, Cambodia, Myanmar and Bangladesh, have expressed the desire to adopt certain Korean laws.[54]

48 Robert Osei-Kyei, Dansoh Ayirebi and JK Ofori-Kuragu, 'Reasons for Adopting Public-Private Partnership (PPP) for Construction Projects in Ghana' (2014) 14(4) *International Journal of Construction Management* 227–238.

49 Bruno Werneck and Mário Saadi, 'Brazil' in Bruno Werneck and Mário Saadi (eds.), *The Public-Private Partnership Law Review*, 3rd Ed. (London: Law Business Research Ltd, 2017) 33.

50 Sunil Seth and Vasanth Rajaskekaran, 'India' in Bruno Werneck and Mário Saadi (eds.), *The Public-Private Partnership Law Review*, 3rd Ed. (London: Law Business Research Ltd, 2017) 112.

51 Fred Onuoha, Okechukwu J Okoro and Bibitayo Mimiko, 'Nigeria' in Bruno Werneck and Mário Saadi (eds.), *The Public-Private Partnership Law Review*, 3rd Ed. (London: Law Business Research Ltd, 2017) 157.

52 National Treasury PPP Unit, *op cit* (note 42) 12.

53 YS Lee, 'General Theory of Law and Development' (2017) 50(3) *Cornell International Law Journal* 433.

54 Ibid.

While Brazil, India and Nigeria are all federations with a federal government and federating states, South Africa is not. Although South Africa's governing structures provide the formal appearances of a federation, the country is indeed more unitary than federal in its day-to-day operations. Thus, while federating states in Brazil, for example, may make their own PPP laws and set up their own PPP units, this is not so in South Africa as the same PPP Unit housed in the Treasury administers all PPP projects in the entire country. This is one area of marked difference. The argument in support of having one PPP unit in charge of the entire country may be that it allows for specialisation and maintenance of the same standards nation-wide. On the other hand, having PPP units in the various states in a country may encourage the growth of PPP expertise nationwide. What is important is that the PPP units function effectively.

Whereas Brazil and Nigeria have specialised PPP laws, India does not. In place of a PPP legislation, India has the 2011 Department of Economic Affairs (DEA) Published Guidelines for PPP. South Africa, on its part, does not have dedicated PPP legislation. Instead, the country's PPP projects are administered mostly via Treasury Regulation 16 and some uniformed guidelines. Again, what is important is for clarity in the process and strict compliance to the rules or guidelines set for PPP projects in the country. However, in a jurisdiction such as Nigeria, where there is a web of laws that overlap in so far as public procurement is concerned, the need to have clear PPP legislation indicating which law should prevail in the PPP process cannot be overemphasised.

Whereas the frameworks in Brazil, India and South Africa allow for the private finance initiative (PFI) type of PPP, it is safe to assume that, at least at the federal level in Nigeria, no PFI arrangement can be made under the substantive PPP law in the country. What this means is that, as far as the federal government of Nigeria is concerned, only a concession (i.e. an arrangement in which private citizens pay to use public facilities) can be implemented. Therefore, a project that is only suitable for PFI arrangements, such as the construction or rehabilitation of libraries or prisons, cannot be arranged between the federal government and the private sector as a PPP.

Furthermore, while Brazil, India and Nigeria have compact institutional frameworks for PPP, Nigeria operates a rather complex institutional framework for PPP. For example, the same National Treasury provides the various treasury approvals for both the national and provincial PPP projects in South Africa. Where there is a need to offer guarantees or indemnities, the Ministry of Finance is required to authorise any such transaction.[55] By implication, if there is no need for the issue of guarantee or indemnity by the public authority, then there is no need for any such approval by the Ministry of Finance. This arrangement helps to expedite projects, unlike the Nigerian case where all national PPP projects must, at one point or another, have the approval of the Federal Ministry of Finance.

55 S. 66 of the Public Finance Management Act of 1999.

Brazil, unlike the other countries studied, has enabled the participation of the public sector in the ownership of project companies. This innovation is significant and could be studied for implementation in other emerging economies. The rationale for this is that with the public sector participating in the ownership structure of project companies, the fear that PPP is a means to merely transfer the government's responsibility will be assuaged. The effect of this is less antagonism of PPP projects by some sections of the public. It is argued that Brazil's dynamism and forward-thinking characteristics have also provided investors with new opportunities to do business.[56]

8.3 Innovations and good practice

In this section, the discussion focuses on the various initiatives adopted by the four countries studied to improve on their PPP processes and to attract investors. The aim here is to provide examples that can be adopted by other emerging economies.

8.3.1 Brazil

Brazil has been able to offer local-currency financing options to check currency exchange risks. This is one area that emerging economies must improve upon in order to ensure successful PPP outcomes. The reliance on foreign finance for the private funding of private infrastructure has been a challenge for emerging economies. Thus, innovation by policymakers in Brazil is commendable. As such, other developing economies must seek ways to unlock domestic funding for their PPPs

Further, the ownership structure of the project company with regard to some projects in Brazil that allow for public-sector participation is worth emu lating by other developing economies. For example, in the Rio de Janeiro Airport Project Company, the Brazilian government maintains a 49 per cent stake in the ownership structure of the company.

Some mechanisms have been introduced by law to ensure PPP success in Brazil. These come in the form of state guarantees.[57] The payment obligations undertaken by the government may be guaranteed by any of the following forms:

1 The pledge of revenues;
2 The creation or use of special funds contemplated by law;
3 The purchase of guarantees from insurance companies that are not under public control;

56 World Finance, 'Navigating Public Private Partnerships in Brazil' (2014) available at <www.worldfinance.com/infrastructure-investment/project-finance/navigating-public-private-partnerships-in-brazil> accessed 4 July 2017.

57 Thiago Fernandes Moreira and Thiago Luís Sombra, *op cit* (note 43).

4 Guarantees by international organisations or financial institutions not controlled by any government authority; or
5 Guarantees by guarantor funds or state-owned companies created especially for that purpose.

8.3.2 India

India offers a structure that allows for the streamlining of the procedures for systematic appraisal and approval of projects. This helps to remove bottlenecks that usually characterise procurement in developing economies. The Government of India maintains a simple structure for administering PPP, including:

1 Setting up the PPP Appraisal Committee (PPPAC) to simplify the appraisal process and to eliminate administrative hurdles;
2 Setting up the India Infrastructure Project Development Fund (IIPDF) for extending financial assistance in infrastructure projects;
3 Formulating the viability gap fund (VGF) for making infrastructure projects commercially viable;
4 Setting up institutions, such as the Infrastructure Finance Company Limited, to provide long-term financial support and act as a catalyst in the stream; and
5 Standardise bidding and contractual documents, such as requests for qualification (RFQs), requests for proposal (RFPs) and model concession agreements (MCAs), for making the process swift.

It is important that developing economies adopt measures such as these to make the PPP process seamless and attractive. This is more so as one of the banes of progress in developing economies is the issue of administrative bottlenecks.

8.3.3 Nigeria

Even though the government of Nigeria has been slow in terms of law reforms, there have been several policy changes to make PPP attractive to the private sector and to unbundle local finance for PPP. One of the areas that may ensure the attraction of local finance for PPP is the pension market in Nigeria. The pension funds contributed under the Nigerian Pension Scheme could potentially fund several people-oriented public-infrastructure projects in the country.

Despite the challenges that followed the execution of the Lekki-Epe Concession Toll Road PPP project, which has now been bought back by the Lagos State Government,[58] the arrangement of the concession was considered world class as the project attracted various international awards, including the *Africa*

58 The failure of the project was due to political reasons and a lack of consultation with community stakeholders at the initial stage of the project.

Investor 2008 Transport Deal of the Year, the Euromoney International 2008 Africa PPP of the Year and the Reuters 2008 African Infrastructure Deal of the Year.[59]

The setting up of some local infrastructure funds by asset-management firms in Nigeria to provide private-sector capital for public infrastructure is a plus and worthy of emulation by other developing economies. For example, the ARM-Harith Infrastructure Fund is a pioneering, indigenously developed infrastructure fund with over US$250 million being managed by the fund managers.[60] Another example is the Infracredit Fund, which is a US$50 million callable funding facility for the first Nigerian-based credit guarantor focused on credit-enhancing infrastructure bonds to target pension-fund investors in the country.[61] These funds, which have been approved by the Securities and Exchange Commission (SEC), will help to augment other sources of domestic funding for private infrastructure in the country. The SEC has set up guidelines and rules for the establishment and management of infrastructure funds in the country. The effect of this is to create room for more private-sector funds for infrastructure. Considering that Nigeria, as well as other developing economies, has a problem of an undeveloped local capital market, the setting up of infrastructure funds is an opportunity to create long-term funding for domestic infrastructure development.

8.3.4 South Africa

While there may be no perfect PPP framework anywhere in the world, some are better than others, and South Africa's PPP structure and process can serve as a template for other developing economies. The country's practice of PPP dates to 1994, and with many successes in different sectors, including toll roads, ports, prisons, water supply, hospitals and tourism, there is much that other emerging economies can learn from South Africa. Although it is argued that there is still a shortage of skilled personnel in government departments and provinces to match the pace at which the government of South Africa can roll out PPPs,[62] compared to public-service staffing size elsewhere in Africa, the staffing of the unit is moderate.

The institutional framework for PPP in South Africa is clear-cut. A prospective investor, or anyone interested in the framework for PPP in South Africa, is not left confused about the number of agencies that are to be dealt with

59 Lekki Concession Company Ltd, 'International Awards' (2019) available at <www.lcc.com.ng/> accessed 20 March 2020.

60 ARM-Harrith, 'More About Us' (2014) available at <http://armharith.com.ng/> accessed 20 March 2020.

61 Infracredit, 'Portfolio' (2020) available at <https://guarantco.com/portfolio/infracredit/> accessed 20 March 2020.

62 Philippe Burger, 'The Dedicated PPP Unit of the South African National Treasury' (2014) available at <www.oecd.org/mena/governance/37147218.pdf> accessed 31 October 2017.

when negotiating or executing a PPP project. Furthermore, the country has a well-developed financial market, compared to other emerging economies. The access to credit in South Africa places it ahead of its peers.

There is also a strong commitment on the part of the political class in South Africa to support PPP. For example, the N4 toll road and the Gautrain project received tremendous public-sector support. There are also several projects that have outlived the administrations that started them. This is a rare attribute for developing economies, in Africa especially.[63]

Worthy of mention is the protection for investors' and lenders' funds. This is at the core of South Africa's PPP framework. A watertight project preparation process is required to prove the merit of the project to potential funders.[64] Other critical components of the feasibility study under Module 4 of the PPP Manual include project due diligence, value assessment, economic valuation and a procurement plan. The procedure involves the engagement of advisors on behalf of the sponsors and the lenders to provide advice on technical, market, financial, legal and incidental matters.[65] This is fundamental to achieving financial closure for the project. South Africa is ranked 10th out of 189 countries for good practice in protecting investors in business.[66] The funding of specific projects in South African currency offers protection against currency-fluctuation risk. For example, the Sasol Natural Gas project is an R8.6 billion project aimed at developing the gas fields and processing facility in Mozambique and operating a gas pipeline from the processing plant to facilities in South Africa.[67]

The 1996 Constitution of the Republic of South Africa states that when an organ of state in the national, provincial or local sphere of government or other institution identified in the national legislation contracts for goods or services, it must do so in accordance with a system that is fair, equitable, transparent and cost-effective.[68] It follows that South African law emphasises transparency and accountability, which are key to ensuring that funds are protected and not wasted. This philosophy happens to be the driving force behind the Public Finance Management Act and the Municipal Finance Management Act. Examples abound in South Africa of projects structured in such a way as

63 For example, see Ed Stoddard and TJ Strydom, 'South Africa's Stock Market Defies Recession, Scales Record Highs' *Reuters Business News*, 31 July 2017.

64 See National Treasury PPP Unit, *PPP Project Cycle: Reflecting Treasury Regulation 16 to the Public Finance Management Act, 1999 National Treasury PPP Manual: Module 1* (Pretoria: National Treasury PPP Unit, 1999).

65 Helge Switala, 'Project Finance and Obtaining Sufficient Funding for the Successful Completion of your Project' a presentation by the Project Manager, Development Bank of South Africa available at <www.dbsa.org/EN/About- Us/Publications/Documents/Project%20finance%20and%20obtaining%20sufficient%20funding%20for%20the %20successful%20completion%20of%20your%20project.pdf> accessed 9 May 2017.

66 The World Bank, *Doing Business Report* (Washington DC, The World Bank 2014).

67 Helge Switala, *op cit* (note 66).

68 Gazette No. 39514 of 15 December 2015.

to ensure that there are sufficient revenue streams accruing in the short to long term. The aim is to optimise the performance of the PPP and encourage private participation. Two examples are worth mentioning here. The City of Johannesburg contracted with a consortium of international operators led by Suez. The project was structured in such a way that Johannesburg Water purchased some biogas-fuelled generators, and the contractor invested in other required capital infrastructure. The contract recovered its cost from the sale of bio-gas generated from the operations.[69] A second example is the city of Tshwane's PPP with Magalies Water Board, ABSA Bank and Bigen Africa. The arrangement was structured to ensure sustainable revenue flows to Tshwane as the city was the main beneficiary of the R500 million project.[70] The protection of investments is vital to the sustainability of PPP arrangements in any economy. This is the spirit behind the passing into law of the Protection of Investment Act 22 of 2015. The Act was passed to replace the bilateral investment treaties (BITs) with European countries and to make direct investment in the country attractive to foreign investors.[71]

The Protection of Investment Act No. 22 of 2015 defines an investor as 'an enterprise making an investment in the Republic of regardless of nationality.'[72] It follows that the protection afforded indigenous investors will be extended to foreign investors as well. The purpose of the Act is threefold: first, to protect investment in accordance with and subject to the Constitution; secondly, to affirm the Republic's sovereign right to regulate investments in the public interest and thirdly, to confirm the Bill of Rights in the Constitution and the laws that apply to all investors and their investments in the Republic.[73] The Act stipulates that foreign investors must not be discriminated against.[74] The Republic must accord foreign investors and their investments a level of physical security equivalent to that enjoyed by domestic investors, in accordance with minimum standards of customary international law.[75] Investors have the right to property in consonance with Section 25 of the Constitution of South Africa.[76] Furthermore, the Act provides that a foreign investor may, in respect of an investment, repatriate funds subject to taxation and other applicable legislation.[77]

69 Cornelius Ruiters and Maselaganye P Matji, 'Public Private Partnership Conceptual Framework and Models for the Funding and Financing of Water Services Infrastructure in Municipalities from Selected Provinces in South Africa' (2016) 42(2) *Water SA*. DOI: 10.4314/wsa.v412i2.13.

70 Ibid.

71 In 2012, South Africa terminated its BITs with European countries such as Denmark, Spain, Germany, Belgium, Luxembourg, Switzerland and Holland. It maintained the BITs with Russia and China.

72 S. 1 of the Protection of Investment Act of 2015.

73 S. 4 of the Protection of Investment Act of 2015.

74 S. 5 of the Protection of Investment Act of 2015.

75 S. 9 of the Protection of Investment Act of 2015.

76 S. 10 of the Protection of Investment Act of 2015.

77 S. 11 of the Protection of Investment Act of 2015.

Regarding disputes, when an investor has a dispute in respecttof action taken by the government, the action having affected an investment of said investor, the investor may within six months of becoming aware of the dispute request the Department to facilitate its resolution by appointing a mediator.[78] A foreign investor is not precluded from approaching any competent court, independent tribunal or statutory body within South Africa for the resolution of the dispute. When all domestic remedies have been exhausted and the dispute persists, the South African government may consent to international arbitration, with such arbitration conducted between South Africa and the home state of the foreign investor. Thus, an investor who feels wronged by an action of the South African government or any of its agencies is clearly empowered by the law to seek redress. It is submitted, however, that what the South African government is giving with the right hand, it seeks to take away with the left, through the provision that the state must only consent to arbitration when domestic remedies have been exhausted and international arbitration becomes the option.

8.4 Weaknesses of the frameworks in the selected jurisdictions

The weaknesses of the jurisdictions studied can serve as a lesson for their contemporaries. A study of these areas of deficiencies can provide opportunities for improvements. Having already noted the areas where the selected countries have their strong points, this study next deals with areas of weaknesses.

8.4.1 Brazil

The law for PPP in Brazil is now little over a decade and has been tested in the courts.[79] The lack of a dedicated single agency to administer PPP at the federal level needs to be reconsidered. What is obtainable is that there are several agencies tasked with administering different aspects of the country's PPP programme. These agencies include the Ministry of Finance, the Ministry of Planning, Budget and Management, the National Treasury Secretariat and the Partnership Steering Committee. The impact of this is that there is no single agency that takes direct ownership of the PPP process.

Some of the challenges faced in the PPP programme in Brazil are due to its mirroring of the UK's framework for PPP.[80] The UK experience was used

78 S. 13 of the Protection of Investment Act of 2015.

79 Thomas Benes Felsberg, Maria da Graca de Brito Vianna Pedretti, Andrea Machado Costa and Fabrizio de Oliveira Sasdelli, 'Brazil' in Jeffrey Delmon and Victoria Rigby Delmon (eds.), *International Project Finance and PPP: A Legal Guide to Key Growth Markets* (Hoevelaken: Kluwer Law International, 2010) 20.

80 Cesar Queiroz and Gaston Astensiano, 'An Overview of the Brazilian PP Experience form a Stakeholders' Viewpoint' (2014) available at <https://publications.iadb.org/publications/english/document/An-Overview-of-the-Brazilian-PPP-Experience-from-a-Stakeholders-Viewpoint.pdf> accessed 20 March 2020.

a reference point for the establishment of the Brazilian framework.[81] Hence, several projects in Brazil were arranged as PFIs. Given the fact that the Brazilian environment is different from that of the UK, several issues have arisen as these projects mostly require payments by the public authority for the use of facilities by citizens, hence the need for a review of the PPP legal framework in Brazil.

Another area of weakness in the Brazilian PPP market is the lack of flow of information to external stakeholders.[82] There is a need to maintain a steady flow of communication, such as a regular update of websites. In a study conducted in Brazil, some respondents identified, among others, inadequate PPP staff training as problem for successful PPP arrangements in the country.[83]

8.4.2 India

Despite being the largest PPP market in the world, India still struggles with a number of issues. One is a lack of flexibility in contractual arrangements.[84] There have been cases of former infrastructure powerhouses weighed down by a huge debt profile and, as a result, can no longer compete in the market.[85]

Another clog in the wheel of progress of the PPP environment in India is the vexed issue of failure to understand the meaning of 'partnership' in PPP.[86] This results in poor risk sharing and in inappropriate business models.[87] Other significant issues bedevilling the PPP framework in India include a poor regulatory environment, lack of comprehensive data, lack of institutional capacity to undertake large and complex projects and a lack of domestic funding for projects.[88]

8.4.3 Nigeria

Nigeria's PPP framework is weighed down by several challenges. Chief of the issues in Nigeria is a not-so-clear framework. The current PPP law does not provide for much except for information regarding the creation of the Infrastructure Concession Regulatory Commission (ICRC), which is the country's

81 Ibid.

82 Ibid.

83 Ibid.

84 Shantanu Nadan Sharma, 'What Ails India's PPP Model and Why it Doesn't Bode Well for Modi Government's Infrastructure Push' *The Economic Times*, 5 July 2015 available at <https://economictimes.indiatimes.com/news/economy/infrastructure/what-ails-indias-ppp-model-and-why-it-doesnt-bode-well-for-modi-governments-infrastructure-push/articleshow/47940200.cms?from=mdr> accessed 19 March 2020.

85 Ibid.

86 M Shivalingegowda and MC Girisha, 'Challenges for Public Private Partnership in India' (2019) available at <www.researchgate.net/publication/330506526_CHALLENGES_FOR_PUBLIC_PRIVATE_PARTNERSHIP_IN_INDIA_final> accessed 20 March 2020.

87 Ibid.

88 Ibid.

PPP unit. There is a web of laws that overlap and makes it difficult for an investor to get a full grasp of the PPP process in the country.

Sourcing finance for PPP projects in Nigeria is another area of major concern. In recent years, the Nigerian government attempted to arrange a PPP deal for a new national carrier for the country. It was shocking that no investor indicated interest in the project. This may be a result of a distrust of the Nigerian government and the inability of the political class in the country to show the will to allow PPP projects to succeed.

Several cases of unilateral cancellations of projects and failure to respect court orders portray the government in Nigeria as lacking any regard for the rule of law. The protracted court cases between Bi-Courtney Aviation Services Limited and the Federal Airports Authority of Nigeria as well as the cancellation of the Lagos Ibadan Expressway Project by the federal government of Nigeria are very good examples.

8.4.4 South Africa

Despite South Africa's PPP successes, there have been errors and pitfalls that could have been avoided. Other emerging economies studying the framework in South Africa and wishing to borrow from it may be able to learn from these.

South African PPP rules require that before a project is arranged as a PPP, the institution sponsoring the project must register the project with the relevant treasury for a project officer and a transaction advisor to be appointed.[89] What the rule omits to state is that public consultation is fundamental. This omission in the rules could lead to avoidable challenges. For instance, Stephen criticises the Gautrain Rapid Rail Link project for insufficient public consultation and legislative debate before the project was approved and put to tender.[90] Although the Gautrain project was a success, the need to consult with stakeholders before embarking on PPP projects is essential. Fombad has argued that a lack of transparency could negatively affect PPPs in South Africa, referring to superficial and inconsistent disclosure of PPP information online via the PPP Quarterly.[91] The argument here is that with little information being made available to the public, the principle of transparency is compromised. No matter how successful a project is, it often remains tainted where there are questions of ethical and procedural irregularity in concluding the contract and executing the project.

This author is of the firm belief that insisting on a Black Economic Empowerment (BEE) Code for PPP, as is currently the case in South Africa is an extreme burden at this emerging stage of PPP in the country. PPP is a partnership between the public and private sectors. Putting a burden on the private

89 See the 2004 PPP Manual.

90 J Stephen, 'Fears Gautrain Will Be a Large, Expensive White Elephant' *The Star*, 9 November 2005.

91 Madeleine C Fombad, 'Accountability Challenges in Public-Private Partnerships from a South African Perspective' (2013) 7(1) *African Journal of Business Ethics* 11.

party to deal with domestic inequality issues could deter foreign direct interest or even encourage corrupt practices. Companies who have the experience and wherewithal to promote and execute flawless projects may find it difficult to meet the BEE targets and be ruled out of the reckoning in favour of less-experienced sponsors who may just superficially appear to be BEE-compliant. It is pertinent that the government deal with issues of inequality in such a way as not to deter legitimate private-sector ventures, which must be allowed to manage their businesses as best as they can. PPPs are very complex arrangements, and anything that can make a PPP arrangement less complex should be welcomed.

8.5 Conclusion

This chapter discussed comparatively the law and practice of PPP in the selected countries of the study, namely, Brazil, India, Nigeria and South Africa, with the aim of showing how emerging economies can learn from their peers in order to improve on their own PPP markets. The PPP frameworks were briefly examined with a dissection of the areas of similarities and divergence in the respective PPP systems.

The areas of strength and weakness in the various systems were also highlighted in the chapter. While Brazil has introduced an opportunity for the public to participate in the ownership structure of project companies and has enabled state-issued guarantees for projects, India fancies a more simplified PPP process with less administrative bottlenecks. On its part, Nigeria hopes to explore the potentials of huge contributions from pension funds and local infrastructure funds to unlock her domestic financial market. In the case of South Africa, its framework to protect investors' and lenders' funds make the PPP framework of the country's PPP market standout among peers. There are significant areas for improvement in all the selected countries studied. The lessons learnt can serve as a turning point for PPP practice in those countries and other emerging economies.

References

American Chamber of Commerce for Brazil. (2016). How to Understand Public-Private Partnership in Brazil. Retrieved December 31, 2019, from https://ticaret.gov.tr/data/5b8a43345c7495406a226f96/9da1bbb8390e8484fe4aa7ae0167c027.pdf.

APMG International. (2017). Establishing a PPP Framework. Retrieved October 12, 2017, from https://ppp-certification.com/ppp-certification-guide/152-legal-and-administrative-approaches-establishing-ppp-frameworks.

ARM HArrith. (2014, March 31). Welcome to ARM-Harith. Retrieved March 20, 2020, from https://armharith.com.ng.

Axis Consulting. (2013). PPP Country Paper: South Africa. Retrieved from www.sadcpppnetwork.org/wp-content/uploads/2015/02/south_africa_27012014.pdf.

BRICS. (2018). Good Practices on Public-Private Partnership Frameworks. Retrieved December 31, 2019, from www.treasury.gov.za/comm_media/press/2018/2018113001%202nd%20Publication%20of%20BRICS%20PPP%20Frameworks.pdf.

Burger, P. (2014). The Dedicated PPP Unit of the South African National Treasury. Retrieved October 31, 2017, from www.oecd.org/mena/governance/37147218.pdf.

Felsberg, T.B., & Pedretti, M.B. (2010). Brazil. In J. Delmon & V.R. Delmon (Eds.), *International Project Finance and PPPs: A Legal Guide to Key Growth Markets* (p. 20). Hoevelake: Kluwer Law International.

Fombad, M.C. (2014). Accountability Challenges in Public – Private Partnerships from a South African Perspective. *African Journal of Business Ethics*, 7(1). doi:10.15249/7-1-33.

IDB Invest. (2019). *Brazil's Challenges and Opportunities inn Infrastructure: A Public-Private Perspective*. Washington, DC: Author.

Infracredit. (2020). Portfolio. Retrieved March 20, 2020, from https://guarantco.com/portfolio/infracredit/.

The International Institute for Sustainable Development. (2014). *Value for Money in Infrastructure Procurement: The Cost and Benefits of Environmental and Social Safeguards in India*. Manitoba: Author.

Izuwa, C. (2017). Financing Nigeria's Infrastructure: The PPP Imperative. Retrieved March 28, 2020, from www.globalinfrafacility.org/sites/gif/files/GIF%20AC%20Meeting%20-%20Big%20Movers%20Panel%20-%20Nigeria.pdf.

Kateja, A. (2012). Building Infrastructure: Private Participation in Emerging Economies. *Procedia – Social and Behavioral Sciences*, *37*, 368–378. doi:10.1016/j.sbspro.2012.03.302.

Lee, Y. (2018). General Theory of Law and Development. *Law and Development*, *50*(3), 38–62. doi:10.4324/9781315150253-3.

Lekki Concession Company Ltd. (2019). International Awards. Retrieved March 20, 2020, from www.lcc.com.ng/.

Ministry of Finance, Government of India. (2020). Overview of PPP in India. Retrieved January 2, 2020, from www.pppinindia.gov.in/toolkit/ports/module1-oopi-india-lffpii.php?links=tables1.

National Treasury Unit. (1999). *PPP Project Cycle: Reflecting Treasury Regulation 16 to the Public Finance Management Act, 1999*. Pretoria: National Treasury PPP Unit.

National Treasury Unit. (2007). *Introducing Public Private Partnerships in South Africa*. Pretoria: National Treasury PPP Unit.

Onuobia, F., & Mimiko, B. (2017). Nigeria. In B. Werneck & M. Saadi (Eds.), *The Public-Private Partnership Law Review*. London, Business Law Research.

Petersen, O.H. (2011). Public-Private Partnerships as Converging or Diverging Trends in Public Management? A Comparative Analysis of PPP Policy and Regulation in Denmark and Ireland. *International Management Review*, *12*(2), 1.

PPIAF. (2007). Public Private Partnership: Value for Money and the Public Private Partnership Procurement Process. Retrieved March 28, 2020, from https://ppiaf.org/sites/ppiaf.org/files/documents/toolkits/highwaystoolkit/6/bibliography/pdf/value_for_money_and_the_public_private_partnership_procurement_process.pdf.

Queiroz, C., & Astensiano, G. (2014). An Overview of the Brazilian PP Experience form a Stakeholders' Viewpoint. Retrieved March 20, 2020, from https://publications.iadb.org/publications/english/document/An-Overview-of-the-Brazilian-PPP-Experience-from-a-Stakeholders-Viewpoint.pdf.

Robert, O., Dansoh, A., & Ofori Kuragu, J.K. (2014). Reasons for Adopting Public – Private Partnership (PPP) for Construction Projects in Ghana. *International Journal of Construction Management*, *14*(4), 227–238. doi:10.1080/15623599.2014.967925.

Ruiters, C., & Matji, M.P. (2016). Public – Private Partnership Conceptual Framework and Models for the Funding and Financing of Water Services Infrastructure in Municipalities from Selected Provinces in South Africa. *Water SA*, *42*(2), 291. doi:10.4314/wsa.v42i2.13.

Seth, S., & Rajaskekaran, V. (2017). India. In B. Werneck & M. Saadi (Eds.), *The Public-Private Partnership Law Review*. London: Business Law Research.

Sharma, S. N. (2015, July 5). What Ails India's PPP Model and Why It Doesn't Bode Well for Modi Government's Infrastructure Push. Retrieved March 19, 2020, from https://economictimes.indiatimes.com/news/economy/infrastructure/what-ails-indias-ppp-model-and-why-it-doesnt-bode-well-for.

Shivalingegowda, M., & Girisha, M. C. (2019, January 20). Challenges for Public Private Partnership in India. Retrieved March 20, 2020, from www.researchgate.net/publication/330506526_CHALLENGES_FOR_PUBLIC_PRIVATE_PARTNERSHIP_IN_INDIA_fina.

Smith, A. (2012). Policy, Legal and Regulatory Frameworks for Successful PPPs. Retrieved October 5, 2017, from www.unescap.org/sites/default/files/4a-Policy-legal-regulatory-frameworks.pdf.

Stephen, J. (2005, November 9). Fears Gautrain Will Be a Large, Expensive White Elephant. *The Star*.

Stoddard, E., & Strydom, T. J. (2017, July 31). South Africa's Stock Market Defies Recession, Scales Record Highs. *Reuters*.

Switala, H. (2017). *Project Finance and Obtaining Sufficient Funding for the Successful Completion of Your Project*. Retrieved from www.dbsa.org/EN/About- Us/Publications/Documents/Project%20finance%20and%20obtaining%20sufficient%20funding%20for%20the%20successful%20completion%20of%20your%20project.pdf.

TLR. (2019). Brazil – The Public-Private Partnership Law Review – Edition 5 – TLR. Retrieved March 28, 2020, from https://thelawreviews.co.uk/edition/the-public-private-partnership-law-review-edition-5/1189691/brazil.

Wang, N., Chen, X., & Wu, G. (2019). Public Private Partnerships, a Value for Money Solution for Clean Coal District Heating Operations. *Sustainability*, *11*(8), 2386. doi:10.3390/su11082386.

Werneck, B., Saadi, M., & Saadi, M. (2017). *The Public-Private Partnership Law Review*. B. Werneck (Ed.). London: Business Law Research.

The World Bank. (2014). *Doing Business Report*. Washington, DC: The World Bank.

World Finance. (2014). Navigating Public Private Partnerships in Brazil. Retrieved July 4, 2017, from www.worldfinance.com/infrastructure-investment/project-finance/navigating-public-private- partnerships-in-brazil.

9 Conclusion

The future of public-private partnerships in emerging economies

9.1 Introduction

This study examines the framework for PPP in emerging economies. At the heart of the discussion is the need to make emerging economies investor-friendly for the purpose of attracting funding for PPP projects. The major areas where answers are needed include the following:

1 What is PPP, and how does it serve as an alternative to traditional public procurement?
2 What are the challenges being posed to the successful arrangements and completion of PPP projects in emerging economies?

A clear point emerging from the literature is that the law is an instrument for economic development and can be used to strengthen government policies, particularly when those policies are geared towards specific goals. For example, the governments of Brazil, India, Nigeria and South Africa all intend to use the PPP model as a means for bridging their respective infrastructure gaps. However, in order to achieve the goal of building public infrastructure through the financial support and expertise of the private sector, the governments of emerging economies must do more than just produce policies. Sectors such as energy, transport, water supply and power are critical areas emerging economies.[1] This chapter discusses the role that national governments must play in emerging economies to strengthen their PPP frameworks and to stimulate the interests of investors.

9.2 A clear understanding of what PPP is and how it works

In the first place, it is important that governments in emerging economies understand what PPP is and what they intend to achieve using the model. PPP plays an important role in the global search for 'the expanded and better quality

1 Augustine Edobor Arimoro, 'Institutional Framework for Public-Private Partnerships in Nigeria: Is it a Case of Too Many Cooks for One Pot of Broth?' (2019) 40(2) *Business Law Review* 73.

delivery infrastructure.'[2] It is a long-term contractual relationship between the public sector and a private entity whereby the latter delivers and funds public services using a capital asset, sharing the associated risks with the public sector.[3] While the PPP concept has evolved and the terminologies used to describe the model depend on the nomenclature chosen by policy drafters, countries must be clear of what they actually intend to achieve by using PPP rather than a system where the public sector raises funds from the private sector as investments to support the development of public infrastructures built, maintained and operated by the government. If this is the case, the public authority does not need to arrange a PPP but to make bonds available or use other money-market instruments to raise funds for the project. For example, the federal government of Nigeria recently received ₦132 billion for a ₦100 billion *sukuk* bond.[4] The funds received from investors was to be used for the financing of road projects across the six geo-political zones in the country.[5] This shows that the government can raise funds from investors for public-infrastructure projects without having to make a PPP arrangement, which is a complex form of contract. The government is free to appoint a private-sector partner to manage the project upon completion by entering a service contract agreement with the private entity.

This analysis is clearer when policymakers and public administrators understand that not all contracts between the public sector and the private sector dealing with infrastructure are PPPs. The sale or divesture of a government's interest in a public enterprise is not a PPP. Such an arrangement is better referred to as privatisation.[6] The mere hiring of a service (such as a cleaning service or a security-guard service) although a partnership between the government and a private entity is outsourcing and not a PPP.[7]

It is therefore necessary that for an arrangement to be considered a PPP within the context of this study, irrespective of the nomenclature used by the policymaker, the arrangement must consist of certain elements. First, the public-sector party[8] to a PPP contract deals with a private entity (the project company) for the construction or rehabilitation of a public facility. Second, the private party is responsible for the design, construction, maintenance and

2 EBRD, 'Public-Private Partnerships (PPPs)' (2020) available at <www.ebrd.com/infrastructure/infrastructurePPPs.com> accessed 30 March 2020.

3 Ibid.

4 Premium Times, 'Nigeria's Sukuk Bon Oversubscribed, Receives N132bn for N100bn Offer' *Premium Times*, 22 December 2018 available at <www.premiumtimesng.com/business/business-news/302415-nigerias-sukuk-bond-oversubscribed-receives-n132bn-for-n100bn-offer.html> accessed 30 March 2020.

5 Ibid.

6 Alimi M Abiola and RO Abiola, 'Impact of Privatisation on the Growth of Nigerian Public Enterprises: A Case Study of Selected Enterprises in Nigeria' (2015) available at <dspace.futa.edu.ng/jspul/handle> accessed 10 April 2015.

7 Public Private Partnership Commission Malawi, 'PPP' available at <www.pppc.mw/faq.html> accessed 12 April 2015.

8 Sometimes referred to as 'public entity,' 'public party,' 'institution,' or 'public authority'.

operation of the facility. Third, the duration of the contract must be long-term and at the end of the contract period, the facility is transferred back to the public authority.[9] If the intention of the public authority is not consistent with this, a separate arrangement could be made to achieve the object in place of terming the arrangement a PPP.

For a PPP to be arranged, the public authority identifies a need for the project, which could be a greenfield or brownfield project. The public authority will then advertise for private-sector parties to make bids. A preferred bid will then be chosen and a project company formed. A contract is signed and contracts are moved to site. At the completion of the project, the private company is responsible for operating and maintaining the facility.

9.3 The challenge facing emerging economies

Emerging economies grapple with the challenge of a shortage of infrastructure facilities vis-à-vis supply.[10] According to the World Investment Report (2014), developing economies face an infrastructure deficit estimated at US$1.6 trillion from 2015 to 2030.[11] PPP can be used as a tool to help realise the United Nations 2030 Sustainable Development Goals.[12] A number of issues bedevilling private-sector participation in PPP arrangements across emerging economies and especially in the selected areas of this study have been identified. The main issues include the fact that these countries are still in the experimental phase of PPP. Countries like the United Kingdom, Canada and Australia had their own challenges while trying out the model. For example, when the PPP model was first introduced in Canada, critics referred to it as 'problem, problem, problem.'[13] It is therefore not strange that some of the issues facing PPP in emerging economies are largely due to the fact that it is a teething phase for several countries. There are few experts available and issues with novel areas of contract law and practice. A typical example is the contract signed between the federal government of Nigeria and Bi-Courtney Highway Services Limited for the construction of the Lagos Ibadan Expressway. That arrangement has been unilaterally cancelled by the Nigerian government. Of note is that while

9 ER Yescombe, *Public- Private Partnerships: Principles of Policy and Finance* (London: Butterworth-Heinemann, 2007) 3.

10 Nathan Hayes, 'Public-Private Partnerships in Emerging Markets' (2017) available at <https://blogs.lse.ac.uk/internationaldevelopment/2017/05/08/ppps-in-emerging-markets/> accessed 30 March 2020.

11 United Nations, *World Investment Report 2014: Investing in the SDGs: An Action Plan* (United Nations, 2014) available at <https://unctad.org/en/PublicationsLibrary/wir2014_en.pdf> accessed 30 March 2020.

12 Eghosa Ekhator, *Barriers to implementation of SDGs in Africa: The Need for Effective Business and Government Collaboration* (2019) available at <https://www.researchgate.net/publication/337622369_Barriers_to_implementation_of_SDGs_in_Africa_the_need_for_effective_business_and_government_collaboration> accessed 2 September 2020.

13 Graeme Hedge and Carsten Greve (eds.), *The Challenge of Public Private Partnerships: Learning from International Experience* (Cheltenham: Edward Edgar Publishing, 2007) 8.

the concessionaire considered itself a mere arranger, the federal government expected the concessionaire to finance the deal.

Corruption is also a serious problem for PPP in emerging economies. One obvious advantage of PPP over traditional public procurement is that the private sector is a better manager of resources than the public sector. It is also trite that traditional public procurement, especially in developing countries, is often marred by allegations of over-inflation of the cost of contracts, kick-backs for payment and poor execution of contracts with the connivance of public officials.[14] While PPP aims to deliver good-quality projects through a transparent and competitive process, there are, regrettably, cases of corruption in PPP contracts. For example, government officials may just initiate a PPP project for the sake of illicit profit to commence a white elephant project. A contractor may make use of substandard materials in the execution of a project. Bidders may also be treated differently by the authorities to favour a crony company.[15] There are also cases where the whole political system is corrupt and discouraging for private enterprise.

A weak business environment can give rise to problems.[16] Weak business environments stem from poor regulatory environments, poor ease of doing business ranking and difficulties in getting permits. Political instability may also be considered a major cause of a weak business environment. In the same vein, there are cases where governments in developing countries do not continue with the programmes of their predecessors in office. The mentality is that completing the projects of your predecessor does not account for an incumbent as it is considered that incumbent never initiated any project. In addition, problems with power supply in many developing countries directly hamper with the growth of local businesses and add to the overall costs of doing business as the private sector seeks alternative means of power supply.

The cost of acquiring finance and the scarcity of long-term domestic funding for infrastructure is problematic. Apart from South Africa in Sub-Saharan Africa, and indeed among several other developing economies, the local financial markets are not well developed. With the scarcity of domestic sources of funding and a heavy reliance on foreign funds, PPP in emerging economies are greatly exposed to foreign currency–exchange risks. This makes it even more difficult to attract foreign investors, as payments for the use of facilities are made in the local currency and not in the currency that the finance for the project was obtained.

More worrisome is the issue of PPP governance in emerging economies. Governance refers to the manner in which the public authority's institutional capacity or lack thereof, intentionally or unintentionally affects the performance

14 Augustine Arimoro, 'Corruption and Public-Private Partnership in Nigeria: Good Governance and Ethical Considerations' in Agada Akogwu (ed.), *Combating the Menace of Corruption in Nigeria* (Awka: Black Tower Publishers, 2019) 135.

15 Ibid.

16 Nathan Hayes, *op cit* (note 10).

of PPP.[17] Governance problems could be counter-productive to successful PPP arrangements. Where the government shows a lack of interest in PPP success, it sends the wrong signals to future promoters and PPP investors.[18]

9.4 How to ensure successful PPP regimes in emerging economies

Having previously discussed the issues that militate against the successful practice of PPP in emerging economies, this study next attempts to provide measures to address challenges that emerging economies face as they practise PPP in their various jurisdictions.

9.4.1 Regulating PPP

One area of shortcoming for many emerging economies has to do with weakness in their regulatory mechanisms for PPP. This can be attributed to the problem of weak institutions that characterise developing countries.[19] The institutional framework for PPP provides the responsibilities of the agencies of state in the PPP process. It defines which institution plays what role at every point.[20] The institutional framework for PPP should include provisions for a PPP unit,[21] standard procedures, and guideline tools to identify, structure, evaluate, award and monitor PPP projects.[22] The institutional framework for PPP in any jurisdiction, therefore, is made up of the specialised unit(s) or programmes structured to develop and supervise PPP projects.[23] They play an important role in the promotion of PPP solutions.[24] Worthy of note is that the PPP unit, which is in most cases the main institutional actor in the regulation and administration of PPP, does not initiate projects.[25] The responsibility for initiating projects is the task of the line ministry, department or agency that has direct oversight function for the facility proposed. Similarly, the guidelines on the operation of the institutions regulating PPPs must be clear to ensure a fair

17 James Leigland, 'Public-Private Partnerships in Developing Countries: Emerging Evidence-Based Critique' (2018) 33(1) *The World Bank Research Obersver* 103–134.

18 Alpana Kateja, 'Building Infrastructure: Private Participation in Emerging Economies' (2012) 37 *Procedia – Social and Behavioural Sciences* 368–378.

19 The Institute for Public-Private Partnership Inc (IP3), *Development of Policy, Legal, and Institutional Framework for the Public-Private Partnership Programme in Malawi* (Washington, DC: IP3, 2007) 38.

20 Ibid.

21 This may be known by another nomenclature.

22 The Institute for Public-Private Partnerships, *op cit* (note 18).

23 Augustine Edobor Arimoro, *op cit* (note 1) 75.

24 Economic and Social Commission for Asia and the Pacific, *PPP Policy, Legal and Institutional Frameworks in Asia and the Pacific* 7 (2017) available at <www.unescap.org/stites/default/files/S4_PPP-Policy-Legal-Institutional-Frameworks_0.pdf> accessed 21 March 2018.

25 Augustine Edobor Arimoro, *op cit* (note 1) 75.

and transparent and competitive bidding process.[26] To make PPP regulation effective in emerging economies, the following steps should be implemented:

1 The PPP unit, although a government agency, must be made independent as much as possible and must not be subservient to other government agencies. Otherwise, it will be difficult for the unit to enforce compliance against public-sector agencies.
2 Dispute-resolution mechanisms should be put in place to deal with differences that will inevitably arise between the public authority and private partners during the lifetime of the PPP contract.
3 It is important that there is a dedicated PPP law or guidelines for PPP. The use of old structures in place before the PPP model was implemented to regulate PPP is an invitation for failure since PPP was not envisaged at the time when the structure was put in place.[27] To do otherwise amounts to putting new wine in old bottles.
4 To ensure efficiency, it might be appropriate under given circumstances for the government to appoint an independent specialist to work with the PPP unit to act as a compliance monitor and to ensure that parties respect the terms of the PPP contract.[28]

9.4.2 Unlocking the domestic financial market

One of the distinct challenges governments face in arranging PPP in emerging economies is that of finding domestic investors with the resources to invest in infrastructure. Foreign exchange risks mean that foreign investments may be hard to come by because investors recoup their investments through payments that local citizens make from the use of the public-infrastructure service. The payments are usually in the domestic currency, and if it happens that the local currency is devalued, it will be difficult for the investor to make commensurate return on investment. This is the more reason why emerging economies must take steps to build their local financial markets. Some of the steps that emerging economies may take to unlock domestic financial market to fund PPP include:

1 Upgrading their credit infrastructure framework. This can be done by providing support for local banks and putting into use credit-information systems. There is a need to reform or review regulation dealing with collateral and registries for liens and on moveable assets.[29]

26 Ibid.
27 Ibid.
28 Jeffrey Delmon, *Creating a Framework for Public-Private Partnership (PPP) Programs: A Practical Guide for Decision Makers* (Washington, DC: The World Bank, 2014) 9.
29 Olufemi Soyeju, 'Public Assets Financing in Nigeria: The Imperatives for Legal Reforms. To Unlock Domestic Financial Resources and Foreign Capital for Infrastructure Development' (Unpublished LLD Thesis, University of Pretoria, Pretoria, 2012) 366.

2 Encouraging the establishment of domestic infrastructure funds to support the infrastructure market. It is important that the government lays down guidelines and approves private-sector fund managers with requisite experience to manage such funds. It is also important that low-entry threshold funds are created to encourage participation of low-income-earning citizens.[30] This will also make ordinary citizens support PPP initiatives, as they would benefit from the returns on investment and consider themselves co-owners of PPP projects.
3 Channelling pension funds towards supporting PPP projects. Such funds are usually held for the long term, and since PPP contracts last usually between 15 and 30 years, assets held in pension instruments may be channelled towards PPP investments.

9.4.3 Respect for rule of law and sanctity of contract

Many developing countries are notorious for their disregard of the rule of law and the sanctity of contract. This makes a country unattractive to investors. The rule of law is essential to every society.[31] It envisages a society organised according to laws that guarantee a good degree of objectivity in dispensing justice while at the same time promoting peace and prosperity. Based on the foregoing, Tamanaha states that government officials must abide by the valid laws in force at the time of any given government action.[32] Furthermore, officials must remain within eir established legal bounds when exercising the power attached to their public positions.[33] Forsyth and Wade similarly argue that all acts must be in accordance with the law to be valid and that government activity must be conducted within a framework of defined rules and regulations.[34]

As a corollary, government officials must abide by laws regulating PPP and ensure transparency and accountability. Following the law will stem corrupt practices and ensure clarity. It is therefore required that government officials respect court orders and abide by the law. The government must ensure that no public official disregards the orders of court. At the same time, the government must show the political will to respect the law.

Because of the emergence of the private sector in the provision of infrastructure, the notion of the sanctity of contract has become more compelling.

30 Augustine Arimoro, 'Law as a Catalyst for Stimulating Investor Sentiments among Low to Middle-Income Individuals in the Development of Infrastructure in Nigeria' (2017) available at <www.lawanddevelopment.net/img/2017papers/Augustine.Arimoro.pdf> accessed 31 March 2020.

31 Elijah Okon, 'The Rule of Law in Nigeria: Myth or Reality?' (2011) 41 *Journal of Politics and Law* 211.

32 Brian Z Tamanaha, 'A Concise Guide to the Rule of Law' in Gianluigi Palombella and Neil Walker (eds.), *Relocating the Rule of Law* (Portland: Hart Publishing, 2008) 3.

33 Ibid.

34 CF Forsyth and William Wade, *Administrative Law* (Oxford: Oxford University Press, 2014).

In the first place, a contract is an 'agreement made between two or more parties which is legally binding on them.'[35] It is an agreement enforceable by the law, between two or more parties to do or to abstain from doing some act or acts, their intention being to create legal relations and not merely to exchange mutual promises.[36] Sanctity of contract is the principle of law that once parties enter into a contract, they must honour their obligations under that contract. The essence of the doctrine of the sanctity of contract has been re-emphasised by Sagay in the following words:

> We must next consider why the law does enforce agreements at all. The commercial and economic life of modern society consists very largely of agreements. Trade and commerce would be chaotic, if not impossible, if the law permitted a promisor to break his promise without at least placing him under an obligation to pay compensation for the loss occasioned by his default.[37]

This position of the law was restated in the Nigerian case of *Arjay Limited & Ors v Airline Management Support Limited*,[38] where the Supreme Court of Nigeria per Niki Tobi JSC (of blessed memory) stated as follows:

> It is an elementary law that where parties have entered into a contract or an agreement, they are bound by the provisions of the contract or agreement. Accordingly, a party cannot ordinarily resile from a contract or agreement just because he later found out that the conditions of the contract or agreement are not favourable to him. This is the whole essence of the doctrine of the sanctity of contract or agreement. The court is bound to construe the terms of the contract or agreement and the terms only in the event of an action arising therefrom.[39]

The Supreme Court of Nigeria was firm in upholding the duty to honour obligations involving the public sector or governments in their sovereign might as illustrated in *Attorney General Nassarawa State v Attorney General Plateau State*.[40] At the creation of Nasarawa State out of the former Plateau State, the Military Administrators had a meeting with General Abacha, the then head of state, during which some areas of Plateau State were by agreement allocated to Nasarawa State. Later, the government of Plateau Sate failed to abide by the

35 Lucy Jones, *Introduction to Business Law* (Oxford: Oxford University Press, 2011) 83.

36 Agbonika John Alewo, 'The Prinicple and Nature of Law of Contract in Nigeria: Formation of Binding Contract' (2012) 5(4) *Journal of Politics and Law* 123.

37 IE Sagay, *Nigerian Law of Contract*, 2nd Ed. (Ibadan: Spectrum, 2000) 1.

38 (2003) LPELR 555 (SC) 67.

39 Supra 67 paras A-E.

40 (2012) 10 NWLR (Pt 1309) 419.

agreement, and the Nasarawa State government instituted action to enforce the agreement. The Supreme Court noted:

> If mutual agreement entered by the parties to it shall be treated lavishly and any party shall be allowed to unilaterally resile from the commitment both parties have signed to bind themselves, then the essence of any agreement or mutual contract is woefully defeated.[41]

Further deprecating the attitude of the Plateau State government in seeking to unilaterally resile from its agreement with the Nasarawa State government, Peter-Odili JSC said:

> This attempt by the defendant is reckless with capacity to encourage lawlessness and disobedience to constituted authority and the Rule of Law which outcome would not rule out chaos. People or those in charge of institutions or government at every level should be cautious and wary of taking steps that are definitely not in keeping with the peace and order of this nation. The defendants are bound and stopped from going against the agreement.[42]

Thus, a valid contract is binding on the parties to that contract, and it may only be modified or terminated by consent of the parties or if provided by the law. The principle is the expression of the legal theory of 'good faith,' without which international contract law (including PPP contracts) would be a mere mockery. While the principle does not apply when it would result in unfair hardship or lead to illegality, the performance of a contractual obligation is sacrosanct to legitimate commercial activity.[43] The doctrine of sanctity of contract, *pacta sunt servanda*, is established as one of the fundamental pillars of the modern law of contract.[44]

It has been noted that for a prospective investor who wishes to enter into a contract with the public sector in a developing economy, the following questions may arise:[45]

1 Would such a contract in writing be respected?
2 Can the investor enforce the terms in case of default?
3 Would an investor have remedy?

41 *Attorney General Nasarawa State v Attorney General Plateau State* Supra 458 *per* Muhammad JSC.
42 Supra 489.
43 Dale Hutchison and Chris-James Pretorius (eds.), *The Law of Contract in South Africa*, 2nd Ed. (Oxford: Oxford University Press, 2012) 8.
44 Ibid.
45 Olatunde Ayeni, 'The Need for Sanctity of Contracts for the Success of the Power Sector Reform: An Investor's Experience' *The Lawyer* (2016) a ThisDay Weekly Pull Out 24 April 8–9.

4 Where there is a remedy, would the government honour the remedial measures?
5 If there is a change in government, would a previous administration's commitments be respected by the succeeding administration?

Emerging economies must therefore consider these questions and take steps to ensure that there is protection for investors in order to attract investors to their projects. The importance of respect for contracts by the government came into question in the United States as far back as the 1930s when, in *Perry v United States*,[46] the court per Chief Justice Hughes held as follows:

> The United States are as much bound by their contracts as are individuals. . . . When the United States, with constitutional authority, makes contracts, it has similar rights and incurs responsibilities similar to those of individuals who are parties to such instruments. . . . The [contrary] argument . . . is in substance that Government cannot by contract restrict the exercise of a sovereign power. But the right to make biding obligations is a competence attaching to sovereignty. . . . The binding quality of the promise of the United States is of the essence of the credit which . . . is pledged. The fact that the United States may not be sued without its consent is a matter of procedure which does not affect the legal and binding character of its contracts.[47]

It is pertinent to note that sanctity of contract is enshrined in the Constitution of the United States under Article I, Section 10. It provides, in the relevant part, that 'No state shall . . . pass any Bill of Attainder, ex post facto Law, or Law impairing the obligation of contracts.' What this means is that the US government is prohibited by the Constitution from taking any action that may retroactively alter the terms of a contract.

It is imperative that the state and its individuals are subject to the law. The law must also be in consonance with the times to support development and protect commerce. All promises intended to have legal obligations must be honoured to the letter, except in cases where it is impossible to perform the obligations or where it is illegal to do so. This is important because every investor considers profit before investing capital. In the case of foreign investors, it is not enough for there to be a prospect of good RoI; the law must also provide a guarantee for the repatriation of profits made from legitimate business concerns. Importantly, it is also not enough to make good laws to encourage investments; the institutions of state have a corresponding duty to ensure that

46 272 US 330 (1934).

47 Ibid 551–554. See the case of the *Attorney General of Nasarawa State v Attorney General Plateau State supra*.

the laws are implemented and respected. It is only in this way that the law can have a positive impact on the economy.

9.4.4 Offering incentives

The governments of emerging economies can introduce some incentives to make PPP arrangements attractive to private-sector investors. Some of the measures that governments in emerging economies can use to incentivise PPP project companies include:

1 Releasing capital grant to PPP project companies in the form of a one-time capital grant;
2 Providing revenue guarantees to assure investors that the projects will become profitable ventures where projects are considered to be high-risk projects;[48]
3 Granting tax holidays to PPP project companies until at least when the facility becomes operational. These may include exemption from registration tax on the acquisition of real property for PPP projects or exemption from value added tax (VAT) for the purchase of construction materials for projects.
4 The government may also consider the buyout of a project in the event of a force majeure or other regrettable circumstances. For example, the Lagos State government in Nigeria bought back the Lekki Concession Toll Road project from the concessionaire. It was not because the project was not successful but because of community rejection of the project and other political considerations, as the ruling party became jittery as the gubernatorial elections approached and for fear that the opposition party would take advantage of the situation.

9.4.5 Regular training of public officials

Public-sector officials handling PPP should undergo regular training.[49] One of the shortcomings in the administration of PPP in emerging economies is a shortage in the number of PPP experts. There is need for staff of the various PPP units to be trained and for them to engage in research on models that fit their local environments. Furthermore, ministries, departments and agencies of government that are responsible for identifying and initiating PPP projects need to identify PPP champions in their various establishments who should undergo continuous training.

48 UNESCAP, 'Types of Government Support and Incentives' (2008) available at <www.unescap.org/ttdw/ppp/ppp_primer/351_types_of_government_support_and_incentives.html> accessed 31 March 2020.

49 Several of the stakeholders interviewed by the author in both South Africa and Nigeria identified the need to provide training for officials dealing with PPP.

9.4.6 Making guarantees available

Brazil and India have implemented strategies to provide guarantees for PPP project companies. This strategy should be adopted by other emerging economies as it will make their PPP programme attractive to both domestic and foreign investors.

9.5 Conclusion

Adopting a PPP policy and implementing such is not enough. Emerging economies need to do more than that if they desire to have successful outcomes as far as PPP arrangements are concerned. The future of PPP in emerging economies will be brighter if certain steps are taken to avoid the pitfalls that have given rise to failed projects. The more success achieved gives rise to increased interest from PPP investors. In the same vein, the more failures in PPP projects, the less interest investors will show to that jurisdiction.

Steps must be taken to engage in the regular review of PPP laws and guidelines. The law-reform process in emerging economies is slow, and most times the laws are not in tune with the reality of the times. For example, the Brazilian PPP law came into force over a decade ago. The law itself mirrors the UK system, which has proven not to be suitable for the Brazilian environment, however, the law is yet to be reviewed. In the case of Nigeria, the PPP law was passed in 2005. Even though the law is deficient, it is still in operation several years later. If emerging economies desire to make a difference with PPP and other areas of commerce, the law must reflect current situations. This is not to say that the law needs to be reviewed every year. The point here is that for sectors that determine the well-being of the citizenry, such as the delivery of infrastructure services, the government needs to be proactive.

References

Aibola, A. M., & Abiola, R. O. (2015). Impact of Privatisation on the Growth of Nigerian Public Enterprises: A Case Study of Selected Enterprises in Nigeria. Retrieved April 20, 2015, from dspace.futa.edu.ng/jspul/handle.

Alewo, A. J. (2012). The Principle and Nature of Law of Contract in Nigeria: Formation of Binding Contract. *Journal of Politics and Law*, *5*(4). doi:10.5539/jpl.v5n4p123.

Arimoro, A. E. (2017). Law as a Catalyst for Stimulating Investor Sentiments Among Low to Middle-Income Individuals in the Development of Infrastructure in Nigeria. Retrieved March 31, 2020, from www.lawanddevelopment.net/img/2017papers/Augustine.Arimoro.pdf.

Arimoro, A. E. (2019a). Corruption and Public-Private Partnership in Nigeria: Good Governance and Ethical Considerations. In A. Akogwu (Ed.), *Combating the Menace of Corruption in Nigeria* (p. 135). Awka: Tower Publishing.

Arimoro, A. E. (2019b). Institutional Framework for Public-Private Partnerships in Nigeria: Is It a Case of Too Many Cooks for One Pot of Broth? *Business Law Review*, *40*(2), 73–75.

Ayeni, O. (2016, April 24). The Need for Sanctity of Contracts for the Success of the Power Sector Reform: An Investor's Experience. *This Day*.

Delmon, J. (2014). *Creating a Framework for Public-Private Partnership (PPP) Programs: A Practical Guide for Decision Makers*. Washington, DC: The World Bank.
EBRD. (2020). Public-Private Partnerships (PPPs). Retrieved March 30, 2020, from www.ebrd.com/infrastructure/infrastructurePPPs.com.
Forsyth, C., & Wade, W. (2014). *Administrative Law*. Oxford: Oxford University Press.
Hayes, N. (2017, May 8). Public-Private Partnerships in Emerging Markets. Retrieved from https://blogs.lse.ac.uk/internationaldevelopment/2017/05/08/ppps-in-emerging-markets.
Hodge, G. A., & Greve, C. (2007). *The Challenge of Public-Private Partnerships: Learning from International Experience*. Cheltenham: Edward Elgar Publishing.
Hutchison, D., & Pretorius, C. (2012). *The Law of Contract in South Africa*. Oxford: Oxford University Press.
John, E. O. (2011). The Rule of Law in Nigeria: Myth or Reality? *Journal of Politics and Law*, *4*(1). doi:10.5539/jpl.v4n1p211.
Jones, L. (2011). *Introduction to Business Law*. Oxford: Oxford University Press.
Kateja, A. (2012). Building Infrastructure: Private Participation in Emerging Economies. *Procedia – Social and Behavioral Sciences*, *37*, 368–378. doi:10.1016/j.sbspro.2012.03.302.
Leigland, J. (2018). Public-Private Partnerships in Developing Countries: The Emerging Evidence-Based Critique. *The World Bank Research Observer*, *33*(1), 103–134. doi:10.1093/wbro/lkx008.
Premium Times. (2018, December 22). Nigeria's Sukuk Bond Oversubscribed, Receives N132bn for N100bn Offer. Retrieved from www.premiumtimesng.com/business/business-news/302415-nigerias-sukuk-bond-oversubscribed-receives-n132bn-for-n100bn-offer.html.
Sagay, I. E. (2000). *Nigerian Law of Contract*. Ibadan: Spectrum Books.
Soyeju, O. (2012). *Public Assets Financing in Nigeria: The Imperatives for Legal Reforms. To Unlock Domestic Financial Resources and Foreign Capital for Infrastructure Development* (Unpublished doctoral dissertation). University of Pretoria, Pretoria.
UNESCAP. (2008). Types of Government Support and Incentives. Retrieved March 31, 2020, from www.unescap.org/ttdw/ppp/ppp_primer/351_types_of_government_support_and_incentives.html.
United Nations. (2014). World Investment Report 2014: Investing in the SDGs: An Action Plan. Retrieved March 30, 2020, from https://unctad.org/en/PublicationsLibrary/wir2014_en.pdf.
Yescombe, E. R. (2007). *Public-Private Partnerships: Principles of Policy and Finance*. London: Butterworth-Heinemann.

Index

Note: Page numbers in **bold** indicate a table on the corresponding page.

For Product Safety Concerns and Information please contact our EU
representative GPSR@taylorandfrancis.com
Taylor & Francis Verlag GmbH, Kaufingerstraße 24, 80331 München, Germany

www.ingramcontent.com/pod-product-compliance
Ingram Content Group UK Ltd.
Pitfield, Milton Keynes, MK11 3LW, UK
UKHW020010200926
475702UK00015B/2570
* 9 7 8 0 3 6 7 6 1 6 0 6 9 *